Contracts:
Law in Action

Second Edition

Volume II
The Advanced Course

Stewart Macaulay
*Malcolm Pitman Sharp Professor and
Theodore W. Brazeau Professor
University of Wisconsin Law School*

John Kidwell
*Kathleen M. & George I. Haight Professor and
Associate Dean for Academic Affairs
University of Wisconsin Law School*

William Whitford
*Professor Emeritus
University of Wisconsin Law School*

LexisNexis
Matthew Bender®

Library of Congress Cataloging-in-Publication Data

Macaulay, Stewart, 1931–
    Contracts: law in action / Stewart Macaulay, John Kidwell, William
Whitford.–2nd ed.
      p. cm.
    Rev. ed. of: Contracts / Stewart Macaulay...[et al.]. c1995.
    Includes bibliographical references and indexes.
    Contents: v. 1. The introductory Course—v. 2. The advanced course
    ISBN 0-8205-5721-8 (set)
      1. Contracts–United States–Cases. I. Kidwell, John, 1945-II. Whitford, William C., 1940-
III. Title.
KF801.A7M3145 2003
346.7302–dc.21

                                            2002037107

Editorial Offices
744 Broad Street, Newark, NJ 07102 (973) 820-2000
201 Mission St., San Francisco, CA 94105-1831 (415) 908-3200
701 East Water Street, Charlottesville, VA 22902-7587 (804) 972-7600
www.lexis.com

(Pub.3025)

PREFACE TO THE SECOND EDITION

We revised our book for a number of reasons. Most importantly, our original book and this revision reject the idea that contract law is no more than a small collection of timeless principles. Contracts problems change as the society changes. Corporate lawyers also have been busy, seeking ways to use the form of contract to ward off liability to employees and consumers. Fashions in scholarly work reflect changes in the academy as we move through cycles of classical contract, realist judging in the grand style, dedication to the consumer movement, reductionist pursuits of efficiency, default rules and formalism, and, perhaps, the coming new realism that reflects a law and society perspective. We have reviewed the entire book to see where we should reflect these changes and new developments, but the major effort has been devoted to bringing up to date our materials on such matters as unconscionability, form contracts printed in fine print or hidden in other ways (particularly in the area of computer programs), and the growing uses of arbitration to repeal the reform statutes of earlier decades. These are the interesting and important matters coming before the courts when this revision was prepared, and we expect these topics to have a fairly long shelf life.

At the same time, those who have used *Contracts: Law in Action* in the past will find much of the book unchanged or only slightly modified. After teaching *Contracts: Law in Action* and earlier photocopied versions for about twenty years, the authors think that the book works. Moreover, it has worked for instructors who emphasize very different approaches in their teaching. The original book and the revision both take the "Law in Action" part of the title seriously. Putting contract problems in context makes the course both more theoretical and more practical at the same time. Whatever one's theoretical outlook, there is a high price to be paid if he or she forgets such things as that law is not free, most disputes end in settlement, crafting nice sounding legal standards is one thing but finding evidence to establish a cause of action is another, and all institutions, including the market, are flawed. American contract law is messy and often contradictory. Even when the form of the rules stay more or less the same, their application varies from court to court over time. Yet our contract law's flaws have not blocked great economic progress or caused recessions. We quote Wittgenstein near the beginning of the course: "Is it even always an advantage to replace an indistinct picture by a sharp one? Isn't the indistinct one often exactly what we need?" At the very least, the answer to this question cannot just be assumed away. We also have been pleased to discover that many of our former students find that our course prepares them to hit the ground running when they begin practice. We have tried to focus on live contracts problems that our students will face when they become lawyers.

We are heavily in debt to contracts teachers at schools other than Wisconsin who have used *CLA*. We have had an e-mail list for those interested in the book. Our friends at other schools have contributed ideas and suggestions, and they have asked us to explain why we did certain things. Sometimes we have been able to explain choices we made long ago, and when we could not we rethought what we had done. We have learned a great deal from these friends. While we risk leaving out people who deserve mention, we wish to thank particularly Tom Russell, Tom Stipanowich, Sandy Meiklejohn, Alan Hunt, Jean Braucher, Peter Linzer and Carolyn Brown. In addition, we staged a conference in the fall of 2001. We gathered many who had used the book and other friends whose contributions we wanted to hear. The papers were later published in 2001 Wisconsin Law Review 525-1006. The papers, discussions and final articles helped us in the revision process.

The authors are not the only people at Wisconsin who have taught from the book. We have a small group program in which each first year student gets one class of around twenty students, and Contracts 1 often has been that class. This means that we have many contracts teachers at Wisconsin. Those teaching the course have met for lunch once a week during the semester. The authors have been challenged by the experiences and questions of their colleagues. In addition to Joe Thome who was thanked in our original preface and who continued to teach from the materials until recently, we should acknowledge the many contributions of Kathryn Hendley, Lawrence Bugge, Gordon Smith and Lori Ringhand (now at the University of Kentucky Law School). Lori was a beginning law teacher when she joined us, and she helped us re-write the employment-at-will material and paid particular attention to the teaching notes that we have made available to those who used the book. She has revised them, pulling together the one set created by Kidwell and the other by Macaulay. Our colleague Marc Galanter decided not to participate in the second edition of *Contracts: Law in Action*. He has not taught contracts for some time. However, he did present a paper at our 2001 contracts conference, and the revision still reflects his many contributions to the original version of the book. Also, Nicole Denow (J.D., Wisconsin, 2001) was a talented and hard working research assistant in the revision of the materials dealing with policing contracts, and Nora Kersten (J.D., Wisconsin, 2002) did many memos which were helpful in expanding some of the notes, or in verifying that no changes were required.

We also owe a debt to the thousands of law students who have worked their way through *Contracts: Law in Action* and its photocopied predecessors. For example, Donovan Bezer, then a student at Rutgers Law School, sent us his reactions that we found provocative. Other students have known one or more of the parties who appear in the cases in the book or they have known much about the kinds of transactions involved. We have been reassured that the book has prompted students to see the hard choices lurking behind what seem to be the simple rules of contract law. Americans, of course, always want to have their cake and eat it too. One student, who identified herself as a liberal, sent us an e-mail, saying, "this class has put me in touch with my inner Republican, and I am not sure that I like *him*." Students have also reminded us that most of them are twenty something, and what we see as things "everyone knows" are but ancient history to them. Students stay about the same age while authors age. Thus, we have tried to change examples so that they will not date too fast and explain a little about such "commonplace things" as the Vietnam conflict, OPEC and the consumer movement and other manifestations of Pre-Reagan politics as well as what were ice houses, dial telephones and typewriters. While we find it hard to believe, many of our students have never heard of Shirley MacLaine, Lee Marvin or Bette Davis. We, on the other hand, are not great followers of River Phoenix. All of these stars, of course, play the parts of litigants in contracts cases.

During the past decade or so, the National Conference of Commissioners on Uniform State Law and the American Law Institute has attempted to revise Article 2 of the Uniform Commercial Code. We debated what to do with the proposed revisions. Then our friend Dick Speidel found the process intolerable and felt that he had to resign as the Reporter after twelve years of work. At the time this is being written, it seems unlikely that there will be ambitious changes to Article 2, with the possible exception of the addition of a highly controversial separate statute dealing with computer-related transactions. There is a risk that states may end up moving in the direction of creating "Ununiform Commercial Codes." As a result, we decided not to include material on the proposed revisions. Instructors, of course, may want to offer their classes particular proposals as a way to raise policy questions about the current law. However, we think that it is hard enough finding your way around Article 2 without having to navigate two or more versions.

TABLE OF CONTENTS

Chapter 1

FORMATION OF CONTRACT

The major focus of the following chapters is performing contracts. We consider questions such as the effect of a seller's only slightly defective performance. Must the buyer accept it with, perhaps, an offset for its flaws? Or does close count only in horseshoes and hand grenades? Suppose a seller tenders defective goods. Can it have a second chance and cure its performance or does the buyer have a right to call off the deal? Should courts consider whether the buyer really was hurt by the defective tender or whether it wants out only because it can get the goods cheaper? Suppose a seller is almost certain that buyer will not be able to pay for the goods when the day for performance comes. Must seller continue performance or can seller stop unless buyer can offer assurances that it will pay when the time comes?

However, we cannot begin the course with these questions. We need to establish familiarity with two opposed models of the contracting process; judicial answers to questions of performance often reflect assumptions about how deals are made. The first model sees the parties' contract as a blueprint for performance. It is assumed that buyers and sellers do or should attempt to fashion an agreement in which they specify obligations very precisely and allocate all the risks of possible contingencies. Contract drafters bring the future back to the present. Since we cannot know the future in advance, the drafter deals with the possibility of a war, a depression, a strike and so on. Ideally, if something goes wrong as parties perform a contract, all the parties, lawyers, and judges need do is read a written document and discover what is to happen in this event.

The second model acknowledges that many contracts reflect long term continuing relationships with a rich history that take place in a business and social context. Instead of a magic moment when everything is defined, the contours of the parties' bargain emerge as they perform it through time. While they may have agreed to terms at the outset, everything is always subject to formal or tacit renegotiation. Moreover, those accepting this second model of bargaining processes understand that a written document signed by the parties is not necessarily their bargain-in-fact. For example, the contract may be drafted by elite lawyers at the home office, but the actual agreement is negotiated and performed by people in the field. In this world, we should be surprised when there is no gap between the real deal and the paper deal.[1]

Those who feel more comfortable with the first image of bargaining are likely to solve questions concerning performance by looking to what the parties agreed at the point they made their deal. They will be uneasy when the parties left too much unprovided for. Those who are more comfortable with relational contracts will view written documents signed by the parties as but one factor to consider in

---

[1] Some might opt for a third model, in which it is acknowledged that people don't really thoroughly embody their intentions in advance of an exchange, but which nevertheless endorses the appealing fiction that they do, in order to increase predictability and social order.

solving problems. They will seek fair results in light of the way things turned out, with risk assumption being just one factor among many which are relevant to what is fair.

Because questions of performance often turn on whether the parties made a deal and what its terms were, we must begin with some of the classic dilemmas concerning how courts know whether the parties closed a deal and how they discover what the bargain means. People often communicate in a sloppy fashion. They sign documents that say things they don't mean. While every bargain rests on what the parties assume about the world, at times buyer and seller assume very different things, or things that turn out to be wrong. Courts must respond to all these situations.

Thus, we begin with questions that law teachers often call issues involving formation and interpretation of contracts. Then we consider performance questions. As we do, we discover that formation and interpretation issues influence the solutions. Finally, we return to unpleasant surprises in a different context. One party discovers she has made a very bad deal and seeks relief, arguing that she shouldn't be required to absorb the losses associated with what has happened.

We begin this part of the materials by considering how the American legal system legitimates holding people bound to what judges, lawyers, and scholars call contracts. Why do we care? The reasons judges accept as common sense may influence how they decide cases. Judges and lawyers form a community with a common language. Judges want to explain their decisions so that lawyers will understand and accept them. Sometimes other audiences may respond to a judge's explanations. For example, newspapers and television may attack a decision. Judges are like the rest of us; they do not like to appear foolish or stupid before any audience.

The relationship between law and legitimacy is unclear. Law contributes something to our view that we live in a just, decent, or tolerable society. Americans tend to regard their legal system as at least acceptable, particularly when they compare it with those found in totalitarian states. It is less clear that Americans honor the results in particular cases. Nonetheless, the legal system itself may have enough prestige so that any norms applied by legal officials seem just. In part, this claim rests on our assumption that the legal system is autonomous enough from other centers of power so that it can apply its procedures, make decisions, and enforce them impartially. Both the King and the Chase Manhattan Bank are under the law. Moreover, legal officials are selected in ways Americans find acceptable. They are experts, selected by Presidents or governors in recognition of their skill or, alternatively, elected and seen as expressing the will of the people. This view suggests that politics should play no role in judicial selection.

Finally, some see particular norms as the law because they naturally flow from legal science, reflect common sense, and are dictated by wise policy choices. We should not, under this view, question the result in a particular case. Experts, far removed from power and politics, have decided. Their decisions reflect legitimate rules.

You probably noticed a few problems with this account. Many, if not most, Americans do not believe that the legal system is autonomous and free from the influence of those who hold power in society. On one hand, some think that legal officials use their power to favor the wealthy and influential. On the other hand, some think those with wealth can play the legal game better even if the rules are applied evenly and fairly by officials. Then, too, some think that a judge is a lawyer who knew the governor. Some see nothing wrong with assigning "seats" to assure that a Catholic, a Jew, a Black and a Woman will sit on the highest courts. It is a way of symbolizing that a particular group is both worthy and powerful.

Many challenge the idea that law reflects common sense. Any book which collects quotations will offer the classics. For example, " '[i]f the law supposes that,' said Mr. Bumble, 'the law is an ass, a[n] idiot.'" (Dickens, *Oliver Twist*, ch. 51); "In a thousand pounds of law there is not an ounce of love." (John Ray, English Proverbs); "The law is a sort of hocus-pocus science, that smiles in yer face while it picks yer pocket; the glorious uncertainty of it is of main use to the professors than the justice of it." (Charles Macklin, *Love a la Mode*, Act ii, scene 1 (1759)); "Laws are spiders' webs, which stand firm when any light and yielding object falls upon them, while a larger thing breaks through them and escapes." (Solon).

We face a major problem in specifying the link between a claim to legitimacy and the attitude of a particular audience. Most people, after all, know very little about particular laws or the legal system. We can wonder whether those who lose when they come before the courts are impressed by the majesty of the law. Few convicted murderers, for example, comment favorably on the skill with which the judge instructed the jury. Indeed, perhaps the major audience for the law's claims to legitimacy are lawyers. Whatever the impact of law on our views about legitimacy, do these attitudes affect our behavior? Do people obey or disobey law because they think it just or unjust?

Having said all this, we can observe that lawyers and judges do make legitimacy claims. Much of the business of law school consists of studying this rhetoric. Although the legitimacy claim often is assumed, law professors, lawyers and judges exert great effort to show that a rule or procedure reflects some version of the good, the true, and the beautiful. The problem comes when we recognize that each side usually can claim plausibly that a decision in its favor will carry out an important value. If this is true, how do we persuade judges and legislators? How do we predict what they will do? If both sides had equally able lawyers, would all cases end in ties?

In the pages that follow we will first look at explanations offered for holding or refusing to hold people to obligations which might be called contracts. We will try to select problems important to modern business. We will also set the stage for the remaining materials which raise problems of performing contracts. We will see that the two questions are closely related. Whether or not I have performed my promise often turns on what, if anything, the courts will say that I promised to do.

A. CHOICE, FAULT, OR SOMETHING ELSE?

EMBRY v. HARGADINE, MCKITTRICK DRY GOODS CO.
Court of Appeals of Missouri
127 Mo. App. 383, 105 S.W. 777 (1907)

GOODE, J. . . . The appellant was an employee of the respondent company under a written contract to expire December 15, 1903, at a salary of $2,000 per annum. His duties were to attend to the sample department of respondent, of which he was given complete charge. It was his business to select samples for the traveling salesmen of the company, which is a wholesale dry goods concern, to use in selling goods to retail merchants. Appellant contends that on December 23, 1903, he was re-engaged by respondent, through its president, Thos. H. McKittrick, for another year at the same compensation and for the same duties stipulated in his previous written contract. On March 1, 1904, he was discharged, having been notified in February that, on account of the necessity of retrenching expenses, his services and that of some other employees would no longer be required. The respondent company contends that its president never re-employed appellant after the termination of his written contract, and hence that it had a right to discharge him when it chose. The point with which we are concerned requires an epitome of the testimony of appellant and the counter-testimony of McKittrick, the president of the company, in reference to the alleged re-employment. Appellant testified that several times prior to the termination of his written contract on December 15, 1903, he had endeavored to get an understanding with McKittrick for another year, but had been put off from time to time; that on December 23d, eight days after the expiration of said contract, he called on McKittrick, in the latter's office, and said to him that as appellant's written employment had lapsed eight days before, and as there were only a few days between then and the first of January in which to seek employment with other firms, if respondent wished to retain his services longer he must have a contract for another year, or he would quit respondent's service then and there; that he had been put off twice before and wanted an understanding or contract at once so that he could go ahead without worry; that McKittrick asked him how he was getting along in his department, and appellant said he was very busy, as they were in the height of the season getting men out—had about 110 salesmen on the line and others in preparation; that McKittrick then said: "Go ahead, you're all right; get your men out and don't let that worry you;" that appellant took McKittrick at his word and worked until February 15th without any question in his mind. It was on February 15th that he was notified his services would be discontinued on March 1st. McKittrick denied this conversation as related by appellant and said that, when accosted by the latter on December 23d, he (McKittrick) was working on his books in order to get out a report for a stockholders' meeting, and, when appellant said if he did not get a contract he would leave, that he (McKittrick) said:

> "Mr. Embry, I am just getting ready for the stockholders' meeting tomorrow, I have no time to take it up now; I have told you before I would not take it up until I had these matters out of the way; you will have to see me at a later time. I said: 'Go back upstairs and get your men out on the

road.' I may have asked him one or two other questions relative to the department; I don't remember. The whole conversation did not take more than a minute."

Embry also swore that when he was notified he would be discharged, he complained to McKittrick about it, as being a violation of their contract, and McKittrick said it was due to the action of the board of directors, and not to any personal action of his, and that others would suffer by what the board had done as well as Embry. Appellant requested an instruction to the jury setting out, in substance, the conversation between him and McKittrick according to his version, and declaring that those facts, if found to be true, constituted a contract between the parties that defendant would pay plaintiff the sum of $2,000 for another year, provided the jury believed from the evidence that plaintiff commenced said work believing he was to have $2,000 for the year's work. This instruction was refused, but the court gave another embodying in substance appellant's version of the conversation, and declaring it made a contract "if you (the jury) find both parties thereby intended and did contract with each other for plaintiff's employment for one year from and including December 23, 1903, at a salary of $2,000 per annum." Embry swore that on several occasions when he spoke to McKittrick about employment for the ensuing year, he asked for a renewal of his former contract, and that on December 23d, the date of the alleged renewal, he went into Mr. McKittrick's office and told him his contract had expired and he wanted to renew it for a year, having always worked under year contracts. Neither the refused instruction nor the one given by the court embodied facts quite as strong as appellant's testimony, because neither referred to appellant's alleged statement to McKittrick that unless he was re-employed he would stop work for respondent then and there.

It is assigned for error that the court required the jury, in order to return a verdict for appellant, not only to find the conversation occurred as appellant swore, but that both parties intended by such conversation to contract with each other for plaintiff's employment for the year from December, 1903, at a salary of $2,000. If it appeared from the record that there was a dispute between the parties as to the terms on which appellant wanted re-employment, there might have been sound reason for inserting this clause in the instruction; but no issue was made that they split on terms; the testimony of McKittrick tending to prove only that he refused to enter into a contract with appellant regarding another year's employment until the annual meeting of stockholders was out of the way. Indeed, as to the proposed terms McKittrick agrees with Embry; for the former swore as follows: "Mr. Embry said he wanted to know *about the renewal of his contract*; said if he did not have the contract made he would leave." As the two witnesses coincided as to the terms of the proposed re-employment, there was no reason for inserting the above mentioned clause in the instruction in order that it might be settled by the jury whether or not plaintiff, if employed for one year from December 23, 1903, was to be paid $2,000 a year. Therefore it remains to determine whether or not this part of the instruction was a correct statement of the law in regard to what was necessary to constitute a contract between the parties; that is to say, whether the formation of a contract by what, according to Embry was said, depended on the intention of both Embry and McKittrick. Or, to put the question more precisely, did what was said constitute a contract of re-employment on the previous terms irrespective of the intention or purpose of McKittrick?

Judicial opinion and elementary treatises abound in statements of the rule that to constitute a contract there must be a meeting of the minds of the parties, and both must agree to the same thing in the same sense. Generally speaking this may be true; but it is not literally or universally true. That is to say, the inner intention of parties to a conversation subsequently alleged to create a contract cannot either make a contract of what transpired, or prevent one from arising, if the words used were sufficient to constitute a contract. In so far as their intention is an influential element, it is only such intention as the words or acts of the parties indicate; not one secretly cherished which is inconsistent with those words or acts. . . .

In *Smith v. Hughes*, L. R. 6 Q. B. 597, 607, it was said:

> If, whatever a man's real intention may be, he so conducts himself that a reasonable man would believe that he was assenting to the terms proposed by the other party, and that other party upon that belief enters into the contract with him, the man thus conducting himself would be equally bound as if he intended to agree to the other party's terms.

. . . In view of those authorities we hold that, though McKittrick may not have intended to employ Embry by what transpired between them according to the latter's testimony, yet if what McKittrick said would have been taken by a reasonable man to be an employment, and Embry so understood it, it constituted a valid contract of employment for the ensuing year.

The next question is whether or not the language used was of that character; namely, was such that Embry, as a reasonable man, might consider he was re-employed for the ensuing year on the previous terms, and act accordingly. We do not say that in every instance it would be for the court to pronounce on this question, because, peradventure, instances might arise in which there would be such an ambiguity in the language relied on to show an assent by the obligor to the proposal of the obligee, that it would be for the jury to say whether a reasonable mind would take it to signify acceptance of the proposal. . . . In *Lancaster v. Elliott*, 28 Mo. App. 86, 92, the opinion, as to the immediate point, reads:

> The interpretation of a contract in writing is always a matter of law for determination by the court, and equally so, upon like principles, is the question what acts and words, in nearly every case, will suffice to constitute an acceptance by one party, of a proposal submitted by the other, so that a contract or agreement thereby becomes matured.

The general rule is that it is for the court to construe the effect of writings relied on to make a contract, and also the effect of unambiguous oral words. . . . However, if the words are in dispute, the question of whether they were used or not is for the jury. . . . With these rules of law in mind, let us recur to the conversation of December 23d between Embry and McKittrick as related by the former. Embry was demanding a renewal of his contract, saying he had been put off from time to time, and that he had only a few days before the end of the year in which to seek employment from other houses, and that he would quit then and there unless he was re-employed. McKittrick inquired how he was getting along with the department and Embry said they (i.e., the employees of the department) were very busy getting out salesmen. Whereupon McKittrick said: "Go ahead, you are all right. Get your men out, and do not let that worry you." We think no reasonable man would construe that answer to Embry's demand that he be employed for another year, otherwise than as an assent to the demand, and that Embry had the right to rely on it as an assent. The natural inference is, though we do not find it testified to, that Embry was at work getting samples ready for the salesmen to use during the ensuing season. Now, when he was complaining of the worry and mental distress he was under because of his uncertainty about the future, and his urgent need, either of an immediate contract with respondent, or a refusal by it to make one, leaving him free to seek employment elsewhere, McKittrick must have answered as he did for the purpose of assuring appellant that any apprehension was needless, as appellant's services would be retained by the respondent. The answer was unambiguous, and we rule that if the conversation was according to appellant's version, and he understood he was employed, it constituted in law a valid contract of re-employment, and the court erred in making the formation of a contract depend on a finding that both parties intended to make one. It was only necessary that Embry, as a reasonable man, had a right to and did so understand. . . .

The judgment is reversed, and the cause remanded. All concur.

NOTES AND QUESTIONS

1. *Individual choice and freedom*: Some see the legitimacy of contract resting on its connection with individual choice. People have rights, and they do not lose them unless they freely choose to do so. However, the court in the *Embry* case abridges Thos. H. McKittrick's freedom. It exposes his business to liability even if, upon retrial, a jury were to find he did not intend to make a contract. Does this mean that assertions about contract and free choice are largely mystification?

2. *A consent theory of contract*: Professor Barnett advocates what he calls a consent theory of contract.[2] He says "contract law concerns enforceable obligations arising from the valid *transfer* of entitlements that are *already vested* in someone, and this difference is what makes consent a moral prerequisite to contractual obligation." Law has a boundary-defining function. As a result, courts must protect the reliance of others. However, he continues, "[t]he consent that is required is a *manifestation of an intention* to alienate rights. In a system of entitlements where manifested rights transfers are what justify the legal enforcement of agreements, any such manifestation necessarily implies that one intends to be 'legally bound,' to adhere to one's commitment. Therefore, the phrase 'a manifestation of an intention to be legally bound' neatly captures what a court should seek to find before holding that a contractual obligation has been created."[3] Under Barnett's theory, would the *Embry* case be decided differently? Would a reasonable person in the employee's position have understood that his boss intended

---

[2] Barnett, *A Consent Theory of Contract*, 86 Colum. L. Rev. 269, 297 (1986).
[3] *Id.* at 304.

to be legally bound to the employee? Suppose that I manifest an intent to be legally bound to a contract, but, in fact, I do not intend subjectively to be legally bound. If a court holds me to what a reasonable person can take as my intention, in what sense does liability rest on consent or choice?

Tiersma[4] argues for a different intention. He relies on speech act theory, a widely used approach to the philosophy of language. Offer and acceptance are not matters of expression or manifestation of intent. They are acts that commit a speaker to a particular course of content. Thus, "[l]oosely stated, the speaker must intend to create in the hearer the perception that in saying the words, the speaker is committing himself to a particular proposal." Under this theory, would the *Embry* case be decided differently? Tiersma asserts it would not. He bases this on the conversational maxims of Grice, a philosopher of language. Most parties will interpret an utterance as being relevant to what went before. Considering the *Embry* case, Tiersma says:

> The primary reason that "Don't worry about it" can constitute acceptance of the employee's implicit offer has to do with Grice's conversational maxim of relevance. A literal interpretation of the employer's statement would not be a relevant answer to the employee's concern. Therefore, this possible interpretation can be eliminated. All that remains is the more idiomatic meaning of the phrase as a promise to dispose of the employee's concern. The employer's response was relevant only as an acceptance.[5]

Does Tiersma's analysis just quoted establish that the employer intended to create in the employee the perception that the employer was committing himself to a year's renewal of the contract?

By the way, how likely is it that either Embry's or McKittrick's recollection of the December 23, 1903 conversation was entirely accurate? How should the reliability of the evidence affect the legal rule, if at all?

3. *Contract as a variety of tort: committing contracts*: In *Hotchkiss v. National City Bank of New York,*[6] Judge Learned Hand said:

> A contract has, strictly speaking, nothing to do with the personal, or individual, intent of the parties. A contract is an obligation attached by the mere force of law to certain acts of the parties, usually words, which ordinarily accompany and represent a known intent. If, however, it were proved by twenty bishops that either party, when he used the words, intended something else than the usual meaning which the law imposes upon them, he would still be held, unless there were some mutual mistake, or something else of the sort. Of course, if it appear by other words, or acts, of the parties, that they attribute a peculiar meaning to such words as they use in the contract, that meaning will prevail, but only by virtue of the other words, and not because of their unexpressed intent.

[4] Comment, *The Language of Offer and Acceptance: Speech Acts and the Question of Intent*, 74 Cal. L. Rev. 189, 189 (1986).
[5] *Id.* at 210.
[6] 200 F. 287, 293 (S.D. N.Y. 1911).

Hand is expressing what Professor Grant Gilmore called the Holmes-Williston construct. Holmes offered the idea in the late 19th century, and Williston developed it in the early 20th century. It certainly had great influence on the vocabulary of generations of law students. Often they talked about the objective theory of contracts.[7]

> [T]he "objective theory of contract" became the great metaphysical solvent—the critical test for distinguishing between the false and the true. . . . [T]he post-Holmesian "objectivists," led by Williston, made no attempt to argue that their principle had any common law past. Perhaps the attempt would have overtaxed even their own very considerable ingenuity. On the contrary, the emergence and triumph of the "objective theory" was put forward as one of the great accomplishments of recent times—the apprehension of a fundamental truth which had long been hidden in a deep morass of error. . . .
>
> The effect of the application of the objective theory to such areas of law as mistake was of course to narrow the range within which mistake could be successfully pleaded as a defense. That is, it is no longer enough that I was subjectively mistaken, even with respect to a fundamental term of the contract. . . . With the narrowing of the range of availability of such excuses as mistake, we move toward the ideal of absolute liability which . . . was one of the basic ideas of the great theory.[8]

4. *A theory about the rise of objective theory*: Holmes's lectures on "The Common Law" were first published in 1881; Williston's great treatise on the American law of contracts was first published in 1920. Why did an objective theory of contracts appeal to men such as Holmes and Williston? Why were they able to sell it to the elite of the American bar at this period? Professor Morton Horwitz, a legal historian on the Harvard Law School faculty, argues that Holmes and Williston merely reflected a battle largely won earlier. This battle served distinct social ends. Horwitz tells us,

---

[7] In contrast, a subjective theory of contract would require that both offeror and offeree actually intend to make a bargain. The classic way of putting this is that there must be a "meeting of the minds." Judges and lawyers still use the phrase. For example, it appears in over 500 cases reported by LEXIS from January 1, 2001 to December 31, 2001. Of course, many of these decisions could be explained on the basis of an objective theory as well. An advocate must watch for misleading dicta selected from only part of an opinion. For example, in Midway Airlines, Inc. v. Northwest Airlines, Inc., 180 B.R. 851 (N.D. Ill. 1995), the court says: "[I]t is essential that the parties to the agreement have a meeting of the minds, and that they truly assent to the same things in the same sense on all of the [agreement's] essential terms and conditions." But then, several pages later, the court comments: "A literal meeting of the minds, however, is not required for an enforceable contract. . . . In determining the intent of the parties, the Court focuses on the parties' objective manifestations of intent and not on their subjective beliefs." Can an advocate arguing for a meeting of the minds standard ethically quote the first statement to a court without quoting the second?

Whenever the law makes a state of mind relevant, someone must prove it. Almost always we infer a state of mind from external manifestations. Thus, even if courts adopted a true meeting of the minds standard, they would look to objective manifestations of intent.

See Joseph M. Perillo, *The Origins of the Objective Theory of Contract Formation and Interpretation*, 69 Fordham L. Rev. 427 (2000).

[8] Grant Gilmore, THE DEATH OF CONTRACT 42-44 (1974).

For seventy or eighty years after the American Revolution the major direction of common law policy reflected the overthrow of eighteenth century pre-commercial and anti-developmental common law values. As political and economic power shifted to merchant and entrepreneurial groups in the post-revolutionary period, they began to forge an alliance with the legal profession to advance their own interests through a transformation of the legal system.

By around 1850, that transformation was largely complete. Legal rules providing for the subsidization of enterprise and permitting the legal destruction of old forms of property for the benefit of more recent entrants had triumphed. Anti-commercial legal doctrines had been destroyed or under-mined and the legal system had almost completely shed its eighteenth century commitment to regulating the substantive fairness of economic exchange. Legal relations that had once been conceived of as deriving from natural law or custom were increasingly subordinated to the disproportionate economic power of individuals or corporations that were allowed the right to "contract out" of many existing legal obligations. Law, once conceived of as protective, regulative, paternalistic and, above all, a paramount expression of the moral sense of the community, had come to be thought of as facilitative of individual desires and as simply reflective of the existing organization of economic and political power.

This transformation in American law both aided and ratified a major shift in power in an increasingly market-oriented society. By the middle of the nineteenth century the legal system had been reshaped to the advantage of men of commerce and industry at the expense of farmers, workers, consumers, and other less powerful groups within the society. Not only had the law come to establish legal doctrines that maintained the new distribution of economic and political power, but, wherever it could, it actively promoted a legal redistribution of wealth against the weakest groups in the society.

The rise of legal formalism can be fully correlated with the attainment of these substantive legal changes. If a flexible, instrumental conception of law was necessary to promote the transformation of the post-revolutionary American legal system, it was no longer needed once the major beneficiaries of that transformation had obtained the bulk of their objectives. Indeed, once successful, those groups could only benefit if both the recent origins and the foundations in policy and group self-interest of all newly established legal doctrines could be disguised. There were, in short, major advantages in creating an intellectual system which gave common law rules the appearance of being self-contained, apolitical, and inexorable, and which, by making "legal reasoning seem like mathematics," conveyed, "an air . . . of . . . inevitability" about legal decisions. . . .

Contract law provides another excellent illustration of the deep pressure towards formalism in nineteenth century law. During the first half of the century, legal writers and judges were largely successful in banishing fair price conceptions from the law of contract and in shifting the focus of contract law to the determination of whether there had been a "meeting of minds." As a result, one of the central problems of the "new" contract law was the development of supposedly "non-political" criteria for distinguishing between "free" and "unfree" wills, while at the same time barring any substantive inquiry into the equivalency of an exchange, which now had come to be regarded as "subjective" and "political." This proscription against examining "consequences" or "outcomes" eventually led to the creation of a disembodied conception of "unfree" states of mind which measured the impairment of "will" by criteria entirely detached from concrete social or economic forms of coercion. . . .

These efforts during the first half of the nineteenth century to disengage the contract system from substantive criteria of fairness produced internal pressures to generate "objective" and "non-political" doctrinal measures of "free will" and "meeting of the minds." These pressures were generalized still further beginning in the 1850's into an "objective" theory of contract. What most distinguished the "objective" theory was its insistence upon establishing uniform and general rules of law with reference to which contracting parties would be required to shape their conduct. With this change, contract law was no longer conceived of as simply implementing the parties' "wills," but rather its categories were often treated as existing somehow prior to individual bargains. . . .

[E]conomic pressures towards uniformity and predictability, as well as the efforts to restrict the scope of jury discretion, also ultimately contributed to this shift toward formal and objective legal rules. But it is important to see as well that this trend towards uniformity necessarily required doctrines of greater abstraction and generality, which in turn had the effect of detaching contract doctrine from the particularities of individual cases and of creating internal logical pressure to conceive of the law of contract as a system of disembodied logical interrelationships. This tendency throughout the second half of the nineteenth century to seek higher levels of generality and inclusiveness of legal doctrine is one of the more important characteristics associated with the development of legal formalism. One of the most important results of this trend in thought was to prevent particularized equitable inquiries into the circumstances of individual cases and to destroy more particular legal rules in the name of promoting the "rule of law." . . .

There were, in short, extremely deep and powerful currents which moved American law to formalism after 1850. . . . A scientific, objective, professional, and apolitical conception of law, once primarily a rhetorical monopoly of a status-hungry elite of legal thinkers, now comes to extend its domain and to infiltrate into the every day categories of adjudication. . . .

For the paramount social condition that is necessary for legal formalism to flourish in a society is for the powerful groups in that society to have a great interest in disguising and suppressing the inevitably political and redistributive functions of law.[9]

Horwitz's positions on many issues have been criticized sharply. For example, Professor A.W.B. Simpson responds,

> No doubt certain aspects of contract law pressed on the poor— imprisonment for debt is surely the principal villain here. But . . . it was their misfortune to be outside the world in which such luxuries as legal actions at common law or bills in equity much mattered.[10]

Scheiber also questions interpretations that ignore what he sees as the complexities of American history.

> [T]he courts *did not* inexorably devolve advantage upon industrial interests at the expense of agrarian interests (the very dichotomy is inapplicable in the West except on fundamentally different terms). Nor did the courts predictably mobilize either "instrumentalist" or "formalist" doctrine to defend and advance large scale industrial aggregates. Both judicial defenses of "rights of the public" and judicial surprises, in choosing between contending economic interests, are prominent enough to cast doubt on any simplistic model of unilinear and monolithic doctrinal innovation. There is ample room for agreement that law was often, if not to say usually, mobilized to provide effective subsidies and immunities to heavily capitalized special interests without leaping to the simplistic corollaries that some scholars have advanced.[11]

Remember that an application of the objective theory favors an employee over an employer in the *Embry* case. Does this, combined with Simpson's and Scheiber's comments, suggest that Horwitz's position can be ignored safely?

5. *Value conflict in contract law*: Modern contract law contains many inconsistent goals. If we accept Horwitz's explanation for the appeal of the objective theory, we also must explain legal realism and its attacks on formalism that began about World War I. We then would have to turn to reactions to realism. Scholars searched for neutral principles for decision in the early 1960s. Law and economics offers another attack on appeals to fairness and case-by-case reactions to situations in the 1970s.

The following excerpts from Professor Macaulay's article attempt to sketch some of the conflicting goals set for contract law. Notice that Macaulay's discussion is empirical and descriptive. Unlike Horwitz, Macaulay does not link any of the approaches he identifies with the interests of particular classes or groups. Nonetheless, do some of the approaches he identifies seem to serve some interests more than others? Might an approach serve manufacturers at one time but, say, consumers at another?

---

[9] Morton J. Horwitz, *The Rise of Legal Formalism*, 19 Am. J. Legal Hist. 251, 251-52, 259, 261-262, 264 (1975). Reprinted by permission.

[10] Simpson, *The Horwitz Thesis and the History of Contracts*, 46 U. Chi. L. Rev. 533, 601 (1979).

[11] Harry N. Scheiber, *Regulation, Property Rights, and Definition of "The Market": Law and the American Economy*, 41 J. Econ. Hist. 103, 109 (1981). Published by Cambridge University Press. Reprinted with the permission of Cambridge University Press.

Private Legislation and the Duty to Read—Business Run by IBM
Machine, the Law of Contracts and Credit Cards
Stewart Macaulay[12]

An analytical scheme I find helpful calls for first separating out the substantive policies that contract and restitution may serve and then identifying at least some of the goals related to the proper or efficient operation of the legal system. For example, we might want our legal system to aid the operation of the insurance industry in order to minimize premium costs (a substantive policy), but we also might want our legal system, insofar as reasonably possible, to reflect the policy choices of a community consensus or those made by an elected legislature rather than those of an appointed judge (a system policy).

Substantive policies primarily can be classified on two dimensions. The first concerns a choice of a market or non-market orientation, in which contract law and restitution can either (a) be tools to facilitate the operation of a market economy—focusing on the needs of those exchanging goods, services, labor and capital or (b) serve to blunt the impact of the unregulated market by refusing to recognize some socially undesirable business practices or by giving aid to people or groups seeking to get out from under onerous contracts. The second dimension concerns the approaches by which contract law and restitution can proceed, tending *toward* either (a) relatively precise general rules or (b) a case-by-case approach.[13] This classification yields four primary categories which must be explained in some detail. The categories, and their somewhat arbitrary names, can be represented as follows:

	Market Goals	**Other than Market Goals**
Generalizing approach ("rules")	a. market functioning policy	c. social (or economic) planning policy
Particularistic approach ("case-by-case")	b. transactional policy	d. relief-of-hardship policy

a. *Market functioning policy* calls for rules of general application in relatively specific terms which minimize (but never eliminate) the creative role of judge and jury or administrators. Predictable law is to be preferred to results that satisfy

---

[12] 19 Vand. L. Rev. 1051, 1056-65 (1966). Reprinted with permission.

[13] Of course, my transactional and market functioning categories differ from the orthodox learning about the meeting of the minds (subjective theory) and the objective theory of contracts. I would view a meeting of the minds approach as entirely a non-market approach; it usually operates as a rationalization for relief-of-hardship. Moreover, there are many kinds of objective theories which fall on the scale that ranges from transactional to market functioning. At one extreme, an objective theory can mean that a contract neither party intended but both appear to have made will be enforced. At the other extreme, transactional policy can call for imposing liability on one who has, without using due care, misled another by his language and conduct, even though the careless person did not "intend" to make a contract. As is apparent from this discussion, my categories are not dichotomies but extreme points on a range: a given rule or standard is *more or less*, say, transactional or market functional, or *more or less*, say, transactional or based on relief-of-hardship.

in particular cases. Thus the parties can consider the impact of contract law both in planning their bargains and in settling disputes. Legal results will not turn on vague abstractions such as "good faith" but on specific conduct such as signing a contract. In addition to certainty, the rules should tend to reward rational assessment of risks in the market and penalize unbusiness like conduct. One can usefully identify at least three products of market functioning policy: increased self-reliance, rewards to the crafty, and advantages to the operation of bureaucratic organizations.

The duty to read in a fairly strict form carries out the substantive goal. The legal system should enforce contracts "as written" and ignore pleas that one party did not read or understand, that the parties agreed that some of the written terms would not apply or that additional ones which were never reduced to writing would apply, and that the words used should be read in some unusual fashion, or in light of some general abstraction such as "reasonableness." On the basis of common sense but not much evidence, some have assumed that this tack will promote self-reliance. If one knows he will be legally bound to what he signs, he will take care to protect himself (or so it is said). And this would be a good thing. People will recognize risks, allocate them in their bargains and plan to deal with them rationally. As a result, more bargains will approach the economists' ideal where both leave the bargaining table in a better position than when the negotiations began. Moreover, disputes during the life of the transaction should tend to be minimized since the process of reading and understanding should make clear who is to do what and who is to take what loss if a particular risk occurs. Also where the legal result is clearly that documents will mean what they say, there is less chance that in settlement negotiations one party's rights must be discounted because of the risk of what a jury might do or because of delay.

Such rules reward those who plan and are careful. In one view those who can drive the best bargains, short of gross fraud, are entitled to their winnings. Perhaps one who can slip into a contract with terms highly favorable to himself which are undetected by the other party, is to be praised for his skill rather than censured. This is just good salesmanship. In this view, a bargain is not an exchange of mutual advantage but a game where each party is to maximize his own gains at the expense of the other. Some may feel that the ability to do well in this game is a skill to be rewarded. A strict duty-to-read rule often will help supply this reward.

Another product of market functioning policy—advantages to the operation of bureaucratic organizations—often derives from people being treated as if they had read and understood a written contract even when it is probable they have not done so. Large economic organizations frequently promulgate rules to govern their exchanges with other organizations and individuals. Typically these rules are cast, or can be cast, in the form of a contract. The other unit's representative or the other individual signs a printed form document or accepts a contractual symbol (say, delivery of a document or goods) although he has little chance or incentive to read, understand, bargain to change the rules or do any or all of these things. Larger firms operate this way for a number of reasons. They must deal through a corps of agents in a myriad of transactions. As a result, there is a need to standardize and formalize procedures. On one hand, the large organization must control its agents who deal with the outside world and limit their power to "give the company away." These agents are under many pressures to treat their customers as individuals and tailor the particular deal to suit their customers' needs; most obvious is the pressure to make sales to earn commissions or promotions. Also, "the customer is always right" in the salesman's world. A rigid form contract which the customer must sign without alteration often is thought to be an efficient way to exercise control over salesmen. The customer is "on notice" of the salesman's limited authority, and the firm wants to avoid being legally bound to expectations its salesman has created by his conduct that are inconsistent with company policy. On the other hand, the written document signed by the customer becomes the obligation within the larger organization because of the problems of internal communication. It specifies what must be produced or shipped, and it indicates the full extent of future payments to be received and contingent obligations assumed. If a salesman has made a promise inconsistent with the formal written contract which is highly standardized, it is difficult to communicate this to those who must perform and to those who must make plans based on cash flow and risk assumption. Even if the inconsistent promise is communicated, it poses a problem for a rational bureaucratic organization which tends to thrive on routine. Large organizations are helped if they can control and plan their exposure to risks; if they can do so, their accounting and pricing will be more accurate, and they will not have to set up large reserves to cover a host of unpredictable contingencies. Arguably, this kind of certainty will foster their activities in the market which in turn should yield more jobs and more products at lower prices. A rather strict duty to read, rather than attacking the balance of economic power in the society, supports the operations of large organizations that have this power. This tends to promote rational business affairs, whatever the impact on the individual who assumed he could rely on what he was told rather than what he signed. . . .

Usually these bureaucratic considerations are coupled with the self-reliance idea—the large organization can deal through standardized forms and the prudent individual will protect himself by reading and taking appropriate action—although at times the likelihood of self protection is slim indeed. Occasionally, bureaucratic policy is coupled with a requirement designed to help self-reliance. For example, a Virginia statute demands that a written contract be set in a certain size type to be legally enforceable, the Uniform Commercial Code requires some warranty disclaimers to be conspicuous to be effective.

b. *Transactional policy*, the second policy category, also seeks to aid the operation of the market, but with a case-by-case strategy rather than by rules that ignore particular circumstances. The courts ought to take steps to carry out the particular transaction brought before them—they should discover the bargain-in-fact and enforce it with appropriate remedies cut to fit the facts of the case. If this discovery is not possible, the court should work out a result involving the least disruption of plans and causing the least amount of reliance loss in light of the situation at the time of the dispute. In short, courts should seek to implement the "sense of the transaction," and thus solve the problem in the particular case in market terms—assumption of the risk, reasonable reliance, and so on.

Transactional policy calls for a duty to read and understand only where the one who has failed to do this is responsible for misleading the other into believing that the document has been read and approved or that the careless one is willing to sign and assume the risk of whatever might be found in the document. Suppose seller sends buyer an offer quoting a price in a letter which also very clearly spells out a number of conditions the seller says are most important to him. The buyer reads the first few sentences of the letter and the price quoted but not the seller's important conditions. The buyer writes on the bottom margin of the seller's letter, "We accept your offer," and signs it; he then mails this back to the seller who begins production of the items in question. The buyer later wants to back out and asserts he did not read the seller's conditions and would not have agreed to them if he had. The buyer has been negligent in conveying his agreement, resulting in disappointed plans and at least the probability of a good deal of reliance loss. A court following a transactional approach would treat the buyer *as if* he had read and understood the seller's letter. But the decision would turn on the rather extreme facts of the case—the buyer's communication was careless and caused either very probable or actual injury.

Perhaps more often transactional policy will call for overturning or modifying a written document (by reforming or construing it) in the light of the bargain-in-fact of the parties. While a case can be made for self-reliance, part of decent social and business conduct is trust. In many negotiation situations all of the pressures push for friendly gestures rather than a suspicious line-by-line analysis of the writing. The buyer of home siding can believe the president of the home remodeling company when he says his siding will not rust or crack; the buyer does not have to parse the text of the lengthy and technical printed form and spot the integration clause at his peril. In cases such as this, the writing was drafted to run counter to the likely agreement-in-fact. If a court is seeking the actual sense of the transaction, it will not let such a writing get in its way. . . .

c. *Social planning policies* can be reflected in contracts and restitution, as well. In one sense, rather than enforcing the bargain that was made, in this third type of policy the courts will enforce the bargain which the parties should have made. Conversely, the courts may refuse to take any action when the actual bargain is found offensive. This policy is something of a catchall, as social planning can call for a variety of things ranging from wealth redistribution to the regulation, or even promotion, of particular types of people, industries or transactions. The most obvious examples involve a change in the market context by removing certain types of bargains from the kinds that will be enforced by the legal system or by requiring or prohibiting particular terms in some bargains. Again, this is a generalizing approach stressing specific rules, so it parallels market functioning policy in strategy—but the goals of the two are very different since social planning policies, by definition, seek to blunt the impact of the market.

A social planning rule relevant to our topic would be one that said certain classes of people could not be held to contracts they signed or accepted, despite their careless failure to read and protect themselves. One could conceive of a rule protecting such people as consumers, illiterates, those of limited mental ability or minors. In effect, the power of a minor to disaffirm even contracts that he has read and understood is such a rule. Since, in theory, the minor cannot guard his own interests, the legal system protects him from his own carelessness and improvident bargains. Consumers may get some of the same treatment under Uniform Commercial Code section 2-719's provisions on limiting remedies for breach of warranty; perhaps consumers need not read and protect themselves since limitations of liability for personal injury caused by a breach of warranty are prima facie unconscionable. It is difficult to offer many examples of this kind of social planning rule since the legal system has preferred a more case-by-case (relief of hardship) approach, rather than letting a whole class of people out of certain kinds of contracts. On the other hand, social planning goals often enter as the price for following the bureaucratic type of market functioning policy. For example, the standard fire insurance policy is set by statute in many states. One side of the coin involves the setting of terms deemed fair to the consumer by the legislature—removing the insurance contract from the area of self-reliance and the exercise of market power. The other side of the coin, however, involves telling insurance companies that if they follow the statute, certain practices have been validated. An insurance company can know where it stands, and this certainty may be extremely important to it. The insurers get certainty at the cost of following fair terms imposed by the legal system.

d. *Relief-of-hardship* is the fourth policy. It calls for the legal system to let one party out of his bargain in exceptional cases where enforcement would be unduly harsh, or, where the content of the bargain is in doubt, to place the burden on the party best able to spread the loss or absorb it. This case-by-case approach is based not upon considerations of market functioning or protecting actual expectations but upon ethical ideals and emotional reactions to the plight of the underdog, to pressing an advantage too far, to making too much profit, or to inequality of resources. To a great extent, this is the policy that is not expressed openly in contract doctrine, but courts can construe language and stretch the innocent misrepresentation or mistake doctrines to help out when the facts are particularly appealing. When done with a deft hand, a relief-of-hardship approach will leave little trace of a precedent to embarrass the court in the next case, where the facts are not quite so appealing.

It is hard to offer a pure example of this policy in operation, but it can be suggested that a good deal of it lurks in the insurance release cases where a duty to read and understand sometimes is and sometimes is not applied. Also the Supreme Court of Wisconsin in several cases has stressed the lack of education of the person seeking to be relieved from a written contract he signed or accepted. On one hand, this factor tracks with transaction-al policy and the degree of care one could expect from a particular individual. Arguably, an illiterate is not responsible for misleading one who knows the illiterate cannot read the document he signed. But on the other hand, the party seeking to uphold the contract, especially the home office of a corporation that deals through salesmen in the field, may have no way accurately to gauge the education and literacy of the man who signed the printed form. Its expectations and potential reliance remain despite the literacy of the man it dealt with. Still the factor may lead to the overthrow of the written treaty. We can speculate that the inability to read and understand is correlated with a generally low socio-economic status, and such people may be the best candidates for relief-of-hardship in the eyes of many.

B. THE RISK OF AMBIGUITY OR MISUNDERSTANDING

People make a number of different kinds of mistakes in entering contracts. Sometimes the law lets a mistaken party back out. Sometimes it doesn't. A true Holmes-Williston objective theory draws sharp lines. The cases, however, are blurred.

Suppose I write a letter saying that I will sell my house to you for $200,000. You accept my offer. However, I own two houses. One is located in the city where I work. The other is located about 100 miles away in a resort area. I always refer to the house in the city as "my house." I call the one in the resort area "my cottage." However, the cottage is an architect-designed large house built on the shore of a beautiful lake. I thought I was selling my house in the city. You, however, thought you were buying my house in the resort area. You did not know that I usually called one the house and the other the cottage. If courts are concerned with my free choice, they will hesitate before deciding that I sold a house I did not want to sell. Of course, I did use language that could refer to two different structures, but this is not the same thing as choosing to sell my house. Nonetheless, you also made a choice, and my letter prompted you to create certain expectations. A court cannot simultaneously protect both my choice and yours.

Suppose, to change the case, both of us correctly understand my letter to refer to my house in the city. You accept my offer to sell the house for $200,000. Later you discover that the house is worth no more than $150,000. If you had known this, you would not have bought it. Is this kind of error different from that suggested by our conflicting interpretations of the term "house"?

Suppose, instead, I submit a bid to you. I propose to do all the electrical work involved in constructing a large building which you are erecting. When I was compiling the information needed to make my bid, the piece of paper on which my assistant had calculated the cost of wiring the third floor fell into my wastebasket. I did not notice this. As a result, I neglected to take the cost of the work on the third floor into my calculations. My bid is much lower than it would have been had I not made a mistake. Is this a kind of mistake different from those involved in the examples about ambiguity and value of an asset?

Suppose we applied an objective theory of contract to all of these cases. A reasonable person hearing or reading the offer and acceptance would assume a deal had been closed. Outward manifestations look as if there were a deal. All of the mistakes are subjective. To recognize them, a court would have to look past the form of bargain to the actual situation. We can defend holding seller and buyer to a contract in all three cases. Such a rule promotes reliance and protects reasonable expectations. Such a rule punishes mistakes and thus offers an incentive for care to avoid them. The person making an error will be taught a lesson. Moreover, others learning of the result will shape up or take the consequences. Not insignificantly, this rule makes the court's job much easier too. We will often hear this song played loudly in the cases. However, there also is a powerful counter theme which we cannot ignore, reflecting our sensitivity to the harsh consequences of applying such an approach.

1. CHOICE AND THE CARELESS USE OF LANGUAGE

Sharp and Fox offer an ethical analysis of the problem of mistake.

The rule for interpretation of ambiguous promises and contracts was laid down by William Paley in the classical discussion of the subject . . . . It will be found in his *Moral Philosophy* (1785), Book III, Part I, Chapters 5 and 6, and reads as follows: "Where the terms of the promise admit of more senses than one, the promise is to be performed in that sense in which the promiser apprehended at the time that the promisee received it." . . . [M]orality is a matter of intent. My obligations to the promisee accordingly depend on the answer to this question: What expectations did I intend to arouse in him? And since . . . desired results may sometimes be obtained by silence as effectively as by any other means, we must go farther and say: I am responsible not merely for those expectations which I actively strove to create, but also for those which I knowingly allowed the promisee to entertain at the time of the promise. And this is precisely what Paley's definition means. . . .

Where, as the result of my negligence in formulating or accepting a contract, the words in which it is incorporated misrepresent my intention, and where at the same time its provisions affect my interests adversely, then, according to what we have termed Paley's principle, I am not morally bound to perform. But this does not mean that I am released from all obligations to my co-contractor. . . . An honorable man will pay for all losses which are due to his negligence in formulating or accepting a contract; he should not be expected to do more. . . .

What ought to be done when both parties are negligent? Where the negligence is, as far as can be judged, equal, the loss should be equally divided; otherwise, in proportion to the amount of fault, in so far as this proportion can be estimated. . . .

The principle that in negligence the damages are to be paid by the party through whose negligence the loss takes place ought to be tempered in morals—whatever may be true in law—by another principle. This is that burdens should be carried by those who can bear them most easily. . . .[14]

To what extent, if at all, does the law reach the same conclusions as Sharp and Fox? Insofar as it does not, does this mean that the law is immoral—that Sharp and Fox have overlooked something—or that what is moral and what is legal are two distinct questions with little or no connection? Keep these questions in mind as you consider the legal rules in the materials that follow. We begin with one of the classics of contracts folklore. Remember as you read the opinion, the objective theory is still largely in the future.

---

[14] Frank Chapman Sharp and Philip G. Fox, BUSINESS ETHICS 110, 116, 117 (1937). Copyright © Appleton, Century, Crofts.

RAFFLES v. WICHELHAUS[15]
Court of the Exchequer
2 Hurl. & C. 906, 159 Eng. Rep. 375 (1864)

[The plaintiff sued the defendant for failing to accept delivery of 125 bales of Surat cotton, pursuant to a contract which specified that defendant was to buy cotton "to arrive ex 'Peerless' from Bombay." Defendant argued for dismissal of the claim on the ground that there were two ships named "Peerless", both bringing cotton from Bombay, and that it appeared that the plaintiff intended to *sell* the cotton which was on a "Peerless" which was to leave Bombay in December, while the defendant intended to *buy* cotton on a "Peerless" which was to sail in October. The defendant had refused to accept the cotton tendered by the plaintiff.]

[The report of the case begins with Milward arguing for the plaintiff.] . . .

The contract was for the sale of a number of bales of cotton of a particular description, which the plaintiff was ready to deliver. It is immaterial by what ship the cotton was to arrive, so that it was a ship called the "Peerless." The words "to arrive ex 'Peerless,' " only mean that if the vessel is lost on the voyage, the contract is to be at an end. [At this point, Lord Chief Baron Pollock interrupted: "It would be a question for the jury whether both parties meant the same ship called the 'Peerless.' "] That would be so if the contract was for the sale of a ship called the "Peerless"; but it is for the sale of cotton on board a ship of that name. [Pollock interrupted again: "The defendant only bought that cotton which was to arrive by a particular ship. It may as well be said, that if there is a contract for the purchase of certain goods in warehouse A., that is satisfied by the delivery of goods of the same description in warehouse B.] In that case there would be goods in both warehouses; here it does not appear that the plaintiff had any goods on board the other "Peerless." [At this point, Baron Martin chimed in: "It is imposing on the defendant a contract different from that which he entered into." Baron Pollock added: "It is like a contract for the purchase of wine coming from a particular estate in France or Spain, where there are two estates of that name."] The defendant has no right to contradict by parol evidence a written contract good upon the face of it. He does not impute misrepresentation or fraud, but only says that he fancied the ship was a different one. Intention is of no avail, unless stated at the time of the contract. [Baron Pollock again: "One vessel sailed in October and the other in December."] The time of sailing is no part of the contract.

[Mellish, who was presenting the case for the defendant, then began to make arguments for defendant's position.]

There is nothing on the face of the contract to shew that any particular ship called the "Peerless" was meant; but the moment it appears that two ships called the "Peerless" were about to sail from Bombay there is a latent ambiguity, and parol evidence may be given for the purpose of shewing that the defendant meant

---

[15] English opinions can be difficult to read. In order to focus your attention on the substantive issue, we offer an edited version of the opinion, with some clarifications noted by [. . .], which don't appear in the original report. Purists may consult the original.

one "Peerless," and the plaintiff another. That being so, there was no *consensus ad idem*, and therefore no binding contract.

[At this point, apparently the Court had heard enough, and Mellish was instructed he need not continue.]

PER CURIAM. There must be judgment for the defendants.

NOTES AND QUESTIONS

1. *Legal history*: Professor A.W.B. Simpson, in his paper *Contracts for Cotton to Arrive: The Case of the Two Ships Peerless*,[16] concluded that traditional contracts scholarship has misinterpreted the *Raffles* case.[17] Accepting Simpson's research and conclusions, the conventional interpretation of the case has a life of its own (like *Hadley v. Baxendale*). It is a part of American, and probably common law, legal culture. You can talk to most lawyers and judges about the two ships named *Peerless*, and they will know what you are talking about; most would not remember that there was no opinion in the case.

2. *The Restatement (Second) Contracts and the Raffles case*: The modern statement of the rule follows neither the 1864 opinion nor Holmes. You should consult, at this point, § 20 (Effect of Misunderstanding) and § 201 (Whose Meaning Prevails) of the Restatement (Second) of Contracts in your statutory supplement.

In *Lamb Plumbing & Heating Co. v. Kraus-Anderson of Minneapolis, Inc.*,[18] Lamb sued a general contractor for the value of work done on a large project which Lamb said was not covered by its bid but which the general contractor had demanded Lamb do. The general contractor learned of a problem in the specifications before bids were submitted. Another subcontractor pointed out that different interpretations of the specifications were possible concerning which the subcontractor was to furnish and install certain valves. The general contractor notified several mechanical subcontractors it knew were likely to bid on the job that the mechanical contractor must supply and install the valves. Plaintiff had obtained the plans and specifications on its own, and the general contractor did not know it would bid. Plaintiff reasonably interpreted the contract documents as not

---

[16] 11 Cardozo L. Rev. 287 (1989).

[17] The *Raffles* case has been read by almost every American first-year contracts student during much of the past century. The case was decided without opinion but is usually read, and taught, as if it had to do with the parties' misunderstanding of which ship Peerless was to carry the cotton for which they contracted a sale. In fact, as Simpson's elaborate historical research revealed, the case is a rare glimpse into the dawn of the market in cotton futures and of judicial acceptance of arbitration. Through examination of shipping records in England and the United States, Simpson demonstrated that the transaction was one that Liverpool cotton merchants of the time would have understood well.

While the volume in such "contracts for cotton to arrive" was large, *Raffles* was one of the only judicial cases to arise from trading in them. The plaintiff was a relative outsider to the closely knit group of cotton brokers and not a regular trader in the contracts. His lawsuit was a breach of the uniformly observed custom of broker arbitration over failures of such contracts. The judgment for the defendant may thus reflect an equally rare common-law decision enforcing, if without opinion, a customary requirement of resort to arbitration. (Cornell L. F., February 1986, at 16.)

[18] 296 N.W.2d 859 (S. Ct. Minn. 1980).

requiring it to supply and install the valves. Its officials did not see the ambiguity in the contract documents. It submitted a bid on this basis, and the general awarded it the contract. The general demanded Lamb install the valves, Lamb did this, and sued for extra compensation for work beyond that required by the contract. Under the Restatement (Second) of Contracts §§ 20, 201, how should a court decide this case? What more, if anything, do you need to know to answer this question?

3. *Professor Sharp and carelessness in communication*: Professor Malcolm Sharp offered an explanation for the position later taken in the Restatement (Second) of Contracts. Essentially, he argued that a promise is a dependable statement about the statement maker's future behavior that may predictably lead to reliance by the person to whom it is made. The actual intentions of the maker are not important. What is important is that language be used carefully, and that losses resulting from the careless use (or understanding) of language be shifted to the person who has been careless. Since our social system is largely built on the protection of private property interests, one must protect those whose business interests suffer as the result of the carelessness of others. Analogizing losses arising from confusion in business situations to losses arising from automobile accidents, Sharp suggests that loss can intelligibly be allocated in terms of fault.[19] That is, one can analyze contractual liability in terms of fault rather than consent. One can rely on an analysis of the meaning of the language used measured against what is "more or less normal in the business community" rather than against the actual intentions of either party to the communication.

> It will be noted that we have now said that care must be used by both parties to communications. If the promisor is careful and the promisee careless, the promisor's understanding will control, in the event of misunderstanding. If both are careful or both careless, neither understanding will control, and there will be no effective communication in the event of misunderstanding.[20]

Does Professor Sharp's explanation of promissory liability support Professor Horwitz's position? Does it make a substantial change in the claim for legitimacy one puts forward for contract law? Has Sharp reduced contract to a specific application of tort—liability for the negligent use of language? Does this matter?

Part of Sharp's position is that a person hearing or relying on what she thinks is a promise must be justified or reasonable. Barnett[21] asserts that this does no more than pose the crucial question it is supposed to answer. He says,

> [W]hether a person has "reasonably" relied on a promise depends on what most people would (or ought to) do. We cannot make this assessment independently of the legal rule in effect in the relevant community, because what many people would do in reliance on a promise is crucially affected by their perception of whether or not the promise is enforceable. . . .

---

[19] How successful is the system for allocating accident costs on the basis of fault? Would the same problems bedevil a contract model?

[20] Malcolm Pitman Sharp, *Promissory Liability I*, 7 U. Chi. L. Rev. 1, 7 (1939).

[21] Barnett, *A Consent Theory of Contract*, 86 Colum. L. Rev. 269, 275-76 (1986).

Unlike the subject of the prediction required by foreseeability analysis in tort law—the physical consequences that follow from physical actions—the subject of the prediction required by foreseeability analysis in contract law is the actions of a self-conscious person. A prediction that a promise can reasonably be expected to induce reliance by a promisee or third party will unavoidably depend upon whether the promisee or third party believes that reliance will be legally protected. The legal rule itself cannot be formulated based on such a prediction, however, without introducing a practical circularity into the analysis. . . .

In short, a person, rather than being entitled to legal enforcement because reliance is justified, is justified in relying on those commitments that will be legally enforced.

Does Barnett's objection require us to disregard Sharp's position? What does Barnett assume about bargaining? Where does he get his data?

4. *Other theories of liability*: Choice and fault are not the only possible principles for decision in contracts cases. We could frame rules designed to support the market or the process of contracting. Is the following case an illustration of such a rule? Why does Barnett find Sharp's position troubling? Note the title of his article.

2. FLAT RULES TO ALLOCATE LOSSES

WPC ENTERPRISES, INC. v. UNITED STATES
United States Court of Claims
323 F.2d 874 (1964)

DAVIS, J. This is a study in the toils of ambiguity. The parties put their names to a contract which, on the point crucial to this lawsuit, could reasonably be read in two conflicting fashions. Each signatory seized in its own mind upon a different one of these contradictory versions. Compounding that confusion, they discussed the issue with each other in such a way that each thought, but this time without good reason, it had obtained the other's acquiescence in its chosen reading. The impasse became unmistakably plain when it was too late. Our task is to determine on whom should fall the risk of such mutually reinforced obscurity.

The Government set out to procure, through bids, a large number of complex generator sets—called the MD-3 set—used to calibrate the electronic systems of the B-47 and other aircraft and to start the engines when an electric starter is required. Beech Aircraft Corporation, which had previously made these elaborate devices for the Air Force on a negotiated basis, had prepared specifications and drawings of various of the component parts which the Government acquired and incorporated in the bid invitations. Plaintiff was the low bidder, lower than Beech and another company which had also provided the sets under a negotiated contract. After a period of consideration and some discussion, the award was made to plaintiff and it performed the contract as required by the Government.

The only dispute now before us is whether five components of these generator sets had to be manufactured by (or with the authorization of) certain named companies, as the Government urges, or whether plaintiff was entitled under the contract to furnish identical components made by other firms (presumably at lower prices). After the award, defendant insisted that the products of the specified companies had to be furnished. Plaintiff complied but, claiming that this directive constituted a contractual change, sought review by the Board of Contract Appeals under the Changes and Disputes articles. The Board turned down the appeal on the ground that plaintiff had been told before the award of the defendant's position and had acquiesced.

For the five components now involved, the textual provisions of the specifications (borrowed from Beech) gave general descriptions, without naming any manufacturer; however, the drawings (also from Beech) listed the part numbers given to the item by a particular firm and declared that that manufacturer was the "approved source," or that the component "may be purchased" from that company, or indicated "make from" a part furnished by a particular company, or simply said that the component was a certain part number of a specific firm. There are also other, slighter, indications of contractual meaning on which the parties rely; the details are set forth in the findings.

Each side urges that its position is sustained by the invitation as a whole—without any need to go beyond the bounds of the contractual instruments. The defendant stresses the references to specific part numbers, designated by particular fabricators, as necessarily showing that only parts made under the aegis of that manufacturer would be acceptable; this use of exact part numbers is said to be equivalent to a mandatory direction to incorporate only those very items. Defendant also points out that: (i) the drawings and specifications for the five components were not adequate for a new manufacturer to make those articles in the relatively short time allotted for completion of the procurement; (ii) the defendant was satisfied with components made from parts supplied by the named manufacturers (because they had been fully tested in the past), but would be required before acceptance to test components made by others; and (iii) this burdensome and time consuming testing would not be practicable within the scheduled period of delivery. It should have been clear, defendant concludes, that the contract called for items supplied by or through the specific companies named in the drawings. (Defendant's witnesses testified to this effect before the Board and at the trial in this court.)

The plaintiff, on the other hand, emphasizes the lack of express mandatory language in the references to particular manufacturers for the five disputed components—in contrast to certain other components which the specifications very plainly declared "shall be" or "shall consist of" an identified part made by a named manufacturer. A command to use only materials or elements made by a specific firm is not frequent in government procurement; it can be expected to be phrased explicitly and not left to inference. Moreover, the references to particular part numbers are not read as mandatory because of a specification provision (labeled "Identification of Parts") which stated:

> "Beech and vendor part numbers will be shown on all items except those items supplied by other than Beech Aircraft Corporation or vendors to

Beech. On items supplied by other than present sources Beech part numbers will be used with a suffix to indicate a different supplier."

To plaintiff, this clause implicitly authorized the use of identical components made by other companies than those named in the Beech drawings. It thought that it could obtain such qualified substitutes by combining the knowledge gained from three sources: the drawings and specifications (insufficient though they might be); a careful breakdown of the sample models supplied plaintiff by the defendant; and general engineering competence. Plaintiff was satisfied that the proper components could be produced in this way within the time allowed. (The contractor's position was likewise supported by evidence before the Board of Contract Appeals.)

This summary of the opposing contentions is enough to show that no sure guide to the solution of the problem can be found within the four corners of the contractual documents. As with so many other agreements, there is something for each party and no ready answer can be drawn from the texts alone. Both plaintiff's and defendant's interpretations lie within the zone of reasonableness; neither appears to rest on an obvious error in drafting, a gross discrepancy, or an inadvertent but glaring gap; the arguments, rather, are quite closely in balance. It is precisely to this type of contract that this court has applied the rule that if some substantive provision of a government drawn agreement is fairly susceptible of a certain construction and the contractor actually and reasonably so construes it, in the course of bidding or performance, that is the interpretation which will be adopted—unless the parties' intention is otherwise affirmatively revealed. . . . This rule is fair both to the drafters and to those who are required to accept or reject the contract as proffered, without haggling. Although the potential contractor may have some duty to inquire about a major patent discrepancy, or obvious omission, or a drastic conflict in provisions . . . he is not normally required (absent a clear warning in the contract) to seek clarification of any and all ambiguities, doubts, or possible differences in interpretation. The Government, as the author, has to shoulder the major task of seeing that within the zone of reasonableness the words of the agreement communicate the proper notions—as well as the main risk of a failure to carry that responsibility. If the defendant chafes under the continued application of this check, it can obtain a looser rein by a more meticulous writing of its contracts and especially of the specifications.[22] Or it can shift the burden of ambiguity (to some extent) by inserting provisions in the contract clearly calling upon possible contractors aware of a problem interpretation to seek an explanation before bidding. . . .

If there were nothing more, the case would end here with a ruling for the plaintiff. But the defendant argues, and the Board of Contract Appeals found, that be-

---

[22] [2] It was a clear mistake to borrow the Beech specifications and drawings for the Government's procurement without more editorial revision and adaptation. Those specifications and drawings were tailored to manufacture and procurement by Beech, a private concern—not by the United States. The trouble came about because the defendant's contracting officials failed to modify the documents, which may have been adequate for a private procurement, so as to make them entirely suitable for a public procurement through bidding.

fore the award was made or the contract signed the plaintiff learned the Government's view of the disputed point and accepted that position. . . .

At the trial in this court, Commissioner McConnaughey had the benefit, with respect to the pre-award meetings between the parties, of testimony by Sugarman[23] (who did not appear before the Board) and of other representatives of both sides, as well as of certain documentary materials (notably an internal memorandum by a Government contracting official made after the December 19, 1956 meeting with Sugarman). He also had the evidence before the Board. . . .

[W]e agree with the Trial Commissioner that (i) both parties became aware of the other's interpretation; (ii) neither acquiesced knowingly in the other's interpretation; (iii) both thought, however, that the other had acquiesced; (iv) without either having reasonable grounds for so thinking; and, finally, that (v) neither took the proper steps to clarify the pertinent terms of the transaction until after the award was made. On both sides ambiguous utterance was piled on unwarranted assumption and laced together by unspoken premise. In the end, the Government officials thought they had made it quite clear that the named manufacturers would have to be used for all components, while the plaintiff's people felt that they had successfully stood their ground at least as to these five components. Both were wholly wrong in their understanding of the other's understanding. The discussions had been one prolonged minuet of cross purposes.

In these circumstances should the onus of the original ambiguity in the specifications still rest on the defendant? We can see no other conclusion. As the author of the defect in the drafting which led plaintiff to the reasonable supposition that it could obtain the five components elsewhere than from the named companies, the Government was under the affirmative obligation (if it wished its own view to prevail) to clarify the meaning of the contract in definitive fashion before the plaintiff was bound. It did make such an attempt, and it did reveal its own view. But when the plaintiff demurred the Government did not adequately indicate that it stood steadfast by its announced opinion. There was a fatal insufficiency in the defendant's effort to communicate to plaintiff that the contract was to be interpreted as the Government understood it. Largely because of this lapse, the plaintiff was left with the mistaken impression that the defendant, rather than insisting, would accept plaintiff's rendering of the contract. The Government, in a word, was very lax in seeing the matter through. Since the burden of clarification was the defendant's, it must bear the risk of an insufficient attempt, even though the plaintiff's obtuseness likewise contributed to the continuance of the misunderstanding. If there had been no communication by defendant to plaintiff between the receipt of the bids and the making of the award, the defendant would have had to suffer the consequences of its poorly drafted specifications. The ineffective attempt to put things right does not place the defendant in a better position. Only an adequate effort to reach the plaintiff's mind could have that result.

Two objections may be made to our taking this ground. The inconclusive discussions between the parties show, it may be said, that there was no "meeting of the minds" on the issue which concerns us, and therefore no valid contract. There

---

[23] Eds. note: Cecil Sugarman was WPC's sales manager.

was no subjective coming together, it is true, but an enforceable agreement came into being nevertheless. The design of the contract can be picked from the terms and words of the invitation, objectively read with the aid of rules of contract construction (which are distillates of the common experience and the common sense of justice). It is a normal characteristic of the class of cases in which the courts have held ambiguities against the drafter that the parties' minds have failed to meet on the specific point in dispute. That gap has not been permitted to swallow the whole contract except perhaps where the gulf is far closer to the bounds of the entire consensual perimeter than here. For a contract to exist there does not have to be, and rarely is, a subjective "meeting of the minds" all along the line. . . .

The other objection is that the plaintiff is bound by the opposing view of the contract because it twice extended the defendant's time to make the award (on February 8 and 18, 1957) after the Air Force's representatives had told plaintiff of their attitude. This contention must be rejected for the reason given above. Although it had the burden, the defendant simply did not make it clear enough that it stood by its position despite the plaintiff's disagreement. When the latter extended the time for the award it did not comprehend that the Government was insisting on its own construction. This state of affairs was attributable, in substantial measure, to defects in the defendant's course of communication to plaintiff on the subject of the source of the five components. Plaintiff was also at fault, but the risk of a failure to clarify lay largely upon the Government and could have been averted only by a more sufficient effort than was made.

We hold, therefore, that the defendant was wrong in demanding that only products of (or authorized by) the named manufacturers could be used for the five components. The contract did not so require. The issue of the amount of damages or recovery has not been tried and we are not called upon to pass upon any aspects of that question. We leave all such problems to the trial under Rule 38(c), including the issue of which party has the burden of showing that the components plaintiff planned to use would or would not have been available, and would or would not have qualified under this contract.

The plaintiff is entitled to recover and judgment is entered to that effect The amount of recovery will be determined under Rule 38(c).

NOTES AND QUESTIONS

1. *Limits on the rule of thumb*: The Court of Claims has been unwilling to resolve all ambiguities in favor of the contractor.[24] In *National By-Products, Inc.*

---

[24] In Beacon Construction Co. v. United States, 314 F.2d 501, 504 (Ct. Cl. 1963), a contractor bidding on a government construction job noticed an ambiguity in the bid documents, but did not inquire of the government contracting officer—choosing instead to bid on the basis of the Maine trade practice. A dispute subsequently arose, and the Court of Claims ruled against the contractor, noting that, "A prime purpose of these contractual provisions relating to ambiguities and discrepancies is to enable potential contractors (as well as the Government) to clarify the contract's meaning before the die is cast." When a contractor "is presented with an obvious omission, inconsistency, or discrepancy of significance, he must consult the Government's representatives if he intends to bridge the crevasse in his own favor."

v. United States,[25] the Court refused to apply the rule of the *WPC* case, even though the parties had "two contrary understandings of the 'deal' [which] were both objectively reasonable in the totality of the circumstances." The court noted that, "Here, there was no root fault on the part of the Government from which the later misunderstanding flowered." Would the test be different in a case involving a supplier and a private non-governmental buyer? *See* Restatement (Second) of Contracts §§ 20, 201.

3. WHEN IS IT TOO LATE TO DISCOVER A MISTAKE AND AVOID THE CONTRACT

a. Introducing the Problem of the Mistaken Bid

People often make offers based on mistakes. When should we let them back out of contracts formed when the other party accepted the mistaken offer? Professor Fuller, in his classic article exploring the reliance and expectation interests,[26] justified holding people to contracts and protecting their expectation interests because of the difficulty of proving reliance. For example, when I think I have a deal with you, I am likely to stop looking for other suppliers of the same item. At the least, your failure to perform costs me the chance to find other bargains. This explanation for holding people to promises suggests several problems. On one hand, buyer may rely on seller's promise even before they make a legally binding contract. Seller, however, wants to withdraw because it made a mistake. Should buyer's reliance be protected? On the other hand, the injury actually or likely caused by buyer's reliance after the parties made a legally binding contract may be very small as compared to the burden on the seller if it is held to its mistaken promise. Should this matter?

Legal formalism would ignore both situations. Under this theory, a bargainer was free to back out of any transaction before the magic moment of closing the deal took place. Conversely, once a deal was closed, absent fraud or a *mutual* mistake going to the essence of the transaction, a bargainer had to live with any mistakes. However, the solutions offered by legal formalism fail to track with much of business life. Many transactions involve an incremental process of give and take. It is hard to find any magic moment of bindingness that matters to the parties. After parties work together, either may suffer losses if the other backs out. Expectations of fairness and good faith grow as the transaction progresses.

Should the law recognize these business practices or should judges demand that parties go through formalities that mark when the parties make a contract? Alternatively, how much weight should courts give to contract formalities? Suppose a seller submits an offer that the buyer accepts. This creates a legally binding contract. Shortly afterward, the seller discovers he made a substantial mistake in calculating the price he quoted. The buyer has done little in reliance. Should the law offer relief from the mistake?

---

[25] 405 F.2d 1256 (Ct. Cl. 1969).
[26] Fuller and Perdue, *The Reliance Interest in Contract Damages: Pt. 1*, 46 Yale L. J. 52 (1936).

We must keep several questions distinct. First, we might ask as a matter of ethics whether a person who has made a promise based on a mistake should stand behind it. Would the good person back out if her lawyer told her that no legally binding agreement was made under the rules of contract law? Second, we might ask whether the ethical person would hold another to a contract once she discovers their agreement was based on the other's mistake. Third, we can ask whether legal rules should reflect whatever moral decisions we reach. We might conclude that most people will offer to stand behind their promises based on mistakes. Most who might benefit from such errors may refuse to accept the benefits of these promises. Most people are ethical or they are subject to private sanction systems that offer all the regulation that is needed.

We will look at several situations in which one party makes a promise based on a mistake. In each situation, the other party has no reason to know that a mistake has been made. In some cases courts enforce the agreement in other cases enforcement is denied. In some cases relief is given to a party even though the formalities of a contract were not met. Can we formulate a principled and coherent explanation of these cases?

Buyers of goods or services often use competitive bidding. Statutes may require governmental units to operate this way to save money and minimize favoritism and kickbacks. Plans and specifications are drawn by architects, and engineers and owners make them available to interested general contractors. General contractors then ask subcontractors and suppliers to make bids. A bid is a statement that the firm making it will do some part of the project for a certain amount. Typically subcontractors and material suppliers give general contractors bids shortly before the generals must submit their prime bids to the corporation or governmental unit having the work done. Though some bids may be submitted in writing, more typically the bidder telephones them to the general contractors just before the deadline. Often the process is hectic and chaotic.

Each general contractor then takes the best bids, adds its own estimates for work its crew will do, and then includes a sum to cover the expense of coordinating the work and taking the risks involved. A general must both keep the amount of the bid as low as possible to get the job and keep it high enough to make money on the project. The owner then makes a contract with the lucky general contractor. Then the general usually makes contracts with selected subcontractors and material suppliers to assure itself of getting the goods and services at guaranteed prices.

Clearly, there is a great deal of room for error in this process. Some building contractors, subcontractors and material suppliers are highly professional and use the most advanced methods of preparing bids. Others operate in a more seat-of-the pants fashion, scorning paperwork. A general or a subcontractor may misread plans and specifications. These documents may be ambiguous or conflict with one another. A contractor may assume that it may make something in a customary way, but an owner's architect may demand a special and more costly procedure in a clause buried in lengthy and poorly organized specifications. A contractor may fail to add a column of figures correctly or a number can be transposed when copied. A component (sometimes a room, or a whole floor) can be inadvertently omitted during the last minute calculations.

Mistakes can hurt everyone involved. If a subcontractor must perform a mistaken bid, it may go broke. But a general may have relied on that bid in computing its offer to the owner and if the subcontractor backs out, the general contractor must cope with the loss. If the owner calls for new bids because of the mistakes, this may increase the price of the building. Ideally, bidders would avoid mistakes; however, this is easier said than done.

We will explore the range of choices open to courts in these cases, and the advantages and disadvantages of each. The cases will expose the eternal tension between a desire for orderly, clear, certain rules and the urge to give relief when those clear rules seem to work a hardship. We begin with the war horses of traditional contract courses—the mail box rule, and the firm offer—and then move to other rules which implicate the same policies. Throughout, we will ask whether courts are protecting free choice, holding people to the consequences of their negligence, or making decisions based on ideas of social engineering or sympathy. Keeping in mind Professor Horwitz's arguments, we will ask whether developments in these areas favor general or subcontractors systematically.

b. The Mailbox Rule

The classic common law "mailbox rule" closes deals quickly without requiring communication. *Acceptances create legally binding contracts when they are mailed.*[27] Nothing happening between the time of mailing and receipt affects the formation of the contract. (All *other* communications—offers, rejections, and revocations—take effect only when they are received.)

Suppose, for example, after a bid, a governmental unit sends the low bidder a purchase order. The purchase order is an offer to be accepted by the contractor that made the bid. The contractor signs the "acknowledgment of order" copy of the purchase order form. This document is an acceptance. The contractor then deposits it in the mail. Then the contractor discovers a major error. Its representative telephones a government official, saying the government should ignore the acceptance because of the mistake. Under the common law rule, it would be too late. One cannot withdraw an acceptance after the parties' actions create a contract.

---

[27] There are a number of wonderful subproblems. The offeree must have addressed the letter of acceptance properly. It must have adequate postage. The person relying on the existence of a contract must prove both that he mailed the acceptance and when he did this. While there are presumptions that help, sometimes it is not easy to prove you mailed a letter. We can worry whether the rule applies to modern methods of communication such as computer systems linked by telephone lines. At least judged by appellate reports, the rule is not a pressing modern problem. Perhaps this makes it good material for bar examinations.

The common law is clear.[28] The attempted revocation is too late. The rule has been rationalized in terms of protecting an offeree's likely reliance. Once it mails a letter of acceptance, it must take that contract into account in its planning from that point onward. It will not seek other contracts to fill the needs involved in the one created by mail. The mailbox rule means that the offeree need not wait for the offeror to learn of the acceptance before the offeree can begin to rely on the contract's existence. The offeror knows that it is in an uncertain situation once it makes an outstanding offer; an offeror who wished to be free from this uncertainty could specify, in the offer, that an acceptance was effective only when received by the offeror. An offeree's possible reliance is a necessary part of making contracts by correspondence, if the mailbox rule is applicable. Notice that the rule applies and there is a contract although the offeree cannot show that it suffered any reliance loss. As you might expect, in many situations offerees will not assert their contract rights. Buyers often allow sellers to back out when they believe that the reason for the attempted revocation is a mistake rather than a desire to sell to another buyer at a higher price.

Notwithstanding the venerability and widespread acceptance of the mailbox rule, in 1949 the Court of Claims announced an acceptance when received rule. *Dick v. United States*,[29] involved the following sequence of communications:

(1) After an extended exchange of telegrams, a manufacturer sent the Coast Guard a bid to supply propellers for an ice-breaking vessel.

(2) The Coast Guard mailed its purchase order to the manufacturer, offering to buy the propellers.

(3) The manufacturer mailed its acceptance of the order to the Coast Guard.

(4) While the letter of acceptance was in transit, the manufacturer discovered that the order was for two *sets* of two propellers and not one set of two propellers as it had assumed. (That is, the Coast Guard ordered four propellers while the manufacturer's representatives thought they were agreeing to supply only two for the price they quoted.) The manufacturer telegraphed the Coast Guard, informing it of the mistake and saying that the price quoted should be doubled. This telegram arrived *before* the Coast Guard received the letter of acceptance.

(5) The Coast Guard's contracting officer told the manufacturer that they would make a new contract. Relying on this, the manufacturer supplied the four propellers (two sets) the Coast Guard wanted. However, the Comptroller General ruled that the contracting officer had no authority to give away the government's rights. A contract was formed when the manufacturer placed a letter of acceptance in the mail. As a result, the government paid the manufacturer only the price set forth in the purchase order. This was the price the manufacturer mistakenly had calculated for only one set of propellers instead of the two sets ordered.

On these facts, the United States Court of Claims changed its rule to acceptance-when-received. It found that the Government should pay the manufacturer

---

[28] The United Nations Convention on the Sale of Goods rejects the common law rule. Article 15 § 1 provides that an acceptance is effective when it reaches the offeree. Even the putatively irrevocable offer can be so revoked.

[29] 82 F. Supp. 326 (Ct. Cl. 1949).

for both sets of propellers supplied. We are almost certain there was no reliance by the offeror on the letter of acceptance. The first thing the Coast Guard received in response to its offer was a communication telling it to disregard the earlier mailed acceptance because of a mistake. Thus, the *Dick* case reached the right result in terms of protecting expectations and reliance, but violated the mailbox rule.

Six years later, the Court of Claims decided *Rhode Island Tool Co. v. United States*.[30] It applied its acceptance-when-received rule and found no contract. An offeror tried to revoke its offer after the offeree had mailed a letter of acceptance but before the offeror had received it. The court assumed there could be but one rule covering both the *Dick* and *Rhode Island Tool* situations. It had to adopt an acceptance-when-mailed or an acceptance when received rule for all situations.

Several writers suggest that we need different rules for different situations. To oversimplify, in the *Dick* situation the rule should be acceptance-when-received. In the *Rhode Island Tool* situation, it should be acceptance-when-mailed. This makes sense if the primary goal is to protect likely reliance. In the *Dick* situation, the Coast Guard's officials did not know that the manufacturer had mailed an acceptance before they learned it had made a mistake. An offeror cannot rely on an acceptance its officials have never seen or heard of. In the *Rhode Island Tool* case, however, an offeree who deposits a letter of acceptance in the mail is entitled to start relying from that point on. Other writers worry about binding one party to a contract when the other party is not bound. However, they concede that perhaps courts should give relief in the *Dick* situation on the ground of mistake. Consider the mistake possibility after we have studied traditional and modern views about such relief.

Would the mailbox rule apply to an acceptance sent by e-mail or by fax?[31] The short answer is that we don't know. Courts have not faced cases involving this problem. Both forms of communication usually are fast, and so parties do not face the delays involved in letters being mailed, carried to another city and being delivered. It is this delay that makes it possible for the offeree to put a letter of acceptance in the mail, and the offeror to attempt to revoke after the mailing but before the letter is received. Some contracts are made when customers go to a web site such as those run by catalog merchants like Land's End or Eddie Bauer. These merchants typically give catalog customers the right to return goods within a reasonable time. This policy avoids many of the problems of the mailbox rule.

---

[30] 128 F. Supp. 417 (Ct. Cl. 1955). The United States Court of Claims has continued to follow its acceptance when received rule. *See, e.g.,* Romala Corp. v. United States, 20 Cl. Ct. 435 (1990). However, other courts have continued to apply the common law acceptance when mailed rule and rejected the Court of Claims position. *See, e.g.,* Soldau v. Organon, Inc., 860 F.2d 355 (9th Cir. 1988); Morrison v. Thoelke, 155 So. 2d 889 (Fla. App. 1963). Under the Court of Claims acceptance when received rule, an offeree could post a letter of acceptance, estimate when it would arrive, and make the final decision as to whether to accept at the last minute before the letter was delivered. In this way, the offeree could watch market fluctuations that much longer before making a final commitment. Is this a reason for rejecting the Court of Claims rule?

[31] *See* Paul Fasciano, *Internet Electronic Mail: A Last Bastion for the Mailbox Rule,* 25 Hofstra L. Rev. 971 (1997); Tuma & Ward, *Contracting Over the Internet in Texas,* 52 Baylor L. Rev. 381, 393 (2000).

Of course, to trigger the mailbox rule, the communication must be properly addressed. The Uniform Electronic Transactions Act (UETA) §15 provides that if e-mail is misaddressed, it is not "sent." UETA has been adopted in 37 states and is pending in at least 10 more.

c. The Firm Offer

Another change in traditional contract rules affects responsibility for mistaken bids and offers. Since the 1960s courts and legislatures have created more liability where parties have not followed procedures for forming contracts. Again we must understand the consequences and ask who benefits and who suffers by the changes.

Suppose Seller offers to sell goods to Buyer at a specified price. Buyer neither accepts nor rejects the offer. Seller, eager to make a sale, says, "Take your time and think about this deal. You'll find it is a good price for goods of this quality." Seller leaves. Buyer then gets another offer for the same type of goods from Competitor, but the price is higher. Buyer rejects Competitor's offer, planning to accept Seller's proposal. However, before Buyer can communicate, Seller revokes its offer. (Seller may have found another customer for the goods it has or may have discovered an error in its calculations upon which it quoted a price or may simply have changed its mind.) Buyer has lost its possible deal with Competitor. May Buyer recover from Seller? The traditional common law rule was clear. Offers are revocable until they are accepted. Buyer had no right to rely on an unaccepted offer. It should have known it did not have a contract. Thus, Buyer could not recover.[32]

Suppose Seller was very eager to make a sale. She says, "Take your time and think about this deal. You'll find it is a good price for goods of this quality. I promise not to revoke this offer for one week." Under the common law rules, the case for Buyer is no stronger. Seller's promise not to revoke lacks consideration. It would not be enforceable, and Seller could revoke without liability to Buyer. Buyer could make a promise not to revoke enforceable by paying for an "option."[33]

There have been changes in these rules. Section 2-205 of the Uniform Commercial Code offers a very limited change in the rules. It provides:

> An offer by a merchant to buy or sell goods in a signed writing which by its terms gives assurance that it will be held open is not revocable, for lack of consideration, during the time stated or if no time is stated for a

---

[32] Some writers would explain this result in terms of mutuality of obligation. Buyer is free to reject Seller's offer or ignore it. If Buyer has this freedom, Seller should have it too. Equal treatment is an important value in our legal system. However, there is no requirement that our law treat people who have done different things equally. Thus, the question remains whether Seller's actions warrant courts treating the Seller differently than they treat the Buyer. Seller has made an offer. Buyer has done nothing. Does this difference in their behavior call for different treatment by the courts? Mutuality does not answer the question.

[33] In some jurisdictions, Seller's promise would be enforceable if it were stated in a sealed instrument. In the United States, few people, other than those advised by lawyers, are likely to use this method of making binding promises.

reasonable time, but in no event may such period of irrevocability exceed three months; but any such term of assurance on a form supplied by the offeree must be separately signed by the offeror.

Notice that the rule applies only to merchants. The promise to hold open an offer must be in writing and signed. The statute limits the duration of the option. Moreover, the Code imposes a special rule for a form contract supplied by the offeree.

This cautious relaxation of the consideration doctrine stands in contrast to the court-fashioned rule applicable to subcontractor bids in building construction. Think about bidding in building construction. Typically, an owner invites bids on the plans and specifications for a project. Several general contractors plan to bid on the job. They calculate their bids from their own estimates of the costs of that part of the work they plan to carry out with their own crew as well as sub-bids from subcontractors and suppliers of machinery and materials. Sub-bids may be written but often they are transmitted at the last minute by telephone.

The owner usually awards a contract to construct the building to the low-bidding general contractor. Suppose one of the subcontractors refuses to stand behind its bid and enter a contract. Assume the subcontractor revokes its offer (its bid) before the general contractor accepts it and forms a contract. The common law rule would allow subcontractors to back out if they did it before their bids were accepted.

The general contractor relied on the subcontractor's bid. The general used this sub-bid in calculating its bid on the contract. Moreover, this reliance is foreseeable and reasonable. Can general contractors find a theory of liability to hold subcontractors or suppliers? Soon after the first Restatement of Contracts was published, a lawyer for a general contractor sued a supplier of materials that had submitted a bid based on mistaken calculations. The lawyer tried to use Section 90. It provides "[a] promise which the promisor should reasonably expect to induce action or forbearance of a definite and substantial character on the part of the promisee and which does induce such action or forbearance is binding if injustice can be avoided only by enforcement of the promise." It was not clear whether it applied to reliance on bids.

Judge Learned Hand of the United States Court of Appeals for the Second Circuit was a member of the American Law Institute. He helped draft the Restatement of Contracts. He wrote the opinion in this first attempt to use Section 90 in a bidding case. He refused to apply it to block withdrawal of a bid. "[A]n offer for an exchange is not meant to become a promise until a consideration has been received. . . . In the case at bar the defendant offered to deliver the linoleum in exchange for the plaintiff's acceptance, not for its bid, which was a matter of indifference to it. . . . There is no room in such a situation for the doctrine of 'promissory estoppel.' "[34]

There were a number of cases suggesting that Judge Hand was wrong. However, the major breakthrough came in an opinion of Justice Roger Traynor of the Supreme Court of California in 1958. His opinion in *Drennan v. Star Paving*

[34] *See* James Baird Co. v. Gimbel Bros., 64 F.2d 344, 346 (2d Cir. 1933).

Co.[35] is cited often, and represents the prevailing view. In the *Drennan* case, a paving subcontractor telephoned an oral bid to a general contractor. The subcontractor's representative did not promise to keep the bid open. There was no finding that this was the custom among subs and generals in that area. The subcontractor refused to enter a contract based on its bid to the general. Justice Traynor found an implied secondary promise in the bid that the subcontractor would keep its offer open for a reasonable time. This implied promise became irrevocable under Section 90 once the general relied on it by using the sub-bid in its prime bid.

Was Justice Traynor's decision based on choice or fault? Is liability imposed for some purpose? While some suppliers of materials have more bargaining power than the general contractors with whom they deal, in the usual situation a large general contractor is seeking to hold a smaller subcontractor to its bid. Subcontractors as a group have a stake in the bidding process. Most will stand behind their bids and eat their losses when they make mistakes. Generals may not ask subcontractors who refuse to honor their bids to submit them in future transactions. However, there is no guarantee that the general who receives the prime contract will award a contract to the subcontractor with the lowest bid. Even if a general does offer the contract to the low bidding subcontractor, the general may seek to bargain for an even lower price.

Is the firm offer rule just another example of the law being twisted in the interests of the powerful behind apolitical-seeming abstractions? None of the judges writing opinions applying Restatement § 90 to subcontractor bids explain why "injustice can be avoided only by enforcement of the promise." Scholars and politicians tell us that judges should not make major political choices but should leave them to the legislature. Why don't they leave this choice to legislation? Organized lobbying groups represent many general contractors, subcontractors, and material suppliers. Isn't their failure to seek legislation significant? If courts can hold subcontractors to their bids under Section 90, they must then consider whether to offer relief for mistake under other provisions. Wouldn't it be easier just to continue the common law position? Are subcontractors who back out and refuse to honor bids likely to hurt general contractors often? How do we know that reputational sanctions are not enough?

How should jurists answer questions such as these? Most of these questions are normative, but they rest on assumptions about the likely consequences of various rules courts could adopt. Facts alone cannot answer normative questions. Nonetheless, data can sharpen normative issues when they let us see how various proposals might operate. The study discussed below fills in some of the blanks, though it cannot establish once and for all "the facts" relevant to subcontractor

---

[35] 51 Cal. 2d 409, 333 P.2d 757 (1958). For a discussion of the Hand and Traynor positions, see Alfred S. Konefsky, *Freedom and Interdependence in Twentieth-Century Contract Law: Traynor and Hand and Promissory Estoppel*, 65 U. Cin. L. Rev. 1169 (1997) ("In *Baird*, Learned Hand viewed the commercial transaction at issue through the lens of individualism and formalism. Traynor, however, impatient with the traditional application of individualism to contract law, sought to transform that law by sanctioning the increasingly interdependent activities of market place actors.").

bids.[36] It does offer far more information than legal decision-makers usually have about a problem. Begin by assessing the quality of this information. Flawed data can mislead, or be suggestive. Once you have some confidence about the facts, you still have to decide what they mean.

The Virginia Law Review Study of Construction Bidding

[This is a paraphrase of a study conducted and published by the Editors of the Virginia Law Review;[37] For reasons of length we have summarized it. For purposes of preserving the accuracy of the summary, some sentences may appear in our paraphrase nearly as they originally appeared in the Virginia Law Review Note. It is included with the permission of the Board of Editors of the Virginia Law Review, who hold the copyright.]

Questionnaires and cover letters explaining their purpose were sent to generals and subs doing business in Virginia. Fifty-three of ninety-four subs and sixty-seven of 100 generals responded to the questionnaires.

Both subcontractors and generals were asked a question regarding the timing of subcontractor bid submissions. A few subcontractors responded that they submitted their bids to the general twenty-four hours or more before the general's bid. Several others represented that their bid was submitted within twelve to twenty-four hours of the general's bid. However, most subs said that they submitted their bids within one to four hours of the general's bid. Moreover, the responses of generals to this question largely coincided with those given by subs. The clear conclusion is that most subs engage in last-minute bidding to exert time pressure on the general to minimize bid-shopping.

Responding to a question about the medium of communication that bids use, over 20% of subs and approximately 10% of generals indicated that *written bids* were submitted to the generals which stated that they would not be withdrawn for a certain period of time. Further, over 40% of the subs indicated that they present *oral bids* which state that they will not be withdrawn for a certain length of time. About 20% of the generals stated that the bids were in this form. More significantly, 37% of subs indicated that their bids say nothing about whether they will remain open, whereas 70% of the generals responded that the bids they received were in this form. Even with the inconsistency, the responses indicate that section 2-205 of the code does not cover a large percentage of bids made to generals.

A clear majority of subs expressed that they had difficulties with generals who bid-shop before awarding a subcontract. They also believed that it was unethical for a general contractor to bid-shop either before or after the award of the prime contract. Further, even subs who indicated that they had never experienced trouble with bid-shopping felt that it was unethical. Subs are not only concerned with

---

[36] At best it is a snapshot of the situation in Virginia in the mid-1960s. We cannot be sure the information would hold for other states today. Moreover, the respondents are not an ideal random sample of the relevant population. As is true whenever respondents are asked questions, we cannot be sure that all of them understood the questions or told the exact truth.

[37] Note, *Another Look at Construction Bidding and Contracts Formation*, 53 Va. L. Rev. 1720 (1967). Reprinted by permission of the Virginia Law Review.

the general's superior bargaining power after the award of the prime contract, but also with disclosure of their bids to competitors at any time.

Though none of the generals specifically said that they engaged in bid-shopping, only about half indicated that they always use the low bid from among those submitted by the subs. Many generals qualified their answer by stating that they used the low bid unless the low bidder had a poor reputation, had performed unsatisfactorily on previous jobs, or was in financial trouble. Thus forty-nine of sixty-six responding generals volunteered that they would use the lowest bid unless the sub was untrustworthy.

Eleven of sixty-five generals responded that it is their practice to use a sub's bid as an estimate of what that portion of the job should cost, with an eye perhaps to doing that part of the work themselves or finding a better price. From the responses it was not possible to tell which generals use bids as estimates and which shop for bids. On the other hand, several generals who indicated that they do not engage in either practice stated that it would be unfair to request a sub to expend the time and money to compute a bid, only to have the general do the work himself. Many noted that such practices were unethical under the Associated General Contractors code of ethics.

Generals were also asked if it was customary to conduct further negotiations with subs before concluding a satisfactory working agreement. Of those responding, twenty-five reported that they usually conduct further negotiations. Of this twenty-five, twenty indicated that negotiations are undertaken only to clarify terms other than price. Only two indicated that they did bargain about price. As to the timing of negotiations, the largest group of generals indicated that they negotiate after they have secured the prime contract. Since generals are under time pressure before bid opening, this is probably the only time such clarifications can be made. Twenty-eight generals responded that they do not conduct further negotiations. Although some generals may have been less than candid in their responses, it seems probable that the great majority do not bid-shop. This coincides with the conclusion of most subs that bid-shopping is not a common practice among reputable generals.

Most subs responded that they have felt compelled to take measures to counteract bid-shopping. In qualifying their response, thirty-one of forty-five subs indicated that they would stop submitting bids to a bid-shopping general. Seven reported they had tried a bid depository, and six indicated they would "puff" their bids to that general. Four subs said they would publicize the general's actions to other subs. Strangely, only three listed late bidding as a weapon, although the vast majority in fact follow this procedure, as indicated by the response to a previous question. Other methods to counteract bid-shopping included "trapping" the general by first quoting a low price and then withdraw-ing. One sub said that he would "do nothing," another reported that the best method to counteract bid-shopping was to submit bids only to honest and competent generals since "bid-shoppers are most always the poorest contractors and credit risks." Significantly, no sub mentioned the possibility of taking the general to court.

Subs were unanimous in expressing that they would feel bound to go ahead and perform the work at their original bid price if it was discovered that the sub made a mistake in the bid but that the general had used the bid in their own bid. It is surprising that none of the subs stated that they felt they were free to withdraw their bid. Of course, it is easy to be magnanimous when answering a questionnaire. Since several generals reported being faced with a situation such as this, we must assume that the subs' responses are not completely representative. Of generals, fifteen of sixty-six indicated that they considered a sub bound to perform the work at the bid price after using the sub's bid in computing their own bid price. Five of sixty-six generals indicated that they considered neither party bound to a sub's bid until there were further negotiations or a formal contract. The vast majority of generals however considered both parties bound to each other as of the time that the general used the bid. Considering the sub bound at this point would seem to be commercially reasonable.

Neither subs nor generals attribute much significance to whether or not a bid is "firm." The important factor in either case is the general's exposed position during the post-bid, pre-award stage. One sub stated that whether or not a bid is "firm" is irrelevant. "Our word is our bond and our reputation paramount." Responses of subs suggest that it is the relative position of the parties rather than the presence of a firm bid that causes subs to feel they must stick to their bids as originally submitted. Most subs stated that they felt compelled to do the job once the general had relied because they felt morally or legally bound. Two subs also indicated that "past experience with a particular general would be important," and one maintained that professional responsibility was the prime factor. On the other side, most generals indicated that they would feel that a sub was being unjust if the sub withdrew his bid after the general had been awarded the prime contract.

When a general decides to use a sub's bid in his own bid to the awarding authorities, rarely is the sub notified that the general is using it prior to the general's bid. More frequently, a sub is notified immediately after the general has used a sub's bid in his own bid. Moreover, around 35% of subs and over 60% of generals indicated that the sub was notified as soon as the general was awarded the prime contract. However, about half of the subs indicated that they were notified at some later time. Less than 20% of the generals indicated that their notification was done at this time.

One sub stated that "the better generals notify subs as soon as possible." Seven generals who said they would notify the sub immediately after using the bid volunteered that they believe the sub is "entitled" to know. Similarly, three others said that notification at this time "establishes better relations with the sub." The great majority of subs, however, hear nothing until the general has been awarded the prime contract. The reasons given for this delay are significant for their lack of uniformity. A couple of generals attributed the delay to the rush of bidding. Other generals stated that the delay either gave them time to evaluate the sub, complete the paperwork, place orders for materials or schedule a place in the order of construction. A few generals stated that the delay was "accepted ethical practice." Two said that late notification helped prevent "mistakes," another said it kept "the subs from worrying us," and still another said that earlier notice was "premature." Yet twelve said that they would tell the sub if the sub called "anytime after bid opening." Of great importance, delay in notification can lead to serious enforcement problems if a contract is deemed to exist as of the time the general uses the sub's bid.

Finally, generals and subs were both asked what objection, if any, they would have if a court found that a contract was formed so that the parties were bound to perform as of the time the sub's bid was used by the general in his own bid. This contract would only take effect if the general received the prime contract. This was the most important question, and the responses were predictable. The only surprise was that complete unanimity among subs was not achieved. Forty-eight subs expressed their approval. Many added comments, such as "Wonderful!" or "I think this is the way it should be." Of the five subs who expressed reservations about finding a contract at this point, none was strongly opposed. Two felt that a general should not be forced to deal with a sub he discovers to be unsatisfactory after bid opening. Another stated that escalator clauses would have to be taken into account. The two remaining were not satisfied that such a finding alone would stop bid-shopping.

Of generals, twenty-eight objected to a court's finding of a contract while thirty-five did not. That a majority of the generals did not object seems remarkable in view of the fact that the change in the law posited by the question would bind the general at an earlier time than is the case under present law. Unreserved acceptance of the proposal was voiced by twenty-one generals. Comments ranged from "All for it" to "Excellent law" and "No objections whatever" to the following statement by one general: "None. We consider we have a contract under those conditions. If such a law were in effect it might serve to eliminate bid-shopping." However, it must be noted that one non-objector added that half his work was performed as a sub.

Many generals, both objecting and non-objecting, commented that the reliability of the sub was all important. One stated that "a sub's ability to perform is a big cost factor to the general contractor." Likewise, another said that he had no objection "so long as we have the right to use the second low bid if for some reason we do not wish to work with the low bidder." Most generals qualified their answers along these lines. Thus if this single objection can be satisfied, and if the votes are realigned accordingly, the result would be thirteen objecting and fifty not objecting—certainly an overwhelming response.

Lastly, nine objected because they did not have time to check the items included in the sub's bid during the hectic bid-opening period and did not want to be bound until after they had the opportunity to make such a check. Three non-objectors similarly qualified their answers.

Although 75% of the generals believed that both parties were obligated to each other as soon as the general used the sub's bid, many of these objected to being bound automatically at this point. Several generals agreed that a general often has to revise prices quoted by subs to fit the contract requirements. In such a situation there can be no contract since no sub's actual bid has been used.

Another objection raised by both generals and subs concerns the difficulty of proving whose bid was used. This practicality argument does not address itself to the wisdom of finding a contract. It merely adds an administrative difficulty and should not be allowed to shield unethical generals. Moreover, solutions are available. As in certain public contract bidding, the general could protect himself by posting the names of his subs with his own bid. This procedure has been recommended by at least one trade association.

A more substantial objection raised concerns the vagueness of some bids, undoubtedly caused by time pressures. As one general stated:

> None of them get their final bids to us until shortly before bid time—when the estimators must, within about three hours, take (over the phone) the sub's bid, get from him what he has covered—and evaluate all sub-bids—which entails adding to or deducting from a sub-bid, whatever he can find is the right price, for the work not included in some, and the extra work included by others. In a job in which there may be thirty-five sub-bid items the estimators may have 150 to 200 sub-bids to evaluate, choose one in each category, transfer the unit prices (which are part of so many bids) onto our sheets, then if there are alternates, add those bids up, add the alternates up, put them in our bid, say a prayer, and submit our bid.

The extent of this problem is uncertain. If plans and specifications are used, the sub's bid must comply with them. The uncertainties in the sub's bid may be of several different kinds. The sub simply may have failed to specify all the details, such as delivery and payment terms, which would be expected to be included in a final agreement. The responses indicated that this was generally the case. . . .

On the other hand, the sub's bid may be unresponsive to the general's request. In the hectic period prior to the submission of the general's bid, it is understandable that the general might inadvertently use such a bid, only to discover his error at some later time. Since the sub has failed to comply with the general's plans and specifications, he should not be allowed to reap the benefit of the general's error.

The principal concern of most objecting generals is the specter of being forced to deal with the "unknown" bidder. Bids may be received from subs that the general is not familiar with. Under this circumstance, a general would want to investigate the sub before awarding the subcontract. Further, a sub may not be registered and therefore not qualified to do the work. Moreover, a sub may be deemed by a general to not have a sufficient labor force to do the job. All of these circumstances are grounds for objection by a general. The problem is dramatically illustrated by the comments of a general who reported receiving a bid ten minutes before his own bid was due which was $85,000 lower than the next lowest bid. There simply was not sufficient time to investigate the bid or the bidder, yet since his competitors most likely had received the same bid, he was torn between using it or discarding it.

A possible solution was suggested by the generals themselves. Although no question dealt with this possibility, twelve generals volunteered that they treated solicited bids differently than unsolicited bids. If a general solicits bids, he should know in advance the financial position and reliability of the sub. Thus if a sub's bid is solicited and is responsive to the specifications, it is likely a trade usage exists that at the time a bid is used, a contract is formed. It is also likely that this usage exists if the general knows the sub's qualifications in advance. This necessarily introduces the problem of proving the general's prior knowledge, a task which would not seem overly burdensome.

At about the same time as the Virginia study, Richard Lewis did a study of the firm offer problem in England, in connection with an effort by the Law Commission for England and Wales.[38] He concluded by noting, "The refinement of the general principles of contract has been the concern of lawyers steeped in classical contract theory. The working paper [of the Commission] rests on an assumption of classical theory that formally available legal opportunities will be exploited in practice. This article together with earlier empirical studies has suggested that in the particular areas investigated such an assumption is not warranted."[39] Does this suggest that things in the United Kingdom are not too different from things in Virginia?

Consider the following decision in light of the Virginia study. How does the court know that the Wisconsin courts would hold that a subcontractor cannot withdraw a mistaken bid once the general contract has used that bid in computing its bid on the prime contract?

JANKE CONSTRUCTION CO. v. VULCAN MATERIALS CO.
United States District Court, Western District of Wisconsin
386 F. Supp. 687 (1974), *aff'd*, 527 F.2d 772 (1976)

ROSENSTEIN, J. In this action, plaintiff, a general contractor, alleges that defendant, a producer of construction materials, including reinforced concrete pipe, agreed to provide plaintiff with pipe and fittings at a per unit cost, for a marine construction project at the University of Wisconsin at Milwaukee, Wisconsin; that defendant expressly warranted and represented to plaintiff that defendant's products would meet the specifications required for that project; that plaintiff, in reliance thereon, used defendant's prices in bidding on the marine project and was awarded the contract; that following the award, defendant proposed to provide plaintiff with pipe and fittings which did not meet the specifications and which were rejected by the project engineers; and that plaintiff was thereby compelled to purchase the specified materials from another supplier at a higher cost, sustaining damages of $40,442.40.

Jurisdiction is based on diversity of citizenship and the parties do not contest that Wisconsin law applies. The case was tried to this Court without a jury, briefs were submitted, and the matter is now ripe for disposition.

Plaintiff, a Wisconsin corporation with its principal offices near Wausau, Wisconsin, has been engaged in various types of construction work, including highway, sewer, airport and marine projects. Defendant, a New Jersey corporation, operates quarries and has sand, gravel, aggregate, and redimix concrete plants in several states. In 1970, it also operated a concrete pipe plant located in Illinois which produced only AWWA (American Water Works Association) Specification C302 pipe.

---

[38] Lewis, *Contracts Between Businessmen: Reform of the Law of Firm Offers and an Empirical Study of Tendering Practices in the Building Industry*, 9 J. Law & Soc'y 153 (1982).
[39] *Id.* at 170-71.

In February 1970, the State Bureau of Engineering, on behalf of the Regents of the University of Wisconsin, publicly invited submission of sealed bids for the construction of condenser water transmission lines, lake piping and a pumping station for the University of Wisconsin-Milwaukee campus. The project was intended to provide the University with its own cooling system. The bids were to be opened at 2:00 P.M., on March 10, 1970, in Madison, Wisconsin.

The general construction, land, marine, and electrical work portions of the project were to be bid on separately, each portion requiring a separate lump sum bid. The marine portion of the work included the furnishing and installation of water intake and return lines into Lake Michigan. The materials required for marine piping included concrete subaqueous pipe in full compliance with either AWWA Specification C300 or AWWA Specification C301. The main contract also contained an "or equal" clause, permitting use of nonspecified materials of equal quality to those specified if they were considered equally acceptable to and approved by the project engineers.

Plaintiff, intending to bid on the marine work, obtained price quotations from suppliers of the various materials required for that portion of the project. On March 5, 1970, Jerry Janke, then vice-president of plaintiff, received by telephone from a Vulcan representative price quotations for the various concrete pipe items to be used in the marine work. Janke made a memorandum of the prices quoted, but did not inquire during this conversation whether defendant proposed to supply C300 or C301 pipe, nor did the caller specify the quality or type of pipe Vulcan intended to furnish.[40] Defendant's prices were $40,000 below that quoted by Interpace, another subaqueous concrete pipe supplier.

On the evening of March 9, 1970, Jerry Janke and his brother, James Janke, owner of plaintiff, checked in at a Madison hotel for the purpose of submitting their bid the next day. Around midnight they were visited in their hotel room by Alex Barry, then general manager of Vulcan's Wisconsin operation, and Peter W. Fox, a salesman for defendant's sand, gravel, crushed limestone, and redi-mix concrete.

While it is not clear whether the visit was only social or included some discussion of Vulcan's ability to furnish the pipe for the project, all parties present at that visit agree that there was no reference to the particular specifications or type of pipe that Vulcan proposed to supply. The next day, shortly prior to submitting his bid, James Janke met Barry in the hallway of the State Office Building. Janke was concerned because of the disparity in the prices quoted by Vulcan and Interpace. He requested and received assurance from Barry that Vulcan could furnish the pipe for the project. During that meeting Barry also placed a telephone call to someone at Vulcan who confirmed his statement.

According to Barry, Janke merely inquired at this meeting whether Vulcan could reduce its quoted prices on the pipe, and his telephone call to Vulcan's

---

[40] [1] Janke stated: "Pipe suppliers or any supplier giving quotations on projects normally don't bother to call you with a price or quotation unless they know they are going to be able to furnish the material, so I normally don't ask. If they call up and say I have some prices for you on this job, we want to sell it, I take the prices."

vice-president was made only to confirm his statement that prices would not be reduced.

Janke, who had relied upon Vulcan's quoted pipe prices in calculating his prime bid, thereupon submitted it and was subsequently awarded the contract.

Within the week after the bid opening plaintiff received a written quotation from Vulcan setting forth the same prices that were quoted to Jerry Janke over the telephone on March 5, but stating that the quotation was for AWWA C302 pipe. The writing is dated March 6, but it is not known when it was mailed.

The record does not indicate the date when plaintiff discovered that defendant was offering to supply C302 pipe and not the pipe listed in the specifications. However, between March 10 and March 23, James Janke met three times in Milwaukee and in Madison with the engineers for the State of Wisconsin, a representative from the University, Alex Barry, and Art Littva of Vulcan's engineering department in an effort to persuade the State to accept the C302 pipe. Littva then sent Janke specifications and shop drawings showing use of the C302 pipe on the marine project, and requested Janke to submit them under the "or equal clause." The plans were submitted as requested, and were rejected by the State's consulting engineers as not approved.

In response to James Janke's inquiry as to why the pipe did not meet specifications the engineers stated that the pipe was not AWWA C300 or C301 as specified; was not steel cylinder type; was not designed for an internal pressure of 5 psi; and did not have a beam strength equal to the pipe specified.

The engineers subsequently requested Janke to submit shop drawings using design conditions and materials as specified, stating that time was critical to the completion of the project. Plaintiff was then forced to buy the specified pipe from Interpace at a cost of $197,093.50, which was $39,942.40 [sic $39,992.40] over the $157,101.10 it would have paid for Vulcan's pipe in accordance with the latter's quotation. James Janke considered $150 to $200 per day to be the reasonable and fair value of his time spent in attending the meetings at Madison and Milwaukee with the state engineers on Vulcan's pipe. . . .

Plaintiff has had previous dealings with defendant, having purchased C302 pipe from it for a project in Racine, Wisconsin.

Evidence was adduced at the trial as to the normal bidding practices in the construction industry in the area. The contemplated project is generally listed or advertised in trade magazines and in the "Dodge Reports," a daily construction news service which lists proposed construction activity for various areas of the country. A subscriber to the "Dodge Reports" for a particular area may inspect the plans for a project in any Dodge plan room located in that area. The University of Wisconsin-Milwaukee project plans were available in Dodge plan rooms located in Milwaukee, Madison, Green Bay, and Eau Claire, Wisconsin.

An interested materials supplier checks the plans and specifications to determine if he can supply any of the required materials. He then submits a quotation by telephone, mail, or both to the contractors interested in bidding on the project. It is in this manner that contractors usually obtain quotations from the competing suppliers and subcontractors. These quotations are used by the contractors to estimate their own costs in preparing their bids. Normally, the twenty-four hour period preceding the prime bid deadline is one of great activity, with the subcontractors and suppliers making the rounds of the contractors who are still preparing their bids. By this time the first quotations have generally become known and the prices are often revised downward at the last minute, with the prime contractors revising their bids accordingly.

The contractor usually purchases the materials from the supplier whose prices he relied upon in preparing his bid. However, the contract is not entered into until after the contractor has been awarded the contract and the project engineers have approved the material, if such approval is needed. The supplier then prepares the shop drawings for the project after the successful bidder signs a letter of intent to purchase the material.

The Janke brothers testified that the supplier normally submits a price on material that will meet the specifications. However, Jerry Janke stated, if the supplier were offering non-specified material under the "or equal" clause he would, in the normal course of trade, alert the contractor to that fact so that the latter, if he relies upon this quotation, would note on his [the general's] bid that he proposed to supply alternate material under the "or equal" clause and that his bid is based on the substitute material.

In this manner the contractor would protect himself from having to perform on the bid, if it were accepted, in the event that the project engineers rejected the non-specified material as unsuitable.

Jerry Lapish, a marine contractor appearing for defendant, testified that when a quotation is received it is customarily the contractor's responsibility to check the specifications listed for the material on the quotation with the material specifications listed in the project contract to determine for himself whether the supplier is offering non-specified material.

Plaintiff views this action as one grounded in contract and governed by the Uniform Commercial Code which was adopted by Wisconsin (Wis. Stat. chs. 401-409). It contends that (1) defendant breached an alleged contract to furnish suitable and acceptable materials for the project, and (2) knowing that plaintiff relied upon its skill and judgment in furnishing the materials for the project, defendant had impliedly warranted their fitness for that particular purpose.

I agree with defendant that no binding contractual obligation existed under the Code. The mere use of Vulcan's bid was not an acceptance in law which gave rise to a contract with plaintiff. *N. Litterio & Company v. Glassman Construction Company,* 115 U.S. App. D.C. 335, 319 F.2d 736 (1963); . . . ; *Drennan v. Star Paving Company,* 51 Cal. 2d 409, 333 P.2d 757 (1958); . . . .

Defendant had not offered to make its bid irrevocable, nor was there an option supported by consideration. Thus its bid does not meet the "firm offer" requirement of section 402.205 Wis. Stat., which states:

> An offer by a merchant to buy or sell goods in a signed writing which by its terms gives assurance that it will be held open is not revocable, for lack of consideration, during the time stated or if no time is stated for a reasonable time, . . .

However, the absence of a contractual basis to plaintiff's claim is not fatal to its action. The facts which plaintiff has pleaded and relied upon to support its claim and to which defendant has responded in entering its defense give rise to the application of the doctrine of promissory estoppel. This doctrine is expressed in the Restatement of the Law of Contracts § 90 as follows:

> A promise which the promisor should reasonably expect to induce action or forbearance of a definite and substantial character on the part of the promisee and which does induce such action or forbearance is binding if injustice can be avoided only by enforcement of the promise.

In *Hoffman v. Red Owl Stores, Inc.*, 26 Wis. 2d 683, 696, 133 N.W.2d 267, 274 (1965), the Supreme Court of Wisconsin, in a significant and what may prove to be far reaching opinion, expressly adopted the doctrine of promissory estoppel, stating:

> Because we deem the doctrine of promissory estoppel, as stated in § 90 of Restatement, 1 Contracts, is one which supplies a needed tool which courts may employ in a proper case to prevent injustice, we endorse and adopt it.

In *Hoffman*, the court found that defendants had promised to establish plaintiffs as franchise operators of one of their stores in a certain town if they would invest a specific amount of capital and fulfill other conditions. During a two year period of negotiations, plaintiffs, relying upon defendants' promise, and in fulfillment of the conditions, sold their bakery and grocery businesses and a building, moved to another town, incurred moving expenses, made a down payment on a lot, and paid one month's rent on a home in the town where they had been led to believe that a franchised store would be available. Negotiations finally broke off after defendants demanded a larger capital investment than originally requested. The Court found that the factual elements of promissory estoppel were present and concluded that injustice would result if plaintiffs were not granted some relief because of defendants' failure to keep their promises which induced plaintiffs to act to their detriment.

The opinion is significant in that the Court clearly distinguished between an action on a promise based on promissory estoppel and one based on breach of contract.[41] The Court further held that a promise actionable under § 90 need not have all the elements of an offer that would result in a binding contract between the parties if the promisee were to accept the same. . . .

Having gained a firm foothold in Wisconsin, the doctrine has been extended there to third persons and held applicable as a basis for relief in actions by employees to receive pension benefits. *Scheuer v. Central States Pension Fund*, 358 F. Supp. 1332 (E.D.Wis.1973).

---

[41] [4] As the Court observed in N. Litterio & Company v. Glassman Construction Company, supra 319 F.2d at 738, the authorities do not "always keep clear the distinction between traditional rules of contract law and the principles of promissory estoppel." For a more extensive treatment of this subject, see Henderson, "Promissory Estoppel and Traditional Contract Doctrine," 78 Yale L.J. 343 (1969).

Although the Wisconsin authorities have not had occasion to consider the applicability of promissory estoppel to construction bidding cases, the doctrine has found increasing acceptance in other jurisdictions as a basis for a cause of action in litigation involving construction bids. . . .

[T]here is no logical reason, particularly in light of the language used in *Hoffman*, why § 90 of the Restatement should not apply to the situation herein. "It is only right and just that a promise a promisor knows will induce action of a substantial character be enforced if it is in fact relied on." *E. A. Coronis Associates v. M. Gordon Construction Co.*, *supra*, 216 A. 2d at 251.

The rationale for application of promissory estoppel to construction bidding cases is perhaps best expressed in *Drennan v. Red Star Paving Company*, *supra*. That case involved an oral bid by a subcontractor for certain work at a school project on which plaintiff, the general contractor, was about to bid. As defendant's bid was the lowest, plaintiff computed his own bid on the basis of defendant's bid price. Plaintiff was the successful bidder but was informed the next day by defendant that it would not do the work at its quoted price. The California Supreme Court, applying the promissory estoppel rule to prevent defendant's revocation of its bid stated (333 P.2d at 760):

> The very purpose of section 90 is to make a promise binding even though there was no consideration "in the sense of something that is bargained for and given in exchange."(See 1 Corbin, Contracts 634 et seq.) Reasonable reliance serves to hold the offeror in lieu of the consideration ordinarily required to make the offer binding.
>
> When plaintiff used defendant's offer in computing his own bid, he bound himself to perform in reliance on defendant's terms. Though defendant did not bargain for this use of its bid neither did defendant make it idly, indifferent to whether it would be used or not. On the contrary it is reasonable to suppose that defendant submitted its bid to obtain the subcontract. It was bound to realize the substantial possibility that its bid would be the lowest, and that it would be included by plaintiff in his bid. It was to its own interest that the contractor be awarded the general contract; the lower the subcontract bid, the lower the general contractor's bid was likely to be and the greater its chance of acceptance and hence the greater defendant's chance of getting the paying subcontract. Defendant had reason not only to expect plaintiff to rely on its bid but to want him to. Clearly defendant had a stake in plaintiff's reliance on its bid. Given this interest and the fact that plaintiff is bound by his own bid, it is only fair that plaintiff should have at least an opportunity to accept defendant's bid after the general contract has been awarded to him.
>
> It bears noting that a general contractor is not free to delay acceptance after he has been awarded the general contract in the hope of getting a better price. Nor can he reopen bargaining with the subcontractor and at the same time claim a continuing right to accept the original offer.
>
> . . .

Under the guidelines set down in *Hoffman*, if plaintiff is to prevail in an action under § 90 of the Restatement, it must establish that a definite promise was made by defendant with the reasonable expectation that it would induce action of a definite and substantial character on plaintiff's part; that plaintiff had acted in justifiable reliance upon the promise to its detriment; and that injustice can be avoided only by enforcement of the promise.

I find substantial evidence to support each of the afore-described elements of promissory estoppel.

Jerry Janke received a definite offer by telephone on March 5, 1970, from Vulcan to supply the concrete subaqueous pipe required for the University of Wisconsin-Milwaukee project at the quoted prices. At no time prior to the awarding of the contract was plaintiff informed that defendant was proposing to furnish anything other than the pipe specified in the project plans. Furthermore, I find that throughout its course of dealing with the Janke brothers on this particular bid, defendant intentionally, and successfully, represented to plaintiff through its agents that it "would supply the pipe for the job" (R. 34), that is, the pipe specified in the plans.

The Janke brothers, not unreasonably, had relied upon the representations of Vulcan's Wisconsin representative, Alex Barry, whom they knew from previous business dealings, and who continued to assure them up to the bid deadline that Vulcan could and would supply the required pipe.[42] Accordingly, the Jankes, men of limited formal education and with no engineering or technical experience in concrete subaqueous piping, were never alerted to the fact that they were relying upon a bid which was based on non-specified material. If they had known that defendant was offering pipe under the "or equal" clause, they would have conditioned their bid in like manner if they still wanted to use Vulcan's pipe.

I find that plaintiff acted with reasonable care and prudence in relying upon Vulcan's offer, and that this offer included, as represented to plaintiff, a proposal to furnish the specified concrete subaqueous pipe.

Plaintiff suffered substantial detriment by acting in reliance upon defendant's bid. It was compelled to go forward on the contract and supply the specified pipe when defendant's products were rejected as unsuitable. Upon defendant's refusal or inability to furnish the required material, plaintiff had to purchase it from Interpace, the other pipe supplier, at a price which was $39,992.40 over defendant's bid. Injustice can be avoided only by enforcement of the promise; accordingly, plaintiff is entitled to reliance damages.

[The court found that Barry had both real and apparent authority to make representations on behalf of Vulcan. It is worth noting that the "apparent authority rule in agency law seems to embody an objective theory of contract formation."]

One question remains. Can the statute of frauds, raised by defendant as a defense in the context of plaintiff's contractual claim, be raised as a defense to a claim for damages based on the theory of promissory estoppel? The issue has not

---

[42] [5] Barry's recollection that his last minute meeting with James Janke on March 10 and his confirming phone call to Vulcan's vice president concerned an attempt by Janke to get a lower price on the pipe seems scarcely credible in view of the fact that Vulcan's price was $40,000 below the quote Janke had received from Interpace.

been raised in the Wisconsin courts and there is a split of opinion in other juris-dictions where this question has been considered.

[The court noted that some courts, like New York, have declined to use prom-issory estoppel to defeat a statute of frauds defense. Other states, like Hawaii, in *McIntosh v. Murphy*,[43] have no such reservations. The District of Columbia, in the *Litterio* case, *supra*, held that promissory estoppel could be used in cases of oral promises.]

I agree with the statement in *Litterio* as to the inapplicability of the statute. The statute of frauds relates to the enforceability of *contracts*; promissory estoppel relates to *promises* which have no contractual basis and are enforced only when necessary to avoid injustice. The Wisconsin Supreme Court clearly stated in *Hoffman* that a promise which could not meet the requirements of an offer that would ripen into a contract if accepted by the promisee is nonetheless enforce-able to avoid injustice if the other elements of promissory estoppel are present. To allow defendant to raise the statute of frauds herein as a defense to prevent enforcement of a promise that is actionable under § 90 of the Restatement would defeat the spirit and intent of *Hoffman*. Accordingly, I find the statute is not ap-plicable in an action based on promissory estoppel.

Turning now to plaintiff's claimed damages, the rule in Wisconsin is that "Where damages are awarded in promissory estoppel instead of specifically en-forcing the promisor's promise, they should be only such as in the opinion of the court are necessary to prevent injustice." *Hoffman, supra*, 26 Wis. 2d at 701, 133 N.W. 2d at 276. I find that the sum of $39,942.40 [*sic;* should be $39,992.40], which represents the difference between what would have been paid for the pipe under defendant's bid and the actual cost to plaintiff in purchasing it from Inter-pace is a proper item of damages. However, the damages claimed for the time James Janke spent in attending meetings with the state engineers after the con-tract was awarded and with the knowledge that defendant would not supply the required pipe are not recoverable under the promissory estoppel doctrine. These actions were not taken in reliance upon defendant's promise but were part of an effort to get the State to accept defendant's nonspecified pipe. In other words, they were not induced by defendant's bid.

It is hereby ordered that judgment be entered in favor of plaintiff in the amount of $39,942.40 [sic $39,992.40] plus costs.

NOTES AND QUESTIONS

1. *The Restatement (Second) of Contracts solution*: At this point, you should consult § 87 of the Restatement (Second) of Contracts. Those drafting the Restatement (Second) of Contracts were aware of cases such as *James Baird Co. v. Gimbel Bros.*[44] and *Drennan v. Star Paving Co.* Rather than adopting a strin-gent rule wherein *no* firm offers, or *all* firm offers, were enforceable against a bidder, they fashioned an intermediate position, embodied in § 87. Consider the adequacy of the Restatement's solution in light of the Virginia survey.

---

[43] 52 Haw. 29, 469 P.2d 177 (1970).
[44] 64 F.2d 344 (2d Cir. 1993).

2. *The legislative decision*: Suppose you were a legislator considering a bill to deal with the legal enforceability of bids by subcontractors submitted to general contractors. Thus, you are free to decide how to vote entirely on the merits of the proposal. In light of the Virginia survey, would you have adopted the solution of the court in the *Janke Construction* case, the Restatement of Contracts,[45] or something else?

3. *Equality and the subcontractor's rights*: Suppose a general contractor uses a subcontractor's bid, and under cases such as *Janke Construction Co., Inc. v. Vulcan Materials Co., Inc.*, the subcontractor cannot withdraw it. The general contractor then receives the award from the state agency or owner. Now can the subcontractor successfully sue the general contractor if it does not award the subcontractor the contract? The Minnesota Supreme Court, which had followed *Drennan v. Star Paving Co.*, decided that symmetry did not require that the subcontractor gain rights. In *Holman Erection Co. v. Orville E. Madsen & Sons, Inc.*,[46] a general contractor declined to award a contract to a subcontractor whose bid it had used (and had listed on its own winning bid). In a suit brought by the disappointed sub, the court directly addressed the apparent unfairness of allowing the general to choose another sub, while at the same time refusing to allow subs to refuse to accept contracts at the general's option. The court reasoned that the general has, and must, rely on the subcontractors, while the subs have no reciprocal need to rely on getting a contract. In addition,

> The bidding process puts the subcontractor and the general in very different positions as to the content of the subcontract. The subcontractors have the luxury of preparing their bids on their own timetable, subject only to the deadline for submitting their bids to the general contractors. The same bid goes to all the general contractors and covers the same work. The generals, on the other hand, are dealing with all the various construction aspects of the project and with numerous potential subcontractors. They compile their bids, as the various subcontractor bids are received, within a few hours of the deadline for submission of the prime bid. Specifics are necessarily given less than thorough consideration and are left for future negotiations. . . .

> Although supplying some certainty and symmetry to the construction industry, . . . a decision [in favor of subcontractors whose bids have been used by generals] would also impose a rigidity on the process and result in greater cost to awarding authorities and potential detriment to general

---

[45] For an attack on the approach of the Restatement, see Kniffin, *Innovation or Aberration: Recovery for Reliance on a Contract Offer, as Permitted by the New Restatement (Second) of Contracts*, 62 U. Det. L. Rev. 23, 39 (1984). She says, "before the general is bound or has bound the sub, the general cannot reasonably expect to be protected from risk." Kniffin also suggests that while the sub can better predict the probability that a loss will occur, the general has better ability to insure against losses caused by subs withdrawing their bids. Generals will increase the amount they bid to cover such risks. Furthermore, under the Restatement rule, offerors (subcontractors) will be uncertain whether they are bound to contracts for some time after they submit their bids. Do you find her arguments persuasive?

[46] 330 N.W.2d 693 (Minn. 1983).

contractors. If such a change is to take place, it is one properly brought before the legislature.[47]

4. ***Representing the bidder who wants out***: Suppose you are retained to represent a bidder who does not want to perform under the terms and conditions of the bid it made. First, you establish that the general contractor seems willing to sue your client. In other words, the damages claimed are substantial, and your client has sufficient assets to make it worth seeking a judgment. Second, the other-than-legal sanctions are not strong enough to prompt your client to perform and swallow its losses. Third, your client probably made a mistake in preparing its bid so that it is far too low.

What can you do to defend your client? Of course, you would like to win a total victory, but remember that if you can fashion a plausible theory, you might be able to settle the case for far less than the general's total damages. The following strategies are worth considering.

(a) ***Attack the firm offer rule***: You might try to persuade the court in your state to reject the firm offer rule reflected in Restatement (Second) of Contracts § 87. This would be playing a long shot. Court after court has adopted the rule. Many of these decisions fail to offer convincing arguments justifying holding bidders once generals have used their bids. Nonetheless, you would have to be very persuasive to convince a court that Justice Traynor's *Drennan v. Star Paving* opinion, the Restatement (Second) of Contracts, almost all writers in the law reviews and the great weight of authority were wrong.

(b) ***Construe the bid***: Lawyers, seeking a way out for clients caught in contracts that have turned out unfavorably, know that they may find legal ammunition if they read written documents or carefully consider testimony about the deal. If the case can be made, it always is nice to say that your client is ready, willing, and able to perform its side of the bargain. However, it never promised to do A, B, and C, as the plaintiff contends. Rather, it only promised to do A, B, and D. (This tactic is feasible only if your client is willing to perform A, B, and D.) Plans and specifications for building construction often are ambiguous if not contradictory.

A few cases have said that the bidder can reserve a right to withdraw the bid after a general has used it. However, if you want to use such language, you face all the fine print problems. For example, in *Lyon Metal Products, Inc. v. Hagerman Construction Corp.*,[48] a general contractor sued a manufacturer of athletic lockers which had made a mistaken bid. The manufacturer's bid was submitted on its quotation form. On the reverse side a clause printed in very small type stated "this quotation may be withdrawn and is subject to change without notice after 15 days from date of quotation."[49] The general relied on the supplier's bid, but it did not make a contract with the manufacturer before 15 days had passed. The manufacturer attempted to withdraw its quotation, arguing that it was entitled to withdraw the bid unless it was accepted within 15 days. Nonetheless, the

---

[47] *Id.* at 698-699.
[48] 391 N.E.2d 1152 (Ind. Ct. App. 1979).
[49] *Id.* at 1153.

court found the general's reliance reasonable and held the manufacturer to the bid. It noted that the bid was in small print on the back of the quote, was not brought to the attention of the general, and was arguably inconsistent with terms in the specifications.

(c) *Use the rules of mistake and Restatement § 90*: To trigger Restatement § 90, reliance must be reasonable. If a general knew or should have known that a bid was based on a mistake, then it cannot reasonably rely on it. For example, in *Maurice Electrical Supply Co., Inc. v. Anderson Safeway Guard Rail Corp.*,[50] the court found that "plaintiff's reliance was not reasonable because of the great difference in price quotes received from defendant and the other two potential suppliers. . . . While the price quotes obtained from the other two suppliers were quite similar to each other, they were anywhere from 50 to almost 100 percent higher than the price quotes given by defendant. In such circumstances, plaintiff's reliance was not justifiable."[51] The court noted "[w]hile a party may reasonably rely on an unusually low price quote if it reconfirms the price quote prior to reliance, here the Court found plaintiff did not reconfirm the price quote prior to bidding on the resale contract."[52]

To similar effect, the Supreme Court of Utah, in *Tolboe Construction Co. v. Staker Paving & Construction Co.*,[53] found that a general contractor's reliance was not reasonable although its estimator telephoned the subcontractor and asked it to review its bid. Defendant's bid was 290 percent below that of the next lowest bid and 350 percent below the other bid submitted. Experts testified that they had never seen a disparity in bids for asphalt paving as large as the one in this case. Another general contractor who bid on the project received the same erroneous bid from defendant and rejected it, assuming that it must be mistaken. The telephone call did not alert defendant to the problem.[54]

In an earlier decision, *Union Tank Car Co. v. Wheat Bros.*,[55] the Utah Supreme Court described the firm offer rule as one involving a balancing of the equities. Wheat Brothers bid $22,500 to paint four steel tanks, based on the erroneous assumption that they could use ordinary paint which cost $6/gallon. Their bid was $6,000 lower than any others because in fact the specifications required "phenoline" paint which cost $26/gallon. Union Tank's representative had called John Wheat to invite a bid and Wheat had phoned in a bid later in the day. A document subsequently sent to Wheat described the job, listed the Wheat Brother's price, and noted that the job was to be done "as per attached specifications"; the specifications referred to "phenoline" paint, but there was no indication that the paint

---

[50] 632 F. Supp. 1082 (D. D.C. 1986).

[51] *Id.* at 1090.

[52] *Id.* at 1091, n.14.

[53] 682 P.2d 843 (1984).

[54] The court said that "According to plaintiff's own version of the request, defendant's estimator was merely informed, as would be any bidder whose bid was 10 to 15 percent below the next lowest bid, that his bid was substantially low, and further was asked to reconfirm it. Nothing was mentioned by plaintiff with respect to the large disparity between defendant's bid and the others, or of any other apparent error. Thus we conclude that plaintiff's request for verifica-tion did not validate the erroneous bid nor justify plaintiff's reliance." *Id.* at 848.

[55] 15 Utah 2d 101, 387 P.2d 1000 (1964).

was extraordinarily expensive. Wheat Brothers signed the document. They then discovered the cost of the paint and sought to withdraw the offer. However, Union Tank had used the Wheat Brothers bid, and had been awarded the contract. The Utah court found that the balance of equities favored Wheat Brothers. Union Tank was in control of the situation. It could have warned Wheat Brothers about the high cost of phenoline paint; it was obvious that Wheat Brothers' bid was based on the price of ordinary paint. Union Tank called twice to verify the bid, but did nothing to alert Wheat Brothers to the high cost of phenoline paint.

(d) *Try to prove bid shopping and chopping*: Most of the states that have adopted the position of Justice Traynor's *Drennan* decision have followed his suggestion that a general contractor loses the right to hold a sub to its bid if the general engages in bid shopping or chopping. That is, the general cannot negotiate with other subcontractors for a cheaper offer after it gets the award and still hold the sub whose bid the general used. Nor can the general negotiate with the sub whose bid the general used and still hold the sub to the original bid.[56]

(e) *Assert the Statute of Frauds*: Often bids of subcontractors and material suppliers are made orally by telephone at the last minute before a general must submit its bid. Contracts for the sale of services need not be in writing unless they cannot be performed within one year. Contracts for the sale of goods for a price of $500 or more, however, come under § 2-201 of the UCC. Furthermore, § 2-205 provides that merchants can make firm offers "in a signed writing which by its terms give assurance that it will be held open."

Remember that the *Janke Construction Co.* case finds that the Statute of Frauds applies to enforcing contracts but not to claims based on promissory estoppel. Thus, Restatement (Second) of Contracts § 90 makes an oral bid of a supplier of goods irrevocable once a general has used it. The court notes in a footnote that Restatement (Second) of Contracts § 217A[57] provides that a court can enforce a promise because of reliance to avoid injustice despite the Statute of Frauds. This provision calls for a case-by-case balancing of factors.

But the court in *C.R. Fedrick, Inc. v. Borg-Warner Corp.*,[58] came to a different result. The federal court decided that the Supreme Court of California would not apply promissory estoppel in a case involving a bid to supply goods for a price of $500 or more. While California had recognized that equitable estoppel might be used to overcome the provisions of the Statute of Frauds, the court declined to apply the doctrine in this case. It decided that equitable estoppel required either a promise not to assert the Statute of Frauds or a representation that a writing was not required; mere reliance on the alleged oral contract was not enough. The Court of Appeals further decided that equitable estoppel to assert the Statute of Frauds requires a greater degree of detrimental reliance than does promissory estoppel. Finally, the Court of Appeals found that the California legislature had resolved the policy questions by passing § 2-201 of the UCC. Section 2-201(3)

---

[56] *See, e.g.,* N. Litterio & Co., Inc. v. Glassman Construction Co., Inc., 319 F.2d 736 (D.C. Cir. 1963); Haselden-Langley Constructors, Inc. v. D.E. Farr & Associates, Inc., 676 P.2d 709 (Colo. App. 1983).

[57] This section is now § 139 in the published version of the Restatement.

[58] 552 F.2d 852 (9th Cir. 1977).

itself offers limited exceptions to the writing requirements of subsections (1) and (2) and it was not proper for the court to create new exceptions.

While firm offers and consideration may have been the issue of the 1950s and 1960s, today oral firm offers and the Statute of Frauds provoke more dispute. Slightly more courts have followed the *Fedrick* approach than the one found in the *Janke Construction Co.* case. The argument in many of these decisions refusing to apply promissory estoppel is very simple: UCC §§ 2-201and 2-205 demand writings and make only limited exceptions. Thus, there is no room for Restatement § 90 to apply to oral bids to supply goods. If this doctrine were recognized, the UCC provisions would be meaningless. If there are to be any further exceptions, it is for the legislature to create them.

How should courts reconcile the competing goals of protecting the reliance of generals on bids from material suppliers and the Statute of Frauds' demand for writings? It is clear that oral bids are common in the construction industry. However, notice that UCC § 2-201 applies only to transactions in goods and not to bids to supply services mixed with goods incidental to the transaction. Thus, if promissory estoppel does not override the UCC Statute of Frauds, bids from suppliers of materials such as the Borg-Warner Corporation will not be enforced unless they are in writing. Oral bids from small asphalt paving contractors, as in Justice Traynor's *Drennan* case, will be enforced since they are not governed by the UCC.

Does this distinction make sense? On one hand, large corporations are bureaucratic, and they typically deal through written documents as a way for those at the top of the chain of command to control salespeople and others who deal with outsiders. From this perspective, is it reasonable for a general contractor bidding on a job to rely on oral bids from a salesperson representing a large corporation? Even if it is reasonable, perhaps the courts are trying to make it easier to run large bureaucratic corporations. On the other hand, the position of the *Fedrick* case means that large corporations need not stand behind their bids while small contractors must.

5.   *Mistakes, bids, and government contracts*: Governmental agencies cannot give away the taxpayer's money. Contracting officers seldom are authorized to be sympathetic, or to compromise to preserve a relationship. If contracting officers are given too much discretion, some might sell it for bribes. Hard and fast rules may also help ward off political influence. These reasons suggest governments could justifiably have the benefit of different rules than commercial enterprises. However, bidding mistakes are a recurrent problem and seem to call for some relief. Cases and statutes have attempted to deal with it by creating standards for relief. How should the balance be struck? The following case provides one court's effort.

MARANA UNIFIED SCHOOL DIST. NO. 6 v. AETNA CASUALTY AND SURETY CO.
Court of Appeals of Arizona
144 Ariz. 159, 696 P.2d 711 (1985)

BIRDSALL, C.J. This appeal arises from a complaint filed by the appellee, Marana Unified School District, seeking judgment on a bid bond given by appellants, L.G. Lefler, Inc., doing business as Defco Construction Company, principal, and the Aetna Casualty and Surety Company, surety. The bond was provided pursuant to A.R.S. § 34-201(A)(3) because Defco submitted a bid proposal to construct a junior high school building for the appellee. The statute provides:

> 3. That every proposal shall be accompanied by a certified check, cashier's check or a surety bond for five per cent of the amount of the bid included in the proposal as a guarantee that the contractor will enter into a contract to perform the proposal in accordance with the plans and specifications, or as liquidated damages in event of failure or refusal of the contractor to enter into the contract. The certified check, cashier's check or surety bond shall be returned to the contractors whose proposals are not accepted, and to the successful contractor upon the execution of a satisfactory bond and contract as provided in this article.

Although Defco was the low bidder, it refused to enter into a contract with the appellee because it had made a mathematical mistake in its proposal.

The trial court entered summary judgment in favor of the Marana District. . . . The appellants' cross motion for summary judgment was denied.

The facts considered in the light most favorable to the appellants may be summarized as follows. The appellee gave notice of its intent to receive sealed bids for the construction of the school pursuant to A.R.S. § 34-201. The bids were required to be submitted by 4 p.m., February 2, 1982, at which time they were opened. The appellant's bid was for $4,890,000 together with alternates, all of which totalled $5,936,500. The bid bond attached to the proposal was "in the sum of five per cent of contract bid." No actual figures were set forth on the bond but the proposal referred to the required bid bond amount as five per cent of the "base bid" which would have been $244,500. Nine other contractors submitted bids. Defco's was the lowest base bid. The next lowest base bid was $5,447,000. The architect's estimated cost for the construction without alternates was $4,900,000. Defco's bid was within two-tenths of one per cent of that estimate.

After all bids were opened, the architect and school district officials reviewed them and a written recommendation was made that day to accept Defco's base bid together with two alternates totalling $5,253,080.

At about the same time, Defco personnel were rechecking their figures since it appeared that a mistake may have been made. The employee who had tabulated Defco's bid sheet then discovered that she had used $42,000 as the bid for the structural steel when the correct figure was $412,000, a mistake of $370,000.

According to the employee's affidavit attached to the appellants' cross-motion for summary judgment, she was still receiving telephone bids from subcontractors and suppliers and working on Defco's bid up until 3:30 on February 2; she found a mistake in her first tabulation of some 170 items on the bid sheet and did a second tabulation, then added the figures six times. Since this brought her so close to the time the bid had to be submitted, there was no time to have another employee check her figures.

Defco advised appellee by telephone within one and one-half hours of the bid opening of the mistake which came to $398,752 with the addition of other items based on percentages of the $370,000 error. A letter containing the same information was delivered to the school within three hours after the bid was opened at 4 p.m. In the letter Defco asked to meet with the school officials to show them the calculator tapes and bid sheet which revealed how the error had occurred.

[After two school board meetings, and confirmation that Defco was unwilling to perform if awarded the contract, the architect was instructed to re-bid the job.]

The important issue presented by this appeal is whether a low bidder for a public contract may refuse to enter into a contract because of a mistake in the bid without forfeiting the bid bond. Although this question has never been decided in Arizona, it has been the subject of numerous opinions in our sister states and federal courts. . . .

It is the appellee's position that the statute permits no escape from forfeiture. There is authority to support such a result. These decisions are cited by the appellees: *Board of Edn. v. Sever-Williams Co.*, 22 Ohio St.2d 107, 258 N.E.2d 605, cert. denied, 400 U.S. 916, 91 S. Ct. 175, 27 L. Ed.2d 155 (1970), and *A.J. Colella, Inc. v. County of Allegheny*, 391 Pa. 103, 137 A.2d 265 (1958). . . . The reasoning in these decisions is generally the same, that this is the purpose of the statute and to permit exceptions would materially weaken the purpose of the bidding procedure for public contracts and make the bid bond requirement meaningless. In *Colella* the court opines that plea of a clerical mistake would make the system of sealed bids a mockery. *Sever-Williams* speaks of possible abuse of the bidding procedure, i.e., favoritism or fraud. . . .

We do not agree with the reasoning or result in those cases. Nor do we believe that the Arizona legislature intended that there be no relief from forfeiture of the bid security for equitable reasons. We agree with the appellants that unless the legislature clearly indicates an intention to do so, its enactments shall not be construed so as to change established common law. *Terry v. Lincscott Hotel Corp.*, 126 Ariz. 548, 617 P.2d 56 (1980); . . . The doctrine of rescission for unilateral clerical mistake was set forth by the United States Supreme Court as early as 1900. *See Moffett, Hodgkins, & Clarke Co. v. City of Rochester*, 178 U.S. 373, 20 S. Ct. 957, 44 L. Ed. 1108 (1900).

We believe the trial court erred in granting summary judgment in favor of the appellee. We follow those decisions which hold that when relief from the forfeiture is legally justifiable, statutes like Arizona's do not mandate the forfeiture. The cases upon which we rely all arise under a statute or bid solicitation which, on its face, prohibits a withdrawal of bids. . . . In these cases the bidder notified the public authority of the mistake prior to acceptance of the bid. Clearly this notice was promptly given by Defco before the appellee had accepted the bid. [The Arizona statute also prohibited bidders from withdrawing their bids for 45 days.]

A starting point is the decision in *Moffett, Hodgkins, & Clarke Co. v. City of Rochester, supra.* The mistake in *Moffett* resulted from mathematical errors committed by an extremely nearsighted engineer working in great haste with a voluminous number of specifications. Affirming a decree in favor of the contractor, the Supreme Court said that the contractor was not endeavoring to withdraw or cancel a bid or bond in contravention of the city charter, since the contractor was proceeding upon the theory that the bid read at the meeting of the board was one which it had never intended to make, and that the minds of the parties had never met. The Court added that if the city was correct in its contention that the charter provision barred any remedy, then there would be no redress for a bidder on a public work, no matter how aggravated or palpable his blunder. A material mistake of fact in a bid justifies a conclusion that there has been no meeting of the minds because the bidder did not intend to make the erroneous bid. . . .

What appear to be the majority decisions rely upon the equitable remedy of rescission. In these decisions the courts have held or recognized that the bidder who had notified the public authority of the mistake prior to acceptance of the bid was entitled to a decree rescinding the bid, or to similar equitable relief, despite a statute similar to A.R.S. § 34-201(A)(3). . . .

These cases generally set forth certain criteria to be satisfied before a forfeiture can be avoided. The criteria are summarized in yet another especially comprehensive decision, *City of Baltimore v. De Luca-Davis Construction Co.*, 210 Md. 518, 524, 124 A.2d 557, 562 (1956).

> 1, the mistake must be of such grave consequences that to enforce the contract as made or offered would be unconscionable; 2, the mistake must relate to a material feature of the contract; 3, the mistake must not have come about because of the violation of a positive legal duty or from culpable negligence; 4, the other party must be put in status quo to the extent that he suffers no serious prejudice except the loss of his bargain.
>
> . . . .

Other cases have added as an additional reason for permitting rescission that the public body knew or had reason to know that a mistake had been made. . . . We do not understand that to be a requirement for rescission. It is indeed difficult to envisage a fact situation where the public body would know that a sealed bid contained a mistake prior to its opening unless the bidder discovered and gave notice of the mistake. After that, unless the bid is accepted and a contract made, it seems immaterial whether upon opening the bid the public body knew or should have known. At least in the instant case, where the appellant notified the appellee within three hours and before any attempted acceptance of the bid, it does not appear to be material.

Other courts admonish that a bidder should not be able to withdraw a bid under circumstances profitable to the bidder or which would permit any collusion or connivance among bidders to the detriment of the public. . . . Nothing suggests any such problems in the record before us.

Turning to the four conditions required by *DeLuca* and other decisions, we believe they are all satisfied by the undisputed evidence before the trial court. We consider them in order.

First, was the mistake of such consequence as to make enforcement of the contract unconscionable? From our analysis of the reported decisions this refers not to the bid bond, since it contains no mistake, but to the mistake in the bid. That mistake was in the amount of almost $400,000. This was approximately eight per cent of the base bid of $4,890,000. Although we believe this to be unconscionable on its face, we compare it to the amounts involved in other reported cases. Thus we find: [The court then cited 10 cases finding mistakes of unconscionable size. Rounding off the amounts, they can be summarized as follows: Mistake of $34,000 on bid of $464,000; mistake of 14% on bid of $141,000; mistake of $150,000 on bid of $883,000; mistake of $590,000 on bid of $1,769,000; mistake of $100,000 on bid of $1,367,000; mistake of $301,800 on bid of $780,000; mistake of $35,000 on bid of $173,000; mistake of $50,000 on bid of $145,000; mistake of $145,000 on bid of $1,242,000 and mistake of $182,000 on bid of $3,547,000.]

Although some of these are proportionately greater than the mistake of Defco, some are smaller in proportion to the bid, and we believe the amount of the mistake was of such grave consequence that it would be unconscionable to enforce it.

The appellee argues, however, that forfeiture of the 5 per cent bid bond is not unconscionable because it is the very bid contract which was bargained for and made by the parties. This argument does not go to the issue of unconscionability but rather to the principal issue, i.e., must the bid bond be forfeited despite the presence of legal justification for the refusal to enter into the contract. In all of the cases cited above, the discussion of unconscionability concerns the amount of the mistake in the bid and not the bid security. In each case it appears that the bid security sought to be forfeited was required by statute or by the bidding documents. Thus if unconscionability was to be determined by reference to the fact that the parties knew the amount of the penalty to be exacted, we believe that would have been decisive in many of those cases. We find no such holding. Assuming, arguendo, that we should look to the forfeiture of the bid bond rather than the amount of the mistake, one quarter of a million dollars is still, in the vernacular, a lot of money, and we believe it would be unconscionable to require even this forfeiture in the instant case.

The second condition, that the mistake must relate to a material feature of the contract, cannot be disputed. The amount to be paid for the construction is clearly a material feature of the contract.

The third condition concerns the question of whether the mistake constituted culpable negligence or the violation of a positive legal duty. If either, then this third requirement is unsatisfied. Since there is no contention that the appellant violated any legal duty, we must determine only whether there was "culpable negligence." Generally a mechanical, clerical, or mathematical error satisfies this condition whereas an error in judgment does not. In fact this distinction highlights the inequitable result of the trial court's decision in this case. The mistake was not one of judgment, as for example, underestimating the cost of labor or materials. It was not intended. We believe this distinction also serves to show the real purpose for the statute requiring forfeiture of the security. The bidder who makes an error in judgment should be penalized if he then refuses to execute the contract. On the other hand, the bidder who submits a bid which is different than that which he intended to make is entitled to relief. . . . The type of mistake satisfying this condition has been variously referred to as resulting from some reasonable excuse, . . . based upon an erroneous omission and not involving gross negligence, . . . and honest and not gross negligence, ...

At least one jurisdiction, Illinois, requires that the party seeking rescission prove that the mistake occurred notwithstanding the exercise of reasonable care. Thus in the present case the appellee argues there was lack of reasonable care. Deposition testimony revealed that the normal procedure would have been to have a second person total the figures on the bid spread sheet and run a tape on those prices as a check on the work of the original clerk. This procedure was not followed. Likewise the original clerk notified one of the estimators working on the project just prior to the bid deadline that her work had not been double-checked. *See also John J. Calnan Co. v. Talsma Builders, Inc.*, 67 Ill. 2d 213, 10 Ill.Dec. 242, 367 N.E.2d 695 (1977) where the court considered the failure of a subcontractor to utilize its own bid procedures. Despite finding this to be less than the exercise of reasonable care, the case is distinguishable since the mistake was not discovered until performance under the contract had begun and it was impossible to return the general contractor to status quo.

We reject the reasonable care standard since it appears to be nothing more than a test for negligence. We agree with the rationale appearing in the comment to § 157 of the Restatement, Second, Contracts. Section 157 concerns the effect of the fault of the party seeking relief from a mistake and provides:

> A mistaken party's fault in failing to know or discover the facts before making the contract does not bar him from avoidance or reformation under the rules stated in this Chapter, unless his fault amounts to a failure to act in good faith and in accordance with reasonable standards of fair dealing.

The comment to the section states:

> The mere fact that a mistaken party could have avoided the mistake by the exercise of reasonable care does not preclude either avoidance or reformation. Indeed, since a party can often avoid a mistake by the exercise of such care, the availability of relief would be severely circumscribed if he were to be barred by his negligence. Nevertheless, in extreme cases the mistaken party's fault is a proper ground for denying him relief for a mistake that he otherwise could have avoided. Although the critical degree of fault is sometimes described as "gross" negligence, that term is not well defined and is avoided in this Section as it is in the Restatement, Second, of Torts. Instead, the rule is stated in terms of good faith and fair dealing.

Defco's burden of showing good faith and fair dealing is satisfied and not in dispute. No facts are suggested by affidavit, deposition, or otherwise from which it could be inferred that there was a lack of good faith or fair dealing.

Another method of testing the mistake to determine if it could be "culpable negligence" is comparing it to the other mistakes for which the courts have granted relief. Such a comparison shows several factual situations which are strikingly similar to the instant case. . . .

Thus we are left with the question of whether the appellee has been placed in status quo so that it suffers no serious prejudice except loss of bargain.

The minutes of the Marana school board meeting of February 4 show that the board rejected all bids and instructed the architect to prepare to rebid the construction contract. All of the rejected bids including the bid the appellant intended to make exceeded the architect's estimate by over $350,000. Obviously the board decided to try again. These facts were before the court for its consideration on the cross-motions for summary judgment. The appellants contend that they established that the school had been put in status quo. The appellee offered nothing to refute this conclusion. No evidence shows that the appellee contends that it suffered serious prejudice, or, in fact, any prejudice except the loss of a bargain which was never intended by the appellants.

We reverse the judgment and direct the trial court to enter judgment in favor of the appellants. HATHAWAY, J., and WILLIAM N. SHERRILL, Superior Court Judge, concur.

NOTES AND QUESTIONS

1. *Mistaken bids on public projects*: As the *Marana Unified School District* case indicates, some courts require that the bond be forfeited despite clerical errors. See, e.g., *J.D. Graham Const., Inc. v. Pryor Public Schools,*[59] where the court distinguished the *Marana* decision because of the differences in the text of the Arizona and Oklahoma statutes dealing with public bidding. Other courts offer relief under a number of theories with many qualifications. See, e.g., *Powder Horn Constructors, Inc. v. City of Florence,*[60] where the court, by a 4 to 3 vote, followed the approach of the *Marana* case. The majority and dissenting opinions review the law review writing and the Restatement (Second) of Contracts position. The Arizona and Colorado courts refuse to require that the public body knew or should have known of the mistake. Thus, we are considering whether there should be a remedy for a unilateral mistake by the bidder when officials of the public body had no reason to recognize that a mistake had been made.

2. *Private construction and mistaken bids*: Suppose the owner seeking bids for construction is not a unit of government but a business corporation. Would the doctrine of *Marana Unified School District v. Aetna* offer relief for bidding mistakes in such a case? If not, are there any avenues open to a bidder who has made a serious error? Many cases say that I cannot snap up your offer, knowing it to be mistaken. The difficulty, of course, comes in deciding that I knew or

---

[59] 854 P.2d 917 (Okla. App. 1993).
[60] 754 P.2d 356 (Colo. 1988).

should have known of your error. It is not necessarily enough that your bid is the lowest one I received. It is not necessarily enough that it is entirely out of the range of the other bids. Your very low bid might rest on a mistake, but also it might rest on efficiency or competitive conditions. Assuming that you cannot show that I knew or should have known your bid to rest on a mistake, can you recover for your mistake that I did not share?

Many states have statutes dealing with mistakes in bidding on public construction. You must always check to see if such a statute controls if you are faced with this problem.

d. Unilateral Mistakes in Communicating: I Meant "X" But Said "Y"

A note on unilateral mistake: Courts have always been reluctant to grant relief to a bargainer who makes a mistake in entering a contract. In part, this reflects our view that a deal is a deal. A court will not relieve a life insurance company of liability because it did not expect the insured to die so soon. A trader on a commodities exchange cannot claim an excuse because he thought the market would go up but it went down. A consumer may want a red car instead of the black one he bought, but has no right to insist the seller exchange automobiles. You have a right to rely on the deal, even if I made a mistake. Furthermore, taking responsibility for my errors should give me reason to be careful and avoid them.

Nonetheless, many writers have advocated more relief for bargainers' mistakes—at least when relief would not hurt the other party. In recent years courts have moved in this direction. However, most of the cases where they have been willing to grant relief involve different kinds of mistakes than the ones we've mentioned.

Section 503 of the first Restatement of Contracts reflects the common law core rule. It says a "mistake of only one party that forms the basis on which he enters into a transaction does not of itself render the transaction voidable. . . ." The Comment says "[t]here is a contract formed by the acceptance of an offer even though the offer is made under a mistake or fails to express what the offeror intends. The objective appearance of his acts is controlling. . . ." Under this classic view, my mistake would be the basis for relief only if my error was caused by your fault or where you know or have reason to know of my error.[61]

The first Restatement reflects an objective theory of contracts. I am bound by my actions and not my intentions. You have a right to rely on what a reasonable person would think I meant. My errors in judgment and communication are no excuse unless you caused or should have known of them. If, however, we share a mistake, then there is a chance for relief.

---

[61] Section 504 of the original Restatement provides "where *both parties* have an identical intention as to the terms to be embodied in a proposed written conveyance, assignment, contract or discharge, and a writing executed by them is materially at variance with that intention, either party can get a decree that the writing shall be reformed so that it shall express the intention of the parties, if innocent third persons will not be unfairly affected thereby."

This core position is much less forgiving than the results of the cases. Few would state the law this way today without a long list of exceptions. While we still think a deal is a deal, we want to be sure what the deal really was. People make mistakes calculating and communicating constantly. We are more willing to ask whether there is good reason to give one party the benefit of another's error. We can see some of the problems with unilateral mistake by tracing the struggles of the Supreme Court of Wisconsin with the issue.

In *Miller v. Stanich*,[62] the Supreme Court of Wisconsin found a unilateral mistake warranted reworking a lease. In 1922, Michael Stanich leased a butcher shop for $75 a month. The term of the lease was five years and there was an option to renew the lease at the same rent for an additional five years. In 1926, S. Miller bought the property from Stanich's lessor, subject of course to the lease to Stanich.

As the first five-year term was coming to an end, Stanich went to his lawyer to talk about negotiating an extended renewal of his lease. Stanich wanted to renew the lease at $75 a month for five years from 1927 to 1932 and wanted another option to renew at the same rent for a third five-year term (from 1932 to 1937). Stanich's lawyer drafted a lease reflecting his client's wishes, sending two copies of this lease to Miller's building manager. The manager telephoned Stanich's lawyer and told him "I don't think that Mr. Miller will sign those leases." Stanich's lawyer responded that to save time, he would also send Miller two copies of a lease which ran from 1927 to 1932 but which had no option to renew for the third term. Stanich's lawyer drafted such a lease. The two leases were the same except one contained twenty-three additional words granting an option to renew from 1932 to 1937. Both sets of leases (two copies of each version) were sent to Miller, at his home in Marshfield, Wisconsin.

Although Miller was the president of a wholesale fruit and cold storage business, he could neither read nor write English. His son read the leases to him. They discovered that one set contained an additional five-year renewal option while the other did not. Miller did not want to renew Stanich's lease at all because he thought that the $75 a month rent was far too low, and he clearly did not want to give Stanich an option to renew for an additional five years at that rent.

Miller drove to Wisconsin Rapids to see his lawyer, R. B. Graves. Miller asked if he had to renew the lease. Graves told him that Stanich had a right to renew the lease from 1927 to 1932. There was no discussion about granting Stanich a right to renew again from 1932 to 1937. Apparently, Graves read only one copy of the lease—one that did not have the additional twenty-three words granting Stanich an option to renew from 1932 to 1937. Apparently, he assumed there were four copies of the same lease. Graves dated two copies of the lease and gave them to Miller. Miller took all four copies back to Marshfield. He signed the two copies Graves had dated and sent them to his building manager who passed them along to Stanich. Graves, of course, had dated the wrong set. As a result, Miller had

---

[62] 202 Wis. 539, 230 N.W. 47 (1930). Much of our description of the case is taken from the briefs and record on appeal.

mistakenly signed the copies that gave Stanich an option to renew for the third five-year term.

In late June 1927, Miller had a chance to sell the building. To make the sale, he had to buy out Stanich's lease. Miller and Stanich met in Milwaukee. Stanich asked $9000 to surrender his rights under the lease. Miller said that this was too much for only a five-year term. Stanich said, "No, it is not five. It is ten." Miller and Graves then tried to persuade Stanich that a mistake had been made. However, Stanich insisted that he had a lease for five years with an option to renew at the same rent for another five.

Miller then sued to have a court reform the lease and cancel the option to renew for an additional five years from 1932 to 1937. The trial court reformed the lease, striking out the option to renew. It found "at no time was there a meeting of the minds . . . to execute a lease for five years with the privilege to renew the same for another period of five years."

On appeal, the Supreme Court of Wisconsin *first* issued an opinion by Justice Fritz, joined by four other justices. Justice Fritz stated:

> Although plaintiff may have made a mistake in signing and sending to defendant the copies of the lease which contained the provision giving defendant an option for a further renewal, nothing had occurred because of which the defendant had reason to believe that plaintiff did not intend to agree to that provision, or that plaintiff had made a mistake. Defendant, in good faith, had submitted two forms. Without being misled by any trick or artifice on the part of any one, plaintiff signed and sent the two copies, containing the clause for another option, to defendant for his signature. When defendant also signed those copies, he was entitled to assume that the minds of the parties had met as to all terms embodied in the signed instruments, and that the plaintiff, by signing, had evidenced his intention to agree to all of those terms. Nothing had been done by plaintiff, on which defendant had knowledge, that indicated an intention of plaintiff's part not to consent to the option for the additional extension. Nothing had occurred which can be said to evidence a meeting of the minds of the parties to another contract, which plaintiff is now entitled by reformation to have expressed in the lease which he voluntarily signed. There was no mutual mistake. At best, it was merely a unilateral mistake, without any fraud on the part of the defendant. Under the circumstances there was no ground for reformation.[63]

Justice Fowler, joined by Justice Stevens, dissented:

> The case is so simple that to my mind the mere statement of it proves the decision of the court wrong. . . . [P]laintiff promptly, and before defendant had taken any steps whatever in reliance upon the provision for a five-year extension, comes into a court of equity and asks relief on the ground of mistake. . . . There was . . . no meeting of the minds of the parties in respect to the extension. . . . Mere inadvertence in signing the wrong lease is not such negligence as should bar plaintiff from relief. . . .

---

[63] 202 Wisc. at 542, 230 N.W. at 48.

Where no one is injured by a mistake except the party making it, and no one has changed his position in consequence of it, relief may be granted, although a high degree of care was not exercised. . . .

It is true . . . that equity does not reform instruments for mistake unless the mistake is mutual, and the mistake here involved is not mutual, but unilateral. But equity rescinds written instruments for unilateral mistakes. . . . The complaint in terms erroneously asks for reformation of the lease by striking out the clause for extension. The plaintiff, strictly speaking, is not entitled to the particular form of relief he asks for, because the defendant did not by signing the lease returned to him agree to a lease without the extension. But the fact is proved and found by the court that entitles plaintiff to rescission of the lease signed by him. Striking from that lease the provision for extension, and letting the lease stand as so changed, affords the plaintiff precisely the same relief that he would have were the lease declared canceled and the defendant adjudged to have the right to hold the premises for the extended term provided for by the original lease. Strictly speaking, that is the relief that should have been adjudged. But the error of decreeing reformation instead of rescission did not affect the substantial rights of the defendant. . . .[64]

The supreme court granted a motion for rehearing, and the case was reargued.[65] This time Justice Fowler wrote an opinion for the new majority, and Justice Fritz dissented. The court changed its decision. It ordered a judgment canceling the lease if plaintiff executed and filed with the clerk of the court a lease with the terms he had intended to sign and deliver.

Miller v. Stanich could have marked a real retreat by the Wisconsin court from an objective theory of contract or the beginning of a general relief-of-hardship doctrine. However, in retrospect, it seems but an odd instance in Wisconsin jurisprudence—since one could argue that it has been overruled implicitly or at least limited to a very narrow exception. On the other hand, it is a resource available in the event a future court chooses to use it.

The Supreme Court of Wisconsin first cited its *Miller v. Stanich* decision eight years later in *Willett v. Stewart.*[66] The facts of the *Willett* case are complicated because of the tangled relationships among the parties. In June of 1929, Mr. and Mrs. Willett, both of whom then were in their seventies, owned property mortgaged to Mr. Garland. About ten acres of this land were referred to as the Bristol Tile Works, consisting of a factory, machinery and land from which workers took clay as a raw material. The Willetts' home occupied another acre or more and was part of the same tract of land. The description in the Willetts' deed covered both the Bristol Tile Works and their home.

The Willetts wanted to convey the portion of their land which contained the Bristol Tile Works to John and Zelba Runge. Zelba was the Willetts' daughter and John was her husband. William Runge, John's brother, practiced law in the

---

[64] *Id.* at 544-546, 230 N.W. at 49-50.

[65] 202 Wis. 548, 233 N.W. 753 (1930).

[66] 227 Wis. 303, 277 N.W. 665 (1938). Again, we have taken much of the information about the case that follows from the briefs and record on appeal.

same office as Calvin Stewart; Stewart was the Municipal Judge for Kenosha County. An associate in their law office drafted the conveyance from the Willetts to John and Zelba. He mistakenly used the same description of the property he found on the original deed. The Willetts signed the conveyance which they were not aware conveyed *both* the Bristol Tile Works *and their home* to their daughter and son-in-law.

Judge Stewart had some money to invest. William Runge suggested that Stewart loan John and Zelba about $7,000, secured by a mortgage on the Bristol Tile Works. Judge Stewart agreed. The same associate drafted the mortgage securing Judge Stewart's loan to John and Zelba and used the same mistaken description of the property he had used in the original conveyance. This subjected the Willetts' home to Judge Stewart's mortgage.

John and Zelba Runge failed to make payments and failed to keep the Bristol Tile Works insured. In 1936, Judge Stewart began foreclosure procedures. The Willetts sued for reformation so that the mortgage would not apply to their home.

The trial court reformed the mortgage to exclude the Willetts' home. It relied on Judge Stewart's testimony:

> William Runge did not tell me there were any buildings on the property used for residential purposes. I was not told that anyone lived in any of the buildings on the land that was mortgaged to me. At the time I loaned the money, . . . I didn't have the Willett home in my mind. The first time I knew the Willett home was included in the description was after we started to foreclose. Prior to that time I never thought anything about whether or not the Willett home was included in my mortgage.

Stewart did not see the premises before making the loan. The trial court said "if the defendant Calvin Stewart was in any way misinformed as to the extent or value of the property on which he was to be given a mortgage to secure the loan he was making to the defendants, John and Zelba Runge, it was because of statements made to him by William Runge, a brother of John Runge, an attorney sharing an office with Mr. Stewart at the time. . . ." While some of the proceeds of the loan had gone to pay off the Garland mortgage on the home, Mr. and Mrs. Willett were not responsible for anything said by William Runge.

The case was appealed to the Supreme Court of Wisconsin. Neither side mentioned *Miller v. Stanich* in its briefs. Both sides offered rather weak legal analyses. Both attorneys tried to convince the supreme court that the equities favored their clients. Judge Stewart's lawyer pointed out that if the Willetts gained reforma-tion of the mortgage, they would own their home free and clear of security interests while Judge Stewart would have loaned over $7,000 on the property now valued at no more than $2,500. His brief spoke of a conspiracy between William Runge, Judge Stewart's former associate in practice, and Runge's relatives. The Willetts' lawyer responded that the low value of the Bristol Tile Works was caused by the depression and not by any fault of the Willetts. Moreover, he objected to the expression of personal anger "against a young lawyer who had the moral courage to testify against his former office associate, who at the time happened to be a judge before whom the lawyer would have occasion to appear from time to time."

The Supreme Court of Wisconsin reversed the decree reforming the mortgage. It said, "no doubt, there was a mutual mistake as between the Willetts and the Runges." However, Judge Stewart loaned money on the representation that it would be secured by a mortgage on about 11½ acres of land. Without the Willetts' homestead, there would be less than 11 acres included. The court quoted language from *Jentzsch v. Roenfanz*:[67] "If the mistake has not been mutual but has been made inadvertently on one side and yet in good faith by the other, if any amendment or reformation of the contract can, under any circumstances, be made, it cannot be made so as to make the agreement conform merely to the views of the party seeking reformation, but only to the original views of both parties."[68] The court then cited *Miller v. Stanich* as supporting this proposition, but it did not discuss the case. Finally, the court concluded "there was no mutual mistake such as is necessary for reformation on the part of the Stewarts."[69]

How does the *Willett* case differ from *Miller v. Stanich*? Both involve drafting mistakes made by lawyers concerning documents related to real estate.[70] It is likely that neither Stanich nor Judge Stewart relied on a literal reading of the rights granted to them by the documents in a way related to their economic interests. Stanich thought he had a five-year renewal plus an option to renew for five more years at a very favorable rent. Judge Stewart thought he had a mortgage on 11½ acres of land, but he did not think he had a mortgage on any residential property. Stanich lost only his expected gain as a result of the decision in his case.[71] Judge Stewart would have found himself with security worth only $2,500 to cover a $7,000 debt if the Willetts had won.

Does the distinction between the *Miller* and the *Willett* cases turn on the remedy? In *Miller* the court could rescind and rely on the option to renew contained in the original lease to put the parties where they should have been. In *Willett*, rescission would have ended Judge Stewart's security interest in the Bristol Tile Works as well as the Willett home. Reformation to exclude the home was

---

[67] 185 Wis. 189, 201 N.W. 504 (1924).

[68] 277 N.W. at 668.

[69] *Id.* We can notice another odd fact about the case. Judge Stewart benefits from a mistake made by a lawyer working in Stewart's law office. Today we might consider fiduciary duty and agency theories if we were representing the Willetts. Indeed, Judge Stewart's firm seems to have represented both sides to the transaction. Lawyers cannot benefit from such a conflict of interest. None of this was raised at trial or on appeal.

[70] In the 2000s, we can consider malpractice actions as solutions to the problems presented by the cases. In the 1930s, it is unlikely that any of the lawyers involved carried insurance or had enough money to pay any judgments that anyone might gain from malpractice actions in these cases.

[71] However, consider Fuller and Perdue's comment in light of Stanich's position:

The difficulties in proving reliance and subjecting it to pecuniary measurement are such that the business man knowing, or sensing, that these obstacles stood in the way of judicial relief would hesitate to rely on a promise in any case where the legal sanction was of significance to him. To encourage reliance we must therefore dispense with its proof. For this reason it has been found wise to make recovery on a promise independent of reliance, both in the sense that in some cases the promise is enforced though not relied on (as in the bilateral business agreement) and in the sense that recovery is not limited to the detriment incurred in reliance.

Fuller and Perdue, *The Reliance Interest in Contract Damages: Pt. 1*, 46 Yale L. J. 52, 62 (1936).

needed. However, why can't judges rewrite legal documents to arrive at what they see as appropriate results? In the *Willett* case would reformation of the mortgage be anything more than making the paper deal conform to the real deal? Or to the deal Judge Stewart would have made had he known the facts in 1929?

Wisconsin appellate courts had cited *Miller v. Stanich* in only six other decisions concerning mistake as of 2001. In a 1994 opinion,[72] a Court of Appeals dismissed the appellant's contention that Wisconsin had adopted the Restatement (Second) of Contracts view of unilateral mistake, finding no evidence of this. It commented on appellant's citation to the *Miller* case by observing in a footnote: "The [appellant] offers only a 1930 case, *Miller v. Stanich* in which the court stated that a party might be entitled to rescission based on unilateral mistake if he or she can establish 'fraud' on the part of the other party, or that the other party knew that the first party 'was laboring under a mistake.' " The two most recent cases cite the *Miller* decision for the proposition that you can get recovery for mutual mistake. Have the Wisconsin intermediate appellate courts overruled *Miller v. Stanich* by just misreading it? Would you expect that judges in other states be just as resistant to accepting the Restatement (Second) of Contracts' position on unilateral mistake?

Why has *Miller v. Stanich* had such a limited application? If we read the decision narrowly, it may be that it applies only to a situation very unlikely to occur. One can get relief for a unilateral mistake which a court views as innocent only when a court can be almost certain there has been no reliance. In addition, perhaps it must be a situation in which a court can bring about a proper result by rescission rather than reformation. If a court calls off the mistaken transaction, some other transaction must exist that defends the rights of both parties.

In the *Miller* case, an illiterate could not protect himself by reading the lease, and he relied on his lawyer. The lawyer made an error that anyone might make. (Indeed, Stanich's lawyer has some responsibility for creating a situation in which it was easy to make a mistake. He drafted two detailed and complex commercial leases that differed only in twenty-three words which were easy to overlook.) Stanich could not argue that he had relied in any substantial way on a lease to begin five years in the future. Stanich clearly wanted to renew for five years whether he got an option to renew for an additional five beyond that. Finally, since the original lease stood, all a court had to do was rescind the mistaken renewal.

In the *Willett* case, however, the Supreme Court of Wisconsin could not be sure that Judge Stewart had not relied on representations about the total number of acres of land that would be security for his loan. Moreover, rescission of the mortgage would have left Judge Stewart without any security. Reformation was needed, but the court was unwilling to write a contract for the parties that parties ought to have written.

Is there reason to have an expansive unilateral mistake doctrine which would allow reworking of contracts and other legal documents to achieve good ends?

---

[72] Erickson by Wightman v. Gunderson, 515 N.W.2d 293 (Wis. Ct. App. 1994). (The case name is correct; it involved a suit brought on behalf of Erickson.)

Consider the following, and ask how Sharp, Kessler and Fine, and the authors of the Restatement would have dealt with *Miller* and *Willett*. As you read the selections, ask yourself how easy the criteria they suggest would be to apply.

Promissory Liability II
Malcolm Pitman Sharp[73]

The extreme and simple case of unilateral mistake is indeed the case where one signs the wrong paper and sends it off to his correspondent by way of the acceptance of an offer already made; discovering the mistake at once, and notifying the correspondent before the communication has in any way affected his conduct. Here it appears persuasively that the same reasons which require relief in cases of mutual error may also require relief in any case of unilateral mistake.

The objective theory of contracts is not really threatened by such a suggestion, for relief from the consequences of the transaction will be allowed subject only to equitable limitations. Thus it is commonly said that change of position on the part of the person relying on the transaction will defeat relief for mistake. The mistaken person has perhaps merely by making a promise assumed some risk. He seems, however, in no worse a position than one who negligently misstates a fact. Apart from odd decisions about the measure of damages for deceit, a consistent treatment of liability would, it seems, require the mistaken party at most to make good the loss of the other party from the transaction as a whole, as a condition of relief against other consequences of the transaction. The mistaken party would thus of course make restitution and compensate the other party normally for expenses incurred in reliance on the promise as made; but the mistaken person would be relieved from liability for expectation damages.

Culpa in Contrahendo?

[What follows is *our summary* of the arguments of Friedrich Kessler and Edith Fine, advanced in an important article entitled *Culpa in Contrahendo, Bargaining in Good Faith, and Freedom of Contract: A Comparative Study.*[74] We offer the summary *in lieu* of their more extended comments.]

The German doctrine of *culpa in contrahendo* provides that parties to a prospective contract have a legal duty to negotiate the contract in good faith. If a party fails to negotiate in good faith and this prevents the parties from reaching their ultimate contractual objective, the blameworthy party can be legally required to compensate the injured party for expenses incurred in relying on the prospective contract. Though American contract law has not [at least at the writing of the Kessler and Fine article] adopted a doctrine equivalent to *culpa in contrahendo*, good faith and fair dealing are expressed in the laws pertaining to preliminary agreements, firm offers, mistake and misrepresentation. Further, doctrines such as negligence, estoppel, and implied contract have served many of the same functions of *culpa in contrahendo*.

---

[73] 7 U. Chi. L. Rev. 250, 267 (1939). Reprinted with permission.
[74] 77 Harv. L. Rev. 401 (1964).

Culpa in contrahendo developed, in large part, as an attempt to deal with the problem of unilateral mistake. Civil law countries, such as Germany, had previously followed the subjective theory of contract because it was widely believed that the objective theory provided too much protection for the promisee and resulted in waste. The subjective theory of contract formation, however, which might imply a broad right of avoidance in the case of unilateral mistake, seemed also to be problematic. Neither the objective nor subjective theory seemed to strike the right balance in allocating the burden of unilateral mistake. Therefore, *culpa in contrahendo* emerged in German law as a middle ground between accepting either theory. *Culpa in contrahendo* created an incentive to avoid careless promises and at the same time gave some protection to those who might rely on the promises.

Under German law a unilateral mistake entitles the mistaken party to void a legal exchange only when certain requirements are met. First, the mistaken party must not have agreed to the contract terms if the party had known the true facts and thus appreciated the significance of assent. Second, the mistake must fall within one of three enumerated (but hard to capture in a summary) categories. The errors generally must be either errors in "purport" or intention, or mistakes as to the characteristics of persons or subject matter that are characterizable as essential. Errors in calculation have been considered to be errors in purport, and so operative and excusing—so long as the negotiations brought home to the other party that the mistaken price, for example, was intended to be the result of accurate calculations. Under these circumstances the mistaken party is allowed to rescind the contract. However, the mistaken party is still liable for the amounts expended by the non-mistaken party in relying on the contract unless the non-mistaken party either knew or should have known of the mistake.

Some American writers have been critical of the German law treatment of unilateral mistake. First, they criticize the German law for not providing a remedy for intangible injuries suffered by a promisee that relies on a promise. The fact that non-economic injuries are difficult to calculate was the driving force behind common law rulings allowing recovery for the full expectation interest. Second, American commentators contend that adhering to the objective theory of contracts and allowing a promisee to recover the full expectation interest (rather than merely the reliance interest) is a strong incentive for parties to avoid careless manifestations of assent.

The first Restatement of Contracts, which can be taken to represent the conventional view of the matter in the United States, states that the mistake of one party does not automatically render a transaction voidable even when the mistake formed the basis for the mistaken party to enter into the contract. But there is a growing body of case law that offers relief for mistake, and which emphasizes some of the same factors that are important under the doctrine of *culpa in contrahendo*. Exceptions in the American law have been carved out for fraud and misrepresentation. Courts are also increasingly considering notions of good faith and fair dealing even at the expense of creating unpredictability in the market place. This has led to exceptions being made for unconscionability and for mistakes of which the other party should have been aware. Relief is also available for material mistakes as to essential terms. Usually when relief is denied, the unilateral nature of the mistake is only one of a number of factors considered. Often courts, in denying relief, stress the immateriality of the mistake, the fact that parties could not be restored to their prior positions and negligence on the part of the mistaken party. Also while miscalculations of price, or errors as to quantity, are generally sufficient, several decisions denying relief in such cases have emphasized the fact that the goods had already changed hands or the parties had materially altered their positions. As Kessler and Fine put it:

> To sum up, in attempting to find acceptable solutions mediating between the legitimate interests of both promisor and promisee, traditional doctrine in this country has been redefined by a body of case law too large to be ignored. In this process of refinement of our law of contract, *culpa in contrahendo* and notions of unjust enrichment have played a significant role. While in the civil law countries *culpa in contrahendo* has been used in large measure to mitigate the will theory, the common law starting from the other end has employed it as one of its weapons to soften the rigor of the objective theory of contracts. In this country the process of mitigation has found further manifestation in the notion that a mistaken party should be protected against oppressive burdens when rescission would impose no substantial hardship on the party seeking enforcement of the contract. Thus a link has been established between operative mistake and unjust enrichment. Here is an instance where the common law will look into adequacy of consideration. This variance from the general rule is not surprising, since the ordinary interest in protecting a price mutually arrived at is not present here.[75]

The Restatement's Synthesis of Common Law Rules

The Restatement (Second) of Contracts contains a number of rules dealing with unilateral mistakes. Those who drafted it were influenced by cases such as *Miller v. Stanich* and the Kessler and Fine article. As a way to give some content to the Restatement's abstractions, ask yourself how a court adopting the Restatement (Second) of Contracts would decide the *Miller* and *Willett* cases. You also should ask what the likely impact of the Restatement might be on bargaining to settle cases. At this point you should consult Restatement §§ 153-55, 157-58 and 204. The following case does not cite the Restatement provisions on unilateral mistake. Nonetheless, does it take the approach advocated by the second Restatement?

---

[75] Kessler and Fine, *supra*, at 436.

S.T.S. TRANSPORT SERVICE, INC. v. VOLVO WHITE TRUCK CORP.

United States Court of Appeals, Seventh Circuit
766 F.2d 1089 (1985)

CUDAHY, J. Plaintiff appeals from a finding of unilateral mistake and rescission of a contract of sale. We affirm the judgment of the district court. . . .

Plaintiff-appellant S.T.S. Transport Service, Inc. ("S.T.S.") is an Illinois corporation whose principal place of business is located in Alsip, Illinois. Since its incorporation in 1978, S.T.S. has leased tractor trucks and trailers to other companies and has also hauled freight for customers. Volvo White Truck Corporation ("Volvo White") is a Virginia corporation with its principal place of business in Greensboro, North Carolina. There is a branch dealership of Volvo White in Alsip, Illinois. In 1979 and 1980 S.T.S. bought trucks and heavy equipment from White Motor Company ("White Motor"), a truck manufacturer whose assets were purchased in 1981 by Volvo White.

Early in 1981 S.T.S. expressed an interest in purchasing eight new tractor trucks from White Motor in Alsip. In order to avoid a down payment, S.T.S. wanted to trade in trucks it already owned and use its equity in those trucks as a down payment. After appraising the trucks S.T.S. intended to trade in, and after some negotiations concerning the appraised value, White Motor offered to sell S.T.S. eight 1981 Road Commander trucks on the following terms:

(a) The 1981 Road Commander trucks would be sold to S.T.S. for a price of $58,749 each;

(b) S.T.S. would trade White Motor one used truck for each new truck purchased;

(c) S.T.S. would continue to make payments (to financing companies) on the used trucks through July, 1981;

(d) White Motor would value six of the used trucks at the same amount that S.T.S. would owe on them in July, 1981; $26,560 each;

(e) White Motor would give S.T.S. a credit of $25,000 on another of the trucks;

(f) White Motor would arrange financing for S.T.S.

Provision (d) meant that S.T.S. would receive no credit for any equity in six of the trucks it owned, but that White Motor would simply pay off the amount still owed by S.T.S. on those trucks. The list price of the Road Commander trucks was $80,784. The offer price of $58,749 was reached by adding a profit of $2,200 to the Alsip branch's base cost of $56,549 for the trucks. These terms were confirmed in a March 10, 1981 letter from White Motor to S.T.S. Apparently they were not satisfactory to S.T.S., and negotiations were suspended.

In August, 1981, while White Motor [remember—the assets of White Motor were later bought by Volvo-White] was the subject of bankruptcy proceedings,

S.T.S. solicited a new offer from them. White Motor recalculated its costs and sent a letter, dated August 17, 1981, which set out the specifications of the eight Road Commander Trucks, and which concluded with the following paragraphs:

> Net delivered price F.O.B. Alsip, including preparation, but excluding state/local taxes is . . . $273,176.00.

> We will pay off balance due to White Motor Credit Corporation on the (6) 1979 Western Stars. We assume you will make your payment to White Motor Credit Corporation on December 14, 1981, and then begin a new note with White Motor Credit Corporation effective January 30, 1982, as your first payment on the new equipment. There will be no prepayment return to you, that figure ($9,035) is included in the above figures.

> We will also pay off the "estimated" money owed to I.T.T. of $31,755 once your trades are turned in. This is the estimated balance after your November 30, 1981 payment to I.T.T. We will receive the 1978 Freight-liner and 1977 Peterbilt as trades and we will also receive the 1979 Western Stars.

> Hope this isn't confusing. I just net'd everything out and gave you the bottom line. It's a good deal for you for 2 reasons, there is a $3,500.00 U.T.A. on this deal, and we expect 6% 1982 increase by September 1, 1981. You are actually purchasing 1982 units at 1981 prices with $3,500 off on top.

> What do you think!!!!!!!

A moment's calculations makes clear how widely the price suggested in the August 12 letter diverges from the earlier price. Eight trucks at the March 10 price of $58,749 would total $469,992; there was to be no credit for the equity of any of the trucks traded in, except for one, and the credit for that one was to be $25,000. Subtracting that credit from the total for the eight trucks would result in a net price of something just under $445,000. The new net price named in the August letter is some $170,000—over $20,000 a truck—less.

Appellee Volvo White claims that the August figure was the result of a miscalculation. Intending to offer the eight new trucks for the lower price of $56,530 each, for a total of $452,240, White Motor subtracted from that figure not only $42,000 in credit that it was now willing to allow on the trade-in of two trucks, but the $137,064 in assessed value on six other trucks, an amount which equalled the outstanding debt on the trucks. Since S.T.S. was to be credited with no equity on those six used trucks, the assessed value should not have been subtracted from the price of the new trucks. White Motor merely intended to wipe out S.T.S.'s remaining debt on those trucks. By subtracting the amount they did from the price of the new trucks, White Motor in effect offered to credit S.T.S. with an amount equal to the amount of the debt remaining on each truck.

In response to further inquiries by S.T.S, White Motor sent out a second letter on September 2, 1981. This letter was in all respects identical to the August 17 letter, except that in place of the last line of the August letter the September 2 letter contained the following paragraph regarding interest rate charges:

If prime rate increases from todays [sic] rate of 20.5%, your rate to be charged will be 2.5% below the existing prime on date of delivery. If prime decreases, your rate will be the then existing add on rate charged by White Motor Credit Corporation.

Both letters were sent out by Joseph LaSpina, manager of the Alsip branch. LaSpina admitted at trial that he did not review the August 17 letter before it went out, and that he did not review or sign the September 2d letter; his name was signed on the first page by his secretary.

S.T.S. accepted the offer. In December, 1981, S.T.S. turned over to Volvo White all of the trade-in vehicles. S.T.S. also entered into a new lease agreement with Suburban Truck & Trailer, under the terms of which Suburban would lease five of the new trucks from S.T.S. for three years. S.T.S. expected the lease to produce gross income before expenses of $37,876.49 per truck per year.

In January, 1982, [before the eight new trucks were delivered to S.T.S.] the parties became aware of the problem. Volvo White informed S.T.S. that the net purchase price for the new trucks was $452,000, and S.T.S. insisted that under the contract the purchase price was $273,176. On January 15, 1982, Volvo White sent a letter admitting that it had made a clerical error in the contract. It offered to go ahead at the $452,000 price or to call off the transaction, and it confirmed that the eight trade-ins, now in Volvo White's lot, would remain the property of S.T.S. until the deal was closed. Maintaining that it could not use the trade-in vehicles in its new leasing contract with Suburban, and maintaining that under the terms of the contract Volvo White should have taken over payments of the used trucks, S.T.S. neither reclaimed the trucks nor kept up payments on them. They were repossessed and sold later in the year for approximately $20,000 per truck. [The eight new trucks were never delivered to S.T.S.]

S.T.S. claims that it lost an equity of $70,900 which it had built up in those trade-in units. It also claims that it lost a profit of $372,352 that it would have earned under its lease with Suburban.

S.T.S. had apparently been experiencing some financial difficulty in the latter half of 1981. In January and February, 1982, it sold its remaining tractor trucks. This lawsuit was commenced on June 11, 1982. A trial in the Northern District of Illinois was held during the week of June 13, 1983. S.T.S. sought as damages its lost profits under the Suburban lease. Volvo White counterclaimed for an unpaid balance on parts and materials Volvo White had provided to S.T.S.

The district court found first that S.T.S. had a duty to mitigate its damages. It found that S.T.S. should have gone ahead with the purchase at the higher price, so that it might fulfill its own commitment to provide trucks for Suburban, reserving the right to sue Volvo White for the difference under the UCC It found that since the plaintiff did not mitigate in that way, it could not realize any of the damages it claimed.

But the district judge also found that the contract contained a mistake with respect to the price term, a mistake that would not have been discovered by merely proof-reading the document. Since she found a mistake, she also found that the mistake could be excused and the contract rescinded if the plaintiff could be returned to the *status quo ante*. She found that the costs of the parts and labor which were the subject of Volvo White's counterclaim were incurred in the process of getting the trucks ready for the trade-in, so that the *status quo* could be restored with respect to those obligations by excusing them. On the other hand, she was persuaded by the testimony of witnesses that S.T.S. intended to go out of business at the end of 1981, and that "there is nothing really to restore it to in that regard." Accordingly, she entered judgment for the plaintiff on the counterclaim [denying Volvo-White's claim for parts and materials] but against the plaintiff on its principal claim. [The S.T.S. claim for lost profits and equity on trade-in trucks.]

On the question of equity, the district judge found that the used trucks probably could have been sold by S.T.S. for more than they were sold for after repossession, but that since S.T.S. had not taken advantage of the opportunity to reclaim the trucks, it was stuck with the price the trucks had actually been sold for. At that price, there was no equity, since the trucks were sold for less than the amount owed on them.

If the contract is void because of a mistake, then there is no question of mitigation, since the duty to mitigate (if there is such a duty) arises out of the breach of a valid contract. Where the court applies the doctrine of mistake, the parties are excused from the contract and consequently there is no breach. Thus, if the district court properly found a mistake concerning the price term and properly voided the contract, we need not reach the issue of mitigation.

The parties have stipulated that Illinois law governs. The sale of the trucks would be governed by the Uniform Commercial Code, chapter 26 of the Illinois Revised Code; but under § 1-103 of the Code, mistake and certain other questions are governed by the common law. 26 Ill.Rev.Stat. § 1-103.

Although the traditional case in which a contract is found to contain a mistake is one in which the parties understand a key term differently (hence, a case in which the mistake is mutual), the cases have also voided contracts—though more reluctantly—where only one party is mistaken as to the facts. In the typical case of this sort, a seller or contractor will miscalculate in adding up a list of items. Under the appropriate circumstances courts will now recognize a right to avoidance of this sort of mistake. . . .

[The court excludes errors of judgment from the kinds of errors which may permit avoidance of the contract.]

As the law now stands, three conditions must be fulfilled before a contract can be rescinded: (1) the mistake must relate to a material feature of the contract; (2) it must have occurred despite the exercise of reasonable care; and (3) the other party must be placed in the position it was in before the contract was made. . . .

The mistake in this case relates to the price, which must be conceded to be material. The mistake must also have occurred in spite of the exercise of reasonable care. Although reasonable care is as difficult to be precise about in this sort of case as it is elsewhere, there are some fairly clear groupings of mistake cases that can serve as guideposts. Most helpful is the knowledge that Illinois courts will generally grant relief for errors "which are clerical or mathematical." *Cummings v. Dusenbury*, 129 Ill. App.3d 338, 84 Ill. Dec. 615, 619, 472 N.E.2d 575, 579 (1984) (citing *WilFred's, Inc. v. Metropolitan Sanitary District, supra*). The reason for the special treatment for such errors, of course, is that they are difficult to prevent, and that no useful social purpose is served by enforcing the mistaken term. No incentives exist to make such mistakes; all the existing incentives work, in fact, in the opposite direction. There is every reason for a contractor to use ordinary care, and, if errors of this sort—clerical or mathematical—slip through anyway, the courts will generally find it more useful to allow the contract to be changed or rescinded than to enforce it as it is. Naturally there are cases of extreme negligence to which this presumption should not apply; and there is an exception of sorts where the contract has been relied upon. We will have something to say about this last at a later point.

Although it would be wrong to suppose that "merely" mathematical or clerical errors are easily distinguished from other errors such as those of judgment—a miscalculation about the economic climate, say—the distinction is clear enough for ordinary purposes. A merely mathematical or clerical error occurs when some term is either one-tenth or ten times as large as it should be; when a term is added in the wrong column; when it is added rather than subtracted; when it is overlooked.

The error involved here is of that sort, but if anything more difficult to detect. The Alsip manager, LaSpina, made the crucial calculations. The assessed value of the used trucks was subtracted from the price of the new trucks. Such a procedure is perfectly appropriate, ordinarily; whoever buys a new car expects to have the price reduced by the value of the trade-in. Here, however, the assessed value was set so as to match the outstanding debt on the trucks. Even so, had the offer been for S.T.S. to pay off the remaining debt on the trucks before they were traded in, the calculation would have been correct. But that was not the offer; Volvo White offered to take over the remaining debt on the trade-ins, so that there was nothing in the way of trade-in value to be subtracted from the purchase price. The assessed value was completely offset by the outstanding debt.

However foolish this mistake, once made it would not easily have been detected. S.T.S. points out that Volvo White conceded in testimony that neither of the two letters containing the term in question were reviewed by LaSpina before going out. But such an omission ought to bar rescission only if it would have resulted in the error's being detected. Here, the mistaken calculations were made by LaSpina, and there is little reason to suppose that he would have detected the error had he proof-read the errors before they went out. The error involved, therefore, was not one that would have been detected by the exercise of ordinary care, and we do not think that the trial judge erred in rejecting the defense of negligence.

The question of reliance is no different from the question whether the parties can be put into the position they were in at the time the contract was signed. Here, S.T.S. claims that it lost the equity it had in the trucks traded in. If it did in fact lose those trucks because of reliance on the contract; and if in fact there was equity in the trucks—that is, if the market value of the trucks exceeded the remaining debt; then S.T.S. is entitled to claim that equity as the price of putting it back into the position it would have been in had it not relied on the contract.

The district court found that S.T.S. could have reclaimed its trucks at any time. At the time it became apparent that Volvo White was not going to honor the contract as written, sometime in January, 1982, S.T.S. could have arranged to sell the trucks on its own. A party to a contract cannot be allowed to create damages by continuing to rely on a contract which has either been breached, or been void from the start. As of January, 1982, S.T.S. was on notice that one of those two situations applied. . . .

Instead, S.T.S. refused to make further payments, and the trucks were repossessed and sold for amounts less than the amounts still owed on each. S.T.S. might have complained of the reasonableness of these sales, but it did not; in any case the sales do not appear to have been unreasonable.[76] The district court therefore correctly found that any loss of equity—if there was equity to begin with— was due to conduct of S.T.S., and that restoring S.T.S. to the *status quo* did not require payment for lost equity.

S.T.S. also incurred certain obligations in preparing the trucks for the trade-in; Volvo White has counterclaimed for repayment of approximately $9500 for parts and services priced during this period. The district judge found that these obligations were legitimately incurred in reliance on the contract and that before the contract can be rescinded those obligations must be excused. She therefore dismissed the counterclaim and rescinded the contract. Volvo White does not reassert its counterclaim on appeal.

Since the district court properly rescinded the contract, the question of mitigation does not arise. The judgment of the district court is affirmed.

NOTES AND QUESTIONS

1. *Mistaken calculations*: The Volvo White dealer's initial offer was calculated as follows:

Price for 8 at $58,749 each:	$469,992
Less credit for 1 used truck:	*$ 25,000*
Total to be paid by S.T.S.:	$444,992
[*6 trucks traded in and dealer pays off amounts due*]	

The second mistaken offer was calculated as follows:

Price for 8 at $56,530 each:	$452,240
Less credit for 2 used trucks:	*$ 42,000*
Subtotal:	$410,240 [Correct amt.]
Less assessed value of 6 trucks:	*$137,064* [☞ Mistake]
Mistaken total:	$273,176

---

[76] [1] The trucks were sold for $20,000 each. Volvo White had appraised the trucks at $22,000-23,000; testimony for S.T.S. would have set the value at $30,000. Considering the conditions under which the trucks were sold, the selling price does not appear unreasonable, whichever estimate of market value we choose.

2. ***The buyer's interest***: Why does the buyer lose the benefit of the bargain? Should it have seen the mistaken calculation? At the time the second offer was made, the court tells us "White Motor was the subject of bankruptcy proceedings." Could the buyer reasonably assume that it was getting a great deal as part of clearing out the inventory of an almost bankrupt manufacturer? However, the next to last sentence of the second offer says "You are actually purchasing 1982 units at 1981 prices with $3,500 off on top." Was this enough to alert the buyer that the calculations were mistaken?

3. ***The authority of the STS case:*** In *Chicago Litho Plate Graining Co., Ltd. v. Allstate Can Company*,[77] the court read the *STS* decision as an example of rescission for unilateral mistake "in the limited circumstances as suggested by the Restatement (Second) of Contracts, § 153(a). . . ." *STS* purported to be an application of Illinois law in a diversity of citizenship case. The case was recognized as a proper reading of Illinois law in *Estate of Blakely v. Federal Kemper Life Assur. Co.*[78] In the *Blakely* decision, an insurance company had charged too large a premium for the deceased's life insurance because it made the wrong calculation. The policy had lapsed before the insured's death. The executor argued that the overpayments extended the duration of the policy so that it would have been in effect when the insured died. Summary judgment for the estate was affirmed. This was not an appropriate case to grant either reformation or restitution for the insurance company's unilateral mistake. Giving the estate back the premiums paid would not give the estate the insurance that the insured thought that he had bought. See also, *Prudential Ins. Co. of America v. S.S. American Lancer*,[79] which cites the *STS* decision with approval in a case involving a clerical error.

C. UNENFORCEABLE CONTRACTS, RESTITUTION AND RELIANCE

People can make mistakes about whether they made a contract or if they did, what its terms are. If the mistake is discovered soon enough, all that is lost is the chance that they might have made as good, or better, a bargain elsewhere. However, in some situations reliance losses may be much greater. You will not be surprised when we tell you that restitution serves to clean up the mess in some cases. Suppose that buyer and auto dealer think they have made a contract, but are mistaken. Dealer delivers the car to buyer before discovering that there was no contract. When the mistake is discovered, the buyer won't go through with the deal. The buyer has been unjustly enriched, and the seller can recover the car in a restitution action. Things are less clear when there has been a reliance loss that does not create an economic benefit for the other party. Furthermore, even where there is a benefit, there are problems when the buyer reasonably thought she was buying something else or that the deal had not yet been closed. The seller has suffered a loss, but it may not be clear that the buyer should pay for it.

[77] 838 F.2d 927 (7th Cir. 1988).
[78] 267 Ill. App. 3d 100, 640 N.E.2d 961 (1994).
[79] 870 F.2d 867 (2d Cir. 1989).

We have placed this material here for teaching reasons. It relates both backwards and forwards. That is, we considered situations where people have been mistaken about whether they made contracts or what the terms were. The material in this section suggests that the question is more than the choice between "contract" or "no contract."

This material also forms part of the context within which problems in the coming sections occur. Up to this point, we did not want to raise restitution and reliance questions because we thought you had enough on your plate. However, we do not want to wait until the end of the course to look at this material either. Those who accept realist jurisprudence insist that judges and lawyers do not decide (1) is there a contract or can it be rescinded for mistake?, and then (2) if there is no contract, can some or all of the reliance losses be recovered? Rather, anyone considering a close question concerning whether a contract was formed may be influenced by the consequences of deciding one way or the other. Judges and lawyers may approach things backwards, asking whether the best solution to a tangled transaction may be to allow expectation or reliance damages, reformation, restitution for benefits conferred or some combination of these forms of relief.

VICKERY v. RITCHIE
Supreme Judicial Court of Massachusetts
202 Mass. 247, 88 N.E. 835 (1909)

KNOWLTON, C.J. This is an action to recover a balance of $10,467.16, alleged to be due the plaintiff as a contractor, for the construction of a Turkish bath house on land of the defendant. The parties signed duplicate contracts in writing, covering the work. At the time when the plaintiff signed both copies of the contract, the defendant's signature was attached, and the contract price therein named was $33,721. When the defendant signed them the contract price stated in each was $23,200. Until the building was completed, the plaintiff held a contract under which he was to receive the larger sum, while the defendant held a contract for the same work, under which he was to pay only the smaller sum. This resulted from the fraud of the architect who drew the contracts, and did all the business and made all the payments for the defendant. The contracts were on typewritten sheets, and it is supposed that the architect accomplished the fraud by changing the sheets on which the price was written, before the signing by the plaintiff, and before the delivery to the defendant. The parties did not discover the discrepancy between the two writings until after the building was substantially completed. Each of them acted honestly and in good faith, trusting the statements of the architect. The architect was indicted, but he left the commonwealth and escaped punishment.

The auditor found that the market value of the labor and materials furnished by the plaintiff, not including the customary charge for the supervision of the work, was $33,499.30, and that their total cost to the plaintiff was $32,950.96. He found that the land and building have cost the defendant much more than their market value. The findings indicate that it was bad judgment on the part of the defendant to build such a structure upon the lot, and that the increase in the market value of the real estate, by reason of that which the plaintiff put upon it, is only $22,000. The failure of the parties to discover the difference between their copies of the contract was caused by the frequently repeated fraudulent representations of the architect to each of them.

The plaintiff and defendant were mistaken in supposing that they had made a binding contract for the construction of this building. Their minds never met in any agreement about the price. The labor and materials were furnished at the defendant's request and for the defendant's benefit. From this alone the law would imply a contract on the part of the defendant to pay for them. The fact that the parties supposed the price was fixed by a contract, when in fact there was no contract, does not prevent this implication, but leaves it as a natural result of their relations. Both parties understood and agreed that the work should be paid for, and both parties thought that they had agreed upon the price. Their mutual mistake in this particular left them with no express contract by which their rights and liabilities could be determined. The law implies an obligation to pay for what has been done and furnished under such circumstances, and the defendant, upon whose property the work was done, has no right to say that it is not to be paid for. The doctrine is not applicable to work upon real estate alone. The rule would be the same if the work and materials were used in the repair of a carriage, or of any other article of personal property, under a supposed contract with the owner, if, through a mutual mistake as to the supposed agreement upon the price, the contract became unenforceable. . . .

The principle has often been applied when the ground for an implication of an agreement to pay was much less strong than in the present case. In *Butterfield v. Byron*, 153 Mass. 517, . . . where the owner was to do a part of the work in the erection of a building, and a contractor was to do the rest, under an express contract for an agreed price, it was held that, when the building was destroyed by lightning, so that the contract became impossible of performance, the contractor might recover, on a *quantum meruit,* the fair value of the labor and materials that he had furnished. This was on the ground that, when the contract came to an end without the fault of either party, there was an implication that what was furnished was to be paid for, and if it could not be paid for under the contract it should be paid for on a *quantum meruit.* . . .

If the law implies an agreement to pay, how much is to be paid? There is but one answer. The fair value of that which was furnished. No other rule can be applied. Under certain conditions the price fixed by the contract might control in such cases. In this case there was no price fixed.

The defendant contends that because the erection of a Turkish bath house on Carver street was not a profitable investment, and therefore, through a seeming error of judgment on the part of the defendant, the building did not add to the value of the land so much by a large sum as it cost, the plaintiff must suffer the consequences of the defendant's mistake and be precluded from recovery. . . .

[N]owhere, so far as we have been able to discover, does the law, as applied to such cases in other jurisdictions, make the right of the contractor depend in any degree upon the profit or loss to the owner, arising from his wisdom or folly, or good fortune or bad fortune, in erecting the building upon his land. . . .

In this case there was no express contract. The plaintiff's right is to recover upon an implied contract of an owner to pay for labor and materials used upon his [owner's] property at his [owner's] request. . . . [I]n cases of the class to which the present one belongs the right does not depend upon the ultimate benefit received by the owner. . . .

In all cases to which this general principle has been applied, the recovery has been upon a *quantum meruit* for that which was furnished, subject to diminution of the amount by the price named in the contract, if that was very low. The right of recovery depends upon the plaintiff's having furnished property or labor, under circumstances which entitle him to be paid for it, not upon the ultimate benefit to the property of the owner at whose request it was furnished. . . .

It follows that the plaintiff is entitled to recover the fair value of his labor and materials.

Exceptions sustained.

NOTES AND QUESTIONS

1. *The AIA treatment of the problem*: Architects, builders and owners make many building contracts today using standard forms drafted by the American Institute of Architects (AIA). Under the 1987 version of the AIA Standard Form of Agreement Between Owner and Architect § 2.4.2, "[t]he Architect shall assist the Owner in the preparation of the necessary bidding information, bidding forms, the Conditions of the Contract, and the form of Agreement between the Owner and Contractor." Section 2.5.1 provides: "[t]he Architect, following the Owner's approval of the Construction Documents and of the latest preliminary estimate of Construction Cost, shall assist the Owner in obtaining bids or negotiated proposals, and assist in awarding and preparing contracts for construction." Section 2.6.4 provides: "The Architect shall be a representative of and shall advise and consult with the Owner (1) during construction until final payment to the Contractor is due, and (2) as an Additional Service at the Owner's direction from time to time during the correction period described in the Contract for Construction. The Architect shall have authority to act on behalf of the Owner only to the extent provided in this Agreement unless otherwise modified by written instrument."[80]

In almost all building contracts, the owner and not the builder selects the architect. Principals usually are liable for contracts made by their agents acting within the scope of their actual or apparent authority. They are liable also for their agents' torts committed in the scope of their employment. In light of that, shouldn't the owner who selected the architect be responsible for the architect's fraud and mistakes?

2. *Calculating the amount of restitution*: If liability is based on restitution, how much should the builder in *Vickery v. Ritchie* be able to recover? Consider the possibilities, rounding off the sums:

---

[80] AIA Document B141, OWNER-ARCHITECT AGREEMENT, 14th ed. Copyright © The American Institute of Architects.

(a) Increased value of owner's land	$22,000
(b) Owner's contract price	$23,000
(c) ½ the difference between construction cost and the added value to the land, or ($32,750 - 22,000 = 10,750; ½ x 10,750 = 5,375 + 22,000)	$27,375
(d) Cost of construction	$32,750
(e) Market value of labor & material, but not including supervision	$33,500
(f) Builder's contract price	$33,721

Does your answer turn on choice, fault, benefit, loss sharing or some form of social engineering?

3. *The Restatement of Restitution's solution*: Section 155 of the Restatement of Restitution offers still another solution to the *Vickery v. Ritchie* problem:

> (1) Where a person is entitled to restitution from another because the other, without tortious conduct, has received a benefit, the measure of recovery for the benefit thus received is the value of what was received, limited, if the recipient was not at fault or was no more at fault than the claimant, to its value in advancing the purposes of the recipient, except as limited by the statement in Subsection (2).

> (2) Where a transaction is rescinded solely because of a mistake as to price, the recipient's duty of restitution is to pay not less than he expected to pay nor more than the claimant expected to receive.

Thus, the Restatement of Restitution would award the "value of what was received, limited . . . to its value in advancing the purposes of the recipient . . ." or $22,000. However, under Subsection (2), the recipient must "pay not less than he expected to pay . . ." or $23,000. Does this solution appeal to you? Given the difficulty in establishing the values in question, shouldn't we just presume that the builder's cost is the owner's benefit? Is the cost of establishing the facts worth the effort?

4. *Recovering for reliance expenses and calling it restitution*: The *Vickery* case deals with the situation in which the work done by the builder, in the mistaken belief that there was a contract, was clearly received by the landowner. The *Vickery* case is interesting because the cost incurred by the builder so substantially exceeded the increase in the value of the land—which we might expect to be an unusual occurrence. (Do you see why?) Nevertheless, it is undeniable that plaintiff's work had really enriched the defendant; the question was, how much, and whether to focus on increases in asset value or the imputed value of work done at one's request. This undeniable fact of enrichment apparently provides the justification for a recovery on a restitution theory. But the court seems candid in admitting that the benefit recovered by the defendant, though the ground for the claim, is not the measure of the recovery. In contrast, the Restatement of Restitution suggests that the award cannot exceed its ". . . value in advancing the purposes of the recipient." The measure of recovery seems more clearly constrained by the substantive rationale for the claim, which is said to be the avoidance of unjust enrichment.

But what happens when a person, mistakenly believing herself to be party to an enforceable contract, incurs expenses which seem not to benefit the other party to the *un*enforceable contract at all? Remember the next to the last paragraph in *S.T.S. Transport, Inc. v. Volvo White Truck Corp.?* It appears that in preparing the used trucks to be traded in, S.T.S. repaired them, buying parts and services from Volvo White on credit. Volvo White had asked to be paid for these parts and services. The trial court had dismissed Volvo White's claim (for reasons that are either ill-considered or unclear), and Volvo White had not pressed the claim on appeal. But what if Volvo White *had* insisted that the court address its counterclaim?

First, it is not clear that the delivery of parts and services to S.T.S. should even have been regarded as part of the ill-fated transaction involving the sale of the eight new trucks. Second, even if S.T.S. was obliged to repair the trucks, and to buy services and parts from Volvo White, S.T.S. may have received the benefit of those parts and services when the used trucks were subsequently resold after being repossessed. The repairs and parts may have increased the liquidation value of the trucks. *But let's assume* that, perhaps because the trucks sat unused on the Volvo White lot for several months, the parts and services were never of any measurable economic benefit to S.T.S. Should Volvo White receive nothing? Or should it be paid something because it provided goods and services to another upon the request of that other? Is this like *Vickery?*

The 1928 Connecticut case of *Kearns v. Andree*[81] allowed recovery of reliance expenses. In *Kearns* the seller incurred expenses in remodeling a house to suit the tastes of a buyer who then refused to complete the transaction. The buyer was held to be entitled to refuse, since the court held the contract to be insufficiently definite. The court concluded, however, that the disappointed seller was entitled to recover expenses it had incurred ". . . in good faith and in the honest belief that the agreement was sufficiently definite to be enforced,"[82] subject to a deduction to the extent that any of those expenses were of any benefit to the seller. The court said, "He has performed those services at the request of the other party to the contract, and in the expectation, known to the other, that he would be compensated therefor. Here is a sufficient basis for an implication in law that reasonable compensation would be made."[83] The court disallowed a claim for additional remodeling to meet the needs of a second buyer, on the ground that to allow such recovery would be to permit recovery upon an unenforceable contract. *Kearns v. Andree* was distinguished in 1941 in *R.F. Baker & Co. v. P. Ballentine & Sons.*[84] Finally, in *Automobile Insurance Co. v. Model Family Laundries*[85] the Connecticut court asserted that the true ground for recovery in cases like *Kearns v. Andree*

---

[81] 107 Conn. 181, 139 A. 695 (1928).
[82] 139 A. at 698.
[83] *Id.*
[84] 127 Conn. 680, 20 A.2d 82 (1941).
[85] 133 Conn. 433, 52 A.2d 137 (1947).

was quasi contract for unjust enrichment, and that quasi contract required that defendant receive a benefit.

In *Ramsey v. Ellis*,[86] the Supreme Court of Wisconsin attempted to clear up the confusion. The court said, "quantum meruit is a distinct cause of action from an action for unjust enrichment, with distinct elements and a distinct measure of damages." Quantum meruit is based upon an implied contract to pay reasonable compensation for services rendered at the defendant's request. Unjust enrichment is based on a benefit conferred on the defendant. If the defendant has asked for the services in a situation where she knows they are not a gift, the plaintiff can recover in quantum meruit whether or not providing the requested services has resulted in a tangible economic gain to the defendant. The defendant has made a choice to request the services.[87] Courts, however, often confuse restitution and quantum merit and deny any remedy when there is no tangible economic benefit even if the defendant has requested the services.[88] The hard cases are, of course, those where the defendant requested the services as part of what the parties thought was a contract, but where the contract is not enforceable. Defendant made a choice to gain plaintiff's services under the terms of the unenforceable contract but she might not have made that choice had she known that she would have to pay the reasonable price of those services.

The paradox was addressed head-on in the California case of *Earhart v. William Low Co.*,[89] Earhart Construction Co. made a contract with William Low Co. to construct the Pana Rama Mobile Home Park. The contract was subject to the conditions that William Low Co. obtain the needed financing and that Earhart Construction Co. secure a performance bond. Neither condition ever was fulfilled. The park was to be built on land owned by William Low Co. and an adjoining tract owned by Ervie Pillow. There was a special use permit altering the zoning regulations that allowed a mobile home park to be built on Pillow's land. However, it would expire on May 27th, without possibility of renewal unless work on the property was "diligently underway" by that date. William Low Co. made a contract to buy the Pillow tract subject to financing. On May 25th, William Low's representative telephoned Fayette L. Earhart and said it had obtained the necessary financing. It urged Earhart to move the necessary equipment onto the property and begin work immediately to save the special use permit. Earhart's crew began work at once. It worked for a week, often in the presence of William Low. On June 1st, Earhart Construction Co. submitted a request for a progress payment. Fayette Earhart then learned that William Low Co. had not obtained the needed financing. William Low Co. refused the bill, and it later signed a contract with another construction company to build the park.

---

[86] 168 Wis. 2d 779, 484 N.W.2d 331 (1992). *See* Midcoast Aviation, Inc. v. General Electric Credit Corp., 907 F.2d 732 (7th Cir. 1990).

[87] *See also*, Kovacic, *A Proposal to Simplify Quantum Meruit Litigation*, 35 Am. U. L. Rev. 547 (1986).

[88] *See* Peter Linzer, *Rough Justice: A Theory of Restitution and Reliance, Contracts and Torts*, 2001 Wis. L. Rev. 665, 764-72 (discussing the unreported opinion in Shore v. Motorola, 210 F.3d 376 (7th Cir. 2000)).

[89] 158 Cal. Rptr. 887, 600 P.2d 1344 (1979).

The trial court awarded Earhart Construction Co. the reasonable value of the work done on William Low Co.'s tract but refused to award anything for the work done on the land owned by Ervie Pillow. It explained, "[a]ll he pays for is the value of what he got, notwithstanding how much it cost the plaintiff to produce it."[90] In other words, work done on the Pillow land at the request of the William Low Co. was not a benefit to it. The trial court followed several California decisions. They held that there must be a direct benefit to justify restitution and the satisfaction of obtaining compliance with a request was not enough.

The Supreme Court of California reversed. Justice Tobriner relied on a dissenting opinion of former Chief Justice Roger Traynor that "urged that we abandon the unconscionable requirement of 'benefit' to the defendant and allow recovery in *quantum meruit* whenever a party acts to his detriment in reliance on another's representation that he will give compensation for the detriment suffered."[91] Traynor argued that benefit conferred was a pure fiction. Allowing recovery would place the loss where it belongs—on the party whose requests induced performance in justifiable reliance on the belief that the requested performance would be paid for. It was enough that plaintiff performed the work on the Pillow property at the urgent request of defendant. Plaintiff reasonably relied, believing that defendant would pay for the work.

Justice Clark dissented on this point. He said, "[a]bsent promise of payment, a person who does no more than request an attorney to consult with a potential client does not incur an obligation to pay the attorney for the consultation."[92] Justice Clark said that William Low Co. might have benefited from saving the special use permit. This increased the time William Low Co. had to obtain financing. However, "[b]y commencing work to maintain the permit, thereby increasing the time to obtain financing, plaintiff also increased the likelihood that his contract would be effective. Because the benefits to plaintiff are substantially similar to those to defendant company, there is no unjust enrichment, and no basis for finding an implied in fact promise to pay."[93]

5. *Same result—different theory*: Is there another way in which one could provide relief to those who rely on unenforceable contracts? If there is, it might be possible to apply it, and avoid the potentially unfortunate effects of stretching the concept of benefit in restitution cases (if not, as some might assert, eliminating it altogether). What about using Restatement § 90? The Wisconsin Supreme Court held in *Hoffman v. Red Owl*[94] that Hoffman was entitled to recover the losses he had reasonably incurred in relying on Red Owl's promise even though that promise was not definite enough to support a contract. Should cases of indefiniteness be treated differently than cases of unilateral mistake? Would the utilization of Section 90 as a theory allow courts to get to just outcomes without doing violence to existing restitutionary doctrines? Or doesn't it matter? What

---

[90] *Id.* at 890, 600 P.2d at 1347.

[91] *Id.* at 892-93, 600 P.2d at 1359-50, *citing* Citizens Engineering Co. v. North American Aviation, Inc., 65 Cal. 2d 396, 410, 420 P.2d 713, 723 (1966).

[92] *Id.* at 897, 600 P.2d at 1354.

[93] *Id.* at 897, 600 P.2d at 1355.

[94] 26 Wis. 2d 683, 133 N.W.2d 267 (1965).

difference does it make so long as the courts are able to arrive at results which square with our sense of justice?

DUNNEBACKE v. PITTMAN
Supreme Court of Wisconsin
216 Wis. 305, 257 N.W. 30 (1934)

NELSON, J. . . . Did the court err in permitting Pittman to recover from the defendants Gilligan upon quasi contract for work performed and materials furnished by him in erecting a breakwater upon certain premises belonging to defendant Lena B. Gilligan?

. . . The defendants Gilligan were residents of Chicago. Mrs. Gilligan taught school there. She owned a parcel of real estate in Kenosha county which abutted upon Lake Michigan. It extended about 140 feet along the lake. The side of the property which sloped abruptly toward the lake was subject to erosion. The defendant Pittman was a local contractor. Prior to the fall of 1932 he had been employed at various times by the Gilligans to perform small jobs in and upon the premises. One of such jobs was the erection of a concrete wall across the slope of the bank for the purpose of protecting it from erosion. That wall as constructed did not extend very far into the soil, and the Gilligans feared that it might give way and fall down unless it was in some manner protected. The Gilligans talked to Pittman at different times about building another wall to protect it. In the spring of 1932 the Gilligans and Pittman met on the beach of the property and at that time discussed what could be done to protect the existing wall. Mr. Pittman testified that at that conference Mrs. Gilligan stated that she would like to put in a wall to protect the first wall; that at that time she walked out to the water's edge, extended her arms, and indicated where the wall which she had in mind should be located; that she asked him whether it should run straight along the bank parallel with the water's edge; that he expressed the opinion that it should not, but should be constructed in the form of a V; that he marked a point near the water's edge to which the end of the proposed wall should reach; that he told her it was his opinion that the structure should be 7 feet high, 4 feet thick at the bottom and 3 or 3½ feet thick at the top; that he told Mrs. Gilligan that it would cost her 25 cents per cubic foot; and that Mrs. Gilligan told him to go ahead and get it in as quickly as he could.

Mrs. Gilligan testified that in the spring of 1932 she discussed with Mr. Pittman the advisability of constructing a wall; that she then told him that she would like to have something constructed about 12 feet in front of the existing wall that would extend into the soil four feet and be level with the bank, for the purpose of protecting the first wall; that she asked him to give her a figure on it and that he promised to do so; that she talked about a wall which would extend across the bank, parallel with the first wall, and that Pittman suggested a V-shaped wall; that Mr. Pittman judged that the wall proposed by him would be about 40 feet from the ends of the old wall to the apex of the triangle; that she asked him how much that would cost; that he said he did not just know, but that he would figure it up and let her know. She further testified that during the summer of 1932 several other conversations regarding the proposed wall were had;

that she saw Mr. Pittman upon the property on September 25 and talked to him about finishing up the different jobs that he had not completed; that she never gave Mr. Pittman orders to go ahead with the construction of the V-shaped wall, but told him to go ahead and finish the things that he had already begun; that thereafter she and her husband went back to Chicago and did not again visit the property until two weeks later, when she discovered that Mr. Pittman had erected a massive V-shaped wall extending from the bank across the beach, a distance of about fifty feet, to the water's edge (the wall is about 7 feet high, 4 feet thick at the bottom, and about 3 feet thick at the top); that upon discovering the wall she was greatly excited because she had never given him any orders to build it; that she told him that the structure was a monstrosity and that she wanted it removed from her property; that after a heated discussion he told her that, if she would pay his workmen, he would blow the damn thing into the lake; that she told him to go ahead and do it as it did not do her any good. The testimony of Mrs. Gilligan was in all respects corroborated by her husband. The breakwater, as constructed, completely blocked travel along the beach and made it impossible to go from one side of the property to the other along the beach without stepping into the water. Testimony was adduced to show that the structure as completed was a benefit to the property and also to the effect that the erection of the wall had greatly damaged it.

At the conclusion of the testimony the court said: "I do not think I can find under the evidence here that the minds of these parties ever met on this subject, there was never more than a discussion about it. I do not believe the plaintiff was warranted in doing the work he did there. That is the way it impresses me. In important work like this the minds of the parties certainly should meet as to what it is to be and the payments and everything. It illustrates a careless way of doing business, that is what it is, very careless. I cannot see how a contractor would go ahead and do a piece of work like this without having something more, something to show for it. It seems he did it. I cannot imagine why he did it if he did not suppose he was doing what he should do. But the evidence is not satisfactory. The burden is on them to show that there was a contract entered into here with the owner of the property as to what it was to be."

Pittman's attorney thereupon asked leave to amend the cross-complaint to conform to the proof so that it would state a cause of action based upon the theory of unjust enrichment. . . .

The court allowed the amendment. The court said: "These parties had business dealings with one another and it is undisputed that they talked about some improvement of this kind being made. The mistake is that the defendant went ahead with this great expense without getting specification and contract, of course, as it should have been done; but it cannot be said that he did not go in there and make all of this expenditure in good faith." . . .

The real question therefore is whether the judgment entered may be upheld under the law of quasi contracts. . . .

Quasi contracts "are legal obligations rather than equitable in the sense that they originated in the courts of law and are enforced by means of so-called legal as distinguished from equitable remedies." They rest "solely upon the universally recognized moral obligation of one who has received a benefit, the retention of which would be unjust, to make restitution." Woodward, The Law of Quasi Contracts, § 6(4), ...

In this case, although the court found that the property was benefitted, it appears that the breakwater was constructed during the absence of the Gilligans; that they had not contracted with Pittman to build it; that they had never contemplated building that kind of a structure; that they did not desire to retain it, but insisted rather that it should be removed from the property. The only sense in which it may be said that the Gilligans are retaining the breakwater is that it continues to exist upon the property against their will. It therefore appears that there is no unjust or inequitable retention of a benefit by them. Had the Gilligans been present during the time that the construction work was going on and had they made no protest, we should have a different situation with which to deal. If, after the breakwater was constructed, the Gilligans had in some manner manifested an intention to retain it, a recovery on the basis of quasi contract might be sustained. It is our opinion that neither the evidence, the findings of fact, nor the conclusions of law sustain a recovery based on the law of quasi contracts. . . . *Reversed.*

NOTES AND QUESTIONS

1. *Distinctions*: How is *Dunnebacke* different from *Vickery v. Richie*? How is it different from *Kearns v. Andree* (discussed in Note 4, *supra*)? In all three cases, construction work is done in the apparent good faith belief that the one doing it will be fairly compensated according to a contract, and in all three cases courts find that no contracts arose. Can you rationalize the no-recovery result in *Dunnebacke* with the recoveries in the other two cases? If not, which one reaches the better result?

2. *Material from the briefs and record*: While the case appears to be a suit between the builder of the wall and the property owners, the record indicates that the supplier of the cement used in the wall was never paid. It was attempting to assert the builder's rights. Pittman, the builder of the wall, did not have sufficient assets to pay for the cement. He was a small handy-man builder, and the case took place in the middle of the Great Depression. The supplier was seeking to assert Pittman's claim, if any, against the property owner. We can wonder whether the case might have been decided differently had Pittman himself been the real party in interest. As between a supplier of materials and an owner who received little tangible benefit, who should take the loss of the value of the cement?

Those who work on the property of others or supply materials often are protected by statutes giving them liens on property that has been improved. However, these statutes require the mechanic or materialman to follow certain procedures. For example, Wis. Stat. § 779.41(1) provides, "Every mechanic and every keeper of a garage or shop, and every employer of a mechanic who transports, makes, alters, repairs or does any work on personal property *at the request of the owner or legal possessor of the personal property*, has a lien thereon for his just and reasonable charges therefor, . . . and may retain possession of the personal property until the charges are paid." They also protect those who have a recorded security interest. Several cases involve attempts by those who otherwise would have been protected by these statutes but who failed to follow procedures to assert a right to recover for unjust enrichment. The Supreme Court of Wisconsin has been unsympathetic to attempts to get around the statutory requirements for liens. The restitutionary end-run has not worked.[95]

---

[95] *See, e.g.*, Gebhardt Bros., Inc. v. Brimmel, 31 Wis. 2d 581, 143 N.W.2d 479 (1966); Industrial Credit Co. v. Inland G.M. Diesel, Inc., 51 Wis. 2d 520, 187 N.W.2d 157 (1971).

Chapter 2

INCOMPLETE PLANNING, FLEXIBILITY AND ENFORCEABILITY

A. SPECIFYING ENDS BUT NOT MEANS: "WE CAN WORK IT OUT!"

1. BUILDING CONSTRUCTION AND ORDINARY PEOPLE

KLIMEK v. PERISICH
Supreme Court of Oregon
231 Or. 71, 371 P.2d 956 (1962)

PERRY, J. This is an action brought by the plaintiff to recover damages from the defendant for breach of contract to remodel an old dwelling house into a rooming house.

The jury returned a verdict for the plaintiff which was set aside and judgment entered notwithstanding the verdict for the defendant. The plaintiff has appealed.

[Much of the court's opinion consists of extracts from the trial court testimony. We offer a summary of it here, At the beginning of the opinion, the court observed that "Both plaintiff and defendant were born in Yugoslavia, and while they now speak and understand English, the record discloses limitations in this regard." It seems that Mrs. Klimek, the plaintiff, had purchased an old building with hopes of turning it into a boarding house. She had conversations with Mr. Perisich, a builder, about the remodeling. Apparently, Mr. Perisich told Mrs. Klimek that he was not sure how many rooms she could get out of the house but that the cost of refurbishing would run $8,000, $9,000 or at the most $10,000.

Blueprints for the remodeling were obtained but no specifications covering materials to be used were ever drafted. The parties did not enter into a formal contract; Mr. Perisich simply began remodeling the building. Although Mr. Perisich was supervising the job, he was paid the same as the other carpenters. Mr. Perisich received no compensation for helping Mrs. Klimek obtain plans and building permits. Mrs. Klimek herself testified that no arrangements were made between the parties as to who would do the required plumbing, heating or electrical wiring, but as these items became necessary both she and Mr. Perisich would search for the most reasonable price. Mrs. Klimek took care of paying bills for materials, services and the workmen's wages. Mrs. Klimek ran out of money before the work was done, was unable to get financing, and sued Mr. Perisich to recover damages.]

We have set forth only the evidence of the plaintiff, as this is an action at law, and if there is substantial evidence of the formation of a contract, as sued upon, the finding of the jury must be sustained. . . .

To constitute a contract such as here present, there must be an offer and an acceptance. . . .

An offer must be certain so that upon an unqualified acceptance the nature and extent of the obligations of each party are fixed and may be determined with reasonable certainty. . . .

As to an acceptance of an offer: "It is well settled that when a contract is to be founded on offer and acceptance, it must be shown that the latter coincides precisely with the former. Unless this appears, there is no agreement." . . . *Northwestern Agencies v. Flynn*, 138 Or 101, 106, 5 P2d 530.

In other words, there must be a meeting of the minds as to the obligations each assumes under the contract before it can be said that a contract exists.

In the matter before us the plaintiff agreed to pay money and the defendant agreed to render services, therefore both the amount to be paid and the services to be rendered must be reasonably certain.

As stated by . . . Corbin on Contracts, § 100, p. 315:

> It is not always the price in money that is left uncertain in an agreement; sometimes it is that for which the price is to be paid. If no method is agreed upon for rendering this subject matter sufficiently definite for enforcement, the agreement must nearly always fail of legal effect; it is not customary for courts to fill the gap by finding that a "reasonable" amount of goods or land or labor has been agreed upon as the exchange for the money.

> . . .

The trial court, in granting judgment for the defendant, notwithstanding the verdict of the jury, based its opinion upon the indefiniteness of the subject matter of the offer. The plaintiff contends that the subject matter of the offer is sufficiently definite in that the parties agreed upon a maximum amount to be paid by the plaintiff for the remodeling of a certain building; that the extent and requirements for remodeling were certain, although no specifications were agreed upon; that the minimum requirements of the building code of the city of Portland required certain materials to be used, and this supplied the lack of specifications as to the work to be done and the material to be used by the defendant. Defendant contends that no agreement existed other than to perform labor at an hourly rate and there was no agreement as to the extent of remodeling or the materials to be used, and therefore no contract existed between the parties.

The difficulty with plaintiff's contentions that the minimal requirements of the city building code are sufficiently definite as a substitute for specifications is that there is no evidence that the parties agreed that compliance with the minimal requirements of the building code would constitute a satisfactory execution of the purported contract, and also there is no evidence that the building code specifies the extent of the remodeling, or the kinds or types of materials that could be satisfactorily used in the remodeling of this particular. Also there is no evidence of what the parties agreed was necessary to constitute a remodeling of the structure.

The building code of the city of Portland was not introduced into evidence, and therefore the jury could not determine whether the building code covered these requirements. . . .

The plaintiff cites and relies upon a number of cases, such as *Helm v. Speith*, 298 Ky. 225, 182 S.W.2d 635. [There] the parties agreed that the building should be contracted to comply with the minimal requirements of the Federal Housing Administration, and the Federal Housing Administration requirements were introduced into evidence. . . . [Here] as previously stated, there is no evidence that the parties agreed that the minimal requirements of the Portland building code were agreed upon as a basis of their negotiations, nor was it introduced into evidence.

The trial court correctly held that there was no contract.

There is additional reason why the judgment of the trial court should be affirmed. An examination of the evidence of the plaintiff, in our opinion, is such that reasonable minds could reach only the conclusion that at all times the plaintiff knew that the statements made by the defendant with relation to the cost of remodeling of the structure were only estimates and that the plaintiff knew this to be such, therefore the words and actions of the defendant could only be construed as not an offer to remodel the building to the satisfaction of the plaintiff at a fixed maximum amount, nor as an acceptance of such an offer.

The judgment of the trial court is affirmed.

NOTES AND QUESTIONS

1. *An additional argument from defendant's brief*: In his brief, defendant argued that a promise to guarantee the cost of a construction project is enforceable only if there is consideration for it. In this case, the defendant received only a carpenter's wages for the work that he did. There was no mechanism by which defendant could share in any cost-savings on component parts of the project:

> There is no question but what a contractor can guarantee a maximum cost of construction, but before that is done there must be an allegation and proof that the agreed figure which is the ceiling price must be a guaranteed maximum cost. In the case at bar, it is clear that the parties merely agreed that this "would be the cost." There is no allegation or proof that the defendant guaranteed this to be the maximum cost and there is no allegation or proof that defendant agreed to be liable for any costs in excess of $10,000. Nor is there any consideration for the alleged guarantee.

2. *The building code as a gap filler*: Should the Supreme Court of Oregon have found that the contract was too indefinite to be enforced in view of the jury's verdict for the plaintiff? Plaintiff argued in her brief that the parties impliedly agreed that the building code provided minimum specifications. Apparently, the jury was not charged that it needed to decide this issue. If we assume that plaintiff had raised this question at trial and in her request for jury instructions, should the appellate court have remanded the case for a new trial on this question? Would this depend on the degree to which the Portland building code specifies what is required in a rooming house?

3. *How formal must a building contract be?* In *Lichty v. Merzenich*,[1] Dr. Merzenich hired Mr. Lichty to build a residence. Under the original contract, Lichty was paid by the hour for his services, plus $0.25 for each hour of additional labor employed on the job. A year later the project proved slower and more costly than expected. Dr. Merzenich prepared a list of things he thought necessary to finish the job. He asked Lichty what it would cost to complete them. Lichty argued that Dr. Merzenich asked for an estimate. Dr. Merzenich contended that he asked for a bid.

A few days later they met at the building site and discussed matters. Lichty suggested that they each write a figure on pieces of paper and turn them over simultaneously. They did. Dr. Merzenich's figure was $5,000; Lichty's was $6,500. Merzenich testified,

> [W]e agreed that he would do it. He agreed to do it for [$]6500 with a provision that we allow plus or minus 10%, not to exceed $6800 total.
>
> In other words, if it came in under [$]6200, I was to receive the benefit of the doubt on the 10%. If it came in over, I would pay him over.[2]

Dr. Merzenich also testified that Lichty would not sign the slip because he did not have a contractor's license, but they shook hands on it.

The trial court found there was a contract for a specific sum. The Supreme Court of Oregon affirmed. Justice Linde said, "the manner of arriving at the remaining costs by turning over slips on which each party had proposed a sum would seem an odd way for a builder and a dentist to arrive at an estimate of labor and materials; it appears more consistent with an attempt to negotiate an agreed price."[3] The court continued,

> Plaintiff also contends that the terms of the parties' discussion of the work to be completed, while adequate as an estimate, were too indefinite to form the essential elements of a contract, citing *Klimek v. Perisich* . . . . The decision [in the Klimek case] illustrates the relevant principles but also the limited usefulness of matching facts among individually unique, nonformalized personal transactions. . . . Dr. Merzenich's list of work to be completed, which in another setting might have left a contractor's commitment too undefined, here drew meaning from the parties' collaboration on the project for a full year.[4]

While Justice Linde may be able to avoid contrasting these cases because he is a judge, the rest of us cannot put aside the point so easily. Is there a difference between the *Klimek* and *Lichty* cases? Does the difference turn on the definiteness and completeness of the agreement or something else?

---

[1] 278 Or. 209, 563 P.2d 690 (1977).
[2] *Id.* at 211, 563 P.2d at 692.
[3] *Id.* at 213, 563 P.2d at 692.
[4] *Id.* at 213, 563 P.2d at 692-93.

4. *The real consequences of the case?* What can you say for and against the following statement?

> The *Klimek* case illustrates the poverty of our legal system in dealing with real human problems. It is likely that neither party came away from their adventure before the Oregon courts with a sense that justice had been done. Of course, Mrs. Klimek could have gone to an architect and a large construction company. They would have given her a firm price as part of a form contract which would have protected their interests and few of hers. Mr. Perisich could have hired a lawyer to draft an agreement limiting his liability so he would never have been sued. However, these solutions ignore the real situations of people such as Mrs. Klimek and Mr. Perisich. These solutions reward education, experience, wealth and social status. They also serve the economic interests of middle class professionals.

Suppose that you agree with the preceding statement? What consequence? What program for change?

2. THE UCC AND INDEFINITENESS: TRANSACTIONS IN GOODS BETWEEN MAJOR CORPORATIONS

BETHLEHEM STEEL CORP. v. LITTON INDUSTRIES, INC.
Superior Court of Pennsylvania
321 Pa. Super. 357, 468 A.2d 748 (1983)

WICKERSHAM, J. The central issue in this case is whether a certain written option agreement is a contract. [The trial judge, sitting without a jury, had ruled that the plaintiff-appellant had failed to meet its burden to show the parties intended to be contractually bound.]

Basically the complaint alleged that on or about April 25, 1968 Litton entered into an agreement with Bethlehem whereby Litton would construct and deliver and Bethlehem would purchase a one thousand foot self-unloading ore vessel. The vessel constructed under the agreement was delivered, accepted, and the price paid therefor.

The complaint further alleged that Litton extended to Bethlehem by letter dated April 25, 1968 "a written offer good until December 31, 1968 for the entry into an option agreement for five vessels." Furthermore, it was alleged that on or about December 31, 1968 Bethlehem accepted Litton's offer to enter into an option agreement under which Bethlehem was granted the right for a period of five years after the execution of the option agreement to obtain from Litton from one to five vessels for prices varying between $22,400,000 and $18,400,000 each. Further, the complaint alleged that Bethlehem, pursuant to the option agreement, by letter dated November 16, 1973 exercised its option for two vessels and thereby ordered the first and second vessels in accordance with the option agreement. On December 26, 1973 Bethlehem, pursuant to the option agreement, exercised its option for an additional (third) vessel.

Finally, the complaint alleged that Litton expressly and unequivocally refused to perform in accordance with its obligations under the option agreement; that Litton demanded the payment of a price for each vessel many millions of dollars in excess of the price provided for in the option agreement and indicated delivery dates substantially later than the delivery provided in the option agreement. Damages were sought in a sum in excess of $95,000,000.00 together with interest and costs. . . .

In its defense, Litton responded, *inter alia*: (1) PX-1 (the letter of December 31, 1968) was never intended to be and was not a contract; (2) no contract was formed in any event because the vital terms left for later negotiation could not be filled by the court on a reasonably certain basis; (3) any purported "option agreement" had been rejected prior to exercise by Bethlehem's assertions that it would "never" order another vessel from Litton; (4) since an "option" unsupported by consideration is revocable at will, any purported "option agreement" had been revoked prior to exercise by Litton's notice to Bethlehem that the Erie shipyard was to be closed; (5) any purported "option" had never been properly exercised; and (6) Litton had never breached or repudiated any "agreement" which might have existed.

On June 28, 1978 a non-jury trial began and Judge Louik filed his adjudication on June 6, 1979 which provided, in part, as follows:

[Beginning of an extended excerpt from the *trial court opinion*.]

After a protracted trial of approximately nine months with over 12,000 pages of testimony and some 500 exhibits, this matter is now before the Court for determination. The claim in excess of 95 million dollars, together with a counterclaim, is based on a two-page letter between two giant corporations. . . .

For background purposes, it should be noted that on April 25, 1968, at a formal signing ceremony, the plaintiff and defendant entered into a ship-construction contract for a newly designed 1,000 foot self unloading ore vessel. This vessel, known as Hull 101, was commissioned "The Cort." . . .

In addition, there is in evidence as PX-4 a document which was executed on that very same day, April 25, 1968, together with a document dated December 31, 1968, in evidence as PX-1. These are the documents in issue in the instant case.

The primary and fundamental question now before the Court is whether or not there has been an option contract. The plaintiff's claim is based upon the following two-page letter:

ERIE MARINE, INC.
ERIE, PENNSYLVANIA

April 25, 1968

Bethlehem Steel Corporation
Bethlehem, Pennsylvania
Attn: Ralph K. Smith

Gentlemen:

Reference is made to the ship construction contract signed by our companies this date for the construction by us of a 1,000-foot self-unloading ore vessel for you. Reference is also made to my letter to you of this date extending to you an option to purchase either one or two additional vessels upon the terms therein set forth.

We hereby extend to you an offer to enter into an option agreement to have us construct for you from one to five additional vessels in accordance with "Specifications covering the Construction of a Self-Unloading Bulk Carrier for Bethlehem Steel Corporation" (Number Y 917) dated March 1968, addendum number 1 thereto dated March 28, 1968 and addendum number 2 thereto dated April 17, 1968. This offer to enter into an option agreement shall be firm and irrevocable until December 31, 1968 at 5:00 P.M. E.S.T.

The terms of the option agreement are to be as follows:

(a) The specifications for the vessels shall be the specifications referred to above, except for mutually agreeable reduced test schedules of the vessels, if the testing of the vessel to be delivered under the contract executed this date proves successful.

(b) Bethlehem to have the right at any time within five years after the effective date of the option agreement to order from one to not more than a total of five vessels, for delivery within 24 months from the date of the order for the first vessel ordered and for delivery within 24 months plus 4 months for each additional vessel ordered within any one calendar year; provided however no vessel shall be scheduled for delivery between November 31 and March 31.

(c) The price of the vessel shall be as follows:

1st vessel ordered	*$22,400,000.00*
2nd " "	*$21,400,000.00*
3rd " "	*$20,400,000.00*
4th " "	*$19,400,000.00*
5th " "	*$18,400,000.00*

(d) The vessel prices are subject to escalation for both labor and material for a base price of $20,400,000.00 for each vessel and based upon Fourth Quarter 1968 mutually agreed upon index such as:

> *Material—"Material index for Bureau of Ships steel vessel contracts" furnished to the Naval Ship Systems Command by the Bureau of Labor Statistics of the U.S. Department of Labor.*

> *Labor—"Index of changes in straight-time average hourly earnings for selected shipyards" (June 1962 = 100) for steel ship construction, furnished to the Naval Ship Systems Command by the Bureau of Labor Statistics of the U.S. Department of Labor.*

At the time of exercise of the option for any vessel, the escalation shall be computed to the date of contract execution, and an appropriate contract clause will be included therein providing for quarterly escalation thereafter. We will furnish you the labor and material percentages subject to escalation by May 15, 1968.

(e) The terms and conditions of the ship construction contracts to be in accordance with the attached terms and conditions and any other mutually agreed to terms and conditions and shall contain a clause giving to Bethlehem the right to cancel at any time upon the payment of all of our costs incurred to date of cancellation, including similar vendor and subcontractor cancellation charges, plus 15% of such costs.

> *Very truly yours,*
>
> *George K. Geiger*

In response to this letter, a letter dated December 31, 1968 was sent by Bethlehem to Erie which stated in part "We hereby accept your offer of an option to have you construct for us from one to five additional vessels." In all other respects, the letter of December 31, 1968 is merely identical repetition of the language in the letter of April 25, 1968. . . .

On November 16, 1973, plaintiff sent a letter to defendant stating that it exercises its option to order two vessels and then on December 26, 1973, plaintiff sent another letter to defendant stating that it exercises its option to order a third vessel. . . .

Defendant did not enter into any ship construction contract with plaintiff and did not construct any vessels under the letters of November 16, 1973 and December 26, 1973. . . .

CONCLUSION OF LAW

1.   Bethlehem has not sustained its burden of proof, either in law or in fact, of imposing liability on Litton-Erie, and a finding accordingly will be entered in favor of Litton-Erie on Bethlehem's claim. . . .

[End of excerpt from trial court opinion.]

SCOPE OF REVIEW

It is quite clear that the scope of appellate review of a finding on contractual intent is limited—indeed narrowly circumscribed.

The "intent to contract" is a question of fact for the trier-of-fact. . . . It is axiomatic that a trial judge's findings of fact, sustained by the Court *en banc*, have the weight of a jury verdict and cannot be disturbed on appeal if supported by competent evidence in the record. . . .

We have reviewed the entire trial record and viewing the evidence in the light most favorable to the victorious party below, a fair distillation of the evidence would indicate the following scenario.

This controversy arose out of ship construction on the Great Lakes. Litton, a newcomer to the Lakes, tried unsuccessfully through its subsidiary, Erie, to develop a market for a unique and revolutionary supertanker-type ore vessel, 1,000 feet long with novel self-unloading features. In seven years of effort (from 1967 to 1973), however, Litton sold only one ore vessel ("Hull 101" [the Cort])—to Bethlehem.

In 1968, Litton and Bethlehem exchanged two incomplete letters, one dated April 25, 1968 (PX-4) and the other dated December 31, 1968 (PX-1), concerning an offer to negotiate a long-term option agreement for construction of up to five novel multimillion dollar vessels at Litton's new shipyard. In the words of Judge Louik: "If anything, there is one matter that is absolutely clear, and that is that the writing provides that further agreements between the parties are necessary." (Ad 13.) During the ensuing years, Litton repeatedly attempted to interest Bethlehem in commencing the negotiations contemplated. These efforts were in vain, however, and from late 1972 through early 1973 Litton repeatedly informed Bethlehem of its intention to close the Erie shipyard unless ship construction orders were immediately forthcoming. When Bethlehem disclaimed interest in purchasing any additional ships and no other contracts were obtained, Litton began closing its Erie yard and disbanding its workforce.

Thereafter, however, Bethlehem notified Litton that it wished to negotiate a ship construction contract pursuant to PX-1. When the parties were unable to agree on contractual terms, Bethlehem commenced this action, contending that despite the parties' failure to agree upon the myriad terms explicitly left for future negotiations, the mere exchange of the letters in 1968 bound the parties to a "contract" for the construction of novel ships worth millions of dollars.

The April 25, 1968 Letter (PX-4)

After four months of careful negotiation and drafting and redrafting of contract terms, representatives of Litton and Bethlehem met on April 25, 1968 for the ceremonial exchange of a contract for the immediate construction of Hull 101, the only one thousand foot vessel actually sold by Litton, for the firm fixed price of $17,994,138.00 ("Hull 101 Contract"). Bethlehem's Board of Directors had insisted upon "great precision" in every aspect of the sale, especially price. The Hull 101 Contract was fully performed and is not at issue here.

During the two to three hours that the parties were together on April 25, 1968, primarily for the exchange of the Hull 101 contract, they jointly drafted a two-page letter (PX-4), extending a last minute sales promotional offer to negotiate a long-term option agreement for up to five additional Hull 101 type vessels. The parties clearly understood that PX-4 was not part of the consideration for the Hull

101 Contract. With one exception, none of the representatives at the April 25 meeting even was aware before that meeting that such an offer was to be made or drafted that day. On its face, PX-4 clearly was not an option agreement; rather, it expressly provided for future negotiations which, if successfully completed, would have resulted in an option agreement which, in turn, if properly exercised, would have resulted in formal execution of a formal written ship construction contract.

In hurriedly drafting PX-4 during a part of their short meeting on April 25, the parties explicitly agreed that price escalation would be included in any long-term option agreement and ship construction contract upon which they might subsequently agree. The parties further expressly acknowledged, however, that because escalation was so critical and so complex, they would postpone the negotiations necessary for agreement upon that vital subject.

PX-4 thus was jointly drafted during the less than three-hour meeting on April 25 in the form of a two-step offer to enter into a future option agreement in order to provide until the end of the year for the parties to investigate and develop the terms of an appropriate escalation clause and the other important matter intentionally left for future negotiation and agreement.

Having taken more than four months to negotiate a contract for a single vessel (Hull 101), on which construction was to begin immediately for a fixed price with no escalation, the parties recognized that negotiation of a long-term option agreement for up to five novel multimillion dollar vessels providing for price escalation would be infinitely more complex and time consuming.

On several occasions from May through November of 1968, Litton sought to negotiate the terms of an option agreement. On each occasion, Bethlehem replied that it was not yet willing to spend the time and effort required for such negotiations, since it would not even consider additional 1000 foot ore vessels until the revolutionary Hull 101 had been successfully operated for at least one season.

By December of 1968, aware that the PX-4 offer was about to lapse, but still unwilling to devote the time necessary to negotiate the terms essential for a definitive option agreement and ship construction contract, Bethlehem sought to preserve the status quo.

Between April 25 and December 31, 1968, there were no discussions, negotiations or agreements between the parties with respect to any of the terms, including escalation, expressly left for future negotiation and mutual agreement under PX-4.

In short, whatever the parties had intended by drafting PX-4 was unchanged by PX-1. In PX-4 the parties had explicitly contemplated negotiations and agreements necessary to create a binding option contract. PX-1 did not resolve any of the substantive terms left open for negotiation in PX-4; as the record clearly reveals, it was adopted as an accommodation to Bethlehem's request for a "holding pattern."

From 1968 through 1973, Litton attracted no other customers to its Erie shipyard. Indeed, by early 1973, Litton officials warned Bethlehem that the Erie yard would be closed unless Bethlehem ordered additional ships. Bethlehem officials had previously stated, however, that they were "disgusted" by the "slow" construction of Hull 101, and by 1973, rather than express any objection to the closing of the Erie yard, repeatedly insisted that they would never order any additional ships from Litton. Thus, without any hope of future business from Bethlehem, Litton "mothballed" its Erie yard.

Thereafter, in full knowledge of the fact that the Erie Shipyard had dismissed most of its labor force for lack of business, Bethlehem notified Litton by letter that it was planning to "exercise its options" for ore vessels. Significantly, however, Bethlehem expressly acknowledged that the terms of an option agreement had to be negotiated before Bethlehem could exercise any option.

At subsequent meetings, Litton advised Bethlehem that although it had closed down its shipyard in reliance upon Bethlehem's representations, it was willing to build vessels if the parties could reach agreement on a ship construction contract (Ad-9), which Litton was at all times willing to negotiate. The parties, however, never agreed on any of the material terms left open in PX-4 and PX-1, including escalation—found by the trial judge to be "one of the most critical provisions of a ship construction contract" (Ad-26). Nor would Bethlehem accept any of Litton's alternative proposals.

Judge Louik carefully considered all the relevant factors under the common law and under the Uniform Commercial Code—the letters themselves, the discussions at the time of the exchange of the letters, the surrounding circumstances, subsequent conduct, the nature of the contemplated construction contract, and the parties' prior dealings—and found that the parties did not intend to enter a binding agreement until they mutually agreed on the critical terms intentionally deferred, including the terms of a price escalation clause, and reduced those terms to a formal ship construction contract. The Court alternatively found that under § 2-204(3) of the UCC, no contract had been formed—because the Court simply could not, on "a reasonably certain basis," fill in the price escalation terms and other missing contract provisions in order to provide for "an appropriate remedy." . . .

Returning now to relevant portions of the adjudication of Judge Louik dated June 6, 1979, our review of the record supports the correctness of the court's conclusions, as follows:

[The court again quotes from the trial court opinion.]

DISCUSSION

While a great many legal issues have been presented by both parties in this trial, their determination and even their relevance depend upon the resolution of one elementary factual dispute: Did both Bethlehem and Litton intend a legally binding option to arise from the two-page letter of April 25, 1968? . . .

UNIFORM COMMERCIAL CODE

One of the contentions of Bethlehem is that these agreements come within the Uniform Commercial Code and, therefore, gaps, (if any appear in the documents), may be filled in by the Court. . . .

Even if the Uniform Commercial Code is applicable, the Court must first find that there was intent to enter into a contract by the two letters (PX-4 and PX-1). The same criteria has to be used in this regard as is used in determining whether or not there is a contract at common law. Even if the Court had found that there was such an intent, there then arises the matter of ability of the Court to fill in the gaps because, if anything is clear in PX-4 and PX-1, it is that gaps exist which must be filled in.

If a contract did exist, there are three general areas in which gaps appear which would require the Court's intervention to fill.

The first term obviously left open was the original escalation index which would be used to calculate the increase in cost per vessel over the time between PX-1 to the date of contract execution.

The only aspect of this stage of escalation that the documents provided is that an index method of escalation shall be used for this portion of escalation, and that the index shall be mutually agreed upon, as evidenced by the language "mutually agreed upon index such as." Because the parties established the method of arriving at the index as mutual agreement, and because of the complexity of negotiations of escalation clauses in the shipbuilding industry, the Court cannot fill in such a gap in light of Code § 2-305(4).

The second gap relates to "second stage escalation" which PX-4 and PX-1 establishes as the escalation from the execution of the construction contract to the end of the escalation period:

> "an appropriate contract clause will be included therein providing for quarterly escalation thereafter."

An escalation clause is a complex, detailed contractual provision negotiated between parties to provide a means necessary to calculate and pay escalation. It is an equitable concept that escalation clauses must be such as not to give the builder a windfall nor to have the builder suffer losses due to inflation. Because of inflation since the middle 1960's, the escalation clauses became one of the most critical provisions of a ship construction contract. There are many essential elements to be negotiated in an escalation clause, some of which are very critical, such as the indexes to be used, the escalatable amount, the amount escalatable each computation period, the duration of escalation, payment, and the method of computation. These elements can have numerous possible variations resulting from negotiations between the parties. One of the most critical elements and perhaps the heart of an escalation clause is the amount escalatable each computation period. This is called the "apportionment" which can have an infinite number of possible variations and will vary from ship to ship depending upon the time of construction, the place of construction, needs and desires of the parties.

The third gap which the Court would have to fill if it found a contract otherwise existed, arises from the language indicated that the terms and conditions were to be in accordance with the sample contract and "any other mutually agreed upon terms and conditions." In view of the fact that the sample form of contract was for a fixed price contract, there must of necessity be changes required since the writings clearly indicate that the parties contemplated an escalation contract. Such a contract would require additional terms and conditions from those that appear in the sample form.

In addition, there are numerous other terms which might be expected to be in a ship construction contract of this magnitude. Evidence of this can be found in the contract (DX-12) proposed by the plaintiffs at the September 24, 1973 meeting with defendants. This proposed contract varied substantially from the sample contract in at least twelve separate items (See Finding 28). These altered or added terms strongly suggest that, at least in the mind of Bethlehem, there were many items left out of the sample contract, or left to be negotiated at a later time.

The breadth of these gaps can only be appreciated in light of the nature of the vessel. According to David Klinges, Bethlehem's Senior Maritime Attorney:

> As you can appreciate this was to be a new departure for maritime transportation for Great Lakes. It contemplated a new revolutionary way of building ships and a new revolutionary way of transporting and discharging.

The apportionment in quarterly escalation, if nothing else, must be one to be negotiated between the parties. Apportionment does not depend upon the actual use of labor or material in a particular quarter, but is an item negotiated between the parties depending upon what the parties are aiming at, either for the purpose of securing payments earlier during the construction period or for a later payment, but higher escalation. The extent of the escalation period can also vary, the payment of escalation amounts can vary, and a host of factors can move the parties to a variety of allocation of apportionment. This is also recognized by plaintiff in its Request for Findings, Point 30.59 where they ask the Court to find:

> In the shipbuilding industry, a party entering a contract would, in negotiating an escalation clause, submit to the other party the form of escalation clause desired, and if the owner submitted a proposal that the builder did not like, the builder would make his feelings known to the buyer. Point 30.59.

All of the expert testimony indicated that such clauses could not be materialized from the air by the Court. Because of the nature of negotiations in shipbuilding and the extreme complexity of the undertaking, such a clause would require careful negotiations between the parties and would need to be custom tailored to fit the project. There is nothing in the record upon which the Court could extract such a clause.

Because of the nature of the gaps as has been discussed in this Option, it would appear that only the parties are the exclusive entities capable of filling in the gaps. Because these gaps are so wide, the Court cannot make a new contract for the parties.

When we consider all of the above elements and the fact that the parties involved here are two of the largest corporations in this country, and PX-4 is only a two-page letter, the language of Mr. Justice Cohen in the case of *Essner v. Shoemaker*, 393 Pa. 422, [143 A.2d 364 (1958)] is most appropriate:

It is difficult to believe that the principals, experienced in real estate dealings as they were, would intend to . . . [assent unequivocally] to an oral agreement in a transaction involving more than a quarter of a million dollars, [and] complicated by assignments, mortgages and taxes.

[End of second extended extract from trial court opinion.]

. . . .

In summary, we agree with the finding of the lower court that there was no enforceable contract between the parties. . . . Order affirmed.

[JUDGE HESTER's dissent follows. ROWLEY and WIEAND, JJ. joined in it.]

. . . .

For the reasons that follow, I would reverse and remand to the lower court for further proceedings consistent with this Opinion. . . .

The threshold issue to be resolved in the instant appeal concerns the contractual intent of the parties. Unlike the majority, which views this issue as a question of fact, I believe the issue of contractual intent is a question of law or ultimate fact. Undeniably, the basic findings of fact of the lower court should not be disturbed if these findings are based upon competent evidence, unless the lower court committed an abuse of discretion or error of law in admitting the evidence from which the findings of fact were derived. However, the contractual intent of the parties as an ultimate fact or conclusion of law is subject to independent appellate scrutiny. . . .

[I]t is clear that the Code applies to the instant case. The issue, as refined by the language of the Code, thus becomes, "Did the parties intend to enter into a contract for sale, whereby Bethlehem would have the right to exercise its option to order specially-manufactured future goods from Litton, resulting in a contract to sell future goods?" . . .

The Code states: [under the heading, "Options and cooperation respecting performance"]

(a) Specifying particulars of performance—An agreement for sale which is otherwise sufficiently definite (§ 2204(c)) to be a contract is not made invalid by the fact that it leaves particulars of performance to be specified by one of the parties. Any such specification must be made in good faith and within limits set by commercial reasonableness." 13 Pa. C.S.A. § 2311(a).

In the instant case, the time of performance, and whether performance would be required at all, was specifically left to Bethlehem as an option. The time within which Bethlehem was required to exercise its option was specified, so there is no issue concerning "commercial reasonableness.". . .

The lower court did not specifically decide whether the Code applies. Rather, the trial court improperly relied upon numerous pre-Code decisions and other authority not involving a contract for the sale of goods.

For instance, the lower court repeatedly cited *Upsal Street Realty Company v. Rubin*, 326 Pa. 327, 192 A. 481 (1937), involving an application for a lease, which along with location, term and rental amount, provided, "Selection of colors will be made after lease is signed." Citing a comment to § 26 of the RESTATEMENT OF THE LAW OF CONTRACTS, the Court in *Upsal* found that this language was evidence that the parties intended no binding agreement by stating:

> if the preliminary agreement is incomplete, it being apparent that the determination of certain details is deferred until the writing is made out; or if an intention is manifested in any way that legal obligations between the parties shall be deferred until the writing is made, the preliminary negotiations and agreements do not constitute a contract.

Id. at 330, 192 A. at 483. Referring to the above-quoted section of *Upsal*, the lower court reasoned:

> In light of the formality of the signing of the first fixed price contract for Hull 101 [the Cort], this language dictates that a final writing be signed before the parties intended to be legally bound . . . Another aspect of this language indicates a conclusion that [the letter of April 25, 1968] was merely an expression of preliminary accord.

As will be further discussed *infra*, the lower court's reliance on *Upsal* is misplaced, since the principles stated therein were specifically displaced by particular provisions of the Code. 13 Pa.C.S.A. § 1103. . . .

From § 2204 of the Code, it is clear that the existence of a contract is initially dependent upon the intent of the parties. If the parties have intended to contractually obligate and benefit each other, their contract is enforceable even if certain terms are left open or are left to be agreed upon in the future. In other words, the Code specifically contemplates that the parties may "agree to agree" with respect to certain terms. The comment to § 2204 acknowledges that, depending upon how many terms are uncertain, an agreement may be defeated due to "indefiniteness" if there is no reasonably certain basis for granting an appropriate remedy. However, the Code specifically provides "gap-filling" so as to avoid defeating a contract which the parties otherwise intended. . . .

Under the Code, parties can expressly agree to be contractually bound, even though certain terms are left open to be negotiated or agreed upon at a future time. It does not matter whether the original agreement is "a preliminary accord," "an agreement to agree," or "an agreement to negotiate." The crucial inquiry is whether the parties intended to enter into an agreement; and, if the parties left certain terms to be negotiated at a future time, then those parties contemplate that those terms will be filled in, on a reasonable basis, through the mutual good-faith negotiations of the parties. . . .

The Code also states "Every contract or duty within this title imposes an obligation of good faith in its performance or enforcement." 13 Pa.C.S.A. § 1203. Therefore, if parties agree to agree concerning certain open contractual terms, then both parties must attempt to negotiate those terms, on a reasonable basis and in good faith.

As evinced by the letter of April 25 and December 31, 1968, as well as other discussions, negotiations, communications and "course of dealing" between the parties, it is clear that the parties intended to enter into an agreement which would give Bethlehem the right to exercise its option to order as many as five one thousand foot, self-unloading ore vessels from Litton at any time during a five year period.

The letter of April 25, 1968, from Litton to Bethlehem states, *inter alia*:

> We hereby extend to you an offer to enter into an option agreement to have us construct for you from one to five additional vessels . . . this offer to enter into an option agreement shall be firm and irrevocable until December 31, 1968 at 5 p.m. E.S.T.

This correspondence expressly represents itself to be "an offer to enter into an option agreement," which is "firm and irrevocable." See 13 Pa.C.S.A. § 2205.

The letter of December 31, 1968, from Bethlehem to Litton states "We hereby accept your offer of an option to have you construct for us from one to five additional vessels." Said letter of December 31, 1968, was executed by George K. Geiger on behalf of Litton and Erie under a heading "AGREED TO."

These two letters are "sufficient to show agreement" for the purposes of 13 Pa.C.S.A. § 2204(a). The letter of December 31, 1968, operated as an acceptance of Litton's offer to enter into an option agreement, for the purposes of 13 Pa.C.S.A. § 2206(a).

Furthermore, the conduct of the parties manifests that they both recognized the existence of such a contract. [Judge Hester then enumerated several letters in which representatives of Litton and Bethlehem seemed to acknowledge that a binding agreement was in force.]

In determining that the parties had not intended to create a legally-binding option agreement, the lower court heavily relied on "the fact that the parties involved here are two of the largest corporations in this country, and [the letter of April 25, 1968] is only a two-page letter," citing *Essner v. Shoemaker*, 393 Pa. 422, 143 A.2d 364 (1958).

I cannot agree with the majority that this reasoning is supported by the evidence. The letters of April 25 and December 31, 1968, incorporate by reference the detailed specifications concerning the construction of the self-unloading ore carrier for Bethlehem Steel Corporation, which were used by the parties in connection with the construction of the Cort. These specifications serve the purposes of identifying the specially-manufactured vessels, as contemplated by the parties at the inception of their agreement.

Furthermore, both letters incorporated by reference the *pro forma* Ship Construction Contract which consists of 26 pages and 21 articles and which was also used as the basis of the agreement between the parties for the construction of the Cort. This *pro forma* contract sets forth in detail many contractual terms including specifications, approval and inspection, delivery schedule and manner of delivery, terms of payment, manner of inspection, trial runs, schedule of trial runs, place of delivery and acceptance, allocation of risk of loss, allocation of insurance proceeds, events of default, remedies in the event of default, manner of modification of the agreement, responsibility to defend alleged patent infringements, confidential information, passing of title, schedule of payments, selection of vendors and subcontractors, choice of materials and manufacturers, manner of assignment, governing law, settlement of disputes by arbitration, indemnification against third-party personal injury claims, manner of notice, a "no oral modification" clause and an integration or "zipper" clause.

As stated in the letters of April 25 and December 31, 1968, "the terms and conditions of the ship construction to be in accordance with the attached terms and conditions and any other mutually agreed to terms and conditions." Thus, the parties specifically agreed that any ship construction contract concerning any vessel ordered by Bethlehem pursuant to its option would be based upon the detailed *pro forma* contract as drafted by Mr. Davis, an attorney for Litton.

[Judge Hester then catalogued certain additional terms which supplemented the *pro forma* agreement.]

The use of the *pro forma* contract by the parties as the basis of the Ship Construction Contract of April 25, 1968, sharply brings into focus the relevancy of the "course of dealing" between the parties. 13 Pa.C.S.A. § 1205. It is apparent from the documentation of the transaction between the parties which occurred on April 25, 1968, that Litton's offer to Bethlehem to enter into an option agreement was part of this overall transaction, perhaps a contract "sweetener." The course of dealing between the parties with respect to the construction of the Cort amplifies the intentions of the parties to be legally bound to each other on the basis of the option agreement. Litton obviously desired to enter the shipbuilding industry as evinced by its construction of a ship for Bethlehem. Clearly Litton was hopeful that it would be able to build additional vessels for Bethlehem in the future and granted options to Bethlehem accordingly. As part of the ship construction contract for the Cort, Litton specifically gave Bethlehem a right of first refusal to purchase any of the ships described in its quarterly shipbuilding schedule.

By letter of July 10, 1968, Litton gave notice to Bethlehem of its projected ship-building schedule, offered Bethlehem the right of first refusal on projected Hull 102, and submitted to Bethlehem a proposed form of contract which was identical to the *pro forma* contract referenced in the letters of April 25, 1968, and December 31, 1968. The suitability of these basic contractual terms was therefore repeatedly recognized by Litton. The fact that the letters of April 25 and December 31, 1968, specified that the ship construction contract might also contain "any other mutually agreed to terms and conditions" does not indicate that the parties did not intend to be legally bound *unless* such additional terms were agreed upon. The parties were obviously able to agree to terms concerning the construction of the Cort and consented to similarly negotiate in good faith at some future time regarding any additional terms.

This "course of dealing" between the parties was not considered by the court below. However, Litton itself recognized the relevancy of this course of dealing and interrelationship between the construction of the Cort and the option agreement. The letter of April 25, 1968, which was drafted by Litton, began as follows:

> Reference is made to the ship construction contract signed by our companies this date for the construction by us of a one thousand self-unloading ore vessel for you. Reference is also made to my letter to you of this date extending to you an option to purchase either one or two additional vessels upon the terms therein set forth.

Thus did Litton make references to the "course of dealing" between the parties. This evidence cannot be ignored, for under the Code, "course of dealing" is always relevant. . . .

As author of the letter of April 25, 1968, Litton was in control of the terms of the offer. Litton also offered and controlled the attached *pro forma* contract. I cannot understand how Litton, as a large corporation, could conceivably have delivered the letter of April 25, 1968, to Bethlehem without intending to be legally bound by the terms stated herein. The letter of April 25, 1968, created a power of acceptance by Bethlehem, which was exercised by the jointly-executed letter of December 31, 1968, was prepared by both the parties and was intended to be a final expression of the terms included therein. "The official commentary to [13 Pa.C.S.A. § 2203] recognizes that the parties may condition their assent on formalities, but must do so expressly. Official commentary to § 203, 1 Uniform Laws Annotated, Uniform Commercial Code 107 (West, 1968)."...

In addition to the previously mentioned course of dealing between the parties, the following conduct by both parties additionally supports the existence of a contract, for the purposes of 13 Pa.C.S.A. § 2204(a):

[Judge Hester then catalogued 16 instances in which, in letters or corporate documents, either Litton or Bethlehem or both seemed to acknowledge the existence of a contract. This list includes, for example:]

> 6. In February, 1973, before Bethlehem notified Litton of the exercise of its option, Litton internally listed "Bethlehem Steel Corporation's option to purchase five additional vessels" as one of its "Contractual Obligations."

> 9. In its financial plan of July, 1973, Litton acknowledged the outstanding option as follows: "It should be noted that Bethlehem has an option for construction of up to five (5) new vessels. That option will not expire until December 31, 1973. The terms of the option, if exercised by Bethlehem, would result in substantial losses by Litton."

. . . .

Finally, and perhaps most importantly, my review of the record does not indicate a single instance whereby Litton denied Bethlehem's right to exercise its option, nor did Litton ever deny that the letter of December 31, 1968, was intended to be a legally-binding agreement, prior to the expiration of the option period on December 31, 1973. . . .

Having concluded that the parties intended to make a contract, the next question to be addressed is whether "there is a reasonably certain basis for giving an appropriate remedy." 13 Pa.C.S.A. § 2204(c).

In addition to the previously-mentioned contractual terms contained in the specifications and *pro forma* contract, the letters of April 25 and December 31, 1968, contain definite terms relating to the period of the option, time of delivery of the vessels, base prices for the vessels, a base index of "Fourth Quarter 1968," "quarterly escalation" of price during construction, specific labor and material percentages (supplied by Litton's letter of May 8, 1968), and a clause providing for Bethlehem's right to cancel subject to liquidated damages.

The terms which were left open by the parties are as follows:

(1) The index by which the material and labor cost escalation would be computed;

(2) "an appropriate contract clause . . . providing for quarterly escalation thereafter";

(3) "any other mutually agreed to terms and conditions," in addition to the terms and conditions of the *pro forma* ship construction contract.

Concerning "any other mutually agreed to terms and conditions," the word "any" implies that the failure of the parties to agree to any such additional terms would not affect their intention to be legally bound pursuant to the option agreement. Litton repeatedly recognized the suitability of the *pro forma* contract for the construction and purchase of the vessels in question. . . .

At the meeting on September 24, 1973, Bethlehem submitted to Litton a proposed contract containing additional terms and conditions which were not included in the pro forma contract. However, many of these proposed additional terms and conditions were previously included by the parties in the ship construction contract relating to the Cort. Therefore, it would appear that Bethlehem did attempt to negotiate in good faith concerning any additional terms and conditions, based upon the course of dealing between the parties relating to the construction of the Cort.

The other open terms directly relate to the ultimate price for the construction of the vessels. The Code, [at 13 Pa.C.S.A. § 2305], specifically addresses this issue as follows:

OPEN PRICE TERM

(a) General rule—the parties if they so intend can conclude a contract for sale even though the price is not settled. In such a case the price is a reasonable price at the time for delivery if:

(2) the price is left to be agreed by the parties and they fail to agree;

(d) Intent not to be bound without established price.—Where, however, the parties intend not to be bound unless the price be fixed or agreed and it is not fixed or agreed there is no contract.

The parties intended to be bound by the option agreement of December 31, 1968. Therefore, the ultimate price of the vessels was "left to be agreed by the parties and they fail[ed] to agree." 13 Pa.C.S.A. § 2305(a)(2).

Under the circumstances, the price for the vessels "is a reasonable price at the time for delivery." However, the parties did specifically agree to stated base prices for the vessels. Therefore, the "reasonableness" of the ultimate price term must be related to the stated base prices, as escalated by a "reasonable" index (using a base of "Fourth Quarter 1968").

The lower court bifurcated this case and received only evidence relating to the issue of liability. Since the lower court improperly held that the parties had not intended a binding agreement, and since the lower court did not address the various sections of the Code cited herein, this case should be remanded for additional findings of fact, conclusions of law and on the development of an appropriate record on matters not already in the record. I would reverse.

NOTES AND QUESTIONS

1. *The end of the appellate story*: Bethlehem Steel Corporation appealed to the Supreme Court of Pennsylvania. Three justices of that court did not participate in the case. The remaining four justices were evenly divided, and so the order of the Superior Court was affirmed.[5] Eleven appellate judges considered the case. Six found enough evidence in the record to support the trial court's conclusion that no contract was formed while five would have reversed. We can only speculate about what might have happened if some or all of the three Pennsylvania Supreme Court Justices who did not consider the case had participated in the decision. How would you have voted?

2. *Relationship to the Klimek case*: Instead of a woman seeking to run a rooming house and a builder, the *Bethlehem Steel* case involves two of the largest corporations in the world. The parties in each case intended some commitment to one another. Do the Supreme Court of Pennsylvania's opinions serve the interests of Bethlehem Steel and Litton Industries any better than the opinion of the Supreme Court of Oregon served Klimek and Perisich?

3. *A different court, a different contract, a different result:* *Oglebay Norton Co. v. Armco, Inc.,*[6] concerned a 1957 contract for shipping iron ore on the Great Lakes. Oglebay was to provide ore boats if and when Armco wished to transport ore from Lake Superior to the lower Great Lakes. Armco was to pay "the regular net contract rates for the season in which the ore is transported, as recognized by the leading iron ore shippers in such season for the transportation of iron ore."[7] If there was no recognized regular net contract rate, "the parties shall mutually agree upon a rate for such transportation, taking into consideration the contract rate being charged for similar transportation by the leading independent vessel operators engaged in transportation of iron ore from The Lake Superior District."[8] The contract was modified four times during the period from 1957 to 1980. In 1980 the contract was amended so that Oglebay Norton was required to provide vessels with self-unloading capability. Armco was to pay an extra twenty-five cents per ton shipped in self-unloading ore boats. Oglebay Norton began a $95 million capital improvement program to meet this provision of the amended contract.

---

[5] Bethlehem Steel Corp. v. Litton Industries, Inc., 507 Pa. 88, 488 A.2d 581 (1985).

[6] 52 Ohio St. 3d 232, 556 N.E. 2d 515 (1990).

[7] *Id.* at 232, 556 N.E. 2d at 516.

[8] *Id.*

The parties had a complex long-term continuing relationship. Armco held a seat on Oglebay Norton's Board of Directors and owned Oglebay Norton stock. They were partners, owning and developing the Eveleth iron ore mine in Minnesota.

From 1957 to 1983 the parties established shipping rates by referring to those indicated in "Skillings Mining Review." After 1983, such information was no longer available from this source. The parties failed to negotiate mutually acceptable rates in 1984 and 1985—Oglebay Norton billed at one rate but Armco paid at a much lower rate which Oglebay Norton was forced to accept. In 1986, Oglebay Norton filed a declaratory judgment action, asking the court to declare the rate demanded in its 1985 invoices as the contract or to declare a reasonable rate for its services. The trial court found that the parties intended to be bound to a contract even if they could not agree on a price for Oglebay Norton's services. It then set a reasonable rate based on expert testimony, Oglebay Norton's past charges for carrying Armco's iron ore, and evidence of what others were charging for those services. Finally, the trial court ordered that "if the parties were unable to agree upon a rate for the upcoming seasons, then the parties must notify the court immediately. Upon such notification, the court, through its equitable jurisdiction, would appoint a mediator and require the parties' chief executive officers . . . to meet for the purpose of mediating and determining the rate for such season, i.e., that they mutually agree upon a rate."[9]

The Ohio Supreme Court affirmed the judgment. It relied on Restatement (Second) of Contracts § 33. Section 33 provides that if the parties intend to conclude a contract and the pricing mechanism fails, the contract will be enforced and the price will be a reasonable price. (This section, in substance, applies UCC § 2-305 to contracts that are not transactions in goods). The Ohio court rejected old cases that found agreements to agree to be unenforceable. It said that there was sufficient evidence to support the trial court's findings of fact about the intent to be bound and the reasonable price.

How did Oglebay Norton establish a reasonable price? It was not a thing existing in the world. The trial court, sitting as trier of fact, had to create it by exercising judgment. In 1996, a magazine story[10] pointed out that there was not much competition among shipping companies on the Great Lakes because the steel companies owned their own fleets or were closely associated with particular operators of ore boats. The story noted: "Rates in the later trade are difficult to get hold of. Published rates are nothing more than a starting point, and with such an incestuous relationship between shippers and carriers, no one talks about what they actually pay." Oglebay Norton tried to subpoena information about rates from independent vessel operators and captive fleets, but the trial court quashed these subpoenas before the trial because Oglebay Norton had no right to this proprietary information. The appellate court noted that the trial court could have allowed Oglebay Norton to gain the information but imposed a protective order so that those rates would not be disclosed to others.

---

[9] *Id.* at 234, 556 N.E. 2d at 518.

[10] Paul F. Conley, *A Long Season Ends for Great Lakes Fleet*, J. Com., Feb. 29, 1996, at 18.

The dispute between Oglebay Norton and Armco came at a time when the American steel industry was in decline. The contract called for Oglebay Norton to supply Armco's requirements of carrying iron ore on the Great Lakes. Despite the order to mediate price, Armco could decrease its needs for such iron ore. At one point in the 1990s, Armco bought much of its iron ore from Brazil. It was shipped by barge up the Mississippi and then the Ohio River to Armco's plants. Obviously, this supply of iron ore was not covered by the contract with Oglebay Norton.

The court said that the trial court's order for mediation "neither added to nor detracted from the parties's significant obligations under the contract." Its order "would merely facilitate in the most practical manner the parties' own ability to interact under the contract." A trial court "may exercise its equitable jurisdiction and order specific performance if the parties intend to be bound by a contract where determination of long-term damages would be too speculative." The court stressed the "unique and long-lasting business relationship between the parties."[11]

Suppose you agree with the dissenting judges in *Bethlehem Steel Corp. v. Litton Industries, Inc.*, and conclude that the parties in that case intended to be bound whether or not they agreed on an escalator clause. Would the mediation approach taken by the Ohio trial court have solved the problem of fashioning an appropriate escalator clause? Suppose the mediator fails to lead the parties to an agreement on a reasonable price or reasonable escalator clause. Then what happens?

4.   *The UCC and indefiniteness*: The fact that the parties did not agree to a term that most of us think essential to a deal is some evidence they had yet to make a commitment. However, the UCC says that is all it is—some evidence. The two-page signed letter may have been drafted at the last-minute, but which party is responsible for that? The long-term continuing relationship between the two firms was not last minute and casual. Why wasn't Bethlehem's reliance on the option reasonable and foreseeable? The UCC tells courts to work things out if there is enough so that a court can fashion a remedy. The standard is no more than that the courts should fashion reasonable terms. How should they do this? Must the remedy reflect risk assumption and choice or can judges engage in rate making when the parties have failed to do it?

The late Professor Edwin W. Patterson, a distinguished contracts scholar at Columbia Law School, studied Article 2 of the Uniform Commercial Code for the New York Law Revision Commission. In reviewing § 2-305, he wrote:

> The last sentence of subsection (4) provides for restitution in case the "agreement" fails to be a contract. It is well to have this sentence to show that an alleged buyer and seller may *think* they have a contract and *act* as if they had one, and yet not have one. The "buyer" is, in such a case, required to make *specific* restitution if able to do so. Perhaps this is the simplest solution; yet the *remedy* of specific restitution is limited in other cases to *unique* chattels. While this sentence does not cover all the prob-

[11] *Id.* at 238, 556 N.E. 2d at 521.

lems of restitution, it will serve as a guidepost to the case law on that subject.

Does or should the adequacy of available restitutionary remedies have any bearing on a court's determination as to whether the parties have made a contract enforceable under UCC § 2-305?

5. *The effect of reliance on indefiniteness:* In *Dawson v. General Motors,*[12] a Cadillac dealer wanted to invest in expanding the service facilities on the Chicago premises that it subleased from General Motors. General Motors leased the building from the owner of the property. The dealer did not want to invest its money unless it could be assured that it would receive renewals of its lease. In response to Dawson's letter, an official of Cadillac wrote: "It is . . . Cadillac Motor Car Division's plan to exercise the remaining five year options extending through 2011. . . . While Cadillac cannot guarantee the annual lease rate will not increase, it is anticipated the percent of increase will be a maximum of three percent for each five year option which is to be exercised." Dawson went ahead with the remodeling and it informed Cadillac about the investments that it was making. Cadillac discovered that Dawson was selling cars made by manufacturers other than General Motors at the dealership. It then raised the rent beyond the amount specified in the letter. The trial court granted Cadillac's motion to dismiss the dealer's complaint because Cadillac's letter was too vague to constitute an offer that could be turned into a contract. The United States Court of Appeals for the Seventh Circuit reversed. It said: "The Illinois courts have not been shy about enforcing promises made in the context of ongoing negotiations and often involving preliminary or 'incomplete' agreements . . . . It is particularly noteworthy in this regard that one party's acquiescence in the other's reliance on the preliminary agreement is a factor that supports enforcement." To what extent, if at all, does the *Dawson* opinion help distinguish the *Bethlehem Steel* case from *Oglebay Norton v. Armco*?

6. *Judicial enforcement of agreements to agree*: Classic doctrine dismisses agreements to agree as illusory and unenforceable. What about an obligation to bargain in good faith? In *Thompson v. Liquichimica of America, Inc.,*[13] the parties stated "it is understood that all parties will exercise their best efforts to reach an agreement on or before May 15, 1979."[14] The court found an obligation to negotiate in good faith. "Such an agreement does not require that the agreement sought be achieved, but does require that the parties work to achieve it actively and in good faith." Compare *Reprosystem, B.V. v. SCM Corp.*[15] The Second Circuit found that since no contract was formed, there was no obligation to act in good faith. If the United States District Courts' analyses were accepted as the law, how, if at all, would it affect the result in the *Bethlehem Steel* case? On one hand, Bethlehem attempted to exercise its option after it knew that Litton had taken significant steps to close its shipyard. Moreover, Litton had told Bethlehem that the shipyard would close unless it got more orders for the self-unloading ore

---

[12] 977 F.2d 369 (7th Cir. 1992).
[13] 481 F. Supp. 361 (S.D. N.Y. 1979).
[14] *Id.* at 362.
[15] 522 F. Supp. 1257 (S.D. N.Y. 1981), *rev'd* 727 F.2d 257 (2d Cir. 1984).

carriers. On the other hand, Litton's construction of the first ore carrier was long delayed, and Bethlehem's officials doubted Litton's ability to produce these ore carriers efficiently.

B. FLEXIBLE PRICE AND QUANTITY: "I'LL BUY WHAT I WANT AT A FAIR PRICE"

From the 1920s to the 1960s, a classic problem in the contracts courses involved what business people call flexibility. Buyer and seller make what they see as a contract. However, their agreement gives buyer discretion as to how much it will order. Seller, in turn, has discretion as to the price which it will charge. Many judges and legal scholars saw such bargains as offending contract theory because the parties had not made specific commitments to buy a specified amount for a stated price. Nonetheless, despite questions about legal enforceability, business people continued to make these arrangements. Since almost every state has adopted Article 2 of the UCC, the classic problems about flexibility have been transformed. Some of the old struggles remain, but we must discuss them with a new vocabulary. However, since the UCC's provisions are a response to older law, we must consider a little history to understand the statutory scheme.

While much legal thought assumes discrete transactions between strangers, many important economic transactions involve long-term continuing relationships, almost bordering on joint ventures or partnerships. For example, Sellerco is Buyerco's supplier; Buyerco is Sellerco's account. There may be no document establishing and regulating their relationship. When Buyerco needs to restock its inventory, it simply orders from Sellerco. Both parties often assume some obligation to each other. In times of shortage, Sellerco will take care of Buyerco as best it can. Buyerco may cancel orders for goods it cannot use. However, its officials feel some obligation to place additional orders later or to be reasonable when Sellerco is late on deliveries of future orders. There are advantages to dealing this way. Buyers can cut the costs of finding reliable high quality performance at an acceptable price by dealing with a small group of suppliers whose reputation cements the relationship. The loss of the status of regular supplier would be costly, and so the threat of turning elsewhere serves as a sanction pressing for good performance.

As long as parties leave matters to customary patterns, it is unlikely that they will create a legally binding contract until the buyer orders goods and the seller accepts the order. While parties may feel ethical obligations to continue to place and fill orders, most lawyers would think the parties are legally free to walk away at any time. They do not make definite commitments for the future. They assume tacitly that their relationship will continue.

Instead of leaving matters to custom or practice, parties may draft what they call contracts covering their long-term relationship. However, the world of business involves fluctuating demand and rising prices. Business people are likely to seek flexibility. Buyers cannot be sure how many parts #123 they will use in the coming quarter or year. Sellers, in turn, hesitate to promise to fill all orders for part #123 at 50 cents each for several months or more. If the price of the special type of steel needed to make part #123 jumps 20% during the course of the year, a fixed-price contract could be disastrous.

There are a number of techniques for dealing with these risks. A seller may make a continuing offer subject to a series of acceptances by the buyer. For example, suppose the seller promises to supply all the #123s that buyer orders at 50 cents each.[16] Each time buyer orders this would close a contract for the amount ordered at that price. If the seller made a promise in writing to hold such an offer open for a specific term, it might be enforceable under UCC § 2-205. However, absent such a firm offer, seller could withdraw the offer as to future deliveries. Sellers also may promise to fill all orders at a specified price, but reserve the right to withdraw their offer at any time. Buyers may order their projected needs for, say, the first quarter of the year, but reserve the right to cancel their order for convenience—perhaps agreeing to pay a specified cancellation charge. Sellers also may promise to supply part #123 for six months as ordered by the buyer but at "seller's price in effect at the time and place of shipment" or at "market price." The parties may use elaborate price escalation clauses so that the contract price tracks some index of prices in the trade. Buyers may agree to buy all or part of their requirements from seller. They can draft this clause to limit the obligation— for example, buyer may promise to take "33% of the requirements of its Austin, Texas plant, but no less than 1000 units and no more than 10,000 units." We will consider these and other techniques to gain flexibility in the materials that follow.

Flexible quantity and price terms created problems for courts applying the common law of contracts. For example, some judges asked whether a seller who had the power to change the price had really promised to do anything. Seller might want to back out of the deal to serve another preferred customer. Seller then could set a price at $1 million per item, forcing buyer to back out. On the other hand, many courts found requirements contracts to lack mutuality of obligation. It was not certain that a buyer would have any requirements, and the amount of requirements was largely within the control of the buyer. Some courts adopted a middle position: they would enforce contracts calling for a seller to supply the requirements of an existing business, but they would not enforce new business requirements contracts since the needs of a new business offered no standard by which to measure a commitment.

The jobber or distributor requirements contract was particularly troublesome. Suppose a producer agrees to supply all of a distributor's requirements of the producer's product. The distributor makes no promise to have any requirements of that product. If the distributor's customers want the product, then the distributor will order some from the producer. If a producer had to fill orders but a distributor did not have to place any, the arrangement seemed to lack mutuality.

---

[16] You must be careful to distinguish the situation in the text where the seller promises to fill orders at a quoted price from one where the seller merely announces that its price is 50 cents a unit. Typically, an advertisement or a catalog is not an offer committing a seller to supply goods at the quoted price. Sellers seldom take the risk of promising to supply anyone with all of #123s they care to order. Sometimes it is difficult to decide whether a seller's communication is a promise or only information.

For example, before the days of mass marketing of beer by television, there were many local or regional brewers. Suppose Ace Beer Co. agreed to supply Acme Distributors with all of its requirements of Ace beer. Acme also distributed King, Queen, and Jack beers which were made by Ace's competitors. On one hand, if Ace beer were not very popular, Acme's sales people would spend their time promoting King, Queen, and Jack beers. They would do little more than take any orders for Ace which tavern and liquor store owners wanted to place. Indeed, Acme might not order any Ace beer under this contract. On the other hand, if Ace beer suddenly became the rage with drinkers, Acme could make almost unlimited demands on the brewer to supply the needed product. To make matters worse, suppose that Ace had agreed to supply Acme with beer at $1.00 per case. Because of unanticipated increases in prices of raw materials, the cost to all brewers to produce a case of beer jumped to at least $1.25 a case. Acme Distributors had no requirements contracts with the other breweries, and they all increased their prices to cover the increase in their costs. Acme then might offer Ace beer to taverns and liquor stores at an extremely favorable price. Now they would promote it with great efforts. The demand could grow for a product on which the brewer lost at least 25 cents a case. Courts in many states refused to enforce jobber or distributor requirements contracts, saying they lacked mutuality.

Many writers, notably Yale's Professor Arthur Corbin, attacked the refusal of courts to keep up with modern business practices. These writers noted that sellers could not name just any price they pleased—"seller's price in effect at time and place of shipment" meant the price the seller was quoting to the trade. This was at least influenced, if not controlled, by the market. Moreover, the mutuality requirement was an unnecessary addition to the requirement of consideration. A promise to buy one's requirements satisfied the consideration doctrine whatever the likelihood there would be any requirements. The buyer gave up its freedom to buy elsewhere whatever the likelihood that it would buy anything. Courts said they were interested in the existence and not the adequacy of consideration. If a seller thought a promise to buy requirements had value, why should courts refuse to enforce the contract when the buyer was a new business? The seller's business judgment may have been poor, but courts seldom recognize this as a reason for relief. Moreover, courts could push jobber or distributor requirements contracts into the consideration mold simply by implying a promise to use reasonable efforts to promote and sell the product.

The UCC changed the common law response to flexibility in long term contracts. Its drafters were aware of the academic criticism of the case law and modern business practices. Rather than asking whether a contract was formed when the parties left issues of quantity and price open, the Code usually finds a binding contract and then directs courts to interpret the obligation assumed in light of standards such as commercial reasonableness or good faith. First, we will look at flexible pricing and then we will consider flexible quantity. However, we must recognize that often both go together. A seller may agree to supply the buyer's requirements only if there is a clause in the contract protecting the seller against rising costs of production.

1. FLEXIBLE PRICING

We can consider arrangements under which the price fluctuates from the perspective of the policy maker considering a legal response or that of a lawyer drafting an escalator clause. First, to what extent, if at all, are flexible pricing clauses socially desirable? Should the likely or possible consequences of these clauses affect the judgments of courts about whether a particular clause is legally enforceable?

Escalator clauses may increase prices beyond actual increases in costs. For example, some sellers may be able to set high base prices that reflect estimates of increasing costs. Then on top of this amount, they provide for an increased price if certain costs increase. Thus, they may be able to justify increasing prices beyond an amount that reflects their actual costs. Other sellers have substantial control over their costs of labor and materials. An escalator clause may weaken their resistance to cost increases that they can pass along directly to their customers without renegotiation. Sellers' escalator clauses may have an "upward bias" as well. A drafter must weigh components of cost in the formula used. How does she deal with items drawn from old inventories purchased at lower prices or from fixed costs that do not increase? How does the clause deal with changes in methods of production that may, at least in part, offset increased raw material costs? How does the clause deal with an industry-wide index of costs which fits a particular seller's costs poorly?

Of course, sellers may have little freedom to draft escalator clauses or to put into effect the prices called for by such clauses in their contracts. In a highly competitive market, buyers may be able to negotiate for fixed prices based on the threat to take their business elsewhere. Or buyers may refuse to honor contracts if sellers exercise the option to raise prices. Of course, a seller always could sue, but this threat is often a paper tiger. Suing a customer jeopardizes future sales. Such litigation is costly, and uncertain.

Professor Daniel A. Farber[17] argues that there are high costs when businesses rely on flexible long-term continuing relationships. He says:

> [T]hese informal incentives are costly; to the extent that inadequate legal incentives cause excessive use of informal incentives, economic efficiency suffers. . . . Customers will tend to deal with sellers with whom they have dealt before and will tend not to engage in a widespread search for sellers. As a result, their willingness to shop for better prices can decrease. Furthermore, entry by new sellers becomes more difficult, because a reputation for reliability cannot be immediately established. Although these effects on behavior are difficult to quantify, they nevertheless represent real costs, because they impede the market's movement toward equilibrium.

Farber is obviously right when he suggests that not all markets are highly competitive, but do the costs of flexible long-term relationships outweigh the benefits? The late Dr. Arthur Okun was the Chairperson of President Lyndon

---

[17] Farber, *Reassessing the Economic Efficiency of Compensatory Damages for Breach of Contract*, 66 Va. L. Rev. 1443, 1465-66 (1980).

Johnson's Council of Economic Advisors and a scholar at the Brookings Institution. He suggested that long-term continuing relationships are a major part of why we can have falling demand and rising prices at the same time.[18] Structures fashioned by lawyers such as flexible pricing clauses and requirements contracts can foster these relationships.

Okun points out there are a number of "auction markets" where supply and demand affect prices directly. Stocks and bonds, agricultural commodities, some primary metals, and things such as cotton and lumber are sold this way. However, most product transactions take place in *customer markets* rather than *auction markets*. Okun explains, "[a]s long as there are costs associated with shopping and limited information about the location of the lowest price in the marketplace, buyers do not find it worthwhile to incur all the costs required to find the seller offering the lowest price."[19] (It is worth wondering whether the development of the Internet will lead to some customer markets looking more like auction markets. If you have a choice between an on-line transaction or a transaction requiring a trip to the store, what factors would cause you to choose one rather than the other?)

Firms discourage customers from shopping by convincing them of the continuity of their policies on price, quality and service. Buyers rely on the experience of their last shopping venture. Even professional buyers prefer continuing relationships with suppliers and will pay premiums for dependability.[20] Sellers who have adopted this customer market strategy are inhibited from exploiting increases in demand by raising prices. This commitment introduces upward stickiness of prices. These sellers limit price increases to certain periods, give notice before they act, and often promise to meet competition. Furthermore, when firms raised prices often they tell customers that higher costs have forced them to do so. This legitimates their action and makes it seem inevitable rather than exploitative of their customers' situations.

Dr. Okun notes that prices are more responsive to changes in costs than to shifts in demand. "I suggest that the asymmetry stems, in part, from implicit contracts or conventions that introduce a concept of fairness in the relations between suppliers and customers whereby price increases based on cost increases are generally accepted as fair, but many that might be based on demand increases are ruled out as unfair." The customer-market view "does not regard the inflexibility of prices as necessarily an adverse consequence of oligopoly. On the contrary, it accepts the attachment between buyer and seller as an inherently desirable institutional arrangement that economizes on the expenses of shopping, trying out products, and otherwise engaging in transactions. . . ."

Whether or not these clauses are socially desirable, lawyers often are asked by clients to draft them. It is difficult to write a contract which parties are to perform

---

[18] Okun, PRICES & QUANTITIES: A MACROECONOMIC ANALYSIS (The Brookings Institution 1981).

[19] *Id.*

[20] While it may be less true than in the past, business people know the expression, "no one ever got fired for buying computers from IBM."

over time if the drafter anticipates inflation. The following law review articles discuss many of the problems.

Drafting Contracts in an Inflationary Era
Thomas R. Hurst[21]

[In periods of inflation the] climate of economic uncertainty poses significant risks for the businessman who has contracted to supply goods or services without allowing for the effects of such instability. A large rise in the cost of labor or materials required to fulfill a contractual commitment could easily turn a contract that was apparently profitable at the time of execution into a losing proposition. Similarly, these adverse effects could also result from a change in currency values.

Even more serious problems may result if the materials necessary to fulfill the contractual commitment are unavailable at any price because of an embargo or shortages resulting from price controls. In such a situation, the seller's liability may include the difference between the contract price and the market price on the date of delivery as well as substantial consequential damages.

In some of these situations, the law provides relief to the seller either through the doctrine of frustration of purpose or through the doctrine of impossibility of performance. The doctrines of impossibility and frustration, as codified in § 2-615 of the Uniform Commercial Code, discharge the seller from his obligation if performance becomes "commercially impracticable" as the result of the "occurrence of a contingency, the nonoccurrence of which was a basic assumption" on which the contract was made. Nonetheless, exclusive reliance on the impossibility doctrine as a tool to cope with inflationary disruptions is undesirable for two reasons. First, the impossibility defense will not operate to release the promisor from his contractual obligation in every situation in which changed circumstances might conceivably warrant a discharge. Second, the doctrine operates to release the seller or buyer from his obligation of performance entirely. In many situations the parties would prefer to modify the contract so that performance would become feasible despite changed circumstances. Thus, drafting sufficient flexibility into the contract to allow for prevailing economic realities is preferable to exclusive reliance on the impossibility doctrine.[22]

---

[21] 28 U. Fla. L. Rev. 879, 880-893 (1976). Reprinted with permission of the University of Florida Law Review, Copyright © 1976. We have removed many of the footnotes from this article, leaving only those that we thought served a teaching purpose.

[22] [24] In many situations, of course, whether the contract contains provisions that either excuse or modify the promisor's duty in a situation in which performance as originally called for would be burdensome is of little consequence. In the context of an ongoing business relationship in which the parties to the contract anticipate doing business with one another over a period of years, the buyer's long-term interests will not be best served by insisting on strict enforcement of his contractual rights in situations in which the contract has become unduly burdensome on the seller. Thus, regardless of whether the contract contains any provisions exculpating or modifying the seller's obligations, it is likely that the parties will voluntarily agree on a modification of the seller's duty of performance in such situations. *See generally* L. Friedman, Contract Law in America (1965). Nevertheless, for a variety of reasons, there will be situations in which voluntary renegotiation may not

The balance of this article examines the techniques that may be utilized within the confines of existing contract law to protect the parties to a contract from various changes resulting from economic instability. The article briefly describes the history of the development of each technique, the situations in which each technique is most appropriately used, and the dangers or problems involved in its use.

Protecting Against Changes in Price or Cost of Performance

The Open-Price Contract. Perhaps the most obvious means by which the parties to an executory contract can protect themselves against changes in the cost of performance between the time the agreement is made and the time performance is called for is to postpone the determination of the contract price until the time of performance. This technique, which is known as the open-price contract, is advantageous to the seller when inflation is anticipated and to the buyer when deflation is feared.[23]

In the past, courts have been hostile to the open-price contract and seldom, if ever, have enforced an executory contract that did not contain a specified price. The courts have generally justified this hostility on the grounds that a mere "agreement to agree" is unenforceable or that the Statute of Frauds bars enforcement of an open-price contract.

This judicial reluctance to enforce open-price contracts is curious, especially when it is contrasted with the willingness of the courts to imply an obligation of reasonableness into contracts in other contexts. For example, in one well-known case in which defendant gave plaintiff the exclusive right to market dresses and millinery under her trademark, the court upheld the agreement over defendant's claim that it lacked mutuality of obligation by reading into the contract an implied obligation of reasonable effort on the part of the plaintiff to promote and market dresses under plaintiff's trademark. Similarly, in situations in which contracts have appeared to give the defendant the absolute right to personal satisfac-

---

occur. First, the contract in question may be an isolated transaction in which there is no incentive for the buyer to behave leniently toward the seller. Second, the possible windfall resulting to the buyer from insisting on full performance of the contract may be so great that the buyer is willing to risk alienating the seller by insisting on full performance of the contract as written. Third, even if a voluntary renegotiation of the contract is likely, the contract may contain some exculpatory language that places the party seeking modification or termination in a stronger bargaining position. Finally, even if voluntary renegotiation of a contract seems likely in the event of unexpected occurrences, there inevitably will be some cases in which the parties simply will fail to reach a satisfactory renegotiation of the agreement; thus, litigation will result. Since the defenses of impossibility of performance and frustration of purpose have been raised frequently in recent litigation, the parties to the contract should, for the above reasons, provide at the outset for discharge or modification of an agreement in the event that performance becomes impossible or unduly burdensome.

[23] [25] There are various categories of open-price contracts. Among the more commonly used are the following: (1) Nothing whatsoever is said about price. (2) A provision stipulates that the price is "to be agreed upon" by the buyer and seller at the time of performance. (3) The price shall be the market price at the time of performance. (4) The price shall be the seller's cost plus a specified percentage or absolute dollar markup. (5) The price shall be no more than that charged by the seller's competitors at the time of performance. (6) The price shall be that charged by the seller to other buyers on the date of performance. (7) The price shall be determined by one of the previous methods but with specified maximum and minimum limitations. (8) The price shall be the buyer's resale price less a specified absolute or percentage discount. (9) The price shall be determined by an impartial third party or by reference to a specified trade journal or formula.

tion, courts have upheld such contracts against the defense of lack of considera-tion on the grounds that the "personal satisfaction called for is that of a reason-able man and that such approval cannot be unreasonably withheld."

In a similar vein, a strong argument can be made that an open-price contract should be sustained by reading into the agreement an implied obligation of the parties to agree to a reasonable price. Few courts, however, have found this ar-gument persuasive. Instead, the majority of jurisdictions appears to regard the contract price as an extremely critical provision and thus feels that judicial recon-struction of the parties' presumed intent should not extend to the determination of the price. Also, the courts frequently find difficulty in determining exactly how the parties intended to establish the price; therefore, any judicial interference would run the risk of contravening the intent of the parties.

Notwithstanding such reluctance, the courts have been willing generally to enforce executory open-price contracts that contained a formula by which the price could be determined at the time of performance. Typically, such formula would be the price established in the market place, or the price published in some specified trade journal, or the price charged by some competitor, or a price based on the seller's cost. By presently agreeing on the formula to be applied in deter-mining the contract price, any future agreement of the parties is not required.

Section 2-305 of the Uniform Commercial Code has further encouraged the use of the open-price contract by providing that "if they so intend," the parties can conclude a contract even if nothing is said about the price and no means is provided by which the price can be determined. The comments accompanying § 2-305 provide that the intent of the section is to overrule prior case law to the effect that an agreement to agree is unenforceable and that a contract with an open-price term is void for indefiniteness. The comments also indicate that § 2-305 is not intended to give the seller unfettered discretion to establish any price that he may wish but that the price must be reasonable. Comment 3 states that the "posted price," "market price," "price in effect," or "given price" would all be considered to be a reasonable price for purposes of § 2-305.

The usefulness of § 2-305, however, is extremely limited. As with all of article 2 of the Uniform Commercial Code, § 2-305 is only applicable to contracts for the sale of goods. Therefore, contracts other than for the sale of goods may con-tinue to be held unenforceable for want of mutuality or for indefiniteness if they do not contain a price or a definite formula for agreeing on a price.

Despite the increasing acceptance of the open-price contract evidenced by Uni-form Commercial Code § 2-305 and, to a lesser extent, by the courts at common law, its usefulness is mitigated by the following considerations. First, the open-price contract may be unsatisfactory to the buyer if his main purpose in entering into the contract is to protect himself against future increases in price or to the seller if he wishes to lock into a sale at the prevailing market price to protect himself against future price declines. Thus, to the extent that a contract provides for *future* determination of the price, it fails to accomplish these objectives.[24] If,

---

[24] [43] This will be true in situations in which the price is left totally open—the price is to be the market price or a reasonable price. The open-price contract, however, cannot be criticized on these

however, the major purpose for entering into a contract for future delivery is to assure the buyer a supply of an essential product or the seller a market for his output and the parties are content that the contract price be determined at the time of delivery, then the open-price contract should be satisfactory.

Second, the open-price contract is of limited utility when it is difficult to find a formula by which the price will be determined. For this reason, open-price contracts are most commonly used in agreements for the sale of homogeneous commodities or for services that are regularly bought and sold in an active market. Conversely, a contract for a manufactured product involving a variety of materials and substantial labor costs in its production will not normally be suitable for an open-price contract.

Third, in using an open-price contract, considerable care should be exercised in specifying the manner in which the price is to be determined. For example, if the contract specifies that the price is to be the "market price," there is often considerable room for argument as to just what is the market price. Disputes that may arise include what price is meant when trading is inactive, whether customary discounts from listed market prices should be taken into account, and whether the prices of one or two sellers who habitually undercut the majority of sellers in a given market should be taken into account.

Finally, in some situations a contract calling for payment of the current "market price" or a "reasonable price" at the time of delivery might be subject to challenge if the market is severely distorted by shortages, strikes, or price-wars. Hence, if the parties decide that the use of the open-price contract is desirable, they should specify as precisely as possible the manner in which the price is to be determined and the circumstances, if any, that would render the formula inapplicable.

Cost-Plus Contracts. Another method by which the seller may protect himself against inflationary increases in his cost of materials or labor is through the use of the cost-plus contract.[25] In this type of contract, the contract price is computed by determining the seller's cost of production and adding to that the seller's profit, which may be either a fixed sum agreed on in advance or a percentage of the total cost of production.

The cost-plus contract has been used most commonly in the defense industry. Rather than protecting against inflation, this contract has been used in the defense industry because of the inability of contractors to estimate accurately the cost of developing new weaponry. Since most contractors would refuse to enter into a fixed-price contract in this situation, the cost-plus contract has become virtually a necessity. Although cost-plus contracts, as such, have not met with the hostility that has been accorded open-price contracts, they have on occasion been held

---

grounds when the contract contains a predetermined formula for determining the price so that there is little or no room for negotiation between the parties.

[25] Eds. note: For example, while a contract for the sale of coffee or lumber would be suitable subject matter for an open-price contract, a contract for the sale of an airplane would not. The problems of the use of the open-price contract in such a case are similar to the difficulties associated with the cost-plus contract.

unenforceable because of uncertainty in situations in which the court was not able to determine what the parties meant by "cost."

While use of the cost-plus contract may be a necessity in research and development contracts, it is not the most desirable contractual device when the parties's main concern is protecting against inflation or deflation. First, the cost-plus clause is not likely to be viewed with favor by the buyer because it removes the incentive for the seller to minimize his costs of production; indeed, if the seller's profit is to be determined by taking a specified percentage of the total cost, the seller actually has an incentive to *maximize* his cost of production. Theoretically, the buyer could guard against this possibility by providing in the contract that only those costs that are "reasonable and necessary" to perform the contract shall be allowed in computing the contract price. In practice, however, the buyer inevitably encounters difficulty in establishing that a particular item claimed by the contractor was not reasonable and necessary.

In addition, it is extremely difficult to draft a cost-plus contract that contains a definition of "cost" that will be sufficiently clear to avoid controversy in its application. A glance at the extensive provisions of the Armed Services Procurement Regulations dealing with the determination of cost illustrates the magnitude of this problem.[26] If the contract involves the sale of goods in their present state—for example, a contract between a wholesaler and a retailer—the problem may be relatively simple since the seller's cost will consist of the cost of goods purchased plus associated incidental costs of transportation, storage, and insurance. By contrast, however, the determination of "costs" for a manufacturing contract will require the parties to resolve many complex problems of cost accounting. Overhead expenses must be allocated to the contract. The hiring of additional labor to perform the contract may be a source of controversy as may be the employment of workers at overtime wages. The hiring of additional managerial and front office personnel may be even more difficult to allocate to a particular contract, and the decision on the valuation of inventory on a LIFO or FIFO basis is open to question.

In summary, the cost-plus contract should be used only as a last resort when other methods of protecting against economic fluctuations are unavailable. In situations in which the parties' primary concern is providing protection against price changes in critical costs of production, a much simpler solution than the cost-plus contract is to include a price-adjustment clause providing for the contract price to be increased in proportion to any increases in the costs of materials and labor above the current market price for such materials and labor. This technique avoids the complex cost determination problems that are involved in the cost-plus contract; furthermore, it provides some protection for the seller's profit margin in times of economic uncertainty. In any event, the attorney who decides to draft a cost-plus contract would be wise to consult the Armed Services Procurement Regulations for guidance in drafting the agreement.

---

[26] [55] 32 C.F.R. § 7.203-04 (1972). The basic provision defining "cost" in the Armed Services Procurement Regulations continues for more than 4 pages in the Code of Federal Regulations.

Price Indexing and Price Escalator Clauses. One of the most commonly employed methods of protecting against inflation and deflation in contracts is the use of price indexing or price escalator clauses. Generally, these clauses provide for periodic adjustments in the contract price based on the change in a price index or the change in the price of materials or labor that constitutes a significant portion of the seller's cost of performance. Both indexing clauses and escalator clauses are commonly found in such diverse types of contracts as collective bargaining agreements, Social Security and other pension benefits, various government welfare programs, long-term bank loans, residential mortgage loans by savings and loan associations, commercial office leases and shopping center leases, insurance policies, and long-term commercial purchase contracts. Several foreign countries have even indexed personal income tax rates and government bond interest rates.

In contrast to the judicial reluctance to enforce open-price contracts, the courts generally have had no difficulty in upholding contracts containing indexing provisions. . . . As long as the indexing formula is drafted so that the method of price calculation can be determined by the courts with reasonable certainty, the contract will likely withstand judicial scrutiny. This conclusion is strengthened by the adoption of Uniform Commercial Code § 2-305, which relaxes the common law requirements of definiteness and certainty.

While the use of the price indexing clause presents no serious conceptual difficulties, a number of practical problems must be surmounted if an indexing clause is to be acceptable and fair to both parties. The first problem is the selection of an appropriate price index for use in a given contract. Most parties contemplating the use of an indexing clause automatically turn to the Department of Labor's Consumer Price Index (CPI) or Wholesale Price Index (WPI). In many contexts, however, neither of these indices will provide an accurate measure of the effect of inflation on a particular contract. The CPI is designed to measure the effects of inflation on the income of urban, blue-collar wage earners. It does so by measuring monthly the price changes of approximately 400 goods and services.[27] The WPI measures the monthly changes in the wholesale prices of a representative group of 2700 industrial and agricultural commodities. While providing a reasonably accurate overall picture of inflation, both of these indices are too broad to accurately measure the effect of inflation on many types of contracts.[28] For example, use of the CPI as an indexing tool in a commercial office lease or a contract for the sale of farm machinery would be inappropriate since the Index will not accurately measure the change in the promisor's costs. Despite these limitations, many persons appear to be utilizing the CPI in precisely those situations because of the lack of knowledge of what the CPI does measure or because of the lack of a more accurate index.

---

[27] [75] See generally, The Price Statistics of the Federal Government (National Bureau of Economic Research, Inc. N.Y. 1961).

[28] [77] The Consumer Price Index can be considered a proper indexing device for use in contracts for the sale of consumer goods if the parties are concerned with the buyer's ability to pay rather than the seller's cost of production. Ordinarily, however, this is not the case. In collective bargaining agreements, the CPI is an accurate measure of the seller-worker's cost of maintaining himself and his family, but this is one of the few situations in which this will be true.

Fortunately, a multitude of other, more accurate indices are readily available. In addition to the CPI and WPI, the Department of Labor's Bureau of Labor Statistics also publishes specific price indices for the output of selected Standard Industrial Classification industries. The Department of Agriculture publishes an Index of Prices Paid by Farmers and an Index of Prices Received by Farmers. In addition, various indices dealing with prices in particular industries are published by trade associations.

In short, indexing is an accurate means of compensating for inflation only if the indexing device is an accurate measure of the changes in the cost of performing a contract. To the extent that such an index is unavailable and cannot be calculated by the parties, indexing may not be a satisfactory answer to the problem at hand.

The problem of finding a suitable index that will accurately represent the true change in the contract price can be solved at least partially by including in the index only those elements of the total contract price that can be accurately measured. Although the formulation of an index that would accurately measure the change in rental value of commercial real estate over a long period of time would be difficult and impractical, a long-term commercial lease can provide for an automatic adjustment of the rent on the basis of certain changes in the landlord's costs that can be easily measured, such as property taxes, utility expenses, and custodial fees. Similarly, in the case of a contract for the manufacture of goods, the price could be indexed to labor costs or to the cost of one or more crucial commodities involved in the manufacturing process.

The second problem confronting potential users of a price indexing clause is to be certain that the index is carefully and accurately compiled, preferably by an impartial source. A trade association publishing an index may have a vested interest in making prices appear as high as possible, which would render such an index unfair to the buyer. For this reason, indices compiled by impartial sources, such as the government or an independent business publication, are generally more desirable.

The third problem lies in attempting to assess the reliability and continuity of the index. Litigation has occasionally resulted when the index on which a contract was based was no longer compiled.[29] Again, government indices would generally seem to be the most reliable, although even these are occasionally changed. To guard against drastic modification or termination of an index, the contract should contain a provision designed to protect the parties from this contingency. An arbitration clause, for example, would be one solution to the problem. Finally, to enable appropriate adjustments in the contract price to be timely made, the parties should take care to select an index that will be published with reasonable speed.

Assuming the seller is able to find an appropriate index that satisfies the above criteria, he may encounter problems in using such an index. Although the seller's

---

[29] [82] Domhoff & Joyce Co. v. Hamilton Furnace Co., 108 Ohio St. 25, 140 N.E. 485 (1923). See generally, Dawson & Coultrap, Contracting by Reference to Price Indices, 33 Mich. L. Rev. 685 (1935).

cost of production may increase in a given situation, the buyer's ability to pay will not necessarily increase commensurately, the seller may find the buyer reluctant to agree to an open-ended indexing clause. In the case of a labor contract, although the cost of living may have increased so that the wage earner feels himself entitled to a wage adjustment, the employer's revenues may not have increased sufficiently to enable him to pay the increase.

Another problem with indexing in a period of constantly changing prices is that it may necessitate frequent and inconvenient revision of the contract price. This problem may be minimized by including a triggering clause providing that adjustments in the contract price shall be made only if the index increases by a certain specified minimum percentage in a given time period. Furthermore, the indexing clause can provide for adjustments to be made semi-annually or yearly rather than monthly.

To summarize, indexing is perhaps the most useful device that can be employed to safeguard the parties from the effects of changes in the price level. Price indexing clauses are well accepted by the judiciary, can be tailored to suit the needs of the particular parties involved, and can provide near total protection to the parties against changes in the price level. On the other hand, because it eliminates the certainty provided by a fixed-price contract, indexing may not always be acceptable to both parties. When utilized, indexing clauses must be carefully drafted to avoid problems in application and to fairly represent actual, relevant changes in costs and prices.

NOTES AND QUESTIONS

1. *Some more thoughts on techniques for drafting "inflation-guard" provisions:* (This note is a short summary of some of the arguments made by Stephen A. Chaplin in his article, *Redistributing the Cost of Inflation.*[30] All of the quotations are from that article and the balance is paraphrase.) Chaplin begins by explaining that lawyers should gain a proper understanding of inflation in order to advise their clients of the risk of a "decrease in the value of performance in a contractual relationship before it is rendered," due to inflation. Lawyers should understand how this risk can be shifted or shared in a contractual relationship.

The risk of receiving a decreased value of performance when it is actually rendered is a type of risk that is rarely shifted in the negotiation process. Usually the risk is borne by the party that has agreed to postpone the receipt of the other's performance. Thus "it has been said that one party to an agreement bears the entire risk of fluctuation in the value of performance because he has agreed to bear it." This commonly occurs when "money, goods or services are transferred in exchange for a promise of future payment. By agreeing to discharge the obligation in a fixed number of dollars with knowledge that the purchasing power of those dollars will probably change, the contracting parties implicitly agree that the recipient of those dollars bears the risk that they may decease in value due to inflation." However, "the risk of changes in the value of promised future performance is by no means limited to decreases in the value of money owed. A

---

[30] 34 U. Miami L. Rev. 301 (1980).

contracting party who agrees to deliver goods or render services in the future, in exchange for present payment, bears the similar risk that the cost of future performance may increase substantially before it is due. Thus, because so many variables affecting the value of future performance are out of the parties's control, it seems unfair that the entire burden of losses due to value fluctuations should fall arbitrarily on one of the parties."

"Parties may redistribute the risk of changes in the value of performance in a number of ways." In long-term relationships, one of the most effective ways of redistributing the risk of inflation is through "periodic revaluation of the goods, services or money bargained for, to reflect their value to the party receiving them. In this end, index clauses are one of the most effective ways of dealing with significant fluctuations in prices over the long term. This is because "[i]ndex clauses link the price of goods and services to their current market values." Yet, the use of an index clause which is not appropriate to the particular needs of the parties can have grave consequences.

For an indexing clause to be useful to the parties it should be appropriate to their needs, but also, it must be reliable and easily accessible. Currently there are a wide variety of indices which are published regularly by government and private institutions. Particular indices may be published in a number of different versions. For example, some indexes have both a regional and a national version. Others are composite indexes with various subgroups which could be used separately if desired. Some indices also have seasonally and nonseasonally adjusted versions. With all of the possible variations available, it is vital for the lawyer to specify the exact form of the index which is being used. Moreover, the lawyer should check to see what the lag time is in the publishing of a particular index to see that it is current when it is published.

The most common method of indexing is where "one party bears the risk of value fluctuations up to an agreed point, and the other party bears the risk over and above that point." Thus no adjustments would be made in the obligation unless "the index moves more than a certain number of points within a specified period." For this method to work, it is important to clearly specify what event triggers adjustment and how often the adjustment is supposed to be made. One of the purposes of having a trigger is to maintain the administrative costs. Thus, the parties will have to consider the administrative costs of the clause in the context of the overall agreement.

It is also important that the index formula is not amenable to multiple interpretations. Thus, the formula should be as simple and as clear as is possible under the circumstances. The clause should also stipulate which parts of the agreement are subject to the clause and which items are excluded.

Provisions should be made for all reasonably foreseeable contingencies. Even when the probability of a particular event occurring seems small, the event may have a large impact on performance. The index clause should account for events which affect the goods and services bargained for as well as events which affect the index itself. Many of the contingencies such as changes in price controls or taxes are government related. Others are controlled by general market forces. In the case of governmental or market changes that significantly affect the value of the agreement, the clause should allow for renegotiation or arbitration of the price structure or the agreement.

The way in which the index clause works can also be significantly affected by events which affect the index itself. For example, the meaning of the terminology used in the index clause could change. Changes could also occur in the way in which the index is calculated. And most importantly, the clause should be drafted to protect against the discontinuation of the index. Oftentimes a successor index will replace an index which is discontinued. In this case, the parties may specify that they will use the replacement index as long as it substantially similar to the original. Otherwise, again the parties may wish to protect against the discontinuation of an index by providing for renegotiation or arbitration of the contract.

Whenever the agreement involves security, the secured party should insist that the security agreement and the index clause grant them an interest in the amount including adjustments which may be made under the index clause.

2. *Specific examples of flexible pricing:* Consider the following examples of flexible pricing clauses. As to each, ask first whether the clause is legally enforceable under the UCC.[31] Ask also whether the clause creates a workable governance structure so that the parties can perform under the contract.

—Acknowledgment of order form of a major American producer of steel:

> Our base prices, together with related lists of Extras and Deductions, are subject to changes without notice, and all orders and contracts are accepted subject to price in effect at time of shipment.

—Requirements contract between a major American producer of aluminum and a major American automobile manufacturer:

> The price for primary aluminum pig, ingot and billet sold by [the aluminum company] and purchased by Buyer [the automobile company] hereunder shall be [the aluminum company's] current published price (including transportation allowance, if any) in effect at the date of delivery for the products involved, unless the price as quoted in "American Metal Market"[32] (or, in the event that "American Metal Market" quotations shall be unavailable or inapplicable, as quoted in some other recognized trade publication) is lower, in which case the price quoted in the "American Metal Market" shall apply.

> If Buyer receives a legitimate offer from some other domestic United States supplier source to sell to Buyer aluminum of the same quality as sold by [the aluminum company], Buyer may communicate to [the aluminum company] the quantity, price and terms so offered to Buyer and if [the aluminum company] is unable or unwilling to meet such price and terms for such quantity, Buyer may, without such action constituting a breach of this agreement, purchase from such other source such quantity at the price and terms so quoted.

---

[31] Consider UCC §§ 2-204, 2-305, 2-311. Do not overlook § 204(3) and the first official comment to § 2-305.

[32] This is a trade publication which reports market prices of metals.

—Long-term contract for sale of paper used by one of the largest American manufacturers of this product:

> 3.   The price(s) to apply to shipments made on this contract during each calendar quarter . . . shall be specified by the Seller not less than fifteen (15) days in advance of the first day of the calendar quarter for which such price(s) is/are specified. In the event that the Seller shall not have thus specified such price(s), the price(s) for the preceding calendar quarter shall continue in effect for the calendar quarter as to which no price(s) shall have been so specified.

> 4.   In case the Seller shall, as to any such calendar quarter, specify a revision in price(s) and the price(s) so specified for such calendar quarter is/are higher than the price(s) at which Buyer can secure an equivalent grade and quality of paper to be delivered by a responsible person during such calendar quarter, the price(s) shall be subject to a satisfactory adjustment by mutual agreement.

—Purchase order of a manufacturer of automobile components such as brakes and transmissions:

> Buyer may at any time make changes in writing relating to this order including changes in the drawings or specifications, method of shipment, quantities, packing, or time, or place of delivery. If such changes result in an increase or decrease in cost of, or time required for, the performance of this contract, an equitable adjustment shall be made in the contract price, delivery schedule or both.

Consider the following comments, made in the course of an interview with a partner in a large law firm with a business practice:

> Many courts are hostile to clauses calling for negotiation or settlement on a fair basis. Yet this is just what the parties want at the time they draft the contract, and a lawyer often cannot get them to be more specific. They are unwilling to work out standards for settlement since there are too many facts that are uncertain and too much remains that cannot be foreseen. Businessmen do not like to deal with hypothetical cases.

What is a lawyer to do in a situation in which the client wants more flexibility than the rules seem to permit?

2. FLEXIBLE QUANTITY

a. Blanket Orders

Major American automobile manufacturers and some other firms with a great deal of bargaining power use blanket order purchasing. The arrangement allows a buyer to separate two functions of contract: an elaborate document drafted by a team of lawyers helps parties plan their transaction, but the buyer makes the minimum commitment possible to purchase anything from the seller. The following article describes practices as of the early 1970s. As automobile manufacturers in the 1980s attempted to follow Japanese methods of management, they often dealt with far fewer suppliers and gave them real commitments so they could invest in new technology.[33] Also, this way they were able to hold much smaller inventories and counted on suppliers delivering just enough to keep the assembly lines moving. Nonetheless, blanket order purchasing continues to be used widely.

The Standardized Contracts of United States Automobile Manufacturers
Stewart Macaulay[34]

. . . 21. The automobile industry in the United States is large, very complex and has great economic power. The major manufacturers are run as bureaucratic structures designed to operate efficiently at all levels. Those people and organizations that deal with the manufacturers have patterned their conduct to accommodate this model of economic efficiency. However, new models of automobiles must be designed several years before they are offered to the public and the demand for new automobiles fluctuates significantly. Bureaucratic operation in the service of economic efficiency, time-span and fluctuating demand are all critical factors which are reflected in many different kinds of exchange transactions found in this industry. In this paper we will consider some of the exchange relationships between the manufacturers, and their suppliers, their dealers and their customers in order to generalize about contract as it is found in this kind of large scale industry.

A. CONTRACTS TO BUILD AND SELL CARS

i.   *The Manufacturers and Their Suppliers*

a. Description of the Relationship

22.   Although the manufacturers can and do make in their own plants some of almost all of the parts which go into an assembled automobile, they also buy many of these parts from suppliers. There are a number of reasons why they purchase from outside suppliers. First, the manufacturer gets a product without investing additional capital in buildings, machines and a trained work force. Second, the manufacturer gets a yardstick which can be used to measure the efficiency of its own division making the same item. If a division making grease seals can produce them at 2 cents each, but an outside supplier can make them for 1 ½ cents each, the manufacturer knows he must re-examine the efficiency of his internal operation. Third, the manufacturer increases the chance that he may benefit from technological innovation. The supplier's designers and engineers may be able to suggest a different design or an improved manufacturing process. On the other side, most businesses, but not all, that can produce parts for automobiles want to sell their output to the automobile manufacturers because of the possibilities for extremely high volume production which, in an efficiently managed firm, can be highly profitable.

There are three additional factors influencing the course a manufacturer-supplier relationship takes: First, the mass production techniques of American automobile manufacturing require that the assembly line not be stopped. When,

---

[33] *See* NEW YORK TIMES, August 8, 1985, at 25, cols. 3-5.
[34] 7 INTERNATIONAL ENCYCLOPEDIA OF COMPARATIVE LAW, Ch. 3, sec. 3-21 to 3-30, 3-51 (1973). Reprinted with permission.

for example, a particular Ford sedan arrives at a certain point on the assembly line four hubcaps must be there ready to be installed. It would be extremely costly to the manufacturer if the line had to be stopped because the supplier's machines that stamp out hubcaps broke down, because a supplier's inventory was not great enough to meet the demand or because the parts were lost in shipment. However, demand for automobiles and even for particular types of automobiles fluctuates. To a great extent, this second factor offsets the first. The easiest way to avoid stopping assembly lines would be to produce large quantities of parts far in advance of need. Yet this approach increases costs because of the possibility of waste and the loss of the use of funds thus devoted to inventories. If, for example, the demand for station wagons declines during the year, exhaust pipes that fit only station wagons that will never be produced are mere scrap metal. Third, component parts can be defective, the defect can cause injury to property or person, and in United States law the injured party in such cases has increasingly been gaining rights against manufactures. Not surprisingly, one finds that manufacturers wish to hold suppliers responsible for such claims, and the suppliers must defend themselves against the costly results of seemingly minor defects in the parts they make.

b. The Blanket Order System

aa.   The System Described

23.   The *manufacturers* have accommodated all of these economic and legal factors in an imaginative piece of transaction architecture which is usually called a "blanket order."[35] Coupled with the suppliers's great desire to do business with the automobile manufacturers, the blanket order system almost always insures that parts will arrive at the assembly plants at the right time, that the suppliers will take the risk of scrapped parts caused by fluctuations in demand, and that the suppliers will be responsible for claims caused by defects. Moreover, the system gives the manufacturers great leverage to ward off price increases caused by the suppliers's increased costs.

This is how it works: Some time before the beginning of the model year, the manufacturer will issue a blanket order to a supplier of, for example, tail pipes designed specifically for one of the manufacturer's station wagons. The blanket order states a number of "agreements." One of the most important is the price per unit. This price is computed on the basis of an estimated number of units to be ordered, and it will not be increased if fewer are actually ordered. Thus, the manufacturer has made the supplier run the risk that he will not even recover his cost of producing the items actually shipped to the manufacturer in the event that the manufacturer uses substantially fewer than the estimated number. And the blanket order does not oblige the manufacturer to take and pay for *any* of the

---

[35] [78] Many divisions of the General Motors Corporation use what are called requirements contracts rather than blanket orders. However, because of the way the General Motors's requirements contracts are written and administered, the two systems are essentially the same in operation. The General Motors's standard agreement form for production requirements calls for it to "purchase . . . approximately the percentage shown on the attached exhibit (of) the Buyer's requirements." Legally, the key word would be "approximately" since it might be interpreted to undercut any commitment to buy.

parts described in it. That obligation comes only when the manufacturer sends the supplier documents called "releases." The idea seems to be that the blanket order creates a force which is held back until released little by little.

Each month, sometimes more often, the manufacturer sends the supplier a release, ordering him to manufacture and ship a specified number of the parts each week. On the release form, the manufacturer also will estimate the number of parts he will require for the next two or three months, but this estimate, to quote one manufacturer's form, "is for planning purposes only and does not constitute a commitment." Typically, manufacturers do not send releases calling for more parts than they will need in a month since their monthly estimates of sales are fairly accurate. However, sometimes they do order too few or too many parts. If there is an increase in public demand for a particular model, the blanket order allows the manufacturer to send another release form to the supplier calling for increased deliveries. Such sudden increases may be a great strain on the supplier if he does not have unused capacity for production. Moreover, a supplier must always guard against a break-down of his machinery, which temporarily destroys his ability to meet the manufacturer's demands. As a result, the supplier usually makes more than the number of parts ordered by the manufacturer so that the supplier will have an inventory to cover anticipated future demands. He builds this inventory at his own risk since the blanket order clearly provides that "Seller shall not fabricate any articles covered by this order, or procure materials required therefor, or ship any articles to Purchaser, except to the extent authorized by . . . written releases . . . Purchaser will make no payments for finished work, work in process or raw material fabricated or produced by Seller in excess of Purchaser's written releases."

If a manufacturer has "released" too many parts in light of a sudden decrease in demand, the blanket order gives it the right to cancel the amount ordered in whole or in part. It then is obligated to pay the contract price for each part finished and "the cost to Seller (excluding profit or losses) of work in process and raw material, based on any audit Purchaser may conduct and generally accepted accounting principles.[36]

bb. Blanket Orders and American Contract Law

(1) Legal Enforceability

24.   American contract law would likely support the manufacturer's plan for the transaction so that, when the law is combined with the market situation, the manufacturer's interests would be favored. Under the law there must be an exchange of promises or of performances to create a legally enforceable contract. In a blanket order the manufacturer makes no promise until it sends a "release," and so until then there has been no exchange and contract rights have not been created. In effect, at the manufacturer's request, the supplier makes an offer—a promise to supply certain goods if they are ordered—which the manufacturer accepts every time it sends a release. The continuing offer and the many accep-

---

[36] [79] General Motors's requirements contract reserves no such right. Interviews, however, indicate that General Motors occasionally does cancel these contracts and pays what it deems reasonable cancellation charges. These charges would be no more than those stated in the text.

tances create a series of contracts. It is possible that two developing doctrines in the Common Law of the United States might be applied in the future to offer remedies despite the absence of a contract. Reliance by the manufacturer on the supplier's promise to fill all orders might receive legal protection, in the unlikely event it were needed, by the growing "firm offer" doctrine. Reliance by the supplier on any assurances (most likely implied ones) of the manufacturer that it would order a reasonable quantity might be protected by the development of rules requiring fairness in negotiations.

25.   One can only speculate about the legal situation in light of general principles of contract law and the Uniform Commercial Code, since litigation testing these conclusions is unlikely.[37] The large automobile manufacturers try to avoid placing total reliance on any one supplier, and other suppliers usually can increase production so that a manufacturer's assembly line is not stopped for lack of an item. Thus manufacturers tend to avoid injury rather than litigate for compensation. On the other hand, no automobile parts supplier is likely to bring a case against a manufacturer; the loss on any one order is very unlikely to be large enough to justify jeopardizing future business. Of course, the trustee of a bankrupt supplier would be free of this constraint. However, in light of the uncertainty of the supplier's legal position, many trustees would think it unwise to risk the cost of legal action against a manufacturer.

26.   What are the consequences of the legal situation? If we assume that the developing reliance and fairness doctrines would not apply, the parties get legal rights only after the manufacturer has issued a release and only as to the goods ordered in that release. This means that there can be a great deal of reliance by the supplier which is unprotected by contract rights. On the other hand, legally the supplier would be free to refuse to continue the relationship by revoking his outstanding offer to supply the parts as ordered by the release forms. As we have said previously, few suppliers who were not going out of business could afford to exercise such a right; very few situations short of bankruptcy would justify losing the good will of General Motors, Ford, Chrysler or American Motors. Most importantly for the manufacturer, it does get legal rights once a release is issued. As a result, it manages to avoid any question that the supplier will bear liability for injuries caused by defective parts which it ships. Once the parts are ordered by a release there is a contract which the manufacturer has written, and the disclaimers and limitations of remedy so typically found in documents drafted by sellers are thus avoided. As between Chrysler and its suppliers, the responsibility for

---

[37] Eds. note: As of 1973, when this article was written, there was only one case involving a manufacturer-supplier dispute. This case arose shortly after General Motors started using the blanket order system, and the supplier claimed he was misled. The court was very critical of the General Motors's blanket order system. *See* Streich v. General Motors Corp., 5 Ill. App. 2d 485, 126 N.E.2d 389 (1955). Another case arose in the 1980s, and led, after 5 years of litigation with GM, to a three paragraph opinion by the Sixth Circuit. The opinion represented a victory for General Motors's assertion that its blanket order did not obligate it to order any specific number of parts from a supplier. Pro-Par Industries, Inc. v. General Motors Corp. 884 F.2d 580 (6th Cir. 1989) The major point still seems valid. Pro-Par was an inexperienced supplier. At the time of the litigation it was in bankruptcy, and so had no continuing relationship to protect. And it lost.

compliance with federal safety and air pollution regulations is also clearly placed on the supplier.

(2) Remedies

27.   The standard blanket order documents drastically limit the remedies to which a supplier would otherwise be entitled under American contract law once a legally binding contract is created by the issuance of a release. Typically, the manufacturer reserves a right to cancel the goods ordered by its release, either in whole or in part. Under American contract law such a cancellation would be a breach if not authorized by the agreement, and, absent a contract provision to the contrary, the seller would be entitled to recover what he had spent in performance before the buyer's notice of cancellation plus the profit he would have made had he been allowed to complete his performance. Most blanket order cancellation clauses, however, exclude a right to profit except as to those parts which have been completed before cancellation. Thus even when a contract is formed by a release, the supplier's rights in most situations will be minimal. The manufacturer gains a practical commitment from the supplier to meet the demands of its assembly line. It retains maximum flexibility by making no commitment to buy any parts until a release is given and making only a very limited payment if it wishes to cancel after one is sent.

c. The Absence of a Reform Movement

28.   There are no statutes attempting to regulate this relationship, and no movement seeking such legislation has been discovered. Insofar as statutes in the United States are the result of pluralistic struggle and compromise, one essential element of pluralism seems lacking. It would be hard to form a group of suppliers to seek legislation. Supplying the manufacturers is very profitable for a firm that can accept all of the risks allocated to it by the blanket order system. Such successful firms would hesitate to jeopardize their standing with the manufacturers by supporting an organization taking a stand antagonistic to the manufacturers's interests. Without the most successful firms, such a group would lack political power. Firms that do not wish to assume the risks of the blanket order system can easily seek other customers since their facilities are not limited to producing original-equipment automobile parts. "Exit" is a relatively cheap remedy for dissatisfaction in this case.[38] The facilities devoted to producing original-equipment parts can be converted readily to producing parts for repairing automobiles—the so-called "after market"—or to supplying related industries such as truck or industrial engine manufacturers which, generally, do not have the bargaining power to use the blanket order system. "Voice"—using private or legal power to change the allocation of risks—would entail high costs and the chances of success would not be great in light of the many resources of the manufacturers.

Moreover, insofar as statutes flow from the efforts of those with access to the communications media attempting to enhance their status and power by acting as champions of the deserving underprivileged, this seems an unpromising area. The auto parts suppliers typically are not small businessmen but only smaller organizations than the giant auto manufacturers. The image of the suppliers is that of

---

[38] [87] See the analysis in Hirschman, Exit, Voice and Loyalty (Cambridge, Mass. 1970).

junior partners who are well-paid for taking large but acceptable risks: it would be hard for an ambitious United States Senator to champion them as the exploited victims of the corporate system.

Finally, insofar as one explains United States legislation as an instrument of the powerful to further their interests, no statutory action is needed in this area. The Common Law of contracts serves to legitimate and support the manufacturers's procedures by minimizing or denying rights to the suppliers.

29.   In summary, the manufacturers have tailored a relationship whereby they get most of the advantages of producing parts in a division of their own firms while preserving most of the advantages of dealing with an outside organization. The suppliers are offered a chance to make high profits in exchange for assuming great risks. Most suppliers are eager for the chance to play the blanket order game.[39] The public may get better automobiles at a lower price as a result of the system, but one cannot be sure. There are important parallels to the contract system used by the United States government to procure military equipment such as tanks and aircraft. Since experience may change the need for a weapon or call for a modification in its design, the government retains great power to change or terminate its orders to private industry while paying less than the damages specified in general contract law. . . . It is thought that the risks in dealing with the United States government are reflected in higher prices paid to the weapons industry on government contracts. The automobile manufacturers may also pay for the flexibility in the blanket order system. However, unlike the United States government, the manufacturers make some of their own needs of each type of part. They can turn to their own divisions if prices are too high, and they can ne-

---

[39] [88] The blanket order system may not be very different from the pattern of expectations which would exist if the manufacturers made contracts for fixed quantities of parts with their suppliers. Study of the contract documents typically used in other industries and interviews with businessman and their lawyers disclose that in many situations purchasers assume they may "cancel" their orders when a change in demand causes them to no longer need the items ordered; suppliers usually accept this as one of the risks of business, particularly if the item in question is not being made specially for the buyer but is what the seller offers in the normal course of his business. At times the contract documents contain cancellation clauses, but even where they do not, the right to cancel is widely but not always assumed to exist. After cancellation, the key question is what the buyer must pay to the seller to use this privilege. The obligation is not always clear. Many purchasers think that the supplier is not entitled to his full anticipated profit on the transaction. Many would limit cancellation charges to payment at the contract rate for items completed before cancellation and payment for the raw materials which cannot be salvaged in partially completed items. Thus, the conventional measure of contract damages in the United States contract law awards an aggrieved party more than many businessmen think appropriate. Of course, the possibility of a breach of contract action with its damage measure defined as the net profit on the entire transaction had it been performed plus expenditures in part performance, may serve indirectly as one factor in inducing industrial buyers to cancel only when suppliers would accept as legitimate the reasons for not wanting the goods. It may be that it is legitimate to cancel an order for steel when there is no demand for the product which the buyer planned to manufacture with the steel; it would not be legitimate to cancel because another supplier of steel offered a lower price. Another way of viewing the matter is that businessmen recognize far broader impossibility and commercial frustration excuses for nonperformance than does the law. In summary, the pattern of risk allocation found in the blanket order system may deviate far more from the contract lawyer's model of business than from the actual expectations of those managing the relationships between large business corporations. See *Macaulay*, Non-Contractual Relations in Business. A Preliminary Study: 28 Am. Soc. Rev. 55 (1963).

gotiate about prices with suppliers in the light of detailed knowledge about what it costs to make the item. Moreover, unlike the government's, the manufacturers's decisions and negotiations are not directly subject to a political process.

ii. *Evaluation: Benefits at What Price?*

a. The Balance of Gains and Costs

51.   Undoubtedly, this kind of rationalized planning has advantages. It is not an insignificant part of a system which has produced great wealth for executives of automobile manufacturers, stockholders in these companies, automobile dealers, parts suppliers, and even, to some extent, for workers employed by this industry and its satellites. The high demand for automobiles produces opportunities for profit and jobs in many related industries and has a major impact on the total American economy. The system may have produced less expensive automobiles than could be made by any other, since one can assume that if the manufacturers had had to assume all of the risks they avoid by these contracts, they would have passed on these costs to buyers in the form of higher prices for new cars.

NOTES AND QUESTIONS

1. *Understanding the arrangement's functions*: Creating a blanket order system costs major buyers something. Why don't they avoid these costs by buying their needs on the market? Why are suppliers interested in blanket orders? Why don't they sell on the market to those who want to buy rather than accept arrangements under which buyers make so little commitment to them? Does the blanket order system help minimize the costs of production or does it increase those costs and contribute to inflation when they are passed along to consumers by higher prices?

2. *Blanket orders when a seller has superior bargaining power*: Sellers with superior bargaining power will use a different structure for blanket orders than those of the automobile manufacturers described by Macaulay. For example, in *Franklin v. Demico, Inc.*,[40] Demico, Inc. contracted to supply electronic circuit boards to Python Corporation under the "Demico Blanket Order Policy." Python agreed to purchase large quantities of circuit boards. However, it could give 90 days notice and increase or decrease the amounts called for. If it decreased the amounts called for, there would be a "bill back" to reflect a higher price per unit. This arrangement, of course, reflects the usual practice of charging less per unit when goods are ordered in large quantities. Under the Demico policy, it bills a buyer on the assumption that it will order enough units in the future to qualify for a quantity discount. If it does not, it owes additional amounts for those units it has received and paid for. The Georgia court upheld this arrangement. It found that the supplier had proved its damages with reasonable certainty under the bill back system.

[40] 347 S.E.2d 718 (Ga. Ct. App.1986).

b. Requirements and Output Contracts

Requirements and output contracts are one of the places where classic contracts scholarship touches modern business practices. A requirements contract is one under which a seller agrees to supply all the part #123 that buyer requires, and buyer agrees to buy all its requirements of that part from seller.[41] An output contract is one under which a seller agrees to deliver to buyer all the output of a particular factory or farm. These contracts raise a number of practical and legal questions. Most were recognized in a classic article written in the 1930s. Havighurst and Berman[42] dealt with the problems of mutuality and enforceability found in the common law cases. The Uniform Commercial Code solves or transforms most of these problems. We will survey the transformation of the requirements and output contract problem from mutuality to UCC interpretation.

Havighurst and Berman also pointed out that lawyers and judges had to interpret the risks taken by each side as a result of promises to supply all the buyer's requirements. The seller risks that the buyer will have either no requirements or too many requirements. In a falling market for seller's goods, buyer can get them elsewhere cheaper. Thus, buyer has an incentive to look for ways out of the requirements contract. First, buyer may change the design of the product in which it used what seller was to supply so buyer no longer has any requirements for seller's goods. Suppose buyer had a contract to buy its requirements of fuel oil from seller. Can buyer switch to natural gas to heat and power its factory? Second, mergers and consolidations can affect requirements contracts. Suppose a contract calls for buyer to purchase "all requirements for the Seattle, Washington plant" from seller. Buyer then is merged into a multinational corporation which closes the Seattle plant. However, multinational makes the same product at its Houston, Texas Plant, free of labor unions and state regulation. Has seller any rights against multinational? Third, suppose buyer goes bankrupt and ceases doing business. Has seller a claim in the bankruptcy proceedings on the theory of an implied promise to have requirements?

Suppose, on the other hand, the requirements contract calls for a fixed price and the market price for the goods in question increases rapidly. Now the buyer may demand too many goods from the seller. Suppose buyer ordered the goods for use in buyer's own manufacturing process. Once the market takes off, may buyer order additional items and resell them at a higher price? Suppose buyer is merged into a multinational corporation that uses its marketing skills and capital to double the demand for buyer's product. Must seller supply these additional requirements at the lower contract price?

Those who drafted Article 2 of the UCC were well aware of Havighurst and Berman's article. Sections 2-306, 1-201, 2-103(1)(b) and the Official Comments to these sections tell us something about how the Code proposes to solve these problems. (Of course, those drafting requirements and output contracts can and do deal with these problems explicitly. Indeed, we raise them, in part, so that you

---

[41] A buyer also may agree to buy a specified percentage of its requirements, the requirements of a particular plant, or the units needed to produce a particular product.

[42] *Requirement and Output Contracts*, 27 Ill. L. Rev. 1 (1932).

will see them if you are ever called on to draft such documents.[43]) However, what are the requirements and output contracts problems which are likely to extend into the future?[44] We will look at a case considering the Code's resolution of one of the problems raised by Havighurst and Berman. Then we will study two of the most common problems involving requirements contracts today—whether a distributorship is a requirements contract governed by the UCC and the impact of UCC § 2-201(1) on provisions for flexible quantity. That section, you may recall, says that a "writing is not insufficient because it omits or incorrectly states a term agreed upon but the contract is not enforceable under this paragraph beyond the quantity of goods shown in such writing." How does UCC § 2-306 track with this apparent demand that parties show the quantity in writing?

EMPIRE GAS CORP. v. AMERICAN BAKERIES CO
United States Court of Appeals, Seventh Circuit
840 F.2d 1333 (1988)

POSNER, CIRCUIT JUDGE. This appeal in a diversity contract case presents a fundamental question—surprisingly little discussed by either courts or commentators—in the law of requirements contracts. Is such a contract essentially a buyer's option, entitling him to purchase all he needs of the good in question on the terms set forth in the contract, but leaving him free to purchase none if he wishes provided that he does not purchase the good from anyone else and is not acting out of ill will toward the seller?

Empire Gas Corporation is a retail distributor of liquefied petroleum gas, better known as "propane." It also sells converters that enable gasoline-powered motor vehicles to operate on propane. The sharp rise in gasoline prices in 1979 and 1980 made American Bakeries Company, which operated a fleet of more than 3,000 motor vehicles to serve its processing plants and bakeries, interested in the possibility of converting its fleet to propane, which was now one-third to one-half less expensive than gasoline. Discussions between the companies resulted in an agreement in principle. Empire Gas sent American Bakeries a draft of its standard "Guaranteed Fuel Supply Contract," which would have required American Bakeries to install a minimum number of conversion units each month and to buy all the propane for the converted vehicles from Empire Gas for eight years. American Bakeries rejected the contract and Empire Gas prepared a new one, which was executed on April 17, 1980, and which was "for approximately three thousand (3,000) [conversion] units, more or less depending upon requirements of Buyer, consisting of Fuel Tank, Fuel Lock Off Switch, Converter & appropriate Carburetor & Small Parts Kit," at a price of $750 per unit. American Bakeries agreed "to purchase propane motor fuel solely from EMPIRE GAS CORPORATION at all locations where EMPIRE GAS has supplied carburetion and dispensing equipment as long as EMPIRE GAS CORPORATION remains in a reasona-

---

[43] See Note, *Requirements Contracts: Problems of Drafting and Construction*, 78 Harv. L. Rev. 1212 (1965).

[44] See Caroline N. Bruckel [now Brown], *Consideration in Exclusive and Nonexclusive Open Quantity Contracts Under the UCC: a Proposal for a New System of Validation*, 68 Minn. L. Rev. 117 (1983).

bly competitive price posture with other major suppliers." The contract was to last for four years.

American Bakeries never ordered any equipment or propane from Empire Gas. Apparently within days after the signing of the contract American Bakeries decided not to convert its fleet to propane. No reason has been given for the decision.

Empire Gas brought suit against American Bakeries for breach of contract and won a jury verdict for $3,254,963, representing lost profits on 2,242 conversion units (the jury's estimate of American Bakeries' requirements) and on the propane fuel that the converted vehicles would have consumed during the contract period. . . .

The heart of this case is the instruction concerning American Bakeries' obligation under the contract. If there were no legal category of "requirements" contracts and no provision of the Uniform Commercial Code governing such contracts, a strong argument could be made that American Bakeries agreed to buy 3,000 conversion units or *slightly* more or *slightly* less, depending on its actual needs, and hence that it broke the contract by taking none. This is not only a semantically permissible reading of the contract but one supported by the discussions that the parties had before the contract was signed (and these discussions are admissible to explain though not to change the parties' undertakings), in which American Bakeries assured Empire Gas that it was planning to convert its entire fleet. American Bakeries insisted on adding the phrase "more or less depending upon requirements of Buyer" just in case its estimate of 3,000 was off, and this is quite different from supposing that the phrase was added so that American Bakeries would have no obligation to buy any units at all.

The parties agree, however, that despite the negotiating history and the inclusion in the contract of a specific estimate of quantity, the quoted phrase sorted the contract into the legal bin labeled "requirements contract" and thereby brought it under the governance of § 2-306(1) of the Uniform Commercial Code, ... Over American Bakeries' objection the judge decided to read the statute to the jury verbatim and without amplification, ... [However,] the law is [not] what a jury might make out of statutory language. The law is the statute as interpreted. The duty of interpretation is the judge's. Having interpreted the statute he must then convey the statute's meaning, as interpreted, in words the jury can understand. If § 2-306 means something different from what it seems to say, the instruction was erroneous.

The interpretive question involves the proviso [in § 2-306(1)] dealing with "quantity unreasonably disproportionate to any stated estimate." This limitation is fairly easy to understand when the disproportion takes the form of the buyer's demanding more than the amount estimated. If there were no ceiling, and if the price happened to be advantageous to the buyer, he might increase his "requirements" so that he could resell the good at a profit. . . . This would place him in competition with the seller—a result the parties would not have wanted when they signed the contract. So the "unreasonably disproportionate" proviso carries out the likely intent of the parties. The only problem is that the same result could easily be reached by interpretation of the words "good faith" in the preceding clause of § 2-306(1), thus making the proviso redundant. But redundancies designed to clarify or emphasize are common in legal drafting, and anyway the Uniform Commercial Code has its share of ambiguities, see *Wisconsin Knife Works v. National Metal Crafters*, 781 F.2d 1280, 1288 (7th Cir. 1986).

The proviso does not distinguish between the buyer who demands more than the stated estimate and the buyer who demands less, and therefore if read literally it would forbid a buyer to take (much) less than the stated estimate. Since the judge did not attempt to interpret the statute, the jury may have read it literally, and if so the judge in effect directed a verdict for Empire Gas. The stated estimate was for 3,000 units; American Bakeries took none; if this was not unreasonably disproportionate to the stated estimate, what buyer shortfall could be?

So we must decide whether the proviso should be read literally when the buyer is demanding less rather than more than the stated estimate. There are no cases on the question in Illinois, and authority elsewhere is sparse, considering how often (one might think) the question must have arisen. But the clearly dominant approach is not to construe the proviso literally, but instead to treat the overdemanding and underdemanding cases differently. . . . We think this is right. . . .

Granted, there is language in the Official Comments (not official in Illinois, be it noted) which points to symmetrical treatment of the overdemanding and underdemanding cases: "the agreed estimate is to be regarded as a center around which the parties intend the variation to occur." UCC § 2-306, comment 3. But there is no elaboration; and the statement is in tension with the statement in comment 2 that "good faith variations from prior requirements are permitted even when the variation may be such as to result in discontinuance," for if that principle is sound in general, why should it cease to be sound just because the parties included an estimate of the buyer's requirements? A tiny verbal point against the symmetrical interpretation is the last word of the proviso—"demanded." The statement that "no quantity unreasonably disproportionate to any stated estimate . . . may be . . . demanded" is more naturally read as applying to the case where the buyer is demanding more than when he is reducing his demand below the usual or estimated level.

More important than this verbal skirmishing is the fact that the entire proviso is in a sense redundant given the words "good faith" in the main clause of the statute. The proviso thus seems to have been designed to explicate the term "good faith" rather than to establish an independent legal standard. And the aspect of good faith that required explication had only to do with disproportionately *large* demands. If the buyer saw an opportunity to increase his profits by reselling the seller's goods because the market price had risen above the contract price, the exploitation of that opportunity might not *clearly* spell bad faith; the proviso was added to close off the opportunity. There is no indication that the draftsmen were equally, if at all, concerned about the case where the buyer takes less than his estimated requirements, provided, of course, that he does not buy from anyone else. We conclude that the Illinois courts would allow a buyer to reduce his requirements to zero if he was acting in good faith, even though the contract contained an estimate of those requirements.

This conclusion would be greatly strengthened—too much so, as we shall see—if the only purpose of a requirements contract were to give the seller a reasonably assured market for his product *by forbidding the buyer to satisfy any of his needs by buying from another supplier.* . . . The buyer's undertaking to deal exclusively with a particular seller gives the seller some, although far from complete, assurance of having a market for his goods; and of course he must compensate the buyer for giving up the opportunity to shop around for a better deal from competing sellers.

There was no breach of *this* obligation. . . . If the obligation were not just to refrain from buying a competitor's goods but to buy approximately the stated estimate (or, in the absence of any estimate, the buyer's "normal" requirements), the contract would be altogether more burdensome to the buyer. Instead of just committing himself not to buy from a competitor even if the competitor offered a better product or terms of sale, he would be committing himself to go through with whatever project generated the estimate of required quantity, no matter what happened over the life of the project save those exceptional events that would excuse performance under the related excuses of *force majeure*, impossibility, impracticability, or frustration. This would be a big commitment to infer from the inclusion in the contract of an estimated quantity, at least once the parties concede as they do here that their contract really is a requirements contract and not a contract for the estimate itself—not, in other words, a fixed-quantity contract.

Both extreme interpretations—that the buyer need only refrain from dealing with a competitor of the seller, and that the buyer cannot go significantly beneath the estimated quantity except in dire circumstances—must be rejected, as we shall see. Nevertheless the judge should not have read the "unreasonably disproportionate" proviso in § 2-306(1) to the jury. The proviso does not apply, though the requirement of good faith does, where the buyer takes less rather than more of the stated estimate in a requirements contract.

This error in instructions requires reversal and a new trial on liability unless it is clear either that American Bakeries acted in good faith or that it acted in bad faith, since the statute requires the buyer to take his "good faith" requirements from the seller, irrespective of proportionality. The Uniform Commercial Code does not contain a definition of "good faith" that seems applicable to the buyer under a requirements contract. Compare § 2-104(1) with § 2-103(1)(b). Nor has the term a settled meaning in law generally; it is a chameleon. . . . Clearly, American Bakeries was acting in bad faith if during the contract period it bought propane conversion units from anyone other than Empire Gas, or made its own units, or reduced its purchases because it wanted to hurt Empire Gas (for example because they were competitors in some other market). Equally clearly, it was not acting in bad faith if it had a business reason for deciding not to convert that was independent of the terms of the contract or any other aspect of its relationship with Empire Gas, such as a drop in the demand for its bakery products that led it to reduce or abandon its fleet of delivery trucks. A harder question is whether it was acting in bad faith if it changed its mind about conversion for no (disclosed) reason. There is no evidence in the record on why it changed its mind beyond vague references to "budget problems" that, so far as appears, may have been nothing more than a euphemism for a decision by American Bakeries not to allocate funds for conversion to propane.

If no reason at all need be given for scaling back one's requirements even to zero, then a requirements contract is from the buyer's standpoint just an option to purchase up to (or slightly beyond, i.e., within the limits of reasonable proportionality) the stated estimate on the terms specified in the contract, except that the buyer cannot refuse to exercise the option because someone offers him better terms. This is not an unreasonable position, but it is not the law. Among the less important reasons for this conclusion are that option contracts are dealt with elsewhere in the Code, see § 2-311, and that the Official Comments to § 2-306 state that "a shut-down by a requirements buyer for lack of orders might be permissible where a shut-down *merely to curtail losses* would not." UCC § 2-306, comment 2 (emphasis added). More compelling is the Illinois Code Comment to § 2-306 which states that "this section . . . is but a codification of prior Illinois decisional law," which had made clear that a requirements contract was more than a buyer's option. "By the original agreement, appellant was entitled to order all the coal which was required or needed in its business for the season named; by the modified contract, appellant was restricted to the privilege of ordering twelve thousand tons. It was not the intention here to contract for the mere option or privilege of buying coal at a future time, but simply to limit the quantity to be bought. . . . It was not intended to be an option contract." *Minnesota Lumber Co. v. Whitebreast Coal Co.*, 160 Ill. 85, 96-97, 43 N.E. 774 (1896). "Requirements" are more than purely subjective "needs," which would be the equivalent of "wants." [citations omitted].

These cases are old, but nothing has happened to sap their strength, ... The statement of an estimate invites the seller to begin making preparations to satisfy the contract, and although no reliance expense was incurred by the seller in this case, a seller is entitled to expect that the buyer will buy something like the estimated requirements unless it has a valid business reason for buying less. More important than the estimate (which was not a factor in the Illinois cases just cited) is the fact that ordinarily a requirements contract is terminated after performance has begun, rather than before as in the present case. Whether or not the seller can prove reliance damages, the sudden termination of the contract midway through performance is bound to disrupt his operations somewhat. The Illinois courts interpret a requirements contract as a sharing of risk between seller and buyer. The seller assumes the risk of a change in the buyer's business that makes continuation of the contract unduly costly, but the buyer assumes the risk of a less urgent change in his circumstances, perhaps illustrated by the facts of this case where so far as one can tell the buyer's change of mind reflected no more than a reassessment of the balance of advantages and disadvantages under the contract. American Bakeries did not agree to buy conversion units and propane for trucks that it got rid of, but neither did Empire Gas agree to forgo sales merely because new management at American Bakeries decided that its capital would be better employed in some other investment than conversion to propane.

The general distinction that we are trying to make is well illustrated by *Southwest Natural Gas Co. v. Oklahoma Portland Cement Co.*, 102 F.2d 630 (10th Cir. 1939), which to the drafters of the Uniform Commercial Code exemplified "reasonable variation of an extreme sort" (at least in the absence of an estimate, but that is irrelevant, for reasons we have explained). UCC § 2-306, comment 2. A cement company agreed to buy all of its requirements of gas from the seller for 15 years. Seven years later, the cement company replaced its boiler, which had worn out, with more modern equipment; as a result its need for gas fell by 80 percent. The court deemed this a bona fide change in the cement company's requirements. It would have been unreasonable to make the company replace its worn-out plant with an obsolete facility.

It is a nice question how exigent the buyer's change of circumstances must be to allow him to scale down his requirements from either the estimated level or, in the absence of estimate, the "normal" level. Obviously it need not be so great as to give him a defense under the doctrines of impossibility, impracticability, or frustration, or under a *force majeure* clause. Yet, although more than whim is required, . . . how much more is unclear. There is remarkably little authority on the question. This is a good sign; it suggests that, while we might think it unsatisfactory for the law to be unclear on so fundamental a question, the people affected by the law are able to live with the lack of certainty. The reason may be that parties linked in an ongoing relationship—the usual situation under a requirements contract—have a strong incentive to work out disagreements amicably rather than see the relationship destroyed by litigation.

The essential ingredient of good faith in the case of the buyer's reducing his estimated requirements is that he not merely have had second thoughts about the terms of the contract and want to get out of it. . . . Whether the buyer has any greater obligation is unclear, . . . but need not be decided here. Once it is decided (as we have) that a buyer cannot arbitrarily declare his requirements to be zero, this becomes an easy case, because American Bakeries has never given any reason for its change of heart. It might seem that once the district judge decided to instruct the jury in the language of the statute, American Bakeries was foreclosed from arguing that it had scaled down its requirements in good faith; a reduction to zero could never be proportionate if, as the instruction implied, the proviso on disproportion applies to reductions as well as increases in the buyer's takings. But the judge did not make this decision until the instructions conference. Until then American Bakeries had every opportunity and incentive to introduce evidence of why it decided not to convert its fleet to propane. It introduced none, and even at the argument in this court its counsel could give no reason for the change of heart beyond a hint that it was due to a change in management, which would not be enough by itself to justify a change in the buyer's requirements.

Even though Empire Gas had the burden of proving breach of contract and therefore (we may assume) of proving that American Bakeries acted in bad faith in reducing its requirements from 3,000 conversion units to zero . . . , no reasonable jury could have failed to find bad faith, and therefore the error in instructing the jury on proportionality was harmless. Empire Gas put in evidence, uncontested and incontestable, showing that American Bakeries had not got rid of its fleet of trucks and did have the financial wherewithal to go through with the conversion process. After this evidence came in, American Bakeries could avoid a directed verdict only by introducing some evidence concerning its reasons for reducing its requirements. It not only introduced no evidence, but as is plain from counsel's remarks at argument it has no evidence that it would care to put before the jury—no reasons that it would care to share with either the district court or this court. It disagrees with the standard of good faith, believing that so long as it did not buy conversion units elsewhere or want to hurt Empire Gas it was free to reduce its requirements as much as it pleased. It does not suggest that it has a case under the standard we have adopted, which requires at a minimum that the reduction of requirements not have been motivated solely by a reassessment of the balance of advantages and disadvantages under the contract to the buyer. . . .

The jury's finding of liability must stand; but was there error in the assessment of damages? American Bakeries objects violently to the assumption made by Empire Gas's expert witness that the vehicles converted by American Bakeries, had it honored what Empire Gas contends were its obligations under the contract, would have run 100 percent on propane. The conversion units would have been dual units, which permit the driver by a flick of a switch in the engine to run his vehicle on either gasoline or propane. But since the parties agree that the price of propane was lower than that of gasoline throughout the entire contract period, a driver would have switched his conversion unit to gasoline only when he was low on propane and too far away from a propane station to reach it before he ran out. This factor was not big enough to upset the expert witness's calculations significantly. The calculation of damages is estimation rather than measurement, and it is foolish to prolong a lawsuit in quest of delusive precision.

The other complaints about the damage assessment are equally inconsequential, and do not require discussion. A great weakness of American Bakeries' case was its failure to present its own estimate of damages, in the absence of which the jury could have no idea of what adjustments to make in order to take account of American Bakeries' arguments. American Bakeries may have feared that if it put in its own estimate of damages the jury would be irresistibly attracted to that figure as a compromise. But if so, American Bakeries gambled double or nothing, as it were; and we will not relieve it of the consequences of its risky strategy. . . .

The judgment is affirmed . . . . [Judge KANNE's dissent is omitted.]

NOTES AND QUESTIONS

1. *Practical problems*: A seller faces some real difficulty in determining just when requirements have become "unreasonably disproportionate." Parties face similar practical problems in asserting that demands are not made in good faith. Cheryl R. Guttenberg[45] asserts:

> The distinction between good and bad faith reductions in requirements that the Seventh Circuit adopted in *Empire Gas* is of no . . . practical use. . . . The court stated that seller assumes the risk of changes in buyer's circumstances that make continuation of the contract unduly costly, but does not assume the risk of less urgent changes. It is unclear when a change in circumstances makes performance of the contract un-

---

[45] *And Then There Were None: Requirements Contracts and the Buyer Who Does Not Buy*, 64 Wash. L. Rev. 871 (1989).

duly costly and when a change is less urgent. The court offered no guide-lines other than that something more than whim is required. . . . [T]his distinction leaves an expansive middle ground where a court's applica-tion of the distinction would be wholly unpredictable.[46]

She advocates a business reason rule: "[i]t would define good faith as buyer pro-viding seller with a business reason for a reduction. 'Business reason means an economic reason, such as business losses or a more profitable alternative invest-ment."[47] She asserts this rule "would provide contracting parties with definite guidelines."[48] This would be efficient because the parties will not have to expend resources bargaining for a more explicit allocation of risk.

Contrast Judge Posner's explanation of why there are few cases construing § 2-306(1):

There is remarkably little authority on the question. This is a good sign; it suggests that, while we might think it unsatisfactory for the law to be unclear on so fundamental a question, the people affected by the law are able to live with the lack of certainty. The reason may be that parties linked in an ongoing relationship—the usual situation under a require-ments contract—have a strong incentive to work out disagreements ami-cably rather than see the relationship destroyed by litigation.[49]

2. *Two examples applying the "good-faith" test*: Zisk[50] offers two examples of the application of this concept:

(i) [T]he controversy in *Orange & Rockland Utilities, Inc. v. Amerada Hess Corp.*,[51] concerned the alleged breach of a fixed-price contract for the oil requirements of a utility. Both parties expected the oil to be used as a supplement to the utility's primary fuel, natural gas, but a rapid rise in fuel prices made it more profitable for the utility to sell its natural gas reserves and substitute for the gas the cheap oil it could obtain under the fixed price Amerada Hess contract. Additionally, the company's access to cheap oil enabled it to increase dramatically its sales of electricity to other utilities, thereby further increasing its own needs for oil. Under these circum-stances, the trial court found that all of the utility's increased requirements were incurred in bad faith. By selling greater amounts of electricity to other utilities, Orange & Rockland was forcing the oil company to supply indirectly the needs of those other utilities at low prices; by selling its re-serves of gas and substituting oil, it was seizing an opportunity to reap substantial profits at the expense of the oil company.

(ii) In contrast, in *Eastern Air Lines, Inc. v. Gulf Oil Corp.*,[52] a supplier's assertion of the buyer's bad faith was rejected. Eastern had been "fuel

---

[46] *Id.* at 882.

[47] *Id.* at 880, 882.

[48] *Id.* at 883.

[49] Empire Gas Corp., 840 F.2d at 134.

[50] Note, *Requirements Contracts, "More or Less," Under the Uniform Commercial Code*, 33 Rutgers L. Rev. 105 (1980). Reprinted by permission.

[51] [47] 59 A.D.2d 110, 397 N.Y.S.2d 814 (1977).

[52] [66] 415 F. Supp. 429 (S.D. Fla. 1975).

freighting"—obtaining fuel in excess of its known requirements at low-priced refueling stations [run by other companies] and thereby obviating the need to obtain fuel at higher-priced stations [run by Gulf]. Gulf attacked fuel freighting as a bad-faith practice,[53] but because fuel freighting was an established practice in the industry, the court found that it had probably been taken into consideration during contract negotiations, and held that Eastern had not breached its obligation of good faith.

If increases under a contract that contains no estimate develop slowly and steadily over a long period, they are arguably allowable on the theory that the parties to a long-term contract should anticipate such increases. A slow and steady increase also means that each year's requirements are not unreasonably disproportionate to the prior year's orders. No such case has yet been decided under the Code, though similar facts were presented in the pre-Code case of *Ehrenworth v. George F. Stuhmer & Co.*,[54] where buyer's 8,000% increase in orders over a seven year period under an exclusive distributorship requirements contract was allowable.

c. Distributorships—Is a Distribution Contract a Requirements Contract?

As you know, a very common commercial arrangement involves a manufacturer who contracts with a distributor to promote and deliver the manufactured goods within a defined territory. The distributors often provide warehousing and delivery services, as well as acting as a sales force. A distributor may carry several "lines" from several different manufacturers. A distributor generally prefers to be the exclusive source for a manufacturer's product in the region. Only if the distributor "has an exclusive" can the distributor be sure of capturing all of the value of its promotional efforts, and developing long-term loyal customers. The distributor acts as a conduit for the goods. The contracts between manufacturers and distributors involve duties that make the distributors look, for some purposes, as if they were the part-time employees or agents for the manufacturer, but for other purposes as if they were buyers of goods for resale. What difference does the characterization of the agreement make? One important difference is that if the transaction between a manufacturer and a distributor is characterized as a sale of goods, the UCC applies. And the application of the UCC may yield different results from the application of common law.

An example of such a question arose in the case of *Famous Brands, Inc. v. David Sherman Corp.*[55] In the course of Famous Brands' purchase of a liquor wholesaler (Midland), Famous sought reassurance that Sherman would continue to supply it with Everclear, and other liquor brands. Sherman's representative replied that, "If [the proposed sale] happens, I want you to know that we will be more than happy to have you distribute Everclear alcohol and any other brands that Midland will be selling for us." Later, Sherman said that Famous could

---

[53] [67] Gulf contended that slight changes in its prices vis-a-vis those of companies operating refueling stations in other cities led to drastic alterations in Eastern's refueling patterns.

[54] 229 N.Y. 210, 128 N.E. 108 (1920).

[55] 814 F.2d 517, 519 (8th Cir. 1987).

"count on" Sherman. Shortly thereafter, Sherman terminated the distributorship, apparently because Famous refused to carry a full line of Sherman's products. Famous sued to enforce the distributorship agreement. The trial court granted Sherman's motion for summary judgment on the grounds that (1) the terms of the contract were too indefinite, and (2) there was no mutuality of obligation.

The Eighth Circuit reversed, finding that since the parties had operated under the agreement for over a year there was a jury issue as to whether an implied contract had arisen. In addition, the court found that the "no mutuality" objection was not well-founded. First, the arrangement could be regarded as a "requirements" contract, recognized as valid in South Dakota's adoption of § 2-306 of the UCC. In addition, the plaintiff had a plausible promissory estoppel argument, based on reliance by Famous on Sherman's reassurance that it could continue as a distributor.

Section 2-306(2) of the UCC says that a "lawful agreement by either the seller or the buyer for exclusive dealing in the kind of goods concerned imposes unless otherwise agreed an obligation by the seller to use best efforts to supply the goods and by the buyer to use best efforts to promote their sale." But how much effort is "best" efforts? If either the buyer or the seller does nothing, this would seem to violate the obligation. However, if either of them takes some action, it will be difficult to judge if they should have done more.[56] How much must a seller invest to see that goods get to its distributor quickly? How much must a distributor spend on advertising and promotion? We would not be surprised to see litigation about this issue turn into a battle of experts. The seller's expert would find the buyer's judgments less than best efforts while the buyer's expert would find them more than enough. What is a court to do then? The burden of proof would help in some cases, but we should expect real difficulty in others.

The next case discusses in an extended fashion the implications of the characterization of a distributorship. In *Famous Brands*, characterizing the contract as governed by the UCC imposes an obligation of good faith, and since the UCC validates requirements contracts, arguably avoids some common law challenges which are based on the higher standard of definiteness which may apply if the common law rule applies.

The UCC, however, is a two-edged sword. In the next case the distributor seeks to avoid application of the Code, since the Code may require a signed writing in cases where the common law would not.

---

[56] In Bloor v. Falstaff, 601 F.2d 609 (2d Cir. 1979), the contract required Falstaff to use best efforts to promote and maintain a high volume of sales of Ballantine beer. The court decided that Falstaff did not use best efforts. However, Victor Goldberg, *Great Contracts Cases: In Search of Best Efforts: Reinterpreting* Bloor v. Falstaff, 44 St. Louis L. J. 1465 (2000), argues that the court was mistaken in light of the nature of the deal and the purposes of the clause. Goldberg concedes that the lawyers did not frame the issue for the court properly, and they did not create a record that would have helped the court see the purposes of the clause. His article reinforces the idea that "best efforts" is an extremely difficult concept to apply.

LORENZ SUPPLY CO. v. AMERICAN STANDARD, INC.
Supreme Court of Michigan
419 Mich. 610, 358 N.W.2d 845 (1984)

LEVIN, J. The principal question presented is whether the distributorship agreement[57] between Lorenz and American Standard is a "contract for the sale of goods" within the meaning of § 2-201 of the Uniform Commercial Code.[58] We hold that it is not and affirm the decision of the Court of Appeals affirming the judgment entered by the circuit court on the jury's verdict in favor of Lorenz.

I.   Lorenz pleaded and the jury found that Lorenz entered into a distributorship agreement with American Standard. The only written evidence of this agreement was a letter from American Standard to Lorenz that "welcome[d]" Lorenz "to the numbers of American Standard distributors across the country."

Section 2-201 does not require that the terms of a contract for the sale of goods, other than the quantity term, be expressed in writing.[59] The requirements of § 2-201 are satisfied if the writing indicates that "a contract of sale has been made between the parties" and "specif[ies] a quantity." 2 Anderson, Uniform Commercial Code (3d ed.), § 2-201:97, p. 61.[60]

The concurring opinion recognizes that the quantity term of a distributorship agreement is generally uncertain, and to require that it be stated with certainty would put most distributorship agreements out of compliance with § 2-201 and, hence, if a distributorship agreement is a "contract for the sale of goods," make them unenforceable. The concurring opinion seeks to avoid this dilemma by in-

---

[57] [1] Plaintiff Lorenz Supply Company and defendant American Standard, Inc., entered into an agreement whereunder Lorenz agreed to purchase $420,000 worth of plumbing inventory from American Standard. The jury found that, at the same time, the parties agreed that Lorenz was to become a distributor of American Standard products in the Detroit area. The terms of the inventory sale agreement, but *not* the distributorship agreement, were set forth in writing.

Subsequently, a dispute arose concerning the performance of the inventory sale agreement. Lorenz withheld payments totaling $65,100 for goods received because it believed that it was owed over $70,000 for alleged errors pertaining to the inventory sale. American Standard then refused to supply additional products under the distributorship agreement unless Lorenz paid cash in advance.

Lorenz filed the instant action claiming breach of both the written inventory sale agreement and the oral distributorship agreement. The complaint sought $2,000,000 in damages. American Standard counterclaimed for approximately $72,000 for products delivered under the inventory sale agreement.

[58] [2] M.C.L. § 440.2201; M.S.A. § 19.2201.

[59] [3] The Official Comment to § 2-201 provides, in part:

> The required writing need not contain all the material terms of the contract and such material terms as are stated need not be precisely stated. All that is required is that the writing afford a basis for believing that the offered oral evidence rests on a real transaction. . . . *The only term which must appear is the quantity term* which need not be accurately stated but recovery is limited to the amount stated. The price, time and place of payment or delivery, the general quality of the goods, or any particular warranties may all be omitted.

(Emphasis added.)

[60] [4] It appears that most, if not all, commentators agree with Anderson's observation that § 2-201 requires that a writing must specify a quantity. See, *e.g.*, Calamari & Perillo, The Law of Contracts, § 313, p. 486; White & Summers, Uniform Commercial Code (2d ed.), § 2-4, pp. 59-60; 3 Duesenberg & King, Uniform Commercial Code Service (Bender), § 2.04[2][a], p. 2-59.

ferring a quantity term. The quantity term must, however, under § 2-201, be specifically stated.[61]

A requirements or output term of a contract, although general in language, nonetheless is, *if stated in the writing*, specific as to quantity, and in compliance with § 2-201.[62] However, not all distributorship agreements are requirements or output contracts. The jury was not asked to decide whether the instant distributorship agreement contained a requirements or output term, and this Court would exceed its role if it were to imply a provision akin to a requirements term.[63] Under the construction advanced in the concurring opinion, American Standard could maintain an action against Lorenz for failure to purchase its requirements whether the parties agreed thereto or not.

Because many distributorship agreements are not requirements or output contracts and in such cases the quantity term is generally uncertain, we conclude that the drafters of the Uniform Commercial Code did not intend that all distributorship agreements be regarded as "contract[s] for the sale of goods."[64]

II. A writing that satisfies § 2-201 does not prove the terms of a contract; such a writing merely removes the statutory bar to the enforcement of the contract whether its terms—other than the quantity term which alone must be specified in writing—be written, oral, or partly written and partly oral. In the instant case, the letter from American Standard to Lorenz welcoming him as a distributor indicates that a contract was made between the parties. If one concludes, as would the author of the concurring opinion, that the letter satisfies the requirements of § 2-201, then the terms of the instant agreement, whatever those terms might be, are enforceable. Because the terms of a contract for the sale of goods, other than the quantity term, need not be stated in writing, the declaration in the concurring opinion that § 2-201 applies to distributorship agreements does not bear on the disputed terms of the instant distributorship agreement. . . . *Affirmed.*

BRICKLEY, J. (concurring). This case presents for the first time in this state the question whether the Uniform Commercial Code, MCL § 440.1101 *et seq.*; MSA § 19.1101 *et seq.*, and its Statute of Frauds, MCL § 440.2201; MSA § 19.2201, are applicable to a distributorship agreement, and whether the Statute of Frauds' quantity requirement can be satisfied by a writing stating that one party is a distributor of another's products. I would answer yes to both questions.

---

[61] [5] . . . [Official Comment to UCC 2-201] and Doral Hosiery Corp. v. Sav-A-Stop, Inc., 377 F. Supp. 387, 389 (E.D. Pa. 1974). . . .

[62] [6] See Cox Caulking & Insulating Co. v. Brockett Distributing Co., 150 Ga.App. 424, 426, 258 S.E.2d 51 (1979); 3 Duesenberg & King, Uniform Commercial Code Service (Bender), § 2.04[2][a], p. 2-59; 2 Anderson, Uniform Commercial Code (3d ed.), §§ 2-201:113, 2-201:114, p. 70.

[63] [7] Other courts have refused to hold that a distributorship agreement contains an implied term that the seller will supply the buyer with its requirements. See, e.g., Eastern Dental Corp. v. Isaac Masel Co., Inc., 502 F. Supp. 1354, 1364 (E.D. Pa. 1980); Cavalier Mobile Homes, Inc. v. Liberty Homes, Inc., 53 Md. App. 379, 395, 454 A.2d 367 (1983).

[64] [8] We express no opinion on the question whether a distributorship agreement may fall within the broader category of "transactions in goods" within the meaning of § 2-102 of the UCC, MCL § 440.2102; MSA § 19.2102. See Farnsworth, Contracts, § 8.16, p. 612; 3A Corbin, Contracts, § 700, p. 309.

I.   In July of 1972, plaintiff Lorenz Supply Company was engaged in a family-owned and operated business selling "in the wall" plumbing items, such as pipes and valves, in the Detroit area. Defendant American Standard, Inc., a major manufacturer of diversified products, was planning to close out a heating and plumbing distribution outlet in Troy, run by its Amstan supply division.

Plaintiff's president, Robert Lorenz, desirous of expanding his plumbing line to "out of the wall" fixtures, such as sinks and faucets, entered into negotiations with defendant's local management. These negotiations resulted in an agreement whereby Lorenz would purchase $420,000 worth of inventory from defendant's Troy warehouse and take responsibility for its outstanding delivery orders. As part of the inducement for the inventory sale, Lorenz was to be made a "preferred" distributor of defendant's products. Plaintiff's president testified at trial that defendant promised to use its best efforts to supply items on a regular basis as they were needed and that plaintiff could distribute defendant's products for as long as it desired.

The arrangement for the inventory sale was reduced to a specific writing which set forth the details for transfer of the goods. The goods were to be transferred from the defendant's warehouse in August 1972. When Mr. Lorenz inquired as to the distributorship part of the arrangement, he was advised that it was the policy of defendant not to have written distributorship agreements. However, in the following month plaintiff received a confirmation letter from an official of defendant corporation. It expressed "happiness with the way our whole negotiations turned out with regard to your purchase of the Amstan inventory and, more importantly, to welcome you to the numbers of American Standard distributors across the country." Lorenz immediately began to enlarge his facilities and augment his staff in preparation for the distributorship and its expected enhancement of his business.

Unfortunately, happiness did not become a hallmark of the relationship. Lorenz first became concerned that defendant was not honoring the terms of their agreement at the time of the inventory transfer in August of 1972, when he received reports that some of the fastest-selling inventory from the Troy warehouse was seen departing for destinations other than plaintiff's business. Lorenz would later testify that some of the fastest-selling items from the inventory were sold to other distributors. Lorenz also testified that defendant overcharged him for some of the items he received from the sale, and charged for some items not received at all. Lorenz further testified at trial that, when he complained to defendant about these various errors, he was told on several occasions that restitution would be made for the missing inventory, and that he should keep track of the billing errors so that the total amount could be offset against his account at a later date.

The dispute between the parties and efforts to resolve it continued through the remainder of 1972 and into 1973. Finally, in December 1973, plaintiff, claiming that it was owed $72,000 by defendant as a result of the alleged errors, refused to pay approximately $65,000 otherwise owing to defendant.[65] Defendant, disputing

---

[65] [1] Plaintiff was to pay defendant $420,000, in six $70,000 monthly installments, for the inventory in defendant's Troy warehouse. Plaintiff was also purchasing additional materials from the defendant under the distributorship arrangement. The record is not clear as to precisely how much

these assertions, advised plaintiff that it would be cut off from further products if it did not pay on its account. When the payment was not received by January 1974, defendant placed plaintiff on "credit hold," meaning that plaintiff could receive additional products only by paying cash in advance.

Meanwhile, plaintiff filed suit for breach of contract. Defendant denied a breach and counterclaimed for the monies due according to defendant's accounting. Robert Lorenz testified at trial that he secured additional financing, at great personal cost, in order to continue to buy essential items from defendant in cash. This in turn compounded his financial problems. Finally, in June 1974, defendant advised plaintiff that because of "restrictions placed on your orders by the credit department . . . we are cancelling all open orders as of June 15, 1974." Plaintiff filed for bankruptcy in March 1975, and at the time of trial was a defunct corporation.

Plaintiff offered evidence at trial that it was saddled with a quarter-million dollar "dead" inventory because it was denied essential related products by defendant, both because it did not receive promised material from the Troy warehouse and because of the refusal of the defendant to continue to furnish products under the distributorship agreement. Lorenz further testified that, in spite of contracting for $420,000 worth of inventory from the Troy warehouse, he received only $260,000 worth of products.

The trial judge instructed the jury that there were "two separate issues that are at issue in this case; one, an issue with respect to the sale of the inventory at the Troy warehouse of American Standard, and the second issue being permitting Lorenz Supply Company to distribute American Standard's products in the Detroit area."

[The jury found a breach of the inventory sale, and damages to plaintiff of $45,000. The jury also found plaintiff had been the victim of a breach of the distributorship agreement with damages of $255,000. After the trial judge ordered a new trial on defendant's counterclaim, the parties stipulated to plaintiff's liability of $69,873.40 and avoided a retrial on that issue.]

Defendant argued before the Court of Appeals, as it does here, that the distributorship agreement was a "transaction in goods" under Article 2 (Sales) of the Uniform Commercial Code and, therefore, was subject to the Statute of Frauds of that article, thus making it unenforceable since the letter welcoming the plaintiff as a distributor did not satisfy the "writing" requirement. Defendant also contested the admission of certain evidence relating to lost profits and argued that the jury's erroneous verdict on the counterclaim invalidated the entire verdict and should have entitled them to a new trial on all issues. Finally, defendant argues that even if it is enforceable, the distributorship agreement was terminable at will, thus precluding any damage award for lost profits.

The letter from defendant to plaintiff, which is the only written evidence of the distributorship aspect of the arrangement between the parties, reads as follows:

---

of the disputed credits or debits between the parties was attributable to the inventory sale as opposed to ongoing purchases of non-inventory merchandise. It is likely the accounts were combined.

Dear Bob:

Now that you have officially joined the family of American Standard distributors, I want to record with you my extreme happiness with the way our whole negotiations turned out with regard to your purchase of the Amstan inventory and, more importantly, to welcome you to the numbers of American Standard distributors across the country.

Ed and I are most enthusiastic about your ability to help us participate in larger measure in the Detroit market and I hope the opportunity will soon present itself when I can express my sincerest welcome to those other Lorenz personnel who I have not yet met but on whom we are counting for the strongest possible support in a very difficult market.

It is a pleasure to have you with us and I trust that our association will be mutually beneficial for many years to come.

Sincerely yours,

Bren O'Connell

The Court of Appeals, 100 Mich. App. 600, 608, 300 N.W.2d 335 (1980), found that the distributorship agreement did not come within the purview of the UCC since the "agreement did not require Lorenz to buy a certain quantity of goods or, indeed, to buy *any* goods from the defendant in the future." Rather, they said, "[t]his agreement envisioned an ongoing economic relationship." The Court did allow that "Lorenz was granted the status of a 'preferred distributor' who would be entitled to purchase plumbing fixtures manufactured by the defendant in the future." Based on that relationship—that plaintiff need not buy but defendant must sell—the Court found the distributorship agreement to be outside of the Uniform Commercial Code and its Statute of Frauds and therefore enforceable.

The Court of Appeals further said that even if it had found the UCC to be applicable, the letter from the defendant to the plaintiff was a "sufficient written memorandum of the previous oral agreement to satisfy the requirements" of the Statute of Frauds. The Court further stated that "Lorenz never undertook to buy any of defendant's products, so the $500 statutory amount was never triggered." Finally, it said, "[a]lthough the quantity term is omitted, in the context of a distributorship agreement such an indefiniteness is inherent to the relationship and would not defeat the validity of the contract where the parties agreed. *See* MCL 440.2204(3); MSA 19.2204(3); MCL 440.2306(1); MSA 19.2306(1)." The Court did not deal with the counterclaim verdict question.

I disagree with both the analysis and conclusion of the Court of Appeals.

Dealing first with the Court of Appeals dictum that the $500 limit of the Statute of Frauds was not triggered, I see nothing in the record or arguments of the parties that would indicate that there was to be a $500 limit on what was to be covered by the distributorship agreement. To the contrary, the record reflects that thousands of dollars's worth of products were sold by defendant to plaintiff. The other two points of the Court' holding, that the UCC was not applicable to this type of distributorship agreement and the question of the satisfaction of the quantity term, are important issues, largely novel to our jurisprudence.

II. On the applicability of the UCC, the Court of Appeals did not distinguish between the "transaction in goods" criteria for the general application of Article 2 and the more specific finding of a "contract for the sale of goods," critical for the applicability of the Statute of Frauds. Instead, the Court of Appeals opined that the distributorship agreement did not fit the Statute of Frauds "contract for the sale of goods" definition and therefore held that the UCC, seemingly in its entirety, does not apply.

Appellants argue forcefully that such an interpretation would leave a major and fast-growing type of commercial activity outside the code. I agree.

Section 2-102 of the UCC, MCL § 440.2102 *et seq.*; MSA § 19.2102 *et seq.*, provides "[u]nless the context otherwise requires, this article applies to *transactions in goods*" (emphasis added), whereas the Statute of Frauds of the UCC, MCL § 440.2201, MSA § 19.2201 provides:

> [A] *contract for the sale of goods* for the price of $500 or more is not enforceable by way of action or defense unless there is some writing sufficient to indicate that a contract for sale has been made. . . . A writing is not insufficient because it omits or incorrectly states a term agreed upon but the contract is not enforceable under this paragraph beyond the quantity of goods shown in such writing. (Emphasis added.)

MCL § 440.2106; MSA § 19.2106 defines "contract for sale" as both a "present sale of goods and a contract to sell goods at a future time."

"Transaction in goods" is a broad term and on its face would seem to cover an agreement that has as its purpose the ongoing transfer of title to goods between the parties. The UCC is to be "liberally construed," MCL § 440.1102; MSA § 19.1102, and is designed to "provide its own machinery for expansion of commercial practices. It is intended to make it possible for the law embodied in this act to be developed by the courts in the light of unforeseen and new circumstances and practices." UCC § 1-102, Official Comment 1.

The predominant holdings among those states which have considered this issue are to the effect that a distributorship agreement is subject to the UCC, although there is anything but a consistent rationale for the holdings. Because cases involving distributorship agreements have involved different sections of Article 2, the courts have variously focused on the words "transaction in goods," "contract for the sale," or "goods." We have found nowhere a case which is precisely on point with the facts of this case, nor has our research disclosed a case with the exact legal analysis which we think is required to properly resolve the issue before us.

Our conviction that Article 2 itself contemplates a distributorship agreement is buttressed by our observation that sections of Article 2 other than the Statute of Frauds quite clearly include distributorship agreements within their scope. Section 2-306, MCL § 440.2306; MSA § 19.2306, which validates contract terms which measure quantity by the output of the seller or the requirements of the buyer, clearly encompasses agreements that contemplate ongoing commercial arrangements such as are involved in a normal distributorship. Indeed, Official Comment No. 1 to this section states that "[i]t applies to such contracts of non-producing establishments such as dealers or distributors as well as to manufacturing concerns." Similarly, § 2-309, MCL § 440.2309; MSA § 19.2309, which deals with a "contract . . . for successive performances [that] is indefinite in duration," clearly lends itself to a distributorship arrangement.

Cases from other jurisdictions support this conclusion. . . .

The more difficult and separate question is the applicability of the Statute of Frauds, MCL § 440.2201; MSA § 19.2201, to the distributorship agreement. I see it as a separate question because the term "contract for the sale of goods" is clearly more restrictive than the term "transaction in goods."

The prevailing authority clearly favors holding a distributorship agreement to be a "contract for the sale of goods." . . .

My observation of the conflicting views represented in the . . . cases is that the majority of holdings implicitly say that a distributorship agreement is subject to the Statute of Frauds because it is a contract *dealing* with the sale of goods (or, stated differently, a contract for the sale of goods once removed). The minority view, adopted by our Court of Appeals in this case, says that, because the distributorship does not itself bind the parties to a specific transfer of specific goods, it is not a "contract for the sale of goods"; rather, as defendant characterizes it, it is "akin to an umbrella underneath which there were a series of commercial transactions between merchants." [66]

I think it wise when interpreting a uniform act, to join what is developing as a clear majority on this question, especially because of our previously mentioned conviction that it furthers the overall intent and scope of the UCC, and to consider the arrangement a contract for the sale of goods.

III. This does not end the inquiry, however. The key factual question in this case is whether the letter from defendant's agent to plaintiff's president satisfied the quantity requirement necessary for a contract to be enforceable under the Statute of Frauds.

In *Cavalier, supra*, the majority view of the Statute of Frauds is applied for the first time in combination with the "quantity" requirement of the Statute of Frauds

---

[66] [4] We are not troubled by the relatively indefinite nature of most distributorship agreements; we believe that both the requisite consideration and mutuality can be found to exist despite the inherently imprecise terms. The UCC, with its provisions for successive performances, MCL § 440.2309; MSA § 19.2309, and indefinite quantity terms, MCL § 440.2306; MSA § 19.2306, envisions very loose arrangements that are reinforced by the code with its requirement of "good faith." MCL § 440.1203; MSA § 19.1203. See J.W. Knapp Co. v. Sinas, 19 Mich. App. 427, 172 N.W.2d 867 (1969). Furthermore, in the typical distributorship arrangement, an agreement by one party to sell without a corresponding agreement by the other to buy, as the Court of Appeals suggests exists in the instant case, is usually accompanied by other forms of consideration, such as exclusive territories, best efforts by the distributor to market the manufacturer's products, and the like. As such, these arrangements are distinguishable from those agreements whose quantity term is totally unascertainable.

The Michigan court does not enforce contracts calling for the purchase or sale of such goods as may be "desired," "ordered," or "wished." Such contracts are distinguishable from the usual output or requirements contracts because the promisor is not bound to deliver or accept any sufficiently definite quantity.

MCLA § 440.2306 practice commentary, p. 247.

with the result that unless a distributorship agreement writing specifies a quantity it is unenforceable.

I cannot, as did the Court of Appeals, completely dismiss the quantity requirement even though I agree that "in the context of a distributorship agreement such an indefiniteness is inherent in the relationship." 100 Mich. App. 600, 300 N.W.2d 335. Indeed, if the quantity term was construed to require a numerically specific quantity of goods, the net result would be that most distributorships by their nature could never comply with the Statute of Frauds. It would indeed be an anomalous result to hold such contracts subject to the UCC and its Statute of Frauds and then proceed to hold them all unenforceable for lack of a sufficiently definite quantity term.

The code obviates such an interpretation in § 2-306, which provides:

> (1) A term which measures the quantity by the output of the seller or the requirements of the buyer means such actual output or requirements as may occur in good faith, except that no quantity unreasonably disproportionate to any stated estimate or in the absence of a stated estimate to any normal or otherwise comparable prior output or requirements may be tendered or demanded.

While this provision does not specifically refer to § 2-201, it would be difficult to argue that it does not impliedly define quantity as it is used in § 2-201. As previously noted, the official comment to § 2-306 states specifically that it applies to "contracts of nonproducing establishments such as dealers or distributors as well as to manufacturing concerns."

In *Kubik v. J & R Foods of Oregon, Inc.*, 282 Or. 179, 187-188, 577 P.2d 518 (1978), the Oregon Supreme Court, in interpreting an exclusive dealing contract, stated:

> As noted, ORS 72.3060 [the counterpart of § 2-306] is a statute designed, among other things, to define 'quantity'—as that item is required by the UCC's own Statute of Frauds—in those situations in which, because of the nature of the contract, a particular quantity cannot be identified in advance with certainty.

I may not go so far as to suggest that § 2-306 is intended to define quantity in § 2-201, but I think it indicates at least that Article 2 of the UCC does not contemplate any rigid definition of the term quantity as it is used anywhere in Article 2, including § 2-201. If it did not refer to the word quantity in § 2-201, then § 2-306 would be without purpose.

Traditional restrictions on requirements contracts and the need to have the quantity term ascertainable have been based on the need to supply consideration in such contracts. The UCC, particularly § 2-306, makes it clear that the code intends contracts to be upheld even where the terms are indefinite by reading into such contracts "good faith" requirements, thus allowing a quantity term as imprecise as an agreement to furnish the distributor with his needs.

The obvious purpose of the Statute of Frauds is to require the understanding of the parties regarding the quantity of goods involved to be spelled out in the writing. Even if the quantity is as imprecise as an agreement to furnish the goods that the plaintiff needs to serve his customers, it is important to have that understanding in writing. As the Maryland court stated in *Cavalier Mobile Homes, Inc. v. Liberty Homes, Inc.*, 53 Md. App. 379, 395, 454 A.2d 367 (1983):

> The Statute of Frauds requires that even where the quantity term is not numerically stated, there must be some writing which indicates that the quantity to be delivered under the contract is a party's requirements.

The letter in question was signed by the party "against whom enforcement is sought"—an agent of the defendant. The only question remaining is whether the language of the letter shows that the parties intended that defendant was obliged to supply plaintiff with its requirements, indefinite though it was.

The letter from defendant to plaintiff stated, "[n]ow that you have officially joined the family of American Standard distributors," and "more importantly, to welcome you to the numbers of American Standard distributors across the country," and "Ed and I are most enthusiastic about your ability to help us participate in larger measure in the Detroit market."

It is perfectly clear from this writing that plaintiff was to be a distributor for defendant, who would supply plaintiff with products to sell "in the Detroit market"; it is equally obvious that in a distributorship the manufacturer must furnish the distributor with sufficient goods to be a successful distributor. The specific quantity of goods to be delivered under the distributorship agreement could have been determined only by the demand generated, and could not have been calculated in advance. Rather, the quantity term was as specific as necessary under these circumstances. The only thing left unsaid in the letter are the words "we will supply those goods necessary for you to represent us in your area." It would have been redundant to do so because the words of welcome to the "family of American Standard distributors" told it all. The word distributorship means the practice of a manufacturer furnishing its distributor with the products it needs to fill its orders. The parties have never, throughout the course of this litigation, disputed the fact that the defendant was required to furnish those goods ordered by the plaintiff, subject to certain conditions. The disagreement is over whether the defendant was justified in cutting off the plaintiff from further deliveries because plaintiff refused to pay its bill.

I conclude that the agreement between the parties was a contract for the sale of goods under the UCC and its Statute of Frauds and that there was a writing satisfying the quantity requirement of that statute. The distributorship agreement should be enforceable.

NOTES AND QUESTIONS

1. *Requirements contracts vs. distributorships and franchises*: The *Lorenz Supply* case suggests some of the problems courts have faced when those who hold distributorships and franchises try to bring their relationship within the Uniform Commercial Code. Many modern cases raise this issue. Remember that many states have passed statutes regulating distributorships and franchises. Should the courts add to this regulation the obligations imposed by UCC § 2-306? What should courts do in states that have no distributorship or franchise statute? Consider the implications of the text of UCC § 2-306(2) on this question.

2. *Requirements contracts and the Statute of Frauds*: The *Lorenz Supply* case also suggests some of the difficulties courts have faced in reconciling §§ 2-306 and 2-201 of the UCC. In *Cox Caulking & Insulating Co. v. Brockett Distributing Co.*,[67] Cox Caulking & Insulating Co. was the insulation subcontractor on a construction project. It made an oral agreement to buy the needed insulating material from Brockett Distribution Co. A Brockett official wrote a letter saying that it had "submitted a price of $2.62 a bag for the above project." The letter earlier defined the project as the "Cardinal and Hunt Joint Venture in Hinesville, Georgia." The Court of Appeals of Georgia acknowledged "the quantity need not be designated numerically where the memorandum evidences a requirements or output contract." However, it said, "we reject appellant's contention that the phrase, 'for the above project,' was sufficient as a term of quantity. We conclude, instead, that the phrase merely designated the project which was the subject of the letter and that the letter contained no such 'term which measure[d] the quantity by the output of the seller or the requirements of the buyer.' Code § 109A-2-306(1)."[68] As a result, the court affirmed summary judgment in favor of Brockett Distributing Co.

Professor Caroline N. Brown[69] writes that the *Cox Caulking & Insulating Co.* case "is perhaps the most notorious example of § 2-201's potential for thwarting the effects of the Code sections that approve open quantity contracts." She continues, "the difficulty was the omission of such a magic word as 'all' or 'requirements' which would allow a *certain* quantitative determination by reference to the project." She notes that UCC § 2-306 does not require these magic words. Professor Brown says:

> The cornerstone of the difficulty concerning quantity lies in the initial determination that the statute requires quantity to "appear." This rule is almost universally accepted, despite the absence of any clear statutory direction to that effect. As construed in cases like *Cox Caulking*, the test imposed for quantity is stricter than the test recognized for the writing's sufficiency to show that the asserted transaction is genuine.[70] The sufficiency requirement which is clearly *central* to the purpose and language of the statute, may be satisfied by merely an "indication." Quantity, on the other hand, must "appear," according to the language of the official comment to § 2-201. The court in *Cox Caulking* apparently took this language to mandate that the quantity term be mechanically ascertainable solely from the face of the writing (together with any reference indicated as necessary to quantify it). In accordance with many courts, the *Cox Caulking* court effectively ruled that if *any* inferences must be drawn from circumstances outside the writing to establish quantity, the memorandum is insufficient.

---

[67] 150 Ga. App. 424, 258 S.E. 51 (1979).

[68] *Id.* at 426, 258 S.E. at 52.

[69] Bruckel [now Brown], *The Weed and the Web: Section 2-201's Corruption of the UCC's Substantive Provisions—The Quantity Problem*, 1983 U. Ill. L. Rev. 811, 819, 820, 822, 856-57. Copyright © 1984 by the Board of Trustees of the University of Illinois. Reprinted by permission.

[70] Eds. note: See the first sentence of § 2-201(1).

This standard is highly inappropriate, for it subordinates the central issue of sufficiency to the peripheral one. It can, and does, result in a refusal of recovery to a plaintiff who clearly establishes a legitimate agreement. This plaintiff will lose even after producing a written memorandum sufficient to "indicate" quantity as well as the agreement's legitimacy, if the written term requires even an obvious inference to give it substance. . . .

The official comment to § 2-201 . . . begins by echoing the drafters' primary concern to reverse the prior rule requiring all essential terms to be stated; it then notes that the only goal of the writing requirement is to establish a credible evidentiary basis for a real transaction. Two sentences later, however, the comment falls into confusion, seeming to recognize a requirement that quantity be stated. . . .

[T]he *single* statutory standard to determine the sufficiency of a memorandum should be its indication of a real transaction. No quantity term need be shown or even indicated in the writing; thus, the only standards affecting quantity are the Code's substantive standards. Consequently, the quantity term may be established by an unsigned writing or by oral allegations sufficient to satisfy the trier of fact, or supplied by implication from usage or conduct, or by law under § 2-306.

When the writing *does* contain a quantity term, § 2-201(1) directs that it serve as a ceiling on enforceability. Even this limitation, however, should give way to avoid manifest injustice when no statutory purpose is served by maintaining it. In cases where granting the plaintiff relief seems especially compelling, the statutory guideline properly yields to the overriding purpose of avoidance of fraud. Safety for the defendant *must* be weighed against injustice to the plaintiff before any coherent place for § 2-201 may be discovered in the Code.

Can you defend the courts against Professor Brown's attack? Can you answer her arguments? As she notes, there are many cases involving the relationship between UCC §§ 2-306 and 2-201, and most courts have insisted that the quantity term be stated in writing. In answering Professor Brown, assume that it is not enough to argue that her position does not follow the majority view.

This is not the only time we will consider a substantive doctrine alongside the statute of frauds. Compare, for example, *Janke Construction Co. v. Vulcan Materials Co.*, *supra*. Might judges comfortable with classic contract law seek to reach the old results by using the Statute of Frauds to offset legal realist innovations such as the firm offer and the enforceability of requirements contracts? Professor Henderson, for example, in his article on promissory estoppel, discussed those decisions that denied "any basis whatsoever for operation of the doctrine [of promissory estoppel] in opposition to the Statute of Frauds." He said, "these decisions surely reflect some lingering doubts about the general legitimacy of the reliance ground of enforcement of promises."[71] Could the same thing be said about the judicial reaction to oral flexible quantity terms?

C. BUSINESS DOCUMENTS AND FORMING CONTRACTS

Businesspeople often sign written agreements. Sometimes a business contract is signed with a formal ceremony. The signatures of high officials representing both sides are symbolic acts of commitment, marking a sharp line between being free to back out and being bound. However, on other occasions a deal is closed by a handshake or phone call. Papers are signed to keep accountants and lawyers happy. The parties may be in the midst of performing before anyone thinks about a formal ceremony.

Even where written documents are used, the situation may be unclear. For example, a letter may convey information with no intention of commitment. "I wouldn't think of selling for less than $500,000, and I might get more if I put the property on the market. Furthermore, unless you are thinking of buying for cash, I would need adequate security for your obligation." Contrast this with a letter saying, "I am willing to sell the Jones Farm to you for $500,000, payable in cash now." On the other hand, we may have a single commitment but too many documents. Seller may send its proposal and Buyer may respond with its purchase order. However, the two forms contain terms that do not match. Often the parties do not notice the inconsistency and start to perform. Is there a legally enforceable contract? If so, what are its terms?

Business patterns do not always neatly fit the categories of contract law. Judges and legislators could demand that businesspeople change their ways, and sometimes they do. However, generally judges, lawyers and law professors see contract law as facilitative and supportive of the market. When business reality does not fit into legal categories, many think that the legal categories should be changed. As we have noted before in these materials, Professor Duncan Kennedy points out that older teachers of common law subjects explained many problems in terms of the core and a periphery of exceptions to deal with hard cases. In the core situations, many lawyers assume the theories work, but there always will be a few peripheral situations that cause difficulty. Kennedy, however, asserts that the periphery tends to swallow the core in area after area. We are about to consider an area where we can ask about the status of core and periphery. Once again we encounter our familiar questions: Is liability based on choice, responsibility for careless use of language, social planning to serve the market or something else? Furthermore, do the rules favor larger, more bureaucratically organized businesses, the underdog consumer or small business, or are the impacts random?

Should the law insist on a signed written document as a kind of magical symbol dividing obligation from freedom or should it try to give effect to the understandings of the parties? Two Uniform Commercial Code provisions indicate conflicting views. UCC § 2-204(1) says "[a] contract for sale of goods may be made in any manner sufficient to show agreement, including conduct by both

---

[71] Henderson, *Promissory Estoppel and Traditional Contract Doctrine*, 78 Yale L. J. 343, 381-82 (1969).

parties which recognizes the existence of such a contract." Subsection (2) says "an agreement sufficient to constitute a contract for sale may be found even though the moment of its making is undetermined." Nonetheless, if the price of the goods is $500 or more, UCC § 2-201 requires "some writing sufficient to indicate that a contract for sale has been made between the parties and signed by the party against whom enforcement is sought." While these provisions can be reconciled, they point in different directions. How do business people regard the practice of documenting transactions?

—Interview with the Purchasing Agent of a large manufacturer of small electric appliances:

Mr. X does make orders at times by telephone, but he always confirms them later by a written purchase order. For example, recently he was buying a complete new appliance to be marketed under his firm's brand name and to be manufactured by one of the large well-known appliance manufacturers. So far only an order to buy the tooling necessary to make the appliance has been issued. In order to have the manufacturer ready to go, Mr. X has called and told it to begin buying materials. He has given them the number of the purchase order which will be sent to the manufacturer, over the telephone. The formal purchase order for the materials is now in the process of being written and approved. Mr. X is sure that the manufacturer has gone ahead and started buying materials at this point because once it has a purchase order number it is safe.

—Interview with the General Counsel of an automobile parts manufacturer:

Mr. Y remarked that, unless something is unusual about a transaction, the house counsel is seldom called in until after a contract has been made and problems develop in performance. People in this corporation often write "letters of intent" in purchasing situations without going through either the purchasing department or the house counsel. In his view these letters of intent often go far towards creating binding offers or contracts. In one case, Mr. Y found that nothing was in the file indicating any commitment on the part of a manufacturer as to how a $50,000 machine would perform, and his company's engineers seemed to have made a binding contract through a fairly vague letter of intent. The engineers said they had intended to refer the matter to the purchasing department to have a formal contract drafted but had overlooked the matter as they were anxious to get started.

—Interview with the General Counsel of a manufacturer of a well-known small consumer item:

Most people would rather not put things in writing. It is amazing how in casual conversations people will agree to one thing after another and will reach almost complete agreement. Then one asks for a signature on a document embodying that agreement. That seems to be a very disruptive act. At this point, many people back out and say, "No, I'd better think about that before I sign," even though they have orally agreed to everything in the written contract.

—Smith, *How a Great Corporation Got Out of Control—The Story of General Dynamics:*[72]

Convair's [the Convair Division of the General Dynamics Corporation] first target was United, which it had listed as a prospect for thirty aircraft. For a time things seemed to be going Convair's way in its pursuit of this critical $120-million sale. Boeing, Douglas, and Convair were all in competition for the United contract, but Convair had the edge with its 880, for it was then the only true medium-to-long-range jet aircraft being offered. All Boeing could offer was essentially the long-range 707, too big and, for its seating capacity, 50,000 pounds too heavy to suit United. The size could be reduced, of course, and some of the weight chopped out, but not 50,000 pounds unless Pratt & Whitney could substantially lighten the engines, the JT3C-6's used on the 707 aircraft. With Pratt & Whitney unwilling to make this effort, United's board decided in favor of the 880 on September 27, 1957, subject to a final going-over by United engineers.

Soon thereafter, United's President William Patterson called G.D.'s Executive Vice President Earl Johnson . . . out of a board meeting to tell him Convair was "in." But perhaps the most consequential call was one Pratt & Whitney's Chairman H. Mansfield "Jack" Horner then made on Patterson himself. Spurred on by Boeing, Horner had been galvanized into action, and now he wanted to know whether something couldn't be done about getting Boeing back into the competition, if Pratt & Whitney could come up with a lighter engine. Patterson referred him to United's engineers, who made very encouraging noises. They themselves had been pushing Pratt & Whitney for just that. Both Boeing and Pratt & Whitney then went into a crash program the former to scale down the 707, the latter to develop a lighter engine than the JT3C-6.

On or about October 10, 1957, Convair's Sales Vice President Jack Zevely and United's Financial Vice President Curtis Barkes had happily worked out eighteen articles of a nineteen-article contract and in fifteen minutes more would have finished the nineteenth, merely a statement of where the notices were to be sent, when a call came through for Barkes. As Zevely recalled this fall: "He came back, shaken, and said, 'Sorry, Boeing's back in the competition.' "

It was indeed. Pratt & Whitney engineers had managed to get 750 pounds out of the JT3C-6 engine . . . Boeing engineers had shortened the fuselage of the 707, reduced the weight of such heavy items as the landing gear, and improved its cost per mile. Within a few weeks Boeing had come up with a new medium-range aircraft—the 720—45,000 pounds lighter than the 707. United then invited Boeing and Convair to cut their prices and both did. . . . In November, United's chief engineer John Herlihy compared Convair's 880 and Boeing's 720 and then strongly recommended the latter. . . . [T]he 720 with its lower operating costs per

---

[72] Part II, FORTUNE, February 1962, at 120, 121-22.

passenger-mile was a better buy than the 880 with a $200,000 cheaper price tag. On November 28, 1957, United's board approved purchase of eleven Boeing 720's, with options for eighteen more.

—Interview with the Vice President in Charge of Merchandising of a firm in the textile industry:

> Things can be worked out informally, you decide to close and do, and then something comes up and you change your mind. You look for something that has been omitted, argue that things really hadn't been closed but there was another point remaining for negotiation, and then you back out. You just simply refuse to go through with things. It is more just to end things at this point, if you change your mind, than to string the other guy along or to maneuver in your performance of the contract to minimize what he gets out of it. At times it is better to break off. It is nice to find a subject of negotiation which has not been completed to save a little face when you do this. Of course, it is not absolutely necessary.

1. FORMATION DOCTRINE AND CORPORATE TAKEOVERS: A CAUTIONARY TALE

Questions of offer and acceptance delight law professors and first year contracts students. However, they seldom come to the attention of most people. The legal battle between Texaco and Pennzoil was a dramatic exception. A Texas jury awarded Pennzoil a judgment of $10.53 billion on November 19, 1985. At that time, Texaco's net worth was $13.5 billion. The *Wall Street Journal* called the verdict the "Texas Common Law Massacre."[73]

In 1988, Texaco paid Pennzoil about $3 billion to settle the dispute. We will look at an analysis of the case by Professor Richard Epstein of the University of Chicago Law School. First, however, we will tell you about an earlier case which might influence your views about the *Pennzoil v. Texaco* litigation.

In *Itek Corp. v. Chicago Aerial Industries, Inc.*,[74] Itek sued Chicago Aerial Industries (CAI) for breach of contract. The trial court granted summary judgment for CAI. Itek appealed, and the Supreme Court of Delaware reversed the decision. Itek wanted to acquire CAI. It offered to purchase all of CAI's assets under a pricing formula which would have given CAI's shareholders about $13 per share. On January 4, 1965, CAI's board agreed, subject to four conditions: (1) Itek was to obtain the necessary financing; (2) An informal letter of intent was to be executed; (3) The details were to be worked out, and (4) Formal documents would be prepared to the satisfaction of the parties.

The parties signed a letter of intent which specified how the purchase price was to be computed. It stated "Itek and CAI shall make every reasonable effort to agree upon and have prepared as quickly as possible a contract providing for the foregoing purchase by Itek and sale by CAI. . . . If the parties fail to agree upon

---

[73] WALL STREET JOURNAL, Dec. 12, 1985, at 32, cols. 1-2.
[74] 248 A.2d 625 (Del. 1968).

and execute such a contract they shall be under no further obligation to one another." [75]

Early in February of 1965, a representative of CAI's shareholders negotiated with Bourns, Inc. It offered to purchase CAI for $16 a share. CAI and Itek agreed on three new conditions at a meeting on February 23. Upon the departure of Itek's representatives, the CAI committee met with Bourns' representative. They told him that the CAI-Itek negotiations had reached an impasse and they were free to go ahead with Bourns. On March 2, CAI notified Itek that it was terminating the transaction as the result of unforeseen circumstances. Bourns, Inc. then acquired CAI.

The Supreme Court of Delaware said that whether an enforceable contract is created by conduct or, on the other hand, must await the signing of a formal agreement depends upon the intention of the parties. There was evidence which, if accepted by the trier of fact, would support a verdict for Itek. The trier of fact could find that both Itek and CAI intended to be bound. Also there was evidence that CAI willfully had failed to negotiate in good faith and to make "every reasonable effort" to agree upon a formal contract as the letter of intent required CAI to do.

The following article by Professor Epstein of the University of Chicago Law School sets forth his version and view of *Pennzoil v. Texaco*. As always, you should read critically. For example, does Professor Epstein ignore or undervalue the benefits of trust within the community of large corporations and financial institutions?

The Pirates of Pennzoil
A Comic Opera Made Possible by a Grant
from the Texaco Corporation
Richard A. Epstein[76]

"You can trust your car to the man who wears the star" was Texaco's slogan for many years. Now the question of trust has come back to haunt the giant oil company, to the tune of ten and a half billion dollars—the size of a judgment that, while not approaching the federal deficit, is nearly enough to wipe out Texaco's net worth.

Even in an era jaded by sky-high legal judgments, Texaco's ill-fated encounter with Pennzoil Corporation in a Texas courtroom has caught the fancy of the public at large and has raised the fears of the financial community. The day the judgment came out, Texaco's stock lost more than $714 million in value. All told, those shareholder losses have now exceeded $2.8 billion since December 10, 1984, when Judge Solomon Casseb decided not to disturb the jury verdict of $7.53 billion in actual damages and $3 billion dollars in punitive damages. (Pennzoil's stock, for its part, surged $7.375 to $57.25 per share on the day of the judgment, a gain to shareholders of $300 million.)

---

[75] *Id.* at 627.
[76] 32 THE [UNIVERSITY OF CHICAGO] LAW SCHOOL RECORD 3 (Fall 1986).

The consequences continue to mount. Texaco's lenders have become nervous, and the firm's previously impregnable credit rating has been slashed for both long- and short-term borrowing. Suppliers, customers, and joint venturers are wondering whether Texaco will be forced into bankruptcy, and where its business dealings stand in the meantime. Texaco has obtained temporary relief from its Texas bond requirement in (of all places) the federal district court at White Plains, New York, on grounds that legal experts find mysterious. Secret and inconclusive settlement talks drag on, while public comments by the parties are alternatively cryptic, confusing, or corrosive. The size of the stakes and the uncertainty of the legal issues have left both sides with ample, indeed too much, room for maneuvering.

As is common knowledge by now, Pennzoil's suit against Texaco arose out of the battle between the two firms over the takeover of the Getty Corporation. Getty Corporation had two dominant stockholders. The Sarah Getty Trust, controlled by Gordon P. Getty, its sole trustee, owned 40.2 percent of the total 79.1 million shares of Getty stock outstanding. The J. Paul Getty Museum controlled another 10.8 percent of the company. The remaining 49 percent was in widely separate hands, ostensibly represented by the Getty management.

When it became clear that Gordon Getty and management did not see eye to eye on a wide variety of business issues, the stage was set for a possible takeover. Enter J. Hugh Liedtke, chief executive officer of Pennzoil. Liedtke saw in the demoralization at Getty Oil an opportunity for Pennzoil to become a major player in the oil industry by gaining control of Getty Oil's extensive reserves.

The two companies reached a deal, the gist of which was that Pennzoil and the Getty Trust were to establish a new corporate vehicle to purchase the Getty shares from the museum and the public at large for a price set at $110 per share, plus $5 in deferred compensation. Pennzoil would wind up with about a 43 percent stake, and the Trust with a 57 percent stake. In essence Pennzoil and the Getty Trust engineered a squeeze play meant to displace present management while providing a handsome profit for the museum and the public shareholders.

Champagne glasses tinkled in celebration, press releases were duly issued, and on January 4, 1984, the deal was reported in the newspapers. Much detailed drafting of complex corporate documents remained to be done. But that was never to come to pass. Within hours of the original announcement Texaco stepped in with an offer to purchase all shares of Getty at $125 per share (later raised to $128), for a total price of just over $10 billion. That offer was accepted with great alacrity by Gordon Getty and the museum on January 5, but only after Texaco agreed to indemnify the Getty interests for any liability they might have had to Pennzoil.

Five days later, on January 10, 1984, Pennzoil sued to block the merger in Delaware court. Its claim was that Texaco's actions had interfered with its own previous contract. The Delaware court refused to enjoin Texaco from the merger (which, as we shall see, should be a matter of great sorrow to Texaco). Pennzoil then shifted the battle to its home turf in Houston, Texas, suing Texaco for the common law tort of inducement of breach of contract. The rest is history.

At one level the ensuing Pennzoil/Texaco litigation seems like just another skirmish in the corporate takeover wars. But the playing field here is rather different. Most merger battles take place in the corporate law—the land of two-tier offers, leveraged buyouts, greenmail, and poison pills. But *Pennzoil v. Texaco* marks the revenge of the common law. Contracts and torts no longer form an inert backdrop to creative corporate maneuvers. With this case they move to center stage.

The core of the dispute is a body of nineteenth-century law that passes under the technical name of intentional (or malicious) inducement of breach of contract. This branch of law envisions a game in which a minimum of three must play. As the law is generally formulated, a defendant will have engaged in wrongful conduct when the following conditions are met. First, there must be a contract between two other parties (as between Getty shareholders and Pennzoil). Second, there must be efforts by the defendant (Texaco) to induce one party under the contract (the Getty shareholders) to break the contract. Third, the inducer must have notice of the existence of the contract between the other two parties. Fourth, the jilted party must suffer damages that follow from the commission of the wrong.

The origins and the rationale of this tort are found in the seminal case of *Lumley v. Gye*, decided by the English courts in 1854. Benjamin Lumley was an opera impresario who held a long-term contract with Johanna Wagner, a singer of evident operatic skills. Frederick Gye, the operator of a rival establishment, prevailed on her to desert her original employment. The contract between Lumley and Wagner was unquestionably binding, and it contained an express provision whereby the diva agreed that she would not sing for another company. Wagner was successfully enjoined from singing for Gye, but she refused to return to her original employment with Lumley. Lumley then brought a second suit against Gye asking for damages because of the deliberate interference with his contract with Wagner.

Lumley's novel suit occasioned a good deal of difficulty in the English courts, for inducement of breach of contract differs in a number of ways from the ordinary torts to person or property. Most torts are actionable on principles either of ordinary negligence or of strict liability—the latter of which means that the defendant can be liable whether or not he acted with negligence or with an intent to harm the plaintiff. The British court was evidently reluctant to say that any defendant can be held liable (even on a theory of negligence) for inducing the breach of contract of which he had never heard. Yet ignorance of the harm caused is not normally a reason to withhold liability in a tort case. The defendant who chops down the plaintiff's trees, reasonably and honestly thinking them his own, normally must pay the owner for the loss. The majority of judges did not give a convincing theoretical explanation why this tort should be different from cutting trees. A powerful dissent by Judge Coleridge made just this point and argued that Lumley's sole remedy should be a damage action against Wagner.

Recently modern writers have echoed Coleridge's concern on economic grounds. The now fashionable theories of "efficient breach" say that inducing a breach of contract is a good thing, so long as it moves the labor or property of the contract breaker to a higher-valued use. The proper response, therefore, the argument continues, is for the breaker to pay "expectation damages," that is, damages that leave the party jilted in the same position that he would have been in if the contract had been fully performed. Those damages being paid, the contract breacher and the inducer can then split the efficiency gain between them. Any rule that allows the innocent party to block the second contract (as happened with Lumley's injunction against Wagner) is said to thwart the reallocation of resources to their best social use.

The case against the tort of inducement of breach of contract thus rests on two propositions: the want of parity with ordinary torts to property, and the theory of efficient breach. Yet neither point carries the day. As to the first, the law contains many areas where liability turns not on negligence or simple wrongful conduct, but on notice. . . .

There is, in fact, no real reason to worry that the use of tort liability to enforce contracts will impede useful social exchanges. If someone wants "out" of a contract, he can negotiate his release. In fact, a framework for such negotiations can be made part of the original deal. Such contracts are not farfetched: it had been reported, for example, that Lou Holtz's coaching contract with the University of Minnesota allowed him to terminate without breach in the event of an offer from Notre Dame, which did come. In short, good contract drafting and sensible renegotiation form a far more "efficient" system than the deliberate breach of contract. No innocent party should be limited to an uncertain contract action solely against the original contracting party, who may be insolvent or beyond the jurisdiction of the court, when there is another party available that knowingly induced and profited from the breach.

This quick sketch of the law of inducement of breach of contract suggests that there is nothing in principle wrong with the basic legal theory on which Pennzoil relied. Nonetheless, there is many a slip between a sound legal theory and its proper application. The normal lay response to the $10.5 billion verdict has been to call it "ridiculous" or "absurd." A *New York Times* editorial called the case a "sad farce." In both cases the size of the damage award attracted far more attention than the fact of liability itself. There is good sense in this popular perception.

To understand what is going on it is necessary to comment on four separate issues: first, was there a deliberate inducement of breach of contract? Second, what remedy is appropriate, damages or injunction? Third, if damages, how should they be calculated? Fourth, should punitive damages be awarded, and in what amount?

Liability. Pennzoil's case for liability rests on its ability to show that the Getty interests breached a valid contract with it. The critical question therefore becomes the traditional one of deciding whether the contract is valid. Normally this sort of decision is straightforward legal business. But the elusive line between preliminary negotiations and a completed and binding contract has generated extensive litigation. The problem has proved to be intractable enough in real estate transactions, for example, that there is widespread support for the requirement, everywhere embodied in the Statute of Frauds, that contracts for the sale of land or buildings (aside from short-term leases) are binding only if evidenced in writing and signed "by the party to be charged." In an area where deals often take surprising twists, where critical conditions can be added or subtracted from an agreement at a moment's notice, this requirement of written contracts provides a nice "bright line" test that obviates many (though by no means all) acrimonious disputes over contract formation that otherwise might arise.

Strange as it might seem, there is no parallel writing requirement for the sale of common stock.[77] The enforcement of oral contracts is strictly necessary for the ordinary telephone brokerage business, but matters are quite different when the sale of corporate assets amounts to the sale of a billion-dollar business, many of whose assets are in real estate—as oil and gas assets are generally classified. The want of the legal writing requirement for merger cases gave rise to the murkiness of contract formation that led to Texaco's undoing.

Texaco argued that Pennzoil and the Getty interests showed no clear intention to create legal relations. It might be that the custom in the mergers and acquisition business is such that, as Yogi Berra says, "It ain't over 'till it's over"—in which case signing on the dotted line would be the only step that matters. But there is always the lurking exception. Could that custom (if it is a custom) be displaced by a joint handshake, smile, and toast? Or are these lesser formalities only evidence of substantial progress on the long road to contractual union?

Texaco might have fared better if it had downplayed the question of intention and argued instead that even if the parties had a clear intention to create a legally enforceable agreement, they had in fact not done so. Normally contracts are enforceable only when their terms are sufficiently definite. Here the basic transaction was a complex reverse triangular merger necessarily containing countless terms that were nowhere captured by a champagne toast or a handshake. If squads of lawyers still had hours of paperwork in front of them, many hidden issues were sure to surface. If some of these proved insurmountable, then the deal would be off, without either side's being in breach. There are many cases on the books where courts have been exceedingly strict—often too strict—in requiring that a contract be definite before declaring it valid. Texaco surely had a shot on these grounds—and on an issue that is normally decided by judge rather than jury. It is hard for an outsider to the case to be confident about either the question of intention or the question of definiteness. But it would surely not be remarkable for the jury to have erred on this point.

The harder question is whether there would still be a case against Texaco for inducement of breach if Pennzoil's preliminary agreement were unenforceable against the key Getty shareholders. Here the basic case law is divided, with some courts holding that the third party will not be liable unless a second party is too, and a majority holding the contrary. There is a good deal to be said for the position that the tort vanishes if the contract is not enforceable. If a buyer can walk away from an unwritten real estate sale because he entertains general prospects of a better deal, why worry if one such concrete prospect makes a flesh-and-blood appearance and induces him to back out? When agreements are fully binding and

---

[77] Eds. note: UCC § 8-319 does set out a Statute of Frauds requirement for contracts for the sale of securities. In this case, an unsigned agreement plus the official record of the Board of Directors probably met the requirement.

enforceable, it generally does not make a difference whether the inducer approaches the contracting party or the contracting party approaches the outsider. If Getty were free to walk, then Texaco should be free to induce Getty to walk with it without having to face any legal sanctions. To take the other side is to assume that both parties have made implied interim promises not to deal with third parties while still negotiating with each other, a plausible but unlikely state of affairs.

Nonetheless, the dominant doctrine holds otherwise. The authoritative Restatement (Second) of Torts notes that "by reason of the statute of frauds, formal defects, lack of mutuality, infancy, unconscionable provisions, conditions precedent to the obligation or even uncertainty of particular terms the third person [here, key Getty shareholders] may be able to avoid liability for any breach. The defendant actor [here, Texaco] is not, however, for that reason free to interfere with performance of the contract before it is avoided." The Restatement does not, unfortunately, give any reasons for its broad conclusion. Instead it merely analogizes the situation to one in which there is a contract "at will," that is, one in which either party is entitled to terminate at any time for any reason. It notes that while the contracting party may terminate for no reason at all, a third party may not induce such a breach. If that is literally the law, then American business should tremble in its boots, for ordinary worker recruitment in which one firm seeks to lure away the at-will employees of a rival becomes presumptively illegal. Do executive headhunters engage in illegal behavior when they ply satisfied employees with tempting offers? It is imperative that the lines of liability be clear throughout this area, and the simplest and most logical rule is: if there was no contract enforceable between the original parties, then there should be no action for inducement of any asserted breach.

What the law should be, however, is perhaps less relevant that what the law is. Texaco is in deep trouble on liability if the unwise Restatement rule governs. On the other hand, it is far from out of the woods even if a binding contract is a prerequisite to breach.

Choice of Remedy. The issues become much less evenly balanced when we move to the remedial aspects of the case. Initially, the plaintiff in such a case is faced with the question of whether it wants to enjoin the breach (as did Lumley with Wagner) or to seek damages. In principle Pennzoil should have been granted a preliminary order requiring Texaco to keep the Getty operations separate from its own until the suit was resolved. If Pennzoil won the underlying suit, it could have gotten its Getty shares back directly, along with additional monetary damages (perhaps in the millions) to "clean up" any residual losses. The great advantage of such injunctive relief is that it reduces the need to make accurate assessments of monetary losses later on. So long as Pennzoil can get the shares, it will necessarily ride up and down with the value of the oil in place, just as it would have done if Texaco had never intervened.

What Damages? Pennzoil received a stroke of good fortune when its original request for an injunction was denied, because it was then free to claim damages. But how should they be calculated? Texaco was reticent about introducing evidence on this point, for fear that quibbles about damages would have been taken as tantamount to an admission of guilt. (In a sense it need not have worried, because the jury took the indemnity agreement between Texaco and the Getty interests as powerful evidence on that point.) So it staked its case on the question of liability where its position, though not without merit, was surely at its weakest.

Left a relatively clear field, Pennzoil grabbed for the brass ring and got it. It insisted that it had acquired its Getty interest largely for the sake of obtaining Getty's proven oil reserves. Now that Texaco's conduct had denied it those reserves, Pennzoil asked for actual damages equal to the cost of developing comparable reserves *by exploration*, less the cost of its Getty acquisition. The cost of such development was estimated at $10 billion, while the purchase price of its Getty shares was $2.5 billion, leaving a bottom line of $7.5 billion.

Breathtaking, but wrong. Arguably, the right figure for damages is zero. One critical fact is that the price of oil dropped after the original Pennzoil/Getty deal was struck. If the deal had gone through, therefore, Pennzoil would have come out of it a loser, for there would have been no way it could have unloaded the Getty reserves before the market broke. No one doubts that Pennzoil was no longer bound by the deal once Getty repudiated it. Why does Pennzoil need damages in addition to that welcome escape? It is therefore perfectly respectable to argue that Pennzoil should not receive any damages to augment its good fortune. If Pennzoil would have sustained a loss by acquiring the Getty shares, then why should it turn a profit when Texaco's wrong worked to its advantage?

The general rule of expectation damages is, however, more favorable to Pennzoil. On the critical question of timing, it measures the plaintiff's loss not by the subsequent movement in the marketplace, but solely by the anticipated profit on the day of the deal. Yet even on this conventional view the right question to ask is, how much more would Pennzoil have had to pay *to buy* comparable reserves from another oil company? To take an analogy, suppose company A refuses to make you a custom chair for $100, as it had promised. If you can get company B to make that chair for $125, then your damages are $25, even if it would cost you (clumsy you) $500 to make the chair yourself. Drilling for oil is the wrong measure because Pennzoil could have searched for oil reserves by searching for another seller.

Looked at the right way, then, the correct damages are a lot less than the $7.5 billion claimed. If the oil reserves were worth as much to Pennzoil as it claimed, then why did the Getty interests give them away for a song? Look at some rough calculations. If Texaco paid $10 billion for the entire business, then (assuming that all shares are worth the same regardless of who controls them) it would have paid about $4.3 billion for Pennzoil's 43 percent interest. Pennzoil had bid about $3.8 billion to acquire that same interest. The damages look to be at most on the order of $500 million, so long as we ignore the subsequent decline in the value of the Getty assets. It might be possible to eke out a slightly larger number, on the theory that Texaco got a bargain at the higher price it bid. If Texaco had overpaid, on the other hand, then a lower number would be in order. All in all it is instructive, though not conclusive, that in an industry of informed and active bidders, Pennzoil did not raise its original offer, while no third party was prepared to intervene at a higher price.

To accept Pennzoil's story, therefore, is to assume that first it and then Texaco had ripped off the Getty interests by an enormous sum. It is, however, very odd to assume massive ignorance and incompetence on one side of a competitive bidding situation involving such sophisticated players. The stock markets did not discern any enormous increase in the value of Texaco's assets when the merger went through. Neither should we.

A half billion dollars is a big number, and one that admits a lot of refinement, up or down. But Texaco could survive such a judgment. As matters now stand the jury verdict does not just give Pennzoil the equivalent of the 43 percent stake in Getty it planned to buy; it gives it a 100 percent stake in Getty and most of Texaco to boot. Does anyone really think that Pennzoil would rather have its original deal than this damage award? With awards like these, all contracting parties should pray continuously for breach by their opposite numbers.

So what will happen to the damage award on appeal? At this writing it is anyone's guess. Since the wrong formula has been used to calculate the damages, appellate courts should be able to set the matter right. But actual litigation is never as clear as legal theory. The moment that the trial judge loses control over the case, the odds shift in favor of the party with the verdict in hand. If the question of the measure of damages is (mistakenly) regarded as one of fact, then the presumption swings more strongly in favor of the jury once the case passes out of the hands of the trial judge to an appellate court. If the question is one of law, then on appeal it can be raised only if the point had first been argued at trial, which Texaco might not have done. Again a lot turns on the state of the record, but in close cases much could turn on the attitude of judges, which on these procedural issues varies enormously. Some judges take a hard line, and will not be swayed by the magnitude of the judgments. Yet even if the damage question is decided on its merits, nothing says that Pennzoil's audacity will not win out on appeal as it did with Judge Casseb at trial.

Punitive Damages. Punitive damages amounted to $3 billion. Why? Normally, punitive damages are awarded to punish and deter deliberate and outrageous forms of conduct. The exact formulation of the rule has been the subject of intense, if inconclusive, judicial debate. It is clear that simple negligence and even gross negligence is not enough to trigger such awards. Yet the consensus breaks down as to what kind of deliberate misconduct—that is, acts done with substantial knowledge of the consequences in question—is needed for punitive damages. Here the verbal niceties matter, because the issue of punitive damages is a natural in any action for inducement of breach of contract. Recall that sometimes the tort is called *maliciously* inducing a breach of contract. If the defendant has to act maliciously in order to commit the tort at all, it is tempting to conclude that punitive damages should be allowed routinely in these cases. Nonetheless, this case is a poor candidate for such an award.

First, malice in ordinary language connotes the ideas of personal spite and ill will. Here it connotes at most the knowledge of another contract, clearly a lesser wrong.

Second, the basic uneasiness on the issue of liability should count heavily against any award of punitive damages. If Texaco thought in good faith that it was acting within its rights—that there was no binding or no enforceable contract between Pennzoil and Getty—then wherein lies the terrible intent that would justify punitive damages?

Third, punitive damages seem here to be an unattractive way of reinforcing the underlying tort law. There is little chance that Texaco could escape detection, since its wrongful behavior consists of a public offer. Nor is there much reason to think that personal ill will and spite against Pennzoil motivated its takeover: on the contrary, it wanted the reserves to recoup from some serious drilling failures.

Finally, it seems odd to think that $3 billion in damages is needed to compensate for corporate pain and suffering. There is no reason whatsoever to compound the error in the contract damages by an excessive award of punitive damages. If actual damages should have been around $500 million, then the $3 billion in punitive damages is off by a factor of fifteen or twenty or more, even on the dubious assumption that these damages should be allowed at all.

With so many serious doubts attached to every aspect of the Pennzoil/Texaco litigation, how was it that Pennzoil was able to succeed before the jury? The secret of its success, I think, was that it imported to the world of corporate takeovers the trial techniques that have proved so successful in product liability litigation, where frail consumers are pitted against huge corporations. It is no accident that Pennzoil's chief counsel was Joseph Jamail, who has won many large product liability cases. His key appeal was made on moral grounds, where he presented the issue in stark terms of black and white. The central point pounded into the jury's head was that Texaco had acted not only improperly but immorally by placing greed and self-interest above the ordinary scruples of commercial dealing. Jamail's theme was captured in the single most expensive sentence in tort history: "Send corporate America a message." And since big damage awards are the only message that corporate America understands, why worry about precise financial calculations? The larger the number, the more unmistakable the message. The strategy worked.

In one sense, this case amounts to little more than a freak incident. One can guess that all future takeover and merger negotiations will be conducted under a clear legal understanding that no contract for acquisition is final until it is signed on the dotted line. The decision might be regarded as unimportant in another sense, too: the assets in question have not been extinguished, even if they have shifted from one set of shareholders to another. Yet the short-term losses from dislocation are substantial, for acquisition by litigation does not have the same consequences as acquisition by purchase.

It is sobering that the increase in the value of Pennzoil stock in the month after the verdict came down was smaller than the decline in value of Texaco stock. As of early January, 1985, for example, the Texaco stock had lost well over $2 billion in value, while the Pennzoil stock had gained only between $800 and $900 million in value. (Days later Pennzoil stock spiked by 19 points while Texaco remained unchanged, so there has been a lot of movement in the market.) Many other factors may have worked to influence the market value of the two firms, but even after these are taken into account, the loss in the *combined* value of the two firms is one rough measure of the social losses that arise when a large corporation is forced to litigate for survival. The legal uncertainty works to depress the value of the Texaco stock below the most accurate estimate of the gain. Uncertainty therefore magnifies losses and reduces gains.

The uncertainty will also affect the behavior of third parties. Texaco will lose business opportunities because others fear dealing with it, while Pennzoil will not gain comparable opportunities until the dust settles. If bankruptcy were costless and without harmful effects on the business opportunities of third parties, the social concern would be negligible. But as frictions dominate social life, the possible extinction of a major corporation, like the sinking of an ocean liner, can easily bring others down in its wake. What is disturbing here is that no one can point to any substantial social gains from this suit that might make the substantial losses worth bearing. We should all hope for a quick resolution—any resolution—that reduces the struggle to more manageable terms. A quick appellate decision that eliminates punitive damages, and reduces actual damages to around $500 million, is not a bad place to start.

NOTES AND QUESTIONS

1.   *Distinctions*: Are there important distinctions between the situation in the *Itek* case and the transaction between Getty, Pennzoil, and Texaco? Pennzoil originally sued in Delaware for an injunction. In denying its demand, the Delaware judge said, "I am convinced that Pennzoil has demonstrated a likelihood that it will be able to establish . . . that a contract came into being." He noted "a binding contract can be formed despite material open issues."

Contrast the negotiations for commercial jet aircraft between United Airlines, the Convair Division of General Dynamics Corporation and the Boeing Corporation, noted previously. Did this situation differ from the *Itek* and the *Pennzoil v. Texaco* cases? Should contracts be easy, or hard, to make in these situations?

2.   *Letters of intent*: Business people, particularly in international trade, often deal on the basis of letters of intent. Ralph Lake says:

> In general, letters of intent can be classified into four types: letters designed to provide information; framework agreements intended to govern only the negotiation process; memorializations of partial agreements during a negotiation process; and documents erroneously entitled letters of intent that are, in actuality, legally enforceable contracts.[78]

Why write a letter of intent? Lake, who is the Europe and Middle East Legal Counsel of Holiday Inns, Inc., says that modern business transactions are becoming increasingly complex. Contracts contain hundreds or thousands of pages.

> The negotiation of such contracts can be a lengthy process and often requires the resolution of numerous details. Participation of financial institutions, government agencies, subcontractors, consultants, and other pro-

---

[78] Lake, *Letters of Intent: A Comparative Examination Under English, U.S., French, and West German Law*, 18 Geo. Wash. J. Int'l L & Econ. 331, 331-32 (1984).

fessionals is essential. Therefore, precontractual agreements that have moral, if not legal effect, are useful in bringing order to the complexity.[79]

Also, letters of intent serve to exclude lawyers from the negotiation process until the final stages. Writers of letters of intent sometimes believe they will incur no obligations but obtaining a commitment from the other party. Lake tells us:

> [G]enerally, English law does not recognize precontractual liability. United States courts have the doctrine of promissory estoppel at their disposal and increasingly impose an obligation to negotiate in good faith. French law imposes liability in tort for actions prior to contractual execution. West German law uses the doctrine of *culpa in contrahendo* to impose precontractual liability.[80]

Marvin Leon[81] reports:

> Litigation over letters of intent fills libraries. In the *Federal Practice Digest* from January 1, 1994, to December 31, 1996, more than 75 reported appellate decisions deal with the attempted enforcement of letters of intent. From January 1, 1997, through December 31, 1999, 31 reported appellate cases appear. These disputes are only the reported ones litigated in the federal court system.

Letters of intent are often used in bringing together directors, actors, scripts and financing to make motion pictures. *See, e.g., Roth v. Garcia Marquez.*[82] A prominent entertainment lawyer offered a continuing legal education program about "the negotiation game." He said that sometimes a lawyer for an actor or producer will want enforceability but often such a lawyer will not. Sometimes the lawyer will want uncertainty about whether a contract has been formed. Sometimes the lawyer will want to be able to claim that the producer is bound in some situations, but in other situations involving the same negotiations and exchange of documents she wants to be able to claim that the actor is not. For example, if the client may have a real chance to go elsewhere for more money or a better part, the lawyer will keep matters as part of an agreement to agree. The entertainment lawyer said that some of the factors to consider are: (1) How committed is your client to making the picture? (2) How crazy is your client (that is, does he change his mind frequently and does he irritate people)? (3) Why would your client like to back out (the nature of the script, the person named as director, changes in the cast, other opportunities)? (4) Is the producer of the picture good for the money? (5) Why would the producer back out (better talent becomes available, money falls through, creative differences)? (6) How replaceable is your client? (7) What is the exposure if your client walks from a binding agreement? The lawyer listed fifteen steps between written evidence that clearly essential points are open to a fully signed written agreement. Those steps in the middle leave matters in more or less doubt.

---

[79] *Id.* at 332.
[80] *Op. cit.*
[81] *Lessening the Risk of Letters of Intent*, LOS ANGELES LAWYER, November 2001, at 20, 24.
[82] 942 F.2d 617 (9th Cir. 1991).

3. *Intent to close a deal and bad faith negotiations*: As Professor Epstein indicates, the transaction between Getty and Pennzoil was complicated. Gordon Getty was trustee of a family trust created by his father, J. Paul Getty. The J. Paul Getty Museum in Malibu, California was the second largest shareholder. Gordon Getty was unhappy with the management of Getty Oil Co. Harold Williams, the head of the museum, wanted to diversify his portfolio, and may have needed to cash out his position in Getty stock to do so. Gordon Getty saw a way to get rid of the Getty Oil Co. management when Pennzoil Chairman J. Hugh Liedtke wanted to buy control of Getty Oil to gain its oil reserves. The takeover would also have served the museum's interests. Getty and Williams signed a "memorandum of agreement" with Pennzoil, but it was contingent on approval by the Getty board of directors. It is a four-page document apparently drafted by one or more lawyers.[83]

The board met on January 2, 1984. Martin Lipton, "one of the acknowledged master tacticians of the corporate takeover bar,"[84] represented the museum and attended the meeting as a board member, and Arthur Liman represented Pennzoil but waited outside the meeting room for a decision. Mr. Lipton came out of the meeting and asked that the deal be sweetened. Mr. Liman said that he didn't want to go back to Pennzoil's president for more money, but if the Getty board would approve a "firm deal" at the higher price, Mr. Liman would sell the deal to Pennzoil's president. Mr. Lipton wrote a note which was introduced into evidence in the case. It said "[b]elieve if we go back *firm* at $5 instead of $3, will accept." Mr. Lipton went back into the meeting and later came out and said, "Congratulations. The board has voted 15 to 1 to accept the proposal . . . provided that your minimum guarantee goes from $3 to $5." Pennzoil's president approved, and Mr. Liman went into the room in which the directors had been meeting. He shook everyone's hand.

The WALL STREET JOURNAL reports,[85] "[s]tanding in a sumptuous suite in New York's Pierre hotel, Mr. Liedtke, chairman of Pennzoil Co., shook hands and hoisted a glass of champagne with Gordon P. Getty, toasting an apparent decision by Getty Oil Co.'s board under which Pennzoil would assume management control of Getty Oil." Getty Oil Co. then issued a news release stating that it had reached an agreement in principle with Pennzoil on the buyout. The release stated that it was "subject to the execution of a definitive merger agreement, approval by the stockholders of Getty Oil and completion of various governmental filing and waiting period requirements." Mr. Liedtke testified that he thought this meant that the parties had a duty in good faith to negotiate the "technical details." The WALL STREET JOURNAL continued, "[i]n Los Angeles, an attorney for Mr. Getty in another case stood up in a courtroom and called the transactions . . . 'an agreement which has been entered into after extremely careful consideration.' "

At trial, Mr. Liedtke was cross-examined for five days. Texaco's lawyer pointed out each discrepancy between the language of the press release and the

---

[83] *The "Memorandum of Agreement" is reproduced in Baron and Baron, The Pennzoil-Texaco Dispute: An Independent Analysis*, 38 Baylor L. Rev. 253, 282-85 (1986).

[84] NATIONAL LAW JOURNAL, Sept. 30, 1985, at 42, col. 1.

[85] WALL STREET JOURNAL, June 13, 1985, at 6, cols 1-6.

memorandum of agreement signed by the museum, Gordon Getty, and Mr. Liedtke. Texaco Board Chairman John McKinley was called as hostile witness by Pennzoil. He acknowledged that he believed that executives and directors could make binding deals before lawyers were called in to work out the drafting wrinkles.[86]

While Pennzoil and Getty lawyers were working on the written contract, Texaco officials met with representatives of Getty Oil and Gordon Getty. The Getty lawyers slowed down their work. Getty's lawyers kept the Pennzoil legal team waiting an entire afternoon. A deposition from an associate in the firm representing Getty, who was in charge of drafting the written contract, said that Martin Lipton had told her to stay away from the drafting sessions.

Gordon Getty agreed to go along with Texaco's deal to avoid being left as a minority shareholder with no power. Mr. Lipton insisted that Texaco indemnify the museum against any Pennzoil breach of contract suit, limited the museum's warranty that it owned its shares to exclude claims by Pennzoil and guaranteed the museum a price of $112.50 per share—Pennzoil's price—if the Texaco deal ultimately fell through. Texaco also agreed to indemnify Gordon Getty against Pennzoil's claims.

The jury was asked whether "at the end of the Getty Oil board meeting of January 3, 1984, Pennzoil and each of the Getty entities . . . intended to bind themselves to an agreement." The jury found they did. The trial court refused Texaco's request to ask the jury whether the parties intended to bind themselves to a contract before a merger agreement was executed.

4.   *The reactions of the jurors*: The jury foreman said, "We won't tolerate this sort of thing in corporate America. . . . We learned quite a bit about the oil business and we were surprised at the loose ethics. . . . The message we wanted to send was that we didn't want to see anyone else do the things that were happening in this case."

Did the jury create a duty to negotiate in good faith? Without ever reading Kessler and Fine, *Culpa in Contrahendo*, *supra*, did they apply the ideas in that article?

The NEW YORK TIMES[87] reported:

> James J. Shannon, Jr., a 34-year-old juror who works as a public information writer for the city of Houston, said in an interview that the jury regarded the issuance of the press releases the following morning as strong evidence that Getty Oil's directors believed they had sold the company.

> "We asked ourselves, if what the board approved was not the memorandum of agreement [signed by Pennzoil, Gordon Getty, and Harold Williams], then how did all the terms of that memo get into the press release?" he recalled. He noted that Getty Oil's outside lawyer, Barton Wi-

---

[86] NATIONAL LAW JOURNAL, Sept. 30, 1985, at 42, 44, col. 2.
[87] Copyright © New York Times, Dec. 19, 1985, sec. II, at 5, col. 3.

nokur, and its chief in-house lawyer, Ralph D. Copley, had both approved the press release.

"All this talk about handshakes and oral agreements does not square with what we saw and heard in the courtroom," the jury's Mr. Shannon said. "I'm not sure what handshake they are talking about, but there was a signed memorandum of agreement—signed by Pennzoil, by Gordon Getty, and by Harold Williams."

Does this suggest that the jury may have decided a case different from the one assumed by Professor Epstein and most who have commented on *Pennzoil v. Texaco*? While the Getty Board and Pennzoil may not have closed a deal, did Pennzoil, Gordon Getty, and the J. Paul Getty Museum have a contract? If they did, then it would have been a tort for Texaco to have knowingly interfered with it. Would it matter that the Pennzoil, Trust, and Museum contract was contingent on approval of the Getty Oil Company Board of Directors? Is there a difference between an agreement to agree and a contract subject to a condition which must take place before a duty to perform arises?

5.   *Extra-legal factors*: Those who have written about the trial, including juror James Shannon, all seem to report that some of the New York financial operatives alienated the jury. They were described as pompous, and unwilling to look the jurors in the eye. At one point Marty Lipton, the museum's lawyer, suggested on cross-examination that there were different rules for $10 billion deals, and contracts between "us ordinary people." Juror Shannon seemed to find this idea astonishing and offensive. Skilled trial lawyer, and archetypal Texan, Pennzoil's counsel Joe Jamail did all he could to paint the New York financiers and their lawyers as alien, ruthless, and dishonorable. He urged the jury to "send a message" to Wall Street that honor and square dealing were expected of them as well as of common working people.

6.   *New York law*: Whatever we might say about the functions of signing a formal agreement generally, Pennzoil and Texaco agree that the law of New York is applicable to the transaction. Baron and Baron[88] point out that the United States Court of Appeals for the Second Circuit reviewed New York law on the formal agreement point in 1984. They say:

Reviewing the claims of the plaintiff in *Horn & Hardart*[89] in order to glean the intention of the parties, the court looked to several important factors: (1) the explicit statements made by the parties; (2) whether or not one or both parties had performed some part of the consideration underlying the contract; (3) whether or not there was literally nothing left to negotiate or settle so that all that remained was to sign a document having been otherwise completely finalized; and (4) whether or not the agreement concerned complex and substantial business matters requiring that it be reduced to a writing.[90]

---

[88] *The Pennzoil-Texaco Dispute: An Independent Analysis*, 38 Baylor L. Rev. 253 (1986).

[89] R.G. Group, Inc. v. Horn & Hardart Co., 751 F.2d 69 (2d Cir. 1984).

[90] 38 Baylor L Rev. at 272.

Applying these tests, Baron and Baron conclude that the Texas trial court did not properly apply New York law in the *Pennzoil v. Texaco* case.

The *Horn & Hardart* case which sets out the United States Court of Appeals' view of New York law involved an alleged oral agreement by a franchisor to award a franchise to a partnership. The franchise document itself stated it was the total agreement between the parties and could be modified only in writing. Plaintiff's own internal memorandum stated "[t]he exact geographic limits of the market area are subject to final agreement . . . and will be set forth in the Development Franchise Agreement to be executed by the General Partner on behalf of the Partnership."[91] Gillman, a representative of the partnership, talked with Schupak, a lawyer for the franchisor. They reached agreement on all disputed points except the territorial boundaries. Gillman asked Schupak, "Do we have a handshake deal?" Schupak answered, "Yes, we have a handshake deal today and right now."[92] No writing was ever signed. The court found that no contract was formed since this was not done. It stressed the language in the standard franchise form which was the basis for all the negotiations. It pointed to the partnership's understanding as indicated in its internal memorandum. It found that the lawyer's handshake agreement comment came when a material item was still unresolved. Furthermore, "it occurred at the end of months of bargaining where there were repeated references to the need for a written and signed document, and where neither party had ever, as far as the record before us shows, even discussed dropping the writing requirement."[93] Finally, with eighty million dollars at stake, "a requirement that the agreement be in writing and signed simply cannot be a surprise to anyone."[94]

7. *Damages*: The jury awarded a very large sum as damages. Many have commented about Texaco's trial strategy. Pennzoil used expert witnesses to testify about the high cost of finding new oil reserves. Pennzoil's damages theory was that in order to preserve its bargain, it was entitled to be put in the same position as if it had drilled wells and discovered such reserves. There were a number of ways in which the Pennzoil experts could have been challenged but Texaco's lawyer Richard Miller largely ignored the Pennzoil damages claim. In doing so he relied on a belief common among many trial lawyers that putting on witnesses to deny Pennzoil's damages' claim would substantially weaken the "no liability at all" theory. The argument is that though law students and lawyers are very comfortable with the argument in the alternative—"I don't owe you anything, and even if I do I don't owe you very much,"—such an argument confuses the jury and causes them to find for plaintiff on the liability issue.

8. *Reactions to the case*: Louis Harris & Associates, Inc. surveyed 600 senior business executives for BUSINESS WEEK.[95] Slightly more than a third of the executives thought that Texaco was "more right" in the case, slightly fewer favored Pennzoil, and about a fourth were unsure. The executives were also about

---

[91] *Id.* at 72.

[92] *Id.* at 73.

[93] *Id.* at 76.

[94] *Id.* at 77.

[95] Copyright © Business Week, December 30, 1985, at 51.

equally divided on the question of whether Texaco and Getty had behaved unethically. Nearly two thirds felt that Texaco's shareholders had been ill-served by the actions of Texaco management.

9. *The tactical significance of procedure*: Under Texas law, Texaco was required to post a bond to guarantee payment of the $11.1 billion judgment if it wanted to appeal the decision of the trial court. Texaco applied to a United States district court in New York to enjoin the application of the requirement. The court found that the requirement denied due process to Texaco, and its judgment was affirmed.[96] The Supreme Court of the United States decided to review the case. Both sides hired famous law professors to debate the propriety of a federal court overturning a state's procedures for appeals on questions of the application of state law. The Supreme Court reversed the two lower federal courts.[97]

The trip through the federal courts provided delay which affected the negotiating position of the parties. The NEW YORK TIMES MAGAZINE published a lengthy article praising David Boies, Texaco's lawyer who had sought the injunction and defended it before the Second Circuit.[98] It says, "[e]ven if Pennzoil appeals the ruling to the United States Supreme Court, that appeal, should the justices agree to hear arguments, probably wouldn't be heard for at least a year, in Boies's estimation. Meanwhile, Texaco has bought precious time for itself—time enough, probably, to work out a settlement. 'I think Liedtke will negotiate now,' Boies predicts, referring to Pennzoil's chairman, J. Hugh Liedtke."

Law professors defend traditional legal education by saying that it teaches students to "think like lawyers." Usually, however, it attempts to teach them to think as law professors do. Notice that David Boies thinks as a lawyer. His immediate goal was not a victory on the merits. Rather he sought to affect settlement negotiations. Later, he attacked the judgment on a variety of grounds before the Texas appellate courts. Pennzoil's lawyers had to defend the award successfully on each claim of error. Pennzoil had to invest in extraordinarily large attorneys' fees and risk losing the award it had won at trial. However, the case proved to be difficult to settle.

Lynn M. Lopucki and Walter O. Weyrauch, *A Theory of Legal Strategy*,[99] discuss the lawyers' strategic moves in the *Texaco v. Pennzoil* litigation at length. They argue that the merits of a case are only one of many factors that lead to the final result. "The legal strategist manipulates those . . . [factors] in a game of skill, expanding and developing the array of decisions, issues, and problems in a manner calculated to confuse and ultimately overwhelm the opponent. Even if the "merits" should ever reach a decisionmaker, it will be a decisionmaker identified by the game, and the "merits" will reach that decisionmaker in a form determined by the game." In the Texaco case, the outcome "was highly serendipitous, and . . . each side had more than one opportunity to win by taking the right action at the right time." They continue: "The challenge to the lawyers in *Texaco*

---

[96] Texaco, Inc. v. Pennzoil Co., 784 F.2d 1133 (2d Cir. 1986).

[97] Pennzoil Co. v. Texaco, Inc., 481 U.S. 1, 95 L. Ed. 2d 1, 107 S. Ct. 1519 (1987).

[98] Reich, *The Litigator: David Boies, The Wall Street Lawyer Everyone Wants*, NEW YORK TIMES MAGAZINE, June 1, 1986, at 19.

[99] 49 Duke L. J. 1405 (2000).

was to determine how best to respond in a context in which the rules were highly ambiguous and the conditions not entirely knowable."

10. *Interference with advantageous relations:* Professor Epstein offers one view about whether the tort should be limited to persuading a party to a legally enforceable contract to breach it. He is very skeptical about extending legal protection to ongoing continuing relations that are not legally enforceable. He comes close to saying that people always should be seeking the best deal because this will send goods and services to their best use as measured by who will pay the most for them. William J. Woodward, Jr.[100] challenges the view that contract law should set the boundaries of the tort. He points to the social benefits of greater relational stability. "Looking at the interference tort from the perspective of the wider community underscores the fact that very little contract analysis—and nearly no economic analysis—takes an expanded view of the winners, losers, and costs involved in forming and ending business relationships." Tort law may be needed to supplement the very limited nature of contract remedies. Finally,

> Setting aside contract doctrine as supplying the principles for deciding the range of tort liability for interference with relationships permits us more easily to attend to the policy issues that might be implicated in a given interference case. How important was the relationship both to the parties and to others? Were there justifications for the interference? If the defendant had a better offer to make, what justification was there in going to the promisor rather than to the promisee?

12. *The end of the story*: Boies also sought to have the Texas courts overturn the judgment and rule in Texaco's favor. However, he failed. The court of appeals affirmed most of the trial court's decision for Pennzoil in a 98-page opinion. However, it cut the jury's award by two billion dollars, leaving an award of $7.53 billion in compensatory damages and $1 billion in exemplary damages.[101] The Supreme Court of Texas denied certiorari, allowing the court of appeals decision to stand. Texaco vowed to take the case to the Supreme Court of the United States, but we cannot be sure that the Supreme Court would have agreed to hear the matter. Texaco would have to have found a substantial federal question to have prompted review by that court.

Texaco went into bankruptcy to cope with Pennzoil's judgment. In late 1987, Texaco and Pennzoil reached a settlement of the claim for approximately $3 billion.

13. *What does it all mean*? How should we judge the *Pennzoil v. Texaco* case? Joseph D. Jamail, Jr., Pennzoil's lawyer, presented the case to the jury as one involving the obligation to honor a promise. Texaco's defense was that despite all the handshakes, champagne, press releases and the like, the contract wasn't final until all the details were worked out and the documents signed. In essence, Texaco's position resembled that of Litton Industries in *Bethlehem Steel Corp. v. Litton Industries, Inc., supra*. Do you see any difference in the cases?

---

[100] *Contractarians, Community, and the Tort of Interference with Contract*, 80 Minn. L. Rev. 1103 (1996).

[101] Texaco, Inc. v. Pennzoil, Co., 729 S.W.2d 768 (Tex. App. 1987).

Pennzoil's expectations certainly were defeated. It is hard to imagine it suffered any material losses relying on its assumption that it had a deal to buy Getty Oil. Does its claim rest on something such as the Continental European doctrines of *culpa in contrahendo*, as described by Kessler and Fine, *supra*? Some have argued that a substantive theory which established a duty to bargain in good faith, with a remedy tailored to that theory, would be more likely to produce a just outcome in cases like that involving Pennzoil and Texaco than the traditional law of contracts or torts.

Furthermore, does the classic response to cases such as *Bethlehem Steel Corp. v. Litton Industries, Inc.* and *Pennzoil v. Texaco* rest on unrealistic assumptions about the process of contracting? Can we say that there is a magic moment when a contract is formed? Before this moment, everyone understands there is no liability. After it, everyone knows that a deal is closed. Or do expectations gradually build as the result of relationships so that there is no single moment when everyone recognizes that a contract is formed? Even if we accept that people other than lawyers build relationships gradually, is the magic moment idea a useful fiction? Should we have a rule defining when people lose the right to back out of a relationship without legal consequences? For example, consider the negotiations between the Convair Division of General Dynamics Corporation and United Airlines, described *supra*. United's President had called General Dynamics's Vice President out of a board meeting to tell him that Convair was "in." Nonetheless, before a written contract was signed, United backed out and staged a new competition between Boeing and Convair. Convair lost and Boeing got the $120-million sale. Should United have been able to do that without liability to Convair? Wasn't there a relationship between Convair and United? Didn't Convair have reasonable expectations as a result of United's conduct? Do these cases differ? If so, how?

2. BUSINESS DOCUMENTS AND COMMERCIAL PRACTICES

People can make contracts many ways, but those who repeatedly make agreements often follow patterns. Lawyers for larger firms attempt to structure these patterns so that they fit into the models favored by the legal system. Some business people, however, pay little attention to lawyers' advice. Usually, business agreements are carried out well enough so that commercial life goes on. Now and again, however, deals collapse. Businesspeople and their lawyers may then look in their files to determine their legal position—assuming enough is involved to make an inquiry, or a struggle, worthwhile. Sometimes business practices have offset all or most of what the lawyers who drafted the documents tried to achieve.

People can draft detailed blueprints of their transactions. While we may wish that parties would do this in all situations, human behavior is flexible and sloppy. Businesspeople write letters that cover some, but usually not all, of the terms of their deal. The provisions in my letter may not match those in your letter. We may not notice this or we may ignore it. Businesses may use printed form documents designed for routine transactions for complex and unusual bargains. Lawyers may attempt to create careful procedures which business people find cumbersome and ignore. We will review some of the forms frequently used and then turn to the legal problems created by business behavior and business forms.

Business forms: The documents for exchanges serve both business and legal functions. When these functions conflict we should not be surprised that the commercial function usually wins out. First, let's look at *documents used by sellers*. Price lists and catalogs usually give information to potential customers about standard items (often called "shelf goods"). A firm's sales department usually has a *proposal or quotation form*. Sellers use this form to state that they will supply some item at an indicated price. Proposals tend to be made for sales of specially made items or large orders of standard items. A proposal form serves as a checklist so that a seller will not fail to cover important matters by oversight and usually must be signed so that someone in the seller's organization will take responsibility for the transaction.

A sales department also may use an *acknowledgment of order form*. Buyers place orders after they have looked at a seller's price list or catalog, talked with a salesperson, or asked for a formal proposal. Most sellers routinely acknowledge these orders for a number of reasons. The form is to control the sale within the seller's organization. Some copies go to the seller's production or shipping department. Some go to the financial department so that the buyer will be billed. The *acknowledgment of order* copy goes to the customer. It serves to tell the buyer that the order was received and what the seller thinks should be shipped and how much it will charge.

A sales department also may use a sales representative's *order form*. Salespeople visit potential customers and talk with them. If they get an order, they fill in the blanks on this form. This serves as a checklist. The sales representative must determine such things as the necessary sizes, speeds, where the product will be shipped, and how the customer will pay for it.

Buyers, if their organizations are big enough, also have form documents. Purchasing departments may have a *request for quotation form* which is sent to sellers asking for bids. If sellers fill out the form, the buyer gains information needed to choose between competitors. Obviously, the functions of this form and sellers' forms overlap. Both buyer and seller may prefer their own forms. A buyer's form, for example, is likely to demand more precise specifications of delivery dates than will be given on a seller's form.

A company big enough to have a purchasing department is likely to have a printed *purchase order*. This form commits the company to buy and gives the transaction an internal control number. It tells the financial department that the company will be billed by the seller, and tells the buyer's receiving department to accept the shipment when it arrives. Some buyers send with their purchase orders their own *acknowledgment of order form*, asking sellers to sign and return it. Obviously, the functions of this form and sellers' acknowledgments overlap.

Selling and buying patterns: If any of several patterns of behavior are followed, there will be little question about when or whether the parties have agreed to sell and buy and what is to be supplied at what price. For example:

(A)   The engineers and purchasing agents of the buyer may negotiate with the seller's engineers and sales representatives for a machine made for the buyer's purposes—for example, the buyer wants a machine that automatically cleans, fills, and seals glass jars at a given rate per hour. Preliminary ideas are exchanged. Seller drafts a proposal, either in a letter or on a proposal form, which contains detailed specifications, prices for alternatives and a delivery date and two lines for signatures. Authorized representatives of both seller and buyer sign the form. While engineers, corporate officers, and even lawyers might have to interpret the terms, it is likely that the parties have a deal and they can determine what it is.

(B)   The purchasing agent of a corporation seeking to buy glass jars wants to discover which manufacturer will furnish the corporation at the best price with the best delivery date. The purchasing agent sends a request for quotation form to several manufacturers. The form states "THIS IS NOT AN ORDER." Each manufacturer fills in the blanks that ask for a description of the product, prices, delivery schedules and the like, and signs it. The purchasing agent selects a lucky supplier. The purchasing department prepares a purchase order and sends it to that seller. Again, the parties have a deal and they probably can determine what it is.

(C)   A purchasing agent seeking to buy glass jars may study products and prices from catalogs. She selects a supplier and sends a purchase order which has an acknowledgment of order copy. The supplier's authorized agent signs the acknowledgment of order copy and returns it. There is a deal.

(D)   A sales representative calls on a purchasing agent, and they discuss the price of glass jars. The salesperson fills out an order form, and the purchasing agent signs it. Typically, this form states, "this order is subject to acceptance at Seller's home office." Sellers may want to check a buyer's credit, inventory or production capacity. Sales representatives seldom are given power to make these decisions. The home office personnel approve the order. The seller may send the buyer an acknowledgment of order form or it may just ship the goods. Again, there is a deal.

Often businesspeople follow these patterns. If the buyer is a large corporation, its suppliers may be smaller organizations. Large corporations with many employees with the power to make contracts may insist that their employees follow standardized procedures. The small suppliers often go along with a large buyer's procedures since a good customer is always right!

Life does not always run smoothly. Anyone who has worked for a major corporation knows there always is some give in the rules. Moreover, while those at the lower levels may follow routines, those higher in the organization often assert their independence and discretion. For example, lawyers and others may plan and draft careful procedures which both serve business procedures and limit liability for breach of warranty. Sales representatives use the proper forms and get buyers' signatures. Then a Vice President writes a letter to one of a buyer's officials.

The Vice President explains the meaning of the deal or says that his firm never would use its rights against a customer such as the buyer.

Suppose a seller sends buyer a quotation form, stating a price for a particular product. The buyer immediately sends a purchase order back to the seller. Does this create a legally enforceable contract? The answer turns in large part on whether a court would classify the quotation as an offer or only a preliminary negotiation. Catalogs and advertisements directed at the world usually are not offers. Buyers are held to understand that sellers do not guarantee to have sufficient inventory or productive capacity to supply the world at the listed price. Catalogs and advertisements are useful ways to convey information, but some of this usefulness would be lost if sellers had to proofread them with great care to avoid being held to mistaken prices. Finally, a seller may be willing to supply the item subject to a credit check.

Some price quotations are similar to advertisements. A quotation, however, which is directed to a particular buyer and is for a specified quantity is another matter. If the quotation is sent in response to a buyer's inquiry, the seller can foresee that the buyer is likely to rely. Clearly, the surrounding circumstances and the words used in the quotation will be important. Many proposal forms attempt to answer the question by their express terms. For example, the proposal form used by one major corporation states in large print, "This proposal will become a binding contract when signed by the purchaser and thereafter accepted by an officer of the . . . [seller corporation] at its home office in Boston, Massachusetts, U.S.A."

a. The Battle of the Forms: Magic Through Contract Drafting

The "Battle of the Forms" has been a pet of contracts scholars for thirty years. Casebook authors dwell on it, and scholars write articles about it. You should ask whether it is a sufficiently large problem for businesspeople to justify all the attention. The Uniform Commercial Code has an elaborate section designed to solve these problems; you should ask whether it does so.

The Business vs. The Legal Model of Contract. Many business transactions follow patterns which involve the exchange of inconsistent business forms. In some instances a lawyer will have to determine whether any contract has been made or what its provisions are. An all too common transaction would proceed as follows:

(A) Buyer has a seller's catalog, or a seller's web address, which gives access to what amounts to an on-line catalog. Buried in the catalog, whether electronic or paper, along with tables of equivalent weights and measures and other handy bits of information, are the seller's terms of sale. They are written in legal language and printed in small type. Buyer's purchasing agent has dozens, if not hundreds, of catalogs, or web addresses, provided by her suppliers. She has never read the terms and conditions in seller's particular catalog, although she has a general idea of what most sellers put on their forms. She finds the item she wants in the catalog, notes its price, and telephones seller's office to ask if the item is available at the catalog price. Seller's agent says "Yes."

(B)   The purchasing agent tells a typist to prepare a purchase order. He types it, she checks it, and may or may not sign it. Buyer's purchase order form is a printed set of documents. There are many terms and conditions on the reverse side of the copy that is sent to the seller. The purchasing agent has read these terms and conditions in the past, but she now has only a general idea of what they say and mean. Buyer's purchase order protects its interests; its terms almost certainly add to or conflict with any seller's conditions of sale. For example, buyer may demand a broad warranty while sellers will offer a narrow warranty. The second copy of the purchase order is an acknowledgment form. Sellers are asked to sign and return it, thus "agreeing" to all of buyer's terms and conditions.

(C)   The purchase order and acknowledgment copy are sent to seller.

(D)   An assistant sales manager receives the purchase order and acknowledgment copy from buyer. He reads only the face of the document, ignoring the fine print on the back as is customary. He decides to fill the order. (Of course, his decision is based on seller's capacity to make the items, its inventory, its backlog of orders and, importantly, buyer's credit rating.)

(E)   The assistant sales manager tells a secretary to write up the order. She types a description of the item ordered, the price, an estimated delivery date, and any other necessary information on a set of business forms. Several copies from this set will go to the accounting or billing department for use as an invoice and for financial records. Several will go to production or shipping to get the item ordered, made, and shipped. One copy of this set is marked "Customer's Acknowledgment." On the reverse side of this document all of the seller's terms and conditions of sale are restated—which are not necessarily the same as those stated in seller's catalog! The document reads, "We accept your order subject to the terms and conditions on the face and reverse side of this acknowledgment." Of course, the sales manager has not read his firm's terms and conditions for a number of years, but he has a general idea of what is covered.

(F)   Seller sends the acknowledgment copy of the seller's set of business forms to buyer. Buyer's acknowledgment of order copy of its purchase order is not signed and returned. It is filed with buyer's purchase order. (Or, to really complicate matters, seller sends *both* its acknowledgment form and buyer's acknowledgment form back to buyer.)

(G)   When buyer receives seller's acknowledgment, the material typed on its face is checked against the face of the purchase order to see that the order has been interpreted correctly. No one at the buyer's office reads the fine print on the reverse side of seller's form.

(H)   The purchase order and the seller's acknowledgment copy are filed away by buyer.

(I)   One of two things happens:

(1) Most commonly, the goods are delivered on time, seller is paid in full, and the goods work perfectly, OR

(2) The goods are not delivered at all or arrive late, buyer does not pay seller, or the goods prove to be defective.

In most instances the inconsistent or additional terms and conditions on buyer's and seller's forms will not matter to anyone. The seller may not deliver the goods at all or they may arrive late, the goods may be defective, or the buyer may not pay on time. Nonetheless, buyer and seller will negotiate a settlement without reading what is said on the face or backs of business forms. They will not involve the lawyers. However, in those few instances where there is a major problem which cannot be resolved easily, someone may begin to read purchase order clause 1(a)(ii)(cc)(5) and wonder whether it is part of a binding contract.

The traditional common-law answer seemed easy; it is often called the "mirror image" rule. As was said in *Clark v. Burr*,[102] "The acceptance of an offer upon terms varying from those of the offer, however slight,[103] is a rejection of the offer."[104]

The Wisconsin court further explained that "[a]n attempted acceptance of an offer, if coupled with any condition that varies or adds to the offer, is not an acceptance, but a counter-proposition or counter-offer. . . . [T]here must be an acceptance of the counter-offer in order to complete the contract. . . . [A]cceptance of a counter-offer can be inferred from any conduct on the offeree's part indicative thereof, but . . . mere silence bears no such significance."

Exemplifying the traditional common-law approach is *Russell v. The Falls Mfg. Co.*,[105] the buyer ordered flour to be shipped between May 27th and July 1st on buyer's request. Payment was due 30 days after shipment. Seller accepted the order but stated that the deal was for shipment "sometime" in June of 1898, apparently at seller's option. Furthermore, the terms were stated as "30 days acceptance without interest, and if longer time wanted 8% interest after thirty days." About twelve days after the order was placed, buyer canceled it. Seller resold the flour at a $267 loss and sued for this amount. The court denied recovery. The seller's response contained substantial modifications and thus it was a rejection of the buyer's offer and a counter-proposal. Buyer's silence was not an acceptance. However, "had [buyer] ordered any of the flour after receiving plaintiffs' letter, that would have sufficed"[106] to accept the counter-offer.

These common-law rules are substantially modified by § 2-207 of the Uniform Commercial Code. However, Article 2 of the Code applies only to "transactions in goods." The common-law rules may still apply to all other kinds of transactions such as sales of real estate and services. These kinds of transactions are less

---

[102] 85 Wis. 649, 55 N.W. 401 (1893).

[103] There are dicta suggesting that a purported acceptance with a "slight," "insubstantial," or "immaterial" variation would not defeat the formation of a contract and make the purported acceptance a counter-offer. However, the point is not considered in any of these cases. *See, e.g.*, Hess v. Holt Lumber Co., 175 Wis. 451, 185 N.W. 522 (1921); Russell v. The Falls Mfg. Co., 106 Wis. 329, 82 N.W. 134 (1900). In light of UCC § 2-207, a lawyer seeking to overcome or limit the common law rule in non-Code situations might draw on this dicta as the basis for arguing that the Code only restates and clarifies the common law rule in Wisconsin. The lawyer would have to overcome the phrase "however slight" in the *Clark* case and some of the discussion in Leuchtenberg v. Hoeschler, 271 Wis. 151, 72 N.W.2d 758 (1955).

[104] 85 Wis. At 655, 55 N.W. at 403. *See also* Morris F. Fox & Co. v. Lisman, 208 Wis. 1, 237 N.W. 267, 240 N.W. 809, 242 N.W. 679 (1932).

[105] 106 Wis. 329, 82 N.W. 134 (1900).

[106] *Id.* at 332, 82 N.W. at 135.

likely to be conducted by the exchange of forms with inconsistent terms, but the problem can arise here as well as in sales of goods. For example, in *Leuchtenberg v. Hoeschler*,[107] the buyer offered to buy a lot with a depth of "about 150 feet." The owner tried to accept the offer but drew a line through the number 150 and substituted "120." The purported acceptance was a counteroffer and no contract was formed.

The common-law solution to the battle of the forms meant that even after an exchange of documents which both buyer and seller assumed formed a contract, either might be able to back out without legal liability. Thus, there was a chance that the law would leave reliance unprotected, which contracts scholars assumed was a significant problem. If we assume the opinions expressed by businesspeople and their lawyers in the excerpts which follow are typical, is there a problem? Does the UCC solve it? Keep your answers to these questions in mind. After you have studied § 2-207 of the UCC, consider whether the problems with that section are worse than those which businesspeople faced under the common law.

—Interview with the purchasing agent of a manufacturer of heavy industrial and construction equipment:

> The company is willing to rely on a supplier's acknowledgment form. The purchasing department is concerned primarily about whether the vendor received the order and entered it properly. Moreover, the purchasing department wants the vendor's number for the transaction to help the company in expediting matters in case of delay. Perhaps we are a bit lax in not following up and insisting that vendors send us our own acknowledgment forms, but the legal department has never made an issue of the matter. The purchasing department's job is to get material here on time; not to arrange for improbable lawsuits. The company never has trouble on terms and conditions, and so it doesn't spend any time on the matter.

—Interview with the purchasing agent of a manufacturer of nationally advertised electrical appliances:

> The purchasing department is too busy getting the items needed to spend its time reading and checking terms and conditions. The company does not need legal sanctions since in every case it gets what it wants. We have never referred to the back of a buying or selling form to get performance from a supplier. A telephone call stressing the agreed schedule for delivery and the specifications is far more effective. All of the company's vendors have been doing business with the firm for years.

—Interview with the purchasing agent of a large manufacturer of industrial and residential electrical equipment:

> The purchasing department will review all of a vendor's terms of acceptance, and if it finds any disagreement with the company's way of doing business, it will take the matter up with the vendor. It does not mind if the vendor simply adds items as long as they are not contrary to the usual way of doing business. This is true although additional items might

---

[107] 271 Wis. 151, 72 N.W.2d 758 (1955).

prevent the formation of a legally binding contract. It is interested in a legally binding contract only in the case of building construction or large capital items such as automation machinery. In normal business one does not pay any attention to the problem of legal enforceability.

—Interview with the owner of a small manufacturer of sporting goods:

We buy a great deal of metal from a large supplier. The supplier has many terms and conditions on its acknowledgment form, but this company is a good one to do business with and would never refer to all this fine print to weasel out. If they did refer to terms and conditions and surprised us with some gimmick, they would lose our account. Moreover, I would comment about this when I went to business meetings. One behaves decently in business and doesn't run to lawyers or contract clauses.

—Interview with the sales and production managers of a manufacturer of packaging machinery:

The company has recently redrafted its standard contract for selling its machines. It now insists that its contract be signed or any modifications be carefully approved. Before these forms were drafted and this procedure was installed, the company often was on the edge of trouble. It is easy to fail to deliver on time when you are manufacturing machinery engineered for the customer's product and his factory. It takes five months or more, to design and build this machinery. You cannot always predict how long it will take to solve some special problem. Yet customers' purchase orders tend to demand firm delivery dates. At present, a competitor is being sued for $600,000 for missing a delivery date on a packaging machine. The customer had arranged a TV presentation to promote a packaging idea that was to be produced on the machine. He had committed his production to the machine and had torn his plant down to install it. Our competitor did not get the machine there on time. The customer had to put his factory back together again and use the old machinery. The customer claims it suffered a loss of reputation when it could not supply its distributors with the item it had advertised. This suit has caused a lot of rethinking in this industry.

—Interview with the purchasing agent of a manufacturer of machine tools:

Terms and conditions might have significance in 1 or 2 percent of all cases. We do not read them. I have been purchasing agent for 11 years and with the company for 16. During that time we've had only 3 or 4 disputes on terms and conditions, and we've never lost much money. Our experience shows that elaborate procedures to check the 8000 to 15,000 purchase orders and acknowledgments which pass through here each year would not be justified.

—Interview with the General Counsel of a manufacturer of machinery which puts products into containers. He supplied letters written by him to be sent out by his firm's sales manager to indicate how the company takes exception to a customer's conditions of purchase:

The sales manager first acknowledges "your most valued purchase order." Then he states, "we have followed the practice for years of selling our machinery under a uniform type of contract under which our liabilities are limited. For those liabilities for which we are responsible under the contract, we purchase insurance so that our annual cost can be anticipated and our selling prices adjusted accordingly." He goes on to discuss the warranties demanded by the customer. Next he states, "we are certain that we can arrange an acceptable contract that will protect you. Our insurance companies, however, have asked us to obtain additional information so that they can advise us whether our present coverage is sufficient and what costs would be involved in acquiring additional protection." Then he states, "in making such comments we want you to know that we are desirous of meeting every reasonable request and that our only objection will be to situations where insurance protection is not reasonably available or the cost thereof was not anticipated in the selling price of the equipment, or where the condition is contrary to a long established and desirable policy of the company." He next makes a show of accepting as many of the customer's conditions as he can. He objects to conditions dealing with warranty, excuses for failure to perform and inspections. He makes, in the course of his argument, several references to the fact that his terms and conditions have been accepted by the customer's major competitors. He ends his letter by saying, "we regret the length of this discussion and hope that we have not in any manner indicated an intention to avoid reasonable responsibility to provide and install a first class unit of equipment. However, it becomes impossible for us to operate under a different contract in the plant of each customer and we have, therefore, established our selling prices on the basis of our uniform contract provisions."

In another letter, the sales manager argues that if the extensive guaranties demanded by the customer are given, it will only be a bonanza for the insurance companies and an additional cost for the seller and its customers. "This kind of protection is not necessary when dealing with a company of our standing. We fear that making an exception in a few cases will lead to a general breakdown of our rule."

—Interview with the General Counsel of a manufacturer of machinery which puts products in containers:

Typically, our purchasing agent's authority to buy is limited to signing for 5 to 10,000 dollars on any one purchase order. The extent of exposure on any order is trivial. There are so many purchase orders that we have many small risks spread over many transactions. If we are buying a more expensive item, the transaction must be approved by an official of the company. He will, as a matter of regular procedure, route the matter to the legal department for approval. Then we can see that the company is protected.

—Interview with the Secretary and General Counsel of a manufacturer of heating and cooling equipment:

You must ask how much time is justified in checking the terms and conditions on customers' forms and seeing that a contract is negotiated in every case. You could get agreement in every case, but this is not practical. Until I came to the company six months ago, someone, but not a lawyer, checked every order. I have set a check point so that only the more important transactions are subject to a careful reading and negotiation for agreement with the customer. The breakdown is designed to catch messy situations and to take a chance on the rest. First, all orders involving more than $25,000 are checked. Second, orders under this amount are not checked unless: (1) they involve government contracts, (2) they involve a retainage provision which allows the customer to retain, say, 10% of the price until the transaction is completed (with many customers you can never get that 10% no matter how well you perform), or, finally, (3) they involve aircraft products which always involve special problems of products liability. Of course, if you have trouble with a particular account, you deal on a tailor-made contract with the best security you can get, if you deal at all. This is an insurance-like approach. You must balance the risk and degree of difficulty against the cost of avoiding all possible liability. You should not spend $100 to save $50.

—Interview with a partner in a law firm in a large city with a corporate practice:

I can think of many disputes where it was wonderful to find that the back of the documents protected my client and not the other party although perhaps there was no enforceable contract. You need arguments for negotiating a settlement. What are you going to say on the telephone?

—Interview with the General Counsel of a large manufacturer of paper and paper products:

The important thing about a contract is not its legal enforceability but its meaning when read by the other side. There is a moral sanction. You can look at the man on the other side of the table and say, "you have agreed to this. Are you going to back out and not honor your word?" But this is a business where buyers and sellers know each other very well.

Before the Uniform Commercial Code was passed, many lawyers relied on "the last shot principle" in planning for their firm in its role as seller. Normally, the last document sent in a battle of the forms situation is a seller's acknowledgment of a buyer's order. Under pre-Code law, if a seller sent an acknowledgment with additional or different terms from those on the buyer's purchase order, it would be a counter-offer rather than an acceptance. No contract would be formed at this point. However, if the seller shipped goods and the buyer accepted them, the buyer's action also accepted the counteroffer and formed a contract on the seller's terms. Of course, the buyer might get the last shot. Suppose a seller offered goods on a proposal form, the buyer sent a purchase order with inconsistent terms and conditions, and the seller responded by shipping the goods. Now the shipment probably would be the acceptance of buyer's counteroffer.

Lawyers drafting forms for buyers and sellers tried to cope with the common law's last shot approach. For example, the selling forms of the Anaconda American Brass Company provided that "seller's failure to object to provisions contained in any communications from buyer will not be deemed as an acceptance of such provisions or as a waiver of the provisions hereof." On the other hand the purchase order of the Pabst Brewing Company provided that "you accept all the terms and conditions on the front and reverse sides of this order . . . by failing to make prompt written objection to these terms and conditions, even if you fail to sign or return the acknowledgment copy to us." Several major corporations used clauses on their purchase orders that read "buyer recognizes that seller may for operating convenience desire to utilize its own form of acknowledgment, contract, or other document in connection with this transaction. Therefore, it is agreed that any provisions in the form of acceptance used, which modify, conflict with, or contradict any provision of this contract or order, shall be deemed waived." Of course, the legal effect of these clauses is debatable, but they gave lawyers something to argue about as part of negotiations.

b. Section 2-207 of the Uniform Commercial Code

Section 2-207 of the UCC purports to wipe out the common-law approach to the battle of the forms and start over. We begin by looking at the text of the statute. As always, one must consider the structure of the legislation and touch all the bases rather than rip a phrase or paragraph out of context. Then we'll turn to some appellate opinions to highlight problems.

Subsections (1) and (2) of § 2-207 go together. If a case does not fit within them, then you must go on to subsection (3). Subsection (1) deals with whether a contract has been formed. If a contract has been formed under subsection (1), then we look to subsection (2) to determine its terms. If a contract has not been formed under subsection (1), then we turn to subsection (3) and not the common law or the last shot doctrine.

Subsection (1) asks whether there is a contract. It says that a "definite and seasonable expression of acceptance" closes a deal and creates a contract. Notice that we must have a communication which a court will classify as an acceptance. Reading the statute literally, a preliminary negotiation, an offer or a counteroffer does not come under UCC § 2-207(1). However, if we have an acceptance, it creates a contract although it states "terms additional to or different from those offered or agreed upon." Clearly, this overturns much of the common-law rule. Under the common law, a purported acceptance that stated "terms additional to or different from those offered or agreed upon," is only a counteroffer. Under the UCC, it can close a contract. However, it does not have this effect if "acceptance is expressly made conditional on assent to the additional or different terms." Courts have had great difficulty interpreting this last clause.

What are the terms of a contract created under subsection (1)? Additional terms are proposals for additions to the contract. In effect, the Code says that we treat the communication as if it said, "I accept your offer and we have a deal now. However, I propose we also add term XYZ to our contract." Between merchants these proposals become part of the contract unless any of the three qualifications in subsection (2) apply. Notice that the "materially alter it" provision goes to the terms of a deal formed under subsection (1) and not to whether there is a contract formed under subsection (1).

Suppose instead of additional terms, the acceptance contains different terms that do not alter the contract materially and to which there is no objection. Do added terms become part of the deal while different terms drop out? Courts and writers have struggled with this question.

Assume the buyer's and seller's forms do not create a contract under subsection (1). Now we turn to subsection (3). "Conduct by both parties which recognizes the existence of a contract is sufficient to establish a contract for sale although the writings of the parties do not otherwise establish a contract." Suppose the seller offered goods on its proposal form. The buyer accepted the offer by sending a purchase order to seller, but the terms printed on the purchase order expressly made acceptance conditional on assent to the additional or different terms found there. Thus, under UCC § 2-207(1), the writings of the parties would not create a contract. However, seller then ships the goods ordered, and buyer accepts and pays for them. This seems to be conduct by both of them which "recognizes the existence of a contract." If a court finds it does, a contract is established.

What are its terms? Subsection (3) says that they are those on which the writings of the parties agree "together with any supplementary terms incorporated under any other provisions of this Act." The proposal and purchase order are likely to agree on the description of the goods and their price. Often the seller's form disclaims warranties and limits remedies while the buyer's form claims these rights. The warranty and remedy provisions found in these documents would drop out of the deal. The UCC provisions on warranties and remedies would fill the gap. Notice that this is not the last shot principle where the party which last submitted a document gets its terms and conditions as the contract.

McCARTY v. VERSON ALLSTEEL PRESS CO.
Appellate Court of Illinois, First District
89 Ill. App. 3d 498, 411 N.E.2d 936 (1980)

ROMITI, J. [A Nash Bros. employee was injured using a machine manufactured by Verson. The employee sued Verson, who settled. Verson then sued Nash Bros. for indemnification under a clause in the form which accompanied its price quotation.] The trial court, after a bench trial, found that the clause was part of the contract and entered judgment for [Verson] in the amount of $322,745.44. We disagree and reverse.

In early 1971, Nash Bros. Co. (hereinafter called buyer), and Verson Allsteel Press Company (hereinafter called seller), entered into oral negotiations regarding the sale of a punch press from the seller, Verson, as a manufacturer, to Nash, the buyer. These negotiations centered almost completely around the technical specifications of the subject punch press. At no time during this period of oral negotiation were any discussions had regarding the indemnification of seller by buyer for injuries caused by defects in seller's presses.

On May 19, 1971, seller sent buyer a document entitled Proposal No. 5575-1-RB. It stated: "In accordance with your request, we are pleased to offer the following press brake equipment for your consideration. . . ." A detailed list of "General Specifications" and "Items Included" followed. The proposal concluded:

> Point of operation guards are not included with this equipment. It is the employer's responsibility to provide guards, devices, tools, or other means to effectively protect all personnel from serious injury which may otherwise occur as a result of any particular machine use or activity. Thank you for this opportunity to offer our equipment. Should you require any additional information, please let us know.

This offer was subject to thirty days' acceptance.

At the foot of the first page of the proposal was the legend: "All quotations, orders and contracts are subject to acceptance of home office."

Enclosed with the May 19th proposal was a copy of seller's form "Conditions of Sale—Machinery." In pertinent part, these provided:

. . .

> 7. WARRANTY—WARRANTY LIMITATIONS—INDEMNITY, . . .
>
> (c) Customer assumes and shall bear all responsibility for providing adequate and sufficient safeguards, work handling tools and safety devices to protect fully the operator and any other users of the goods at all times, in accordance with the prevailing federal, state, and local codes and industry-accepted standards. Verson shall bear no liability whatsoever for the failure of customer to order, install, or use such safeguards, work handling tools or safety devices.
>
> Customer shall establish and use, and require all persons operating the equipment to use, all proper and safe operating procedures, including but not limited to procedures set forth in any manuals or instruction sheets relating to the equipment. Customer shall not remove or modify any devices, warning sign, or manual furnished with, or installed upon or attached to the goods.
>
> NOTWITHSTANDING ANY PROVISION OF THESE TERMS AND CONDITIONS, THE WARRANTY CONTAINED IN THIS PARAGRAPH, AS LIMITED HEREIN, IS THE ONLY WARRANTY EXTENDED BY VERSON IN CONNECTION WITH ANY SALE BY IT AND IS IN LIEU OF ALL OTHER WARRANTIES, EXPRESS OR IMPLIED, INCLUDING WARRANTIES OF MERCHANTABILITY AND FITNESS FOR PURPOSE.
>
> 8. INDEMNITY, Customer hereby (1) waives, releases and discharges any and all claims of any and every kind (including but not limited to injury to or death of any person or damage to property), which it may have at any time against Verson, its agents or employees, by reason of or arising out of any claimed improper design, specifications or manufacture of the goods sold hereunder, or of devices; and (2) covenants to indemnify and hold-harmless Verson, its agents and employees of, from and against any and all loss, damage, expense, claims, suits or liability which Verson or any of its employees may sustain or incur at any time for or by reason

of any injury to or death of any person or persons or damage to any property, arising out of any claimed improper design or manufacture of the goods sold hereunder, or of any claimed inadequate or insufficient safeguards or safety devices. . . .

14.   ACCEPTANCE-WHOLE AGREEMENT,

ALL ORDERS ARE VALID AND BINDING UPON VERSON ONLY UPON ACKNOWLEDGMENT BY A DULY AUTHOR- IZED OFFICER OR DEPARTMENT MANAGER OF VERSON, BY ANY ACKNOWLEDGMENT OR ACCEPTANCE BY CUS- TOMER IN ANY MANNER OF VERSON'S PROPOSAL, OR BY THE SUBMISSION OR ISSUANCE OF CUSTOMER'S OWN PURCHASE ORDER BASED ON SUCH PROPOSAL, CUS- TOMER UNCONDITIONALLY ACCEPTS AND AGREES TO BE BOUND BY THE TERMS AND CONDITIONS HEREIN, SUCH TERMS AND CONDITIONS SHALL CONSTITUTE THE COM- PLETE AGREEMENT BETWEEN CUSTOMER AND VERSON AND SHALL NOT BE SUPERSEDED BY ANY CONDITIONS OR PROVISIONS IN CUSTOMER'S ORDER WHICH MAY CON- FLICT WITH, BE CONTRARY TO OR OTHERWISE VARY FROM THOSE HEREIN CONTAINED. ALL PREVIOUS COM- MUNICATION BETWEEN THE PARTIES HERETO, WHETHER VERBAL OR WRITTEN, WITH REFERENCE TO THE SUB- JECT MATTER HEREOF, IS HEREBY ABROGATED, IT BEING UNDERSTOOD THAT THERE ARE NO OTHER AGREE- MENTS, UNDERSTANDINGS, GUARANTEES OR WARRAN- TIES WHATEVER, EXPRESS OR IMPLIED, EXCEPT AS CON- TAINED IN VERSON'S PROPOSAL, AND THESE CONDITIONS.

Verson Allsteel Press Co.

On or about May 28, 1971, seller sent buyer its Proposal No. 5575-1-RB Revised. This document contained language almost identical to the May 19, 1971, proposal in its opening and conclusion. It also provided that the prices were subject to thirty days' acceptance and that all quotations, orders and contracts were subject to the acceptance of the home office. The enclosures included another copy of seller's "Conditions of Sale—Machinery." Various changes were made, however, in the "General Specifications" and "Included Items."

On June 8, 1971, seller sent buyer a letter, on its own stationery, reducing the price of the press which was the subject of its proposals. On the face of this letter was printed:

All quotations, orders and contracts are subject to acceptance of home of- fice and are contingent upon strikes, fires or other causes beyond our control.

Seller's "Conditions of Sale" were not included with this document and did not appear therein.

On June 16, 1971, buyer sent seller its form "PURCHASE ORDER." On its face was typed:

IN ACCORDANCE WITH YOUR QUOTATION PROPOSAL NO. 5575-1-RB REVISED AND LETTER DATED 6-8-71, WE WISH TO PURCHASE THE FOLLOWING:

A detailed list of "General Specifications" and "Included Items" was then typed on each of 7 pages. On the front of each page was printed the following:

This Purchase Order Is Subject To The Terms and Conditions Below and On The Reverse Side.

PLEASE ACKNOWLEDGE THIS ORDER AT ONCE UPON AT-TACHED COPY. This order is not binding until accepted. This order shall become a binding contract when Vendor executes and returns the attached Acknowledgment copy or ships any of the items, or renders any of the services, ordered herein. When accepted, the terms and conditions on the face and reverse sides of this order will constitute the complete agreement between Purchaser and Vendor. No additional or different terms that may be contained in Vendor's forms or otherwise proposed by Vendor will be binding upon Purchaser unless accepted in writing signed by Purchaser.

On the back of each page were buyer's "Terms and Conditions." In pertinent part these provided:

PURCHASE ORDER

Terms and Conditions

1.   ACCEPTANCE OF ORDER. This order is an offer to purchase upon the conditions and terms below and on the reverse side hereof and at the prices stated herein and may be withdrawn at any time prior to the actual receipt by Purchaser of Vendor's unconditional, written acceptance hereof. No modifications of, or exceptions to, any of the terms, conditions, or provisions of this order by Vendor shall be of any effect unless and until accepted in writing by Purchaser. Any delivery (complete or partial) by Vendor pursuant hereto prior to actual receipt of Vendor's unconditional, written acceptance hereof, shall constitute Vendor's acceptance of this order in accordance with all terms, conditions, and provisions thereof. . . .

On June 25, 1971, seller responded to the buyer's Purchase Order by returning a copy of the buyer's Acknowledgment form, signed by Walter C. Johnson, Vice-President of Verson, as follows:

ACCEPTED:

Verson Allsteel Press Company
(Vendor)

_____
Date
/s/ Walter C. Johnson
Walter C. Johnson
Vice-President—Marketing
Industrial Products

The cover letter accompanying the Acknowledgment provided:

Gentlemen:

We acknowledge and express our sincere gratitude for your subject order, covering a # B-1110-250 and a # B-3010 Verson Major Series Press
Brakes. The order has been entered in our production schedule for shipment of the B-1110-250 during the month of October, 1971, and the B-
3010 during the month of November, 1971.

Based upon the previous correspondence, our formal proposal and your
purchase order, the enclosed acknowledgment copies of our production
orders give our terms, specifications, and pricing.

Point of operation guards are not included with these equipments. It is
the employer's responsibility to provide guards, devices, tools, or other
means to effectively protect all personnel from serious injury which may
otherwise occur as a result of any particular machine use or activity.
Again, please accept our thanks for your purchase order.

The maintenance manual delivered with the machine also stated that "Providing safe working conditions and safety devices are the sole responsibility of the
user."

In 1974 an employee of the buyer was injured while operating the press, allegedly because of defects in the sufficiency of safety guards and warning devices
on the press. He collected workmen's compensation benefits from the buyer and
then sued the seller which settled for $300,000. Seller in turn sued buyer on the
alleged indemnification agreement.[108]

At trial Johnson, seller's vice-president, testified the price of the machinery did
not vary with the inclusion or exclusion of the indemnification agreement. He
also volunteered the statement that they would not sell the machine without such
an agreement. Buyer's contracting officer testified that he was familiar with the
purchase of this type of machine and that when some other press manufacturer
had wanted a similar indemnification agreement, they refused. He could recall no
other occasion in his eight and one half years of employment at buyer's where a
manufacturer had required an indemnification agreement as a condition of sale.

The trial court held that the buyer was bound by the indemnification agreement.

I.   The rights of the parties are governed by § 2-207 of the Uniform Commercial Code. . . .

The seller, relying on *Alan Wood Steel Co. v. Capital Equipment Enterprises,
Inc.* (1976), 39 Ill. App. 3d 48, 349 N.E.2d 627, contends that the price quotation
was an offer, although any contract was subject to approval by the home office;

---

[108] [1] Prior to 1977 Illinois did not permit a manufacturer held liable for a products liability injury to a buyer's employee to seek common-law indemnification from the employer of the employee for its negligence in maintaining or altering the machine. This rule was overturned in 1977
by the Illinois Supreme Court in Stevens v. Silver Manufacturing Co. (1977), 70 Ill.2d 41, 374
N.E.2d 455, which held, however, that its ruling was prospective only. Accordingly, since the injury occurred in 1974, the seller cannot recover from the buyer unless it can prove a contractual
right to indemnification.

that since the price quotation was an offer the order must have been an acceptance of the offer; and that, therefore, the terms in the price quotation are binding.

We are not convinced, however, that *Alan Wood* is controlling. It is true that that case stated that the price quotation, which, like the price quotation in the present case, provided that no order was binding until acceptance by the seller, was an offer. However it does not appear from the case that this question had been litigated by the parties. Furthermore, the court in *Alan Wood* stated that the buyer orally accepted the offer by telephone before mailing the purchase order. Obviously, therefore, both parties in that case were treating the price quotation, not the purchase order, as the offer.

A price quotation, if sufficiently detailed as was the price quotation in the present case, may constitute an offer. . . . It does not follow, however, that a price quotation which is not binding when accepted by a buyer but only becomes binding if and when accepted by the seller, who is under absolutely no obligation to accept it, can by itself be treated as an offer. . . . It follows that where the so-called offer is not intended to give the so-called offeree the power to make a contract there is no offer. . . .

In *West Penn Power Co. v. Bethlehem Steel Corp.* (1975), 236 Pa. Super. 413, 348 A.2d 144, *allocatur refused*, the court refused to treat a proposal requiring acceptance by its home office as an offer since the clause was clearly intended to prevent formation of a contract by the unilateral action of the other party, saying at 236 Pa. Super. 426, 427, 348 A.2d 152:

> The first legal issue involved in this conclusion concerns the validity of the "Acceptance" clause. There can be no doubt about appellee's right to include this clause in its proposal to appellants, nor about the effect of the clause. The clause kept the proposal in effect for seven days but precluded the formation of a contract except upon approval by appellee's home office. Such a clause is valid in Pennsylvania under the common law of contracts. If the seller does not authorize the contract or accept the order within a reasonable time, the buyer may revoke its order, but there is no contract until the terms of the clause are met. *McCrea v. Automatic Heat, Inc.*, 161 Pa. Super. 545, 55 A.2d 564 (1947). "The purpose of [the inclusion of such a standard acceptance clause] is that the negotiating agent shall have no power to bind his principal, and that expressions of agreement on the paper shall therefore be no more than an offer to be accepted or rejected by the principal at his pleasure." 1 Corbin Contracts, § 33, at 128-29 (1963).

II.   Even if we were to treat the seller's price quotation as an offer and the buyer's purchase order as an acceptance . . . it does not follow under the facts in the present case that the provisions in the seller's proposal would control. The seller unconditionally signed the buyer's acknowledgment form sent with the purchase order. The purchase order retained by the seller provided on its face above the purchaser's signature, in fairly large sized print, that when the order was accepted, the terms and conditions on the face and reverse sides of this order would constitute the complete agreement between the purchaser and vendor and that no additional or different terms contained in the vendor's forms would be binding on the purchaser. Where the seller signs the buyer's acknowledgment without expressly conditioning that signature, the seller accepts the conditions in the buyer's forms . . . even though the price quotation contained a provision that the buyer by ordering any of the listed merchandise agreed to the enumerated conditions of sale. . . . The seller could, of course, have avoided this result by not signing the acknowledgment at all or by expressly conditioning the signature as did the seller in *Lincoln Pulp & Paper Co. v. Dravo Corp.* (D. Me. 1977), 445 F. Supp. 507, where the seller said on the acknowledgment that it was accepted in accordance with the accompanying letter, and the letter said conditions on back of form were not acceptable.

III.   Furthermore, even if we were to treat the price quotation as an offer, it does not follow that the purchase order was necessarily an acceptance of that offer, despite the provision in the seller's condition of sale which, apparently, attempts to make any purchase order, regardless of its terms, an acceptance of all of the seller's terms. (Absent proper punctuation, it is impossible to decipher the precise meaning of paragraph 14.) While it is true that the offeror has total control over its own offer and may condition *acceptance* to the terms of the offer (Ill. Rev. Stat. 1969, ch. 26, par. 2-207(2)(a)), as apparently the seller did here, nevertheless it is not true that the first party to a sales transaction will always get his own terms. In most commercial transactions which party processes its terms first is purely fortuitous . . . and "it must be recognized that the offeree should not be compelled to accept the terms of the offer if he does not want them, and he ought also to be free to respond with a counteroffer." 3 R. Duesenberg & L. King, Uniform Commercial Code Service (MB) § 3.06[3] (1977).

Under § 2-207(1) of the Uniform Commercial Code . . . any definite and seasonable expression of acceptance operates as an acceptance even though it is not a mirror image of the offer unless the acceptance is expressly made conditional on assent to the additional or different terms. However that section still requires a definite expression of acceptance and does not change the basic common-law requirement that there must be an objective manifestation of mutual assent. . . . No contract can be found where the offeror could not reasonably treat the response of the offeree as an acceptance (*Air Products and Chemicals, Inc. v. Fairbanks Morse, Inc.* (1973), 58 Wis.2d 193, 206 N.W.2d 414), and parties may initially exchange printed forms which differ so radically that the second cannot be treated as an acceptance of the first. (*Koehring Co. v. Glowacki* (1977), 77 Wis.2d 497, 253 N.W.2d 64.) Here the purchase order clearly, expressly and repeatedly stated that it was an offer to be accepted by the seller and that no contract existed until it was accepted by the seller. We cannot distort this definite expression of an offer into a "definite and seasonable expression of acceptance."

IV.   Seller's signing of the purchase order acknowledgment acted as an acceptance of the order. Indeed, the seller admitted this in its request to admit that "Verson Allsteel Press Company by Walter C. Johnson, Vice-President, accepted the purchase order and signed it on Page 1." Nor did seller dispute this point in its brief, although it was raised by the buyer. The mere fact that the seller enclosed its "Conditions of Sale" with the accompanying letter merely stating that enclosed copies gave its terms, specifications and pricing was not sufficient to make the acceptance a counteroffer instead of an acceptance, since to prevent such an assent from being an acceptance under § 2-207(1) it must be *expressly* made conditional on assent to the additional or different terms. This provision is construed narrowly to apply only to an acceptance which clearly reveals that the offeree is unwilling to proceed without agreement to the additional terms. . . . [See] *Dorton v. Collins & Aikman Corp.* (6th Cir. 1972), 453 F.2d 1161, which held that even a statement that acceptance subject to all the terms and conditions on reverse side was not "expressly made conditional on assent to the additional or different terms."

Under § 2-207(2) of the Commercial Code the terms enclosed with the letter were merely to be construed as proposals for additions to the contract. They did not, however, become part of the contract since, as the seller admits, they materially altered it. . . .

V.   If we were to assume, contrary to the cases, that seller's acceptance was expressly made conditional on assent to the conditions set forth in its "Conditions of Sale," the result would still be the same. In that case, under § 2-207(1) of the Commercial Code the acknowledgment would act as a counteroffer, not an acceptance. . . . Following this reasoning, since the only contract formed would be that formed by the parties' conduct, their rights would be controlled by § 2-207(3) of the Code. . . . This section provides that the terms of the particular contract consist of those on which the *writings* of the parties agree and the code provisions. It is well established that under this provision terms contained only in one of the party's forms are not part of the contract. . . .

VI.   The seller argues, however, that the court's finding was proper because the parties intended to make the indemnity clause part of the contract, pointing to the testimony of seller's marketing vice-president that seller would never have sold the press without the indemnity provision. There is absolutely no evidence in the record that this intent was communicated to the buyer. To the contrary, the only evidence in the record is that there was no discussion between the parties regarding the indemnification of the seller. . . .

Seller, however, contends that the terms of the "Conditions of Sale" were incorporated into the buyer's order by the language "in accordance with your quotation Proposal No. 5575-1-RB Revised and letter dated 6-8-71," relying on the well-established axiom that typewritten provisions prevail over printed ones. This rule is applicable only where there is a conflict between typed and printed portions of a document. . . . A contract must be read as a whole . . . and neither the printed portion nor the typewritten portion should be disregarded unless there is a conflict between the two. Rather, a typewritten provision of a contract should prevail over inconsistent printed stipulations only as far as it is apparent that the parties intended to modify or disregard such printed stipulations, and where the antagonism is merely apparent, the difference should be reconciled, if possible, by any reasonable interpretation. . . . Reading the purchase order as a whole it is clear the general phrase "in accordance with" was intended only to identify the pertinent price quotations and not to incorporate the "Conditions of Sale" attached to only one of those quotations in direct conflict with the many provisions of the purchase order specifically stating that the seller's conditions were not binding.

The seller also contends that the buyer is bound by the indemnity provision because it failed to object to it. The indemnity provision only appeared in the "Conditions of Sale" which, as we have already determined, did not become part of the contract. The other notices sent to the buyer repeatedly informed the buyer that the responsibility for installing safety devices was on the buyer but did not contain an indemnification clause. Such unobjected-to notice might be construed as modifying the contract so as to remove any warranties relating to the safety of the machine, but obviously could not be considered to change the contract to add an indemnification clause never referred to in such notice. To the contrary, an indication that the seller was not relying on any indemnification clause is the fact that while the notices reaffirmed the buyer's duty to install safety devices, a duty first mentioned in the "Conditions of Sale," they failed to make any reference to the indemnification clause also in the same conditions. Since the accident occurred before the decision in *Stevens v. Silver Manufacturing Co.* (1977), 70 Ill.2d 41, 374 N.E.2d 455, the claim does not and cannot arise out of the buyer's failure to install effective devices. It can arise only if the buyer did in fact agree "to indemnify . . . Verson . . . against any and all loss, damage, expense, claims, suits or liability which Verson . . . may sustain or incur at any time for or by reason of any injury to or death of any person or persons or damage to any property, arising out of any claimed improper design or manufacture of the goods sold hereunder, or any claimed, inadequate or insufficient safeguards or safety devices."

Since we believe it is clear as a matter of law that the indemnification clause cannot be found to be part of the contract agreed upon by the parties, the judgment of the trial court is reversed.

Reversed.

NOTES AND QUESTIONS

1. *Section 2-207 and substantive policy concerning the clauses in question*: The seller tried to convince the court that the safety obligation was that of the buyer who was to use the machine in a particular setting for a particular purpose. It said that the buyer's "safety device obligation was not an overlooked item in a 'battle of forms,' but a prime point expressly reiterated at least 10 different times in the documents exchanged between the parties."

2. *The buyer's views about indemnity*: The buyer responded that the case "remains one in which Verson, as seller, is attempting to foist a hold harmless clause (which is contrary to the policies embodied in the UCC) on its buyer, Nash, after the fact of sale, and without procuring any agreement, written or otherwise, from Nash with respect to the clause." The buyer pointed out that the parties had never discussed the clause during negotiations. It continued:

> This court is asked to decide whether the manufacturer of an unreasonably dangerous machine can attempt to enforce a hold-harmless clause in the "contract" of sale of the machine, and, thereby, escape liability for its failure to equip the machine with safety devices. It is submitted that to allow such a practice would be to effectively remove a manufacturer's obligation to create its products safely. Certainly, if one

realizes that he will be reimbursed for any damages he may be required to pay on account of his responsibility for another's injuries, he will no longer be as inclined to take precautions which will prevent the injury. It is the prevention of this injury with which the law of products liability is concerned. . . .

Thus, Verson has marketed a product which is unreasonably dangerous due to its lack of safety devices, and has, simultaneously attempted to transfer its liability for injuries caused thereby to Nash. A minute clause on the back of Verson's printed form is the means by which Verson seeks to effectuate this transfer. Verson's attempted transfer of the financial responsibility for its violation of a duty which it could not delegate cannot, and should not, be tolerated if the policies embodied in the doctrine of strict tort liability are to be preserved.

3. _Sneaking provisions into deals_: Professor John E. Murray asserts "[i]f a party would not reasonably understand that certain terms were included in the contract ab initio, they will not be included, because their inclusion would unfairly surprise and oppress the party against whom they would have operated. Section 2-207, therefore, may be viewed as addressing incipient unconscionability—its philosophy is identical to 2-302's."[109] Suppose the seller's representative had called the attention of buyer's officials to the hold-harmless clause and to the problem of installing safety devices on the machine. Is it likely that this would have made a difference in the negotiations or other behavior of the parties?

STEINER v. MOBIL OIL CORP.
Supreme Court of California
20 Cal. 3d 90, 569 P.2d 751 (1977)[110]

TOBRINER, J. In this case, over one year after apparently accepting plaintiff's offer, the Mobil Oil Corporation sought to impose upon plaintiff the very contractual terms which plaintiff expressly rejected in his offer. As justification for its conduct, Mobil asserted that the crucial provision of plaintiff's offer was lost in the labyrinth of the Mobil bureaucracy, and thus that Mobil decisionmakers had no opportunity to pass on plaintiff's offer as

---

[109] Murray, _The Chaos of the "Battle of the Forms": Solutions_, 39 Vand. L. Rev. 1307, 1322 (1986).

[110] Eds. note: It is interesting to note that Mobil Oil was represented by McCutchen, Black, Verleger & Shea, a firm which had an office on Wilshire Boulevard and had 25 partners and 33 associates. Steiner was represented by Mr. Lazaroni and Mr. Sapiro, who were solo practitioners. Mr. Lazaroni had been in practice over fifty years at the time of this case; Mr. Sapiro had been in practice over thirty years.

Marc Galanter, _Contract in Court; Or Almost Everything You May or May Not Want to Know About Contract Litigation_, 2001 Wis. L. Rev. 577, 621, distinguishes what he calls uphill from downhill litigation. An individual suing a corporation is an example of uphill litigation; a corporation suing an individual is downhill. He finds that uphill litigation does not succeed as often as downhill. He also points out that contracts casebooks tend to feature an atypical selection of uphill cases where the plaintiff wins. He comments: "The casebooks reflect the uphill struggle and magnify its success—perhaps both encouraging those eager to engage in that struggle but also offering reassurance that the law embodies a benign balance, so that it doesn't really matter which side one is on."

such. As we shall see, however, the trial court correctly concluded that § 2207 of the California Uniform Commercial Code bars Mobil from in this way converting its own error into plaintiff's misfortune.

Section 2207, subdivision (1), provides that parties may form an agreement, even if the terms of offer and acceptance do not entirely converge, if the offeree gives a definite expression of acceptance, and if the terms of acceptance do not explicitly condition agreement upon the offeror's consent to the offeree's new proposed terms. In this case, as the trial court found, defendant Mobil did not condition its acceptance of plaintiff's offer upon plaintiff's agreement to Mobil's alteration of plaintiff's offer and thus a contract was formed. Section 2207, subdivision (2), provides in turn that, if the terms of the offer and acceptance differ, the terms of the offer become part of a contract between merchants if the offer expressly limits acceptance to its own terms, or if the varying terms of the acceptance materially alter the terms of the offer. As the trial court found, under either of these clauses, the terms of Steiner's offer must prevail, because Steiner's offer was expressly conditional upon Mobil's agreement to provide a guaranteed discount, and Mobil's substitution of a discount terminable at its discretion materially affected Steiner's interests.

Accordingly, the trial court did not err in granting judgment for plaintiff, and we shall thus affirm its judgment.

1. The facts in this case

. . . Joseph R. Steiner is an independent service station operator. . . . [leasing his station from a third party and buying gasoline from Mobil].

In 1971, the third party who leased the service station property to Steiner informed him that the property was for sale. Steiner contacted Mobil sales representative Tony Montemarano. Montemarano informed Steiner that Mobil would not purchase the property, but that Mobil was interested in assisting Steiner in making the purchase.

Thereafter, Steiner entered into extended negotiations with J.S. Chenen, Mobil's area manager and Montemarano's superior. Steiner and Chenen agreed that Mobil would supply the down payment on the property, amounting to $30,000. In return, Steiner would enter into a 10-year contract with Mobil. The contract would treat the cash advance as a prepaid competitive allowance, to be amortized over the 10-year period through Steiner's purchase of 5.8 million gallons of gasoline.

The negotiations did not terminate with the agreement concerning the down payment. Steiner had concluded that he would not be able to do business successfully if he were compelled to purchase gasoline from Mobil at the standard tank wagon price. As the trial court found, Steiner told Chenen that he, Steiner, "needed a firm competitive allowance for the length of his distributor's agreement to make his cash flow adequate to meet the payments on the property." Steiner and Chenen agreed that a satisfactory arrangement with Mobil would include not only the $30,000 prepaid competitive allowance, but also a further competitive allowance reducing Mobil's tank wagon price by 1.4 cents per gallon. Mobil would also supply Steiner with $3,000 worth of improvements.

As Chenen made clear to Steiner, neither Chenen nor his immediate supervisor, district manager D.L. Dalbec, possessed the authority to accept the negotiated terms on Mobil's behalf. The negotiations therefore did not culminate in an agreement as such but rather in a proposal to be submitted to R.D. Pfaff, the division general manager, who did possess authority to agree to the proposal on Mobil's behalf.

Moreover, the proposal did not take the form of a documented single contract. Chenen and Steiner utilized a series of standard Mobil forms in putting together the proposal, modifying the forms where necessary. Steiner signed those of the forms, such as the basic retail dealer contract, which required his signature. The package of documents which comprised the proposal, therefore, needed only Pfaff's approval to become effective.

Near the close of the process of negotiating and assembling the proposal, Steiner obtained a copy of the standard Mobil form which would embody the 1.4 cents per gallon competitive allowance. This form, which did not require Steiner's signature, stated: "This allowance may be changed or discontinued by us at any time upon notice to you in writing. . . ." Upon receipt of the form Steiner immediately contacted Chenen by telephone, told Chenen that he would not go ahead with the deal if Mobil could revoke the competitive allowance at any time, and demanded assurances that no such revocation would occur.

In order to placate Steiner, Chenen, after consultation and authorization from Dalbec, sent Steiner a letter, dated December 2, 1971, which declared "[¶] The ten-year Retail Dealer Contract dated December 15, 1971, effective January 1, 1972, is signed by you on the basis that Mobil grant a $30,000 Prepaid Competitive Allowance, and a *$.014 Competitive Allowance at time of delivery.* [¶] If Mobil management does not accept in full the above conditions outlined in your competitive offer, the above mentioned contract will be void." (Italics added.)

[The trial court found that Chenen was authorized to write Steiner and that Chenen and Dalbec's knowledge of Steiner's firm insistence on a competitive allowance was attributable to Mobil. Chenen and Dalbec, under the circumstances, "were obligated in the exercise of good faith and ordinary care and diligence" to inform Pfaff of the terms of Steiner's offer.]

In fact, however, Chenen and Dalbec did *not* transmit to Pfaff the letter which Chenen had sent to Steiner; Mobil's copy of that letter remained in the district office files. In preparing the proposal for submission to Pfaff, Chenen and Dalbec assembled a package which included the various documents that Steiner had executed, the standard form providing the revocable 1.4 cents per gallon competitive allowance, and various memoranda explaining the advantages of the deal for Mobil. Early in 1972, several months after Chenen and Dalbec had transmitted the proposal to him, Pfaff approved it as submitted.

Chenen informed Steiner of Pfaff's approval by telephone. Steiner had called Chenen to find out what was happening with the proposal which they had negotiated. Chenen told Steiner that Mobil had a check for him, and that the next thing for Steiner to do was to *open an escrow account* and *proceed with the purchase of the property.*

Subsequently, Montemarano delivered to Steiner at his service station a manila folder containing the documents approved by Pfaff. These documents, the trial court found, were "numerous and complex in nature." Nonetheless, there was no cover letter describing the contents of the folder. Although the folder included Mobil's standard competitive allowance form, with its clause providing for revocation at will, Montemarano did not call this fact to Steiner's attention.

Thus, as the trial court found, at no time after Chenen sent Steiner the December 2 letter "did Mobil advise [Steiner] that a non-cancellable allowance would not be part of the agreement." Moreover, Steiner "did not at any time reread all of the documents delivered to him by Mobil, particularly the form letter . . . setting forth the provision regarding the 1.4 cents per gallon competitive allowance being cancellable." Mobil did not "specifically bring" to Steiner's attention "the statements made in the form letter . . . concerning the cancellable condition of the competitive allowance."

By April 1972, Steiner had completed the process of acquiring the service station property. Beginning in March, Mobil afforded Steiner the benefit of the 1.4 cents per gallon competitive allowance in billing him for gasoline and continued to do so until the summer of 1973. On July 16, 1973, Chenen informed Steiner by letter that, in accordance with the provisions of Mobil's notice of competitive allowance, Mobil would reduce Steiner's discount to 0.5 cents per gallon as of August 1, 1973.

Steiner brought this suit in the Los Angeles County Superior Court, seeking declaratory and monetary relief. The trial court, sitting without a jury, found that Mobil "had reason to know" that Steiner would not enter into an agreement unless Mobil agreed that he "was to have a non-cancellable . . . competitive allowance . . . to run as long as the distributor agreement was in force." Moreover, the trial court found, in returning the package of documents to Steiner, "Mobil intended to make a contract, not to make a counter offer." The trial court concluded that "in the exercise of good faith and reasonable care and diligence Mobil was required to specifically bring to the attention of plaintiff the statements made in the form letter sent by Dalbec concerning the cancellable condition of the competitive allowance."

The trial court ruled that, under California Uniform Commercial Code § 2207, Mobil had entered into a contract with Steiner which guaranteed Steiner a 1.4 cents per gallon discount for 10 years. "Mobil made a definite and seasonable expression of acceptance of plaintiff's offer, although its reply contained a material term different from that offer." Moreover, "[i]n accepting plaintiff's offer Mobil did not either orally or in writing expressly condition its acceptance upon plaintiff's assent to the different terms as to the competitive allowance in Mobil's acceptance." The trial court granted Steiner a declaratory judgment to that effect, and awarded Steiner damages of $4,953.63. Mobil appeals the trial court's judgment.

2.   *Under California Uniform Commercial Code § 2207, Steiner's contract with Mobil grants Steiner a 1.4 cents per gallon discount for the duration of the contract.*

[The California UCC applies to this dispute, and § 2-207 (§ 2207 in the Cal. code) is the critical section.]

Under traditional common law, no contract was reached if the terms of the offer and the acceptance varied. . . . This "mirror image" rule of offer and acceptance was plainly both unfair and unrealistic in the commercial context. . . . [since it ignored the parties' mutual and reasonable understandings that there was a deal.]

Section 2207 rejects the "mirror image" rule. (*See, e.g., Roto-Lith, Ltd. v. F. P. Bartlett & Co.* (1st Cir. 1962) 297 F.2d 497, 500.) "This section of the Code recognizes that in current commercial transactions, the terms of the offer and those of the acceptance will seldom be identical." (*Dorton v. Collins & Aikman Corp.* (6th Cir. 1972) 453 F.2d 1161, 1166.)

Under § 2207, for example, the parties may conclude a contract despite the fact that, after reaching accord, they exchanged forms which purport to memorialize the agreement, but which differ because each party has drafted his form "to give him advantage." (White & Summers, Uniform Commercial Code (1972) p. 23; *see, e.g., Rite Fabrics, Inc. v. Stafford-Higgins Co., Inc.* (S.D.N.Y. 1973) 366 F. Supp. 1.) Similarly, the parties may form a contract even if the terms of offer and acceptance differ because one or the other party, in stating its initial position, relies upon "forms drafted to cover the majority of [its] transactions in a uniform, standard manner" (Duesenberg & King, Sales and Bulk Transfers under the Uniform Commercial Code (1976) § 3.02, p. 3-9), and subsequently fails to amend its form to reflect the deal which the other party claims was actually negotiated. (*See, e.g., Ebasco Services Inc. v. Pennsylvania Power & L. Co.* (E.D. Pa. 1975) 402 F. Supp. 421, 434-435.)

In place of the "mirror image" rule, § 2207 inquires as to whether the parties intended to complete an agreement . . . . If the parties intend to contract, but the terms of their offer and acceptance differ, § 2207 authorizes a court to determine which terms are part of the contract, either by reference to the parties' own dealings (*see* § 2207, subds. (1), (2)), or by reference to other provisions of the code. (*See* § 2207, subd. (3).)

Section 2207 is thus of a piece with other recent developments in contract law. Instead of fastening upon abstract doctrinal concepts like offer and acceptance, § 2207 looks to the actual dealings of the parties and gives legal effect to that conduct. Much as adhesion contract analysis teaches us not to enforce contracts until we look behind the facade of the formalistic standardized agreement in order to determine whether any inequality of bargaining power between the parties renders contractual terms unconscionable, or causes the contract to be interpreted against the more powerful party, § 2207 instructs us not to *refuse* to enforce contracts until we look below the surface of the parties' disagreement as to contract terms and determine whether the parties undertook to close their deal. Section 2207 requires courts to put aside the formal and academic stereotypes of traditional doctrine of offer and acceptance and to analyze instead what really happens. In this spirit, we turn to the application of § 2207 in this case.

Section 2207, subdivision (1), provides: "A definite and seasonable expression of acceptance or a written confirmation which is sent within a reasonable time operates as an acceptance even though it states terms additional or different from those offered or agreed upon, unless acceptance is expressly made conditional on assent to the additional or different terms."

In this case, as the trial court found, Mobil provided "[a] definite and seasonable expression of acceptance." Steiner offered to enter into a 10-year dealer contract with Mobil only if Mobil, among other things, agreed to advance Steiner $30,000, and to give Steiner a 1.4 cents per gallon competitive discount on the price of Mobil gasoline for the duration of the contract. When Steiner telephoned Chenen, Mobil's employee, to inquire as to the fate of Steiner's offer, *Chenen told Steiner that Mobil had a check for him, that he should open an escrow account, and that he should go ahead with the purchase of the service station property*—in context a clear statement that Mobil had approved the deal.

Moreover, through Montemarano, another Mobil employee, Mobil returned to Steiner various executed documents in an envelope unaccompanied by any cover. The documents provided written confirmation of the deal. The fact that Mobil returned the documents without in any way calling Steiner's attention to them is further evidence that Mobil regarded the process of negotiation as over and the deal as complete.

As the trial court also found, Mobil did not in any way make its acceptance "expressly . . . conditional" on Steiner's "assent to the additional or different terms." Chenen, in telling Steiner to go ahead with the purchase, did not suggest that Mobil had conditioned its acceptance. In returning the executed documents, Mobil enclosed no cover letter; again, it did not use the occasion in any way to condition expressly its acceptance.

Thus, neither of the restrictions which limit § 2207, subdivision (1)'s application are relevant in this case. Despite the fact that the terms of Mobil's acceptance departed partially from the terms of Steiner's offer, Mobil and Steiner did form a contract. To determine the terms of this contract, we turn to § 2207, subdivision (2).

Section 2207, subdivision (2), provides: " . . . additional terms are to be construed as proposals for addition to the contract. Between merchants such terms become part of the contract unless: [¶] (a) The offer expressly limits acceptance to the terms of the offer; [¶] (b) They materially alter it; or [¶] (c) Notification of objection to them has already been given or is given within a reasonable time after notice of them is received."

Under § 2207, subdivision (2), Mobil's revocable discount provision does *not* become part of the agreement between Steiner and Mobil. In order to become part of the agreement, Mobil's provision must not fall within *any* of the categories defined by § 2207, subdivision (2), subsections (a), (b), and (c). Mobil's term, however, clearly comes within subsections (a) and (b).

Subsection (a) provides that no additional term can become part of the agreement if Steiner's offer "expressly limit[ed] acceptance to the terms of the offer." (§ 2207, subd. (2)(a).) Mobil concedes that Steiner's offer provided that the competitive allowance of 1.4 cents per gallon would run for the full length of the 10-year dealer contract. Chenen's December 2 letter to Steiner explicitly acknowledges Mobil's awareness that "[i]f Mobil management does not accept in full the above conditions outlined in your competitive offer, the above mentioned contract is void."

Moreover, Mobil's acceptance falls within subsection (b) since without question the acceptance "materially alter[ed]" the terms of Steiner's offer. (*See* § 2207, subd. (2)(b).) The Uniform Commercial Code comment notes that a variation is material if it would "result in surprise or hardship if incorporated without express awareness by the other party . . . . " (§ 2-207, U. Com. Code, com. 4.) Here, Steiner clearly indicated to Mobil in the course of the negotiations that, without the 1.4 cents per gallon discount, he could not economically operate the service station. Mobil's alteration, therefore, amended the terms of the offer to Steiner's significant detriment; accordingly, the alteration was necessarily "material."

To reiterate, subsections (a), (b), and (c) of § 2207, subdivision (2), operate in the alternative. If any one of the three subsections applies, the variant terms of an acceptance do not become part of an agreement. Here, as we have seen, the provisions of both subsections (a) and (b) are met. Mobil's declaration that the 1.4 cents per gallon discount was terminable at Mobil's discretion did not become part of the contract. Instead, Steiner and Mobil formed a contract incorporating the terms of Steiner's offer: Under this contract, Steiner was guaranteed a 1.4 cents per gallon discount throughout the 10-year period of the dealer contract.[111]

---

[111] [5] The parties do not challenge the finding of the trial court that both Steiner and Mobil are" merchants" within the meaning of § 2104, subdivision (1), and thus within the meaning of § 2207, subdivision (2), as well. Moreover, the parties do not argue that the applicability of § 2207, subdivision (2), subsections (a), (b), and (c) turns upon whether the terms of Mobil's acceptance were additional to, or instead different from, Steiner's offer. Despite the parties' agreement in this case, however, the question of the relevance of the distinction between "additional" and "different" terms has become a matter of some controversy among courts and commentators.

Section 2207, subdivision (1), refers to acceptances in which terms are either "additional to or different from" the terms of an offer. Section 2207, subdivision (2), however, expressly concerns itself with only "additional terms." Noting this difference, several courts and commentators have concluded that § 2207, subdivision (2), applies if an acceptance *adds* terms to an offer, but does not apply if an acceptance *alters* the term of an offer. (See, e.g., American Parts Co., Inc. v. American Arbitration Ass'n (1967) 8 Mich. App. 156 [154 N.W.2d 5, 11]; Duesenberg & King, supra, § 3.03[1], pp. 3-33 to 3-38.) Other courts and commentators, however, suggest that § 2207, subdivision (2), applies without regard to whether the varying terms of an acceptance differ from or add to an offer. (See, e.g., Ebasco Services Inc. v. Pennsylvania Power & L. Co., supra, 402 F. Supp. 421, 440 & fn. 27; Comment, Section 2-207 of the Uniform Commercial Code--New Rules for the "Battle of the Forms" (1971) 32 U. Pitt. L. Rev. 209, 211.)

We conclude that the applicability of § 2207, subdivision (2), should not turn upon a characterization of the varying terms of an acceptance as "additional" or "different." First, Uniform Commercial Code comment 3 specifically states that "[w]hether or not additional *or different* terms will become part of the agreement depends upon the provisions of subsection (2)." (Italics added; see also UCC com. 2.) Second, the distinction between "additional" and "different" terms is ambiguous. Since an offer's silence with respect to a particular issue may indicate an intent to adopt the code's

Thus, on their face, subdivisions (1) and (2) of § 2207 confirm the trial court's conclusion that Mobil breached its agreement with Steiner. We now turn to Mobil's opposing argument that we should adopt an interpretation of § 2207 which conflicts with the trial court's conclusion.

3. *Contrary to Mobil's argument, California Uniform Commercial Code §§ 2204 and 2207 do not incorporate the traditional rule that parties to a contract must mutually assent to all essential terms.*

We set forth Mobil's contentions, which, although elaborately developed, can be simply stated. Section 2207 does not apply if the general contract formation rules of § 2204 are not met. Section 2204 does not change the traditional rule that, in order to create an enforceable contract, the parties must mutually assent to all essential terms of the supposed agreement. In order to square § 2207 with § 2204, Mobil argues, we must construe § 2207, subdivision (1), to provide that there is no "definite" acceptance unless the parties agree to all essential terms. Moreover, Mobil contends, we must also hold that, under the same section, an acceptance which alters an essential term of an offer is an acceptance "expressly made conditional on assent" to the variant term. Finally, Mobil concludes that, since its acceptance, in changing the duration of the discount, modified an essential term of Steiner's offer, i.e., price, we must find that Steiner cannot claim a continued discount.

As we shall explain, Mobil's arguments do not survive scrutiny. The official comments accompanying § 2204, other provisions of the code, and the case law interpreting § 2204, all support the conclusion that § 2204 does not require mutual assent to all essential terms. Mobil's interpretations of the definite agreement and conditional acceptance provisions of § 2207, subdivision (1), likewise conflict with other subdivisions of § 2207.

[a.] *California Uniform Commercial Code § 2204 does not incorporate the traditional requirement of mutual assent to all essential terms.*

Section 2204 incorporates three subdivisions. The third of these subdivisions directly refutes Mobil's claims. "Even though one or more terms are left open a contract for sale does not fail for indefiniteness if the parties have intended to make a contract and there is a reasonably certain basis for giving an appropriate remedy." (§ 2204, subd. (3).)

Section 2204, subdivision (3), does not, by its terms, require parties to a contract to assent to *all* essential terms. Instead, this provision states that a court, if it is to enforce a contract, must first make two findings. Initially, the court must find some basis for concluding that the parties engaged in a process of offer and acceptance, rather than inconclusive negotiations. Second, the court must find

---

gap-filling provisions, even an acceptance term which at first glance appears to be plainly "additional" is at least arguably "different." (See Air Products & Chem., Inc. v. Fairbanks Morse, Inc. (1973) 58 Wis.2d 193 [206 N.W.2d 414, 424].) Third, the distinction between additional and different terms serv es no clear purpose. If additional and different terms are treated alike for purposes of § 2207, subdivision (2), an offeror does not, as some contend, lose "the ability to retain control over the terms of his offer." (Duesenberg & King, supra, at p. 3-37.) Under § 2207, subdivision (2), if the offeror wishes to retain such control, he may do so by framing his offer so that it "expressly limits acceptance to the terms of the offer. . . ." (§ 2207, subd. (2)(a).)

that it possesses sufficient information about the parties' incomplete transaction to apply the provisions of the California Uniform Commercial Code which fill in the gaps in parties' contracts.[112] As we have already seen, both of these minimal requirements are met in this case: the parties did not engage in inconclusive negotiations, and § 2207 readily fills in the terms of their contract.

To overcome the literal language of § 2204, subdivision (2), Mobil argues that the traditional requirement of "a meeting of the minds upon the essential features of the agreement" (*Ellis v. Klaff* (1950) 96 Cal. App.2d 471, 478 [216 P.2d 15]; ...) is so fundamental that the code could not conceivably have rejected it. The California code comment, however, explicitly states: "'[A] meeting of the minds on the essential features of the agreement' is not required .... " (§ 2204, com. 2.)

Other code provisions sustain the comment's view. As we have already pointed out, § 2207, subdivision (2)(b), expressly acknowledges the possibility that parties may reach a contract without agreeing to all "material" terms. Mobil does not attempt to distinguish "material" from "essential" terms; in any event, we do not think that it could successfully do so. Section 2305, subdivision (1), provides an even more dramatic refutation of Mobil's argument. As we have noted, Mobil treats price as an "essential" term. Nonetheless, this section states: "The parties if they so intend can conclude a contract for sale even though the price is not settled." (§ 2305, subd. (1).)

The case law interpreting § 2204 reinforces the interpretation offered by the code comment and the implication of other code provisions: the rules of contract formation under the California Uniform Commercial Code do not include the principle that the parties must agree to all essential terms in order to form a contract. Courts have held that, under § 2204, subdivision (3), parties may form a contract even though they do not agree as to the terms of payment ... , the time or place for performance ... , or the quantity of the goods sold ...—all terms which might appear to be "essential" to an agreement.

More significantly, in view of Mobil's emphasis on the essential character of price terms, a number of courts have held that, under § 2204, subdivision (3), the parties may frame a contract without fully agreeing as to price. ... Concededly, one court has suggested in dictum that § 2204, subdivision (3), incorporates the requirement of assent to essential terms. (*See Blackhawk Heat. & P. Co., Inc. v. Data Lease Fin. Corp.* (Fla. 1974) 302 So.2d 404, 408.) We think, however, that the Delaware Supreme Court stated the prevailing view: "[T]he omission of even an important term does not prevent the finding under [section 2204, subdivision (3)] that the parties intended to make a contract." (*Pennsylvania Co. v. Wilmington Trust Co.* (1960) 39 Del. Ch. 453, 463 [166 A.2d 726].)[113]

---

[112] [7] These provisions, of course, include § 2207; they also include, for example, § 2305, which deals with open price terms, § 2307, which fixes otherwise open delivery provisions, and § 2309, which sets a duration for otherwise indefinite contracts.

[113] [8] In the instant case, Steiner and Mobil, at Mobil's instigation, arranged their dealings in a way that clearly distinguished preliminary bargaining from the process of offer and acceptance as such. As we have seen, Steiner and Chenen initially negotiated the terms of Steiner's offer. Chenen and Dalbec then submitted the offer to Pfaff, who accepted it on Mobil's behalf. Other Mobil em-

[b.] *California Uniform Commercial Code § 2207, subdivision (1), should not be narrowly read to conform to the principle of mutual assent to all essential terms.*

As we have seen, § 2204 quite clearly does *not* incorporate the rule that parties must mutually assent to all essential terms. Mobil has thus failed to establish the premise that it would postulate as justifying a narrow reading of § 2207, subdivision (1). We shall, however, briefly consider Mobil's other and further arguments concerning the construction of § 2207, and show that these arguments, taken in isolation, are consistent neither with the language of § 2207, subdivision (1), nor with the logic of § 2207 as a whole.

Initially, Mobil focuses on § 2207, subdivision (1)'s requirement of a "definite . . . expression of acceptance." Mobil would define "definite" by reference to the extent of the difference between offer and acceptance: the more significant the divergence, the less definitely a response is an acceptance. This construction suffers from two flaws. First, in § 2207, subdivision (1), "definite" modifies "expression" and not "acceptance," and thus refers to the *process* of offer and acceptance and not to the *terms* of the acceptance itself. Second, in any event, § 2207 as a whole bars any interpretation of "definite" which, as Mobil urges, would exclude from the ranks of acceptances all but collateral variations on the terms of offers. Section 2207, subdivision (2)(b)'s concern with material variations necessarily implies that acceptances incorporating such variations can satisfy the requirements of subdivision (1).

Mobil would also construe the final clause of § 2207, subdivision (1), which provides that, if acceptance "is expressly made conditional on assent to . . . additional or different terms," the "acceptance" does not operate as an acceptance but as a counteroffer. Specifically Mobil argues that we should read this provision broadly, by adopting the interpretation advanced in *Roto-Lith, Ltd. v. F. P. Bartlett & Co., supra,* 297 F.2d at page 500: "a response which states a condition materially altering the obligation solely to the disadvantage of the offeror is an 'acceptance . . . expressly . . . conditional on assent to the additional . . . terms.'"

Again, however, Mobil's construction does not accord with the language of the section. Such an interpretation of the conditional acceptance clause would transform acceptances into counteroffers without regard to whether the acceptance is in fact, as § 2207, subdivision (1), requires, "expressly made conditional on assent to . . . additional or different terms." Moreover, under Mobil's reading, the conditional acceptance clause of § 2207, subdivision (1), would largely duplicate the function of the material variation clause of § 2207, subdivision (2)(b).

---

ployees treated Pfaff's decision as terminating negotiations: Chenen told Steiner to go ahead with the service station purchase; Montemarano delivered the contract documents to Steiner without comment or cover letter. Thus, because of the hierarchical structure which Mobil imposed on the bargaining, the trial court could conclude, as it did, that Mobil intended to accept Steiner's offer and not merely to continue negotiations.

In this case, thus, the serious nature of the contract provision in dispute does not preclude a finding that they intended to conclude a contract; the parties' negotiating procedure itself reveals their intent. In other cases, in which negotiations are not so well organized, the importance of a term which the parties leave open may very well be a decisive measure of whether the parties intended to enter into a contract. . . .

As Mobil concedes, courts and commentators alike have repeatedly criticized the *Roto-Lith* interpretation of § 2207, subdivision (1). . . . Most courts have rejected *Roto-Lith*, and have instead interpreted the conditional acceptance clause literally, as we did earlier. . . . Recognizing the superiority of the majority view, we reject Mobil's attempt to advance the *Roto-Lith* interpretation of § 2207, subdivision (1).

4. *Conclusion.*

In this case, as we have seen, the trial court correctly concluded that under § 2207 the guaranteed discount included in the terms of Steiner's offer, and not Mobil's standard revocable discount provision, became part of the agreement between Mobil and Steiner. Mobil cannot assert as a defense the failure of its own bureaucracy to respond to, or even fully recognize, Steiner's efforts to modify the standard Mobil dealer contract.

The judgment is affirmed. [Bird, C. J., Mosk, J., Clark, J., Richardson, J., Manuel, J., and Jefferson, J., concurred.]

NOTES AND QUESTIONS

1. *Of offers and acceptances*: Suppose the court had found that the package of forms created by Chenen and Steiner and submitted to Pfaff was a proposal and not an offer. Then assume the court found that the manila folder containing the documents approved by Pfaff was an offer. Finally, assume that Steiner's actions in acquiring the service station property and running the business under the competitive allowance were deemed an acceptance. Would a court decide the case for Mobil?

Remember that UCC § 2-207(1) applies only to a "definite and seasonable expression of acceptance." However, does anything of substance turn on whether a court classifies Mobil's documents in the manila folder as the offer or as an acceptance of Steiner's offer? Justice Tobriner wrote "[i]nstead of fastening upon abstract doctrinal concepts like offer and acceptance, § 2207 looks to the actual dealings of the parties and gives legal effect to that conduct. . . . Section 2207 requires courts to put aside the formal and academic stereotypes of traditional doctrinal offer and acceptance and to analyze instead what really happens." Can a court put aside the "formal and academic stereotype" of an acceptance when § 2-207(1) says it applies to an acceptance? Should the section be amended to avoid this problem?

In light of the fact that Steiner had objected in the strongest possible way to giving Mobil the right to change the competitive allowance, could we make an argument for him based on UCC §§2-204, 1-201(3)?

2. *Section 2-207 and "a written confirmation"*: As we have discussed, § 2-207 applies to the exchange of two or more forms. However, it also applies to a different situation. Suppose the buyer and seller made an oral contract in a telephone conversation. Then the seller sends the buyer a printed form confirming that order. There are terms on the confirmation form additional to or different from the oral order. We could read the *Steiner* case as involving a variation of this situation. Steiner and the lower ranking Mobil officials put together an offer.

Then Chenen, Mobil's area manager, told Steiner that the deal had been approved and that Steiner should buy the property. The folder with all the Mobil standard terms was a written confirmation of that telephone call. (Of course, this reading requires us to assume that under the law of agency that Chenen had apparent authority to pass along a commitment by Mobil). If we read the forms in the folder as a written confirmation, would the result in the case change?

Suppose a buyer telephones a seller and orders a computer or computer software. The seller's employee takes the order. Nothing is said about warranties, remedy limitations, arbitration or any other terms beyond a description of the goods and the price. The goods are shipped to the buyer along with a seller's document (an invoice or a page in the instruction manual) which contains a disclaimer of warranties, a remedy limitation and an arbitration clause. Does § 2-207 apply? In *ProCD, Inc. v. Zeidenberg*,[114] Judge Easterbrook said "Our case has only one form; UCC 2-207 is irrelevant." Judge Wisdom applied § 2-207 to a situation somewhat like our hypothetical; he did not think that you must have two documents for this section to apply.[115] Which United States Circuit Judge reads statutes the best?

3. *Why did the middle managers create the mess*? Unfortunately, the briefs cast no light at all on the most interesting question raised by the case: Why did the middle managers of Mobil create the problem by not telling their supervisor about the competitive allowance provision? Compare the role of the architect in *Vickery v. Ritchie, supra.*

4. *The interpretation of § 2-207(2)—"additional vs. different" terms*: In one of the long footnotes in *Steiner* the court addresses an argument which arises in the course of interpreting § 2-207(2). The question is whether there is an important distinction between "different" and "additional" terms. The question arises because § 2-207(1) refers to acceptances in which terms are either "additional to or different from" the offered terms, whereas § 2-207(2) seems to concern itself only with "additional" terms. The court mentions, in that footnote, the case of *Air Products & Chemicals, Inc. v. Fairbanks Morse, Inc.*,[116] the facts of which may serve not only to illuminate that issue, but as a useful review and drill concerning the difficulties of applying § 2-207.

It seems that Air Products wanted to buy some large electric motors from Fairbanks Morse. After discussions about the specifications of the motors, Air Products verbally agreed to buy several. Air Products then submitted a purchase order. Fairbanks Morse returned an executed copy of the purchase order together with Fairbanks Morse's acknowledgment of order form. Air Products asserted that the motors failed to perform properly, and brought suit against Fairbanks Morse. (The complaint alleged 43 causes of action; they must have been really mad!) Fairbanks Morse interposed as a defense a limitation of liability term contained on its acknowledgment of order form. The front of the Fairbanks form contained the following language, which the Wisconsin Supreme Court described as being printed "in reasonably bold face type at the bottom." We have tried, as

---

[114] 86 F.3d 1447 (7th Cir. 1996).

[115] *See* Step-Saver Data Systems, Inc. v. Wyse Technology, 939 F.2d 91 (3d Cir. 1991).

[116] 58 Wis. 2d 193, 206 N.W.2d 414 (1973).

nearly as we could, to reproduce the type size of the form itself. You might note that § 2-207 contains no explicit requirement of conspicuousness. Does this mean the appearance of the clause is irrelevant?

> WE THANK YOU FOR YOUR ORDER AS COPIED HEREON, WHICH WILL RECEIVE PROMPT ATTENTION AND SHALL BE GOVERNED BY THE PROVISIONS ON THE RE-VERSE SIDE HEREOF UNLESS YOU NOTIFY US TO THE CONTRARY WITHIN 10 DAYS OR BEFORE SHIPMENT WHICHEVER IS EARLIER.

> BEFORE ACCEPTING GOODS FROM TRANSPORTATION COMPANY SEE THAT EACH ARTICLE IS IN GOOD CONDITION. IF SHORTAGE OR DAMAGE IS APPARENT REFUSE SHIPMENT UNLESS AGENT NOTES DEFECT ON TRANSPORTATION BILL. ACCEP-TANCE OF SHIPMENT WITHOUT COMPLYING WITH SUCH CONDITIONS IS AT YOUR OWN RISK.

> THIS IS NOT AN INVOICE. AN INVOICE FOR THIS MATERIAL WILL BE SENT YOU WITHIN A FEW DAYS.

ACKNOWLEDGEMENT OF ORDER

The reverse side of the "acknowledgment of order" contained six printed provisions that were immediately preceded by the following statement:

> The following provisions form part of the order acknowledged and accepted on the face hereof, as express agreements between Fairbanks, Morse & Co. ("Company") and the Buyer governing the terms and conditions of the sale, subject to modification only in writing signed by the local manager or an executive officer of the Company:

Provision 6, which became the subject of the dispute between the parties, provided:

> 6.—The Company nowise assumes any responsibility or liability with respect to use, purpose, or suitability, and shall not be liable for damages of any character, whether direct or consequential, for defect, delay, or otherwise, its sole liability and obligation being confined to the replacement in the manner aforesaid of defectively manufactured guaranteed parts failing within the time stated.

Fairbanks Morse asserted that Paragraph 6 became part of the contract, and effectively limited its liability. Air Products asserted that Paragraph 6 did NOT become part of the contract and therefore, that Air Products was entitled to rely on the Code's provisions governing the implied warranties of merchantability, fitness for a particular purpose, and providing for recovery of consequential damages. The trial court had concluded, apparently without thoroughly considering UCC § 2-207(2)(b) that, since the terms limiting damages were completely new and additional proposed terms, and since the parties were merchants, the terms became part of the contract.

Air Products advanced two arguments to seek to avoid Paragraph 6. They first argued that § 2-207(2) only applies to "additional" terms; that is, that only terms which can be characterized as "additional" can become part of the contract by reason of the application of § 2-207(2). Air Products then, of necessity, argued that Paragraph 6 was a "different, as opposed to an "additional" term, and so was not included *via* § 2-207(2). They argued that terms are "additional" if they concern a subject matter not addressed in the offer, and that they are "different" if they concern a subject matter which was covered but dealt with in a variant way.

Air Products then argued that their offer must be regarded as including the terms expressly included AND the terms implied by law—such as the implied warranty and damages claims. *Voila!* By this logic the Fairbanks Morse confirmation contains a "different" term because it is at variance with the terms of the offer, which included the implied terms concerning warranty and liability.

Fairbanks Morse sought to parry the thrust of this argument by asserting that recovery of consequential damages is not included in every contract by implication, since they are only recoverable "in a proper case" (§ 2-714(3)). As a result, even if you accept the first steps of the Air Products' argument, Paragraph 6 is okay because recovery of consequential damages is not among the terms which could fairly be implied in a contract otherwise silent on the topic.

The court expressed doubt about the basic premise of the entire debate, suggesting that the Code should not be interpreted as creating an important distinction between "different" and "additional" terms. But in addition to suggesting the argument was perhaps irrelevant, the court rejected Fairbanks Morse's counter-argument by carrying it one step farther. The court noted that the Comment to § 2-715 observes that sellers are liable to buyers for consequential damages in cases in which the seller "had reason to know of the buyer's general or particular requirements at the time of contracting." In this case Fairbanks Morse was aware of the needs of Air Products, making it a "proper case" for recovery of consequential losses—and so a recovery of consequential loss was implicit in the contract.

Air Products' second argument was more direct, since it was not based on the argument that "additional" terms and "different" terms should be treated differently—an argument which has been widely criticized. Air Products argued that the disclaimer in the Fairbanks Morse acknowledgment was a material alteration of the agreement and could become a part of the contract only if expressly agreed to. To quote from the Court's decision:

> Hartford and Air Products contend that the eradication of a multimillion dollar damage exposure is per se material. Fairbanks bases its argument on the ground that consequential damages may not be recovered except in "special circumstances" or in a "proper case." (§§ 2-714(2) and (3)). As already stated, these "special circumstances" would seem by comment 3 to § 2-715 to be referring to situations which concern instances where the seller [had] reason to know of buyer's general or particular requirements at the time of contracting. "Consequential damages resulting from the seller's breach include (a) any loss resulting from general or particular requirements and needs of which the seller at the time of contracting had reason to know and which could not reasonably be prevented by cover or otherwise; . . . ." UCC § 2-715(2)(a).

> While the comment 4 clearly indicates that a disclaimer of an implied warranty of merchantability is material, there is no good reason to hold that a disclaimer that has the effect of eliminating millions of dollars in damages should become a part of a contract by operation of law.

We conclude that the disclaimer for consequential loss was sufficiently material to require express conversation between the parties over its inclusion or exclusion in the contract.[117]

5. *An additional argument in Air Products v. Fairbanks Morse*: The lawyers for Fairbanks Morse made an argument in their brief which seems not to have been confronted in the court's opinion. The argument, essentially, was that the Code, in § 2-719(3), provides that limitations on consequential damages are valid unless unconscionable. This goes to whether a limitation on consequential damages should be regarded as a material alteration of the offer. In the commercial world in which Air Products and Fairbanks Morse were resident, such limitations were, allegedly, quite common, and in the words of the Fairbanks Morse brief, "effectuate the very purpose of § 2-719 which is to encourage and facilitate the allocation of risks associated with the sale of goods, particularly those occurring in a commercial setting."

Suppose Fairbanks Morse's lawyers commissioned a survey of machinery manufacturers and purchasers, and this survey showed that in, say, 92.66% of all contracts for the sale of machinery consequential damages were ruled out. Would, or should, this information change the court's decision? Suppose the clause was found in 60% of all contracts? In 40%? Would an attitude survey be better? Suppose businesspeople were asked whether they expected to be able to recover consequential damages, and 85% said that they would not in the ordinary case. Would this be relevant to the application of § 2-207 to the Fairbanks Morse situation? How does the Supreme Court of Wisconsin get its data on whether the remedy limitation materially alters the contract created by F-M's acceptance? Or is it a question of data?

6. *Once burned, twice shy*: You might be interested to learn that as a result of the litigation with Fairbanks Morse, Air Products adopted the following language in its purchase order form. This is the fifteenth clause printed in small type on the back of the form:

> This Order shall be binding upon the parties either upon receipt of Seller's acknowledgment of its acceptance hereof or commencement of its performance of the work contemplated by this Order. No terms or conditions in Seller's order acknowledgment form or in any other form of acceptance of this Order, shall bind Buyer or modify Seller's obligations hereunder, unless accepted in writing by Buyer.

7. *Additional or different terms*: UCC § 2-207(1) finds a contract created by an acceptance "even though it states terms additional to or different from those offered. . . ." Subsection (2), however, talks about "additional terms" but says nothing about "different" ones. The courts in both the *Steiner* and *Air Products* cases seem to think that the distinction between additional and different terms should not matter. Professor Murray argues that we should begin by looking to the purposes of the section. He notes that "if a material term became part of the contract contrary to the reasonable understanding of the offeror, the result would be oppression, hardship, or unfair surprise to the offeror—the essential evil to be

---

[117] *Id.* at 213-14, 206 N.W.2d at 424-25.

avoided." He thinks the drafters made a reasonable distinction, and that the distinction can be drawn in a way that supports the Code's policy objectives. He tells us:

> [N]o illustration of a nonmatching term in an acceptance is both material and additional without being different. If a so-called additional term is also material in that it creates hardship and unfair surprise to the offeror, it is by definition different. . . . If a term in the acceptance properly is characterized as additional and not different, this additional term necessarily is an immaterial term that, between merchants, would become part of the contract.[118]

8. *One more example*: Given the complexity of § 2-207, it should not be a surprise that courts adopt different, and sometimes apparently inconsistent, ways of applying it. One more example is *Northern States Power Co. v. International Telephone and Telegraph Corp.*[119] NSP contracted with ITT for anchors used in erecting power line towers. Each anchor consisted of a 10-foot long section capable of being augered into the ground. Guy wires were attached from the anchors to points near the top of the tower. Welds on some anchors were defective, and towers fell. NSP had to replace all of the anchors. NSP sued for damages of over $2,400,000. ITT moved for summary judgment, arguing that NSP's claim was barred by ITT's remedy limitation.

The court denied the motion. The trier of fact could find that the remedy limitation was part of the contract. NSP had sent a request for quotation to ITT. ITT responded with a proposal containing a detailed remedy limitation. During the negotiations the parties did not discuss limitation of liability. NSP issued a purchase order which did not specifically mention the remedy limitations in ITT's proposal. It did say "[c]onfirming Verbal Order of 8-11-78 Per Your Proposal #780049 of 7-16-78."[120] ITT then issued a sales acknowledgment which again included the remedy limitation. NSP did not respond, and the parties proceeded to perform the contract.

While the court cited § 2-207, it did not discuss the terms of the statute. It said only:

> The purchase order (offer) makes no express reference to the limitation of liability clause. The sales acknowledgment (acceptance) does contain the clause, but this reference to the clause does not necessarily mean the acknowledgment varies from the terms of the purchase order. Prior to the purchase order Meyer [a division of ITT] had submitted a proposal that included a special reference to the limitation of liability clause, and NSP had placed a verbal order during discussions between the parties. The subsequent purchase order could be merely a written verification of the verbal order; it made express reference to Meyer's proposal. . . . On this

---

[118] Murray, *The Chaos of the "Battle of the Forms": Solutions*, 39 Vand. L. Rev. 1307, 1359, 1361, 1364, 1365 (1986).

[119] 550 F. Supp. 108 (D. Minn. 1982).

[120] *Id.* at 110.

record the trier of fact could find the limitation of liability clause part of the contract between the parties.[121]

The court also decided that the trier of fact could find that ITT's remedy limitation "failed of its essential purpose" and was ineffective under § 2-719. Is the result consistent with *Steiner* and *Air Products*?

C. ITOH & CO. (AMERICA) INC. v. JORDAN INTERNATIONAL CO.
United States Court of Appeals, Seventh Circuit
552 F.2d 1228 (1977)

SPRECHER, J. The sole issue on this appeal is whether the district court properly denied a stay of the proceedings pending arbitration under § 3 of the Federal Arbitration Act, 9 U.S.C. § 3.

I.   C. Itoh & Co. (America) Inc. ("Itoh") submitted a purchase order dated August 15, 1974 for a certain quantity of steel coils to the Jordan International Company ("Jordan"). In response, Jordan sent its acknowledgment form dated August 19, 1974. On the face of Jordan's form, the following statement appears:

> Seller's acceptance is, however, expressly conditional on Buyer's assent to the additional or different terms and conditions set forth below and printed on the reverse side. If these terms and conditions are not acceptable, Buyer should notify seller at once.

One of the terms on the reverse side of Jordan's form was a broad provision for arbitration.[122] Itoh neither expressly assented nor objected to the additional arbitration term in Jordan's form until the instant litigation.

Itoh also entered into a contract to sell the steel coils that it purchased from Jordan to Riverview Steel Corporation, Inc. ("Riverview"). The contract between Itoh and Riverview contained an arbitration term which provided in pertinent part:

> Any and all controversies arising out of or relating to this contract, or any modification, breach or cancellation thereof, *except as to quality*, shall be settled by arbitration. . . .

After the steel had been delivered by Jordan and paid for by Itoh, Riverview advised Itoh that the steel coils were defective and did not conform to the standards set forth in the agreement between Itoh and Riverview; for these reasons, Riverview refused to pay Itoh for the steel. Consequently, Itoh brought the instant suit against Riverview and Jordan. Itoh alleged that Riverview had wrongfully refused to pay for the steel; as affirmative defenses, Riverview claimed that the steel was defective and that tender was improper since delivery was late. Itoh alleged that Jordan had sold Itoh defective steel and had made a late delivery of that steel.

---

[121] *Id.* at 112.

[122] [1] The arbitration clause provides:

Any controversy arising under or in connection with the contract shall be submitted to arbitration in New York City in accordance with the rules then obtaining of the American Arbitration Association. Judgment on any award may be entered in any court having jurisdiction. . . .

Jordan then filed a motion in the district court requesting a stay of the proceedings pending arbitration under § 3 of the Federal Arbitration Act, 9 U.S.C. § 3. The district court concluded that, as between Itoh and Riverview, the issue of whether the steel coils were defective was not referable to arbitration because of the "quality" exclusion in the arbitration provision of the contract between Itoh and Riverview. Since arbitration would not necessarily resolve all the issues raised by the parties, the district court, apparently assuming *arguendo* that there existed an agreement in writing between Jordan and Itoh to arbitrate their dispute, denied the stay pending arbitration. In the district court's opinion, sound judicial administration required that the entire litigation be resolved in a single forum; since some of the issues—those relating to quality between Itoh and Riverview—were not referable to arbitration, this goal could only be accomplished in the judicial forum.

It is from this denial of a stay pending arbitration that Jordan appeals. . . .

III. Having concluded that the district court had no discretion under § 3 of the Federal Arbitration Act, 9 U.S.C. § 3, to deny Jordan's timely application for a stay of the action pending arbitration *if* there existed an agreement in writing for such arbitration between Jordan and Itoh, the remaining issue is whether there existed such an agreement. . . .

In support of its contention that there exists an agreement in writing to arbitrate, Jordan places some reliance on certain New York decisions interpreting § 2-201 of the Uniform Commercial Code, the UCC Statute of Frauds provision. That section provides in pertinent part:

> (1) Except as otherwise provided in this section a contract for the sale of goods for the price of $500 or more is not enforceable by way of action or defense unless there is some writing sufficient to indicate that a contract for sale has been made between the parties and signed by the party against whom enforcement is sought . . .

> (2) Between merchants if within a reasonable time a writing in confirmation of the contract and sufficient against the sender is received and the party receiving it has reason to know its contents, it satisfies the requirements of subsection (1) against such party unless written notice of objection to its contents is given within ten days after it is received.

Several New York lower court decisions have apparently held that under § 2-201, where there has been an oral offer or agreement followed by a written confirmation containing an additional arbitration term and where the merchant recipient of the confirmation has reason to expect that a provision for arbitration would be included in any written confirmation of an oral offer or agreement, the arbitration provision becomes a part of the parties' agreement unless notice of objection is given within the prescribed period. . . .

These decisions are premised on a fundamental misconception of the purpose and effect of § 2-201. *See generally* Duesenberg & King, Sales and Bulk Transfers Under the Uniform Commercial Code § 308[1] at 97-99 (1976). The *only* effect of a failure to object to a written confirmation of an oral offer or agreement under § 2-201 is to take away from the receiving merchant the defense of the Statute of Frauds. . . . Although § 2-201 may make *enforceable* an oral agreement which was in fact reached by the parties, it does not relieve the party seeking enforcement of the alleged oral agreement of the obligation to prove its existence. Official Comment 3 to § 2-201. Section 2-201 obviously cannot be relied on to make a particular term, such as a provision for arbitration, binding on a party if that section does not even serve to establish the *existence* of an agreement.

The Official Comments make clear that, while under § 2-201 the failure to object to a written confirmation of an oral agreement has the limited effect of removing the Statute of Frauds as a bar to the enforceability of an oral agreement, under § 2-207 a failure to object to a term in a written confirmation may, *under the circumstances specified by that section*, have the effect of making that term a part of whatever agreement is proved to have been reached by the parties. Official Comment 3 to § 2-201. Hence, once the existence and terms of an alleged oral agreement have been established, it is necessary to refer to § 2-207, Additional Terms in Acceptance *or Confirmation*, not § 2-201, to ascertain whether a term included in a written confirmation but not in the parties' oral agreement is binding on the recipient of the written confirmation. . . .

However, even if we assume that New York's highest court would adhere to those lower court decisions and their extremely questionable application of the Statute of Frauds to situations where a party has added an arbitration term to a written *confirmation* of an oral offer or agreement, this is not such a situation. Jordan does not suggest that its acknowledgment form was simply a *confirmation* of a prior *oral* offer or agreement. Rather, Jordan's argument is that *the exchange of forms* between itself and Itoh *created* a contract, which includes the additional arbitration term in Jordan's form.

The instant case, therefore, involves the classic "battle of the forms," and § 2-207, not § 2-201, furnishes the rules for resolving such a controversy. Hence, it is to § 2-207 that we must look to determine whether a contract has been formed by the exchange of forms between Jordan and Itoh and, if so, whether the additional arbitration term in Jordan's form is to be included in that contract. . . .

IV. . . . Under § 2-207 it is necessary to first determine whether a contract has been formed under § 2-207(1) as a result of the *exchange of forms* between Jordan and Itoh.

At common law, an acceptance which contained terms additional to those of the offer constituted a rejection of the offer and thus became a counter-offer. Thus, the mere presence of the additional arbitration term in Jordan's acknowledgment form would, at common law, have prevented the exchange of documents between Jordan and Itoh from creating a contract, and Jordan's form would have automatically become a counter-offer.

Section 2-207(1) was intended to alter this inflexible common law approach to offer and acceptance. . . .

However, while § 2-207(1) constitutes a sharp departure from the common law "mirror image" rule, there remain situations where the inclusion of an additional term in one of the forms exchanged by the parties will prevent the consummation of a contract *under that section*. Section 2-207(1) contains a proviso which operates to prevent an exchange of forms from creating a contract where "acceptance is expressly made conditional on assent to the additional . . . terms." In the instant case, Jordan's acknowledgment form contained the following statement:

> Seller's acceptance is . . . *expressly conditional* on Buyer's *assent* to the additional or different terms and conditions set forth below and printed on the reverse side. If these terms and conditions are not acceptable, Buyer should notify Seller at once.

The arbitration provision at issue on this appeal is printed on the reverse side of Jordan's acknowledgment, and there is no dispute that Itoh never expressly assented to the challenged arbitration term.

The Court of Appeals for the Sixth Circuit has held that the proviso must be construed narrowly:

> Although . . . [seller's] use of the words "subject to" suggests that the acceptances were conditional to some extent, we do not believe the acceptances were "expressly made conditional on [the buyer's] assent to the additional or different terms," as specifically required under the Subsection 2-207(1) proviso. In order to fall within this proviso, it is not enough that an acceptance is expressly conditional on additional or different terms; rather, an acceptance must be expressly conditional on the offeror's *assent* to those terms (emphasis in original).

. . . [I]t is clear that the statement contained in Jordan's acknowledgment form comes within the § 2-207(1) proviso.

Hence, the exchange of forms between Jordan and Itoh did not result in the formation of a contract under § 2-207(1), and Jordan's form became a counteroffer. "[T]he consequence of a clause conditioning acceptance on assent to the additional or different terms is that *as of the exchanged writings, there is no contract*. Either party may at this point in their dealings walk away from the transaction." Duesenberg & King, *supra*, § 3.06[3] at 73. However, neither Jordan nor Itoh elected to follow that course; instead, both parties proceeded to performance—Jordan by delivering and Itoh by paying for the steel coils.

At common law, the "terms of the counter-offer were said to have been accepted by the original offeror when he proceeded to perform under the contract without objecting to the counter-offer.". . . Thus, under pre-Code law, Itoh's performance (*i.e.*, payment for the steel coils) probably constituted acceptance of the Jordan counter-offer, including its provision for arbitration. However, a different approach is required under the Code.

Section 2-207(3) of the Code first provides that "conduct by both parties which recognizes the existence of a contract is sufficient to establish a contract for sale although the writings of the parties do not otherwise establish a contract." . . . . Thus, "[s]ince . . . [Itoh's] purchase order and . . . [Jordan's] counter-offer did not in themselves create a contract, § 2-207(3) would operate to create one because the subsequent performance by both parties constituted 'conduct by both parties which recognizes the existence of a contract.' " . . .

What are the terms of a contract created by conduct under § 2-207(3) rather than by an exchange of forms under § 2-207(1)? As noted above, at common law the terms of the contract between Jordan and Itoh would be the terms of the Jordan counter-offer. However, the Code has effectuated a radical departure from the common law rule.[123] The second sentence of § 2-207(3) provides that where, as here, a contract has been consummated by the conduct of the parties, "the terms of the particular contract consist of those terms on which the writings of the parties agree, together with any supplementary terms incorporated under any other provisions of this Act." Since it is clear that the Jordan and Itoh forms do not "agree" on arbitration, the only question which remains *under the Code* is whether arbitration may be considered a supplementary term incorporated under some other provision of the Code.

We have been unable to find any case authority shedding light on the question of what constitutes "supplementary terms" within the meaning of § 2-207(3) and the Official Comments to § 2-207 provide no guidance in this regard. We are persuaded, however, that the disputed additional terms (*i.e.*, those terms on which the writings of the parties do not agree) which are necessarily excluded from a Subsection (3) contract by the language, "terms on which the writings of the parties agree," cannot be brought back into the contract under the guise of "supplementary terms." This conclusion has substantial support among the commentators who have addressed themselves to the issue. As two noted authorities on Article Two of the Code have stated:

> It will usually happen that an offeree-seller who returns an acknowledgment form will also concurrently or shortly thereafter ship the goods. If the responsive document [sent by the seller] contains a printed assent clause, and the goods are shipped and accepted, Subsection (3) of § 2-207 comes into play. . . . [T]he terms on which the exchanged communications do not agree drop out of the transaction, and reference to the Code is made to supply necessary terms. . . . Rather than choosing the terms of one party over those of the other . . . it compels supplying missing terms by reference to the Code.

Duesenberg & King, *supra*, § 3.06[4] at 73-74. Similarly, Professors White and Summers have concluded that "contract formation under subsection (3) gives neither party the relevant terms of his document, but fills out the contract with the standardized provisions of Article Two." White & Summers [Uniform Commercial Code 30 (1972), at 29].

Accordingly, we find that the "supplementary terms" contemplated by § 2-207(3) are limited to those supplied by the standardized "gap-filler" provisions of Article Two. *See, e.g.*, § 2-308(a) ("Unless otherwise agreed . . . the place for delivery of goods is the seller's place of business or if he has none his residence"); § 2-309(1) ("The time for shipment or delivery or any other action under a contract if not . . . agreed upon shall be a reasonable time"); § 2-310(a) ("Unless otherwise agreed . . . payment is due at the time and place at which the buyer is to receive the goods even though the place of shipment is the place of

---

[123] [8] Jordan relies on Roto-Lith [Ltd. v. F.B. Bartlett & Co., 297 F.2d 497 (1st Cir. 1962)], in support of its contention that Itoh's payment for the steel coils constituted acceptance of all the terms in Jordan's counter-offer. In Roto-Lith the court ignored § 2-207(3) and simply applied the common law rule. . . . [W]e adopt the consensus of the courts and commentators that Roto-Lith, in reading § 2-207(3) out of the Code, evidences an incorrect interpretation and application of § 2-207.

delivery"). Since provision for arbitration is not a necessary or missing term which would be supplied by one of the Code's "gap-filler" provisions unless agreed upon by the contracting parties, there is no arbitration term in the § 2-207(3) contract which was created by the conduct of Jordan and Itoh in proceeding to perform even though no contract had been established by their exchange of writings.

We are convinced that this conclusion does not result in any unfair prejudice to a seller who elects to insert in his standard sales acknowledgment form the statement that acceptance is expressly conditional on buyer's assent to additional terms contained therein. Such a seller obtains a substantial benefit *under § 2-207(1)* through the inclusion of an "expressly conditional" clause. If he decides after the exchange of forms that the particular transaction is not in his best interest, Subsection (1) permits him to walk away from the transaction without incurring any liability so long as the buyer has not in the interim expressly assented to the additional terms. Moreover, whether or not a seller will be disadvantaged *under Subsection (3)* as a consequence of inserting an "expressly conditional" clause in his standard form is within his control. If the seller in fact does not intend to close a particular deal unless the additional terms are assented to, he can protect himself by not delivering the goods until such assent is forthcoming. If the seller does intend to close a deal irrespective of whether or not the buyer assents to the additional terms, he can hardly complain when the contract formed under Subsection (3) as a result of the parties' conduct is held not to include those terms. Although a seller who employs such an "expressly conditional" clause in his acknowledgment form would undoubtedly appreciate the dual advantage of not being bound to a contract under Subsection (1) if he elects not to perform and of having his additional terms imposed on the buyer under Subsection (3) in the event that performance is in his best interest, we do not believe such a result is contemplated by § 2-207. Rather, while a seller may take advantage of an "expressly conditional" clause under Subsection (1) when he elects not to perform, he must accept the potential risk under Subsection (3) of not getting his additional terms when he elects to proceed with performance without first obtaining buyer's assent to those terms. Since the seller injected ambiguity into the transaction by inserting the "expressly conditional" clause in his form, he, and not the buyer, should bear the consequence of that ambiguity under Subsection (3).

Moreover, even were we to assume *arguendo* that, in a simple diversity case, a disputed additional term, while not becoming part of a § 2-207(3) contract as a consequence of the writings exchanged by the parties (which is clearly precluded by the language of Subsection (3)), could be brought into that contract as a "supplementary term" by implication from custom and usage, the district court's denial of the stay application must still be affirmed. After the Supreme Court's decision in *Prima Paint [Corp. v. Flood & Conklin Mfg. Co.,* 388 U.S. 395 (1967),] it is clear that "this action is not a simple diversity suit, but involves federal rights asserted under the Federal Arbitration Act." *Commonwealth Edison Co. v. Gulf Oil Corp.,* 541 F.2d 1263 (7th Cir. 1976). Accordingly, "[f]ederal courts are bound to apply rules enacted by Congress with respect to matters—here, a contract involving commerce—over which it has legislative power." *Prima Paint, supra*, 388 U.S. at 406. Under § 3 of the Federal Arbitration Act, 9 U.S.C. § 3, federal district courts may issue a stay order only where there is an agreement in *writing* for arbitration. While the arbitration provision need not be signed to come within § 3, the Act requires that there be a *written* agreement to arbitrate. *See Fisser v. International Bank*, 282 F.2d 231 (2d Cir. 1960). As noted above, there is no *written* arbitration provision included in the contract created under § 2-207(3) when Jordan and Itoh proceeded to performance.

Accordingly, for the reasons stated in this opinion, the decision of the district court is affirmed.

NOTES AND QUESTIONS

1.   *The real dispute and making a case*: The briefs and record suggest that the legal proceedings were a game far removed from the assumptions and understandings of the real parties to the dispute. Itoh, the buyer, submitted a purchase order for steel coils. Jordan, the seller, confirmed the order on its own form. The terms on this confirmation included a standard American Arbitration Association clause calling for arbitration of disputes. Itoh then contracted to sell the steel coils to Riverview. Riverview submitted a purchase order, and Itoh accepted the order on its form that included the same standard American Arbitration Association clause calling for arbitration of disputes. Jordan pointed out that arbitration clauses are the custom in the steel brokerage industry, Itoh regularly used them, and Itoh knew that Jordan regularly used them. Moreover, the exact arguments based on UCC § 2-201 (the Statute of Frauds section) asserted here by Jordan, had been asserted successfully by Itoh in *Klockner, Inc. v. Itoh & Co.*[124] to bring an arbitration clause into a bargain on the same facts as were before the court in this case. Is such a triumph of legal technicality justified? Or does the case represent a failure of legal technique?

2.   *Other provisions of this Act*: The court in the *Itoh* case says that § 2-207(3) governs, and that if the parties' documents fail to create a bargain but their conduct recognizes the existence of one, then the terms are those upon which they agree plus all of the gap-filling provisions of Article 2. Furnish[125] argues that the terms of a § 2-207(3) contract should be based on agreement plus Article 1 as well as Article 2. If this view were accepted, then a court could look to sections such as § 1-205, which deals with course of dealing and usage of trade. If arbitration could be shown to be the usage of the steel brokerage trade, then it could "supplement or qualify terms of an agreement." For this approach to change the result in the *Itoh* case, the seller would have had to show "any practice or method of dealing having such regularity of observance in a place, vocation or trade as to justify an expectation that it will be observed with respect to the transaction in question." Official Comment 5 to § 1-205 provides in part:

> 5.   A usage of trade . . . must have the "regularity of observance" specified. The ancient English tests for "custom" are abandoned in this

---

[124] 17 U.C.C. Rep. Serv. 915 (N.Y. Sup. Ct. 1975).

[125] *Commercial Arbitration Agreements and the Uniform Commercial Code*, 67 Cal. L. Rev. 317 (1979).

connection. Therefore, it is not required that a usage of trade be "ancient or immemorial," "universal" or the like. . . . [F]ull recognition is thus available for new usages and for usages currently observed by the great majority of decent dealers, even though dissidents ready to cut corners do not agree.

We will consider course of dealing, usage of trade, and course of performance under § 2-208 in some detail later in this course.

Many modern § 2-207 cases deal with arbitration clauses. On one hand, the Court of Appeals of New York almost never will use UCC § 2-207 to add an arbitration clause to a contract.[126] On the other hand, other courts have found an obligation to arbitrate as a result of the battle of the forms.[127]

c. Lawyers Cope with § 2-207: Business Procedures and Drafting Practices

Lawyers have struggled with the problems posed by the need to anticipate the application of § 2-207. For every controversy which has ripened into a lawsuit, requiring lawyers to figure out how to apply § 2-207 after a transactional breakdown, there are many instances in which lawyers have struggled to draft forms which will either avoid problems, or give their clients an edge if a problem arises. We can set the stage with an interview with the General Counsel of a manufacturer of heating and cooling equipment:

> The battle of the forms is the most important contracts problem the firm faces. Our ordering and billing processes still are back in the days of the Uniform Sales Act when the last shot decided which set of terms and conditions governed. In the process we will fire our terms and conditions more than our customers or vendors, but the other party may have objected under UCC § 2-207.
>
> When we order goods, our form has an acknowledgment copy. When we sell goods we acknowledge purchase orders from our customer or sign their acknowledgment copies, but we stamp their acknowledgment saying that we accept the order in accordance with our terms. There is no

---

[126] In Matter of Marlene Industries Corp., 45 N.Y.2d 327, 380 N.E.2d 239 (1978), the court stressed its long-standing policy that one should not be subject to arbitration in the absence of an express, unequivocal agreement to arbitrate. Receiving a form and doing nothing would not be enough. In Schubtex, Inc. v. Allen Snyder, Inc., 49 N.Y.2d 1, 399 N.E.2d 1154 (1979), the court conceded that an agreement to arbitrate could be implied from a prior course of dealing or usage of trade. However, it demanded clear evidence that the parties agreed to arbitrate their disputes. In the Schubtex case the buyer had retained without objection seller's forms containing arbitration clauses in a number of transactions. The court found this not enough to show a course of dealing. It said that repeated use of an ineffective form does not show an agreement to arbitrate.

[127] For example, in Schulze & Burch Biscuit Co. v. Tree Top, Inc., 831 F.2d 709 (7th Cir. 1987), the court noted, "Tree Top's agent Brady had sent a confirmation form containing the same arbitration provision to Schulze in each of the previous nine transactions he brokered between the two parties. Schulze had ample notice that the tenth confirmation would be likely to include an arbitration clause." Thus, Schulze could not claim "unfair surprise" when its past course of dealing created an obligation to arbitrate. *See also*, Genesco, Inc. v. T. Kakiuchi & Co., Ltd., 815 F.2d 840 (2d Cir. 1986).

real working out of each contract. It would be a hard task since there are 100s if not 1000s of orders passing through the office daily. We have never tried to sit down and negotiate a deal on a routine basis with each customer. It would be impossible.

However, we face special problems in one air conditioning application. We produce what we call a "computer room air conditioning unit." It is a top of the line system with a sophisticated humidity control. It costs a great deal more than a normal installation, but its very name and the way we sell it involves express if not implied warranties that it will protect computers and their software. Suppose one of our units were to fail without a backup available. Someone could lose an entire computer program and all the data. We can foresee this—indeed, the point of our expensive air conditioning installation is to avoid just this. I understand that in an as yet unreported case, a major airline lost 60 days of reservations when an auxiliary power unit for its computer went out. It sued the manufacturer and was successful. We must be concerned because our liability insurance does not cover this. It would cover a case where the unit blew up and the explosion damaged the property of a customer or it would cover water leaking from our unit that caused damage. But "passive" damage isn't covered and cannot be at a reasonable cost.

Our practice with this machine is as follows: if the customer's purchase order has no inconsistent terms, we will treat the situation as one where there is no notice of objection to our disclaimer which will be on our acknowledgment of the order. If the customer's document has an inconsistent requirement, then our sales representative must go to the customer and get a document that says our remedy limitation governs. The sales rep must do this personally and explain that the customer must get its own insurance. Even though there are a lot of equities in our favor since we are warning customers and who can expect us to guarantee a unit forever against any defect, we have had a lot of trouble getting these agreements. As a result of all this trouble, we are now offering an option to our customers. They can buy consequential damages protection. Our approach is to introduce this matter into the negotiations for the contract itself because the exposure is just too great. If the customer does not want to pay for insurance, great, but then don't expect us to underwrite a machine forever.

However, an important problem may remain. Suppose we sell our air conditioner to a mechanical contractor who then installs it in a building. Does the limitation and the opportunity to buy insurance help us now? We had a lawyer in our office work several days at a major university law library, but he could not find a case on the impact of the chance to buy insurance on a third party purchaser. How do you ward off liability to third parties you cannot negotiate with? As a practical matter, you cannot control how your machine is used and maintained, but it is hard to prove that the third party buyer's own fault produced the breakdown that destroyed a computer program and data being processed or stored.

Purchasing agents for mechanical contractors object to our attempts to negotiate contracts since they must bid on terms that come down the chain to them which they cannot modify. Many of them are thinly capitalized, and they will sign anything to get the job. If a job goes bad, they will go bankrupt and lose only a minute book and a corporate seal. As a result, they pay little attention to things that are vital to us.

Matters usually are different when you are dealing with industrial users of our equipment. They are used to being careful, and they see liability as just a simple business problem. You buy just as much warranty as you want. Moreover, typically if air conditioning fails, all that happens is that people get hot. Usually, all that results is unhappiness and not monetary damages. However, if one of our heat exchangers is used in a process where a great deal of money is involved, we try hard to negotiate questions of liability. Then we are careful.

In our role as purchaser, usually we get what we want without question. Our purchase order form is fairly innocuous. We feel that we will get plenty of rights under the UCC if we ever have to look for them. We are a good customer, and other firms treat us well. Generally, all of our suppliers sign our acknowledgment of order form, and this binds them to our terms. In one case, we settled an argument with the president of a supplier by sending him a photocopy of our form with his signature on the bottom. On the other hand, we buy a lot of motors from General Electric, but GE won't just sign our acknowledgment of order form.

The following is taken from a major corporation's acknowledgment of order form, drafted in response to UCC § 2-207:

If your order is an acceptance of a written proposal on the regular Company proposal form without the addition of any other terms and conditions of sale or any other modification, this document shall be treated solely as an acknowledgment of such order. If your order is not such an acceptance, then this document is not intended as an acceptance on the part of our Company, but an offer to provide the goods ordered solely in accordance with the following terms and conditions of sale. If we do not hear from you within two weeks from the date hereof, we shall rely upon your silence as an acceptance therewith. Your acceptance of goods shipped by our Company on this order will in any event constitute an acceptance by you of these terms and conditions of sale.

The drafting effort in the selling form attempts to solve the § 2-207 dilemma by making the buyer's silence an acceptance of the seller's terms and conditions. Will this work? It introduces another constraint into the mix. In most situations I cannot force you to speak to avoid making a contract with me. You can ignore my letters and demands. However, this is not always true. Consult, at this point, the Restatement (Second) of Contracts § 69.

Does the Restatement validate the approach used in the selling forms quoted above? Would the attempt to use silence, or the act of accepting goods, overcome the provisions of UCC § 2-207(3)? Recall §2-206(1)(b). We will encounter another aspect of the "silence as acceptance" rule in just a few pages, when we discuss the "subject to approval of the home office" clause.

On Winning the Battle of the Forms:
An Analysis of Section 2-207 of the Uniform Commercial Code
Frederick D. Lipman[128]

The victorious attorney in the battle of forms must direct his strategy toward making the first offer. The Code favors the party who makes the first offer by giving him the best opportunity to have his terms of sale become part of any subsequent contract. The offeror need only wait and hope that the offeree will do any one of the following things:

(1)   expressly accept the offer or do so by actions which are a reasonable mode of acceptance (e.g. commencing work);

(2)   send an Expression of Acceptance document which does not make the acceptance expressly conditional on assent to the additional or different terms; or

(3)   send a Confirmation document which does not make the acceptance expressly conditional on assent to the additional or different terms.

In either of the three events, the first offeror has obtained a contract with his opponent, without negotiation, containing his own terms of sale and, at worst, only the non-material additions of the offeree's form. The Code's favoritism of the first offeror is reminiscent of the favoritism shown by the common law "last shot doctrine" to the last offeree.

If the seller is to make the first offer, the seller must have a quotation form in his arsenal of weapons and be prepared to "fire it" off to the buyer before the buyer can make the first offer. If the buyer is to make the first offer, the buyer must be prepared to send the seller either a request for quotation form or a purchase order form before the seller can "fire off" his quotation form. It is difficult, but not impossible, to make an offer out of the buyer's request for quotation form, since the buyer will generally use the request for quotation form merely to request an offer from the seller with respect to certain goods described in the buyer's form. Therefore, the buyer must rely heavily on the purchase order form. In the natural sequence of events, if a quotation form is issued by the seller, it will be issued before the buyer's purchase order is issued, and thus the buyer generally has a built-in disadvantage in this regard. Of course, the buyer was also disadvantaged under the common law "last shot doctrine," whereby the buyer was usually deemed to have accepted the seller's last offer when the buyer accepted or used the goods.

If your client is not the first offeror, but in fact the offeree, do not despair; all is not lost, provided certain defensive strategy is employed. Your client must scrupulously avoid engaging in any of the three actions previously set forth and immediately "fire of" a rejection and counteroffer. Of course, your client would not want to call the document "a rejection and counteroffer" since these terms are

---

[128] BUSINESS LAWYER, Vol. 24, No. 789, pp. 802-805 (1969). Reprinted by permission of the American Bar Association.

too harsh and legalistic in tone and might arouse the suspicions of the offeror. Rather the document must have that effect without really saying it.

If your client is the seller who has just received the buyer's purchase order, you can advise him to "fire off" his sales acknowledgment. If your client is the buyer who has just received the seller's quotation form, you can advise him to "fire off" a purchase order. In both cases, however, the form must contain either and preferably both of the following clauses to constitute a rejection an counteroffer:

(1)   a clause negating the fact that it is an Expression of Acceptance or Confirmation document.

(2)   a clause expressly making any acceptance contained in the form conditional on the offer's assent to your additional or different terms.

All defensive moves in a battle have certain inherent risks. The risk of making a rejection and counteroffer is that no contract is thereby formed and, if nothing more is done, either party can with legal immunity walk away from the transaction. The advantage is that by sending the counteroffer, the offeree avoids being bound by all the terms of sale of the offeror. In addition, although there is a risk that a contract will never be formed, the likelihood is that the parties will commence performance and will be deemed to have formed a contract under paragraph (3) of § 2-207. Such a contract will be deemed to contain only those terms on which the forms of the two parties agree, plus such other terms as are read in by the Code. On balance, the risk of not having a contract ultimately formed is very small in the normal transaction and the defensive move previously described is generally well worth the risk.

The Arsenal

Since the prime purpose of engaging in the battle of forms is to save the time and expense of negotiating terms, the attorney had best prepare his arsenal of forms by contemplating all eventualities in the battle. Thus, in preparing the sales acknowledgement form, the seller's attorney must anticipate the possibility that a contract has already been formed between the parties by virtue of the exchange of the quotation form and purchase order form. On the other hand, the buyer's attorney must realize that the purchase order may in any given transaction be either the first offer or the Expression of Acceptance or Confirmation document sent in response to the seller's quotation form. The following are a few thoughts in drafting documents in the arsenal of forms:

(a)   Buyer's request for quotation form—Print the buyer's terms of purchase on this form. Insert a clause stating that any quotation sent in response to the request for quotation is deemed subject to the buyer's terms of purchase, unless seller specifically states the contrary in the typewritten portion of seller's quotation form.

(b)   Seller's quotation form—Insert the clauses contemplated by clauses (a) and (c) of § 2-207(2). State that the dispatch of buyer's purchase order is an acceptance of the quotation if the purchase order agrees with the quotation with respect to certain basic terms, e.g. description of goods, quantity, price and delivery schedule.

(c)   Buyer's purchase order form—Insert the clauses contemplated by clauses (a) and (c) of paragraph (2) of § 2-207 and add the following clause: "Any acceptance contained herein is expressly made conditional on seller's assent to the additional or different terms contained herein." State that the seller's commencement of work or shipment is a mode of acceptance of the purchase order if the sales acknowledgement agrees with the purchase order with respect to certain basic terms, e.g. description of goods, quantity, price and delivery schedule.

(d)   Seller's sales acknowledgement form—State that the form is to be disregarded if a contract has already been formed on seller's terms of sale and insert the following clause: "Any acceptance contained herein is expressly made conditional on buyer's assent to the additional or different terms contained herein."

Training the Manpower

The victor in the battle of the forms will not satisfy himself merely with a well-stocked forms arsenal. The manpower who will use the forms, i.e. the purchasing and selling agents, must also be trained in their use and misuse. Purchasing agents must be trained to avoid making verbal agreements with respect to goods they wish to purchase. Such verbal agreements could convert the purchase order subsequently sent from an offer into a Confirmation document. In such situations, the terms of the verbal agreement of the purchasing agent and, at best, the non-material alterations made to that verbal agreement by the purchase order form would constitute the terms of the contract. If it is absolutely necessary for the purchasing agent to make a verbal agreement, the purchasing agent should be trained to make the terms of the purchase order form part of the verbal agreement, where feasible. Of course, purchasing agents must also be advised to never verbally accept the seller's quotation form. Likewise, selling agents must be cautioned against making verbal agreements or verbally accepting purchase orders.

Certain limits must also be placed upon the extent to which the purchasing and selling agents can automatically use their respective forms without consulting an attorney. Very large orders or contracts containing unusual terms must, by standard operating procedure, be reviewed by an attorney.

The degree of sophistication of the manpower using the forms may well determine the ultimate victor in the battle of the forms.

NOTES AND QUESTIONS

1.   *Drafting drawbacks*: Is the drafting suggested by Lipman always a good idea? In *Salt River Project Agricultural Improvement & Power District v. Westinghouse Electric Corp.*,[129] such drafting caused problems for a buyer.

In the early 1970s, Westinghouse sold power plant equipment to SRP. In May of 1976, there was an explosion causing $1,900,000 damage to the SRP power plant. SRP alleged that the damage was caused by a malfunction of a $15,000 control device it had purchased from Westinghouse in 1973. It sued Westinghouse, alleging causes of action in strict products liability, breaches of express

---

[129] 143 Ariz. 437, 694 P.2d 267 (Ct. App. 1983), modified en banc, 143 Ariz. 368, 694 P.2d 198 (1984).

and implied warranties, and negligence in design, manufacture and installation of control device. Westinghouse moved for summary judgment on the strict products liability and warranty theory and partial summary judgment on the negligence theory which would limit SRP's recovery to $15,000, the price of the control device. The Court of Appeals affirmed the grant of summary judgment to Westinghouse.

The transaction under which the control unit was purchased involved a battle of the forms. SRP's purchase order stated:

> This Purchase Order becomes a binding contract, subject to the terms and conditions hereof, upon receipt by Buyer at its Purchasing Department of the acknowledgement copy hereof, signed by Seller, or upon commencement of performance by Seller, whichever occurs first. Acceptance of this Purchase Order must be made on its exact terms and if additional or different terms are proposed by Seller such response will constitute a counter-offer, and no contract shall come into existence without Buyer's written assent to the counter-offer. Buyer's acceptance of or payment for material shipped shall constitute acceptance of such material subject to the provisions herein, only, and shall not constitute acceptance of any counter-offer by Seller not assented to in writing.[130]

Westinghouse returned an acknowledgment form. On its face it said "SEE REVERSE SIDE FOR TERMS AND CONDITIONS." There, Westinghouse gave a warranty that the goods would be as described in the acknowledgment and would be free of defects in workmanship and materials. All other warranties were disclaimed in a provision printed in capital letters. It also limited its liability, stating that it would not be liable for consequential damages nor for more than the price of the product sold in this transaction.

The Court of Appeals found "as a matter of law that the exclusions of warranty and limitation of liability set forth in Westinghouse's Acknowledgement form are enforceable against SRP." It explained:

> Paragraph I of the "Terms and Conditions of [SRP's] Purchase Order" dictated how the SRP order could or could not ripen into a binding contract by expressly providing: (1) that it could only be accepted on its "exact terms"; (2) that any contrary document would constitute only a "counter-offer," and (3) that no contract would result from such an exchange unless SRP assented to the counter-offer in writing.

> The Westinghouse Acknowledgement did not accept SRP's Purchase Order on its "exact terms." The Acknowledgement's warranty exclusions and limitation of liability clauses are substantially different from those contained in the SRP Purchase Order; therefore, the Acknowledgement became a "counter-offer" as was contemplated by the express terms of SRP's Purchase Order. The pivotal question before us then is whether SRP accepted the Westinghouse counter-offer.

> The record reveals that SRP failed to object to the changed terms contained in the Acknowledgement. SRP took delivery of the LMC [Lo-

---

[130] *Id.* at 440, 694 P.2d at 270.

cal Maintenance Controller], paid for it and made extended use of it. . . . A contract for the sale of goods may be made in any manner sufficient to show agreement, including *conduct* by both parties which recognizes the existence of a contract. . . . UCC § 2-204(1). Furthermore, an offer to make a contract shall be construed as inviting acceptance in any manner and by any medium reasonable in the circumstances. . . . UCC § 2-206(1). The "counter-offer" embodied in the Westinghouse Acknowledgement was accepted by SRP's conduct manifested through SRP's acceptance, payment for, and use of the LMC. This was true even in the absence of SRP's express assent. Where, as here, an offeree uses a seller's goods for his own purposes, that action will be deemed to constitute an acceptance of the terms of the counter-offer or offer. . . . While SRP's Purchase Order specifically states that any counter-offer can only be accepted by SRP when that acceptance is in writing, the SRP Purchase Order terms concerning the acceptance of the counter-offer do not control. Because SRP's original offer was rejected, the rejected offer could not govern how the new Westinghouse "counter-offer" could or would be accepted. Absent any limiting language in the counter-offer which would restrict the manner of acceptance, the acceptance of the counter-offer would be governed by the general provisions of the UCC . . .

We find no support for SRP's argument that . . . UCC § 2-207, the so-called "battle of the forms" provision, applies in this case because SRP's own Purchase Order rejected in advance its possible application. The SRP order distinctly stated that a responsive document containing any different or additional terms would operate as a counter-offer and could not be an acceptance of the SRP offer. . . . [Section 2-207] comes into play when there has in fact been a "definite and seasonable expression of acceptance." The Westinghouse Acknowledgement was not such an "expression of acceptance" because the SRP Purchase Order would not permit it to be one. Thus, the exchange of documents which occurred in this case is wholly outside the scope of. . . . [Section 2-207].[131]

Professor Murray comments:

The first reaction to this bizarre situation may be to regard the buyer's draftsman as a classic illustration of one who, in Llewellyn's words, tried to "draft to the edge of the possible" and was hoisted on his own excessively drafted petard. Further reflection, however, reveals a more troubling analysis. . . . In *Salt River* the seller's form is not a counter-offer by its own language. Instead, it becomes a counter-offer by *unread* language in the buyer's purchase order. Section 2-207 has no application. *Salt River* thus provides the most recent example of the "last shot" principle. . . . [T]his kind of analysis may appear at any time because of chaotic judicial interpretations in this area.[132]

---

[131] *Id.* at 444-45, 694 P.2d at 267.

[132] Murray, *The Chaos of the "Battle of the Forms": Solutions*, 39 Vand. L. Rev. 1307, 1354 (1986).

Would a careful application of § 2-207(3) produce a different result in the *Salt River* case? See Official Comment 7 to that section. Moreover, could we say that in this case a remedy limited to the amount of the purchase price "failed of its essential purpose" under § 2-719(2) because it "operates to deprive . . . [the buyer] of the substantial value of the bargain"?

2. *Arguing the Salt River case as a matter of policy*: Assuming a good technical argument could be made for liability under §§ 2-207(3) and 2-719(2), did the court, nonetheless, reach the right result? Consider the policies sought by the courts in *McCarty v. Verson Allsteel Press Co.*, *Steiner v. Mobil Oil Corp.*, *Air Products & Chemicals, Inc. v. Fairbanks Morse, Inc.*, and *C. Itoh & Co. v. Jordan Intl. Co.* Would they favor Westinghouse in this case? Make a case that they would . . . and then make a case that they would not. Remember the policies justifying the *Hadley v. Baxendale* rule in carrying out this exercise.

3. *What do you tell the client*? Should lawyers drafting form contracts be able to fashion forms that they know will protect their clients whatever the actual negotiations between representatives of the parties? In seeking the actual expectations of the parties, does UCC § 2-207 undercut a lawyer's ability to structure transactions?

4. *Evaluations of § 2-207*: Professor Alexander M. Meiklejohn[133] points out that § 2-207 is based on Karl Llewellyn's idea that business people give blanket assent to all of the terms and conditions that they do not read except those that are unreasonable or unconscionable. As an empirical matter, Meiklejohn doubts that this is true. As a result, § 2-207 produces results different from the likely real expectations of the parties. Instead of the complexities of § 2-207, courts should look to the agreement of the parties. It is likely that they assume that the usages of their business will control unless they really negotiate for something different.

Professor Victor Goldberg[134] also would abandon § 2-207. He advocates a rule calling for courts faced with conflicting forms to enforce all the terms found on one form based on which one was the most fair expression of the deal. This would give drafters an incentive to take account of the interests of the other side.

Do you see any problems with either of these approaches? If neither satisfies you, could we defend the common law "last shot" rule on the basis that it is close to a random flipping a coin solution to the problem? If no means-ends solution works well, what is wrong with leaving the matter to chance?

d. Remember the UN Convention on Contracts for the International Sale of Goods

You should, at this point, have a fair appreciation for the difficulties both with the perceived problem which the Code sought to "solve" in § 2-207, and the problems with the solution. A certain measure of consternation would not be an unusual reaction upon a first reading of the previous pages. Unfortunately, the

---

[133] *Castles in the Air: Blanket Assent and the Revision of Article 2*, 51 Wash. & Lee L. Rev. 599 (1994).

[134] *The "Battle of the Forms": Fairness, Efficiency, and the Best-Shot Rule*, 76 Ore. L. Rev. 155 (1997).

picture is just slightly more confusing still. Though you might face a dispute concerning your domestic client's purchase or sale of goods, requiring an analysis of incomplete or contradictory paperwork, the answer might not be in the Uniform Commercial Code. Another body of law might apply. We introduced this topic earlier in these materials, but a brief review might be wise.

The development of trade across state boundaries led to the need for a code of commercial law which was more or less uniform from one state to another; this led to the Uniform Sales Act, and later the UCC Similarly the growth of international trade led to a felt need for a code which would govern international sales of goods. Hence the Convention on Contracts for the International Sale of Goods (CISG). The Convention was approved by a diplomatic conference in Vienna in 1980, and the process of adoption by individual countries began immediately. As of 2000, fifty-eight nations, including the United States, Australia, China, France, Mexico, and Sweden had already subscribed to the Convention. Contracts for the international sale of goods which are entered into by parties in countries which have ratified the convention are subject to CISG unless the contract for sale explicitly designates another law (such as the UCC) as the governing law. Many of the rules of the Convention are the same as those of the U.S. common law, or the UCC, but there are important differences.

The Convention excludes a number of contracts that would be covered under the UCC. First, the Convention is not applicable to consumer sales. Second, the Convention does not apply when a government is a party to the contract. Further, the Convention excludes transactions pertaining to securities, the sale of ships, aircraft and electricity. In addition, claims for personal injury or death caused by goods are not covered. Finally, parties to an international contract are free to exclude the application of the Convention or vary the effects of the provisions unlike parties to a contract arising under the UCC.

We will, on occasion, call your attention to the Convention when we think it would be useful or interesting to do so; we do not intend, however, to provide an exhaustive summary of the Convention's rules. It is important that you know that the Convention provides the default standards for international sales of goods involving participating nations, and that the rules may be different from those you might otherwise expect to apply.

We are calling your attention to the Convention at this point because the manner in which the CISG deals with the battle of the forms is different from the UCC solution. Article 19(1) of the Convention is analogous to the common law "mirror image" rule. It provides that "a reply to an offer which purports to be an acceptance but contains additions, limitations or other modifications is a rejection of the offer and constitutes a counter offer." But, paragraph (2) states that unless the offeror objects, a reply is an acceptance if the additional or different terms do not materially alter the terms of the offer. The terms of a contract thus formed would incorporate the modifications included in the acceptance of the offer. Paragraph (3) goes on to furnish a non-exclusive list of terms that are considered material. These relate to price, quality and quantity of goods, place and time of delivery, means of settling disputes, and the extent of a party's liability. The impact of Article 19 is likely to be that fewer enforceable contracts will result under the Convention than under the UCC, so long as the parties have not performed. If there is performance, Article 18 provides that the "conduct of the offeree indicating assent to an offer is an acceptance." Therefore when one party has met its contractual obligation, the "last shot" doctrine would indicate what the terms of the contract are.

D.   CLOSING THE DEAL BUT LEAVING A WAY OUT

Bargainers often want to close a deal but, at the same time, leave a way out. I want you committed, but I want to be able to call things off. I may not be sure whether it is a good deal, and I may want some time to think about it. I may want to control my salespeople who dealt with you. I may want to investigate your credit or my ability to perform. I may want time to seek financing to pay for my purchase, but I may not be sure I can find a lender willing to put up the money on acceptable terms.

If the parties are willing to put their cards on the table and have good legal advice, legally enforceable contracts can be created that achieve these purposes. An *option* is perhaps the easiest way to preserve a business opportunity while buying time. For example, a TV producer thinks she may want to fashion a television show or series based on a novel. She can buy an option from the novelist or the publisher. In exchange for money, the novelist or publisher agrees not to sell the rights to anyone else for a specified time. On the other hand, a bargainer can make its performance *subject to a condition*. We can agree we have a contract provided I am awarded a government contract.

As always, things can be more complicated. A common problem is created by a practice sellers have long used to limit the authority of their salespeople to close contracts.[135] The sales person calls on a customer and writes an order on the seller's standard form. The customer and the sales person sign, and the customer is likely to think that the deal is closed. However, the form states "[a]ny quotation by Seller on the face hereof or on any attachment hereto is merely an invitation for an offer from potential customer(s). All resulting customer offers (orders) are thus subject to acceptance at Seller's offices at the address shown on the face here, before any contract is formed." The customer, thinking there is a deal, is not likely to back out, but the seller can decide whether or not to accept the order. We can view this as a condition, but it is a condition that goes to creating a contract. Furthermore, it is a condition left in the hands of the seller. It has said no more than it will perform if it wants to.

Such clauses usually work as their drafters plan. There are many cases saying that if an order is subject to acceptance at the home office, no contract is formed until such acceptance is given.[136] However, these clauses raise all the problems of fine print, duty to read, and even the battle of the forms. Can the buyer reasonably rely on such a transaction when seller has not accepted its order? In some situations sellers try to have it both ways. They want buyers to think they are

---

[135] *See* Cole-McIntyre-Norfleet Co. v. Holloway, 141 Tenn. 679, 214 S.W. 817 (1919).

[136] *See, e.g.*, Foremost Pro Color, Inc. v. Eastman Kodak Co., 703 F.2d 534 (9th Cir. 1983); Meekins-Bamman Prestress, Inc. v. Better Construction, Inc., 408 So. 2d 1071 (Fla. App. 1982).

bound, but they want the power to back out if it suits their purposes. Do sellers have a duty to approve or reject orders within a reasonable time? Can the seller's conduct create an obligation even when it has not accepted the order?

HILL'S, INC. v. WILLIAM B. KESSLER, INC.
Supreme Court of Washington
41 Wash. 2d 42, 246 P.2d 1099 (1952)

MALLERY, J. The plaintiff, Hill's, Inc., ordered thirty-four men's suits from the defendant, using a printed form supplied by defendant through its salesman. The printed form provided that the order would not become a binding contract until it had been accepted by an authorized officer of the defendant at its office in Hammonton, New Jersey.

The defendant's salesman procured the order on May 16, 1950, and on May 23, 1950, the defendant, by form letter, advised the plaintiff that "You may be assured of our very best attention to this order." What occurred next is shown by the trial court's finding of fact:

> . . . but notwithstanding, on or about July 18, 1950, defendant intention-ally and deliberately, at the instigation of a large retail store selling de-fendant's clothing in the downtown Seattle area, wrongfully cancelled said order and breached its agreement with plaintiff to deliver said suits as ordered, or at all. That at the time defendant cancelled said order and breached its agreement, the period for placing orders for delivery of fall suits had passed, and it was impossible for plaintiff to thereafter procure comparable suits from any other source to meet its fall trade. . . .

Thereupon, plaintiff brought this action for loss of profits in the amount of a 66 2/3 percent markup aggregating $815.83. From a judgment in favor of the plaintiff, the defendant appeals.

The defendant contends that its letter of May 23, 1950, in which it said "You may be assured of our very best attention to this order," was not an acceptance of the plaintiff's order.

In *Bauman v. McManus*, 75 Kan. 106, 89 P. 15, 18, the court said:

> The promise that the order shall receive prompt and *careful* attention seems to imply something more than that the manufacturers will quickly and cautiously investigate the advisability of accepting it. The care they might expend in that direction—in looking up the defendants' financial standing, for instance—is not presumably a matter in which any one but themselves would be greatly interested. The engagement to use care seems more naturally to relate to the manner of filling the order than to the settling of a doubt whether to fill it at all. The expression of thanks for the favor has some tendency in the same direction. We incline strongly to the opinion that the letter, standing by itself, was as effectual to close a contract as though in set phrase it had said that the goods would be shipped; that to permit any other construction to be placed upon it would be to countenance the studied use of equivocal expres-

sions, with a set purpose, if an advantage may thereby be derived, to keep the word of promise to the ear and break it to the hope.

Notwithstanding that the *Bauman* case is exactly in point, it is not necessary to rely upon it exclusively, for the reason that the intention of the defendant to accept the offer is shown by subsequent correspondence with the plaintiff in this case.

On July 18, 1950, defendant wrote plaintiff the following letter:

> *This is to inform you we find it will be impossible to ship the Fall order which you placed with Mr. Jacobus on May 16, order #8585. We dislike very much having to inform you of this, but we trust that you will understand when we say that because of previous commitments to other stores in town it is necessary to cancel this order.*
>
> *We are certainly sincerely sorry if this action on our part inconveniences you at all.* [Italics added by court.]

This letter recognizes the existence of a contract, which it undertakes to cancel.

The defendant contends that the correspondence in this case was not signed by an authorized officer of the defendant corporation. The treasurer of the corporation testified that Glenda Fitting was a clerk in the office; was not an officer of the corporation; was not authorized to accept orders; and that the only persons who were authorized to accept orders were the president, the secretary, and the treasurer.

From a large amount of correspondence in this record, all signed by Glenda Fitting, which the trial court examined, it was justified in not believing the foregoing testimony. The testimony does not go so far as to make out that Glenda Fitting intruded herself into the affairs of the defendant corporation without its knowledge or over its protest.

In such a case, " ... where a principal has, by his voluntary act, placed an agent in such a situation that a person of ordinary prudence conversant with business usages and the nature of the particular business is justified in assuming that such agent has authority to perform a particular act and deals with the agent upon that assumption, the principal is estopped as against such third person from denying the agent's authority; he will not be permitted to prove that the agent's authority was, in fact, less extensive than that with which he apparently was clothed." ... 2 Am. Jur. 86, Agency, § 104.

The defendant contends that the court erred in allowing loss of profits as the measure of damages, in this case, and complains that the plaintiff made no effort to procure similar suits elsewhere by way of mitigating the damages. The plaintiff, however, showed that the cost of going east to fill such an order would have been greater than his lost profits, and, hence, would not have been justified.

We think that the defendant understood that the plaintiff was purchasing the thirty-four suits for resale at a 66 ⃞ per cent markup; that the order was specifically placed for the plaintiff's fall trade; and that the suits, of the defendant, were of a quality that was unobtainable in the west. Loss of profits, in such a case, is a correct measure of damages. . . .

The judgment is affirmed.

[Concurrence by Donworth, J. omitted.]

NOTES AND QUESTIONS

1. *Background from the briefs*: The briefs submitted to the court clarify the parties' arguments and some facts in the case. The lawyers for the manufacturer (William B. Kessler, Inc.) argued that the "letter is merely a courteous acknowledgment of the order, and an assurance to respondent that its order will receive attention." They continued, saying:

> This letter was apparently written immediately upon receipt of the order without any time having elapsed which would have permitted appellant to consider the order and to decide whether it should be accepted or rejected. Mr. Chester Kessler, the treasurer and sales-manager of appellant, testified that the above letter was a form letter which was sent to each customer upon receipt of an order before the order was processed through the Credit, Manufacturing, Sales and other departments for the purpose of making a decision as to the acceptance or rejection of the order. He further testified that it usually takes about two weeks to process an order and arrive at a decision as to the acceptance or rejection of same in the case of appellant's regular accounts, or where there are special problems, it would take a considerable length of time to assemble the information on which the decision would be based.

> The order, among other things, constituted a request for the extension of credit by the provision "terms net 30 days." It is inconceivable that appellant would have accepted the order immediately upon its receipt without having had an opportunity to investigate the credit of respondent.

What argument(s) was appellant making? Why is it relevant that it is "inconceivable that appellant would have accepted the order immediately upon its receipt without having had an opportunity to investigate the credit of respondent"?

2. *Offer and acceptance as a surrogate for the antitrust laws*: The retailer's brief offers the following version of the facts:

> Respondent is a small retail men's clothing store located in the University District of Seattle. Among other lines of merchandise it stocked appellant's Hammonton Park suits, which, by direction of appellant, it sold under respondent's own label. The same line of suits was stocked by Prager's, a large retail store located in downtown Seattle, and sold under the Hammonton Park label. These suits are recognized and accepted as having exceptional quality and style for ready-made clothing.

> In March, 1950, the ownership of respondent changed hands, Charles Shapiro and Morris Shapiro, father and son, purchasing all of the corporation stock, and in this fashion acquiring all of the corporate assets. One of the factors motivating the purchasers to acquire the business was that it constituted an outlet for appellant's quality suits. There were 13 of appellant's suits in stock from a previous order at the time the respondent changed ownership, and these suits were readily sold within two or three weeks thereafter.

Immediately following acquisition of respondent, the Shapiros communicated with appellant concerning further purchases of its Hammonton Park Suits. Appellant's West Coast salesman and representative, Herbert Jacobus, answered respondent's communications and arrangements were made to display appellant's line of fall suits to the Shapiros when Jacobus called at Seattle to solicit fall orders. On May 16, 1950, the Shapiros, both father and son, in response to the invitation of Mr. Jacobus, examined the display of appellant's clothing set up by Jacobus at the Olympic Hotel in Seattle, and at that time placed an order for 34 suits. Mr. Jacobus attempted to secure a larger order from respondents, but it was explained that respondent's small operation did not warrant a larger order at that time, and Mr. Jacobus assured the Shapiros that they could place fill-in orders from time to time. Mr. Jacobus advised that delivery could be had commencing July 1st, and the order specially provided for shipment "as soon as possible July 1st" with a delivery date "thru Nov. 15th." A provision such as this means, in the clothing industry, that the merchandise ordered, if not shipped all at one time, may be shipped in units during the period July 1st to November 15th.

Nothing was said by Mr. Jacobus concerning the order being subject to confirmation. The order form . . . contained . . . [the requirement of confirmation of an authorized officer] in one of many provisions in small print appearing on the reverse side thereof. . . .

[The retailer received the letter of July 18th, quoted in the court's opinion, purporting to cancel the order.]

The uncontradicted testimony established and the trial court found that this letter cancelling the accepted order resulted from threats and pressure exerted upon appellant by Prager's, a large outlet for appellant's merchandise in downtown Seattle. On May 25, 1950, Sidney Portner, manager and buyer for Prager's, had written appellant making a completely unjustified charge of price cutting against respondent, and threatening to withdraw Prager's business if appellant persisted in selling suits to other outlets in the Seattle-Bremerton area. The matter referred to in this letter was also the subject of personal discussions between Mr. Portner and Chester Kessler, one of appellant's officers. Appellant offered no other explanation for the cancellation of the accepted order whatever. . . .

Cancellation came 16 days after the initial date specified for the shipment of the order, and so late that the time for placing any other order for the delivery of fall suits had passed, so that it was impossible for respondent to obtain substitute suits to meet its fall trade. As a result respondent was forced to do business for the 1950-51 fall and winter season without a stock of goods of the type it had ordered from appellant for sale to its customers.

If the retailer's theory about the threats from Prager's could have been established beyond a reasonable doubt, this conduct probably was criminal, and if it were established under a lesser burden of proof, it probably would be tortious and justify punitive damages. The naive can wonder why the Shapiros did not seek to have a prosecutor bring criminal charges or why they did not sue Prager's in a tort action. Whatever we speculate about such issues, it seems likely that the trial judge was influenced by the wrong being done by the big manufacturer and retailer to the small men's store in the university area.

3. *Tough rhetoric but bad tactics*: The manufacturer's response may have been technically correct, but consider whether it was the right thing to say tactically:

> Both respondent and the trial court have discussed at length their versions as to why appellant would not ship the goods ordered by respondent. We do not believe the reason for appellant's failure to accept the order is material. Appellant was under no obligation to sell goods to respondent until it accepted its order. It had the right to reject respondent's offer for any reason of any kind, or for no reason at all.

4. *A cross-reference to agency law*: Much of the debate in the briefs concerned the power of Glenda Fitting to bind William B. Kessler, Inc. to contracts. Agents can be given express authority to make contracts, but they also can have apparent authority if the principal is responsible for putting them in a position where others reasonably will assume that they have this power. The reasons for the rule are similar to those underlying an objective theory of contract; in an exchange-based society, people find it easier to deal in light of reasonable assumptions and appearances.

The trial court found that Chester Kessler, the manufacturer's treasurer and sales-manager, had testified falsely in several respects. The judge said "and then the question is whether he told the truth or not in regard to the authority of Glinda Fitting. And it is my opinion that he didn't tell the truth under oath in that respect." Notice that the court could have found that Fitting had apparent authority since she signed a wide variety of correspondence directed to William B. Kessler's customers and there was no indication on the letter of her position in the company.

5. *What constitutes an "acceptance at the home office"?* In *Nordyne, Inc. v. International Controls & Measurements Corp.,*[137] the seller sent a price quotation for an improved version of a control panel which buyer had been purchasing for a number of years. The quotation provided that any action brought under this agreement would be tried in Onondaga, New York. The document also stated: "All orders are subject to acceptance by the Seller at its home office in Cicero, New York." Buyer asked to see samples of the new control panel. Seller supplied them on September 12, 1997, along with a letter that said "Full blown manufacturing of this device is awaiting your sign off of these check samples as approved for production. Please review the samples and 'sign off' this document and send it back by return fax so that we may fulfill your production requirements in a timely manner." The buyer signed the seller's production approval form, and then two days later it issued a purchase order for 20,000 units at the quoted price. This purchase order said nothing about the place of trying any lawsuit. Buyer

---

[137] 262 F.3d 843 (8th Cir. 2001).

alleged that the control panels were defected and sued in a federal court in Missouri. The trial court dismissed the complaint for improper venue because the forum selection clause in the seller's proposal governed. Buyer argued that there had been no approval. The appellate court affirmed. It said: "The fact that ICM's home office issued the letter of September 12, 1997, asking for Nordyne's production approval, i.e., Nordyne's acceptance of ICM's offer, undermines Nordyne's argument that the quotation was not an offer because it required ICM's home office approval. This approval in fact occurred, and thereafter Nordyne approved the beginning of production." Do you see any problem with the court's analysis? Was the buyer's request for manufactured samples of the new control panel an offer? Wouldn't the buyer be free to look over the samples and decide not to buy? When the buyer signed the production approval form and faxed it back to the seller, was this an offer? Would seller be reasonable in thinking that buyer had made a commitment before buyer issued a purchase order?

6. *Silence as acceptance*: "Subject to approval at the home office" clauses raise the classic problem of "silence" as acceptance of an offer. The older black letter rule was that silence could not be taken as an acceptance. This position seems to have been an over-generalization of the idea that I cannot force you to act to ward off a contract. Suppose I park my ten-year-old Ford Taurus in your driveway and send you the keys with a letter saying that unless you reject my offer within three days, I will deem you to have agreed to buy the car for $1,000. Individualistic contract law refused to allow me to force you to act; your inaction would not be taken by courts to be an agreement to buy the car.

However, courts were never easy with a rule saying that "silence" never could be an acceptance. On the one hand, a person receiving such an offer could rely on it and get hurt. On the other hand, a person receiving such an offer could try to play it both ways. If she or he desired to enforce the contract, inaction could be called an acceptance. If she or he desired not to be bound, inaction could be called a rejection. The cases cannot be explained in terms of whether silence was a manifestation of acceptance—one must turn to other factors.

For example, in *Kukuska v. Home Mutual Hail-Tornado Ins. Co.*,[138] a farmer filed an application for insurance on July 3; the insurance company gave notice of rejection of the application at 11:00 a.m. on August 1; and the crops were destroyed by a storm later that afternoon. The court found the insurance company liable. It said that three theories support such a conclusion: silence as acceptance; an implied contract to act promptly; and a duty arising from the franchise created by being licensed as an insurance company in the state. The court observed that, "[i]f the insurer is under such a duty and fails to perform the duty within a reasonable time and, as a consequence, the applicant sustains damage, it is not vastly important that the legal relationship be placed in a particular category."[139]

Later, in *Sell v. G.E. Supply Corp.*,[140] the same court found that inaction had not created liability. The plaintiff applied to become a distributor for Hotpoint refrigerators and ordered five. The order, written on a G.E. Supply Corporation

---

[138] 204 Wis. 166, 235 N.W. 403 (1931).
[139] 235 N.W. at 405.
[140] 227 Wis. 242, 278 N.W. 442 (1938).

form, was "subject to approval" by G.E. Supply. Seventeen days later, General Electric Contracts Corporation notified plaintiff that it would purchase his customers' installment payment contracts. However, nineteen days later plaintiff received a telegram saying that the application to become a distributor had been disapproved. It explained that there was a shortage of refrigerators, and it had decided to allocate production to the existing distributors rather than add new ones. The Supreme Court of Wisconsin, finding no liability, pointed out that there was a good reason for rejecting the application, the decision was relatively prompt, and plaintiff's reliance was not particularly great.

The "silence cannot be acceptance" rule was further shaken in *Morris F. Fox & Co. v. Lisman.*[141] Here, plaintiff made an offer on a form drafted by defendant which stated that a contract was "subject to approval at home office." Defendant considered the deal and plaintiff's credit and made a note on plaintiff's offer indicating that defendant had accepted the contract. However, this letter was filed away, and no notice of acceptance was ever given to plaintiff. While other things were communicated by defendant to plaintiff, the court stressed that the letter showed defendant's intention to accept and found that a contract had been made. Compare *International Filter Co. v. Conroe Gin, Ice and Lt. Co.,*[142] reaching a similar result.

All in all, cases such as *Hills v. Wm. B. Kessler, Inc.* and the three Wisconsin decisions just discussed suggest that some courts have been willing to regulate the reservation of a right of approval after the business adopting the practice creates a situation where an applicant can be hurt by reliance. Regulation appears particularly likely when the one reserving the right does not use it for legitimate business purposes or, as in the *Morris F. Fox & Co.* case, where the legitimate business purposes of the procedure have been served. Compare Restatement (Second) of Contracts § 69.

7. *Estoppel and good faith in bargaining*: In *Iacono v. Toll Brothers,*[143] the plaintiffs sued for specific performance of a contract to purchase real property. Defendants were developers. They listed units in Colts Neck Estates with a real estate broker. The broker sold buyers a house to be built by the developers on a contract form provided by the developers. This form provided:

> This Agreement has been obtained by Seller's salesman or agent who has no authority to bind Seller to this Agreement. This Agreement shall not be binding upon Seller unless signed by Seller within thirty (30) calendar days from the date below. Otherwise, the deposit money will be returned to the Buyer without interest. . . .[144]

Buyers conceded that they were aware of the clause and understood it. They paid a deposit, but defendants never signed the form. Almost two months after buyers signed the contract, defendants notified them there was no deal. The trial court found that a binding contract had been formed. The appellate court reversed this judgment. However, it remanded the case for findings necessary to determine

---

[141] 208 Wis. 1, 237 N.W. 267, 240 N.W. 809, 242 N.W. 679 (1932).

[142] 277 S.W. 631 (Tex. Civ. App. 1925).

[143] 217 N.J. Super. 475, 526 A.2d 256 (1987).

[144]*Id.* at 477, 526 A.2d at 257.

whether the defendants were equitably estopped. The defendants had not returned the deposit, and they had waited almost two months before writing plaintiffs, rejecting the agreement of sale. Plaintiffs requested several modifications in the design of the house defendants were to build, and defendants agreed to these changes. Plaintiffs tendered checks in partial payment for construction charges which defendants accepted and deposited. The defendants' construction superintendent referred to the house as "your home" or "your new home." Plaintiffs were not in the real estate market looking for another house at a time of sharply rising real estate values.

The court said there were a number of unresolved issues:

> [W]hether Toll Brothers' [the defendants] silence or conduct or both following April 13, 1985 [30 days after the agreement was signed by the buyer] induced reliance by plaintiffs that Toll Brothers had accepted the agreement of sale; whether such reliance, if found factually, was reasonable and in good faith in the light of plaintiffs' concessions that they knew of and understood the import of the home office acceptance clause in the agreement of sale; whether plaintiffs, relying upon Toll Brothers' silence or conduct or both, changed their position to their detriment by staying out of the rising real estate market as purchasers for a significant time interval after April 13, 1985.[145]
>
> Plaintiffs would be entitled to judgment on remand only if the determination of all the foregoing fact questions is in the affirmative. If so, there should be a further factual determination as to whether the Statute of Frauds was met.

Notice that while the buyers and the developers may not have entered a binding contract, they did enter a continuing relationship. Can we explain the court's decision in terms of a duty of good faith in negotiations? That is, the developers would have several acceptable reasons for not wanting real estate brokers to have the power to bind them to contracts. For example, the developers had only a certain number of lots, and various brokers might sell more than the total available. Developers might want to investigate the credit of buyers or institutions providing financing for buyers. However, developers also might want to be able to reject buyers in order to discriminate on the grounds of race or religion. In the *Iacono* case, the buyers argue that the developers tried to back out so they could benefit from a rapidly rising housing market. Can we view these cases as finding at least a possible liability despite "subject to approval" clauses as American versions of *culpa in contrahendo*? See Kessler and Fine, *supra*.

8. *Subject to financing clauses*: Buyers of real estate and other expensive items often insist that contracts be drafted with a "subject to financing" clause. Buyers must shop for the property they want to purchase and shop for a loan on terms they find acceptable. This way of closing a deal while leaving a way out provokes several problems for courts. Does the buyer have any obligation to look for financing seriously? Must the buyer accept a reasonable offer of credit from a lending institution or is its acceptability left to the buyer's discretion?

---

[145] *Id.* at 480-81, 526 A.2d at 259.

Some courts solve such problems by refusing to consider them. They refuse to enforce contracts subject to financing or they refuse to enforce them unless the parties have agreed to the amount, terms and conditions of the loan which the buyer will seek.[146] They explain that such clauses leave buyers too much discretion. Furthermore, courts would be burdened by trying to judge the reasonableness of financing buyers could have obtained. On one hand, financing could be reasonable in the sense that the loan was what most lenders were offering. On the other hand, such a loan could burden a particular borrower greatly in light of his or her personal situation. Courts would have to decide whether a reasonable person in the buyer's position would have made the sacrifices of lifestyle needed to produce enough money to make the monthly payments. For example, perhaps a buyer would be reasonable in rejecting a loan which would make him unable to pay for his child's college education. Would he be reasonable in rejecting one that would require him to sell his sports car?

Finally, this position may serve to protect inexperienced buyers, who must first shop for a house and then shop for financing. They may overestimate their ability to make loan payments out of a modest income. Classic mistake doctrine would offer them little relief. However, if their lawyer can attack their contract with the seller, a court can overturn the deal without being forced to craft a new mistake rule. For example, in *Perkins v. Gosewehr*,[147] a contract for the sale of a house for $65,000 provided "[t]his offer is contingent upon buyer obtaining a first mortgage loan commitment for $52,000." The appellate court found "the statement of the amount of the loan does not fill the evidentiary void, and does not establish that the parties reached a meeting of the minds concerning the primary objective of the 'subject to financing' clause, i.e., what financing would be affordable or desirable to the buyers and acceptable to the sellers. In the absence of such evidence, the contract is void for indefiniteness."[148] The trial court had concluded that the buyers "were in over their heads" and could not afford the monthly payments needed to buy the house.

Courts do, however, usually uphold such conditions.[149] Compare the outcome in *Perkins* with that in *Wiggins v. Shewmake*.[150] In that case, the buyers agreed to

---

[146] *See, e.g.*, Gerruth Realty Co. v. Pire, 17 Wis. 2d 89, 95, 115 N.W.2d 557, 560 (1962).

[147] 98 Wis. 2d 158, 295 N.W.2d 789 (1980).

[148] *Id.* at 164-65, 295 N.W.2d at 792.

[149] Professor Farnsworth notes:

A surprisingly wide variety of matters can be left to the satisfaction of one of the parties without making the agreement unenforceable. Courts have, for example, allowed the buyer of real estate to condition its obligation on its satisfaction with governmental action on zoning and development plans and engineers' and architects' feasibility studies. They have even allowed the parties to leave the precise nature of the financing obtained by the buyer to its own satisfaction. While it scarcely can be sound practical advice to say merely "subject to financing," such language has passed muster. Courts have been equally tolerant with similar conditions commonly found in commitments to lend that leave matters to the lender's discretion. Thus it has been held that the commitment of a lender that had agreed to finance a shopping center was not illusory although it was conditioned on leases in the shopping center not being "unsatisfactory or otherwise unacceptable" to the lender.

Courts, however, have been less tolerant of terms that condition the agreement on approval by a party's lawyer, a kind of term that often appears if there is a division of repurchase a house provided they were able to obtain a "13% conventional loan." The buyers were denied a loan by one lender. The seller got a commitment from a bank for such a loan to the buyers, but they refused to accept it. They obtained a loan on another home which they purchased shortly thereafter. Seller sued, and the trial court found that the buyers had failed to use due diligence in carrying out their good faith duty to obtain financing. Seller was awarded consequential damages. The South Dakota Supreme Court affirmed, saying:

> . . . the circumstances surrounding the contract can make the clause sufficiently certain enough to grant specific performance. . . . Enforcement by specific performance of a residential real estate purchase contract does not require an expansive recitation of mortgage financing details.
>
> Excessive detail may be counter productive to enforcement of the contract by unwarrantedly narrowing the contingency clause to an extent that makes its fulfillment improbable. It also ignores the fiscal realities that the total effect of the financing terms is often more important than the variation in individual details which often offset each other. For the latter reason, financing clause terms are better stated in essentials so that inconsequential variances resulting from current financial market conditions do not preclude consummation of the transaction. . . .
>
> [T]he trial court found that "conventional loan," as used in the agreement, is a loan directly through a local lending agency not guaranteed by a governmental agency. Several local banking officials testified that this was the common understanding of the term. . . .
>
> [A] purchaser, such as the Shewmakes, is under an implied promise to use his best efforts to bring about the happening of the condition. . . . Shewmakes did indeed fail to exercise their best efforts when they refused to accept offered financing which comported with the exact language of the purchase agreement.[151]

Does this result better protect the expectations of the parties than those found in the Wisconsin cases? Does it reflect an American approach to *culpa in contrahendo*? *See* Kessler and Fine, *supra*. Do you see any problems with the approach of the South Dakota court?

---

sponsibilities between managers and lawyers. The key is the extent of responsibility given to the lawyer under the term. Sometimes the agreement is conditioned on the lawyer's approval of the agreement itself. Such a provision invites the inference that the lawyer's responsibility includes a review of the advisability of the deal, and courts have held that this makes the party's obligation illusory. Sometimes, however, the agreement is conditioned on the lawyer's approval of documents such as guarantees or closing papers. Here, even though the lawyer's discretion may be said to extend to "substance" or "content" as well as form, it is easier for a court to reject the argument that the lawyer's responsibility includes a review of the advisability of the deal.

Farnsworth, *Precontractual Liability and Preliminary Agreements: Fair Dealing and Failed Negotiations,* 87 Colum. L. Rev. 217, 247-48 (1987).

[150] 374 N.W.2d 111 (S.D. 1985).

[151] *Id.* at 115-16.

Chapter 3

THE DEAL IS CLOSED—BUT WHAT IS IT?

A. INTRODUCTION

A great many judicial opinions deal with giving meaning to contracts. This suggests there are two important lawyering tasks that students should know something about: first, you should know how to write contracts that are sufficiently clear to avoid unnecessary disputes about their meaning. Second, you should know something about how courts give meaning to those contracts that come before them. Obviously, these questions are related.

Law schools have not done well teaching about either of these problems. Teaching contract drafting is difficult.[1] Many, if not most, Americans are not skilled writers or speakers of English. Few students come to law school able to state what they mean and no more or less. Probably we have to play the game to learn how. That is, we have to write, have our drafts ripped apart, redraft in light of criticism and so on. This requires individual instruction which is not generally available—certainly not in most introductory contracts courses. Law schools are funded largely on the assumption that a single teacher armed only with a case book can instruct 50 to 100 students or more. Legal writing classes, which tend to be under financed, rarely devote their resources to contract drafting.

Law school contracts courses do not do much better in teaching how courts give meaning to contracts. The rules of construction are vague. While students might draw analogies, each case turns on its own facts. Furthermore, many cases involving interpretation age poorly. Lawyers draft around a problem in later contracts so that the original case offers solutions to a problem unlikely to occur again.

While some lawyers are masters at contract drafting, many do a poor job. For example, Suchan and Scott[2] studied 196 collective bargaining agreements between managements and unions. They used three formulas to test how understandable these documents were—Rudolph Flesch's Reading Ease Formula, Robert Gunning's Fog Index, and Farr-Jenkins-Patterson's Reading Ease Index. These tests use sentence and clause length as well as the number of single-and polysyllabic words in a passage as variables to measure readability. According to the Flesch and Farr-Jenkins-Patterson formulas, 95 to 99 percent of these collective bargaining agreements would be "difficult" or "very difficult" to understand. The Gunning Fog Index indicated that these contracts had an average score of 18.73. "What this figure means is that the rank and file would need more than 18 years of education—a college degree plus two years of graduate school—to unscramble a typical union-management agreement."

---

[1] *See* Felsenfeld and Siegel, WRITING CONTRACTS IN PLAIN ENGLISH (West Publishing Co. 1981); Burnham, THE CONTRACT DRAFTING GUIDEBOOK (Michie 1992).

[2] Suchan and Scott, *Unclear Contract Language and Its Effect on Corporate Culture*, 29 Bus. Horizons 20 (1986).

Suchan and Scott seek to explain why collective bargaining agreements are so hard to read. They suggest that those who draft the contracts may inhabit different semantic worlds from rank and file workers. "Accustomed to reading drawn-out sentences filled with passive constructions and polysyllabic, Latin-based words, negotiators have little trouble translating the 'cognizants,' 'ascertains,' and 'hereinafters' into language they can understand." Those who draft contracts also may take the easy way out and copy stock clauses from form books. The legalese and convoluted sentences of earlier contracts set the standard for appropriate style. People may want these documents to look legal so others will honor them.[3] Few drafters consider the audience for the agreements and ask if they can understand them. At times, drafters deliberately use unclear language. Those negotiating may want to avoid being pinned down on an issue or may think it is better to agree to something rather than not agree at all. If I'm too clear about a point, the other side may object or may call off the entire transaction. On the other hand, those negotiating may not be clear on what they are trying to say. Contracts often reflect the rushed and confused thinking of fatigued negotiators. Skilled negotiators may not be skilled drafters. Those who are insecure about their writing ability often try to hide behind jargon, complicated sentences, and endless paragraphs. People write "to *impress* rather than *express*, often with disastrous results."

Collective bargaining agreements may be extreme examples of a common problem. While we think that labor negotiations are conducted between management and the union, many different people are involved. For example, the Vice President for Labor Relations may negotiate the contract, working under guidelines set by the Chief Executive Officer and the Board of Directors. The actual drafting will be done by management lawyers. Workers are represented by their union. They, too, will have their lawyers. To make matters more complicated, the lawyers for one or both sides may write primarily for officials of regulatory agencies or judges who might review the document in the future. Furthermore, labor negotiations are more adversarial than many business bargains. There is some incentive to try to slip things past the other side.

When a question arises during the life of the collective bargain, the document may be read by a foreman, a shop steward or a rank-and-file worker. Many times these people will ignore the text and work matters out on a common sense basis. This will create expectations and working interpretations of the real deal which may or may not reflect what is written on paper.

Commercial contracts between business people may share many features of collective bargains. Those who perform a deal often are not the ones who wrote it. People often copy form clauses to save time. Business people dictate docu-

---

[3] Lawyers know that some clients, even sophisticated ones, are disappointed if a lawyer drafts a contract or will in simple and clear language. They wonder what they got for their money. They mistakenly think that anyone could have written a clear document in simple language. They want "whereas" clauses, and "parties of the first part" along with a dash of legal Latin so that the document will have magical properties. Of course, in some situations the client may be right. If others honor a document because it looks legal and thus is something out of the ordinary, then this is a form of power. As always, a major part of a lawyer's stock in trade is judgment about when to do what.

ments and don't revise them. They use vague words to deal with problems they think are unlikely to occur, or don't want to call attention to, or to avoid upsetting the other side. Language which makes sense in one context may be ambiguous when it is applied to a problem the drafter did not foresee. Furthermore, English is not a precise language. It is filled with synonyms with different shades of meaning. Ordinary conversation relies heavily on context and common patterns. There often is a wide gap between what I said and what I meant.

This is the reality lawyers and judges confront when they have to give meaning to words and phrases in contracts. Remember what you know about communication when you read that courts interpret contracts to find "the intention of the parties" or to find the "plain meaning" of a writing. Remember to ask who is going to read what *you* write and what they are likely to make of it. It is not always easy to communicate to judges and lawyers. It is harder to communicate to those unaccustomed to reading legal documents.

As you will see, there are two related issues in all this material. First, we can ask how judges give meaning to words. Second, we must confront rules that define what judges can look at in this process. We can think of the issues as how do judges interpret contracts, and what are the boundaries of the communications to be interpreted? For example, suppose buyer and seller sign a written contract. Seller tells buyer that clause 28 doesn't apply to him. Will courts read only the written document or will they take account of this inconsistent statement? For now, all we can say is that it depends. This problem is put in the category called the parol evidence rule.[4] Long ago, Professor Thayer commented, "[f]ew things are darker than this [the parol evidence rule], or fuller of subtle difficulties."[5] We will try to shed some light on this dark subject, but the subtle difficulties remain.

We begin our discussions of interpretation, and of the parol evidence rule, by reproducing excerpts from several articles. A first reading should give you an idea about the nature of the problems involved in giving meaning to words in a written document. You also should begin to recognize common judicial responses to these problems and difficulties with them. Cases are offered to serve as examples of what you have read.

---

[4] Do not spell parol "parole." Please.
[5] Thayer, A PRELIMINARY TREATISE ON EVIDENCE 390 (1898).

B. INTERPRETATION AND CONSTRUCTION OF CONTRACTUAL LANGUAGE

The Interpretation and Construction of Contracts
Edwin W. Patterson[6]

I. Interpretation, Construction, and Inference Distinguished

A. *Interpretation.* What is interpretation? It is the process of endeavoring to ascertain the meaning or meanings of symbolic expressions used by the parties to a contract, or of their expressions in the formative stage of arriving at the creation of one or more legally obligatory promises. Since most contracts are temporary in their effects, the process of interpretation often consists merely of the direct application of the symbols used to the factual situation that gives rise to controversy. For example, if *S*, a farmer, has agreed for a stated price to sell and deliver to *B*, a grocer, four dozen egg-plants, and on the appointed day *S* tenders as his performance to *B* four dozen eggs, an objective observer could, without formulating any *general* conception of the genus and species of "egg-plant," give a *particular* interpretation that the tender was not within the terms of the contract; and this interpretation might well support a *particular* legal evaluation that *B* was under no duty to accept the eggs in performance, and possibly that *S* has breached his contractual duty. Interpretation, then, goes on without the framing of *generalities* about the symbols, such as the definitions one finds in a dictionary of the Anglo-American language. These "definitions" are synonyms (logical equivalents) of the terms defined, expressed in other words (*i.e.*, other than the word to be defined) that are, in turn, to be defined elsewhere, or, as "primitive terms," left undefined (in a particular realm of discourse).

However, the process of interpretation of a contract may be used to establish a *general* meaning of the symbols used. This may occur in the case of a long-term contract (*e.g.*, a 99-year lease) or a contract affecting the interests of many people, such as a collective labor agreement, or a standardized contract used by a large number of individuals or corporations. Among the oldest examples of the last is the British marine insurance contract, the quaint language of which has been judicially interpreted often enough to establish a body of esoteric meanings familiar only to specialists. . . .

The process of interpretation may be applied to the spoken words or other symbolic utterances expressed by the party, or his authorized agent, as terms of an oral contract, or it may be applied to the written (handwritten, typed, printed, or otherwise inscribed) words of a written contract, or to an offer or purported acceptance, in the formative stage of contracting. Interpretation may be aided by the nonverbal conduct of one or both parties . . . .

B.   *Construction.* Construction, which may, in this writer's opinion, be usefully distinguished from interpretation, is a process by which legal consequences are made to follow from the terms of the contract and its more or less immediate context, and from a legal policy or policies that are applicable to the situation. Construction may be applicable along with interpretation, or it may take over when interpretation wholly or partly fails. Take three possible cases:

1.   An action has been brought upon an alleged contract which has vague and meaningless expressions of what would normally be important terms; *e.g.*, the quality and quantity of goods are vague, and so is the price. In such a case the symbolic conduct will ordinarily be adjudged to be too indefinite to be enforced. "The court cannot make a contract for the parties," is the basic policy. Yet if goods have been delivered and accepted, the context may show that no gift was intended, as the recipient knew, and the court will construe (imply) a duty to pay the reasonable value of the goods. The policy seems to be to prevent unjust enrichment, yet the duty construed is contractual, not quasi-contractual.

2.   An action has been brought by *P* upon a written contract, partly printed and partly typed, the terms of which are chosen and drafted by *D* defendant. On interpretation of the terms it appears that a crucial term, such as a condition precedent of *D*'s promise, is ambiguous, that is, has two possible meanings, one of which is more favorable in its effect to *D*, and the other of which is more favorable to *P*. If the latter interpretation will signify that *P* has fulfilled the condition, then the court will usually construe the crucial term *contra proferentem*, that is, unfavorably to the party drafting the contract, *D*, and favorably to the other party, *P*. This construction may be based upon the inference that *D* in drafting the instrument intended only the meaning favorable to *P*, otherwise it would have excluded that meaning by more explicit drafting; or it may be based upon a policy of equalizing the inequality of the one-sided bargain. This principle of construction is frequently applied to insurance contracts (where sometimes, it seems, the court conjures up the ambiguity) and to other "contracts of adhesion."

3.   An action is brought by *P* upon a contract which contains an unconscionable condition of *D*'s contractual duty or an unconscionable limitation or extension of the measure of damages for a breach by *D*. In such a case the court may, under exceptional circumstances, and in direct denial of the meaning that interpretation properly would give, construe the unconscionable term to be unenforceable in this action and in this sense "void." Here construction overrides interpretation. Such uses of construction are exceptional.

Other examples of construction of conditions will be given below, yet the process is inexhaustible.

Can we say that interpretation is a matter of "pure fact" and construction a matter of "pure law"? No, because interpretation (of a *legal* instrument) is meaningless without some one or more possible legal consequences as ends-in-view; and because construction does not operate without regard to some facts, including not only the terms of the contract but also its transactional context. The latter, be it noted, is properly available for use in the process of construction, but part of it is ordinarily excluded in the process of interpretation of a contract embodied in a single written memorial by a legal doctrine known as the "parol evidence" rule.

Aside from the utterances of the parties that are not expressed in the written memorial, the "surrounding circumstances," it is commonly said by courts, may be considered by the court in interpreting the written contract. Since all circumstances are "surrounding," we avoid tautology by referring to the transactional circumstances or, more broadly, the transactional context.

C. *Inference.* Inference of fact plays an important part in the interpretation and construction of contracts. An example . . . is the process by which the court infers some purpose or purposes of the parties and then interprets the language of the contract in such a way as to be consistent with the purpose or purposes. Still another example is the so-called "practical construction" of the parties; that is, their conduct during the course of performance may support inferences as to the meaning of language in the contract, or as to their intentions with respect to gaps and omissions in the contract. Here inference may aid either a genuine interpretation, or a policy of avoiding unjust enrichment or of favoring the creation of a contract, or it may aid both.

D. *Court and Jury.* Even in a case in which a jury is the trier of issues of fact, the interpretation and construction of a written contract is within the exclusive province of the judge. While the judge may be called upon, in this process, to determine several issues of "fact," such as those inferences referred to above, the relevant dictionaries, and relevant circumstances, yet the meaning of a written instrument is often called "a question of law." This characterization of the rule is a surviving fiction (or semi-fiction). The continuance of the rule is justified by the judge's superior equipment—his education and legal experience—to interpret written instruments and to give them reliability. As a determination of law, the trial judge's interpretation of the meaning of a written contract is not as conclusive upon an appellate court as his "findings of fact" would be and hence may be set aside as an "error of law."

Where the contract is partly oral and partly written, the judge may instruct the jury as to the meaning of the written part and, with other instructions, leave the remaining issues of interpretation to be determined by the jury. If the jury is directed to bring in a general verdict (*i.e.*, for the plaintiff or for the defendant), it may in so doing exercise its views of jury equity and thus impair the reliability of written instruments. This possibility may account for the reluctance of courts to admit parol evidence and other extrinsic aids to interpretation, and for their adherence to the "plain meaning" of the contract.

E. *Reasons for Distinction.* The distinction between interpretation and construction of contracts has been doubted or rejected, principally, it is believed, for two reasons: First, because it is difficult or impossible to draw the line between the two in many problematic cases, and secondly, because many courts in many cases have ignored the distinction. However, as exemplified in the three illustrations given above it is believed by the present writer to be a workable and useful distinction for the following reasons, among others:

1. To say that all determinations by a judge of the meaning of a contract are *merely* his legal evaluations is at least a gross exaggeration. The judge (or judges) must start with the symbols (and other manifestations of intention) expressed by the parties in order to arrive at a proper judicial determination. If every "contract"

were "interpreted" as if it were a (signed) blank sheet of paper, the usefulness of contract would vanish. The careful drafting of contracts is commonly rewarded by smooth performance, or by an expected and justified judicial interpretation. When the court knows what the symbols mean but regards this meaning as "unconscionable," they go beyond the meaning of symbols and enforce a special kind of legal policy. Of this, too, the canny draftsman should be aware. In ordinary cases the meanings of symbols and the manifestations of intention provide the operative facts upon which the legal consequences depend.

2.   An expert witness may be called to testify to the meaning of a term in a trade or technical dictionary. But no expert can be called to tell the court when it should find a term or a clause unfair or unconscionable. That is the court's exclusive function.

3.   A trial court's construction of a contract may be set aside by an appellate court as an error of law; yet its finding as to the meaning of a trade or technical term would more likely be deemed conclusive on appeal.

II. "Plain Meaning" and the Several Dictionaries

The ideal result that legal draftsmen seek to attain and that judicial interpreters commonly seek to find in a written contract is that a judge should be able, by reading the contract without lifting his eyes from the page, to determine its one and only "true" meaning in relation to the issues being litigated. Once this "true" meaning has been ascertained, no other evidence should be permitted to fritter away the meaning and thus make written contracts unreliable. What I have called the "true" meaning is transformed into "plain meaning" in the standard set of maxims of interpretation. In accordance with this ideal, if the court finds a "plain meaning" of the relevant terms of the writing, it will exclude various kinds of proof, discussed in this and the next two sections, which would contradict or qualify the plain meaning. If, however, the written contract on its face contains an ambiguity, then evidence extrinsic to the contract will be admitted. . . .

How seriously . . . should one take the "plain meaning" rule that is stated in many judicial opinions? Seriously enough to induce the counselor to draft every contract as clearly as he knows how and as the other party (or perhaps his own client) will let him. While he can not always foresee the contingencies that will arise to frustrate his best efforts, he may still be able to state clearly the rights and duties, powers and privileges, risks and immunities that will arise under the terms of the contract. He cannot exclude all latitude of interpretation of terms, yet, to quote the words of a brilliant judge, [Learned Hand] "there is a critical breaking point . . . beyond which no language can be forced. . . ." This breaking point is the limit of "plain meaning." It serves to fulfill one or more of the basic purposes of the law of contracts.

Yet the plain meaning rule must be taken with reservations. The first one is that it does not apply in case of an "ambiguity," which may be cleared up by extrinsic aids; only the courts can say when there is an ambiguity. A second one, less important, is that a "plain meaning" provision may be deemed unconscionable and thus unenforceable. A third one is more important than either of these: the term of a contract that at first sight seems to have only one "plain" meaning may have two to a dozen meanings in a standard or universal dictionary of the vernacular. From among these the court, if it looks at the universal dictionary, has to *select* the one meaning that is "plainly" *appropriate* in this case. Usually, however, the crucial interpretation is not dependent on a single word but is dependent upon a phrase or a sentence which is not listed in a dictionary and to which the court gives its own interpretation.

A fourth reservation to the "plain meaning" rule is that a local, trade, or other special usage may give to a term a meaning very different from that given to it by the common or universal dictionary, and when one reads the contract terms with the proof of the usage, of which both parties knew or should have known, the appropriate meaning is no longer merely the "plain" one. A striking example is the old English case involving a suit by a lessee of a rabbit warren against his lessor, who by the terms of the written lease agreed to pay the lessee, at the expiration of the lease, "£60 per thousand" of rabbits left in the warren, and the lessor proved that by local usage, of which the lessee had reason to know, the term "thousand" meant "1,200," so that for 19,200 rabbits, the lessee was entitled to recover just 16 times £60. It is not easy to match this case with one in which the contract term, unaided by a special usage, had as "plain" a meaning as "thousand," and the special usage had a "plain" and plainly contradictory meaning. Does the admission of the usage for such a purpose contradict the late Judge Learned Hand's statement that there is a "breaking point" beyond which no language can be forced? And what of the famous dictum of Judge Oliver Wendell Holmes, Jr.? "It would open too great risks if evidence were admissible to show that when they [the parties] said "five hundred feet" they agreed that it should mean "one hundred inches," or that "Bunker Hill monument" should signify the "Old South Church."

The late Professor John H. Wigmore, who first developed the notion that there are several "dictionaries," besides the ordinary lexicon, in which symbols may have meaning (*e.g.*, trade or technical usages), apparently thought there was a contradiction. Yet Learned Hand certainly, and Holmes probably, was referring to the latitude of discretionary interpretation of words taken in their "ordinary dictionary" sense. This restrictive view would, it is believed, be appropriate if, as in the case of a recorded deed to land, third persons had innocently relied upon the ordinary meaning. If a trade or local usage can be proved and if it was known to both parties at the time when the written instrument was signed, then a different case is presented and the special usage should control. . . . [For example] a promise by *R*, a seller of books by subscription, was to pay his salesman, *E*, a commission on "every order," yet *R* was allowed to prove that "every order" meant, in the subscription book business, "every order where five volumes were taken and paid for by the subscriber." In such cases there is a substantial variance between the contract term in its ordinary sense and the usage meaning; yet the contract term does not manifest an intention not to be "bound" by the usage. On the other hand, an extreme case, such as the "1,000 rabbits" case, might be taken to express such an intention, and the court should require stricter than usual proof that there was such a linguistic usage, that the objector may fairly be charged with knowledge of it, and that the contract term was not intended to exclude it.

If the interpretation of the contract requires ascertainment of the meaning of a scientific or technical term that the court cannot find in any standard dictionary, the scientific or technical linguistic usage as to the meaning of the term may be proved by the testimony of expert witnesses who are familiar with it. For instance, a contract in litigation contained a promise to purchase dyes, "Amacid Blue Black KN," and expert testimony was admissible to prove the meaning of the quoted term. Here the term had no "plain meaning" to the court, and not even ambiguous meanings—it was meaningless. Hence the "plain meaning" rule was not applicable. Cases of this type give no difficulty.

Despite numerous dicta that a "plain meaning" cannot be explained by a special usage, it is believed that the law as laid down in judicial precedents is otherwise. A contract to sell 125,000 "chickens, 2 ½-3 lbs." was, by the aid of expert testimony and of terminology derived from the U.S. Department of Agriculture, interpreted by the court to include "stewing chickens," as the seller interpreted it, and not limited to "broilers or fryers," as the buyer argued it should be. The *Restatement*, which does not recognize the "plain meaning" rule, states as the standard of interpretation of a contract contained in a single written instrument ("integrated") "the meaning that would be attached to the . . . [instrument] by a reasonably intelligent person acquainted with all operative usages. . . ."

The term, "operative usages," includes the linguistic usages here referred to and also the additive usages that add to the terms of a contract. The latter are discussed below.

Still another kind of dictionary may be used to interpret the terms of a contract: a private code agreed upon by the parties, in advance of making the contract, as their means of communication with each other. Such private codes are used by and between persons who frequently have dealings with each other, in order to prevent others from learning valuable business information. They are used, for instance, by and between stockbrokers trading on the various stock exchanges and brokers on commodity exchanges. If litigation arises over a contract made in this way, the code book may be produced in evidence to translate the apparently meaningless language, or the language whose "plain" meaning would be at variance with its code meaning. To emphasize his position that one can not reliably determine the meaning of a contract in the way described above, Wigmore told of a young man who, before going on a pleasure trip to Europe, agreed with his father to use a certain code book in cabling. Later the father was startled to receive from his son by cable the single word, "laugh," which he found, on looking it up in the code book, to mean, "send $500."

Besides all these dictionaries there is the law dictionary, which gives the established meanings of legal terms or phrases. If an instrument embodying a contract has been drafted by a lawyer or lawyers, a legal term in it would presumably be interpreted in its legal sense, and in the absence of fraud or mistake this meaning would be given it regardless of the unfamiliarity of the term to one or both parties. Such terms are most often found in our archaic vocabulary of real property law. However, this interpretation is not conclusive; by the transactional context it may be shown that the established legal meaning was not intended. Thus where two laymen draw up their contract and use words having a technical-legal and also an ordinary meaning (such as, for instance, "consideration," "condition") they are not to be entrapped by this inadvertent use of legal lingo.

The "plain meaning" rule serves as a last resort, to guide a court that has found no aids to interpretation nor signs of intention in the transactional context and no basis for an "equitable construction," and thus falls back upon the literal wording of the contract for which the court does not see any rational basis. Either poor drafting of the contract or supervening unforeseen circumstances have made the contract scarcely intelligible, and the court refuses, under the guise of "equitable interpretation," to make a new contract for the parties.

III. Extrinsic Aids: Relevant Circumstances

An extrinsic aid is anything outside of the written instrument in which the terms of a contract are embodied ("integrated") and which may be used in ascertaining the meaning of these terms. The ideal process of interpretation outlined in Part II can rarely, if ever, be realized: the contra-document usually does not "speak for itself." In suggesting that such a document *may* carry its own meaning I refer only to the *interpretation* of the contract, not to its validity or to the proof of its performance. In case of dispute as to the genuineness of the signatures, the authority of agents to sign on behalf of their principals, or the identity of agents and principals, extrinsic proof may be used. So, if a claim is made that the contract was induced by fraud or duress and is therefore voidable, proof of conduct of the parties and other facts outside the contract are admissible. The same is true when a dispute arises as to the facts of performance of the contract. A written contract *may* be so carefully drawn with explicit provisions, definitions of terms, and recitals of fact, that, as to some disputes that *do* arise (but not as to all disputes that *might* arise) its meaning is clear in relation to the particular dispute without the aid of extrinsic proof.

Yet proof of many of the circumstances of the transaction that would tend to show how the contract came to be made, the motivation or purposes of the parties in making it, the particular characteristics of the subject matter, and the like, are admissible to show its meaning. Even courts which profess to follow the "plain meaning" rule generally recognize an exception for "relevant circumstances." For instance, in an action by a railroad company against a motor-vehicle manufacturer the court first said the switch-track agreement between them was so clear that there could be no "right of construction," and then said:

> The greatest latitude should be given in developing the surrounding situations and conditions attending the negotiations for the consummation of a contract, and the language employed in a contract should be construed in the light of circumstances surrounding the contracting parties at the time. Circumstantial evidence is as competent to prove a contract as it is to prove a crime.

A. *Course of Performance.* The conduct of both parties to a contract in the course of its performance is, if it indicates that they gave a particular meaning to its terms, provable as evidence of that meaning. This kind of proof is frequently called the "practical construction" of the parties. The basis of inference in such cases is often an admission by one party, by his conduct, that the contract has a certain meaning. For instance, the fact that *P*, a trucking company, did not in its monthly billings to the other party, a freight forwarder, make any claim for certain alleged "receiving charges" referred to in the contract, was deemed sufficient zevidence of the meaning of the provision concerning "receiving charges" to justify a denial of a later claim for such charges. . . .

A party's course of performance in a manner against his interest, as he now claims it to be, is primarily an admission by that party, and as such it is not conclusive or legally binding on that party, but may be withdrawn or corrected by him. Mere forgetfulness or ignorance of a claim does not discharge the claim. However, the position taken by one party in the course of performance may signify to the other a representation or a promise on which he relies and acts to such an extent as to create an estoppel, and when this occurs the representation can not be corrected nor the promise revoked. An example appears in an action by *S*, a subcontractor for painting, against *G*, a general contractor for the erection of 175 dwelling units at an air force base. After *S* had completed the exterior and interior painting in accordance with contract specifications, weather damaged the outside paint and defective lumber spoiled the interior paint. *G* told *S* that he would be paid for repainting the houses; *S* did so and then sought recovery of 96,000 dollars for this additional work. In affirming a judgment for *S* the court treated the conduct of the parties as a "practical construction" of the contract. The decision might, it seems, have been based on estoppel, or on a new and independent contract.

One party's performance in accordance with his interpretation, favorable to his own interests, may, if the other party consents to or acquiesces in this interpretation, create a practical construction unfavorable to the latter. If the latter gives an *express* assent to the former, who afterward acts in reliance on it, an estoppel may be created. Hence practical construction may entrap a party who is not alert to detect and repudiate practical interpretations with which he disagrees. "Self-serving" interpretations by one party are not often given effect. At least they should be limited to cases of knowledge and acquiescence by the other party.

For contracts to sell goods the Uniform Commercial Code gives a clearer and more restrictive meaning of course of performance than can be found in judicial opinions: [§ 2-208(1)]

> Course of Performance or Practical Construction. . . . Where the contract for sale involves repeated occasions for performance by either party with knowledge of the nature of the performance and opportunity for objection to it by the other, any course of performance accepted or acquiesced in without objection shall be relevant to determine the meaning of the agreement.

This language avoids the pitfalls of the doctrine.

B. *Prior Utterances and Thoughts.* [We have omitted Patterson's brief summary of the parol evidence rule, since we take up that topic somewhat later, in more detail.]

C. *Recitals.* Recitals are statements of a factual character inserted in written contracts for the purpose of explaining and clarifying their terms. They are frequently worded as "whereas" clauses, and are useful aids to interpretation.

IV. Extrinsic Aids: Course of Dealing and Trade Usages

"Custom conquers all" is a maxim that had somewhat greater reliability in previous centuries than in this one. Still, it may serve to remind us that the transactions with which lawyers and judges have to deal take place in an ordered and established society for the most part, and that the social matrix envelops every word that the parties may utter, or every sentence that they may sign. What is this social matrix? It includes, above all, the common or universal language of the community, for which no dictionary is ordinarily needed by parties, lawyers, judge, or jury. It includes the vocabulary of lawyers when relevant. It includes a previous course of dealing (if any) between these same parties to this contract. It includes the linguistic usages discussed in Part III above that give meaning to special terms in the contract, and also those *additive* usages which may add terms to the contract where the contract itself is silent and does not exclude such usages.

A. *Course of Dealing.* A prior course of dealing between the parties to a contract has long been recognized by courts as relevant to the interpretation of their contract. A contract by D to supply P with chemicals at "ruling market rates" was followed by deliveries, monthly rendition of accounts by D to P, and payment by P. Then P discovered he had been paying jobber's rates, rather than the lower exporter's rates, and sued for the difference. Prior dealings between P and D (and also their prior conversations) were relied on by the court to show that P had not been overcharged. A course of dealing may, it seems, consist of a repeated practice of one party that was known to the other, which the jury might find helpful in determining their rights—here a buyer's belated claim for breach of warranty. Yet one party's practice, unknown to the other, can not establish a course of dealing. The regular accounts rendered by one party to another and acquiesced in by failure to object within a reasonable time may be held effective against the latter on the basis of two older doctrines, estoppel or account stated. Course of dealing, sometimes confused with "custom" or "usage," has seldom been relied upon in reported case law.

The Uniform Commercial Code defines the term: [§ 1-205(1)]

> A course of dealing is a sequence of previous conduct between the parties to a particular transaction which is fairly to be regarded as establishing a common basis of understanding for interpreting their expressions and other conduct.

This definition, far superior to any previous judicial attempts, gives some objectivity ("sequence of conduct establishing") to the term, yet the requirement of knowledge of the sequence, "between the parties," is left to "fairly" and "common basis of understanding." The trier of fact will, it seems, have considerable discretion; yet it is somewhat limited by the hierarchy of persuasiveness discussed below.

B. *Additive and Linguistic Usages.* American case law as to customs and usages shows a good deal of confusion. To the present writer it seems that some clarification results from distinguishing *linguistic* or translative usages from *additive* usages. The former merely give special meanings to the words or other expressions or symbols of a contract, as explained in Part II above. The latter add something to the terms of the contract, some regular practice in a trade, locality, or class which implies an obligation to do or not to do something in a particular way. For instance, a theatrical producer by a telegram offered an actor employment, on the road and in stock, with some terms specified but no mention of the period of employment. The actor accepted by telegram. After four months the producer gave the actor two weeks notice of termination and paid him accordingly. The actor claimed he was employed according to an oral agreement with the producer's agent for a year. The producer's proof that in the theatrical profession a usage, well understood by both parties, was to the effect that either party had a right to terminate the contract on two weeks notice was excluded by the trial court. On appeal it was held error not to let this evidence go to the jury. A trade usage may prescribe what should be done by one party with respect to a matter not mentioned in the contract. Thus, whether a buyer of fine granulated sugar had inspected it within a reasonable time was determined partly by proving a usage that a buyer who resold the sugar in the original containers would not inspect it until he received some complaint from his customers. A usage in this sense has two elements: (1) a pattern of prevailing human conduct, and (2) a conviction or belief that the pattern *ought* to be followed. . . .

Although a trade or class usage resembles a custom, such usages are not required to have existed "from time immemorial," as are English local customs. The original of a trade usage need not be veiled in mystery. It may be embodied in regulations adopted by a trade association, of which one party is a member, if the regulations are known to the other party. However, if the nonmember was not aware of the trade rule when the contract was made, he is not bound by it. American courts have been less careful than English courts in requiring proof from which it might be inferred that one party knew, or had reason to know, of a usage relied on by the other. Under a contract by a seller to deliver potatoes f.o.b. railroad cars in Virginia, a jury found that the seller was aware of a usage by which payment by the New York buyer was to be deferred until after the potatoes arrived in New York and were inspected by him. On the other hand, a court in Arkansas held that a remote nonresident, dealing with a New York buyer, was not charged with knowledge of a New York usage, and a New York court held a usage of fruit buyers in New York was not so long and well established as to be imputed to a fruit-grower shipping fruit from Oregon to the New York market. Ordinarily the "insider" tries to impute knowledge of his group's usage to the "outsider." However, on the principle of reciprocity, the "outsider" should not be allowed to claim the benefit of the "insider's" usage if the "outsider" was not aware of it when the contract was made, and in Virginia it was so held. With respect to *knowledge* by a party of a trade usage so as to make it binding upon him the Uniform Commercial Code seems to provide three categories: (1) parties engaged in the vocation or trade, (2) parties who are aware, and (3) parties who should be aware are deemed to have knowledge. . . .

C. *"Unreasonable" Usages and the Hierarchy of Authority.* While usage may often be used to smooth the channels of commercial transactions, yet parties to contracts sometimes seek to prove usages with which their lawyers may mislead juries. There has thus grown up the judicial doctrine that a court will not permit proof of an "unreasonable" or an unlawful usage. [For example, a] Missouri court held that a usage of used-car dealers to turn back the speedometer mileage on used cars, after making "improvements" on them, was deceptive and contrary to the public good. On the whole judicial supervision of usages has been salutary.

The Commercial Code seeks to express the requirement of reasonableness along with a statement as to which source of interpretation prevails when they are in conflict with each other: "The express terms of an agreement and an applicable course of dealing or usage of trade shall be construed wherever reasonable as consistent with each other; but when such construction is unreasonable express terms control both course of dealing and usage of trade and course of dealing controls usage of trade." An alleged usage which contradicts express terms of the contract is to be rejected. A course of dealing between these two parties is more likely to express their expectations than a conflicting usage that may be the practice of other persons.

D. *Notice of Intention To Prove Usage.* As another safeguard against the false usage as an escape hatch for delinquents the Uniform Commercial Code provides that one party's evidence of a usage shall not be admissible "unless and until he has given the other party such a notice as the court finds sufficient to prevent unfair surprise to the latter." The Code will, it is believed, have good effects in two ways: in clarifying the legitimate role of usage in commercial contracts, and in preventing some of the abuses of usage-evidence that prior case law revealed.

V. Secondary Maxims of Interpretation and Construction

In addition to or in conjunction with the principles of interpretation and construction of contracts set forth above, courts rely upon and purport to use a number of maxims of interpretation some of which are very broad but most of which are applicable only to special situations. There is some doubt whether they have reliable guidance value for judges, or are merely justifications for decisions arrived at on other grounds, which may or may not be revealed in the opinion. This rather cynical view is supported by two observations. One is that for any given maxim that would persuade a judge to a certain conclusion a contrary maxim may be found that would persuade him to the opposite (or contradictory) conclusion. For instance, the courts often quote the maxim, "the court cannot make a contract for the parties," and, somewhat less frequently, they make statements such as: "The law does not favor, but leans against, the destruction of contracts because of uncertainty; and it will, if feasible, so construe agreements as to carry into effect the reasonable intentions of the parties if that [*sic*] can be ascertained."

[The author then provides other possibly contradictory maxims.]

The second reason, referred to above, for believing that the maxims of interpretation are ceremonial rather than persuasive is that in many instances the court will set forth in its opinion the whole battery of maxims and then proceed to decide the case on the basis of an analysis of the terms of the contract and the facts of the dispute, without indicating which maxim or maxims, if any, were applied or invoked in reaching that decision. In a system of law based on judicial precedents, a clear statement of the operative facts and the legal reasons is a part of judicial responsibility. However, the court's awareness of the quoted maxims is a part of the context of its reasoning. Moreover, the lawyers on each side of a controversy would do well to quote to the court the relevant maxims for their positions. . . .

In this brief treatment we can only quote a list of standard maxims, which may not be complete. The ones most often phrased in Latin are given first:

1. *Noscitur a sociis*. The meaning of a word in a series is affected by others in the same series; or, a word may be affected by its immediate context. The example for the next maxim may be taken to illustrate this one.

2. *Ejusdem generis*. A general term joined with a specific one will be deemed to include only things that are like (of the same genus as) the specific one. This one if applied usually leads to a restrictive interpretation. *E.g., S* contracts to sell *B* his farm together with the "cattle, hogs, and other animals." This would probably not include *S*'s favorite house-dog, but might include a few sheep that *S* was raising for the market.

3. *Expressio unius exclusio alterius*. If one or more specific items are listed, without any more general or inclusive terms, other items although similar in kind are excluded. *E.g., S* contracts to sell *B* his farm together with "the cattle and hogs on the farm." This language would be interpreted to exclude the sheep and *S*'s favorite house-dog.

4. *Ut magis valeat quam pereat*. By this maxim an interpretation that makes the contract valid is preferred to one that makes it invalid.

5. *Omnia praesumuntur contra proferentem*. This maxim states that if a written contract contains a word or phrase which is capable of two reasonable meanings, one of which favors one party and the other of which favors the other, that interpretation will be preferred which is less favorable to the one by whom the contract was drafted. This maxim favors the party of lesser bargaining power, who has little or no opportunity to choose the terms of the contract, and perforce accepts one drawn by the stronger party. Such "contracts of adhesion" are discussed below. However, the maxim is commonly invoked in cases that do not reveal any disparity of bargaining power between the parties.

6. *Interpret contract as a whole*. A writing or writings that form part of the same transaction should be interpreted together as a whole, that is, every term should be interpreted as a part of the whole and not as if isolated from it. The maxim expresses the contextual theory of meaning, which is, perhaps, a truism.

7. *"Purpose of the parties."* "The principal apparent purpose of the parties is given great weight in determining the meaning to be given to manifestations of intention or to any part thereof." This maxim must be used with caution. In fact, the two parties to a (bargain) contract necessarily have different purposes, and if these are apparent, then the court can construe a principal or common purpose from the two as a guide to the interpretation of language or the filling of gaps. Thus a contract to sell, buy, and export scrap copper was construed to make the buyer's obtaining of an export license a condition of the seller's promise to deliver. However, if the purposes of the parties are obscure the court may well fall back upon "plain meaning."

8. *Specific provision is exception to a general one.* If two provisions of a contract are inconsistent with each other and if one is "general" enough to include the specific situation to which the other is confined, the specific provision will be deemed to qualify the more general one, that is, to state an exception to it. A lease of a truck-trailer provided that the lessee should be absolutely liable for loss or damage to the vehicle, yet another clause stated that no party's liability should be increased by this contract. It was held that the former was more specific and therefore controlled the general provision, hence the lessee was liable. A careful draftsman would have stated the former as an exception to the latter, and the court in effect does it for him.

9. *Handwritten or typed provisions control printed provisions.* Where a written contract contains both printed provisions and handwritten or typed provisions, and the two are inconsistent, the handwritten or typed provisions are preferred. This maxim is based on the inference that the language inserted by handwriting or by typewriter for this particular contract is a more recent and more reliable expression of their intentions than is the language of a printed form. While this maxim is used in interpreting insurance contracts and other contracts of adhesion, it is also applicable to all contracts drawn up on a printed form.

10. *Public interest preferred.* If a public interest is affected by a contract, that interpretation or construction is preferred which favors the public interest. The proper scope of application of this rule seems doubtful. It may have some appropriate uses in construing contracts between private parties. However, as applied to government contracts it would, if applied, be used to save the taxpayers' money as against those contracting with the government. But this is not, it is believed, a standard of interpretation or construction uniformly applied to government contracts.

This battery of maxims is never fired all together. The judge or other interpreter-construer of a contract may, by making prudent choices, possibly obtain some useful guides for his reasoning and justifications for his conclusion.

VI. Contracts of Adhesion and Compulsory Contracts

[We have omitted Patterson's treatment of this topic. Briefly, Patterson notes that if the drafter of a contract was in a stronger bargaining position than the other signer, a court under the influence of twentieth century views might favor the weaker party whenever possible. This is consistent with the general rule of interpretation which suggests construction against the drafter, but is an extension of it. The origins of the idea that there are some contracts—contracts of adhesion—which are in some respects "pretended contracts" seemed to originate in France. The French scholar suggested that those contracts in which are the expression of the intentions of only one party (the drafter) should be treated, in a sense, as private legislative enactments. There may be sound reasons, grounded in efficiency concerns, to enforce such contracts, but they do threaten the assumptions about contract as the expression of two or more parties sharing some common intention. Whether the adhesion contract is subject to different interpretive rules is a question that neither courts nor scholars have answered with any clarity.]

NOTES AND QUESTIONS

1. *Another Patterson, another view*: Professor Edwin Patterson's article is written in what we might call the "authoritative" voice. But we must always remember that there can be more than one side to nearly any assertion. In Section IV. C. of his article, *supra*, Professor E. Patterson asserts that, under the Code, "An alleged usage which contradicts express terms of the contract is to be rejected." This statement is a part of the argument which he presents concerning the hierarchies of authority which bear on interpretation. Professor Dennis Patterson, in an article which seeks, in part, to examine the jurisprudence of Code-architect Karl Llewellyn,[7] suggests that at the very least Edwin Patterson's assertion was antithetical to Llewellyn's purpose, if not the presumed purpose of the Code's drafters; he labels the assertion we have just quoted as "simply fantastic." He first notes that Llewellyn was seeking, in the Code, to integrate trade usage and course of dealing with the written terms of the parties, giving effect to each. Dennis Patterson argues:

> Llewellyn's conceptual revolution was not universally embraced. After the completion of the New York Law Revision Commission hearings, Professor Edwin Patterson of the Columbia University Law School prepared a report recommending "amendment of § 1-205(4) to insure that express terms would always dominate usage of trade and course of dealing." No published discussion of Patterson's recommendation exists; however, neither the New York Law Revision Commission nor the Code Editorial Board adopted the recommendations.

> Having failed in his attempt to influence the Law Revision Commission in New York to adopt a totem-pole approach to § 1-205, Professor Patterson never gave up in his attempt to reorient judicial thinking to the classical model. In 1964, fully eight years after having his perspective rejected by the New York Law Revision Commission, Patterson wrote the following:

> [Dennis Patterson then quotes from a paragraph from the article you have just read which includes the contested assertion concerning the hierarchy of express terms and trade usage.]

> Patterson's assertion . . . [that trade usages must be rejected if they contradict express terms] is simply fantastic. It represents an unabashed attempt to subjugate Llewellyn's creation, the Code concept of agreement, to the classical model of contract. Lest one think that the classical orthodoxy has been eclipsed, a review of current treatises on the Code reveals that at least one influential authority proffers the argument that the proper interpretation of § 1-205 results in a totem-pole approach in the analysis of the meaning of agreement. . . . [Dennis Patterson then quotes Chancellor Hawkland as supporting the view that express terms control course of performance, which in turn dominates course of dealing, which trumps usage of trade, which triumphs over statutory terms.]

---

[7] *Good Faith, Lender Liability, and Discretionary Acceleration: Of Llewellyn, Wittgenstein, and the Uniform Commercial Code*, 68 Tex. L. Rev. 169, 192-94 (1989).

Hawkland's methodological approach to § 1-205 is sure to mislead initiates to the Code. This flatly literal reading of § 1-205 is completely at odds with Llewellyn's concept of agreement and with the overall architecture of the Code. . . . Instead, the logic of § 1-205 is that "if a contract can be defined by shared expectations, and if those expectations were created by trade usage, then the contract should be defined by trade usage."

At the risk of opening the door to a deconstructionist debate, should we accept the proposition that the Code means what Llewellyn intended it to mean, because he wrote it? Professor Dennis Patterson may think that Professor Edwin Patterson's "totem-pole" approach runs counter to Llewellyn's intentions. However, as a matter of statutory construction, could you fashion an argument that would support Dennis Patterson? Without abandoning the words of the Code, can you avoid reading UCC §§1-205(4), 2-208(2) as legislating such a "totem-pole" approach?

"Meaning" in the Law of Contracts
E. Allan Farnsworth[8]

 "Interpretation" will be used here . . . to refer to the process by which courts determine the "meaning" of the language. We are not concerned with overriding legal rules which may render contract language ineffective after it has been interpreted. Nor are we concerned with "gap filling" by which the absence of contract language is remedied. Our concern is exclusively with contract language and its "meaning."

The object of contract law is to protect the justifiable expectations of the contracting parties themselves, not those of third parties, even reasonable third parties.

"Meaning" for the purpose of contract interpretation should therefore be defined as: (1) that to which either party refers, where it can be determined and where it can be established that it is the same as that to which the other party refers, or believes or has reason to believe the first party to be referring; and, only failing this, (2) that to which either party has reason to believe the other to be referring. Interpretation then becomes the process applied to the language of the parties by which this meaning is determined. It is sometimes supposed, however, that language can be so clear that no recourse need be had to external circumstances to determine its meaning. Are there circumstances under which the meaning of language is so "plain" that some other definition of that term is appropriate?

---

[8] Reprinted by permission of The Yale Law Journal Company and Fred B. Rothman & Company (now William S. Hein Company) from The Yale Law Journal, Vol. 76, pp. 939-957 (1967).

The Search for Plain Meaning

In Semantics. The very concept of plain meaning finds scant support in semantics, where one of the cardinal teachings is the fallibility of language as a means of communication. Waismann lamented that,

> Ordinary language simply has not got the "hardness," the logical hardness, to cut axioms in it. It needs something like a metallic substance to carve a deductive system out of it such as Euclid's. But common speech? If you begin to draw inferences it soon begins to go "soft" and fluffs up somewhere. You may just as well carve cameos on a cheese *soufflé.*

. . . . Quine has built upon Skinner's theory of language learning to explain the concept of vagueness. According to Quine, "stimulations eliciting a verbal response, say 'red,' are best depicted as forming not a neatly bounded class but a distribution about a central *norm*." The idea of a central norm is useful in explaining the concept of vagueness, for a word is vague to the extent that it can apply to stimuli that depart from its central norm.

Contract language abounds in perturbing examples of vagueness. The parties provide for the removal of "all the dirt" on a tract; may sand from a stratum of subsoil be taken? An American seller and a Swiss buyer agree upon the sale of "chicken"; is stewing chicken "chicken"? Vagueness may even infect a term that has an apparently precise connotation. The parties contract for the sale of horsemeat scraps "Minimum 50% protein"; may evidence be admitted to show that by trade usage scraps containing 49.5% or more conform?

Ambiguity, properly defined, is an entirely distinct concept from that of vagueness. A word that may or may not be applicable to marginal objects is vague. But a word may also have two entirely different connotations so that it may be applied to an object and be at the same time both clearly appropriate and inappropriate, as the word "light" may be when applied to dark feathers. Such a word is ambiguous.

Whether an ambiguity arises may depend upon the medium of communication. Some ambiguities (ordinarily homonyms), such as "beer" and "bier" arise only in speech and disappear in writing; others such as "tear" (a rip or a drop), arise only in writing and disappear in speech. Speech will do much to remove the ambiguity from sentences such as, "Do you think that one will do?" which can be read aloud in a variety of ways by stressing a different word each time. Gestures also play a part in normal face-to-face conversation, and habits of speech have been shown to change when conversation is over a telephone and normal gesture reinforcement is lost. Ambiguity may arise in a telegram because of the lack of punctuation which would ordinarily be supplied in a letter. And even given an ambiguity, it may be resolved by its context: one drinks a beer, not a bier, and sheds a tear (drop) not a tear (rip).

Ambiguities may be classified into those of term and those of syntax. As Young has pointed out, true examples of ambiguity of term are rare in contract cases. A contract specifies "tons"; are they to be long or short tons? A charter party provides that a vessel must be "double-rigged," which by usage can refer to either two winches and two booms per hatch, or four of each per hatch; how many must the vessel have? An important variety of ambiguity of term, for our purposes, is proper name ambiguity, the kind of ambiguity that plagued Shake-speare's Cinna,[9] the kind of ambiguity that we deliberately create when we name a child after someone. It was this kind of ambiguity that was involved in the celebrated case of the ships "Peerless."

An ambiguity of syntax is, in the strictest sense, an ambiguity of grammatical structure, of what is syntactically connected with what. A classic example is, "And Satan trembles when he *sees* / The weakest saint upon his knees," in which the ambiguity is that of pronominal reference.

Ambiguity of syntax is probably a more common cause of contract disputes than is ambiguity of term. An insurance policy covers any "disease of organs of the body not common to both sexes"; does it include a fibroid tumor (which can occur on any organ) of the womb? A contract provides that, "Before the livestock is removed from the possession of the carrier or mingled with other livestock, the shipper . . . shall inform in writing the delivery carrier of any visible injuries to the livestock"; is it enough that he notify before mingling although after re-moval?

Syntactical ambiguity is often the result of inadequate punctuation. Note, for example, the confusion that sometimes results from contracts concluded by an unpunctuated telegram. Sometimes the ambiguity is caused by the dropping of words to make shorthand expressions. A contract for the sale of "approx. 10,000" heaters adds "All in perfect condition"; is this, as buyer contends, an express warranty ("All *to be* in perfect condition") or, as seller contends, a limitation on the quantity ("All *that are* in perfect condition")?

Particularly hazardous as a source of ambiguity for the contract draftsman are the words "and" and "or."

Ambiguity in contracts may also result from inconsistent or conflicting lan-guage. A buyer agrees to pay "at the rate of $1.25 per M" for all the timber on a designated tract, and that "the entire sale and purchase price of said lumber is $1400.00"; how much must he pay for 4,000 M feet? In many of these cases the conflict is between language in a form contract and that added by the parties for the particular transaction. A printed warranty in the sale of a house requires the owner to give notice of breach "within one year from . . . the date of initial occu-pancy" and also provides that "notice of nonconformity must be delivered no later than January 6, 1957," the date having been inserted by hand; when must the buyer give notice if he moves in on May 16, 1955?

It would be wrong to assume that the failure of contract language to dispose of a dispute that later arises is invariably due to some inherent fallibility of language as a means of communication. The parties may simply not have foreseen the problem at the time of contracting. An insurance contract on a motor vessel cov-ers "collision with any other ship or vessel"; is a collision with an anchored fly-ing boat included? Or one or both may have foreseen the problem but deliber-ately refrained from raising it during the negotiations for fear that they might

---

[9] [66] "(Cinna): I am Cinna the poet. I am not Cinna the conspirator! (Second Plebeian): It is no matter, his name's Cinna; pluck but his name out of his heart and turn him going." Julius Caesar, III, iii.

fail—the lawyer who "wakes these sleeping dogs" by insisting that they be re-solved may cost his client the bargain. An elderly lady enters a home for the aged, paying a lump sum, to be returned to her "if it should be found advisable to discontinue her stay" during a two-month probationary period; must the home refund her money if she dies within that time? Or both may have foreseen the problem but chosen to deal with it only in general terms, delegating the ultimate resolution of particular controversies to the appropriate forum. A contract for the sale of wool requires "prompt" shipment from New Zealand to Philadelphia; does shipment in 52 days conform? It is interesting to note that while either am-biguity or vagueness may result from the other causes just suggested, only vagueness is suitable for use in such a conscious attempt at delegation. . . .

[We have omitted Farnsworth's discussion of the parol evidence rule, but you should keep his discussion of ambiguity and vagueness in mind, since parts of the parol evidence rule require characterizations of a contractual term as ambiguous, or not ambiguous.]

FEDERAL EXPRESS CORP. v. PAN AMERICAN WORLD AIRWAYS, INC.
United States Court of Appeals, Eighth Circuit
623 F.2d 1297 (1980)

MCMILLIAN, J. Appellant Federal Express Corporation, which operates an air express cargo service, appeals from a judgment of the district court dismissing its claim of damages for breach of contract in a diversity action against appellee Pan American World Airways, Inc. For the reasons stated below, we affirm.

This case involves contracts for the sale of a particular kind of jet aircraft called the Falcon 20 Jet, manufactured by Avions Marcell Dassault and marketed at the time of the contracts in the United States by the Business Jets division of appellee. The controversy is over a provision in the sales contracts calling for appellee to provide to appellant (the buyer) "initial training" for flight personnel on a "flight simulator," a machine designed to recreate conditions that might be encountered in flight and to test the responses of the trainee. While we do not attempt to detail the facts of the case, which are admirably set forth in the district court's opinion, some background is required for an understanding of the parties' dispute.

Appellant Federal Express came into existence after Frederick W. Smith, a young but experienced pilot and aircraft industry businessman, sought to set up a new kind of air express delivery service. He planned to use Falcon 20 Jets for this purpose, an inventive idea which created a new function for what had been pri-marily a "corporate jet," normally used by large enterprises for transportation of personnel. Smith took his plan to Mr. C. C. Flemming, an executive officer of the Business Jets division of appellee, who was supportive, and the parties arranged in 1971 for a sale of a total of twenty-five jets, two at once and the other twenty-three for future delivery. After some delays while appellant obtained financing and while regulatory changes were made which enabled appellant to go into business, the twenty-three aircraft were delivered between October, 1972, and May, 1973.

The contracts called for delivery of the aircraft in a "green" condition, that is, without modifications for appellant's particular needs and without finished instruments or interiors. Appellant subsequently modified the aircraft as they were delivered, with the modifications on the last aircraft completed by December, 1974.

The contracts also called for appellee to provide certain training for appellant's personnel, including the "initial training" for aircraft crews on the flight simulator which is at issue in this case. In regard to this training, the schedule provided by appellee with the first two aircraft purchased in 1971 varied from that provided under the contract for the twenty-three aircraft delivered in 1972-73. The training schedule covering the first two aircraft provided,

> Seller shall arrange to provide, at its expense, initial training of flight and maintenance personnel of buyer as follows: . . . Flight Simulator Training. . . . Up to 30 hours per crew. . . .

A similar printed training schedule was appended to the subsequent contract for the twenty-three with a typed alteration in the first sentence to read,

> Seller shall arrange to provide, at its expense, for each Aircraft, initial training of flight and maintenance personnel. . . .

A modification of this provision occurred in September, 1972, when appellant had encountered delays in obtaining financing which postponed the delivery dates envisioned under the contract, and the parties negotiated a letter agreement under which appellant agreed to waive all rights to training under the original contract except the simulator time.

The only flight simulator for the Falcon 20 aircraft in existence at the time of the contract was owned by a firm called Flight Safety, Inc., which had purchased the simulator from appellee. Under terms of the simulator sale, Flight Safety agreed upon notice of appellee to supply to customers of the Business Jets division who purchased Falcon 20 aircraft "initial training" of flight personnel, "including use of the Simulator as necessary," without charge to Business Jets or the customer. Business Jets, however, apparently did not notify Flight Safety, Inc., of the sale to appellant.

Nor did appellant request training until July, 1975. In the meantime, appellant made certain other arrangements for training. It set up a Veterans Administration approved school for veterans who could make use of federal training funds and trained about 400 Falcon Jet pilots, about 200 of whom appellant employed. In 1973, it ordered its own Falcon simulator, a $1.25 million machine, but its financial sources balked and appellant transferred the simulator to Flight Safety, Inc., where it was installed in early 1975. On July 3, 1975, having sold its flight school, appellant contracted with Flight Safety, Inc. to provide simulator training for flight personnel on a continuing basis, allowing appellant 1,000 hours of training a year and covering Falcon Jets as well as other aircraft.

A week later, on July 10, 1975, appellant requested from appellee the "30 hours per crew, per aircraft, for initial flight simulator training" appellant considered itself entitled to under the sales contracts. Appellee refused, and this lawsuit ensued.

The result below hinged upon the meaning of "initial training" of flight personnel in the sales contracts. Appellant urged that the meaning of "initial training" must be taken from the Federal Aviation Administration regulations covering training of flight crew members, which defines "initial training" as that "required for crew members" in order to qualify them for service on a type of aircraft. 14 C.F.R. § 121.400(c)(1) (1979). Under appellant's interpretation, therefore, the phrase "initial training" refers to the status of the crew to be trained, and the "initial training" for pilots provided under the contracts would be available to appellant to train two crew members per aircraft at appellee's expense at any reasonable time upon appellant's demand. The district court found that, under the contracts for the first two aircraft, this interpretation would be proper.

The court also found, however, that the phrase, "for each aircraft, initial training," which appeared in the contract for the additional twenty-three aircraft, was on its face susceptible of a second interpretation which appellee advanced: whatever training of crew the buyer needed at the time of the purchase to put the aircraft into its initial operation. Under appellee's interpretation, therefore, "initial training" refers to the status of the aircraft, and under the contract training would be available for two crew members per aircraft only as required at the time of purchase to provide an initial crew for appellant to operate the aircraft.

The court concluded that the phrase "initial training" was ambiguous. Applying the law of New York, which has adopted the Uniform Commercial Code, New York Uniform Commercial Code Annotated (McKinney 1964) (hereinafter NYUCC), the court resolved the ambiguity by interpreting the writing in light of trade usage. NYUCC §§ 1-205(4), 2-208(2). Finding that the trade usage was for the seller of this kind of aircraft to provide only initial training for an original crew to put a particular aircraft into service for a buyer, the court interpreted the writing as consistent with this usage. . . .

Appellant argues that the district court erred on three points, each of which requires reversal: (1) appellant contends that the contract was not ambiguous and clearly referred to initial training in the sense of the training required to qualify any crew member; (2) appellant contends that trade usage for sale of a single aircraft as a "corporate jet" does not apply to this sale of a fleet of aircraft intended to be used as cargo vehicles; . . . . [We omit discussion of appellant's third point.]

As a preliminary matter, we note that the parties agree that New York law controls, and we note also that because the contract was primarily for the sale of goods, NYUCC § 2-105(1), the Uniform Commercial Code applies to it. . . . We note that the district court decided the case under the Code and neither party challenges the applicability of the Code to this transaction.

Turning to the ambiguity issue, appellant's own argument suggests that the contract was ambiguous. Although appellant contends that the regulation of the Federal Aviation Administration controls the meaning of the parties' written agreement, there is a facial difference between the regulation which defines "initial training" of flight crew and *dispatchers*, 14 C.F.R. § 121.400(c)(1) (1979), and the written sale agreement which calls for "initial training" of flight crew and *mechanics*. On this basis alone, we would consider some doubt justified that the contract phrase referred to the same thing the FAA regulations referred to. Furthermore, we think it would do violence to the plain sense of the words to read the phrase "for each aircraft, initial training" without understanding the phrase to refer at least ambiguously to the training required for initial use of the aircraft. We therefore fully agree with the district court's conclusion that the contract was ambiguous. . . .

Next, appellant asserts that usage of trade in sales of "corporate jets" was inapplicable to this case, because sale of a whole fleet of aircraft for cargo service is unique and fundamentally different than other sales of single aircraft for personnel transport purposes.[10] In particular, appellant urges that when used as a "corporate jet" the Falcon would only require one flight crew for relatively infrequent use, while the use of Falcons in a cargo business required five or six different flight crews for each aircraft because of much more frequent use. Therefore different training provisions would be anticipated under this sale.

Whatever the validity of this distinction, it does not avail appellant. The critical point is that this transaction involved the same aircraft and virtually the same written agreement as the "corporate jet" sales. The usage in those cases therefore had some relevance to this transaction, and the trial court clearly was correct in considering it. NYUCC § 1-205, ... The existence and scope of trade usage is a matter of fact. NYUCC § 1-205(2); 1 R. Anderson, Uniform Commercial Code § 1-205-6. "In case a dominant pattern has been fairly evidenced, the party relying on the usage is entitled to go to the trier of fact on the question of whether such dominant pattern has been incorporated into the agreement." Draftsmen's Comment 9, NYUCC § 1-205. The dominant pattern in this case was the pattern that buyers of Falcon aircraft had a contract right to certain training for the first crew to fly the aircraft. We find no error in the conclusion of the trial court that usage of trade shown by other sales of Falcon Jets was applicable to this contract to explain the meaning of the indefinite term "initial training," and we certainly see no reason to find this conclusion clearly erroneous. Fed.R.Civ.P. 52(a).

Appellant argues that in any event New York law requires construction of ambiguities in a writing against the drafting party. It is true that New York courts have shown some tendency to do so where the party who drafted the agreement takes a position which has little support outside some verbal ambiguity. . . .

But the Uniform Commercial Code specifically requires the written language of the parties' agreement to be construed consistently with applicable trade usage, and this statutory rule of construction must prevail. NYUCC § 1-205. . . .

Accordingly, the judgment of the district court is affirmed.

---

[10] [4] Appellant suggests that it was misled at trial by the district court which indicated at one part of the trial in passing that custom of trade would not be determinative. Appellant asserts that thereafter it considered the case to depend entirely upon the "clear language of the contract." If so, appellant should have looked more closely at the Uniform Commercial Code, which rejects the law of *custom of trade* as a guide to contract meaning, and instead adopts the approach that the language is to be read in light of *trade usage*, a very different approach according to the comments of the code draftsmen. See NYUCC § 1-205 and draftsmen's comments 4 and 5 to § 1-205. See generally, Levie, Trade Usage and Custom Under the Common Law and the Uniform Commercial Code, 40 N.Y.U.L.Rev. 1101 (1965); R. Nordstrom, Handbook of The Law of Sales 157 (1970). Consideration of trade usage was not only consistent with, but also required for, termination under the Code of the meaning of the contract language. NYUCC §§ 1-205, 2-208.

NOTES AND QUESTIONS

1. *Ambiguity*: Judge McMillian assumes that terms in a contract must be ambiguous before a court can consider evidence such as UCC §§ 1-205, 2-208. In *Paragon Resources, Inc. v. National Fuel Gas Distribution Corp.,*[11] the court looked to UCC § 2-202, Official Comment 1. It says that the Code "definitely rejects" the requirement that the court determine that contract language is ambiguous before admitting evidence of course of dealing, usage of trade, or course of performance. The court in the *Paragon Resources* case then concluded:

> The UCC thus adds a third level to a traditional two-level inquiry. Instead of asking, "Were the contract terms ambiguous" and then, "If they were ambiguous what do they mean in light of extrinsic evidence" the Code poses three inquiries:
>
> 1.   Were the express contract terms ambiguous?
>
> 2.   If not, are they ambiguous after considering evidence of course of dealing, usage of trade, and course of performance?
>
> 3.   If the express contract terms by themselves are ambiguous, or if the terms are ambiguous when course of dealing, usage of trade, and course of performance are considered (that is, if the answer to either of the first two questions is yes), what is the meaning of the contract in light of all extrinsic evidence?[12]

Is this a proper reading of the UCC comment? The rules about ambiguity rest on an assumption that contract clauses can have a plain meaning apart from evidence about the context in which they were used. That is, an unambiguous provision is one with a plain meaning. Is this consistent with Patterson's and Farnsworth's discussions?

2. *Usage of trade*: Judge McMillian says "[w]e find no error in the conclusion of the trial court that usage of trade shown by other sales of Falcon Jets was applicable to this contract to explain the meaning of the indefinite term 'initial training.'" He points to no evidence that Frederick W. Smith (the CEO of Federal Express) knew of the usage of the executive jet trade. Under the UCC does this matter? Remember Professor Patterson's discussion of this point.

The Federal Express brief did not raise the question of Mr. Smith's knowledge of the usage. Indeed, it does not deal with the UCC in any way.[13] However, Mr. Smith was asked whether airline crews flew only particular aircraft. He responded:

> A.   No. In that regard, it would probably be the most dramatic difference between corporate and airline-type flying, and *I am very familiar with both of those fields*. In the case of corporate aviation, with a few notable exceptions of some major companies . . . generally the business operate has a specific crew for a specific aircraft, and as long as these peo-

---

[11] 695 F.2d 991 (5th Cir. 1983).

[12] *Id.* at 996.

[13] It cites the Code only once. The brief relies entirely on pre-UCC cases and a legal encyclopedia. The UCC was adopted in New York in 1964.

ple are employed, they fly the aircraft. . . . In the airline business, on the other hand, because of the considerably higher utilization of the aircraft . . . the crews are never married to the aircraft. They rotate among all of the given aircraft of a given type in the airline's fleet. So the unusual nature of this contract [between Federal and Pan Am] . . . was the fact that the Falcon aircraft for the first time was going to be put into the regime of airline operations.

Does the Italicized sentence solve the problem of Mr. Smith's knowledge of trade usage? Until this sale, there had never been a purchase of more than five Falcon jets by one corporation. Federal Express ordered 23, and its crews rotated among them. Does this suggest that there was no usage in the trade of selling Falcon jets for airline use? Suppose we agreed with Federal Express's argument on this point. How, then, would the case have been decided?

All of the questions in this note address the reasons why usage of trade is relevant to finding given meaning to contract language. How many reasons are there? Is trade usage relevant because I am so likely to know of the trade usages that the usages are evidence of my actual intentions? Or is it because it is reasonable for you to assume that these usages form the context of my words and conduct? Or is it because if courts hold people to the usages of their trades, this lowers the cost of transacting business, and saves valuable court time? All of these reasons? Are the reasons consistent? Are there other reasons for believing trade usage relevant?

3. *Proof of usage*: How do you prove a usage of trade? Does this require a social science survey? Would the testimony of an expert witness be enough? How would a person qualify as an expert on the usages of a particular trade? Notice that Mr. Smith testified about his knowledge of practices in corporate and commercial aviation. Pan American did not question his qualifications to do this.

How common must an understanding be to qualify as a usage? Suppose people in the trade usually understand expressions in a certain way, but occasionally they do not. Can you defeat a claimed usage by showing it does not hold in every case? Mr. Smith qualified his observations about corporate aviation. He used the word "generally" and said "with a few notable exceptions of some major companies." Can you have a usage "with a few notable exceptions?" What does UCC § 1-205(2) say about this?

4. *Construction against the drafter*: Judge McMillian refuses to construe the contract against Pan American, the firm that drafted it. He says "[b]ut the Uniform Commercial Code specifically requires the written language of the parties' agreement to be construed consistently with applicable trade usage, and this statutory rule of construction must prevail." Does Official Comment 6 to § 1-205 indicate that this particular maxim of construction should no longer be applied but that tests of good faith and unconscionability must be used? Does it make any difference?

5. *Course of performance*: The opinion addresses the question of trade usage, but does not discuss whether or not the behavior of the parties themselves was relevant to the contract's interpretation. Read UCC § 2-208, and ask whether such an argument could have been made. What facts would have been relevant to such a claim? Which of the parties could profitably have asserted it?

6. *Default rules:* The preceding materials considered how custom and trade usage could be used by judges as tools of contract interpretation or construction. Sometimes, however, a contract will contain a "gap" because the parties didn't think about an issue that later becomes important to performing their deal. What should courts do when they find such a gap? They could fashion what contracts scholars now call default rules. For example, unless the parties agree otherwise, a merchant seller impliedly warrants that the goods it sells are merchantable—such as pass in the trade under the contract description without objection. Sellers who do not want to give such a warranty can bargain it out of their deals, but if they don't deal with the subject in their contracts, the law imposes such a warranty. Some scholars have advocated what they call penalty default rules. The default rule should be designed to induce good behavior on the part of a bargainer.

Remember *Hadley v. Baxendale*? The court in *Hadley* had to decide whether a carrier that was unreasonably tardy in its delivery of a mill shaft was responsible for consequential damages caused by the delay. The contract between the parties didn't address the issue, so the court created a *default rule*—in that case, a rule saying that undisclosed consequential damages are not recoverable. Such a rule offers an incentive to one party to let the other know the risks of the deal. If the potential consequential damages were disclosed, the carrier could disclaim responsibility in the contract, charge more for taking the risk or exercise greater care in seeing that it made timely delivery.

All contracts, at least those written in the real world, have gaps. Some gaps are easy to fill: If two farmers in Ames, Iowa make a contract to sell 100 bushels of wheat for $100, a court will find that the contract called for payment in *US dollars*, even though no contractual provision specified which national currency was to be used. While we cannot be absolutely certain what the two farmers meant, it is highly likely that two American farmers did not mean Canadian, Australian or New Zealand dollars.

But what if the gap to be filled is complex? What criteria should a court use when fashioning default rules? There are several contenders. Advocates of the law and economics approach argue that default rules should be "efficient"—that is, they should be designed to maximize the aggregate welfare.[14] But defining "efficiency" in this context is no easy task: choosing defaults that "most" parties would choose themselves, if they had the time, money or foresight to do so, saves those parties the expense of contracting those terms for themselves, but contracting parties have different preferences, and any efficiency analysis must include the increased costs those parties must incur to discover and contract around the default. Moreover, why should the contractual agreement of any *particular* pair of contracting parties be sacrificed to increase the aggregate welfare of the world at large? Efficiency-based default rules are rarely concerned with what the parties before the court actually would have agreed to, if they had had the time, fore-

---

[14] For a discussion of the merits of this approach, see C.A. Riley, *Designing Default Rules in Contract law: Consent, Conventionalism, and Efficiency*, 10 Oxford J. Legal Stud. 367, 382 (2000).

sight, or money to "fill the gap" on their own. If there are good indicators of what these parties would have agreed to, why shouldn't those indicators be considered by the court?

In response to this last concern, some contract scholars propose the use of custom and trade usage to fill contractual gaps. This is the approach taken by the UCC, which encourages using industry custom and trade usage to interpret contracts, and thereby to gradually incorporate industry-specific default rules into contract law. Under this approach, a court looking for a default rule will fashion the rule in accordance with the customs or expectations of those in the trade.

Of course, using trade customs to fill contractual gaps also presents real problems. Often, there is no commonly understood trade usage available to fill the relevant contractual gap.[15] Professor Lisa Bernstein, in demonstrating this point, has considered the different meanings of the term "bale" as used to measure quantities of hay.[16] Thus, there is a risk that those buying and selling hay might face a *Raffles v. Wichelhaus* problem—the seller might have meant the Texas meaning of the term bale while the buyer might have meant the Oklahoma meaning.

A third contender for the role of best gap filling mechanism is to refuse to fill gaps at all. This approach advocates a return to *contractual formalism,* in which contract terms are interpreted literally and courts are expected to enforce only "verifiable express terms."[17] Under this theory, courts should simply refuse to "complete" the parties' agreement by filling in any gaps left after the express terms of the contract have been applied. Advocates of this approach argue that restricting the court's role to enforcement of express contractual terms will, in the long run, result in better, more predictable contracts.[18] At least parties who negotiate contracts advised by lawyers or other experts will know that they must invest in careful planning which they reduce to clearly drafted written documents. The disadvantage, of course, is that more contracts will be deemed incomplete or ambiguous, and thus unenforceable. From the law and economics perspective, this is a bad result because it may fail to maximize the potential economic value of the contract. It seems likely that investing resources in drafting contracts that attempt to provide for all conceivable although improbable contingencies will often be a waste of money. From the law and society perspective, it is undesirable because it often will fail to acknowledge the full scope of the real agreement between the parties.

So how should courts fill contract gaps, if indeed they should fill them at all? Law and economics theory is useful in that it forces us to acknowledge the cost of legal rules and contract drafting, but as a gap filler, it too often ignores the real circumstances of the parties actually before the court. Moreover, often courts will

---

[15] *See, e.g.,* Lisa Bernstein, *The Questionable Empirical Basis of Article 2's Incorporation Strategy: A Preliminary Study,* 66 U. Chi. L. Rev. 710 (1992).

[16] *Id.* Bernstein found at least 4 different usages of the term: New England, New York, Virginia, and western bales—all of which were different sizes.

[17] *See* Robert E. Scott, *The Case For Formalism In Relational Contracts,* 94 Nw. U. Law Rev. 847 (2000).

[18] *Id.*

lack enough information about the consequences of adopting various rules to determine which one would be the most efficient. Custom and trade usage will be helpful in filling some gaps—although there may not always be an agreed upon trade usage available to the court. In the end, perhaps we must rely on judges to *judge*—to use the various tools available to them to reach what they feel is the fairest solution under the circumstances. This is a messy answer, of course, with its own set of risks, such as judicial subjectivity and the possibility of error. Do you think that these risks are more or less significant than the risks of using the other suggested methods of filling contractual gaps?

Would you advocate different approaches for different types of contracts? For example, on one hand, when one major corporation makes a contract to buy another, we can expect both sides to be represented by lawyers and investment bankers who are experts in mergers and acquisitions. These transactions are sufficiently common that the documents used in past transactions can serve as a checklist of the issues to resolve for the current deal. On the other hand, a transaction between a consumer and a sales person working for a corporation usually has very different characteristics. While there may be a standard form contract drafted by a lawyer working for the seller, neither the consumer nor the sales person is likely to read and understand its provisions. Do you see any difficulty if courts try to tailor approaches to transaction types?

C.   THE PAROL EVIDENCE RULE

The parol evidence rule is not easy to understand. This short note and the next essay should help sort the cases that follow. While the rule may be difficult for judges, lawyers and law students, it is clear that it is an important doctrine in modern contract law.

Let's begin with the easiest case. Seller and Buyer are negotiating a complicated contract. They have been exchanging oral and written communications for weeks. As a result, both have file folders filled with formal drafts of provisions, scraps of paper with handwritten proposals, notes and letters. They have tried to consider matters one by one. However, the bargaining about, say, point five has reopened their tentative agreement about point three. Of course, there also have been oral concessions and proposals. Some of these are reflected in the notes in the files and some remain only imperfectly in the memories of the parties.

Finally, Seller confesses that she is uncertain just where they stand. She says she thinks they really have agreed on everything and have a contract. However, it is not written down anywhere from beginning to end. She proposes that she draft a clean text from which they can work. Buyer thinks this is a good idea. Two days later, Seller and Buyer meet again. Seller presents Buyer with a detailed written contract. She says, "I think this is our deal. Look it over. If I've left out anything, tell me. If I've got something wrong, we can change it. If there's more to negotiate, at least we'll know where to start." A day later Buyer returns and says, "You've done a remarkable job in capturing just what we have agreed. I have one small problem in clause 2, but if we can solve that, we have a contract." Together they work out the problem in clause 2. Seller then says to Buyer, "Now, you are sure that this writing expresses your understanding of our deal? We haven't left anything out? I don't want any misunderstandings or mistakes." Buyer responds, assuring Seller that the writing reflects perfectly his understanding of their agreement. He says, "My lawyer and I have been through all of the earlier material. Of course, you made some changes to harmonize the entire deal, but I can live with them in order to close a contract. The document is our deal." They have the document retyped to reflect the few corrections to clause 2. Then they both sign it.

A year later, Buyer sues Seller for breach of contract. Buyer offers as evidence the text of a preliminary draft of clause 23 which both Buyer and Seller had initialed. This draft is dated a week before Buyer and Seller signed the writing to close their deal. Clause 23 in the preliminary draft declares that if X occurs, then Buyer shall have right Y. Clause 23 in the writing they signed to create a contract declares, on the other hand, if X occurs, then Buyer shall not have right Y but only right Z.

The parol evidence rule would bar admission of evidence of the preliminary draft of clause 23. Here, it is just a matter of free contract. Buyer and Seller agreed that their entire agreement was expressed in the writing they signed to create a contract. Implicitly, they also agreed that the final writing superseded and overturned all prior inconsistent agreements—after all, this was the point of starting with a clean draft. If parties agree that a particular document states their entire agreement and amends or repeals all prior bargains, then courts will give effect to their choice. In short, if we agree that version 2 of our written agreement repeals version 1, then it does. We can wipe the slate clean and start over. This is not a rule of evidence, but simply a rule of contract law calling for courts to enforce parties' agreements.

However, our story, while understandable, is atypical. People seldom agree expressly that a writing they sign is the final crystallization of their contract.[19] They just sign written documents called contracts. We could presume that everyone understands, or should understand, any writing which he or she signs. However, we know this will not be the case in many instances. Whatever the wisdom of doing business this way, people do assume that *both* a formal writing labeled "CONTRACT" and their prior oral statements and letters *together* constitute the deal. If clause 23 in a prior letter and clause 23 in the written contract conflict, it is likely to be the product of mistake. Courts could approach the situation much as the British judges did in *Raffles v. Wichelhaus*. On the other hand, perhaps it is just easier for courts to presume that formal later writings supersede whatever is said in earlier correspondence and conversations. Many people see writings as a form of magic, and it may help bureaucratically run organizations to ignore choice and hold people to whatever they signed.

A more typical case is even more difficult. Buyer offers in evidence a letter from Seller. It was written before their final contract was signed. In it, Seller agrees to something which is not covered in the final document. Should courts view the omission of this provision as an implied agreement that there should be

---

[19] Lawyers drafting form contracts may sneak clauses saying this into documents which they should understand are not likely to be read. Is this a type of fraud? Should you feel a personal sense of guilt if you use guile, and legal knowledge, to take advantage of the trusting or unwary?

no such clause in the contract? Should courts recognize that people may put some but not all of their bargain in a final writing? Should courts seek the actual intentions of the parties or create presumptions to protect writings?

Matters get more uncertain. Suppose Buyer offers a preliminary draft of clause 23 in evidence. Buyer does not seek to have it enforced as part of the contract. Rather Buyer argues that the preliminary draft is relevant to interpreting the meaning of clause 23 in the final agreement. The written document says that if X occurs, Buyer shall have right Z. However, what are the boundaries of right Z? Buyer argues that it should be interpreted in light of the definition of right Y in the preliminary draft—in effect, what is not Y is Z. Should courts consider this evidence? Must they first determine that the scope of right Z is ambiguous?

Suppose, on the other hand, Buyer wants to show that clause 23 never was supposed to be effective. Rather, it was written into the contract to comply with requirements of the Mexican government. Buyer and Seller agreed in a prior letter that the clause was to have no effect. Should this evidence be admitted? Suppose, instead, Buyer wants to show that Buyer and Seller agreed in a side agreement that clause 23 would be effective only if the Mexican government could not be persuaded to waive its regulation in the case of this transaction. Should this evidence be admitted?

Finally, suppose Buyer wants to have the court *reform* the final written contract to change the term "right Z" to "right Y." Buyer wants to offer evidence of prior agreements to show that Seller's word processor was mistakenly programmed so that it produced the wrong clause when a typist entered "ALT 25." "ALT 25" should have produced language giving Buyer "right Y." Instead, it produced language giving the Buyer "right Z." Neither Buyer nor Seller discovered the error before they signed the document. Is an action for reformation different than one for damages for breach of contract? Can Buyer contradict the writing in a reformation action? Is the claim really different from the original case where Buyer wanted to contract a final writing with preliminary draft?

Obviously, a great deal turns on whether courts seek to carry out real choices. They may seek other goals without announcing them openly. We can now turn to consider what courts have done with such cases.

A Plea for a Uniform Parol Evidence Rule and Principles of Contract Interpretation
John D. Calamari & Joseph M. Perillo[20]

Any reader of advance sheets is well aware that most of the contract decisions reported do not involve offer and acceptance or other subjects usually explored in depth in a course in contracts but rather involve the parol evidence rule and questions of interpretation, topics given scant attention in most courses in contracts. Although a number of articles have appeared recently on these subjects, for the most part they tend to express the individual view of the writer as to what the law should be. While the authors of this paper will state their views, their principal purpose is to set forth the basic problems involved and to offer a guide for com-

---

[20] 42 Ind. L. J. 333 (1967). Reprinted with permission.

prehending the reasons for the many contradictory decisions in these areas. Much of the fog and mystery surrounding these subjects stems from the fact that there is basic disagreement as to the meaning and effect of the parol evidence rule and as to the appropriate goals to be achieved by the process of contractual interpretation. The cases and treatises of the contract giants tend to conceal this conflict. While frequently masking disagreement by using the same terminology, Professors Williston and Corbin are often poles apart in the meaning they attach to the same term. Often starting from what superficially appear to be the same premises, they frequently advocate different results in similar fact situations. The polarity of their views reflects conflicting value judgments as to policy issues that are as old as our legal system and that are likely to continue as long as courts of law exist. Although many writers and courts have expressed their views on the subject and have made major contributions to it, concentration on the analyses of Professors Williston and Corbin will point up the fundamental bases upon which the conflicting cases and views rest.

I. The Parol Evidence Rule

The Area of Substantial Agreement

There is a rule of substantive law which states that whenever contractual intent is sought to be ascertained from among several expressions of the parties, an earlier tentative expression will be rejected in favor of a later expression that is final. More simply stated, the contract made by the parties supersedes tentative promises made in earlier negotiations. Consequently, in determining the content of the contract, the earlier tentative promises are irrelevant.

The parol evidence rule comes into play only when the last expression is in writing. Professor Corbin states the rule as follows: "When two parties have made a contract and have expressed it in a writing to which they have both assented as the complete and accurate integration of that contract, evidence, whether parol or otherwise, of antecedent understandings and negotiations will not be admitted for the purpose of varying or contradicting the writing." Professor Williston's formulation is not to the contrary: "Briefly stated," he writes, "this rule requires, in the absence of fraud, duress, mutual mistake, or something of the kind, the exclusion of extrinsic evidence, oral or written, where the parties have reduced their agreement to an integrated writing." Both agree that this, too, is a rule of substantive law that also operates as an exclusionary rule of evidence merely because prior understandings are irrelevant to the process of determining the content of the final contract. The similarity between the parol evidence rule and the rule stated in the preceding paragraph is obvious. The main and important difference is that where the last expression is not in writing the jury determines whether the parties intended the second expression to supersede the first. This is to say that this question of intention is determined as is any other question of intention stemming from oral transactions. Where the later expression is in writing, however, this question is usually determined by the trial judge. At an early date it was felt (and the feeling strongly remains) that writings require the special protection that is afforded by removing this issue from the province of unsophisticated jurors.[21]

While it is unanimously agreed that the parol evidence rule applies to *prior* expressions, and has no application to an agreement made *subsequent* to the writing, there is no unanimity as to expressions *contemporaneous* with the writing. Williston and the *Restatement* take the position that contemporaneous expressions should be treated the same as prior expressions except that contemporaneous writings should be deemed to be a part of the integration. Corbin appears to argue that expressions are either prior or subsequent to the writing and that therefore the word "contemporaneous" merely clouds the issue. Everyone agrees that the parol evidence rule does not apply to a separate agreement; that is, an agreement that has a separate consideration.

A distinction is drawn between a total and a partial integration. Where the writing is intended to be *final* and *complete*, it is characterized as a total integration and may be neither contradicted nor supplemented by evidence of prior agreements or expressions. But where the writing is intended to be *final* but *incomplete*, it is said to be a partial integration; although such a writing may not be *contradicted* by evidence of prior agreements or expressions, it may be *supplemented* by evidence of consistent additional terms. Thus, in approaching a writing, two questions must be asked: (1) Is it intended as a final expression? (2) Is it intended to be a complete expression?

Is the writing intended as a final expression? Writings that evidence a contract are not necessarily "final" embodiments of the contract. Exchanges of letters or memoranda that show the conclusion of a contract may have been intended to be read in the light of more far-ranging conversations and documents. Or, the parties may have intended their writing to be tentative and preliminary to a final draft. In these cases, the parol evidence rule does not bar enforcement of the entire agreement as proved by the writing read in the context of prior and contemporaneous expressions. It is agreed that any relevant evidence is admissible to show that the writing was not intended to be final. Although the question of finality is frequently characterized as one of law in order to remove it from the province of unsophisticated jurors, it is actually a question of fact—one of intention—which the trial judge determines. To be considered final the writing need not be in any particular form and need not be signed. The crucial requirement is that the parties have regarded the writing as the final embodiment of their agreement.

Sometimes confused with this question of finality, but clearly distinguishable, is the frequently raised question of whether parties who have made a tentative written agreement intended that no contract would exist until a final writing was executed. On this issue of the existence of the contract, the parol evidence rule is

---

[21] [10] "It is often assumed that the parol evidence rule protects the "haves" against the "have nots," since it is the former who ordinarily draft written contracts and the latter who receive the sympathy of the jury. See McCormick, The Parol Evidence Rule as a Procedural Device for Control of One Jury, 41 Yale L. J. 365, 427-28 (1932). Surprisingly, however, a substantial number of the reported cases dealing with the rule involve sizable transactions between persons with apparently strong bargaining power.

even more clearly inapplicable. This question is treated as a normal question of intention. . . . The determination is frequently made by the jury.

Is the writing a complete or partial integration? Once it is determined that the writing is intended to be final and therefore an integration, it becomes necessary to ascertain whether the integration is complete (so that it cannot be contradicted or supplemented) or only partial (so that it cannot be contradicted but may be supplemented by evidence of consistent additional terms). It seems to be generally agreed that this is a question of law in the sense that it is determined by the trial judge.

The Parol Evidence Rule: The Major Area of Conflict

Apparent agreement by Professors Williston and Corbin, except as noted, on the rules stated above conceals real conflict. The battleground upon which they express disagreement is a major one: the concept of total integration. This, of course, is the area in which most of the cases arise. Both assert that the existence of a total integration depends on the intention of the parties. Williston does so primarily in a section entitled, "Integration Depends Upon Intent." Corbin's emphasis on intent runs throughout his entire discussion of the rule. It appears, however, that in this context they use the term "intent" in ways that are remarkably dissimilar. A typical fact situation will illustrate this. *A* agrees to sell and *B* agrees to purchase Blackacre for $10,000. The contract is in writing and in all respects appears complete on its face. Prior to the signing of the contract *A*, in order to induce *B*'s assent, orally promises him in the presence of a number of reputable witnesses that if *B* will sign the contract, *A* will remove an unsightly shack on *A*'s land across the road from Blackacre. May this promise be proved and enforced? This depends upon whether the writing is a total integration.

Williston argues that if the intention to have a total integration were to be determined by the ordinary process of determining intention, the parol evidence rule would be emasculated. He points out that the mere existence of the collateral oral agreement would conclusively indicate that the parties intended only a partial integration and that the only question that would be presented is whether the alleged prior or contemporaneous agreement was actually made. This would be a question of fact for the jury, thus eliminating the special protection which the trial judge should afford the writing.

Williston, therefore, suggests that the issue of partial or total integration should be determined according to the following rules.

(1) If the writing expressly declares that it contains the entire agreement of the parties (what is sometimes referred to as a merger clause), the declaration conclusively establishes that the integration is total unless the document is obviously incomplete or the merger clause was included as a result of fraud or mistake or any other reason exists that is sufficient to set aside a contract. As previously indicated, even a merger clause does not prevent enforcement of a separate agreement supported by a distinct consideration.

(2) In the absence of a merger clause, the determination is made by looking to the writing. Consistent additional terms may be proved if the writing is obviously

incomplete on its face or if it is apparently complete but, as in the case of deeds, bonds, bills and notes, expresses the undertaking of only one of the parties.

(3) Where the writing appears to be a complete instrument expressing the rights and obligations of both parties, it is deemed a total integration unless the alleged additional terms were such as might naturally be made as a separate agreement by parties situated as were the parties to the written contract.

Thus in the hypothetical case given, Williston's view is that the collateral promise to remove the unsightly shack could not be enforced. The writing was apparently complete on its face and contracting parties would ordinarily and naturally have included such a promise in the writing. Many might agree with this result, but can it be seriously argued that this result is based on the parties' intent that the agreement be integrated? How can a rule based on the intention of the parties be emasculated by seeking to determine their actual expressed intent? It is quite clear that the expressed intent shown by overwhelming evidence is at variance with an intent to have the writing serve as their complete agreement.

Professor Corbin takes a contrary view as to the proper result in our hypothetical case: "It can never be determined by mere interpretation of the words of a writing whether it is an 'integration' of anything, whether it is 'the final and complete expression of the agreement' or is a mere partial expression of the agreement." Elsewhere, he states: "Since the very existence of an 'integration' . . . is dependent on what the parties thereto say and do (necessarily extrinsic to the paper instrument), at the time they draw that instrument 'in usual form,' are we to continue like a flock of sheep to beg the question at issue, even when its result is to 'make a contract for the parties,' one that is vitally different from the one they made themselves?" When Professor Corbin speaks of the intent of the parties he emphatically means their actual expressed intent.

Thus, two schools of thought are on the scene, one determined to seek out the intent of the parties, the other speaking of intent but refusing to consider evidence of what the intent actually was. . . .

Fictions have been enormously important in the development of our law. In an era when the law was deemed unchangeable and eternal, they provided almost the only mechanism for avoiding the impact of rules deemed unwise. Their use today serves only to obfuscate what should be clear. Shorn of language indicating a fictitious search for intent, the courts and writers who adopt a Willistonian approach are saying this: *When parties adopt a written form that gives every appearance of being complete and final, they are required to incorporate in that form their entire agreement. If they fail to do so, unincorporated agreements relating to the same subject matter are void.*

That the intention of the parties is not relevant in courts adopting the same approach as Williston has been recognized in a number of opinions. In a California case, testimony in violation of the parol evidence rule was admitted without objection. The question presented was whether the rule could be invoked despite the lack of objection. The court held that the rule could be invoked, stating that the parol evidence rule did not merely prohibit the proof of contemporaneous oral agreements; rather it prohibited the making of such agreements.

Professor Corbin has an easy task in demolishing the Willistonian approach. In treating the matter of integration as a question of intent, as Professor Williston purports to do, he shows the absurdity of excluding all relevant evidence of intent except the writing itself. But, as we have seen, Williston . . . [is] unconcerned about the true intention of the parties. Rather, shorn of rote language of fiction indicating a search for intention . . . [he is] advocating and applying a rule of form. Since (and even before) the common law had its genesis, there has been a deeply felt belief that transactions will be more secure, litigation will be reduced, and the temptation to perjury will be removed, if everyone will only use proper forms for his transactions. The Statute of Wills and the Statute of Frauds are but examples of this belief. Professor Corbin, by attacking the apparent arguments of Williston's position has not expressly come to grips with the substance of his position. This is not to suggest that either he or Professor Williston have been unaware of the true nature of their disagreement. Rather, they seem for the most part to have been content not to make explicit the basis of their differing views. The purpose of the above discussion is to bring their differences into bold relief so that the debate on this matter can break away from the bland assumption that everyone agrees as to the statement of the parol evidence rule and that there is merely some confusion as to its application.

The debate involves the question: is the public better served by giving effect to the parties' entire agreement written and oral, even at the risk of injustice caused by the possibility of perjury and the possibility that superseded documents will be treated as operative, or does the security of transactions require that, despite occasional injustices, persons adopting a formal writing be required, on the penalty of voidness of their oral and written side agreements, to put their entire agreement in the formal writing.

The conflict is an old one. Rules excluding evidence on the ground that it is likely to be false are not strangers to the law. Formerly, parties and interested third persons were incompetent to testify on the ground that their testimony would be unworthy of belief. The Statute of Frauds and Statute of Wills embody similar considerations. The authors believe, however, that the possibility of perjury is an insufficient ground for interfering with freedom of contract by refusing to effectuate the parties' entire agreement.

The whole thrust of our law for over a century has been directed to the eradication of exclusionary rules of evidence in civil cases. Thus parties may now testify, their interest in the outcome affecting only the weight and not the admissibility of the evidence. Dissatisfaction with rigid application of the parol evidence rule has resulted in the strained insertion of fact situations into the categories where the parol evidence rule is inapplicable. Thus, to circumvent the rule fraud has been found and reformation has been granted in situations where these concepts are not ordinarily deemed applicable. Moreover, whole categories of exceptions have been carved out; for example, a deed absolute may be shown to be a mortgage. Professor Thayer's summation of the parol evidence problem warrants repetition: "Few things are darker than this, or fuller of subtle difficulties." When any rule of law is riddled through with exceptions and applications difficult to reconcile, it is believed that litigation is stimulated rather than reduced. If the policy of the parol evidence rule is to reduce the possibility of judgments predicated upon perjured testimony and superseded documents, it may be effectuated to a large extent by continuing to leave control over determining the question of intent to integrate in the hands of the trial judge. Finally, the trend of modern decisions, as Williston suggests, "is toward increasing the liberality in the admission of parol agreements." This tendency of the courts is in no small measure due to the influence of Professor Corbin's treatise.

It is of little moment whether the views of the authors of this article as to what the law should be are convincing. The essential point being made here is that there is no uniform parol evidence rule. Rather, there are at least two rather dissimilar rules which, for convenience, may be denominated the Corbin Rule and the Williston Rule. In view of the confusion engendered by having two contradictory rules expressed in the same terminology, it is remarkable that a few states have shown a degree of consistency. New York, despite some inconsistent cases, generally maintains a rigorously Willistonian approach. Rhode Island seems recently to have adopted the Corbin approach with a Willistonian touch, admitting extrinsic evidence out of the presence of the jury to determine whether a total integration exists; the trial judge decides this question on the Willistonian test of whether the alleged collateral agreement "is such that the parties would naturally or normally" have included it in the writing. This seems to be a sound indicia of intent, but not a conclusive one. If the norm is that of the "reasonable man," this good citizen would probably insist that the entire agreement be reduced to writing. The end result would seem to be pure Williston. Some states, such as Connecticut, reach results consistent with Corbin's test, while utilizing the most varied reasoning. Perhaps most states are consistently erratic. Such is the confusion that in any state a decision may be reached which is ludicrous in result and analysis or sensible in result but strained in analysis.

It is hoped that once the source of confusion is comprehended, courts will achieve a greater degree of consistency by consciously choosing one of the competing rules. The widespread adoption of the Uniform Commercial Code may give impetus to a consistent and enlightened approach if it is applied to cases not specifically under its coverage. An official comment to § 2-202 states:

> [C]onsistent additional terms, not reduced to writing, may be proved unless the court finds that the writing was intended by both parties as a complete and exclusive statement of all terms. If the additional terms are such that, if agreed upon, they would *certainly* have been included in the document in the view of the court, then evidence of their alleged making must be kept from the trier of fact. (Emphasis added.)

Thus, the Code requires the court to ascertain the intention of the parties, and it can be assumed that the codifiers meant a true expressed intention and not a fictitious intention. The trial judge has an important function in making this determination. If he finds that it is certain the parties would have incorporated the additional term into the writing if they had agreed upon it, he excludes evidence of the alleged term from the jury's consideration. If it is merely improbable that the parties would have agreed to the term without incorporating it into the writing, the jury must determine whether the additional term was agreed upon. The Code, of course, does not propose to affect the power of the court to set aside or direct a verdict where the evidence supporting an alleged supplementary term is flimsy. Thus, the writing is protected at two stages. First, there is a preliminary finding, based on an external standard, as to whether any evidence will be heard by the jury. Second, the court contains its control over the quality and quantity of evidence required to support a verdict. . . .

III. The Relationship Between the Parol Evidence Rule and Rules and Standards of Interpretation

Before the parol evidence rule may be invoked, the judge must determine that the parties intended the writing to be final. The question of intent is determined according to the standards and rules of interpretation discussed above. Conversely, the parol evidence rule should have no effect on the question of interpretation—the *meaning* of language. Stated otherwise, before the parol evidence rule can be invoked to exclude evidence, the *meaning* of the writing must be ascertained since one may not determine whether a writing is being contradicted or supplemented until one knows what the writing means.

This should mean that evidence of prior and contemporaneous expressions is always admissible to aid in determining the meaning of the integration, and Corbin so states. Williston is cautiously in accord. Such evidence may be introduced, he grants, but not to prove that the intention of the parties is at variance with the appropriate local meaning of the words. The evidence may be considered only on the question of whether the parties contracted with reference to a local or trade usage or, if this local or trade meaning is ambiguous, on the question of what meaning the parties attached to the words. Even accepting his premise that the true intention of the parties is usually irrelevant, there are two difficulties with Williston's position on the admissibility of this evidence. First, it assumes that the court can successfully ignore the parties' real intention when it is shown by the evidence. Second, it involves a great deal of tension with the exclusionary aspects of his version of the parol evidence rule. If evidence of prior and contemporaneous expressions is not admissible to prove terms supplementary to or at variance with a total integration, but is admissible to show the meaning of the integration, the astute trial lawyer will characterize his evidence on what are really supplementary or contradictory terms as evidence on the true meaning of the contract. Although the function of this evidence is to demonstrate the "meaning of the writing," once it is admitted the court may find it difficult (and unjust) to disregard what may be clear and convincing proof that the writing is not the complete agreement of the parties. Williston's grand structure meticulously separating the parol evidence rule, standards of interpretation, and primary and secondary rules of interpretation seems to collapse into this procedural pitfall.

It is little wonder, then, that many courts that share Williston's concern for the "security of transactions" have retreated even further from the intention of the parties to the almost universally condemned "plain meaning rule," holding that if a writing appears clear and unambiguous on its face, its meaning must be determined from the four corners of the instrument without resort to extrinsic evidence of any nature. This approach excludes evidence of trade usage and prior dealings between the parties as well as evidence of surrounding circumstances and prior and contemporaneous expressions. The latest legislative ruling on the matter, the

Uniform Commercial Code, explicitly condemns the plain meaning rule and explicitly allows use of evidence of a course of dealing or course of performance to explain the agreement "unless carefully negated."

1. THE PAROL EVIDENCE RULE: SEARCH FOR TRUTH . . . OR DEFENSE OF FORM?

BINKS MANUFACTURING CO. v. NATIONAL PRESTO INDUSTRIES, INC.
United States Court of Appeals, Seventh Circuit
709 F.2d 1109 (1983)

COFFEY, J. This appeal involves a contractual dispute concerning the manufacture and sale of an "industrial spray finishing and baking system." Binks Manufacturing Company, the System's manufacturer, brought an action in federal district court to collect the purchase price of the System. Presto Manufacturing Company counterclaimed alleging damages resulting from defective design and manufacture of the System as well as late delivery. The jury returned verdicts in favor of Binks on its purchase price claim and against Presto on its counterclaims. We affirm.

I. Presto is engaged in the manufacture and sale of electrical appliances, including hamburger cookers. Binks Manufacturing Company is a leading manufacturer of industrial spray finishing equipment. In 1975, Presto management decided to increase its production capacity of electric hamburger cookers and as part of its expansion plan, determined to purchase an automatic system designed to coat aluminum castings (the principal components of hamburger cookers) with a non-stick "teflon-like" coating for installation at its Alamogordo, New Mexico plant. Presto entered into negotiations with Binks Manufacturing Company for the design and manufacture of the system.

The negotiations between Binks and Presto continued from October 1975 through March 1976, resulting in a contract with Binks agreeing to manufacture "a custom designed, custom built automatic spray application and oven curing system intended to apply coatings to various Presto products" (hereinafter the "System"). The System was to consist of one continuous conveyor 858 feet long, designed to carry an aluminum casting through a six-step manufacturing process: (1) a booth in which the castings would be sprayed with a primer; (2) an oven where the primer would be baked on to the aluminum castings; (3) a cooling area; (4) a booth where the castings would be sprayed with a non-stick coating; (5) three progressively hotter ovens in which the non-stick coating would be baked on to the aluminum castings over the primer; and (6) a final cooling area. . . .

[The contract provided for delivery of the system not later than June 2, 1976; the contract contained a clause providing that "time is of the essence." In fact, due to unforeseeable and apparently unavoidable problems encountered by a Binks' subcontractor (Radiant Products), delivery was not accomplished until July 19, 1976.]

Binks offered to supervise installation of the System, but Presto chose not to accept the offer and hired their own local independent contractors to install the System. According to Binks, Presto's independent contractors committed installation errors of major proportions, including a failure to properly align and anchor the conveyor equipment. Binks further contends that Presto insisted upon initially operating the System at maximum capacity, thereby ignoring Binks' advice that the System be brought up to full capacity only gradually.

After installation of the System had been completed, Presto personnel made several unsuccessful attempts to operate the System's conveyor. In the ensuing weeks representatives of Presto, Binks and Radiant [the oven subcontractor] made other attempts to operate the System, but experienced a myriad of problems. Binks contends that Presto's independent contractors failed to properly synchronize the electric motors used to run the conveyor causing the conveyor to run sporadically and jam. These problems in conveyor synchronization continued for some two months causing the System to operate at less than half capacity.

Binks and Presto disagree as to the underlying cause of the System's faulty performance. Presto alleges that the System was defectively manufactured in that the conveyor, contrary to the contract specifications, was totally enclosed in the System's ovens, causing the conveyor components to overheat, contributing to the twisting, bending and eventually breakage of the conveyor chain.

Binks, on the other hand, contends Presto: (1) improperly installed the System; (2) inadequately lubricated the conveyor; (3) operated the System's oven at excessive temperatures; (4) ignored Binks' advice in initially operating the System at maximum capacity; and (5) ran defective castings through the System, resulting in pieces breaking off the castings and jamming the conveyor.

Binks also asserts that Presto abused the System by "double loading" the castings used to make upper components of the hamburger cookers, thereby exceeding the System's maximum capacity set forth in the contract. According to Binks, "double loading" the System resulted in twice as many upper burger castings being loaded into the System per hour as specified in the contract (2,250 "upper double burger" castings per hour instead of the 1,125 castings per hour outlined in the contract and 4,500 "upper square burger" castings per hour rather than 2,250 castings per hour set forth in the contract). . . .

. . . Binks and Presto made several unsuccessful attempts to reach a negotiated settlement and failing to achieve this, on November 4, 1977, Binks filed a complaint seeking recovery under the contract for the balance of the purchase price. Presto answered by filing a $9.5 million counterclaim against Binks alleging late delivery of the System, breach of contractual warranties, breach of implied warranties, negligence and misrepresentation in connection with the design, manufacture and sale of the spraying and baking system. . . .

The case came to trial on March 1, 1982, and after the four-week jury trial, judgment was entered in favor of Binks on its claim for the balance of the purchase price and [against Presto's counterclaims].

On appeal, Presto contends that the district court erred:

1. In granting Binks' pre-trial motion in limine, precluding Presto from introducing parol and extrinsic evidence to attempt to show that the parties intended to define the maximum capacity of the System in terms of pounds of castings per hour, rather than the number of castings per hour. . . .

II. The Motion in Limine Concerning the Issue of Maximum Capacity

Presto's counterclaim against Binks alleged that the System designed and manufactured by Binks was defective, resulting in repeated breakdowns and loss of production. Binks answered that the System's breakdowns were not a result of defective design or manufacture, but rather were caused by Presto's abuse of the System, particularly Presto's practice of "double loading" the System.

Therefore, to establish this "double loading" theory at trial, it became necessary to determine the System's "maximum capacity" as defined in the parties' contract. The parties agree that the following provision of the contract sets forth the System's maximum capacity:

One Item of Equipment designed to coat any one of the following parts on one and/or both sides in quantities, as listed at the conveyor rate of 25 fpm with either 16 or 18 inch spindle spacing:

#60-001* Upper Double Burger at (13 oz.)	1,125 pcs./hr.
#60-002* Lower Double Burger at (24 oz.)	1,125 pcs./hr.
#60-003* Upper Square Burger (9.5 oz.)	2,250 pcs./hr.
#60-004* Lower Square Burger (12 oz.)	2,250 pcs./hr.
#60-121* Upper Round Burger (7 oz.)	2,250 pcs./hr.
#60-120 Lower Round Burger (5 oz.)	2,250 pcs./hr.

#28-006 Fry Pan at 3.8#—Quantities as later established.

*Asterisk to indicate item coated on both sides. Hinges on 60-001 and 60-003 coated both sides.

The maximum capacity of the system is limited to the above parts or parts of similar size and cross section with a maximum loading of 4,500 pounds per hour and 4,500 #/hr. of work holders, which would pass through each oven.

Based on the foregoing contractual language, Binks takes the position that the "maximum capacity" of the System for the castings specified in the contract is defined in terms of the *number* of castings that the System can handle per hour consistent with the design of the machine. Presto, however, contends that extrinsic evidence concerning negotiation and performance of the contract demonstrates that the parties intended the maximum capacity of the System to be defined in terms of *pounds* of castings run through the System per hour; i.e., 4,500 pounds of castings per hour. Presto further argues, and Binks concedes, that Presto never loaded the System with more than 4,500 pounds of castings per hour.

Presto, in support of its contention that the parties intended the System's maximum capacity to be defined in *pounds* per hour, sought to introduce extrinsic evidence pertaining to the negotiation and performance of the contract.[22] On February 25, 1976, four days before trial, Binks presented a motion in limine seeking an order precluding Presto from presenting extrinsic evidence to show that the parties intended to define the maximum capacity of the System in terms of pounds per hour rather than number of castings per hour. After hearing arguments, the court ruled in favor of Binks on the motion in limine and stated:

> I conclude that so far as the six identified parts are concerned, the specified maximums of the system are those numbers appearing opposite each of the items [in the contract provision quoted above] and not the number of items which would aggregate 4,500 pounds.

Presto contends the court committed reversible error in ruling that Presto could not introduce extrinsic evidence to show that the parties intended to define the System's maximum capacity in pounds per hour.

In evaluating Presto's challenge to the district court's ruling, we must bear in mind that our role as an appellate court is not to consider a case *de novo*. Rather, our role in reviewing the district court's ruling on the motion in limine is limited as "decisions regarding the admission and exclusion of evidence are peculiarly within the competence of the district court and will not be reversed on appeal unless they constitute a clear abuse of discretion." *Ellis v. City of Chicago*, 667 F.2d 606, 611 (7th Cir. 1981). . . .

Guided by these principles, we turn to the issue of whether the court abused its discretion by precluding Presto from introducing extrinsic evidence to establish that the parties intended the System's maximum capacity for "Upper Double Burger" and "Upper Square Burger" castings to be defined in pounds per hour, rather than number of castings per hour. The admissibility of extrinsic evidence to interpret the contract in this case is governed by Ill.Rev.Stat. ch. 26, § 2-202 [Uniform Commercial Code § 2-202]. . . .

Thus, it is evident that under UCC § 2-202, evidence of a prior agreement or a contemporaneous oral agreement must be excluded if (1) the writing (here the contract between the parties) was intended as the final expression of the parties agreement with respect to the maximum capacity term; *and* (2) the proffered evidence *contradicts* or is *inconsistent* with the terms of the written contract. *See* Nordstrom, Law of Sales 161-66 (1970). It is evident from the record that both Binks and Presto agree that their written contract was intended to be the final expression of their agreement; therefore, the crucial question is whether the interpretation urged by Presto (i.e., that the parties intended the System's maximum capacity for "Upper Square Burger" and "Upper Double Burger" castings to be a function of pounds of castings per hour) contradicts or is inconsistent with the terms of the written contract.

---

[22] [6] This extrinsic evidence included *inter alia*: (1) a quotation submitted by Binks several days prior to formation of the contract stating "approximately 4,500 pounds of aluminum work pieces . . . will pass through each oven per hour;" (2) a March 9, 1976 letter from Binks' project engineer to Presto reciting "The System capacity increased from 1500 to 4500 #/Hr.;" and (3) that Binks participated in designing the work holders in which castings were placed, and allowed for "double loading" of castings.

Although the Uniform Commercial Code itself fails to delineate or set forth when extrinsic evidence contradicts or is inconsistent with written terms of a contract, this court recently defined "inconsistency" for the purpose of UCC § 2-202 as "the absence of reasonable harmony in terms of the language and respective obligations of the parties." *Luria Bros. & Co. v. Pielet Bros. Scrap Iron*, 600 F.2d 103, 111 (7th Cir. 1979). Applying this definition of "inconsistency" to this case, it is clear that if the court were to allow the admission of extrinsic evidence tending to show that the maximum capacity of the System for "Upper Square Burger" and "Upper Double Burger" castings was defined in terms of pounds per hour it would necessarily lead to an "absence of reasonable harmony" between the terms of the written contract and the proffered extrinsic evidence of the parties' purported intent. Presto's theory that the System's maximum capacity for the upper burger castings was defined as 4,500 pounds of such castings per hour would render almost meaningless the express language of the written contract which, after reciting a specified number of each particular casting, states "the maximum capacity of the System is limited to the above parts. . . ." On the other hand, the district court's well reasoned interpretation of the written contract gave meaning to each and every provision of the contract; for each of the six castings listed, the maximum capacity of the System was defined in number of parts per hour, while for other unspecified castings which Presto might decide to run through the System in the future, the maximum capacity was defined in pounds of castings per hour. Thus, the court's decision to exclude the extrinsic evidence of the parties intent is amply supported by the basic principles of contract interpretation that a written contract should be given a construction that "harmonizes all the various parts" of the contract so that no provision is "conflicting with, or repugnant to, or neutralizing of any other." *Zannis v. Lake Shore Radiologists, Ltd.*, 73 Ill.App.3d 901, 29 Ill.Dec. 569, 392 N.E.2d 126, 129 (1979).

Furthermore, the district court's decision to preclude Presto from introducing extrinsic evidence regarding the maximum capacity issue pays credence to the policy underlying the parol evidence rule as set forth in UCC § 2-202. This court in *Luria Bros.*, 600 F.2d at 110 n. 5, stated:

> The parol evidence rule . . . is a rule of substantive law. Evidence is excluded not because it is not credible or not relevant but because of a policy favoring the reliability of written representations of the terms of a contract.

This policy of upholding the integrity of written contracts and favoring written terms over extrinsic evidence is particularly relevant in cases of this nature involving a written contract between two large corporations presumably represented by competent counsel. Such parties should be held to the terms of their written contract whenever it is reasonable to do so, as it is incumbent upon courts to uphold the dignity of a contract whenever possible by preventing parol evidence from being used to negate the terms of written contracts. The First Circuit's words in *Intern. Business Machines v. Catamore Enterprises*, 548 F.2d 1065, 1073 (1st Cir. 1976), *cert. denied*, 431 U.S. 960, 97 S.Ct. 2687, 53 L.Ed.2d 278 (1977) are particularly apt in this case:

The morass of business dealings between two companies described on this record, their promises oral and written, the disparity of their understandings, the frustration of expectations, the inevitable recriminations and conflicting memories—all this is not unique, new, or infrequently encountered. The law in its effort to facilitate just resolutions of such controversies has, over the centuries, developed certain aids or guides to decision. . . . The first is the substantive principle that when, in the course of business transactions between people or corporations, free and uncoerced understandings purporting to be comprehensive are solemnized by documents which both parties sign and concede to be their agreement, such documents are not easily bypassed or given restrictive interpretations.

Additionally, as this lawsuit involved a lengthy and complicated fact situation, admitting extrinsic evidence would have increased the possibility of unnecessarily confusing the jury, a possibility § 2-202 is designed to avoid:

But the way [§ 2-202] is worded, the trial is certainly not to be a freewheeling affair in which the parties may introduce before the jury all evidence of terms, including the writing, with the jury then to decide on terms. Rather, it is plain from the rule and from prior history of similar rules that some of the evidence is to be heard initially only by the judge and that he may invoke the rule to keep this evidence from the jury.

White & Summers, The Law Under the Uniform Commercial Code 77 (2d ed. 1980). *See also* McCormick, The Parol Evidence Rule as a Procedural Device for Control of the Jury, 41 Yale L.J. 365 (1932).

In summary, we conclude that the district court's order barring Presto from introducing extrinsic evidence regarding the intended maximum capacity of the System was not an abuse of discretion as it properly held the parties to the written terms of their contract, accorded with the basic principle of law favoring the dignity of a written contract, and avoided unnecessarily confusing the jury. . . .

Conclusion

We agree with the rulings of the trial court and hold that: (1) the district court did not err in precluding Presto from introducing extrinsic evidence to attempt to prove that the parties intended the maximum capacity of the System to be defined solely in terms of pounds of castings per hour. . . .

NOTES AND QUESTIONS

1. *Interpretation as a surrogate for the real dispute*: Presto's small hamburger cookers were very successful, and a large Christmas market was anticipated in 1976. Seller's delivery was six weeks late. The trial court ruled that it was excused by the delay of an oven subcontractor caused by a supplier's strike and an injury to a key employee. The trial court also suggested that Presto had waived any damages arising from late delivery by accepting delivery, not terminating the contract, and not making a written claim at that time. Presto was in a tough spot once Binks announced it would be late. What should they have done? What are the risks of complaining, and threatening a suit? On the other hand, what are the risks of remaining silent? The minutes of a November 15, 1976 meeting of the seller's officials said that "Presto has made commitments on their products and they cannot make their commitments. Presto is desperate. Their frying pans are a commitment to Sears for the Christmas rush." We will return to the issue of what victims of breach can do when we look at waiver and the required notices of an intention to hold a seller for damages under the Uniform Commercial Code. Notice that in this case, however, the issue of the interpretation of the contract as to the capacity of the unit is largely a surrogate for the responsibility for the delay and the efforts made to overcome the lost time. For example, the seller's brief tells us:

> Binks and its suppliers recommended that Presto break in the System gradually after installation. Presto started up the system "full bore" and thereby increased the chance that the conveyor later would drag and the ovens would not seal properly. When the K was made, the parties assumed the ovens would run 8 hours a day 5 days a week, but Presto decided to operate it 24 hours per day 6 days a week. Presto had no program of preventive maintenance until 6 months after installation.

2. *The excluded parol evidence*: The key item of parol evidence excluded by the trial court was the second of three quotations submitted to Presto by Binks. This quotation provided that:

> The equipment is designed to process approximately 2250 work pieces per hour on 8" *centers at a conveyor speed of 25 fpm or the same* number of pieces held two per work holder on 16" *centers.*

> Approximately 4500 pounds of aluminum work pieces, and 4500 pounds of steel work holders will pass through each oven per hour.

Binks's letter of a day after the second proposal said that under it "the system capacity increased from 1500 to 4500 #/hr." The third proposal, which became the contract was written within four days after this letter.

Presto also argued that the trial court should have looked at the course of performance to indicate the proper construction of the contract. The work holder was designed to allow two parts per holder and thus a load more than what the trial court found to be the maximum weights under the contract. The system was operated with Binks's knowledge, and Presto double-loaded the system at the 24-hour test run, and Binks's officials did not object.

3. *Explaining the way the contract was drafted*: Binks responded, arguing:

> There was an important reason for expressing the maximum capacity of the System in terms of specific hourly quantities for the identified parts. The ovens in the System baked Presto's coatings by "impinged high velocity hot air" —jets of hot air directed at the parts as they progressed through the ovens. An increase in the number of parts passing back and forth through the ovens would obstruct the impinged air and, therefore, decrease the efficiency of the ovens. On the other hand, the "maximum loading" provision in the contract established the weight above which the loading of the parts (4500 pounds) and the workholders

(4500 pounds) would exceed the weight-bearing tolerances of the entire System, including the conveyor and conveyor drives. . . .

Binks has never contended that it was improper to load 2 parts per workholder, so long as the applicable pieces-per-hour limitation was not exceeded. These overall limits could have been observed even when workholders were being doubleloaded simply by doubling the distance between workholders.

4. ***Construing a contract against the party that drafted it***: Apparently Binks's engineers drafted the less than clear language in the proposal form that became the contract between the parties. Why didn't the court in the *Binks* case admit the parol evidence to resolve the ambiguities in the contract or construe the language most strongly against Binks, the party that drafted it? To what extent, if at all, do you think the answer to that question involves National Presto's claim for $9.5 million dollars in damages against a smaller machinery supplier?

5. ***Extending the Binks principle***: In *Air Line Stewards and Stewardesses Assoc. v. Trans World Airlines*,[23] the Seventh Circuit Court of Appeals applied the *Binks* case to a dispute between TWA and a union concerning an agreement in which TWA agreed to reinstate flight attendants who had been fired when they became pregnant. The dispute concerned whether the attendants were entitled to be reinstated only if vacancies developed, or were to be reinstated whether or not there were vacancies. The district court had ruled for the union. The court of appeals reversed, finding that the language of the contract was plain and unambiguous and required reinstatement only when vacancies arose. The dissent argued that the contract was sufficiently ambiguous and imprecise to warrant consideration of extrinsic evidence in resolving the question of its meaning. The majority responded:

> As we recently stated in Binks Manufacturing Co. v. National Presto Industries, Inc.:
>
>> The policy of upholding the integrity of written contracts and favoring written terms over extrinsic evidence is particularly relevant in cases of this nature involving a written contract between two large corporations presumably represented by competent counsel. [*Brinks* at 116.]
>
> Although *Binks* involved the interpretation of . . . UCC § 2-202 concerning extrinsic evidence, the general policy of "upholding the integrity of written contracts" appears to apply equally as well to the present agreement between a labor association and a corporation which were both represented by competent counsel.[24]

Is the Seventh Circuit's position based on a policy of carrying out choice, fault, facilitating bureaucracy, giving lawyers incentives for care in drafting, easing judicial burdens, or something else? How can the majority say that the contract is unambiguous in light of the contrary reading by both the district court and the dissenting judge? In finding the agreement unambiguous, isn't the Seventh

---

[23] 713 F.2d 319 (7th Cir. 1983).
[24] *Id.* at 321-22.

Circuit saying that readings contrary to its own are totally implausible? How does it establish this?

Other factors may have influenced the majority. The agreement in question was a settlement in a former case, and had been approved by the Seventh Circuit. The union had argued against the settlement, contending that the reinstatement provisions would adversely affect the seniority rights of TWA's current flight attendants. The Seventh Circuit had responded to this argument by interpreting the agreement so no current TWA attendant would lose employment because "providing positions for these reinstated attendants would normally be possible as a result of normal attrition of workers." The majority in the second case said that if it accepted the district court's construction of the settlement, TWA would either have to fire flight attendants to make places for those it reinstated, or pay the reinstated workers for doing nothing. "There was no language in the Settlement Agreement requiring TWA to accept this 'featherbedding' approach advocated by the plaintiffs."[25] Is this argument more than just the adoption of the plain meaning of an unambiguous document?

2. OF PARTIAL INTEGRATIONS AND SIDE AGREEMENTS

MITCHILL v. LATH
Court of Appeals of New York
247 N.Y. 377, 160 N.E. 646 (1928)

Appeal, by permission, from a judgment of the Appellate Division of the Supreme Court in the second judicial department, entered May 27, 1927, unanimously affirming a judgment in favor of plaintiff entered upon a decision of the court on trial at Special Term in an action to compel specific performance of an alleged contract to remove an ice house. . . .

ANDREWS, J. In the fall of 1923 the Laths owned a farm. This they wished to sell. Across the road, on land belonging to Lieutenant-Governor Lunn, they had an ice house which they might remove. Mrs. Mitchill looked over the land with a view to its purchase. She found the ice house objectionable. Thereupon "the defendants orally promised and agreed, for and in consideration of the purchase of their farm by the plaintiff, to remove the said ice house in the spring of 1924." Relying upon this promise, she made a written contract to buy the property for $8,400, for cash and a mortgage and containing various provisions usual in such papers. Later receiving a deed, she entered into possession and has spent considerable sums in improving the property for use as a summer residence. The defendants have not fulfilled their promise as to the ice house and do not intend to do so. We are not dealing, however, with their moral delinquencies. The question before us is whether their oral agreement may be enforced in a court of equity.

This requires a discussion of the parol evidence rule—a rule of law which defines the limits of the contract to be construed. (*Glackin v. Bennett*, 226 Mass.

---

[25] *Id.* at 324.

316.) It is more than a rule of evidence and oral testimony even if admitted will not control the written contract (*O'Malley v. Grady*, 222 Mass. 202), unless admitted without objection. (*Brady v. Nally*, 151 N.Y. 258.) It applies, however, to attempts to modify such a contract by parol. It does not affect a parol collateral contract distinct from and independent of the written agreement. It is, at times, troublesome to draw the line. Williston, in his work on Contracts (§ 637) points out the difficulty. "Two entirely distinct contracts," he says, "each for a separate consideration may be made at the same time and will be distinct legally. Where, however, one agreement is entered into wholly or partly in consideration of the simultaneous agreement to enter into another, the transactions are necessarily bound together. . . . Then if one of the agreements is oral and the other is writtem, the problem arises whether the bond is sufficiently close to prevent proof of the oral agreement." That is the situation here. It is claimed that the defendants are called upon to do more than is required by their written contract in connection with the sale as to which it deals.

The principle may be clear, but it can be given effect by no mechanical rule. As so often happens, it is a matter of degree, for as Professor Williston also says where a contract contains several promises on each side it is not difficult to put any one of them in the form of a collateral agreement. If this were enough written contracts might always be modified by parol. Not form, but substance is the test.

In applying this test the policy of our courts is to be considered. We have believed that the purpose behind the rule was a wise one not easily to be abandoned. Notwithstanding injustice here and there, on the whole it works for good. Old precedents and principles are not to be lightly cast aside unless it is certain that they are an obstruction under present conditions. New York has been less open to arguments that would modify this particular rule, than some jurisdictions elsewhere. Thus in *Eighmie v. Taylor* (98 N.Y. 288) it was held that a parol warranty might not be shown although no warranties were contained in the writing.

Under our decisions before such an oral agreement as the present is received to vary the written contract, at least three conditions must exist, (1) the agreement must in form be a collateral one; (2) it must not contradict express or implied provisions of the written contract; (3) it must be one that parties would not ordinarily be expected to embody in the writing; or put in another way, an inspection of the written contract, read in the light of surrounding circumstances must not indicate that the writing appears "to contain the engagements of the parties, and to define the object and measure the extent of such engagement." Or again, it must not be so clearly connected with the principal transaction as to be part and parcel of it.

The respondent does not satisfy the third of these requirements. It may be, not the second. We have a written contract for the purchase and sale of land. The buyer is to pay $8,400 in the way described. She is also to pay her portion of any rents, interest on mortgages, insurance premiums and water meter charges. She may have a survey made of the premises. On their part the sellers are to give a full covenant deed of the premises as described, or as they may be described by the surveyor if the survey is had, executed and acknowledged at their own expense; they sell the personal property on the farm and represent they own it; they agree that all amounts paid them on the contract and the expense of examining the title shall be a lien on the property; they assume the risk of loss or damage by fire until the deed is delivered; and they agree to pay the broker his commissions. Are they to do more? Or is such a claim inconsistent with these precise provisions? It could not be shown that the plaintiff was to pay $500 additional. Is it also implied that the defendants are not to do anything unexpressed in the writing?

That we need not decide. At least, however, an inspection of this contract shows a full and complete agreement, setting forth in detail the obligations of each party. On reading it one would conclude that the reciprocal obligations of the parties were fully detailed. Nor would his opinion alter if he knew the surrounding circumstances. The presence of the ice house, even the knowledge that Mrs. Mitchill thought it objectionable would not lead to the belief that a separate agreement existed with regard to it. Were such an agreement made it would seem most natural that the inquirer should find it in the contract. Collateral in form it is found to be, but it is closely related to the subject dealt with in the written agreement—so closely that we hold it may not be proved.

Where the line between the competent and the incompetent is narrow the citation of authorities is of slight use. Each represents the judgment of the court on the precise facts before it. How closely bound to the contract is the supposed collateral agreement is the decisive factor in each case. . . . Attention should be called also to *Taylor v. Hopper* (62 N.Y. 649), where it is assumed that evidence of a parol agreement to remove a barn, which was an inducement to the sale of lots, was improper.

We do not ignore the fact that authorities may be found that would seem to support the contention of the appellant. . . . But the fixed form of a deed makes it inappropriate to insert collateral agreements, however closely connected with the sale. This may be cause for an exception. Here we deal with the contract on the basis of which the deed to Mrs. Mitchill was given subsequently, and we confine ourselves to the question whether its terms may be modified.

Finally there is the case of *Chapin v. Dobson* (78 N.Y. 74, 76). This is acknowledged to be on the border line and is rarely cited except to be distinguished. Assuming the premises, however, the court was clearly right. There was nothing on the face of the written contract, it said, to show that it intended to express the entire agreement. And there was a finding, sustained by evidence, that there was an entire contract, only part of which was reduced to writing. This being so, the contract as made might be proved.

It is argued that what we have said is not applicable to the case as presented. The collateral agreement was made with the plaintiff. The contract of sale was with her husband and no assignment of it from him appears. Yet the deed was given to her. It is evident that here was a transaction in which she was the principal from beginning to end. We must treat the contract as if in form, as it was in fact, made by her.

Our conclusion is that the judgment of the Appellate Division and that of the Special Term should be reversed and the complaint dismissed, with costs in all courts.

LEHMAN, J. (dissenting). I accept the general rule as formulated by Judge Andrews. I differ with him only as to its application to the facts shown in the record. The plaintiff contracted to purchase land from the defendants for an agreed price. A formal written agreement was made between the sellers and the plaintiff's husband. It is on its face a complete contract for the conveyance of the land. It describes the property to be conveyed. It sets forth the purchase price to be paid. All the conditions and terms of the conveyance to be made are clearly stated. I concede at the outset that parol evidence to show additional conditions and terms of the conveyance would be inadmissible. There is a conclusive presumption that the parties intended to integrate in that written contract every agreement relating to the nature or extent of the property to be conveyed, the contents of the deed to be delivered, the consideration to be paid as a condition precedent to the delivery of the deeds, and indeed all the rights of the parties in connection with the land. The conveyance of that land was the subject-matter of the written contract and the contract completely covers that subject.

The parol agreement which the court below found the parties had made was collateral to, yet connected with, the agreement of purchase and sale. It has been found that the defendants induced the plaintiff to agree to purchase the land by a promise to remove an ice house from land not covered by the agreement of purchase and sale. No independent consideration passed to the defendants for the parol promise. To that extent the written contract and the alleged oral contract are bound together. The same bond usually exists wherever attempt is made to prove a parol agreement which is collateral to a written agreement. Hence "the problem arises whether the bond is sufficiently close to prevent proof of the oral agreement." *See* Judge Andrews' citation from Williston on Contracts, § 637.

Judge Andrews has formulated a standard to measure the closeness of the bond. Three conditions, at least, must exist before an oral agreement may be proven to increase the obligation imposed by the written agreement. I think we agree that the first condition that the agreement "must in form be a collateral one" is met by the evidence. I concede that this condition is met in most cases where the courts have nevertheless excluded evidence of the collateral oral agreement. The difficulty here, as in most cases, arises in connection with the two other conditions.

The second condition is that the "parol agreement must not contradict express or implied provisions of the written contract." Judge Andrews voices doubt whether this condition is satisfied. The written contract has been carried out. The purchase price has been paid; conveyance has been made, title has passed in accordance with the terms of the written contract. The mutual obligations expressed in the written contract are left unchanged by the alleged oral contract. When performance was required of the written contract, the obligations of the parties were measured solely by its terms. By the oral agreement the plaintiff seeks to hold the defendants to other obligations to be performed by them thereafter upon land which was not conveyed to the plaintiff. The assertion of such further obligation is not inconsistent with the written contract unless the written contract contains a provision, express or implied, that the defendants are not to do anything not expressed in the writing. Concededly there is no such express provision in the contract, and such a provision may be implied, if at all, only if the asserted additional obligation is "so clearly connected with the principal transaction as to be part and parcel of it," and is not "one that the parties would not ordinarily be expected to embody in the writing." The hypothesis so formulated for a conclusion that the asserted additional obligation is inconsistent with an implied term of the contract is that the alleged oral agreement does not comply with the third condition as formulated by Judge Andrews. In this case, therefore, the problem reduces itself to the one question whether or not the oral agreement meets the third condition.

I have conceded that upon inspection the contract is complete. "It appears to contain the engagements of the parties, and to define the object and measure the extent of such engagement;" it constitutes the contract between them and is presumed to contain the whole of that contract. (*Eighmie v. Taylor*, 98 N.Y. 288.) That engagement was on the one side to convey land; on the other to pay the price. The plaintiff asserts further agreement based on the same consideration to be performed by the defendants after the conveyance was complete, and directly affecting only other land. It is true, as Judge Andrews points out, that "the presence of the ice house, even the knowledge that Mrs. Mitchill thought it objectionable, would not lead to the belief that a separate agreement existed with regard to it;" but the question we must decide is whether or not, *assuming* an agreement was made for the removal of an unsightly ice house from one parcel of land as an inducement for the purchase of another parcel, the parties would ordinarily or naturally be expected to embody the agreement for the removal of the ice house from one parcel in the written agreement to convey the other parcel. Exclusion of proof of the oral agreement on the ground that it varies the contract embodied in the writing may be based only upon a finding or presumption that the written contract was intended to cover the oral negotiations for the removal of the ice house which lead up to the contract of purchase and sale. To determine what the writing was intended to cover "the document alone will not suffice. What it was intended to cover cannot be known till we know what there was to cover. The question being whether certain subjects of negotiation were intended to be covered, we must compare the writing and the negotiations before we can determine whether they were in fact covered." (Wigmore on Evidence [2d ed.], § 2430.)

The subject-matter of the written contract was the conveyance of land. The contract was so complete on its face that the conclusion is inevitable that the parties intended to embody in the writing all the negotiations covering at least the conveyance. The promise by the defendants to remove the ice house from other land was not connected with their obligation to convey, except that one agreement would not have been made unless the other was also made. The plaintiff's assertion of a parol agreement by the defendants to remove the ice house was completely established by the great weight of evidence. It must prevail unless that agreement was part of the agreement to convey and the entire agreement was embodied in the writing.

The fact that in this case the parol agreement is established by the overwhelming weight of evidence is, of course, not a factor which may be considered in determining the competency or legal effect of the evidence. Hardship in the particular case would not justify the court in disregarding or emasculating the general rule. It merely accentuates the outlines of our problem. The assumption that the parol agreement was made is no longer obscured by any doubts. The problem then is clearly whether the parties are presumed to have intended to render that parol agreement legally ineffective and non-existent by failure to embody it in the writing. Though we are driven to say that nothing in the written contract which fixed the terms and conditions of the stipulated conveyance suggests the existence of any further parol agreement, an inspection of the contract, though it is complete on its face in regard to the subject of the conveyance, does not, I think, show that it was intended to embody negotiations or agreements, if any, in regard to a matter so loosely bound to the conveyance as the removal of an ice house from land not conveyed.

The rule of integration undoubtedly frequently prevents the assertion of fraudulent claims. Parties who take the precaution of embodying their oral agreements in a writing should be protected against the assertion that other terms of the same agreement were not integrated in the writing. The limits of the integration are determined by the writing, read in the light of the surrounding circumstances. A written contract, however complete, yet covers only a limited field. I do not think that in the written contract for the conveyance of land here under consideration we can find an intention to cover a field so broad as to include prior agreements, if any such were made, to do other acts on other property after the stipulated conveyance was made.

In each case where such a problem is presented, varying factors enter into its solution. Citation of authority in this or other jurisdictions is useless, at least without minute analysis of the facts. The analysis I have made of the decisions in this State leads me to the view that the decision of the courts below is in accordance with our own authorities and should be affirmed.

Cardozo, Ch. J., Pound, Kellogg and O'Brien, JJ., concur with Andrews, J.; Lehman, J., dissents in opinion in which Crane, J., concurs.

Judgment accordingly.

NOTES AND QUESTIONS

1. *Background from the briefs and record*: The buyers sued for specific performance. On December 20, 1926, the trial court issued a decree ordering the seller to remove the ice house by December 25th or to pay the buyers $8,000. The court found that the sellers orally promised to remove the ice house by the spring of 1924. Relying on this promise, buyers bought the farm for $8,400. The deed was delivered on December 19, 1923. Buyers made extensive repairs and improvements, spending over $23,000, "during the course of some of which the defendants were employed." The presence of the ice house and the operation of the ice business decreased the value of the property by $8,000.

2. *The likely impact of the decision*: What lessons might the decision teach the rest of us? Are future buyers in Mrs. Mitchill's position likely to learn that they cannot trust sellers but must get these promises in writing? Can we count on real estate brokers and lawyers to tell her? What is likely to happen in cases where parties deal without brokers or lawyers? To what extent is a demand to put promises such as this one in writing an attack on the integrity of the other party?

3. *1928 sexism?* Can we explain the court of appeals' decision as sexist? Did the court, a group of older male middle- or upper-class lawyers, assume that concern with aesthetics is feminine and thus frivolous and unimportant? Property values are conventionally tangible and part of the male sphere. Legal institutions respond only to this male world of deeds and dollars. Recall that the formal written contract was made between Mrs. Mitchill's husband and the sellers. The men took care of business, and only then was she able to assert her concerns. She gained a promise that prompted her to agree to the deal, but it was treated as of little consequence—as a woman's whim. To the extent that women trust others more than men and assume cooperation rather than conflict, the court of appeals penalizes this desirable tendency. Is the foregoing a plausible, likely, or fair analysis of the case? Or is this note sexist insofar as it assumes that Mrs. Mitchill was not the business brains of the family and perfectly capable of taking care of herself in the world of business?

4. *Social class and the Mitchill case*: Suppose we speculated on the relationship between Catherine Mitchill and Charles Lath and their families. The Mitchills were able to spend $23,000 in 1923 for improvements on a farmhouse on a lake which was to be a summer residence. Apparently, the Laths were farmers who ran an ice business. (On the other hand, they could afford to fight a case to the court of appeals.) The Mitchills hired the Laths to work on remodeling what once was their house. They went from owner to worker subject to the commands of others. It is easy to imagine that the Laths could have harbored resentments about the circumstances which caused them to sell the property, or to the way in which they were treated by the Mitchills. Should there be an inquiry into such questions? If not, can justice be done?

Justice Andrews said "[w]e are not dealing . . . with their [the Laths'] moral delinquencies." How might Charles Lath justify failing to remove the ice house to himself and his friends? Remember that Mrs. Mitchill found a plain and practical building where work was done offensive. The Laths were able to win by asserting their legal rights. Is such an assertion a form of moral delinquency?

5. *Is the Mitchill standard still good law in New York?*: Judge Andrews's opinion spoke of additional terms "that parties would not ordinarily be expected to embody in the writing." Official Comment 3 to UCC § 2-202 talks of "additional terms . . . such that, if agreed upon, . . . would certainly have been included in the document. . . ." Is the difference between these two formulations of the standard significant? In what setting? To whom?[26]

---

[26] A lower New York court suggested in George v. Davoli, 91 Misc.2d 296, 299, 397 N.Y.S.2d 895, 897 (City Ct. Geneva 1977), that the *Mitchill* case "does not apply herein as its application to the instant case [a transaction in goods covered by Article 2 of the UCC] has been changed by legislative enactment (Uniform Commercial Code § 2-202, sub (b)) which took effect in 1964." In the case of Braten v. Bankers Trust Co., 60 N.Y.2d 155, 162, 456 N.E.2d 802 (1983), the court of appeals indicated that the *Mitchill* case is alive and well, at least outside the area covered by Article 2 of the UCC, finding in that case that evidence of an oral promise to delay enforcing foreclosure rights contradicted the document since it did not appear in the writing and "such a fundamental condition would hardly have been omitted."

6. *A way around Mitchill?*: In *Plum Tree, Inc. v. N.K. Winston Corp.*,[27] a commercial tenant sued the lessor of space in a large shopping center. The tenant alleged oral promises to advertise, select other tenants whose businesses would complement those of existing lessees, provide security measures, and maintain and clean the center. It also alleged that these were fraudulent misrepresentations. The court applied *Mitchill v. Lath* and ruled that the tenant could not offer evidence of the oral promises. It said, "[o]ne would expect the promise if made to be written down along with the other written promises." However, the court said that making promises with no intention to perform would be fraud. The parol evidence rule does not bar proof of fraudulent statements that prompt a person to enter a contract. The court allowed the tenant to amend its complaint to proceed on this theory. While this allowed the tenant to survive a motion for summary judgment, the tenant faced real problems proving such a case.

MASTERSON v. SINE
Supreme Court of California
68 Cal.2d 222, 436 P.2d 561 (1968)

Action for declaratory relief to establish plaintiff's right to enforce an option to repurchase certain real property. Judgment declaring plaintiff's right to exercise the option reversed.

TRAYNOR, C.J.—Dallas Masterson and his wife Rebecca owned a ranch as tenants-in-common. On February 25, 1958, they conveyed it to Medora and Lu Sine by a grant deed "Reserving unto the Grantors herein an option to purchase the above described property on or before February 25, 1968" for the "same consideration as being paid heretofore plus their depreciation value of any improvements Grantees may add to the property from and after two and a half years from this date." Medora is Dallas' sister and Lu's wife. Since the conveyance Dallas has been adjudged bankrupt. His trustee in bankruptcy and Rebecca brought this declaratory relief action to establish their right to enforce the option.

The case was tried without a jury. Over defendants' objection the trial court admitted extrinsic evidence that by "the same consideration as being paid heretofore" both the grantors and the grantees meant the sum of $50,000 and by "depreciation value of any improvements" they meant the depreciation value of improvements to be computed by deducting from the total amount of any capital expenditures made by defendants grantees the amount of depreciation allowable to them under United States income tax regulations as of the time of the exercise of the option.

The court also determined that the parol evidence rule precluded admission of extrinsic evidence offered by defendants to show that the parties wanted the property kept in the Masterson family and that the option was therefore personal to the grantors and could not be exercised by the trustee in bankruptcy.

The court entered judgment for plaintiffs, declaring their right to exercise the option, specifying in some detail how it could be exercised, and reserving jurisdiction to supervise the manner of its exercise and to determine the amount that

---

[27] 351 F. Supp. 80, 84 (S.D. N.Y. 1972).

plaintiffs will be required to pay defendants for their capital expenditures if plaintiffs decide to exercise the option.

Defendants appeal. They contend that the option provision is too uncertain to be enforced and that extrinsic evidence as to its meaning should not have been admitted. The trial court properly refused to frustrate the obviously declared intention of the grantors to reserve an option to repurchase by an overly meticulous insistence on completeness and clarity of written expression. . . . It properly admitted extrinsic evidence to explain the language of the deed . . . to the end that the consideration for the option would appear with sufficient certainty to permit specific enforcement. . . . The trial court erred, however, in excluding the extrinsic evidence that the option was personal to the grantors and therefore nonassignable.

When the parties to a written contract have agreed to it as an "integration"—a complete and final embodiment of the terms of an agreement—parol evidence cannot be used to add to or vary its terms. . . . When only part of the agreement is integrated, the same rule applies to that part, but parol evidence may be used to prove elements of the agreement not reduced to writing. . . .

The crucial issue in determining whether there has been an integration is whether the parties intended their writing to serve as the exclusive embodiment of their agreement. The instrument itself may help to resolve that issue. It may state, for example, that "there are no previous understandings or agreements not contained in the writing," and thus express the parties' "intention to nullify antecedent understandings or agreements." (*See* 3 Corbin, Contracts (1960) § 578, p. 411.) Any such collateral agreement itself must be examined, however, to determine whether the parties intended the subjects of negotiation it deals with to be included in, excluded from, or otherwise affected by the writing. Circumstances at the time of the writing may also aid in the determination of such integration. . . .

California cases have stated that whether there was an integration is to be determined solely from the face of the instrument, . . . and that the question for the court is whether it "appears to be a complete . . . agreement. . . ." . . . Neither of these strict formulations of the rule, however, has been consistently applied. The requirement that the writing must appear incomplete on its face has been repudiated in many cases where parol evidence was admitted "to prove the existence of a separate oral agreement as to any matter on which the document is silent and which is not inconsistent with its terms"—even though the instrument appeared to state a complete agreement. . . . Even under the rule that the writing alone is to be consulted, it was found necessary to examine the alleged collateral agreement before concluding that proof of it was precluded by the writing alone. (*See* 3 Corbin, Contracts (1960) § 582, pp. 444-446.) It is therefore evident that "The conception of a writing as wholly and intrinsically self-determinative of the parties' intent to make it a sole memorial of one or seven or twenty-seven subjects of negotiation is an impossible one." (9 Wigmore, Evidence (3d ed. 1940) § 2431, p. 103.) For example, a promissory note given by a debtor to his creditor may integrate all their present contractual rights and obligations, or it may be only a minor part of an underlying executory contract that would never be discovered by examining the face of the note.

In formulating the rule governing parol evidence, several policies must be accommodated. One policy is based on the assumption that written evidence is more accurate than human memory. . . . This policy, however, can be adequately served by excluding parol evidence of agreements that directly contradict the writing. Another policy is based on the fear that fraud or unintentional invention by witnesses interested in the outcome of the litigation will mislead the finder of facts. . . . McCormick has suggested that the party urging the spoken as against the written word is most often the economic underdog, threatened by severe hardship if the writing is enforced. In his view the parol evidence rule arose to allow the court to control the tendency of the jury to find through sympathy and without a dispassionate assessment of the probability of fraud or faulty memory that the parties made an oral agreement collateral to the written contract, or that preliminary tentative agreements were not abandoned when omitted from the writing. (*See* McCormick, Evidence (1954) § 210.) He recognizes, however, that if this theory were adopted in disregard of all other considerations, it would lead to the exclusion of testimony concerning oral agreements whenever there is a writing and thereby often defeat the true intent of the parties. (*See* McCormick, *op. cit. supra*, § 216, p. 441.)

Evidence of oral collateral agreements should be excluded only when the fact finder is likely to be misled. The rule must therefore be based on the credibility of the evidence. One such standard, adopted by § 240(1)(b) of the Restatement of Contracts, permits proof of a collateral agreement if it "is such an agreement as might *naturally* be made as a separate agreement by parties situated as were the parties to the written contract." (Italics added; *see* McCormick, Evidence (1954) § 216, p. 441; *see also* 3 Corbin, Contracts (1960) § 583, p. 475, § 594, pp. 568-569; 4 Williston, Contracts (3d ed. 1961) § 638, pp. 1039-1045.) The draftsmen of the Uniform Commercial Code would exclude the evidence in still fewer instances: "If the additional terms are such that, if agreed upon, they would *certainly* have been included in the document in the view of the court, then evidence of their alleged making must be kept from the trier of fact." (Com. 3, § 2-202, italics added.)[28]

The option clause in the deed in the present case does not explicitly provide that it contains the complete agreement, and the deed is silent on the question of assignability. Moreover, the difficulty of accommodating the formalized structure of a deed to the insertion of collateral agreements makes it less likely that all the

---

[28] [1] Corbin suggests that, even in situations where the court concludes that it would not have been natural for the parties to make the alleged collateral oral agreement, parol evidence of such an agreement should nevertheless be permitted if the court is convinced that the unnatural actually happened in the case being adjudicated. (3 Corbin, Contracts, § 485, pp. 478, 480; cf. Murray, The Parol Evidence Rule: A Clarification (1966) 4 Duquesne L. Rev. 337, 341-342.) This suggestion may be based on a belief that judges are not likely to be misled by their sympathies. If the court believes that the parties intended a collateral agreement to be effective, there is no reason to keep the evidence from the jury.

terms of such an agreement were included.[29] (*See* 3 Corbin, Contracts (1960) § 587; 4 Williston, Contracts (3d ed. 1961) § 645; 70 A.L.R. 752, 759 (1931); 68 A.L.R. 245 (1930).) The statement of the reservation of the option might well have been placed in the recorded deed solely to preserve the grantors' rights against any possible future purchasers, and this function could well be served without any mention of the parties' agreement that the option was personal. There is nothing in the record to indicate that the parties to this family transaction, through experience in land transactions or otherwise, had any warning of the disadvantages of failing to put the whole agreement in the deed. This case is one, therefore, in which it can be said that a collateral agreement such as that alleged "might naturally be made as a separate agreement." *A fortiori*, the case is not one in which the parties "would certainly" have included the collateral agreement in the deed.

It is contended, however, that an option agreement is ordinarily presumed to be assignable if it contains no provisions forbidding its transfer or indicating that its performance involves elements personal to the parties. . . . The fact that there is a written memorandum, however, does not necessarily preclude parol evidence rebutting a term that the law would otherwise presume. In *American Industrial Sales Corp. v. Airscope, Inc., supra*, 44 Cal.2d 393, 397-398, we held it proper to admit parol evidence of a contemporaneous collateral agreement as to the place of payment of a note, even though it contradicted the presumption that a note, silent as to the place of payment, is payable where the creditor resides. . . . Moreover, even when there is no explicit agreement—written or oral—that contractual duties shall be personal, courts will effectuate presumed intent to that effect if the circumstances indicate that performance by substituted person would be different from that contracted for. . . .

In the present case defendants offered evidence that the parties agreed that the option was not assignable in order to keep the property in the Masterson family. The trial court erred in excluding that evidence.

The judgment is reversed. . . .

BURKE, J.—I dissent. The majority opinion:

(1) Undermines the parol evidence rule as we have known it in this state since at least 1872 by declaring that parol evidence should have been admitted by the trial court to show that a written option, absolute and unrestricted in form, was intended to be limited and nonassignable;

(2) Renders suspect instruments of conveyance absolute on their face;

(3) Materially lessens the reliance which may be placed upon written instruments affecting the title to real estate; and

(4) Opens the door, albeit unintentionally, to a new technique for the defrauding of creditors.

---

[29] [2] See Goble v. Dotson (1962) 203 Cal. App.2d 272 21 Cal.Rptr. 769, where the deed given by a real estate developer to the plaintiffs contained a condition that grantees would not build a pier or boathouse. Despite this reference in the deed to the subject of berthing for boats, the court allowed plaintiffs to prove by parol evidence that the condition was agreed to in return for the developer's oral promise that plaintiffs were to have the use of two boat spaces nearby.

The opinion permits defendants to establish by parol testimony that their grant to their brother (and brother-in-law) of a written option, absolute in terms, was nevertheless agreed to be nonassignable by the grantee (now a bankrupt), and that therefore the right to exercise it did not pass, by operation of the bankruptcy laws, to the trustee for the benefit of the grantee's creditors.

And how was this to be shown? By the proffered testimony of the bankrupt optionee himself! Thereby one of his assets (the option to purchase defendants' California ranch) would be withheld from the trustee in bankruptcy and from the bankrupt's creditors. Understandably the trial court, as required by the parol evidence rule, did not allow the bankrupt by parol to so contradict the unqualified language of the written option.

The court properly admitted parol evidence to explain the intended meaning of the "same consideration" and "depreciation value" phrases of the written option to purchase defendants' land, as the intended meaning of those phrases was not clear. However, there was nothing ambiguous about the granting language of the option and not the slightest suggestion in the document that the option was to be nonassignable. Thus, to permit such words of limitation to be added by parol is to *contradict* the absolute nature of the grant, and to directly violate the parol evidence rule.

Just as it is unnecessary to state in a deed to "lot X" that the house located thereon goes with the land, it is likewise unnecessary to add to "I grant an option to Jones" the words "*and his assigns*" for the option to be assignable. As hereinafter emphasized in more detail, California statutes expressly declare that it *is* assignable, and only if I add language in writing showing my intent to withhold or restrict the right of assignment may the grant be so limited. Thus, to seek to restrict the grant by parol is to *contradict* the written document in violation of the parol evidence rule.

The majority opinion arrives at its holding via a series of false premises which are not supported either in the record of this case or in such California authorities as are offered. . . .

At the outset the majority in the present case reiterate that the rule against contradicting or varying the terms of a writing remains applicable when only part of the agreement is contained in the writing, and parol evidence is used to prove elements of the agreement not reduced to writing. But having restated this established rule, the majority opinion inexplicably proceeds to subvert it.

Each of the . . . cases cited by the majority . . . holds that although parol evidence is admissible to prove the parts of the contract not put in writing, it is *not admissible* to vary or *contradict* the writing or *prove* collateral *agreements* which are *inconsistent* therewith. The meaning of this rule (and the application of it found in the cases) is that if the asserted unwritten elements of the agreement would contradict, add to, detract from, vary or be inconsistent with the written agreement, then such elements *may not* be shown by *parol* evidence.

The contract of sale and purchase of the ranch property here involved was carried out through a title company upon written escrow instructions executed by the respective parties after various preliminary negotiations. The deed to defendant grantees, in which the grantors expressly reserved an option to repurchase the property within a ten-year period and upon a specified consideration, was issued and delivered in consummation of the contract. In neither the written escrow instructions nor the deed containing the option is there any language even suggesting that the option was agreed or intended by the parties to be personal to the grantors, and so nonassignable. The trial judge, on at least three separate occasions, correctly sustained objections to efforts of defendant optionors to get into evidence the testimony of Dallas Masterson (the bankrupt holder of the option) that a part of the agreement of sale of the parties was that the option to repurchase the property was personal to him, and therefore unassignable for benefit of creditors. But the majority hold that that testimony should have been admitted, thereby permitting defendant optionors to limit, detract from and contradict the plain and unrestricted terms of the written option in clear violation of the parol evidence rule and to open the door to the perpetration of fraud.

Options are property, and are widely used in the sale and purchase of real and personal property. One of the basic incidents of property ownership is the right of the owner to sell or transfer it. . . .

The right of an optionee to transfer his option to purchase property is accordingly one of the basic rights which accompanies the option unless limited under the language of the option itself. To allow an optionor to resort to parol evidence to support his assertion that the written option is not transferable is to authorize him to limit the option by attempting to restrict and reclaim rights with which he has already parted. A clearer violation of two substantive and basic rules of law—the parol evidence rule and the right of free transferability of property—would be difficult to conceive. . . .

[The dissent quarreled with the majority's assertion that its decision was consistent with previous cases. The dissent concluded this section by characterizing the example of a promissory note as "obviously specious."] Rarely, if ever, does a promissory note given by a debtor to his creditor integrate *all* their agreements (that is not the purpose it serves); it may or it may not integrate *all* their present contractual rights and obligations; but relevant to the parol evidence rule, at least until the advent of the majority opinion in this case, alleged collateral agreements which would vary or contradict the terms and conditions of a promissory note may not be shown by parol. . . .

Upon this structure of incorrect premises and unfounded assertions the majority opinion arrives at its climax: The pronouncement of "several policies [to] be accommodated . . . *[in] formulating the rule governing parol evidence.*" (Italics added.)[30] Two of the "policies" as declared by the majority are: Written evidence

---

[30] [7] It is the *Legislature* of this state which *did the formulating* of the rule governing parol evidence nearly a century ago when in 1872, as previously noted, §§ 1625 of the Civil Code and 1856 of the Code of Civil Procedure were adopted. And as already shown herein, the rule has since been consistently applied by the courts of this state. The parol evidence rule as thus laid down by the Legislature and applied by the courts *is the policy* of this state.

is more accurate than human memory;[31] fraud or unintentional invention by interested witnesses may well occur.

I submit that these purported "policies" are in reality two of the basic and obvious reasons for adoption by the Legislature of the parol evidence rule as the policy in this state. Thus the speculation of the majority concerning the views of various writers on the subject and the advisability of following them in this state is not only superfluous but flies flatly in the face of established California law and policy. It serves only to introduce uncertainty and confusion in a field of substantive law which was codified and made certain in this state a century ago.

However, despite the law which until the advent of the present majority opinion has been firmly and clearly established in California and relied upon by attorneys and courts alike, that parol evidence may *not* be employed to vary or contradict the terms of a written instrument, the majority now announce that such evidence "should be excluded only when the fact finder is *likely to be misled*," and that "The rule must therefore be based on the *credibility of the evidence*." (Italics added.) But was it not, inter alia, to avoid misleading the fact finder, and to further the introduction of only the evidence which is most likely to *be* credible (the written document), that the Legislature adopted the parol evidence rule as a part of the substantive law of this state?

Next, in an effort to implement this newly promulgated "credibility" test, the majority opinion offers a choice of two "standards": one, a "certainty" standard, quoted from the Uniform Commercial Code,[32] and the other a "natural" standard found in the Restatement of Contracts,[33] and concludes that at least for purposes of the present case the "natural" viewpoint should prevail.

This new rule, not hitherto recognized in California, provides that proof of a claimed collateral oral agreement is admissible if it is such an agreement as might *naturally* have been made a separate agreement by the parties under the particular circumstances. I submit that this approach opens the door to uncertainty and confusion. Who can know what its limits are? Certainly I do not. For example, in its application to this case who could be expected to divine as "natural" a separate oral agreement between the parties that the assignment, absolute and unrestricted on its face, was intended by the parties to be limited to the Masterson family?

Or, assume that one gives to his relative a promissory note and that the payee of the note goes bankrupt. By operation of law the note becomes an asset of the bankruptcy. The trustee attempts to enforce it. Would the relatives be permitted to testify that by a separate oral agreement made at the time of the execution of

---

[31] [8] Although the majority declare that this first "policy" may be served by excluding parol evidence of agreements that directly contradict the writing, such contradiction is *precisely* the *effect* of the agreement sought to be shown by parol in this case.

[32] [9] "If the additional terms are such that, if agreed upon, they would *certainly* have been included in the document in the view of the court, then evidence of their alleged making must be kept from the trier of fact." (Comment 3, § 2-202; italics added.)

[33] [10] Viz., proof of a collateral agreement should be permitted if it "is such an agreement as might *naturally* be made as a separate agreement by parties situated as were the parties to the written contract." (Restatement of Contracts, § 240, subd. (1)(b); italics added.)

the note it was understood that should the payee fail in his business the maker would be excused from payment of the note, or that, as here, it was intended that the benefits of the note would be *personal* to the payee? I doubt that trial judges should be burdened with the task of conjuring whether it would have been "natural" under those circumstances for such a separate agreement to have been made by the parties. Yet, under the application of the proposed rule, this is the task the trial judge would have, and in essence the situation presented in the instant case is no different. . . .

In an effort to provide justification for applying the newly pronounced "natural" rule to the circumstances of the present case, the majority opinion next attempts to account for the silence of the writing in this case concerning assignability of the option, by asserting that "the difficulty of accommodating the formalized structure of a deed to the insertion of collateral agreements makes it less likely that all the terms of such an agreement were included." What difficulty would have been involved here, to add the words "this option is nonassignable"? The asserted "formalized structure of a deed" is no formidable barrier. . . .

To support further speculation that "the reservation of the option might well have been placed in the recorded deed solely to preserve the grantors' rights against any possible future purchasers, and this function could well be served without any mention of the parties' agreement that the option was personal," the majority assert that "There is *nothing in the record* to indicate that the parties to this family transaction, through experience in land transactions or otherwise, had any warning of the disadvantages of failing to put the whole agreement in the deed." (Italics added.) The facts of this case, however, do not support such claim of naiveté. The grantor husband (the bankrupt businessman) testified that as none of the parties were attorneys "we wanted to contact my attorney . . . which we did. . . . The wording in the option was obtained from [the attorney]. . . . I told him what my discussion was with the Sines [defendant grantees] and he wanted . . . a little time to compose it. . . . And, then this [the wording provided by the attorney] was taken to the title company at the time Mr. and Mrs. Sine and I went in to *complete the transaction*." (Italics added.) The witness was an experienced businessman who thus demonstrated awareness of the wisdom of seeking legal guidance and advice in this business transaction, and who did so. Wherein lies the naïve family transaction postulated by the majority? . . .

The statement of the majority opinion that in the absence of a controlling statute the parties may provide that a contract right or duty is nontransferable, is of course true. Equally true is the next assertion that "even when there is no explicit agreement—written *or* oral—that contractual duties shall be personal, courts will effectuate a presumed intent to that effect if the circumstances indicate that performance by a substituted person would be different from that contracted for." But to apply the law of contracts for the rendering of personal services to the reservation of an option in a deed of real estate calls for a misdirected use of the rule, particularly in an instrument containing not one word from which such "a presumed intent to that effect" could be gleaned. Particularly is the holding objectionable when the result is to upset established statutory and case law in this state that "circumstances" shown by parol may *not* be employed to contradict, add to or detract from, the agreement of the parties as expressed by them in writing. . . .

Neither personal skill nor personal qualities can be conjured as a requirement for the exercise of the option reserved in the deed here, regardless of how ardent may be the desire of the parties (the bankrupt husband-optionee and his sister), "to keep the property in the . . . family." Particularly is this true when a contrary holding would permit the property to be acquired by plaintiff referee in bankruptcy for the benefit of the creditors of the bankrupt husband.

Comment hardly seems necessary on the convenience to a bankrupt of such a device to defeat his creditors. He need only produce parol testimony that any options (or other property, for that matter) which he holds are subject to an oral "collateral agreement" with family members (or with friends) that the property is nontransferable "in order to keep the property in the family" or in the friendly group. In the present case the value of the ranch which the bankrupt and his wife held an option to purchase has doubtless increased substantially during the years since they acquired the option. The initiation of this litigation by the trustee in bankruptcy to establish his right to enforce the option indicates his belief that there is substantial value to be gained for the creditors from this asset of the bankrupt. Yet the majority opinion permits defeat of the trustee and of the creditors through the device of an asserted collateral oral agreement that the option was "personal" to the bankrupt and nonassignable "in order to keep the property in the family"![34]

It also seems appropriate to inquire as to the rights of plaintiff wife in the option which she holds with her bankrupt husband. Is her interest therein also subject to being shown to be personal and not salable or assignable? And, what are her rights and those of her husband in the ranch land itself, if they exercise their option to purchase it? Will they be free to then sell the land? Or, if they prefer, may they hold it beyond the reach of creditors? Or can other members of "the family" claim some sort of restriction on it in perpetuity, established by parol evidence?

And if defendants sell the land subject to the option, will the new owners be heard to assert that the option is "personal" to the optionees, "in order to keep the property in the *Masterson* family"? Or is that claim "personal" to defendants only?

These are only a few of the confusions and inconsistencies which will arise to plague property owners and, incidentally, attorneys and title companies, who seek to counsel and protect them.

I would hold that the trial court ruled correctly on the proffered parol evidence, and I would affirm the judgment.

[McComb, J., concurred.]

---

[34] [14] As noted at the outset of this dissent, it was by means of the bankrupt's own testimony that defendants (the bankrupt's sister and her husband) sought to show that the option was personal to the bankrupt and thus not transferable to the trustee in bankruptcy.

NOTES AND QUESTIONS

1. *Justice Traynor*. Roger Traynor was a member of the University of California at Berkeley Law faculty when he was appointed to the Supreme Court of California in 1940. He served on that court until his retirement in 1970. Henry Friendly, a much respected judge, wrote a tribute on the occasion of Justice Traynor's death. He said, "Roger Traynor was the ablest judge of his generation in the United States. I say this without hesitation, qualification, limitation, or fear of successful contradiction."[35]

Walter Schaefer, another famous appellate judge, wrote,[36]

> "Roger Traynor is a law professor's judge," said the late Professor Harry Kalven, pointing out that his own casebook on torts used eight Traynor cases and that "we would have been well advised to have used more." . . .

> That Roger Traynor was also a judge's judge is obvious from the frequent citation of his opinions. A Traynor opinion is always sound currency, always to be reckoned with. His influence on judges was enhanced by his warm personal relationships with so many of them. Over a span of just short of ten years, he served on the faculty of the Appellate Judges Seminar at New York Law University Law School. There he met for two weeks each year with twenty to twenty-five judges of top state courts and federal courts of appeals. The atmosphere was informal; common problems were discussed frankly and lasting friendships resulted. . . .

Justice Traynor's opinions in cases such as *Drennan v. Star Paving*, *supra*, and in areas such as the conflict of laws and products liability have had great influence on courts in other states. Although it has been cited in Alaska, Colorado, Idaho, North Carolina, Oregon, Rhode Island, Utah, Washington, Wisconsin and Wyoming, *Masterson v. Sine* has not had great influence outside of California. Why not?[37]

2. *The interests of others*: One of the plaintiffs in this case was Dallas Masterson's trustee-in-bankruptcy. A trustee acts on behalf of the creditors of the bankrupt debtor. As Justice Burke observes in his dissent, the value of the real estate transferred to the Sines had no doubt appreciated to the point where it exceeded, perhaps by a considerable amount, the price that Dallas and Rebuke Masterson would be required to pay under their option to purchase. If the trustee could have exercised the option held by Dallas to half the property (the option to the other half being held by Dallas' wife, Rebuke, who had not filed bankruptcy), the trustee could have resold the property for more than he or she had paid for it. The profits on the resale would have gone to repay Dallas' creditors, if any remained after deductions for the trustee's costs and profits.

---

[35] Friendly, *Ablest Judge of His Generation*, 71 Cal. L. Rev. 1039, 1039 (1983).

[36] Schaefer, *A Judge's Judge*, 71 Cal. L. Rev. 1050, 1051 (1983).

[37] For a discussion of Justice Traynor's opinions, see Macaulay, *Mr. Justice Traynor and the Law of Contracts*, 13 Stan. L. Rev. 812 (1961).

At the time this case was litigated, the Bankruptcy Act vested in the trustee-in-bankruptcy all "transferable or leviable" property owned by the debtor at the time of the filing of bankruptcy. That is why the Sines were able to defeat the trustee's suit to exercise the option by showing that Dallas' option was personal and not transferable. The trustee did not own the option. Such a showing did not destroy Dallas' option, however. If Dallas later received a discharge of unsecured debts in bankruptcy (most debtors due), he could afterwards exercise the option, resell the real estate, and pocket the profits, probably leaving his unpaid creditors without any ability to obtain repayment from this asset. That is why Justice Burke refers to the parol testimony about the nontransferability of the option as "a device to defeat . . . creditors." (This analysis assumes that the original transfer of the real estate from the Mastersons to the Sines could not be shown to have been done with the intent of defeating the Masterson's creditors, in which case it could have been set aside under the Uniform Fraudulent Conveyances Act. This topic is beyond the scope of this note.)

In 1978, the Bankruptcy Act, which is federal legislation applicable in all states, was extensively revised. The new Bankruptcy Code provides that the trustee-in-bankruptcy becomes vested with all property interests of the debtor even if "a provision in an agreement . . . restricts or conditions transfer of such interest by the debtor." 11 U.S.C. § 541(c)(1). Consequently, if *Masterson v. Sine* were to recur today, the bankruptcy trustee's action to enforce the option against the Sine's would not be defeated by a showing that Dallas' option was nontransferable.

3. ***Justice Traynor on construction of documents***: *Masterson v. Sine* is but one of several decisions written by Justice Traynor concerning interpreting and construing written documents. Roughly, he adopts Professor Corbin's approach. For example, in *Pacific Gas & Elect. Co. v. G.W. Thomas Drayage & Rigging Co.*,[38] there was a contract for repairs on a steam turbine. It provided that G.W. Thomas was to indemnify PG & E "against all loss . . . resulting from . . . injury to property . . . in any way connected with the performance of this contract." PG & E sued to recover damages for an injury to the turbine itself. G.W. Thomas offered evidence that the parties intended the indemnity clause to cover only injury to the property of third parties. The trial court refused to consider this evidence because the contract had a "plain and clear" meaning. The Supreme Court of California reversed. The question was the credibility of this evidence and not its admissibility.

Justice Traynor reinforced (and perhaps even extended?) this view in *Delta Dynamics, Inc. v. Arioto*.[39] In a case in which the trial court refused to hear evidence that the parties intended that cancellation of the contract was the exclusive remedy for a failure by a distributor to sell a specified number of safety devices, the Supreme Court of California reversed.

Justice Traynor wrote "[t]he test of admissibility of extrinsic evidence to explain the meaning of a written instrument is not whether it appears to the court to

---

[38] 69 Cal. 2d 33, 442 P.2d 641 (1968).
[39] 69 Cal. 2d 525, 446 P.2d 785 (1968).

be plain and unambiguous on its face, but whether the offered evidence is relevant to prove a meaning to which the language of the instrument is reasonably susceptible."[40] However, Justice Traynor also suggests that credible evidence does not necessarily mean evidence conforming to an objective standard. That implies that all credible evidence should be admitted provisionally to prove the intentions of the parties. Indeed, he even suggests that the evidence may be credible and establish a meaning to which the language of the document is not reasonably (objectively?) susceptible. If this is the case, then it could be argued that courts must look at all the offered evidence to see if this interpretation is believable.[41]

Contrast Justice Traynor's approach with that of the Seventh Circuit's approach in *Binks Manufacturing Co. v. National Presto Industries, Inc.* What are the advantages and disadvantages of each approach?

4. *Later developments*: For ten to fifteen years after *Masterson v. Sine* and Justice Traynor's other decisions on interpretation of contracts, the California appellate courts generally followed his approach. However, Professor Ralph James Mooney asserted in 1995:

> . . . California judges have largely abandoned Justice Traynor's admonitions that words have no fixed meanings and that courts should interpret contracts in ways that would have made sense to both parties considering the language at the transaction's outset. As always, the principal beneficiaries of the newer, more absolutist interpretations are the economically dominant parties who drafted the language.[42]

Professor Robert A. Hillman characterized Mooney's article as "important and provocative."[43] However, Hillman questions whether there is a trend to favor "economically privileged parties."[44] He says: "I am more comfortable with the proposition that recent reported decisions demonstrate an incremental enhancement of rules that favor the enforcement of written contracts over alleged oral, less formal representations or agreements."[45] He notes, "[r]ules that support written contracts can protect underdogs as well as disadvantage them."[46] Hillman explains the shift as a reflection of a change in public opinion. "[P]eople have become more distrustful of big government, more wary of non-democratic institutions such as the judiciary, and more respectful of market exchange."[47] He concludes: "Law is . . . in part political, subjective, and indeterminate. Lawyers must

---

[40] *Id.* at 528, 446 P.2d at 787, *quoting* Pacific Gas & Elec. Co. v. G.W. Thomas Drayage & Rigging Co., 69 Cal. 2d 33, 37, 442 P.2d 641,644 (1968).

[41] For a discussion, see West, *Chief Justice Traynor and the Parol Evidence Rule*, 22 Stan. L. Rev. 547 (1970).

[42] *The New Conceptualism in Contract Law*, 74 Ore. L. Rev. 1131, 1165 (1995).

[43] *The "New Conservatism" in Contract Law and the Process of Legal Change*, 40 B.C. L. Rev. 879, n. 2 (1999).

[44] *Id.* at 880.

[45] *Id.* at 881-2.

[46] *Id.* at 882.

[47] *Id.* at 883.

be cognizant not only of legal rules, but also of current events and political and social tides."[48]

One of the most colorful attacks occurred in *Trident Center v. Connecticut Gen. Life Ins. Co.*,[49] In that case, a partnership consisting of an insurance company and two of Los Angeles' largest and most prestigious law firms brought an action in federal court for a declaratory judgment. California law governed the transaction. The partnership asserted that it had the right to prepay a loan of more than $56 million. The 12¼ percent rate that had seemed reasonable in 1983 compared unfavorably with 1987 market rates and Trident [the partnership plaintiff] started looking for ways of refinancing the loan to take advantage of the lower rates. The defendant lender brought a motion to dismiss, claiming that the loan documents clearly and unambiguously precluded prepayment during the first 12 years of the loan. The trial court granted the motion and dismissed the plaintiff's complaint. Moreover, the trial court also sanctioned the plaintiff for filing a frivolous lawsuit.

The United States Court of Appeals reversed. Judge Kozinski said:

> The contract documents are lengthy and detailed; they squarely address the precise issue that is the subject of this dispute; to all who read English, they appear to resolve the issue fully and conclusively.
>
> Plaintiff nevertheless argues here, as it did below, that it is entitled to introduce extrinsic evidence that the contract means something other than what it says. This case therefore presents the question whether parties in California can ever draft a contract that is proof to parol evidence. Somewhat surprisingly, the answer is no.[50]

Judge Kozinski analyzed Justice Traynor's opinion in the *Pacific Gas & Electric Co.* case. He was highly critical:

> We question whether this [Justice Traynor's] approach is more likely to divulge the original intention of the parties than reliance on the seemingly clear words they agreed upon at the time. . . .
>
> *Pacific Gas* casts a long shadow of uncertainty over all transactions negotiated and executed under the law of California. As this case illustrates, even when the transaction is very sizeable, even if it involves only sophisticated parties, even if it was negotiated with the aid of counsel, even if it results in contract language that is devoid of ambiguity, costly and protracted litigation cannot be avoided if one party has a strong enough motive for challenging the contract. While this rule creates much business for lawyers and an occasional windfall to some clients, it leads only to frustration and delay for most litigants and clogs already overburdened courts.
>
> It also chips away at the foundation of our legal system. By giving credence to the idea that words are inadequate to express concepts, *Pacific Gas* undermines the basic principle that language provides a mean-

[48] *Id.* at 889.
[49] 847 F.2d 564 (9th Cir. 1988).
[50] *Id.* at 565.

ingful constraint on public and private conduct. If we are unwilling to say that parties, dealing face to face, can come up with language that binds them, how can we send anyone to jail for violating statutes consisting of mere words lacking "absolute and constant referents"? How can courts ever enforce decrees, not written in language understandable to all, but encoded in a dialect reflecting only the "linguistic background of the judge"? Can lower courts ever be faulted for failing to carry out the mandate of higher courts when "perfect verbal expression" is impossible? Are all attempts to develop the law in a reasoned and principled fashion doomed to failure as "remnant[s] of a primitive faith in the inherent potency and inherent meaning of words"? . . .

By holding that language has no objective meaning, and that contracts mean only what courts ultimately say they do, *Pacific Gas* invites precisely this type of lawsuit. With the benefit of 20 years of hindsight, the California Supreme Court may wish to revisit the issue. If it does so, we commend to it the facts of this case as a paradigmatic example of why the traditional rule, based on centuries of experience, reflects the far wiser approach.[51]

Judge Kozinski noted that the defendant could move for summary judgment after completion of discovery. He said that the motion would succeed "unless Trident [the plaintiff] were to come forward with extrinsic evidence sufficient to render the contract reasonably susceptible to Trident's alternative interpretation, thereby creating a genuine issue of fact resolvable only at trial."

The WALL STREET JOURNAL[52] praised Judge Kozinski's opinion in an editorial. The judge was trying to rescue contracts "from high weirdness." The editorial said that challenges to the meaning of language, "undermining the rule of law, is what the deconstructionist theory of the Critical Legal Studies movement is all about." Roger Traynor was an activist judge who advocated "freewheeling judicial reinterpretations of contracts." The editorial concluded:

The freedom to write contracts and the duty to abide by their terms are features of American life so basic that it's hard to believe they could be litigated. Yet this is where the law has now led. Judge Kozinski did his best to embarrass the judicial activists into retreat. We will now see if they have any shame.

Did Judge Kozinski and the WALL STREET JOURNAL read Justice Traynor's opinions correctly or plausibly? Two months after the *Trident* decision was announced, another panel of judges on the United States Court of Appeals for the Ninth Circuit raised this question very politely. In *A. Kemp Fisheries, Inc. v. Castle & Cooke, Inc.,*[53] the court said:

The broad language in *Trident* suggests that under California law courts must always admit extrinsic evidence to determine the meaning of

---

[51] *Id.* at 569, 570.

[52] Crovitz, *Rescuing Contracts from High Weirdness*, WALL STREET JOURNAL, August 3, 1988, at 16, col. 3.

[53] 852 F.2d 493, n. 2 (9th Cir. 1988).

disputed contract language. *Trident* held only that courts may not dismiss on the pleadings when one party claims that extrinsic evidence renders the contract ambiguous. The case must proceed beyond the pleadings so that the court may consider the evidence. If, after considering the evidence, the court determines that the contract is not reasonably susceptible to the interpretation advanced, the parol evidence rule operates to exclude the evidence. The court may then decide the case on a motion for summary judgment.

Does it matter whether a court can dismiss a case on the pleadings when it thinks documents are unambiguous or whether it must allow the parties to develop evidence by discovery and otherwise before considering a motion for summary judgment? Even if allowing the case to go on past the initial pleadings has some costs, does Justice Traynor's position "chip . . . away at the foundations of our legal system"?

3. DOCUMENTS INTENDED TO REPRESENT SOMETHING OTHER THAN THE PARTIES' REAL DEAL

IN RE SPRING VALLEY MEATS, INC.:
DAIRYLAND EQUIPMENT LEASING, INC. v. BOHEN
Supreme Court of Wisconsin
94 Wis.2d 600, 288 N.W.2d 852 (1980)

CALLOW, J. [In April, 1976 Dairyland Equipment Leasing and Spring Valley Meats executed two documents which, on their face, appeared to be leases of equipment to be used by Spring Valley. In May, 1977, upon request of a creditor, Donald Bohen was appointed Receiver of Spring Valley. Spring Valley had, by this time, stopped making payments on the "lease," and Dairyland asked that the equipment be returned to it. A hearing was held.] [T]estimony was introduced to show that the written agreements entered into by Dairyland and Spring Valley were intended only as a partial integration of the parties' agreement and that the agreements were not actually leases but lease-purchase agreements which would give Spring Valley ownership of the equipment upon completion of the payment schedule contained in the agreements. Counsel for Dairyland interposed a parol evidence objection, but immediately withdrew the objection.

On July 18, 1977, the trial court filed a decision which held that the written agreements were not leases but were instead security agreements and that Dairyland was therefore not entitled to the return of the equipment. Findings of fact, conclusions of law, and an order were filed accordingly. Dairyland appeals, arguing . . . that testimony regarding an oral agreement was received in violation of the parol evidence rule. . . .

Dairyland's . . . contention is that evidence presented at the hearing violated the parol evidence rule. The evidence related to an oral agreement between Dairyland and Spring Valley under which Spring Valley would own the equipment at the completion of the payment schedule. The receiver argues that Dairyland cannot raise this issue on appeal, having withdrawn any objections it had to the reception of the testimony. On the merits, the receiver argues that the parol evidence was properly admitted on the question whether the parties intended the written agreements to be the final and complete statement of the agreement between Dairyland and Spring Valley and that, having determined that the parties' agreement was not wholly embodied by the writing, the trial court properly heard testimony as to the oral contract between Dairyland and Spring Valley.

The parol evidence rule can be stated as follows:

> When the parties to a contract embody their agreement in writing and intend the writing to be the final expression of their agreement, the terms of the writing may not be varied or contradicted by evidence of any prior written or oral agreement in the absence of fraud, duress, or mutual mistake. . . .

. . . It is a rule of substantive law and not a rule of evidence. . . . Therefore, even if, without objection, parol evidence of the intention of the parties to a written contract, which conflicts with the express provisions of such contract, gets into the record, the court must disregard it. Thus the merits of Dairyland's contention must be addressed.

The receiver argues that the trial court properly admitted parol evidence on the issue of whether the written agreements constituted the final and complete statement of their agreement. . . .

If a writing is shown to be only a partial integration of the agreement reached by the parties, it is proper to consider parol evidence which establishes the full agreement, subject to the limitation that such parol evidence does not conflict with the part that has been integrated in writing. . . . Thus parol evidence is always admissible with respect to the issue of integration, that is, parol evidence is admissible to show whether the parties intended to assent to the writing as the final and complete (or partial) statement of their agreement. . . .

Dairyland argues, however, that an exception exists to the general rule that parol evidence is admissible with respect to the issue of integration; that evidence of contemporaneous or prior agreements, written or oral, which relate to the same subject matter as the agreement in question is not admissible when the written agreement embodies written terms excluding additional understandings or agreements not contained in the writing, i.e., "merger" clauses. With this much we can agree. Absent claims of duress, fraud, or mutual mistake, a written provision which expressly negatives collateral or antecedent understandings makes the document a complete integration. . . .

Dairyland contends that "merger" clauses are contained in the agreements in question. On the schedule attached to and incorporated by reference in the April 16 agreement, a handwritten "none" follows the phrase "ADDITIONAL TERMS." On the schedule attached to and incorporated by reference in the July 20 agreement, a hand-drawn line evinces the same meaning. Dairyland argues that these provisions expressly negate the existence of terms not contained in the written agreements. However, an alternative reading of the "merger" clause contained on each of the schedules would restrict the effect of the "additional terms" lines to the terms stated on the schedules and would find them inapplicable to the documents denominated "leases." We believe the latter construction must be adopted, for the general rule is that ambiguous contracts are to be construed against the maker or drafter. . . .

Therefore, the trial court's consideration of evidence on the issue of integration was not error. Additionally, the trial court's finding of fact that the written agreements were intended as only partial integrations of their agreements must be accepted, there being no evidence to the contrary. However, reception of parol evidence would be subject to the limitation that the parol evidence received may not conflict with the part of the agreement that has been integrated in writing. This limitation was not observed.

Unless the parties' complete agreement contains provisions, either oral or written, for the vesting of title to the goods in their user, the parties' agreement must be considered a true lease as opposed to a conditional sales contract or a chattel mortgage disguised as a lease. . . . The receiver sought to establish such provisions by use of parol evidence; Spring Valley's directors testified that, under the oral provisions of the Dairyland-Spring Valley agreements, Spring Valley would own the equipment free and clear upon completion of the payment schedules contained in the written agreement. However, the agreements provide that "[t]itle to all equipment shall remain in Lessor" and that "the equipment shall be returned to the Lessor in the same appearance and condition as when received." The directors' testimony stands in conflict with that part of the parties' agreement which had been integrated in writing. Thus, even if testimony was permitted on the issue of integration, the parol evidence rule still barred the directors' testimony as to the nature of their agreement. Accordingly, there is no evidence to support the trial court's conclusion that the agreements constituted anything other than leases.

By the Court.—Order reversed and cause remanded for further proceedings not inconsistent with this opinion.

NOTES AND QUESTIONS

1. *Is the intention to integrate a question of fact*? Does the decision in the *Spring Valley Meats* case rest on the Corbin or the Williston parol evidence rule? Is it consistent with the decision of the Supreme Court of California in *Masterson v. Sine*? The leases were printed forms. They had a schedule attached that described the machine as a "Swiss Vac 'Tandem' Machine w/Stainless Steel Stand," the delivery date, the place of delivery, when the first payment was due, and "ADDITIONAL TERMS: None." Spring Valley Meats argued that the question was whether this form was intended as an integration and cited UCC § 2-202.

The only evidence offered about the parties' intentions in this regard was the testimony of two of Spring Valley Meats directors. Dennis A. Carlson testified: "It was discussed with me before it was signed. It was my understanding that this writing did not contain the entire agreement between us and Dairyland Equipment Leasing, Inc. . . . [I]t was my understanding that at the end of the payments we would own this equipment, would be given title to it." Herbert Severson testified "I did not read this agreement word for word but here again it was our understanding that this machine would be ours upon the completion of the lease, free and clear."

The court says there are two tests: (1) did the parties intend "to assent to the writing as the final and complete (or partial) statement of their agreement?" and (2) if they did intend an integration, does the tendered parol evidence contradict what was integrated? In the *Spring Valley* case, the court asserts that there was a "partial integration," apparently of the term "lease." What is the evidence the parties had agreed that the document's characterization of the transaction as a lease should be "a final expression of their agreement with respect to such term . . ."? Read the applicable text of UCC § 2-202 carefully in light of Official Comment 1 (b) and (c).

2. *The functions of the Spring Valley rule*: Does the decision in the *Spring Valley Meats* case carry out the intentions of the parties to the original contract/lease? Is the court seeking to protect someone against fraudulent claims? Why might parties make the alleged oral contracts? The Spring Valley Meats brief suggested that it was common for equipment sales to be drafted as leases ". . . so that the seller would be able to secure his tax advantage in the meantime." What tax advantage might seller gain if the transaction were a lease rather than a sale with installment payments of the price? Consider depreciation.

Later in law school you may take a course in which you study Article 9 of the UCC; this Article deals with "secured transactions." The parties in *Spring Valley* may have been seeking to structure the transaction as an alternative kind of secured transaction. It is common when adopting the discourse of secured transactions to seek to determine whether the economic effect of the transaction was to create a security interest, and if so, to treat it pursuant to the laws governing such matters. The court in this case didn't refer to Article 9. Perhaps the parties didn't either. But the transaction is arguably susceptible to being analyzed according to another set of rules and vocabulary.

The case is a battle among creditors about the disposition of assets of a failed business. How, if at all, does the difference between the real and the paper deal affect the interests of various creditors? A lessor can recover the property when the lessee stops making payments. A seller's right to the property when the buyer stops paying turns on whether it recorded a security interest. Do these considerations have anything to do with the parol evidence rule as it is conventionally rationalized?

Compare *Kergil v. Central Oregon Fir Supply Co., Inc.*[54] A truck owner sued a wholesale lumber dealer for breach of an equipment lease. At the trial, the defendant introduced evidence that the lease was a sham transaction designed to assist plaintiff in avoiding federal taxes. The trial court gave judgment for the defendant. The Supreme Court of Oregon reversed on the ground that parol evidence should not be admitted to show that a written document was executed to defraud a third party. The court said:

> The courts are not of a single mind on this issue. We confess, the majority of jurisdictions at the present time, based upon pure logic, admit

---

[54] 213 Ore. 186, 323 P.2d 947 (1958).

the evidence on the basis that such testimony is offered, not to vary the terms of the written instrument within the letter of the parol evidence rule, but only to show the parties never intended the written instrument to be a binding agreement.

The difficulty with this view is that it overlooks the moral aspects of the situation. It permits the law to be used to lend its aid to those who would mislead or defraud third parties without providing any restraining penalty upon their immoral actions.[55]

How does the court's decision reflect "the moral aspects of the situation"? Who planned the transaction and benefited from it? Is a deterrence argument convincing? Doesn't any rule which deters one party, in some sense, encourage the other? Remember the complexity and uncertainty of illegality as a defense to contract formation; isn't this an illegality case in disguise?

3. *Another type of misleading document*: People may sign what appears to be a written contract but not intend it to take effect immediately, or at all. For example, in *Merritt v. Walter Pocock Associate Brokers, Inc.*,[56] Pocock asked Merritt, one of the owners of a building, to sign a listing contract. The document set forth the terms on which the owners would sell the building and called for an $8,000 broker's commission to be paid by the seller. Pocock, the broker, and Merritt agreed that the listing contract was subject to the approval of the other owners of the building although they failed to mention this in the writing. Pocock sued to enforce his rights under the writing. Merritt tried to prove that Pocock and he had agreed that the approval of the other owners was a condition to the writing taking effect. The trial court refused to allow Merritt to prove the alleged condition and granted summary judgment in favor of the broker. The Supreme Court of Arizona reversed and remanded the case for trial. It said "[p]roof of such a condition precedent is clearly not a violation of the Parol Evidence Rule since it is not introduced to vary the terms of the writing but rather is intended to show that the contract never came into existence."

This is one of the classic exceptions to the parol evidence rule. Why is proof of this kind of oral agreement allowed? Doesn't it vary the express terms of the written contract?

4. *Omitting terms so no written record of them exists*: Parties may think that a perfectly legal bargain might offend others. For example, in *Zell v. American Seating Co.*,[57] plaintiff Zell was hired by American Seating. He was to attempt to procure contracts for American Seating from the United States Government. Zell was to be paid $1,000 a month for three months. If he were successful, he was to be paid a percentage of the price paid by the United States. The parties executed a written contract that omitted any mention of the agreement to pay a contingent fee, in order to "avoid any possible stigma which might result" from using such a term. Such contingent fee contracts had been criticized in Congress, but were not illegal. Zell got the contracts for American Seating, which then refused to pay the

---

[55] *Id.* at 189, 323 P.2d at 948.
[56] 105 Ariz. 392, 465 P.2d 585 (1970).
[57] 138 F.2d 641 (2d Cir. 1943).

agreed-upon contingent fee. Zell sued; the District Court granted summary judg-ment, but the Second Circuit reversed. Judge Jerome Frank wrote:

> [i]t has been held virtually everywhere . . . that . . . in the absence of any fraudulent or illegal purpose . . . a purported written agreement, which the parties designed as a mere sham, lacks legal efficacy, and that extrin-sic parol or other extrinsic evidence will always be received on that is-sue. . . . [W]hile it may be undesirable that citizens should prepare documents so contrived as to spoil the scent of legislators bent on pro-posing new legislation, yet such conduct is surely not unlawful and does not deserve judicial castigation as immoral or fraudulent; the courts should not erect standards of morality so far above the customary. . . .
>
> The rule, then, does relatively little to deserve its much advertised virtue of reducing the dangers of successful fraudulent recoveries and de-fenses brought about through perjury. The rule is too small a hook to catch such a leviathan. Moreover, if at times it does prevent a person from winning, by lying witnesses, a lawsuit which he should lose, it also, at times, by shutting out the true facts, unjustly aids other persons to win lawsuits they should and would lose, were the suppressed evidence known to the courts. . . .
>
> We are asked to believe that the rule enables businessmen, advised by their lawyers, to rely with indispensable confidence on written con-tracts unimpeachable by oral testimony. In fact, seldom can a conscien-tious lawyer advise his client, about to sign an agreement, that, should the client become involved in litigation relating to that agreement, one of the many exceptions to the rule will not permit the introduction of uncer-tainty-producing oral testimony.[58]

In *American Seating v. Zell*,[59] the Supreme Court of the United States reversed Judge Frank's decision by a vote of 7 to 2. The District Court decision was af-firmed. Four justices thought that proof of the contract was precluded by the ap-plicable state parol evidence rule, and three thought that the contract was con-trary to public policy and void. The Supreme Court wrote only a two-sentence *per curiam* opinion. Do you understand the views of the four justices who thought the evidence was barred by the parol evidence rule? Do you think they understood the rule? Suppose instead of omitting the contingent fee term, the par-ties wrote the contract in code. Most courts would allow parol evidence admitted to interpret the code. Would this situation differ significantly from that in the *Zell* case?

---

[58] *Id.* at 644, 645, 649.
[59] 322 U.S. 709 (1944).

4. THE PAROL EVIDENCE RULE, MISREPRESENTATION, AND PROMISSORY ESTOPPEL

ENRICO FARMS, INC. v. H.J. HEINZ CO.; PALLADINO v. CONTADINA FOODS, INC.[60]
United States Court of Appeals, Ninth Circuit
629 F.2d 1304 (1980)

PER CURIAM: . . . Palladino sought to prove the breach . . . [by Contadina] of two written contracts for the sale and purchase of processing tomatoes by means of parol evidence to interpret or explain the contracts. [The District Court entered a partial summary judgment in favor of defendant Contadina Foods, Inc. The 9th Circuit affirmed.]

Palladino is a California grower, harvester and seller of processing tomatoes. [Contadina] buys and processes tomatoes. The first written contract between Palladino and [Contadina] is for the sale and purchase of tomatoes. The second written contract is for the sale of tomatoes by Edward Pippo to [Contadina]; and Palladino, as a harvester, is a third-party beneficiary of the Pippo contract.

The gist of Palladino's claim is that although both contracts contain written provisions allowing [Contadina], in time of glut, to place quotas on the quantity of tomatoes it would accept, he, Pippo and [Contadina]'s field agent made oral modifications striking these provisions and providing instead that [Contadina] would purchase Palladino's and Pippo's entire outputs.

The District Court dismissed the claim under the Palladino—[Contadina] contract for the reason parol evidence cannot be received to contradict the terms of the written agreement and the Statute of Frauds requires that this agreement be in writing. The District Court dismissed the claim on the Pippo contract because Palladino could not reasonably rely on an oral statement made by Contadina to Pippo since he knew Pippo had also signed a written contract containing the provision for prorate of the crop. The District Court was right.

"Parol evidence may be admitted to prove elements of an agreement not reduced to writing so long as the parties have not intended the writing to be a complete and final embodiment of their agreement and the parol evidence does not contradict the terms of the writing." *James G. Freeman & Associates, Inc. v. Tanner*, 56 Cal. App.3d 1, 9, 128 Cal. Rptr. 109, 114 (1976). We realize that an integration clause in the written agreement is not necessarily conclusive as to the parties' intent to include their entire agreement in the writing. *Masterson v. Sine*, 68 Cal.2d 222, 436 P.2d 561, 65 Cal. Rptr. 545 (1968). Nevertheless, . . . the intent not to embody the complete agreement in the writing is only one condition that must be met before parol evidence may be admitted. The parol evidence must also "not contradict the terms of the writing." We, therefore, need not actually determine to what extent the written contract was integrated. The "threshold integration issue" referred to in *Royal Industries v. St. Regis Paper Co.*, 420 F.2d 449, 452 (9th Cir. 1969), need only be resolved in order to decide whether or not

---

[60] Eds. note: The caption for this case is explained by virtue of the fact that Palladino was an intervenor in an antitrust case involving Enrico Farms and Heinz.

the parol evidence rule precludes admission of oral evidence that would add to or vary the terms of a written agreement. Similarly, *Masterson* is of no help to Palladino; it held that when a writing is not intended to embody the complete agreement of the parties, parol evidence may be admitted to prove a matter "on which the document is silent and which is not inconsistent with its terms." 65 Cal. Rptr. at 548, 436 P.2d at 564. We find no support for and reject Palladino's contention that, absent an integration, parol evidence may be admitted to directly contradict a written agreement.

Palladino's reliance upon this Court's decision in *Bell v. Exxon Co., U.S.A.*, 575 F.2d 714 (9th Cir. 1978), is misplaced. The written contract in *Bell* contained a provision for prorating the agreed gallonage supply of gasoline in the event of a shortage of the defendant-seller's supply of gasoline. Bell claimed that he was fraudulently induced to enter into the contract by relying upon sales representations of Exxon's sales representative "that despite the anticipated fuel supply shortage appellee would supply appellant's gasoline requirements if he entered into the new agreement." . . .

Here Palladino's complaint did not allege that the appellee's field agent's oral statements were fraudulent. At best, he claimed only that the quota purchase provision in time of glut was "waived" and the written contract modified.

We are firm in the conclusion that under the facts here, the parol evidence sought to be introduced by Palladino is in direct contradiction to the terms of the written contract.

The other issues presented by Palladino are without merit.

The Partial Summary Judgment entered by the District Court on October 3, 1977 is . . . affirmed.

Kilkenny, Circuit Judge, dissenting:

I would allow the petition for rehearing and remand the case to the district court for a decision on whether the contracts in question were integrated as required by the decisions in *Masterson v. Sine*, 436 P.2d 561 at 563, 65 Cal. Rptr. 545 at 547 (1968); *In re Wm. Rakestraw Co.*, 450 F.2d 6 (CA9 1971), ... Beyond question, these cases hold that the court must first decide the intention of the parties on integration of the two contracts under consideration. I quote from *In re Wm. Rakestraw Co., supra*, at p. 8, where it is said:

> However, under California law, before the parol evidence rule may be applied, a preliminary determination must be made as to the integration of the contract, based on the parties' intent.

I find nothing in the record which would lead me to believe that the district court passed on the issue dealing with the integration of the contract or contracts. . . .

NOTES AND QUESTIONS

1. *A first mention of third party beneficiary rules*: You might have been puzzled by the fact that Palladino, the harvester, is apparently complaining about the breach of a promise that Contadina made to Pippo. The court assumes, perhaps merely for the sake of argument in this case, that Palladino has a right to complain about Contadina's failure to keep its promise to Pippo. It is clear that since apparently Pippo has arranged for Palladino to harvest the Pippo tomatoes, Palladino has a financial interest in the harvesting of those tomatoes. Courts sometimes allow those who will benefit from a performance of a promise to sue for its enforcement. The rules governing just when non-parties can sue to enforce promises will be taken up in a later section. When we *do* take it up, you might come back to this case and reflect on whether it is a strong case for the acknowledgment of third-party rights.

   2. *Federal courts seek California law*: Does this decision reflect the Williston or the Corbin view of the parol evidence rule? Is it a proper application of California law, following *Masterson v. Sine*?

   3. *Authority to modify the contract*: Contadina Foods' brief raises an issue never decided by the court, but which might explain the result of the case. Palladino and Pippo were members of the California Tomato Growers Association (CTGA), a growers' cooperative. As members, Palladino had given CTGA the exclusive right to negotiate the terms of a standard "Approved Contract" which was to be used by all of the members; the only exception was for additional clauses which were subject to CTGA approval. The standard contract which CTGA had negotiated contained the proration clause. Contadina complained that Palladino should be estopped from claiming an oral agreement at variance with the collectively bargained contract that it had use. To allow Palladino to prevail would give it the benefit of a contract preferential to all of the other tomato growers in the Association.

   4. *Misrepresentations that contradict a written contract*: Notice the court's discussion of *Bell v. Exxon*. Parol evidence generally can be admitted to prove misrepresentations. Palladino alleged that Sal Lucchesi, a field agent for Contadina, had assured Palladino and Pippo that all of their tomatoes would be accepted and they "would not lose a single tomato." He said that it was not necessary to put this in writing and they could trust him to treat them as well as they had been treated in the past. Is this sufficient to raise a claim of fraud in the inducement? Contadina's brief suggests the problem with a fraud approach in the *Enrico Farms* case:

> Palladino, for the first time in his memorandum of law in opposition to Contadina's motion for summary judgment claimed "fraud in the inducement." There is no allegation of fraud in the complaint or in Palladino's affidavit, nor is there evidence to support such an allegation. . . .

> It is just this type of unsupportable assertion of "fraud" that the leading commentators on the UCC warn against permitting to be used in an attempt to avoid the Parol Evidence Rule. . . . [The brief then quotes White and Summer's treatise on the UCC, where they say "A party should not be allowed to introduce his evidence of an alleged extrinsic term merely by alleging fraud."] Allowing introduction of parol evidence on the basis of unsupportable arguments of counsel, such as presented here, would undermine the policy behind the parol evidence rule and the integrity of written contracts.

5. *Parol evidence and estoppel*: In *Ehret Co. v. Eaton, Yale & Town, Inc.*,[61] Ehret, a former manufacturer's sales representative, sued Eaton for breach of contract. Ehret often had to adapt Eaton's products so they would work with customers' finished products or their manufacturing equipment. Ehret often had to work as long as ten years before a sale became final. Eaton proposed a contract under which either party could terminate the relationship upon thirty days' notice. This contract provided that commissions would be paid on orders accepted before termination, provided purchasers would take delivery within three months from the date of cancellation. Ehret objected. Eaton could cancel after Ehret had expended considerable time and money procuring a sale, but before its customer placed an order. Eaton refused to change the written contract. One of its officials wrote a letter, which said:

> [In] those few cases where the contract has been cancelled by us we have always been much more liberal than provided for in the contract. . . . [W]e cannot alter the terms of the contract—the same contract must exist with you as with all of our other representatives and in the very unlikely event of cancellation, you will have to rely on receiving extremely fair treatment.[62]

Ehret signed the contract.

About two years later, Eaton canceled the contract. It first applied the written contract literally and refused to pay commissions on sales to be shipped after three months from termination. Later it agreed to pay commissions on orders received before termination no matter when the goods were shipped. Ehret sued, contending it was entitled to better treatment than called for by the written contract. It relied on the letter which stated that it would receive "extremely fair treatment." Eaton's motion for summary judgment was denied.

The court of appeals affirmed. Eaton was estopped to set up the clause in the written document. Ehret was induced to sign the writing by Eaton's representation that Ehret would receive "extremely fair treatment" in the unlikely event of termination. The court quoted an Illinois decision which said "[f]raud is a necessary element [of estoppel] but it is not essential that there be a fraudulent intent. It is sufficient if a fraudulent effect would follow upon allowing a party to set up a claim inconsistent with his former declarations."[63] The theory of equitable estoppel relied on by the court in this case is a close cousin to promissory estoppel à la Restatement 90. The court noted that if Eaton could disclaim its representations after receiving the benefits of them, "this would have the fraudulent effect that an estoppel was designed to prevent." As a result, the trial court did not err in admitting the letter written and received before the written contract was signed. This letter "is not in conflict with the parol evidence rule as the defendant contends. An estoppel is an equitable remedy which has its own independent force."

Next, the court interpreted the phrase "extremely fair treatment." This phrase is susceptible to numerous interpretations. Thus, parol evidence could be consid-

---

[61] 523 F.2d 280 (7th Cir. 1975).

[62] *Id.* at 282.

[63] *Id.* at 283.

ered to give it meaning. "There was sufficient evidence to establish that it took up to ten years for the plaintiff to develop a customer prior to an order being placed. It was this concern of the plaintiff that prompted the defendant's promise of 'extremely fair treatment' and it was on this basis that the jury awarded damages."[64]

Suppose Palladino had argued that Contadina was estopped to deny the field agent's statements in the *Enrico Farms* case. Might Palladino have won on this theory? *See, generally,* Metzger, *The Parol Evidence Rule: Promissory Estoppel's Next Conquest?*[65]

6. *More on the relationship between the parol evidence rule and the Statute of Frauds*: Contadina argued that if the parol evidence striking the glut clause were admitted, Palladino's alleged oral contract would be unenforceable under the Statute of Frauds. UCC § 2-201 states that "[a] writing is not insufficient because it omits or incorrectly states a term agreed upon but the contract is not enforceable under this paragraph beyond the quantity of goods shown in such writing." Striking the glut clause would have obligated Contadina to take a greater quantity than the writing, and so this provision of § 2-201 would bar enforcement of the oral modification. Palladino, in reply, says that the written contract provides that Contadina agreed to take 875 tons of tomatoes grown from 25 acres at $53.50 per pound, and this is the provision that it was seeking to enforce. The rider provision "has nothing to do with quantity but only specifies the terms of delivery in the event that all plants are glutted." The Ninth Circuit's decision on the parol evidence rule made it unnecessary to decide this issue. However, you should recognize that the parol evidence rule and the Statute of Frauds *both* must be satisfied, and in some instances one may be able to jump the parol evidence hurdle, but fail to clear that of the Statute of Frauds.

7. *Adding the battle of the forms to parol evidence and statute of frauds problems*: In *David J. Joseph Co. v. S & M Scrap Metal Co., Inc.,*[66] buyer's counterclaim was based on a document called a "purchase confirmation." It provided for the sale to buyer of "60 carloads (estimated 2700 gross tons)" of "#2 bundles scrap iron for remelting and recycling." On the back of the confirmation it was stated that "This confirmation constitutes the entire contract between the parties. Receipt of this confirmation by seller shall be deemed to be an acceptance by seller of the terms and conditions of this contract regardless of whether or not the seller has acknowledged this confirmation. Any additional or inconsistent terms or conditions are not binding on [buyer] unless agreed to in writing by [buyer]."[67] Seller admitted receipt of the document and its failure to object to its terms. Seller denied liability to buyer under this contract because the "purchase confirmation" did not reflect the oral agreement reached prior to the receipt of that document by seller, and seller claimed that it had performed the oral agreement.

---

[64] *Id.* at 284.
[65] 36 Vand. L. Rev. 1383 (1983).
[66] 163 Ga. App. 685 (1982).
[67] *Id.* at 685.

The court applied UCC § 2-201(1) and held that the seller was bound by the "purchase confirmation" since it had made no written objection to it. It then turned to § 2-202's provision that "[t]erms with respect to which the confirmatory memoranda of the parties agree or which are otherwise set forth in a writing intended by the parties as a final expression of their agreement with respect to such terms as are included therein may not be contradicted by evidence of any prior agreement or of a contemporaneous oral agreement." The court said: "[c]onsequently, the terms of the Purchase Confirmation are binding on appellee [the seller] and may not be contradicted by prior or contemporaneous parol evidence. . . . [Seller's] position that the Purchase Confirmation was not intended to be the final expression of the parties' agreement directly contradicts the document's express terms, which were not objected to within 10 days of receipt."[68]

How many problems do you see with the court's analysis of the interrelationship of the parol evidence rule and Statute of Frauds section of the UCC? Recall § 2-207, and its relationship with § 2-201 as well.

NANAKULI PAVING AND ROCK CO. v. SHELL OIL CO.
United States Court of Appeals for the Ninth Circuit
664 F.2d 772 (1981)

HOFFMAN, J. Appellant Nanakuli Paving and Rock Company (Nanakuli) initially filed this breach of contract action against appellee Shell Oil Company (Shell) in Hawaiian State Court in February, 1976. Nanakuli, the second largest asphaltic paving contractor in Hawaii, had bought all its asphalt requirements from 1963 to 1974 from Shell under two long-term supply contracts; its suit charged Shell with breach of the later 1969 contract. The jury returned a verdict of $220,800 for Nanakuli on its first claim, which is that Shell breached the 1969 contract in January, 1974, by failing to price protect Nanakuli on 7200 tons of asphalt at the time Shell raised the price for asphalt from $44 to $76. Nanakuli's theory is that price-protection, as a usage of the asphaltic paving trade in Hawaii, was incorporated into the 1969 agreement between the parties, as demonstrated by the routine use of price protection by suppliers to that trade, and reinforced by the way in which Shell actually performed the 1969 contract up until 1974. Price protection, appellant claims, required that Shell hold the price on the tonnage Nanakuli had already committed because Nanakuli had incorporated that price into bids put out to or contracts awarded by general contractors and government agencies. The District Judge set aside the verdict and granted Shell's motion for judgment n.o.v., which decision we vacate. We reinstate the jury verdict because we find that, viewing the evidence as a whole, there was substantial evidence to support a finding by reasonable jurors that Shell breached its contract by failing to provide protection for Nanakuli in 1974. . . . We do not believe the evidence in this case was such that, giving Nanakuli the benefit of all inferences fairly supported by the evidence and without weighing the credibility of the witnesses, only one reasonable conclusion could have been reached by the jury. . . .

---

[68] *Id.* at 687.

Nanakuli offers two theories for why Shell's failure to offer price protection in 1974 was a breach of the 1969 contract. First, it argues, all material suppliers to the asphaltic paving trade in Hawaii followed the trade usage of price protection and thus it should be assumed, under the UCC, that the parties intended to incorporate price protection into their 1969 agreement. This is so, Nanakuli continues, even though the written contract provided for price to be "Shell's Posted Price at time of delivery," F.O.B. Honolulu. Its proof of a usage that was incorporated into the contract is reinforced by evidence of the commercial context, which under the UCC should form the background for viewing a particular contract. The full agreement must be examined in light of the close, almost symbiotic relations between Shell and Nanakuli on the island of Oahu, whereby the expansion of Shell on the island was intimately connected to the business growth of Nanakuli. The UCC looks to the actual performance of a contract as the best indication of what the parties intended those terms to mean. Nanakuli points out that Shell had price protected it on the two occasions of price increases under the 1969 contract other than the 1974 increase. In 1970 and 1971 Shell extended the old price for four and three months, respectively, after an announced increase. This was done, in the words of Shell's agent in Hawaii, in order to permit Nanakuli to "chew up" tonnage already committed at Shell's old price.[69]

Nanakuli's second theory for price protection is that Shell was obliged to price protect Nanakuli, even if price protection was not incorporated into their contract, because price protection was the commercially reasonable standard for fair dealing in the asphaltic paving trade in Hawaii in 1974. Observance of those standards is part of the good-faith requirement that the Code imposes on merchants in performing a sales contract. Shell was obliged to price protect Nanakuli in order to act in good faith, Nanakuli argues, because such a practice was universal in that trade in that locality.

Shell presents three arguments for upholding the judgment n.o.v. or, on cross appeal, urging that the District Judge erred in admitting certain evidence. First, it says, the District Court should not have denied Shell's motion *in limine* to define trade, for purposes of trade usage evidence, as the sale and purchase of asphalt in Hawaii, rather than expanding the definition of trade to include other suppliers of materials to the asphaltic paving trade. Asphalt, its argument runs, was the subject matter of the disputed contract and the only product Shell supplied to the asphaltic paving trade.[70] Shell protests that the judge, by expanding the definition

---

[69] [4] Price protection was practiced in the asphaltic paving trade by either extending the old price for a period of time after a new one went into effect or charging the old price for a specified tonnage, which represented work committed at the old price. In addition, several months' advance notice was given of price increases.

[70] [5] Shell's argument would, in effect, eliminate all trade usage evidence. First, it argues that its own acts were irrelevant as mere waivers, not acts in the course of the performance of the contract. Second, it contends that all acts of price protection by the only other asphalt supplier in Hawaii, Chevron, the marketing division of Standard Oil Company, were irrelevant to prove trade usage because Chevron at one time owned all or part of the paving company it supplied and routinely price protected Hawaiian Bitumuls (H.B.). The court correctly refused to bar that evidence since the one-time relationship between the two went to the weight, not the admissibility, of the evidence. Nanakuli was given permission to offer evidence in rebuttal that Chevron price protected

of trade to include the other major suppliers to the asphaltic paving trade, allowed the admission of highly prejudicial evidence of routine price protection by all suppliers of aggregate. Asphaltic concrete paving is formed by mixing paving asphalt with crushed rock, or aggregate, in a "hot-mix" plant and then pouring the mixture onto the surface to be paved. Shell's second complaint is that the two prior occasions on which it price protected Nanakuli, although representing the only other instances of price increases under the 1969 contract, constituted mere waivers of the contract's price term, not a course of performance of the contract. A course of performance of the contract, in contrast to a waiver, demonstrates how the parties understand the terms of their agreement. Shell cites two UCC Comments in support of that argument: (1) that, when the meaning of acts is ambiguous, the preference is for the waiver interpretation, and (2) that one act alone does not constitute a relevant course of performance. Shell's final argument is that, even assuming its prior price protection constituted a course of performance and that the broad trade definition was correct and evidence of trade usages by aggregate suppliers was admissible, price protection could not be construed as reasonably consistent with the express price term in the contract, in which case the Code provides that the express term controls.

We hold that the judge did not abuse his discretion in defining the applicable trade, for purposes of trade usages, as the asphaltic paving trade in Hawaii, rather than the purchase and sale of asphalt alone, given the unusual, not to say unique, circumstances. . . . Additionally, we hold that, under the facts of this case, a jury could reasonably have found that Shell's acts on two occasions to price protect Nanakuli were not ambiguous and therefore indicated Shell's understanding of the terms of the agreement with Nanakuli rather than being a waiver by Shell of those terms.

Lastly we hold that, although the express price terms of Shell's posted price of delivery may seem, at first glance, inconsistent with a trade usage of price protection at time of increases in price, a closer reading shows that the jury could have reasonably construed price protection as consistent with the express term. . . . Our decision is reinforced by the overwhelming nature of the evidence that price protection was routinely practiced by all suppliers in the small Oahu market of the asphaltic paving trade and therefore was known to Shell; that it was a realistic necessity to operate in that market and thus vital to Nanakuli's ability to get large government contracts and to Shell's continued business growth on Oahu; and that it therefore constituted an intended part of the agreement, as that term is broadly defined by the Code, between Shell and Nanakuli.

I. History Of Nanakuli-Shell Relations Before 1973

Nanakuli, a division of Grace Brothers, Ltd., a Hawaiian corporation, is the smaller of the two major paving contractors on the island of Oahu, the larger of the two being Hawaiian Bitumuls (H.B.). Nanakuli first entered the paving business on Oahu in 1948, but it only began to move into the largest Oahu market, Honolulu, in the mid-1950's. Until 1964 or so, Nanakuli only got small paving

---

other customers in California with whom it had no such relationship in the event Shell tried to impeach that evidence.

jobs, such as service stations, driveways, and small subdivision streets; it was not in a position to compete with H.B. for government contracts for major roads, airports, and other large jobs. In the early sixties Nanakuli owner Walter Grace began to negotiate a mutually advantageous arrangement with Shell whereby Shell, which had a small market percentage and no asphalt terminals in Hawaii, would sign a long-term supply contract with Nanakuli that would commit Nanakuli to buy its asphalt requirements from Shell. On the other hand, Nanakuli would be helped to expand its paving business on Oahu through a guaranteed supply and a discount on its asphalt prices. Nanakuli's growth would expand the market for Shell's asphalt on the island, which would justify Shell's capital investment of a half a million dollars on Oahu, to which asphalt would be brought in heated tankers from Shell's refinery in Martinez, California.

Shell signed two five-year contracts in 1963: a supply contract with Nanakuli itself and a distributorship with Grace, which provided for a $2 commission on all Nanakuli's sales. In fact, almost all Nanakuli's sales were to itself and thus the commission operated, according to Shell's Hawaiian representative, Bohner, primarily as a discount mechanism. Lennox, who succeeded Grace as president in 1965 at Grace's death,[71] testified that its purpose was "to make us competitive in our paving operation with our competitor [H.B.] who is much larger than ourselves because they were a distributor for the Standard Oil Company's asphalt operation." Lennox and Smith, who joined Nanakuli as vice-president in 1965 and eventually succeeded Lennox, both saw Nanakuli's and Shell's relationship as that of partners. That characterization was not denied by Bohner, Shell's Hawaiian representative from 1964 to 1978, who, in fact, essentially corroborated their description of the close relations between the two companies. As a symbol of that relationship, Nanakuli painted its trucks "Shell white," placed Shell's logo on those trucks, chose the same orange as used by Shell for its own logo, and put the Shell logo on its stationary [sic].

In 1966 Pacific Cement and Aggregates (P.C. & A.), Nanakuli's landlord at its rented rock quarry at Halawa, was bought by Lone Star Cement Corporation, which later became Lone Star Industries. Lone Star requested that Nanakuli upgrade its plant facilities at the quarry, which Nanakuli estimated would cost between $250,000 to $300,000. Nanakuli, knowing Shell was eager to build up its paving business on Oahu, approached Shell for direct financing of the plant, an idea to which Shell was initially receptive. Lennox testified that Shell "had a sizeable installation at Iwilei and they didn't think we were selling enough of their product and they wanted us to sell more and that's why we enlarged our plant." Shell management philosophy later changed and it was decided not to finance the plant directly but rather to offer Nanakuli an additional $2 volume discount on all sales over five thousand tons to help finance the plant, according to Bohner. Lennox testified that Shell authorized Nanakuli to tell Lone Star that Shell, with a million-dollar investment in Hawaii, fully supported Nanakuli's plant expansion plans. In 1968 two top Shell asphalt officials came from the mainland to discuss Nanakuli's expansion: Blee from San Francisco and Lewis

---

[71] [11] After Grace died, new supply and distributorship contracts were signed, the latter substituting Nanakuli for Grace as Oahu distributor for Shell.

from New York.[72] Together with Bohner and Nanakuli's Lennox and Smith, they met with officials of Nanakuli's bank to discuss the loan and repayment schedule. The three contracts were finally signed after long negotiations on April 1, 1969. They were to parallel the amortization schedule of the bank loan for the plant: a supply contract, a distributorship contract, and volume discount letter, all three to last until December 31, 1975, at which point each would have the option to cancel on six-months' notice, with a minimum duration of over seven years, April 1, 1969, to July 1, 1976. Such long-term contracts were certainly unusual for Shell and this one was probably unique among Shell's customers, at least by 1974.

Lennox' testimony, which was partially stricken by the court as inadmissible, was that Shell's agreement with Nanakuli in 1969 included a commitment by Shell never to charge Nanakuli more than Chevron charged H.B., in order to carry out the underlying purpose of the agreement to make Nanakuli competitive with H.B. and thus expand its and Shell's respective businesses on Oahu. This testimony was ruled inadmissible as parol evidence.[73] Shell, itself at the end of the trial, read in parts of Smith's earlier deposition in which he made a similar

---

[72] [12] The hierarchical structure was that Bohner reported to Blee, who reported to Lewis.

[73] [14] The judge ruled evidence of prior dealings and additional terms inadmissible at several points. At one point he said, "Well, unless it refers to the trade usage, I don't think I'm going to allow anything prior to the date of the contract," and at another he asked, "Why don't you start with the 1969 contract? Why do you have to go before that?" One exclusionary ruling relied on paragraph H, a boilerplate clause in Shell's printed-form contract in the "Remedies/Waivers" section that evidence of dealings or waivers was disallowed as affecting "Shell's right to require specific performance of buyer's obligations." That limited exclusion should not have operated to exclude all dealings evidence for any purpose, unless the parties had evidenced a clear intent to contract with no reference whatsoever to such evidence. "Writings are to be read on the *assumption* that the course of prior dealing between the parties . . . [was] taken for granted when the document was phrased. Unless *carefully negated* they become an element of the meaning of the words used." Haw. Rev. Stat. § 490:2-202, Comment 2 (emphasis supplied). In our opinion paragraph H did not carefully negate all uses of evidence of prior dealings. The court also relied on paragraph E, a classic integration or merger clause, but such a clause at most might show that the agreement was "a complete and exclusive statement of the terms of the agreement," in which case evidence of additional terms would be excluded but not evidence of prior dealings, which is admitted under subsection (a) and not excluded, even if the court makes a finding of completeness and exclusivity. *Accord*, White & Summers, Uniform Commercial Code, § 2-5 at 67, § 2-10 at 73, § 2-12 at 77 (1972). Even though additional terms evidence is excluded if such a finding is made, a boilerplate merger clause is not enough. The drafters directed the court to look to whether the additional terms are "such that, if agreed upon, they would *certainly* have been included in the document. . . ." Haw. Rev. Stat. § 490:2-202, Comment 3 (emphasis supplied). The only indication that the court was aware of this test was a rhetorical query: "[I]f that point [price protection] is so important, at the time the contract was entered into, why wasn't it stated in the contract?" In fact, however, "the Code presumption seems to be that unless proven otherwise the writing does not include all the terms," White & Summers, supra, § 21-10 at 69-70, and price protection might well not be written into a contract between parties with a long and close relationship. Certainly Shell would not be likely to put its agreement never to charge more than Chevron charged H.B. into writing. The judge also excluded the offer of proof by Lennox that Shell agreed to price protect Nanakuli because, when voir dired by Shell as to the basis of that understanding, he cited Chevron's price protection of H.B., later specifying Chevron's actions in 1970 and 1971, after the 1969 contract was signed. Had his testimony not been cut short, he might have cited earlier acts of price protection by Chevron. In addition, the judge's ruling ignored the second basis he stated for his understanding: "and the general principle of price protection."

point. Smith's deposition testimony was that, although no written provision was included on price protection, he was led to believe by Shell's Bohner that he would get price protection. "I think there was a thought running between the two parties at that time that something would be done." It was only after the fact, he added, that Bohner told Nanakuli that he had to get permission for price protection from the mainland at the time of price increases; before that, "we had no idea how the pricing was done." Smith's comments on additional terms agreed to were not as probative as those of Lennox, who was president and chief negotiator for Nanakuli of the 1969 contract. Nanakuli's offer of proof by Lennox was that Shell agreed "to sustain that price during those contracts in the same way in which Standard Oil Company [Chevron] sustained its price to the principal paving contractor on the island, Hawaiian Bitumuls, if there was any price increase" and to "not exceed Standard Oil's [Chevron's] posted price for asphalt sold to Hawaiian Bitumuls." It was agreed that Nanakuli would have to submit bids on a fixed-price basis and be price protected to compete with H.B. "We understood that Shell gave us the same protection in our bidding and our purchase of asphalt from them to incorporate in our work," Lennox did testify, adding that by that means Nanakuli could compete with H.B. and Shell would thereby benefit. He said Nanakuli understood the price term to mean that Shell would not increase prices without advance notice and would hold the price on work bid for enough time to allow Nanakuli to use up the tonnage bid at the old price. Smith's testimony backed up that of Lennox: the price was to be "posted price as bid as was understood between the parties," further explaining that it was to be Shell's price at time and place of delivery, except for price increases, at which point the price was time and place of bid for a period of time or a specified tonnage.[74]

Much information relevant to the "commercial context" of the agreement, essential to an understanding of the meaning of the terms, was contained in the testimony of Smith and Lennox. *See* Haw. Rev. Stat. § 490:2-202, Comment 2. None of it was flatly contradicted by the evasive responses of Bohner to such inquiries. Smith testified that Bohner was in Nanakuli's offices at least weekly, sometimes was involved in the preparation of bids, and knew when a bid had been submitted or a contract awarded, at times attending the awards himself. The amount of time he spent following Nanakuli's progress was understandable; as he explained, in the 1960's and 1970's Nanakuli "was basically . . . our only customer at this time." Thus Nanakuli felt it had no need to notify Shell in writing of

---

[74] [16] The principal reason the judge initially refused to allow any such testimony and one major reason for his inclination to grant the defendant's motion for a directed verdict, was his belief that there was no ambiguity in the express price term of "posted price at time of delivery." He was reluctantly persuaded to allow the evidence because of Shell's answer to interrogatory 11, asking its understanding of the contract term, that it had never had a posted price although it did have a list price. The court stated its doubts about Nanakuli's case at the time it denied Shell's directed verdict motion: lack of ambiguity in the express term and inconsistency between the trade usage of that term. When first requested to allow evidence of prior dealings the judge asked, "Can you point out what terms [in the written contract] are supposed to be ambiguous?" However, the Code lets in evidence of prior dealings, usage, and performance under § 2-202(a) even if the contract terms are clear: "This section definitely rejects: . . . (c) The requirement that a condition precedent to the admissibility of the type of evidence specified in paragraph (a) is an original determination by the court that the language used is ambiguous." Haw. Rev. Stat. § 490:2-202, Comment 1.

projects awarded; Lennox testified he was only told to do so on one occasion, the award of its first big contract on August 17, 1970. Due to the long shipping time from California, Bohner had to know well in advance Nanakuli's supply needs. Lennox testified that Bohner was "as close to us as any person could be as far as the asphalt supply was concerned. He had to know what we were doing. . . ." Lennox said Bohner was not only aware of Nanakuli's day-to-day progress but knowledgeable about the broader asphaltic paving marketplace in which Nanakuli was competing. Bohner denied having closely delved into the economics of the aggregate trade or even knowing much about the asphalt prices of its chief competitor, Chevron, but he admitted he was interested in Chevron's prices; made inquiries of Chevron's customers, including H.B.; and had a ballpark estimate of aggregate prices. The jury could have inferred that he knew more about Chevron's and the aggregate suppliers' prices than he admitted. The jury could have looked to the importance of aggregate prices to Nanakuli's success in getting large contracts; Bohner's statements that he was "very definitely interested in the construction trades," especially asphaltic paving; his subscription to a local construction journal that listed paving as well as other construction projects on Oahu; his membership in an asphaltic paving institute; and his knowledge about the use of aggregates as a component of asphaltic paving.

II. Trade Usage Before And After 1969

The key to price protection being so prevalent in 1969 that both parties would intend to incorporate it into their contract is found in one reality of the Oahu asphaltic paving market: the largest paving contracts were let by government agencies and none of the three levels of government—local, state, or federal—allowed escalation clauses for paving materials. If a paver bid at one price and another went into effect before the award was made, the paving company would lose a great deal of money, since it could not pass on increases to any government agency or to most general contractors. Extensive evidence was presented that, as a consequence, aggregate suppliers routinely price protected paving contractors in the 1960's and 1970's, as did the largest asphaltic supplier in Oahu, Chevron. Nanakuli presented documentary evidence of routine price protection by aggregate suppliers. . . . The smallness of the Oahu market led to complete trust among suppliers and pavers. . . . None of the aggregate companies had a contract with Nanakuli expressly stating price protection would be given; Nanakuli's contract with P.C. & A. merely set out that P.C. & A. would not charge Nanakuli more than it charged its other customers.

[The court summarized evidence that Chevron had given price protection to H.B., and that there was no mention of price protection in the written contract between H.B. and Chevron.]

In addition to evidence of trade usages existing in 1969 when the contract at issue was signed, the District Judge let in evidence of the continuation of that trade usage after 1969, over Shell's protest. He stated that, giving a liberal reading to § 1-205, he felt that later evidence was relevant to show that the expectation of the parties that a given usage would be observed was justified. The basis for incorporating a trade usage into a contract under the UCC is the justifiable expectation of the parties that it will be observed. That later evidence consisted here of more price protection by the aggregate companies on Oahu, as well as continued asphalt price protection. Chevron after 1969 continued price protecting H.B. on Oahu and, on raising prices in 1979, price protected Nanakuli on the island of Molokai, where Nanakuli purchased its asphalt from Chevron. Additionally, Shell price protected Nanakuli in 1977 and 1978 on Oahu.[75]

III. Shell's Course Of Performance Of The 1969 Contract

The Code considers actual performance of a contract as the most relevant evidence of how the parties interpreted the terms of that contract. In 1970 and 1971, the only points at which Shell raised prices between 1969 and 1974, it price protected Nanakuli by holding its old price for four and three months, respectively, after announcing a price increase. In the late summer of 1970, Shell had announced a price increase from $35 to $40 a ton effective September 1, 1970. When Nanakuli protested to Bohner that it should be price protected on work already committed, Blee wrote Bohner an in-house memo that, if Bohner could not "convince" Nanakuli to go along with the price increase on September 1, he should try to "bargain" to get Nanakuli to accept the price raise by at least the first of the year, which was what was finally agreed upon. During that four-month period, Nanakuli bought 3,300 tons. Shell announced a second increase in October, 1970, from $40 to $42 effective December 31st. Before that increase went into effect, on November 25 Shell increased the raise to $4, making the price $44 as of the first of the year.[76] Shell again agreed to price protect Nanakuli by holding the price at $40, which had been the official price since September 1, for three months from January to March, 1971. Shell did not actually raise prices again until January, 1974, but at several points it believed that increases would be necessary and gave several months' advance notice of those possible increases. Those actions were in accord with Shell's own policy, as professed by Bohner, and that of other asphalt and aggregate suppliers: to give at least several months' advance notice of price increases. On January 14, 1971, Shell wrote its asphalt customers that the maximum 1971 increase would be to $46. On July 9, 1971, another letter promised the price would not go over $50 in 1972. In addition, Bohner volunteered on direct the information that Shell price protected Nanakuli on the only two occasions of price increases after 1974 by giving 6 months' advance notice in 1977 and 3 or 4 months' advance notice in 1978, a practice he described as "in effect carryover pricing," his term for price protection. By its actions, Bohner testified, Shell allowed Nanakuli time to make arrangements to buy up tonnage committed at the old price, that is, to "chew up" tonnage bid or contracted. [Shell offered the evidence to show it acted in good faith, but the jury may have taken it to show what constituted commercially reasonable behavior.]

---

[75] [17] We do not need to decide whether usage evidence after a contract was signed is admissible to show that a party's reliance on a given usage was justifiable, given its continuation, because part of that evidence dealing with asphalt prices was admissible to show the reasonably commercial standards of fair dealing prevalent in the trade in 1974 and the part dealing with the continuation of price protection by aggregate suppliers, after 1969 was not so extensive as to be prejudicial to Shell.

[76] [18] That November letter also announced a "new pricing policy" of Shell, setting out a requirement that firm contractual commitments be made with Shell within 15 days of accepting a bid.

IV. Shell-Nanakuli Relations, 1973-74

Two important factors form the backdrop for the 1974 failure by Shell to price protect Nanakuli: the Arab oil embargo and a complete change of command and policy in Shell's asphalt management. The jury was read a page or so from the World Book about the events and effect of the partial oil embargo, which shortened supplies and increased the price of petroleum, of which asphalt is a byproduct. The federal government imposed direct price controls on petroleum, but not on asphalt. Despite the international importance of those events, the jury may have viewed the second factor as of more direct significance to this case. The structural changes at Shell offered a possible explanation for why Shell in 1974 acted out of step with, not only the trade usage and commercially reasonable practices of all suppliers to the asphaltic paving trade on Oahu, but also with its previous agreement with, or at least treatment of, Nanakuli.

Bohner testified to a big organizational change at Shell in 1973 when asphalt sales were moved from the construction sales to the commercial sales department. In addition, by 1973 the top echelon of Shell's asphalt sales had retired. Lewis and Blee, who had negotiated the 1969 contract with Nanakuli, were both gone.[77] Their duties were taken over by three men: Fuller in San Mateo, California, District Manager for Shell Sales, Lawson, and Chippendale, who was Shell's regional asphalt manager in Houston. When the philosophy toward asphalt pricing changed, apparently no one was left who was knowledgeable about the peculiarities of the Hawaiian market or about Shell's long-time relations with Nanakuli or its 1969 agreement, beyond the printed contract.

Shell had begun rethinking its asphalt pricing policies several years before. Swanson, who succeeded Lewis in New York in 1970, wrote an internal memorandum on April 21, 1970, in which he discussed frankly the advantages and disadvantages of price protection of its asphalt buyers. Such a practice assured Shell of captive-volume sales, he wrote. The practice of granting carry-over pricing at times of price increases, however, had the unfortunate side effect of depressing prices in the asphalt market everywhere else, the memorandum concluded. This rethinking apparently led to a November 25, 1970, letter setting out "Shell's New Pricing Policy" at its Honolulu and Hilo terminals. The letter explained the elimination of price protection: "In other words, we will no longer guarantee asphalt prices for the duration of any particular construction projects or for the specific lengths of time. We will, of course, honor any existing prices which have been committed for specific projects for which we have firm contractual commitments." The letter requested a supply contract be signed with Shell within 15 days of the receipt of an award by a customer.

The District Judge based his grant of judgment n.o.v. largely on his belief that, had Nanakuli desired price protection, it should have complied with Shell's request in that 1970 letter, by which we assume he meant Nanakuli should have made a firm contractual commitment with Shell for each project on which its bid was successful within 15 days of award. That conclusion, however, ignores sev-

---

[77] [19] Lewis had left earlier, his position in New York having been taken over by Swanson. Later a Houston office took charge of asphalt sales for Nanakuli's region.

eral facts. First, compliance by Nanakuli with the letter's demand that a contract be signed within 15 days of an award would have offered Nanakuli little, if any, protection. Nanakuli still would have been stuck with only charging the government the price incorporated into its bid if Shell raised its price between bid and award. The purpose of price protection was to guarantee the price in effect when a paver made a bid because of the often lengthy time span between bid and award. Second, if price protection was a part of Nanakuli's 1969 agreement with Shell, Shell had no right to terminate unilaterally that protection. Third, the letter was addressed to "Gentlemen" with Nanakuli's name typed in at the top; it was apparently addressed to all Shell's Hawaiian customers. Fourth, Nanakuli officials testified that they did not believe the letter was applicable to its unusual situation of already having a long-term contract with Shell. Smith and Lennox both testified that they did not view the letter as applicable to that supply contract but only to sales it might make to third parties under the distributorship contract. Shell characterized that argument as disingenuous, given Nanakuli's infrequent, if not nonexistent, sales to third parties. Nevertheless, the letter does assume that a Shell customer would need to sign a contract or purchase order setting forth the terms of sale as well as the price for any asphalt they would need to buy after an award. Nanakuli, on the other hand, already had a supply contract with all the terms of sales set forth, a point its two officials made repeatedly at trial. For example, Smith testified he saw no need to notify Shell because Bohner knew of each project and because the supply contract was a firm contractual commitment with Shell.[78] Shell had added in the 1970 letter: "All previous contractual commitments made prior to the date of this letter will, of course, be honored." Smith's reading of this was that Nanakuli's supply contract with Shell *was* a firm contractual commitment by Shell and that no further contract was needed. "We felt that this letter was unapplicable [*sic*] to our supply contract, that we already had a contractual commitment with Shell Oil Company which was not to end before 1975." Smith said he did not discuss with Bohner that part of the letter, which also announced the increase in asphalt prices to $44 on January 1, because "[t]here was no need to. The price had been protected before. He knew it. We knew it." There is an additional reason why Nanakuli might have felt that the letter did not apply to its particular situation. The letter announced that Shell would charge "from this date forward . . . the posted selling price on the date of purchase." This was different from the express term of Nanakuli's contract with Shell, which was the price in effect at time of *delivery*. Either Shell's agreement with Nanakuli embraced price protection, in which case Shell could not unilaterally abrogate Nanakuli's rights by this letter, or, as Shell argues, only the words on the written contract counted, in which case the price to Nanakuli was Shell's price at delivery. In the latter case, Nanakuli could safely ignore any attempt by Shell to change the price to that at purchase. Given Nanakuli's particular agreement, as it understood the agreement to be, the jury could have believed that Nanakuli officials reacted reasonably in believing that parts of the letter dealing with the need to notify Shell of awards won did not apply to Nanakuli.

---

[78] [22] "We already had a supply contract. Why would we need another supply contract?" Smith asked. "There was no need to write. We had our supply contract. We didn't need to enter a new contract with the Shell Oil Company with every successful project."

Nanakuli's strongest argument as to its failure to comply with the letter was that there was no need to notify Shell, as Bohner already knew of each project as it was bid and each award as it was made. Lennox testified, "The Shell Oil representative was in our office frequently and knew what jobs we had successfully bid." At another point Lennox said, "The Shell representative was in the office and was fully aware of what we were doing and what jobs we had gotten. He was familiar and was more or less a partner in this thing; he even attended the bid openings at times. He was fully aware and congratulated us every time we got a nice big job because it was more for Shell." Bohner kept his principals informed of Nanakuli's projects, Lennox said. He added, "[W]e had always been protected and our understanding was that we were protected and it wasn't necessary to keep making notices." Smith in his deposition said that Bohner only told him that he lacked the authority to grant price protection "after the fact." Since he knew nothing about how Shell arrived at its pricing, Smith assumed Bohner could carry out Shell's agreement to price protect Nanakuli each time it was needed without consulting the mainland.

After Shell's December 31, 1973, letter arrived on January 4, 1974, Smith called Bohner, as he had done before at times of price increases, to ask for price protection, this time on 7200 tons. Bohner told Smith that he would have to get in touch with the mainland, but he expected that the response would be negative. Smith wrote several letters in January and February asking for price protection. After getting no satisfaction, he finally flew to California to meet with Lawson, Fuller, and Chippendale. Chippendale, from the Houston office, was acknowledged by the other two to be the only person with authority to grant price protection. All three Shell officials lacked any understanding of Nanakuli and Shell's long, unique relationship or of the asphaltic trade in Oahu. They had never even seen Shell's contracts with Nanakuli before the meeting. When apprised of the three and their seven-year duration, Fuller remarked on the unusual nature of Nanakuli's relations with Shell, at least within his district. Chippendale felt it was probably unique for Shell anywhere. Smith testified that Fuller admitted to knowing nothing, beyond the printed page of Nanakuli's agreement with Shell, of the background negotiation or Shell's past pricing policies toward Nanakuli. Chippendale could not understand why Nanakuli even had a distributorship contract giving it a $2 commission on sales; he thought Nanakuli had been paid "illegally." No one had ever heard about Shell giving price protection to Nanakuli before. Instead of asking Bohner directly, Chippendale told Fuller to search the files for something on paper. Fuller testified that Shell would not act without *written* proof of Shell's past price protection of Nanakuli. He admitted he was unable to find anything in the files before 1972 because the departments had been reorganized in that year, about which he informed Chippendale. Chippendale accordingly decided to deny Nanakuli any price protection and wrote a draft of a letter for Fuller to send Nanakuli. He wrote a note to Fuller that he should adopt the "least said" approach with Nanakuli and check any letters with the legal department. When asked at trial if he had ever simply asked Bohner about Shell's past pricing practices toward Nanakuli, Fuller answered, "No, I didn't know we had it, other than the standard policy if we had one which we didn't."[79] Chippendale told Smith in the California meeting that, although 7200 tons represented an infinitesimal amount for Shell, it would set a bad precedent for Shell, since price protection was not Shell's "*current* policy." (emphasis supplied). Shell people told him, Smith testified from contemporaneously made notes, that "any past practice was inapplicable at the present time."[80] Smith testified from those same notes that he had left the meeting under the impression that Shell was going out of business in Hawaii.

We conclude that the decision to deny Nanakuli price protection was made by new Houston management without a full understanding of Shell's 1969 agreement with Nanakuli or any knowledge of its past pricing practices toward Nanakuli. If Shell did commit itself in 1969 to price protect Nanakuli, the Shell officials who made the decisions affecting Nanakuli in 1974 knew nothing about that commitment. Nor did they make any effective effort to find out. They acted instead solely in reliance on the 1969 contract's express price term, devoid of the commercial context that the Code says is necessary to an understanding of the meaning of the written word. Whatever the legal enforceability of Nanakuli's right, Nanakuli officials seem to have acted in good faith reliance on its right, as they understood it, to price protection and rightfully felt betrayed by Shell's failure to act with any understanding of its past practices toward Nanakuli.

V. Scope Of Trade Usage

The validity of the jury verdict in this case depends on four legal questions. First, how broad was the trade to whose usages Shell was bound under its 1969 agreement with Nanakuli: did it extend to the Hawaiian asphaltic paving trade or was it limited merely to the purchase and sale of asphalt, which would only include evidence of practices by Shell and Chevron? Second, were the two instances of price protection of Nanakuli by Shell in 1970 and 1971 waivers of the 1969 contract as a matter of law or was the jury entitled to find that they constituted a course of performance of the contract? Third, could the jury have construed an express contract term of Shell's posted price at delivery as reasonably consistent with a trade usage and Shell's course of performance of the 1969 contract of price protection, which consisted of charging the old price at times of price increases, either for a period of time or for specific tonnage committed at a fixed price in non-escalating contracts? Fourth, could the jury have found that

---

[79] [24] Fuller only found out the background to the Shell-Nanakuli 1969 agreement and Shell's past price protection of Nanakuli in an August 11, 1974, in-house memo from Bohner. Bohner explained in that memo that Shell only built its two terminals in Hawaii in 1963 because of long-time firm commitments from Nanakuli on Oahu and James W. Glover, Ltd., at Hilo. . . .

[80] [25] Other testimony by Smith was thrown out as hearsay: that Chippendale felt that, if Shell deviated from the rule for one, it would have to do so for all. He also testified that Chippendale had said that the loss was a transitional one for Shell's customers who in the future would seek escalation clauses. In testimony that was allowed, Smith testified that Chippendale told him to try to pass on the asphalt price increases, which Nanakuli unsuccessfully tried to do. Smith wrote Chippendale on February 14, "Our attempts . . . have met with utmost resistance and threats of litigation." By December 1973, Nanakuli, in reaction to Shell's November letter, had already begun inserting escalation clauses in its contract bids, which were mostly rejected. By March, 1974, local and state governments allowed such clauses for paving materials, although the federal government still does not allow escalation clauses for asphalt.

good faith obliged Shell to at least give advance notice of a $32 increase in 1974, that is, could they have found that the commercially reasonable standards of fair dealing in the trade in Hawaii in 1974 were to give some form of price protection?

We approach the first issue in this case mindful that an underlying purpose of the UCC as enacted in Hawaii is to allow for liberal interpretation of commercial usages. The Code provides, "This chapter shall be liberally construed and applied to promote its underlying purposes and policies." Haw. Rev. Stat. § 490:1-102(1). Only three purposes are listed, one of which is "[t]o permit the continued expansion of commercial practices through custom, usage and agreement of the parties; . . . ." Id. § 490:1-102(2)(b). The drafters of the Code explain:

> This Act is drawn to provide *flexibility* so that, since it is intended to be a semipermanent piece of legislation, it will provide its own machinery for *expansion of commercial practices*. It is intended to make it possible for the law embodied in this Act to be *developed* by the courts in the light of *unforeseen and new circumstances and practices*. . . .
>
> The text of each section should be *read in the light of the purpose and policy* of the rule or principle in question, as also of the Act as a whole, and the application of the language should be *construed narrowly or broadly*, as the case may be, in *conformity with the purposes and policies* involved. . . . [T]he Code seeks to *avoid . . . interference with evolutionary growth*. . . .
>
> This principle of *freedom of contract is subject* to specific *exceptions* found elsewhere in the Act. . . . [An example being the bar on contractual exclusion of the requirement of good faith, although the parties can set out standards for same.] . . . *In this connection*, § 1-205 incorporating into the agreement *prior course of dealing and usages of trade is of particular importance.*

Id., Comments 1 & 2 (emphasis supplied). We read that to mean that courts should not stand in the way of new commercial practices and usages by insisting on maintaining the narrow and inflexible old rules of interpretation. We seek the definition of trade usage not only in the express language of the Code but also in its underlying purposes, defining it liberally to fit the facts of the particular commercial context here.[81]

The Code defines usage of trade as "any practice or method of dealing having such regularity of observance in a *place, vocation or trade* as to justify an expec-

---

[81] [26] Shell would have us apply the definition of a merchant in the Code, which is defined as "a person who deals in goods of the kind or otherwise by his occupation holds himself out as having knowledge or skill peculiar to the practices or goods involved in the transaction. . . ." Id. § 490:2-104. By that definition, says Shell, it only dealt in or held itself out as knowledgeable about asphalt, not aggregates or even asphaltic paving. Leaving aside the arguable question of whether Shell's Bohner held himself out as knowledgeable about asphaltic paving, see textual discussion supra, the trade usage provisions do not refer to merchants but to "parties." See, e.g. id. 490:1-205(3), (6) & Comments 1, 4, 7 & 9. Probably for that reason Comment 2 to § 2-104, on which Shell relies, does not list the trade usage provision among those to which one definition or another of "merchant" is applicable. . . .

tation that it will be observed with respect to the transaction in question." *Id.* § 490:1-205(2) (emphasis supplied). We understand the use of the word "or" to mean that parties can be bound by a usage common to the *place* they are in business, even if it is not the usage of their particular vocation or trade. That reading is borne out by the repetition of the disjunctive "or" in subsection 3, which provides that usages "in the vocation or trade in which they are engaged *or* of which they are or should be aware give particular meaning to and supplement or qualify terms of an agreement." *Id.* § 490:1-205(3). The drafters' Comments say that trade usage is to be used to reach the ". . . commercial meaning of the agreement. . . ." by interpreting the language "as meaning what it may fairly be expected to mean to parties involved in the particular transaction *in a given locality or* in a given *vocation or trade." Id.,* Comment 4 (emphasis supplied). The inference of the two subsections and the Comment, read together, is that a usage need not necessarily be one practiced by members of the party's own trade or vocation to be binding *if* it is so commonly practiced in a locality that a party should be aware of it. Subsection 5 also shows the importance of the place where the usage is practiced: "An applicable usage of trade in the place where any part of performance is to occur shall be used in interpreting the agreement as to that part of the performance." The validity of this interpretation is additionally demonstrated by the Comment of the drafters: "Subsection (3), giving the prescribed effect to usages of which the parties 'are or should be aware', reinforces the provision of subsection (2) requiring not universality but only the described 'regularity of observance' of the practice or method. This subsection also reinforces the point of subsection (2) that such usages may be either *general to trade or particular to a special branch of trade." Id.,* Comment 7 (emphasis supplied). This language indicates that Shell would be bound not only by usages of sellers of asphalt but by more general usages on Oahu, as long as those usages were so regular in their observance that Shell should have been aware of them. This reading of the Code, in our opinion, achieves an equitable result. A party is always held to conduct generally observed by members of his chosen trade because the other party is justified in so assuming unless he indicates otherwise. He is held to more general business practices to the extent of his actual knowledge of those practices or to the degree his ignorance of those practices is not excusable: they were so generally practiced he should have been aware of them.

No UCC cases have been found on this point, but the court's reading of the Code language is similar to that of two of the best-known commentators on the UCC:

> Under pre-Code law, a trade usage was not operative against a party who *was not a member of the trade unless* he actually knew of it or *the other party could reasonably believe he knew of it.*

J. White & R. Summers, *Uniform Commercial Code,* § 12-6 at 371 (1972) (emphasis supplied) . . . White and Summers add (emphasis supplied):

> This view has been carried forward by § 1-205(3). . . . [U]sage of the trade is only binding on *members of the trade* involved *or persons* who knew or *should know about it.* Persons who should be aware of the trade usage doubtless *include those who regularly deal with members of the*

relevant trade, and also members of a second trade that commonly deals with members of a relevant trade (for example, farmers should know something of seed selling).

White & Summers, *supra*, § 12-6 at 371. Using that analogy, even if Shell did not "regularly deal" with aggregate supplies, it did deal constantly and almost exclusively on Oahu with one asphalt paver. It therefore should have been aware of the usage of Nanakuli and other asphaltic pavers to bid at fixed prices and therefore receive price protection from their materials suppliers due to the refusal by government agencies to accept escalation clauses. Therefore, we do not find the lower court abused its discretion or misread the Code as applied to the peculiar facts of this case in ruling that the applicable trade was the asphaltic paving trade in Hawaii. An asphalt seller should be held to the usages of trade in general as well as those of asphalt sellers and common usages of those to whom they sell. Certainly, under the unusual facts of this case it was not unreasonable for the judge to extend trade usages to include practices of other material suppliers toward Shell's primary and perhaps only customer on Oahu. He did exclude, on Shell's motion *in limine*, evidence of cement suppliers. He only held Shell to routine practices in Hawaii by the suppliers of the two major ingredients of asphaltic paving, that is, asphalt and aggregate. Those usages were only practiced towards two major pavers. It was not unreasonable to expect Shell to be knowledgeable about so small a market. In so ruling, the judge undoubtedly took into account Shell's half-million dollar investment in Oahu strictly because of a long-term commitment to Nanakuli, its actions as partner in promoting Nanakuli's expansion on Oahu, and the fact that its sales on Oahu were almost exclusively to Nanakuli for use in asphaltic paving. The wisdom of the pre-trial ruling was demonstrated by evidence at trial that Shell's agent in Hawaii stayed in close contact with Nanakuli and was knowledgeable about both the asphaltic paving market in general and Nanakuli's bidding procedures and economics in particular.

Shell argued not only that the definition of trade was too broad, but also that the practice itself was not sufficiently regular to reach the level of a usage and that Nanakuli failed to show with enough precision how the usage was carried out in order for a jury to calculate damages. The extent of a usage is ultimately a jury question. The Code provides, "The existence and scope of such a usage are to be proved as facts." Haw. Rev. Stat. § 490:1-205(2).[82] The practice must have "such regularity of observance . . . as to justify an expectation that it will be observed. . . ." *Id.* The Comment explains:

> The ancient English tests for "custom" are abandoned in this connection. Therefore, it is not required that a usage of trade be "ancient or immemorial," "universal" or the like. . . . [F]ull recognition is thus available for new usages and for usages currently observed by the great majority of decent dealers, even though dissidents ready to cut corners do not agree.

Id., Comment 5. The Comment's demand that "not universality but only the described 'regularity of observance' " is required reinforces the provision only giv-

---

[82] [27] Written trade codes, however, are left to the court to interpret. Id.

ing "effect to usages of which the parties 'are or should be aware'. . . . " *Id.*, Comment 7. A "regularly observed" practice of protection, of which Shell "should have been aware," was enough to constitute a usage that Nanakuli had reason to believe was incorporated into the agreement.[83]

Nanakuli went beyond proof of a regular observance. It proved . . . that price protection was probably universal practice by suppliers to the asphaltic paving trade in 1969.[84] It had been practiced by H.C. & D. since at least 1962, by P.C. & A. since well before 1960, and by Chevron routinely for years, with the last specific instance before the contract being March, 1969, as shown by documentary evidence. The only usage evidence missing was the behavior by Shell, the only other asphalt supplier in Hawaii, prior to 1969. That was because its only major customer was Nanakuli and the judge ruled prior course of dealings between Shell and Nanakuli inadmissible. Shell did not point in rebuttal to one instance of failure to price protect by any supplier to an asphalt paver in Hawaii before its own 1974 refusal to price protect Nanakuli. Thus, there clearly was enough proof for a jury to find that the practice of price protection in the asphaltic paving trade existed in Hawaii in 1969 and was regular enough in its observance to rise to the level of a usage that would be binding on Nanakuli and Shell.

Shell next argues that, even if such a usage existed, its outlines were not precise enough to determine whether Shell would have extended the old price for Nanakuli for several months or would have charged the old price on the volume of tonnage committed at that price. The jury awarded Nanakuli damages based on the specific tonnage committed before the price increase of 1974. [The court considers Code Sections and Comments which eliminate the need to prove usages and related damages with "mathematical accuracy."] The manner in which the usage of price protection was carried out was presented with sufficient precision to allow the jury to calculate damages at $220,800.

VI. Waiver Or Course Of Performance

Course of performance under the Code is the action of the parties in carrying out the contract at issue, whereas course of dealing consists of relations between the parties *prior* to signing that contract. Evidence of the latter was excluded by the District Judge; evidence of the former consisted of Shell's price protection of Nanakuli in 1970 and 1971. Shell protested that the jury could not have found that those two instances of price protection amounted to a course of performance of its 1969 contract, relying on two Code comments. First, one instance does not constitute a course of performance. "A single occasion of conduct does not fall within the language of this section. . . ." Haw. Rev. Stat. § 490:2-208, Comment 4. Although the Comment rules out one instance, it does not further delineate

---

[83] [28] White and Summers write that Code requirements for proving a usage are "far less stringent" than the old ones for custom. "A usage of trade need not be *well known*, let alone 'universal.'" It only needs to be regular enough that the parties expect it to be observed. White & Summers, supra § 3-3 at 87 (emphasis supplied). "Note particularly [in §§ 1-205(1) & (2)] that it is not necessary for both parties to be consciously aware of the trade usage. It is enough if the trade usage is such as to 'justify an expectation' of its observance." Id. at 84.

[84] [30] All evidence was that trade usage continued to be universally practiced after 1969, even by Shell.

how many acts are needed to form a course of performance. The prior occasions here were only two, but they constituted the only occasions before 1974 that would call for such conduct. [The court discusses another occasion Shell seemed in discussions to have recognized Nanakuli's right to price protection.]

Shell's second defense is that the Comment expresses a preference for an interpretation of waiver.

> 3. Where it is difficult to determine whether a particular act merely sheds light on the meaning of the agreement or represents a waiver of a term of the agreement, the preference is in favor of "waiver" whenever such construction, plus the application of the provisions on the reinstatement of rights waived . . . , is needed to preserve the flexible character of commercial contracts and to prevent surprise or other hardship.

Id., Comment 3. The preference for waiver only applies, however, where acts are ambiguous. It was within the province of the jury to determine whether those acts were ambiguous, and if not, whether they constituted waivers or a course of performance of the contract. The jury's interpretation of those acts as a course of performance was bolstered by evidence offered by Shell that it again price protected Nanakuli on the only two occasions of post-1974 price increases, in 1977 and 1978.

VII. Express Terms As Reasonably Consistent With Usage In Course of Performance

Perhaps one of the most fundamental departures of the Code from prior contract law is found in the parol evidence rule and the definition of an agreement between two parties. Under the UCC, an agreement goes beyond the written words on a piece of paper. " 'Agreement' means the bargain of the parties in fact as found in their language or by implication from other circumstances including course of dealing or usage of trade or course of performance as provided in this chapter (§§ 490:1-205 and 490:2-208)." *Id.* § 490:1-201(3). Express terms, then, do not constitute the entire agreement, which must be sought also in evidence of usages, dealings, and performance of the contract itself. The purpose of evidence of usages, which are defined in the previous section, is to help to understand the entire agreement.

> [Usages are] a factor in reaching the commercial meaning of the agreement which the parties have made. The language used is to be interpreted as meaning what it may fairly be expected to mean to parties involved in the particular commercial transaction in a given locality or in a given vocation or trade. . . . Part of the agreement of the parties . . . is to be sought for in the usages of trade which furnish the background and give particular meaning to the language used, and are the framework of common understanding controlling any general rules of law which hold only when there is no such understanding.

Id. § 490:1-205, Comment 4. Course of dealings is more important than usages of the trade, being specific usages between the two parties to the contract. "[C]ourse of dealing controls usage of trade." *Id.* § 490:1-205(4). It "is a sequence of previous conduct between the parties to a particular transaction which is fairly to be regarded as establishing a common basis of understanding for interpreting their expressions and other conduct." *Id.* § 490:1-205(1). Much of the evidence of prior dealings between Shell and Nanakuli in negotiating the 1963 contract and in carrying out similar earlier contracts was excluded by the court.

A commercial agreement, then, is broader than the written paper and its meaning is to be determined not just by the language used by them in the written contract but "by their action, read and interpreted in the light of commercial practices and other surrounding circumstances. The measure and background for interpretation are set by the commercial context, which may explain and supplement even the language of a formal or final writing." *Id.*, Comment 1. Performance, usages, and prior dealings are important enough to be admitted always, even for a final and complete agreement; only if they cannot be reasonably reconciled with the express terms of the contract are they not binding on the parties. "The express terms of an agreement and an applicable course of dealing or usage of trade shall be construed wherever reasonable as consistent with each other; but when such construction is unreasonable express terms control both course of dealing and usage of trade and course of dealing controls usage of trade." *Id.* § 490:1-205(4).

Of these three, then, the most important evidence of the agreement of the parties is their actual performance of the contract. *Id.* The operative definition of course of performance is as follows: "Where the contract for sale involves repeated occasions for performance by either party with knowledge of the nature of the performance and opportunity for objection to it by the other, any course of performance accepted or acquiesced in without objection shall be relevant to determine the meaning of the agreement." *Id.* § 490:2-208(1). "Course of dealing . . . is restricted, literally, to a sequence of conduct between the parties previous to the agreement. However, the provisions of the Act on course of performance make it clear that a sequence of conduct after or under the agreement may have equivalent meaning (§ 2-208)." *Id.* § 490:1-205, Comment 2. The importance of evidence of course of performance is explained: "The parties themselves know best what they have meant by their words of agreement and their action under that agreement is the best indication of what that meaning was. This section thus rounds out the set of factors which determines the meaning of the 'agreement'. . . . " *Id.* § 490:2-208, Comment 1. "Under this section a course of performance is always relevant to determine the meaning of the agreement." *Id.*, Comment 2.

Our study of the Code provisions and Comments, then, form the first basis of our holding that a trade usage to price protect pavers at times of price increases for work committed on nonescalating contracts could reasonably be construed as consistent with an express term of seller's posted price at delivery. Since the agreement of the parties is broader than the express terms and includes usages, which may even add terms to the agreement, and since the commercial background provided by those usages is vital to an understanding of the agreement, we follow the Code's mandate to proceed on the assumption that the parties have included those usages unless they cannot reasonably be construed as consistent with the express terms.

Federal courts usually have been lenient in not ruling out consistent additional terms or trade usage for apparent inconsistency with express terms. . . .

Numerous state courts have interpreted their own state's versions of the Code in line with the weight of federal authority on the UCC to admit freely evidence of additional terms, usages, and prior dealings and harmonize them in most instances with apparently contradictory express terms. The only Hawaiian case on the subject dealt with the parol evidence rule in dicta. . . .

Some guidelines can be offered as to how usage evidence can be allowed to modify a contract.[85] First, the court must allow a check on usage evidence by demanding that it be sufficiently definite and widespread to prevent unilateral post-hoc revision of contract terms by one party. The Code's intent is to put usage evidence on an objective basis. J. H. Levie, "Trade Usage and Custom Under the Common Law and the Uniform Commercial Code", 40 N.Y.U.L.Rev. 1101 (1965), states:

> When trade usage adds new terms to cover matters on which the agreement is silent the court is really making a contract for the parties, even though it says it only consulted trade usage to find the parties' probable intent. There is nothing wrong or even unusual about this practice, which really is no different from reading constructive conditions into a contract. Nevertheless the court does create new obligations, and perhaps that is why the courts often say that usage . . . must be proved by clear and convincing evidence. . . .

Id. at 1102. Although the Code abandoned the traditional common law test of nonconsensual custom and views usage as a way of determining the parties' probable intent, *id.* at 1106-07, thus abolishing the requirement that common law custom be universally practiced, trade usages still must be well settled, *id.* at 1113. . . .

Evidence of a trade usage does not need to be protected against perjury because, as one commentator has written, "an outside standard does exist to help judge the truth of the assertion that the parties intended the usage to control the

---

[85] [44] White and Summers write that usage and dealings evidence "may not only supplement or qualify express terms, but in appropriate circumstances may even override express terms." White & Summers, supra, § 3-3 at 84. "[T]he provision that express terms control inconsistent course of dealing and [usages and performance evidence] really cannot be taken at face value." Id. at 86. That reading, although at odds with the actual wording of the Code, is a realistic reading of what some of the cases allow. A better formulation of the Code's mandate is offered by R. W. Kirst, Usage of Trade and Course of Dealing: Subversion of the UCC Theory, 1977 Law Forum 811:

> The need to determine whether the parties intended a usage . . . to be part of the contract does not end if the court finds that the commercial practice is inconsistent with or contradicts the express language of the writing. If an inconsistency exists, the intention of the parties remains unclear. The parties may have intended either to include or exclude the practice. Determining the intent of the parties requires that the court attempt to construe the written term consistently with the commercial practice, if that is reasonable. If consistent construction is unreasonable the Code directs that the written term be taken as expressing the parties' intent. Before concluding that a jury could not reasonably find a consistent construction, the judge must understand the commercial background of the dispute.

Id. at 824.

particular dispute: the existence and scope of the usage can be determined from other members of the trade." Kirst, *supra*, at 839. *Kirst* sets out guards on jury determination of usage evidence:

> Questions of the parties' intentions concerning an asserted trade usage or course of dealing will not always require a jury determination. If the evidence fails to show a practice is regularly observed, the judge can exclude the evidence because it does not show a course of dealing or usage of trade as defined in the Code. If the members of the trade confirm an actual usage but do not support the assertion that the usage applies to the particular facts in litigation, the judge will exclude evidence of the usage as irrelevant. If the parties used new and different language to convey their agreed intention to abandon the past practice, the court will recognize that practice under the old language is irrelevant to the contract containing the new language and, consequently, will exclude the evidence.

> . . . .

Here the evidence was overwhelming that all suppliers to the asphaltic paving trade price protected customers under the same types of circumstances. Chevron's contract with H.B. was a similar long-term supply contract between a buyer and seller with very close relations, on a form supplied by the seller, covering sales of asphalt, and setting the price at seller's posted price, with no mention of price protection. The same commentator offers a second guideline:

> Because the stock printed forms cannot always reflect the changing methods of business, members of the trade may do business with a standard clause in the forms that they ignore in practice. If the trade consistently ignores obsolete clauses at variance with actual trade practices, a litigant can maintain that it is reasonable that the courts also ignore the clauses. Similarly, members of a trade may handle a particular subset of commercial transactions in a manner consistent with written terms because the writing cannot provide for all variations or contingencies. Thus, if the trade regards an express term and a trade usage as consistent because the usage is not a complete contradiction but only an occasional but definite exception to a written term, the courts should interpret the contract according to the usage.

Kirst, *supra*, at 824. Levie, *supra*, at 1112, writes, "Astonishing as it will seem to most practicing attorneys, under the Code it will be possible in some cases to use custom to contradict the written agreement. . . . Therefore usage may be used to 'qualify' the agreement, which presumably means to 'cut down' express terms although not to negate them entirely." Here, the express price term was "Shell's Posted Price at time of delivery." A total negation of that term would be that the buyer was to set the price. It is a less than complete negation of the term that an unstated exception exists at times of price increases, at which times the old price is to be charged, for a certain period or for a specified tonnage, on work already committed at the lower price on nonescalating contracts. Such a usage forms a broad and important exception to the express term, but does not swallow it entirely. Therefore, we hold that, under these particular facts, a reasonable jury could have found that price protection was incorporated into the 1969 agreement between Nanakuli and Shell and that price protection was reasonably consistent with the express term of seller's posted price at delivery.

VIII. Good Faith In Setting Price

Nanakuli offers an alternative theory why Shell should have offered price protection at the time of the price increases of 1974. Even if price protection was not a term of the agreement, Shell could not have exercised good faith in carrying out its 1969 contract with Nanakuli when it raised its price by $32 effective January 1 in a letter written December 31st and only received on January 4, given the universal practice of advance notice of such an increase in the asphaltic paving trade. The Code provides, "A price to be fixed by the seller or by the buyer means a price for him to fix in good faith," Haw. Rev. Stat. § 490:2-305(2). For a merchant good faith means "the observance of reasonable commercial standards of fair dealing in the trade." *Id.* 490:2-103(1)(b). The comment to § 2-305 explains, "[I]n the normal case a 'posted price' . . . satisfies the good faith requirement." *Id.*, Comment 3. However, the words "in the normal case" mean that, although a posted price will usually be satisfactory, it will not be so under all circumstances. In addition, the dispute here was not over the amount of the increase—that is, the price that the seller fixed—but over the manner in which that increase was put into effect. It is true that Shell, in order to observe the good faith standards of the trade in 1974, was not bound by the practices of aggregate companies, which did not labor under the same disabilities as did asphalt suppliers in 1974. However, Nanakuli presented evidence that Chevron, in raising its price to $76, gave at least six weeks' advance notice, in accord with the long-time usage of the asphaltic paving trade. Shell, on the other hand, gave absolutely no notice, from which the jury could have concluded that Shell's manner of carrying out the price increase of 1974 did not conform to commercially reasonable standards. In both the timing of the announcement and its refusal to protect work already bid at the old price, Shell could be found to have breached the obligation of good faith imposed by the Code on all merchants. "Every contract or duty within this chapter imposes an obligation of good faith in its performance or enforcement," *id.* § 490:1-203, which for merchants entails the observance of commercially reasonable standards of fair dealing in the trade. The Comment to § 1-203 reads:

> This section sets forth a basic principle running throughout this Act. The principle involved is that in commercial transactions good faith is required in the performance and enforcement of all agreements or duties. Particular applications of this general principle appear in specific provisions of the Act. . . . It is further implemented by § 1-205 on course of dealing and usage of trade.

Id. § 490:1-203, Comment. Chevron's conduct in 1974 offered enough relevant evidence of commercially reasonable standards of fair dealing in the asphalt trade in Hawaii in 1974 for the jury to find that Shell's failure to give sufficient advance notice and price protect Nanakuli after the imposition of the new price did not conform to good faith dealings in Hawaii at that time.

Because the jury could have found for Nanakuli on its price protection claim under either theory, we reverse the judgment of the District Court and reinstate the jury verdict for Nanakuli in the amount of $220,800, plus interest according to law.

Reversed and remanded with directions to enter final judgment.

[Special concurrence by Judge Kennedy omitted]

NOTES AND QUESTIONS

1. *Expectations vs. bureaucratic control*: Once again the person in the field made a deal with a customer. As often is true, their deal was inconsistent with the "legislation" of the organization, as announced in its printed form contracts. The people in Shell's home office knew little about what was going on in Hawaii. Shell's managers in corporate headquarters wanted to control agents in the field. Their lawyers fashioned lengthy documents protecting Shell's interest, warding off liability, and claiming maximum flexibility.

At the same time, Shell's agents in the field dealt with their own problems. They worked in specific business contexts influenced by the competitive situation. They did not go by the book. They created expectations inconsistent with the literal language of Shell's standard form contracts.

Should courts honor the "real deal" or the "paper deal?" A strict parol evidence rule helps officials of large corporate bureaucracies. They rely on what they find in their files. The court's approach in the *Nanakuli* case places real burdens on the home office. They cannot know for sure what their agents have said and done. Nonetheless, Nanakuli's people were likely to be less cautious about reading and understanding written documents than people in more distant relationships. Nanakuli and Shell were not in an arms-length relationship. They were quasi-partners, and officials of Nanakuli and Shell's local representative worked together for mutual benefit for a long time. In short, we are suggesting that the case reflects far more than a technical construction of the provisions of the Uniform Commercial Code. The court looked to the relationship rather than to the abstractions of formal contract law.[86]

2. *Price protection in the asphalt trade*: The *Nanakuli* case isn't the only dispute arising out of the custom of price protecting distributors of asphalt. When OPEC caused petroleum prices to rise drastically in the early 1970s, the United States government regulated prices charged by major oil companies. Asphalt, however, was largely unregulated. Thus, the oil companies could make up on asphalt pricing some of what they lost under the regulations controlling other petroleum products. When the major oil companies withdrew price protection,

---

[86] For discussions of the problems raised by the *Nanakuli* case, see Kastely, *Stock Equipment for the Bargain in Fact: Trade Usage, "Express Terms," and Consistency Under Section 1-205 of the Uniform Commercial Code*, 64 N.C. L. Rev. 777 (1986); Goetz and Scott, *The Limits of Expanded Choice: An Analysis of the Interactions Between Express and Implied Contract Terms*, 73 Cal. L. Rev. 261 (1985); Hadjiyannakis, *The Parol Evidence Rule and Implied Terms: The Sounds of Silence*, 54 Fordham L. Rev. 35 (1985).

their distributors suffered losses on bids outstanding which they had calculated at the old prices. Some of the distributors sued.[87]

3. *CISG and parol evidence*: A court applying the Convention on Contracts for the International Sale of Goods will have the authority to consider extrinsic evidence which contradicts the "paper deal"; the Convention contains no parol evidence rule. There would be no need to struggle, as the court seemed to in *Nanakuli*, to justify consideration of evidence which it regarded as relevant and probative. In Article 8(3) the Convention states that "[i]n determining the intent of a party . . . due consideration is to be given to all relevant circumstances of the case including the negotiations, any practices which the parties have established between themselves, usages and any subsequent conduct of the parties."

a. Merger and "No Representations" Clauses

ANDERSON v. TRI-STATE HOME IMPROVEMENT CO.
Supreme Court of Wisconsin
268 Wis. 455, 67 N.W.2d 853 (1955)

[Plaintiffs, the Andersons, were husband and wife. He was a machinist with thirty years' experience. She had no business experience. Spector, the president of Tri-State, called on the Andersons. He persuaded them to sign a contract calling for the installation of Perma-loy siding on their home. The jury found that Spector told the Andersons that Tri-State guaranteed the siding against chipping, cracking, rusting, or peeling for at least thirty years. He said that the siding had been tested under all climatic conditions in their area, and the paint on the siding was not affected by snow, ice, or salt water. These statements were false, which Spector did not know but should have known. He made the statements recklessly, having no knowledge about testing. The written contract did not mention a thirty-year guarantee nor did it contain statements about testing and the impact of snow, ice or salt water. The writing did contain a "no representations" clause.]

CURRIE, J. The contract entered into between plaintiffs and defendant company under date of April 6, 1950, contained the following clause:

"The company prohibits the making of any promises, or representations, unless it is inserted in writing in this agreement before signing. . . ."

---

[87] In W.H. Barber Co. v. McNamara-Vivant Contracting Co., Inc., 293 N.W.2d 351 (Minn. 1979), a jury found that supplier's representatives had promised price protection. The Supreme Court of Minnesota affirmed the judgment for the supplier, ruling that there was no writing adequate to show the quantities of asphalt to be supplied, and the contractor did not establish that the supplier was estopped to assert the statute of frauds.

In Lige Dickson Co. v. Union Oil Co. of Calif., 96 Wash. 2d 291, 635 P.2d 103 (1981), the Supreme Court of Washington made a similar ruling. Although a Union Oil official had conceded that "there was an unwritten custom in the liquid asphalt business in the Tacoma area, well known and acted upon by suppliers and users, that any increase in price of liquid asphalt would not be applicable to manufacturers' then-existing contracts," nonetheless, the court said that "we cannot help but foresee increased litigation and confusion as being the necessary result of the eroding of the UCC" if promissory estoppel is held to override § 2-201.

The first question which faces us on this appeal is whether such clause is effective to bar plaintiffs' cause of action grounded upon the alleged false representations of defendant's president and agent which induced the plaintiffs to enter into the contract. . . . [W]e conclude that it is not.

An excellent statement of the policy reasons which have caused courts to refuse to construe so-called "integration" clauses, and contract clauses attempting to bar liability for false representations, as being effective to bar causes of action based upon fraudulent representations inducing a contract, is set forth in *Bates v. Southgate* (1941), 308 Mass. 170, 182, 31 N.E.2d 551, 558, as follows:

> As a matter of principle it is necessary to weigh the advantages of certainty in contractual relations against the harm and injustice that result from fraud. In obedience to the demands of a larger public policy the law long ago abandoned the position that a contract must be held sacred regardless of the fraud of one of the parties in procuring it. No one advocates a return to outworn conceptions. The same public policy that in general sanctions the avoidance of a promise obtained by deceit strikes down all attempts to circumvent that policy by means of contractual devices. In the realm of fact it is entirely possible for a party knowingly to agree that no representations have been made to him, while at the same time believing and relying upon representations which in fact have been made and in fact are false but for which he would not have made the agreement. To deny this possibility is to ignore the frequent instances in everyday experience where parties accept, often without critical examination, and act upon agreements containing somewhere within their four corners exculpatory clauses in one form or another, but where they do so, nevertheless, in reliance upon the honesty of supposed friends, the plausible and disarming statements of salesmen, or the customary course of business. To refuse relief would result in opening the door to a multitude of frauds and in thwarting the general policy of the law.

1 Restatement, Agency, p. 579, § 260, states in effect that a principal, by inserting in a contract that he is not liable for the representations of his agent, may relieve himself from liability in an action for deceit to recover damages for the agent's fraudulent representations inducing the execution of the contract, but cannot by such a clause bar the other party's cause of action for rescission. However, 3 Williston, Contracts (rev. ed.), p. 2283, § 811A, points out that such rule, insofar as it relates to the barring of an action of damages for deceit, is not applicable where the fraud is attributable to the principal. In the case at bar, the defendant did not contend that Spector, its president, was not authorized to make the false representations claimed by the plaintiffs, but denied that any such representations were made by him. It seems to us that, where a corporation clothes its president with authority to execute a contract on its behalf, it is in no position to contend that such president was without authority to make representations of fact for the purpose of inducing the execution of the contract.

It appears that the authorities are divided on the question of whether an action to recover damages for deceit can be maintained against a principal for fraudulent representations of an agent, which induced the entering into of the contract, where the contract contains a clause negativing the existence of any representations not incorporated in the contract. Anno. 127 A. L. R. 132, 143 *et seq.* In a recent case the Iowa supreme court held that such an action could be maintained against the principal. *Hall v. Crow* (1948), 240 Iowa 81, 34 N.W.2d 195. We, however, find it unnecessary here to pass upon the issue of whether an honest principal by proper contract provision cannot protect himself from liability to respond in damages in an action at law for fraud grounded upon the unauthorized fraudulent representations of his agent.

[After a brief discussion of whether the jury's finding was supported by adequate evidence, the court turned to the question of whether a false promise can stand as the premise for a fraud claim.]

[D]efendant contends that the [false representation] constitutes merely an unfulfilled promise as to future events and, therefore, no liability can be grounded thereon. . . .

> The principal contention made here by the plaintiff is that he has sustained damages in reliance upon the promissory misrepresentations made by the defendants. It is a well-established rule of law that fraud must relate to a present or pre-existing fact, and it cannot ordinarily be predicated on unfulfilled promises or statements made as to future events. . . . [*Beers v. Atlas Assurance Co.* 215 Wis. 165, 171, 253 NW 584, 687 (1934).]

. . .

[T]his court in *Alropa Corp. v. Flatley* (1938), 226 Wis. 561, 565, 277 NW 108, 110, adopted the position contended for by Mr. Justice Fairchild . . . [in a concurring opinion in *Beers*] recognizing . . . an exception to the general rule, that an unfulfilled promise to perform a future act cannot be the basis of an action for deceit, and declared:

> To amount to a fraud upon the purchaser the representations must relate to present or pre-existing facts, and it cannot ordinarily be predicated on unfulfilled promises or statements made as to future events. *Beers v. Atlas Assurance.* . . . One of the exceptions to this rule is that *when promises are made upon which the purchaser has a right to rely, and at the time of making them the promisor has a present intent not to perform them, the promises may amount to fraudulent representations and liability result.* (Emphasis supplied.)

. . .

Furthermore, we believe a reasonable construction of the representation, that Spector and his company (the defendant) "*guaranteed the siding against chipping, cracking, rusting, or peeling for at least thirty years,*" to be that the defendant had a policy of so guaranteeing all Perma-loy siding installed on buildings of its customers for thirty years. In other words, the representation had reference to the existence of a general business policy of defendant rather than to a promise which was restricted to the siding to be installed on plaintiffs' home. . . .

We conclude that, whether construed as an unfulfilled promise, which when made defendant had no intention of performing, or as a statement of an existing general business policy, the representation as to the guaranty is sufficient upon which to ground plaintiffs' cause of action for fraud and deceit. . . .

NOTES AND QUESTIONS

1. *Merger clauses and warranty theory*: Suppose that the *Anderson* case had been tried as a breach of an express warranty under UCC § 2-313. Do you see any problems in bringing the case under that section? What would have been the effect of the merger or integration clause in the seller's form contract? *See* UCC § 2-316(1) and Comment 2, § 2-721, § 1-103.

2. *Merger clauses and the parol evidence rule*: A merger clause states that the parties agree that the written document is the final and complete expression of their agreement. If, in fact, the parties agreed that a written document should have this effect, the clause makes their choice clear, and insertion of the clause may serve to protect one, or the other, or both parties. Problems arise when a merger clause does not express the parties' bargain in fact but reflects the drafting skill, craft or even trickery of the lawyer for the more sophisticated party. Do even fairly experienced businesspeople realize that these clauses purport to cancel the legal effect of all a salesperson's representations and promises? Or is it the case that lawyers who insert such clauses in sales contracts to be used in transactions with unsophisticated consumers are structuring fraud? Is it ethically permissible for a lawyer to use his or her training to trick the unsuspecting? Or are lawyers entitled to assume that their clients are ethical people and will use the rights granted by form contracts only to ward off unjustified claims by those who want something for nothing? It could be argued that clients who use clauses hidden in form contracts to injure their customers will be disciplined by the market. Moreover, some would assert that lawyers are hired to implement their clients' not-unlawful wishes, and not to pass moral judgment on them. Lawyers, under this view, are expected to protect their clients by drafting such clauses, not to protect the interests of non-clients. What do you think? How would you respond if asked to draft a potentially crucial provision for a form contract, and were told to "make it as inconspicuous as the law will allow"?

3. *Using contract terms to limit responsibility for the actions of an agent*: To what extent can a company use language in form contracts to immunize itself from liability for responsibility for statements made by its sales force? This is a major problem both for buyers and sellers, as well as for the courts that are confronted with their disputes. First, if contract law seeks to hold people for the expectations they intentionally or negligently create, we need to consider the extent to which the clauses in form contracts serve as meaningful warnings to customers to discount advertising, the seller's reputation, and the "seller's talk" of salespeople and sales engineers. This would seem to be an empirical question. Next, with the answer to that question in hand, we could try to assess the advantages and disadvantages of the consequences we would bring about by enforcing the clauses.

We need to consider these consequences not only from the point of view of those whose potential claims are limited by the form provisions, but from the point of view of those seeking immunity as well. It is important to understand that salespeople deal with potential customers outside the direct supervision and control of the top officials of a corporation. The salespeople have incentives to oversell the product, and this is hard to control. The problem sometimes arises not because of what a salesperson literally said, but because of the impression they created, in combination with the assumptions made by the customers; a customer may be severely disappointed with a product which literally complies with the express promises made about it. Customers may lie about what salespeople said, or shade the truth either deliberately or innocently. In addition, juries may be more sympathetic with retailers or other small businesses than with the Fortune 500 companies that manufacture the products. If we give effect to the liability-denying provisions in form contracts, we may do an injustice to those who have innocently and in good faith relied on the impressions created by the sales force, and we may allow some companies to make sales by painting a rosy picture of their products' capacities, while avoiding the responsibility of living up to the promises implicit in the picture. On the other hand, if we deny to corporations the ability to use this tool, we weaken their control over their sales force, and permit victories by those who can convince a jury that promises were made that really weren't, or enforcement of promises that reasonable buyers should have realized were beyond the authority of the agent to make.

A brief look at some of the litigation involving Burroughs Corp. may serve to make the abstract problem described in the foregoing paragraph more concrete. In the 1960s and 70s Burroughs was a profitable company selling, among other things, computers and installed software to small commercial users.[88] Many of its customers became dissatisfied, and they filed at least 190 cases against Burroughs. Although Burroughs emphasized that this represented only a small fraction of its installed base of users, and that other computer equipment companies had suffered similar problems leading to litigation, no other company faced as many cases as Burroughs did. Burroughs blamed the customers for inexperience in using computers, for neglecting to send operators to Burroughs's training sessions, and for having unrealistic expectations. The customers charged that Burroughs oversold its computers, put products on the market before they were developed properly, and either encouraged or allowed its sales force to misrepresent what the machines could do. Though there is no doubt a fair amount of truth in both sides of the story, a computer consultant said, "Burroughs has a long and colorful history of announcing machines before they are fully developed, shipping them without software, and having hardware breakdowns in the user's shop." Some Burroughs salespeople testified for plaintiffs, and suggested that they only said what they were instructed to say in the sales meeting.

Some of the other computer suppliers adopted a strategy of settling disputes with customers. Burroughs was more litigious. The chief weapon in its defensive strategy was the standard form contract which it required its customers to sign. The terms of the contract were described in *Badger Bearing Co. v. Burroughs Corp.*[89] A provision on the front page of the contract provided that there was a three-month warranty, governed by the terms on the reverse side of the form. On

---

[88] In 1986, Burroughs merged with Sperry to form Unisys Corporation.
[89] 444 F. Supp. 919 (E.D. Wis. 1977), *aff'd without opinion*, 588 F.2d 838 (7th Cir. 1978).

the reverse side were two clauses; the first was a limitation of remedy clause, and the second a merger clause:

> Seller . . . shall not be held responsible . . . in any event under this agreement for more than a refund of the purchase price, less reasonable rental for past use, upon return of the equipment to Seller with Seller's prior written consent. (Purchaser hereby expressly waives all incidental and consequential damages.)
>
> **There are no understandings, agreements, representations, or warranties, express or implied (including any regarding merchantability or fitness for a particular purpose), not specified herein, respecting this contract or equipment hereunder. This contract states the entire obligation of seller in connection with this transaction.**[90]

The express warranty offered by Burroughs was relatively narrow. In addition, the provisions were in many cases accompanied by a provision which cut the time for filing claims from the four or six years provided by most state statutes to just two years. Burroughs sometimes brought cross-actions against its customers, and some lawyers accused Burroughs of delaying the progress of litigation by extensive (and allegedly unnecessary) use of pre-trial procedures.

Burroughs won some, and it lost some. In the *Badger Bearing* case, in which the customer had experienced 76 service calls in 2 ½ years on a $62,590 computer, Judge Gordon, the trial judge found that any warranties which might have been breached had been successfully disclaimed, and that Badger had not established that any material misrepresentations had been made. Although the outcome represented a victory for Burroughs, Judge Gordon did find that the sales agreement was not intended as a final expression of the contract, and so allowed Badger to try to prove the existence of terms which contradicted the sales form. Unfortunately for Badger, he then concluded that the plaintiff had failed to prove that the disclaimer language had been "negotiated out" of the contract. As a result the disclaimers stood. Judge Gordon also ruled that the contractual disclaimers could not be used to prevent Badger from proceeding on the tort theories of negligent misrepresentation or strict responsibility for misrepresentation. Again, it was just that Badger failed to prove those claims. And so in *Badger Bearing* the effort to use the parol evidence clause or merger clause proved ineffective, as it did for similar reasons in *Sierra Diesel Injection Service, Inc. v. Burroughs Corp.*[91] An Arizona court, however, found that "since the contract specifically negated the alleged misrepresentations, Kalil's [plaintiff] claims for negligent misrepresentation, fraud and consumer fraud, based upon statements made prior to the signing of the contract were not actionable because of the parol evidence rule."[92] The Fifth Circuit seemed to follow the same approach in *Earman Oil Co. v. Burroughs Corp.*[93] Other cases, which turned on other factors and other UCC sections, met with similarly mixed success for Burroughs.

---

[90] *Id.* at 920-21.
[91] 874 F.2d 653 (9th Cir. 1989).
[92] Kalil Bottling Co. v. Burroughs Corp., 127 Ariz. 278, 619 P.2d 1055 (Ariz. Ct. App. 1980).
[93] 625 F.2d 1292 (5th Cir. 1980).

(Parenthetically, what can we learn from the fact that different courts, faced with the same contractual language, seemed to come to different conclusions as to its legal effect? How big a problem is the inconsistency? If it is a big problem, what can be done about it? Is the existence of the inconsistency an indictment of the ability of the legal system to live up to its goal of objectivity and uniformity?)

To return to the Burroughs cases themselves, they could be described in at least two different ways. Some might suggest that they represent a situation in which a major company attempted to use its superior market power to abuse its customers, who were not in a position to evaluate the company's promises. The fact that the provisions were available to customers does not mean that the customers assented to them in any meaningful way, especially since they were inconsistent with all of the other signals being sent by the seller. If that is your view, you would probably be disappointed in those courts which seemed to permit Burroughs to use its forms and technical Code sections to escape justice.

On the other hand, some would paint a more benign picture. They would argue that if one wants companies like Burroughs to bring new and innovative products to market, they must be able to free themselves from the burden of claims for consequential damages or compensation for the misrepresentations of sales people. In the long, and even medium, term they would assert that we can rely on the desire to protect commercial reputation to prompt most companies to fix defective machines, or give refunds. Companies that fail to offer good products on fair terms will wither and disappear. In time, the market will correct the situation. In a sense, the relationship between Burroughs and its customers could be seen as a kind of partnership. By trial and error both producer and customer attempt to get a new product to operate properly, sharing the rewards and risks. If we impose liability, we can expect to increase the cost to everyone of spreading the benefits of computers. Much of any damages award will be siphoned off to pay lawyers' fees and litigation costs. In the long run, this argument concludes, enforcing merger clauses and disclaimers is in the best interest of most people in society, even though in the short run firms like Badger Bearing must pay a price.

Do you find either argument convincing? Can you offer others? Strike the balance?

4. *Disclaiming the fraud of your employees*: In the Burroughs cases, to give Burroughs the benefit of the doubt, we may have had a pattern of widespread corporate optimism, unwarranted by the operating characteristics of the computers. Sometimes, however, sellers make knowing misrepresentations. In *City Dodge, Inc. v. Gardner*,[94] the jury found that the seller's salesman had knowingly misrepresented that a used car sold to the buyer had never been wrecked and repaired. The buyer signed a sales agreement which stated, "no other agreement, promise or understanding of any kind pertaining to this purchase will be recognized." In addition, the sales agreement stated that the car was sold "as is." The buyer sued for fraud and deceit, and won a verdict which was affirmed on appeal.

The Supreme Court of Georgia found that UCC § 2-202 was inapplicable to misrepresentation actions. Some earlier Georgia cases had found a disclaimer in a

---

[94] 232 Ga. 766, 208 S.E.2d 794 (1974).

written contract defeated a fraud action because it prevented a buyer from justifiably relying on a misrepresentation. However, in the *City Dodge* case, the Georgia Supreme Court rejected this view, explaining that "[i]t is inconsistent to apply a disclaimer provision of a contract in a tort action brought to determine whether the entire contract is invalid because of alleged prior fraud which induced the execution of the contract. If the contract is invalid because of the antecedent fraud, then the disclaimer provision therein is ineffectual since, in legal contemplation, there is no contract between the parties. In this case, . . . [a]s the antecedent fraud was proven to the satisfaction of the jury, it vitiated the contract."[95] ("Vitiate" means "to contaminate; spoil; corrupt; pollute; debase; pervert; or render ineffective.")

Suppose Salesman knowingly made a false representation that a used car had never been wrecked and repaired and then negotiated a price with Buyer. A form contract with the same provisions as found in the *City Dodge* case was filled out by Salesman. Then the Owner of the dealership talked with Buyer, telling him that "salesmen say a lot of things and buyers hear what they want to hear. You understand that I am selling this car 'as is,' and as this written contract says, I cannot be responsible for whatever Salesman said or you think he said about this car." Buyer said, "understood," and signed the written sales agreement. Under the reasoning of the *City Dodge* case, would Buyer be able to sue the dealership for misrepresentation despite the disclaimer and merger clause in the document? Should Buyer be able to sue even when the Owner gave him such a warning? Would Buyer be able to sue for misrepresentation in such a case under the rule in the *Anderson* decision?

5. *Conspicuousness of merger clauses*: In *Seibel v. Layne & Bowler, Inc.*,[96] there was a "merger clause" in a printed form contract, purporting to bar the buyer from showing representations and warranties not stated in the writing. The court found the merger clause to be inconspicuous. As a result, it said, the parol evidence rule did not prevent the buyer from offering testimony about oral warranties. Is there any requirement of conspicuousness in UCC § 2-202? Such a requirement is stated, of course, in § 2-316(2) for an effective disclaimer in writing of the implied warranty of merchantability and for any disclaimer of the implied warranty of fitness for particular purpose. Can we argue with any chance of success that § 2-202 speaks of a writing "intended by the parties as a final expression of their agreement." UCC § 1-201(3) defines "agreement" as "the bargain of the parties in fact as found in their language or by implication from other circumstances. . . ." If a merger clause in a printed form contract is not conspicuous, then this is evidence that this part of the writing is not "intended by the parties as a final expression of their agreement." Notice that the phrase from the Code is stated in the plural and not singular. It is not enough that the clause is intended by its drafter as a final expression of the deal.

Suppose a merger clause were found to be conspicuous under the tests in § 1-201(10). Would it necessarily then be effective? And what is the authority, in states other than Oregon, of the *Seibel* case? Can it be ignored safely elsewhere?

---

[95] *Id.* at 770, 208 S.E.2d at 797-98.
[96] 56 Ore. App. 387, 641 P.2d 668 (1982).

b. Reformation and Parol Evidence

To what extent, if at all, can a party seeking to contradict a written contract *reform* the document and avoid the parol evidence rule? Classically, this could be done in a few limited situations. For example, suppose Vendor sells Purchaser the house at 123 Main Street. However, the typist made an error, and the written contract describes the house as located at 213 Main Street. Traditionally, courts of equity would reform legal instruments to cure such mistakes. Of course, when a court allows this mistake to be proved, it allows evidence that contradicts a writing that appears complete on its face. We can say that the parties did not intend the writing with the mistaken description to be the final and complete record of their bargain. However, we could say the same thing about the agreement to tear down the ice house in *Mitchill v. Lath.* Perhaps the willingness of courts to allow evidence of this kind of mistake rests on the absence of a jury in an equitable action. Perhaps it rests on the ease of proof in the usual situation—after all, the vendor usually owns the house at 123 Main and not the one at 213 Main.

How far can we go using reformation as a way around the parol evidence rule? If the party seeking to prove an oral agreement is willing to give up a jury, can she add prior agreements and contradict the language of the writing by casting the suit as one for reformation? Courts have been hesitant to attack the parol evidence rule this way, but the possibility remains.

JOHNSON v. GREEN BAY PACKERS
Supreme Court of Wisconsin
272 Wis. 149, 74 N.W.2d 784 (1956)

Action by the plaintiff Clyde Johnson against defendant the Green Bay Packers, Inc., for reformation of contract and to recover damages for breach of contract.

Plaintiff's complaint contained two causes of action stated in the alternative, the first of which prayed for reformation of the contract entered into between the parties on June 30, 1948, and for the recovery of damages by plaintiff for breach of the contract as so reformed; while the second cause of action prayed for recovery of damages by the plaintiff for breach of the contract as originally written without first being reformed. The answer interposed by the defendant . . . contained denials of most of the material allegations of plaintiff's complaint. The action was tried to the court without a jury. . . . A summary of the testimony and evidence adduced at the trial follows.

Johnson, a professional football player, had a contract with the Los Angeles Rams for the 1947 season. This was a "season" contract under which Johnson could not be released during the season at the option of the Rams. The contract also provided that the Rams had the right to renew the contract for the 1948 season. At the end of the 1947 season the Rams informed Johnson that they would employ him for the 1948 season, but not on the basis of a season contract. This was not satisfactory to Johnson and the parties failed to agree on terms. The Rams then traded Johnson to the defendant Packers.

About June first, Lambeau, in behalf of the defendant Packers contacted Johnson by phone and arranged an appointment. . . . At the first meeting between Mr. and Mrs. Johnson and Lambeau at the latter's home contract terms were discussed for the employment of Johnson by the Packers. Johnson testified that he insisted on a "season" contract like he had had with the Rams and that Lambeau agreed thereto. This Lambeau denied.

Later, Lambeau and Johnson met at the Hotel Roosevelt in Hollywood on or about June 30, 1948. Lambeau produced a printed form of contract in blank which was in triplicate (one for the player, one for the Packers, and one for the commissioner of the National Football League). Lambeau wrote in longhand the figure "$7,000" on the face of the contract. Johnson then brought up the fact that a "season" contract had been agreed on, whereupon Lambeau turned over the contract and wrote in longhand on the back:

$7,000 season 1948   Season
                           contracts
Minimum $7,000 1949   E. L. L.

Both Johnson and Lambeau signed the contract in triplicate and Lambeau retained all copies for the purpose of sending them in to the Packers to be typed and made to conform to the verbal understanding of the parties, after which one of the three would be returned to Johnson.

Johnson testified that at the time of these negotiations at the Hotel Roosevelt he asked Lambeau to strike out paragraph 6 on the printed forms of the contract, covering the power of the Packers to release the player, to which Lambeau replied that he would send the contracts in and have them "fixed" as agreed.

Several weeks later Johnson received his copy of the contract which bore the afore-mentioned notations in ink on the back made by Lambeau, but he noted that paragraph 6 had not been stricken. Such paragraph 6 reads as follows:

> The player represents and warrants that he is and will continue to be sufficiently highly skilled in all types of football team play to play professional football of the caliber required by the league and by the club, that he is and will continue to be in excellent physical condition, and agrees to perform his services hereunder to the complete satisfaction of the club and its head coach. (If in the opinion of the head coach the player does not maintain himself in excellent physical condition or fails at any time during the football seasons included in the term of this contract to demonstrate sufficient skill and capacity to play professional football of the caliber required by the league

```
and by the club, or if in the opinion of the head
coach the player's work or conduct in the per-
formance of this contract is unsatisfactory as
compared with the work and conduct of other mem-
bers of the club's squad of players, the club
shall have the right to terminate this contract
upon written notice to the player of such termi-
nation.)
```

As soon as Johnson received his copy, he called Lambeau and protested that the printed portion of the contract which gave the Packers the right to release Johnson during the season (paragraph 6) had not been stricken as agreed. Lambeau replied that Johnson should not worry, that the commissioner did not like the contracts to be cut up or have portions crossed out, that his (Lambeau's) word was as good as gold, and that Johnson had a two-year "season" contract. Johnson accepted this explanation by Lambeau, Johnson's testimony on this point being as follows:

> "Well, as closely as I can remember, I took him at his word, plus the notation on the back of the contract that it was a two-year seasonal."

Johnson later came to Green Bay, went into training, and played two exhibition games. On or about September 16, 1948, the defendant Packers then terminated Johnson's employment by written notice sent by mail, reading as follows:

Notice of Termination
Attention of Clyde Johnson

Dear Sir: *Date: September 16, 1948*

> *You are hereby notified that the Green Bay Packers, Inc., a member of the National Football League, pursuant to paragraph 6 of its contract with you dated June 30, 1948, hereby terminates said contract, effective immediately, for the reason[s] checked below:*
>
> ☐ *In the opinion of the head coach, you are not and have not maintained yourself in excellent physical condition.*
>
> ☒ *In the opinion of the head coach, you are failing and have failed to demonstrate sufficient skill and capacity to play professional football of the caliber required by the league and by the club.*
>
> ☒ *In the opinion of the head coach, your work and conduct in the performance of your contract is unsatisfactory as compared with the work and conduct of other members of the club's squad of players.*
>
> *Remarks:*
>
> *Club*
> *By /s/ E. L. Lambeau*

The only compensation Johnson received from the Packers was $100 travel money for the trip to Green Bay. Johnson played the remainder of the 1948 season with the Los Angeles Dons and his earnings from such source were $6,000. Early in the spring of 1949 Johnson wrote to the Packers and informed them that he was ready, willing, and able to play for them in 1949, but received no answer. The total amount of his earnings and income for the period of August through December, 1949, was $1,007.25. The answer of the defendant raises no issue that Johnson should have attempted to earn more during such period, or to take other action to mitigate damages.

Following the trial, the trial court made and filed a memorandum decision in which he determined that the plaintiff Johnson was entitled to have his contract of employment with the defendant for the football seasons of 1948 and 1949 reformed by striking out paragraph 6 thereof, and that Johnson should recover from the defendant the agreed compensation for said two seasons less his earnings from other sources. . . .

Judgment was . . . rendered . . . in favor of plaintiff and against the defendant. From such judgment the defendant has appealed.

CURRIE, J. The following issues are raised on this appeal:

(1) Whether reformation may be decreed to delete a provision in a contract, where such provision was left in the contract with the consent of the aggrieved party, even though such consent was obtained in reliance upon a contemporaneous oral promise which was not kept;

(2) Whether the judgment in behalf of Johnson can be affirmed on the ground set forth in plaintiff's second cause of action, *i.e.*, that the trial court should have enforced the contract as written giving effect to the written portion over the conflicting printed paragraph 6; . . .

[Issues 3 & 4 deleted.]

Without dispute, it appears from the facts found by the trial court that, when Johnson in the summer of 1948 received back his copy of the contract of employment, he at once discovered that paragraph 6 thereof had not been deleted as agreed between the parties, and that he immediately called the matter to Lambeau's attention. Lambeau then explained to Johnson that paragraph 6 had not been deleted because the league commissioner did not like contracts with parts crossed out, but assured Johnson that the original agreement for a "season" contract for the years 1948 and 1949 would be lived up to. Upon such verbal assurance from Lambeau, Johnson did not renew his request that paragraph 6 be deleted but entered into employment with such paragraph still in the contract.

In *Touchett v. E Z Paintr Corp.* (1953), 263 Wis. 626, 630, 58 N.W.2d 448, 59 N.W.2d 433, this court had before it a cause of action for reformation of contract, and in its opinion stated:

> There is a further rule of law that the court will not insert a provision in a contract which was omitted with the consent of the parties asking for reformation, although such consent was given in reliance on an oral promise of the other party that the omission would not make any difference.

We consider the above-quoted principle to be equally applicable to the facts in the instant case. The fact that here we are concerned with the failure to delete a clause necessary to conform the written contract to the prior verbal understanding of the parties, while in the *Touchett* case the written contract failed to include a paragraph covering a matter previously agreed upon by the parties in parol, we deem to be of no significance. In both situations the aggrieved party accepted the contract as written and entered into performance thereof upon the oral promise of the other party that the failure of the contract to read as agreed would not make any difference. We, therefore, conclude that it was error for the trial court to have decreed reformation of the contract by ordering the deletion of paragraph 6.

Counsel for Johnson urge that, even if the contract be not reformed so as to delete paragraph 6 thereof, the written provisions indorsed on the back of plaintiff's copy of the contract by Lambeau, being in direct conflict with the printed provisions of paragraph 6, must prevail over such printed provisions. In other words, it is urged that the trial court should have reached the same result by a proper interpretation of the contract as written. . . .

We deem that the point under consideration is ruled in plaintiff's favor by the case of *Tollefson v. Green Bay Packers, Inc.* (1950), 256 Wis. 318, 41 N.W.2d 201. Such case involved an action to recover damages for breach of contract of employment by Tollefson, a professional football player, against the same defendant as in the instant case. Most of the provisions of the contract were in printed form, as in the instant case, and Lambeau, manager of the Packers, wrote in longhand in paragraph 1, which covered the matter of Tollefson's compensation, "minimum $3,600 for season." Paragraph 7, one of the printed clauses of the agreement, provided that the contract might be terminated any time by the Packers giving notice in writing within forty-eight hours after the date of the last game in which Tollefson had participated. This court interpreted such words to mean that, unless discharged for cause, Tollefson was entitled to the full sum of $3,600 whether he participated in the games played by the Packers or not. In its opinion, this court stated (p. 322):

> . . . *"Where written provisions are inconsistent with printed provisions* [of a contract], *an interpretation is preferred which gives effect to the written provisions."* Restatement, 1 Contracts, p. 328, § 236(e). . . . [emphasis supplied]

Lambeau in the instant case testified on his adverse examination that if the provision contained in paragraph 6 of the printed form of the contract were deleted then the contract would have constituted that which is known "in the trade" as a "season contract." This corroborates Johnson's testimony that it was verbally agreed between him and Lambeau that he was to have a "season" contract for both years 1948 and 1949 under which the Packers would have no right to terminate the same except for cause, and that the notation placed on the back of Johnson's copy of the contract in longhand by Lambeau, and initialed by him, were in order to comply with Johnson's request that he have a "season" contract for such two years. As we view it, the only material difference in the facts of the *Tollefson* case and the one at bar is that the governing provision written in longhand in the former was written on the face of Tollefson's contract, while in the instant case it was written on the back of the contract. However, inasmuch as the parties intended the provision in the instant case with respect to a "season" contract to be part of the contract, its location, whether on the face or back, is wholly immaterial. . . .

Inasmuch as the provisions of paragraph 6 directly conflict with the provision in Lambeau's handwriting for "season" contracts for each of the years 1948 and 1949, the latter provision must govern. . . .

NOTES AND QUESTIONS

1. *Background from briefs and record*: The record contains Coach Lambeau's testimony about the contract with Johnson. He said:

> Johnson did not insist on a seasonal contract. He mentioned a seasonal contract, and I said, I don't sign players for season contracts, no players, because anyone that doesn't have enough confidence in their ability shouldn't be playing this game of football. I said that we needed big tackles, and you are a big boy [Johnson was 6 feet 6 inches tall and weighed 265 pounds] and all you have to do is your best and you have nothing to worry about.
>
> I remember that he was quite concerned. We agreed to terms and he was quite concerned about being cut. At that time, as you know, there were players—mostly in the All America Conference—that were being signed for tremendous salaries and then asked to take a cut; and Mr. Johnson was quite concerned about the talk around about players being cut, which is true. When I say "cut," I mean and have reference to a reduction in salary, and not being eliminated from the squad. I told him that I was willing to sign anything, that if he played with our ball club that his salary would not be cut for two years. I never made a statement to the effect that at that time or any other time that if he signed with me I would either play him, pay him, or trade him. I don't make statements like that. . . . I did not discuss with him at that time, or at any other time before the contract was signed, that any contract he signed with me would not be subject to his release. . . . The notation "7000 season 1948, minimum 7000 1949," and a bracket and then "season contracts, E.L.L." . . . is in my handwriting. . . . I don't remember anything like Mr. Johnson calling me and complaining after he got his copy [of the contract] from the Commissioner. I don't remember him complaining that his contract was not a season contract. . . . A seasonal contract does not necessarily mean that a player cannot be dismissed. . . . When the portion of the contract that gives the club the right to release them is deleted from the printed portion, that would be a season contract, of course.

2. *A contemporary example:* Today athletes participating in professional sports are usually represented by skilled agents and often are unionized as well. We might expect the "no-cut" issue to belong to the past. But the prob lem can still arise. *See Chuy v. Philadelphia Eagles Football Club.* [97] Berry and Wong [98] note:

---

[97] 595 F.2d 1265 (3d Cir. 1979).
[98] LAW AND BUSINESS OF THE SPORTS INDUSTRY, Vol. 1 at 260 (1986).

Players are always after the "no-cut" contract. We have seen that the term "no-cut" is really inappropriate. . . . What is really sought is a guaranteed salary, whether the player stays on the team or not. But what is meant by a guarantee? That term is only slightly less amibiguous. Is the salary guaranteed even if the player defaults and refuses to play? Obviously, no club would agree to such one-sidedness. Thus, there is a need to specify under what conditions it will not. The National Basketball Association has set forth different approaches in its Allowable Amendments to the Uniform Player Contract. . . These guides should be consulted when contemplating the various possibilities. But even those provisions may not anticipate all grounds for dispute.

3. *Relief for victims of the parol evidence rule*: Suppose the trier of fact believed Clyde Johnson's version of all of the events involved in the case. Suppose, however, that Lambeau had made no notation on the standard National Football League contract. Lambeau told Johnson that when the form came back from the League office with clause 6 still included that Johnson could trust Lambeau because his word was good as gold. Johnson could not get reformation. There would be no handwritten provision to override the printed form. Would Johnson have any remedy?

Today could Johnson assert Restatement (Second) of Contracts § 90 to offset the parol evidence rule? Few courts have faced the problem squarely. Professor Metzger argues that courts are likely to use promissory estoppel to undercut the parol evidence rule. [99] The same reasons for applying promissory estoppel to the Statute of Frauds also suggest its application to the parol evidence rule. He suggests that courts following a Willistonian parol evidence rule because of their desire to defend written documents will resist. Courts following a Corbin parol evidence rule might not need the doctrine. If one party has reasonably relied on a prior or contemporaneous promise or statement, then the parties did not intend the writing to be a final statement of their deal. Nonetheless, he argues:

> Estoppel could enhance the effectuation of the parties' true intent in a written contract, an objective shared by modern formulations of the parol evidence rule, and could minimize the injustice associated with mechanical applications of the rule. Estoppel also could provide a better doctrinal explanation for the results courts reach in many parol evidence cases than the traditional parol evidence rubric that courts currently employ affords. Such doctrinal clarity would result in the focusing of judicial attention in parol evidence cases on the real issues that ultimately will determine whether a court will give legal effect to an extrinsic promise, a consequence likely to provide a much needed measure of clarity and predictability in the administration of the parol evidence rule. Finally, promissory estoppel's application in parol evidence cases would be consonant with the tendency of twentieth century contract law to elevate substance over form in the pursuit of just results, a tendency of which the reliance principle is merely one manifestation.

[99] *See* Metzger, *The Parol Evidence Rule: Promissory Estoppel's Next Conquest?*, 36 Vand. L. Rev. 1383, 1466 (1983).

Compare Restatement (Second) of Contracts §§ 155, 158.

D. CONCLUSIONS ABOUT THE PAROL EVIDENCE RULE

AM INTERNATIONAL, INCORPORATED v. GRAPHIC MANAGEMENT ASSOCIATES, INC.
United States Court of Appeals, Seventh Circuit
44 F.3d 572 (1995)

POSNER, Chief Judge. This diversity breach of contract suit, governed by Illinois law, was brought by AM International ("AM" for short) against Graphic Management Associates (GMA). The district judge entered judgment on the pleadings for GMA. Fed. R. Civ. P. 12(c). The appeal raises surprisingly fundamental questions of contract law.

Both parties are manufacturers of printing machines used in the newspaper business. One of these machines is called a "newspaper inserting machine," and it comes equipped with what is called a Missed Insert Repair System (MIRS). These are complicated and expensive machines, which must be customized to the purchaser's specifications. AM brought a suit against GMA, charging that GMA's newspaper inserting machines with MIRS infringed a patent of AM's. The case was settled on December 27, 1988. The settlement included a license agreement, effective the same day, which entitled AM to a royalty of $ 200,000 on each MIRS-equipped newspaper inserting machine made by GMA and "shipped after . . . [Dec. 27, 1988] and before the expiration of" the patent, which was to expire on July 23, 1991. But there was an exception: "beginning on January 1, 1991 and continuing to July 23, 1991 [the date of the expiration of the patent] royalty shall accrue on the receipt by GMA of a bona fide purchase order for a product, provided that product is shipped prior to December 31, 1991."

In January 1990, the owner of the Philadelphia Inquirer ordered nine MIRS-equipped machines from GMA. Four were not shipped until after December 31, 1991, and AM concedes that no royalty is due on any of those machines. The other five machines were shipped between September and November of 1991, and thus before December 31, and as to those AM contends that royalty is due. The district judge disagreed, thinking the contract too clear against AM's contention to allow the taking of parol evidence to determine the parties' true intentions. The judge did, however, mention some of that evidence, which had been obtained in discovery before GMA moved for judgment on the pleadings, en route to his conclusion that the evidence was inadmissible to alter the apparent meaning of the contract.

When judges say that a contract is "clear on its face," they mean simply that an ordinary reader of English, reading the contract, would think its application to the dispute at hand certain. That describes this case to a T. AM is entitled to royalties on machines shipped by GMA before July 23, 1991, unless the purchase order was received between January 1 and July 23, in which event AM is entitled to royalties on machines shipped by GMA until December 31. The purchase order for the five machines in issue was received before January 1, so the exception did not come into play, and therefore AM would have been entitled to royalties on the machines only if they had been shipped before July 23, which they were not.

The text contains no clue that the contract might mean something different from what it says. GMA says that that is the end of the case; and there is plenty of judicial language, from Illinois cases as from cases from other states, that if the language of a contract appears to admit of only one interpretation, the case is indeed over. . . . This is the "four corners" rule. AM ripostes that the doctrine of "extrinsic ambiguity" entitled it to present evidence that although the contract appears to be clear, anyone who understood the real-world context would know that it does not mean what it seems to mean. And there are many cases which say this, too. . . . Can these lines of cases be reconciled? If so, how? If not, how are we to decide this case?

Rules of law are rarely as clean and strict as statements of them make them seem. So varied and unpredictable are the circumstances in which they are applied that more often than not the summary statement of a rule—the terse formula that judges employ as a necessary shorthand to prevent judicial opinions from turning into treatises—is better regarded as a generalization than as the premise of a syllogism. Take the rule that if a contract is clear on its face, the court will not permit the taking of evidence to contradict that "clear" meaning. The famous contract in *Raffles v. Wichelhaus*, 2 H. & C. 906, 159 Eng. Rep. 375 (Ex. 1864) . . . was clear on its face. It called for the shipment of a specified amount of cotton from one port to another on the ship Peerless. Clear as a bell. Only there were two (if not more) ships Peerless, and it was impossible to tell which one the contract referred to. The contract was unclear because clarity in a contract is a property of the correspondence between the contract and the things or activities that it regulates, and not just of the semantic surface.

Take another example. Suppose the parties to the contract in *Raffles* had been members of a trade in which the term "cotton" was used to refer to guncotton rather than to the cotton used in textiles. The ordinary reader of English would not know about this special trade usage, and so would suppose the contract unambiguous. Again, the ambiguity is in the reference, that is, the connection between the word and the object that it denotes.

There has to be a means by which the law allows these surfaces to be penetrated, but without depriving contracting parties of the protection from the vagaries of judges and juries that they sought by reducing their contract to writing. A review of the doctrines that allow this penetration of semantic surfaces suggests that the key is the distinction between what might be called "objective" and "subjective" evidence of ambiguity. We use these terms informally, rather than with any approach to philosophical precision. By "objective" evidence we mean evidence of ambiguity that can be supplied by disinterested third parties: evidence that there was more than one ship called Peerless, or that a particular trade uses "cotton" in a nonstandard sense. The ability of one of the contracting parties to "fake" such evidence, and fool a judge or jury, is limited. By "subjective" evidence we mean the testimony of the parties themselves as to what they believe the contract means. Such testimony is invariably self serving, being made by a party to the lawsuit, and is inherently difficult to verify. "Objective" evidence is admissible to demonstrate that apparently clear contract language means some-thing different from what it seems to mean; "subjective" evidence is inadmissible for this purpose. AM relies on our decision in *FDIC v. W.R. Grace & Co.*, 877 F.2d 614 (7th Cir. 1989), the principal case in this court dealing with extrinsic ambiguity and a case in which we were, as here, interpreting Illinois law, but overlooks our observation that "the nature of the offer of proof to show an [ex-trinsic] ambiguity is . . . critical." Id. at 622. We said that "a self-serving state-ment . . . that a party did not understand the contract to mean what it says (or ap-pears to say) will not suffice"; only "an offer to show that anyone who under-stood the context of the contract would realize it couldn't mean what an untu-tored reader would suppose it meant will [suffice]." Id. at 622.

There is a further screen to protect the parties from the uncertainties of trial. Objective evidence claimed to show that an apparently clear contract is in fact ambiguous must be presented first to the judge, and only if he concludes that it establishes a genuine ambiguity is the question of interpretation handed to the jury. . . .

There are exceptions to the rule that only objective evidence can be used to alter the meaning of a clear contract, but they are consistent with the underlying principle. If the parties agree to an idiosyncratic meaning, the court will honor their agreement. *Skycom Corp. v. Telstar Corp.*, 813 F.2d 810, 814-16 (7th Cir. 1987). . . . Or if one party charges fraud, the court will go behind the face of the contract—but it will require the party to prove fraud by clear and convincing evi-dence, . . . thus imposing a heightened standard of proof, a device analogous to requiring objective evidence. . . .

So far, so good; but when one speaks in a diversity case of rules of contract law such as the parol evidence or "four corners" rules that erect procedural ob-stacles to a party's efforts to avoid being bound by the words of his contract, questions can arise concerning the seam between the doctrine of *Erie R.R. v. Tompkins*, 304 U.S. 64, 82 L. Ed. 1188, 58 S. Ct. 817 (1938), and the dictates of the Seventh Amendment. Are these "substantive" rules because of their effect on the behavior of contracting parties outside the courtroom—on their decision how to structure their relations (whether even to have contractual relations), what forms of words to use in their written contracts (whether even to have a written contract), and so on? Or are they "procedural" rules because they involve the re-lation between judge and jury, governed in federal courts by the Seventh Amendment? If they were treated as procedural rules, a substantial wedge would be driven between state contract cases and federal diversity contract cases. So it comes as no great surprise that rules of contract interpretation, such as the parol evidence and four-corners rules, are deemed substantive, because of their effect on the conduct of contracting parties outside the courtroom, even though the rules operate through limiting the kinds of evidence that are admissible. . . . No doubt suspicion of juries plays a role in the doctrines that limit the admissibility of evidence by which a party seeks to avoid the consequences of his written words; but the rules do not differentiate between judge and jury; they bind the former as much as the latter.

The rule that a claim of extrinsic ambiguity is to be "screened" by the judge before being submitted to the jury . . . is different. That is a rule about the division of functions between judge and jury, and in federal court that division is governed by the Seventh Amendment rather than by state law. . . . But these cases did not involve a state procedural rule limited to a particular field of law, such as contract law, and arguably motivated by substantive rather than procedural concerns, as in this case. . . . The rule that the judge must be satisfied that extrinsic evidence creates a legitimate ambiguity before he can submit the dispute over the contract's meaning to the jury is a sensible rule, and if not bound to follow it under Erie we can still adopt it as a rule of federal common law to guide procedure in diversity breach of contract suits. We need not consider the extent to which it is already implicit in Rule 56 of the Federal Rules of Civil Procedure (summary judgment). There is a sense in which a motion for summary judgment requires the judge to "screen" the evidence in advance of trial to make sure it creates a genuine issue of material fact.

The principle that allows the court in some but not all cases to search beneath the semantic surface for clues to meaning is not limited to contract cases. Even the strongest devotees of the "plain meaning" rule of statutory interpretation, a rule that resembles the "four corners" rule of contract law, allow it to bend when necessary to avoid absurd results. . . . An absurdity in the application of the plain-meaning rule usually results from a comparison of the apparently plain meaning to the real-world setting in which the contract or statute is to be applied. It is the same point that a clear document can be rendered unclear—even have its apparent meaning reversed—by the way in which it connects, or fails to connect, with the activities that it regulates. Discrepancy between the word and the world is a common source of interpretive problems everywhere.

With this understanding of the law, we can wrap up our discussion of this case in short order. AM presented no objective evidence that the contract means something different from what it seems to mean. No relevant custom or usage of the trade was tendered for the judge's consideration. There is no indication of the sort of "latent" ambiguity, resulting from uncertain reference or correspondence, that was present in the Raffles case. AM points out that the contract does not expressly discuss purchase orders received before January 1, 1991, and not filled till after July 23. But if a contract says "X after January 1," we hardly expect it to say "and not-X until January 1," since that is plainly implied.

AM argues that it is arbitrary—absurd—to distinguish between purchase orders received before or after January 1, 1991, when it is obvious that the parties intended AM to receive royalties on all allegedly infringing machines, and therefore on all machines made before the expiration of the patent. But that is not at all obvious, and in fact is obviously incorrect. AM concedes that no royalty was due on the four machines ordered by the owner of the Philadelphia Inquirer that were shipped after December 31, 1991, even if those machines happened to have been made before July 23, 1991, and therefore infringed the patent, since a valid patent excludes others from manufacturing, as well as selling, the patented device. 35 U.S.C. § 154. So not all infringing machines trigger a royalty obligation; and why should the five shipped after the expiration of the patent but before December 31 do so? If the parties . . . being competitors can be assumed to be knowledgeable about the subject matter of the contract, had wanted AM to obtain royalties on all machines shipped before December 31, whenever ordered—which is AM's position—they could have said so in just those words. They did not; and there is no objective evidence that their failure to do so must be overlooked if the contact is to be enforced in conformity with the parties' intentions when they signed it. Although the January 1, 1991, cut-off date for GMA's obligation to pay royalties on infringing machines is arbitrary, as all such temporal lines are, it is not absurd that there should have been a cut-off date. The obvious reason for extending the royalty expiration date from the patent expiration date to some months later was to discourage GMA from delaying shipment in order to escape having to pay the royalty, which was sizable. The danger of strategic delay would be less acute for orders that GMA received long in advance of the expiration of AM's patent—orders received, for example, before January 1, 1991. Customers will not wait indefinitely for the delivery of the goods that they order, and GMA would be unlikely, therefore, to delay shipment on orders received before 1991 until after the expiration of the patent in late July. The more acute danger was manipulation of the shipment date of last-minute orders, so a cut-off date was chosen that in effect extended the final royalty expiration date for last-minute orders only.

This interpretation of the reason for the January 1, 1991, cut-off date is conjecture. But it shows that interpreting the contract in accordance with its actual language does not produce absurd results. It thus underscores AM's failure to present objective evidence that the apparent clarity of the contract is an illusion. Without such evidence, the interpretation of the contract presents a question of law, for the judge to decide (not ignoring context, *Florida East Coast Ry. v. CSX Transportation*, Inc., 42 F.3d 1125, 1129 (7th Cir. 1994), but ignoring disputed evidence), and judgment on the pleadings is therefore appropriate.

So when GMA, after discovery was completed, moved for judgment on the pleadings on the ground that the contract was unambiguous, AM was required to demonstrate the existence of objective evidence that the contract was not so clear as it seemed to be. In its brief in opposition to GMA's motion for judgment on the pleadings, AM argued that there was evidence demonstrating an extrinsic ambiguity, tendered that evidence in the form of affidavits, and asked the district judge to convert GMA's motion into a motion for summary judgment and deny the recharacterized motion on the ground that there was a genuine issue of material fact concerning the meaning of the contract, precluding summary judgment. Fed. R. Civ. P. 12(c). This was a proper procedure for AM to follow. . . . But its affidavits do not create a factual issue concerning the existence of an extrinsic ambiguity. The strongest of them is the affidavit of a patent expert who opined that "In my 30 years of patent practice, I have never seen, handled or heard of a patent license in which there was a royalty exclusion window [of the kind suggested by GMA]." What does that prove? That such a provision is unusual? That AM was fooled? It is not evidence that the parties were employing a special vocabulary, so that the meaning of the contract is opposite to what an outsider would think. It is not the sort of evidence that would authorize a jury to ignore the language of the contract. So the judge was right to grant GMA's motion, though he should have said that he was ruling on a motion for summary judgment, because the propriety of granting the motion depended on a determination that AM's affidavits did not create a genuine issue of material fact.

AFFIRMED

NOTES & QUESTIONS

1. *Later application in the Seventh Circuit:* In *Central States, Southeast and Southwest Areas Pension Fund v. Central Cartage Co.,*[100] Judge Frank Easterbrook limited Judge Posner's parol evidence rule to contracts with relatively little impact on third parties. He found "a multi-employer pension agreement is not a normal two party contract for which evidence of idiosyncratic meaning may be used to depart from the objective meaning of the words." Judge Flam concurred, but he questioned Judge Easterbrook's rule limiting objective evidence of idiosyncratic meanings to two party contracts. He notes "[w]e have previously expressed this idiosyncratic meaning doctrine as follows: 'Parties, like Humpty Dumpty, may use words as they please. If they wish the symbols, "one Caterpillar D9G tractor" to mean "500 railroad cars full of watermelons," that's fine—provided [the] parties share this weird meaning.' " In *TKO Equipment Corp. v. C & G Coal Co.,*[101] Judge Flam concurred in the result because the affidavit offered in the case contained statements about what parties to the contract believed it meant, "rather than direct evidence of an objective fact observable in the world." He thought that such evidence would be easy to fake and difficult to verify. Thus, under Judge Posner's test, it was subjective.

Is the Seventh Circuit rule consistent with the law of New York? Of Wisconsin? Is there any significant difference in substance between Justice Traynor's views about the California law governing interpretation of contracts and the Seventh Circuit's rule? In *Cole Taylor Bank v. Truck Ins. Exchange,*[102] Judge Posner suggested that failing to distinguish objective from subjective testimony as a way of showing that a seemingly clear contract really is ambiguous, explains the debate between Justice Traynor in cases such as *Masterson v. Sine* and Judge Kozinsky in *Trident Center.* Judge Posner notes: "the risk of erroneous interpretations would be very great if parties could not present even unimpeachable evidence that the clarity of the written contract was illusory."[103]

2. Is the Posner parol evidence rule the law? William C. Whitford, The Role of the Jury (And the Fact/Law Distinction) in the Interpretation of Written Contracts,[104] sees the Posner rule as a compromise with "the potential to have legs." It is a reasonably bright line rule with some potential to introduce greater predictability into the law, and it might narrow historic differences. Nonetheless, Whitford notes that "[e]arly returns . . . do not look promising for Judge Posner's invention." The judge was attempting to make sense out of competing lines of Illinois precedent in a diversity of citizenship case where Illinois law governed. There have been a number of Illinois intermediate appellate court cases that have

---

[100] 76 F.3d 114 (7th Cir. 1996).
[101] 863 F.2d 541 (7th Cir. 1988).
[102] 51 F.3d 736 (7th Cir. 1995).
[103] *Id.* at 737.
[104] 2001 Wis. L. Rev. 931.

not followed the Posner rule, including some that excluded evidence that would clearly be labeled objective under the Seventh Circuit position. "Only one Illinois Appellate Court decision has cited and relied on Judge Posner's decision in AM International. The Illinois Supreme Court has addressed the PER at any length only once since the decision in AM International and it applied a 'four corners' rule, excluding objective extrinsic evidence, without citation of Judge Posner's decision." Air Safety v. Teachers Realty Corp.[105]

3. Professor Whitford and the best of all possible worlds: Professor Whitford concludes his article, saying:

> The prophecy of continued confusion and conflict may be a source of despair for many. But we have lived with this conflict for decades. And maybe life isn't so bad. Undoubtedly things could be better, and it is possible that the unsettled law of contract interpretation is holding us back. It is also possible that it just doesn't make much difference whether we have a coherent and consistent law of interpretation or continued confusion and conflict. If it doesn't make much difference, then the promoters of efficiency in contract performance as an important value will need to reevaluate their position. Their position is premised on the idea that predictability in how a lawsuit will be decided is very important to the efficient performance of transactions. That is the essential rationale for keeping interpretation away from juries, assumed to be unpredictable. That we have persevered for so long with such unpredictability in how courts will decide contract interpretation cases weakens this rationale, and strengthens the case for tilting the balance more toward the pursuit of autonomy values, and perhaps even rehabilitation goals. That probably means, in light of our traditions for drawing the fact/law distinction, giving juries a more consistent rule in contract interpretation.[106]

4. *Dean Robert Scott's approach:* Scott argues that "the state's primary substantive role in uniformly enforcing commercial contracts is to regulate incomplete contracts efficiently."[107] This involves two often inconsistent tasks. Courts must "correctly (or uniformly) interpret . . . the meaning of the contract terms chosen by the parties to allocate contract risk." They also must create "broadly suitable default rules and/or . . . [label] widely used contract terms and clauses with standard meanings." He argues that uniformity requires not just the same substantive standards be adopted by all the American states. For all of the advantages of uniformity, courts must apply those standards in predictable ways.

Scott's solution to the uniformity problem is a return to a plain-meaning approach to interpretation and a strict parol evidence rule. Often, this will defend writings at the cost of defeating actual expectations. Professor Scott seems ready to trade having courts seek the assumptions of the parties for something approaching certainty. He says:

---

[105] 706 N.E.2d 882 (Ill. 1999).

[106] 2001 Wis. L. Rev. at 964.

[107] Robert E. Scott, *The Uniformity Norm in Commercial Law: A Comparative Analysis of Common Law and Code Methodologies,* in THE JURISPRUDENTIAL FOUNDATIONS OF CORPORATE AND COMMERCIAL LAW 127 (Cambridge University Press 2000)

[T]he efficient regulation of contract does not require that every relational norm be judicialized or that the legal mechanism operates efficiently viewed on its own terms, but rather that it operates efficiently in concert with social norms of trust, reciprocity, and conditional cooperation that also regulate relational contracts. Under the formalist approach, these norms would not be legally enforceable contract terms . . . but they nevertheless would be enforced by social sanctions that would effectively constrain the parties' incentives to exploit changed circumstances strategically.[108]

There are costs, as Scott recognizes: "[o]ne who argues for a return to acontextual modes of interpretation has to concede, and I do, that there are real costs to a return to the common law approach." To what extent do Professors Scott and Whitford disagree? Would Judge/Professor Posner be more likely to side with Scott or Whitford? Would he side with neither and march to his own drummer?

Professors Childres and Spitz [109] studied the 149 cases relevant to the parol evidence rule cited in volumes ten through fifteen of West's General Digest, Fourth Series.[110] They found they could order the apparent chaos of the parol evidence rule by classifying the cases in terms of the status of the parties to the contracts in question.

They divided the cases into categories they labeled as (a) formal contracts, (b) informal contracts, and (c) contracts involving an abuse of the bargaining process. Formal contracts are transactions between parties with some expertise and business sophistication. The parties can be regarded as professionals, and the agreements are negotiated fairly and in detail. Informal contracts are agreements between people who lack sophistication in business. Abuse of bargaining power cases include contracts of adhesion and unconscionable contracts as well as other contracts objectionable on public policy grounds.

Courts protect written documents in formal contract situations. They do not allow oral evidence to replace contract language with an alleged prior understanding. They will allow parties to show that the writing was not a complete statement of the contract. For example, parties may not have defined all their obligations because they deal under the assumption that usages of trade will govern. Businesspeople can prove side agreements. However, courts frequently ignored the parol evidence rule in informal contracts. About 27% of the cases in the sample involved these situations. Courts refused to hear extrinsic evidence in only three reported cases involving informal contracts. The approach here was obviously inconsistent with both that in the formal situation and the language of the rule itself. Often courts strained to find terms in the written document to be ambiguous so parol evidence could be admitted. In those cases where courts upheld

---

[108] Robert E. Scott, *The Case for Formalism in Relational Contract*, 94 Nw. U. L. Rev. 847, 861 (2000). *See also,* Robert E. Scott, *Is Article 2 the Best We Can Do?*, 52 Hastings L. J. 677 (2001).

[109] Childres and Spitz, *Status in the Law of Contract*, 47 N.Y.U. L. Rev. 1 (1972).

[110] Roughly, these volumes reported cases decided during the decade of the 1960s.

the written document, the courts frequently indicated that they did not believe the alleged oral agreement had been made. Finally, any person who alleged inferior bargaining position or an abuse of bargaining power usually got his evidence to the trier of fact. A third of the cases in the sample involved an abuse of bargaining power, and the courts in all but seven of them allowed the evidence to be considered.

Childres and Spitz conclude "[o]nce it is made explicit that no single rule can be expected to operate across all status lines, we can get about the business of trying to create new categories and rules." The authors concede that their categories may be crude and imprecise. Their study tells us only about reported appellate cases. Furthermore, some might suspect that the reactions of courts in the 1960s might differ substantially from reactions today. Interestingly, in 1991 Michael Lawrence [111] sought to replicate the Childres and Spitz analysis, using Wisconsin cases. He concluded that the outcomes in the cases supported the Childres and Spitz hypothesis with "striking frequency."

Professor William Whitford [112] labels the Childres and Spitz approach "denial." They find consistency in the application of the parol evidence rule by inventing new categories. Whitford is skeptical.

> My primary quarrel is with the vagueness of their categories. The distinctions between "formal" and "informal," and between "substitution" and "variation," are not precise. The result is a great risk of coder bias, with cases applying a hard PER pushed into the "formal" contract and "substitution" categories and cases admitting extrinsic evidence pushed into the other categories, in order to validate the preconceived hypotheses. Another weakness is that the study cannot show that the same pattern will prevail over time. The hypothesis is that judges bend the black letter rules to achieve what they perceive as the proper result in the cases, and that there is consistency across judges in what is perceived as the just result. Today there is a greater willingness to recognize differences in judges' basic sensibilities than there once was. Some judges will be much more devoted to efficiency in contract performance as a policy goal, others to autonomy values, still others to redistribution values. And judges will differ in what is the best strategy to achieve autonomy values. So even if Childres and Spitz correctly found a consistency in result in the 1960s, there is no guarantee that the consistency would continue over time, nor would I expect it to.

Professor Justin Sweet [113] argues:

> [T]rue integration should be the only basis for any rule that limits provability of prior oral agreements. The desirable objectives now sought through the parol evidence rule can be accomplished more directly

---

[111] Comment, *The Parol Evidence Rule in Wisconsin: "Status in the Law of Contracts" Revisited*, 1991 Wis. L. Rev. 1071 (1991).

[112] *The Role of the Jury (and the Fact/Law Distinction) in the Interpretation of Written Contracts*, 2001 Wis. L. Rev. 931, 959.

[113] Sweet, *Contract Making and Parol Evidence: Diagnosis and Treatment of a Sick Rule*, 53 Cornell L. Rev. 1036 (1968). Copyright © 1968 by Cornell University. All Rights Reserved.

through other accepted legal doctrines. To make the integration concept work, however, there is a need for workable and realistic methods of recognizing the objective trappings of a true integration. A model of a truly integrated contract should be created and criteria developed for identification of truly integrated writings. . . .

The hallmark of a truly integrated contract is that it is put together carefully and methodically. In this sense it resembles the creation of a statute or a treaty. A good deal has occurred before the act of integration. The person preparing the integration, usually the attorney, gathers all the evidence of what has transpired in order to prepare a draft. He will look at letters, wires, memoranda, agreements, contracts and any other data relevant to the final document. . . . Drafts are exchanged and revised. Provisions are traded, eliminated or modified. Each party uses its persuasiveness to support inclusion or deletion of specific clauses. Language is reviewed carefully with a view toward achieving phraseology satisfactory to both parties. Usually, a clause stating that the writing covers the entire transaction is included. Attorneys look over the final draft and confer with the top negotiators in order to iron out final details. The final draft is prepared and the date set for execution. Top executives of the contracting parties and other interested persons gather to sign or to witness the execution of the agreement. . . .

Obviously, the percentage of contracts made in this manner is small. It can be argued that if we protect only true integrations of this sort, we are in effect abolishing the parol evidence rule. But these are the only types of written agreements which can confidently be assumed to integrate the entire transaction in one repository. . . .

Even a contract put together in a manner suggested by the above model would not invariably integrate everything relating to the transaction. Contracts which appear to be integrated contracts *may* not contain everything. Oral agreements may be made simultaneously with the execution of a complete and final-looking written agreement, and may nevertheless be enforceable.

Sweet then lists nine factors a court should consider in deciding whether a written document truly was intended as a final and complete expression of the parties' contract. Two important factors, he lists, are the "bargaining situation" and the "degree of standardization of the writing." He says "[t]he greater the one-sidedness of the bargaining situation, the less likely it is that the bargain was concluded by an integrated writing." Furthermore, "[t]he greater the standardization of the writing, the less likely that the transaction was concluded by an integrated writing."

How might corporate lawyers respond to Childres and Spitz and to Sweet? Are there reasons for defending written documents these authors fail to consider? Arguably, the parol evidence rule reflects an important political position. How would you state the politics of the cases you have read in this section? Would you agree with Professor Patricia J. Williams? She says:

The body of private laws epitomized by contract, including slave contracts, for example, is problematic not only because it endows certain parties with rights, but because it denies the object of contract any rights at all.

The quintessential rule of contract interpretation, the parol evidence rule, illustrates the mechanics by which such constriction is achieved. . . . If this rule is understood as a form of social construction, the words could as well read: "Terms with respect to which the constructed reality (or governing narrative) of a given power structure agree, may not be contradicted, but only supplemented or explained." . . .

One consequence of [a] broader reconfiguration of rights, again in the context of contract, is to give voice to those people or things which, by virtue of their object relation to the contract, historically had no voice.

Chapter 4

PROBLEMS CONCERNING THE ADJUSTMENT OR MODIFICATION OF PERFORMANCE TERMS

It is hard to make a contract of any complexity that will continue to satisfy everyone concerned as it is performed over time. People often expect to make adjustments and changes during the course of performance. Often contracts are written with provisions designed to track with changing conditions. We have already seen flexible quantity and price arrangements.

At times, however, people will write what appear to be flat and absolute contracts with no provisions for changes, but they will understand that there is an implicit obligation to make adjustments as circumstances change. Some American lawyers are surprised to find that Japanese and Chinese negotiators often view an express contract as only the starting place for adjustments. However, the cultural difference is one of degree, not of kind. Americans in many fields recognize the necessity of altering deals as circumstances change.[1] It is not always easy to tell when business culture allows me to hold you to the letter of our bargain and when custom demands that I let you out of what you are literally obligated to do.

While often there are good reasons to adjust bargains to changing situations, sometimes people want out of contracts for opportunistic reasons. Beale, Bishop and Furmston[2] note:

> [a]n agreement running over a period of time may give a party the scope for "opportunism," by taking advantage of the other's circumstances to threaten a breach of contract unless the deal is renegotiated in his favor. Frequently the opportunity for such extortion arises from the operation of the contract itself. Even if the parties met on an equal footing originally, when the time for performance draws near one party may be heavily dependent on the other; he may face serious losses if he does not get the other's performance and has nowhere that he can readily obtain a substitute.

Contract law often is contradictory if not incoherent. This is particularly true in the area of adjustments, modifications and changes to an ongoing bargain. There are a number of issues that have troubled courts, legal scholars and law students. For example, how far can we control the future by clauses in contracts? Suppose we agree that we cannot modify a contract or that we can modify only by following certain procedures. Later can we agree to ignore the provisions of our earlier bargain concerning modifications? Do modifications of contracts require consideration or sufficient reliance to trigger promissory estoppel? Or can we just give up rights voluntarily? Suppose my failure to perform entitles you to certain

---

[1] In some fields of business, form contracts provide that they may be cancelled for convenience and spell out a cancellation charge. Other clauses say that quantities ordered may be decreased subject to an equitable adjustment in the unit price.

[2] Beale, Bishop and Furmston, CONTRACT: CASES AND MATERIALS 491 (Butterworths 1985).

remedies. However, you do not assert them but allow me to continue to perform. Can you lose some or all of your remedies? Does this require bad faith, consideration, reliance, writings or any other conduct or form? The answers to these questions are important but very unclear.

The following material serves as a transition between ideas about forming contracts and performing them. While in theory we can distinguish between making and carrying out bargains, in practice often these things are intertwined.

A.   "WRITTEN MODIFICATIONS ONLY" CLAUSES

UNIVERSAL BUILDERS, INC. v. MOON MOTOR LODGE, INC.
Supreme Court of Pennsylvania
430 Pa. 550, 244 A.2d 10 (1968)

EAGEN, J. [This was an appeal from a final equitable decree ordering the defendant to pay the plaintiff the balance due on a construction contract, plus extras. The plaintiff had sued to have a real estate conveyance set aside on the ground that it was a fraudulent conveyance. Plaintiff also had asked to have a supplemental agreement declared void, alleging it was procured by fraud. Plaintiff also sought money damages for work done under both the basic and supplemental agreement. The defendant had denied the fraud, and had denied it owed plaintiff any money for work which had been done, claiming both a set-off and damages for delay. Except for the decree for the balance due, the trial court had denied all of the claims and counterclaims.]

Briefly, the background facts of this case are as follows. On August 16, 1961, the plaintiff, Universal Builders, Inc. (hereinafter Universal), entered into a written contract with the defendant, Moon Motor Lodge, Inc. (hereinafter Moon), for the construction of a motel and restaurant in Allegheny County. The contract provides, inter alia, that all change orders must be in writing and signed by Moon and/or the Architect and that all requests for extension of time must be made in writing to the Architect. The contract specifications also required that a certain proportion of a reinforcing substance be used in the building walls. The masonry sub-contractor failed to use the specified proportion. When this defect was discovered, Moon magnified its importance, withheld from Universal a progress payment to which Universal was entitled, threatened to expel Universal from the job and thereby induced Universal to enter into the supplemental agreement. The supplemental agreement, dated March 27, 1962, provides, inter alia, that Universal will pay Moon $5000 as damages for the absence of the reinforcing material, that Universal will perform certain additional work at no additional cost to Moon, that the date for completion of the project is extended from April 1, 1962, to July 1, 1962, and that liquidated damages at a specified rate per day will be assessed for delay.

Universal substantially completed performance on September 1, 1962, and left the construction site on October 1, 1962. After filing this suit, Universal went into bankruptcy. The trustee prosecuted this action and won a final decree in the lower court. . . .

. . . Moon urges that the lower court erred in several respects.

First Moon submits that the chancellor erred in not enforcing the contract provision that extras would not be paid for unless done pursuant to a written, signed change order.

Unless a contract is for the sale of goods, see the Uniform Commercial Code—Sales, the Act of April 6, 1953, P.L. 3, § 2-209(2), as amended, 12A P.S. § 2-209(2), it appears undisputed that the contract can be modified orally although it provides that it can be modified only in writing. . . . Construction contracts typically provide that the builder will not be paid for extra work unless it is done pursuant to a written change order, yet courts frequently hold that owners must pay for extra work done at their oral direction. . . . This liability can be based on several theories. For example, the extra work may be said to have been done under an oral agreement separate from the written contract and not containing the requirement of a written authorization. . . . The requirement of a written authorization may also be considered a condition which has been waived. . . .

On either of the above theories, the chancellor correctly held Moon liable to pay for the extras in spite of the lack of written change orders. The evidence indicates that William Berger, the agent of Moon, requested many changes, was informed that they would involve extra cost, and promised to pay for them. In addition, Berger frequently was on the construction site and saw at least some of the extra work in progress. The record demonstrates that he was a keen observer with an extraordinary knowledge of the project in general and the contract requirements in particular. Thus it is not unreasonable to infer that he was aware that extra work was being done without proper authorization, yet he stood by without protesting while the extras were incorporated into the project. Under these circumstances there also was an implied promise to pay for the extras.

C.I.T. Corp. v. Jonnet, 419 Pa. 435, 214 A.2d 620 (1965), does suggest that such non-written modifications are ineffective unless the contract provision requiring modifications to be in writing was first waived. That case, however, is misleading. Although it involved a contract for the sale of movable bar and restaurant equipment, which is a contract for the sale of "goods" controlled by the Uniform Commercial Code—Sales, *supra*, § 2-101 *et seq.*, as amended, 12A P.S. § 2-101 *et seq.*, it overlooks that legislation, in particular § 2-209. . . .

From subsection (5) it can be inferred that a provision in a contract for the sale of goods that the contract can be modified only in writing is waived, just as such a provision in a construction contract is waived, under the circumstances described by Restatement, Contracts, § 224 (1932), which provides: "The performance of a condition qualifying a promise in a contract within the Statute [of Frauds or in a contract containing a provision requiring modifications to be in writing (§ 407)] may be excused by an oral agreement or permission of the promisor that the condition need not be performed, if the agreement or permission is given while the performance of the condition is possible, and in reliance on the agreement or permission, while it is unrevoked, the promisee materially changes his position." Obviously a condition is considered waived when its enforcement would result in something approaching fraud. . . . Thus the effectiveness of a non-written modification in spite of a contract condition that modifications must be written depends upon whether enforcement of the condition is or is not barred by equitable considerations, not upon the technicality of whether the condition was or was not expressly and separately waived before the non-written modification.

In view of these equitable considerations underlying waiver, it should be obvious that when an owner requests a builder to do extra work, promises to pay for it and watches it performed knowing that it is not authorized in writing, he cannot refuse to pay on the ground that there was no written change order. . . . When Moon directed Universal to "go ahead" and promised to pay for the extras, performance of the condition requiring change orders to be in writing was excused by implication. It would be manifestly unjust to allow Moon, which misled Universal into doing extra work without a written authorization, to benefit from nonperformance of that condition.

Next Moon submits that the lower court erroneously dismissed its counterclaim for delay damages. The lower court denied Moon any recovery for the delay because it resulted from Moon's own acts in ordering many changes. There is authority for this position. . . . In this case, however, the contract expressly conditions the allowance of any time extension on the submission of a written request to the Architect. This condition specifically applies to delays caused by the owner's, i.e., Moon's, own acts. Article 18 of the General Conditions provides: "If the contractor be delayed at any time in the progress of the work by any act or neglect of the Owner or the Architect, or of any employee of either, or by any separate contractor employed by the Owner, or by changes ordered in the work . . . then the time of completion shall be extended for such reasonable time as the Architect may decide. No such extension shall be made for delay occurring more than seven days before claim therefor is made in writing to the Architect. . . ."

Consequently the case authority on which the lower court based its decision is not controlling.

The evidence that Universal conformed with the procedure required by Article 18 is slight; what evidence there is has been largely discredited. However a condition precedent such as the one contained in Article 18 can of course be waived . . . and there is evidence to support at least a partial waiver.

By executing the Supplemental Agreement (which extends the time of substantial completion from April 1, 1962, to July 1, 1962) without reference to the procedure established by Article 18, Moon certainly waived Article 18 with reference to that extension. It is not apparent, however, that this waiver applies to subsequent delays. Apart from the execution of the supplemental agreement, there is no evidence that Moon expressly or impliedly promised that the condition precedent contained in Article 18 would not apply to subsequent delays. We think it does so apply. . . .

Finally, we have carefully considered the record and we agree with the lower court that there was sufficient evidence to establish the amount of Universal's claim for extras and that there was not sufficient evidence to establish Moon's set-off claim for uncompleted work.

The decree of the lower court therefore was correct, except insofar as it failed to allow Moon's counterclaim for delay damages, as before indicated, for the period from July 1, 1962, to September 1, 1962.

Decree vacated and record remanded for entry of a decree consonant with this opinion. Each party to bear own costs.

Dissenting Opinion by MUSMANNO, J.:

I believe an injustice is being done the defendant in this case. The lower court awarded the plaintiff $42,283.29, for extras, but the record shows that only $900 of such extras was earned on two signed change orders agreed to in writing. Yet the agreement specifically provides that, except in an emergency endangering life or property, no claim for an addition to the contract price was to be valid unless the work was done pursuant to the owner's written, signed order, and after written notice given by the contractor before proceeding with the work. I am disturbed that the Majority could have reached its conclusion when the record shows that *there was no such writing*.

Even the plaintiff did not contend that the requirement in writing was waived by agreement of the parties. . . . The most that the plaintiff has shown are oral modifications of the work called for under the contract, which is exactly what is prohibited by the solemn agreement entered into between the parties. The oral modification certainly cannot be used as evidence of a waiver, for otherwise, a requirement of writing would become meaningless. This Court clearly pointed out this fundamental proposition of law in *C.I.T. Corp. v. Jonnet*, 419 Pa. 435, 438, where this writer, speaking for the Court, said: "Nowhere, however, do the defendants allege cancellation by the plaintiff of the express term of the original conditional sale contract that 'no waiver or change in this contract or related note, shall bind such assignee (in this case, the plaintiff) unless in writing signed by one of its officers.' "

"This specific condition stands as a stone wall in the path of the defendants' contention. However, they believe they have found a way around this formidable barrier by citing the case of *Kirk v. Brentwood M.H., Inc.*, 191 Pa. Superior Ct. 488, 492 where the Superior Court said that 'Even where the written contract prohibits a non-written modification, it may be modified by subsequent oral agreement.' This is true but there must first be a waiver of the requirement which has been spelled out in the contract. Otherwise, written documents would have no more permanence than writings penned in disappearing ink. If this, the defendants' argument, were to prevail, contractual obligations would become phantoms, solemn obligations would run like pressed quicksilver, and the whole edifice of business would rest on sand dunes supporting pillars of rubber and floors of turf. Chaos would envelop the commercial world." . . .

It was the plaintiff's duty to support its claim for extras with competent evidence which in my opinion it wholly failed to produce. I cannot, therefore, go along with the Majority's conclusions as to recoveries to be permitted. . . .

Mr. Chief Justice BELL joins in this dissenting opinion.

NOTES AND QUESTIONS

1. *Colorful language from the Wagner case*: Both opinions cited *Wagner v. Graziano Construction Co.*[3] There the court said "The most iron-clad written contract can always be cut into by the acetylene torch of parol modification. . . . The hand that pens a writing may not gag the mouths of the assenting parties." The parol evidence rule itself does not apply to parol modifications of writing made *after* a writing is executed.[4] On one hand, we can agree that our written document cancels all prior agreements, and courts will apply the principles of free contract to enforce our choice. On the other hand, we can agree that our written contract cannot be modified or cannot be modified except by a specified procedure. Nonetheless, we remain free to change our minds and agree to make changes apart from this procedure.

The somewhat heated dispute between the majority and Justice Musmanno in *Universal Builders v. Moon Motor Lodge* does not involve this proposition. Rather they battle about whether an oral waiver of the required writing clause must be a distinct step in the process. Justice Musmanno would seem to want the builder to say to William Berger, Moon's agent, "If you want us to perform extras, then you must execute a written change order or tell me now that you are waiving that requirement." Then Berger would have to say, "Go ahead. We hereby waive that requirement." The majority is willing to take the oral request for changes as enough to establish both a waiver and a promise to pay for the extras. Its opinion seems to rely on both the policies of choice and unjust enrichment. Moreover, the court could have talked about a duty of good faith in performing a contract. Berger seemed to be trying to trick the builder into doing work while hiding behind the formal requirement.

2. *Written modifications clauses in modern building contracts*: Building construction projects traditionally involve making detailed plans and specifications, getting bids from contractors, and finally executing a contract to build according to the plans and specifications. Building contracts often require all changes to be approved by the architect in writing.

Professor Halper comments:

> [T]he goal of limiting changes in the scope of the work to those memorialized in formal change orders is a laudatory but usually unattainable ideal. Developers and their field personnel often request changes on the spur of the moment, and they often find it impractical to wait until the architect can actually prepare formal drawings and specifications to describe the change. Thus, the contractor has a dilemma. Should he ignore a change order request until the architect gets around to preparing

---

[3] 390 Pa. 445, 136 A.2d 82 (1957).

[4] Discussed in Chapter 3, Childres and Spitz, *Status in the Law of Contract*, 47 N.Y.U. L. Rev. 1, 16 (1972), studied the 149 cases applying the parol evidence rule found in West's General Digest during the 1960s. They tell us:

> The parol evidence rule is not, at present, well understood. The depth of misunderstanding is indicated by the fact that eight of the fifty-nine cases in the formal category (more than 15%) were concerned with *subsequent* modifications of written documents. This is error at such an elementary level as to be astonishing.

the formal documentation, or should he take a chance and immediately perform the work? A decision to wait may be wasteful because he may be proceeding with work that he will have to demolish or alter later in order to conform to the change order. Furthermore, delay might irritate the developer. On the other hand, a decision to go ahead might result in the developer's refusal to pay for the changed work.[5]

Under modern "design-build/fast track" construction methods, those involved in building complicated structures merge the design and performance steps to minimize delays and cut costs. For example, a builder may make a contract before the plans and specifications are final. Often these contracts contain the standard provisions calling for written change orders signed by the architect. Nonetheless, all involved understand that changes and adjustments to the preliminary plans and specifications will be made as work progresses, difficulties are encountered, and practical solutions found. There often will be a high volume of change orders, and frequently owners, project managers, architects and builders will shortcut procedures for changes written in contract documents and handle modifications informally to avoid delays and paperwork.

Can an owner assert the formal provisions calling for written modifications to be approved by the owner, architect or both to resist paying for extras? While there always is a risk that courts and arbitrators will find that there has not been a waiver of the formal procedure, courts and arbitrators have enforced "the real deal" rather than the "paper deal" in a number of cases.

For example, in *Southern Maryland Hospital Center v. Edward M. Crough, Inc.,*[6] Crough and the hospital entered a construction management contract. Crough was to provide design consultation and direct construction of a major structure. The agreement included the American Institute of Architect forms which called for written change orders to be signed by both the owner and the architect in order to modify the design, the date for completion or the amounts to be paid. Even before the owner signed the construction management agreement, the owner knew that the structural engineer was having a problem with soil borings. The plan called for "spread footings," but Crough and the structural engineer decided that the building needed a mat foundation. This modification of the plan required many other changes in the design as well. Crough, however, never prepared, nor requested anyone else to prepare, a change order reflecting the mat foundation and the other extras. Both the architect and the owner knew of the changes.

There was a six-day arbitration under the procedures established by the AIA form contracts used by the parties. The arbitrators awarded compensation for all extras despite the failure to follow the formal change order procedure. The trial court granted enforcement of the award, and the appellate court affirmed. It noted that the owner was aware of all the changes in the scope of the work and had been advised by Crough of the estimates of the increased costs caused by the changes. There was no suggestion that the changes were not required, not per-

---

[5] Halper, *Negotiating Construction Contracts III*, 18 Real Estate Rev. 45 (Summer 1988).
[6] 48 Md. App. 401, 427 A.2d 1051 (1981).

formed in a workmanlike manner, nor that the prices charged were not fair and reasonable. Finally, the appellate court pointed out that courts would refuse to enforce an award only when it was based on "a completely irrational interpretation of the contract." The arbitrators could find that the owner knowingly permitted noncompliance with the strict terms of the agreement and thus waived its rights.

CENTRAL ILLINOIS PUBLIC SERVICE COMPANY v. ATLAS MINERALS, INC.
United States District Court, District of Illinois
965 F. Supp. 1162 (1997)

MILLS, J. A contract between a coal company and a public utility to supply coal. During the term of the contract, things did not go well for the coal company. Now that the term of the contract has expired, the parties disagree whether each side held up its end of the bargain. To resolve this case, the Court must untangle the parties' extensive dealings and must unravel and apply two provisions of the Uniform Commercial Code.

I. BACKGROUND

A. *Parties and Characters*

Defendants Atlas Minerals, Inc. (Atlas) and Indiana Coal Company (Indiana Coal) are both Indiana Corporations. Indiana Coal is the successor to two merged companies, Buck Creek Coal, Incorporated and Buck Creek Mining, Incorporated. Atlas was the marketing representative for the Buck Creek companies (for simplicity's sake, the Court will call Defendants collectively: Atlas).

Atlas Minerals, Inc. was wholly owned by Walter Pieper. Pieper was also a principal in Buck Creek. From 1986 to 1994, Richard Bartholomew acted as the Vice President of Marketing for Atlas. Charles Schulties became an investor in Buck Creek in 1992, and assumed an active management role in mid-1994 when Pieper became ill.

Central Illinois Public Service Company (CIPS) is an Illinois public utility supplying electricity to central and southern Illinois. CIPS operates several coal-burning power plants in Illinois. CIPS buys coal to burn in its power plants by entering long-term purchase contracts (like the one at issue in this case) and by making "spot" purchases (open market purchases with durations of less than one year).

In 1988-89, CIPS' Fuel Procurement Section handled the utility's purchases of coal. Mark Cochran, an engineer and attorney, headed the Fuel Procurement Section. The Fuel Procurement Section fell within CIPS' Purchasing and Stores Department, headed by James Birkett. John Prier and Bruce Garner worked for Cochran in the Fuel Procurement Section. In 1990, Dennis Kirchner took over Cochran's post when Cochran was promoted.

B. *The Contract*

On June 22, 1989, Atlas and Indiana Coal entered into a Coal Sale and Purchase Agreement (the contract) with CIPS. Through the contract, Atlas agreed to sell coal from the Buck Creek mine near Sullivan, Indiana to CIPS to burn at its Newton, Illinois Generating Station Unit Number 2. Due to a geologic anomaly, the Buck Creek mine produces both high and low sulphur coal. The contract was for the purchase of "compliance coal," coal that produces less than 1.2 pounds of sulphur dioxide per 1,000 BTUs of energy released when the coal is burned. At the Buck Creek mine, compliance coal came from the north section and high sulphur coal from the south section of the mine.

The parties' sixteen page contract specifies delivery schedules and prices for the coal, and describes in detail the properties of the coal to be supplied. It also specifies its term: "This Agreement shall commence on June 22, 1989, and continue through December 12, 1995. No suspension of an obligation under this Agreement by reason of Force Majeure (as hereinafter defined) shall extend the term of this Agreement, except upon mutual consent of the SELLER and BUYER." The parties agreed that Illinois law would govern the contract. For purposes of this litigation one of the most important contract provisions is this: "This Agreement contains the entire agreement between the parties hereto, and no alteration or modification thereof shall be binding unless in writing and signed by the BUYER and SELLER."

The contract specified that from June 1, 1990 to December 31, 1990 Atlas would sell and tender a minimum of 100,000 tons of coal, less any tonnage excused by reason of a force majeure. From January 1, 1991 to December 31, 1995, Defendants were required to sell at least 235,000 tons per year and not more than 250,000 tons per year (the contract allowed CIPS to elect to receive any quantity between 235,000 and 250,000 tons per year). The contract set prices for the coal that started at $22.27 per ton for the first 50,000 tons of coal delivered during the June 1, 1990 to December 31, 1990 period. The final price, for the January 1, 1995 through December 31, 1995 period was either $27.37/ton or $27.85/ton depending on the method of shipment. At the time the parties entered the contract, the prices were below the market price for purchases of coal on the "spot" market. The contract did not contemplate delivery of any coal beyond the specified annual allocations, unless the parties amended the contract.

The contract defined the term "force majeure" as:

> [A]ny causes beyond the reasonable control of the party affected thereby, such as acts of God; acts of the public enemy; insurrections; riots; strikes; labor disputes; fires; explosions; floods; breakdown or damage to plants, equipment, or facilities; accidents of navigation; interruptions to transportation; river freeze-ups; embargoes; orders or acts of military or civil authority (executive, judicial, or legislative), including but not limited to, any regulation, direction, order, or request (whether valid or invalid) made by any governmental authority or person acting therefor, which is complied with in good faith; or other such causes of a similar or dissimilar nature which wholly or partly prevent the mining, delivering, and/or loading of coal by SELLER, or the receiving, transporting and/or delivering of coal by the carrier of the coal, or the accepting, utilizing and/or unloading of the coal by BUYER. The doctrine of ejusdem

generis shall not be applied to exclude any event dissimilar to the enumerated events, but which is beyond the reasonable control of a party.

The effect of a force majeure under the contract was to allow the party suffering the force majeure to cease performance upon notice to the other party. Thus, if one party suffered a force majeure event and gave notice to the other party, the notifying party was excused from performing its obligations under the contract from the beginning of the force majeure until the condition ceased. The contract specified, however, that "[a]ny deficiencies in deliveries of coals hereunder, which are excused by Force Majeure, shall not be made up except by mutual consent of the parties."

C. *The Course of Performance*

The relationship between CIPS and Atlas was troubled, primarily because the Buck Creek mine did not live up to expectations. The mine's disappointing performance has led to bankruptcy for Indiana Coal and, predictably, to this lawsuit.

Problems began early and continued through the life of the contract. In 1990, Buck Creek experienced severe mining difficulties and wrote to CIPS to claim a force majeure. In a November 30, 1990 letter to CIPS, Rick Bartholomew stated that Indiana Coal had encountered mining difficulties and wished to excuse a production shortfall of 69,629 tons.

On December 4, 1990, representatives of CIPS, Atlas, and Indiana Coal met to discuss the 1990 shortfall. On December 21, 1990, Dennis Kirchner of CIPS wrote back to Indiana Coal:

> . . . At this time, [CIPS] does not believe it is appropriate to Force Majeure this tonnage. Our Agreement guarantees CIPS 100,000 tons of coal (less applicable Force Majeure) in 1990 and 250,000 annual tons of coal (less applicable Force Majeure) for the period of January 1, 1991 through December 31, 1995. Accordingly, CIPS would like to further discuss this issue with Atlas [ ] and Buck Creek [ ].

Because of the poor mining conditions experienced by Atlas during the start-up and your discussions regarding the effect it has had on cash flow of the mine, CIPS would be willing to discuss 1) the delivery of the subject tonnage at such time when production levels of compliance coal have stabilized (including delivery after December 31, 1995); and 2) a price or pricing mechanism for the subject coal that is agreeable to both parties.

Representatives of the parties again met on January 25, 1991. At the meeting, Atlas proposed making up the 1990 shortfall in two installments of 15,000 tons each in 1994 and 1995 followed by a third installment of 39,629 in 1996. On February 7, 1991, John Prief wrote to Rick Bartholomew of Atlas and stated:

> During our meeting of January 25, 1991, in Springfield, Illinois, you proposed the following possibilities for making up the shortfall of the 1990 shipments (69,629 tons):
>
> 1) For each of the years 1994 and 1995, deliveries would be accelerated by approximately 15,000 tons. CIPS would pay the applicable price for each year, as stated in our Agreement.

2) For the year 1996, deliveries would be accelerated by approximately 39,629 tons. CIPS would pay the 1995 price, plus any escalation that would be based on an indicator agreed to by both parties.

As stated in our letter of December 21, 1990, CIPS is agreeable to making up the tonnage at an agreed-to price that differs from the contract price. We would, however, prefer to have the tonnage made up as soon as production levels permit. This would afford both parties the possibility of making up tonnage in any future adverse mining conditions.

On February 18, 1991, Rick Bartholomew responded to Prief's letter:

In response to your letter of February 7, 1991, I have listed below for your review our thoughts regarding the 1990 shortfall tonnage-69,629 tons.

(1) 1994—15,000 tons delivered in addition to the 1994 base contract tonnage. This tonnage would be priced at the 1994 contract price.

(2) 1995—15,000 tons delivered in addition to the 1995 base contract tonnage. This tonnage would be priced at the 1995 contract price.

(3) 1996—39,629 tons delivered in addition to the contract tonnage elected by [CIPS]—1996. The 1996 shortfall tonnage would be priced at the 1995 contract price, adjusted (+) by an escalator of 6%. The base contract tonnage for 1996 would follow the pricing guidelines of our agreement.

(4) Tonnage considered as surplus to (1) our operations and (2) our required base contract tonnage, during 1991, 1992, and 1993, will be shipped to satisfy our shortfall tonnage requirement. This coal will be delivered following negotiation of, and approval by [CIPS]. Pricing would be governed by the contract price in effect at the time of delivery.

John, if the above conditions are satisfactory to [CIPS], we are prepared to execute a Memorandum or Letter of Agreement, following these guidelines.

In a February 22, 1991 telephone call, CIPS indicated to Bartholomew that Atlas could ship its excess production to make up the 1990 shortfall. Then, on March 6, 1991, J.L. Lisenbee, CIPS' Vice President for Corporate Services,[7] responded to Bartholomew's February 18, 1991 letter. He wrote:

After reviewing your letter of February 18, 1991, regarding the 1990 delivery shortfall of 69,629 tons, [CIPS] would like to propose the following:

1. During each of the contract years 1994 and 1995, CIPS shall receive, in addition to the contractual tonnage stated in Article III, 15,000 tons at the applicable price for each year as stated in Article X;

2. During 1996, CIPS shall have the option to receive 39,629 tons. The price for this tonnage shall be determined by a mutually agreed to

---

[7] [1] Lisenbee was the CIPS corporate official authorized to enter into a written amendment of the contract.

method of adjusting the 1995 contract price as stated in Article X of the subject Agreement;

3. In the event surplus tonnage of the quality specified in the Agreement is mined prior to 1994, CIPS shall have the right of first refusal to such tonnage. The price per ton shall be at the price stated in Article X for the year in which it was delivered; and

4. The terms and conditions of this Letter Agreement shall not be considered precedential.

If you are in agreement with the above stated, please have the appropriate person sign below and return one executed original of the letter to my attention.

Atlas never executed the proposed agreement.

Also on March 6, 1991, CIPS declared a force majeure with respect to 3,972 tons of coal due to a condenser leak at the Newton power plant. The parties met in March 1991 to discuss CIPS' force majeure claim. In a memorandum of the meeting, Bartholomew indicates that he told CIPS' representatives that he thought their force majeure claim was trivial and made Atlas reconsider its position regarding the 69,629 tons it had proposed to force majeure. The memorandum also indicates that Atlas considered the possibility of selling excess coal produced in 1991 on the open market instead of using it to make up the 1990 shortfall on the CIPS contract. On March 21, 1991, Bartholomew wrote to Walter Pieper to suggest a written response to CIPS' March 6, 1991 proposal. The proposed response was actually sent to CIPS. It stated:

In reference to the proposed letter of agreement dated March 6, 1991 and executed by Mr. J.L. Lisenbee, regarding the 1990 shortfall/force majeure [sic] tonnage, Atlas Minerals-Buckcreek would like to propose the following. The format suggested follows that indicated in my letter to you dated February 18, 1991, and deviates slightly from the method suggested in Mr. Lisenbee's letter.

(1) During each of the contract years 1994 and 1995, CIPS shall receive, in addition to the contractual tonnage stated in Article III, 15000[sic] tons at the applicable price for each year as stated in Article X;

(2) During 1996, CIPS shall have the option to receive 39,629 tons. The price for this tonnage shall be determined by a mutually agreed to method of adjusting the 1995 contract price as stated in Article X of the subject agreement;

(3) Any tonnage considered as surplus to (1) Atlas-Buckcreek operations and (b) our required base contract tonnage, during 1991, 1992, 1993 can be shipped *at the sole discretion* of Atlas-Buckcreek to satisfy our 1990 shortfall/force majeure [sic] tonnage. Pricing would be governed by the applicable contract price in effect at the time of shipments.

Acknowledging all of our previous correspondence and discussion regarding this tonnage, we propose the format indicated above, to resolve this issue. Please consider that we have not altered our position regarding the legitimacy of our original force majeure [sic] claim, however, we wish to resolve the problem in a manner satisfactory to CIPS.

. . . .

John, if Sections I, II and II above represent a satisfactory method of addressing our 1990 force majeure/shortfall [sic] tonnage, please incorporate the language in a letter of agreement, and we will execute the letter to resolve this issue.

These letters did not culminate in a written agreement to dispose of the Force Majeure claims or to make up the 1990 delivery shortfall.

By the end of 1991, Atlas had delivered 274,304 tons of coal. CIPS paid for the first 69,629 tons at the 1990 contract price. CIPS paid the 1991 price for the remaining 204,675 tons, leaving a shortfall for 1991 of 45,325 tons. On October 1, 1991, CIPS informed Atlas in writing that it wished to receive 250,000 tons of coal in 1992. In a December 12, 1991 meeting, the parties discussed shipment schedules for 1992. The parties concurred that any coal delivered in 1991 above the 250,000 tons required by the contract would be applied to the 1990 shortfall.

In January 1992, Atlas sought additional financing for its operations from Old National Bank of Evansville, Indiana. In its loan proposal, Atlas repeatedly indicated that its contract with CIPS expired in 1995. Atlas stated "[t]he bulk of the low sulfur coal is sold under contract with [CIPS] and Pfizer through 1995." Atlas also listed its current contracts and their termination dates. The CIPS contract was listed as expiring on December 31, 1995, "with CIPS having the option to extend for a three-year period. . . ."

In early 1992 Atlas must have been optimistic about the coming year, because on March 19, 1992, Bartholomew wrote CIPS and proposed a delivery schedule for the remainder of 1992 that would not only make up all existing deficits, but would also leave a 41,000 ton surplus at year's end. On his file copy of the letter, Bartholomew wrote a note to Pieper in which he expressed doubt that CIPS would agree to accept 41,000 tons of surplus coal in 1992. Bartholomew indicated that if CIPS refused, Atlas would insist on selling that surplus to another buyer and crediting it against its obligation to CIPS.

CIPS initiated the only written amendment to the contract when, on September 4, 1992, it wrote to Atlas to complain about the coal's moisture content and Gross Calorific Value. The parties resolved CIPS' complaints in a written amendment signed by J.L. Lisenbee and Bartholomew. The amendment provided that "[e]xcept as hereby amended, the Agreement and each and every provision and condition thereof, is and shall remain in full force and effect."

On September 29, 1992, CIPS informed Atlas that it wished to receive 250,000 tons of coal during 1993. During the negotiations about coal quality, Bartholomew wrote CIPS a letter regarding coal shipments for the remainder of 1992. He stated that Atlas had encountered mining problems and anticipated ending 1992 with a "carry-over of 1992 'tonnage due'. Per our discussion, we will deliver any 1992 carry-over tonnage at 1992 contract pricing." On October 28, 1992, Bartholomew wrote CIPS with a proposed delivery schedule for 1993. He estimated that Atlas would deliver between 280,000 to 290,000 tons of coal and said that Atlas would like to ship any excess coal to make up contract deficits.

The parties again met to discuss 1993 shipments on November 9, 1992. At the meeting, CIPS indicated that it wanted to receive 300,000 tons of coal during 1993. In a follow-up letter, CIPS stated:

> With respect to 1990 through 1992 shipments from the Buck Creek Mine to CIPS, it is projected that the cumulative shortfall will equal approximately 134,000 tons (see attached information). It is CIPS' position that this initial 134,000 tons, or whatever the cumulative shortfall might be as of December 31, 1992, shipped during 1993, will be billed at the 1992 price. . . . All remaining tonnage shipped during 1993, up to 250,000 tons, will be billed at the 1993 price. . . .

Atlas delivered 167,387 tons of coal in 1992. CIPS paid for the first 45,325 tons at the 1991 price, and the remaining 122,062 tons at the 1992 price.

1993 was not a good year for Atlas. In April, the United Mine Workers of America, who had just been chosen to represent miners at the Buck Creek mine, began a strike. During all of 1993, Atlas only delivered 83,605 tons of coal, all of which CIPS bought at the 1992 price.

1994 was little better. That year, Atlas shipped 129,756 tons of coal. CIPS paid for the first 44,333 tons at the 1992 price, and the balance (85,423 tons) at the 1993 price. In December 1994, Atlas lost its other major contract for coal. Atlas had previously supplied high sulfur coal from the south section of its mine to Hoosier Energy's Merom generating plant. The contract expired in December 1994, and was not renewed. Upon receiving the bad news, Atlas shut down its entire mine.

The loss of the Merom contract and the subsequent shutdown of the mine triggered a series of events in late 1994 and early 1995. First, Atlas' bank exercised its right under security agreements with Atlas to direct CIPS to forward all payments directly to the bank. When CIPS learned of this development, it sent Atlas two letters on January 13, 1995. The first letter was a notice that CIPS was terminating the contract effective July 13, 1995. The termination was pursuant to a provision in the contract that allowed either party to terminate the agreement if the other failed to deliver or purchase 50% of the tonnage required during a six month period. The second letter demanded adequate assurances of performance pursuant to § 2-609 of the Illinois Commercial Code.

The parties met on January 16, 1995. Charles Schulties (who had stepped in as the manager of the mine) indicated that Old National Bank had been on the verge of providing additional financing, but had backed down when it learned of CIPS' position. In order to obtain financing necessary to reopen the Buck Creek mine, Atlas requested "assurances relative to the marketing of [its] coal" from CIPS. Atlas stated that financing was contingent on such assurances. In a letter sent on January 17, 1995, Schulties proposed to resume deliveries in February 1995 and continue them at a rate of 15,000 to 20,000 per month until December 1995 and then at a rate of 19,000 to 30,000 per month in 1996. On January 27, 1995 CIPS faxed a letter to Atlas at 11:06 a.m. The letter stated that CIPS would accept deliveries during 1995 on a probationary basis, but would not accept any coal past the December 31, 1995 termination date in the contract. The letter also spelled out various other terms and conditions for CIPS to continue buying coal from Atlas. One hour and fifteen minutes after CIPS faxed the letter to Atlas, Bartholomew left a voice mail message for Kirchner. The message stated that Atlas would resume shipments to Newton the following Monday morning.

Atlas resumed shipments to Newton on January 30, 1995. Then, in July 1995, Atlas approached CIPS about the possibility of continuing to contract past December 31, 1995. CIPS refused to do so. In a meeting on October 2, 1995, Schulties told CIPS that he believed that Atlas was entitled to ship all of the coal contracted for under the contract, even it that meant CIPS would have to accept delivery in 1996 and beyond. CIPS disputed that claim. Atlas delivered 250,048 tons of coal in 1995. CIPS paid the 1993 price for the first 164,577 tons and the 1994 price for the remaining 85,471 tons.

D. *The Proceedings Before this Court*

CIPS filed its Complaint for Declaratory Judgment on December 1, 1995. In its Complaint for Declaratory Judgment, CIPS sought a declaration that: (1) the contract between CIPS and Atlas terminated on December 31, 1995; (2) CIPS has no further obligations under that contract after December 31, 1995; and (3) CIPS complied with its obligations under the contract. Defendants answered on January 8, 1996. Defendants also raised as an affirmative defense the claim that the contract was extended by agreement, course of dealing, and waiver. Finally, Defendants asserted a counterclaim for breach of contract. CIPS answered the Counterclaim on January 29, 1996. In February 1996, the Court allowed CIPS to amend its Complaint to include a claim for damages based on Atlas' alleged failure to timely deliver the agreed upon quantities of coal.

On January 19, 1996, creditors of Indiana Coal Company filed an involuntary bankruptcy petition under Chapter 7 of the Bankruptcy Code. On Indiana Coal's motion, the bankruptcy court converted the case to one under Chapter 11. The bankruptcy court also modified the automatic stay to allow this case to proceed.

On March 19, 1996, after informing the Court that they had filed for bankruptcy under Chapter 11, Defendants filed an Amended Answer and Counterclaim. CIPS answered the Amended Counterclaim on March 27, 1996 and raised three affirmative defenses. CIPS added a fourth affirmative defense later. . . .

II. ANALYSIS

The Court will only reach the first two motions for summary judgment and will dispose of this case entirely based on those motions. Specifically, the Court finds that CIPS never waived the December 31, 1995 termination date, so the contract must be enforced as written, at least with respect to the termination date. The Court, however, rejects CIPS' damages claim because CIPS waived its right to enforce the contract's delivery schedule by acquiescing in Atlas' course of performance. Finally, the Court concludes that CIPS was not required to accept more than 250,000 tons of coal during 1995, as Atlas contends. Thus, CIPS is entitled to a declaratory judgment stating that CIPS has done all that the contract required and Atlas is entitled to judgment in its favor on Count II of the Amended Complaint.

A. *The Law*

The contract in this case was one for the sale of goods, namely coal. Accordingly, it is governed by Article 2 of the Illinois Commercial Code, found at 810 ILCS §§ 5/2-101 to 5/2-725 (West 1993). Under the UCC, the instant contract is considered one between merchants. UCC § 2-104 (defining merchants as those "who deal in goods of the kind" or hold themselves out "as having knowledge or skill peculiar to the practices or goods involved in the transaction").

To resolve the dispute in this case, the Court must reconcile and then apply three parts of the UCC. The first is the UCC provision that allows contracting parties to agree that their written contracts may not be modified except by a signed writing. The *second* is the UCC provision that allows "attempts at modification" to waive terms in a written contract, despite a clause in the contract allowing only written and signed modifications. The *third* provision is the UCC's rule on course of performance, which states that although course of performance is generally an interpretive tool, it may also be relevant to show a waiver of any terms inconsistent with the course of performance.

Unlike the common law, which takes a skeptical view of contract provisions requiring modifications to be in writing, *see Williams v. Jader Fuel Co.*, 944 F.2d 1388, 1394 (7th Cir. 1991) (reciting the common law principle that parties may orally modify a contract even after they include a contract provision requiring modifications to be in writing), the UCC strictly enforces such provisions. *See Wisconsin Knife Works v. National Metal Crafters*, 781 F.2d 1280, 1284-85 (7th Cir. 1986), 1 James J. White & Robert S. Summers, Uniform Commercial Code 40 (4th ed. 1995). In § 2-209(2), the UCC states: "A signed agreement which excludes modification or rescission except by a signed writing cannot otherwise be modified or rescinded, but except as between merchants such a requirement on a form supplied by the merchant must be separately signed by the other party."

Not unlike the common law, however, the UCC provides some relief to parties who have agreed in writing that their agreement may not be changed except in writing and who have then performed or orally agreed to perform in a manner different from that specified by the written contract. In § 2-209(4), the Code provides that "[al]though an attempt at modification or rescission does not satisfy the requirements of [§ 2-209(2)] it can operate as a waiver." The leading case on §§ 2-209(2) and (4) is *Wisconsin Knife Works v. National Metal Crafters,* 781 F.2d 1280 (7th Cir. 1986). In that case, the United States Court of Appeals for the Seventh Circuit, applying Wisconsin's Uniform Commercial Code, rejected a claim that delivery dates in a contract had been modified because the party asserting modification had not identified a written modification. *Id.* at 1284-85. The court then examined whether the parties had waived the delivery dates by virtue of an attempted modification. The court concluded that to prove that an attempt at modification led to a waiver, the party asserting waiver must prove not only the existence of an oral modification (or other modification that does not comply with the contract's terms) but must also prove that it relied on the alleged waiver. *Id.* at 1287-88. . . .

To add another layer of complexity, UCC § 2-208 also speaks to the issue. . . .

By its terms, § 2-208 is primarily an interpretive tool. *See* § 2-208(1) (course of performance "shall be relevant to determine the meaning of the agreement"); § 2-208, cmt. 1 ("This section . . . rounds out the set of factors which determine the meaning of the 'agreement'. . . ."); *see also Wagner Excello Foods v. Fearn International, Inc.*, 235 Ill.App.3d 224, 176 Ill.Dec. 258, 264, 601 N.E.2d 956, 962 (1st Dist. 1992) (noting that course of performance is often used to determine the meaning of an agreement). Section 2-208 also permits course of performance to "show a waiver or modification of any term inconsistent with" the contracting parties' course of performance. § 2-208(3). Section 2-208(3), however, states that course of performance can only show waiver or modification of inconsistent terms "[s]ubject to the provisions of" § 2-209. This qualification seems intended to achieve a limited purpose: subjecting waivers by course of performance to § 2-209(5) which allows retraction of a waiver. § 2-208, cmt. 3 ("Where it is difficult to determine whether a particular act merely sheds light on the meaning of a term of the agreement, the preference is in favor of 'waiver' whenever such construction, plus the application of the provisions on reinstatement of rights waived . . . is needed to preserve the flexible character of commercial contracts and to prevent surprise or other hardship.").[8]

Waiver is not defined in the UCC, but its meaning is well established. Generally, "waiver in contract law is the intentional relinquishment of a known right." *Sethness-Greenleaf, Inc. v. Green River Corp.*, 65 F.3d 64, 67 (7th Cir. 1995). . . .

The burden is on Atlas to prove that CIPS waived any provisions of the written contract. *See Wisconsin Knife Works*, 781 F.2d at 1285. Waiver seems like a factual issue. However, when the relevant facts of the case are undisputed and only one possible inference may arise from those facts, waiver is a legal question. *Wagner Excello Foods, Inc.*, 176 Ill.Dec. at 264, 601 N.E.2d at 962. Thus, to win on its waiver claims, Atlas must show, by reference to undisputed facts, that CIPS intentionally relinquished its right under the contract.

B. *The Termination Date*

1. The Contract

In contract law, the place to start is with the written contract, if there is one. In this case, the parties—both sophisticated participants in the coal market—signed a detailed written contract. The contract ended by its terms on December 31, 1995 and it stated that the parties could not modify it unless they did so in a writ-

---

[8] [3] In this case, the only question is whether the parties waived any of the contract's provisions. The contract precluded all modifications except those written and signed by both parties. Section 2-209(4) only allows attempts at modification to constitute waivers. Section 2-208(3) allows course of performance to show either a waiver or a modification of a term inconsistent with the course of performance. But since that section is expressly subject to § 2-209's provisions on modification, it appears that the question here is limited to whether any terms of the contract were waived by course of performance.

Waiver and modification are distinct concepts. "[I]f the court asks whether the conduct of the parties amounted to a 'modification,' it will determine whether there was assent by applying the usual rules for the formation of contracts; if the court asks whether the conduct amounted to a 'waiver,' it may give effect to more dubious manifestations of assent." 2 E. Allan Farnsworth, Farnsworth on Contracts § 8.5 at 375 (1990).

ing signed by both parties. UCC § 2-209(2) provides an easy answer, initially Atlas admits that no written modification exists which alters the December 31, 1995 termination date. Thus, under the terms of the contract (which are fully enforceable under § 2-209(2)) the termination date remained December 31, 1995.

2.   Attempt at Modification?

The Court, then, must pass to the next question under UCC § 2-209: did the parties attempt to modify the contract's termination date, and if so, does their attempt support Atlas' claim that CIPS waived the termination date? From the facts the Court has already recited, it is obvious that the parties did not attempt to modify the termination date of the contract. Additionally, nothing in CIPS' conduct suggests that CIPS intentionally relinquished its right to cease performance on December 31, 1995.

The contract provided for coal deliveries in the years 1990-95. Problems with deliveries began in 1990. At that time, Atlas sought to declare a force majeure with respect to 69,629 tons of coal to be delivered in 1990. CIPS' December 12, 1990 letter shows that CIPS did not want to excuse delivery of that coal under the contract's force majeure clause and instead wanted to work out an alternate schedule for delivery of the 1990 shortfall. Initially, CIPS proposed taking deliveries of coal in 1996. Indeed, the initial proposal was for Atlas to make up the 1990 shortfall by delivering 15,000 tons of coal in both 1994 and 1995 and 39,629 tons in 1996. On February 18, 1991, Atlas wrote to CIPS with a revised proposal for making up the shortfall. In that letter, Atlas suggested the same deliveries for 1994 and 1995 but proposed that CIPS could take 39,629 tons in addition to "contract tonnage elected by [CIPS]—1996." By the time CIPS sent its proposed formal letter agreement to Atlas on March 6, 1991, the proposal was for CIPS to have an option to purchase 39,629 tons of coal in 1996. Atlas' March 21, 1991 response to that proposal stated: "During 1996, CIPS shall have the option to receive 39,629 tons."

Atlas claims that the contract was amended in early 1991 to bar the parties from filing further force majeure claims and to allow Atlas to deliver all 1,350,000 tons of coal contemplated by the agreement, regardless of the year of delivery. The parties' correspondence does not support either claim. Even if the correspondence and discussion of the parties can be considered "an attempt at modification" under UCC § 2-209(4), the attempted modification dealt only with the 1990 tonnage shortfall. Additionally, the best evidence of the extent of the purported attempted modification are the letters of March 6, 1991 and March 21, 1991 and neither letter discusses modifying the contract's termination date or barring the parties from filing force majeure claims. At best, the letters show that the parties agreed to make up the 1990 tonnage shortfall as quickly as possible with CIPS having an *option* to buy coal in 1996.

The overall course of events further limits the impact of the March 1991 letters. By the end of 1991, Atlas had delivered 274,034 tons of coal. CIPS paid the 1990 contract price for the first 69,629 tons. Neither side protested this; therefore, the issue of the 1990 tonnage shortfall was resolved. The discussions regarding the 1990 tonnage shortfall were the last time until early 1995 that the parties expressly discussed the contract's termination date.

Of course, delivery problems did not end with the 1990 tonnage shortfall. As just noted, Atlas came up 45,325 tons short by the end of 1991. To remedy this situation, Atlas proposed a delivery schedule for 1992 that would have made up that deficit and ended 1992 with a delivery *surplus*. By the end of 1992, however, Atlas still lagged behind in deliveries and proposed to deliver any "1992 carryover tonnage at 1992 contract pricing." This routine continued, with Atlas falling farther and farther behind on deliveries, until December 1994. Despite the fact that it was becoming increasingly difficult to do so, it appears from all of the evidence that the parties intended to make up all of the tonnage shortfalls by the end of 1995. And nothing in the record indicates that the parties discussed going beyond that year.

The parties' agreement for 1995 deliveries, the agreement that allowed the Buck Creek mine to stay open, expressly barred deliveries in 1996. When the Atlas mine shut down in December 1994, it reopened only after assurances by CIPS that it would continue to accept coal in 1995. In response to CIPS' notice of termination and demands for adequate assurances, Atlas proposed a delivery schedule that would have spanned 1995 and 1996. In a counteroffer, CIPS said it would accept coal on a probationary basis in 1995 only. Atlas' representative accepted this proposal by leaving a telephone message for CIPS stating that Atlas would resume shipments within the next few days. Again, to the extent the January 1995 negotiations can be considered "an attempt at modification," the modification consisted of reinstating the contract (which would have terminated in July 1995 if CIPS had not agreed to accept deliveries for all of 1995) for the purpose of delivering coal in 1995 only.

The preceding summary demonstrates that the parties never attempted to modify the termination date. At the very least, the evidence shows that modifying the termination date was initially placed on the bargaining table, but subsequently withdrawn. Other evidence—evidence of Atlas' own conduct—shows that Atlas never believed that CIPS had agreed to extend the contract beyond 1995. In its January 1992 financing proposal to Old National Bank, Atlas repeatedly stated that its contract with CIPS terminated at the end of 1995. Atlas alleges that the parties amended the contract to extend beyond December 31, 1995 sometime in early 1991. If so, why didn't Atlas share that information with its bank? Furthermore, in mid 1995, Atlas sought to negotiate a contract extension, another strange act if Atlas believed that CIPS had already agreed to accept deliveries in 1996 and beyond.

Even if the facts could support a claim that the parties attempted to modify the contract's termination date, the facts do not permit a finding that that provision was waived. To prove a waiver, Atlas would have to show that CIPS intentionally relinquished its right to cease performance on December 31, 1995. *See Sethness-Greenleaf, Inc.*, 65 F.3d at 67 (stating that a waiver requires intentional relinquishment of a known right). The evidence reveals no conduct which could possibly show that. Finally, Atlas makes a great deal out of the fact that CIPS never explicitly withdrew its proposal to accept deliveries in 1996. Atlas apparently means to rely on UCC § 2-209(5) but that provision is inapplicable because CIPS never waived the termination date.

3. Course of Performance

The final step under the UCC is to determine whether course of performance might play a role in deciding whether the contract terminated on December 31, 1995. Course of performance is primarily an interpretative tool. UCC § 2-208(1) (stating that course of performance "shall be relevant to determine the meaning of the agreement"); *Sethness-Greenleaf, Inc.,* 65 F.3d at 67 (" '[C]ourse of performance' can be used to flesh out an ambiguous or incomplete agreement."). As far as the termination date is concerned, the contract was neither ambiguous nor incomplete. Thus, course of performance is only relevant to the extent it is evidence of a waiver. § 2-208(3).

The course of performance under the contract was that until 1995, whenever Atlas was unable to deliver a year's tonnage, CIPS allowed Atlas to deliver that tonnage in following years, but at the price stated in the contract for the year Atlas should have delivered the coal. That course of performance has implications for the contract's internal delivery schedule, but not for the termination date. There is no course of performance that might shed light on the validity or meaning of the termination date provision. And even if CIPS had taken coal after December 31, 1995, a single instance of conduct does not amount to course of performance. *See* § 2-208, cmt. 4 ("A single occasion of conduct does not fall within the language of this section. . . .").

Furthermore, to the extent that performance within the contract's term is relevant to interpreting or applying the termination date, the Court must first decide if that course of performance may be reasonably construed consistently with the termination date. § 2-208(2) ("The express terms of the agreement and any such course of performance, as well as any course of dealing and usage of trade, shall be construed whenever reasonable as consistent with each other; but when such construction is unreasonable, the express terms shall control course of performance. . ."). The parties abandoned the internal delivery and price schedules to allow Atlas to make up shortfalls—that much is evident in their conduct and communications. It is not inconsistent with that course of performance to conclude that performance should cease on the contract's termination date. Indeed, the parties' correspondence and conduct demonstrates that they abandoned the internal delivery and price schedules in order to make up shortfalls before the end of the contract. Thus, the Court can construe the termination date and the course of performance (i.e. abandoning the internal delivery and price schedules) consistently with each other, so the Court need not disregard the express term (the termination date). In any event, when the terms of a contract conflict with the course of performance, § 2-208(2) provides that the express terms govern. Accordingly, even if the course of performance and the termination date cannot be construed consis`tently with each other, the termination date would control.

In summary, the Court finds as follows: (1) the parties did not modify the contract's termination date in writing, as the contract required; (2) the parties did not attempt to modify the contract's termination date so that term could not have been waived; and (3) there is no course of performance relevant to interpreting or applying the contract's termination date. Accordingly, the parties' contractual obligations ceased on December 31, 1995. . . .

III. CONCLUSION

The parties in this case entered into a five year contract for the sale and purchase of coal. The contract had both a fixed end date and fixed delivery and price schedules. Because the coal mine could not produce according to the contract, the parties abandoned the delivery and price schedules in the hope that the mine would catch up before the contract terminated. At the beginning of the contract's final year, the mine shut down and reopened only after CIPS agreed to buy only as much coal that year as it had originally promised.

In this lawsuit, Atlas has claimed that the parties modified the contract in various ways. Atlas cannot prove most of those claims. The only alteration the Court finds was of the internal delivery and price schedules, which the parties waived. Accordingly, the Court will enforce the contract's termination date, but will not permit CIPS to recover damages for late deliveries that occurred during the contract's term.

In short, the Court finds that both parties to this contract may simply walk away from the contract. CIPS was not obliged to accept any more coal than it did. Atlas and Indiana Coal performed as required under the contract, as modified by course of performance. Neither side owes the other any damages. This result is no doubt of little comfort to Indiana Coal, which is now in bankruptcy. But in light of the mine's miserable performance during the term of its contract with the utility, the Court cannot justly place blame anywhere but with the mine. . . .

NOTES AND QUESTIONS

1. *CISG and modification-in-writing clauses:* The Convention on International Sale of Goods provides in Article 29 that "[a] contract may be modified or terminated by the mere agreement of the parties." At the same time, the Article gives effect to contract clauses which require that modification be in writing. However, (and we might have expected the however) the Article goes on to provide that "a party may be precluded by his conduct from asserting such a provision to the extent that the other party has relied on that conduct." How different is the approach taken by the CISG from that advocated by Judge Posner in *Wisconsin Knife* (discussed in the *Central Illinois Public Service* opinion, *supra*)?

B. WAIVING CONDITIONS CONTRASTED WITH MODIFYING CONTRACTS

CLARK v. WEST
Court of Appeals of New York
193 N.Y. 349, 86 N.E. 1 (1908)

[Plaintiff, an author, sued defendant, a publisher, for breach of contract. The trial court overruled defendant's demurrer to the complaint. The Appellate Division reversed this decision and sustained the demurrer. But the Court of Appeals reversed the Appellate Division, ruling that the complaint stated a cause of action.

Clark, the plaintiff, alleged that he had entered a contract with the West Publishing Company to write and prepare for publication a series of law books. Manuscripts were to be satisfactory to West. Clark promised "to totally abstain from the use of intoxicating liquors during the continuance of this contract, and the payment to him in accordance with the terms of this contract of any money in excess of $2 per page is dependent on the faithful performance of this as well as the other conditions of this contract." Clark was to be paid $2 a page for each manuscript accepted by West. The contract continued, stating that if Clark "abstains from the use of intoxicating liquor and otherwise fulfills his agreements, . . . he shall be paid an additional $4 per page."

Clark's complaint alleged that West published Clark's three-volume work on corporations. The book was successful, and West received large net receipts. The work contained 3,469 pages. West paid Clark at a rate of $2 per page ($6,938). It refused to pay Clark the additional $4 a page. Clark fully performed the contract, except he "did not totally abstain from the use of intoxicating liquor during the continuance of said contract, but such use by the plaintiff was not excessive and did not prevent or interfere with the due and full performance by the plaintiff of all the other stipulations in said contract."

The complaint stated that the intoxicating liquor condition had been waived. Long prior to the completion of the book, West had full knowledge that Clark drank intoxicating liquor. It did not then terminate the contract. Its agents failed to object. They continued to "exact and require of the plaintiff performance of all the other stipulations and conditions." West continued to receive installments of manuscript and continued to make advance payments. It published the book. At no time did West's agents "notify or intimate to the plaintiff that defendant would insist upon strict compliance, or that defendant intended to take advantage of plaintiff's said breach." "[W]ith full knowledge of plaintiff's said use of intoxicating liquors, defendant repeatedly avowed and represented to the plaintiff that he was entitled to and would receive said royalty payment [the full $6 a page], and plaintiff believed and relied on said representation, and in reliance thereon continued in the performance of said contract."]

WERNER, J. . . . Briefly stated, the defendant's position is that the stipulation as to plaintiff's total abstinence is the consideration for the payment of the difference between $2 and $6 per page, and therefore could not be waived except by a new agreement to that effect based upon a good consideration; that the so-called waiver alleged by the plaintiff is not a waiver, but a modification of the contract in respect of its consideration. The plaintiff, on the other hand, argues that the stipulation for his total abstinence was merely a condition precedent, intended to work a forfeiture of the additional compensation in case of a breach, and that it could be waived without any formal agreement to that effect based upon a new consideration.

The subject-matter of the contract was the writing of books by the plaintiff for the defendant. The duration of the contract was the time necessary to complete them all. The work was to be done to the satisfaction of the defendant, and the plaintiff was not to write any other books except those covered by the contract unless requested to do so by the defendant, in which latter event he was to be paid for that particular work by the year. The compensation for the work specified in the contract was to be $6 per page, unless the plaintiff failed to totally abstain from the use of intoxicating liquors during the continuance of the contract, in which event he was to receive only $2 per page. That is the obvious import of the contract construed in the light of the purpose for which it was made, and in accordance with the ordinary meaning of plain language. It is not a contract to write books in order that the plaintiff shall keep sober, but a contract containing a stipulation that he shall keep sober so that he may write satisfactory books. When we view the contract from this standpoint, it will readily be perceived that the particular stipulation is not the consideration for the contract, but simply one of its conditions which fits in with those relating to time and method of delivery of manuscript, revision of proof, citation of cases, assignment of copyrights, keeping track of new cases and citations for new editions, and other details which might be waived by the defendant, if he saw fit to do so. This is made clear, it seems to us, by the provision that, "in consideration of the above promises," the defendant agrees to pay the plaintiff $2 per page on each book prepared by him, and if he "abstains from the use of intoxicating liquor and otherwise fulfills his agreements as hereinbefore set forth, he shall be paid an additional $4 per page in manner hereinbefore stated." The compensation of $2 per page, not to exceed $250 per month, was an advance or partial payment of the whole price of $6 per page, and the payment of the two-thirds, which was to be withheld pending the performance of the contract, was simply made contingent upon the plaintiff's total abstention from the use of intoxicants during the life of the contract. . . .

It is obvious that the parties thought that the plaintiff's normal work was worth $6 per page. That was the sum to be paid for the work done by the plaintiff, and not for total abstinence. If the plaintiff did not keep to the condition as to total abstinence, he was to lose part of that sum. . . . This, we think is the fair interpretation of the contract, and it follows that the stipulation as to the plaintiff's total abstinence was nothing more nor less than a condition precedent. If that conclusion is well founded, there can be no escape from the corollary that this condition could be waived; and, if it was waived, the defendant is clearly not in a position to insist upon the forfeiture which his waiver was intended to annihilate. The forfeiture must stand or fall with the condition. If the latter was waived, the former is no longer a part of the contract. Defendant still has the right to counterclaim for any damages which he may have sustained in consequence of the plaintiff's breach, but he cannot insist upon strict performance. . . .

The theory upon which the defendant's attitude seems to be based is that, even if he has represented to the plaintiff that he would not insist upon the condition that the latter should observe total abstinence from intoxicants, he can still refuse to pay the full contract price for his work. The inequity of this position becomes apparent when we consider that this contract was to run for a period of years, during a large portion of which the plaintiff was to be entitled only to the advance payment of $2 per page; the balance being contingent, among other things, upon publication of the books and returns from sales. Upon this theory the defendant might have waived the condition while the first book was in process of production, and yet, when the whole work was completed, he would still be in a position to insist upon the forfeiture because there had not been strict performance. Such a situation is possible in a case where the subject of the waiver is the very consideration of a contract . . . but not where the waiver relates to something that can be waived. In the case at bar, as we have seen, the waiver is not of the consideration or subject-matter, but of an incident to the method of performance. The consideration remains the same. The defendant has had the work he bargained for, and it is alleged that he has waived one of the conditions as to the manner in which it was to have been done. He might have insisted upon literal performance, and then he could have stood upon the letter of his contract. If, however, he has waived that incidental condition, he has created a situation to which the doctrine of waiver very precisely applies.

The cases which present the most familiar phases of the doctrine of waiver are those which have arisen out of litigation over insurance policies where the defendants have claimed a forfeiture because of the breach of some condition in the contract . . . , but it is a doctrine of general application which is confined to no particular class of cases. A "waiver" has been defined to be the intentional relinquishment of a known right. It is voluntary and implies an election to dispense with something of value, or forego some advantage which the party waiving it might at its option have demanded or insisted upon. . . . In the recent case of *Draper v. Oswego Co. Fire R. Ass'n*, 190 N.Y. 12, 16, 82 N.E. 755, Chief Judge Cullen, in speaking for the court upon this subject, said: "While that doctrine and the doctrine of equitable estoppel are often confused in insurance litigation, there is a clear distinction between the two. A 'waiver' is the voluntary abandonment or relinquishment by a party of some right or advantage. . . . The doctrine of equitable estoppel, or estoppel *in pais*, is that a party may be precluded by his acts and conduct from asserting a right to the detriment of another party who, entitled to rely on such conduct, has acted upon it. . . . As already said, the doctrine of waiver is to relieve against forfeiture; it requires no consideration for a waiver, nor any prejudice or injury to the other party." . . .

In the . . . complaint, the plaintiff alleges facts and circumstances which we think, if established, would prove defendant's waiver of plaintiff's performance of [the] contract stipulation [calling for total abstinence]. . . .

NOTES AND QUESTIONS

1. *Getting performance from a delinquent*: Suppose the West Publishing Co. editor in charge of Clark's book wanted to get the best book written as close to on time as possible. The editor knows Clark has a problem with alcohol. The editor becomes aware of Clark's drinking. What does the opinion in *Clark v. West* suggest that the editor should do to preserve West's rights to pay only $2 a page for the manuscript? Could the editor do anything less than give Clark formal notice that the publisher would not pay the added $4 a page? What might a reasonable editor fear would be the consequence of such a notice?

Furthermore, the court seems to see the case as one involving forfeiture. West has the book, but now it won't pay the contract price for it. Is the quality of the book necessarily the same as West had hoped for? Is it possible that Clark's book produced while drinking is acceptable but that he could have written an excellent one had he not taken a single drink? The court says West could sue for its damages caused by Clark's drinking. How would you compute them? Or, suppose West's editor discovered Clark's drinking. The editor then told Clark that he would be paid only $2 a page. Clark finished the book. It became a best seller, and West earned a great deal from its publication. Moreover, knowledgeable critics praised the book as well written and thought-out. Should Clark then be able to recover the additional $4 a page?

2. *Consideration and waiver—some history I*: Suppose I owe you $1,000, and I am supposed to pay you today. I tell you that I am in financial trouble and have only $600. You agree to discharge the debt if I will pay you $600 now. Later you discover that I have plenty of money. You can sue me for $400 because your release was not supported by *consideration*. Or suppose I am the captain of a fishing boat. You agree to work on the boat during a trip for a certain wage. When we arrive at the fishing area, you refuse to work unless I double your wage. I agree to do this. When we return to port, I refuse to pay you the additional money. I can defeat your lawsuit for the additional money both because of duress and the lack of consideration for my promise to pay more for the services you promised me.

Of course, as you are aware, courts have sidestepped the pre-existing duty rule in many ways. Suppose, for example, you and I rescind our first contract. I give up my rights against you in exchange for your giving up your rights against me. Now we are free to walk away and have no dealings. However, we are also free to make a new contract, under which you must pay me more to do what I promised to do for less under our original deal. Some courts have found that when we modify a contract we are impliedly rescinding our original deal. Thus, there is consideration for our new bargain. The doctrine of consideration is more than an exercise in abstract logic. The technical rules can be manipulated to reach desired results.

In classic contract theory, modifications of bargains required consideration. However, this did not apply to waivers of certain conditions to duties under contracts. Suppose, for example, a buyer accepts services a week after the contract called for them to be rendered. The buyer says nothing about the delay. Six months later the buyer wants to sue the seller for the delay. The seller argues that the buyer waived its rights by accepting the services a week late. The buyer argues that this would be a modification of the contract unsupported by consideration. Section 88 of the original Restatement of Contracts recognized that there could be a waiver of rights without consideration if, in our example, performance on time was "not a substantial part of what was to have been given in exchange for" the buyer's duty to pay money and if "the uncertainty of the happening of" performance on time "was not a substantial element in inducing the formation of the contract."

Professor Farnsworth explains the fondness courts have had for waiver. It "permits more flexibility in dealing with the conduct of the parties at the performance stage then would the rules of contract law that are designed for the negotiation stage. By characterizing the conduct as a 'waiver' rather than as a 'modification,' a court may avoid three requirements for a modification: the requirement of assent, the requirement of a writing under the statute of frauds, and the requirement of consideration or of detrimental reliance." He notes that "if the court asks whether the conduct amounted to a 'waiver,' it may give effect to more dubious manifestations of assent." "[I]f the court concludes that the conduct amounted to a 'waiver,' the statute [of frauds] is not relevant." Moreover, if there is a waiver that is effective without consideration or reliance, it can be retracted. "If a party, without consideration, has waived a condition that is within the other party's control *before* the time for occurrence of the condition has expired, he can retract the waiver and reinstate the condition unless the other party has relied to such an extent that retraction would be unjust."[9]

Waiver, then, is a useful tool. But why did courts want such a tool? Why did they want to turn off rules such as those dealing with mutual assent, consideration, the Statute of Frauds and the literal reading of conditions?

3.   *Consideration and waiver—some history II*: The opinion in *Clark v. West* tells us that much of the development of waiver came from judicial opinions dealing with insurance contracts. Spencer Kimball studied insurance regulation in Wisconsin from 1835 to 1959.[10] He found that courts regulated the administration of insurance claims. They attempted to balance two policies: they tried to give effect to the reasonable expectations of the parties while at the same time preserve the integrity of the insurance fund by preventing unwarranted raids on it by persons not entitled to share. Major fires destroyed large cities throughout the second half of the Nineteenth Century, and the insurance companies were faced with the threat of serious losses.

> [I]t became industry policy to tighten up loss settlement practices. Suspicion of arson seldom resulted in a defense frankly based on an allegation of criminal incendiarism; instead the companies used whatever technical defenses came to hand. Moreover, to protect the companies against fraudulent and exorbitant claims, and to give time for adequate investigation, it was industry policy to delay settlement as long as possible under the contract. Though insurance men were presumably actuated

---

[9] Farnsworth, Contracts 561-63 (1982).
[10] Kimball, Insurance and Public Policy (Wisconsin Press 1960).

only by creditable motives, no device can be imagined more calculated to harm the industry's public relations than a set policy of arbitrary delay of loss settlement for the maximum period permitted by law.[11]

Loss settlement usually involved two steps which policies made conditions to recovery. First, the insured had to give notice within a certain time. Second, it had to submit proofs of the amount of loss within another specified time after that. Insureds often missed the deadlines. Kimball says "the judges were not willing to forfeit the insured's protection by reason of his failure to perform these technical conditions, so long as they could possibly rationalize a contrary result without overtly discarding the canon that freedom of contract was a basic value."[12] This provoked a game between the courts and insurance company lawyers.

> The industry men saw it as a game, the object of which for them was finding and using language so explicit that the court could find in it no latent ambiguity. Though in fact the courts were less hostile than company men supposed, industry committees frequently made drafting suggestions for making the contracts so airtight that even a judge with a strong bias against insurance companies could not misunderstand. . . . Occasionally someone expressed a more pessimistic view—that the courts were creating liability arbitrarily outside the contract. If that were true, more careful drafting would help little.[13]

Lawrence Friedman[14] developed these ideas further. He argued first that classic contract law was grounded in abstraction; it assumed a system of doctrine that appears to be constructed by the deduction of rules from principles. The principles are universal. That is, they are applicable whether the parties are rich or poor, without regard to the subject matter of the transaction, and are unchanging over time. But, Friedman argued next, it is not really possible for a rapidly developing economy to cope with this abstract law which gave no regard to context and change. How was the idea of abstract contract law applied to serve the needs of a developing economy? Two of the tools which Friedman suggests the courts used to bridge this gap were waiver and estoppel. He notes:

> It might offend a purist to talk in one breath about estoppel, waiver, ratification, election of remedies, laches, and accord and satisfaction. These were all different concepts, with different histories and uses. They had in common, however, that they all related to particular acts of particular parties, subsequent to the formation of a contract but affecting the contract rights of the actors. And they were all ideas that could be used to bend rules of higher generality. Though they themselves could be expressed in terms of rules, they constituted statements of reasons (derived from the facts of particular cases) why some more general rule should not be applied.

---

[11] *Id.* at 215.

[12] *Id.* at 213.

[13] *Id.* at 211-12.

[14] Friedman, CONTRACT LAW IN AMERICA: A SOCIAL AND ECONOMIC CASE STUDY (Wisconsin Press 1965). Reprinted by permission of The University of Wisconsin Press.

. . . A concept like estoppel is in essence antithetical to pure contract abstraction. A party is "estopped" for reasons which are peculiar to his or her opponent's situation. Abstraction, however, abhors the special and the particular. [Friedman then notes that the use of these concepts was common throughout the period he was studying (1836 to 1958) but was perhaps more common at the end of the nineteenth century. The use of the doctrines to give relief in individual cases avoided the "bother or embarrassment" of making radical changes in the formal doctrine.]

Waiver and estoppel were not used only on a case-by-case basis. If the court had a consistent bias of values in a given area of transactions, it sometimes applied one or more of these concepts consistently in handling such transactions. This warping and sliding process was characteristic of the way the common law developed. After a generation or two in which a court consistently found that not the general rule but the "exception" applied to whatever cases was at hand, the original general rule turned into a mummified corpse. Historically the insurance companies were on the losing end of such a process, which, by the use of "estoppel" and "waiver," created what amounted to a set of rules for construing insurance policies so as to aid the insured. This process of attrition took place frequently in the law; and in the twentieth century "legal realism" gave dead rules decent burial in many instances simply by pointing out that the old rules were no longer used even when legal literature still paid them lip service.

4.   *Consideration and waiver—the Restatement (Second) of Contracts provisions*: Modern courts have allowed parties to modify contracts without much concern about consideration. The Restatement (Second) of Contracts reflects this. It deals with both waiving conditions as in *Clark v. West* and modifying more central provisions of contracts. Section 84 provides:

> [A] promise to perform all or part of a conditional duty under an antecedent contract in spite of the non-occurrence of the condition is binding, whether the promise is made before or after the time for the condition to occur, unless
>
> > (a) occurrence of the condition was a material part of the agreed exchange for the performance of the duty and the promisee was under no duty that it occur; or
> >
> > (b) uncertainty of the occurrence of the condition was an element of the risk assumed by the promisor.

The section also allows a party to reinstate a condition that it has waived if a reasonable time to perform it remains, there has been so little reliance that reinstatement would not be unjust, and the promise is not enforceable on some other ground.[15]

---

[15] As we have noted several times in these materials, under the Restatement (Second) more significant changes in contracts also can be made without orthodox consideration. Section 89 provides:

5. *UCC § 2-209(1) and bad-faith modifications*: Section 2-209(1) overturns the pre-existing duty rule for modifications of transactions in goods. Official Comment 2 says:

> [M]odifications made thereunder [the section] must meet the test of good faith imposed by this Act. The effective use of bad faith to escape performance on the original contract terms is barred, and the extortion of a "modification" without legitimate commercial reason is ineffective as a violation of the duty of good faith. Nor can a mere technical consideration support a modification made in bad faith.

The Official Comment adds a good deal of substantive law to the text of the statute. Professor Robert Hillman[16] says that courts are reading the text of § 2-209(1) and ignoring the Official Comment. They are enforcing modifications without considering the issue of good faith.

He proposed an amendment to § 2-209(1) which would add two sentences to it: "An agreement modifying a contract made as a result of economic or other duress is not enforceable. The burden of establishing that a modification involving a material net loss to the party opposing its enforcement was not a product of duress is on the party seeking to enforce the modification." He would add to the Official Comment the following: "Factors relevant to determining whether a material net loss modification was entered into as a result of duress include the reasonableness of entering into the modification, the availability of market substitutes to the party seeking to avoid the modification, the manner of presentation of the modification, the reasons for seeking the modification, and the foreseeability of those reasons." Why haven't courts taken something such as this approach following the invitation in the UCC Comment?

6. *Elections contrasted with waivers*: An "election of remedies" may be seen as different from a "waiver" of right. For example, one of the most important remedies granted buyers by the UCC is the right to reject or return defective goods and have no obligation to pay for them. However, under UCC § 2-606(1)(a), a buyer "accepts" goods when "after a reasonable opportunity to inspect the goods," he signifies to the seller "that he will take or retain them in spite of their nonconformity." If the buyer has no "reasonable assumption that . . . [the] . . . non-conformity would be cured," then the buyer cannot return them. He has given up this remedy and *elected* to do nothing or seek damages. The seller need offer no new consideration nor prove that he relied on the statement. Does

---

A promise modifying a duty under a contract not fully performed on either side is binding
>   (a) if the modification is fair and equitable in view of circumstances not anticipated by the parties when the contract was made, or
>   (b) to the extent provided by statute; or
>   (c) to the extent that justice requires enforcement in view of material change of position in reliance on the promise.

See Lowey v. Watt, 684 F.2d 957 (D.C. Cir. 1982), for a case in which, for reasons analogous to those covered by Restatement (Second) of Contracts § 89, the court gave effect to a unilateral waiver even though there was neither consideration, nor notice.

[16] Hillman, *Policing Contract Modifications under the UCC: Good Faith and the Doctrine of Economic Duress,* 64 Iowa L. Rev. 849 (1979).

this kind of election of remedies significantly differ from a waiver of rights? The `buyer's choice may be less than ideally free when confronted by a delivery of defective but usable goods. She may no longer have time to find substitutes. Of course, she can accept the goods and sue for damages, but often this will not provide an adequate remedy. Yet under the language of the Code read literally, this does not seem to matter.

Chapter 5

PERFORMANCE AND BREACH OF CONTRACT

A. THE MAIN THEMES—PROMISES, CONDITIONS AND THE ROLE OF COURTS

1. THE LOGIC OF "CONDITIONS"

Suppose S and B make a legally enforceable contract under which S contracts to sell an antique car to B for $40,000. They agree in their written contract that S is to rebuild the engine before delivery of the car. After S and B close the deal, many things must happen before the transaction is completed. What happens to B's obligations if S does not perform some or all of his? Does it matter that S comes close to performing all his obligations but does not quite make it? Not surprisingly in a society that gives a high place to individual choice, courts and lawyers attempting to answer these questions give great weight to the parties' agreement. However, often the parties have said little about the details involved in carrying out their contract. In many instances, having just made a deal, they do not want to think about what will happen if one or both fails to perform. Courts often are called on to fill in gaps in planning.

Students may have difficulty with questions of performance and breach of contracts. Part of that difficulty comes from attempting to begin with complex issues before a number of simple matters are understood. Thus, it may help to consider some relatively easy examples in order to establish a vocabulary and see the logic of orthodox conditions analysis.

First, assume seller promises to deliver the car to buyer on April 7th if buyer is then ready, willing and able to pay $40,000 to seller. The buyer, in turn, promises to pay $40,000 on April 7th if seller is then ready, willing and able to deliver the car. Assume further that on April 7th, seller fails to deliver the goods and does not have a legally adequate excuse. Buyer, who was ready, willing and able to pay on April 7th, did not pay because seller failed to make delivery.

Suppose an unlikely event: seller sues buyer for failing to pay $40,000. *Seller would lose because buyer did not breach his promise.* Buyer did not make an unqualified promise to pay $40,000. He promised to pay ONLY IF seller was ready, willing and able to deliver the goods. Seller was not. Putting the matter in the vocabulary of contracts, a *condition precedent* to buyer's duty to perform was not fulfilled, and this failure serves to shield him from liability. Conditions precedent usually are "if" or "when" clauses qualifying promises to perform. If the qualifications are not met, then my promise literally does not bind me to do anything. I cannot be held liable for failing to do what I never promised to do.

Now assume the same contract and facts but add that buyer came to seller's place of business on April 7th with $40,000, asked for delivery of the goods and indicated clearly that he had the money and was ready to pay if seller was ready to deliver. As before, seller refused to deliver. Buyer could sue seller and win a judgment for damages because seller has failed to perform his promise—the conditions on that promise were fulfilled and so there was an obligation to perform.[1]

Notice that in the example, the *condition* to buyer's promise and seller's *promise* are almost the same. Buyer promises to pay *if and when seller delivers*. Seller promises to deliver *if and when buyer pays*. Paying is both a condition and promise; delivering, also, is both condition and promise. But paying is a condition to the promise to deliver and delivering is a condition to the promise to pay. These are simple ideas, but some students look for something subtle and complex. If you find this confusing, perhaps a diagram will help:

Buyer *promises* to pay on *condition* that seller deliver.

Seller *promises* to deliver on *condition* that buyer pay.

Keep one thing clear: *one always sues for breach of promise and not breach of condition*. Although it is not uncommon, the phrase breach of condition is misleading insofar as it connotes that someone did something she was not supposed to do—"failure of condition" is probably a more descriptive term. A failure of condition is a *defense* and often ends the obligation to perform a qualified promise.

Notice, as well, that an aggrieved party often gets rights based on both a breach of promise and a failure of a condition flowing from the same actions by the defaulting party. The buyer refuses to pay if seller refuses to deliver. The buyer can both sue the seller for breach and defend any suit brought by the seller claiming damages because buyer failed to pay the purchase price. When the promise on one side is the same as the condition on the other, lawyers often speak of *concurrent conditions*. While this may be a useful shorthand, it does not describe the situation very well. Paying the money is both promise and condition, as is delivering the goods. What we are talking about is a swap where I do not have to perform unless you do, but you do not have to perform unless I do. In our example, buyer is immune from a successful suit by seller based on the contract since seller failed to deliver and that was a condition on buyer's duty to pay $40,000. Buyer can recover from seller because the condition on seller's duty was met.

Let's change the facts slightly to illustrate another possibility. Assume that seller promises to deliver the car on April 7th, (a) if buyer is then ready, willing and able to pay $40,000, and (b) if the components needed to rebuild the engine arrive from England on or before March 27th. Buyer promises to pay $40,000 on April 7th if seller then is ready, willing and able to deliver. The components fail to arrive from England on or before March 27th. Buyer is at seller's place of business on the 7th ready, willing and able to pay. Seller, of course, fails to deliver. Buyer sues seller for breach of contract. Buyer would lose her suit because seller did not breach the promise to deliver ONLY IF the components arrived on time. Seller did not promise that they would arrive on time, but he negotiated the contract so that he would not assume this risk. Here we have an express condition

---

[1] Put aside for the moment the question of whether buyer could do anything less than engage in the elaborate ceremony we sketched and still meet the conditions of seller's promise. We will get to this later.

precedent to seller's duty to deliver *which is not also a promise*. Of course, seller could not sue buyer for failure to pay $40,000 since that promise to pay was still qualified by a condition that seller deliver the car. In this case, the conditions would give each party a defense to a suit by the other.

Sometimes lawyers talk of a "failure of consideration" in situations such as this one. Notice that this is not the same thing as an "absence" of consideration. Formation and performance of contracts are different things. Buyer and seller made a legally enforceable contract, supported by the consideration of their promises to pay and deliver. However, since seller failed to deliver goods, he cannot sue buyer, and since the components failed to arrive from England, buyer cannot sue seller. "Failure of consideration" is too easy to confuse with "absence of consideration," and so the term is not favored by contracts teachers. This does not stop courts from using it, and so you should both understand the phrase and be careful to avoid confusion.

Finally, let's illustrate a more complicated situation. Suppose buyer wants to purchase a car from a seller who needs first to borrow $30,000 to finance the acquisition of the car and the repair parts. X Bank agrees to provide the needed money. However, it demands that the transaction be structured as follows: seller expressly promises to deliver the car to buyer on April 7th. In exchange, buyer expressly promises to pay $30,000 to the X Bank on May 1st *in any event whether or not seller has delivered the car on April 7th.*[2] As a result of this contract, X bank on March 5th pays $30,000, less its charges for financing the deal, to seller. Seller, however, fails to deliver on April 7th without a legally sufficient excuse. Buyer refuses to pay X Bank on May 1st, asserting seller's non-delivery as a defense.

X Bank would win in a suit against Buyer. Buyer's promise to pay was not conditioned on delivery of the car by seller. The bank was not taking the risk of problems in the seller-buyer transaction. It advanced money to seller and bargained for a right to be repaid by buyer even if seller failed to perform. Buyer's remedy would be to sue seller for failure to deliver the goods. Seller, in turn, might have a cause of action against buyer for any damages caused by buyer's failure to pay X Bank. X Bank likely would have reserved a right to hold seller responsible if buyer failed to pay. Of course, almost certainly suits involving buyer, seller and X Bank would involve setting off damages due one against the other; modern procedure offers devices to avoid multiple lawsuits. In this kind of case, lawyers often speak of *independent promises*—that is, promises that are unqualified by reference to performance by other parties. They are rare in two party situations, but they can serve a function when the deal involves more than two people.

Planning the transaction to minimize risks: So far we've stated the obvious: courts usually enforce promises as made, and if a person puts a qualification on a promise, she hasn't promised to act unless or until something happens. But there is more to the matter than this. Conditions reflect assumptions of risk by the par-

---

[2] X Bank also is likely to keep a security interest in the goods until it is paid so that it can sell them to recover some or all of its money if B fails to pay.

ties. On one hand, they can be geared to allocate risks of events external to the particular deal. For example, our seller promised to perform provided that component parts arrived from England by a certain date. Seller also might provide that it would perform only if its shop were not damaged by some natural disaster before it could do the work. Of course, if buyer had sufficient bargaining power, it might demand that seller *promise* to deliver goods whether or not component parts arrived from England. Under such a contract, seller would have to get parts from England, find substitutes elsewhere, or be liable to pay damages to the buyer for non-delivery of the goods.

Furthermore, conditions reflect a structuring of a relationship so that one person has sanctions to induce the other to perform. For example, often it is advantageous to arrange things so that the other person performs first before you must act (that is, the other's promise is unconditional and must be performed on a certain date. Your promise, however, is to be performed later and is conditioned on receiving the other's full performance). If you have the bargaining power and skill to negotiate such a contract, you take no risk of losing your performance if the other breaches the contract as you would if you had to pay in advance before he was to perform.

Of course, if the contract requires that you pay in advance but the other person fails to perform, you are likely to have a cause of action for breach of contract or restitution. However, you may have to hire a lawyer to evaluate your case, draft documents, gain personal jurisdiction over the other party, win a verdict, and defend it on appeal. And *then* you must find some non-exempt assets owned by the other party to satisfy your judgment, and hope she isn't bankrupt. You avoid all this if you can make her go first.

If the other person must perform before you act, you may have another tactical advantage. If you think that the other person's performance is defective, you can deduct an allowance from your performance and offer it to her in full settlement.[3] Since she has performed, she must accept the offer or take legal action against you to recover the balance. She must make the difficult choice. Moreover, since the other person wants to be sure that you perform after she does, she has some incentive to perform well and on time. Her interest in keeping you happy may grow as she invests more and more effort in her performance and seeks to guard that investment by making you a satisfied customer who feels some obligation to pay for the fine performance.

The person who must perform first may have some countervailing power. If you need her performance by a certain time, you may become more and more dependent on her completing the job as time passes. You no longer can turn elsewhere and get performance on time. In this case, she may ask you to modify the contract and make a payment in order to finance the completion of the performance.

Also certain psychological factors might operate to the disadvantage of the one who has arranged things so that the other person must perform a complex and lengthy task before getting paid. If the risks are out of balance, the other person

---

[3] *See* UCC § 2-717.

may perceive the situation as coercive and feel that she was tricked or forced to accept an unfair deal. This may produce resentment and hostility. If it does, the person who holds the advantage in a hard bargain may lose any moral claim to first-class performance based on customary norms of reciprocity, craftsmanship or an obligation to help others. The one who has driven the hard bargain may get only performance to the letter of the contract most restrictively construed but not first class performance. Furthermore, the disadvantaged person may remember the situation when it comes time to deal again, and what is gained in one contract may be lost in the next. In short, at the bargaining stage it is possible to negotiate too good a deal for yourself when the performance stage arrives. This may not be a problem if the performance is to pay money and one has reasonably good security; it may be critically important if the performance involves judgment, discretion, technical skill or even artistic aspects.

We do not find too many contracts where all the risks in performance rest solely on one side.[4] Rather, leverage is used to provide incentives for both sides to perform.

For example, frequently an owner who wishes a building constructed agrees to pay a down payment and then installments at specified times as the building is erected. In this way, the owner helps the builder finance construction. The builder does not have to provide or borrow all the money needed to purchase labor and materials during the course of performance. The builder also minimizes the risk that she will not be paid for the work which she has done by limiting the amount put into the building before the owner pays. If one or more payments are missed or late, the builder may have the right to suspend working on the job until she is paid for what is due. On the other hand, an owner is likely to negotiate for the right to hold back, say, ten percent of the value of the work done at each installment and this "hold-back" is paid to the builder only upon full completion of the job. Thus, the builder is given an incentive to finish the work and do it well. All of this can be expressed in the language of conditional promises—the builder *promises* to perform *provided* that the down payment and installments are paid on time; the owner *promises* to pay the installments *provided* the builder is performing and *promises* to pay the amount held back *provided* the builder completes the structure on time according to plans and specifications.

People planning a transaction can rely on forms of leverage that only awkwardly conform to a conditions analysis. On one hand, if the transaction is part of a long-term continuing mutually advantageous business relationship, the other's continued satisfaction is a powerful sanction. If she becomes dissatisfied, there is a risk that she will end the relationship and turn to a competitor. On the other hand, where continuing relationships or the right to withhold one's own performance do not seem to offer enough leverage, there may be other things that can be

---

[4] Employment contracts once tended to be out of balance. Today statutes, with some exceptions, require wages to be paid frequently rather than withheld for long periods of time. Still employees usually work first and then get paid. Compare performances of motion pictures, plays, rock concerts and the like. Typically, a member of the audience pays first and then sees the performance. Why is this order of performance customary? Imagine the consequences of a custom in which the audience saw the show and then paid on the way out. However, restaurants manage to collect in all but a few situations when they present the bill after their customers have eaten the food.

done. One can insist that the other person buy a bond to guarantee his performance. One can insist that money be paid to a neutral third party who will hold it until the return performance is completed—an "escrow" arrangement. One selling goods can retain a security interest in them, thereby retaining some right to reclaim the goods if payment is not made as agreed (the threat of losing the machine, the T.V. or the car may induce performance, but a seller who repossesses may be hard pressed to gain much from a resale of used goods). Bonds, escrow arrangements and conditional sales provisions can be expressed in terms of conditions, but they are sufficiently different from the questions of the timing of performance and the right to withhold performance to warrant special mention.

Some problems in applying the law of conditions: Courts must interpret or construe contracts to determine whether promises are to be deemed subject to a condition, and, if so, what that condition is—as must lawyers planning transactions and lawyers engaged in salvage operations after transactions have collapsed.

Even where the parties spell out things, they are likely to leave a few questions unanswered by the express words of their agreement. In the examples we've considered, the parties expressly said that the seller would be ready, willing and able to deliver on April 7th if the buyer was ready, willing and able to pay $40,000 then. As a result, we know that if the buyer cannot pay, the seller need not deliver and cannot be sued for failing to do so.

But even in this simple case questions remain. Suppose buyer refuses to come to seller's place of business with the money but insists that seller bring the car to buyer's place of business and pick up the money there. The contract is silent about where money and goods are to be exchanged. UCC § 2-308, following common law tradition, fills the gap in the contract and tells us that in most instances a buyer must go to a seller's place of business unless they agree otherwise.

Suppose buyer offers seller a personal check calling for a bank to pay seller $40,000. Has buyer met the condition on seller's promise to deliver so that the buyer is entitled to the goods? Or must a buyer tender cash? UCC § 2-511(2) fills this gap and tells us that "tender of payment is sufficient when made by any means or in any manner current in the ordinary course of business unless the seller demands payment in legal tender and gives any extension of time reasonably necessary to procure it."

And suppose it is fairly clear by April 1st that the buyer will be unable to pay for the car on April 7th. Does the seller have to offer it to the buyer on the 7th to put the buyer in default as a necessary step in creating a cause of action? UCC §§ 2-609, 2-610, 2-703(f) suggest that the seller may have other alternatives open.

Contracts frequently, if not typically, are less explicit than our example. People often neglect to spell out who is to do what and when in the event certain contingencies occur. A seller may offer to sell goods for a specified sum, and the buyer may sign a letter saying little more than "I accept your offer." Nothing is said about whether the buyer must pay in advance, whether the seller must deliver before the buyer pays or whether they must pay and deliver at the same time.

And whatever order of performance we select, *when* are these things to take place?

Often courts must supply "constructive conditions" to fill such gaps in contracts, and the process is very much as that when they "imply" promises. Courts can look to the likely expectations of the parties; flat rules which are designed to serve the market; who ought to win, applying sympathy for the underdog; or rules based on achieving some other goal. In the simple situation given here as an example, there are a number of gap-filling rules which probably would control. For example, UCC § 2-511(1) says that, "unless otherwise agreed tender of payment is a condition to the seller's duty to tender and complete any delivery." Section 2-507(1) says that "tender of delivery is a condition to the buyer's duty to accept the goods and, unless otherwise agreed, to his duty to pay for them. Tender entitles the seller to acceptance of the goods and to payment according to the contract." Section 2-310 says that unless otherwise agreed "payment is due at the time and place at which the buyer is to receive the goods even though the place of shipment is the place of delivery. . . ." Section 2-309(1) provides that "the time for shipment or delivery . . . if not . . . agreed upon shall be a reasonable time." Section 2-503(1) provides that "the manner, time and place for tender are determined by the agreement and this Article, and in particular (a) tender must be at a reasonable hour. . . ." Thus, we can see that the Uniform Commercial Code, following common law tradition, fills the gaps by presuming a swap rather than a credit transaction.

However, there is a common law rule, implicit in the UCC, which pushes one party to go first. If a contract calls for one performance which by its nature takes time and another which can be done instantly, the one that takes time must be done first. For example, I promise to work for you for a month. You promise to pay me $1,000 for my services. Under this rule of construction, I must do the work before you must pay me. Why is there such a rule? Does it reflect custom? Does it protect wealth and power at the expense of the dominated? Does it prompt efficient behavior?

A second major problem faced by the courts in the area of performance and breach of contracts is that of fairness and the prevention of forfeitures. The parties, for example, may have provided in their contract that if one fails to perform, the other has no obligation to carry out his or her promise. The default may be relatively minor. Calling off the contract may cause extreme reliance losses, great forfeiture benefiting the one not in default or both reliance loss and forfeiture. For example, suppose a contract calls for a seller to manufacture and install a machine by April 7th which will do certain specified things. The buyer promises to pay $100,000 if the machine is installed by April 7th. The machine cannot be resold to anyone else since it is tailored to the buyer's special needs. The seller spends $85,000 to make and install the machine, and it is in place on April 7th. However, it will not quite do the things specified, but it comes close. On April 8th, seller could make adjustments which would cost $1,000, and they would make the machine perform as specified in the contract. While the buyer would lose the use of the machine for a day, it would be valuable to him on the 8th and thereafter. May the buyer refuse to allow these adjustments on the 8th and be free of any obligation under the contract since the condition to his promise was not met precisely?

On one hand, this could be seen as just a question of interpretation of the contract. We might doubt whether the seller had in fact assumed the risk without a clear showing from the facts that he was aware he was entering into an $85,000 gamble. We might wonder whether the buyer's conduct was in good faith or only was serving as a pretext to bail out of what now seems to be a poor deal. On the other hand, suppose it is clear that the buyer has drafted the contract to put the risk of timely performance on the seller. Will courts accept this allocation of risk, or will they impose some standard of fairness and consider whether or not to enforce the contract as written? Suppose a court accepts the contractual allocation of risk in this example and finds that the condition to the buyer's promise to pay has not been met. Does this mean that the buyer gets a machine without an obligation to pay for it? Can a seller in default on a contract get restitution of any net benefits conferred?[5]

2. CONDITIONS AND FORFEITURES: FREE CONTRACT VS. FAIRNESS AND SYMPATHY?

In the cases that follow, those drafting the written contracts attempted to structure the transactions to gain advantages for their clients. In some cases, the language used could be read one way or another; in others there were gaps; in still others the most plausible literal reading of the language would have produced results that the courts seemed not to want to reach. Consider the role of courts in these cases, and consider the lessons for those planning commercial transactions.

JACOBS ASSOCIATES v. ARGONAUT INSURANCE CO.
Supreme Court of Oregon
580 P.2d 529 (1978)

DENECKE, C.J. Plaintiff is an engineering firm which provided services used in construction of the Portland General Electric (PGE) Company headquarters building in Portland. The services were provided for Target Dredging and Pile-driving Company. Target has since been adjudicated bankrupt without paying plaintiff $10,891.94 due under its subcontract. In accordance with its contract with PGE, Target secured a bond through defendant. After Target was adjudicated bankrupt, plaintiff instituted this action asserting that it was a third party beneficiary on the bond executed by defendant. Defendant demurred to plaintiff's complaint on the ground that it failed to state facts constituting a cause of action. The demurrer was sustained. Plaintiff refused to plead further. Judgment was entered for defendant and plaintiff appealed.

The bond at issue in this case is of standard form. After reciting that Target as principal and defendant as surety are bound to PGE in the sum of $820,771, the bond lists the "conditions" which will void the obligations. The bond recites:

---

[5] See UCC §§ 2-606, 2-602, 2-703, 1-103.

NOW, THEREFORE, THE CONDITION OF THIS OBLIGATION IS SUCH that if the Contractor [Target] shall

(a) Pay all persons, firms and corporations who perform labor or furnish equipment, supplies and materials for use in the work under the Contract; . . .

(d) Fully complete the work as provided in the Contract, free from all liens and claims of any kind whatsoever, and in all other particulars shall faithfully and fully perform the Contract on its part according to all the terms, covenants, and conditions thereof, and within the time specified therein;

(e) Fully indemnify and save harmless the Owner [PGE] against and from all cost and damage which it may suffer by reason of a default in the performance of any of the foregoing provisions, and fully reimburse and repay the Owner all outlay and expense which the Owner may incur in making good any such default; then this obligation shall be void; otherwise the same shall remain in full force and effect.

1. It is clear that the conditions have not all been satisfied and that the bond remains in effect. The question, however, is whether plaintiff is [a] party which may maintain an action on the bond.

Plaintiff candidly admits that the question was squarely answered in the negative by this court in *Tait & Co. v. D. Diamond Corp.*, 228 Or. 602, 365 P.2d 883 (1961). In *Tait* we recognized that our decision followed the minority rule and that our approach had been strongly criticized, but we felt that our prior decisions dictated the result. *Parker v. Jeffrey*, 26 Or. 186, 37 P. 712 (1894), and *Pankey v. National Surety Co.*, 116 Or. 648, 239 P. 808 (1925).

In *Parker* and *Pankey* we held we would not imply a promise to pay the third party plaintiff. We did not interpret the language of the bond to constitute a promise, only a condition.

This is the principal ground for the dissent; that is, that the surety did not promise to pay laborers and the words of condition are irrelevant on the issue of to whom the surety owes the obligation to pay.

The difficulty is caused by the archaic form which continues to be used in surety bonds. Most courts have not interpreted the archaic form literally but consider the words of condition to be words of promise. To do otherwise would be erroneous in instances even more obvious than in this case.

Corbin states:

"... Words of 'condition' are not words of 'promise' in form; but in this class of cases it is sound policy to interpret the words liberally in favor of the third parties. In a majority of states, it is already done; and without question the surety's rate of compensation for carrying the risk is sufficiently adjusted to the law. The compensated surety has become an institution that is well suited to carry the risk of the principal contractor's default, whereas individual laborers and materialmen are frequently very ill prepared to carry the risk. The legislatures have recognized this fact, and in the case of public contracts have required surety bonds to protect the third parties. While this has not been done in the case of private construction, and while the courts should not on their own motion put such a provision into a private surety bond, they may well interpret a bond that is expressly conditioned on the payment of laborers and materialmen as being a promise to pay them and made for their benefit. The words reasonably permit it, and social policy approves it. . . ." [4 Corbin, Contracts s. 800, 177-178 (1951]. . . .

Some sureties have discarded the ancient form and inserted language expressly providing that unpaid laborers shall have a direct action against the bond. In our opinion this was not intended to change the surety's obligation from that stated in the archaic form but to express that same obligation in understandable language.

If the dissent is correct, that language in the bond in this case, "Pay all persons . . . who perform work . . ." does not amount to a promise to pay persons such as plaintiff, the quoted condition is completely superfluous. PGE does not need this condition for protection; it is fully protected by other conditions in the bond. Condition (d), before quoted, includes a requirement that the work shall be completed, free of all liens and claims. Condition (e) provides that the contractor shall fully indemnify PGE against damage suffered by reason of any default in contractor's performance. Because the above-quoted condition is unnecessary to protect PGE, the inference necessarily arises that it is a promise to pay an unpaid laborer or materialman. . . .

We conclude, therefore, that our decisions in *Parker* and *Pankey* were incorrectly decided.

2.   When an express promise to pay a third party has been found the subjective intent of the promisee, in this case PGE, is immaterial; the third party can maintain an action against the promisor surety. The general principle which is the basis for that proposition has always been the law in Oregon. "On the second point, the authorities with us are quite decisive that when A., for a valuable consideration, agrees with B. to pay his debt to C., the latter can enforce the contract against A." *Baker & Smith v. Eglin*, 11 Or. 333, 334, 8 P. 280 (1883).

This same principle applies to contracts of surety:

". . . And thirdly, the third party has an enforceable right if the surety promises in the bond, either in express words or by reasonable implication, to pay money to him. If there is such a promissory expression as this, there need be no discussion of 'intention to benefit.' We need not speculate for whose benefit the contract was made, or wonder whether the promisee was buying the promise for his own selfish interest or for philanthropic purposes. It is a much simpler question: Did the surety promise to pay money to the plaintiff?" 4 Corbin, Contracts, *supra*, at 163-164.

3.   In addition to the lack of persuasive precedents supporting *Tait*, it should be overruled because it failed to follow a recognized rule of the construction of contracts. The defendant in this case is a compensated surety; its business is writing surety bonds for a fee. The universal rule is that a compensated surety is regarded as an insurer and the contract it draws will be construed most strongly against it. . . .

In *Tait* we chose not to repudiate our former decisions because we stated, "an untold number of surety contracts have been entered into in reliance upon the unequivocal holdings of this court," and we could not "judge the repercussions that could occur within the construction industry by an abrupt reversal of the rule." 228 Or. at 604-605.

We are now of the opinion that in *Tait* we were unrealistic in our concern over the possible magnitude of the effect of repudiating our former decisions and since *Tait* the effect of repudiating our former decisions has been lessened by changes in the mechanic's lien laws. The only persons who are vitally interested in bringing an action on the payment provision of a bond are those who have no lien rights in the owner's property or who failed to perfect their lien rights. At the time of *Tait* most persons performing services for or furnishing material to a construction project had statutory mechanic's lien rights. ORS 87.010. Since *Tait* the legislature provided for lien rights for more classes of persons, including engineers such as plaintiff. (Plaintiff did not have lien rights at the time it performed the work for Target.) For these reasons the number of persons affected by a change would be small.

In addition, the defendant and other sureties can change the form of their bonds and clearly provide that unpaid engineers, laborers and materialmen have no right of action. This will not affect outstanding bonds; however, as we observed, this will not be of concern to many sureties or claimants.

If this were a "custom" contract, "tailor made" for these parties for this project, it is very unlikely that we would repudiate the interpretation reiterated in *Tait*. In that situation it would be likely that the parties relied upon our holding in *Tait* and wrote the clause accordingly. But that is not the situation in this case. This is a standard clause in bonds. It is not part of a contract of adhesion but it is not a clause that is normally negotiated. Under these circumstances there is no reason we should not overrule our past decisions interpreting the clause to the contrary if we conclude the past decisions are clearly erroneous. . . .

We hold that the plaintiff has a right of action against the surety. *Tait & Co. v. D. Diamond Corp., supra,* (228 Or. 602), is overruled. Therefore, the demurrer should be overruled.

Reversed and remanded for setting aside the judgment for defendant and for further proceedings.

[Linde concurred, noting that the majority found the bond to contain a promise, while the dissent found the absence of such a promise to be "clear. To decide this case on the pleadings would be to suggest that "the parties clearly understood something, but we disagree on what they clearly understood." The demurrer was improper, since there were factual issues which might have given plaintiff a victory if resolved in favor of plaintiff. Lent J. joined in Linde's concurrence.]

HOLMAN, J., dissenting. [Bryson joined in the dissent.]

The majority takes a condition of a bond and makes it a promise. The surety made no promise to pay parties other than the owner, Portland General Electric Company (PGE). The words of the contract provide that ". . . *if the Contractor* shall (a) Pay all persons, firms and corporations who perform labor or furnish

equipment, supplies and materials for use in the work," there will be no obligation of the surety under the bond. (Emphasis added.) Thus, the language from the
contract quoted by the majority provides no obligation upon the surety to pay but
provides only that *if the contractor* pays, no obligation can exist under the bond.
It is a provision for the benefit of the surety. The words are not words of promise
on the part of the surety but are words which specify a condition which, if fulfilled, nullifies the surety's obligation. *They say nothing about to whom the
surety owes the obligation.*

The words which indicate in whose favor the obligation runs are as follows:

> ... TARGET DREDGING & PILEDRIVING CO ... and ARGO-
> NAUT INSURANCE COMPANY, ... are jointly and severally held and
> *firmly bound unto* PORTLAND GENERAL ELECTRIC COMPANY,
> ... in the sum of ... $820,771.00 ... *for the payment whereof to the
> Owner* the Contractor binds itself, its successors and assigns, and *the
> Surety binds itself,* its successors and assigns firmly by these presents.

... In view of the quoted language from the agreement, I do not understand
how the majority comes to the conclusion that the contracting parties intended
that the bond should also run in favor of someone else. A contract is a matter of
the intention of the parties, and there is no evidence here that this contract was
intended to benefit anyone other than PGE. The contract, although drawn in an
archaic form, is clear and unambiguous. . . .

The purpose of a bond of this kind is to save an owner harmless from the expense of clearing liens which might be filed upon the premises being constructed.
A bond of this kind is given because those in the position of PGE require it for
their protection. The premium on the bond is a cost of doing business and is reflected in the contractor's bid. Neither the contractor nor the owner is interested
in enhancing the premium, and thus the amount of the bids on the property being
constructed, by securing coverage for anyone other than the owner. Unless the
milk of human kindness runs thicker in the veins of public utilities and contractors than is generally apparent, there is no real basis for believing there was an
intention to benefit anyone other than PGE. . . .

If there is an ambiguity, because of the archaic form of the bond, as to what the
parties intended, it would be proper to submit proof showing what the parties did
intend. Whether the parties intended those in the position of plaintiff to be beneficiaries would then be a question of fact. However, even if the contract is treated
as being ambiguous, plaintiff is in no position to recover in the face of the literal
wording of the bond and in the absence of evidence that the parties intended otherwise. The majority not only construes the wording contrary to its literal meaning but it does so *as a matter of law* without the necessity of evidence that the
words of condition were intended as words of promise. I have no quarrel with the
law of third party beneficiary contracts as stated by the majority nor with its application to plaintiff if such was the intent of the parties, but that intent cannot be
conjured out of the language of the contract.

The majority contends it was not necessary that the condition, which it construes as a promise, be in the contract unless it was intended as a promise. I
would counter by contending that if the parties intended to benefit anyone other

than PGE, they would have said so instead of using words of condition. In addition, we know that sureties state everything at least three different ways because courts construe contracts against them if such contracts do not completely cover every possible contingency. We now hold that any duplication arising out of any statements made by sureties will be construed against them.

[The dissent notes the majority's reliance on Corbin. He quotes Corbin, and then observes. . . .] A reading of the text preceding and following the quoted material makes it apparent that his reason for such a statement is that he believes a better social result would follow if sureties were made responsible to all claimants—not because he believes the parties to such a contract usually intend to so agree.

The majority's result is appealing because the bonding company can distribute the risk through premiums and because it is a way of assuring the payment of all workmen and materialmen. Whether one wants to twist the words to reach what is considered a good social result depends upon how important one considers the right of the parties to make their own contract. This is the kind of public policy that is usually handled by legislatures, and the law has been settled in this state for 95 years without any legislative action.

NOTES AND QUESTIONS

1. *An argument from Jacobs Associates' brief:* Jacobs Associates argued that the *Tait* decision ought to be overruled. Much of Jacobs Associates' argument turned on Oregon decisions after 1961, and also on stressing that the *Tait* decision was contrary to the great weight of authority in the United States. However, it also said in its brief,

> Unfortunately, because this case was not allowed to proceed beyond the Demurrer stage, plaintiff did not have the opportunity to engage in any discovery. Plaintiff therefore admittedly does not have actual data to buttress the argument it is about to make but since the Court in the *Tait* case was making certain assumptions sixteen years ago, plaintiff believes it would be proper to suggest some alternative assumptions for application in 1977. In fact, plaintiff will be so bold as to contend that, give the present state of the law on this subject in the country today, plaintiff has great faith that the facts would support the following contentions:
>
> 1. The great majority of jurisdictions in this country would allow plaintiff a right of action against defendant as a third party beneficiary of the type of bond involved in this case.
>
> 2. The bond set forth in Exhibit "A" is probably a standard form of bond employed by defendant in most areas of the country where it does business.
>
> 3. Defendant's actuaries have determined a premium rate for such bonds and have probably based such a premium on an analysis of the risks being covered; and being prudent actuaries have built into their premium structure the risk of the right of recovery by third party

subcontractors which such third parties have under the laws of most jurisdictions.

4. The defendant probably does not discount its standard premium to reflect its reduced exposure in Oregon when it writes Oregon bonds.

Argonaut is a national company licensed in all states, and controlled by the Teledyne Corporation, a diversified company with interests in aviation, electronics, specialty metals and insurance. Argonaut carries out operations through twenty-three division and branch offices located throughout the United States. Approximately 1,800 agents and brokers utilize the facilities of the company. Best's Insurance Reports – Property – Casualty 231 (1983) states "[a]ll business . . . is written at standard rates. . . . The company and four of its property-casualty subsidiaries operate under an inter-company reinsurance agreement . . . whereby all business acquired by the participants is pooled and the combined premiums distributed and the losses and expenses prorated." Does it seem likely that Argonaut's actuaries would calculate a premium specifically for Oregon, taking into account the *Tait* doctrine?

2. A digression on third party beneficiaries: Once the court in the *Jacobs Associates* case found that Argonaut had *promised* the owner to pay all those who had worked on the Portland Headquarters Building, it then allowed *Jacobs Associates* to sue to enforce that promise as a "third party beneficiary."

Nineteenth and early Twentieth Century courts struggled with the idea of allowing a person who was not a party to a contract bring an action to enforce it. Today it is clear that beneficiaries of some contracts between others can sue in almost all states. Moreover, the parties to the contract may not be able to rescind it without the consent of beneficiaries in some circumstances.

As you might expect, there are a core of clear cases and a periphery of uncertain ones. The first Restatement of Contracts divided all beneficiaries of other people's contracts into three kinds: creditor, donee and incidental. Incidental beneficiaries could not sue. For example, owner and builder make a contract to construct a beautiful house on a vacant lot. If the house were built, it would increase the value of neighbor's adjoining property. Builder breaches the contract with owner, and the house is not built. Neighbor would be "an incidental beneficiary" and could not sue the builder.

Creditor and donee beneficiaries could sue. For example, A sells his painting to B for $1,000. Instead of paying the money to A, B is to pay it to C. This will satisfy a debt that A owes C. B fails to pay. C may sue B as a "creditor beneficiary." Or B buys A's painting for $1,000. A is to deliver it to C who is B's mother. It is a birthday gift. A fails to deliver the painting. C can sue A. She is a "donee beneficiary."

However, can A and B in either case rescind the contract without C's consent? The first Restatement distinguished donee and creditor beneficiaries. A donee's right vested immediately and could not be rescinded without the donee's consent. A creditor beneficiary's right vested only when the beneficiary had relied on the promise, and the deal could be rescinded before that. The courts have not always followed the Restatement's distinction between donee and creditor beneficiaries.

Furthermore, they differ on whether the beneficiary's right vests when the contract is made, when the beneficiary learns of it or when the beneficiary relies.

Restatement (Second) of Contracts § 302 abandons the creditor, donee and incidental beneficiary scheme. It keeps the idea that incidental beneficiaries cannot sue. However, those who can sue are called "intended beneficiaries." To be one, a person must show that "recognition of a right to performance in the beneficiary is appropriate to effectuate the intention of the parties." In addition, one must show either:

(a) the performance of the promise will satisfy an obligation of the promisee to pay money to the beneficiary; or

(b) the circumstances indicate that the promisee intends to give the beneficiary the benefit of the promised performance.

Restatement (Second) of Contracts § 311 states a general rule and some exceptions concerning the power of the original parties to change or end a beneficiary's rights. Generally, the parties who made the contract can modify it without the consent of the beneficiary. They do not have this power if their contract provides that the third party beneficiary's rights cannot be changed. Also, if a beneficiary "materially changes his position in justifiable reliance on the promise or brings suit on it or manifests assent to it at the request of the promisor or promisee," the beneficiary's rights cannot be changed.

Martinez v. Socoma Companies, Inc.[6] is an example of third party beneficiary doctrine and modern American history. As part of President Johnson's "War on Poverty," Socoma and two other corporations made contracts with the Secretary of Labor. However, they entered these contracts just three days before President Johnson's term ended and President Nixon would take office. The companies agreed to lease space in a public building, and adapt the space so items could be manufactured. They also promised to train and employ in the facilities for at least 12 months, at minimum wage rates, a specified number of East Los Angeles residents certified as disadvantaged by the government. They further agreed to provide these employees with opportunities for promotion to available supervisorial-managerial positions and with options to purchase stock in the corporation that employed them. The corporations failed to perform, and officials of the Nixon Administration did not assert the government's rights against the corporations.

A legal services program, representing disadvantaged unemployed persons, brought a class action claiming that they were third party beneficiaries of the contract between the United States government and the three corporations. Demurrers to the complaint were sustained, and the Supreme Court of California affirmed by a 4-3 vote.

The majority found that the "benefits to be derived from defendants' performance were clearly intended not as gifts from the government to such persons but as a means of executing the public purposes stated in the contracts and in the underlying legislation. Accordingly, plaintiffs were only incidental beneficiaries

---

[6] 11 Cal. 3d 394, 521 P.2d 841 (1974).

and as such have no right of recovery."[7] The majority relied greatly on the first Restatement of Contracts in its opinion.

What is involved in a case such as this? Do classifications such as "incidental," "donee," or "intended" beneficiaries raise the relevant issues? If the corporations had breached their promises, the United States could sue for contract remedies, settle the case or abandon its rights. Why might government officials decide to allow the corporations to abandon their commitment without being subject to a suit? Should this decision be left in the hands of those appointed by elected officials or should those speaking for the unemployed of East Los Angeles be able to make the decision? Neither the majority nor the dissent in the *Martinez* case discussed this issue.

DAVIS v. ALLSTATE INSURANCE CO.
Supreme Court of Wisconsin
101 Wis. 2d 1, 303 N.W.2d 596 (1981)

DAY, J. . . . The principal question on review is: Did the court of appeals err in overturning the trial court's finding that the Allstate Insurance Company (Allstate), exercised bad faith in the course of handling Ronald D. Davis' (insured's) claim under a contract of fire insurance?

The insured is an attorney who graduated from law school in 1974 and immediately entered the private practice of law in Milwaukee.

In 1975, insured obtained a standard "deluxe" business-owner's fire and extended coverage insurance policy from Allstate in the amount of $8,000. The policy coverage was based on Allstate's inspection of the insured's business personal property, which resulted in a written report placing an approximate value of $7,500 on the property in plaintiff's office. A second Allstate inspection in February, 1976, estimated the value of plaintiff's business property at $11,100. Based on this second estimate, the policy limit was increased to $15,000 on Allstate's recommendation. In October of 1976, Allstate conducted another inspection and recommended that the policy limits be raised to $25,000, however, the policy was not amended.

On February 22, 1977, a fire destroyed all of the contents of insured's law office, including invoices and receipts for purchases of the contents of the office. Allstate was notified of the loss on the day following the fire.

Bruce Piette, an Allstate claims adjuster, was assigned to the claim. He investigated the fire between February 24 and May 15, 1977, and recommended to Allstate a "cash out" settlement of $14,860.04, which was approved by Mr. Piette's supervisor, Larry Peterson, a commercial claims supervisor.

On May 15, 1977, the insured filed a sworn proof-of-loss statement detailing the property destroyed in the fire and the value of each item, claiming losses in excess of the policy limit of $15,000. Internal Allstate memoranda stated that both Piette and Peterson believed the proof-of-loss to be substantially completed in proper form.

---

[7] *Id.* at 397, 521 P.2d at 843.

In a separate internal memorandum, Mr. Piette stated he would offer the plaintiff a lower amount initially, and go up to $14,860 if necessary.

Jerome Mondl, Piette and Peterson's supervisor, rejected their recommendations. He advised Peterson to reject insured's proof-of-loss for lack of documentation of purchase of the individual items of property claimed. Mr. Mondl did authorize settlement of $4,148.53 which Piette offered the insured to satisfy the claim. This offer was rejected.

The insured then brought this action seeking damages for the fire loss and compensatory and punitive damages for bad faith. The case was tried before a jury. The jury returned a special verdict finding that the insured substantially performed the conditions required by the policy to recover his claim and found damages for losses to his personal property of $14,860.04. The jury also found that Allstate exercised bad faith in the course of its handling of the claim and awarded compensatory damages resulting from the defendant's bad faith of $12,103 and punitive damages of $30,000.

Allstate's motions after verdict were denied and the trial court affirmed the jury's verdict and judgment was entered in the amount of the jury's verdict plus costs and disbursements for a total of $57,306.54.

The defendant filed a notice of appeal from the entire judgment.

The court of appeals affirmed the jury's finding that the insured substantially performed his obligations under the insurance contract to recover his claim. The court rejected Allstate's contention that an insured must supply certified invoices or receipts establishing the cost of each item of lost property as a precondition to recover, characterizing that theory as "nonsense." The court of appeals found that an insured need only substantially comply with the proof-of-loss requirements in the insurance contract, which he had done. Accordingly, the jury's verdict finding $14,860.04 as the amount of damage to the insured's personal property was affirmed.

Turning to the bad faith issue, the court of appeals found insured's claim to be "fairly debatable," thus shielding Allstate from charges of "bad faith." Relying on this court's decision in *Anderson v. Continental Ins. Co.*, 85 Wis.2d 675, 691, 271 N.W.2d 368 (1978), the court held the trial court erred in presenting the bad faith issue to the jury and reversed the jury's findings on that issue.

This court granted the insured's petition for review.

The first question on review is: Did the insured satisfy the conditions of the standard fire insurance policy concerning proof of ownership and valuation of property lost in the fire?

The insurance policy was the standard form required by § 203.06, Stats. 1973.[8]

---

[8] [1] The Standard Policy incorporated by reference to § 203.01 provides in lines 90-122:
Requirements In Case Loss Occurs. The insured shall give immediate written notice to this Company of any loss, protect the property from further damage, forthwith separate the damaged and undamaged personal property, put it in the best possible order, furnish a complete inventory of the destroyed, damaged and undamaged property, showing in detail quantities, costs, actual cash value and amount of loss claimed; and within sixty days after the loss, unless such time is extended in writing by this Company, the insured shall

It is clear that insured failed to comply with that part of the insurance contract providing that:

> The insured . . . shall produce for examination all books of account, bills, invoices and other vouchers, or certified copies thereof if originals be lost. . . .

He did, however, provide the company with a sworn proof of loss setting out in detail the items lost and the value of each.

The record shows that Allstate's employees did not demand certified copies of the invoices which were lost in the fire until June 10, 1977, nearly four months after the insured's loss occurred. In fact, the record amply supports the insured's contention that until that date, Allstate agreed to verify ownership and valuation by checking with the vendors of the lost property and later by referring to the insured's tax records. The record also shows that insured cooperated with the defendant in determining ownership and valuation of the property.

Substantial performance with the terms of the contract is necessary for insured to recover under the policy. Where a party has met the essential purpose of the contract, he has substantially performed under the contract. . . .

We conclude that, on this record, the jury correctly found that the insured substantially performed his obligations under the contract. Allstate on this review does not challenge the affirmance by the Court of Appeals of the award of $14,860.04 to the insured for damage to his property.

The second question is: Did Allstate exercise bad faith in the handling of the insured's claim?

The controlling case on the law of bad faith is *Anderson v. Continental Ins. Co.*, 85 Wis.2d 675, 271 N.W.2d 368 (1978). Bad faith is an intentional tort "which results from a breach of duty imposed as a consequence of the relationship established by contract." *Anderson, supra*, 85 Wis.2d at 688. The duty imposed on an insurance company has been characterized as being analogous to that of a fiduciary. *Anderson, supra*, 85 Wis.2d at 688. "Bad faith" is defined as deceit, duplicity or insincerity. *Anderson, supra*, 85 Wis.2d at 692.

---

render to this Company a proof of loss, signed and sworn to by the insured, stating the knowledge and belief of the insured as to the following: the time and origin of the loss, the interest of the insured and of all others in the property, the actual cash value of each item thereof, and the amount of loss thereto, all encumbrances thereon, all other contracts of insurance, whether valid or not, covering any of said property, any changes in the title, use, occupation, location, possession or exposures of said property since the issuing of this policy, by whom and for what purpose any building herein described and the several parts thereof were occupied at the time of loss and whether or not it then stood on leased ground, and shall furnish a copy of all the descriptions and schedules in all policies and, if required, verified plans and specifications of any building, fixtures or machinery destroyed or damaged. The insured, as often as may be reasonably required, shall exhibit to any person designated by this Company all that remains of any property herein described, and submit to examinations under oath by any person named by this Company, and subscribe the same; and, as often as may be reasonably required, shall produce for examination all books of account, bills, invoices and other vouchers, or certified copies thereof if originals be lost, at such reasonable time and place as may be designated by this Company or its representative, and shall permit extracts and copies thereof to be made.

In order to show a claim for bad faith, this court has held that:

"... a plaintiff must show the absence of a reasonable basis for denying benefits of the policy and the defendant's knowledge or reckless disregard of the lack of a reasonable basis for denying the claim." *Anderson, supra*, 85 Wis.2d at 691.

The insurer is, however, entitled to challenge the claim on the basis of debatable law or facts. . . .

Allstate contends that no bad faith issue was presented because the failure of the insured to supply certified invoices or receipts showing the cost of each claimed item of property provided a reasonable basis for denying the claim.

The court of appeals found the issue of valuation to be fairly debatable as a matter of law. We disagree.

The insured submitted upon request a sworn proof-of-loss statement to Allstate, claiming damage to his property under the policy of $15,000. The proof-of-loss statement placed a value on each of nearly four hundred items destroyed by the fire. The testimony of two of defendant's claims personnel considered the statement to be substantially complete. The same Allstate employees recommended a cash payment to plaintiff of nearly $15,000. Allstate investigators had recommended an increase in coverage on plaintiff's property to $25,000 only four months before the fire. Allstate's claims adjuster confirmed the insured's purchase of many of the major items shown on the proof-of-loss statement. After recommending a cash settlement of nearly $15,000, Allstate's claims adjuster noted in his records that:

When I get authorization I will attempt to cashout insured for a complete loss. I will start at a low price and work my way up. I'm not going to offer the full amount at first. There is no harm in offering a lower amount at first. I can always go up.

The insured testified that he spoke with Allstate's Commercial Claims supervisor, after the claims adjuster offered only $4,000 to settle the claim. He testified that the supervisor told him:

We know we owe the money but if you don't take the $4,000, we are not going to offer you anything else and if you don't take the settlement we'll just turn it over to our lawyers and we'll tie you up for the next two or three years in a [sic] litigation and you won't see a dime.

The claims adjuster also wrote to his supervisor stating that:

I don't feel we should drag this out to [sic] much longer. Insured is more than willing to supply us with tax records. [which had been requested by Allstate to verify ownership.]

Allstate introduced evidence at trial showing that the insured had represented the value of his office property at $350 to $3,500 and in one case claimed the property was merely rented by him. These representations were not made to Allstate but in divorce and bankruptcy proceedings and on personal property tax returns.

But whatever the insured's motives were in those proceedings, it is apparent from its inter-office memos that Allstate was not misled as to the property's ownership or value, even if others may have been.

We conclude that the evidence before the trial court was sufficient to submit the bad faith question to the jury and find no error in submitting the question.

The jury was obviously persuaded that the property was worth what insured had claimed. That figure was almost identical to the amount recommended by Allstate's representatives to their superiors to settle the claim and $10,000 less than the coverage limits recommended by Allstate's underwriters four months before the fire. Accordingly, the jury determined that Allstate had no reasonable basis for denying the claim.

Because there is ample evidence to support that conclusion, we reverse that part of the court of appeals' decision overturning the award of damages for bad faith, and reinstate the award for bad faith of $12,103 in compensatory damages and $30,000 in punitive damages found by the jury and approved by the trial court. Accordingly, we uphold the entire judgment of the trial court for $57,306.54. . . .

NOTES AND QUESTIONS

1. *Behavior of lawyers, clients, and insurance companies:* Given the amount involved, a great deal of legal work was devoted to Davis' claim. If courts insisted on literal rather than substantial compliance with the conditions in the insurance policy, we would get easy and quick answers. Why are courts and lawyers willing to spend so much effort on cases such as that of Mr. Davis?

In thinking about exact and substantial performance, consider the third paragraph of Justice Day's opinion carefully. Is it likely that the salespeople from Allstate explained to Mr. Davis the record keeping requirement and the risk that records would be destroyed in the very fire being insured against? What if they had done so? Moreover, consider Allstate's sales tactics in the transaction. What expectations did it create as it sold Davis more and more insurance? Finally, should the jury have been told to consider whether both parties were dealing in good faith?

What is the lesson of the Allstate loss for insurance companies? Would you expect Allstate to change its practices? In what way? Should Allstate be able to use technical defenses when they suspect that a policy holder is making a questionable claim? Should insurance companies be able to drive hard bargains when they question the merit of a policy holder's claim? Would this lead to desirable compromises rather than an all or nothing resolution of the problem? Should courts require lawyers to protect themselves more than other businesspeople? Should they be required to read policy terms and comply with them closely? Should they be left to their own skill and bargaining power?

2. *Regulation of insurance settlement*: Many courts recognize a tort of bad faith performance of an insurance contract. We will consider later how far courts will use this idea outside the insurance area. Why isn't an insurance company privileged to bargain to settle claims? What was wrong with taking advantage of

Mr. Davis' need for money to continue his law practice? Suppose Mr. Piette had made an opening offer of $8,000 (twice the offer he did make). Would the situation have been different? Recall the history of judicial supervision of the insurance contract. Compare the discussions of waiver and estoppel in insurance cases by Kimball and Friedman, *supra* Chapter 4.

The California courts were the first to find insurers liable when they denied or delayed legitimate claims. However, California law now recognizes that when there is a genuine dispute about coverage, courts may conclude as a matter of law that the denial of coverage or delay in payment did not constitute bad faith and may grant summary judgment for the insurance company. Originally, the genuine issue doctrine seemed to be limited to disputes based on interpretation of the policy and insurance law. In *Guebara v. Allstate Ins. Co.*[9], the Ninth Circuit decided that California law also would allow an insurer to deny a claim when there was a factual dispute about items an insured claimed were in a house destroyed by fire. In *Chateau Chamberay Homeowners Ass'n v. Associated International Ins. Co.,*[10] a California intermediate appellate court also decided that the genuine dispute doctrine was not limited to legal issues but also could be applied to factual disputes on a case by case basis. The court said: "the record contains substantial and unrebutted evidence that HOA included in its claim matters that were not covered under the policy and/or related to pre-existing conditions, including design and construction defects, and sought to claim unreasonable repair and professional fees and expenses. AIIC had every right to question these matters and to require HOA to provide full and proper support for its demands. HOA failed to do so." Summary judgment thus was justified.

3. *Substantial performance in building contracts*: Insurance is not the only home of the substantial performance doctrine. Courts also often use substantial performance in contracts to erect or repair buildings. For example, suppose owner promises to pay when builder constructs the building according to plans and specifications. Courts generally read the builder's *promise* as building to plans and specifications. However, they read the *constructive condition* on the owner's promise to pay as requiring only substantial performance of the contract in good faith.

As a result, the owner must pay the full contract sum although he or she did not get exactly what was bargained for. The owner has a cause of action for damages for the builder's failure to perform the promise to meet plans and specifications. This might seem to approximate compensation for loss better than a forfeiture which might result if the condition were construed as full and complete performance. However, at least in some cases, the owner's damages are measured as the difference between the value of the house as it stands and as it would be had the contract been performed exactly. Often this produces only a token sum, leaving the owner's interest in having good craftsmanship unprotected insofar as it is not reflected in market values.

---

[9] 237 F.3d 987 (9th Cir. 2001).
[10] 108 Cal. Rptr. 2d 776 (Ct. App. 2001).

4. *Experts' certificates in building contracts and substantial performance*:
Under many construction contracts, owners are to pay only when the builder obtains an *architect or engineer's certificate* that the work has been done. Suppose
the architect or engineer refuses to grant the certificate. May the builder claim the
contract price less a set-off for the owner's damages on the ground that the
builder has substantially performed? We can contrast two views:

In *Coorsen v. Ziehl*,[11] the court found that the satisfaction of the architect "is a
condition precedent to the right to sue for the contract price, unless the refusal to
certify should be disregarded on the grounds of fraud or bad faith, or clear evidence of mistake, on the part of the architect." In *Wauwatosa v. Jacobus & Wind-
ing Concrete Construction Co.*,[12] the court said that the kind of mistake needed to
overturn the requirement of an architect's certificate must be an "unintentional
misapprehension or ignorance of some material fact, and it must be clearly established by the evidence, and so gross and palpable that it is equivalent in its effects
to dishonest, fraudulent, or merely arbitrary action."

However, in the classic case of *Jacob & Youngs, Inc. v. Kent*,[13] Justice Cardozo found that a builder could recover despite his failure to obtain the required
architect's certificate when the builder had substantially performed and where
"the defect was insignificant in its relation to the project" and denial of recovery
would result in a great forfeiture. One of the specifications for plumbing work
provided that "all wrought iron pipe must be well galvanized, lap welded pipe of
the grade known as 'standard pipe' of Reading manufacture." About nine months
after occupying the country residence, the owner discovered that some of the
pipe "instead of being made in Reading, was the product of other factories."
$3,483 remained unpaid. The builder was directed by the architect to do the work
anew. Carrying out the order would have meant the demolition at great expense
of substantial parts of the completed structure. The omission of Reading pipe
"was neither fraudulent or willful. It was the result of the oversight and inatten-
tion of the plaintiff's subcontractor." The builder sued for the unpaid balance.

The trial court excluded evidence that the pipe installed was of the same quality, appearance and market value as Reading pipe, and it directed a verdict for the
defendant owner. The Court of Appeal reversed and directed a judgment for
Jacob & Youngs by a 4 to 3 vote.

The dissent said that Kent "had a right to contract for what he wanted." "It
may have been a mere whim on his part, but even so, he had a right to this kind
of pipe, regardless of whether some other kind, according to the opinion of the
contractor or experts, would have been 'just as good, better, or done just as well.'
He agreed to pay only upon condition that the pipe installed were made by that
company and he ought not be compelled to pay unless that condition be performed."

Danzig[14] studied the background of the *Jacob & Youngs* case. The contract
was lengthy and detailed. It created a system whereby the builder was to be paid

---

[11] 103 Wis. 381, 79 N.W. 562 (1899).
[12] 223 Wis. 401, 271 N.W. 21 (1937).
[13] 230 N.Y. 239, 129 N.E. 889 (1921).
[14] THE CAPABILITY PROBLEM IN CONTRACT LAW 108-28 (Foundation Press 1978).

when it obtained architect certificates, but it did not expressly state the circumstances under which certificates should be granted or denied. All that was said was that the builder was entitled to a certificate when "in the Architect's judgment the work called for . . . has been satisfactorily executed. . . ." Paragraph 22 of the General Conditions stated that "Where any particular brand of manufactured article is specified, it is to be considered as a standard. Contractors desiring to use another shall first make application in writing to the Architect, stating the difference in cost, and obtain their written approval of the change." Jacob & Youngs, of course, had made no such written application nor received written approval of a substitution of brands of pipe.

Kent was a successful New York lawyer, and there is no evidence that he had any connection with the Reading Pipe Company. There were four major brands of wrought iron pipe on the market, and an informant said that they were of the same quality and price. Wrought iron pipe cost 30% more than steel pipe, it was used in quality construction before World War I, but it is almost never used today. It was normal trade practice to assure wrought iron pipe quality by naming a manufacturer known not to use iron containing steel scrap. The specifications themselves were imprecise. Apparently, it was impossible to make lap welded wrought iron in all of the sizes necessary for the house as called for by the specifications.

Why did Kent object to the pipe? Danzig reports he was told "The old man would go all over town to save a buck." However, he may have used the substitution as an expression of his frustration with Jacob & Youngs' performance of the contract. Completion of the job was long delayed. Jacob and Youngs did additional work that added to Kent's bill.

5. *Free contract and excusing experts' certificates:* John Murray,[15] argues:

> A few courts have taken the position that the condition is excused if the architect's failure to grant the certificate resulted from his mere unreasonableness. Such holdings are unsound since they have the effect of nullifying the condition entirely. In every case in which the certificate is refused and the price not paid, the contractor will claim that the architect was unreasonable, with the result that the whole matter will have to be decided as a question of fact, just as it would be if no condition were stated in the contract. This is contrary to the obvious intent of the parties.

Is Murray right? What does Cardozo's approach do to the power of lawyers to control the future by contract drafting? Are there reasons why a disappointed contractor might accept an architect's determination rather than relitigate the matter in court even when it followed Justice Cardozo's approach?

However, is it realistic to say that the contractor made a choice to accept a private government subject to almost no meaningful review by public government? To what extent is the substantial performance doctrine a covert application of the

---

[15] Copyright 1974, 1965, 1947 The Michie Company. Reprinted from MURRAY ON CONTRACTS, Second Edition, by John Edward Murray, Jr., with permission from The Michie Company, Charlottesville, Virginia.

ideas behind the unconscionability doctrine? Does a rule strictly enforcing the condition permit exploitation of the weak or unwary?

As you think about the advantages and disadvantages of the rules governing using expert certificates, consider the following problem. Shizuko Natsuki is Japan's bestselling mystery writer. In her novel, THE OBITUARY ARRIVES AT TWO O'CLOCK,[16] Natsuki writes about Kosuke Okita, a young businessman who owns Wakashiba Landscaping, Inc. He made a contract with Nansuno, the developer of a golf club, to do the landscaping on the new course. Kosuke thought it would be "a real coup for a small company like his to receive such a contract."

> [Kosuke] started work in June of '81 with a budget of three hundred and fifty million yen, and it was six months before he became suspicious of Nasuno's intentions. When making a golf course, the contractor first prepares the land and then the landscape gardener moves in and plants the trees, which in the Tokyo area usually consist of pine, zelkove, and numerous flowering shrubs. This generally takes quite a while as it is difficult to collect such a large number of trees at one time, but once it is finished, the turf is planted. The greens take a lot of care to shape, and when they are almost ready, the designer comes and gives detailed instructions concerning the gradient. The work was to be done over the course of a year and Kosuke was to receive payments on a monthly basis. According to the agreement, Wakashiba Landscaping, Inc. was to receive ten percent in advance, five percent per month, and the final thirty percent upon completion of the work. However, the payments only came regularly for the first three months. The design had been left up to another small company, and as each hole was finished, the designer would come and give his okay before work was started on the next. There were no problems at first, but then suddenly he started finding fault with everything.
>
> "You should move the green five yards to the left."
>
> "That bunker should be moved forward another twenty yards."
>
> It was easy enough to say, but it meant hours of extra work. If the designer said that he did not like the surface of the green or that the gradient was wrong, all the turf had to be lifted and relaid. Every time the designer made a claim against Wakashiba, Nasuno would make a deduction from the amount that he paid them that month, sometimes paying as little as half of the agreed amount. This was all well and good for him, but Kosuke had to pay for the changes as well as paying for the work on the other greens, and when the next month came around, the designer would simply make another claim and Nasuno would postpone payment even longer.
>
> Despite his loss of income, Kosuke still had to pay the nursery gardeners for the turf and trees that he used and also had to pay the laborers he employed. A large project like a golf course required between forty and fifty workers a day, and, needless to say, these had to be paid on a

---

[16] (Ballantine Books 1988). Copyright by Shizuko Natsuki.

daily basis. In order to pay all his overhead, he was forced to borrow from the bank, and as time passed, the interest on these loans only served to make things worse.

He was about halfway through the job when he began to realize that Nasuno had planned it this way from the beginning. The designer's company was connected to Nasuno and he had obviously been told to find fault with the greens so that Nasuno could delay payment. In July, after the construction was finished, Kosuke's worst fears came true. By this time Nasuno was sixty-five million yen in arrears, and when the designer came up with a whole new batch of complaints, Nasuno announced that instead of paying the remaining thirty percent that was due to Kosuke, he would only pay fifteen. Kosuke had followed the plans faithfully and had all the records to prove it, so if he were to sue Nasuno, he would most probably win, but he knew that the company would not be able to stay solvent until the case came to court.[17]

Nasuno is murdered, and Kosuke becomes the police's main suspect. Natsuki's fiction should prompt you to review the law about expert's certificates. However, suppose Nasuno had not hired an expert, but he had made all the objections to Kasuke's work himself. Assume also that the transaction took place in the United States rather than in Japan. Kasuke, the landscaper, comes to you and asks for legal advice. Using American law, can you suggest a course of action likely to help him short of murdering Nasuno?

VAN IDERSTINE CO. v. BARNET LEATHER CO.
Court of Appeals of New York
242 N.Y. 425, 152 N.E. 250 (1926)

LEHMAN, J. . . . On September 10th, 1920, the parties entered into another contract for the sale of 6,000 vealskins, delivery to be made in September, "to be received by Jules Star & Co. subject to their approval." . . .

. . . Jules Star & Co. rejected the entire quantity of 6,000 skins which the plaintiff tendered in attempted performance of its contract of September 10th, 1920, and defendant refused to accept them.

The plaintiff has brought this action to recover damages suffered because of the defendant's refusal to accept the skins which plaintiff offered to deliver. . . .

. . . In the second cause of action as amended at the trial the plaintiff alleged that any condition for approval by a representative of Jules Star & Co. of the skins to be delivered under the contract of September 10th was waived and excused because the approval was unreasonably withheld, and because defendant prevented Jules Star & Co. from giving such approval and "because defendant and said Jules Star & Co. wrongfully and knowingly colluded to withhold that approval, with intent to avoid defendant's having to accept the said skins." The issues raised by the denial to these allegations were submitted to the jury and decided in favor of the plaintiff. . . .

---

[17] *Id.* at 13-15.

We have pointed out that under both contracts sued upon, the seller agreed to make delivery subject to the approval of Jules Star & Co. The parties chose to stipulate that such approval must be given. It constitutes a condition which, unless waived or excused, must be fulfilled before the buyer can be compelled to accept skins that are tendered. Concededly approval of Jules Star & Co. has not been given. . . .

. . . [T]he condition was waived also in regard to the contract which forms the basis of the second cause of action if refusal of approval by Jules Star & Co. was the result of bad faith on the part of Jules Star & Co. in which the defendant had some share. If by its own interference and wrong the defendant prevented the plaintiff from obtaining the stipulated approval, then the plaintiff may recover without it. We have pointed out that in the second cause of action the plaintiff has pleaded that the condition was waived and excused not only because of wrongful act on the part of the defendant but because approval was "unreasonably withheld," and the serious question raised upon this appeal is whether the plaintiff may recover under its contract upon proof that it offered to deliver skins which in quality complied with the contract requirements, and that the representative of Jules Star & Co. unreasonably withheld its approval of these skins.

The trial judge charged that if "approval was unreasonably withheld, whether Barnet had anything to do with it or not, the plaintiff could recover. Star must have acted honestly. If he showed an honest judgment the defendant is entitled to a verdict." Though the parties have stipulated that the approval of Jules Star & Co. must be obtained for any skins delivered under the contract, under the rule laid down in the charge, the plaintiff may become liable for damages if he insists upon this stipulation being carried out. It places upon the buyer the risk of determining whether Jules Star & Co. have acted reasonably; it makes the buyer determine whether approval should reasonably have been given, though not he but Jules Star & Co. were to approve of the quality of the skins. In effect it makes the buyer a guarantor of both the honesty and the good judgment of Jules Star & Co.

It is said that authority for the rule laid down in the charge may be found in many cases in this and other jurisdictions where the courts have considered the effect of unreasonable or dishonest refusal of architect or engineer to approve of work done or materials furnished, under building contracts when such approval was made a condition precedent to payment. . . . In those cases it must be remembered that by the nature of the contracts, if failure to obtain approval deprived the contractor of right to recover the agreed compensation the result would be that the benefit of work actually performed and materials actually furnished could be appropriated by the owner without payment, though in other respects the contractor had fully complied with his contract. It would cause forfeiture of agreed price for agreed service without any fault on the contractor's part. In the same manner as the courts have evolved the rule that under contracts of that nature there may be recovery for substantial performance, they have evolved a rule which permits recovery without stipulated certificate of approval where the certificate has been wrongfully or unreasonably refused. . . .

So, too, in some cases where the contract shows that the person whose approval is required under the contract is merely an agent of a buyer selected by the buyer to pass upon the goods in the buyer's place, wrong on the part of the agent is imputed to the principal. . . .

Here the contract is of different nature. The parties agree that a designated broker acting as expert and not simply as the buyer's agent must pass upon the goods and delivery must be made subject to the expert's approval. Refusal to approve by the expert does not enable the buyer to obtain property from the seller without payment. According to the terms of the contract it merely permits him to refuse to accept the goods because he stipulated not merely for goods of a certain quality but for goods of that quality approved by a particular expert. To compel him to accept and pay for the goods without such approval is to impose liability upon him which he had not agreed to assume, and gives compensation to the seller for goods not delivered in full compliance with contract. The theoretical soundness of the rule applied to building contracts has not escaped criticism. It rests upon the basis that enforcement of the contract according to its strict terms would cause forfeiture of compensation for work done or materials furnished. The rule should not be extended by analogy where the reason for the rule fails. . . . Unless the certificate has been withheld dishonestly and in bad faith, and the defendant is a party to that bad faith through control of the expert or collusion with him, there may be no recovery under the second cause of action.

There are cases where parties stipulate for the approval or certificate of a third person not as part of the contractual obligation of either party to the contract but rather as machinery for avoiding dispute between the parties as to whether these obligations have been properly performed. Question may then arise as to whether the stipulated approval or certificate constitutes in full sense a condition precedent to recovery, or whether there may be recovery based on substantial performance, upon proof that in other respects the contract has been fully complied with. Such question we do not now decide. Doubtless there are cases where such hardship would be imposed upon a party who performs work or manufactures goods at the special instance of another if payment were withheld merely because approval is wrongfully refused, that argument may well be made that such result was not intended by the parties. Here we have no such circumstances. The plaintiff's obligation is only to deliver certain goods, and by express stipulation there may be no delivery without approval of a third party. It has done nothing for which it might legally or equitably expect compensation until delivery is made. If approval is withheld the plaintiff cannot perform; it loses the profit which it might have otherwise made by delivery of goods at a contract price higher than the then prevailing market price. It assumed this risk. It still retains the goods and may sell them at market price. The defendant should not be required to pay the contract price unless the plaintiff performs according to contract "subject to the approval" of the third party. . . .

The judgments should be reversed and a new trial granted, with costs to abide the event. Cardozo, Pound and Andrews, JJ., concur; Hiscock, Ch. J., McLaughlin and Crane, JJ., dissent.

NOTES AND QUESTIONS

1. *Material from the briefs and record—the buyer's story*: The briefs and record in the case disclose that the jury was presented with two conflicting stories about the transaction. It was agreed that calfskins from farmers and butchers outside of New York City were likely to be of lower quality than New York City skins. Those slaughtering calves in New York City exercised care so that the skins would not be marked, and it was customary in New York City to use a special salt that did not discolor in the tanning process. The Barnet Leather Company, the buyer, offered evidence that before the contract involved in the case was signed, representatives of the seller had tried to sell calfskins to Barnet. Barnet refused because Van Iderstine "does not handle skins that are satisfactory to us, on account of buying outside skins, and our experience has been such that we have refrained from buying from you since last year."

Jules Star & Co. was a broker handling calfskins. It offered seller's skins to buyer on the standard form contract in the industry. The contract provided that the skins were "to be received by Jules Star & Co.'s representative subject to their approval." Star told his employees to bend over backwards to find the skins acceptable if possible, but they found that the skins were not of acceptable quality. Van Iderstine's representatives asked that Jules Star himself look at the skins. He did, and he testified,

> I could not approve of that kind of skins, that is not what the contracts call for. . . . I found that the condition of the skins was very bad, they were . . . in the worst shape I have ever been presented with New York City skins by anybody. I did not trust my eyes when I really saw this lot of poor stuff laying there coming out of that pack, and satisfying myself from all over that they were poor all the way through. . . . [The] custom of the trade is to reject a lot of skins if a proportion of these country and resalted and old outside city skins is mixed in with a supposedly first class New York City first salted skin.

Van Iderstine's representatives then contacted Mr. Barnet, the buyer, and complained about the rejection.

> So I told both of them that Mr. Star was our representative and the skins had been sold subject to his approval and that was final, as it had been final in every other transaction we had ever made through Star with them, or with anybody else, and that we would not have inserted in our contract that they were subject to the approval of Jules Star if it did not mean something. They were not satisfied, nevertheless, with Star's rejection and they begged me to come over. I decided that I would go over in all fairness to determine whether these skins were as Star reported to us or not, but without any obligation of any kind on our part. . . . [It] was a shame to call that [material offered] a first salted New York City skin and try to force him [Star] to take that kind of stuff.

Finally, the buyer offered the testimony of a former Van Iderstine Company employee. He said that Van Iderstine collected many skins from farmers and others outside New York City, including people known in the business to offer lower quality goods. Then Van Iderstine would mix the best of the outside skins in with New York City skins, offering all of them at New York City prices.

2. *Material from the briefs and record—the seller's story*: Van Iderstine, the seller, offered evidence that told a very different story. The salesman who handled the deal testified that in fact the skins offered were clean, fresh New York City calfskins. After Barnet claimed that the skins were badly scored, dirty and not clean and bright as New York City's should be, the salesman said he responded "[t]he reason you do not want these skins, Mr. Barnet, is not because they are not New York City's, but due to the fact that the market has dropped badly."

Jules Star was a stockholder in the Barnet Leather Company. A telegram was introduced in evidence. It was sent by Star representing Barnet Leather Company in a transaction with another seller shortly after Star and Barnet had rejected the skins offered by Van Iderstine. It said, "Barnet agrees to take quantity as per contract not exceeding two thousand. Take as few as possible make strict selection make sure skins sound not slipped salt stained or otherwise damaged." Van Iderstine argued that this showed Star and Barnet were raising the standard for skins to minimize losses in a falling market. In denying Barnet's motion for a new trial, the judge said that he regarded this telegram "to be perfectly competent, especially upon cross-examination, because it was sent so close to the transaction in suit as to give a valuable insight into the motives and actions of defendant's agent."

3. *The trial judge's view of the evidence*: The jury found for Van Iderstine, the plaintiff seller, based on the evidence and instructions quoted. The buyer moved for a new trial in part because it was against the weight of the evidence, but its motion was denied. The trial judge said "the court would not have disturbed the verdict whichever way it went, although its impressions upon the trial were distinctly in favor of the merit of the plaintiff's [seller's] claim, and the impression has not been changed by the further consideration of the testimony."

4. *Van Iderstine under the UCC*: Would the *Van Iderstine* case be decided differently today now that such a transaction in goods is governed by the UCC? Section 2-513 deals with a buyer's right to inspect goods, but it does not mention inspections by experts. Would a sale of calfskins "to be received by Jules Star & Co.'s representative subject to their approval" be governed by § 2-515(b)? It provides:

> In furtherance of the adjustment of any claim or dispute . . . the parties may agree to a third party inspection or survey to determine the conformity or condition of the goods and may agree that the findings shall be binding upon them in any subsequent litigation or adjustment.

Does this section cover only claims or disputes which have already arisen or would it apply to potential claims or disputes that might arise as well?

5. *A hypothetical question:* Imagine that the time is the present. You are a lawyer for a manufacturer who utilizes veal skins to make leather goods. Your client has a contract which obligates it to accept "suitable" veal skins from Seller. The market for veal skins has fallen to substantially below the contract price. Your client has refused to accept a shipment of veal skins, having characterized them as "unsuitable." What will be the standard by which your client's behavior will be judged, should Seller complain? Will it differ importantly from the standard in *Van Iderstine*? Is it relevant that the market price has fallen?[18]

6.   *Can one bargain for discretion under the UCC*? Suppose a buyer wanted to have the final judgment on the quality of the goods offered and avoid debate about the matter. Can its lawyer write a provision in the contract with the seller stating that the buyer's determination of quality cannot be challenged even on the ground of bad faith? UCC § 1-102(3) is an important but often overlooked provision. It says:

> The effect of provisions of this Act may be varied by agreement, except as otherwise provided in this Act and except that the obligations of good faith, diligence, reasonableness and care prescribed by this Act may not be disclaimed by agreement but the parties may by agreement determine the standards by which the performance of such obligations is to be measured if such standards are not manifestly unreasonable.

Thus, a buyer could not contract out of an obligation to use good faith, but it could set "not manifestly unreasonable" standards by which the performance of that obligation was to be measured.

7.   *Personal approval in house building contracts*: In *Haymore v. Levinson*,[19] owners and builder entered a contract for the construction of a house. $3,000 of the purchase price was placed in escrow until the "satisfactory completion of the work." The owners gave the builder a list of things to be done, and after these items were finished, they refused to release the money because they still were not satisfied. The builder recovered $2,739, and the owners appealed, asserting that there had been no "satisfactory completion" of the contract. They argued that the phrase should be given a subjective meaning: "unless they are satisfied and so declare, the money is not payable."

The Supreme Court of Utah affirmed. It said that if the work were reasonable under the circumstances, the builder was entitled to recover. The court said that where the purpose of the contract is "pleasing taste, fancy or sensibility of another" then a subjective standard will be applied. Where, however, the purpose is operative fitness, mechanical utility or structural completion, an objective standard will be applied: "that is, the party favored by such a provision has no arbitrary privilege of declining to acknowledge satisfaction and he cannot withhold approval unless there is apparent some reasonable justification for doing so."

The owners argued that free contract required a subjective standard. "If parties are not legally bound by their contracts, there could be no order or progress in the business world." Moreover, "a house should rank high among those aesthetic things which are dependent upon personal satisfaction and taste." The owners spent a substantial sum to buy a home. "There they would live their lives, and there they would entertain their friends, relatives and social visitors. It would be difficult to say that the finishing and decorating of a house does not contribute to one's personal fancy, taste, and judgment."

---

[18] *See, e.g.,* Neumiller Farms, Inc. v. Jonah D. Cornett, 368 So. 2d 272 (S. Ct. Ala. 1979).

[19] 8 Utah 2d 66, 328 P.2d 307 (1958).

The court rejected this argument. Why? Building contractors often complain that the last installment is difficult to collect. They say that homeowners often cannot visualize what will be built from a set of drawings, and they often have unrealistic expectations about cost, time, progress and quality. Homeowners complain that it is very difficult to get builders to finish a job.[20] In the *Haymore* case, the owners complained of such matters as the dishwasher protruded two inches beyond the rest of the cabinet because it was the wrong size, acoustical tile had started to fall off the basement ceiling, there was a hole in one of the basement bedroom walls, the doors in the house were warped, and cement walls and slabs had cracked. The builder offered experts who said that the defects were minor and not structural, and the builder testified that it tried to make repairs until the owners ordered its workers off the premises.

Do courts seem appropriate places to resolve disputes of this sort?

8. *More conditions of satisfaction:* Conditions of satisfaction are also used in the publishing industry. (Can you see why?) Sometimes, as we might expect, problems arise. For example, in *Doubleday & Co., Inc. v. Curtis*[21] a publisher sued for the return of an advance it had paid actor Tony Curtis, and he counter-claimed for anticipated earnings. In 1976, Doubleday signed a two-book contract with Curtis. On the basis of this, Curtis prepared a draft manuscript for a novel entitled KID ANDREW CODY AND JULIE SPARROW. After examining the manuscript, Doubleday signed a standard publishing contract. It provided that Curtis was to be paid royalties provided that he could deliver a final manuscript which was "satisfactory to Publisher in content and form." A final draft, prepared by Curtis and Larry Jordan (a Doubleday editor) was accepted for publication.

Doubleday then agreed to renegotiate the contract governing the second book. It paid Curtis an advance on future royalties. The contract provided, once again, that the manuscript was to be "satisfactory to Publisher in content and form." Doubleday then made a contract with New American Library which provided for payment to Doubleday of $200,000 for the paperback rights in the second novel, if and when the second novel was accepted for publication by Doubleday.

Curtis delivered a partial first draft of a rags-to-riches story of a Hollywood starlet; the book was entitled STARSTRUCK. The draft was assigned to Adrian Zackheim, a Doubleday editor who was a stranger to Curtis. Four months later Zackheim sent Curtis a seven-page letter which contained both praise and criticism of the manuscript. The letter said Zackheim was "charmed" with the "wonderful possibilities" of STARSTRUCK and that he did not anticipate the need for substantial changes in the basic outlines of the novel. On the other hand, the letter noted numerous inconsistencies and inherent contradictions in the manuscript, and urged Curtis to tighten the plot. Curtis, who had worked closely with Larry Jordan on the first book, was preoccupied with his divorce proceedings, and, apart from a few conversations, did not work with Zackheim on the revision of the book.

---

[20] *See* NEW YORK TIMES, Feb. 25, 1982, at 29, cols. 1-4; WALL STREET JOURNAL, May 17, 1982, at 31, col. 1.

[21] 763 F.2d 495 (2d Cir.), *cert. dismissed* 474 U.S. 912 (1985).

Curtis subsequently delivered what he characterized as a completed manuscript. He had paid little attention to the suggestions and criticisms contained in Zackheim's letter. Zackheim believed the book was unpublishable, but passed it along to Elizabeth Drew, his supervisor. Notwithstanding the fact that rejecting the book would cost Doubleday the NAL reprint arrangement, Drew wrote a memo in which she characterized STARSTRUCK as "junk, pure and simple" and concluded that neither editing nor rewriting could make it publishable. Zackheim suggested to Curtis' agent that the manuscript be submitted to a "novel doctor," but this suggestion was rejected.

At the trial Curtis characterized Zackheim as an apathetic and incompetent editor, as compared to Larry Jordan. He also complained that he had not received any indication from Doubleday that STARSTRUCK would be unacceptable until his agent, Lazar, informed him that Doubleday had made an irreversible decision not to publish it. Zackheim admitted at trial that his letter overstated the strengths of Curtis' first draft, and minimized the weaknesses. But both Zackheim and Drew testified that they sincerely believed the manuscript was irreparable, and that their decision not to publish was motivated by both ethical and artistic considerations.

The trial court judge began by finding that though New York decisions did not make it clear whether a "satisfactory to the publisher" clause required the publisher to offer editorial services, Doubleday had in fact offered such services. Next he concluded that Doubleday's rejection was animated by a genuine belief that the manuscript was unpublishable. But he then found that Doubleday had led Curtis to believe the book would be published, and that this constituted a waiver of the publisher's right to ask that the advance be returned.

There was an appeal and the Court of Appeals ruled that good faith honest dissatisfaction was a prerequisite to assertion of a "satisfaction" clause. It was appropriate to investigate the good faith and honesty of the publisher, since "to shield from scrutiny the already chimerical process of evaluating literary value would render the 'satisfaction' clause an illusory promise, and place authors at the unbridled mercy of their editors." On the other hand, it was important to realize that a requirement that publishers perform honestly was not the same as a requirement that they perform skillfully.

> The possibility that a publisher or an editor—either through inferior editing or inadvertence—may prejudice an author's efforts is a risk attendant to the selection of a publishing house by a writer, and is properly borne by that party. To imply a duty to perform adequate editorial services in the absence of express contractual language would, in our view, represent an unwarranted intrusion into the editorial process. Moreover, we are hesitant to require triers of fact to explore the manifold intricacies of an editorial relationship. Such inquiries are appropriate only where the contracts specifically allocate certain creative responsibilities to the publisher.

The Court of Appeals sustained the trial court finding that Doubleday had acted in good faith. Though Zackheim's revisions may have been offered somewhat belatedly, he did extend numerous offers to discuss the novel with Curtis, which Curtis refused. There is no reason to regard the encouraging notes in Zackheim's letter as prejudicial to Curtis. Doubleday did sacrifice the financial rewards of the NAL contract by choosing not to publish, and the decision could "hardly be said to constitute an act of bad faith."

The Court of Appeals then reversed the trial court on the waiver issue, and remanded with orders that a judgment be entered for Doubleday on that issue. The issue of waiver was not properly before the trial court. Curtis had not raised the issue at trial, and Doubleday had no notice that its claim was subject to challenge on the ground of waiver.

Having offered a brief summary of the controversy, we are left with questions. Why doesn't an obligation to produce a satisfactory manuscript impose a reciprocal obligation on the publisher to supply skillful editorial services? Doubleday editor Larry Jordan had apparently provided skillful services on the first book. Why couldn't Curtis reasonably expect Doubleday to provide the same level of editorial support on the second? Does this decision rest on a determination of what the likely expectations of the parties were? How does the United States Court of Appeals for the Second Circuit know what those expectations were? Does the decision rest on a judgment that the courts should not enter the dismal swamp of attempting to review editorial decisions? Should the Court have considered that the contracts with new authors are generally drafted by the publishers? Won't publishers be largely exempt from supervision when dealing with the works of unknown authors, since only successful authors will have the bargaining power to eliminate the "satisfactory to the publisher" clauses? If this is true, is it a good or bad thing?

Joan Collins, an actress who played a scheming businesswoman on the television series "Dynasty," made a contract to write two books for Random House. Her agent, Irving (Swifty) Lazar, negotiated a clause providing that all she had to submit was a "complete manuscript." In other words, he had sufficient bargaining power to negotiate the standard "satisfactory to the publisher" clause out of the contract. Ms. Collins submitted two manuscripts, but Random House argued that it was not liable to pay her for them because they were unreadable and unpublishable. She sued, and the issue tried to a jury was whether what she had submitted was a "complete manuscript." A Random House lawyer summarized one of her plot lines: "Stephanie has a miscarriage and tells a doctor or nurse not to tell anyone, while she goes about trying to adopt a baby. In the meantime, she pretends for eight months to be pregnant. When the husband of her best friend sees her without her pregnancy disguise, she murders him. Then she runs to the forest to give birth to her imaginary child."[22] The jury found for Ms. Collins on the first manuscript but for Random House on the second. One juror said: "A good editor can virtually take the phone book and turn it into something reasonable."[23]

Publishers have another way to reject books for which they contracted which they later decide they do not want to publish. Typically, publishing contracts set

---

[22] NEW YORK TIMES, February 13, 1996, at A13.
[23] NEW YORK TIMES, February 14, 1996, at A1.

a date by which the author is to submit a manuscript. Authors often fail to meet these submission dates. The publisher can cancel the deal because of the delay. However, authors with reputations usually get an advance payment from the publisher when they sign the contract. While the publisher would have a cause of action to recover the advance in most cases, practically few authors would be able to repay it. The NEW YORK TIMES reports:

> Often by the time a book is canceled, a good bit of . . . [the] advance has been paid to the writer, and the disenchanted publisher wants the money back. Usually, the only practical way to get it is for another publisher to buy the book and give the writer an advance large enough to live on and at the same time pay back at least some of the advance to the first publisher. Since any other method of recovery is largely wishful thinking, trashing the product doesn't help.[24]

B. MY RIGHT TO CALL OFF SOME OR ALL OF THE DEAL BECAUSE OF YOUR FAILURE TO PERFORM: "MATERIAL FAILURE OF PERFORMANCE"

1. A NOTE AND SOME PROBLEMS TO SET THE STAGE

What should a court do when one party fails to perform perfectly but comes close? In Volume I of these materials, we considered the remedial alternatives available to a victim of a breach. In the course of that inquiry, we looked at *Colonial Dodge, Inc. v. Miller*,[25] in which the issue was whether a disappointed purchaser could walk away from the transaction when the seller had tendered a defective performance. We will be revisiting that issue here, but exploring it in greater detail, and emphasizing not only the question of the availability of remedy, but spending more time on the question of the qualitative assessment of performance. Where the seller is to supply a single tangible object, and the buyer is to pay the contract price when the object is delivered, one of the buyer's important rights is to walk away free and clear of obligations to the seller if there is anything wrong with the item. However, it is not so clear that the buyer should be able to walk away free and clear of obligations to the seller where the seller's performance was complex and a great deal but not all of it has been given to the buyer. In some situations, at least, it may make more sense to require the buyer to pay for the less than perfect performance but grant an offsetting claim for damages. In ordinary transactions, at least, buyers cannot expect extremes of perfection. Consider several examples:

---

[24] Martin Arnold, *Making Books; The Many Ways of Saying "No,"* NEW YORK TIMES, April 30, 1998, at E3.
[25] 322 N.W.2d 549 (1982), *reh'g* 328 N.W.2d 678 (1982).

(1) Suppose seller sells her car[26] to buyer for $1,000, and they agree that seller will tender the keys and the title certificate to the buyer in front of the buyer's house between 9:00 and 11:00 a.m. on April 7th. Both are present on that morning at 10:00. Buyer takes the key and tries to start the car unsuccessfully. The battery is dead. A new battery of the type in the car can be purchased for $50 at the service station across the street from where the car is parked. Seller is a regular customer at the service station, and its owner is willing to bring the battery across the street and install it. Seller explains this to the buyer, but he says that he is no longer bound to the contract since the seller failed to perform. Has buyer the right to back out of the deal free from contractual liability? What more, if anything, do you need to know?

(2) Suppose a singer of popular music of some fame agrees to perform at a nightclub. He promises to perform there on the night of April 7th, singing in shows to begin at 9:00 and 11:00 p.m. of no less than 30 minutes and no more than one hour. He is to be paid $10,000 for the performances. Suppose the singer performs for 45 minutes at the 9:00 show, and the audience is enthusiastic. However, the singer cuts the 11:00 show short and sings for only 20 minutes because the audience fails to respond to his act. Assume that the owner of the club is in no way responsible for the reaction of the audience at the 11:00 show. The owner asserts that since the singer did not perform for at least 30 minutes at the 11:00 show, he did not perform his part of the contract, and, as a result, the owner owes the singer nothing. Are the singer's lawyers likely to collect the $10,000? Anything? Could they assert with any real chance of success that since he performed the 9:00 show, he should be paid $5,000 for it? Since he also performed 20/30th of the 11:00 show, should he be paid 2/3 of $5,000 (or $3,333), making a total of $8,333 earned for the night of April 7th? Of course, this would be subject to a set-off of any damages the club owner could prove had been caused by the failure to perform for ten minutes. Suppose the singer cut short the 9:00 show which annoyed many in the audience who might have stayed for the 11:00 show and did not. Would this make a difference?

(3) Suppose seller is to deliver an X, a Y, and a Z in exchange for $2,800. Seller delivers the X and the Y, but fails to produce the Z. Can buyer refuse to accept delivery or return the items and then be free of any obligation under the contract? Suppose the Z is, arguably, a relatively minor part of the total contract as compared to the X and the Y? Suppose that X, Y, and Z are an IBM desktop computer, a Hewlett Packard scanner and the computer program "Adobe Photoshop," respectively. The contract document lists the prices as follows: (1) the computer = $1,700; (2) the scanner = $500; (3) "Adobe Photoshop" = $600. Seller tenders delivery of the computer and the scanner but fails to deliver the computer program. Can buyer reject the computer and the scanner and call off the contract? Should we view this as one contract for three items that are to work

---

[26] Of course, cars are movables, and contracts for their sale are transactions in goods governed by Article 2 of the Uniform Commercial Code. While many courts apply a materiality test to cases not governed by the Code such as our singer and nightclub owner, the UCC's approach is a little different. We will consider it later. We offered the sale of a car as an example here only because most students can understand the facts easily.

together or is it really three contracts that happen to be recorded on one piece of paper? Would it matter if seller had agreed to sell "Photoshop" at about half the price which it normally costs? Would it matter whether the contract called for "Photoshop," a program that is widely available from computer stores or another program that was available only from this seller? Suppose the seller had not listed separate prices for each of the three items but had only quoted the total price ($2,800) for all three?[27]

Courts could solve most of these problems by saying that because one party has not performed precisely, she or he cannot assert any rights under the contract. The one in default could be left to restitution for benefits conferred by partial performance. However, often the defaulting party would not think this a fair solution. Restitution for a party in default will cost the almost-performer his or her expectation interest as well as much of the reliance interest that does not produce tangible economic benefits. In some states, moreover, it is said that a party in default (or perhaps one in "willful" default) cannot recover restitution. The defaulting party may forfeit a great deal, and in some cases, at least, the punishment may be too great for the crime.

Rather than using a strict performance standard, courts have often adopted a test of materiality. If X has performed some but not all of his duties under a contract, Y may walk away free and clear of any obligation other than restitution only if the failure of performance is "material" or "substantial." In the first example which dealt with the delivery of a used car with a dead battery, a new battery could be installed quickly and the contract carried out. It seems unlikely that any failure of performance here would be material or substantial. Contrast a case where seller tenders the keys and the title, but buyer looks under the hood and discovers that there is no engine in the car. Almost certainly the seller's default would be material then; installing a new battery and a new engine are different matters, and we can wonder about the seller's good faith in one situation but not the other.

2. SOLUTIONS OFFERED BY THE RESTATEMENT (SECOND) OF CONTRACTS

So far we've talked about the consequences of finding a failure to give a complete performance to be material or immaterial. How does one decide how important the defect is? To a great extent, materiality seems to turn on whether or not the ultimate consequences of the classification seem appropriate, given the facts of the case. The late Professor Malcolm Sharp wrote that the "best statement of these ordinary tests [for materiality], and perhaps the best portion of the work, is § 275 of the Restatement of Contracts."[28] (Section 275 is now § 241 in the second Restatement.) How would you deal with our three examples (the car and battery; the singer who cut short a show; the delivery of an X, and a Y but not a Z)

---

[27] Just as is true of our first example, this computer transaction would be governed by Article 2 of the UCC. *See* § 2-307. *See, also*, Restatement (Second) of Contracts § 240. Does § 2-307 incorporate the ideas found in § 240 of the Restatement? Reading the text of § 2-307, how would you make an argument that it does?

[28] Sharp, *Promissory Liability II*, 7 U. Chi. L. Rev. 250, 272 (1939).

under the Restatement? To see the structure of the Restatement's approach, you will have to consider the several sections of the work. At this point you should review Restatement §§ 225, 237, 240, 241, and 242.

Professor Eric G. Andersen[29] challenges the Restatement approach to material breach. He says "the relevant *Restatement* provisions seem enigmatic at best." They "resemble a list of ingredients rather than a recipe; no real guidance is provided on the order or proportions in which to combine the provisions." They "fail to identify an underlying, unifying principle more specific than 'fairness' or 'justice. . . .' " Courts can apply these rules only through a "gut-level judgment about how a particular case should be decided."

Professor Andersen offers his solution. Materiality requires us to focus on the appropriateness of courts making cancellation available to the victim under the circumstances of the case. We must seek to protect the victim's expectation interest without imposing needless costs on the defaulting party. A party to a contract has two interests. One is her interest in *present performance*. The defaulting party promised to perform today, but he failed to do so. Usually, courts can protect this interest by allowing the victim to sue for damages. The other is her interest in *future performance*—an interest in the likelihood that the contract will be performed as agreed in the future despite the defaulting party's failure to perform as promised to date. In some cases courts must allow the aggrieved party to cancel to protect this interest. The victim must be sure that she is free of her original contract so she can seek her needs elsewhere. Thus, courts should ask whether it is necessary to allow cancellation to protect this interest and whether the victim could take reasonable steps to eliminate or avoid injury.

Andersen attacks the Restatement's balancing approach. He argues that we should not look at the burden on the defaulting party. Rather he advocates an expanded view of restitution for a party in default to protect any interest of the defaulting party. In this way, we can be sure that the victim will have the right to cancel when she must in order to turn elsewhere to protect her expectation interest.

Finally, Andersen asserts "[c]ancellation should be invoked only when a breach so impairs the interest in future performance that the victim has reasonable cause to bring the contract to an end, so that the bargained-for security [of performance], or its economic equivalent, may be acquired elsewhere." He concludes: "[w]hen the interest it protects is so understood and administered, the cancellation power is effectively harnessed."

Consider Professor Andersen's criticism of the Restatement's balancing test. Does it call for an intuitive approach? If so, why would anyone object to this? Does Andersen's approach significantly limit the amount of judgment and discretion necessary when a court considers whether to allow one party to cancel? To what extent, if at all, does it make a court's task easier?

---

[29] *A New Look at Material Breach in the Law of Contracts*, 21 U.C. Davis L. Rev. 1073 (1988).

3. TRANSACTIONS IN GOODS: THE BASIC SOLUTIONS OF THE UCC

a. The General Pattern

To what extent does the UCC follow the approach of the Restatement (Second) of Contracts for cases coming within Article 2? Standing alone, § 2-601 appears to state what has been called "the perfect tender" rule. With some important qualifications, it says that "if the goods . . . fail *in any respect* to conform to the contract, the buyer may . . . reject the whole. . . ." [Emphasis added]. For example, in *Frankel v. Foreman & Clark*,[30] the court permitted rejection of an entire shipment of coats although the jury found that there was a trivial or inconsequential failure to comply with the contract involving only one or two percent of the coats. Would a court be likely to reach this result under the UCC? White and Summers[31] think not, saying:

> Close examination of the Code reveals that the Code well nigh abolishes the [perfect tender] rule. First of all, section 2-601 renders the perfect tender rule inapplicable to installment contracts, and 2-612 permits rejection in such contracts only if "the non-conformity substantially impairs the value of that installment. . . ." Secondly, the seller's right to cure a defective tender, embodied in 2-508 . . . is a further substantial restriction upon the buyer's apparent right to reject for insubstantial defects under 2-601. Additional restrictions upon the perfect tender rule in 2-601 may be found in 2-504 (an improper shipment contract which causes a late delivery is grounds for rejection only if "material delay or loss ensues")[32] and in the Code's general invitations to use trade usage, course of dealing, and course of performance in interpretation. . . . Finally, the courts have the power to deny rejection for what they regard as insubstantial defects by manipulating the procedural requirements for rejection. That is, if the court concludes that a buyer ought to be denied his right to reject because he has suffered no damage, the court might arrive at that conclusion by finding that the buyer failed to make an effective rejection (for example, because his notice was not timely).
>
> We conclude, and the cases decided to date suggest, that the foregoing changes have so eroded the perfect tender rule that little is left of it; the law would be little changed if 2-601 gave the right to reject only upon "substantial" nonconformity.

The following chart should help you see the pattern of the UCC's sections related to tender, acceptance, rejection, cure, revocation of acceptance, notices and remedies. We will be exploring these issues in greater detail in the pages that follow.

---

[30] 33 F.2d 83 (2d Cir. 1929).
[31] Uniform Commercial Code 304-305 (2nd ed. 1980).
[32] *See* Monte Carlo Shirt, Inc. v. Daewoo Int'l (America) Corp., 707 F.2d 1054 (9th Cir. 1983).

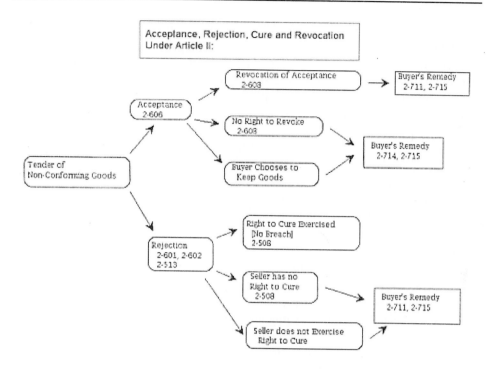

The following decision illustrates the UCC's basic approach to a buyer's right to reject or return a defective performance.[33] Remember, however, that a seller may have a right to cure a defective performance under § 2-508. Furthermore, under § 2-612 installment contracts are treated differently. We will consider these variations later.

b. Inspection and Acceptance of the Goods

ARDEX COSMETICS OF AMERICA v. LOGOTECH, INC.
United States District Court, Northern District of New York
2002 U.S. Dist. LEXIS 1545 (2002)

TREECE,J. This is a civil action for breach of contract involving the sale of adhesive labels by defendant Logotech, Inc. ("Logotech") to plaintiff Ardex Cosmetics of America, Inc. ("Ardex"). . . .

FINDING OF FACTS: Ardex is a New York corporation involved in, inter alia, the manufacturing of perfumes and oils, which are then packaged and sold in labeled bottles to retailers. . . . In 1997, Ardex created anew line of oils called Ancient Oils. These oils would be contained in an ember color, cylinder type bottle approximately two inches in height. On or about April 8, 1997, Ardex received substantial orders for the Ancient Oils line from Family Dollar of Charlotte, North Carolina. The orders were to be tentatively delivered on July 21 and August 18, 1997. To complete the order, Moses Suklijian, [an Ardex manager] entered into negotiations with Logotech, a New Jersey printing company that

---

[33] However, if a defect is a seller's late delivery to a carrier, UCC § 2-504 controls.

specializes in the production of adhesive labels for many types of packages including bottles.

There were various stages to these negotiations, such as, selecting artwork, selecting colors and determining the size of the labels. Ardex sent Logotech several samples of the Ancient Oils' bottle in order to determine the specifications for the labels. Logotech was aware of the urgency of this production due to the Family Dollar order. Logotech quoted the labels at a cost of $ 11.42 per thousand, plus several production costs. On June 27, 1997, Ardex ordered two million labels, but contested the production costs. In July 1997, Logotech shipped the test labels to Ardex. After receiving the first shipment, Ardex began placing the labels on the Ancient Oils' bottles with a label machine. . . . Lorretta Sukljian was in charge of this aspect of production and immediately noticed that the labels did not properly adhere to the bottles.

On or about July 12, 1997, Moses Sukljian advised Logotech's salesperson, Randy Fiorey ("Fiorey"), that the labels were peeling away from the bottles and suggested that Logotech used another type of adhesive for the remaining labels. Logotech informed Ardex that it experienced a similar problem with the sample bottles. Logotech suggested washing and then placing the labels on the bottles, a process Logotech found successful with the sample bottles. Ardex attempted this course of action after attempting to heat the labels and/or heat the bottles and then put the labels on, with the hope of activating the adhesion on the labels, which was to no avail. . . . Indeed, washing the bottles proved to be the soundest solution. . . .

Logotech began delivering the two million labels on or about August 5, 1997, continuing into November 1997. Logotech then billed Ardex $ 30,982.42, which included the production charges that Moses Sukljian challenged. Ardex continued to experience some problems with the labels, notwithstanding the washing of the bottles prior to applying the labels. From the receipt of the initial delivery in July of the test sample-labels and continuing for months thereafter, the parties discussed the problem. Nonetheless, Ardex was concerned about meeting the Family Dollar order and continued the production of their product line. The then-president of Logotech, Tuvia Leibovitz, . . . [said] that the only successful remedy was to wash the bottles.

Moses Sukljian accepted Leibovitz's assertion that it was the bottles that was causing the labels to peel off. Thus, Ardex went through the arduous task of removing the first run of 255,000 labels from the bottles as well as washing and drying 550,000 bottles and then putting on labels. As mentioned earlier, this process worked best, but the labels still did not adhere properly. Ardex continued to complain. Within a week after the August 5, 1997 delivery, Logotech representative Bombardier arrived at Ardex with the hope of resolving the dilemma. Indeed, there were other occasions when Bombardier and/or Fiorey visited Ardex either to determine how things were going or to collect moneys toward the account. The last meeting occurred in February 1998.

Despite the problems, Ardex used approximately 810,000 labels on the Ancient Oils bottles, of which, approximately 660,000 bottles were sent to Family Dollar. On November 5, 1997, . . . Sukljian sent a check to Logotech, . . . in the amount of $25,322.42 ($30,982 minus the challenged production costs), with the notation "payment full" [sic]. A second check was given to Bombardier and Fiorey at the February 1998 meeting in the amount to $1,200 with the same notation. No further negotiations occurred between the parties after February 1998. Replacement of the labels was never offered by Logotech nor any other remedy provided.

Sometime in 1998, Bombardier left Logotech and began working for a competitor, Mid-Atlantic Labels, Inc. ("Mid-Atlantic"). . . . Very interested in gaining Ardex's business, it appears that he approached Moses Sukljian on two accounts: purchase of machinery and purchase of labels for the Ancient Oil line of products. . . .

Eventually Mid-Atlantic secured an order from Ardex for one million labels at a price substantially lower than the contract price for the same labels with Logotech. These labels were used immediately upon their delivery on or about December 17, 1998. The Mid-Atlantic labels adhered to the bottles without the bottles being washed, although approximately 100,000 Mid-Atlantic labels were placed on bottles that had been pre-washed by Ardex. The successful implementation of these Mid-Atlantic labels dispelled the notion for Moses Sukljian that a "film" or "residue" was the caused for the Logotech labels not sticking to the bottles. Rather, this was a "red flag" for him that Logotech's product was defective and the sole cause for this label debacle.

In January 1999, Logotech sent a bill for the balance it believed still due. In the same month, Ardex sent a letter to Logotech advising that "we never accepted these labels as useable merchandise," reiterated the problem with the labels, informed them that they had more than one million "defective" labels remaining and sought a refund for the "unuseable" labels. The unused labels were not returned to Logotech because Ardex felt they were unuseable for anyone and thus worthless.

Ardex commenced this breach of contract action on or about December 13, 1999.

CONCLUSIONS OF LAW: This matter concerns the sale of goods (labels) in New York; therefore, the parties' rights and obligations are governed by Article 2 of the New York Uniform Commercial Code (N.Y. U.C.C.). . . . Under N.Y. U.C.C. § 2-601, upon deliver of goods, the buyer has the right to accept or reject, in whole or in part, such goods that fail to conform to the contract. "Acceptance of the goods occurs when the buyer after a reasonable opportunity to inspect the goods signifies to the seller that the goods are conforming or that he will take or retain them in spite of their non-conformity " N.Y. U.C.C. § 2-606(1)(a).

When a buyer accepts non-conforming goods, he may revoke his acceptance of the goods pursuant to N.Y. U.C.C. § 2-608. . .

Here, Ardex noticed that the test labels did not properly adhere to the bottles and suggested that Logotech use a different adhesive on the remaining 2 million labels. When the first shipment arrived on or about August 15, 1997, the labels again failed to properly adhere to the bottles and again Ardex immediately informed Logotech of the problem. The parties then began negotiating a solution. While the best solution was washing the bottles prior to applying the labels,

Ardex never expressed its satisfaction with the labels, but neither did Ardex unequivocally express its dissatisfaction. Despite these problems, on November 5, 1997, Ardex paid Logotech $25,322.42 for the labels. This payment constitutes acceptance of the non-conforming goods. However, Ardex's continued complaints to Logotech demonstrates that it accepted the non-conforming labels under the reasonable assumption that the adhesion problem would be seasonably cured. Thus, the issues are: whether the non-conformity was a "substantial impairment; and whether Logotech seasonably cured the non-conformity and, if not, whether Ardex revoked its acceptance within a reasonable time.

"Substantially Impaired"

There is no dispute that the labels did not properly adhere to the bottles, regardless of whether the bottles were pre-washed. This defect clearly substantially impaired the value of the labels to Ardex. Logotech, however, contends that Ardex failed to prove that the labels did not stick because of a defect in the labels. Rather, Logotech contends that a residue or film on the bottles may have caused the problem. Ardex, however, sent sample bottles to Logotech for it to determine what adhesive needed to be used on the labels so they would properly adhere to the bottles. Logotech sent the labels to Ardex without indicating that it experienced any problems affixing the labels to the bottles. Therefore, Logotech sent non-conforming goods.

"Seasonably Cured"

The next issue is whether the solution of washing the bottles "seasonably cured" the non-conformity. Washing the sample bottles worked for Logotech and appeared to work relatively well for Ardex. Indeed, more than 600,000 Ancient Oils bottles were sent out to Family Dollar. Nonetheless, Ardex continued to lodge complaints with Logotech and the parties continued to discuss the issue until February 1998. Since Ardex never accepted Logotech's "cure" of pre-washing the bottles, and Logotech did not provide any other acceptable alternative, Logotech failed to "seasonably cure" the non-conforming labels.

Timely Revocation

The final issue is whether Ardex's revocation of acceptance in January 1999 was both timely and reasonable. "Reasonable time is not an inflexible term. It depends commonly on the circumstances of each case." . . .

Here, Ardex continued to discuss the problems with the labels through February 1998. These negotiations were sufficient to extend Ardex's time to revoke its acceptance of the goods. See N.Y. U.C.C. § 2-607(2) & (3). . . . The parties' mutual attempts to cure the non-conformity, however, ended in February 1998. Since no other cure was proffered by Logotech after February 1998, it should have been readily apparent to Ardex that it had to either retain the non-conforming goods or revoke its acceptance. See N.Y. U.C.C. § 2-608(2).

Ardex contends that it did not become aware of the non-conformity until it secured new labels from Mid-Atlantic in December 1998. However, Ardex did not formally notify Logotech of its revocation until it received a bill from Logotech for the balance due on the account. It is this Court's opinion that it was this bill, and not the Mid-Atlantic labels, that raised the ire of Ardex. Thus,

Ardex's contention is unpersuasive and it should have known it had an obligation to provide timely revocation of acceptance in February 1998. . . . Ardex did not send its unequivocal notice of revocation until January 1999. Waiting approximately one year to revoke is unreasonable under these circumstances. This untimely notice precludes Ardex from recovering the contract price. . . .

Damages

Ardex's failure to reject or revoke the acceptance of the labels, however, does not impair any other remedy provided by Article 2 of the N.Y. U.C.C. for nonconformity. See N.Y. U.C.C. § 2-607(2). . . . Moreover, repeated complaints made within a reasonable time upon the receipt of the first shipment of labels is sufficient to recover damages. Since Ardex almost immediately informed Logotech that the labels were not properly adhering to the bottles, Ardex may recover damages pursuant to N.Y. U.C.C. § 2-714, which states in pertinent part:

> (1) Where the buyer has accepted goods and given notification (subsection (3) of Section 2-607) he may recover as damages for any nonconformity of tender the loss resulting in the ordinary course of events from the seller's breach as determined in any manner which is reasonable. . . .

The only issue is whether Ardex has proven damages. . . . Ardex has failed to provide such proof to this Court. Ardex withdrew its claim for loss profits prior to trial. Instead, Ardex seeks recovery for labor costs incurred when its employees spent time removing approximately 250,000 labels and washing approximately 910,000 bottles before securing new labels to them. The only evidence provided to the Court is a pile of payroll records and vague testimony by current and former employees that they spent hours a day for approximately one year peeling labels and washing bottles. This evidence is both qualitatively and quantitatively deficient. [The court found that Ardex' evidence failed to establish the cost of removing the labels and washing the bottles].

It is hereby ordered that judgment be entered for defendant Logotech, Inc.

NOTES AND QUESTIONS

1. *The burden on the aggrieved party:* The court finds that Logotech, the seller, supplied defective labels. Nonetheless, it wins the lawsuit. Ardex certainly complained to Logotech, and Logotech misdiagnosed why the labels would not stick. What did Ardex do that cost it its rights? From a business person's standpoint, did it do anything that was unreasonable? Is the lesson of the case that a business needs legal advice when it faces a breach of contract?

2. *Section 2-601 and acceptance of the goods:* Consider UCC §§ 2-606, 2-602. What did Ardex, the buyer, do that constituted an acceptance of the defective labels? Does a buyer have to know that goods are defective in order to accept them and thus lose its rights to reject them for any defect under § 2-601?

c. Cooperation and Good Faith

ADMIRAL PLASTICS CORP. v. TRUEBLOOD, INC.
United States Court of Appeals, Sixth Circuit
436 F.2d 1335 (1971)

WEICK, J. This appeal arose out of an action for damages filed in the District Court by Admiral Plastics Corporation (Admiral) of New York against Trueblood, Inc. (Trueblood) of Dayton, Ohio, for breach of contract in which Trueblood agreed to design and manufacture for Admiral three injection blow mold machines, at a cost of $39,750.00 per machine. Jurisdiction was based on diversity of citizenship. The case was governed by Ohio law.

The District Court, sitting without a jury, found that both parties failed to act in good faith and failed to cooperate in the performance of the contract, thus rendering the contract void. The District Court entered judgment in favor of Admiral for $29,812.50, which was the amount of its down payment to Trueblood, and dismissed Trueblood's counterclaim. Both parties appeal. We affirm.

In 1965, Admiral was a leading manufacturer and supplier of plastic containers, which were extensively used in the food, beverage and pharmaceutical industries. Admiral could not meet the ever-increasing demand for its product, and as a result, began investigating machine manufacturing companies to determine which company could best supply Admiral with the injection blow mold machines it needed to increase production. Paul Marcus, the chief engineer for Admiral, contacted Trueblood, a manufacturer of injection mold machines, and was informed that Trueblood had never built a blow mold machine, but would consider doing so if Admiral provided the specifications.

Marcus made several trips to Trueblood's plant, the last preliminary meeting being on May 17, 1966. At this meeting Marcus described the features of the machine required by Admiral and stated that it would want Trueblood to build only the rear portion of the machine, in order to protect Admiral's trade secrets. On May 24, 1966, Marcus called Trueblood, and asked for a firm quotation on the price of the machine. Trueblood quoted $39,750.00 per machine, and Marcus ordered three machines to be manufactured by Trueblood. Marcus stated that the written purchase order, the specifications, and a check for 25% of the total purchase price would be forthcoming.

By June 22, 1966, Trueblood had not received the purchase order, specification letter, or check from Admiral. Trueblood advised Marcus of this fact, and on June 28, Marcus informed Trueblood that the purchase order had been written, but would not be sent until the middle of July, at the end of Admiral's fiscal year. Thereafter, on July 20, 1966, Trueblood received from Admiral a check for $29,812.50, a six-page specification letter dated May 24, 1966, and the purchase order.

The specification letter stated that Trueblood would redesign (where necessary), manufacture, assemble and test three injection blow molding machines and furnish all engineering drawings of the machine and that the delivery dates for the machines were November 1, November 15, and December 1, 1966. On July

21, 1966, Trueblood informed Admiral that there were discrepancies between the specification letter and the previous discussions with Marcus. After being assured that the specifications would be revised, Trueblood deposited Admiral's check of $29,812.50, but did not sign the purchase order.

On August 25, 1966, Marcus visited Trueblood's plant, and expressed concern over the lack of progress in the construction of the machines, and the fact that Trueblood had not forwarded the design drawings. Marcus was informed that the component parts had been ordered, and also that Trueblood had not received the revised specifications. Marcus revised the specifications upon his return to New York, and Trueblood received them on September 9, 1966. These revised specifications satisfied Trueblood, except for the terms of payment, and the fact that Trueblood considered the data on the machine's automatic sequence of operation to be inadequate.

On October 19, 1966, an engineer of Admiral visited Trueblood's plant, and discovered that little work had been done on the manufacture of the machines. Only one of the three machines ordered was in any stage of construction, and only to the extent of the basic weldment.

On October 26, 1966, Marcus informed Trueblood that one of the component parts ordered by Trueblood, the Egan reciproscrew, was the wrong size, and that a larger one was required. Trueblood told Marcus that to reorder the part would entail added expense. Marcus instructed Trueblood to order the larger reciproscrew, and that Admiral would bear the added expense.

No design drawings of the machines were furnished to Admiral as of November, 1966. On November 11, 1966, a Trueblood official visited Admiral's plant, to observe Admiral's machines in operation, in order to aid Trueblood in the making of the design drawings. However, no drawings were ever furnished to Admiral.

On December 1, 1966, the Admiral engineer again visited Trueblood's plant, and again observed little progress on the construction of the machines. He was informed that the earliest possible delivery date would be March 1, 1967. Thereafter, on December 8, 1966, Admiral's attorney contacted Trueblood, asserting that Trueblood was in default, and threatened legal action unless Trueblood signed the purchase order. At this same time, Trueblood ceased work on the drawings and on the machines. No machine was ever delivered to Admiral, and Trueblood did not return the $29,812.50 down payment.[34] Both parties claimed substantial damages as the result of the other's alleged lack of performance and breach of contract.

The District Court held that Admiral and Trueblood entered into a valid contract, under UCC 2-204. . . . With this there can be no dispute. The District Court recognized that the contract was one for the manufacture and sale of unique machines, in the designing of which neither company had any experience. It was

---

[34] [1] The difficulty of performing this contract for the custom-made machines is exemplified by the fact that Admiral hired, on November 7, 1966, one Ephraim Natkins as chief engineer, and on January 21, 1967, one Eli Jaffe as engineer. Both men worked almost exclusively on designing the injection blow mold machines that were finally manufactured and delivered by a Connecticut company, between September, 1967 and January, 1968.

understandable therefore, that certain terms were left unspecified and that difficulty was encountered in designing and producing the machines. This in no way detracts from the validity of the contract.

The nature of the contract made it imperative that both parties cooperate to the fullest extent in order for the machines to be successfully designed and built. The UCC recognizes such situations where good faith and cooperation are necessary to the successful fulfillment of a contract. UCC 1-203 and 2-311. The District Court determined that both parties failed to act in good faith and failed to cooperate in the performance of the contract, thus terminating their respective obligations and rendering the contract void.

Each party has urged that whatever its shortcomings were, they were caused by the other party's initial failure to cooperate and subsequent breach of contract. The District Court found that lack of progress on the machines could not be attributed to the conduct of any one party to the contract, and we agree. There was evidence that Admiral was delinquent in furnishing the specifications, as was Trueblood in failing to furnish the machine design drawings.

The evidence is not clear as to who was at fault for ordering the wrong size Egan reciproscrew, but a resolution of this is not necessary, as both parties were sufficiently at fault in other instances which justify the finding of mutual breaching of the contract. In our opinion, the findings of fact adopted by the District Court are supported by substantial evidence and are not clearly erroneous. The District Court was correct in dismissing Trueblood's counterclaim for damages against Admiral, and in not awarding to Admiral any money damages other than the return of its down payment.

The only question remaining is whether the District Court was correct in ordering the refund of Admiral's down payment of $29,812.50. We think it was.

The UCC does not provide a remedy for the specific situation of a mutual breaching of a contract.[35] We must therefore turn to other state principles of law and equity. UCC 1-103.

The rule in Ohio is: "Mutual delinquency gives rise to the presumption of mutual assent to a rescission."

We construe the parties' actions in this case, illustrated by their failure to cooperate and failure to perform tasks called for by the contract within a reasonable time, as evidence of a mutual rescission. . . . In *Brown v. Johnston*, 95 Ohio App. 136, 108 N.E.2d 298 (1952), a contract was mutually rescinded, and the purchaser was allowed to recover the money that he had paid on the purchase price, in excess of the benefits conferred upon him while the contract was in existence. Since Admiral received no benefits from Trueblood during the existence of the contract, it is entitled to the return of its down payment.

The judgment is affirmed in each appeal. Costs will be assessed against each appellant.

---

[35] [2] In our opinion UCC § 2-718 is not applicable to this case. The section bears some resemblance, in that it pertains to a buyer's right to restitution of his payments on the contract. However, the section specifically applies when "the seller justifiably withholds delivery of goods because of the buyer's breach." That is not the case here.

NOTES AND QUESTIONS

1. *Information from the record about the transaction*: Admiral manufactured clear plastic bottles that looked like glass but were much stronger and lighter. It wanted Trueblood to build machines to which it would attach parts which it had developed. Ray Trueblood testified that Admiral's General Manager came to the Trueblood plant at the beginning of the negotiations. "We . . . started to discuss his special machine and he wouldn't tell me too much because he said it was a secret, what produced over the front end was a secret and he wanted us to produce the main part of the machine in the rear." The specifications were written by Admiral's General Manager who had a degree in mechanical and industrial engineering, and they were sent to Trueblood in a seven page letter drafted in outline form. After four pages of specifications, the following appears: "All other details may be worked out between the authorized personnel of Admiral and Trueblood." Trueblood was to design the hydraulic and electrical systems, but Trueblood's engineers never were certain about the sequence of operation. One of Admiral's engineers conceded that Trueblood's engineers could not have been able to prepare the hydraulic and electrical circuitry if they did not understand the sequence of operation. Neither Trueblood nor Admiral ever took steps to clear up the difficulty and get the project underway. Each seemed to assume that the other party was responsible for working out matters. After the dispute arose, Admiral bought machines from another manufacturer. This time, Admiral's engineers designed exactly what they wanted in great detail. Even so, once the machines were delivered it took some effort to adjust them and make modifications so that they would work.

2. *Formation and performance*: The opinion of the trial court in the *Admiral Plastics* case suggests some of the relationships between classical notions of formation and a more relational contract approach based on the UCC:

> This is another one of those disturbing cases caused by the failure of both parties to have the benefit of counsel. This agreement does not pertain to the ordinary purchase of known or advertised machinery but pertains exclusively to a new type, a custom type piece of machinery requiring the intense cooperation of each side in order to manufacture an injection blow mold machine. . . .

> Before the enactment of the Uniform Commercial Code [*See* UCC § 2-204] the evidence presented would be conclusive that no contract ever existed between these parties because there had never been a meeting of the minds regarding the obligations of each party to this transaction. Equity in such a case would restore the parties to the same position that they were on the date plaintiff claims, May 24, 1966.

> Applying the provisions of the Uniform Commercial Code, a consideration of all the evidence shows a contract between plaintiff and defendant which was breached by failure of both parties to cooperate in the performance of the contract. In law and in equity this Court concludes that each party should bear its own losses.

Does it matter whether a court follows the approach of the appellate or the trial court?

3. *Loss sharing*? Why should each party bear its own losses? Trueblood, the manufacturer, expended time and effort designing and beginning production of the machine. Moreover, the Admiral order was placed on the production line in its plant, and this affected its ability to accept other orders and the scheduling of those it did accept. Admiral, however, invested time and effort negotiating the contract and trying to help Trueblood perform. In its complaint it claimed:

> [Admiral had] been damaged and will continue to be damaged in that it will be obliged to expend other and additional monies for the purchase of such machines from other suppliers at prices more expensive than those provided for by the agreement; it has lost and will continue to lose profits on the sale of plastic containers from the dates on which said machines were to have been delivered and in production to and including the dates on which substitute machines may be delivered and be in production; it has lost the value of drawings, materials and parts prepared at its expense specifically for use in said machines and has suffered other and further losses and damages in the aggregate amount of $324,962.50.

Should the parties share all of these losses in some way? How? If you think these losses should be shared, is there a legal theory which accomplishes this purpose?

4. *Good faith and cooperation—one requirement, or two?* The court talks about a duty of good faith and cooperation. Are these words synonymous? Is there a duty of good faith, and a separate duty of cooperation? Does it matter? Are both present in every contract? Do you believe that they provide meaningful standards against which to measure performance? Which interest groups would you expect to lobby for and against the inclusion, of a Code section providing for a duty of good faith?

5. *Good faith, long term continuing relations, and the UCC—quasi-fiduciary obligations*? In *Conoco, Inc. v. Inman Oil Co., Inc.*,[36] Conoco was found to have breached its implied obligation of good faith to one of its distributors. Inman Oil Co. obtained most of the products it sold from Sinclair Oil Co. and Shell Oil Co. from 1967 to 1972. St. Joe Minerals Corp., a lead mining company, was one of its major customers. Conoco had been unable to sell products to St. Joe Minerals. Conoco and Inman held a series of meetings in 1972. Their officials agreed to cooperate in Conoco's attempt to persuade St. Joe to switch from Sinclair products to Conoco products to be supplied by Inman as a distributor. The effort was successful, and there were no problems until 1980.

Conoco operates through two divisions. Conoco Wholesale and Commercial Operations (WCO) sells petroleum products directly to large commercial and industrial users. Conoco Branded Division sells to distributors such as Inman. In 1981, WCO decided to bid directly on the St. Joe Minerals account and bypass Inman Oil. It was successful. The loss of the lucrative, long-time St. Joe account was a significant factor in Inman Oil going out of business in 1982.

---

[36] 774 F.2d 895 (1985).

The Court of Appeals reversed the finding that Conoco had acted in good faith. It found the relationship governed by the UCC It said:

> Conoco had earlier obtained St. Joe as an indirect Branded Division customer through the efforts and good will of Inman Oil. On the basis of its long-standing relationship with and confidence in Inman Oil, St. Joe had agreed to transfer much of its business from Sinclair to Conoco. However, Conoco evidently felt no obligation to repay this substantial favor by continuing to channel its St. Joe business through Inman Oil. Moreover, having acquired St. Joe as a direct customer [by submitting bids below its jobber price quotations], Conoco then refused to permit Inman Oil to serve as the delivery agent. . . .

The Court of Appeals remanded the case, directing a federal magistrate to find Inman Oil's damages as a result of Conoco's direct bids on the St. Joe account.[37]

The Association of American Historians (AAH) is a professional association, and its members are, largely, people who hold positions as professors of history at various universities and colleges. The Bank Royal Hotel (not its real name) in St. Louis offers hotel rooms, meeting rooms and other facilities in which organizations can hold conferences. AAH made a contract in 1998 to hold its 2000 annual meeting at the Bank Royal Hotel in St. Louis. In 1999, the Bank Royal Hotel was charged by the Missouri Civil Rights Commission with discriminating against African American guests and employees. A hearing was held that was covered in both the St. Louis and national press, and the hotel was found to have engaged in many discriminatory practices. As a result of this negative publicity, the AAH found that at least some of its members were unwilling to attend the annual meeting at the Bank Royal Hotel. It was unclear how many of its members would refuse to attend the meeting at that location. Members of its Board of Directors did not want to hold the meeting there, and many thought that moving the meeting to another hotel would make a symbolic statement against discrimination.

The AAH consults an organization of law professors interested in civil rights. One professor suggested that the Bank Royal Hotel has violated an "implied condition of cooperation" in its contract with the professional association. He mentioned *Beuttas v. United States*.[38] There the plaintiff made a contract with the federal government to build part of a large housing project. The contract required plaintiff to pay a specified minimum wage to all those who worked for it on the project. The government then invited bids to build the rest of the project. However, in this bid invitation, it required the winning contractor to pay a specified minimum wage that was significantly higher than the one in the contract with the plaintiff. The effect of imposing a higher minimum wage was to require plaintiff to pay that wage in order to get workers; had it refused to do this, it would be able to get only those workers unable to get jobs with the second contractor. This raised plaintiff's costs and lowered its profit on the project. The plaintiff recov-

---

[37] *Compare* Bloor v. Falstaff Brewing Corp., 601 F.2d 609 (2d Cir. 1979). *See also,* Farnsworth, *On Trying to Keep One's Promises: The Duty of Best Efforts in Contract Law,* 46 U. Pitt. L. Rev. 1 (1984).

[38] 60 F. Supp. 771 (Ct. Cl. 1944).

ered compensation for its increased costs: "It was an implied condition of this contract that the Government would not do any act that as a necessary consequence would make performance by plaintiff's more expensive." The law professor also mentioned the *Conoco* case, where the court said that this implied covenant "imposes upon each party the duty to do nothing destructive of the other party's right to enjoy the fruits of the contract and to do everything that the contract presupposes they will do to accomplish its purpose."[39] Is this implied duty of cooperation a plausible argument for AAH? What would you expect the Bank Royal Hotel's lawyers to say? In *Burger King Corp. v. C.R. Weaver,*[40] the court found that the Florida courts would limit any implied duty of good faith or cooperation. Such an obligation "is not an independent contract term. It is a doctrine that modifies the meaning of all explicit terms in a contract, preventing a breach of those explicit terms *de facto* when performance is maintained *de jure.*" The implied duty cannot vary the express terms of the contract. "A duty of good faith must relate to the performance of an express term of the contract and is not an abstract and independent term of a contract which may be asserted as a source of breach when all other terms have been performed . . .". What term of the contract between AAH and the Bank Royal Hotel could AAH argue involved a duty of cooperation?

d. Notice: § 2-607(3)(a)—and a Note on § 2-608(2)

The next case is an interesting, and instructive one. It raises several issues in addition to that involving the application of § 2-607(3). We say this only to alert you that we will return to the Eastern/McDonnell Douglas dispute again later in this volume.[41]

EASTERN AIR LINES, INC. v. MCDONNELL DOUGLAS CORP.
United States Court of Appeals, Fifth Circuit
532 F.2d 957 (1976)

AINSWORTH, J. This important Florida diversity case involves an appeal from a judgment for damages for breach of contract in favor of Eastern Air Lines against McDonnell Douglas Aircraft, Inc. based on a jury verdict in Eastern's favor for the sum of $24,552,659.11 plus costs of $241,149.02—one of the largest jury verdicts ever reviewed by this Court. Involved is a series of contracts covering the years 1965-1968 by which Douglas Aircraft, Inc.[42] agreed to manufacture and sell to Eastern Air Lines nearly 100 jet planes for approximately a half billion dollars. Suit was filed by Eastern against Douglas on July 31, 1970, based on allegations that 90 of these planes were delivered a total of 7,426 days

---

[39] Conoco, Inc. v. Inman Oil Co., 774 F.2d 895, 908 (8th Cir. 1985).

[40] 169 F.3d 1310 (11th Cir. 1999).

[41] Some may remember that it appears earlier in CONTRACTS: LAW IN ACTION in connection with the requirement that damages be proven with reasonable certainty, and the role of expert witnesses in meeting that requirement.

[42] [1] As will be noted below, Douglas merged with the McDonnell Aircraft Company on April 28, 1967 to become the McDonnell Douglas Corporation. Although we will occasionally refer to "Douglas" in discussing acts which antedated the merger, the company will generally be denominated "McDonnell" or "McDonnell Douglas" during the course of this opinion.

late. It was not until July 12, 1973, after almost three years of pretrial motions and discovery and four and one-half months of trial, that the jury's verdict was rendered in the District Court.

Our review of the case convinces us that the District Court made a diligent effort to resolve the many difficult matters before it. Nevertheless, we conclude that the trial judge committed substantial and prejudicial errors in a number of his rulings and instructions to the jury, which require reversal of the judgment and a new trial. Accordingly, we reverse and remand.

I. *Background*

Eastern Air Lines decided in 1964 to replace what remained of its outmoded propeller-driven fleet in an effort to reverse a serious five-year financial decline. Ever since the advent of the commercial jet age in 1959, Eastern had lagged behind its competitors in the purchase of jet-powered planes. Consequently, the company's decision to order 100 new planes made it the last major trunk carrier to purchase a large number of jet aircraft.

Although Eastern is one of the largest passenger carriers in the world, its route system has historically been composed of relatively short segments. In 1964, only Boeing and Douglas could offer a small, twin-engine, short-range jet suited to Eastern's needs. Eastern's decision to purchase the Douglas DC-9 rather than Boeing's 737 was based in part on Douglas' offer to lease it a number of DC-9-14's as an interim plane until the larger "stretched" DC-9-31's were available.[43] Boeing had been unable to provide Eastern with an equivalent aircraft as a substitute for its short-haul, twin-engine 737 which was not due to be delivered until a year after Douglas was to begin producing the DC-9-31. For its longer range flights, Eastern also ordered a number of DC-8-61 jets which are Douglas' equivalent of the Boeing 707.[44]

Letters of intent providing for Eastern's lease or purchase of DC-9-14's and for its purchase of the "stretched" DC-9-31 and the DC-8 planes were signed in February of 1965. The following July, Douglas and Eastern entered into the first three of what was to be a series of eight contracts providing for the delivery of a total of 99 planes. Five of the eight contracts were amended, some a number of times, between 1965 and 1968.

Although varying in details, all the agreements are basically similar; each required Douglas to manufacture a number of planes at a stipulated price per aircraft to be paid upon the delivery of each plane at Douglas' California plant. Each jet was designated for delivery during a particular calendar month. In addition, every contract contained two provisions which are of special importance to these appeals. One clause is a choice of law provision which requires that the contracts' construction and performance be determined under California law. The

---

[43] [2] The DC-9 is a "second generation" commercial jet with two engines mounted on its tail and is designed for short to medium-haul service. The DC-9-14 is capable of carrying approximately 65 passengers while the "stretched" model DC-9-31 can carry 100 passengers.

[44] [3] The DC-8-61 planes ordered by Eastern are large (200 passenger), medium-range (2,000 miles), four-engine jets. The Model 61 is a larger and more advanced version of the DC-8 introduced in 1959.

other provision is an "excusable delay" clause which exempts Douglas from liability for delays beyond its control and not its fault.

Problems developed in the Douglas-Eastern relationship before even the first plane was scheduled to be delivered. In January 1966, it became evident to both parties that Douglas would be unable to complete its DC-9-14 jets in time to meet the contract delivery dates. In an early exchange of letters on the subject, Douglas attributed the delivery delays to "our nation's rapidly increasing commitments in Southeast Asia," and Eastern replied by expressing concern and noting that "[i]t appears to us that some of this slippage really should have been avoidable."

Subsequently it appeared that the delays could not be confined to the DC-9-14 deliveries. During 1966 and 1967, Douglas repeatedly revised its scheduled delivery of DC-8's and DC-9-31's. These further delays were viewed with "great concern" by Eastern executives who informed Douglas that the late deliveries were imposing a "substantial burden" on the airline.

Throughout this period, Douglas was confronted with a mounting financial crisis which, to some extent, was the result of the DC-8 and DC-9 delivery delays. In the summer of 1966, Douglas forecast a loss of almost $30 million in its operations for the year. By November, Douglas' cash shortage reached such catastrophic proportions that the company's creditors insisted that a solvent merger partner be found. The natural choice was the McDonnell Aircraft Company whose military and space activities effectively complemented Douglas' strength in the commercial aircraft field. After McDonnell infused into Douglas over $68 million in new funds, a merger was consummated on April 28, 1967. The new McDonnell Douglas Corporation assumed all the obligations and liabilities of the former Douglas Aircraft Company.

Delivery delays continued after the merger until the last of the planes was delivered in January 1969. On the average, each of the 90 late planes was delivered 80 days after the month specified in the contract date. Several months after performance had been completed under the last of the eight contracts, Eastern wrote McDonnell on May 29, 1969 presenting a claim for damages resulting from the late deliveries over the previous three years. The airline alleged that these delays could not be deemed excusable under the applicable clause in the agreements. McDonnell rejected the claim and suit was filed in the District Court for the Southern District of Florida.

On the order of the District Judge, the trial was bifurcated with the liability phase to be tried first; to be followed, if necessary, by a trial on damages before the same jury. The greater part of the three-month liability trial was devoted to McDonnell's efforts to prove that the delivery delays were the product of events covered by the excusable delay clause in each contract. Although McDonnell produced evidence that some of the deliveries were late because of strikes and labor shortages, the heart of its defense was that most of the delays were caused by the rapid military buildup occasioned by the war in Vietnam. During the 1966-1968 escalation of the war, the Government asked the aviation industry to accord specific military projects priority over civilian production. Although military priority, in some cases, was gained through written directives and ratings issued pursuant to the Defense Production Act of 1950 ("D.P.A."), the Government often effectively achieved the same result by more informal and less direct means. McDonnell endeavored to show that, because its subcontractors cooperated with this "jawboning" policy of the Government, there were serious delays in the delivery of parts vital to DC-8 and DC-9 production. Throughout the course of this phase of the trial, however, the District Judge took the position that the only excusable delays were those resulting from written government orders issued in strict compliance with procurement regulations. As a result, the trial judge refused to allow the jury to consider evidence of less formal efforts by the Government to expedite military production.

McDonnell Douglas also contended that Eastern had failed to give timely and reasonable notice of the breaches, that one of the contracts was no longer enforceable, and that Eastern should be estopped from pursuing any of its claims. The District Court, however, ruled against McDonnell on all these issues.

At the close of the liability trial, the jury was instructed that McDonnell bore the burden of proving that the delays were caused by events which were excused under the contracts. Furthermore, according to the court's instructions, no event could be an excuse unless it was not reasonably foreseeable at the time the particular contract was entered into. On May 16, 1973, the jury's verdict, in the form of answers to special interrogatories, found that none of the 7,426 days of delay was excusable.

During the six-week damages phase of the trial, each side presented testimony concerning the effect of the delivery delays on Eastern's operations during the 1966-1968 period. Eastern's expert estimated the airline's lost profits to be $23,400,000 while McDonnell's expert witness was of the opinion that no such damages resulted from the delays. The airline so presented evidence to support its claims for damages resulting from surplus pilot time expense, wasted pilot training and wasted schedule expense. In addition to these claims, the District Judge permitted the jury to consider Eastern's contention that, under Florida law, it was entitled to prejudgment interest from the time of the breach. On July 12, 1973, the jury returned a special verdict awarding Eastern a total of $22,219,601 in compensatory damages and $9,650,715 in pre-judgment interest. . . .

In its appeal, McDonnell Douglas' most fundamental contentions concern the District Court's rulings on excusable delay, Eastern's obligation to give reasonable and timely notice of breach, and the enforceability of one of the contracts. . . .

III. *Notice of Breach Under the Uniform Commercial Code*

During the trial and in final instructions to the jury, the District Court held that Eastern need not prove, as a predicate for recovery in this suit, that it had given McDonnell Douglas reasonable and timely notice of the delivery delays. McDonnell strongly contests the trial judge's rulings for Eastern on this issue and argues either that the airline should, as a matter of law, be barred from any recovery or, alternatively, that the issue of timely notice should have been submitted to the jury.

The statute governing this question is section 2-607(3)(a) of the Uniform Commercial Code which provides in part as follows:

(3) Where a tender has been accepted

(a) the buyer must within a reasonable time after he discovers or should have discovered any breach notify the seller of breach or be barred from any remedy; . . . .

McDonnell contends that the trial judge denied it the benefits of this provision, both by ruling that section 2-607 does not apply to late deliveries and by holding in the alternative that Eastern gave adequate notice. Because we are unable to agree with the District Court's ruling on either ground, we hold that the question of timely notice under section 2-607 should have been submitted to the jury.[45]

A. *Applicability of UCC § 2-607(3)(a)*

Even though section 2-607, by its very terms, governs "any breach," the trial court found the notice requirement to be inapplicable to delivery delays because a seller necessarily has knowledge of this sort of contract violation. Relying on the case of *Jay V. Zimmerman Company v. General Mills, Inc.*, E.D. Mo., 1971, 327 F.Supp. 1198, 1204, the District Judge concluded that notice is useless where a breach is apparent to both parties.[46] The trial court apparently was of the view that the sole function of section 2-607 is to inform the seller of hidden defects in his performance. Under this approach, the only purpose of notice is to provide the seller with an opportunity to remedy an otherwise unknown nonconforming tender. . . .

Section 2-607's origins, however, reveal that it has a much broader function. The Code's notice requirement was derived from decisional law in California and several other states which sought to ameliorate the harsh common law rule that acceptance of goods by the buyer waived any and all of his remedies. . . . This approach was codified under section 49 of the Uniform Sales Act which was adopted in California as Civ. Code § 1769.

As Professor Williston, the author of the Sales Act, has noted, section 49 continued the common law rule treating a seller's tender of goods as an offer of them in full satisfaction. 3 S. Williston, Contracts § 714 (rev. ed. 1961). The buyer,

---

[45] [31] Notification under § 2-607 is an integral part of a buyer's cause of action and is not an affirmative defense of the seller. Therefore, the buyer must both plead and prove that the notice requirement has been complied with.

[46] [32] In relevant part, the *Zimmerman* opinion reads as follows:

In the present, as in any case involving late delivery, both the seller and the buyer are necessarily fully aware *prior* to tender that the seller's contract obligation to timely deliver has not been complied with. It would be an unreasonable, if not absurd, construction of the statute to require a renewed notice of breach *after* acceptance of the goods under the facts here involved. A party has notice of a fact when he has actual knowledge of it. Section . . . 1-201(25) of the Uniform Commercial Code. The purpose of a notice in the context of this section . . . is to *inform* the seller of matters which would not normally come to the buyer's attention until *after* the goods came into his possession. The legislative intent was to make provision with respect to the effect of acceptance of allegedly defective or inferior goods or those allegedly not meeting warranted standards of quality. In that situation it is reasonable to require the buyer to inform the seller of the existence of a possible factual dispute relating to matters of which the buyer presumably was not aware prior to his acceptance of a tender of the goods.

Jay V. Zimmerman Company v. General Mills, Inc., E.D. Mo., 1971, 327 F. Supp. 1198, 1204 (emphasis in original).

though, was permitted to accept the offer without waiving any claims if he gave the seller prompt notice to this effect. . . . This approach reconciled the desire to give finality to transactions in which goods were accepted with the need to accommodate a buyer who, for business reasons, had to accept the tendered goods despite unsatisfactory performance by the seller. . . . Pre-UCC decisions in California and elsewhere, therefore, recognized that the primary purpose of notice is to inform the seller that, even though his tender has been accepted by the buyer, his performance is nonetheless considered a breach of contract.

Under section 49 it was irrelevant whether a seller had actual knowledge of a non-conforming tender. Instead, the critical question was whether the seller had been informed that the buyer considered him to be in breach. Consequently, in Professor Williston's words, "the section is applicable not only to defects in quality but to breach of any promise or warranty, as, for instance, *delay in time*." 5 S. Williston, Contracts § 714 at 409 (3d ed. 1961) (emphasis supplied). Pre-UCC decisions, therefore, applied the notice requirement in delivery delay cases. . . .

As the drafters of Article 2 acknowledge, section 2-607 continues the basic policies underlying section 49 of the Uniform Sales Act. Indeed, the notice requirement developed in pre-UCC cases is entirely consistent with the Article 2 goals of encouraging compromise and promoting good faith in commercial relations. As Comment 4 to section 2-607 indicates, the purpose of notice is not merely to inform the seller that his tender is nonconforming, but to open the way for settlement through negotiation between the parties. In the words of the California Supreme Court, "the sound commercial rule" codified in section 2-607 also requires that a seller be reasonably protected against stale claims arising out of transactions which a buyer has led him to believe were closed. *Pollard v. Saxe & Yolles Development Company*, 1974, 12 Cal.3d 374, 115 Cal.Rptr. 648, 525 P.2d 88. . . . Early warning permits the seller to investigate the claim while the facts are fresh, avoid the defect in the future, minimize his damages, or perhaps assert a timely claim of his own against third parties. . . .

Given these undeniable purposes, it is not enough under section 2-607 that a seller has knowledge of the facts constituting a non-conforming tender; he must also be informed that the buyer considers him to be in breach of the contract. The Code's notice requirement, then, is applicable to delivery delays as well as other breaches. . . . Accordingly, we decline to follow the reasoning of the *Zimmerman* decision, and we find that the trial court erred in not applying section 2-607 to the delivery delays at issue in this case.

B. *Adequate Notice Under Section 2-607(3)(a)*

Turning next to the lower court's alternative rationale for ruling against McDonnell on the issue, we must determine whether the notice given by Eastern was both sufficient and timely as a matter of law. Finding the facts "essentially uncontradicted," the trial court concluded that Eastern adequately informed McDonnell that it considered the delivery delays to be an actionable breach:

> Eastern's management repeatedly protested the delays and requested negotiation of the dispute, but they were always put off by McDonnell Douglas with the assurance that the matter would be taken up once the assembly line was back on schedule. When production was again on-line

many months later it became obvious to Eastern that no good-faith settlement negotiations would take place.

Because the court's ruling was, in effect, a directed verdict, it can be sustained only if there is no conflict in substantial evidence and the inferences from these facts "point so strongly and overwhelmingly" in favor of Eastern that reasonable men could not have arrived at a contrary verdict. . . . As will be demonstrated below, the adequacy and timeliness of notice under section 2-607 typically depend upon the reasonableness of the buyer's efforts to communicate his dissatisfaction. . . . Therefore, whether the notice requirement has been complied with is a question which is particularly within the province of the jury. . . . Applying this standard of review to the facts, we find that there was at least one substantial factual dispute before the court and that the trial judge's interpretation of the facts in the case was not the only reasonable inference that could be drawn from them. We, therefore, reverse on this issue as well. We do not agree, however, with McDonnell's contention that, as a matter of law, Eastern's notice was inadequate and untimely.

As we have seen, the contractual relationship between Douglas and Eastern stretched over a number of years and was governed by a series of separate agreements, several of which were amended a number of times. The complexity of these agreements and the large number of planes involved required the parties to be in constant communication with each other. Indeed, throughout this period, Eastern was informed of all significant developments by one of its own engineers who was in residence at the Douglas plant. Eastern, therefore, often knew of anticipated delivery delays before being formally informed of them by Douglas.

By early January of 1966, both parties were aware that production under Contract 65-41-L, the agreement with the earliest delivery dates, was behind schedule. Douglas did not officially notify Eastern of the impending delays until February when it sent several letters ascribing the DC-9-14 production difficulties to delays by subcontractors and a shortage of skilled labor. In Douglas' view, all of these problems were due to "our nation's rapidly increasing commitments in Southeast Asia." Douglas also indicated that it was making every effort to mitigate the impact of its subcontractors' difficulties.

Eastern replied on March 15, stating that it was "most disappointed with the delivery status" of the DC-9-14's. The airline noted that it had repeatedly expressed concern over the lack of early notification by Douglas. Without contesting Douglas' assertions concerning the Vietnam War, Eastern stated that

> It appears to us that some of this slippage really should have been avoidable if corrections had been rigorously pursued when it first became apparent. In light of this, we believe the Douglas Company has a responsibility to assist Eastern wherever possible in the reduction of our own pre-inauguration activities. Some of the areas that assistance would be beneficial [sic] are training (flight crews, cabin attendants, mechanics, and inspectors) and additional introductory service support.

> While it may be too early to evaluate completely, we assume your corrective actions will preserve the presently planned deliveries for the DC-9-31 and the DC-8-61 currently on order by Eastern.

On May 4, Douglas wrote Eastern expressing its willingness to discuss ways of "minimizing the difficulties these delays are causing you." Douglas, however, asked the airline to defer such conversations until production was back on schedule. There was no further correspondence concerning Contract 65-41-L, and, as we have seen, the agreement itself was terminated on July 14, 1966.

By fall of 1966, however, it became apparent that there also would be delays in the delivery of the DC-9-31 and DC-8-61 planes. Between October 1966 and September of 1967, Douglas wrote Eastern at least four times informing the airline of further delays in the production of these two types of aircraft. In a September 28, 1967 letter, written after the April merger, McDonnell Douglas again attributed the delays to "the worker shortage and continuing material and equipment shortages."

Eastern's first formal response to this series of announcements came on October 6, 1967. This letter informed McDonnell that "the delays in aircraft delivery have been very expensive to Eastern Airlines and we must view continuing slippage with great concern." Eastern went on to state that

> the delivery delays have cost Eastern so heavily that it would now appear that we made a mistake in going the DC-9 and DC-8-61 routes. Terms that were offered to us by another manufacturer would have been far less costly and although all aircraft manufacturers have suffered to some degree from common problems, it is apparent that the delivery schedule offered to us by your competitors have been more realistic than those attained by Douglas. . . .
>
> The delivery record of your current series of aircraft must necessarily be taken into account as we evaluate the purchase of the next series of airplanes. Unless there is concrete evidence that we can expect the DC-10 to be delivered in accordance with schedules offered by Douglas, it will be very difficult for us to decide in favor of your product as compared with that of another manufacturer.

On November 7, 1968, Eastern's Chief Financial Officer, Mr. Simons, wrote McDonnell Douglas asking that every effort be made to deliver several planes on schedule because a delay during the peak holiday season would place "a substantial burden on Eastern which is more severe than that imposed on your other customers."

There were no further significant written communications from Eastern until May 29, 1969 when McDonnell was formally presented with a claim for damages, in a letter from Eastern reading, in part, as follows:

> Eastern has made a full study of such delays and their economic impact and has concluded that Eastern has sustained very substantial damages as a result of delays which cannot be deemed "excusable" within the meaning of the definition in the applicable Purchase Agreements. At its meeting on May 27, 1969, our Board of Directors instructed management to present and process a claim for such damages.

In addition to this undisputed documentary evidence, the District Court had before it testimony concerning Eastern's attitude toward the delivery delays.

Eastern's Chairman, Floyd Hall, testified that he "talked with almost every one of the top officials [of Douglas and then of McDonnell Douglas] at one time or another. . . . [E]very time I met them I reminded them of the late delivery of their aircraft.". . .

The record, however, also contains testimony that Eastern informed McDonnell executives that it did not intend to make a claim for the late deliveries. . . . Another McDonnell executive, Jackson R. McGowan, also testified that Eastern's Chairman, Floyd Hall, told him that no legal action was contemplated.[47] We note here that § 2-607 does not require an explicit waiver of legal rights for a buyer's claim to be defeated. McGowan's memorandum, therefore, does not necessarily support the trial court's directed verdict on the notice issue. These allegations were denied by Eastern's witnesses.

Eastern contends that these facts are more than sufficient to constitute adequate notice as a matter of law. The Code, in Eastern's view, does not require the buyer to inform the seller that he is presenting a claim under the contract. This contention is based on Comment No. 4 to section 2-607 which states, in part, that "[t]he content of the notification need merely be sufficient to let the seller know that the transaction is still troublesome and must be watched." Eighth Circuit decisions[48] and at least one commentary[49] have relied on this sentence from Comment No. 4 for the proposition that almost any indication of dissatisfaction on the buyer's part meets the requirements of section 2-607. Under this standard, there would be little doubt that Eastern's letters concerning the delays constituted sufficient notice under the UCC.

It appears that Comment No. 4 was aimed at remedying a rule adopted under section 49 of the Uniform Sales Act by some courts that a mere complaint of a breach was not adequate notice. In California and a number of other states, for example, a buyer was required to indicate that he intended to look to the seller for damages. Several jurisdictions, moreover, required the buyer to specify in detail the basis for his claim that the contract was breached. . . .

---

[47] [42] In a memorandum to Mr. McDonnell, apparently written after Eastern had formally presented its claim in 1969, McGowan wrote concerning this conversation:

> From his remarks I took him to mean that he was trying to be understanding of our problems and did not anticipate taking legal action. On the other hand, I did not get the opinion that he was giving up his legal rights.

[48] [43] Bonebrake v. Cox, 8 Cir., 1974, 499 F.2d 951, 956-67 (letter informing seller that equipment not installed within meaning of contract sufficient notice as a matter of law); Lewis v. Mobil Oil Corporation, 8 Cir., 1971, 438 F.2d 500, 509 (constant communications from buyer concerning his suspicion that improper oil was being supplied sufficient to support jury verdict of adequate notice); Boeing Airplane Company v. O'Malley, 8 Cir., 1964, 329 F.2d 585, 593-96 (failure to perform properly in front of seller's expert and resulting shutdown of buyer's operations sufficient evidence for jury's finding on notice).

[49] [44] J. White & R. Summers, Handbook of the Law under the Uniform Commercial Code 347-48 (1972). The authors of this treatise conclude that

> Quite clearly the drafters intended a loose test; a scribbled note on a bit of toilet paper will do. . . . Under [Comment No. 4], it is difficult to conceive of words which, if put in writing, would not satisfy the notice requirement of 2-607. Indeed a letter containing anything but the most exaggerated encomiums would seem to tell the seller that the transaction "is still troublesome and must be watched."

These technical requirements were dispensed with because they frequently served to deny an uninformed consumer of what was otherwise a valid claim. As is noted in the draftsmen's comments, "the rule of requiring notification is designed to defeat commercial bad faith, not to deprive a good faith consumer of his remedy."[50] Eastern is therefore correct in asserting that notice under section 2-607 need not be a specific claim for damages or an assertion of legal rights. . . .

However, the fact that the Code has eliminated the technical rigors of the notice requirement under the Uniform Sales Act does not require the conclusion that any expression of discontent by a buyer always satisfies section 2-607. As Comment 4 indicates, a buyer's conduct under section 2-607 must satisfy the Code's standard of commercial good faith. Thus, while the buyer must inform the seller that the transaction is "still troublesome," Comment 4 also requires that the notification "be such as informs the seller that the transaction is claimed to involve a breach, and thus opens the way for normal settlement through negotiation."

In arguing that these requirements have been complied with, Eastern cannot rely on the same minimal standards of notice developed for ordinary consumers. The measure of good faith required under the Code varies with a buyer's commercial status. Unlike an ordinary purchaser, a merchant's good faith is measured by "reasonable commercial standards of fair dealing in the trade."[51] Therefore, as the Comments to section 2-607 indicate, what constitutes adequate notice from an inexperienced consumer may not be sufficient in a transaction between professionals.[52] While an ordinary purchaser is generally ignorant of his obligation to give timely notice, a merchant buyer should be well aware that some form of notice is a requirement of his trade. We find merit, then, in those decisions which have indicated that, under section 2-607, merchants will be held to a higher standard than ordinary buyers. . . .

We note, moreover, that the trial judge's rationale for ruling against McDonnell on the notice issue appears to have been based on a single letter written by Douglas in response to Eastern's March 15, 1966 request for aid in reducing its "pre-inauguration activities." In his post-trial memorandum, the District Judge appeared to infer a waiver of Douglas' right to notification concerning any future breaches from its request that this aid be postponed. In our view, though, the March 15 letter from Eastern does not constitute adequate notice as a matter of law. Indeed, a close reading of the communication reveals that Eastern's primary concern was the lack of early notification of impending delivery delays rather than the validity of Douglas' contention that these delays were the product of the Vietnam War. Although Eastern expressed the view that some of the delays should have been avoided, it requested merely that Douglas help to mitigate the

---

[50] [49] Uniform Commercial Code § 2-607, Comment 4.

[51] [51] Section 2-103(1)(b). . . .

[52] [52] Although the following statement concerns the time in which notification must be given, we consider it equally applicable to the issue of the content of adequate notice under § 2-607:

> The time of notification is to be determined by applying commercial standards to a merchant buyer. "A reasonable time" for notification from a retail consumer is to be judged by different standards. . . .

Uniform Commercial Code § 2-607, Comment 4.

delays' impact upon Eastern's operations. A jury, therefore, might reasonably infer from this correspondence that Eastern was not claiming a breach of the particular contract involved.[53]

More importantly, the District Court's reliance on these two particular letters evidences a failure to recognize that the buyer's good faith is the governing criterion under section 2-607. As we have seen, the Code's draftsmen disposed of rigid technical requirements which would frustrate the notice requirement's design of defeating commercial bad faith.[54] Therefore, the fact that dissatisfaction may once have been communicated to the seller should not preclude an inquiry into the buyer's good faith as evidenced by his entire course of conduct. . . . Even though adequate notice may have been given at one point in the transaction, subsequent actions by the buyer may have dissipated its effect. The buyer's conduct, then, taken as a whole, must constitute timely notification that the transaction is claimed to involve a breach.[55]

It is particularly important in continuing contractual relationships—such as the one which bound Eastern and McDonnell Douglas together for almost four years—that all of a buyer's dealings with a seller be evaluated under the good faith standard. An overly mechanical application of the notice requirement to complex or ongoing agreements would frequently frustrate the section 2-607 design of defeating commercial bad faith.

Reviewing Eastern's entire course of conduct during the years 1965-1969, and recognizing that Eastern must be held to a higher standard of good faith than an ordinary consumer, we conclude that a jury could reasonably find, as one of its options, that adequate notice was not given. In analyzing the record before us . . . we give McDonnell the benefit of every reasonable inference.

We note first that even Eastern's most strongly worded communications can reasonably be construed as an effort to prod McDonnell Douglas into minimizing the Vietnam War's impact upon production rather than as a claim for breach. As we have seen, Eastern's March 15, 1966 letter to Douglas—perhaps its single most forceful expression of dissatisfaction—can be viewed as a request for aid in minimizing the impact of the delays rather than an assertion that Douglas had violated the contract.

Eastern, moreover, did not dispute McDonnell Douglas' contention that the delays were caused by the Vietnam War until the airline presented its formal claim for damages in 1969. Indeed, throughout the life of all the contracts, East-

---

[53] [54] The exchange of letters relied on by the trial judge was concerned exclusively with delays arising under Contract 65-4-L which, as we have seen, cannot be the subject of an action by Eastern.

[54] [55] Indeed, the Code focuses so heavily on the buyer's conduct that notice is deemed given merely if the notifying party has taken reasonable steps to give the requisite notice to his counterpart. Uniform Commercial Code § 1-201(26) [Cal. Comm. Code § 1201(26)]. Thus, if a reasonable effort has been made by the buyer, it is not necessary that the seller actually learn of the breach for a buyer's rights to be preserved under § 2-607. . . .

[55] [56] We emphasize that even though a buyer's notification under this test may be adequate in terms of content, it may nonetheless be untimely. See Uniform Commercial Code § 2-607 Comment 4. The jury could have found, for example, that Eastern had given timely notice with regard to only some of the delivery delays.

ern was advising its shareholders,[56] the public,[57] and, in sworn testimony, the Federal Government,[58] that war-related defense priorities were causing the delivery delays. Inasmuch as the "excusable delay" clause found in all the contracts provides that the "[s]eller shall not be . . . deemed to be in default" on account of delays caused by "governmental priorities," Eastern may well have led McDonnell to believe that it was not in breach of the agreements.

We disagree with Eastern's contention that it "had no choice but to accept what Douglas was saying as the truth." Eastern was in constant communication with its own engineer who was in residence at the Douglas plant throughout this period.[59] Furthermore, Eastern and, indeed, the entire aviation industry were aware that Douglas' catastrophic financial crisis was, to some degree, precipitated by internal management difficulties. As early as the summer of 1966, therefore, Eastern had ample opportunity to assert then, as it does now, that the delivery delays were caused by internal problems rather than the Vietnam War. It failed to do so.

Eastern's commercial good faith is subject to further challenge because it continued to negotiate new contracts and amend old ones throughout the period in which the delays occurred. Two of the agreements, in fact, were executed in October of 1967 after 44 of the planes were already late. At no time during the negotiation and execution of any of these contracts did Eastern seek a settlement of its claims or even dispute McDonnell's Vietnam excuse. This may very well have led McDonnell to believe that, even though Eastern was unhappy about the delays, it did not consider them to be a breach of the contract.[60]

In addition to supporting the inference that adequate notice was not given, the record reveals a conflict in the evidence which . . . is sufficiently substantial to preclude a directed verdict for Eastern. As we have seen, both Mr. McDonnell and Mr. McGowan testified that Eastern's management had assured them that no damages would be sought because of the delivery delays. Eastern's witnesses disputed this contention. If such assurances were in fact given, Eastern's conduct

---

[56] [57] Eastern's 1966 Annual Report, for example, stated that the aircraft deliveries were being delayed because of "the war demands on the aerospace industry and its suppliers."

[57] [58] On March 2, 1966, an Eastern press release stated that its "ability to increase available seat miles . . . is being restricted by the slow rate of the new aircraft deliveries by both Boeing and Douglas caused by the military requirements in Viet Nam."

[58] [59] Before the Civil Aeronautics Board, on December 8, 1967, Eastern stated that "Eastern, like other purchasers, has experienced substantial delays in delivery of DC-9-31 aircraft, largely because of military requirements for the Vietnam conflict."

[59] [60] At oral argument, in fact, Eastern's counsel stated that the airline's representative at the Douglas plant "had a better estimate of when the planes were coming out than Douglas did."

[60] [62] We recognize, of course, that once an airline begins to build a fleet with a particular make of airplane it cannot easily switch to a competing manufacturer. Eastern, therefore, is correct in pointing out that as of 1965, it was effectively "married" to Douglas. The conjugal nature of its relationship with Douglas, however, did not relieve Eastern of its obligation of commercial good faith. As we have seen, the notice requirement reconciles the seller's right to early warning of claims for breach with the need to accommodate the buyer who, for reasons of necessity, has to accept a tender which is not in full compliance with the contract. In a continuing contractual relationship, therefore, the buyer must decide whether the benefits of claiming a breach of contract outweigh the need for a close rapport with the seller.

may well have violated the requirements of commercial good faith. This conflict alone, then, is sufficient to render the question of notice an issue for the jury.

The evidence reflected in the record, however, is also insufficient to support a directed verdict in favor of McDonnell Douglas on the issue of notice. There was no evidence at trial concerning the "reasonable standards of fair dealing" in the commercial aviation industry. We, therefore, cannot determine whether Eastern's conduct failed to satisfy contemporary standards of commercial good faith. Additionally, the conflict in evidence described above, the testimony that Eastern in several instances refused to waive its legal rights,[61] and the dissatisfaction with the delays evident in several of the airline's communications with McDonnell, are sufficient to create a jury question. In conclusion, therefore, the issue of notice under UCC § 2-607 should have been submitted to the jury with instructions that it determine whether Eastern's conduct throughout the life of the contracts constituted adequate and timely notice to McDonnell that it was considered to be in breach of the contracts. [To be continued....]

NOTES AND QUESTIONS

1. *The Fifth Circuit elaborates on Eastern Air Lines:* The United States Court of Appeals for the Fifth Circuit explained its *Eastern Air Lines* decision in *T.J. Stevenson & Co. v. 81,193 Bags of Flour.*[62] In a dispute concerning whether or not the nation of Bolivia had given an adequate § 2-607(3)(a) notice of its objection to insect infested wheat flour it was buying, the Fifth Circuit re-affirmed and explained its decision in Eastern. Applying Illinois law, the court observed:

   (i) Notice Under § 2-607(3)(a)

   In Illinois it is well-established that § 2-607(3)(a)'s requirement of notification of breach of warranty need not be in any particular words and is ordinarily a question of fact, looking to all the circumstances of the case. Notice need not be written. It may be given in a single communication or derived from several. It is also well-established that "notice under section 2-607 need not be a specific claim for damages or an assertion of legal rights." *Eastern Air Lines, Inc. v. McDonnell Douglas Corp.*, 532 F.2d 957, 976 (5th Cir. 1976) (Calif.). . . .

---

[61] [63] McDonnell also contends that the District Judge erred in ruling against and not submitting to the jury its contentions that Eastern had waived its claims and was otherwise estopped from pursuing this cause of action. Because they parallel McDonnell's contentions under section 2-607 and are based on the same evidence, the defenses of waiver and estoppel will be effectively decided by the jury's determination of the notice issue. . . . Our holding concerning section 2-607, therefore, obviates the need for any separate consideration of these contentions. However, because we find no reasonable support in the record for McDonnell's contention that Eastern executed an accord and satisfaction with it, we do conclude that the District Judge correctly ruled against McDonnell on this particular issue.

[62] 629 F.2d 338 (5th Cir. 1980).

Beyond these principles, however, Courts have disagreed in their interpretations of § 2-607(3)(a)'s notification requirement. A few decisions, largely from the Eighth Circuit and from Oregon, have held that the seller need only be informed that "the transaction is still troublesome and must be watched." And if the troublesome nature of the transaction is moreover apparent or already known to the seller, no notice at all is required. In *Eastern Air Lines, Inc. v. McDonnell Douglas Corp., supra,* however, this Court decided that for merchant buyers § 2-607(3)(a) requires something more than the minimal notification endorsed by those Courts. 532 F.2d at 970-80. We held that the dual policies of "encouraging compromise" and "promoting good faith in commercial relations," *id.* at 972, underlay the notice requirement of § 2-607(3)(a). Notice consequently must fulfill those policies; merely indicating that the transaction is troublesome is not enough. One way in which the policies are fulfilled is by notice informing the seller that the buyer regards the contract as breached by the seller, though specific legal rights need not be invoked. *Id.* at 973, 976.

The *Eastern Air Lines* interpretation of § 2-607(3)(a) has been adopted by the vast majority of Courts which subsequently have considered the issue. It is also significant that the Eighth Circuit, which decided three cases which we declined to follow in *Eastern Air Lines,* recently decided a case under Illinois law and adopted the *Eastern Air Lines* view of notification. *Southern Illinois Stone Co. v. Universal Engineering Corp.,* 592 F.2d 446, 452 (8th Cir. 1979). Because we regard the Eighth Circuit as very knowledgeable concerning Illinois law and considering the wide acceptance of *Eastern Air Lines'* view of notification, we hold that Illinois law requires application of the *Eastern Air Lines* principles to this case.

Our *Eastern Air Lines* decision grew out of McDonnell Douglas's late delivery over a period from 1965-1969 of aircraft ordered by Eastern. The contract required a high degree of cooperation and communication between the parties. Beginning even before the expected time of the first aircraft's delivery, Eastern continuously expressed dissatisfaction with the delivery schedule. Finally, Eastern sued for damages. The District Judge found that that evidence of Eastern's communications with McDonnell Douglas was sufficient to permit a directed verdict that § 2-607(3)(a) notice had been given. A jury then considered other issues and returned a verdict in Eastern's favor. We reversed, ruling that examination of the "entire course of conduct during the years 1965-1969" revealed enough doubt concerning notification to preclude a directed verdict for either party and to require evaluation by the jury as factfinder. 532 F.2d at 978. We emphasized that Eastern's expressions of dissatisfaction were less than unequivocal in view of the parties' cooperative arrangement and Eastern's failure to cancel future aircraft deliveries. It was not clear to a reasonable certainty that Eastern's alleged notice was sufficient to encourage compromise by McDonnell Douglas. Furthermore, there was evidence which created a jury question concerning the second policy of notification, the encouragement of commercial good faith. For example, Eastern at times praised McDonnell Douglas's performance and made public statements that might "well have led McDonnell to believe that it was not in breach of the agreement." *Id.* at 978. During the 1965-1969 period encompassing the alleged breaches of contract, Eastern negotiated several new contracts with McDonnell Douglas without attempting to raise or settle its claims under the original contract. Added to this were the assurances by Eastern during 1968 that it would not seek delay damages from McDonnell Douglas. All of this, we held, created a question of the adequacy of Eastern's notification which was a fact question calling for resolution by the fact-finder.

Eastern Air Lines therefore teaches two concepts. First, the fact-finder's determination of the mixed law-fact issue of notice, if based on a correct understanding of the law, is to be given great weight. Second, § 2-607(3)(a) notice must be evaluated from the perspective of the policies which it seeks to encourage: compromise by the parties; and conduct within the bounds of commercial good faith.[63]

Applying these concepts to the instant case we first observe that while the District Judge did not make elaborate findings concerning notice, he did treat it as a fact question and recognized that *Eastern Air Lines* requires more than minimal notice:

> A purpose of section 2-607 notice requirement is to inform the seller that his tender is non-conforming, *but also to open the way for settlement* through negotiations between the parties.

449 F.Supp. at 129 (emphasis supplied). Because of this appreciation for the appropriate legal standard, we give great weight to the District Judge's conclusion that "the facts are sufficient to find that Bolivia gave adequate notice under [§] 2-607(3)(a) to ADM. *Id.*

> Second, the record reveals a number of specific communications, as well as additional inferable ones, between Bolivia and ADM, which must be evaluated for adequacy under the § 2-607(3)(a) policies.[64]

The court then proceeded to consider a number of communications between Bolivia and ADM Milling Co., the seller. The wheat flour itself had been shipped

---

[63] [49] While endorsing the *Eastern Air Lines* approach, Standard Alliance Indust. Inc. v. Black Clawson Co., 587 F.2d 813, 824 (6th Cir. 1978) (Ohio) seemingly interprets the second of § 2-607(3)(a)'s underlying policies:

> Notice of breach serves two distinct purposes. First, express notice opens the way for settlement through negotiation between the parties. . . . Second, proper notice minimizes the possibility of prejudice to the seller by giving him "ample opportunity to cure the defect, inspect the goods, investigate the claim or do whatever may be necessary to properly defend himself or minimize his damages while the facts are fresh in the minds of the parties."

587 F.2d at 826 (quoting Note, Notice of Breach and the Uniform Commercial Code, 25 U.Fla.L.Rev. 520, 522 (1973)). But, as J. White & R. Summers, *supra*, § 11-9, at 344, points out, this articulation of the second policy is just the equivalent of the commercial good faith policy, in that "if the court senses that a merchant buyer is lying in the Johnson grass with the thought of increasing his damages, it will not hesitate a moment to cut him off."

[64] *Id.* at 359-362.

from Mobile, Alabama to Arica, Chile. Bolivia initially refused to allow the flour to be unloaded in Chile, but eventually allowed the unloading of the flour; it was eventually sold in Chile at reduced prices. The court concluded its discussion of the notice issue:

> We find four aspects of the record which indicate that Bolivia gave proper notice *after* accepting the flour in Arica: (i) the fact that, as stated above, communications concerning the flour problems were ongoing; (ii) prior communications, including the September 25 telex, indicated Bolivia's staunch position with respect to live infestation; (iii) Bolivia's action in refusing to allow the flour to be discharged in Arica, an action consistent with a position that the contract had been breached; and (iv) Bolivia's October 24, 1974, telex stopping further letter of credit payments and asserting that the flour was contaminated when it left ADM's hands. From these facts and inferences, the District Judge was entitled to conclude that *Eastern Air Lines'* first policy of encouraging compromise was fulfilled, since ADM had full knowledge that the flour was infested and that Bolivia regarded live infestation as a breach of contract.

> Similarly, the second policy of encouraging commercial good faith is fulfilled under the facts and permissible inferences of this case. Bolivia acted in good faith. There was nothing about its conduct that was unreasonable with respect to ADM, although the same may perhaps not be said with respect to Stevenson and the detention of the ships in Arica. For example, Bolivia complained to ADM in Mobile and again after the flour reached South America and was found "reinfested." Unlike the buyer in *Eastern Air Lines*, Bolivia did not try to continue its relationship with ADM; to the contrary, it rejected the *Nedon* flour and stopped payments under the letter of credit. Bolivia never gave ADM any assurances that ADM would not be liable. In contrast, ADM acted less reasonably. For example, the speed with which ADM declared that it had delivered uninfested flour suggests a lack of actual investigation into the condition of its deliveries. That ADM made its declaration recklessly and possibly with knowledge different from that it represented is moreover suggested by its immediate fumigation of the warehouse flour (although ADM now claims that it took that step solely to promote good customer relations).

> We therefore have a situation converse to that in *Eastern Air Lines*. In the instant case, there is a factfinding, not a directed verdict, of adequate notice based on all the evidence. The notice encouraged compromise, notwithstanding ADM's adamant refusal to even consider doing so. And the buyer acted in commercial good faith in contrast to the seller's questionable conduct—as compared to the reverse situation in *Eastern Air Lines*. We cannot say that the District Judge was wrong in finding that Bolivia gave adequate notice of breach to ADM under § 2-607(3)(a). Bolivia's claim for damages for the *Arizona* and *Southwall* flour is therefore not barred under the UCC's notice requirement.[65]

---

[65] *Id.* at 364.

The court went on to find that ADM was not entitled to raise Bolivia's failure to comply with a notice procedure outlined in the ADM contract, since ADM had effectively waived that condition in the course of dealing with Bolivia after the infestation was discovered.

2. *Section 2-607(3)(a) and "good faith":* The Fifth Circuit stated in its *Eastern Air Lines* opinion that:

> The evidence reflected in the record . . . is also insufficient to support a directed verdict in favor of McDonnell Douglas on the issue of notice. There was no evidence at trial concerning the "reasonable standards of fair dealing" in the commercial aviation industry. We, therefore, cannot determine whether Eastern's conduct failed to satisfy contemporary standards of commercial good faith. Additionally, the conflict in evidence described above, the testimony that Eastern in several instances refused to waive its legal rights, and the dissatisfaction with delays evident in several of the airline's communications with McDonnell are sufficient to create a jury question.

Section 2-607(3)(a) itself says nothing about good faith. Section 1-203, however, tells us that "[e]very contract or duty within this Act imposes an obligation of good faith in its performance or enforcement." Section 2-103(1)(b) defines "good faith" in Article 2 "in the case of a merchant" as "honesty in fact and the observance of reasonable commercial standards of fair dealing in the trade."

Burton[66] says:

> Good faith limits the exercise of discretion in performance conferred on one party by the contract. When a discretion-exercising party may determine aspects of the contract such as quantity, price, or time, it controls the other's anticipated benefits. Such a party may deprive the other of these anticipated benefits for a legitimate (or good faith) reason. The same act will be a breach of the contract if undertaken for an illegitimate (or bad faith) reason. Therefore, the traditional focus on the benefits due the promisee is inadequate.
>
> Bad faith performance occurs precisely when discretion is used to recapture opportunities foregone upon contracting—when the discretion-exercising party refuses to pay the expected cost of performance. Good faith performance, in turn, occurs when a party's discretion is exercised for any purpose within the reasonable contemplation of the parties at the time of formation—to capture opportunities that were preserved upon entering the contract, interpreted objectively. The good faith performance doctrine therefore directs attention to the opportunities foregone by a discretion-exercising party at formation, and to that party's reasons for exercising discretion during performance.

Does Burton's suggestion aid in resolving the *Eastern Air Lines* case? Does the Fifth Circuit's opinion help Eastern gain the benefit of its bargain? Does it protect McDonnell Douglas from liability for risks it did not assume?

---

[66] *Breach of Contract and the Common Law Duty to Perform in Good Faith*, 94 Harv. L. Rev. 369, 372-73 (1980).

3. *Proof of good or bad faith:* As the Fifth Circuit notes, the question of good faith never was submitted to the jury in the *Eastern Air Lines* case. For teaching purposes, we can sketch the situation based on reports in business publications as well as opinions in the case, but, of course, a jury might find some of our "facts" not to have been proved. Given this qualification, let's first look at Eastern Air Lines. It was not a healthy corporation. Despite government regulation of competition, it lost money in seven of the ten years from 1960 to 1970. It competed with Delta on many of its routes, and Delta was well managed and, unlike Eastern, many of its employees were not unionized. As the court notes, "Ever since the advent of the commercial jet age in 1959, Eastern had lagged behind its competitors in the purchase of jet-powered planes." It was the "last major trunk carrier to purchase a large number of jet aircraft." On many of its routes it flew the Lockheed Electra, a prop-jet that was both slower than a pure jet and unpopular with passengers because of a number of serious crashes when the plane was introduced. In the early 1960s, Eastern had alienated business passengers and had a reputation for trying to save money by providing poor service. Employee morale was very low. There was an organization of those who had to fly Eastern regularly which had a newsletter called "WHEALs"—the letters stood for "We Hate Eastern Air Lines."

A new management tried to remedy the situation. It ordered 60 Boeing 727s, and it had received about half of them by 1965. It was heavily in debt for these purchases, but the 727 was not well-suited for many of Eastern's routes. Thus, it entered eight contracts for Douglas DC-8 and DC-9 jets between July of 1965 and October of 1967. A major factor in selecting Douglas rather than Boeing planes was Douglas' willingness to lend Eastern the money to buy the DC-8s and DC-9s at favorable rates. When Douglas fell behind on deliveries in mid 1966, it disappointed all of the airlines that had bought planes from it. However, airlines such as TWA, United, Delta and Continental did not have to cancel flights on existing schedules. Eastern had to cancel about 5% of its June service because it had no pilots to fly additional piston aircraft since it had been concentrating on jet pilot training.

Eastern had a profit of $24.1 million in 1967, but it reported a loss of $11.9 million in 1968, and it had a sharp drop in earnings in the first half of 1969. In May of 1969, Eastern's Board of Directors instructed management to bring suit against McDonnell Douglas for the losses caused by the delays in performing the contracts to deliver the DC-8 and DC-9 aircraft. During the course of the litigation in the 1970s, Eastern's fortunes continued up and down. It had unsuccessful merger discussions with Pan American; it ordered the Lockheed L-1011, but it experienced great delays when Rolls Royce defaulted on the contract to produce the engines for that plane; and one of its L-1011s crashed in the Everglades under circumstances that generated negative publicity for both the plane and Eastern's pilots.

The Douglas Aircraft Corporation was the most successful producer of passenger aircraft in the world from the 1930s to the 1950s. However, it lost its position when it decided to produce the DC-7, the last piston engine transport sold in great numbers, rather than manufacture a jet aircraft. The Boeing Corporation developed a plane that could refuel jet bombers in flight so they could continue on patrol for longer periods, and when the United States Air Force bought the tanker, it paid to create the necessary manufacturing facilities. The tanker was converted by Boeing into the 707, the first successful passenger jet aircraft. Douglas found itself two to three years behind Boeing before it could offer the DC-8, and it lost its position as the major producer of commercial aircraft. Douglas saw a market for a smaller plane than either the 707 or the DC-8, and it developed the twin-engined DC-9. Technically, it was a fine aircraft. Douglas worked hard to sell it to the airlines, battling Boeing's 737. In order to make sales, Douglas was willing to tailor the DC-9 to the wishes of its customers, and so production could not be completely standardized.

The WALL STREET JOURNAL,[67] BUSINESS WEEK,[68] and FORTUNE[69] all reported that Douglas was a victim of its own success because it sold more DC-9 aircraft than it could deliver on time. This point was the subject of great controversy in the *Eastern Air Lines* trial. The business journals all reported that Douglas had underestimated the market and accepted orders exceeding its production capacity. It had to hire many new workers whose lack of experience delayed production. Douglas managers were reported to be better aircraft engineers and salespeople than experts in production. Douglas, however, pointed to the expansion of the Vietnam war as the major cause of its problems. It, and Boeing as well, experienced delays caused by Pratt and Whitney's inability to supply all the ordered engines; Douglas also was delayed by its suppliers of landing gear and galleys. Commercial jet aviation was in competition with military production, and war production came first. There was a debate about what part of the problem was caused by Douglas mismanagement and what part by the unexpected demands of the escalation of the war.

Douglas was in great financial trouble, and its major lenders pushed a merger with a profitable corporation to salvage the situation. The McDonnell Aircraft Corporation was primarily a producer of military aircraft, and it had the cash needed to keep Douglas in production. The two firms merged on April 28, 1967. It was clear that McDonnell was the dominant partner in the new firm; its people took over operation of Douglas. They set revised production schedules, and deliveries of DC-8 and DC-9s caught up to the new schedules in late 1967.

Suppose during 1966 to 1969, Eastern had been advised by lawyers who interpreted § 2-607(3)(a) exactly as the Fifth Circuit read it in the *Eastern Air Lines* and *T.J. Stevenson* decisions. What would they have told Eastern's management to do? If Eastern had given a § 2-607(3)(a) notice that would have passed the court's test, what would have been the likely result? Would Eastern have received more planes sooner or fewer planes later? Suppose Eastern had given proper § 2-607(3)(a) notices. Douglas, in response, said that Eastern would have to give up its claims to damages or receive no special favors in the delivery of DC-9 aircraft. Would this be the exercise of economic duress or just the negotiations that the court says § 2-607(3)(a) is designed to bring about? Given Eastern's great need for the planes and Douglas' great difficulties which business

---

[67] Jan. 26, 1967, at 28.
[68] Oct. 22, 1966, at 175-80.
[69] December 1966, at 167-71.

publications attributed in part to bad management, what, if anything, was wrong with trying to get Douglas to perform and then suing for the damages caused by the delays?

4. *McDonnell Douglas' case for bad faith*: McDonnell Douglas' brief is not a cool and dispassionate document. A few excerpts will show its response to the idea that Eastern could "string along" Douglas:

> The acquisition of Douglas by McDonnell . . . occurred only after McDonnell had been assured by Douglas that no claims had been asserted against it as the result of late deliveries of aircraft. True, letters from Eastern and other airlines had expressed concern over the status of future deliveries . . . Eastern, like most of the other airlines, was vitally interested in witnessing the marriage of Douglas to a solvent bridegroom, so as to insure the delivery of the many planes still on order. Hence, Eastern refrained from asserting any claims which might have frightened the groom and cancelled the wedding. . . .

> As late as 1968, Floyd Hall, Eastern's Chairman, and Arthur Lewis, Eastern's President, were assuring McDonnell's top officials that Eastern had no intention of asserting a claim. . . . Mr. James S. McDonnell, defendant's founder and Chairman, testified that . . . he attended a luncheon . . . held during the recess of an Eastern board meeting, at which Arthur Lewis reaffirmed the agreement reached the preceding evening [that Eastern would not pursue its claim for late delivery] but conditioned it upon a satisfactory resolution of the problems resulting from late deliveries of aircraft simulators by Conductron Corporation [a subsidiary of McDonnell Douglas] to Eastern. In accordance with this understanding, Mr. McDonnell instructed David Lewis, defendant's president, to resolve the Conductron dispute. . . .

> Eastern had a change of heart as its financial picture deteriorated. When Charles Simon arrived on the scene [as Eastern's vice president in charge of financial affairs], he reversed the decisions previously made and persuaded Eastern to pursue the "fat-cat" McDonnell in order to brighten its financial outlook. . . .

> Besides being morally suspect and inherently prejudicial, Eastern's conduct is precisely the type prohibited by Section 2-607 of the UCC. . . . Eastern's string-along tactics deprived defendant of an opportunity to enter into meaningful settlement negotiations during the critical period when its entire production program was being disrupted and delayed; to take what steps it could to minimize its own potential damages, by preserving claims against subcontractors or suppliers or otherwise; or to prepare a proper defense to this action. Additionally, defendant's willingness to enter into further contractual arrangements with plaintiff would doubtless have been influenced had it been aware of Eastern's litigious designs. . . .

> Although . . . Eastern stoutly professes that it gave a series of notifications to McDonnell throughout the 1966-69 period, Eastern's true attitude and the philosophy underlying the "string-along" theory is strikingly

conceded . . . [in] its brief, where it acknowledges that by making claims against defendant while some of the planes were still undelivered, it would be "in the awkward position of having to sue the seller to whom [it] must continue to look for further deliveries." Eastern therefore admits, in effect, that it gambled under Section 2-607 . . . and did not alert defendant to its designs for fear of jeopardizing the future deliveries which first Douglas and then McDonnell were working so hard to expedite. It is now time for Eastern to pay the price for that gamble. . . .

5. *The settlement*: Macaulay[70] reports what happened after the Fifth Circuit's reversal and remand for a new trial:

> The delays . . . were an important factor in Eastern's decision to buy Lockheed L-1011 wide-body jets rather than the McDonnell Douglas DC-10. This was a serious loss to McDonnell Douglas. . . . The suit was filed in 1970, and the Fifth Circuit's opinion reversing the district court judgment was handed down almost six years later. Rather than retry the case, McDonnell Douglas and Eastern reached a complicated settlement. Eastern returned nine older model DC-9 jets and leased nine newer model DC-9s at a price lower than usual. . . .
>
> The settlement reached gave Eastern much needed newer planes that were larger, quieter, and burned less fuel; importantly, it did not require Eastern to try to borrow money in order to do this. McDonnell Douglas apparently sought the resumption of close business relations after the earlier divorce.

The Fifth Circuit stressed that promoting compromise was an important objective of § 2-607(3)(a). All in all, the entire process did promote a compromise. However, it took two years of pre-trial proceedings, about 5 months of trial, and almost two years while the case was on appeal. Given that over $30 million was involved, was this a sensible investment of the time of lawyers, paralegals, secretaries, officials of the two corporations and judges? Suppose Eastern had given a proper § 2-607(3)(a) notice when Douglas fell behind on the delivery schedule for the DC-8s and DC-9s. What kind of a settlement could have been reached then?

PAULSON v. OLSON IMPLEMENT COMPANY, INC.
Supreme Court of Wisconsin
107 Wis. 2d 510, 319 N.W.2d 855 (1982)

CALLOW, J. This is an appeal from judgments . . . dismissing this breach of warranty action against defendants Olson Implement Company, Inc., and Super Steel Products Corporation. . . .

The facts generating this litigation may be summarized as follows: The plaintiff corporation, Breezy Prairie Farms, Inc., had two stockholders, Ronald Paulson and Kenneth Wachholz, who are neighboring dairy and grain farmers. . . . In the fall of 1975 the plaintiffs contacted Lawrence Olson, of Olson Implement

---

[70] Macaulay, *Elegant Models, Empirical Pictures, and the Complexities of Contract*, 11 Law & Soc'y Rev. 507, 517-518 (1977).

Company, Inc., to inquire about a grain drying and handling facility for their corn harvest. In January of 1976 Olson, accompanied by David Miller of Super Steel Products Corporation, went to the Paulson home to discuss such a facility with both Paulson and Wachholz. Paulson testified they informed Olson and Miller that they "definitely wanted something to keep up with [their] daily harvesting schedule, and that [they] were harvesting approximately 5000 bushels a day and [they] wanted a dryer that would dry what [they] harvested in one day, or 5000 bushels." After they had looked over Super Steel's literature on drying bins, they testified Miller informed them that Super Steel was experimenting with a new stirating device, a "seven screw, seven auger stirator," and that it would more than double the capacity of the 30-foot drying bin advertised in the brochure (which had three auger stirators and dried 2,400 bushels of corn in twenty-four hours). Paulson testified that Olson and Miller then left the farm to "figure out a facility and come back and give us a price on it."

On March 11, 1976, Olson and Miller returned to the Paulson farm with a written proposal, on a Super Steel form, setting forth the specifications and cost of a seven auger stirator drying bin and a storage bin. No contract was signed or agreement reached on the purchase of the facility, and Olson and Miller left the farm to enable the plaintiffs to discuss the proposal and the financing arrangements. On March 17, 1976, the plaintiffs gave Olson a check for $2,000 as a down payment to hold the price on the bin. Plaintiffs were given a receipt which Paulson described at trial: "It's got our name across the heading, 'Breezy Prairie Farm, Columbus, Wisconsin. Merchandize [sic] Sold.' It's got 'Cash, $2,000.00. Sold by L. Olson. Down Payment on Bin Job. See Order Super Steel. Paid Check 340, $2,000.00.' And my signature is on the bottom."

Throughout the summer of 1976 Paulson and Wachholz had contact with Olson regarding whether they would purchase the bin if they obtained additional acreage and whether their crop was coming along well enough to warrant purchasing the bin. On or about September 20, 1976, Paulson and Wachholz went to Olson's office and signed an agreement to purchase the drying facility. According to the plaintiffs' testimony, at the time of the signing of the purchase agreement, Olson affirmed Miller's earlier representations that the drying equipment would dry 5,000 bushels of corn in a twenty-four-hour period.

After receiving their drying bin, Paulson and Wachholz dried three or four bins containing 5,000 bushels of corn and discovered that instead of twenty-four hours it took approximately forty to fifty hours to dry. Paulson phoned Olson to complain about this, and both Miller and Olson stopped by the farm on several occasions in 1976 to discuss any problems with the facility. On one of these occasions, the defendants recommended increasing the drying temperature to alleviate the problem. This was done, but it provided no improvement in the drying time. Olson then replaced a drying fan with a new one from his shop. Paulson testified this "made no difference."

Paulson testified at trial that in 1977 Miller put a new drying floor in the facility because "[h]e felt the floor was restricting the air flow." Plaintiffs continued to have problems drying corn in 1977 and continued to complain to Olson. Wachholz and Paulson stated nothing was done about their complaints and that it took them forty to fifty hours to dry 5,000 bushels of corn. Plaintiffs' harvest time was delayed, and they were forced to leave 325 acres of corn standing in the field until the spring of 1978.

The failure of the facility to dry 5,000 bushels in twenty-four hours continued into 1978, requiring Paulson and Wachholz to secure storage space for the corn they could not put in the dryer. This involved considerable expense in hauling and securing off-farm storage. On October 5, 1978, Paulson and Wachholz commenced suit against Olson Implement Company, Inc., Super Steel Products Corporation, and Specialized Products, Inc., alleging breach of warranty as the grain drying unit never dried 5,000 bushels of corn in twenty-four hours.

The jury returned a special verdict on August 1, 1980, finding that both Olson Implement Company, Inc., and Super Steel Products Corporation warranted that the drying equipment sold to the plaintiffs had a drying capacity of 4,800 to 5,000 bushels of corn in a twenty-four hour period; that the plaintiffs relied upon this warranty in purchasing the equipment; and that they were damaged as a result of their reliance on the warranty. The trial court, in a decision and order following the verdict, responding to motions by the defendants, dismissed the action against defendants for the following reasons. . . .

[The action was dismissed against Olson Implement because the plaintiffs' pleading did not allege having given notice within § 402.607, Stats., and because the trial court determined "as a matter of law a two year delay in giving notice would be unreasonable."]

Section 402.607(3)(a), Stats., requires that a buyer notify a seller of a breach of contract within a reasonable time or be barred from any remedy. In the instant case, the issue of notice was not presented to the jury. The trial court concluded as a matter of law that the requisite notice had not been provided, and this conclusion we may independently review. The trial court noted that, although the grain drying equipment was installed and used in 1976, the lawsuit was not commenced until October 5, 1978.

Examining the trial court's first proposition that plaintiffs' complaint was defective as it failed to assert notice, we note that, while the plaintiffs' complaint and amended complaint may not have been artfully drafted, under our liberal pleading rules we believe the issue of notice was apparent. At paragraph 11 of plaintiffs' amended complaint the following appears, in part: "That defendants told plaintiff's [sic] agents [Paulson and Wachholz] the reason the bin was not performing properly was caused by poor floor construction and a new floor was constructed by defendants in the summer of 1977." Both Olson Implement and Super Steel's answers to the complaint contain language denying that any drying problems were caused by poor floor construction. Although defendant Super Steel denied in full paragraph 11 of plaintiffs' amended complaint in its answer, it admitted in its answer to plaintiffs' original complaint that a new floor had been installed. Obviously, a new floor would not have been installed without the plaintiffs having informed the defendants of dissatisfaction with the drying equipment. Super Steel alleged as an affirmative defense that plaintiffs had failed to provide notice within a reasonable time of the alleged defect in the grain drying bin. . . .

The defendants and the trial court cite several pre-Code cases for the proposition that notice must apprise the seller that the buyer looks to seller for damages for such breach.

We note that with the adoption of the Uniform Commercial Code, Chapter 401, Stats., this is no longer intended to be a requirement of notice. *See* Annot., 93 A.L.R.3d 363, 367 n. 6 (1979) (The Uniform Sales Act predecessor to the UCC § 2-607(3)(a) required a "claim of damages" which explains why pre-Code cases use this language); Note, *Notice of Breach and The Uniform Commercial Code*, 25 U. Fla. L. Rev. 520, 536 (1973). The official comments to UCC § 206-7 reveal the following:

> The content of the notification need merely be sufficient to let the seller know that the transaction *is still troublesome and must be watched.* There is no reason to require that the notification which saves the buyer's rights under this section must include a clear statement of all the objections that will be relied on by the buyer. . . . *Nor is there reason for requiring the notification to be a claim for damages or of any threatened litigation or other resort to a remedy.*

Comment 4, UCC § 2-607 (emphasis added). While this comment is not law, we find it persuasive authority which we adopt in order to protect purchasers.

In the instant case, the plaintiffs, after they had attempted to dry three or four bins of corn, provided notice within approximately two months following installation of the facility that the grain drying equipment was not performing as expected. This was not unreasonable. *See* Note, *Notice of Breach and The Uniform Commercial Code, supra* at 538-40 ("courts balance the equities in determining what is a reasonable time for the giving of notice, and this time may vary considerably depending upon the facts and circumstances of the particular case"). *Id.* at 540.

The principal reason for requiring notice "is to enable the seller to make adjustments or replacements or to suggest opportunities for cure to the end of minimizing the buyer's loss and reducing the seller's own liability to the buyer." White & Summers, *Handbook of the Law Under the Uniform Commercial Code*, 421 (2d ed. Hornbook Series 1980). Other obvious policies inherent in the notice requirement are to permit the seller to assist the buyer in minimizing the buyer's losses and to expedite the return of the goods to the seller before they have substantially depreciated. *See* Annot., 93 A.L.R.3d 363, 368 (1979).

In the instant case the record contains numerous instances where Olson and Super Steel went to the Paulson and Wachholz farm and attempted to alleviate the grain drying problems about which plaintiffs repeatedly complained. The defendants inspected the equipment, recommended increasing the drying temperature, Olson replaced a drying fan, and Super Steel's representative, Miller, installed a new drying floor facility. It appears to us that the purpose of the notice provision, enabling the seller to cure the defect, has been effected. Only after the seller proved unable to remedy the situation did the plaintiffs commence the instant action. There is nothing in the record to indicate that the plaintiffs were not the good faith purchasers which the Uniform Commercial Code seeks to protect through liberal notice requirements. As we view the record, the defendants ac-

knowledged the warranty and their responsibilities under it by attempting to repair the defects of which Paulson and Wachholz complained. . . . Thus we hold
that Paulson and Wachholz provided the requisite notice to the defendants in this
action. . . .

By the Court.—The judgments of the trial court dismissing the defendants
from this action are reversed, and the jury verdict against the defendants is reinstated.

NOTES AND QUESTIONS

1. *Material from the briefs and record*: The briefs and record on appeal, for
the most part, deal with whether any warranty was given, the effectiveness of a
disclaimer found on the back of the printed form "sales agreement" used in the
transaction, and the liability of Super Steel Products Corporations for representations made by officials of Olson Implement Company. The § 2-607(3)(a) issue
was treated by both parties as a minor one as compared to these other problems.

The sellers' argument concerning the adequacy of notice was as follows:

> Neither complaints nor repairs alone are sufficient notice under
> § 402.607, Wis. Stats. It was held in *Marsh Wood Products Co. v. Bab-
> cock & Wilcox Co.*, 207 Wis. 209, 240 NW 392, that such notice is not
> only a condition precedent to liability of the vendor, but that *the notice
> must fairly apprise the seller that the buyer looks to him for damages.*
> *Ace Engineering Co. v. West Bend Malting Co.*, 244 Wis. 91, 11 NW2d
> 627 (1943). (Emphasis added.) In *Marsh Wood* the Court had stated,
> "Even the fact that the seller knew of the facts constituting the breach
> does not render it unnecessary for the buyer to give the required notice,
> since the notice required is not of the facts concerning the breach, but of
> the buyer's claim that they will constitute a breach." *Id.* at 224. All Ap-
> pellants did was complain to Respondents. There is no evidence in the
> record that they stated at any time that they held Respondents responsible
> for any damages incurred; and knowledge of the facts of an alleged
> breach is not enough.
>
> Moreover, the fact that repairs were done is not sufficient to establish
> notice of breach. . . . [A 1963 Wisconsin decision is next cited and dis-
> cussed.] . . . Respondents should not be penalized for making a good
> faith effort to satisfy its customer by working on the drying system.

Apparently, Justice Callow or one of his law clerks found the annotation in 93
A.L.R.3d cited in the opinion. This annotation does not cite or discuss *Eastern
Air Lines v. McDonnell Douglas Corp.* It briefly summarizes the *T.J. Stevenson*
case as presented in the District Court but does not mention the Fifth Circuit's
opinion in that case. It does not draw the distinction between merchant and consumer buyers found in the *Eastern Air Lines* opinion. All of the law review articles cited in Justice Callow's opinion are cited in this ALR annotation.

What does this information suggest about legal research? Suppose a lawyer for
the sellers had found, cited and discussed the *Eastern Air Lines* and *T.J. Stevenson* decisions of the Fifth Circuit before the Supreme Court of Wisconsin. Might

the case have come to a different conclusion? To what extent, if at all, is the *Paulson* case a choice of one view of the meaning of notice in § 2-607(3)(a) and a rejection of that followed by the Fifth Circuit? Insofar as you conclude that the briefs and research done by the Supreme Court of Wisconsin were inadequate, what do you conclude about the legal process? Would the *Eastern Air Lines* decision have been hard to find? How much time can busy lawyers and judges spend in tracking down all of the possibly relevant authorities? Who pays for legal craft?

2. *Distinctions*: Could the *Paulson* and the *Eastern Air Lines* decisions both exist in the same jurisdiction, assuming its courts were concerned about consistency? Suppose one were to argue that in the *Eastern* opinion the court distinguished consumer from merchant buyers, holding the latter to a much higher burden of giving notice in order to comply with § 2-607(3)(a). However, *Paulson* could be taken to suggest that more refined categories are needed. Consumers may constitute one group and large bureaucratically organized corporations well served by legal staff such as Eastern Air Lines may constitute another. However, Breezy Prairie Farms, Inc. is still a different kind of entity. Much as a consumer, such smaller businesses do not get day-to-day legal advice and are likely to deal less formally. Unlike an Eastern Air Lines, the Breezy Prairie Farms of the world cannot be expected to comply with unknown and hard to discover procedures. Do you see any problems with such an analysis? For example, what does the consumer/business distinction have to do with the Fifth Circuit's position on promoting settlements? Do you see any statutory basis for a distinction based on the type of buyer seeking to assert rights?

3. *The functions of § 2-607 notice—settlement*: In *Shooshanian v. Wagner*,[71] the Supreme Court of Alaska found that a retail consumer gave adequate notice under § 2-607 by filing a complaint to initiate a lawsuit. It noted:

> The majority of courts do not allow the filing of a complaint to serve as notice. We disagree, and are of the opinion that a complaint filed by a retail consumer within a reasonable period after goods are accepted satisfies the statutory notice requirement. The filing of a complaint is certainly not a bar to the negotiation and settlement of claims. To the contrary, the prospect of going to trial is often a powerful incentive to a defendant to investigate the claims against it and arrive at a reasonable agreement. A defendant may more easily and effectively prepare for either settlement or trial when it may compel discovery and so determine for itself the basis for a plaintiff's claims of liability. Allowing a consumer's complaint to serve as notice will not prevent a defendant manufacturer from raising the issue of timeliness if it has been prejudiced by an unreasonable delay. . . .

> In some cases, a consumer may not even know who produced an allegedly defective product until he files a complaint and begins discovery. A rule requiring notice prior to suit could effectively prevent an injured

---

[71] 672 P.2d 455 (Alaska 1983).

consumer from joining a manufacturer as a party defendant in a suit already begun.

Three years earlier, in *Armco Steel Corp. v. Isaacson Structural Steel Co.*,[72] the Supreme Court of Alaska, by a three to two vote, found that filing a complaint was not adequate notice in a business transaction. Should the Alaska court's argument in the *Shooshanian* case be limited to consumer plaintiffs?

Professor John C. Reitz[73] says "[t]he promotion-of-settlement justification for the notice rule depends on the questionable premise that the sooner the parties begin negotiations after breach, the greater the chances of settlement." He continues: "A closely related premise, namely that settlement negotiations started before litigation are more likely to result in settlement than those started after the initiation of litigation, has apparently led some courts to hold that pleadings cannot constitute notice and that notice with or after the pleadings comes too late to satisfy the rule." Reitz thinks both assertions are overgeneralizations. Moreover, suppose a Buyer who has accepted goods gives a proper § 2-607(3)(a) notice. Does this necessarily mean that either seller or buyer will negotiate in good faith for a settlement?

4.   *The functions of § 2-607 notice—standards and predictability*: Professor Reitz argues that a seller should have to show prejudice before a buyer loses rights for failure to give notice of a claim. He points out that § 2-725(1) requires that buyers bring claims within four years. Moreover, that section also provides: "[b]y the original agreement the parties may reduce the period of limitation to not less than one year but may not extend it." He asks why the seller needs more protection that a one-to-four-year statute of limitations.

However, wouldn't such a qualitative balancing rule as advocated by Reitz provoke great uncertainty among those faced with predicting the consequences of a breach of contract? Consider Llewellyn:[74]

> For the fact is that the work of our appellate courts all over the country is reckonable. It is reckonable first, and on a relative scale, far beyond what any sane man has any business expecting from a machinery devoted to settling disputes self-selected for their toughness. It is reckonable second, and on an absolute scale, quite sufficiently for skilled craftsmen to make usable and valuable judgments about likelihoods, and quite sufficiently to render the handling of an appeal a fitting subject for effective and satisfying craftsmanship.

To what extent, if at all, do the § 2-607(3)(a) cases challenge Llewellyn's assertion?

In *United States v. Southern Contracting of Charleston, Inc.*,[75] the court considered whether it should adopt a "lenient standard of notification" or a "strict

---

[72] 611 P.2d 507 (Alaska 1980).

[73] *Against Notice: A Proposal to Restrict the Notice of Claims Rule in UCC § 2-607(3)(a)*, 73 Cornell L. Rev. 534 (1988).

[74] The Common Law Tradition: Deciding Appeals 4 (Little, Brown & Co. 1960).

[75] 862 F. Supp. 107 (D. S.C. 1994).

standard" under § 2-607(3)(a). The court rejected the *Eastern Air Lines* approach. It explained:

> As a policy matter, the lenient standard discourages the use of litigation to settle commercial disputes. Requiring a buyer to use the magic word "breach" does not encourage settlement with a seller who is attempting to cure defects. In fact, it does little more than force buyers to retain lawyers in an effort to preserve their rights and force sellers to hire lawyers as a defensive maneuver.

5. *Sections 2-607(3) and 2-608(2) notices distinguished:* Most of us know very little about Gertrude Stein other than the fact that she authored that immortal line "A rose is a rose is a rose is a rose." Is it true that "A notice is a notice is a notice?" It seems not. Different words may, for some purposes and in some situations, mean the same thing. It is equally true, though sometimes confusing and a bit inconvenient, that the same word may mean different things. UCC § 2-607(3) requires that the buyer notify the seller of the breach "or be barred from any remedy." The very next section of the Code deals with revocation of acceptances, and provides, in § 2-608(2) that "[revocation] . . . is not effective until the buyer notifies the seller of it." We have just seen that what constitutes a notice can prove to be a subject of great (and critical) controversy. Can we carry over to § 2-608 notices the jurisprudence of the meaning of notice under § 2-607? It *is* the same statute, the same Article, the same Part, and the words are only 4-1/2 inches apart in the Wisconsin Statutes. But, asking the question as we have should suggest that the answer may be no.

The court in *Solar Kinetics Corp. v. Joseph T. Ryerson & Son, Inc.*[76] discussed the requirements for a notice of revocation. Solar Kinetics had been awarded damages for breach, but to sustain the award the plaintiff was required to prove that it had revoked its acceptance.

> Since revocation "is not effective until the buyer notifies the seller of it," Conn.Gen.Stat.Ann. § 42a-2-608(2), the third condition is met only if the buyer gives the seller effective notice of revocation within a reasonable time after the buyer knew or should have known of the seller's breach. Plaintiff insists that the jury has already decided this question and seeks to support this claim by reference to the following interrogatory:

>> Do you find the plaintiff has shown by a fair preponderance of the evidence that it gave Ryerson notice of any of its claims within a reasonable time after it knew or should have known of any breach of the contract by Ryerson?

> While the jury did answer this question in the affirmative, its finding does not, contrary to plaintiff's assertion, amount to a finding of notice of revocation. In order to have found that Ryerson was liable to Solar Kinetics for breach of warranty, the jury was only required to find that a notice of breach was given to the seller pursuant to § 42a-2-607(3). The content of the limited notice necessary to preserve a claim for damages need only "be sufficient to let the seller know that the transaction is trou-

---

[76] 488 F. Supp. 1237 (D. Conn. 1980).

blesome and must be watched." UCC § 2-607, comment 4. The official comments to the section on revocation, however, make it clear that the *content* of notice required under § 2-608 is generally more than "the mere notification of breach" required under § 2-607. . . . Consequently, when the jury concluded that adequate § 2-607 notice had been given, it had no occasion to consider and rule on the question of whether or not Solar Kinetics had given the more extensive § 2-608 notice necessary for revocation.

Nor does the language of the question itself suggest that the jury was being asked to make more extensive findings than were necessary to resolve the breach-of-warranty claim. All the question asks is whether notice of "any claim" was given. When the question is considered in light of the oral instructions given to the jury, it is clear that the jury was asked only to find whether Ryerson was given the limited notice required by § 42a-2-607. Thus, it is clear that the jury's affirmative answer to the question concerning adequate notice of breach of contract does not estop this court from reaching a different conclusion with respect to the notice required for revocation. . . .

While the various authorities who have considered the question have uniformly insisted that a notice of revocation must contain more than a mere notice of breach, they differ widely over how much more. Some have suggested that as little as conduct manifesting a buyer's desire to get his money back will suffice. . . . An intermediate position requires the buyer to notify the seller that he considers the seller to be in breach and that he desires to revoke his acceptance as to particular goods. The strictest test was recently set forth in the case of *Lynx, Inc. v. Ordnance Products*, 273 Md. 1, 327 A.2d 502 (1974), where the court held that notice of revocation "should inform the seller that the buyer has revoked, identify the particular goods as to which he has revoked and set forth the nature of the nonconformity. . . ." 273 Md. at 16, 327 A.2d at 513. . . . However, consideration of the cases reveals two significant trends. First, those cases which have found an effective notice of revocation based on minimal communications with the seller are generally cases where the dissatisfied buyer is the ultimate consumer. The notice required for revocation is generally more content-specific in a transaction between merchants. . . .

Second, courts have been reluctant to allow a buyer in litigation to justify his earlier attempted revocation by reference to defects in the goods which he only discovered after the supposed revocation. . . . Both of these trends are in accord with the policy expressed in the UCC official comment 5 to § 2-608, which provides:

> The content of the notice under subsection (2) is to be determined in this case as in others by considerations of good faith, prevention of surprise, and reasonable adjustment. More will generally be necessary than the mere notification of breach required under the preceding section. On the other hand the requirements of the section on

waiver of buyer's objections do not apply here. The fact that quick notification of trouble is desirable affords good ground for being slow to bind a buyer by his first statement. Following the general policy of this Article, the requirements of the content of notification are less stringent in the case of a non-merchant buyer.

The first line of cases is in accord with the code's stricter treatment of interactions between merchants. The second line of cases adopts a rule designed to prevent surprise and to allow the seller to have an opportunity to make a reasonable adjustment with the buyer. Where the seller does not know the grounds for revocation it may be substantially prejudiced in its efforts to respond reasonably and in good faith to a supposed revocation. Thus, both of the rules adopted by other courts serve to highlight aspects of the official comment. . . . [The court discussed the communications between Solar Kinetics and the seller, finding in each instance that though there was a notice of a defect, there was no notice of revocation.]

Effective notice is an absolute prerequisite to the revocation of acceptance. Since Solar Kinetics failed to set forth the particular nonconformity on which it was relying to revoke, its attempted revocation was ineffective.[77] [78]

Consider UCC § 2-608, Comment 5, and § 2-607, Comment 4, second paragraph. What functions should the notices required under these sections serve? That is, if a seller has delivered defective goods, why is it entitled to more notice than that given by the filing of a complaint in a court within the period of the statute of limitations (§ 2-725)? Why should more notice be given in a case where buyer wants to return the goods than where buyer wants to sue for breach of warranty after accepting the goods? What does the interplay between the two notice provisions as explained in the comments suggest about the decision in the *Eastern Air Lines* case?

6. *Written notices*: In *Prompt Electrical Supply Co., Inc. v. Allen-Bradley Co.*,[79] a former distributor sued Allen-Bradley. Allen-Bradley counterclaimed for payment for electrical equipment shipped to plaintiff. Plaintiff said that the goods were defective, Allen-Bradley would not accept their return, and they were destroyed in a fire in a warehouse. In granting summary judgment for Allen-

---

[77] [15] There is substantial evidence to support the jury's finding that the notice of breach required under § 42a- 2-607(3) was given within a reasonable time after the breach was discovered. As early as April, Ryerson was informed that the transaction was "troublesome and must be watched." While the comments to the code indicate that a reasonable time to give notice of revocation is generally longer than a reasonable time to give notice of breach, UCC § 2-608, comment 5, plaintiff was clearly not entitled to wait indefinitely. As early as April 27, 1976, Mr. Pohlman had information which should have put him on notice that the aluminum supplied failed to meet the 80% specular reflectivity requirement. Arguably, by waiting until August to attempt to revoke, plaintiff had already delayed beyond a reasonable time. Certainly, any delay beyond the August meeting constituted an excessive delay. While there was no evidence as to when Ryerson was finally informed of the complaint over specularity, it is worthy of note that the complaint filed by the plaintiff in October of 1976 still did not mention the word "specular."

[78] 488 F. Supp. at 1244-1250.

[79] 492 F. Supp. 344 (E.D. N.Y. 1980).

Bradley, the court noted that while plaintiff gave Allen-Bradley *oral notice* of the alleged defects, Allen-Bradley's terms and conditions of sale required that notice of an alleged defect must be given Allen-Bradley *in writing* promptly upon discovery. The court cited §§ 2-607(3)(a) and 1-102(3) of the UCC to justify the requirement of written notice. Should the court have cited §§ 2-607(3)(a) or 2-608(2)?

Do you see a problem with upholding a written notice requirement which appears in the terms and conditions of a seller's printed form? See §§ 1-102(3) and 1-201(3), referring to varying provisions of the Code by "agreement" and defining that term as "the bargain of the parties in fact."

7. *Section 2-605 demands for specification of defects*: Suppose a seller has supplied goods that are defective in several respects. Buyer and seller negotiate about the problem. Seller demands in writing "a full and final written statement of all defects on which the buyer proposes to rely." Buyer makes such a statement. Later buyer discovers still another serious defect. Suppose seller could not prove that it had changed its position materially in reliance on the statement of defects. Why should buyer lose the right to seek a remedy for the unlisted serious defect in the goods? Wouldn't a contrary rule deter breaches by sellers and increase the level of quality generally?

e. Section 2-508: The Seller's Right to Cure

MCKENZIE v. ALLA-OHIO COALS, INC.
United States District Court, District of Columbia
29 U.C.C. Rep. Serv. 852 (1979)

GASCH, J. [In the first part of the opinion the court concluded, based on a very questionable application of UCC 2-207, that the plaintiff had entered into a contract to sell coal to the defendant. The coal was intended for metallurgical purposes, which required coal with a low ash content; the specified ash content of 7.5%. The price was $34.00 per ton. The contract also contained a term which provided that if the ash content exceeded 7.5%, then ". . . a penalty of $.80 per 1% of ash in excess of 7.5% shall be assessed, fractions in proportion." The defendant inspected the 43 railcars of coal when it arrived in Hampton Roads, and rejected it, since its preliminary test results showed the ash content was at least 13.5% or more. The plaintiff at first insisted that defendant accept the coal, and when defendant refused, plaintiff sold the coal for $26.74 per ton. Plaintiff then sued defendant for the difference between the $26.74 which it received on resale and the $29.20 per ton which would have been the contract price ($34) less the penalty for an ash content higher than that specified.]

This case turns primarily on the issue of whether the penalty clause set out in the purchase order of July 5 was the exclusive remedy for defendant, or whether defendant was entitled to reject coal that did not conform to the specifications. . . .

II. Limitation of Remedies.

Plaintiff argues that the penalty clause was defendant's exclusive remedy in the event that the coal did not conform to the requirements of the contract, and that the parties did not intend to permit the "radical" remedy of rejection. In *Ray Farmers Union Elevator Co. v. Weyrauch*, 238 NW2d 47 [18 UCC Rep 683] (ND 1975), for example, the Supreme Court of North Dakota held that a liquidated damages clause in a contract was so inconsistent with any other damages remedy that it must have been intended to be exclusive. Plaintiff argues for the same result here, contending that rejection is totally inconsistent with a clause penalizing the seller by reducing the price in increments for defective coal.

UCC § 2-719 provides that parties may agree to limit or exclude remedies otherwise available, and it further provides that "resort to a remedy as provided is optional unless the remedy is expressly agreed to be exclusive, in which case it is the sole remedy." The comment to § 2-719 asserts that the section creates the presumption that clauses prescribing remedies are cumulative, and any intention to make them exclusive must be clearly expressed. See J. White and R. Summers, Uniform Commercial Code § 12-9, at 376-77 (1972). The purchase order of July 5 in this case nowhere stated that defendant would be limited solely to the price reduction mechanism set forth in the penalty clause. . . .

In addition, the UCC has codified the "perfect tender" rule of the common law, and provides that goods not sold in installments may be rejected if they "fail in any respect to conform to the contract." UCC § 2-601. There is substantial authority, however, that the perfect tender rule has been greatly diminished, and that, where a buyer has suffered no damage, he should not be allowed to reject goods because of an insubstantial nonconformity. See J. White and R. Summers, supra § 8-3 at 256-57, and cases cited therein. Assuming this approach to be the correct one, in this case the nonconformity was substantial. The July 5 purchase order specified that the ash content of the coal was not to exceed 7.5%. The coal delivered to defendant had ash content of at least 13.5% and up to 16%. Moreover, the UCC provides that if the nonconformity will impair the value of the goods to the buyer because of the buyer's particular circumstances, he is entitled to reject the goods even though the seller had no advance knowledge of the circumstances. UCC § 2-608.[80] The coal ordered by defendant here was intended for use as metallurgical coal. Metallurgical coal must be high quality coal and may have ash content no greater than 8%, or, for marginal grade metallurgical coal, no greater than 12%. See Defendant's Supplemental Memorandum at 9 n. 4. On the basis of the foregoing facts, the court concludes that the coal tendered by plaintiff did not conform substantially to the requirements of the contract. On that basis, defendant was entitled to reject the nonconforming coal.

A troublesome question, however, is the potential capacity for the seller to cure a nonconforming performance. Under UCC § 2-508, a seller may cure after the time for performance has passed if (1) he had reasonable grounds to believe that a nonconforming tender would be acceptable, (2) he seasonably notifies the

---

[80] [4] Although UCC § 2-608 governs revocations after acceptance of goods, and not rejection before acceptance, the analysis applicable to both §§ 2-608 and 2-601 is the same. See J. White and R. Summers, supra § 8-3, at 260.

buyer of his intention to cure, and (3) he cures within a further reasonable time. Addressing these considerations, the court notes that it is unlikely that a reasonable seller in plaintiff's position would be ignorant of such drastic variances in the quality of the coal. Similarly, no evidence of trade custom in the record indicates that coal with such high ash content would be suitable for use as metallurgical coal, the purpose for which it was purchased. Therefore, the court finds that plaintiff did not have reasonable grounds for believing that a nonconforming tender would be acceptable. Furthermore, although there is evidence that plaintiff offered to take a reduced price for the coal, such attempted cure by price allowance is not one of the methods of cure approved by the UCC See UCC § 2-508, Comment 4. Under all of these circumstances, then, plaintiff could make no effective cure short of tendering conforming coal. There was never any offer to do so, and defendant was justified in rejecting the high ash coal.

In sum, the contract between plaintiff and defendant did not limit the parties to accepting a price reduction for coal that did not meet the specifications for ash content that were imposed. The coal actually tendered deviated so substantially from the coal promised that defendant was entitled, after inspection, to reject the whole. UCC § 2-601. Furthermore, defendant is entitled to recover damages incurred in inspecting the coal. UCC § 2-715(1) provides in part that, "Incidental damages resulting from the seller's breach include expenses reasonably incurred in inspection . . . of goods rightfully rejected. . . ." Defendant has by affidavit established that its inspection costs amount to $495.70.

Accordingly, in view of the foregoing, the court will deny plaintiff's motion for summary judgment, grant defendant's motion for summary judgment on plaintiff's claim. . . .

NOTES AND QUESTIONS

1. *Price allowances and UCC § 2-508*: Read Comment 4 to § 2-508 which Judge Gasch cites for the proposition that "attempted cure by price allowance is not one of the methods of cure approved by the UCC." Even if the judge is correct, would Comment 4 indicate another approach to the case? Compare the last sentence in Comment 2.

2. *A revisionist view*: White and Summers[81] say that "[d]espite the modest violence it does to the language of 2-508(2), we believe that the buyer who complains of some insubstantial nonconformity which can be recompensed by a reduction in the price should be made to accept such a reduction as cure even if there is no usage in the trade to accept such reductions." In a footnote to this passage in the first edition that is not included in the second, they go on to say that "[o]ne must remember that there are many defects which cannot be cured by a money allowance. . . . [A] price reduction does not . . . cure a quality defect which makes the goods unusable or unsalable." (See page 269 of the first edition.)

---

[81] UNIFORM COMMERCIAL CODE 322-323 (2nd ed., West Publishing Co. 1980).

T.W. OIL, INC. v. CONSOLIDATED EDISON CO. OF NEW YORK, INC.
Court of Appeals of New York
57 N.Y.2d 574, 443 N.E.2d 932 (1982)

FUCHSBERG, J. In the first case to wend its way through our appellate courts on this question, we are asked, in the main, to decide whether a seller who, acting in good faith and without knowledge of any defect, tenders nonconforming goods to a buyer who properly rejects them, may avail itself of the cure provision of subdivision (2) of section 2-508 of the Uniform Commercial Code. We hold that, if seasonable notice be given, such a seller may offer to cure the defect within a reasonable period beyond the time when the contract was to be performed so long as it has acted in good faith and with a reasonable expectation that the original goods would be acceptable to the buyer.

The factual background against which we decide this appeal is based on either undisputed proof or express findings at Trial Term. In January, 1974, midst the fuel shortage produced by the oil embargo, the plaintiff (then known as Joc Oil USA, Inc.) purchased a cargo of fuel oil whose sulfur content was represented to it as no greater than 1%. While the oil was still at sea en route to the United States in the tanker *M T Khamsin*, plaintiff received a certificate from the foreign refinery at which it had been processed informing it that the sulfur content in fact was .52%. Thereafter, on January 24, the plaintiff entered into a written contract with the defendant (Con Ed) for the sale of this oil. The agreement was for delivery to take place between January 24 and January 30, payment being subject to a named independent testing agency's confirmation of quality and quantity. The contract, following a trade custom to round off specifications of sulfur content at, for instance, 1%, .5%, or .3%, described that of the *Khamsin* oil as .5%.[82] In the course of the negotiations, the plaintiff learned that Con Ed was then authorized to buy and burn oil with a sulfur content of up to 1% and would even mix oils containing more and less to maintain that figure.

When the vessel arrived, on January 25, its cargo was discharged into Con Ed storage tanks in Bayonne, New Jersey.[83] In due course, the independent testing people reported a sulfur content of .92%. On this basis, acting within a time frame whose reasonableness is not in question, on February 14 Con Ed rejected the shipment. Prompt negotiations to adjust the price failed; by February 20, plaintiff had offered a price reduction roughly responsive to the difference in sulfur reading, but Con Ed, though it could use the oil, rejected this proposition out of hand. It was insistent on paying no more than the latest prevailing price, which, in the volatile market that then existed, was some 25% below the level which prevailed when it agreed to buy the oil.

The very next day, February 21, plaintiff offered to cure the defect with a substitute shipment of conforming oil scheduled to arrive on the *S.S. Appollonian Victory* on February 28. Nevertheless, on February 22, the very day after the cure

---

[82] [1] Confirmatorily, Con Ed's brief describes .92% oil as "nominally" 1% oil.

[83] [2] The tanks already contained some other oil, but Con Ed appears to have had no concern over the admixture of the differing sulfur contents. In any event, the efficacy of the independent testing required by the contract was not impaired by the commingling.

was proffered, Con Ed, adamant in its intention to avail itself of the intervening drop in prices, summarily rejected this proposal too. The two cargos were subsequently sold to third parties at the best price obtainable, first that of the *Appollonian* and, sometime later, after extraction from the tanks had been accomplished, that of the *Khamsin*.

There ensued this action for breach of contract,[84] which, after a somewhat unconventional trial course, resulted in a nonjury decision for the plaintiff in the sum of $1,385,512.83, essentially the difference between the original contract price of $3,360,667.14 and the amount received by the plaintiff by way of resale of the *Khamsin* oil at what the court found as a matter of fact was a negotiated price which, under all the circumstances,[85] was reasonably procured in the open market. To arrive at this result, the Trial Judge, while ruling against other liability theories advanced by the plaintiff, which, in particular, included one charging the defendant with having failed to act in good faith in the negotiations for a price adjustment on the *Khamsin* oil (Uniform Commercial Code, § 1-203), decided as a matter of law that subdivision (2) of section 2-508 of the Uniform Commercial Code was available to the plaintiff even if it had no prior knowledge of the nonconformity. Finding that in fact plaintiff had no such belief at the time of the delivery, that what turned out to be a .92% sulfur content was "within the range of contemplation of reasonable acceptability" to Con. Ed., and that seasonable notice of an intention to cure was given, the court went on to hold that plaintiff's "reasonable and timely offer to cure" was improperly rejected (*sub nom. Joc Oil USA v. Consolidated Edison Co. of N.Y.*, 107 Misc.2d 376, 390, 434 N.Y.S.2d 623 [Shanley N. Egeth, J.]). . . .

II.

We turn then to the central issue on this appeal: Fairly interpreted, did subdivision (2) of section 2-508 of the Uniform Commercial Code require Con Ed to accept the substitute shipment plaintiff tendered? In approaching this question, we, of course, must remember that a seller's right to cure a defective tender, as allowed by both subdivisions of section 2-508, was intended to act as a meaningful limitation on the absolutism of the old perfect tender rule, under which, no leeway being allowed for any imperfections, there was, as one court put it, just "no room . . . for the doctrine of substantial performance" of commercial obligations (*Mitsubishi Goshi Kaisha v. Aron & Co.*, 16 F.2d 185, 186 [Learned Hand, J.]. . . .

In contrast, to meet the realities of the more impersonal business world of our day, the code, to avoid sharp dealing, expressly provides for the liberal construction of its remedial provisions (§ 1-102) so that "good faith" and the "observance of reasonable commercial standards of fair dealing" be the rule rather than the

---

[84] [4] The plaintiff originally also sought an affirmative injunction to compel Con Ed to accept the *Khamsin* shipment or, alternatively, the *Appollonian* substitute. However, when a preliminary injunction was denied on the ground that the plaintiff had an adequate remedy at law, it amended its complaint to pursue the latter remedy alone.

[85] [5] These circumstances included the fact that the preliminary injunction was not denied until April so that, by the time the *Khamsin* oil was sold in May, almost three months had gone by since its rejection.

exception in trade (see § 2-103, subd. [1], par. [b]), "good faith" being defined as "honesty in fact in the conduct or transaction concerned" (Uniform Commercial Code, § 1-201, subd. [19]). As to section 2-508 in particular, the code's Official Comment advises that its mission is to safeguard the seller "against surprise as a result of sudden technicality on the buyer's part" (Uniform Commercial Code, § 2-106, Comment 2; see, also, Peters, Remedies for Breach of Contracts Relating to the Sale of Goods under the Uniform Commercial Code: A Roadmap for Article Two, 73 Yale L.J. 199, 210; 51 N.Y.Jur., Sales, § 101, p. 41). . . .

[There are two parts to Section 2-508. The first, which had its counterpart before the enactment of the Code, provides for a cure when the time for performance has not yet expired. The second part, new with the Code, provides an opportunity for cure in some cases even though the time for performance has passed.]

Since we here confront circumstances in which the conforming tender came after the time of performance, we focus on subdivision (2). On its face, taking its conditions in the order in which they appear, for the statute to apply (1) a buyer must have rejected a nonconforming tender, (2) the seller must have had reasonable grounds to believe this tender would be acceptable (with or without money allowance), and (3) the seller must have "seasonably" notified the buyer of the intention to substitute a conforming tender within a reasonable time.

In the present case, none of these presented a problem. The first one was easily met for it is unquestioned that, at .92%, the sulfur content of the *Khamsin* oil did not conform to the .5% specified in the contract and that it was rejected by Con Ed. The second, the reasonableness of the seller's belief that the original tender would be acceptable, was supported not only by unimpeached proof that the contract's .5% and the refinery certificate's .52% were trade equivalents, but by testimony that, by the time the contract was made, the plaintiff knew Con Ed burned fuel with a content of up to 1%, so that, with appropriate price adjustment, the *Khamsin* oil would have suited its needs even if, at delivery, it was, to the plaintiff's surprise, to test out at .92%. Further, the matter seems to have been put beyond dispute by the defendant's readiness to take the oil at the reduced market price on February 20. Surely, on such a record, the trial court cannot be faulted for having found as a fact that the second condition too had been established.

As to the third, the conforming state of the *Appollonian* oil is undisputed, the offer to tender it took place on February 21, only a day after Con Ed finally had rejected the *Khamsin* delivery and the *Appollonian* substitute then already was en route to the United States, where it was expected in a week and did arrive on March 4, only four days later than expected. Especially since Con Ed pleaded no prejudice (unless the drop in prices could be so regarded), it is almost impossible, given the flexibility of the Uniform Commercial Code definitions of "seasonable" and "reasonable," to quarrel with the finding that the remaining requirements of the statute also had been met.

Thus lacking the support of the statute's literal language, the defendant nonetheless would have us limit its application to cases in which a seller *knowingly* makes a nonconforming tender which it has reason to believe the buyer will accept. For this proposition, it relies almost entirely on a critique in Nordstrom, Law of Sales (§ 105), which rationalizes that, since a seller who believes its tender is conforming would have no reason to think in terms of a reduction in the price of the goods, to allow such a seller to cure after the time for performance had passed would make the statutory reference to a money allowance redundant.[86] Nordstrom, interestingly enough, finds it useful to buttress this position by the somewhat dire prediction, though backed by no empirical or other confirmation, that, unless the right to cure is confined to those whose nonconforming tenders are knowing ones, the incentive of sellers to timely deliver will be undermined. To this it also adds the somewhat moralistic note that a seller who is mistaken as to the quality of its goods does not merit additional time (Nordstrom, *loc. cit.*). Curiously, recognizing that the few decisions extant on this subject have adopted a position opposed to the one for which it contends, Con Ed seeks to treat these as exceptions rather than exemplars of the rule. . . .

That the principle for which these cases stand goes far beyond their particular facts cannot be gainsaid. These holdings demonstrate that, in dealing with the application of subdivision (2) of section 2-508, courts have been concerned with the reasonableness of the seller's belief that the goods would be acceptable rather than with the seller's pretender knowledge or lack of knowledge of the defect. . . .

It also is no surprise then that the aforementioned decisional history is a reflection of the mainstream of scholarly commentary on the subject. . . . [Citations omitted.]

White and Summers, for instance, put it well, and bluntly. Stressing that the code intended cure to be "a remedy which should be carefully cultivated and developed by the courts" because it "offers the possibility of conforming the law to reasonable expectations and of thwarting the chiseler who seeks to escape from a bad bargain" (*op. cit.*, at pp. 322-324), the authors conclude, as do we, that a seller should have recourse to the relief afforded by subdivision (2) of section 2-508 of the Uniform Commercial Code as long as it can establish that it had reasonable grounds, tested objectively, for its belief that the goods would be accepted (*ibid.*, at p. 321). It goes without saying that the test of reasonableness, in this context, must encompass the concepts of "good faith" and "commercial standards of fair dealing" which permeate the code (Uniform Commercial Code, § 1-201, subd. [19]; §§ 1-203, 2-103, subd. [1], par. [b]).

As to the damages issue raised by the defendant, we affirm without reaching the merits. At no stage of the proceedings before the trial court did the defendant object to the plaintiff's proposed method for their calculation, and this though the plaintiff gave ample notice of that proposal by means of a preliminary statement and pretrial memorandum filed with the court. . . . And, even after the decision at

---

[86] [8] The premise for such an argument, which ignores the policy of the code to prevent buyers from using insubstantial remediable or price adjustable defects to free themselves from unprofitable bargains (Hawkland, Sales and Bulk Sales Under the Uniform Commercial Code, pp. 120-122), is that the words "with or without money allowance" apply only to sellers who believe their goods will be acceptable with such an allowance and not to sellers who believe their goods will be acceptable without such an allowance. But, since the words are part of a phrase which speaks of an otherwise unqualified belief that the goods will be acceptable, unless one strains for an opposite interpretation, we find insufficient reason to doubt that it intends to include both those who find a need to offer an allowance and those who do not.

nisi prius revealed that the Judge had acted on such an assumption, so far as the record shows, no motion was ever made to correct it. . . .

For all these reasons, the order of the Appellate Division should be affirmed, with costs.

NOTES AND QUESTIONS

1. *Arguments by plaintiff and defendant:* Not surprisingly, Con Edison and Joc Oil emphasized different aspects of the dispute in their arguments to the jury. Mr. Goldstein, lawyer for Con Edison, attempted to describe as unreasonable Joc Oil's conduct upon discovering that the oil had a higher sulphur content than the contract provided. After noting that oil prices had fallen $4.50 per barrel since the contract was formed, Goldstein urged:

What did Joc Oil offer to give us off on the oil that was defective? They offered to give us off at most 80 cents a barrel. . . .

Well, 80 cents a barrel as a reduction is nowhere near the prevailing market price for that oil, 1 percent oil, on February 14th or February 15th or February 20th or February 21st, any of those dates, because on those dates the oil was selling for $13 a barrel, so they wanted to take a price of $17.875 a barrel, which we had agreed to pay for .5 percent maximum sulfur oil and reduce that to not more than $17.075 a barrel, and ask us to pay that price for oil that was selling for $13 a barrel at the time they asked us to accept it. . . .

Joc Oil is the party that put us in the position of having to figure out what to do with the defective product. We didn't ask for .92 percent oil. We asked for .5 percent maximum sulfur oil. They delivered to us a defective product and then they asked us to do something that would make them get paid for it. They asked us to accept the oil at far more than we would have paid for that oil if we went out to buy it on the day that they asked us to buy it.

I don't want to belabor the point, but I think it goes without saying that their position was unreasonable. If they would have come down . . . to the then prevailing price we would have bought it, because we stipulated to that.

They wanted us to swallow a huge chunk of money because of their error. . . .

. . . when you talk about a substitute shipment, you have to consider what is doing with this substitute shipment. It is very nice to say, o.k., we learned that the oil is defective that we delivered to you; we've got another barge and here it is, that is a reasonable way, perhaps, of offering a substitute shipment, because there is no delay there. But Joc Oil didn't do that, it said, we got a ship coming in, this is on February 21st, we have a ship coming in, it is due to arrive February 28th, we will give you that shipment at the old contract price.

And we said we don't want that ship, we ordered a shipload of oil that was supposed to arrive between January 24 and January 30, and although it arrived it didn't meet specifications. Don't tell us you are going to give us a shipload of something that will meet specifications five weeks or six weeks later. We are not going to buy it at the old contract price because the market price is way down. . . .

The argument of Mr. Maloof, counsel for plaintiff, emphasized the cure.

. . . [W]e were in the position to make Con Ed one hundred percent whole according to the contract. They should not have the advantage of a drop in the market that occurred from extraordinary military pressures in the Middle East, why should Con Ed get the benefit of that drop in the market and Joc Oil suffer so badly. . . . Mr. Elias . . . offered 80 cents and Mr. Doyle responded with an arbitrary offer of market value. . . . The market value, according to the papers and the guides was $13 a barrel. This meant that Joc would have taken a bath of 188,000 barrels times more than $4 a barrel, which is over $700,000, and this is what Con Ed wanted them to do because they were innocently surprised when the oil arrived at .92, and Mr. Goldstein admitted, admitted that we didn't know that it was .92, so we are innocent parties. . . .

Now did we offer the conforming shipment on the APPOLLONIAN VICTORY seasonably? Well, on February 20th we had this meeting with Mr. Doyle, it broke up. On the next day we offered the conforming shipment. Seasonably means reasonably. I think that is pretty close. Nobody is going to talk about doing these things in a couple of hours. We were quite fortunate to find it, find that we owned it, and offered it on February 21st to be delivered on February 28th. I don't think there is a big question that and I do hope that you will agree.

2. *Cure in a falling market*: When Joc Oil made its tender, the market price was falling. Section 2-508(2) calls for "seasonable" notice of an intention to cure and a "reasonable time to substitute a conforming tender." The trial court found that there was no showing of prejudice to Con Edison by "the relatively short delay arising from the substitute delivery. . . ." What would Con Edison have to establish to show prejudice?

3. *Revocation of acceptance and cure*: Suppose a buyer accepts a defective performance. Then the buyer revokes acceptance under UCC § 2-608. May the seller then cure under § 2-508?

The Supreme Court of Texas considered this problem in *Gappelberg v. Landrum*,[87] There, the buyer purchased a large screen Advent television set from seller for about $3,700. Buyer had problems with the set and demanded his money back. Seller offered another Advent set as a replacement. Buyer refused this attempted cure and sued Seller.

The Texas court decided that a seller does not have a right to cure under § 2-508 when a buyer revokes acceptance under § 2-608. Seller argued unsuccessfully that under § 2-608(2)(c) a "buyer who so revokes has the same rights and duties with regard to the goods involved as if he had rejected them." One of the

---

[87] 666 S.W.2d 88 (1984).

duties of a buyer who rejects is to accept a cure that meets the requirements of § 2-508.

The Supreme Court of Texas disagreed. "We do not consider paragraph (c) in UCC § 2-608 as having any reference to UCC § 2-508. It is more logically related to UCC § 2-603 and 2-604, as UCC § 2-608(c) makes absolutely no mention of seller's rights." Buyer "had seen one Advent television perform, or fail to perform as the case may be, and there certainly is justification for his not wanting to go through experiences with another Advent." Once a buyer's faith in a product is shaken, the buyer does not have to keep the product after repairs or take another of the same model. The court pointed out that the seller ordinarily is in a better position to maximize the return on the resale of repaired goods.

Often buyers will not have rights to revoke acceptances of goods that prove defective. Sellers usually disclaim warranties and limit remedies successfully. Frequently, buyers must be satisfied with replacement or repair at the seller's option. The Supreme Court of Texas does not explain why Advent large screen televisions sets are sold without effective remedy limitations.

4.   *How much burden can a seller put on the buyer in attempting to cure?* In *Travelers Indemnity Co. v. Maho Machine Tool Corp.,*[88] a complex machine tool had been shipped to Singapore, but it had been damaged by rust. The machine had to be returned to Germany for reconditioning. The seller proposed that the buyer do the following: (1) file a claim with its insurance carrier; (2) return the damaged machine to Germany where it would be reconditioned and resold; (3) accept a replacement machine which would arrived within a month; and (4) use a smaller but similar machine that the seller would loan the buyer in the period between returning the machine and its replacement. The buyer had expected to finance the purchase of the machine by a loan from a Singapore bank which would have been secured by the machine itself. Without the machine, the bank would not loan the money. Buyer did not have available sufficient funds to pack and ship the defective machine from Singapore to Germany. The trial court found that the seller had complied with UCC §2-508(2). The Second Circuit reversed. It said: "The law of sales does not impose upon the buyer any obligation to assume the expenses of the seller in effecting a cure for the delivery of non-conforming goods."

f.   CISG and Imperfect Performance

We have offered, in the preceding chapters, notes which offer a glimpse of the manner in which the Convention on Contracts for the International Sale of Goods deals with the topics of the course. In most cases, the CISG either adopts a rule which tracks the UCC, or chooses a variation which reflects the common law approach, or perhaps an approach which is widespread in other parts of the world. When it comes to the issue of the treatment of breach, notice, cure, and remedy, we have concluded that it is appropriate only to call your attention, in the broadest terms possible to the CISG approach. To do more would require more time and space than we believe appropriate here. Not that the differences

---

[88] 952 F.2d 26 (2d Cir. 1991).

are not significant, but rather the opposite. Professor Reitz[89] suggests that, "The most important . . . [differences between CISG and the UCC] deal with the performance stage of sales contracts, particularly when a performance is late or is qualitatively or quantitatively deficient." The CISG creates, to some extent, a different structure than the Code; it rejects the perfect tender rule as a starting point for defining a buyer's rights, makes distinctions between late performance and the tender of non-conforming goods, provides for a remedy in which a buyer can insist on repair, adopts a concept which it calls "fundamental breach" as the critical point in establishing a right to "avoid" a contract, and generally "seeks to keep troubled contracts going forward despite failings to a greater extent than the rules of the Commercial Code."[90] If you have a transaction governed by the CISG, you should realize that the CISG provides a different structure of rights and remedies. Our brief warning should also stand as more evidence that the rules which we have been discussing represent one set of choices from among competing possibilities, and not the inevitable result of the application of "legal science" to the problem.

4. TWO CLASSIC, BUT TROUBLESOME, PROBLEMS

a. Installment Contracts and the Failure to Perform Part of the Deal

Installment contracts often present several problems to lawyers and courts. Suppose supplier is to perform steps A, B, C and D while buyer is to pay $100,000. UCC § 2-307 states the common law rule: "Unless otherwise agreed all goods called for by a contract for sale must be tendered in a single delivery and payment is due only on such tender. . . ." The same idea is contained in the rule that when one performance takes time while the other can be done all at once, then the performance which takes time must be performed first. In other words, unless they agree otherwise, sellers of goods and services must complete the job before the buyer must pay for it.

Suppose, however, that supplier and buyer's contract looks like this:

Supplier does:	Buyer pays:
Step A	$25,000
Step B	$15,000
Step C	$35,000
Step D	$25,000
Total:	$100,000

Then assume that supplier completes step A, but supplier has not yet begun the other steps. Must buyer pay supplier $25,000 then? UCC § 2-307 continues, pro-

---

[89] *The Uniform Commercial Code and the Convention on Contracts for the International Sale of Goods*, in NEGOTIATING AND STRUCTURING INTERNATIONAL COMMERCIAL TRANSACTIONS (American Bar Association 1991).
[90] *Id.*

viding: "but where circumstances give either party the right to make or demand delivery in lots the price if it can be apportioned may be demanded for each lot." If what we've called steps are orders for goods which are in no way interrelated, supplier may deliver item A without delivering the other three items. Buyer then should pay supplier $25,000. However, if A, B, C and D are interrelated steps necessary to produce the final product for which buyer has promised to pay $100,000, the result may differ. Buyer may have no use for step A without the other three steps. If this is true, then "circumstances [do not] give either party the right to make or demand delivery in lots."

Building contracts often provoke even more difficult problems. For example, suppose a builder has promised to do steps A, B, C and D. The owner has promised in turn to make the four payments indicated as each step is completed. Often the owner is not buying step A for $25,000. Step A may be worth much more or much less than $25,000. Rather, the parties have agreed on a payment schedule which serves several purposes. With such a payment schedule, the builder does not have to finance the entire job until completion. Rather than borrowing money to pay for needed materials, wages and subcontracts, the builder can settle its debts with the money the seller pays at designated times. Furthermore, the builder lessens its credit risk. It does not want to take the chance that it will build an entire structure and then discover that the owner cannot raise enough money to pay for it. In a pay-as-you-go contract, the builder only risks losing its investment of time and materials made between payments. Owners may benefit too from installment contracts. They can appraise the quality of performance at each step before they pay rather than waiting to the end when at least some defects will be harder to cure.

However, what happens when this nice system doesn't work to produce harmony? First, at the negotiation stage, builders often try to "front load" the contract. They seek to have owners pay far more than the builders have invested in the job at the early stages of performance and relatively little as performance is completed. This minimizes their risks as owners are paying in advance of the builders' performance. Moreover, builders can use owners' payments both to finance the particular job as well as pay bills due from past projects. Or builders can finance other projects until they have earned money under them. Owners, however, try to "back load" contracts. In this way, they limit the time during which they must borrow money and pay interest.

Second, what happens when one party fails to perform as called for by the contract? Suppose that builder completes step A and owner pays $25,000. Builder then completes step B, but owner fails to pay the $15,000 which is due. Must builder continue and finish steps C and D? Can it exercise *self-help remedies*? May builder suspend performance until owner pays the $15,000 which is due? May builder call off the entire contract and move its workers to another job? Suppose owner is eager to have builder complete the job and says that it will pay builder just as soon as it can. Should this matter?

Suppose builder sues for its *damages* caused by owner's breach of contract when the $15,000 was not paid when it came due. Should builder recover $15,000? If builder recovers $15,000 in addition to the $25,000 which builder paid when step A was completed, in some cases builder will be far better off than had the contract been performed. Can you imagine such a situation? Suppose that builder's costs to do steps A and B would have been $30,000. However, builder's costs to complete the entire job would have been $95,000. Or should builder recover the contract price less (a) the cost of completing the job and (b) the $25,000 which owner already has paid?

First, we'll look at installment contract problems in the setting of building contracts, and then we'll turn to transactions in goods and one of the Uniform Commercial Code's less satisfactory sections.

PALMER v. WATSON CONSTRUCTION COMPANY
Supreme Court of Minnesota
265 Minn. 195, 121 N.W.2d 62 (1963)

SHERAN, J. The appeal is from an order of the district court denying defendants' motion for judgment notwithstanding the verdict or, in the alternative, a new trial.

The action was instituted by plaintiff to recover progress payments, retained percentages, and damages for breach of contracts for excavation and backfilling, one being dated August 26, and the other September 20, 1960. In response defendant Watson Construction Company asserted default by plaintiff and counterclaimed for damages occasioned by his failure to perform.

The subject matter of the contracts was excavation, backfilling, sodding, and seeding to be performed in connection with the construction of four buildings and connecting tunnels being built at the state hospital at Brainerd pursuant to a prime contract between defendant and the State of Minnesota.

Relevant contract provisions fixing the obligations of these parties included the following:

The Contractor agrees—. . .

h) To pay the Subcontractor on demand for his work or materials as far as executed and fixed in place, less the retained percentage. . . .

The subcontractor's obligations are described as follows:

Section 3. The Subcontractor agrees to complete the several portions and the whole of the work herein sublet by the time or times following: As required by the progress of the job. Sub-Contractor agrees to provide sufficient equipment to complete the excavation of the four buildings this fall and, further agrees that if he does not provide proper equipment to complete his contract, the contractor has the right to bring in additional equipment and charge the cost of same against his contract.

The contracts involved do not contain provisions governing resolution of disputes between the parties as to quantities of work performed for purpose of progress payments where, as here, there was no certification by the architect.[91]

---

[91] [2] Neither party to the contracts insisted upon architect's certificates as to excavation done and hence the provisions of the contracts pertaining to payment upon the architect's certificate were

On October 6, 1960, plaintiff submitted to defendant a statement for work completed as of September 20, 1960, which included a claim for $7,760 for excavation of 19,400 cubic yards of earth at 40¢ per cubic yard. Upon receipt defendant disputed the quantity of excavation for which it had been billed and sent plaintiff a check which included the sum of $5,400, less retained percentage, representing payment for excavation of 13,500 cubic yards of material. Protracted negotiations then ensued during the course of which plaintiff insisted that he was entitled to payment based upon his figures, which represented the quantity of material which he claimed he had in fact removed. Defendant persisted in its refusal to accept these figures on the theory that if the quantity of material claimed by plaintiff had in fact been removed, plaintiff had "overexcavated," i.e., excavated from the foundation grade to the level of the ground at an angle in excess of that prescribed by defendant and by proper and customary standards of workmanship. . . .

Although plaintiff submitted statements for and received payment on account of additional excavation performed during the month of November, the disagreement with respect to the quantity for which he was entitled to payment in connection with the digging done by him and included in the October 6 billing was never resolved. Apparently construction work on the project was resumed in February 1961, but plaintiff declined to perform further under his subcontracts unless he was paid in conformity with his calculations. . . .

Correspondence between defendant and plaintiff and plaintiff's attorney during February, March, and April reveals that the parties had reached an impasse. By letter dated March 2, 1961, which reviews the February correspondence and reflects the persistence of the disagreement, defendant wrote, "Further, we are requesting at this time a definite statement from Mr. Palmer as to whether he intends to complete his contract." By letter dated March 6, 1961, defendant advised plaintiff that it was correcting the grade level in one of the basements and completing the backfilling on this building and would backcharge the expense to plaintiff. On March 16, 1961, defendant wrote to plaintiff, "If we do not hear from you by return mail that you intend to complete your contract on this project, it will be necessary for us to hire another contractor to complete your contract on a time and material basis. Any costs over and above your total contract price will necessarily have to be assumed by your firm." On March 20, 1961, plaintiff's attorney wrote to defendant as follows: "Mr. Palmer has always been willing to complete his contract but he is not going to complete the contract unless you fulfill your obligation to make payment as set forth above." In addition this letter contains a statement that plaintiff was unable to pay another subcontractor and that defendant was placing plaintiff "in a position where he cannot proceed with the contract by reason of this inability to pay."

The jury was instructed that if refusal by plaintiff to continue performance under the contract was justified, he was entitled to recover not only for the excavation and other contract services actually performed, but also for such profits as he

---

waived and neither could insist on strict compliance or payment thereunder. Standard Const. Co. Inc. v. National Tea Co. 240 Minn. 422, 62 N.W.2d 201.

would have realized had performance been completed and payment made according to the agreement. The jury was informed that if plaintiff's refusal to proceed was not justified, defendant was entitled to recover damages on its counterclaim. No instructions were given or requested that plaintiff would be entitled to recover in quantum meruit for the services in fact performed by him up to the point when the disagreement brought work to a halt. . . .

. . . [I]t is our opinion that the evidence does not sustain the verdict in so far as it includes damages for loss of the profit anticipated in the event of full performance. A party to a contract who is entitled to progress payments may treat the failure to make such payments when due as a breach of the contract which will justify him in refusing to perform further and which will give legal basis for a claim for the reasonable value of the services performed or material supplied pursuant to the contract. . . . His alternative course is to continue with performance and recover the contract price in full upon completion. . . . It is true that a party ready, willing, and able to perform may recover damages for breach of contract, as distinguished from the reasonable value of the services rendered or material supplied, if he is *prevented* from performance by an act or omission of the other contracting party. . . . We are committed in this state, however, to the rule that nonpayment of installment obligations is not in and of itself such prevention of performance as will make possible suit for loss of profits even though the party entitled to payment may lack working capital. . . .

Although the letter written by plaintiff's attorney on March 20 stated that non-payment was interfering with the discharge of Palmer's obligation to his subcontractor and thus preventing completion, there is nothing in the testimony of the subcontractor, who was called as a witness in behalf of plaintiff, to support this argument adequately. While the parties to a construction contract could make nonpayment of progress payments such an event as would empower the party entitled to the money to discontinue performance and sue for that which he would have earned had the contract been completed, we find no such provision in the agreements here involved. It is conceivable that refusal to make progress payments without justification and under circumstances where the refusal is intended to make performance by the contractor impossible could be considered such prevention of performance as would justify recovery of profits for breach of an indivisible contract. For the present, it is sufficient to say that this is not such a case.

Reversed and remanded for a new trial.

NOTES AND QUESTIONS

1. *An exercise in alternatives:* As an exercise, craft a list of possible rules to apply in cases like the *Palmer* case. Then critique them, both in terms of the quality of outcomes they would yield (using whatever criteria for evaluating quality you believe appropriate) and then in terms of their administrability. As a second exercise, describe the facts of the *Palmer* case as they might have appeared first, to Palmer, and then to Watson Construction. How could a court, or even the parties themselves, determine which version of the facts was "true?" Is it the case that one of the difficulties of making such an assessment arises because either party may have legitimate, but different, fears of what may happen next? For those familiar with game theory, is there something like a Prisoner's Dilemma here?[92]

2. ***The resources of the parties as affecting the outcome:*** The General Contractor in the *Palmer* case thought that far too much dirt and rock had been taken away. It paid only a portion of the amount claimed by the Grading Contractor, the Grading Contractor then refused to continue until it was paid in full, and ultimately the parties found themselves before the Supreme Court of Minnesota. The General Contractor argued that if the Grading Contractor had performed properly, there was only a breach of the progress payment provisions and not the whole contract. It quoted *New York Life Ins. Co. v. Viglas*[93] as stating that to justify treating a contract as completely broken, a repudiation "must at least amount to an unqualified refusal or declaration of inability substantially to perform according to the terms of its obligation." The brief continued, saying that "[t]he trial judge in his memorandum attempts to distinguish . . . case law . . . on the basis that [the Grading Contractor's] financial resources were insufficient to let him finish the job. . . . [T]his contention has been repeatedly raised, examined on the merits in trial and has been held as a matter of law inapplicable." The General Contractor quoted a passage from *Beatty v. Howe Lumber Co.:*[94]

> It could make no difference with the legal liability of the defendant whether the plaintiffs were rich or poor. If they had been rich, or had ample means, it is evident, from the record, that they would or could have continued to perform the services. . . . [One may recover when another prevents performance] . . . , but . . . this right does not rest in the mere default in payment of an installment when it becomes due, especially when . . . there was no[t] denial of the legal right of the plaintiffs to proceed in the performance of the contract unaffected by the conduct or default of the defendant.

On March 20, 1961, the Grading Contractor's lawyer wrote the General Contractor, "Mr. Palmer has always been willing to complete his contract but he is not going to complete the contract unless you fulfill your obligation to make payment as set forth above." He then said that the General Contractor was placing Palmer in a position where he could not proceed with the contract because he required payments from the General in order to be able to pay the subcontractors. Suppose this were clearly the case. Would the result have been different? Suppose, instead, the *General Contractor* was short of working capital and could not make the progress payments required under the contract. Its managers looked for some item to question in order to delay paying the Grading Contractor. Would the result have been different?

---

[92] A "prisoner's dilemma" arises in a situation in which two persons must decide whether to cooperate or not. If both cooperate, both are slightly better off. If both choose not to cooperate, both are significantly worse off. However, both are tempted not to cooperate because if one chooses to cooperate, and the other chooses NOT to cooperate, the non-cooperating person receives a very significant gain.

[93] 297 U.S. 672 (1936).

[94] 77 Minn. 272, 79 N.W. 1013, 1015 (1899).

Like many legal questions, there is another view of the question of whether late payments constitute cause for a contractor's refusal to proceed. In *Cork Plumbing Co., Inc. v. Martin Bloom Associates, Inc.*,[95] the court stated:

> Because of the nature of construction contracts and the contractor's need for funds to meet expenses and proceed with construction, courts have distinguished construction contracts from other installment contracts with respect to the subcontractors's right to terminate for non-payment of installments. This judicial sentiment is expressed in *Brady Brick & Supply Co. v. Lotito*, 43 Ill. App. 3d 69, 1 Ill. Dec. 844, 848, 356 N.E.2d 1126, 1130 (1976):
>
> > The failure to pay an installment of the contract price as provided in a building or construction contract is a substantial breach of contract and gives the contractor the right to consider the contract at an end, to cease work, and to recover the value of the work already performed. . . .[96]
>
> We recognize that the facts in every construction contract might not warrant a termination upon failure to pay an installment, but the present facts, particularly the repeated failure to keep payments current coupled with M.B.A.'s statements about future payments, permit such a resolution. We must consider the effect of delays on the builder's finances, and "[s]ince the builder's risks depend largely upon the financial resources of the debtor, . . . a non-payment by an obligor who is of doubtful solvency . . . *or who accompanies his non-payment by words of near repudiation is almost certain to be held a vital breach.*" (Emphasis added.) 3A Corbin on Contracts, § 692.

   3. *Legislation by a private government—the American Institute of Architect forms*: The American Institute of Architects (AIA) has drafted form contracts covering most of the building process. These forms, or provisions modeled on them, are widely used in the construction industry. To what extent, if at all, do these provisions affect the resolution of disputes such as those in *Palmer v. Watson*?

AIA Document A401, Contractor-Subcontractor Agreement[97] provides:

> 4.7.1   If the Contractor does not pay the Subcontractor through no fault of the Subcontractor, within seven days from the time payment should be made as provided in this Agreement, the Subcontractor may, without prejudice to other available remedies, upon seven additional days' writ-

---

[95] 573 S.W.2d 947 (Mo. App. 1978).

[96] Eds. note: Does the court mean that the contractor can only recover restitution? Why shouldn't it be able to recover damages based on protection of its expectation interest? CORBIN ON CONTRACTS § 693 (1952) says that if "the nonpayment is held to be a vital breach," the builder has four choices: He may stop performance and bring no suit. He may continue performance while either seeking no remedy or suing for the installment due. He may sue for restitution as an alternative remedy for breach. Or he may sue for damages for total breach. Under this last option, the builder would recover the contract price less the cost of completion and less any payments he has received from the owner.

[97] (12th ed., The American Institute of Architects 1987).

ten notice to the Contractor, stop the Work of this Subcontract until payment of the amount owing has been received. The Subcontract Sum shall, by appropriate adjustment, be increased by the amount of the Subcontractor's reasonable costs of shutdown, delay and start-up.

7.1.1   The Subcontractor may terminate the Subcontract ... for non-payment of amounts due under this Subcontract for 60 days or longer. In the event of such termination by the Subcontractor for any reason which is not the fault of the Subcontractor, Sub-subcontractors or their agents or employees or other persons performing portions of the Work under contract with the Subcontractor, the Subcontractor shall be entitled to recover from the Contractor payment for Work executed and for proven loss with respect to materials, equipment, tools, and construction equipment and machinery, including reasonable overhead, profit and damages.

While this might seem to clarify the situation, the subcontractor must establish that an amount is due or owing to trigger these sections. Section 6.1 provides that "any controversy or claim between the Contractor and the Subcontractor" shall be settled by arbitration. Arbitration is to be conducted as provided in the contract between Owner and Contractor.[98]

The result of the delay built into the agreement, plus the additional delays which accompany the arbitration process, is that a subcontractor may have to wait two months or even much longer before it can invoke the remedies described in the AIA Contractor-Subcontractor Agreement. An undercapitalized subcontractor might find it difficult to pay suppliers and workers while awaiting a decision in situations such as involved in *Palmer v. Watson*. It might have to accept an offer such as the general contractor made in that case. Why do the AIA standard contract forms leave subcontractors in such a weak position?

4. *The measure of damages*: Suppose an owner or general contractor fails to make a progress payment. A court decides that the subcontractor is entitled to stop work on the job and sue for damages as well. What is the measure of recovery? Can the subcontractor recover the installments due or should damages be calculated in some other manner? Courts often distinguish between "partial" and "total" breaches of contract in discussing such questions. Under a *partial breach*, the contract continues despite the default. Nonetheless, the aggrieved party can recover a judgment for the payment that has been missed. Under a *total breach*, the contract is at an end. Now damages are not measured by the installment payments in the contract but are to be calculated in terms of the expectation, reliance

---

[98] Arbitration is governed by a number of provisions in the General Conditions of the Contract for Construction. (AIA Document A201, 14th ed. 1987. Copyright © The American Institute of Architects.) Claims are submitted to the architect who must act within ten days. He or she may reject the claim, recommend approval, suggest a compromise or ask for additional supporting evidence. After the architect's initial response, if the claim has not been resolved, the party making the claim has ten days to respond. Then the architect has another seven days in which to decide the claim. The architect's decision is subject to arbitration under the Construction Industry Arbitration Rules of the American Arbitration Association. A demand for arbitration must be submitted within 30 days after the architect's decision. Pending final resolution of a claim, § 4.3.4 provides "the Contractor shall proceed diligently with performance of the Contract and the Owner shall continue to make payments in accordance with the Contract Documents."

or restitution interests. How do we know whether a breach is "partial" or "total"? Courts often ask whether the breach was substantial or material. To a great extent, the question is whether the aggrieved party should be required to continue to perform in the face of the other's breach.

The problem is reflected in *Fuller v. United Electric Co.*[99] The owner was constructing a new home in Las Vegas. She hired United Electric to do the electrical wiring. The total price was $1,410, and the contract provided that "80% of contract price payable on completion of rough-in and inspection thereof; balance payable on final completion and inspection." Rough-in was completed, and a municipal building inspector approved the work. The owner paid $500 on account but refused to pay more or to allow United Electric to complete the job, asserting that United Electric had breached. The trial court found that United had not breached but that the owner had.

The trial court awarded United Electric $1,048.60. It arrived at that sum by calculating that 80% of $1,410 contract price was $1,128. It then added 20% of $1,128 as a reasonable profit. United Electric was also entitled to $195 for extras. This totaled $1,548.60, and the court subtracted the $500 that had been paid to arrive at the award of $1,048.60. The Supreme Court of Nevada reversed. It explained:

> [T]he breach by defendant was not a partial breach with the contract continuing in effect notwithstanding, in which event an installment or progress payment due under the contract might be claimed in full. The breach was a total breach and was so treated by plaintiff. The contract was thereby terminated. . . .
>
> In our view the contract in this case was clearly an entire one. The specified payment of 80% upon completion of rough-in was but a scheduled part payment upon the specified contract price and was not a full and fixed payment allocated absolutely to that portion of the work done up to completion of rough-in. Upon a total breach, then, damages must be ascertained upon the entire contract and the total contract price without regard to those provisions having to do with the times at which portions of the contract price were to become payable.

The case was remanded for a determination of contract damages. "What is allowed is the profit, if any, which would have been realized had the contract proceeded to completion." United Electric, then, would have to show the difference between the contract price and its total cost of performance had the contract been completed. It would be entitled to this sum plus its reasonable expenditures in part performance. Of course, alternatively, United Electric might also bring a restitution action to recover the reasonable value of the work it had done in part performance.

Courts often discuss this problem in terms of "entire" and "divisible" contracts. Corbin objects to these words as terms of confusion.[100] We can imagine a divisible contract. For example, suppose a lawyer is to draft the documents nec-

---

[99] 70 Nev. 448, 273 P.2d 136 (1954).
[100] *See* 3 CORBIN ON CONTRACTS §§ 694, 695, 955.

essary to incorporate client's business and also draft a will for that client. Both tasks are mentioned in the written contract between lawyer and client. The document states that the incorporation is to be done for a fee of $X payable when the articles of incorporation are filed. It also says that the will is to be drafted for $Y payable when it is presented to the client for execution. The contract then states the total fee to be $X + $Y. Unless a court were to find some relationship between the incorporation and the will, these seem to be distinct tasks and the fees would likely have been set independently for each one. If this were the case, one contract document expresses two "divisible" tasks, and the two sums mentioned are allocated to each one. If the lawyer completes the will, he is entitled to $Y although he has not begun the articles of incorporation. Furthermore, failure to pay $Y when the will was completed would not necessarily give the lawyer the right to abandon his or her work on the articles of incorporation under the contract.

However, suppose the entire purpose of the will was to deal with questions of control of the new corporation if one of its founders died. Furthermore, assume it was clear that the sum named for preparing the articles of incorporation was less than the usual charge for this service while the sum named for the will was a corresponding amount greater. It seems likely that the sums named were a payment schedule. That is, the writing meant that the lawyer was to get $X WHEN he produced the articles of incorporation and $Y WHEN he drafted the will. The parties named the amounts so that the new corporation could delay its need for cash until matters were settled but so that the lawyer would get something during the time he was performing.

Now a court might find that the will and the articles of incorporation were not separate tasks purchased at the named prices. Rather, the payments of $X and $Y were partial payments of the total sum.

Suppose the client repudiates the arrangement and tells the lawyer to stop work. In this event, completion of the will before the repudiation would not entitle the lawyer to $Y. The lawyer would be entitled to expectation damages based on doing the entire job. If there had been no clear repudiation other than the failure to pay, it would be an open question whether the lawyer could stop work on the transaction.

Modern practice and the American Institute of Architects form contracts minimize the entire and divisible problem in building contracts. Contractors are required to allocate the entire contract price to designated portions of the work in a "schedule of values." This document is submitted to the architect for his or her approval before the contractor makes its first application for payment. Then payments are made in terms of the approved schedule. This means that payments are more closely related than in the past to the actual cost of the construction performed during the payment period. The specificity of the schedule of values and the degree to which the contractor can front load it are a matter of negotiation. The contractor makes a proposal and must get the architect to accept it. When a detailed and cost specific schedule of values is established, this practice creates something close to a divisible contract. Each installment payment will be a fair approximation of the contract rate for the work actually done.

b. Installment Contracts and the UCC

Suppose a contract calls for several goods to be delivered at different times. Assume that it is subject to Article 2 of the UCC.[101] Then read the next case, *Midwest Mobile Diagnostic Imaging, L.L.C. v. Dynamics Corp. of America.*[102] After you have read the relevant provisions of the UCC and *Midwest Mobile Diagnostic Imaging*, consider the following hypothetical case. This problem is based on an actual dispute between the University of Wisconsin-Madison (UWM) and Globe Ticket and Label Co. The contract provisions are the actual ones used by UWM. However, a number of details have been changed to pose issues relevant to our purposes here, and so the parties have been given other names. Nonetheless, the question is very close to the problem faced by lawyers representing UWM.

The University of Southern Michigan's Fighting Wasps emerged in the 1990s as a football power. Its men's and women's basketball and men's ice hockey teams, the other three of the four so-called "income sports," also have had success. The University of Southern Michigan (The University or USM) depends on what it earns from these programs to fund all other athletic programs and the maintenance, modernization and construction of stadiums, rinks and courts. It sells "season tickets" to all of these income sports. A season ticket holder buys a ticket to a particular seat (or seats) for all games played by the team for a particular season. The buyer pays in advance, and usually a few weeks to a month before the first game, s/he is sent tickets for each home game the team will play for that particular season. Sales of season tickets in all four sports are critical to the University's ability to plan and count on receiving certain sums of money, and season tickets cut the risks associated with having any team having a very bad year because the seats are sold no matter what the record of the particular team.

USM had purchased the sets of season tickets from WWL Ticket, Corporation for many years. In 2000, USM made a contract to buy all of its season tickets from a new supplier, Ball Ticket and Label Company. Ball bid $200,000, $50,000 less than WWL Ticket, Corporation. Ball was well known in the industry and regularly produced tickets for professional and university football, basketball and hockey teams.

The contract between USM and Ball was made on forms drafted by the University's Purchasing Services Department. It was to send season tickets "directly to the indicated ticket holder by the US Postal Service via Priority Mail."

There were to be 60,000 general public, 15,000 student, and 1,000 limited view **football** season tickets printed and distributed. "All season tickets will be delivered directly to individual ticket holders by Priority Mail. The tickets must be mailed on, or before, August 10, 2001." Each bidder indicated a specified price for printing the football tickets and the cost of distributing them.

There were to be 17,500 general public and 2,500 student men's **basketball** season tickets printed and distributed. "All season tickets will be delivered di-

---

[101] *See* UCC §§ 2-307 and 2-612.
[102] 965 F. Supp. 1003 (W.D. Mich. 1997).

rectly to individual ticket holders by Priority Mail. The tickets must be mailed on, or before, October 30, 2001." Each bidder indicated a specified price for printing the men's basketball tickets and the cost of distributing them.

There were to be 9,500 general public and 2,500 student **women's basketball** season tickets printed and distributed. "All season tickets will be delivered directly to individual ticket holders by Priority Mail. The tickets must be mailed on, or before, October 30, 2001." Each bidder indicated a specified price for printing the women's basketball tickets and the cost of distributing them.

There were to be 14,000 general public series 1, and 14,000 general public series 2, **men's ice hockey** season tickets printed and distributed. Generally, series 1 tickets were for games played on Fridays and series 2 tickets were for games played on Saturdays. "All season tickets will be delivered directly to individual ticket holders by Priority Mail. The tickets must be mailed on, or before, September 15, 2001." Each bidder indicated a specified price for printing the each series of hockey tickets and the cost of distributing them.

The dates for mailing had been established so that season tickets would arrive well before the first game. For example, hockey season tickets were to be mailed on or before September 15th, but the first game was not until October 19th.

The University's Special Conditions of Bid were incorporated into the contract via the bidding process. Among other things, they provided:

8. TIMELINESS OF DELIVERY:

Failure to meet the absolute delivery date(s) may result in cancellation of an award.

> * * *

14. CONTRACT TERMINATION:

14.1   Shall either party fail to perform under the terms of this Contract, the aggrieved party may notify the other party in writing via certified mail of such failure and demand that the same be remedied within 30 calendar days. Should the defaulting party fail to remedy the same within said period, the other party shall then have the right to terminate this Contract by giving the other party 5calendar days written notice. Performance failure can be defined as, but not limited to, less than acceptable printing results, not meeting delivery requirements, or failure to provide any of the conditions of the Specifications or Special Conditions of Bid.

14.2   If at any time the contractors performance threatens the health and/or safety of the University, or causes the University to suffer monetary loss, the University has the right to cancel and terminate the Contract without notice.

> * * *

The University's Standard Terms and Conditions for Requests for Bids also were incorporated into the contract via the bidding process. Among other things, they provided:

11.0   GUARANTEED DELIVERY: Failure of the contractor to adhere to delivery schedules as specified or to promptly replace rejected materials shall render the contractor liable for all costs in excess of the contract price when alternate procurement is necessary. Excess costs shall include the administrative costs.

      * * *

23.0   CANCELLATION: The University of Southern Michigan reserves the right to cancel any contract in whole or in part without penalty . . . for failure of the contractor to comply with terms, conditions, and specifications of this contract.

There was no clause excusing either the University or the successful bidder that won the contract to produce and deliver the various season tickets for impossibility or frustration (that is, there was no *force majeure* clause).

Ball Ticket mailed the 60,000 general public football season tickets in four mailings of 15,000. The first was put in the mail on Friday, August 10, 2001, the second on Saturday, August 11th, the third on Monday, August 13th and the fourth on Thursday, August 16th. The USM Fighting Wasps were to play their first football game against the University of Virginia on Saturday, August 25, 2001. All of the season tickets arrived at the mailing addresses of the general public season ticket holders before the August 25th game. However, many season ticket holders were concerned when their tickets had not arrived as the date for the game approached and called the Athletic Ticket Department. On Wednesday, August 22nd, Ball Ticket's National Sales Manager issued a statement that was reported in the press and on television. He said that a combination of peak season and staffing problems at Ball Ticket's soon-to-be-closed printing and distribution center in Tacoma, Washington, caused the problems. He explained that some disgruntled employees quit when it was announced that the Tacoma plant was to be closed. This left a thin work force that was less than diligent about getting work out on time.

Ball Ticket's representatives traveled to the campus to meet with USM Athletic Department officials on August 22, 2001. Ball Ticket's representatives orally assured USM that there would be no more problems because the account was now being handled at Ball Ticket's new processing headquarters in Pennsylvania. Ball Ticket was to mail all of the two series of general public hockey season tickets before September 15, 2001. Twenty eight thousand season tickets were to be sent to season ticket holders. Twenty thousand were mailed on or before September 15th; 8,000 were mailed over the next four weeks. The first hockey game was on Friday, October 19th. About 2,500 season tickets had not been received by the night of the first game, and the USM Athletic Ticket Office had to issue duplicate tickets for these season ticket holders so that they could get into the October 19th game. These ticket holders had to stand in line at will-call to receive their tickets. The problem was reported and discussed in both local newspapers. All of the delayed 2,500 season tickets arrived in either Saturday's or Monday's mail; that is, all tickets had arrived by Monday, October 22nd.

On Monday, October 22, 2001, the USM Athletic Ticket Department canceled its order with Ball Ticket for men's and women's basketball season tickets. USM sent Ball Ticket a written contract termination notice, and it informed Ball that it could expect breach of contract proceedings under the contract.

Ball Ticket responded in writing on the 23rd. It objected that it had not breached its contract and asserted that it was entitled to print the basketball tickets. It explained that Ball Ticket had its headquarters and a large plant in Franklin, Pennsylvania. The Pennsylvania plant was running near capacity in August and early September of 2001 because this is a peak time when work must be done for the many universities that are Ball Ticket's customers for tickets. Despite paying its workers to work overtime, the Pennsylvania plant was not able to finish distributing all of the USM hockey tickets on time. It argued that its delay was trivial and showed nothing about its ability to deliver the basketball tickets. Late September and October is always a slow time because all of the work for football will have been completed well before then. The Pennsylvania plant would have had adequate capacity and workers to print and distribute USM basketball season tickets by about October 30th.

The University of Southern Michigan placed an emergency order for these tickets with WWL, the firm that had produced season tickets for the University for a number of years before being replaced by Ball Ticket. It had to pay $27,396.03 more for WWL to print and distribute these tickets than it would have paid Ball Ticket for the same work.

You work for USM's legal department. The University's General Counsel asks you to write a detailed memorandum discussing the University's legal position as a result of the problems with the football and hockey tickets and the University's response to these problems. She tells you that she has heard that Ball Ticket is considering suing the University and asserting that the University rather than Ball Ticket breached their contract. She wants to know all the legal theories that Ball Ticket is likely to raise, and, importantly, whether USM has any response to them. The state of Southern Michigan has no special contract law that governs all state contracts, and none of the various specific provisions of its law applicable to state contracts are relevant to this case. The case will be governed by the general contract law of Southern Michigan. That state has passed the Uniform Commercial Code. Write the memorandum.

MIDWEST MOBILE DIAGNOSTIC IMAGING, L.L.C. v. DYNAMICS CORPORATION OF AMERICA
United States District Court, Western District of Michigan
965 F. Supp. 1003 (1997)

ENSLEN, Chief Judge.

I. INTRODUCTION

Plaintiff Midwest Mobile Diagnostic Imagining, L.L.C. [hereinafter "MMDI"] brings this diversity action against defendant Ellis & Watts, d/b/a Dynamics Corporation of America [hereinafter "E&W"], seeking damages for 1) breach of a sales contract for the purchase of four mobile MRI units[103] and 2) misrepresentation. Defendant, the seller, counterclaims for damages, alleging that the buyer is in breach. Having considered the evidence submitted and the legal arguments of the parties made during a three-day bench trial, and having reviewed the exhibits submitted, the Court enters the following Findings of Fact and Conclusions of Law pursuant to Federal Rule of Civil Procedure 52(a). To the extent that any findings of fact also constitute conclusions of law or vice versa, they are so adopted. . . .

III. CONTENTIONS OF THE PARTIES

MMDI contends that, after its rightful rejection of a nonconforming trailer tendered by E&W on December 13, 19995, E& W repudiated the contract in its entirety. E&W's repudiation whether anticipatory or not, destroyed whatever right to cure E&W may have had and gave MMDI the right to cancel the contract, which it then did. MMDI argues it is entitled to damages.

E&W counters that its tender on December 13, 1995 was both timely and in conformity with contract specifications. Consequently, MMDI's rejection was wrongful. E&W continues that, even if the trailer were not conforming, E&W had a right to cure pursuant to Uniform Commercial Code [hereinafter "UCC"] §2-508, and MMDI could not cancel the contract without first requesting adequate assurances from E&W in writing pursuant to UCC §2-609. Since plaintiff did not satisfy §2-609 and a reasonable time for performance had not expired, MMDI's cancellation of the contract on December 18, 1995 constituted anticipatory repudiation.

IV. FACTS

Plaintiff Midwest Mobile Diagnostic Imaging, L.L.C ("MMDI") is a Delaware limited liability company, with offices in Kalamazoo, Michigan, engaged in the business of furnishing equipment and personnel for magnetic resonance imaging (MRI) scans to hospitals in southwestern Michigan. In 1995, MMDI had three mobile MRI units servicing area facilities.

Defendant Ellis & Watts ("E&W") is a New York corporation whose principal place of business is in Cincinnati, Ohio, which engineers, designs, and manufactures trailers for mobile medical uses, including mobile MRI systems.

Under Michigan regulations, the number of mobile MRI scanners which may be licensed is strictly limited. Consequently, companies wishing to provide this service must seek a Certificate of Need from the State. In 1995, the demand for these mobile MRI units exceeded that which MMDI could supply. MMDI, therefore, sought and received a Certificate of Need to begin operating a fourth mobile MRI unit.

In April 1995, plaintiff commenced negotiations with defendant to purchase four mobile MRI trailers, each designed to house a state-of-the-art, ACS NT 1.5T

---

[103] [1] A mobile MRI unit is, in effect, a mobile MRI clinic. It is a semi tractor trailer which contains an MRI scanner and the computer equipment necessary to operate such a machine. It is designed to function as a temporary extension of the hospital which it is serving, with an interior which generally matches the hospital environment.

MRI scanner system, which plaintiff would purchase separately from Philips. During these initial negotiations, E&W became aware that MMDI had an immediate need for the first trailer because of the growing demand for its services.

As a consequence, the parties agreed that delivery of the first trailer would occur in September 1995 with the rest to follow in monthly installments. However, during final negotiations in Kalamazoo on August 10, 1995, the parties agreed to delete a clause in the written contract requiring that all four trailers be delivered in 1995. While no specific delivery dates were ultimately included in the written contract, E&W understood that early delivery of the first trailer was of great importance to MMDI. At the time of signing, the parties expected delivery of the trailers to occur in October, November, December, 1995 and January, 1996. The delivery dates were, however, contingent upon coordination with Philips and agreement of the parties.

In addition to the timing of the project, during negotiations the parties also made representations concerning the design of the trailer. On April 17, 1995, Robert Freudenberger of E&W faxed a signed purchase agreement to Jerry Turowski of MMDI. Attached to the form contract were two drawings. One of the drawings depicted a three-dimensional illustration of the interior of a mobile MRI system trailer upon which was written: "Spacious, efficient layout with clean, aesthetically pleasing interior." (Exh. 2.) In addition, these drawings, and all others reviewed by MMDI both before and after contract signing, did not depict a bracing structure surrounding the scanner magnet.

On August 10, 1995, Mr. Turowski and Mr. Freudenberger executed a purchase agreement for four E&W trailers. (Exh. 9.) With the signing of the contract, MMDI paid E&W a deposit in the amount of $63,000. On August 11, 1995, Mr. Andrew Pike, President of E&W, countersigned the purchase agreement in Cincinnati, Ohio. Under the parties' agreement, E&W was to construct the four trailers in accordance with Philips' specifications. Once certified by Philips, the trailers could be delivered. (Exh. 9, ¶ 3.)

On September 7, 1995, plaintiff and defendant met in Kalamazoo to discuss the delivery schedule. On September 21, 1995, MMDI sent a letter indicating that, as a result of that meeting, MMDI expected delivery of the first trailer on November 6, 1995. The letter also noted the parties' understanding that the trailer would be "show" ready for MMDI's open house in Kalamazoo, Michigan, on November 3, 1995. E&W did not respond to this letter. During the course of construction, the parties discussed several alterations to the trailer and consequently, again renegotiated the delivery date for the first trailer. Ultimately, the parties agreed upon a December 1, 1995 delivery date. Under the expectation that the trailer would be delivered on that date, MMDI scheduled patients assuming the trailer would be ready for use beginning December 4, 1995.

On November 3, 1995, indicating that the trailer was cosmetically complete, E&W presented the trailer to MMDI to show at its open house in Kalamazoo, during which representatives of MMDI and many of its customers, inspected the trailer. At that time, the scanner magnet was free from any metal, bracing structures. The trailer was then returned to E&W for final adjustments and testing.

As of mid-November 1995, the first E&W trailer was fully fabricated and substantially all equipment was installed and ready for testing by Philips. In anticipation of the December 1 delivery date, E&W invoiced MMDI on November 10, 1995 for the full purchase price of the first trailer. (Exh. 20.) On November 16, 1995, E&W sent a follow-up letter requesting payment prior to shipment of the trailer on November 30 in accordance with the purchase agreement. (Exh. 9, 22.) MMDI paid $321,500 to E&W on November 17, 1995. (Exh. 20.)

On November 28, 1995, the first trailer failed to meet contract specifications in a test conducted by Philips. The test indicated that the trailer did not comply with Philips' specifications for magnetic shielding in the side walls of the trailer. This failure occurred despite the fact that, throughout the construction of the trailer, Philips had repeatedly noted the importance of the proper fabrication of this feature in its correspondence with E&W. (Exhs.13, 17, 19.)

When the parties discovered that the trailer had failed the test, they met to discuss potential solutions to the situation. At that time, E&W stated unequivocally that: 1) the trailer was defective; 2) the defect was entirely its fault and responsibility; and 3) it would cure the problem. E&W also indicated a willingness to reimburse MMDI for at least part of the expenses it might incur in renting another trailer to substitute for the one that E&W had not completed. As a result of the need for a cure, E&W failed to tender a conforming trailer on the December 1 delivery date and MMDI was forced to cancel appointments which had been scheduled with patients for December 4, 1995.

During the following two weeks, E&W designed a reinforcement structure to contend with the wall-flexing problem. The solution consisted of multiple, large, steel beams placed around the scanner magnet in a cage-like structure which prevented removal of the magnet's outer covers and dramatically changed its appearance. Such a bracing structure had never been used with a mobile MRI scanner by any manufacturer. During this period, E&W exchanged multiple letters and sketches with Philips in which Philips' representatives indicated several concerns with the bracing structure. E&W made adjustments to address some of these concerns. Ultimately, Philips approved the design as a temporary solution to the wall-flexing problem.

On December 7, 1995, E&W sent MMDI a schedule indicating that the decision whether to proceed with this design would be made on December 12, 1995. The letter indicated: "if no go at this point, alternate plans established." Although MMDI had reviewed drawings of the interior during the course of construction, E&W did not include a sketch of the reinforcement design in this correspondence.

On December 12, 1995, Philips' representatives retested the trailer with the bracing structure in place and found that the flexing problem had been remedied. Thus, the trailer was approved for use on a temporary basis. However, because the structure impaired service of the scanner magnet, Philips would not certify the trailer for permanent use with the structure in place.

On December 13, 1995, Mr. Turowski of MMDI arrived at E&W to inspect the new design for the first time. After viewing the trailer and speaking with Philips' representatives, Mr. Turowski concluded that the bracing structure was unacceptable for several reasons. Mr. Turowski and Mr. Andrew Pike of E&W then placed a telephone conference call to Dr. Azzam Kanaan and Dr. Ilydio Polachini at MMDI. At that time, Mr. Turowski indicated that, with the bracing structure, the trailer did not conform to the contract obligations because: 1) service of the scanner magnet would be impeded and, in cases, would be more dangerous; 2) its appearance was objectionable; and 3) the resale value of the trailer would be diminished.

Mr. Pike countered that the structure in place conformed to the parties' agreement, that this was the design that met the Philips' specification, that it had been approved by Philips, and told MMDI to accept it the way it was. Further, Mr. Pike stated that the materials had already been purchased to install this design in the second trailer, that this was the best design that one could come up with, and that he did not know if it could be done any differently. Finally, Mr. Pike refused to pay rent for a replacement unit or to refund MMDI's previous payment.

The following day, December 14, 1995, Mr. Pike sent a letter to Dr. Kanaan at MMDI (Exh. 29.), indicating that E&W was working with "this design" to see if it could be made more aesthetically pleasing. The letter made no reference to the servicing problems, safety concerns, or concerns about a potential diminution in resale value resulting from the use of the bracing structure. Mr. Pike again asserted the validity of the contract, and refused to refund MMDI's payment for the trailer.

On December 18, 1995, acting in good faith, MMDI advised E&W in writing that the Purchase Agreement was canceled. On December 19, 1995, MMDI rented a mobile MRI unit to replace the one it had expected to receive from E&W. On December 21, 1995, MMDI executed a contract with a third party for the manufacture and construction of two trailers to house two of the Philips 1.5T MRI scanner systems.

On December 22, 1995, Mr. Freudenberger sent a letter to Mr. Turowski, reiterating that the first trailer was ready for shipment and requesting instructions on how to ship it. In addition, the letter indicated that E&W was finalizing the design for an alternative bracing structure which would neither impede the servicing of the magnet components nor negatively impact the aesthetics of the trailer interior. Mr. Freudenberger also suggested that, after final testing and seeking MMDI's input regarding the aesthetics of the design, the design "would be considered the permanent solution" for the trailer. The design would then be incorporated into the second trailer at which time the first trailer would be returned to E&W and retrofitted with the new design at no cost to MMDI. E&W, however, maintained that the purchase agreement was still effective and continued to refuse to refund MMDI's payment. Soon after this correspondence, the parties ceased communication. Ultimately, E&W did remove the offending reinforcement structure and replaced it with an alternative design which was approved for permanent use by Philips. In the time since this replacement solution was fabricated and installed, E&W has sold two of the trailers to a third party.

On January 9, 1996, MMDI filed the instant suit for damages resulting from breach of contract and misrepresentation. E&W retained payments made by MMDI in the amount of $384,500. Further, MMDI incurred expenses in the amount of $185,250 for the lease of a mobile MRI scanner and trailer between December 19, 1995 and April 20, 1996.

V. ANALYSIS

A. Breach of contract

The primary issue for resolution by the Court is whether MMDI rightfully rejected E&W's tender of the first trailer and then subsequently canceled the contract, or if its actions in mid-December constituted anticipatory repudiation of the contract. Having previously determined that Michigan law controls in the instant case, the Court simply notes that the Michigan version of the Uniform Commercial Code [hereinafter the "UCC"] applies to this sales contract. . . .

1. Installment Contract

Before turning to the specific questions of rejection and cancellation, the Court must first resolve a threshold issue. Under the UCC, the parties' rights to reject, cure, and cancel under an installment contract differ substantially from those defined under a single delivery contract. Consequently, resolution of whether the contract is an installment contract is of primary concern. Section 2-612(1) defines an "installment contract" as "one which requires or authorizes the delivery of goods in separate lots to be separately accepted. . . ." The commentary following this section emphasizes that the "definition of an installment contract is phrased more broadly in this Article [than in its previous incarnation as the Uniform Sales Act] so as to cover installment deliveries tacitly authorized by the circumstances or by the option of either party." § 2-612, cmt. 1.

Plaintiff argues that the contract between itself and E&W does not constitute an installment contract because it authorizes delivery in commercial units, and not lots, as required by subsection (1). However, upon review of the Code section defining those terms, it becomes clear that those terms are not mutually exclusive. Section 2-105 defines a "lot" as a "parcel or single article which is the subject matter of a separate sale or delivery, whether or not it is sufficient to perform the contract." The same section defines a commercial unit as "such a unit of goods as by commercial usage is a single whole for purposes of sale and division of which materially impairs its character or value on the market or in use. A commercial unit may be a single article (as a machine) or a set of articles (as a suite of furniture or an assortment of sizes) or a quantity (as a bale, gross, or carload) or any other unit treated in use or in the relevant market as a single whole." Thus, a lot, which is the measure of goods that the contract states will be delivered together in one installment, can be a single commercial unit. Consequently, § 2-612 applies wherever a contract for multiple items authorizes the delivery of the items in separate groups at different times, whether or not the installment constitutes a commercial unit.

The contract between MMDI and E&W for the sale of four trailers authorizes the delivery of each trailer separately. While the written contract does not explicitly state this delivery schedule, it does authorize separate delivery. Paragraph 2 of the contract assumes separate delivery dates by setting out a payment schedule wherein the balance for each unit is due at the time of shipment. Furthermore, based on the parties' testimony it is clear that both parties understood the trailers would be delivered in separate installments. Indeed, neither party disputes that they agreed to have the trailers delivered at four separate times. Therefore, the Court finds that the contract in dispute is an installment contract.

2. Right of Rejection

Section 2-612, therefore, is the starting point for the Court's analysis of MMDI's actions on December 13, 1995. . . . Under § 2-612, the buyer's right to reject is far more limited than the corresponding fight to reject under a single delivery contract defined under § 2-601. Under § 2-601, a buyer has the right to reject, "if the goods or tender of delivery fail in any respect to conform to the contract. . . ." Known as the "perfect tender" rule, this standard requires a very high level of conformity. Under this rule, the buyer may reject a seller's tender for any trivial defect, whether it be in the quality of the goods, the timing of performance, or the manner of delivery. To avoid injustice, the Code limits the buyer's correlative right to cancel the contract upon such rejection by providing a right to cure under § 2-508. § 2- 508, cmt. 2. Under § 2-508, the seller has a right to cure if s/he seasonably notifies the buyer of the intent to do so, and either 1) the time for performance has not yet passed, or 2) the seller had reason to believe that the goods were in conformity with the contract. Thus, § 2-508's right to cure serves to temper the buyer's expansive right to reject under a single delivery contract. . . .

Section 2-612 creates an exception to the perfect tender rule. . . . Under subsection (2), a buyer may not reject nonconforming tender unless the defect substantially impairs the value of the installment. In addition, "if the nonconformity is curable and the seller gives adequate assurances of cure," the buyer must accept the installment. § 2-612, cmt. 5. But even if rejection is proper under subsection 2, cancellation of the contract is not appropriate unless the defect substantially impairs the value of the whole contract. § 2-612(3), cmt. 6. Because this section significantly restricts the buyer's right to cancel under an installment contract, there is no corresponding necessity for reference to § 2-508; the seller's right to cure is implicitly defined by § 2-612.[104]

a. Delivery Date

Before proceeding with the analysis of MMDI's December 13 rejection, the Court initially notes that E&W's tender on December 13 constituted a cure attempt for the wall-flexing defect which delayed the delivery of the first trailer beyond the agreed upon delivery date. Although under § 2-612 the delivery date

---

[104] [6] Courts of other jurisdictions have reached differing conclusions with regard to the interaction between §§ 2-612 and 2-508. See, e.g. Arkla Energy Resources v. Roye Realty & Dev., Inc., 9 F.3d 855 (10th Cir.1993); Bodine, 97 Ill.Dec. at 906, 493 N.E.2d at 713; Bevel-Fold, Inc. v. Bose Corp., 9 Mass.App.Ct. 576, 402 N.E.2d 1104, 1108 (1980); Continental Forest Prods., Inc. v. White Lumber Sales Inc., 256 Or. 466, 474 P.2d 1, 4 (1970). This Court does not find the arguments of these other courts persuasive, however, and notes that their decisions are not binding on this Court. Nevertheless, the Court also notes that, since the time for delivery of the first installment had already passed on December 1, 1995 (see infra § 2(a)) and defendant could not have reasonably believed and, in fact, did not believe that the trailer was in conformity with the contract on that date, defendant had no right to cure under § 2- 508.

does not cut off the seller's right to cure, it does have an effect on the rights of the parties. . . .

In the instant case, the original, written contract included no definite delivery date. Instead, the contract left the delivery term to be agreed upon at a later date. At the time of execution, the parties both expected delivery of the first trailer to take place in October. During the months after the execution of the contract, however, the parties modified the deadline for the first installment of the contract on several occasions. As noted above, upon review of the testimony and documentary evidence, the Court finds that, whatever delivery date the parties had agreed upon prior to November 1995, by early November they had renegotiated their agreement to establish a December 1, 1995 delivery date. See § 2-209 (sales contract may be modified by oral or written agreement without consideration, so long as agreement does not state otherwise).

Defendant argues, however, that, even if the parties had at one point agreed upon a December 1, 1995 deadline, when the first trailer failed the Philips road test on November 28, 1995, the parties renegotiated the delivery term to allow E&W a reasonable time to cure the defect. While E&W is correct that, as of December 1, it had a reasonable time in which to cure the wall-flexing problem, the Court disagrees that MMDI's willingness to wait for a cure constitutes an agreement to extend the delivery deadline. Because the parties believed that the defect was curable and E&W, without solicitation, unequivocally promised to cure it, under § 2-612, MMDI had no choice but to accept an offer of cure. To reject the installment on November 28 would have constituted a violation of § 2-612. The Court, therefore, finds that any negotiations the parties engaged in regarding delivery after discovery of the wall-flexing problem, did not constitute a modification of the delivery date for the first installment, but rather involved negotiation regarding cure. Since no specific date for delivery of a cure was agreed upon during those negotiations, under § 2-309(1), E&W had a reasonable time to effectuate a cure. Although there is some question as to whether further delay would have been reasonable, the Court finds that, as of December 13, 1995, a reasonable time had not yet passed. Therefore, defendant's tender of a cure was timely.[105]

b. Substantial Impairment of the Installment

The Court's conclusion that E&W's December 13 tender was an attempt to cure the November 28 breach raises another question: which standard of conformity applies to cure under an installment contract, perfect tender or substantial impairment? Looking to the rationale behind § 2-612, the Court notes that the

---

[105] [7] Defendant contends that because under ¶ 3 of the purchase agreement (Exh. 9), delivery was conditioned upon certification by Philips and the condition was not yet satisfied, defendant's duty to perform had not yet arisen on December 13. The argument is unavailing, however, given that it was defendant's deficient performance that prevented certification of the trailer both in late November and mid-December 1995. See Kentucky Skilled Craft Guild v. General Electric Co., 431 F.2d 62, 68 (6th Cir.1970) (quoting Gulf Oil Corp. v. American Louisiana Pipe Line Co., 282 F.2d 401 (6th Cir.1960)). (" 'Where liability under a contract depends upon a condition precedent one cannot avoid his liability by making the performance of the condition precedent impossible, or by preventing it.' ")

very purpose of allowing the seller time to cure under this section is to permit it additional time to meet the obligations of the contract. The assumption is that, because the parties have an ongoing relationship, the seller should be given an opportunity to make up the deficiency. This section was not designed to allow the seller to have a never-ending series of chances to bring the item into conformity with the contract. Nor was it enacted to force the buyer to accept a nonconforming product as satisfaction of the contract. Consequently, it is logical that a tender of cure should be required to meet the higher "perfect tender" standard. On its face, however, § 2-612, which generally defines a buyer's right to reject goods under an installment contract, requires only substantial impairment in this context as well. Thus, there is some question as to which is the appropriate standard. The answer is not crucial however, since the trailer in this case fails under both standards. Because a decision on this point will not effect the ultimate outcome in this case, the Court declines to address the issue. Instead, the Court proceeds with the substantial impairment analysis provided by § 2-612.

To establish substantial impairment of the value of an installment, the buyer " 'must present objective evidence that with respect to its own needs, the value of the goods was substantially impaired.' " . . . See also § 2-612, cmt 4. The existence of such nonconformity depends on the facts and circumstances of each case, and "can turn not only on the quality of the goods but also on such factors as time . . . , and the like." § 2-612, cmt. 4. . . . Finally, whether nonconformity rises to the level of substantial impairment may be judged by reference to the concept of material breach under traditional contract law. . . .

In the instant case, plaintiff alleges several aspects in which defendant's December 13 tender failed to conform to contract obligations. Plaintiff contends that the trailer tendered on December 13 with the bracing structure did not conform to the parties' agreement because: 1) it was not and could not be certified by Philips without conditions for use with the 1.5T scanner and 2) its interior design did not conform with the parties' agreements. Because of these defects, MMDI argues that the value of trailer was reduced substantially. Defendant, on the other hand, contends that the contract required only that the trailer meet the technical specifications provided by Philips, and that, therefore, the December 13 trailer was in complete compliance with its terms.

The written contract signed by the parties in this case is relatively skeletal and thus, requires interpretation. The Court's fundamental purpose in interpreting the terms of the contract is to give effect to the intent of the parties as it existed at the time the agreement was made. . . . " 'The meaning of the agreement of the parties is to be determined by the language used by them and by their action, read, and interpreted in the light of commercial practices and other surrounding circumstances.' " 1 WILLISTON ON SALES § 10-2, 431 (quoting 1 CORBIN ON CONTRACTS § 2.9 (rev. ed.)). See also § 1-203 (setting out the requirement of good faith and requiring the Court to interpret "contracts within the commercial context in which they are created, performed, and enforced"). Furthermore, the Code explicitly authorizes courts to look to the parties' course of dealings and performance and to the usage of terms in trade in interpreting the terms of the contract. §§ 1-205, 2-202, and 2-208.

As instructed by the commentary to § 2-612, the Court begins the substantial impairment analysis by looking to the "normal and specifically known purposes of the contract." § 2-612, cmt. 4. Reviewing the evidence presented, the Court finds that the primary purpose of the contract was to provide the plaintiff with four trailers for use with the Philips 1.5T scanner. With that in mind, the parties agreed that the trailers would be constructed in accordance with the specifications provided by Philips and that the trailer would be not be ready for delivery until Philips certification had been received.[106] Philips did not, however, ever certify the trailer for unconditional use with the bracing structure. Because the bracing structure prevented normal service of the scanner magnet, it was only approved as a temporary fix.[107]

The general rule in cases where third party approval is required as a condition of performance is one of strict compliance. . . . Such conditions will only be excused where the third party acts in bad faith or dishonestly. In the instant case, there was no credible evidence presented that Philips acted in bad faith by withholding approval. On the contrary, there was extensive evidence presented detailing the inherent problems with the long-term use of such a bracing solution, which demonstrated the reasonableness of Philips' refusal to certify the trailer. The bracing structure's shape and orientation prevented removal of the outer panels from the scanner magnet and made some repairs to the magnet more difficult and more dangerous. Furthermore, in order to perform certain repairs, the steel brace would have to be unbolted and removed. Once removed, the scanner magnet would have to be recalibrated and retested. Consequently, Philips' decision to refuse certification was entirely justified. Having found no evidence of bad faith or dishonesty on the part of Philips, the Court finds that defendant's failure to meet this condition constituted a breach of the parties' agreement. . . . Given that the central purpose of the trailer was to house a Philips 1.5T scanner, the failure to meet the standard for Philips' certification substantially impaired the value of the trailer. The Court, therefore, finds that this failure to conform to the parties' agreement, in and of itself, constituted a material breach.

In addition to violating the requirement that the trailer receive certification from Philips, plaintiff correctly asserts that defendant breached yet another term of the contract. The Court notes that the bracing structure also violated the parties' implied agreement regarding the design of the interior of the trailer. During the course of the parties' dealings both before and after the contract signing, MMDI reviewed numerous representations of the trailer's interior layout and design. Many of these drawings showed the location of the scanner and detailed the

---

[106] [8] Although the contract does not explicitly state that the trailers must be constructed in accordance with Philips' specifications, the parties have stipulated that the contract so required and the Court, therefore, begins its analysis from this premise. In addition, it is undisputed, indeed the defendant asserted repeatedly in its trial brief, that, under the contract, delivery of the trailer was conditioned upon certification of the unit by Philips.

[107] [9] Defendant argues that Philips did approve the trailer with the structure and that the testimony and documentary evidence reveal this to be so. However, review of the evidence convinces the Court that, in fact, while Philips may have approved the brace as a temporary solution to bring the wall-flexing problem within specification, it never approved the steel brace for permanent use with the Philips scanner.

location of every structure in the trailer. None of them, however, depicted a cage-like brace made up of multiple, large, steel beams surrounding the scanner mag-net. These drawings, when coupled with E&W's own statement that the trailer was cosmetically complete without the brace when it was presented at the open house, convince the Court that there was an implied agreement that the trailer would not have such a structure.

Furthermore, it is clear that, when the contract was executed, the parties both understood that the trailer's interior was meant to be aesthetically pleasing. It is the very nature of a mobile MRI trailer to function as an extension of the hospital it services. Since E&W was in the business of constructing trailers for mobile medical uses, it no doubt understood that the appearance of the trailer's interior could impact the comfort of MMDI's patients. Indeed, it is apparent that E&W realized such aesthetics were important to the value of the trailer, since, in its initial negotiations with MMDI, E&W included a cut-away drawing of the inte-rior of a mobile unit which read: "Spacious, efficient layout with clean, aestheti-cally pleasing interior." The Court, therefore, finds that the agreement between the parties required that the interior of the trailer be aesthetically pleasing.

Such a condition of satisfaction by one of the parties to the contract will only be excused if approval is withheld unreasonably. . . . In the instant case, upon review of photographs of the bracing structure and testimony of those experi-enced in this industry, and in light of the fact that the interior of the trailer should match that of a hospital and not a construction site, the Court finds that plaintiff's refusal to approve the aesthetics of the design was commercially reasonable. Given that an integral aspect of the trailer's function is to serve as a clinic for patients undergoing medical procedures, and given MMDI's clients' expectations after having viewed the trailer at the open house, such a defect in the trailer's interior also reduced the value of the trailer substantially.

Upon review of the evidence, the Court finds that the bracing structure sub-stantially impaired the value of the first trailer. Although the trailer met the ex-press technical Philips' specifications for wall-flexing, it was never certified by the manufacturer. The failure of this condition does not relieve defendant of li-ability because it was defendant's failure to properly construct the trailer that prevented certification. In light of the specific facts and circumstances of this case, the Court finds that this deficiency substantially impaired the value of the installment. When coupled with the trailer's failure to conform with the aesthetic requirements of the contract and the delay caused by the cure attempt, the Court holds that the cure attempt clearly constitutes a substantial breach within the meaning of § 2-612(2).

Substantial impairment, however, does not in itself justify rejection of the in-stallment. As noted above, the buyer must still accept tender if the defect can be cured and the seller gives adequate assurances. Under § 2-612, as opposed to § 2-609, it is incumbent upon the seller to assure the buyer that cure would be forth-coming. . . . Defendant has failed in this regard. The Court notes that neither E&W's statements during the December 13 conference call nor the letter sent the following day constituted adequate assurances. On the contrary, during the De-cember 13 conference call, Andrew Pike, the President of E&W denied the existence of a defect, disclaimed any continuing obligation to cure under the contract, and stated that he did not believe a better design could be made which would remedy the wall-flexing problem. Furthermore, on December 14, Mr. Pike again ignored the servicing problems that the bracing structure had caused, ignored the fact that the bracing structure had not been approved for permanent use by Philips, and reiterated his doubt that the design could be constructed in a more aesthetically pleasing manner. Under these circumstances, the Court finds that MMDI's rejection of E&W's cure on December 13 constituted a rightful rejection under § 2-612(2).[108]

3. Cancellation

a. *Substantial Impairment of Contract as a Whole*

The fact that rejection of one installment is proper does not necessarily justify cancellation of the entire contract. Under § 2-612(3) the right to cancel does not arise unless the nonconforming goods substantially impair the value of the entire contract. Indeed, as noted above, the very purpose of the substantial impairment requirement of § 2-612(3) is to preclude parties from canceling an installment contract for trivial defects. . . .

Whether a breach constitutes "substantial impairment" of the entire contract is a question of fact. Bill's Coal Co. v. Board of Public Utilities, 887 F.2d 242, 247 (10th Cir.1989). To make such a determination, the Court should consider "the cumulative effect of [the breaching party's] performance under the contract, based on the totality of the circumstances. . . ." . . . Ultimately, "[w]hether the non-conformity in any given installment justifies cancellation as to the future depends, not on whether such non-conformity indicates an intent or likelihood that future deliveries will also be defective, but whether the non-conformity substantially impairs the value of the whole contract." § 2-612, cmt. 6. Thus, the question is one of present breach which focuses on the importance of the nonconforming installment relative to the contract as a whole. If the nonconformity only impairs the aggrieved party's security with regard to future installments, s/he "has the right to demand adequate assurances but not an immediate right to cancel the entire contract." § 2-612, cmt. 6. The right to cancel will be triggered only if "material inconvenience or injustice will result if the aggrieved party is forced to wait and receive an ultimate tender minus the part or aspect repudiated." § 2-610, cmt. 3 (noting the test for anticipatory repudiation under § 2-610 is the same as the test for cancellation under § 2-612(3)).

---

[108] [10] Defendant argues that, as of December 13, it still had a right to cure under § 2-508 and that it was not required to give assurances unless plaintiff requested them in writing under § 2-609. The Court reiterates that, under § 2-508, defendant's right to cure was cut off on December 1. Furthermore, § 2-612, unlike § 2-609, does not require the aggrieved party to request assurances. In an installment contract, where the seller's right to cure is more expansive it stands to reason that the burden would fall on the seller to show that it had the present ability and the intent to cure any remaining defect. Allied Semi-Conductors Int'l Ltd. v. Pulsar Components Int'l, Inc., 907 F. Supp. 618 (E.D. N.Y. 1995). In the instant case, defendant gave no indication that it either had the capability to satisfy the contract or the will to do so. On the contrary, E&W's President, gave MMDI the impression that cure was not possible and indicated clearly that he was not required to do anything more under the contract. Under such circumstances, MMDI's rejection was rightful.

In the instant case, there is substantial evidence that one of the primary purposes of this contract was to provide MMDI with a fourth mobile MRI trailer so that it could meet the growing demand for its services. Thus, impairment of one of the four installments would have a substantial negative impact on MMDI. Moreover, an early delivery time was of primary importance to MMDI, as E&W was well aware. By failing to cure the November 28 breach on the first installment, E&W substantially delayed completion of the remainder of the contract which delayed MMDI's ability to begin use of the 1.5T MRI trailer it had promised to its customers at the open house on November 3. Having found that substantial injustice would be done to plaintiff if it were required to accept the remaining three trailers after substantial delay as satisfaction of the contract, the Court finds that plaintiff rightfully canceled the contract on December 18, 1995. . . .

4. Damages

Having found that plaintiff rightfully rejected defendant's tender of cure on December 13, 1995, and subsequently properly canceled the contract, the Court finds that plaintiff is entitled to damages. Plaintiff has requested reimbursement of the amount it already paid for the nonconforming installment in the amount of $384,500 as well as damages in the amount of $185,250 incurred for the lease of a rental mobile MRI trailer between December 19, 1995 and April 20, 1996, to replace the trailer E&W failed to produce. Under § 2-711, a buyer who has rightfully canceled a contract may recover, among other things: 1) the amount that has already been paid, 2) damages for "cover" as defined in § 2-712, and 3) any damages of nondelivery, including consequential and incidental damages, as defined by § 2-715. Under § 2-715, incidental damages include "any reasonable expense incident to the delay or other breach." Thus, plaintiff is clearly entitled to return of the amount already paid for the item it never received. Plaintiff is also entitled to recover the amount paid for a replacement rental unit. Though this amount does not constitute cover it is allowable as incidental to the delay produced by E&W's breach. Had E&W made conforming tender on December 13, 1995, plaintiff would not have been forced to contract with another company for the trailers and to wait until spring for the first one. The Court, therefore, finds plaintiff is entitled to both expectation and consequential damages under the Code and awards plaintiff a sum total of $569,250 for the breach of contract claim. . . .

VI. CONCLUSION

For the foregoing reasons, plaintiff is awarded expectation and incidental damages in the amount of $569,250. Plaintiffs claim of misrepresentation is deemed waived and dismissed. Defendant's counterclaim for damages is denied and its motion for judgment on partial findings pursuant to Federal Rule of Civil Procedure 52(c) is deemed moot.

NOTES AND QUESTIONS

1. *Cure under § 2-612:* The court decides that we need look only to § 2-612 to deal with cure in an installment contract. If we confine ourselves to the language of this section, what do we learn about "cure"? For example, could the seller argue that, under subsection (2), a buyer does not have the right to reject an installment even if its non-conformity substantially impairs the value of that installment, in cases where the non-conformity can be cured? The text says only "and cannot be cured." Literally, the statute seems to say that there is no right to reject if a non-conformity can be cured, *whether or not the seller cures it.* Section 2-612 leaves much unsaid about the subject of cure in installment contracts. However, look at Official Comment 5. Here we find a small essay about cure. It goes far beyond the text of § 2-612. To what extent is Official Comment 5 the law? Did it seem to influence the court's decision in *Midwest Mobile Diagnostic Imaging*?

The court says that we do not need to look at § 2-508 which deals with cure. However, it finds that the seller would not win if § 2-508 were applied. Suppose § 2-508 were applied to installment contracts. Would it make any substantial difference?

2. *Needy buyers and defective installments***:** Suppose MMDI needed these units immediately. The seller delivered the first one in the same condition as in the case. MMDI, however, took the first unit and put it into service to avoid breaching its contracts with the various local hospitals that were going to make use of the machine. MMDI also communicated with the seller and stressed its need for the rest of the units although it said they must comply with the contract specifications. Notice § 2-612(3)'s last sentence: "But the aggrieved party reinstates the contract if he accepts a non-conforming installment without seasonably notifying of cancellation or if he brings an action with respect only to past installments or demands performance as to future installments." Official Comment 7 is another essay that expands a great deal on the text of the statute. However, if you were serving as MMDI's lawyer, what would you tell its officials to do when the seller tendered the first defective unit when MMDI needed it to avoid breaching its own contracts with the hospitals? How much help does the text plus Official Comment 7 give you?

3. *The gaps in the drafting of § 2-612:* Peters, *Remedies for Breach of Contracts Relating to the Sale of Goods Under the Uniform Commercial Code: A Roadmap for Article Two,*[109] is still an often quoted important analysis of this part of the Code. Professor, and then Justice, Peters says that § 2-612

is reasonably clear at the extremes.

[A] If the breach is trivial and curable, the buyer must accept the installment and cannot categorically refuse further installments. He may, however, be able to reduce or postpone payments otherwise due upon delivery. . . . [She cites §§ 2-609 and 2-717 for this idea.]

[B] On the other hand, incurable breaches so substantial as to impair the value of the contract as a whole will privilege total rejection of installment and contract. . . .

[C] It is the middle ground which remains unnecessarily uncertain. Consider the following cases:

---

[109] 73 Yale L.J. 199, 225-227 (1963).

(1)   the defect is trivial and incurable;

(2)   the defect is trivial, curable, but not cured;

(3)   the defect is substantial as to the installment only and not curable;

(4)   the defect is substantial as to the installment only, curable, but not cured;

(5)   the defect is substantial as to the installment, and as to the contract, and seller actually tenders adequate cure. . . .

The present language of 2-612 is a law professors' delight. Introduced at the proper moment, when the class in commercial law needs to be shaken up, it guarantees at least two class hours of wandering through a maze of inconsistent statutory standards and elliptical cross references. . . .

Would the *Midwest Mobile Diagnostic Imagine* case be an example of the third, the fourth or another of Peters' categories?

c.   The Long Wait: Delay and Calling Off the Deal After One Has Given Extensions

FAIRCHILD STRATOS CORP. v. LEAR SIEGLER, INC.
United States Court of Appeals, Fourth Circuit
337 F.2d 785 (1964)

BELL, J. [The Hufford Corporation Division of Lear Siegler, Inc. [hereafter Hufford], appealed from a judgment awarding Fairchild Stratos Corporation [hereafter Fairchild], damages upon a finding that Hufford breached a special warranties contract. The court affirms the finding of a breach but not the amount of damages.]

The background facts of this case are rather complex; the legal issues are reasonably simple. Generated by Fairchild's invitation to bid, Hufford on January 4, 1960, submitted proposals to design, fabricate, and install a stretch wrap forming press in Fairchild's Hagerstown, Maryland, plant. The press, according to the district court, was to be "a sophisticated piece of machinery, the purpose of which was, with a high degree of automation, to pull and stretch a sheet of aluminum to conform to dies for half sections of boat hulls so as to cause the formation of aluminum half-boat hulls which could be thereafter welded together to make a complete hull for certain aluminum pleasure boats that [Fairchild] desired to manufacture and sell." In its proposals, Hufford made certain affirmations of fact which are germane to the present controversy.

Hufford stated that "the equipment will be designed and built so that *no hand work* will be required in the formation of parts." (Emphasis in original.) Hufford further stated that "the stretch forming equipment will be capable of producing formed boat hull halves at a rate of ten (10) parts per hour or six (6) minutes per part on existing dies constructed by Fairchild. . . ." This statement was qualified in two respects: first, by the statement that it could not be expected that the press would, immediately after installation, be capable of producing parts at the guaranteed rate until operators had been trained and the machine's functions refined, and second, as a consequence, Hufford was "to provide a qualified operating crew for a period of three (3) months to bring this facility to a full scale production capacity, simultaneously training [Fairchild's] personnel in operational procedures, maintenance, tooling, etc." The cost of providing the crew was to be borne by Fairchild.

Hufford agreed to manufacture and ship components in the order required for installation, so that installation could proceed concurrently with the latter stages of machine manufacture. Shipments were to start approximately four months from the date of receipt of the proposals and were to be completed two months thereafter. The purchase price was to be paid in six installments, five during the time that Hufford was shipping parts to Fairchild and installing them at Fairchild's plant and the sixth upon the completion of shipment, installation, and acceptance of the parts by Fairchild.

Fairchild issued a purchase order on January 21, 1960, accepting Hufford's proposals. Fairchild, in the purchase order, suggested that the cost of the operating crew be prorated, so that if less than three months was required, Fairchild's obligation would be accordingly reduced. Fairchild also suggested that shipments begin within four months from January 15, 1960, (the date of Fairchild's acceptance of the proposals by telephone) and be completed two months thereafter. Hufford agreed to these suggestions on February 2, 1960, and as of that date the terms and conditions of the contract were made explicit.

By the terms of the contract, Hufford was obligated to begin shipment of the components of the press on May 15, 1960, and to complete deliveries by July 15, 1960. This schedule was not met. Hufford's first shipment, that of rails for the press, was not made until July 12, 1960; the final shipment was not made until September 8, 1960; and not until November 21, 1960, did the press become operable. Thus, Hufford from the beginning was late in deliveries and acknowledged this fact in inter-company correspondence. For instance, a July 1, 1960, memorandum from Hufford's president stated:

> We are badly behind schedule on this machine. Our customer is in serious need for production from the machine to introduce their new line of boats in time to meet the marketing season.

The operating crew which was to be provided for a three month period arrived at Fairchild's plant and began work on the press on October 31, 1960. Initial attempts to stretch matching half hulls failed. Some measure of success was achieved on December 22, 1960, when a matching pair of half hulls was stretched; but it was found that when the half hulls were trimmed and put on the assembly jig, the tumble home area[110] lacked any formation at all. It was this area that was to present the major difficulties in the press' operation right up until Hufford's breach. After the December experience, Hufford undertook to redesign the machine assembly used in forming the tumble home area.[111] Discussions were

---

[110] [3] Described by the district court as the area in the stern of the boat "where the sides bend inward to join. It may be likened to the base of an isosceles triangle."

[111] [4] Formation of the tumble home area was to be achieved by imposing localized pressure on the aluminum sheets by the use of heavy pressure rubber rollers.

held within the period between January 6, 1961, and February 10, 1961, between representatives of the two companies to discuss problems in connection with the press and to try to work out an agreement as to what would constitute an acceptable half hull. Fairchild requested a completion date for the press' qualification, and Hufford's representative stated that Hufford expected the press to be ready for acceptance by April 7, 1961. Fairchild, waiving any claim it may have had to hold Hufford in breach at a prior date, orally advised Hufford that June 1, 1961, was the deadline for qualification.

Hufford, purporting to confirm the oral agreements between the parties, submitted a written memorandum in which it agreed to redesign and modify the machine element to provide configuration in the tumble home area and proposed a set of standards to determine whether the half hulls were in conformity with the die and with each other. Fairchild replied in writing, suggesting specific tolerances of stand off from the die in both the tumble home and forward areas of the boat and gave formal notice of the June 1, 1961, deadline. Hufford wrote and declined to accept specific tolerances as dimensional limitations, but it reiterated its memorandum position that the stand off in the tumble home area would be no more than that which could be pushed into position against the die by hand pressure. Hufford again acknowledged, without guaranteeing, its target date of April 7, 1961. On April 5, 1961, Hufford stretched two half hulls on the press. Although there was marked improvement in conformation on the second half hull, the stern area stood approximately two feet from the die, and it was impossible to force it into position by hand. Under these circumstances, Fairchild refused to give written confirmation that the machine was functioning properly.

Additional corrective work was done on the press by Hufford representatives and on April 15, 1961, they began stretching half hulls with Fairchild personnel as onlookers or helpers in loading and unloading the press. On April 24, 1961, Hufford representatives stretched three half hulls, and the third, as the most satisfactory, was left on the die for Fairchild's inspection. The following day, April 25, 1961, Hufford's representative advised Fairchild that he was ready for the qualification test. That same day, upon Fairchild's inquiry, Hufford's representatives prepared a test procedure and delivered it to Fairchild. It was agreed by the parties that the qualification run would consist of six half hulls of each hand rather than the ten upon which they had previously agreed.

The qualification run was never undertaken. Instead, Fairchild and Hufford reached an impasse. Hufford insisted that Fairchild accept the standards for forming sequence and procedures as set forth in Hufford's memorandum of April 25, 1961, and further insisted that if these standards were met by the qualification test, Fairchild must accept the press without regard to whether or not it could produce acceptable boat hulls. Fairchild adamantly refused, advising Hufford that it might undertake the qualifying test at any time but that Fairchild would accept or reject the press only on the basis of its operating characteristics and that there was no substitute for actual demonstration. This impasse came to a head on May 26, 1961, when Fairchild sent a telegram to Hufford stating that:

Fairchild awaits proof of press by actual operation by Hufford. June 1st nearly here. If Hufford fails to heed our warning regarding this firm deadline litigation will undoubtedly follow shortly.

Although duly warned, Hufford failed to meet the June 1, 1961, deadline, and on May 31, 1961, stated its willingness to "start acceptance test on June 5." Fairchild on June 2, 1961, notified Hufford not to send test personnel and on June 23, 1961, formally rescinded the contract. Thereafter, Fairchild brought this declaratory judgment action.

I. BREACH OF CONTRACT

In its memorandum opinion the district court exhaustively delineated the pre-contract negotiations between the parties, the causes for delay in shipment of the component parts, and the problems attending the installation and functioning of the press. We need not cover the same ground. Suffice it to say that the district court had ample support in the record to conclude that whatever delay in the final performance of the contract could be attributable to Fairchild, it "was considerably less than the extension of the date for performance granted by Fairchild" and that failure to meet the June 1, 1961, deadline was the fault of Hufford alone. Applying the law of Maryland, conceded by the parties to govern, the district court found the ultimate facts and conclusions of law to be as follows:

1. Hufford agreed to build and install a stretch press *and to complete shipment thereof* by July 15, 1960, and especially warranted the press to be capable of producing within three months from that date "... boat hulls halves at a rate of ten (10) parts per hour or six (6) minutes per part on existing dies constructed by Fairchild," and that the stretch press would be "... designed and built so that *no hand work* will be required in the formation of the parts."

2. Hufford failed to perform the contract or to fulfill its special warranty by June 1, 1961, notwithstanding that Fairchild waived performance by Hufford prior to that date, and had agreed to a less rigorous test to determine the acceptability of the stretch press.

3. Fairchild's refusal to extend Hufford's date of performance beyond June 1, 1961, was fair and reasonable under all of the circumstances.

4. Whether the boat press is capable of performance in accordance with the special warranty is unknown, but, in view of the repeated failure of the stretch press to perform, the conclusion is inescapable that it is extremely unlikely that the boat press possesses this capability, absent an actual demonstration that it possesses this capability.

5. Hufford had an obligation to demonstrate the production capability of the stretch press on or before June 1, 1961, and its refusal to meet that obligation was arbitrary, unreasonable and without legal justification, so that Hufford's refusal constituted a material legal breach of the contract.

6. Fairchild had a legal right to refuse to accept the stretch press and to rescind the contract. Fairchild *refused further performance of* the

contract on *and after* June 2, 1961, *and formally rescinded it by notice dated June 23, 1961,* because of Hufford's breach of warranty and Hufford's unjustified refusal to perform.

7. Fairchild is entitled to judgment on Hufford's counterclaim and to damages and supplementary declaratory relief, as hereafter discussed. (Italics represent modifications in initial findings by the district court.)

On appeal, Hufford makes three basic contentions with respect to the above ultimate findings: (1) that Hufford had no contractual obligation to demonstrate the press' capabilities by June 1, 1961; (2) that Hufford's failure to demonstrate by June 1, 1961, was not such a material breach of the contract as to warrant Fairchild's rescission; and (3) that Fairchild's failure to perform its own contractual obligation prevented rescission. We discuss these contentions *seriatim.*

(1) *Hufford's Contractual Obligations* Hufford strenuously contends that it had no contractual obligation to demonstrate the press' warranted capabilities by performing an acceptance test. While it is true that the contract did not provide by express language that Hufford must conduct such a test, the contract did provide that Hufford guaranteed a press that would produce ten parts an hour of such conformation to existing dies that no hand work would be required in their formation. These warranties, clearly spelled out in the contract, of necessity required Hufford to demonstrate their fulfillment. These warranties constituted the contractual standard that Hufford was required to meet by an acceptance test. Fairchild properly rebuffed Hufford's attempts to superimpose additional parts standards that were neither expressly provided for nor implicit in the terms of the contract. Fairchild was concerned with a satisfactory finished product; the method by which Hufford was to establish the press' capabilities was not Fairchild's concern. Fairchild had a right to expect a press of a guaranteed production rate producing parts of such quality as to require no hand work in their formation. Under the contract Fairchild could not insist upon more, but conversely, it had a right to demand no less.

(2) *The Materiality of Hufford's Breach* The district court, after finding that Hufford's failure to demonstrate the press' warranted capabilities by June 1, 1961, constituted a breach of the contract, further found that the breach was material and justified Fairchild's rescission. Hufford contends, however, that even if it be assumed that Hufford's failure to demonstrate the press' warranted capabilities amounted to a breach of the contract, such breach may not be deemed so material as to defeat the parties' just expectations. Hufford points to its willingness to tender performance on June 5, 1961, and argues that its purported breach resulted in only two lost working days—by no reasonable standard a material breach.

Hufford's argument carries some force. Generally "in the contracts of merchants, time is of the essence," *Norrington v. Wright,* 115 U.S. 188, 203, 6 S.Ct. 12, 29 L.Ed. 366 (1885), and the failure of the seller to meet a promised day of performance permits the buyer to rescind. We think, however, that the present contract may not be viewed as an ordinary mercantile contract. It is more akin to the contract discussed in *Beck & Pauli Lithographing Co. v. Colorado Milling & Elevator Co.,* 52 F. 700 (8 Cir. 1892). There, in considering a seller's action for the purchase price of custom-made stationery, the Eighth Circuit reversed a directed verdict for the buyer. The court declined to accept the buyer's contention that the seller's delay of one day in delivery constituted a material breach of the contract, for as the court stated:

> "[I]n contracts for work or skill, and the materials upon which it is to be bestowed, a statement fixing the time of performance of the contract is not ordinarily of its essence, and a failure to perform within the time stipulated, followed by substantial performance after a short delay, will not justify the aggrieved party in repudiating the entire contract, but will simply give him his action for damages for the breach of the stipulation. *Tayloe v. Sandiford*, 7 Wheat. 13, 17 [5 L.Ed. 384]; *Hambly v. [Delaware, M. & V.] Railroad Co.*, 21 Feb.Rep. 541, 544, 554, 557." 52 F. at 703.

We think that this was, as in the *Beck* case, a contract for "work or skill" and "time [was] not . . . of its essence." Thus, Hufford's delay of two working days in demonstrating that the press performed in accordance with its warranted capabilities, nothing else appearing, would not have justified Fairchild's rescission. But ours is a different case. It will be recalled that the contract contemplated that shipment of component parts of the press was to begin May 15, 1960, and was to be completed by July 15, 1960, at which time Hufford was given three months to bring the press up to its warranted capabilities. By October 15, 1960, Hufford was to have completed its contractual obligations and was to receive the final installment payment, and Fairchild was to begin mass production and distribution of aluminum pleasure boats. This schedule was not met, and in view of the sophistication of the press, the first of its kind, it seems improbable that the parties expected the schedule to be met to the day. Significantly, Fairchild waived a demonstration of the press' warranted capabilities until June 1, 1961. This date seemed an eminently reasonable deadline in view of Hufford's assurance, repeated in correspondence, that it would have the press ready by April 7, 1961. Thus, we are not faced here with the situation where a seller in a contract for "work or skill" fails to meet a specified day for performance. Rather we are faced with a seller who failed to meet a contract performance date, failed to meet a subsequent date set by himself, and then failed to meet an even later date set by the buyer. Even in out-of-the-ordinary mercantile contracts, there must come a day when a long suffering buyer may demand performance or opt rescission. In our case that day came on June 1, 1961. . . .

We conclude that the district court correctly held that Hufford's failure to demonstrate the warranted capabilities of the press by June 1, 1961, constituted a material breach of the contract and entitled Fairchild to rescind. . . .

NOTES AND QUESTIONS

1. *The reasons for Fairchild's actions*: Why did Fairchild let matters drag on for so long? Why did it then insist on calling off the deal? Lear Siegler contended that in July 1960 Fairchild was under pressure from its bankers to eliminate money losing projects. Its brief tells the story this way:

In January, 1960, plaintiff was negotiating to become the sole source of supply for aluminum boats for Sears, Roebuck & Company and was interested in launching a program of boats of its own design. Plaintiff was also building F27 airplanes and radar antennas. For use in these projects, plaintiff requested and received from defendant a quotation on the desired stretch press, and on January 25, 1960, issued to defendant a purchase order for it. On February 3, 1960, the plaintiff's Directors voted . . . to approve the purchase of the press. The basis of this approval was that a contract to assemble 1,300 boats for the 1960 Sears season had been received; and although the press was not involved in the Sears program for 1960, it would be required for the production for 1961 and subsequent years, as well as for plaintiff's own line of boats, its airplane and radar programs. The Sears program for 1961 contemplated a minimum of 10,800 and a maximum of 13,800 boats.

On February 23, 1960, the plaintiff entered into a contract with Miracle Marine, Inc., Theodore Cromp, President, under which Miracle Marine, Inc. was to participate in design, development, advertising, sales promotion, and the establishing of dealerships for a line of marine products to be manufactured by plaintiff. . . .

Commencing in February, 1960, while the stretch press was being manufactured, plaintiff undertook the manufacturing of boats for Sears and Miracle Marine using boat hull halves from a Sears inventory and those purchased from Allied Products Incorporated. This effort was pursued vigorously until a Sears request for stop work was received on June 17, 1960, because of structural failure of plaintiff's boats in tests at the Sears Test Center, Fort Meyers, Florida. Manufacturing for inventory was allowed to continue until July 19, 1960, on the assumption that structural fixes would resolve the problem. Subsequent testing of the structural fixes showed that the problem was not resolved, therefore, a management decision was made on July 19, 1960, to stop work on the boat program. . . .

On September 14, 1960, the Directors were told that the cooperative attitude of Sears would reduce by approximately one-half the indicated loss on the boat program and that expenses on the boat program had been written off as incurred. An attempt was then made to sell the boat program, including the press but the prospective purchaser, Miracle Marine, could not finance the purchase. Finally, on November 28, 1960, Fairchild advised all distributors that a decision had been reached not to renew their agreements at their expiration and immediate termination was invited. . . .

[Thus, when Fairchild canceled the contract on June 1, 1961, its] boat program had terminated much earlier. . . . No practical or production use was to be made of the parts [produced at the demonstration of the machine] and they were nothing more than test pieces to be run for demonstration purposes.

As we might expect, Fairchild's brief sees the story differently:

The 1960 Sears boat program had absolutely no connection with or relevance to the pending lawsuit.

Difficulties with the Sears boats did not mean abandonment by Fairchild of its own boat program, based on mass production from the Hufford press. Fairchild's own program was only abandoned after June 1, 1961, when the Hufford press failed to prove out. The Hufford [Lear Siegler] brief fails to differentiate between the Sears boat program and the Fairchild boat program which was geared to the boat press.

The trial judge responded to Lear Siegler's argument by saying that "Fairchild's activities can only be characterized as those of prudence and caution, because it was obvious to Fairchild throughout the period that it was communicating with its distributors and seeking to sell the stretch press that Hufford was badly in default under the contract. That Fairchild sought to minimize its damages does not mean that it caused a breach of the contract. At most, Fairchild had a motive in failing to waive all of Hufford's defaults under the contract, but if, as is hereafter concluded, Hufford breached the contract, Fairchild's motive in asserting the breach is immaterial."

2.   *Waiver and notice*: Is this decision consistent in reasoning and result with *Eastern Air Lines v. McDonnell Douglas, supra*? If Fairchild had given notice of its intention before it canceled the contract, would that have set the stage for the kind of negotiation so valued in the *Eastern Air Lines* case?

3.   *The Fairchild case under the UCC*: How would the *Fairchild* case be decided under the UCC? Under § 2-601, Fairchild would have had a right to reject the defective delivery. Under § 2-606(1)(b), Fairchild may have accepted the goods by failing to make an effective rejection. However, it is questionable whether Hufford ever made a delivery or tender to start the reasonable time for inspection running.[112] Under § 2-503(1), "[t]ender of delivery requires that the seller put and hold conforming goods at the buyer's disposition. . . ." This was not done.

Perhaps under § 2-208(3), the course of performance showed a waiver of the original delivery date. Section 2-209(5) allows a retraction of a waiver "by reasonable notification . . . that strict performance will be required of any term waived. . . ." Yet Fairchild probably cannot demand that Lear Siegler meet the original contract date after Fairchild waived it. Section 2-209(5) blocks retractions of waivers when they would be "unjust in view of a material change of position in reliance on the waiver."

Could Fairchild, after such a waiver and reliance, then set a reasonable deadline for completion of the machine and declare the contract at an end if Lear Siegler failed to meet it? Section 2-309(1) provides that the "time for shipment or delivery or any other action under a contract if not provided in this Article or agreed upon shall be a reasonable time." We might think that after a waiver which has been relied upon, the time has not been "agreed upon." Then Lear Siegler would have a reasonable time in which to perform. Official Comment 1 tells us "[i]t thus depends upon what constitutes acceptable commercial conduct

---

[112] *See* UCC § 2-602(1).

in view of the nature, purpose and circumstances of the action to be taken." However, this comment continues, saying "[a]greement as to a definite time, however, . . . may be found in a term implied from the contractual circumstances, usage of trade or course of dealing or performance as well as in an express term. Such cases fall outside of this subsection since in them the time for action is 'agreed' by usage." Fairchild's action in setting a new time and Lear Siegler's acceptance of it could be viewed as an agreement by course of dealing or performance.

The Code seems written to deal with contracts for delivery of "shelf goods." It does not seem too helpful when a seller and buyer enter a "quasi-partnership" to assemble a large custom-made machine in the buyer's plant and to work out difficulties as part of an ongoing process. We can always fall back on notions of agreement and the reasonable expectations of the parties. However, once the buyer allows the seller to miss deadlines for completion and gives the seller second and third chances in this kind of relationship, it is often hard to determine the reasonable expectations of the parties.

The following decision involves specially made goods, but something less than the long-term continuing relationship we found in the *Fairchild* case. The opinion was written by Justice and Professor Ellen Peters, an expert on the Uniform Commercial Code. (Be sure to notice her comments about the lawyers' "total disregard" of Article 2 of the UCC; this kind of lawyering before state appellate courts is much too common—at best, a client wins a case in spite of his or her lawyer.) We can ask whether Justice Peters reaches a sensible result and whether she finds adequate authority and help in the text of Article 2 of the Code to deal with a long-delayed performance.

BEAD CHAIN MANUFACTURING CO. v. SAXTON PRODUCTS, INC.
Supreme Court of Connecticut
183 Conn. 266, 439 A.2d 314 (1981)

PETERS, J. This is an action for the breach of a contract for the purchase of specially manufactured electronic parts. The plaintiff, The Bead Chain Manufacturing Company, the seller, sued the defendant, Saxton Products, Inc., the buyer, for failure to accept delivery of goods tendered pursuant to the contract of sale, and for failure to pay related costs and damages. The defendant denied the plaintiff's allegations and entered both special defenses and a counterclaim. After a trial to the court, judgment was rendered for the plaintiff on the complaint and on the counterclaim, and this appeal followed.

The underlying facts are not, on this appeal, in dispute. After more than a year of discussion, negotiation, and examination of handmade samples, the defendant Saxton in January, 1973, sent to the plaintiff Bead a purchase order for five million electrical components known as female contacts. The contract called for the production of special new tooling for these newly designed parts. The purchase order described the material out of which the goods were to be made and specified that they were to conform to "Sketch S-1318." A month later, a superseding design drawing was prepared by Bead and approved by Benjamin Jarmolow,

Saxton's chief engineer and vice president. The idea for and the design of the female contacts was initially provided by Jarmolow who made some changes in it subsequent to the original submission. After receipt of the initialed drawing from Jarmolow in February, 1973, Bead began to prepare for production, by manufacturing the necessary tooling and producing preproduction samples in conformity with the initialed drawing.

Although the contract called for the first installment of 250,000 contacts to be delivered by the middle of June, 1973, Bead first sent 100 preproduction samples to Saxton for its approval in August of that year. These samples were lost. When this loss came to light upon inquiry by Bead, further preproduction samples were delivered in October, 1973, and February, 1974. Small installments, 1000 each, of finished contacts were delivered in April and May of 1974. Until July, 1974, Saxton neither rejected any of these tenders nor made any complaint about their conformity with Jarmolow's design or about their timeliness. In July, confronted with a bill for the costs of tooling, Saxton for the first time stated that the contacts were defective because they lacked "memory" characteristics, i.e., the ability to return to their original shape after having been deformed. "Memory" characteristics were, according to Saxton, essential to the incorporation of this component in the electrical products which Saxton intended to market and to sell. Saxton never suggested what specific design modifications would be required to make the contacts acceptable. Further discussions proved fruitless, and this lawsuit ensued.

The trial court, after extensive proceedings, found all of the issues for the plaintiff, the seller Bead. It concluded that the contract required Bead to provide electrical contacts in accordance with the specifications in the initialed design drawing, rather than requiring Bead to design the contacts subject to the buyer Saxton's approval. Essentially, the court concluded that the basic responsibility for design rested with Jarmolow, Saxton's engineer, while Bead's responsibility was to manufacture goods in conformity with that design. . . . Finally the court determined that Saxton could not rely on contract provisions making time of the essence with regard to Bead's performance, when Saxton by its conduct, had waived compliance with the delivery dates specified in the purchase order. Having thus concluded that Saxton was in breach in refusing to accept the tendered female contacts and in refusing to pay the tooling charges stipulated in the purchase order, the court awarded the plaintiff Bead damages in the amount of $8411 plus interest and costs. The defendant Saxton's appeal challenges each of these conclusions, in whole or in part.

Before we address the merits of the defendant's claims of error, we must observe that this case has been presented with virtually total disregard of the relevant provisions of our statutes, in particular Article 2 of the Uniform Commercial Code, General Statutes § 42a-2-101 et seq. While it is true that the Code incorporates, by reference, supplementary general principles of contract law and of the law merchant, § 42a-1-103, such supplemental bodies of law cannot displace those provisions of the Code that are directly applicable. Article 2 applies to all contracts for the sale of goods, whether those goods be existing at the time of sale or whether, as in this case, they are to be specially manufactured. See, e.g., §§ 42a-2-106(1); 42a-2-201(3)(a); 42a-2-704(2).

The defendant's first claim of error challenges the court's conclusion that the defendant waived contract provisions concerning the time for delivery. The defendant's purchase order made time of the essence, providing, "The dates of delivery in quantities herein specified are of the essence of this order, and delivery must be effected within the time specified. If deliveries are not made on time and in the quantities specified, Buyer reserves the right to cancel and to purchase elsewhere and hold Seller accountable therefor." At the trial, the defendant relied on this provision both as a defense to the plaintiff's claim for damages and as the basis of its counterclaim. We agree with the trial court that this clause, in the circumstances of this case, neither excused the defendant's nonperformance nor supported its own cause of action "because the defendant did not exercise its right to cancel in a timely fashion."

Under the Uniform Commercial Code, "[r]ejection of goods must be within a reasonable time after their delivery or tender. It is ineffective unless the buyer seasonably notifies the seller." General Statutes § 42a-2-602(1). Although a buyer must be afforded a reasonable opportunity to inspect goods to determine whether they should be rejected; §§ 42a-2-606(1)(b); 42a-2-513(1); he must exercise his right to inspect in a timely fashion. Section 42a-2-602 establishes a policy that requires the buyer to act with reasonable speed in determining whether to reject and requires prompt implementation of rejection by notification to the seller. See White & Summers, Uniform Commercial Code (2d Ed) § 8-3, p. 309. The parties, in their contract, may establish guidelines to determine whether any action required by the Code has been taken within a reasonable time, but their agreement may only fix a time period "which is not manifestly unreasonable." § 42a-1-204(1).

Applying these statutory provisions to the case before us, we conclude that Saxton's protracted delay in rejecting the contacts tendered by Bead, coupled with its delay in notifying Bead of their alleged nonconformity, obligated Saxton to accept those deliveries. It would be manifestly unreasonable, in the circumstances of this case, to permit a printed time-is-the-essence clause in Saxton's contract form to extend for six months or more its opportunity to inspect and to reject.

As White and Summers point out (p. 312), one of the relevant factors in determining timeliness is the course of performance between the parties after the sale but before the formal rejection. This course-of-conduct factor in effect incorporates the common law principles of waiver which the trial court found persuasive in this case. . . .

Contrary to the defendant's assertion, Saxton's silence in the face of Bead's deliveries now precludes it from complaining about defects, such as delay in delivery, that were readily apparent at the time of tender. . . .[113]

The defendant's third claim of error is that the trial court could not reasonably have concluded that the defendant's conduct constituted a breach of the contract.

---

[113] [1] The defendant also adverts to a printed contract provision reserving to the buyer "The right to reject any material which does not fulfill the specifications of the order or time of delivery." This clause is as vulnerable as is the time-of-the-essence clause to the implications of §§ 42a-2-602 and 42a-1-204.

The court found the defendant in breach for refusing to accept the parts shipped to it in 1974 and for refusing to pay the tooling charges. We have already noted that Saxton failed effectively to reject the goods tendered to it. Saxton's rejection was wrongful[114] because, as the trial court found, the contacts that were tendered conformed to the design drawing initialed by Saxton's engineer, Jarmolow. Saxton might have bargained for a sale on approval; the trial court found that it had not done so.[115] A manufacturer of parts does not impliedly warrant that his goods will meet a buyer's special requirements unless, "at the time of contracting, the seller has reason to know any particular purpose for which the goods are required and that the buyer is relying on the seller's skill or judgment to select or furnish suitable goods." § 42a-2-315. No such implied warranty was alleged or proven in this case. Absent a statutory warranty or definitive contract language, the determination of what the parties intended to encompass in their contractual commitments is a question of the intention of the parties, unless the trial court could not reasonably have arrived at the conclusion that it reached. . . .

NOTES AND QUESTIONS

1. *The background as disclosed by the briefs*: Saxton issued a purchase order for 1 million female contacts to be delivered in four installments. The first was to be delivered on June 18, 1973, the second on September 17, 1973. The contacts were to be part of a solderless connector which had been designed by B. Jarmolow, who was the Chief Engineer of Saxton. Bead Chain Mfg. Co. did not assume any responsibility for the electrical or mechanical properties of the connector since Jarmolow did not disclose how it was to be used by Saxton. Jarmolow left Saxton before the pre-production samples were delivered in August of 1973. It is likely that no one at Saxton saw the solderless connector project as of great importance once Jarmolow left the firm.

Bead Chain received no response to the August delivery of pre-production samples and inquired about the matter. It was told they had been lost. It then sent samples on October 31st, but again it heard nothing. On February 27, 1974, again Bead Chain sent additional samples. It received no response until May 16, 1974, when Saxton's President wrote stating that after testing in Singapore, the part

---

[114] [2] The Uniform Commercial Code makes a distinction between a rejection that is ineffective and a rejection that is wrongful. An ineffective rejection is a rejection that is procedurally defective, the buyer having improperly delayed in rejecting the goods or, more typically, in notifying the seller. § 42a-2-602(1). The consequence of an ineffective rejection is that the buyer is held to have accepted the goods, § 42a-2-606(1)(b), and thereafter becomes liable for their purchase price. § 42a-2-607(1). A wrongful rejection is a rejection that is substantively incorrect, the buyer having improperly asserted that a tender is nonconforming when in fact the tender meets the specifications of the contract of sale. The consequence of a wrongful rejection is that the buyer is in breach and the seller is entitled to invoke any of the remedies available to a seller aggrieved by a buyer's breach. § 42a-2-602(3); § 42a-2-703. White & Summers, Uniform Commercial Code (2d Ed) § 8-3, pp 314-15. Operationally, the substantive scope of the buyer's right to reject is limited, and his rejection therefore more likely to be wrongful, when the contract of sale is, as here, an instalment contract. § 42a-2-612. Further exploration of these highways and byways must await another day.

[115] [3] Under the provisions of General Statutes §§ 42a-2-326 and 42a-2-327, dealing with the sales on approval, it is, furthermore, doubtful whether the right to disapprove an otherwise conforming tender would have survived the protracted delay in its exercise.

needed modification. This prompted unsuccessful negotiations, and Bead Chain sued.

2. *"Time is of the essence" clauses*: Lawyers often draft clauses that attempt to give their client the right to cancel a contract if there is any delay in performance. Consider a few examples used by major corporations:

a. *Buyers' Clauses*

(i)   The purchase order of Trane, a manufacturer of heating and air conditioning equipment provides:

DELIVERY DATE. Time is of the essence and if delivery of items or rendering of service is not completed by the time promised, the Buyer reserves the right without liability, in addition to its other rights and remedies to terminate this contract by notice effective when received by Seller, as to stated items not yet shipped or services not yet rendered, and to purchase substitute items or services elsewhere and charge the Seller with any loss incurred. Any provisions herein for delivery of articles or the rendering of services by installments shall not be construed as making the obligations of the Seller severable.

(ii)   The purchase order of Allis-Chalmers, a manufacturer of heavy machinery provides:

DELIVERY DATE. Shipment must be made to meet the required date specified. Time is of the essence. Production schedules established or commitments made to satisfy the required date must not contemplate production or procurement in advance of the current lead or procurement time required to meet such date, without the specific written approval of Buyer. On premature shipments, Buyer may return the goods at Seller's expense, and in any event payment will be withheld and any discount period will begin to run from the required date specified. Buyer, without waiving any other legal rights, reserves the right to cancel without charge or to postpone deliveries of any of the goods or services covered by this order which are not shipped in time to meet the required delivery date. . . .

b. *Sellers' Clauses*

The following clauses are used by the Xerox Corporation on their standard forms:

1.   DELIVERY—Customer shall accept delivery of . . . equipment at the installation address(es) indicated herein in accordance with the delivery schedule quoted by Xerox and in no event later than fifteen (15) days after notification by the appropriate Xerox branch that the Equipment is available for delivery. In case of multiple unit purchases, Xerox shall have the right to make separate deliveries. Xerox shall deliver the Equipment within 120 days of acceptance of this Agreement, provided that if Xerox fails to make timely delivery of any individual installation of Equipment, the Customer may treat this Agreement as breached as to such individual installation only. If at the time of execution of this Agreement, Customer requests delivery more than thirty (30) days later

than the delivery date quoted by Xerox, the Equipment Purchase Price shall be Xerox' Equipment price in effect at the time of actual delivery.

2.   DEFAULT—Time is of the essence hereof and if Customer shall fail to pay when due any installment, or otherwise fail to observe, keep or perform any provisions of this Agreement required to be observed, kept or performed, or if Customer ceases doing business as a going concern, or if a petition is filed by or against Customer under any of the provisions or chapters of the Bankruptcy Act or any amendment thereto, or if Customer shall make an assignment for the benefit of creditors or call a general meeting of creditors, or attempts an informal arrangement or composition with creditors or if a receiver or any officer of a court be appointed to have control of any of the property or assets of Customer or if Customer makes or has made any misstatement or false statement of fact in connection with this transaction, or if any of the foregoing occurs with regards to any guarantor, the unpaid time balance hereunder shall become immediately due and payable at Xerox' option and without notice.

If any of the foregoing occurs, Xerox shall have all of the rights and remedies of a secured party upon default under the Uniform Commercial Code or any similar law as enacted in the state where the equipment is located.

To the extent permitted by law, Xerox may recover the balance of all amounts due hereunder, enter upon the premises where the Equipment may be and render the Equipment unusable and/or take possession thereof and hereunder. In addition, Customer agrees at Xerox' request to assemble the Equipment and make it available to Xerox at a place designated by Xerox.

All rights and remedies of Xerox shall be cumulative and may be exercised successively or concurrently without impairing Xerox' security interest in the Equipment. Customer agrees to pay to Xerox reasonable attorneys' fees and legal expenses in exercising any of its rights and remedies upon default up to 15% of the unpaid balance and if such percentage is not so permitted, such other percentage or amount as is permissible under law. All the foregoing is without limitation or waiver or any other rights or remedies available to Xerox according to law.

One might ask, to what extent do Trane, Allis-Chalmers and Xerox Corporations gain greater rights by using these clauses than they would have if they said nothing about timely delivery or payment? To answer, one would begin by consulting UCC §§ 2-507, 2-503, 2-601, 2-602(1), 2-612; 2-508, 1-201(3), 2-309(1), 1-204(1) and 1-208. Xerox' rights as a secured creditor, and its rights in a bankruptcy or other insolvency proceeding are, of course, beyond the scope of this course.

The Restatement (Second) of Contracts deals with delayed performance in § 242. Two of the comments to that section suggest the Restatement's approach to common problems concerning delay that are found in the cases.

Substitute arrangements. It is often said that in commercial transactions, notably those for the sale of goods, prompt performance by a party is essential if he is to be allowed to require the other to perform or, as it is sometimes put, "time is of the essence." The importance of prompt delivery by a seller of goods generally derives from the circumstance that goods, as contrasted for example with land, are particularly likely to be subject to rapid fluctuations in market price. Therefore, even a relatively short delay in a rising market may adversely affect the buyer by causing a sharp increase in the cost of "cover." *See* Uniform Commercial Code §§ 2-712, 2-713. A less rigid standard applies to contracts for the sale of goods to be delivered in installments or to be specially manufactured for the buyer. On the other hand, considerable delay does not preclude enforcement of a contract for the sale of land if damages are adequate to compensate for the delay and there are no special circumstances indicating that prompt performance was essential and no express provisions requiring such performance. . . .

Effect of agreement. The agreement of the parties often contains a provision for the time of performance or tender. It may simply provide for performance on a stated date. In that event, a material breach on that date entitles the injured party to withhold his performance and gives him a claim for damages for delay, but it does not of itself discharge the other party's remaining duties. Only if the circumstances, viewed as of the time of the breach, indicate that performance or tender on that day is of genuine importance are the injured party's remaining duties discharged immediately, with no period of time during which they are merely suspended. It is, of course, open to the parties to make performance or tender by a stated date a condition by their agreement, in which event, absent excuse . . . delay beyond that date results in discharge . . . Such stock phrases as "time is of the essence" do not necessarily have this effect, although . . . they are to be considered along with other circumstances in determining the effect of delay. . . .

3. *Delays in building contracts*: Delays in building construction contracts raise special problems. *Marshall & Ilsley Bank*[116] points out that building construction often involves lenders. It also reminds us that completion dates often are waived.

On one hand, a builder or subcontractor's delay can be a material breach of contract. The owner or the general can terminate the contract and get someone else to complete the job. If the aggrieved party must pay more to complete construction, it can recover its increased costs as damages. On the other hand, an owner's failure to make payments may give the builder a right to suspend performance and in some situations to cancel and sue for damages. However, owners can delay performance in other ways as well. Often, they cannot get the necessary financing when they expected to have it, and they postpone the starting date until all the lenders have agreed to finance the project.

---

[116] 88 Wis. 2d 323, 276 N.W.2d 295 (1977).

Professor Halper notes that builders can be hurt by such delays:

> A contractor bids for work in the expectation that he will not be pre-
> vented from organizing it efficiently. He expects to have the freedom to
> determine the methods by which the project will be constructed and the
> sequence of thousands of tasks that comprise the construction of a build-
> ing. Within the framework of his bargain with the owner, he plans to per-
> form the work during advantageous times of the year. If the starting date
> is postponed or the progress of the work is delayed unexpectedly, the de-
> lay may affect the seasons during which the work is scheduled, the con-
> struction methods, the construction sequences, or any combination of
> them.
>
> For example, a contractor may have assumed that the construction
> period would start in the spring of one year and end in the summer of the
> following year. Thus, he would be building during two spring seasons,
> one winter, and two summers. A six-month delay in the starting date
> might change that work period to two winters, two springs, and one
> summer. Pouring concrete in the winter is more expensive than doing it
> in the spring or summer. In fact, severe cold and snow will make almost
> any kind of outdoor operation go more slowly. The cost differences may
> be substantial. . . .
>
> Notwithstanding the potential damage to the general contractor aris-
> ing from excusable delays, relatively few construction contracts provide
> for an increase in the contract price when such delays occur. Most con-
> tractors are content to take the risk of short interruptions of the work
> schedule caused by an excusable delay. That is, they are willing to settle
> for an extension of the time period in which they are required to perform.
> On the other hand, if the interruption lasts for a significant period of
> time, contractors usually seek much more drastic relief—the right to can-
> cel the contract altogether. . . .[117]

However, suppose *both parties* are responsible for the delay. In *United States
v. Klingensmith, Inc.,*[118] a subcontractor sued a general contractor for damages
caused by the general's failure to coordinate the work of its subcontractors. The
subcontractor contended that this caused delays which injured it. The trial court
found that the subcontractor's own actions also contributed to the delays. The
court concluded that neither party could collect delay damages from the other.
The Court of Appeals reversed this decision. It said that each party should be
able to recover to the extent of the injury caused by the other's delay. The subcontractor could recover whatever damages it proves that the general caused minus the amount of damages the general proves the subcontractor to have caused.

Such a rule protects each party from losses due to the delay of the other
throughout the period of performance. It also induces each party to avoid

---

[117] Copyright © 1988 by Warren, Gorham & Lamont, One Penn Plaza, New York, NY 10119-
4098 (1-800-999-9336). All rights reserved. Reprinted by permission of Warren, Gorham, & Lamont from Halper, *Negotiating Construction Contracts III*, 18 Real Estate Review 45, 48 (Summer
1988).
[118] 670 F.2d 1227 (D.C. Cir. 1982).

imposing losses on the other at any time during the period of performance. . . . Therefore, when both parties to a contract breach their contractual obligations by delaying performance, a court must assess the losses attributable to each party's delay and apportion damages accordingly.

Courts that follow this view still insist that the evidence must enable them to allocate the losses caused by each party's delay. Often this cannot be done, and the court will reject any claim for damages.[119] Other courts, however, say that when each party proximately contributed to the delay, "the law does not provide for the recovery or apportionment of damages occasioned thereby to either party."[120]

Some construction contracts contain "no-damage-for-delay" clauses. Often such clauses are found in standard form construction contracts entered as the result of competitive bidding on government contracts. Such a clause might provide: "The Contractor agrees to make no claim for damages for delay in the performance of this contract occasioned by any act or omission of the City or any of its representatives, and agrees that any such claim shall be fully compensated for by an extension of time to complete performance of the work as provided herein."

Professor Halper comments:

> Contractors who agree to such a clause carry a heavy burden. They are already vulnerable to the risk of cataclysmic events that neither they nor the owners can control. The no-damages-for-delay clause adds the risk of delays caused by the owner's behavior (subject to possible relief from a court or arbitration panel). This risk would be best left to an insurance company or a Mississippi riverboat gambler.
>
> Nevertheless, contractors routinely agree to execute contracts that include a no-damages-for-delay clause. The nature of the competitive bidding process and the need of contractors to provide work to cover overhead and keep their supervisory staffs employed causes contractors to take such risks.[121]

Courts have upheld these clauses, but they have intervened to regulate them. In New York such a clause will not "excuse or prevent the recovery of damages resulting from the contractee's grossly negligent or willful conduct, i.e., conduct which 'smacks of intentional wrongdoing.' "[122] Moreover, the New York courts allow a contractor to recover damages despite such a clause when the damages resulted from "uncontemplated delays caused by the contractee [the building owner]." They also will allow recovery when the contractee "is responsible for delays which are so unreasonable that they connote a relinquishment of the con-

---

[119] *Id.*

[120] *See, e.g.*, J.A. Jones Const. Co. v. Greenbriar Shopping Center, 332 F. Supp. 1336 (N.D. Ga. 1971).

[121] Halper, *supra*, at 49.

[122] Kalisch-Jarcho, Inc. v. City of New York, 58 N.Y.2d 377, 461 N.Y.S. 746, 448 N.E.2d 413 (1983).

tract by the contractee with the intention of never resuming it."[123] Why have the courts created these exceptions to no-damages-for-delay clauses?

5. "ANTICIPATORY BREACH" AND "REASONABLE GROUNDS FOR INSECURITY"

a. Repudiation and the Power to Walk Away From the Deal

B. M. FREEDMAN v. THE RECTOR, WARDENS AND VESTRYMEN OF ST. MATTHIAS PARISH OF LOS ANGELES
Supreme Court of California
37 Cal.2d 16, 230 P.2d 629 (1951)

Action for specific performance of contract to sell real property or for damages. Judgment for defendant reversed insofar as it denied plaintiff restitution of any part of his down payment, with directions to retry issue of amount thereof to which he was entitled; affirmed in all other respects.

TRAYNOR, J.—On October 8, 1947, plaintiff signed a deposit agreement with Clarence Urban, a real estate broker, for the purchase of two lots owned by defendant. He paid $2,000 down and agreed to pay the balance of $16,000 into escrow within 30 days. Both parties signed the escrow instructions a few days later. Although the deposit agreement was ambiguous with respect to title requirements, the escrow instructions provided that the property should be free of encumbrances except "covenants, conditions, restrictions, reservations, rights, rights of way, [and] easements . . . now of record." There was evidence that at the time plaintiff signed the escrow instructions he was informed of all covenants and easements affecting the property, but he took the position thereafter that he was under no obligation to purchase the property until the title had been cleared. On November 20th the escrow agent informed plaintiff that the title was clear except for an easement held by the water and power department across the rear 5 feet of one of the lots. This easement was abandoned the following April. On November 28th plaintiff wrote defendant and the escrow agent repudiating the contract and demanding the return of his deposit. He stated that the property had been misrepresented to him and that defendant had failed to clear the title as required by the contract. On December 19th plaintiff wrote defendant that he would take title and pay the balance of the purchase price as soon as the easement had been cleared. Defendant, however, on December 27th cancelled the escrow and thereafter sold the property to a third party for $20,000. Early in January plaintiff indicated his willingness to purchase the property and shortly thereafter brought this unit for specific performance. The trial court entered judgment for defendant and plaintiff appeals.

Plaintiff's main contention is that the contract was still in effect when he sought to perform in January after defendant had cancelled the escrow and ar-

---

[123] *See* Corinno Civetta Const. Corp. v. City of New York, 67 N.Y.2d 297, 502 N.Y.S.2d 681, 493 N.E.2d 905 (1986). *Compare* Wes-Julian Const. Corp. v. Commonwealth, 223 N.E.2d 72 (S.J.Ct. Mass. 1967).

ranged for the sale of the property to a third party. He bases this contention on the theory that time was not of the essence of the contract and that therefore defendant could not terminate his rights under it without giving him notice to perform within a reasonable time after the closing date, November 10th, fixed in the escrow instructions. This contention overlooks the fact, however, that plaintiff unconditionally repudiated the contract by his letters of November 28th. Even if it is assumed that under the terms of the escrow instructions plaintiff had a reasonable time to perform after November 28th, his repudiation on that date if acted upon by defendant before it was retracted, would excuse performance on defendant's part and make plaintiff's repudiation a total breach of contract. . . .

Although plaintiff made various oral proposals to continue with the purchase on terms other than those provided in the contract, he did not unconditionally withdraw his repudiation until after defendant, in reliance thereon, had sold the property to another. Plaintiff's letter of December 19th expressed willingness to perform the contract only after the easement held by the water and power department had been abandoned. The escrow instructions provided, however, that the title should be subject to easements of record. There was evidence that plaintiff read the instructions and was informed of the easement at the time he signed them. Since his letter of December 19th contained a condition with respect to the clearance of the easement that he had no right to impose, it did not constitute a withdrawal of the earlier repudiation. . . .

Accordingly, the judgment must be affirmed insofar as it denies plaintiff specific performance or damages for breach of contract.

NOTES AND QUESTIONS

1. *The conceptual problem of anticipatory breach*: On January 2nd, Businessperson hires Linguist to accompany her as an interpreter on an extended trip to various Eastern European countries. The trip is to begin on August 1st. On January 25th, Businessperson is promoted to a new position and the trip is canceled. She immediately notifies Linguist that their contract is canceled. Linguist files suit on February 10th, alleging a breach of contract. Can he sue in February or must he wait until August 1st when the contract was to begin? After all, Businessperson has only said that she will not perform in the future, and she might change her mind between February and the end of July. Reading the contract literally, Businessperson has promised to perform in August, and she cannot fail to perform in August until it is August. However, in *Hochster v. De La Tour*,[124] the English court allowed an immediate suit to be brought, and this rule is followed by almost all American jurisdictions. The Queen's Bench said that this rule would encourage employees to get other employment as soon as they could. However, the employee did not have to sue but could await the day of the employer's performance.

The Queen's Bench could have dealt with the problem without allowing a suit for "anticipatory breach" to be brought before performance was due. All the employee really needs in most instances is to be sure that he or she can take another

---

[124] 2 El. & B. 678, 118 Eng. Rep. 922 (Q.B. 1853).

job between January and August in our example without breaching the obligation to perform under the original contract. If Businessperson repudiates the contract before her performance is due, Linguist is free to walk away from their contract at that point. In the language of Restatement (Second) Contracts § 253(2): "Where performances are to be exchanged under an exchange of promises, one party's repudiation of a duty to render performance discharges the other party's remaining duties to render performance." Clearly, this kind of self-help to avoid or mitigate damages is important, and in all but a few instances it is more important than the right to bring a lawsuit before the time for performance arises.

   2. *Anticipatory and present breaches distinguished*: Suppose seller agrees to deliver one car on April 1st, ten on May 1st, and ten more on June 1st, and buyer promises to pay in specified installments for them. First, assume on March 20th, seller tells buyer that the deal is off and that no cars will be delivered. This would be an anticipatory breach since the repudiation came before the time specified for seller's performance. Second, assume there was no repudiation on March 20th, and seller delivered the first car on April 1st. However, seller fails to deliver the ten cars on May 1st and it is clear that seller will not deliver the ten cars due on June 1st. This would be a present breach of contract. (Anticipatory breaches are dealt with in UCC §§ 2-610 and 2-611, while present breaches of installment contracts are governed by § 2-612.) Why is *Freedman v. The Rector, etc.* an anticipatory breach case? The contract fixed the closing date as November 10th, and the repudiation came on November 28th. However, Justice Traynor's opinion assumes that performance would be required only when the owner demanded it. "Time is not of the essence" in real estate contracts, and since the owner had not demanded a closing before the repudiation on November 28th, it was anticipatory.

   Does the distinction between anticipatory and present breaches make a difference? For many purposes a breach is a breach. The aggrieved party may sue or walk away free of obligation. However, there are a few distinctions. Suppose that seller changes his or her mind and decides to perform the contract after repudiating it. Under § 2-611(1), the seller can reinstate the contract by retracting the anticipatory repudiation "unless the aggrieved party has since the repudiation canceled or materially changed his position or otherwise indicated that he considers the repudiation final."[125] After a present breach of contract, however, seller can reinstate the deal only with buyer's agreement. Seller, acting alone, cannot withdraw the repudiation even in the absence of reliance. Furthermore, § 2-725(1) provides that "[a]n action for breach of any contract of sale must be commenced within four years after the cause of action has accrued." A repudiation that is a present breach of contract starts the four year period running. However, § 2-610(a) says that after an anticipatory repudiation the aggrieved party may "for a commercially reasonable time await performance by the repudiating party." Would the cause of action accrue to trigger the statute of limitations before "a commercially reasonable time?"

---

[125] Restatement (Second) of Contracts § 256 states a similar rule for contracts other than those involving transactions in goods.

3. *Anticipatory breach under the UCC*: Suppose Mr. Freedman had contracted to purchase a recreational vehicle (RV) from Mr. Sam Rector for $18,000. Rector promised to clear several outstanding liens against the RV held by mechanics who had worked on it. $2,000 was paid as a downpayment by Freedman when the contract was signed in mid-October. Rector cleared the liens in mid-November. However, Freedman wrote Rector on November 28th, demanding his money back and saying that the condition of the RV had been misrepresented to him. On December 19th, Freedman wrote Rector saying he would pay the remaining $16,000 due just as soon as he could be sure that all the liens really had been cleared. On December 27th, Rector sold the RV to a third party for $20,000. The third party knew of the transaction with Freedman, and so the third party would take title subject to whatever rights Freedman might have. Freedman sues for replevin of the RV under UCC § 2-716(3), asserting that cover would be impossible since this model of RV is no longer made and Rector's vehicle has particular features which would be difficult, if not impossible, to find on available used RVs. Assume that Freedman's performance (payment of the price) was not yet due on November 28th because he would have had a reasonable time in which to establish that all liens had been discharged. Under UCC §§ 2-610 and 2-611 would the result be the same as reached in *Freedman v. The Rector, etc.*? If not, is there any reason to have results different under a contract for the sale of land from those under a contract for the sale of goods?

4. *What is a repudiation?* Suppose seller, before the time for delivery arrives, writes buyer and says, "I doubt whether I shall be able to perform, and indeed, the way prices are going I doubt whether if I am able I shall care to do so." Restatement (Second) of Contracts § 250, Comment *b*, says that "mere expression of doubt as to his willingness or ability to perform is not enough to constitute a repudiation. . . ."[126]

A more difficult issue is posed when one party insists on her rights under a contract as she sees them. Can a person repudiate a contract by insisting on an erroneous interpretation of a contract? Suppose that she honestly believes that her interpretation is the correct one, but a court later finds that she is wrong. Suppose most lawyers would say that the party's interpretation was plausible. To the extent that you can breach by insisting on a mistaken understanding of a contract, how can you maintain your position and avoid repudiating the deal? Consider the following cases:

---

[126] However, the Restatement (Second) suggests that courts should expand UCC § 2-609 to all contracts and allow a party who has "reasonable grounds for insecurity . . . with respect to the performance of . . . [the other party]" to demand adequate assurance of performance and to suspend performance until it is received. We will turn to this section of the Code later in these materials.

b. Insisting on My Interpretation of the Contract as Repudiation

BILL'S COAL CO., INC. v. BOARD OF PUBLIC UTILITIES OF SPRINGFIELD, MISSOURI
United States Court of Appeals, Tenth Circuit
682 F.2d 883 (1982), *cert. denied*, 459 U.S. 1171 (1983)

LOGAN, J. . . . [Bill's Coal Company, Inc. had entered into a long-term contract in 1970 to supply all of the requirements of coal of the Board of Utilities of Springfield, Missouri ("Utility"). The contract provided for minimum and maximum amounts. The contract provided that before the end of each calendar year, Bill's Coal was to notify Utility as to the price for the next year, the price to take effect on April 1. The contract also contained an interesting termination clause. Utility was entitled to solicit bids from other coal companies. If Utility received a bid at least 25% under Bill's Coal's price, then Utility could terminate the contract effective March 31. If the bid was at least 15% less, then Utility could terminate, but not until the following March 31. The contract required Bill's Coal to quote its price F.O.B. its Garland, Kansas mine. Utility paid the cost of transportation from the mine to Springfield.

In March 1980 Utility notified Bill's Coal it was invoking the termination clause. Bill's Coal responded by bringing suit for breach of contract, and requesting both damages and injunctive relief. The trial court held that Bill's Coal had committed a bad faith breach by repeatedly urging an interpretation of the termination clause which it knew was contrary to the intentions of the parties. During discovery Bill's Coal had inadvertently given Utility a document which outlined an attorney's plan to assert that the contract required a comparison of the Bill's Coal price at its mine-head with the competitor's bid for coal delivered to Springfield. This interpretation would have given Bill's Coal a huge cost advantage with respect to other suppliers. The trial court had held that Bill's Coal had adopted this position in bad faith, and that such a position amounted to a repudiation of the contract because it manifested an intention not to be bound by the terms of the agreement. Bill's Coal argued (1) that Missouri would not recognize a claim grounded in a failure to abide by the UCC's good faith provision, (2) that Bill's Coal's interpretation was plausible and therefore could not be made in bad faith and, finally, (3) that even if the interpretation was made in bad faith, this did not interfere with any act of performance and so did not constitute a repudiation.]

. . . We do not address the first two arguments Bill's Coal makes since we agree that this type of bad faith behavior is not to be regarded as a contract breach or repudiation. In urging an interpretation of the termination clause it knew did not reflect the parties' intent, Bill's Coal did not affect either party's performance under the contract. A breach of a contract is a failure to provide the other party with the goods or services as the contract requires. *See* 20A *Mo.Ann.Stat.* §§ 400.2-601 to 608, 400.2-612; *Restatement (Second) of Contracts* §§ 235, 241, 243, 245 (1981). A repudiation is a party's manifestation that it is not going to provide those goods or services when they will be due at some future date. *See* 20A *Mo.Ann.Stat.* § 400.2-610; *Restatement (Second) of Contracts* § 250 (1981). The bad faith urging of a particular interpretation of a termination clause is neither a failure to perform contract obligations (breach) nor an indication those obligations will not be performed in the future (repudiation).

We can envision situations in which bad faith conduct might be actionable: for instance, if the Utility solicited bids from competing coal companies and Bill's Coal in some way coerced competitors into not submitting bids. That might constitute such a breach of Bill's Coal's good faith obligation as to allow the Utility to cancel the contract.[127] But the mere urging of a particular interpretation is quite different. If a seller's interpretation of a termination clause is ludicrous, the buyer should ignore it; if the interpretation might prevail in a court of law, the seller has the right to urge it. If the party that wishes to invoke the termination clause is unsure of the merits of the other party's interpretation, it can either accept that interpretation, rely on its own interpretation, or obtain a declaratory judgment as to the meaning of the contract language.

Since we have found the trial court erred in its application of the law on the only issue it found against Bill's Coal in Phase II of the trial, the injunction we ordered reinstated should be continued in effect. . . .

Our review of the trial court's rulings has been restricted to the one issue treated in this opinion. We express no view on its other rulings in Phase I or II of the trial. The Utility raises questions in its motion for clarification and instructions concerning price to be paid and whether additional bond should be required. These should be addressed by the trial court after remand, in light of the conclusions in this opinion and the trial court's other rulings interpreting the contract.

The case is hereby remanded for further proceedings consistent with this opinion.

[BARRETT, J.'s dissenting opinion, published at 685 F.2d 360 (1982)]

It is my view that the District Court correctly concluded that Bill's Coal's demand for more than it was entitled under the contract with Utility constitutes a repudiation under § 2-610 of the Missouri Uniform Commercial Code (20A U.A.M.S. § 2-610), fully justifying the Court's January 29, 1982, order dissolving the injunction. Thus, I would affirm the District Court.

The main issue generating this litigation involves the "take-out" provision of the 1979 amendment to the coal contract. That provision states, *inter alia*, that if Utility can secure a bid . . . "at a delivered price of at least 25% less than the price quoted by [Bill's Coal] (adjusted to eliminate the depreciation credit referred to in paragraph 6) . . . [Utility] may by written notice cancel this agreement as of the end of the then current fiscal year."

---

[127] [2] The only case the Utility cites that recognizes a cause of action for bad faith in connection with a termination clause, Baker v. Ratzlaff, 1 Kan.App.2d 285, 564 P.2d 153 (1977), is distinguishable. *Baker* holds that a party invoking a clause permitting termination in the event of non-payment committed a breach of the good faith obligation if the party did not first request payment. A party's taking such affirmative acts is quite different from a party's urging a particular interpretation of the termination clause.

Utility had until March of the year to exercise the take-out provision. At a meeting later in the same day that the 1979 amendment was drafted, an attorney representing Bill's Coal noted that the contract language could be viewed to require a comparison of Bill's Coal quoted f.o.b. mine price to any competitor's delivered price. However, this attorney stated then that such was not the intention of the parties; rather, the parties agreed and intended that a comparison under the take-out clause would be delivery price versus delivery price.

In December, 1979, Bill's Coal became aware that Utility was going to solicit bids and attempt to utilize the "take-out" provision. Bill's Coal then formulated a "plan" to block a take-out by insisting that Utility make a comparison of Bill's Coal's f.o.b. mine price to competitors' delivered price. When Bill's Coal supplied Utility with its f.o.b. mine price for 1980, it also "demanded" that Utility make the bid comparison in accordance with Bill's Coal's "plan." An agent of Utility vehemently rejected Bill's Coal's proposed comparison formula and informed Bill's Coal if it insisted on the formula that Utility would see Bill's Coal in court.

Inasmuch as Bill's Coal's mine is located substantially closer to Springfield's power plant than any of its competitors, a comparison between Bill's Coal's f.o.b. mine price to competitor's delivery price could hardly, if ever, result in a bid sufficient to trigger the take-out provision. Bill's Coal's f.o.b. mine price was substantially higher than any competitor's f.o.b. mine price.

Utility proceeded to solicit bids and to compare Bill's Coal's f.o.b. mine price to competitors' f.o.b. mine price. On March 27, 1980, Utility gave Bill's Coal notice of termination under the take-out clause. Utility thereafter filed a declaratory judgment action against Bill's Coal seeking a declaration of the relative rights and liabilities of the parties under the 1979 amendment. Bill's Coal filed a separate action against Utility for breach of contract. Bill's Coal's action was subsequently consolidated with Utility's action. In all of its pleadings, Bill's Coal held fast to its interpretation of the comparison language of the take-out clause.

The parties agreed that the litigation should be divided into three phases. Phase I involved the interpretation of the take-out clause. The Court concluded that the take-out provision called for a delivery price versus delivery price comparison. It was only after this court finding that Bill's Coal finally abandoned its interpretation of the take-out clause. *It amended its pleadings to assert that the contract language was ambiguous and that the parties had always intended a delivery versus delivery price comparison. In response, Utility amended its complaint to allege anticipatory repudiation and bad faith on Seller's part.*

Phase II was conducted to determine liability. The Court found anticipatory repudiation by virtue of Bill's Coal's demand that Utility use a different price comparison than that which the parties had agreed to. The District Court recognized that although this is an unusual case on its facts, for anticipatory repudiation, the law appears clear that if a party, in bad faith, demands performance of the other party beyond the terms of the contract, and the demanding party conditions his own performance on the injured parties' performance of the additional terms, then there is an anticipatory repudiation by the demanding party. The District Court thus found anticipatory repudiation. It specifically found that Bill's

Coal's interpretation of the take-out provision was the result of bad faith in that it was not an honestly held interpretation because Bill's Coal had agreed to a different interpretation. The Court also found a separate cause of action for bad faith.

Based upon these conclusions, the District Court dissolved the injunction, and rendered detailed findings of fact and conclusions of law with which I agree. Specifically, the Court found that because Bill's Coal admitted that it knew at all times that the parties had in fact agreed to the delivery price versus delivery price interpretation of the "take-out" provision of the 1979 amendment, Bill's Coal did not entertain an honest mistake of contract interpretation when it insisted on its f.o.b. versus delivery price position. This, the Court concluded, was a bad faith contention. I agree.

When a party practices fraud, *i.e.*, assertion of a position it knows to be absolutely contrary to the agreement, it repudiates the contract if this false assertion, as here, impairs the value of the contract. This principle applies here inasmuch as the practical effect of Bill's Coal's false interpretation was to block any "take-out" and thus lock Utility into Bill's Coal's price. It follows that by forcing Utility to pay what may well be exorbitant prices under the contract, Bill's Coal impaired the value of the contract to Utility.

The majority opinion anchors its holding, it seems to me, on the proposition that Bill's Coal has "performed" under the contract because it has, at all times, delivered coal to Utility. This holding does not meet the issues addressed by the District Court relating to performance. What was the full performance promised? In terms of money values, it had to be Bill's Coal's promise to permit Utility to exercise the "take-out" provision in good faith by obtaining bona fide competitive bids based on delivery price versus delivery price. This plain intent was absolutely frustrated by the bad faith practiced by Bill's Coal. This bad faith could not be corrected. Accordingly, we are not here dealing with mere "deviations" from full performance which are inadvertent or unintentional. The "deviation" here is all pervasive and due to Bill's Coal's bad faith. It impaired the structure of the contract as a whole. It cannot be "repaired" and thus the contract must be terminated.

We have here an admitted, acknowledged manifestation on the part of Bill's Coal to frustrate the "termination" clause of the contract. The intention is unequivocal. *Restatement of Contracts*, (First), §§ 314, 315 and 318 (1932), as supplemented, states that in a bilateral contract, one who has failed, without justification, to perform all or any part of what is promised in a contract has breached it (here, Bill's Coal's refusal to recognize the right of Utility to receive proper competitive bids) and, further, that one who, like Bill's Coal, has prevented or hindered Utility from determining whether it is bound to the condition of further purchases of coal from Bill's Coal (performance of a return promise to purchase) is guilty of an anticipatory breach which constitutes a total breach of contract. Under § 318(a) it is stated that ". . . a positive statement to the promisee or other person having a right under the contract, indicating that the promisor will not or cannot substantially perform his contractual duties" constitutes an anticipatory breach.

UCC § 2-610, Comment 1 states that "anticipatory repudiation centers upon an overt communication of intention or an action which renders performance impossible or demonstrates a clear determination not to continue with performance." In *Neal-Cooper Grain Co. v. Texas Gulf Sulphur Co.*, 508 F.2d 283 (7th Cir. 1974), relied upon by the trial court, it was held that although a demand by a party to a contract for more than the contract calls for in the way of counter-performance is not in itself a repudiation, when a fair reading leads to the conclusion that it amounts to a statement of intention not to perform except on conditions which *go beyond the contract, it becomes a repudiation.* "In order to constitute an anticipatory breach of contract, there must be a definite and unequivocal manifestation of intention on the part of the repudiator that he will not render the promised performance *when the time fixed for it in the contract arrives.*" 4 Corbin on Contracts, § 973, p. 905. [Emphasis supplied]. And, "Where the two contracting parties differ as to the interpretation of a contract . . . an offer to perform in accordance with his own interpretation . . . [will] constitute such a breach, [if] the offer . . . be accompanied by a clear manifestation of intention not to perform in accordance with any other interpretation." 4 Corbin on Contracts, § 973 at p. 911.

I would . . . affirm the District Court.

NOTES AND QUESTIONS

1. *A duty to negotiate in good faith about modifying a contract*? In *Missouri Public Service Co. v. Peabody Coal Co.*,[128] Peabody and Missouri Public Service entered a contract in 1967, under which Peabody agreed to supply the requirements of coal at certain power plants for ten years. Even though the contract contained an escalator clause, it became very unprofitable for Peabody Coal. Peabody Coal asked to renegotiate, but was not satisfied with the price adjustment which Missouri Public Service offered. Missouri Public Service brought an action to require that Peabody Coal honor its contract. Peabody Coal showed its losses to be in excess of $3.4 million dollars (though the same inflationary events had caused a threefold increase in the value of its coal reserves).

Peabody asserted that Missouri Public Service had acted in bad faith in refusing to agree to a reasonable modification of the price under the contract. In rejecting this argument, the appellate court said:

> [T]he fact that foreseeable economic trends or developments resulted in loss of anticipated profits or, as here claimed, actual financial loss, does not prevent Public Service from refusal of a modification of price and to take advantage of a good bargain. Such is particularly true here, for the reason that Public Service is a utility impressed with public interest and any increase in its cost in producing electricity would reflect in its rates to its public and private consumers. For this reason, its good faith, if it had agreed to a gratuitous modification upward of its costs, might properly be called into question.

The court also rejected Peabody's claim that it was excused under UCC § 2-615. It provides for an excuse "if performance as agreed has been made impracti-

---

[128] 583 S.W.2d 721 (Mo. Ct. App. 1979), *cert. denied* 444 U.S. 865 (1980).

cable by the occurrence of a contingency the nonoccurrence of which was a basic assumption on which the contract was made." Peabody was an experienced bargainer in long-term coal contracts. It had agreed to the escalator clause based on a particular price index, and thus it had assumed the risk of the index' adequacy. We will consider § 2-615 in more detail later. Of course, if Peabody had been excused by this section, then it would have had no duty to supply coal under the original contract. Its demands then would be just bargaining about a new contract rather than the repudiation of an old one.

2. _A demand for a modification as an anticipatory breach_: In _Unique Systems, Inc. v. Zotos International, Inc._,[129] Duane Lilja was the chief officer of Unique Systems, Inc. which held a patent on a multi-station hair spray system intended for use in beauty salons. However, Unique lacked the resources needed to manufacture and market the systems. Zotos International, Inc. is a major manufacturer and distributor of shampoos, permanents and setting lotions for the professional hair dressing field.

Unique and Zotos entered a contract. Lilja was to develop, manufacture, and place in inventory hair spray systems. Zotos was to buy 15,000 systems over a two-year period, and it had an option to buy 7,500 systems a year for the following two years. The actual stocking and distribution of the systems would begin with what the contract called "month one," a "mutually agreed date in the year 1974."

During 1974, several unanticipated delays occurred, some of which were the fault of Lilja, some the fault of Zotos, and some the fault of third parties. By January of 1975, "month one" still had not been set. In early 1975, Lilja told Zotos that he was ready to receive an order. However, other firms had introduced similar systems, and Zotos feared that the market had softened. Zotos demanded that Lilja demonstrate that its system would work. In July of 1975, a test was held, and Zotos' officials agreed that the system complied with the warranties in the contract. However, they refused to put their approval in writing or set "month one" unless Lilja would agree to a test marketing of the systems. There were proposals and counter-proposals, but Zotos insisted on test marketing before it would place orders.

Lilja notified Zotos that the contract had been repudiated and sued. The trial court entered a judgment in favor of Lilja and Unique Systems for $398,760, and Zotos appealed. The judgment was affirmed. The court found there was a repudiation under UCC § 2-610. "If a party to a contract demands of the other party a performance to which he has no right under the contract and states definitely that, unless his demand is complied with, he will not render his promised performance, an anticipatory repudiation has been committed. . . . When Zotos told Lilja . . . that it would not proceed until market tests were performed with results subject to Zotos's approval, Zotos repudiated the contract and was in total breach. No market tests were required by the contract, a fact that Zotos admits that it knew."

---

[129] 622 F.2d 373 (8th Cir. 1980).

c. Anticipatory Repudiation and the Calculation of Damages

Suppose Buyer and Seller make a contract on November 1st for the sale of goods which are to be delivered several years later in installments. On December 1st, Buyer tells Seller that it will not perform the contract because the project for which the goods are to be purchased has been cancelled. Seller's officials are angry because they have invested engineering and selling effort in negotiating the deal and turned down other business opportunities. They seek to persuade Buyer's officials to reconsider and to reinstate the contract. On March 1st of the next year, Buyer's representatives tell Seller that the deal is off and there is no chance to going forward with it. How would damages be calculated under the Uniform Commercial Code? Consider the following case:

COSDEN OIL & CHEMICAL CO. v. KARL O. HELM AKTIENGESELLSCHAFT
United States Court of Appeals, Fifth Circuit
736 F.2d 1064 (1984)

REAVLEY, J. We must address one of the most difficult interpretive problems of the Uniform Commercial Code—the appropriate time to measure buyer's damages where the seller anticipatorily repudiates a contract and the buyer does not cover. The district court applied the Texas version of Article 2 and measured buyer's damages at a commercially reasonable time after seller's repudiation. We affirm, but remand for modification of damages on another point.

I. CASE HISTORY

This contractual dispute arose out of events and transactions occurring in the first three months of 1979, when the market in polystyrene, a petroleum derivative used to make molded products, was steadily rising. During this time Iran, a major petroleum producer, was undergoing political turmoil. Karl O. Helm Aktiengesellschaft (Helm or Helm Hamburg), an international trading company based in Hamburg, West Germany, anticipated a tightening in the world petrochemical supply and decided to purchase a large amount of polystyrene. Acting on orders from Helm Hamburg, Helm Houston, a wholly-owned subsidiary, initiated negotiations with Cosden Oil & Chemical Company (Cosden), a Texas-based producer of chemical products, including polystyrene.

Rudi Scholtyssek, general manager of Helm Houston, contacted Ken Smith, Cosden's national sales coordinator, to inquire about the possibility of purchasing quantities of polystyrene. Negotiating over the telephone and by telex, the parties agreed to the purchase and sale of 1250 metric tons of high impact polystyrene at $.2825 per pound and 250 metric tons of general purpose polystyrene at $.265 per pound. The parties also discussed options on each polystyrene type. On January 18, 1979, Scholtyssek met with Smith in Dallas, leaving behind two purchase confirmations. Purchase confirmation 04 contained the terms for high impact and 05 contained the terms for general purpose. Both confirmations contained the price and quantity terms listed above, and specified the same delivery and payment terms. The polystyrene was to be delivered during January and February in one or more lots, to be called for at Helm's instance. Confirmation 04 specified that Helm had an option for an additional 1000 metric tons of high impact, and confirmation 05 expressed a similar option for 500 metric tons of general purpose. The option amounts were subject to the same terms, except that delivery was to be during February and March. The options were to be declared, at the latest, by January 31, 1979.

On January 22, Helm called for the first shipment of high impact under order 04, to be delivered FAS at a New Jersey port to make a January 29 shipment date for a trans-Atlantic voyage. On January 23, Helm telexed Cosden to declare the options on purchase orders 04 and 05, designating the high impact option quantity as order 06 and the general purpose option quantity as order 07. After exercising the options, Helm sent purchase confirmations 06 and 07, which Cosden received on January 29. That same day Helm Houston received confirmations 04 and 05, which Smith had signed.

Cosden shipped 90,000 pounds of high impact polystyrene to Helm on or about January 26. Cosden then sent an invoice for that quantity to Helm Houston on or about January 31. The front of the invoice stated, "This order is subject to the terms and conditions shown on the reverse hereof." Among the "Conditions of Sale" listed on the back of the invoice was a force majeure provision. Helm paid for the first shipment in accordance with the agreement.

As Helm had expected, polystyrene prices began to rise in late January, and continued upward during February and March. Cosden also experienced problems at two of its plants in late January. Normally, Cosden supplied its Calumet City, Illinois, production plant with styrene monomer, the "feed stock" or main ingredient of polystyrene, by barges that traveled from Louisiana up the Mississippi and Illinois Rivers to a canal that extended to Cosden's plant. Due to the extremely cold winter of 1978-79, however, the Illinois River and the canal froze, suspending barge traffic for a few weeks. A different problem beset Cosden's Windsor, New Jersey, production plant. A new reactor, used in the polystyrene manufacturing process, had recently been installed at the Windsor plant. A manufacturing defect soon became apparent, however, and Cosden returned the reactor to the manufacturer for repair, which took several weeks. At the time of the reactor breakdown, Cosden was manufacturing only general purpose at the Windsor plant. Cosden had planned on supplying Helm's high impact orders from the Calumet City plant.

Late in January Cosden notified Helm that it was experiencing problems at its production facilities and that the delivery under 04 might be delayed. On February 6, Smith telephoned Scholtyssek and informed him that Cosden was cancelling orders 05, 06, and 07 because two plants were "down" and it did not have sufficient product to fill the orders. Cosden, however, would continue to honor order 04. Smith confirmed the cancellation in a letter dated February 8, which Scholtyssek received on or about February 12. After Helm Hamburg learned of Cosden's cancellation, Wolfgang Gordian, a member of Helm's executive board, sent an internal memorandum to Helm Houston outlining a strategy. Helm would urge that Cosden continue to perform under 04 and, after receiving the high impact polystyrene, would offset amounts owing under 04 against Helm's damages for nondelivery of the balance of polystyrene. Gordian also instructed Helm

Houston to send a telex to Cosden. Following instructions, Scholtyssek then requested from Cosden "the relevant force majeure certificate" to pass on to Helm Hamburg. Helm also urged Cosden to deliver immediately several hundred metric tons of high impact to meet two February shipping dates for which Helm had booked shipping space.

In mid-February Cosden shipped approximately 1,260,000 pounds of high impact to Helm under order 04. This shipment's invoice, which also included the force majeure provision on the reverse side, specified that Helm owed $355,950, due by March 15 or 16. After this delivery Helm requested that Cosden deliver the balance under order 04 for shipment on a vessel departing March 16. Cosden informed Helm that a March 16 delivery was not possible. On March 15, citing production problems with the 04 balance, Cosden offered to sell 1000 metric tons of styrene monomer at $.41 per pound. Although Cosden later lowered the price on the styrene monomer, Helm refused the offer, insisting on delivery of the balance of 04 polystyrene by March 31 at the latest. Around the end of March, Cosden informed Scholtyssek by telephone that it was cancelling the balance of order 04.

Cosden sued Helm, seeking damages for Helm's failure to pay for delivered polystyrene. Helm counterclaimed for Cosden's failure to deliver polystyrene as agreed. The jury found on special verdict that Cosden had agreed to sell polystyrene to Helm under all four orders. The jury also found that Cosden anticipatorily repudiated orders 05, 06, and 07 and that Cosden cancelled order 04 before Helm's failure to pay for the second 04 delivery constituted a repudiation. The jury fixed the per pound market prices for polystyrene under each of the four orders at three different times: when Helm learned of the cancellation, at a commercially reasonable time thereafter, and at the time for delivery.

The district court, viewing the four orders as representing one agreement, determined that Helm was entitled to recover $628,676 in damages representing the difference between the contract price and the market price at a commercially reasonable time after Cosden repudiated its polystyrene delivery obligations and that Cosden was entitled to an offset of $355,950 against those damages for polystyrene delivered, but not paid for, under order 04.

II. TIME FOR MEASURING BUYER'S DAMAGES

Both parties find fault with the time at which the district court measured Helm's damages for Cosden's anticipatory repudiation of orders 05, 06, and 07.[130] Cosden argues that damages should be measured when Helm learned of the repudiation. Helm contends that market price as of the last day for delivery—or the time of performance—should be used to compute its damages under the contract-market differential. We reject both views, and hold that the district court correctly measured damages at a commercially reasonable point after Cosden informed Helm that it was cancelling the three orders.

---

[130] [5] The damages measurement problem does not apply to Cosden's breach of order 04, which was not anticipatorily repudiated. The time Helm learned of Cosden's intent to deliver no more polystyrene under 04 was the same time as the last date of performance, which had been extended to the end of March.

Article 2 of the Code has generally been hailed as a success for its comprehensiveness, its deference to mercantile reality, and its clarity. Nevertheless, certain aspects of the Code's overall scheme have proved troublesome in application. The interplay among §§ 2.610, 2.711, 2.712, 2.713, and 2.723, Tex. Bus. & Com. Code Ann. (Vernon 1968), represents one of those areas, and has been described as "an impossible legal thicket." J. White & R. Summers, *Uniform Commercial Code* § 6-7 at 242 (2d ed. 1980). The aggrieved buyer seeking damages for seller's anticipatory repudiation presents the most difficult interpretive problem.[131] Section 2.713 describes the buyer's damages remedy:

Buyer's Damages for Non-Delivery or Repudiation

   (a) Subject to the provisions of this chapter with respect to proof of market price (§ 2.713), the measure of damages for non-delivery or repudiation by the seller is the difference between the market price *at the time when the buyer learned of the breach* and the contract price together with any incidental and consequential damages provided in this chapter (§ 2.715), but less expenses saved in consequence of the seller's breach. (emphasis added).

Courts and commentators have identified three possible interpretations of the phrase "learned of the breach." If seller anticipatorily repudiates, buyer learns of the breach:

   (1) When he learns of the repudiation;

   (2) When he learns of the repudiation plus a commercially reasonable time; or

   (3) When performance is due under the contract.

. . . We would not be free to decide the question if there were a Texas case on point, bound as we are by *Erie* to follow state law in diversity cases. We find, however, that no Texas case has addressed the Code question of buyer's damages in an anticipatory repudiation context. . . .

We do not doubt, and Texas law is clear, that market price at the time buyer learns of the breach is the appropriate measure of § 2.713 damages in cases where buyer learns of the breach at or after the time for performance. This will be the common case, for which § 2.713 was designed. *See* Peters, *Remedies for Breach of Contracts Relating to the Sale of Goods Under the Uniform Commercial Code: A Roadmap for Article Two*, 73 Yale L.J. 199, 264 (1963). In the relatively rare case where seller anticipatorily repudiates and buyer does not cover, *see* Anderson, *supra*, at 318, the specific provision for anticipatory repudiation cases, § 2.610, authorizes the aggrieved party to await performance for a commercially reasonable time before restoring to his remedies of cover or damages.

In the anticipatory repudiation context, the buyer's specific right to wait for a commercially reasonable time before choosing his remedy must be read together with the general damages provision of § 2.713 to extend the time for measure-

---

[131] [6] The only area of unanimous agreement among those that have studied the Code provisions relevant to this problem is that they are not consistent, present problems in interpretation, and invite amendment.

ment beyond when buyer learns of the breach. Comment 1 to § 2.610 states that if an aggrieved party "awaits performance beyond a commercially reasonable time he cannot recover resulting damages which he should have avoided." This suggests that an aggrieved buyer can recover damages where the market rises during the commercially reasonable time he awaits performance. To interpret 2.713's "learned of the breach" language to mean the time at which seller first communicates his anticipatory repudiation would undercut the time that 2.610 gives the aggrieved buyer to await performance.

The buyer's option to wait a commercially reasonable time also interacts with § 2.611, which allows the seller an opportunity to retract his repudiation. Thus, an aggrieved buyer "learns of the breach" a commercially reasonable time after he learns of the seller's anticipatory repudiation. The weight of scholarly commentary supports this interpretation. *See* J. Calamari & J. Perillo, *Contracts* § 14-20 (2d ed. 1977); Sebert, *Remedies Under Article Two of the Uniform Commercial Code: An Agenda for Review*, 130 U. Pa. L. Rev. 360, 372-80 (1981); Wallach, *Anticipatory Repudiation and the UCC*, 13 U.C.C. L.J. 48 (1980); Peters, *supra*, at 263-68.

Typically, our question will arise where parties to an executory contract are in the midst of a rising market. To the extent that market decisions are influenced by a damages rule, measuring market price at the time of seller's repudiation gives seller the ability to fix buyer's damages and may induce seller to repudiate, rather than abide by the contract. By contrast, measuring buyer's damages at the time of performance will tend to dissuade the buyer from covering, in hopes that market price will continue upward until performance time.

Allowing the aggrieved buyer a commercially reasonable time, however, provides him with an opportunity to investigate his cover possibilities in a rising market without fear that, if he is unsuccessful in obtaining cover, he will be relegated to a market-contract damage remedy measured at the time of repudiation. The Code supports this view. While cover is the preferred remedy, the Code clearly provides the option to seek damages. *See* § 2.712(c) & comment 3. If "[t]he buyer is always free to choose between cover and damages for non-delivery," and if 2.712 "is not intended to limit the time necessary for [buyer] to look around and decide as to how he may best effect cover," it would be anomalous, if the buyer chooses to seek damages, to fix his damages at a time before he investigated cover possibilities and before he elected his remedy. *See id.* comment 2 & 3. . . .

Moreover, comment 1 to § 2.713 states, "The general baseline adopted in this section uses as a yardstick the market in which the buyer would have obtained cover had he sought that "relief." *See* § 2.610 comment 1. When a buyer chooses not to cover, but to seek damages, the market is measured at the time he could have covered—a reasonable time after repudiation. *See* §§ 2.711 & 2.713.

Persuasive arguments exist for interpreting "learned of the breach" to mean "time of performance," consistent with the pre-Code rule. *See* J. White & R. Summers, *supra*, § 6-7; Anderson, *supra*. If this was the intention of the Code's drafters, however, phrases in §§ 2.610 and 2.712 lose their meaning. If buyer is entitled to market-contract damages measured at the time of performance, it is difficult to explain why the anticipatory repudiation section limits him to a commercially reasonable time to await performance. *See* § 2.610 comment 1. Similarly, in a rising market, no reason would exist for requiring the buyer to act "without unreasonable delay" when he seeks to cover following an anticipatory repudiation. *See* § 2.712(a).

The interplay among the relevant Code sections does not permit, in this context, an interpretation that harmonizes all and leaves no loose ends. We therefore acknowledge that our interpretation fails to explain the language of § 2.723(a) insofar as it relates to aggrieved buyers. We note, however, that the section has limited applicability—cases that come to trial before the time of performance will be rare. Moreover, the comment to § 2.723 states that the "section is not intended to exclude the use of any other reasonable method of determining market price or of measuring damages. . . ." In light of the Code's persistent theme of commercial reasonableness, the prominence of cover as a remedy, and the time given an aggrieved buyer to await performance and to investigate cover before selecting his remedy, we agree with the district court that "learned of the breach" incorporates § 2.610's commercially reasonable time[132]. . . .

VI. "COVER" AS A CEILING

At trial Cosden argued that Helm's purchases of polystyrene from other sources in early February constituted cover. Helm argued that those purchases were not intended to substitute for polystyrene sales cancelled by Cosden. Helm,

---

[132] [11] We note that two circuits arrived at a similar conclusion by different routes. In Cargill, Inc. v. Stafford, 553 F.2d 1222 (10th Cir. 1977), the court began its discussion of damages by embracing the "time of performance" interpretation urged by Professors White and Summers. *Id.* at 1226. Indeed, the court stated that "damages normally should be measured from the time when performance is due and not from the time when the buyer learns of repudiation." *Id.* Nevertheless, the court conclude[d] that under § 4-2-713 a buyer may urge continued performance for a reasonable time. At the end of a reasonable period he should cover if substitute goods are readily available. If substitute goods are available and buyer does not cover within a reasonable time, damages should be based on the price at the end of that reasonable time rather than on the price when performance is due. *Id.* at 1227. The *Cargill* court would employ the time of performance measure only if buyer had a valid reason for not covering.

In First Nat'l Bank of Chicago v. Jefferson Mortgage Co., 576 F.2d 479 (3d Cir. 1978), the court initially quoted with approval legislative history that supports a literal or "plain meaning" interpretation of New Jersey's § 2-713. Nevertheless, the court hedged by interpreting that section "to measure damages within a commercially reasonable time after learning of the repudiation." *Id.* at 492. In light of the unequivocal repudiation and because cover was "easily and immediately . . . available . . . in the well-organized and easily accessible market," *id.* at 493 (quoting Oloffson v. Coomer, 11 Ill. App.3d 918, 296 N.E.2d 871 (1973)), a commercially reasonable time did not extend beyond the date of repudiation.

We agree with the *First National* court that "the circumstances of the particular market involved should determine the duration of a 'commercially reasonable time.'" 576 F.2d at 492; *see* Tex. Bus. & Com.Code § 1.204(b). In this case, however, there was no showing that cover was easily and immediately available in an organized and accessible market and that a commercially reasonable time expired on the day of Cosden's cancellation. We recognize that § 2.610's "commercially reasonable time" and § 2.712's "without unreasonable delay" are distinct concepts. Often, however, the two time periods will overlap, since the buyer can investigate cover possibilities while he awaits performance. *See* Sebert, *supra*, at 376-77 & n. 80.

Although the jury in the present case did not fix the exact duration of a commercially reasonable time, we assume that the jury determined market price at a time commercially reasonable under all the circumstances, in light of the absence of objection to the form of the special issue.

however, contended that it did cover by purchasing large amounts of high impact polystyrene from other sources late in February and around the first of March. Cosden claimed that these purchases were not made reasonably and that they should not qualify as cover. The jury found that none of Helm's purchases of polystyrene from other sources were cover purchases.

Now Cosden argues that the prices of polystyrene for the purchases that Helm claimed were cover should act as a ceiling for fixing market price under § 2.713. We refuse to accept this novel argument. Although a buyer who has truly covered may not be allowed to seek higher damages under § 2.713 than he is granted by § 2.712, *see* § 2.713 comment 5; J. White & R. Summers, *supra*, § 6-4 at 233-34, in this case the jury found that Helm did not cover. We cannot isolate a reason to explain the jury's finding: it might have concluded that Helm would have made the purchases regardless of Cosden's nonperformance or that the transactions did not qualify as cover for other reasons. Because of the jury's finding, we cannot use those other transactions to determine Helm's damages. . . .

d. Uncertainty about the Other Side's Performance—The Code's Framework

AMF, INC. v. MCDONALD'S CORP.
United States Court of Appeals, Seventh Circuit
536 F.2d 1167 (1976)

CUMMINGS, J. . . . AMF seeks damages for the alleged wrongful cancellation and repudiation of McDonald's Corporation's ("McDonald's") orders for sixteen computerized cash registers for installation in restaurants owned by wholly-owned subsidiaries of McDonald's and for seven such registers ordered by licensees of McDonald's for their restaurants. In July 1972, McDonald's of Elk Grove, Inc. sued AMF to recover the $20,385.28 purchase price paid for a prototype computerized cash register and losses sustained as a result of failure of the equipment to function satisfactorily. . . . [T]he district court rendered a memorandum opinion and order in both cases in favor of each defendant. The only appeal is from the eight judgment orders dismissing AMF's complaints against McDonald's and the seven licensees. We affirm. . . .

In 1966, AMF began to market individual components of a completely automated restaurant system, including its model 72C computerized cash register involved here. The 72C cash register then consisted of a central computer, one to four input stations, each with a keyboard and cathode ray tube display, plus the necessary cables and controls.

In 1967, McDonald's representatives visited AMF's plant in Springdale, Connecticut, to view a working "breadboard" model 72C to decide whether to use it in McDonald's restaurant system. Later that year, it was agreed that a 72C should be placed in a McDonald's restaurant for evaluation purposes.

In April 1968, a 72C unit accommodating six input stations was installed in McDonald's restaurant in Elk Grove, Illinois. This restaurant was a wholly-owned subsidiary of McDonald's and was its busiest restaurant. Besides functioning as a cash register, the 72C was intended to enable counter personnel to work faster and to assist in providing data for accounting reports and bookkeeping. McDonald's of Elk Grove, Inc. paid some $20,000 for this prototype register on January 3, 1969. AMF never gave McDonald's warranties governing reliability or performance standards for the prototype.

At a meeting in Chicago on August 29, 1968, McDonald's concluded to order sixteen 72C's for its company-owned restaurants and to cooperate with AMF to obtain additional orders from its licensees. In December 1968, AMF accepted McDonald's purchase orders for those sixteen 72C's. In late January 1969, AMF accepted seven additional orders for 72C's from McDonald's licensees for their restaurants. Under the contract for the sale of all the units, there was a warranty for parts and service. AMF proposed to deliver the first unit in February 1969, with installation of the remaining twenty-two units in the first half of 1969. However, AMF established a new delivery schedule in February 1969, providing for deliveries to commence at the end of July 1969 and to be completed in January 1970, assuming that the first test unit being built at AMF's Vandalia, Ohio, plant was built and satisfactorily tested by the end of July 1969. This was never accomplished.

During the operation of the prototype 72C at McDonald's Elk Grove restaurant, many problems resulted, requiring frequent service calls by AMF and others. Because of its poor performance, McDonald's had AMF remove the prototype unit from its Elk Grove restaurant in late April 1969.

At a March 18, 1969, meeting, McDonald's and AMF personnel met to discuss the performance of the Elk Grove prototype. AMF agreed to formulate a set of performance and reliability standards for the future 72C's, including "the number of failures permitted at various degrees of seriousness, total permitted downtime, maximum service hours and cost." Pending mutual agreement on such standards, McDonald's personnel asked that production of the twenty-three units be held up and AMF agreed.

On May 1, 1969, AMF met with McDonald's personnel to provide them with performance and reliability standards. However, the parties never agreed upon such standards. At that time, AMF did not have a working machine and could not produce one within a reasonable time because its Vandalia, Ohio, personnel were too inexperienced. After the May 1st meeting, AMF concluded that McDonald's had cancelled all 72C orders. The reasons for the cancellation were the poor performance of the prototype, the lack of assurances that a workable machine was available and the unsatisfactory conditions at AMF's Vandalia, Ohio, plant where the twenty-three 72C's were to be built.

On July 29, 1969, McDonald's and AMF representatives met in New York. At this meeting it was mutually understood that the 72C orders were cancelled and that none would be delivered.

In its conclusions of law, the district court held that McDonald's and its licensees had entered into contracts for twenty-three 72C cash registers but that AMF was not able to perform its obligations under the contracts (see note, 1, *supra*). Citing § 2-610 of the Uniform Commercial Code (Ill. Rev. Stats. (1975) ch. 26, § 2-610) and Comment 1 thereunder, the court concluded that on July 29,

McDonald's justifiably repudiated the contracts to purchase all twenty-three 72C's.

Relying on § 2-609 and 2-610 of the Uniform Commercial Code (Ill. Rev. Stat. (1975) ch. 26, §§ 2-609 and 2-610), the court decided that McDonald's was warranted in repudiating the contracts and therefore had a right to cancel the orders by virtue of § 2-711 of the Uniform Commercial Code (Ill. Rev. Stats. (1975) ch. 26, § 2-711). Accordingly, judgment was entered for McDonald's.

The findings of fact adopted by the district court were a mixture of the court's own findings and findings proposed by the parties, some of them modified by the court. AMF has assailed ten of the 124 findings of fact, but our examination of the record satisfies us that all have adequate support in the record and support the conclusions of law.

Whether in a specific case a buyer has reasonable grounds for insecurity is a question of fact. Comment 3 to UCC § 2-609; Anderson, Uniform Commercial Code, § 2-609 (2d Ed. 1971). On this record, McDonald's clearly had "reasonable grounds for insecurity" with respect to AMF's performance. At the time of the March 18, 1969, meeting, the prototype unit had performed unsatisfactorily ever since its April 1968 installation. Although AMF had projected delivery of all twenty-three units by the first half of 1969, AMF later scheduled delivery from the end of July 1969 until January 1970. When McDonald's personnel visited AMF's Vandalia, Ohio, plant on March 4, 1969, they saw that none of the 72C systems was being assembled and learned that a pilot unit would not be ready until the end of July of that year. They were informed that the engineer assigned to the project was not to commence work until March 17th. AMF's own personnel were also troubled about the design of the 72C, causing them to attempt to reduce McDonald's order to five units. Therefore, under § 2-609 McDonald's was entitled to demand adequate assurance of performance by AMF.

However, AMF urges that § 2-609 of the UCC is inapplicable because McDonald's did not make a written demand of adequate assurance of due performance. In *Pittsburgh-Des Moines Steel Co. v. Brookhaven Manor Water Co.*, 532 F.2d 572, 581 (7th Cir. 1976), we noted that the Code should be liberally construed and therefore rejected such "a formalistic approach" to § 2-609. McDonald's failure to make a written demand was excusable because AMF's Mr. Dubosque's testimony and his April 2 and 18, 1969, memoranda about the March 18th meeting showed AMF's clear understanding that McDonald's had suspended performance until it should receive adequate assurance of due performance from AMF. . . .

After the March 18th demand, AMF never repaired the Elk Grove unit satisfactorily nor replaced it. Similarly, it was unable to satisfy McDonald's that the twenty-three machines on order would work. At the May 1st meeting, AMF offered unsatisfactory assurances for only five units instead of twenty-three. The performance standards AMF tendered to McDonald's were unacceptable because they would have permitted the 72C's not to function properly for 90 hours per year, permitting as much as one failure in every fifteen days in a busy McDonald's restaurant. Also, as the district court found, AMF's Vandalia, Ohio, personnel were too inexperienced to produce a proper machine. Since AMF did not provide adequate assurance of performance after McDonald's March 18th demand, UCC § 2-609(1) permitted McDonald's to suspend performance. When AMF did not furnish adequate assurance of due performance at the May 1st meeting, it thereby repudiated the contract under § 2-609(4). At that point, § 2-610(b) (note 3 *supra*) permitted McDonald's to cancel the orders pursuant to § 2-711 (note 6, *supra*), as it finally did on July 29, 1969. . . .

. . . McDonald's could cancel the orders under §§ 2-610 and 2-711 because of AMF's failure to give adequate assurance of due performance under § 2-609. . . .

Judgment Affirmed.

NOTES AND QUESTIONS

1. *Materials from the briefs of the parties*: AMF argued that McDonald's Corporation had no grounds for insecurity since the machine with the defects was a prototype model, McDonald's knew of all the defects when it placed its order for the machines, and then McDonald's decided it could buy more advanced technology for less money and so it looked for a way out. If it had made a written demand for assurances, AMF could have responded by giving appropriate assurances.

McDonald's cited an internal AMF memo that stated:

> On Tuesday, March 18, we had a meeting with McDonald's at which time they expressed their unhappiness with the last 2 months performance of the equipment and stated that they intended to cancel the order unless we could give them a warranty or assurance on the reliability of the production units, which reliability would have to be "considerably" better than the recent experience with the prototype.

What, if anything, would a formal written demand for assurances have added? Compare the approach of the court in *Eastern Air Lines v. McDonnell Douglas Corp.*, *supra*.

2. *Section 2-609 as the all-purpose tool*: Professor White[133] points out that the court used § 2-609 to avoid considering whether the failure to perform the installment contract met the tests for breach in § 2-612. "In effect, the court applied § 2-609 to one party's routine negotiating behavior and gave it significant legal consequence—namely, repudiation by the other."

In another case in which the court declined to require a written demand for assurance,[134] White says that the court used § 2-609 to magnify the importance of particular immaterial breaches and change them into material ones. "The analysis short-circuits the agonizing found in many common-law cases in which a court attempts to determine whether a breach in one installment so affects the expectations or behavior for other installments as to constitute a material breach."

---

[133] *Eight Cases and Section 251*, 67 Cornell L. Rev. 841 (1982).
[134] ARB (American Research Bureau), Inc. v. E-Systems, Inc. 663 F.2d 189 (D.C. Cir. 1980).

In a third case,[135] a buyer of specialized industrial burners for a plant in Yugo-slavia discovered that similar burners in use in Syria and Sri Lanka had devel-oped problems in operation. The buyer, before installation of the burners, asked that the seller take the burners back, or failing that guarantee they would operate properly, with the guarantee secured by a letter of credit. Seller refused, and buyer was awarded a full refund of the purchase price. The court held that seller had failed to provide meaningful assurances. Notice that by using UCC § 2-609, buyer never had to prove that the burners would not meet the agreed specifica-tions when they were installed in the Yugoslavian ammonia plant which had yet to be completed and put into operation at the time of the hearing on the motion for summary judgment. Of course, it looks as if neither buyer nor seller thought the burners would meet specifications if they had been installed. Buyer did not have to deal with questions of whether it had accepted the burners and whether seller still could cure or whether buyer was entitled to revoke its acceptance be-cause of a defect that substantially impaired the value of the burners to the buyer.

3. ***The relation among UCC §§ 2-609, 2-610, and 2-611***: In the *AMF* case the court said "[w]hen AMF did not furnish adequate assurance of due perform-ance at the May 1st meeting, it thereby repudiated the contract under § 2-609(4). At that point, § 2-610(b) . . . permitted McDonald's to cancel the orders pursuant to § 2-711. . . ." If § 2-609(4) is applicable, must one also meet the requirements of and be subject to the qualifications in §§ 2-610 and 2-611? For example, could AMF have withdrawn its repudiation under § 2-611?

CHERWELL-RALLI, INC. v. RYTMAN GRAIN CO., INC.
Supreme Court of Connecticut
180 Conn. 714, 433 A.2d 984 (1980)

PETERS, J. This case involves a dispute about which of the parties to an oral instalment contract was the first to be in breach. The plaintiff, Cherwell-Ralli, Inc., sued the defendant, Rytman Grain Co., Inc., for the nonpayment of moneys due and owing for accepted deliveries of products known as Cherco Meal and C-R-T Meal. The defendant, conceding its indebtedness, counterclaimed for dam-ages arising out of the plaintiff's refusal to deliver remaining instalments under the contract. The trial court, *Bordon, J.*, trial referee, having found all issues for the plaintiff, rendered judgment accordingly, and the defendant appealed.

The trial court's unchallenged finding of fact establishes the following: The parties, on July 26, 1974, entered into an instalment contract for the sale of Cherco Meal and C-R-T Meal on the basis of a memorandum executed by the Getkin Brokerage House. As modified, the contract called for shipments accord-ing to weekly instructions from the buyer, with payments to be made within ten days after delivery. Almost immediately the buyer was behind in its payments, and these arrearages were often quite substantial. The seller repeatedly called these arrearages to the buyer's attention but continued to make all shipments as requested by the buyer from July 29, 1974 to April 23, 1975.

---

[135] Creusot-Loire International, Inc. v. Coppus Engineering Corp., 585 F. Supp. 45 (S.D. N.Y. 1983).

By April 15, 1975, the buyer had become concerned that the seller might not complete performance of the contract, because the seller's plant might close and because the market price of the goods had come significantly to exceed the contract price. [Do you see why this latter fact might cause plaintiff to worry about future deliveries?] In a telephonic conversation between the buyer's president and the seller's president on that day, the buyer was assured by the seller that deliveries would continue if the buyer would make the payments for which it was obligated. Thereupon, the buyer sent the seller a check in the amount of $9825.60 to cover shipments through March 31, 1975.

Several days later, on April 23, 1975, the buyer stopped payment on this check because he was told by a truck driver, not employed by the seller, that this shipment would be his last load. The trial court found that this was not a valid reason for stoppage of payment. Upon inquiry by the seller, the buyer restated his earlier concerns about future deliveries. Two letters, both dated April 28, 1975, describe the impasse between the parties: the seller again demanded payment, and the buyer, for the first time in writing, demanded adequate assurance of further deliveries. The buyer's demand for assurance was reiterated in its direct reply to the seller's demand for payment. The buyer, however, made no further payments, either to replace the stopped check or otherwise to pay for the nineteen accepted shipments for which balances were outstanding. The seller made no further deliveries after April 23, 1975, when it heard about the stopped check; the buyer never made specific requests for shipments after that date. Inability to deliver the goods forced the seller to close its plant, on May 2, 1975, because of stockpiling of excess material.

The trial court concluded, on the basis of these facts, that the party in breach was the buyer and not the seller. The court concluded that the seller was entitled to recover the final balance of $21,013.60, which both parties agreed to be due and owing. It concluded that the buyer could not prevail on its counterclaim because it had no reasonable grounds to doubt performance from the seller and had in fact received reasonable assurances. Further, the buyer had presented no reasonably accurate evidence to establish the damages it might have sustained because of the seller's failure to deliver.

The buyer on this appeal challenges first the conclusion that the buyer's failure to pay "substantially impaired the value of the whole contract," so as to constitute "a breach of the whole contract," as is required by the applicable law governing instalment contracts. General Statutes § 42a-2-612(3). What constitutes impairment of the value of the whole contract is a question of fact. . . .

The record below amply sustains the trial court's conclusion in this regard, particularly in light of the undenied and uncured stoppage of a check given to comply with the buyer's promise to reduce significantly the amount of its outstanding arrearages. . . .

The buyer argues that the seller in an instalment contract may never terminate a contract, despite repeated default in payment by the buyer, without first invoking the insecurity methodology of General Statutes § 42a-2-609. That is not the law. If there is reasonable doubt about whether the buyer's default is substantial, the seller may be well advised to temporize by suspending further performance until it can ascertain whether the buyer is able to offer adequate assurance of future payments.

. . . But if the buyer's conduct is sufficiently egregious, such conduct will, in and of itself, constitute substantial impairment of the value of the whole contract and a present breach of the contract as a whole. An aggrieved seller is expressly permitted, by General Statutes § 42a-2-703(f), upon breach of a contract as a whole, to cancel the remainder of the contract "with respect to the whole undelivered balance.". . . Nor is the seller's remedy to cancel waived, as the buyer argues, by a law suit seeking recovery for payments due. While § 42a-2-612(3) states that a contract is reinstated if the seller "brings an action with respect *only* to past instalments" (emphasis added), it is clear in this case that the seller intended, as the buyer well knew, to bring this contract to an end because of the buyer's breach.

The buyer's attack on the court's conclusions with respect to its counterclaim is equally unavailing. The buyer's principal argument is that the seller was obligated, on pain of default, to provide assurance of its further performance. The right to such assurance is premised on reasonable grounds for insecurity. Whether a buyer has reasonable grounds to be insecure is a question of fact. *AMF, Inc. v. McDonald's Corporation*, 536 F.2d 1167, 1170 (7th Cir. 1976). The trial court concluded that in this case the buyer's insecurity was not reasonable and we agree. A party to a sales contract may not suspend performance of its own for which it has "already received the agreed return." At all times, the buyer had received all of the goods which it had ordered. The buyer could not rely on its own nonpayments as a basis for its own insecurity. The presidents of the parties had exchanged adequate verbal assurances only eight days before the buyer itself again delayed its own performance on the basis of information that was facially unreliable. Contrary to the buyer's argument, subsequent events proved the buyer's fears to be incorrect, since the seller's plant closed due to a surplus rather than due to a shortage of materials. Finally, it is fatal to the buyer's appeal that neither its oral argument nor its brief addressed its failure to substantiate, with probative evidence, the damages it alleged to be attributable to the seller's nondeliveries.

There is no error.

NOTES AND QUESTIONS

1. *Material from the briefs and record*: Rytman, in its brief, asserts that in addition to the truck driver's statements about his "last load," Rytman had heard that Cherwell-Ralli was selling to others at the higher market price. Rytman had heard rumors that C-R was going to close the plant because "they were held to a fast contract price with him and had problems with fuel and environmental protection." Rytman's lawyer wrote Cherwell-Ralli on April 28th, as follows:

> As I understand it, deliveries on this contract are quite late and there is some question in our client's mind as to whether your company is willing and able to comply with the terms of the contract. Our client requests delivery of this material and I hereby make formal demand for same. I can advise you that if we receive either delivery of the material or ade-

quate assurance that the material will be delivered in accordance with the contract we will make satisfactory arrangements for payment of all present and future sums which may be due under the terms of the contract. In the meantime, our client will be damaged if you do not deliver the balance of the contract in accordance with its terms and this letter will give you notice that our client will seek compensation from your company for any and all damages which may result from your violation of the contract and will withhold all payments until this matter is resolved.

Cherwell-Ralli stockpiled the meal produced to supply Rytman, and on May 2, the New Jersey plant stopped production.

2. *"Reasonable grounds for insecurity"*: Do you agree that Rytman's concern did not give it reasonable grounds for insecurity? Suppose Rytman had come to you for advice in late April of 1975. What would you have told him to do? Suppose, instead, Rytman's lawyer had showed you a draft of the letter of April 28th. Would you have advised him to change anything?

Justice Peters says that "subsequent events proved the buyer's fears to be incorrect. . . ." Can one's fears be incorrect but reasonable within the meaning of § 2-609(1)?

3. *Does a demand for assurances rewrite the contract?* Professor Larry Garvin[136] argues that a § 2-609 demand for assurances may upset the allocation of risk in the contract. He says:

> Adequate assurance is a first cousin to contract modification. If the party demanding assurances actually gets them, it has in essence secured a change in the express terms. Even the promisor's unsupported promise that it will in fact perform goes beyond the bargain, in that the parties could have, but did not, arrange for periodic assurance. Any greater assurance--paying in advance or granting a security interest, or giving progress payments--gives the promisee more than it had when the contract was made. In essence, then, the promisee uses the mechanism of adequate assurance to secure a new contract, one that it had not bargained for and that, almost by definition, it could not get voluntarily from the promisor.

Would the drafters of § 2-609 concede Professor Garvin's point? What does the statutory text say about the proper reading of a contract for sale?

e. Uncertainty About Performance—At Common Law

Suppose a case does not involve a transaction in goods and so Article 2 is inapplicable. Can a party who has "reasonable grounds for insecurity" suspend performance and demand assurances? The traditional common-law position is not clear, but there is little clear authority for this course. Consider the following case:

---

[136] *Adequate Assurance of Performance: Of Risk, Duress, and Cognition*, 69 U. Colo. L. Rev. 71, 130 (1998).

LOUIS KEPPELON v. W.M. RITTER FLOORING CORP.

Court of Errors and Appeals of New Jersey
97 N.J.L. 200, 116 Atl. 491 (1922)

TRENCHARD, J. . . . [Plaintiff won a verdict and judgment at trial. Defendant appealed.] We are of the opinion that the judgment must be affirmed. . . .

The complaint averred that the plaintiff was building an apartment-house in East Orange; that the defendant contracted to furnish the labor and materials necessary to lay, scrape and finish the floors for a stated price to be paid in stated installments as the work progressed; that when the time arrived for the defendant to begin performance, the plaintiff requested performance, but the defendant stated to the plaintiff that it, the defendant, refused, and thereafter would refuse, to perform the contract; and that the defendant has wholly repudiated and refused to perform the contract.

The defendant's answer in the "second separate defence" averred that since the execution of the contract the credit of the plaintiff had become impaired, so he was no longer a good credit risk, and that he had failed to meet other obligations between him and the defendant, and that by reason of the plaintiff's poor financial condition the defendant was warranted in not performing the terms of the contract.

At the trial the plaintiff moved to strike out that "defence" on the ground that it disclosed no defence, and that motion was granted with permission, however, to the defendant to amend the answer. This the defendant did by adding to the above-stated "second separate defence" the averment that the plaintiff, when the time for the defendant to perform arrived, "was in fact insolvent." This defence, also, the trial judge struck out. . . .

The fact that the credit of a party to a building contract (to whom by the terms of the contract labor and material are to be furnished) has become impaired, so that he is no longer a good credit risk, and that he has failed to meet other independent obligations, does not relieve the other party from performance, and is no defence to an action for the breach of such contract, for it does not appear therefrom that he cannot and will not perform his part when his time for performance comes.

It has been held that mere doubts of the solvency of a party to a contract, or mere belief that he will be unable to perform when the time for his performance comes, will not excuse performance by the other party. . . . If contracts could be repudiated upon the mere allegation that the credit of the other party had become impaired, there would indeed be much consternation in the business world, for contracts are made in view of the fact that credit fluctuates, and it is common knowledge that contracts are frequently fully performed by those whose credit has become impaired.

It has also been held that the mere failure of a party to a contract to perform an independent contract will not excuse performance by the other party. . . . To adopt any other rule would result in the admission of so much extraneous matter as to make trials a hopeless procedure. It would involve in the trial of a single action evidence concerning every other contract between the same parties, to determine whether there was performance, or perchance cancellation, or rescission, or satisfaction, or a counterclaim, in order to determine whether there was, as a matter of fact, a breach of other obligations of the plaintiff.

It is also clear that the "second separate defence" as amended discloses no defence to the action.

It sets forth the same matters contained in the original defence and adds that, when the time for the defendant to perform arrived, the plaintiff was in fact insolvent, and avers that by reason thereof "the defendant was warranted in not performing the terms of the said contract."

But we think that the mere insolvency of a party to a building contract (to whom by the terms of the contract labor and materials are to be furnished) does not terminate the contract, in the absence of provisions to that effect therein, nor does it justify the other party in refusing altogether to perform, for it does not follow therefrom that the insolvent party could not and would not perform his part even though insolvent. . . .

It might well be that the insolvent party might find it advantageous and possible to carry out his part of the contract, since insolvency does not necessarily mean a total lack of assets. To hold that mere insolvency of a party puts an end to a contract, and excuses the solvent party from the obligation altogether, would be intolerable. If the mere fact of insolvency terminates a contract every insolvent contractor would automatically be shorn of all property rights and beneficial interests in contracts. Of course, this cannot be. . . .

The defendant, however, contends that it was relieved of its obligation to do the work and furnish the materials "upon credit" when the plaintiff had become insolvent and that it could "only be obliged to proceed with its contract in case payment is assured it in cash by some satisfactory indemnity," and refers us to cases said to support that proposition.

But that question is not presented in the case at bar and will not be considered. Neither the defendant's pleading, as originally stated, nor as amended, raises that question, because it does not assert that defendant's refusal to proceed was due either to plaintiff's failure to pay in advance or to plaintiff's refusal to give assurance of payment, the pleader merely attempting to justify defendant's failure to proceed because of plaintiff's alleged poor financial condition and insolvency when the time arrived for defendant to begin performance.

The judgment will be affirmed, with costs.

NOTES AND QUESTIONS

1. *The attempt of the Restatement (Second) to expand the law*: Restatement (Second) of Contracts § 251, provides:

> (1) Where reasonable grounds arise to believe that the obligor will commit a breach by non-performance that would of itself give the obligee a claim for damages for total breach . . . the obligee may demand adequate assurance of due performance and may, if reasonable, suspend any performance for which he has not already received the agreed exchange until he receives such assurance.

(2) The obligee may treat as a repudiation the obligor's failure to provide within a reasonable time such assurance of due performance as is adequate in the circumstances of the particular case.

The language of § 251(1) differs from that of § 2-609. Might anything turn on this difference?[137]

Will the courts take the Restatement's invitation to expand UCC §2-609 to other-than-Code cases? In *C.L. Maddox, Inc. v. Coalfield Services, Inc.*,[138] the court said:

> The principle of § 2-609 is generalized to all contracts in § 251 of the Restatement (Second) of Contracts (1981). . . . The Restatement, of course, is not law, and we cannot find any Illinois cases discussing § 251. But the principle strikes us as a sound one, and we have no reason to doubt that it would be so regarded by the courts of Illinois.

The New York Court of Appeals was more cautious. In *Norcon Power Partners, L.P. v. Niagara Mohawk Power Corp.*,[139] it said that it would only decide that § 251 should apply "to the type of long-term commercial contract between corporate entities entered into by Norcon and Niagara Mohawk here, which is complex and not reasonably susceptible of all security features being anticipated, bargained for and incorporated in the original contract."

2. *Contractual drafting to expand or make clear the rights granted by UCC § 2-609 and Restatement § 251*: A large manufacturing corporation uses the following clause on its purchase order:

> Buyer shall have the right to cancel and terminate this contract forthwith upon the happening of any one or more of the following events: (1) Seller's insolvency; (2) filing of a voluntary or involuntary petition in bankruptcy by or against the Seller; (3) the execution by the Seller of an assignment for the benefit of creditors; (4) appointment of a receiver or trustee for the Seller by any court of competent jurisdiction, or (5) if at any time, in the judgment of the Buyer, the Seller's financial condition shall be such as to endanger its performance hereunder. The acceptance of goods or performances after the occurrences of any of the above events shall not waive the right of the Buyer to cancel and terminate this contract, nor shall cancellation, hereunder waive the Buyer's right to any damages to which the Buyer is otherwise entitled.

To what extent does Buyer gain greater rights under this clause than under UCC § 2-609? Are there limits to the extent to which one can use a contract term to alter the result reached by § 2-609?[140] What if, in a situation in which the

---

[137] *See* Note, *A Right to Adequate Assurance of Performance in All Transactions: UCC 2-609 Beyond Sales of Goods*, 48 S. Cal. L. Rev. 1358 (1975).

[138] 51 F.3d 76, 80-81 (7th Cir. 1995).

[139] 92 N.Y.2d 458, 705 N.E.2d 656 (1998).

[140] *See* UCC §§ 1-102(3), 1-208.

preceding clause is contained in the agreement, Buyer makes an honest unreasonable judgment about seller's financial condition.[141]

C. SELF-HELP IN THE FACE OF DEFAULT

Often an aggrieved party facing a breach of contract will want to take some form of self-help rather than sue for breach of contract. If one can protect her interests without going to court, she is likely to come out better off. UCC §2-702(1), for example, allows a seller who discovers that the buyer is insolvent to refuse to deliver the goods "except for cash including payment for all goods theretofore delivered under the contract. . . ." The WALL STREET JOURNAL[142] reported that a software developer had included a "drop dead" function in a program. When the buyer refused to pay $40,000 that was due, the seller activated the function and blocked the buyer's access to vital data. The newspaper reported that a federal district judge in Tulsa, Oklahoma ruled that this action was "abhorrent" and ordered that it not be used again. The article also talked about "time bomb" functions in computer programs. These functions block use of the program unless they are deactivated. Probably, a seller of computer software could include such functions in its programs if it provided for these rights in the contract.

What about buyer's rights to self-help? We will look at a buyer's right to deduct damages from what she or he owes a seller, checks "in full satisfaction of all claims," and a buyer's right to use the goods to avoid loss.

1. DEDUCTING DAMAGES FROM WHAT IS DUE

Section 2-717 gives a buyer a very limited right to deduct damages from what it owes a seller. First, the buyer can only deduct "damages resulting from any breach." This means that the buyer must determine the damages accurately. Second, the buyer may deduct damages only from "any part of the price still due under the same contract." Suppose the buyer has two contracts with the seller. The buyer has paid the price for goods which the buyer later discovers are defective. Nonetheless, the buyer may not deduct its damages under the first contract from what it owes on the second. Third, the buyer must give the seller notice that it is deducting its damages from any part of the price still due.[143] You should notice how § 2-609 can work with § 2-717 when buyer and seller have two or more contracts. The buyer cannot deduct damages for breach of contract number one from what is due on contract number two. However, the default on contract number one can give the buyer reasonable grounds for insecurity about whether it will receive the performance called for by contract number two. As the Official

---

[141] *See, generally,* Havighurst, *Clauses in Sales Contracts Protecting the Seller Against Impairment of the Buyer's Credit,* 20 Minn. L. Rev. 367 (1936). Although written long before the UCC was drafted or enacted, this article is still relevant if read in light of the changes made by the Code.

[142] May 8, 1989, at B1.

[143] *See* William J. Geller, *The Problem of Withholding in Response to Breach: A Proposal to Minimize Risk in Continuing Contracts,* 62 Fordham L. Rev. 163 (1993).

Comment to § 2-609 says: "a ground for insecurity need not arise from or be directly related to the contract in question."

2. CHECKS IN FULL SATISFACTION OF ALL CLAIMS

When buyer and seller dispute the quality of goods supplied or the amounts due, often the buyer will send seller a check for an amount which the buyer asserts is all that is due. The check is restrictively endorsed and states that cashing it will constitute a full settlement of all claims. The common-law rule was that a creditor could not cash the check and disown the condition upon which it was tendered.[144] UCC § 1-207 may change the common-law rule and allow a creditor to cash the check if the creditor explicitly reserves her rights. The courts have divided on this issue. For example, in *Flambeau Products Corp. v. Honeywell Information Systems, Inc.*,[145] where the Supreme Court of Wisconsin split 4 to 3 on the proper interpretation of UCC § 1-207, the majority found that a creditor cannot cash the check without accepting the debtor's offer of an accord and satisfaction. However, there must be consideration for the settlement of the claim. In *Kelly v. Kowalsky*,[146] the court held that merely retaining the checks did not settle the claim when the debtors failed to ask that the checks be returned.[147]

3. USING THE GOODS TO AVOID LOSS AFTER REVOCATION OF ACCEPTANCE

JOHANNSEN v. MINNESOTA VALLEY FORD TRACTOR CO., INC.
Supreme Court of Minnesota
304 N.W.2d 654 (1981)

PETERSON, J. The defendants, Ford Motor Co. and Minnesota Valley Ford (dealer), appeal from the judgment entered in favor of the plaintiff, Harvey Johannsen, the buyer of a defective tractor manufactured by Ford and sold to him by the dealer. After a trial in which the jury found that Johannsen had effectively revoked his acceptance of a Ford Model 9700 tractor (9700), the district court entered judgment for the plaintiff in the amount of the purchase price of the tractor less an offset for use and depreciation. Defendants appeal from the order denying post-trial motions for judgment notwithstanding the verdict or a new trial and also appeal from the judgment. We affirm.

. . . On July 13, 1977, plaintiff, together with his wife, went to the premises of the dealer to pick up his 1974 Ford Model 9600 tractor (9600), which had been taken to the dealer for repairs. Johannsen had experienced a number of problems with the fourth gear and hydraulic system of his 9600. The tractor had jumped out of fourth gear on a number of occasions while Johannsen was plowing. Jo-

---

[144] *See* Restatement (Second) of Contracts §281.
[145] 116 Wis. 2d 95, 341 N.W.2d 655 (1984).
[146] 186 Conn. 618, 442 A.2d 1355 (1982).
[147] *See* Rosenthal, *Discord and Dissatisfaction: Section 1-207 of the Uniform Commercial Code,* 78 Colum. L. Rev. 48 (1978).

hannsen expressed his concern to Brian Gaard, one of the dealer's employees, that the 9600 would again jump out of gear.

Gaard told Johannsen that the transmission of the new 1977 Ford Model 9700 had been redesigned to avoid the transmission defects of the 9600 and that he could solve his tractor transmission problems by purchasing a new 9700 for $26,000. Gaard did not tell Johannsen that Ford had sent a letter to its tractor dealers in May of that year detailing transmission defects in the 9700. Dealers were informed that some 9700's jumped out of fourth and/or eighth gear. They were instructed to check all 9700's in stock for the defect and to sell defective tractors only if they would lose a sale. Johannsen purchased a 9700 from the dealer and traded in his 9600.

The dealer delivered the tractor to Johannsen's farm in late July. The tractor jumped out of fourth gear upon its first use, and at about the same time the frost plugs blew out of the engine, causing a loss of all the coolant. The dealer sent a repairman to plaintiff's farm on that day who told Johannsen to see the dealer about the transmission defect. On August 3, 1977, the tractor developed a fuel restriction problem and a hydraulic leak, which made it difficult to lower the implements into the soil. The dealer informed Johannsen that it could not fix the hydraulic defect until replacement parts became available in April, 1978. Johannsen told every serviceman who called at his farm that he wanted to return the tractor.

On September, 1977, Johannsen, by his attorney, formally notified the dealer in writing of his revocation of acceptance due to transmission, hydraulic and fuel line defects, and he directed the dealer to pick up the tractor immediately.

Johannsen continued to use the tractor after the written revocation and called the dealer on September 28 because the tractor continued to exhibit the same problems. The dealer made service calls on September 28, October 2, and October 9 in response to Johannsen's complaints. Ray Chaik, an employee of the dealer, told Johannsen that he could finish his fall work and bring the tractor in for winter servicing. Johannsen used the tractor for a total of 120 hours but was able to plow or disk only 150 acres of his farm with it. Approximately 90 of those hours were put on the tractor after the revocation letter of September 19. Johannsen put the tractor in storage in late October, 1977.

The defendants contend that the plaintiff did not effectively revoke his acceptance of the 9700 tractor because . . . the plaintiff continued to use the tractor after revocation of acceptance. . . .

Defendants additionally contend that plaintiff's use of the tractor after he gave written notice of revocation of acceptance constitutes a second acceptance. Although the revoking buyer's continued use of defective goods may be wrongful under some circumstances, we think that there can be no blanket rule which prohibits such a buyer from continuing to use the goods. A blanket rule prohibiting a revoking buyer from continuing to use the goods would contravene the code's rule of reasonableness and its underlying purpose of modernizing commercial transactions. We agree with those jurisdictions that have so held. . . .

The reasonableness of the buyer's use of a defective good after revocation is a question of fact for the jury that is to be based on the facts and circumstances of each case. Several factors that the jury may consider include the seller's instructions to the buyer after revocation of acceptance; the degree of economic and other hardship that the buyer would suffer if he discontinued using the defective good; the reasonableness of the buyer's use after revocation as a method of mitigating damages; the degree of prejudice to the seller; and whether the seller acted in bad faith.

We hold, limited to the facts and circumstances of this case, that the jury could find that plaintiff's continued use of the 9700 tractor was reasonable and did not constitute a waiver of his revocation of acceptance. The defects in the 9700 tractor were major. Employees of the dealer knew that Johannsen specifically purchased the 9700 to avoid the transmission defect in the 9600, knew of the possibility of the identical defect in the 9700, and yet they led Johannsen to believe that buying the 9700 would solve all of his tractor transmission problems. In addition, evidence in the record tends to show that Johannsen used the tractor only to perform necessary tasks.

We note that the trial court, based upon expert testimony, allowed the defendants to setoff for use and depreciation of the tractor. . . .

Defendants contend that the trial court improperly excluded for lack of foundation a warranty which limited a buyer's remedies to repair or replacement. Defendants asserted that plaintiff had been given a copy of Ford's standard warranty, but they were unable to produce an executed copy of the warranty. Plaintiff denied that he had executed any such warranty. We conclude that the trial court did not err in the exclusion of the alleged warranty. . . . Affirmed.

NOTES AND QUESTIONS

1. *Material from the briefs:* Johannsen argued:

> [i]n the present case, Johannsen's use of the tractor after revocation was reasonable. The 9700 tractor was the only tractor Johannsen had which was even capable of pulling much of Johannsen's equipment. Johannsen only used the tractor to finish out the 1977 crop season. However, because of the defects, he could not use the tractor for all the purposes which he wanted and as extensively as he would have liked. . . . To punish Johannsen for using the tractor for the remainder of the 1977 crop year when the sellers had his $26,000 in money and machinery and would not return them; when the only tractor that was capable of pulling much of his machinery was the new tractor is unreasonable. Offset is the reasonable appropriate remedy for Johannsen's use of the tractor rather than to invalidate his revocation of acceptance.

Ford responded:

> Buyer in this case did more than simply continue using the tractor. His actions and words led Seller to believe he had changed his mind about revoking acceptance. Buyer requested additional service on the tractor . . . allowed Ray Chaik to field test the tractor . . . and agreed to allow Valley Ford to repair the tractor during the winter . . . [E]ach time Ray Chaik called him about bringing the tractor in for repairs in November

through January, Buyer indicated that it was too cold then to start the tractor or that he could not get the tractor out because of the snow. In those conversations, Buyer did not, however, inform Chaik that he never wanted the repairs made. . . . Had Sellers realized that Buyer would later change his mind and file suit, they could have made the necessary repairs immediately to avoid litigation, or they could have removed the tractor before Buyer made further use of it. The Sellers, not Buyer, would be punished for their good faith efforts to accommodate a customer if Buyer is allowed to revoke his acceptance of the tractor. A buyer should not escape the consequences of his continued use of goods following a revocation of acceptance by arguing, after the fact, that this use constituted mitigation of damages. Unless a buyer makes it clear to a seller at the time of his continued use that this use is only for the purpose of mitigating damages or is only because he has absolutely no other alternative, the seller is placed in the awkward position of not knowing whether the buyer intends to revoke acceptance or intends to honor his contract.

Compare the court's argument in the *Eastern Air Lines* case, *supra*.

2. *Another example of continued use*: In *McCullough v. Bill Swad Chrysler-Plymouth, Inc.*,[148] Deborah McCullough bought a 1978 Chrysler LeBaron from the dealer in May of that year. Following delivery she noticed problems with the brakes, lack of rust proofing, paint and seat panels, transmission and air conditioning. She returned the car for repairs. The brakes were not fixed and none of the other work was done. A month later she returned the car for correction of its defects. The dealer had the car for over three weeks, but many of the former problems persisted. Moreover, the dealer's attempts at repair had damaged the car's stereo system and exterior. Still a month later, the car had to be towed to the dealer's shop for repair. On a honeymoon trip, the brakes failed again. By the end of October of 1978, few of the problems had been remedied. A successor dealer attempted to repair the car several times, but in May of 1979 refused to continue, stating that the vehicle was in satisfactory condition.

On January 8, 1979, McCullough wrote the original dealer, rescinded the contract and demanded a refund of the purchase price plus expenses. The dealer did not respond to the letter. McCullough continued to operate the car. By the time of the trial in June of 1980, the car had been driven about 35,000 miles. About 23,000 miles had been logged after she mailed her notice of revocation. The court awarded McCullough $9,376.82, ruling that she had properly revoked her acceptance despite her continued use of the vehicle, which was reasonable.

The court pointed out that a "young clerical secretary of limited financial resources, was scarcely in position to return the defective automobile and obtain a second in order to meet her business and personal needs. A most unreasonable obligation would be imposed upon [her] were she to be required, in effect, to secure a loan to purchase a second car while remaining liable for repayment of the first car loan." It also said that whether the dealer acted in good faith throughout the transaction "is highly problematic, especially given the fact that whenever

---

[148] 5 Ohio St. 3d 181, 449 N.E.2d 1289 (1983).

repair of the car was undertaken, new defects often miraculously arose while previous ones frequently went uncorrected." The buyer's brief stated:

> On August 24 the car was taken in again for repairs. While in the dealer's possession, Mr. McCullough [the buyer's husband] and a friend, Hector Drost, saw three persons in the McCullough auto southbound on Hamilton Road. The front seat occupants were wearing the stereo head-phones. When the car was returned there were 266 miles on the trip odometer, the gas tank which had been full was nearly empty and there was a marijuana "roach" in the rear seat ashtray. The stereo radio was tuned to a country music station to which Mr. McCullough, a rock musi-cian, would not have been listening.

> Although the witnesses in testimony were unsure of the date, Mr. McCullough did testify that after one of the service trips during this pe-riod . . . he was informed by Swad employee Lloyd Nickey that the hood of McCullough's car had been removed by the dealer and placed on an-other car which needed a hood. Plaintiff's car now sported a "new" hood with dents, nicks, scratches, pry marks at the cowl and did not match the rest of the car in color . . .

The dealer argued, "[a]lthough Mrs. McCullough had many complaints about the automobile, her continued use of it demonstrated that any claimed non-conformity did not substantially impair its value to her." McCullough responded that "[e]conomic necessity, aggravated by defendant's incompetence and bad faith, required her to drive the impaired vehicle, or nothing."[149]

3. *Sections 2-608 and 2-508*: Ford argued that § 2-608(3) of the UCC says that a "buyer who so revokes has the same rights and duties with regard to the goods involved as if he had rejected them." It continued by asserting that one of the duties imposed upon *revoking* buyers by this statute is the duty to allow a seller to cure under § 2-508(2) which grants sellers this right in certain cases when a buyer *rejects* a non-conforming tender. The Supreme Court of Minnesota rejected this argument. It said that "any right to cure should be limited to cases in

---

[149] Customers of the various Bill Swad dealerships have sued them in a number of cases reported on LEXIS. For example, in Freitag v. Bill Swad Datsun, 3 Ohio App. 3d 83, 443 N.E.2d 988 (1982), a customer ordered a 1979 Datsun. Swad's sales person filled out a purchase order indicating that the customer was to receive a $4,850 allowance on his trade-in. When the car arrived three months later, Swad asserted that the trade-in allowance expired after thirty days although the written con-tract said nothing about this. The customer recovered treble damages under the Ohio Consumer Protection Act.

In Haygood v. Bill Swad Datsun, 729 F.2d 1461 (6th Cir. 1984), the trustee in bankruptcy of a buyer of a used car recovered damages against Swad. Swad neglected to repair an oil leak covered under warranty, and the engine was damaged. In BancOhio Nat'l Bank v. Cousins, 1984 Ohio App. LEXIS 10021 (Ohio Ct. App. 1984), Cousins accompanied his girlfriend when she bought a car from Swad. Cousins co-signed her promissory note. A Swad salesman came to Cousins' place of employment. The salesman told Cousins that he had to sign a life insurance form, and Cousins signed the document. Actually, the form was a second promissory note calling for $1,000 more than the original amount agreed. Cousins discovered the situation and went to Swad's sales man-ager. The salesman admitted that he had made a $1,000 mistake in figuring the deal and was hoping to offset it this way. The sales manager ripped up Cousins' copy of the note. However, Swad later sold the original note to BancOhio National Bank. The trial court found for Cousins, and this deci-sion was affirmed.

which the defects are minor, and we hold that the seller has no right to cure defects which substantially impair the good's value." Is § 2-508(2) by its terms limited to defects that do not substantially impair the value of the goods?

D.   A CRITICAL REVIEW OF THE ISSUES

Contract Performance: Promises, Conditions and the Obligation to Communicate
Arthur I. Rosett[150]

Every morning the businessmen of America learn to their chagrin that their suppliers will not be delivering what they want when they want it. The goods will not arrive on time, they will be short count, and the only ones in stock are avocado green. If that were not bad enough, the same businessmen discover daily that their customers will not take and pay for what the businessmen think they ordered. Unfortunately, despite several centuries of effort by legal scholars and jurists, the businessman who has just learned that his order will be late or who did not receive exactly what he expected will not be given much useful advice by the common law as to what he should do next. Traditional contract law provides no comprehensive set of principles to supply clear answers to the central questions in most contract disputes: has there been performance; has there been a breach; has there been a discharge of obligation?

There are at least three reasons why the carefully tooled doctrines of Lord Mansfield, Williston, Corbin and the notables of the American Law Institute have failed to help the very individuals whose experiences are the raw material for those doctrines. First, in formulating contract law, the lawmaker must fashion objective rules to govern what is essentially subjective—the expectations of the parties when they reached agreement. These expectations are rarely thought through, and inherent limitations on the process of drafting agreements make it certain that they will be incompletely and imperfectly expressed. Any effort to make rules to encompass the vagaries of agreement is inevitably unsuccessful. Unfortunately, too, the effort produces a varied and confusing vocabulary. A contract term may be a promise, a dependent or independent covenant or a promissory condition; if it is a condition, it may be subsequent or precedent. A breach may be material or immaterial, or performance may be nonexistent, partial, or substantial. Consideration—whose adequacy the law never questions—may nonetheless fail partially or totally. Contracts may be unilateral or bilateral, express or implied in law or fact. It is no wonder that the businessman, faced with this formidable array of terms, does not keep treatises or the Restatement at his elbow, but instead considers contract law an incomprehensible lawyers' game. The confusion of overlapping sets of vocabulary could be dispelled if lawyers would settle on one set as the vehicle for expression and stick to it through more than one generation. This is unlikely, given the predilection of legal scholars for rejecting the sensible but somewhat imperfect work of those who have gone be-

---

fore. Even if a standard vocabulary did exist, the businessman's dilemma would not be solved, although at least he could discuss it intelligently.

A second and more important failure of traditional doctrine is that it has concentrated on helping a judge decide a breach of contract lawsuit at the expense of telling a businessman how to handle a breakdown in contract relations. Contract law is a common law system responsive to the needs of appellate courts. Even the most recent embodiment of contract doctrine—the tentative drafts of the Second Restatement—focuses on the time, probably some years after the businessman has received that first unsettling news, when the parties face one another in court.

The third shortcoming of traditional legal analysis is its tendency to treat unusual situations as prototypical and to underemphasize more usual transactions. In part this tendency may reflect the lawyer's inexperience with the business world, or it may simply be that the legal profession has been fascinated with the occasional exotic case or the professor's hypothetical. In any event, the result of this tendency is a distortion of the rules; they lavish attention on resolving far-fetched problems rather than providing simple solutions to common disputes.

The effects of these deficiencies are evident when we look at the way traditional doctrine deals with a basic contract dispute: The parties have exchanged promises, committing themselves to future performance. But prior to or during performance one party finds its expectations are not being fulfilled: The promised building is not completed or does not conform to plans; the goods delivered may not be quite what was expected or they are late, etc. The disappointed party will ask two questions: (1) shall I continue to perform my half of the contract or will the deal be terminated, and (2) how will I be compensated for the loss associated with my disappointment?

In answering these questions, traditional theory makes four inquiries. First, it asks whether one or both parties breached a promise; if so, the breaching party is liable to the other for damages. Second, it asks whether one or more of these breaches was material, that is, whether the breach was so serious that it justified the other side in suspending and ultimately terminating his own performance. Since most ruptures involve an interrelated set of failures on both sides, the answer to the last question is likely to require analysis of a third inquiry: the relationship between the promises the parties have exchanged. If it is concluded that the promise of performance of one was given in exchange for the performance of the other, then the failure of one performance affects the obligation to render the return performance. On the other hand, if the promises are deemed independent, any disappointment with performance does not relieve the obligation of counterperformance. The answers to the last two inquiries are likely to provide the resolution of the fourth—the determination of who committed the first material breach. That party is liable, not only for losses associated with the partial breach, but for damages measured by the value of the entire contract.

This brief description is unlikely to explain conventional contract law analysis to anyone not already familiar with it. However, it does make explicit the traditional approach, which is to sort out the conflicting claims that have arisen long after the contractual relationship has gone sour. From the standpoint of the businessman, this four-step analysis is likely to be of little use. It assumes that the crucial need is to advise judges and lawyers how to dispose of litigation. This assumption is misguided, for at the time of litigation courts are engaged in salvage operations at best, seeking to raise the hulk or to apportion blame for the sinking. At worst, courts serve a function analogous to that of the men with brooms who follow the passage of the circus parade.

This Article will suggest an expansion in the focus of contract rules to include the businessman's decisions during performance as well as the court's resolution of litigation. This widening of perspective is hardly a radical suggestion; it is implicit in the Restatement II and more evident in the Uniform Commercial Code. In amplifying upon this suggestion, I must first look at the structure of contract terms and their contributions to problems of contract performance. Secondly, I will explore some of the reasons why contracts fail, emphasizing that there is an opportunity to cure most instances of defective performance, and that in virtually all cases the parties will be able to define the consequences of the failure to perform by communications between them. If this proposed expansion is accomplished, the ephemeral conceptual problems that have preoccupied legal scholars become more manageable.

I. Basic Contract Structure

In simplest terms, a contract demands that each party do what he promised. If a party fails to do what he promised, his failure is a breach; the universal consequence is that a court may require him to pay money damages sufficient to provide the nonbreaching party with the financial equivalent of performance. However, not all promises are absolute; most obligations are limited by their terms. The promise is likely to be conditioned on an event, so that until the event occurs, the obligation to perform does not arise.

This simple framework can become complicated. The categories of promise and condition are not mutually exclusive. A performance event may be promised, it may be a condition to a promised performance, or it may be both. Both promises and conditions are defined in terms of the legal consequences which a breach of one or a failure of the other entails: A promise is that which produces damages for its breach; a condition is that which may require or may excuse or discharge further performance. The consequences of defining an event will therefore have quite different impact depending on which label is selected. Damages for breach of contract are generally conservative, and the burden on the breaching party is likely to be relatively light or at least bearable. In contrast, the result of finding a discharging condition is that one side will lose the entire benefit of the contract without any compensation whatsoever.

It is essential that the businessman have some idea what will be considered a promise or a condition in order that he may predict the likely legal consequences of a disappointment during performance. However, if these differences can be explained at all, it is only through use of an example, in this case, a quasi-historical vignette.[151]

---

[151] Eds. note: Professor Rosett's example and cast of characters may be easier to understand if we recognize that Rosett's article is a contribution to a *festschrift* in the UCLA Law Review mark-

As is well known, Addison Mueller was a successful lumber merchant in Milwaukee, Wisconsin before he began his legal career. During the period he was in business, "Mueller's Planks" was a prime purveyor of specialty marine items built of Wisconsin hardwood. The qualities of his laminated spars were toasted in all the best yacht clubs. Therefore, when after years of teaching Admiralty Law, Grant Gilmore decided to build his own racing yawl, he naturally turned to Mueller to supply the spars. We now join the contract in progress.

On September 1, Mueller agrees to provide specially designed laminated spars to Gilmore. The spars are to be delivered in installments, since only a few can be constructed at a time; the first installment is to arrive by March 1, with delivery and payment for each set of spars due on the first of each succeeding month. Among the several pages of tightly printed terms and specifications are the following conditions:

(a) Mueller agrees that each spar will not exceed 170 pounds in weight;

(b) Mueller agrees that the spars will be laminated with a special dichloryl polymer glue;

(c) The Stewards of the America's Cup Race approve the yawl's design for the challenging rounds of the race by January 15th.

The clearest promissory aspects of this transaction are that Mueller promises to provide the spars, that they will weigh no more than 170 pounds, that he will use the dichloryl glue for lamination, and that Gilmore promises to pay the purchase price and take the spars. The most obvious condition which will affect Gilmore's promise to perform is whether the Stewards of the America's Cup Race approve the yawl plans. In addition, Mueller's promise of the spars and Gilmore's promise of the price are conditional as well as promissory in nature because Gilmore's obligation to pay will not become due until Mueller tenders the spars and vice versa. In addition to these explicit promises and conditions, there may be implicit ones as well. The approval of the plans by the Stewards is primarily a conditioning event outside the control of either party, but one may imply a promise by Gilmore to make sure at least that the design is one which meets the Stewards' basic specifications, and to submit the plans for approval.

We can see the significance of the promise/condition distinction by examining the contract term in which Mueller promised to provide spars weighing no more than 170 pounds. Suppose that instead the spars weigh 172 or 168 pounds but are

---

ing the retirement of Professor Addison Mueller from the faculty of the UCLA Law School. Mueller wrote a number of important articles in the field. In addition, he edited a casebook called "Contract in Context." Students learned contracts by working through problems encountered during the construction of a house. Professor Rosett is a co-editor of later editions of the casebook. Before joining the UCLA faculty, Mueller was a law professor at Yale.

The late Grant Gilmore was a member of the Yale Law School faculty. He was the author of important works in many fields. His THE DEATH OF CONTRACT was widely discussed during the 1970s. Professor Gilmore called his contribution to the *festschrift*, "The Truth About Addison Mueller." He began by saying, "Not the whole truth, of course—we reserve that for our enemies. In 1941 Addy and I had both belatedly undertaken the study of law at the Yale Law School. For the ten years before that I had been teaching French and Addy had been running a lumber business in Milwaukee. Conceivably there are even worse ways of preparing for law school than teaching French or running a lumber business but, offhand, I cannot think what they would be."

nonetheless usable in a racing yawl. Assume also that regardless of the weight, the price for the spars remains the same. If it is concluded that Mueller has merely promised to provide lightweight spars which will efficiently hold the sails during the stress of a race, the deviation in contract terms created by the variation in weight gives rise to damages but does not relieve Gilmore of his obligation to take the spars and pay for them. Various measures of damages are possible, but in no case would the total amount be substantial. In contrast, if the term is found to be a condition as well as a promise, Gilmore will be entitled to refuse the spars. This result is likely to follow even if the spars would not impair the racing ability of the yawl. Then Mueller's loss is likely to be substantial and disproportionate to the impact of the deviation on Gilmore. In fact, if we assume further that there is no ready market for the specially laminated spars, Mueller's loss may be catastrophic.

Such extreme results are undesirable. Precisely because of this, courts as well as businessmen have recognized gradations in defining consequences for breach of promise. The failure of some promises will have a de minimis effect, some will give rise to a claim for partial damages, but others will result in payment of compensation for the loss of the entire contract. As we return to old Milwaukee, Mueller has promised to laminate the spars using the special dichloryl glue. If instead he uses trichloryl glue, Mueller will be liable for damages even if the trichloryl glue is in every respect as satisfactory and in some respects is superior to dichloryl glue. But what damages? The probable answer is that either Mueller will be required to pay what it will cost to reglue the spars or Gilmore may be given the financial equivalent of performance by awarding him the difference in value between the spars as promised and those provided. If the first measure is applied, Gilmore will receive partial damages for the cost of regluing. If the latter diminished value measure is used, the amount of compensation is likely to be inconsequential and to fall within the de minimis category.

In contrast, suppose that Mueller, studying law at night rather than supervising construction of the spars, is late delivering the first set of spars, and they do not arrive until April. The losses associated with this failure of performance are likely to be more than de minimis. In some circumstances the damages may be substantial. Assuming, however, that construction of the yawl is going forward, although slowly, and the delays can be made up eventually, it seems most likely that the default will be considered a partial breach, giving rise to a claim for compensation but not one measured by the loss of the entire contract. Finally, if the spars arrive but they are the wrong size and do not fit the rig, partial breach damages are inadequate; Gilmore will have to look elsewhere for spars, and the damages will be measured by the failure of the entire expectancy.

The concepts of de minimis, partial and total breach are effective in resolving breach of promise conflicts. Unfortunately, there has not been a similarly effective delineation of the consequences with respect to conditions. The difficulty is in deciding whether a condition discharges or merely suspends performance obligations. For example, Mueller's tender of the spars conditions Gilmore's obligation to pay for them. If Mueller is only fifteen minutes late in delivering, there may be a failure of a condition, but it is one that in most circumstances would be insignificant and is unlikely to justify termination. If delivery is delayed several days, Gilmore will be justified in suspending his duty to pay until the spars arrive, but once they are delivered, it is likely that Gilmore's duty to pay will then become due. But at some point the suspension becomes a discharge. If Mueller has gone off to Yale Law School and the spars therefore never arrive, he cannot come around with the spars after graduation and demand payment in order to pay for his bar review course. At some point, Gilmore's duty can no longer be revived by occurrence of the condition. It is discharged, and the possibility of performance is terminated.

The Uniform Commercial Code and the Restatement II recognize the existence of this gradation between suspending and discharging conditions[152] but there are few court opinions or classical treatises which attempt to differentiate clearly between the two. As a result, a party is likely to be uncertain whether and when his obligation is discharged. Moreover, the risks and burdens of decision are placed on the innocent party, rather than on the party who created the insecurity. If Gilmore fails to pay on time, Mueller must make the risky decision whether to seek another buyer immediately or wait until payment is forthcoming. When Gilmore is only three days late, Mueller will be uncertain whether he *may* sell the spars to someone else and if he does, whether he will be liable for damages to Gilmore if Gilmore eventually tenders the money. It is also unclear when Mueller *must* attempt to sell elsewhere. If he moves too quickly, this change of position may itself be deemed a repudiation, and he will be liable for breach if Gilmore later demands the spars Mueller can no longer deliver. If several months go by and Gilmore has not come up with the money and Mueller has not tried to sell to another buyer, his eventual damages might be reduced under the avoidable consequences rule because he failed to mitigate them. To the degree that a contract is for goods readily available in the market, it makes sense to allow the disappointed seller to treat a rather brief delay in performance as a contract terminating event, allowing him to go into the market and engage in a compensating transaction. When one party repudiates before performance is due, it also makes sense to require the disappointed party to cover after a "commercially reasonable" time rather than to let him sit around waiting for performance forever. But to the extent that the contract covers specially manufactured goods or is a construction contract, and covering transactions are more difficult and wasteful, it is harder to decide when the disappointed party *may* terminate by cover or other change of position and when the party *must* terminate.[153]

The attempt to delineate consequences of failures of conditions is complicated by the variety of events that may suspend performance. In addition to present breaches, such as the failure to deliver or pay on time, there are all sorts of events that will give the parties legitimate cause for uncertainty and justify a suspension until that uncertainty is removed. Many of these events are likely to have only a temporary impact. If the scuttlebutt among the yachting crowd is that the Stewards have tentatively decided to eliminate yawls from America's Cup races, the resulting uncertainty might justify either Gilmore, Mueller, or both in suspending

---

[152] [12] Uniform Commercial Code §§ 2-609, 2-615; Restatement II §§ 266D, 277.
[153] [15] These difficulties are presented in equally troubling form in land sales and personal services contracts.

performance. The contract is explicit that the construction of the yawl is contingent on the Stewards' approval of the plans. It is likely to be wasteful for Mueller to continue laminating the spars in the face of this doubt. But the duration of the justified suspensions is uncertain. Assuming that there is a real chance that the Stewards may change their minds prior to the date performance is due, Mueller may want to wait until the January 15 deadline for approval of the plans before he considers the deal terminated. In any event, it seems unlikely that Mueller will be able to claim successfully that the October rumors permanently discharge his obligation or that his duty would not be revived by a change of mind by the Stewards prior to January 15 and subsequent approval of the plans.

II. Causes of Contract Failure

In the preceding section we saw that inherent in the structure of contract is the potential for the creation of uncertainty. As a result, a party is unable accurately to predict whether his performance disappointment has terminated the contract and whether his damages will be measured on the basis of partial or total breach. Unfortunately, as the hypothetical case suggests, conventional doctrine is of little help; in fact, it sometimes adds to the innocent party's anxiety by suggesting that he might be guilty of repudiation or failure to mitigate damages if his timing is poor. This portion of the article will discuss whether such uncertainty can be resolved by measures short of contract termination. In part this will depend on the causes of contract failure and the feasibility of communications between the parties and cure to enable the contract to continue in force.

A virtually infinite variety of contingencies may arise during contract performance to disturb the parties' expectations. It would be futile to attempt to catalog these disturbing events in detail, but in general, most performance difficulties are the product of:

(a) *Failure to perform.* One of the performing parties simply fails to act as he could have and should have acted;

(b) *External supervening event.* A party's ability to perform as promised is impaired by catastrophe, the unforeseen acts of individuals or governments, death, or the destruction of specific objects;

(c) *Market change.* A variation in the price or in supply makes the agreement much less attractive to one side than obtaining the same performance in the open market;

(d) *Agreement failure.* The process of agreement is defective because of mistake, ambiguity, incompleteness, or misunderstanding;

(e) *The Bad Marriage.* Some transactions degenerate into an interrelated series of escalating mutual breaches, each of which is quite minor viewed alone. The cause of the perturbation is less the troubling events themselves than the parties' responses to them. The deal is going sour, and that, rather than specific incidents, is the central problem.

Failure of performance, the situation in which the party could have performed but failed to do so without justification, is the clearest case for casting the burden of failure on the breaching party. However, the party in trouble is likely to be able to cure most failures of performance. If he cannot cure or cannot provide assurances of future performance, his material failure to perform is appropriately treated as a discharging event. The nonbreaching party is relieved from all further obligations of performance under the contract and is awarded damages measured by the total breach.

When the failure to perform, current or prospective, is the result of some *supervening event* outside the control of either party, the problem is not so easily handled by assigning fault or risk to one side. A strict application of conventional doctrine would leave the parties with all the risks they failed to avoid by expressly conditioning their promises. It would not necessarily matter that the cause of the trouble was beyond the party's control or even that performance as promised was literally impossible or illegal. One might not be able to perform, but one could almost always pay damages. However appealing this analysis may have been in an earlier, sterner age, it does not satisfy the expectations and realities of modern contract-making. Contract would not be a usable tool if the parties were required to state explicitly every assumption underlying their agreement and every conceivable contingency limiting it. When a person agrees to work for another he assumes he will be alive and well to perform; when specific goods are bought and sold it is assumed that they will remain in existence and that there will be money in circulation to pay for them. Ordinary people would think it strange, to say the least, if they were told that such assumptions must be expressed. When one of these basic assumptions of the contract has been weakened or destroyed it no longer makes sense to assign fault or impose on one side all the burdens associated with nonperformance. In an ongoing commercial relationship when such external event occurs, it is necessarily an excuse. The realistic choice is between modifying the agreement to conform to changed circumstances or relieving both sides of their obligations.

In contrast, because the possibility of *market change* is a primary and essential risk of all promise-making, when the failure of performance is traceable primarily to such change, the losses associated therewith should be left where they lie. It is likely that one party to almost any deal will feel that he sold too cheaply or bought too dearly. A judgment regarding the extent to which market change is an assumed contract risk must be made on the basis of the parties' agreement, trade usage, and community expectations. If the change is beyond assumed risk, the only practical choices are likely to be contract modification or discharge.

When there is *agreement failure*, it becomes apparent during the course of performance that the parties did not make the deal they thought they did. This failure may be the result of mistake, misunderstanding, ambiguity, erroneous information, or simply failure of the parties to think through and reach agreement on likely contingencies. Contract law is based on the premise that an agreement which results from the parties' intentional and consensual acts warrants enforcement since it is presumed to be serious, worthwhile and socially desirable. If there has, in fact, been no agreement, this rationale for enforcement no longer applies. However, abandoning the contract altogether may work a real hardship on the parties. If the failure resulted from an honest mistake and not pettifogging, poor judgment, or fraud, some compromises may have to be made. It seems apparent that the parties are in a position to sort the problem out far superior to that of any court. Often the parties can cure their original agreement failure or can restate their deal in mutually satisfactory terms, while the best a court could hope to do is to impose some synthetic "reasonable" solution by "interpretation" of the agreement.

Bad contract marriages resemble the family disputes upon which the metaphor is based. Court efforts to untangle such situations on the basis of fault or risk are likely to prove futile or to create more problems than they solve. Again, the important point is that the parties are in a better position than a court to untangle the mess.

Conventional legal doctrine would deal with the parties in all the above-described situations as if they were strangers, isolated from one another. Too little weight is given the likelihood that most failures of performance are curable when, or soon after they occur. Breaches and failures become material in part because they are treated that way rather than promptly adjusted. When a party is faced with present or threatened failure of performance, the Restatement II analyzes the issue in terms of whether this behavior is a breach and whether that beach is material. The party who is guilty of the first uncured material breach bears the loss. The Restatement emphasis is on characterizing the performance of the parties, not upon guiding them in determining whether to continue with the contract. Although the Restatement II recognizes the possibility of communication, assurance, and cure, little emphasis is placed on whether the parties have tried to communicate to adjust the difficulties. No duty to communicate candidly is improved, nor are the parties bound by what they say if they do communicate. Not only are the parties not required to communicate, but there seems to be a real danger that candid communication advising the other side of the circumstances jeopardizing performance and requesting a modification to accommodate the changed circumstances, unless carefully phrased, will be interpreted as a repudiation—a material breach by the communicating party.

This traditional orientation is unrealistic, because most business transactions are part of an ongoing relationship between people who are or can easily be in direct communication. The first thing a contracting party in difficulty should do is contact the other party, explain the situation, and give assurances that the defect will be cured, or if that is not possible, seek to modify the agreement so that it can be performed, or else terminate it altogether. If Mueller fails to deliver the spars on time, Gilmore will undoubtedly call or write to find out why. If Gilmore is uncertain whether to treat Mueller's failure to deliver as a delaying suspension or a discharging termination he will ask what is going on. The quality of the communications between Gilmore and Mueller should be given equal weight with the reason for failure of performance in defining the parties' rights, options and obligations.

The following hypothetical scripts will demonstrate what is meant by "quality of the communications." Suppose that when Gilmore, the insecure party, asks Mueller why the spars have not arrived, Mueller says to him, "Contract is dead,"[154] and will not even talk about the possibility of cure. Under these circumstances, the contract does not appear to be dead, and Gilmore seems to have few

---

[154] [22] Cf. G. Gilmore, The Death of Contract (1974).

options. If Gilmore does not engage in a covering transaction, he may impair his right to receive full damages since he could be accused of failure to mitigate his losses. Mueller's breach must be considered material, further performance on Gilmore's part is discharged, and Gilmore has a cause of action for damages measured by the total value of the contract.

In the second script, the forever insecure Gilmore receives a credible promise from the apologetic Mueller who explains that he has temporarily run out of the dichloryl glue, but he has just received word that it is on its way. He assures Gilmore that the spars will be completed and the contract will be performed in the future. In this case the agreement continues in force, and Gilmore is not justified in terminating. However, depending on the credibility of Mueller's assurances, Gilmore may be justified in suspending performance or otherwise protecting himself until Mueller's intentions are confirmed. To the extent that the assurances are credible and cure is possible, the legal consequences of the failure are inevitably limited to those denominated as immaterial or partial breach. Once performance is resumed, and the failure cured, damages are confined to those losses associated with partial breach.

In a third scenario, Gilmore is informed that performance is indefinitely suspended because of a supervening event—an infestation of the nefarious Wisconsin hardwood beetle which makes it unclear whether there will be sufficient wood of the type needed to construct the spars. Although Gilmore's lawyer may be uncertain what factual circumstances provide legally valid excuses for nonperformance, Gilmore may accept delays or excuses which a court would not. He and Mueller are likely to agree to a modification of the performance to reflect the new situation, or they might consider that the wisest course is to abort the deal, with or without compensating payments. The point is that since the parties are in a better position than courts to determine what to do, they would best be served by rules which encourage them to solve the problem themselves. If they are unable to do so, and litigation results, the Court's resolution of the difficult question of excuse would be easier if it knew whether the injured party was willing to accept a modified or curing performance. Furthermore, by leaving primarily to the parties the characterization of the incident as one that terminates the agreement or merely suspends performance, any ultimate litigation will be limited to questions relating to damages or other forms of relief appropriate in cases of frustrated contracts.

Another possibility is that the communications following the insecurity-producing event are marked by disagreement, indefiniteness, equivocation or avoidance. The breaching party may express his intention to perform and the hope that he will be able to, but at the same time he may express doubt whether he will be able to perform. Or, as in the classic case of *Norrington v. Wright*,[155] the lawyers may get into the act, supplanting the parties' attempts to communicate with evasive pettifogging. In *Norrington*, a British merchant sold scrap rails to a Philadelphia buyer through a local broker. The goods were to be delivered in monthly installments of a specified quantity, but the seller's early shipments were

---

[155] [23] 115 U.S. 188 (1885).

late and fell short. At the same time the market price declined sharply. The insecure buyer wanted out of the contract now made unattractive both by the market change and the imperfect installments. The communications which ensued between the lawyers for buyer and seller are models of equivocation, the flavor of which is conveyed by the following:

> You ask us to determine whether we will or will not object to receive further shipments because of past defaults. We tell you we will if we are entitled to do so, and will not if we are not entitled to do so. We do not think you have the right to compel us to decide a disputed question of law to relieve you from the risk of deciding it yourself. You know quite well as we do what is the rule and its uncertainty of application.[156]

When, as here, both sides are intentionally evasive, it is hard to determine after the fact which side is responsible for the first uncured material breach or for making the other side insecure. If the law encouraged candid communications between parties, a court would be aided in evaluating the parties' competing claims. For example, the buyer in *Norrington* might simply have said that the falling market and the seller's failure to deliver timely and complete installments suggested to him that the seller was speculating on the falling market at the buyer's expense, and therefore the buyer wished to terminate the contract. Under the Restatement II, however, these statements by the buyer might be interpreted not as an attempt to resolve problems but as a repudiation and therefore as a material breach. This approach, however, discourages candid dispute settlement. The buyer should not be penalized without first examining the seller's response. The seller might have recognized the validity of the buyer's point and agreed to compensate him for market losses associated with the failure to deliver the full installments on time. It seems likely that the seller would try to keep the transaction alive because he had a profitable contract. However, if the seller were unable or unwilling to provide the buyer with substantial assurances of future performance or compensation for defaults, it would be easier for a court to find that these defaults were contract-terminating events.

In another scenario, closely related to the situation in *Norrington*, we find Gilmore awaiting the third shipment of spars from the delinquent Mueller. When he calls Mueller to find out why the spars are late, Mueller is not at all apologetic and says merely that the spars were not sent because Gilmore failed to pay for the last installment and further, that no more spars will be forthcoming, because of Gilmore's material breach. Gilmore is surprised, to say the least, because not only did he send a check, which apparently became lost in the mails, but he also assumed that if Mueller were upset about nonpayment, he would have let Gilmore know. A significant advantage of emphasizing the importance of communication and cure is that the accusing party's previous failure to communicate at the time of the first alleged failure gives rise to the inference that he did not consider the deviation an insecurity-producing event. If communication were required upon the occurrence of an insecurity-producing event, a party seeking assurance who is himself accused of breaching first would have an external standard (that

---

[156] [24] Id. at 192.

is, whether the other side complained of the earlier breach and sought assurances and cure) against which to evaluate the claim that *his* failure was the cause of the mutual failure. He would also have the option of continuing the transaction or abandoning it, which he would exercise by characterizing the other side's behavior as either an immaterial or material breach.

In a final possible script we find Gilmore struggling to install the spars but they will not fit in the gumpals. He calls Mueller to complain and asks for assurances that Mueller will cure the defects. Mueller airily replies that there is no problem and that he constructed the spars in accordance with specifications. Now Gilmore has few options. He can accept Mueller's assurances that all is well, he can press further in an effort to communicate his concerns, or, recognizing the futility of that choice he can return the spars, terminating the contract, and prepare for litigation. If he selects this last option, the relevant considerations are not those regarding communications. Rather, in this situation traditional doctrine applies, and the answers to the questions whether there was a material breach, who committed it, and were the promises dependent or independent, will determine the outcome of the dispute.

III. Conclusion

In summary, when trouble arises during the life of a contract as a result of a present or threatened failure of performance, an insecure party should be justified in suspending his performance long enough to communicate with the other side to seek cure of past failures and to receive assurances of future compliance with the contract. A party who communicates candidly should not be considered to have repudiated unless he unequivocally refuses to perform or to give assurances of future performance. The quality of communications between the parties should be a major factor in the court's evaluation of their competing claims. Failure of a party to seek cure or assurances promptly creates a strong inference that the party did not regard the trouble a threat to the contract relationship. In such a case, the trouble would not condition either party's further performance; that is, it would not be a potential contract terminating event. Of course, the aggrieved party would always be able to press a claim for damages measured by a partial breach.

In suggesting that contract law should place greater emphasis on advising the businessman in the course of performance, I am aware that there may be some who would question whether this is a proper task for the law to undertake. Some reassuring comments can be addressed to those who see this proposal as an unwarranted extension of present law.

First, the approach suggested is not a great departure from the substance of existing law embodied in statutes and cases. However, new emphasis is placed on the availability and importance of communication and cure when trouble arises in the course of contract performance. As suggested earlier, the requirement that parties communicate is implicit in current bodies of contract doctrine and is therefore hardly an unheard of innovation. Second, the central assumption of contract law has always been that all interests are best served if the force of law is used to sanction the arrangements people make for themselves rather than to structure their relationships by externally imposed rules. Consequently, the law allows contracting parties to set limits on remedies for breach, to liquidate damages, and to opt out of the legal system's method of dispute resolution by arbitration. The same approach would support encouraging the parties to resolve their differences themselves by reinforcing the duties of communication and cure before turning to the institution of last resort, the courts.

The sanctity of traditional doctrine is difficult to defend when one considers that it painstakingly advises the owner of a bull which escapes his pasture whether he owes anything to the man who takes care of the beast; tells the home-buyer whose builder installed the wrong brand of pipe whether he has a cause of action; and assists the cotton broker whose cotton was delivered on the wrong ship "Peerless" in deciding whether he may recover damages. To require the law also to advise the businessman would not seem to entail a great philosophical leap.

Chapter 6

ADJUSTING TO CHANGED CIRCUMSTANCES: RISKS ASSUMED AND IMPOSED

A. LARGE ORGANIZATIONS AND GREAT EVENTS: CONTRACT DOCTRINE, RESTITUTION, AND COPING WITH THE PROBLEMS

People making contracts can be mistaken about the present situation, and can make wrong predictions of the future. Some mistakes are just the risks of the deal. For example, Seller, a used book dealer, sells an old book to Buyer for $5.00, and Buyer makes no misrepresentations. The book is a rare first edition, worth $25,000. Or Buyer thinks the value of land or corporate securities will increase after their purchase, but their value falls sharply. The risk of some mistakes, however, is not implicit in the deal, and our sense of fairness may require intervention and adjustment. While situations at the extremes may not present too much difficulty, often arguments can be made both that a risk was assumed and that it was not.

Legal culture at times distinguishes mistakes concerning existing facts from assumptions and predictions about the future. Typically, the law of mistake focuses on errors about facts at or before the contract was made. However, things may happen in the future that make it very difficult, impracticable, or virtually impossible to perform contractual duties. Lawyers often speak of this situation as one involving "impossibility." However, I may be able to perform my duties under a contract without difficulty, but events may rob my performance of any value to you. In the classic situation, I rent to you a place from which you plan to watch an elaborate parade. The parade later is canceled. You can still stand or sit there and watch whatever passes by, but this right is far less valuable to you than what you assumed you were buying. Lawyers label this as a problem of "frustration of purpose."

There is much discussion of frustration of purpose in some quarters. However, Professor Wladis surveyed the cases and concluded: "The *Krell* case [which established the frustration doctrine and involved the rental of space overlooking the planned parade to celebrate the coronation of King Edward VII] can be deleted or reduced to the status of a footnote case. For all the trouble it has caused generations of law students, and law professors, *Krell* has had virtually no influence upon the law.[1]"

UCC § 2-615 excuses sellers whose performance "has been made impracticable by the occurrence of a contingency the non-occurrence of which was a basic assumption on which the contract was made." However, the text of the section says nothing about buyers whose purposes have been frustrated. Official Comment 9 suggests that when a seller knows that a buyer's order is based on a defi-

---

[1] Wladis, *Common Law and Uncommon Events: The Development of the Doctrine of Impossibility of Performance in English Common Law*, 75 Geo. L. J. 1575, 1630-1631 (1988).

nite and specific venture "the reason of the present section may well apply and entitles the buyer to the exemption." Professor Wladis is right that there are few successful frustration defenses, but the issue still can trouble a lawyer from time to time. We will see that the threat of international terrorism may give new life to the old doctrine.[2]

While these distinctions-between impossibility, and frustration, for example-can be drawn, as always we must ask whether the distinctions make any difference that matters. Many modern writers see mistake, impossibility and frustration as involving essentially similar problems, although the doctrinal tests may be stated in different terms.

Suppose, for example, Seller contracts with Buyer to deliver a machine built according to plans and specifications. Buyer is to pay on the date specified for delivery. The contract, however, says nothing about the effect of strikes, floods, fires and the like that delay production. Assume:

(a) seller needs a special type of steel to build the machine. Seller's supplier's employees strike, and this kind of steel cannot be obtained elsewhere in time so that Seller can perform; or

(b) seller's own employees strike; or

(c) there is a flood in Seller's plant, stopping production.

Seller fails to deliver on time. Buyer sues Seller for breach of contract. Does Seller have a defense in any, all or none of these situations?

Suppose, instead, Seller completes the machine a month after the delivery date. Seller's delay was caused by the strike or flood we've assumed. Seller then tenders the machine to Buyer. Buyer refuses to accept it. May Seller successfully sue Buyer for breach of contract or does Buyer have a defense? (These problems, of course, all raise issues of *impracticability* or *impossibility* since the seller cannot get the machine there on time.)

Suppose, finally, Seller could deliver on time, but Buyer is prevented from using the machine because of environmental protection regulations issued after the contract was made. The issue now is whether there is an excuse because of *frustration of purpose*.

1. CONTRASTING LEGAL APPROACHES

Consider the approaches taken by the common law in the 17th and 19th centuries and by the Uniform Commercial Code today. We can ask whether the legal system has gained any ground in 300 years. Whatever the reasons offered, we can see the spirit of *Paradine v. Jane* in some decisions interpreting the Uniform Commercial Code or applying contract doctrine to other than transactions in goods.

---

[2] For a recent case in which the court applied the frustration of purpose doctrine, see Chase Precast Corporation v. Paonessa Company Inc., 566 N.E.2d 603 (Mass. 1991), where a subcontractor which had contracted to supply concrete median barriers to a highway construction contractor was denied a claim for lost profits when the state, acting in response to strong community protests, eliminated the use of median barriers on the project. The court characterized the frustration doctrine as a "companion rule" to the doctrine of impossibility

PARADINE v. JANE
King's Bench
Mich. 23 Car. Banco Regis.[3] Hil. 22 Car. Rot. 1178, & 1179

In debt the plaintiff declares upon a lease for years rendring rent at the four usual feasts; and for rent behind for three years, ending at the Feast of the Annunciation, 21 Car. brings his action; the defendant pleads, that a certain German prince, by name Prince Rupert, an alien born, enemy to the King and kingdom, had invaded the realm with an hostile army of men; and with the same force did enter upon the defendant's possession, and him expelled, and held out of possession from the 19 of July 18 Car. till the Feast of the Annunciation, 21 Car. whereby he could not take the profits; whereupon the plaintiff demurred, and the plea was resolved insufficient. . . .

3.   It was resolved, that the matter of the plea was insufficient; for though the whole army had been alien enemies, yet he ought to pay his rent. And this difference was taken, that where the law creates a duty or charge, and the party is disabled to perform it without any default in him, and hath no remedy over, there the law will excuse him. As in the case of waste, if a house be destroyed by tempest, or by enemies, the lessee is excused. [S]o of an escape. So in 9 E. 3. 16. a supersedeas was awarded to the justices, that they should not proceed in a cessavit upon a cesser during the war, but when the party by his own contract creates a duty or charge upon himself, he is bound to make it good, if he may, notwithstanding any accident by inevitable necessity, because he might have provided against it by his contract. And therefore if the lessee covenant to repair a house, though it be burnt by lightning, or thrown down by enemies, yet he ought to repair it. Now the rent is a duty created by the parties upon the reservation, and had there been a covenant to pay it, there had been no question but the lessee must have made it good, notwithstanding the interruption by enemies, for the law would not protect him beyond his own agreement, no more then in the case of reparations; this reservation then being a covenant in law, and whereupon an action of covenant hath been maintained (as Roll said) it is all one as if there had been an actual covenant. Another reason was added, that as the lessee is to have the advantage of casual profits, so he must run the hazard of casual losses, and not lay the whole burthen of them upon his lessor; and Dyer 56. 6. was cited for this purpose, that though the land be surrounded, or gained by the sea, or made barren by wildfire, yet the lessor shall have his whole rent: and judgment was given for the plaintiff.

NOTES AND QUESTIONS

1.   *Historical context*: Some very simplified history may help make the case more understandable. Who was Prince Rupert who invaded the land with an

---

[3] 23 Car. refers to 1647, the 23d year of the reign of King Charles I.

army and prompted this case? The phrase "an alien, and an enemy of the King" is misleading. King James I had several children. One was Charles I, the King at the time of the *Paradine* case. Charles' sister, Elizabeth, married Frederick, the Elector of the Palatine (then a state in central Europe). In 1619, Prince Rupert was born to Frederick and Elizabeth in Prague. Thus, Rupert was Charles' nephew.

In 1618, a revolt in Bohemia began the Thirty Years' War. In 1619, Frederick became King of Bohemia. The Bohemians were defeated in 1620, and Frederick, Elizabeth and Rupert fled to Holland. James I attempted to aid his son-in-law by sending an army of 12,000 men to march to the Palatine, and it was landed in Holland. However, the army disintegrated because of sickness and lack of supplies. Frederick continued to fight in the Thirty Years' War, and Rupert joined him in battle when he was fourteen.

Paradine v. Jane is a product of the English Civil War which overthrew Charles I and brought Oliver Cromwell and the Parliamentarians to power. Several events produced this conflict. In 1603, James I asserted the absolute power to tax in order to finance his role in international affairs. Parliament resisted, asserting that only it could tax. Charles I became king in 1625. Soon he was involved in wars with Spain and France and needed money. In 1628, Parliament responded to Charles' actions with the Petition of Right which asserted that the King's power to tax, imprison and quarter soldiers was limited legally. Charles responded by dismissing Parliament in 1629.

Charles I also was involved in the religious battles of the time. Actions taken in his name drove the Puritans out of the Church of England to North America. In 1638, Charles tried to impose the Church of England on Scotland and prompted a revolt. The tensions between Catholics and Protestants were involved in the Thirty Years' War on the continent and in the conflicts in England as well.

Parliament met in 1640. It attacked the King's policies, and it seized some of his ministers. The King came to Parliament and tried to arrest its leaders, but he failed. The Civil War began in August of 1642. The King held the territory from Oxford to the North; the Parliament held London.

At the outbreak of the Civil War, Rupert came to England to join his cousin Charles at Nottingham in 1642. Although he offended various courtiers by "his rough manner and arrogance," he commanded the King's forces to a number of victories and proved himself one of the King's few able military leaders. He was named Earl of Holderness and Duke of Cumberland in 1644. In 1645, he became Governor of Bristol, but he surrendered it to Parliamentary forces. The King was angered by the surrender and banished Rupert, but Rupert brought about a reconciliation during that same year.

During most of the Civil War, neither side could win. Troops on both sides looted the estates of the nobility. This is the way armies of the time were paid and gained needed supplies. *Paradine v. Jane* involves one of the many minor actions in the war. Rupert's forces held the land from 1642 to 1645. Finally, in 1645, Cromwell organized what, for the time, was a professional army. It defeated the King's forces in a number of battles. In 1646, the King surrendered. The Parliamentary forces captured Rupert when Oxford surrendered. He was ordered to leave the country. Charles I was beheaded in 1649. Cromwell took power and ruled until his death in 1657. Charles II gained power in 1660. Rupert returned with him. He fought in the wars against the Dutch, and he was First Lord of the Admiralty from 1673 to 1679. He died in 1682.[4]

2. *Grant Gilmore on Paradine v. Jane*: Professor Gilmore comments on the significance of the case:[5]

> No legal system has ever carried into practice a theory of absolute contractual liability. Our own system, during the nineteenth century, may be the only one which has ever proclaimed such a theory. The proclamation was made in this country long before Holmes came on the scene and, at least in this country, was steadfastly adhered to, mostly as a matter of ritual incantation, throughout the century. The source of the absolute liability idea in English law was always confidently stated to be the seventeenth century case of *Paradine v. Jane*. In that case, a landlord's action to recover rent, the tenant had pleaded that he should be excused from payment because, during the term of the lease, he had been evicted from the land by a royalist army under the command of Prince Rupert. The plea was held bad: "Though the whole army had been alien enemies, yet he ought to pay his rent." Two hundred years later we find Morton, J., for the Massachusetts court, explaining the "general rule" on excuse by reason of impossibility in this fashion:

> . . . [W]here the party by his agreement voluntarily assumes or creates a duty or charge upon himself, he shall be bound by his contract, and the nonperformance of it will not be excused by accident or inevitable necessity; for if he desired any such exception, he should have provided for it in his contract.

> This language was copied, almost word for word, from one of the seventeenth century reports of *Paradine v. Jane*—a case which, in all probability, Judge Morton had never read and which he did not cite.

> The story of the transmission of the *Paradine v. Jane* language from mid-seventeenth century England to mid-nineteenth century America is one of the curiosities of the legal literature. In its own day *Paradine* does not seem to have been a particularly celebrated case, nor does its seventeenth century meaning, so far as we can determine it, necessarily have much or anything to do with what came to be its nineteenth century meaning. One possibility is that the seventeenth century court meant merely that the tenant could not interpose his plea in the landlord's action for the rent but could bring an independent action against the landlord to recover whatever damages he had suffered as the result of his eviction by Prince Rupert; indeed, *Paradine* is cited to that proposition in a case decided in 1723. Another possibility is that the court looked on the leasehold as a fully executed transaction, with the tenant bearing the risk of

---

[4] *See* Cook and Wroughton, English Historical Facts 1603-1688 (Rowman & Littlefield 1980).

[5] Grant Gilmore, The Death of Contract 44-47 (1974). Copyright © 1974 by the Ohio State University Press. Reprinted by permission.

eviction in the same way that a buyer of chattels would bear the risk of their loss or destruction after receiving delivery of them from the seller. The modern vogue of *Paradine* dates from Serjeant Williams's edition, first published in 1802, of Saunders, which was a collection of late seventeenth century cases. One of the cases in Saunders, *Walton v. Waterhouse*, involved a covenant by a tenant to rebuild after a fire. In a lengthy note to *Walton v. Waterhouse*, Williams paraphrased the language used in the Aleyn report of *Paradine* and it was Williams' note which Judge Morton, in the Massachusetts case just referred to, cited and copied out. Indeed, there are several early nineteenth century references to *Paradine v. Jane* which assume that the case, given the context in which Williams had put it, involved a tenant's covenant to rebuild.

However, all this is mere bibliographical amusement. The importance of the story lies in the facts that the Williams edition of Saunders was highly successful—having been many times reprinted both in England and in the United States—and that the Note to *Walton v. Waterhouse* became celebrated—the apparent meaning of the Note being that English law for two hundred years past had steadfastly adhered to a theory of absolute contractual liability. Such a theory evidently made sense to the judges—particularly the American judges—of a hundred years and more ago. It would take us too far afield to inquire into the reasons for the success of such a theory; we might perhaps speculate that the Puritan ethic was somehow involved. . . . Let me repeat a point I have already made: the absolute liability idea was often preached but rarely practiced. . . . This comment makes the ideas themselves no less significant; it is always a matter of the highest interest when courts—like people generally—say one thing while doing its opposite. . . .

Professor Gilmore invites us to speculate about the appeal of an absolute liability rule. In that spirit, we can ask whether the impact of such a rule would be random or would systematically benefit one group and disadvantage another? Recall Professor Horwitz's views, *supra* Chapter 1.

Professor Wladis reviews the history of the English law of impossibility. He says that law and history "are often incorrectly taught to law students. *Paradine*, for example, is usually cited for a proposition for which the case does not stand and which the judge had no intention of establishing." Wladis points to Aleyn's report which says: "when the party by his own contract creates a duty or charge upon himself, he is bound to make it good, *if he may*, notwithstanding any accident by inevitable necessity, because he might have provided against it by his contract." The key phrase is "if he may." And "*Paradine* was not a case in which the defendant's dispossession made payment of the rent impossible."[6] Wladis continues, noting "[f]ar from reflecting a general rule of the common law at the time, both the result and the reasoning in *Paradine* struggled for acceptance for some 150 years." He finds the first explicit recognition of the *Paradine* reasoning

---

[6] Wladis, *Common Law and Uncommon Events: The Development of the Doctrine of Impossibility of Performance in English Contract Law*, 75 Geo. L. J. 1575, 1576, 1583-4 (1987).

as a general principle in 1858, although he finds the decision used often in lease cases.

3. *Rule and counter-rule*: Whatever the force of the ideas associated with *Paradine v. Jane*, it was possible to fashion a counter-rule well within the traditions of the common law. A court could find that what appeared to be an absolute unqualified promise was in fact a promise subject to an implied condition. Again, in the spirit of speculation, recall Professor Horwitz' views. Consider the text of what in the late-20th century is a better known case than *Paradine v. Jane*.

TAYLOR v. CALDWELL
King's Bench
3 B. & S. 826, 122 Eng. Rep. 309 (1863)

The declaration alleged that by an agreement . . . the defendants agreed to let . . . The Surrey Gardens and Music Hall, Newington, Surrey, for . . . Monday the 17th June 1861, Monday the 15th July, 1861, Monday the 5th August, 1861, and Monday the 19th August, 1861, for the purpose of giving a series of four grand concerts and day and night fetes, at the Gardens and Hall on those days respectively, at the rent or sum of 100£. for each of those days. It then averred the fulfilment of conditions &c., on the part of the plaintiffs; and breach by the defendants, that they did not nor would allow the plaintiffs to have the use of The Surrey Music Hall and Gardens according to the agreement, but wholly made default therein, &c.; whereby the plaintiffs lost divers moneys paid by them for printing advertisements of and in advertising the concerts, and also lost divers sums expended and expenses incurred by them in preparing for the concerts and otherwise in relation thereto, and on the faith of the performance by the defendants of the agreement on their part, and had been otherwise injured, &c. . . .

[The defendants answered:] That at the time of the agreement there was a general custom of the trade and business of the plaintiffs and the defendants, with respect to which the agreement was made, known to the plaintiffs and the defendants, and with reference to which they agreed, and which was part of the agreement, that in the event of the Gardens and Music Hall being destroyed or so far damaged by accidental fire as to prevent the entertainments being given according to the intent of the agreement, between the time of making the agreement and the time appointed for the performance of the same, the agreement should be rescinded and at an end; and that the Gardens and Music Hall were destroyed and so far damaged by accidental fire as to prevent the entertainments, or any of them, being given, according to the intent of the agreement, between the time of making the agreement and the first of the times appointed for the performance of the same, and continued so destroyed and damaged until after the times appointed for the performance of the agreement had elapsed, without the default of the defendants or either of them. . . .

On the trial, before Blackburn, J., at the London Sittings after Michaelmas Term, 1861, it appeared that the action was brought on the following agreement:—

"Royal Surrey Gardens,

"27th May, 1861.

"Agreement between Messrs. Caldwell & Bishop, of the one part, and Messrs. Taylor & Lewis of the other part, whereby the said Caldwell & Bishop agree to let, and the said Taylor & Lewis agree to take, on the terms hereinafter stated, The Surrey Gardens and Music Hall, Newington, Surrey, for the following days, viz.:—

"Monday, the	*17th June, 1861,*
"	*15th July, 1861,*
"	*5th August, 1861,*
"	*19th August, 1861,*

for the purpose of giving a series of four grand concerts and day and night fetes at the said Gardens and Hall on those days respectively at the rent or sum of 100£. for each of the said days. The said Caldwell & Bishop agree to find and provide at their own sole expense, on each of the aforesaid days, for the amusement of the public and persons then in the said Gardens and Hall, an efficient and organised military and quadrille band, the united bands to consist of from thirty-five to forty members; al fresco entertainments of various descriptions; coloured minstrels, fireworks and full illuminations; a ballet or divertissement, if permitted, a wizard and Grecian statues; tight rope performances; rifle galleries; air gun shooting; Chinese and Parisian games; boats on the lake, and (weather permitting) aquatic sports, and all and every other entertainment as given nightly during the months and times above mentioned. And the said Caldwell & Bishop also agree that the before mentioned united bands shall be present and assist at each of the said concerts, from its commencement until 9 o'clock at night; that they will, one week at least previous to the above mentioned dates, underline in bold type in all their bills and advertisements that Mr. Sims Reeves and other artistes will sing at the said gardens on those dates respectively, and that the said Taylor & Lewis shall have the right of placing their boards, bills and placards in such number and manner (but subject to the approval of the said Caldwell & Bishop) in and about the entrance to the said gardens, and in the said grounds, one week at least previous to each of the above mentioned days respectively, all bills so displayed being affixed on boards. And the said Caldwell & Bishop also agree to allow dancing on the new circular platform after 9 o'clock at night, but not before. And the said Caldwell & Bishop also agree not to allow the firework display to take place till a 1/4 past 11 o'clock at night. And, lastly, the said Caldwell & Bishop agree that the said Taylor & Lewis shall be entitled to and shall be at liberty to take and receive, as and for the sole use and property of them the said Taylor & Lewis, all moneys paid for entrance to the Gardens, Galleries and Music Hall and firework galleries, and that the said Taylor & Lewis may in their own discretion secure the patronage of

*any charitable institution in connection with the said concerts. And the
said Taylor & Lewis agree to pay the aforesaid respective sum of 100£.
in the evening of the said respective days by a crossed cheque, and also
to find and provide, at their own sole cost, all the necessary artistes for
the said concerts, including Mr. Sims Reeves, God's will permitting.*

(Signed)	*"J. Caldwell.*
"Witness	*"Chas. Bishop.*
(Signed)	*"S. Denis."*

On the 11th June the Music Hall was destroyed by an accidental fire, so that it became impossible to give the concerts. Under these circumstances a verdict was returned for the plaintiff, with leave reserved to enter a verdict for the defendants on the second and third issues. . . .

H. Tindl Atkinson shewed cause [to enter a verdict for the plaintiffs].—First. The agreement sued on does not shew a "letting" by the defendants to the plaintiffs of the Hall and Gardens, although it uses the word "let," and contains a stipulation that the plaintiffs are to be empowered to receive the money at the doors, and to have the use of the Hall, for which they are to pay 100£, and pocket the surplus; for the possession is to remain in the defendants, and the whole tenor of the instrument is against the notion of a letting. . . .

Secondly. The destruction of the premises by fire will not exonerate the defendants from performing their part of the agreement. In *Paradine v. Jane* (Al. 26) it is laid down that, where the law creates a duty or charge, and the party is disabled to perform it without any default in him, and hath no remedy over, there the law will excuse him; but when the party, by his own contract, creates a duty or charge upon himself, he is bound to make it good, if he may, notwithstanding any accident by inevitable necessity, because he might have provided against it by his contract. And there accordingly it was held no plea to an action for rent reserved by lease that the defendant was kept out of possession by an alien enemy whereby he could not take the profits.

Pearce, in support of the [defendant theater owner:].—First. This instrument amounts to a demise. It uses the legal words for that purpose, and is treated in the declaration as a demise.

Secondly. The words "God's will permitting" override the whole agreement.

The judgment of the Court was now delivered by BLACKBURN, J. In this case the plaintiffs and defendants had, on the 27th May, 1861, entered into a contract by which the defendants agreed to let the plaintiffs have the use of The Surrey Gardens and Music Hall on four days then to come, viz., the 17th June, 15th July, 5th August and 19th August, for the purpose of giving a series of four grand concerts, and day and night fetes at the Gardens and Hall on those days respectively; and the plaintiffs agreed to take the Gardens and Hall on those days, and pay 100£. for each day.

The parties inaccurately call this a "letting," and the money to be paid a "rent;" but the whole agreement is such as to shew that the defendants were to retain the possession of the Hall and Gardens so that there was to be no demise of them, and that the contract was merely to give the plaintiffs the use of them on those days. Nothing however, in our opinion, depends on this. The agreement then proceeds to set out various stipulations between the parties as to what each was to supply for these concerts and entertainments, and as to the manner in which they should be carried on. The effect of the whole is to show that the existence of the Music Hall in the Surrey Gardens in a state fit for a concert was essential for the fulfilment of the contract,—such entertainments as the parties contemplated in their agreement could not be given without it.

After the making of the agreement, and before the first day on which a concert was to be given, the Hall was destroyed by fire. This destruction, we must take it on the evidence, was without the fault of either party, and was so complete that in consequence the concerts could not be given as intended. And the question we have to decide is whether, under these circumstances, the loss which the plaintiffs have sustained is to fall upon the defendants. The parties when framing their agreement evidently had not present to their minds the possibility of such a disaster, and have made no express stipulation with reference to it, so that the answer to the question must depend upon the general rules of law applicable to such a contract.

There seems no doubt that where there is a positive contract to do a thing, not in itself unlawful, the contractor must perform it or pay damages for not doing it, although in consequence of unforeseen accidents, the performance of his contract has become unexpectedly burdensome or even impossible. The law is so laid down in 1 Roll. Abr. 450, Condition (G), and in the note (2) to *Walton v. Waterhouse* (2 Wms. Saund. 421 a. 6th ed.), and is recognized as the general rule by all the Judges in the much discussed case of *Hall v. Wright* (E. B. & E. 746). But this rule is only applicable when the contract is positive and absolute, and not subject to any condition either express or implied: and there are authorities which, as we think, establish the principle that where, from the nature of the contract, it appears that the parties must from the beginning have known that it could not be fulfilled unless when the time for the fulfillment of the contract arrived some particular specified thing continued to exist, so that, when entering into the contract, they must have contemplated such continuing existence as the foundation of what was to be done; there, in the absence of any express or implied warranty that the thing shall exist, the contract is not to be construed as a positive contract, but as subject to an implied condition that the parties shall be excused in case, before breach, performance becomes impossible from the perishing of the thing without default of the contractor.

There seems little doubt that this implication tends to further the great object of making the legal construction such as to fulfill the intention of those who entered into the contract. For in the course of affairs men in making such contracts in general would, if it were brought to their minds, say that there should be such a condition.

Accordingly, in the Civil law, such an exception is implied in every obligation of the class which they call obligatio de certo corpore. The rule is laid down in the Digest, lib. XLV., tit. 1, de verborum obligationibus, l. 33. "Si Stichus certo die dari promissus, ante diem moriatur: non tenetur promissor." The principle is more fully developed in l. 23. "Si ex legati causa, aut ex stipulatu hominem certum mihi debeas: non aliter post mortem ejus tenearis mihi, quam si per te stete-rit, quominus vivo eo eum mihi dares: quod ita fit, si aut interpellatus non dedisti, aut occidisti eum." The examples are of contracts respecting a slave, which was the common illustration of a certain subject used by the Roman lawyers, just as we are apt to take a horse; and no doubt the propriety, one might almost say ne-cessity, of the implied condition is more obvious when the contract relates to a living animal, whether man or brute, than when it relates to some inanimate thing (such as in the present case a theatre) the existence of which is not so obviously precarious as that of the live animal, but the principle is adopted in the Civil law as applicable to every obligation of which the subject is a certain thing. The gen-eral subject is treated of by Pothier, who in his Traite des Obligations, partie 3, chap. 6, art. 3, § 668 states the result to be that the debtor corporis certi is freed from his obligation when the thing has perished, neither by his act, nor his ne-glect, and before he is in default, unless by some stipulation he has taken on him-self the risk of the particular misfortune which has occurred.

Although the Civil law is not of itself authority in an English Court, it affords great assistance in investigating the principles on which the law is grounded. And it seems to us that the common law authorities establish that in such a contract the same condition of the continued existence of the thing is implied by English law.

There is a class of contracts in which a person binds himself to do something which requires to be performed by him in person; and such promises, e.g. prom-ises to marry, or promises to serve for a certain time, are never in practice quali-fied by an express exception of the death of the party; and therefore in such cases the contract is in terms broken if the promisor dies before fulfillment. Yet it was very early determined that, if the performance is personal, the executors are not liable; *Hyde v. The Dean of Windsor* (Cro. Eliz. 552, 553). See 2 Wms. Exors. 1560, 5th ed., where a very apt illustration is given. "Thus," says the learned au-thor, "if an author undertakes to compose a work, and dies before completing it, his executors are discharged from this contract: for the undertaking is merely per-sonal in its nature, and, by the intervention of the contractor's death, has become impossible to be performed.". . . In *Hall v. Wright* (E. B. & E. 746, 749), Cromp-ton J., in his judgment, puts another case. "Where a contract depends upon per-sonal skill, and the act of God renders it impossible, as, for instance, in the case of a painter employed to paint a picture who is struck blind, it may be that the performance might be excused."

It seems that in those cases the only ground on which the parties or their ex-ecutors, can be excused from the consequences of the breach of the contract is, that from the nature of the contract there is an implied condition of the continued existence of the life of the contractor, and, perhaps in the case of the painter of his eyesight. In the instances just given, the person, the continued existence of whose life is necessary to the fulfillment of the contract, is himself the contractor, but that does not seem in itself to be necessary to the application of the principle; as is illustrated by the following example. In the ordinary form of an apprentice deed the apprentice binds himself in unqualified terms to "serve until the full end and term of seven years to be fully complete and ended," during which term it is covenanted that the apprentice his master "faithfully shall serve," and the father of the apprentice in equally unqualified terms binds himself for the performance by the apprentice of all and every covenant on his part. (See the form, 2 Chitty on Pleading, 370, 7th ed. by Greening.) It is undeniable that if the apprentice dies within the seven years, the covenant of the father that he shall perform his covenant to serve for seven years is not fulfilled, yet surely it cannot be that an action would lie against the father? Yet the only reason why it would not is that he is excused because of the apprentice's death.

These are instances where the implied condition is of the life of a human being, but there are others in which the same implication is made as to the continued existence of a thing. For example, where a contract of sale is made amounting to a bargain and sale, transferring presently the property in specific chattels, which are to be delivered by the vendor at a future day; there, if the chattels, without the fault of the vendor, perish in the interval, the purchaser must pay the price and the vendor is excused from performing his contract to deliver, which has thus become impossible.

That this is the rule of the English law is established by the case of *Rugg v. Minett* (11 East, 210), where the article that perished before delivery was turpentine, and it was decided that the vendor was bound to refund the price of all those lots in which the property had not passed; but was entitled to retain without deduction the price of those lots in which the property had passed, though they were not delivered, and though in the conditions of sale, which are set out in the report, there was no express qualification of the promise to deliver on payment. It seems in that case rather to have been taken for granted than decided that the destruction of the thing sold before delivery excused the vendor from fulfilling his contract to deliver on payment.

This also is the rule in the Civil law, and it is worth noticing that Pothier, in his celebrated Traite du Contrat de Vente (see Part. 4, § 307, &c.; and Part. 2, ch. 1, sect. 1, art. 4, § 1), treats this as merely an example of the more general rule that every obligation de certo corpore is extinguished when the thing ceases to exist. See Blackburn on the Contract of Sale, p. 173. . . .

It may, we think, be safely asserted to be now English law, that in all contracts of loan of chattels or bailments if the performance of the promise of the borrower or bailee to return the things lent or bailed, becomes impossible because it has perished, this impossibility (if not arising from the fault of the borrower or bailee from some risk which he has taken upon himself) excuses the borrower or bailee from the performance of his promise to redeliver the chattel. . . .

In none of these cases is the promise in words other than positive, nor is there any express stipulation that the destruction of the person or thing shall excuse the performance; but that excuse is by law implied, because from the nature of the contract it is apparent that the parties contracted on the basis of the continued existence of the particular person or chattel. In the present case, looking at the whole contract, we find that the parties contracted on the basis of the continued existence of the Music Hall at the time when the concerts were to be given; that being essential to their performance.

We think, therefore, that the Music Hall having ceased to exist, without fault of either party, both parties are excused, the plaintiffs from taking the gardens and paying the money, the defendants from performing their promise to give the use of the Hall and Gardens and other things. Consequently the rule must be absolute to enter the verdict for the defendants.

Rule absolute.

NOTES AND QUESTIONS

1. *Application to production delayed by a strike*: Would *Taylor v. Caldwell* excuse late delivery or nondelivery of goods caused by a strike? The early cases which considered this question drew distinctions based on whether the strike was of the promisor's own employees, or involved a strike by the employees of a third party. If the strike involved the promisor's own employees, there were many cases which held that the promisor was expected to yield to the demands, at least if they were reasonable and if the strike was a peaceful one; failure to yield to a reasonable and peaceful strike destroyed any defense of impossibility. These cases, however, though reasonably numerous are of doubtful authority and pre-date modern labor law and labor practices. In light of the uncertainty associated with the early cases, it is usual for the parties to expressly address the question of strikes in their agreements.

Again, recall Professor Horwitz's views. Do these early cases on the impact of strikes reflect the domination of a capitalist ideology or do they reflect some counterview?

2. *The UCC and strikes*: Apply UCC §§ 2-615 and 2-616 to the simple case of a delivery delayed by a strike by the employees of a manufacturer. Be sure to consider the Official Comments as well as the text of the statute. It is unlikely that you will find certain answers in the text or comments of the Code, but the exercise should make you sensitive to the questions that must be answered in order to use the Code's provisions. Does the UCC reflect *Paradine v. Jane, Taylor v. Caldwell*, or both?

3. *The destruction of a specific thing necessary for performance of a contract:* Read UCC §§ 2-613, 2-615. Often these sections are triggered when there has been a crop failure. In *ConAgra, Inc. v. Bartlett Partnership*,[7] a partnership entered four contracts for the sale of 300,000 bushels of corn in June 1992. The partnership had approximately 2,800 acres planted in corn. In 1992, the partnership undertook an extensive manure-spreading operation to improve the soil. To keep costs down, the partnership hauled corn to ConAgra's elevator in Grand Island and the on the way back hauled manure from Hastings to the land the partnership farmed. This unusual arrangement prompted the partnership's interest in selling its corn to ConAgra, a fact known to ConAgra.

On August 13, 1992, the partnership's crop was severely damaged by a hailstorm. One of the partners notified a ConAgra manager. The partnership delivered the corn it could salvage and bought some corn on the market which it tendered to ConAgra. Nonetheless, it was some 61,500 bushels short of the quantity it had promised to deliver. ConAgra sued and recovered a directed verdict. The

---

[7] 248 Neb. 933, 540 N.W.2d 333 (1995).

Supreme Court of Nebraska affirmed. If a farmer had made a contract to sell crops to be grown on designated land, and if they were destroyed without the farmer's fault, then he or she would be excused either because of the destruction of identified goods or because of the failure of a basic assumption of the contract. However, here the written contracts "did not identify the corn in any way other than by kind and amount. Nor did the contracts make any reference to corn grown or to be grown by the partnership on any identified acreage. The only limitation the contracts placed on the source of the corn was that it be grown in the continental United States." The language of the contracts was not ambiguous, and so they must be enforced according to their terms. Thus, the contract did not limit the partnership to corn grown on its land, and so neither § 2-613 nor § 2-615 applied. Although the court's opinion does not talk about the point, it seems likely that the contracts would be written on a ConAgra standard form. Would the partnership have known that it would get no relief if the corn were destroyed by a hailstorm? Does it seem likely that the partnership planned on delivering corn grown on its own land? Suppose the partnership regularly engaged in agricultural futures trading. Would this affect your judgment about the case?

4. *The mistake parallel*: Compare the famous "cow" case, *Sherwood v. Walker*,[8] with *Paradine v. Jane*, and *Taylor v. Caldwell*. Sherwood, the buyer, sued for replevin of a cow and won in a Justice's Court. Walker, the seller, appealed. He argued that he was entitled to rescind because of a mutual mistake of fact. The judgment was reversed, with one judge dissenting. The majority opinion said that Sherwood, a banker, had called on Walker, a businessman,[9] seeking to buy some blooded cattle. "He was asked to go out and look at . . . [some on Walker's Greenfield farm] . . . with the statement at the time that they were probably barren, and would not breed." A few days later Sherwood called on Walker to buy a cow known as Rose 2d of Aberlone. The price was set at $80. Walker told Graham, his employee, to deliver the cow at King's cattle yard. Graham then discovered that the cow was with calf, and Walker refused to deliver her. The cow had cost Walker $850, and if it were not barren, it would be worth between $750 and $1,000. The majority of the Michigan Supreme Court said that there had been a "mutual mistake of a material fact as to the substance of the thing bargained for." "[T]he mistake was not of the mere quality of the cow but went to the very nature of the thing. A barren cow is a substantially different creature than a breeding one." The cow was "evidently sold and purchased on the relation of her value for beef, unless the plaintiff had learned of her true condition, and concealed such knowledge from defendants." A new trial was ordered to consider whether the cow was sold upon the understanding of both parties that she was barren.

The dissenting judge said that there was nothing in the record indicating that the cow was sold as beef. The buyer was told by the seller that the cow was barren, but the buyer thought she could be made to breed. The mistake went only to the quality of the animal rather than to the substance of the contract. "As to the

---

[8] 66 Mich. 568, 33 N.W. 919 (1887).

[9] We are told that this was Hiram Walker, a man whose business may be known to some readers.

quality of the animal, and as to this each party took his chances. If this were not the law, there would be no safety in purchasing this kind of stock."

How, if at all, does the right to rescind for mutual mistake about a material fact differ from the defense of an implied condition excusing performance when there has been the destruction of a specific thing essential for that performance? One could say that the theater owner promised to have a theater available on certain dates and that Walker had promised to sell Rose 2d of Aberlone; neither qualified his promise expressly. Yet both courts were willing to look to what they saw as the real deal behind the formal one.

Nonetheless, are there differences as to when which doctrine would apply? Presumably, Rose 2d of Aberlone was with calf when Walker sold her to Sherwood. However, the theater was standing and available for performances when Caldwell agreed to let it to Taylor. The fire came about fifteen days later. Do we need different rules of law to cover these two situations or is the problem essentially the same? (Whatever your view on whether the difference as to when an event occurs makes a difference, you must recognize that, at least in form, mistake and impossibility are distinct doctrines.)

If you are troubled by the result of *Sherwood v. Walker*, you will be relieved to learn that as is true so often there is a matched offsetting case usually considered with it.[10] We, therefore, ask you to wait to consider a summary of *Wood v. Boynton*, the Wisconsin "diamond" case, *infra*, before you make a final judgment on what the law is and ought to be.

2. COPING WITH FLOODS, STRIKES AND THE LIKE

a. Business Practices

Businesspeople often cope with unanticipated events that make performance of a contract very difficult or rob performance of its value. There is a great deal of negotiation and concession, but sometimes one party insists that the other assumed the risk:

—Interview with the Purchasing Agent of a manufacturer of heavy industrial items:

> It does not seem that a clause in a contract excusing delivery because of impossibility is really necessary. Any reasonable customer should not expect that material would be supplied if a supplier's plant is struck or under six feet of water.

---

[10] Sherwood v. Walker may no longer be the law of Michigan. In Lenawee Co. Bd. of Health v. Messerly, 417 Mich. 17, 331 N.W.2d 203 (1982), the court said "[w]e find that the inexact and confusing distinction between contractual mistakes running to value and those touching the substance of the consideration serves only as an impediment to a clear and helpful analysis for the equitable resolution of cases in which mistake is alleged and proven. Accordingly, the holding . . . of *Sherwood* with respect to the material or collateral nature of a mistake [is] limited to the facts of [that] case." The court called for a case by case analysis. Rescission is not available "to relieve a party who has assumed the risk of loss in connection with the mistake." The court said that had a risk of loss analysis been undertaken in *Sherwood*, "we believe that the result might have been different." *Compare* Florida v. Treasure Salvors, Inc., 621 F.2d 1340 (5th Cir. 1980).

—Interview with the Secretary-General Counsel of a maker of heating and cooling equipment:

> When we are purchasing, we often help a supplier in difficulty. We will not penalize him in monetary terms. We think a strike or fire is a justifiable impossibility excuse whether or not the courts would think so. Our suppliers work with us when we need to delay deliveries or cancel, and we work with them. You don't worry about legal niceties.

—Interview with the Purchasing Agent of a large manufacturer of agricultural machinery:

> We have gone to great lengths to help our suppliers when they face situations beyond their control. A number of years ago there was a flood in the Connecticut Valley that put many electrical manufacturers out of business. . . . Our Boston works sent in men and equipment to help clean up the mess so our suppliers could get back in operation. . . . You don't kick a man when he is down. Someday you may need help yourself.

—Interview with the Purchasing Agent of a manufacturer of automobile parts:

> On important raw material items we keep a careful record of the vendor's labor contracts. We know when they expire and we try to keep up on the labor problems faced by all our vendors. When the contract approaches the expiration date, we may ask for a monthly, or even weekly, report on negotiations with the union, and we may ask for an appraisal of the likelihood of a strike. . . . We may buy from nonunionized plants. . . . We may buy from two vendors who deal with two different unions. . . . We like vendors who have several plants so that production can be transferred to the one still in operation.

b. Allocations: Solutions With a High Potential for Dispute

A fire, strike or flood may destroy part but not all of a supplier's productive capacity. It is able to make some of its product but not enough to fill all of the claims on its supply. What can or must it do with what it has? Suppose, for example, a fire destroys part of a manufacturer's plant under circumstances that justify an impossibility excuse. It will be two months before the plant is back in full production. However, the manufacturer can still operate at exactly one-half of its former capacity—that is, before the fire it could produce 1,000 units a week but after the fire it can produce only 500 units. What can or must it do with the 500 units?

Before the fire, for example, the manufacturer had five contracts with five customers each calling for 100 units a week.

(1) One of these five contracts is legally unenforceable because of uncertainty as to price and quantity, but the parties have performed under it for six months before the fire.

(2) In addition to these five contract customers, the manufacturer had two regular customers who had purchased 100 units a week for five years but had no contract with the manufacturer at the time of the fire.

(3) Moreover, a division of the manufacturer's own company regularly took 100 units a week for use in its own operations.

(4) Shortly after the fire, the manufacturer received an order for 100 units a week from a large firm, but it has not yet accepted this order. The manufacturer had been trying to sell to this firm for years, and its business is more important to the manufacturer's continued success than that of any of its older customers.

(5) The manufacturer also received an order after the fire from a hospital that needs 100 units a week for purposes directly related to the treatment of seriously ill patients.

(6) One of the five customers that has a legally enforceable contract with manufacturer for 100 units a week is a race track. Another customer with a contract has an inventory of these units large enough to supply its needs for at least three months. The units are not readily available on the market at the present time.

You are the manufacturer's general counsel. Which actual and potential customers get how many units per week?[11]

Some of the answers are fairly easy; many are not. Suppose that a manufacturer allocates its available goods in a manner that does not comply with Section 2-615(b). A buyer who did not get enough sues. What is the consequence of the improper allocation? Does the manufacturer lose its entire impossibility excuse or will the buyer be limited to damages based on the difference between its allocation and what it would have received had an improper allocation not been made? See Section 2-615(a) granting an excuse in certain cases to a seller "who complies with paragraphs (b) and (c)." May we assume that a seller who does not comply does not get the excuse granted by paragraph (a)?

Professor James J. White, of the University of Michigan Law School, studied contract administration in the chemical industry during a time of shortage.[12] There were widespread shortages and allocations in 1974 and 1975. White interviewed about 30 people at 10 chemical and pharmaceutical companies.

He found that no company had a written allocation plan or a fixed plan concerning all products. The predominate method of allocating production was on a pro rata basis in accordance with actual purchases over a historic period. This allowed allocations to both contract and spot purchase customers. Some contracts had clever clauses, but businesspeople did not refer to them, and often seemed not to know about them.

There were some deviations from pro rata allocations that seem justifiable. Some firms gave more product to military orders, to buyers who would otherwise have suffered extraordinary losses if all they received was their pro rata share, and to customers of a product not thought part of the pool such as a customer who had built a plant next door to the supplier's production facility.

---

[11] *See* U.C.C. §§ 2-615(b)(c), 2-616, 2-615, Official Comment 11.

[12] White, *Contract Law in Modern Commercial Transaction, An Artifact of Twentieth Century Business Life?*, 22 Washburn L. J. 1 (1982).

There also were some deviations from pro rata allocations that seem unjustifiable. There were upstream diversions. The basic chemicals could be combined to produce a variety of products, but some firms found a product mix that produced the greatest yield for themselves. Often allocations were made only after all the internal needs were filled. One business person explained that he might be working next year for the president of the division that he had shorted this year, and he did not want to take this risk. Sales were made to new customers. "One should have a right to 'salt the market' because times of shortage were when one 'added to his market share.' We might serve new customers where in prior times we 'never got beyond the lobby.' " Extra allocations also were given to particularly good customers.

White concludes that "a large part of the behavior a lawyer might conceive as in response to the dictates of the law is in fact taken in ignorance or disregard of it." Lay agents of the seller ration subject to the sanctions within the corporations. Their decisions are largely based on immediate profitability and long-term relationships with buying companies. Furthermore, buyers are unlikely to discover or be able to prove that suppliers have not complied with the UCC allocation rules. Other buyers who got more than they should have often are competitors and are unwilling to share information. Even if a misallocation were discovered, fighting could be costly; buyers might hesitate to lose what relationship they do have with a seller.

c. Restitution After an Excuse

Impossibility or frustration may excuse performance, but a contract that has been stopped in mid-course will likely cause many reliance losses. Who should take these losses? How far can doctrines such as restitution be used to shift some or all of them? If one party to a contract confers a clear tangible benefit on the other before the contract is discharged for impossibility, most courts will allow its recovery in a restitution action. The one receiving the benefit has been unjustly enriched—something has been handed over on the assumption that it would be paid for when the contract was fully performed and now the contract will not go forward to completion. However, many writers find the case more difficult when the alleged benefit was itself destroyed by the event that provoked the impossible excuse. At best, the unjust enrichment was temporary.

Suppose, for example, a court decides that one who is to construct a machine or make repairs or alterations on another's building is excused because of, say, a fire that has destroyed the partially built machine or the structure on which the builder was to make alterations or repairs.[13] This means that the buyer cannot sue the seller for failure to perform. However, usually the seller's performance also will be a condition to the buyer's promise to pay, and so the seller will be unable

---

[13] Typically, a builder will not be excused if a partially constructed structure is destroyed by fire. The structure is under the builder's control, and placing the burden on builders gives them an incentive to insure or to insist that the owner buy insurance. Those repairing buildings, however, usually are excused if a building is destroyed making it impracticable for them to do their job. Of course, builders can contract for excuses in case of fire and place the burden on owners to obtain insurance; indeed, this is commonly done.

to recover on the contract. Suppose, however, the person trying to build the machine or make repairs has done a great deal of work trying to perform the contract before the fire. Can this seller of services or goods recover the value of that lost effort from the buyer? The answer is uncertain.

A seller whose duties were discharged by impossibility can recover for any benefits conferred in a restitution action.[14] As always, the difficult question is what courts will call a benefit and how they will value it. Comment b to § 377 states:

> Usually the measure of reasonable value is appropriate. A benefit may be found if it was conferred before the occurrence of the event even though the event later resulted in its destruction, and in that case recovery may be limited to the measure of increase in wealth prior to the event, if this is less than reasonable value. . . . A party cannot, however, recover his reliance interest under the rule stated in this Section, and his expenditures in reliance are not subtracted from what he has received in calculating benefit for which he is liable. . . . Furthermore, to the extent that the contract price can be roughly apportioned to the work done, recovery will not be allowed in excess of the appropriate amount of the price.

To what extent does this comment reflect the cases? More particularly, suppose Owner and Painter contract to have Painter paint three rooms in Owner's house. The house is destroyed by fire. Before the fire, the Painter has completed painting one room. He has also masked woodwork in another room with plastic sheets and tape so that painting the walls would not damage the woodwork. He has purchased the paint needed for the third room, and he has tinted it so that it is the proper color for the job. Paint so tinted cannot be sold to others. All of this paint remains in cans at Painter's place of business. Painter sues Owner for restitution of benefits conferred trying to perform the contract. For what items, if any, can he recover from the Owner? How will these items be valued?

The English common law view: In contracts discharged by impossibility, the English courts left all losses where they found them. Painter could recover nothing in restitution against Owner. A few early American cases also refused to allow either owner or contractor to recover for essential reliance expenditures which, arguably, had produced a benefit to the owner. Whether or not these old cases would be followed today in these states is uncertain.

The American view: While many states have no cases dealing with the problem, a number have allowed restitutionary recovery after a contract is discharged by impossibility. Owners have been allowed to recover advance payments made to builders. However, courts have used the "entire" and "severable" concepts to divide the losses. If the contract is entire, the contractor is entitled to the contract price only when the job is done, and the installment payments do not reflect equivalents for the work to date. However, the contract might be severable—that is, several contracts in a single document. Then the contractor would earn an amount specified in the contract as each step was completed. Suppose, for example, a painting contract is to paint a house. However, the owner is to pay speci-

---

[14] *See* Restatement (Second) of Contracts § 377.

fied sums as each room is completed. The court might construe the contract so that, for example, Painter would be entitled to keep any installments paid as the price of painting each room he had completed before the fire.

Does Painter have a restitutionary claim for work done before the fire? Many are troubled by the idea that Owner has been benefited by an attempt to perform the contract. Any benefit would seem to have gone up in smoke. Nonetheless, property concepts produce what some are willing to see as benefits. Suppose Painter finished the last room, doing the job perfectly. However, five minutes after Painter leaves with the money, the house burns to the ground. Painter is in no way responsible for the fire. The risk that the value of a coat of paint will be destroyed by fire, a leaking roof or a falling tree that crashes into the house are just part of the risk of owning property. Indeed, Painter handed over a tangible "thing." He left a thin layer of paint in the right places in the house, and this "thing" belongs to Owner. Thus, we can call it a benefit although it is destroyed immediately after the job is completed.

If we accept this property analysis, we can use it to tell us when a benefit has been conferred. When the paint is applied to the wall it becomes Owner's property, and thus he is benefited in a tangible way. Before the paint is applied, however, it still "belongs" to Painter, and thus the risk that it will be destroyed or rendered valueless is his. Painter could, for example, take paint purchased for Owner and sell it to a third party. On the other hand, Painter might take it to another job, add additional tinting pigments to modify the color, and apply it to the walls of another house. Thus, all these reliance expenditures by Painter will not become Owner's property until the paint is applied to the walls, and we could say that Owner will be benefited only at that point. A number of courts have taken just this approach.[15]

Massachusetts and reliance: In *Young v. Chicopee*,[16] a contractor agreed to repair a wooden covered bridge by replacing timber wherever it had decayed. The contractor was to be paid compensation based on a sum per 1,000 feet of lumber actually used. However, so that public travel would not be stopped, the contract required that no work be begun until material for at least half the repairs was on the job site. The contractor stacked lumber on the bridge and on the riverbank. It was possible that some or much of this lumber never would have become part of the bridge. The bridge and all the lumber were destroyed by fire. The

---

[15] Carroll v. Bowersock, 100 Kan. 270, 164 P. 143 (1917) draws distinctions based on this theory. A builder sued to recover for part performance of a contract to tear out an old reinforced concrete floor in owner's warehouse and construct a new one. The warehouse was destroyed before the job was completed. The court allowed the builder to recover for tearing out the old floor and for new concrete footings which had been completed when the building was destroyed. However, the court refused recovery for wooden forms into which concrete was to have been poured which were nailed in place and for steel reinforcing rods which were wired in place and would have become a part of the structure when the concrete was poured. Both could have been removed by the builder. The court said that "the liability of the owner . . . should be measured by the amount of the contract work done which, at the time of the destruction of the structure, had become so far identified with it as that but for the destruction it would have inured to him as contemplated by the contract."

[16] 186 Mass. 518, 72 N.E. 63 (1904).

court held that the contractor could not recover for the timber which had not been "actually wrought into the bridge" at the time of the fire.

The law of Massachusetts seemed to follow the property notions we have described—as each board was nailed into the bridge, it became the bridge owner's property and at that point the risk of loss changed from the contractor to the bridge owner. However, the Supreme Judicial Court of Massachusetts reconsidered the matter in the 1950s. That court overturned a contract between John Bowen Co. and the Commonwealth of Massachusetts to build the Chronic Disease Hospital and Nurses Home in Boston. John Bowen Co., although in good faith, had failed to comply with the statutory procedure for bidding on public work.[17] However, the court's decision came after subcontracts had been awarded by John Bowen Co. and work had begun. All of these subcontractors were discharged since it became impossible to continue the work. The court said that John Bowen Co. was discharged since, although it caused the impossibility by its method of bidding, "it must appear . . . that, except for the defendant's conduct, there would have been in existence valid and enforceable contracts" in order for the subcontractors to hold John Bowen Co. in breach. Had John Bowen Co. complied with the correct procedure, it would not have been the low bidder and could not have been awarded the general contract. Hence, Bowen's obligations under the subcontracts were excused by impossibility.[18] Are you impressed with this argument? Why do the subcontractors have to take the risk of John Bowen Co.'s command of bidding procedures?

Though relieved of liability for expectation damages suffered by subcontractors, John Bowen Co. soon found itself defendant in a series of suits seeking to recover for the work that had been done before the general contract was overturned in the *Gifford* case.

In *M. Ahern Co. v. John Bowen Co.*,[19] the plumbing subcontractor sued for labor and materials furnished before it was ordered to stop work. The court allowed recovery. The opinion, however, does not indicate whether the labor and materials had been "incorporated" into the structure, but the court did not seem to regard this as important. Bowen argued that it had received no "benefit" since it no longer held the general contract and would not be paid for this work by the Commonwealth. The court rejected this argument, saying that recovery in cases of excusable impossibility is *not* based "in the ultimate analysis on the principle of unjust enrichment . . . wherein recovery is limited to benefits received."

The court allowed recovery, explaining:

> [I]t is no longer necessary to find implications of a contract to support recovery. The implications are undoubtedly found in each case in accordance with what the court holds to be fair and just in the unanticipated circumstances and it is in order to proceed at once to that issue.

---

[17] *See* Gifford v. Commissioner of Public Health, 328 Mass. 608, 105 N.E.2d 476 (1952).

[18] Boston Plate & Window Glass Co. v. John Bowen Co., 335 Mass. 697, 141 N.E.2d 715 (1957).

[19] 334 Mass. 36, 133 N.E.2d 484 (1956).

This is not a case where the defendant stands fully apart, as the plaintiff does, from the circumstances which caused the unexpected destruction of the subject matter of the contract. The defendant did those things with respect to the subbids discussed in Gifford v. Commissioner . . . which caused its bid to appear the lowest, although in fact it was not. The Gifford decision has held that what the defendant did was not properly done. Even though we assume, as the defendant urges here, that it acted in good faith, and in respects as to which the prescribed course was not clear, the fact is that its actions, in a field where it had a choice, had a significant part in bringing about the subsequent critical events—the awarding to it of an apparent contract which turned out to be void and the ensuing decision of this court. In the circumstances it is plain that this is not a case of fully excusable impossibility. The defendant's part in the train of events is amply sufficient to offset the consideration that it has suffered uncompensable loss. Whatever might be said against the application of our established rule (and we do not intend any suggestion) to a case where the contract subject matter is destroyed by an event completely unconnected with either party and where both parties were equally interested in making the contract for mutual profit, and neither, by insurance or otherwise, could have provided against the risk of the unexpected loss and there is no final benefit, it is clearly fair and just to say in the instant case that "It is enough that the defendant has actually received in part performance of the contract something for which when completed he had agreed to pay a price." Williston, Contracts (Rev. Ed.) Section 1976, page 5551.[20]

The Massachusetts court squarely faced the question of recovery for reliance losses in preparation for performance in *Albre Marble and Tile Co. v. John Bowen Co.*[21] There, the subcontractor was allowed to recover for "preparation of samples, shop drawings, tests and affidavits" which were required by the contract's provisions. John Bowen Co. relied on *Young v. Chicopee* and its requirement that work be "wrought into" the structure before recovery would be given. The court said that the "wrought into" test was merely a "variant" of the "enured to the benefit of the owner" requirement, and the term "benefit" could not be taken literally as was pointed out in the *M. Ahern* decision. The court considered Fuller and Perdue, *The Reliance Interest in Contract Damages.*[22] It pointed out that John Bowen Co.'s responsibility for the impossibility was greater than the subcontractor's although John Bowen Co.'s conduct was not so culpable as to render it liable for breach of contract. Later in its opinion, the court speaks of John Bowen Co.'s "fault."

The court noted that the efforts in preparation for performance involved in the case were not solely within the discretion and control of the subcontractor as they were to be approved by John Bowen Co. These samples, shop drawings and tests, by their very nature, could not be "wrought into" the structure. Under all these

---

[20] *Id.* at 40-41, 133 N.E.2d at 486-87.
[21] 338 Mass. 394, 155 N.E.2d 437 (1959).
[22] 46 Yale L.J. 52, 373 (1936-37).

circumstances, the court was not disposed to "extend" the rule of *Young v. Chicopee* and deny recovery. The court concluded:

> A combination of factors peculiar to this case justifies such a holding without laying down the broader principle that in every case recovery may be had for payments made or obligations reasonably incurred in preparation for performance where further performance is rendered impossible without fault by either party. . . . [T]he damages to be assessed are limited solely to the fair value of those acts done in conformity with the specific request of the defendant as contained in the contract. Expenses incurred prior to the execution of the contract, such as those arising out of preparing the plaintiff's bid, are not to be considered.

The Supreme Judicial Court of Massachusetts returned to the problem of restitution and reliance in impossibility cases in *R. Zoppo Co., Inc. v. Commonwealth*.[23] Here, a construction company agreed to build a sewer for a sewage treatment plant in Boston. The contract called for a deep marine trench excavation, and the installation of "forty linear feet of sixty-inch precast reinforced concrete subaqueous pressure diffuser pipe between designed stations on the outfall sewer line." The work involving this pipe was subcontracted to the Perini Corporation. The pipe was specially designed and required fabrication of special forms for its manufacture. It had no salvage value since the only possible use for it was in performance of this contract. Perini, following the requirements of the prime contract, submitted to the Metropolitan District Commission's engineer detailed drawings for the sixty-inch pipe, and they were approved.

After the pipe was manufactured and delivered to the job site, tidal actions were discovered which in the opinion of the engineer required the final twenty-four linear feet of pipe to be deleted from the job. The Commission stored the deleted pipe.

The Massachusetts court found that performance in full was excused by impossibility. It then said:

> We hold that this case is governed by Albre Marble & Tile Co., Inc. v. John Bowen Co., Inc., . . . There, as here, preliminary samples, shop drawings, and so forth, were prepared under a clause similar to that appearing in the contract we discuss. There, as here, the labor and materials for which action was brought were not actually wrought into the structure but the preparatory efforts of the contractor were under the supervision of the defendant. . . . [I]t appears just, having regard to all the circumstances of the case . . . that the petitioner here may recover for those expenditures which it made pursuant to the specific request of the Commission.

Is the *Zoppo* case just an application of the doctrine of *Albre Marble* or is it a major extension? Does it overrule whatever *Albre Marble* left of *Young v. Chicopee*?

Valuing the recovery under contracts discharged by impossibility: Suppose a court decides that impossibility excuses performance under a contract. It also

---

[23]353 Mass. 401, 232 N.E.2d 346 (1967).

decides that a party can recover for preparation or part performance under a reliance or benefit theory. How should it value the work? The Restatement (Second) of Contracts § 371 says that "as justice requires" a court may measure "benefit" either by what it would have cost to buy the performance elsewhere or by "the extent to which the other party's property has been increased in value or his other interests advanced."

Few cases deal with this issue. In a New Hampshire case,[24] the court awarded a portion of the contract price measured by a fraction comprised of the ratio of the costs of completing the work to the anticipated total cost. Is this formula either of those suggested by the Restatement (Second)? By contrast, in *R. Zoppo Co., Inc. v. Commonwealth*,[25] mentioned earlier, the court found that plaintiff, who had performed work in good faith that was rendered valueless by tidal action, to be entitled to the costs incurred in doing the work, including a reasonable profit.

Loss splitting as the solution: A number of writers have suggested that "benefit" and "reliance loss" are inappropriate concepts when a contract has been excused by impossibility. Losses should be shared in such cases.[26] The writer of a Comment in the University of Chicago Law Review gives the following example:

> Plaintiff has agreed to install an elevator in defendant's building. The contract price is $2,500. Nothing has been said about time or terms of payment. When the plaintiff has expended $800 in preparing to install the elevator, but before any part of the installation has been made, the building is destroyed by accidental fire. The preparations have consisted primarily of procuring and readying specialized materials which were to be used in the installation and which because of their specialized nature and adaptation have a present market value of only $100. While it is clear that further performance on the contract would be excused, under present loss distribution schemes . . . the plaintiff would probably bear the complete loss for the materials purchased and work done. Under a principle of equal sharing of essential reliance losses, since the net loss is $700 [$800 expenditures less the $100 salvage], the plaintiff could recover $350 from the defendant.[27]

To what extent does this note on restitution actually offer a variety of loss sharing schemes when a contract's value is destroyed by an unanticipated event? On the facts of the example in the Chicago Comment, why shouldn't the elevator contractor share some of the owner's loss from the fire that destroyed the building? Why should the elevator contractor be entitled to add to the loss suffered by

---

[24] Anderson v. Shattuck, 76 N.H. 240, 81 A. 781 (1911).

[25] 353 Mass. 401, 232 N.E.2d 346 (1967).

[26] *See* Comment, *Loss Splitting in Contract Litigation*, 18 U. Chi. L. Rev. 153, 157 (1951); Sharp, *Promissory Liability II*, 7 U. Chi. L. Rev. 250, 269 (1940); Corbin, *Frustration of Contract in the United States of America*, 29 J. Comp. Legis. & Int'l L. (3rd Series, Part III-IV) 1, 8 (1947); Note, *Less Distribution in War-Time Impossibility of Performance*, 59 Yale L.J. 1511; Comment, *Quasi-Contract—Impossibility of Performance—Restitution of Money Paid or Benefits Conferred Where Further Performance Has Been Excused*, 46 Mich. L. Rev. 401, 421 (1948).

[27] 18 U. Chi. L. Rev. 153, 157 (1951).

the owner? From this perspective can we view the "wrought into" test as a kind of rough loss sharing scheme that also has the virtue of some degree of certainty as compared to the Massachusetts recovery of some essential reliance loss in some cases?

A British solution to the problems: In *Fibrosa Spolka Akcyjna v. Fairbairn Lawson Combe Barbour, Ltd.*,[28] the House of Lords considered the impact of World War II on a commercial contract. In July 1939, Fairbairn, an English manufacturer of textile machinery, contracted to supply machinery to Fibrosa, a Polish textile manufacturer. Fairbairn was to build specially designed flax-hackling machines in England and install them in Gdynia in Poland. Fibrosa paid £1,000 as a downpayment and was to pay £3,800 on delivery.

In August 1939, Germany invaded Poland, and Great Britain declared war against Germany. On September 7, 1939, Fibrosa's English representative asked for return of the £1,000 downpayment since delivery of the hackling machines could not take place in Poland because of the German occupation and the English statutes prohibiting trading with the enemy. Fairbairn refused to return the downpayment because considerable work had been done on the machines.

Fibrosa sued for the downpayment. Fairbairn defended, asserting that performance of the contract was excused because it was frustrated by the German occupation of Gdynia. It said that Fibrosa had no right to the downpayment because of several 1900 British decisions that said that an excuse did not wipe out the contract retroactively but only relieved the parties from further obligations. The Court of Appeal said that it hoped that the House of Lords would overrule these earlier decisions and adopt "the more civilized rule of Roman and Scottish law." The Court of Appeal assumed that it would have to determine how much of the £1,000 Fairbairn should be allowed to retain to compensate it for its reliance losses and how much of the sum was "a pure windfall" and should be returned to Fibrosa.

The House of Lords did overrule the earlier cases, but it awarded Fibrosa the entire £1,000. It said that the consideration had failed totally, and, as a matter of quasi-contract, Fairbairn had no claim to the money since its expenditures had not benefited Fibrosa at the time performance was excused. The House of Lords conceded that its position might work an injustice where there had been great reliance expenses which had not produced a benefit, but the common law did not furnish the court with a yardstick with which to apportion losses. "It must be for the legislature to decide whether provision should be made for an equitable apportionment of prepaid moneys. . . ." However, we should note that Lord Roche mentioned that according to Fairbairn, the machines as far as completed were "realizable without loss."

Parliament reacted to the *Fibrosa* by enacting The Reform [Frustrated Contracts] Act of 1943.[29] We can summarize a complicated statute as follows:

---

[28] [1943] A.C. 32.

[29] 6 & 7 Geo. 6, c. 40. Swan and Reiter, CONTRACTS 470-471 (3rd ed. 1985), tell us that the Frustrated Contracts Act "was adopted by the Uniform Law Conference of Canada, and formed the basis for the legislation of all common-law provinces except Nova Scotia, Saskatchewan, and British Columbia. The latter province has legislation that is special to it; the others have retained the

(1) The Act provides for recovery measured by benefits conferred (restitution) where there have been such benefits.

(2) The Act has no provision for equitably apportioning reliance losses if the seller has not received a down payment or if the buyer has not yet become liable to make payments.

(3) If there has been a down payment, the Act provides that a court "may, if it considers it just to do so having regard to all the circumstances of the case," apportion the losses following frustration or impossibility although these losses produce no increase in the assets (tangible benefit) to the other party.

(a) Little direction is given for the exercise of this discretion.

(b) The court is directed not to give weight to whether either party has secured insurance.

The only reported case involving the Frustrated Contracts Act is *B.P. Exploration Ltd. v. Hunt*.[30] Nelson Bunker Hunt owned a concession giving him the right to drill for oil in Libya. He was required to start drilling by December of 1960, but he lacked the resources and experience needed to explore and develop the concession. He entered an agreement under which B.P. Exploration Co., a wholly owned subsidiary of British Petroleum, would explore and develop the concession. The Court described the arrangement:

> Obviously the expenditure incurred in the exploration and development of an oilfield can be enormous. Under the agreement, however, up to the time when the field came on stream, all funds had to be advanced by B.P. Half such expenditure would be incurred for Mr. Hunt's account; but under the contract B.P. had no right of recoupment in respect of Mr. Hunt's share of the expenditure until the oil came on stream. All oil produced from the field belonged to both B.P. and Mr. Hunt, and was to be shared equally between them, subject to the provision that B.P. was entitled to take and receive a portion of Mr. Hunt's share of the oil, such proportion being called reimbursement oil, in order to recoup both the expenditure incurred by them for Mr. Hunt's account before the field came on stream . . . plus 25 per cent. Once the field came on stream, Mr. Hunt had to bear half the cost of production, and of further development of the field.

A large and very valuable oil field was discovered and developed at great expense. A large amount of oil was taken from the field, but Mr. Hunt's obligation to B.P. for exploration and development had not been covered. In 1969, a revolution overthrew the Government of King Idris of Libya and substituted the Government of the Revolutionary Command Council led by Colonel Gaddafi. In 1971, the Libyan Government expropriated B.P.'s assets, and in 1973, it expropriated Mr. Hunt's.

---

common law. The model act was largely adopted in the other Canadian provinces." Swan and Reiter also note that the British Columbia Act differs principally in the definition of the term "benefit." The British Columbia statute defines it as something done under a contract whether or not a benefit is received by the other party.

[30] [1979] 1 W.L.R. 783, aff'd [1982] 1 All ER 925.

The court found that the work in exploration and development was a benefit to Mr. Hunt. It then awarded B.P. an amount which was "just." It considered Mr. Hunt's offsetting claims against B.P. B.P. was awarded a balance of $15,575,823 and 8,922,060£.

Justice Goff wrote a 67-page opinion. He noted:

> . . . in addition to difficult and novel questions of law, the case involves substantial questions of fact and of accounting procedure. The sums involved are enormous; B.P.'s claim was advanced in a number of alternative ways, the sum claimed varying from nearly $45,000,000 to nearly $230,000,000. Furthermore, allegations made by Mr. Hunt relating to the manner in which B.P. developed the oil field led to an investigation of almost the entire history of the exploration, appraisal, and development of the field, and the production of oil from the field. This investigation required a substantial body of evidence, much of it technical; and the documents before the court, which were very largely concerned with these allegations by Mr. Hunt, were very numerous—I was told that there were over 15,000 documents in court. Many of these were of a technical nature; and in any event they represented only the tip of the iceberg of documents disclosed on discovery. Only by reason of the good sense and restraint shown by counsel on both sides, and the efficiency of their instructing solicitors, was it possible for a so substantial piece of litigation to be kept under control and for the hearing to take no longer than 57 days.

In dealing with whether the statute authorized the court to take into account the time value of money, Justice Goff noted that the lawyers described the consequences as involving "only $10 million."

Justice Goff was very critical of the Act itself, saying:

> . . . all these difficulties would have been avoided if the legislature had thought it right to treat the services themselves as the benefit. [That is, to allow compensation for essential reliance whether or not defendant ultimately gained from it.] In the opinion of many commentators, it would be more just to do so; after all, the services in question have been requested by the defendant, who normally takes the risk that they may prove worthless, from whatever cause. In the example I have given of the building destroyed by fire, there is much to be said for the view that the builder should be paid for the work he has done, unless he has (for example by agreeing to insure the works) taken upon himself the risk of destruction by fire. But my task is to construe the Act as it stands. On the true construction of the Act, it is in my judgment clear that the defendant's benefit must, in an appropriate case, be identified as the end product of the plaintiff's services, despite the difficulties which this construction creates, difficulties which are met again when one comes to value the benefit.

How should losses caused by expropriation of a joint venture of this sort be allocated among the parties? Does the Frustrated Contracts Act give a court adequate guidance in solving the problem? Recall that one may look to essential reliance losses only when there has been a down payment or the buyer has become liable to pay a sum of money. In other cases, a court must find a benefit, value it, and then determine a "just" allocation of this amount among the parties. Beale, Bishop and Furmston[31] note:

> As [Justice] Robert Goff points out, the Act does not enable the court to put the parties into the position they would have been in if the contract had been performed (eg, no recovery of lost profit), nor to restore them to their pre-contractual position. Thus the licensees in *Taylor v. Caldwell* would still get nothing for the wasted advertising. . . . Perhaps this is right: the court has already determined that neither party was better able to prevent the frustrating event, and maybe each is the best insurer of his own expenses, since he alone knows the amount of them.

Furthermore, we can ask whether courts have the capability to carry out the task given them by the statute. Even concluding that Justice Goff did a splendid job, we must consider spending 57 days of court time plus all the lawyering that went into this process. We may wonder about the impact of the case on contracts to develop oil concessions in the future. Should we expect parties to provide in their contracts ways to deal with the consequences of expropriation or are answers to this possibility so complex that parties will tend to avoid them by using vague and general phrases about equitable adjustments?

How would cases such as *Fibrosa* and *B.P. Exploration* be decided in the United States? There is no clear answer. Indeed, Nelson Bunker Hunt argued that the contract in the *B.P. Exploration* case was governed by the law of Texas rather than the British statute.[32]

Generally, American courts have looked for a tangible benefit conferred by performance before it was excused. However, outside of the area of building repair contracts, there is little authority. Nonetheless, in *Angus v. Scully*,[33] plaintiffs were to move a house from where it stood to another lot several blocks away. The house was moved about halfway and then left at the end of the workday. That night the house burned and was destroyed. The services rendered in moving the house part of the way to its new location were held to be a benefit to the owner, and plaintiffs recovered their fair-market value.

Official Comment 6 to § 2-615 of the UCC says, "[i]n situations in which neither sense nor justice is served by either answer when the issue is posed in flat terms of 'excuse' or 'no excuse,' adjustment under the various provisions of this Article is necessary, especially the sections on good faith, on insecurity and assurance and on the reading of all provisions in light of their purposes, and the general policy of this Act to use equitable principles in furtherance of commercial standards and good faith." Could a court reach results similar to the British Frustrated Contracts Act under UCC § 2-615 and its official comments?

Notice that § 2-615 as such does not cover the typical frustration situation where delivery can be made on time but, because of changed circumstances, it

---

[31] Beale, Bishop and Furmston, CONTRACT: CASES AND MATERIALS 311 (London 1985).
[32] *See* [1976] 1 W.L.R. 788.
[33] 176 Mass. 357, 57 N.E. 674 (1900).

has lost its value to the buyer. The text of § 2-615 speaks only of a seller's excuse. Official Comment 9, however, says:

> Even where notice is given by the buyer that the supplies are needed to fill a specific contract of a normal commercial kind, commercial understanding does not see such a supply contract as conditioned on the continuance of the buyer's further contract for outlet. On the other hand, where the buyer's contract is in reasonable commercial understanding conditioned on a definite and specific venture or assumption as, for instance, a war procurement subcontract known to be based on a prime contract which is subject to termination, or a supply contract for a particular construction venture, the reason of the present section may well apply and entitle the buyer to the exemption.

Harris, Campbell and Halson[34] are very critical of the British Frustrated Contracts Act and the decision in the *B.P. Exploration* case. They comment:

> One might wonder why a position as unsatisfactory as that left by LR(FC)A[35] 1943 has been allowed to remain the law, and part at least of the answer has been that to a significant degree parties do not have recourse to the formal law to govern these aspects of economic action. Competent commercial parties, faced with the absurdity of the law of common mistake at common law or the weakness of the remedies for frustration, have included modification provisions in contracts of sufficient value and complexity to make this worthwhile. These clauses provide for non-binding alternative dispute resolution or arbitration . . . which give the parties far more flexibility to apportion loss than any conceivable restitutionary recasting of the frustration rules might do. Should provisions of this sort not prove adequate, such empirical evidence as is available shows that the parties ignore the terms of their contracts to reach superior outcomes than those contracts provide. The extremely limited scope of and the very inadequate remedies for common mistake and frustration provide a great incentive for parties to follow either or both of these courses, and the absolute paucity of cases on LR(FC)A 1943 would appear to be evidence that they are doing so.

Practical solutions to the problems: Typically, businesses use some type of "impossibility clause" on their contract forms if they use any legal provisions at all. However, the common clause is very brief. By far the most usual wording is no more than that the contract or order is "subject to" or "contingent on" certain specified events (such as "fire, strike or other circumstances beyond our control"). This simple phrase is found on the business documents of both large and small firms. One businessperson told us that only a simple clause was needed. "If you tried to cover every possible contingency in a contract, you wouldn't have time to get any other work done."

Larger firms with legal staffs often attempt to spell out matters in much more detail. A major producer of metal uses a form providing:

---

[34] REMEDIES IN CONTRACT AND TORT 253-254 (Butterworths 2002).
[35] Law Reform (Frustrated Contracts) Act.

Seller will not be liable for any delay or failure in performance of this order or in the delivery or shipment of products hereunder, or for any damages suffered by Buyer by reason of such delay or failure, when such delay or failure is, directly or indirectly, caused by or in any manner arises from acts of God, or of public enemies, fires, floods, explosions, accidents, epidemics, quarantine restrictions, riots, mobilizations, war, rebellion, revolutions, blockades, hostilities, governmental regulations, requirements, restrictions, interference or embargoes, strikes, lockouts, differences with workmen, inadequate transportation facilities, delays or interruptions in transportation, shortages of labor, fuel, raw materials, supplies or power, accidents to, breakdowns to or mechanical failure of plant machinery or equipment arising from any cause whatsoever or any other cause or causes (whether or not similar in nature to any of those hereinbefore specified) beyond Seller's control. In no event will Seller be liable for any consequential damages for delay in or failure of performance, whether or not excused by the foregoing.

There are a number of questions to be raised in drafting and considering an elaborate excuse clause. Some of the many can be suggested by an outline:

(1) Who gets what excuse?

    (a) Who is excused, the buyer, the seller or both?

    (b) What excuse is given?

        (i)   If a party is "not liable" for delay or failure to perform, must the other accept a partial or delayed performance?

        (ii) If a party is given an extension of time, is there any limit on how long the other must await performance?

        (iii) If one party has an option to cancel, what happens to the other's reliance losses?

(2) How is the excusing event defined?

    (a) Are they defined generally or in detail?

    (b) Does the contract attempt to expand the "other causes" to include "similar or dissimilar" ones?

(3) What must the consequences of the event be in order to trigger an excuse? How serious an impact on the ability to perform? What about problems of multiple causation?

Realize also that courts may use their interpretive authority to avoid construing contracts that seem to undercut the spirit of the bargains the parties have made. That is, a court may strain to avoid literal application of a provision which allows a buyer to avoid risks which seemed inherent in the overall bargain the parties had made.[36] While we sometimes joke that, "The large print giveth, and the small print taketh away," the courts, like all the rest of us, seek to avoid such consequences if it seems inconsistent with what the parties expected and bargained for.

---

[36] *See, e.g.*, Monolith Portland Cement Co. v. Douglas Oil Co., 303 F.2d 176 (9th Cir. 1962).

B. CONTRACTS INVOLVING LARGE ORGANIZATIONS AND GREAT EVENTS OF OUR TIME

Typically contracts are performed. Most problems can be anticipated and in long-term relationships other-than-legal sanctions serve to hold parties together. However, disaster can strike, and good faith may not be enough when millions or the very life of a multinational corporation are at stake. In the last thirty years or so there have been many important events which have upset assumptions held by those in business—the Suez Canal was closed; the Vietnam war escalated; OPEC changed the price of energy suddenly; Japanese competition changed the way Americans had to do business. Cases arising out of these events prompt lawyers to bring forth many of the doctrines we have considered to this point, but these atypical cases tend to put the whole structure of contract law to the test.

We will begin by reminding ourselves that the spirit of *Paradine v. Jane* is still alive and well as we begin the 21st Century. We can offer quaint examples from the past, but both the person on the street and the commercial lawyer in an expensively appointed office accept the idea that a deal is a deal and those who lose bets have to pay up. Nonetheless, when losses get too big, other ideas are asserted. Perhaps, as has been said, the idea of capitalism without bankruptcy is like Christianity without Hell. Yet when Penn-Central, Lockheed and Chrysler are threatened, some begin to think of the impact of their failure on jobs and the economy as a whole. As we will see, the legal system and contract doctrine—the spirit of *Taylor v. Caldwell*—can be turned to salvage operations. There are lessons in these materials about doctrine, the legal system and lawyering, as well as questions of politics in the face of crisis cases.

1. THE SPIRIT OF *PARADINE v. JANE*

We will begin with a classic statement of individualistic ideology. Although the case is 100 years old, the ideas are alive and well today. But before we begin to discuss "the diamond case," as it has been called by generations of law students, a reminder that we earlier read a brief summary of "the cow case," as *Sherwood v. Walker* is often known. In that case, you recall, the Michigan court excused the seller from delivering Rose, the cow, on the ground that the bargain had been for a barren cow and there was no barren cow—Rose being discovered to be with calf. Just two years earlier the Wisconsin Supreme Court had struggled with a case which many have believed posed a similar dilemma. In *Wood v. Boynton*,[37] Mrs. Wood sued to recover an uncut diamond alleged to be worth $1,000 from Samuel B. Boynton, who operated a jewelry store in Milwaukee. She had sold the stone, which was "about the size of a canary bird's egg" and straw colored, to Boynton for $1. The trial court directed a verdict for Boynton, and the Supreme Court affirmed. "When this sale was made the value of the thing sold was open to investigation of both parties, neither knew its intrinsic value, and, so far as the evidence in this case shows, both supposed that the price paid was adequate."

---

[37] 64 Wis. 265, 25 N.W. 42 (1885).

Mrs. Wood made five trips to Boynton's store: (1) In September or October of 1883, she went to get a pin mended. While in the store, she showed Boynton the stone and asked what it was. "He took it in his hand and seemed some time looking at it. I told him I had been told it was a topaz and he said it might be." Boynton offered then to buy it "as a specimen" for $1, but she refused to sell. He asked where she found it, and she told him she found it in Eagle, Wisconsin.

(2) About December 28th, "I needed money pretty badly, and thought every dollar would help, and I took it back to Mr. Boynton and told him I had brought back the topaz, and he says, 'Well, yes; what did I offer you for it?' and I says, 'One dollar;' and he stepped to the change drawer and gave me the dollar, and I went out."

(3) She went into the store to get a clock repaired. Boynton questioned her about where she had found the stone. It came out of gravel thrown up when a well had been dug in Eagle, Wisconsin. Boynton then purchased the land where the stone was found.

(4) Boynton testified that "he sent word to her by her husband, that he wished to see her. She came to the store, and he told her, the stone he had purchased from her, proved to be of a good deal more value than he paid for it, and he intended to make her a nice present, not in jewelry, but in cash, when he got around to it. She said, 'Mr. Boynton, you do not owe me anything, . . . you gave me more for the stone than I could get anywhere else. . . .'" He replied that he did not propose to be a hog, supposed that he did not owe her anything according to law, but was going to make it all right with her, because the stone proved to be worth more than he paid for it. Mrs. Wood denied that such an offer had been made and denied that she said he did not owe her anything. (5) After an account of the diamond recovery appeared in the newspapers, she demanded return of the stone, tendering $1.10, which Boynton refused.

The day Boynton purchased the stone, he took a file and tried to cut it but could make no impression on it. He said to his son and partner, "Charlie, this is a diamond!" His son responded, "Pshaw!" His son then took it to several dealers who set diamonds, but they thought it was a sapphire. Boynton took it to Chicago and had it tested on a diamond wheel. Afterward he showed it to an expert from New York who said it was a diamond.

Mrs. Wood's lawyer's brief to the Supreme Court of Wisconsin concludes:

> Clearly there was in the minds of the defendants no such uncertainty or speculation as will justify them in claiming that they bought a diamond or anything which might turn out to be a diamond. The uncertainty in their minds was limited to a narrow range of species of inferior crystals of values ranging from fifty cents to forty dollars. Their uncertainty or speculation did not in any event include a diamond of any value, and it is just as clear that this stone was bought and sold under a material misapprehension of an existing fact going to the very substance of the sale, as it would be if they had bought it supposing it to be a diamond and it had turned out to be a topaz, and the plaintiff's right to rescind is just as clear as their's would have been in that case.

Boynton's counsel struck a very different note:

The effort of counsel [for Mrs. Wood] to get this case before a jury is appreciated. Some of the phrases evidently conned for use before that body, are deftly fired at this court, on many pages of counsel's brief. Such as "the poor woman became pressed for money, so that even a dollar came to be regarded by her as an essential addition to her funds." "She felt too poor to purchase jewelry at any price;" "a woman in desperate want of money;' etc., etc. Is Mrs. Wood, by reason of these conditions, entitled to any more remedies against the defendants, than Vanderbilt would have been, if he had sold us the stone? "A woman in desperate want of money," on one side, and two full grown men on the other, with the disparity in value and price shown by this case, without a scintilla of proof of fraud, and without any mistake recognizable in the law, are the circumstances under which, counsel claims, that the case should have been submitted to the jury. The jury room has become the only legal refuge of the Commune in this country. Its jurisdiction ought not to be extended. Balancing the scales of justice with an eye to a "desperate want of money" by one party, is no better practice than a verdict based on color, sex or religion.[38]

The "deal is a deal" principle is a powerful one. Judge Jerome Frank, a famous liberal judge, invoked it in 1951 in *Guttman v. Illinois Central RR. Co.*[39] The dispute concerned the rights of preferred stockholders in the railroad to dividends. Between 1937 and 1947, the railroad had chosen not to declare any dividends, though it would have been possible for them to do so. In 1950, the company declared dividends for both the preferred and common stockholders. The applicable rules required that preferred stockholders receive their dividend before common stockholders can be paid a dividend. Guttman, the holder of a stock designated as "non-cumulative preferred," sued to require that the preferred stockholders be paid all of the dividends which could have been paid to them from 1937-47 before the common stockholders be paid any. The trial court dismissed the complaint, and Judge Frank, writing for the Second Circuit, affirmed:

Here we are interpreting a contract into which uncoerced men entered. Nothing in the wording of the contract would suggest to an ordinary wayfaring person the existence of a contingent or inchoate right to arrears of dividends. The notion that such a right was promised is, rather, the invention of lawyers or other experts, a notion stemming from considerations of fairness, from a policy of protecting investors in those securities. But the preferred stockholders are not—like sailors or idiots or infants—wards of the judiciary. As courts on occasions have quoted or

---

[38] Eds. note: The Eagle Diamond became part of the collection at the J.P. Morgan Hall of Gems and Minerals at the American Museum of Natural History. In the late evening of October 29th or the early morning of the 30th of 1964, twenty-four famous gems were stolen from the Museum. On January 8, 1965, nine of the gems were returned as part of a plea agreement with the robbers. Nine other stones had been sold to illegal gem dealers so that the robbers could pay for lawyers and bondsmen. The NEW YORK TIMES reported "authorities had virtually abandoned hope of recovering the 15.37 carat Eagle Diamond and four smaller stones." (NEW YORK TIMES, Jan 13, 1965, at 74). The Eagle Diamond never was recovered, and it probably was cut into many smaller stones.

[39] 189 F.2d 927, 930 (2nd Cir. 1951).

paraphrased ancient poets, it may not be inappropriate to paraphrase a modern poet, and to say that "a contract is a contract is a contract."[40] To be sure, it is an overstatement that the courts never do more than carry out the intentions of the parties: In the interest of fairness and justice, many a judge-made legal rule does impose, on one of the parties to a contract, obligations which neither party actually contemplated and to which the language of the contract is silent. But there are limits to the extent to which a court may go in so interpolating rights and obligations which were never in the parties' contemplation. In this case we consider those limits clear.

Does the following decision indicate that the "a deal is a deal" ideology was still alive and well in 1983? Restatement (Second) of Contracts § 262 provides that "[i]f the existence of a particular person is necessary for the performance of a duty, his death or such incapacity as makes performance impracticable is an event the non-occurrence of which was a basic assumption on which the contract was made." Such events excuse performance. However, what should courts interpret "incapacity" to mean?

HANDICAPPED CHILDREN'S ED. BD. OF SHEBOYGAN CO. v. LUKASZEWSKI
Supreme Court of Wisconsin
112 Wis. 2d 197, 332 N.W.2d 774 (1983)

CALLOW, J. This review arises out of an unpublished decision of the court of appeals which affirmed in part and reversed in part a judgment of the Ozaukee county circuit court, Judge Warren A. Grady.

In January of 1978 the Handicapped Children's Education Board (the Board) hired Elaine Lukaszewski to serve as a speech and language therapist for the spring term. Lukaszewski was assigned to the Lightfoot School in Sheboygan Falls which was approximately 45 miles from her home in Mequon. Rather than move, she commuted to work each day. During the 1978 spring term, the Board offered Lukaszewski a contract to continue in her present position at Lightfoot School for the 1978-79 school year. The contract called for an annual salary of $10,760. Lukaszewski accepted.

In August of 1978, prior to the beginning of the school year, Lukaszewski was offered a position by the Wee Care Day Care Center which was located not far from her home in Mequon. The job paid an annual salary of $13,000. After deciding to accept this offer, Lukaszewski notified Thomas Morrelle, the Board's director of special education, that she intended to resign from her position at the Lightfoot School. Morrelle told her to submit a letter of resignation for consideration by the Board. She did so, and the matter was discussed at a meeting of the Board on August 21, 1978. The Board refused to release Lukaszewski from her contract. On August 24, 1978, the Board's attorney sent a letter to Lukaszewski

---

[40] Eds. note: The reference is to a line from Gertrude Stein's poem *Sacred Emily*: "Rose is a rose is a rose is a rose." Note that there are 4 roses, and not just 3, and no indefinite article to begin the line.

directing her to return to work. The attorney sent a second letter to the Wee Care Day Center stating that the Board would take legal action if the Center interfered with Lukaszewski's performance of her contractual obligations at the Lightfoot School. A copy of this letter was sent to the Department of Public Instruction.

Lukaszewski left the Wee Care Day Care Center and returned to Lightfoot School for the 1978 fall term. She resented the actions of the Board, however, and retained misgivings about her job. On September 8, 1978, she discussed her feelings with Morrelle. After this meeting Lukaszewski felt quite upset about the situation. She called her doctor to make an appointment for that afternoon and subsequently left the school.

Dr. Ashok Chatterjee examined Lukaszewski and found her blood pressure to be high. Lukaszewski asked Dr. Chatterjee to write a letter explaining his medical findings and the advice he had given her. In a letter dated September 11, 1978, Dr. Chatterjee indicated that Lukaszewski had a hypertension problem dating back to 1976. He reported that on the day he examined Lukaszewski she appeared agitated, nervous, and had blood pressure readings up to 180/100. It was his opinion that, although she took hypotensive drugs, her medical condition would not improve unless the situation which caused the problem was removed. He further opined that it would be dangerous for her to drive long distances in her agitated state.

Lukaszewski did not return to work after leaving on September 8, 1978. She submitted a letter of resignation dated September 13, 1978, in which she wrote:

> I enclose a copy of the doctor's statement concerning my health. On the basis of it, I must resign. I am unwilling to jeopardize my health and I am also unwilling to become involved in an accident. For these reasons, I tender my resignation.

A short time later, Lukaszewski reapplied for and obtained employment at the Wee Care Day Care Center.

After Lukaszewski left, the Board immediately began looking for a replacement. Only one qualified person applied for the position. Although this applicant has less an educational background than Lukaszewski, she had more teaching experience. Under the salary schedule agreed upon by the Board and the teachers' union, this applicant would have to be paid $1,026.64 more per year than Lukaszewski. Having no alternative, the Board hired the applicant at the higher salary.

In December of 1978 the Board initiated an action against Lukaszewski for breach of contract. The Board alleged that, as a result of the breach, it suffered damage in the amount of the additional compensation it was required to pay Lukaszewski's replacement for the 1978-79 school year ($1,026.64). A trial was held before the Court. The trial court ruled that Lukaszewski had breached her contract and awarded the Board $1,249.14 in damages ($1,026.64 for breach of contract and $222.50 for costs).

Lukaszewski appealed. The court of appeals affirmed the circuit court's determination that Lukaszewski breached her contract. However, the appellate court reversed the circuit court's damage award, reasoning that, although the

Board had to pay more for Lukaszewski's replacement, by its own standards it obtained a proportionately more valuable teacher. Therefore, the court of appeals held that the Board suffered no damage from the breach. We granted the Board's petition for review.

There are two issues presented on this review: (1) whether Lukaszewski breached her employment contract with the Board; and (2) if she did breach her contract, whether the Board suffered recoverable damages therefrom.

I.   It is undisputed that Lukaszewski resigned before her contract with the Board expired. The only question is whether her resignation was somehow justified. Lukaszewski argues that, because she resigned for health reasons, the trial court erred in finding a breach of contract. According to Lukaszewski, the uncontroverted evidence at trial established that her employment with the Board endangered her health. Therefore, her failure to fulfill her obligation under the employment contract was excused.

We recognize that under certain conditions illness or health dangers may excuse nonperformance of a contract. This court held long ago that "where the act to be performed is one which the promisor alone is competent to do, the obligation is discharged if he is prevented by sickness or death from performing it." *Jennings v. Lyons*, 39 Wis. 553, 557 (1876). *See also* Restatement (Second) of Contracts § 262 (1981); 18 S. Williston, *A Treatise on the Law of Contracts* § 1940 (3d ed. 1978). Even assuming this rule applies to Lukaszewski's failure to perform, we are not convinced that the trial court erred in finding a breach of contract.

A health danger will not excuse nonperformance of a contractual obligation when the danger is caused by the nonperforming party. *See Jennings v. Lyons*, 39 Wis. at 557-58. Nor will a health condition or danger which was foreseeable when the contract was entered into justify its breach. *Id.* It would be fundamentally unfair to allow a breaching party to escape liability because of a health danger which by his or her own fault has precluded performance.

In the instant case the trial court expressly found that the danger to Lukaszewski's health was self-induced. Lukaszewski testified that it was stressful for her to return to the Lightfoot School in the fall of 1978 because she did not want to work there and because she resented the Board's actions to compel her to do so. Citing this testimony, the court concluded: "The Court finds that the defendant's medical excuse was a result of the stress condition she had created by an attempted repudiation of her contract, and was not the product of any unsubstantiated, so-called, harrassment [sic] by the plaintiff's board." Lukaszewski further complained about the hazard of driving 45 miles to and from Sheboygan Falls each day. She alone, however, caused this commute by choosing to live in Mequon. The trial court pointed out in its decision from the bench that she could have eliminated this problem by simply moving to Sheboygan Falls. Thus the court clearly found that any health danger associated with performance of the employment contract was the fault of Lukaszewski, not the Board. This factual finding alone is enough to invalidate the medical excuse for Lukaszewski's breach.

The medical excuse is defective for a second reason. In order to excuse Lukaszewski's nonperformance, the trial court would had to have made a factual finding that she resigned for health reasons. The oral decision and supplemental written decision of the trial court indicate that it found otherwise. In its written decision the court stated:

"[Lukaszewski's] reasons for resignation were succinctly stated in her testimony, upon cross-examination . . . as follows: '. . . I had found a job that was closer in proximity to my home and it offered a different type of challenge, . . . also that the pay was, was more, and I asked them if I could be released from my contract.' "

The trial court did not include the health danger. Indeed, the court appeared to doubt that Lukaszewski resigned for health reasons. The trial judge observed that Lukaszewski had a history of hypertension dating back at least five or six years. Her blood pressure would fluctuate at the slightest provocation. He further noted that she was able to commute between Sheboygan Falls and Mequon from January, 1978, through the middle of the following summer. In short, the decisions indicate that the court believed Lukaszewski resigned for reasons other than her health.

These factual findings by the trial court invalidate Lukaszewski's medical excuse and thereby establish a breach. . . . We conclude that the trial court's findings of fact are not against the great weight and clear preponderance of the evidence and, therefore, must be upheld. Accordingly, we affirm that portion of the court of appeals' decision which affirmed the circuit court's determination that Lukaszewski breached her employment contract. . . .

By the Court.—The decision of the court of appeals is affirmed in part and reversed in part.

DAY, J. *(dissenting).* I dissent. The majority opinion correctly states, "The only question is whether her resignation is somehow justified." I would hold that it was.

Elaine Lukaszewski left her employment with the school board. She suffered from high blood pressure and had been treated for several years by her physician for the condition. She claimed her hypertension increased due to stress caused when the Board refused to cancel her teaching contract. Stress can cause a precipitous rise in blood pressure. High blood pressure can bring on damage to other organs of the body.

She was upset over what she perceived was the unreasonable attitude of her employer in refusing to cancel her contract. Following an unpleasant exchange with the Board's Director of Special Education, Mr. Morrelle, she went to her physician. He found her blood pressure to be 180 over 100 which he testified was very high. He advised her to rest and to get out of the situation that was causing her symptoms which she properly interpreted to mean "quit the job." He also told her that her elevated blood pressure made it dangerous for her to drive the ninety miles round-trip each day, that commuting from her home in Mequon to Sheboygan Falls entailed.

The trial court and the majority of this court conclude she could have obviated the danger of driving by moving to Sheboygan Falls. But the fact is that would not have eliminated her illness nor the hazards to her health that her condition posed. There is not a shred of medical evidence that her blood pressure problems would be cured or appreciably alleviated if she moved from her home to Sheboygan Falls.

Once the dangerous hypertension is established, and here the only medical testimony did just that, it should follow that one should be relieved of a contractual obligation for services unless malingering is shown. In this case no one denies she has the condition. But, the trial court says, the condition was one "she had created," which the majority on this court refer to as "self induced." The majority here seized on the rationale that illness that is "self induced" is somehow less worthy of judicial consideration than illness caused by others, or by outside forces over which the patient has no control.

It seems clear from the trial judge's comments that if he had found her physical condition had been caused by the Board's "harassment," he would have let her out of the contract. This is the only logical conclusion from the statement by the trial judge that, "The Court finds that the defendant's medical excuse was a result of the stress condition she had created by an attempted repudiation of her contract, and was not the product of any unsubstantiated, so-called, harrassment [sic] by the plaintiff's board."

In either instance, whether "caused" by the Board or "self induced" because of her gnawing feeling of being unfairly treated, the objective symptoms would be the same.

Either, in my opinion, should justify termination of the contract where the physical symptoms are medically certifiable as they admittedly are here.

The majority makes the following assertion, "It would be fundamentally unfair to allow a breaching party to escape liability because of a health danger which by his or her own fault has precluded performance."

Happily no authority is cited for this sweeping statement which means that it will be easier to ignore it, gloss over it, "distinguish" it or overrule it in the future. Under this new found axiom, could a concert violinist under contract be sued to cover any added costs of his replacement if he lost an arm in an accident where he was found 100 percent negligent? Or could another party to a personal service contract be held liable if he was unable to perform because of a debilitating illness clearly caused by negligent health habits?

The majority cites a hundred year old case, *Jennings v. Lyons*, 39 Wis. 553 (1876), for two propositions:

> A health danger will not excuse non-performance of a contractual obligation when the danger is caused by the nonperforming party. *See Jennings v. Lyons*, 39 Wis. at 557-58. Nor will a health condition or danger which was foreseeable when the contract was entered into justify its breach.

Jennings is cited by the majority to bolster its position. The case is not really in point. In that case a husband and wife contracted to work on a farm for one year for the sum of $300. He was to do outside work and she to do housework. After four and one-half months she had to leave to have a baby and the husband had to go with her. The employer refused to pay either of them anything and they brought suit to recover for the time they had worked. The trial court instructed the jury that if at the time the plaintiff and his wife quit working for defendant, the wife was sick and unable to do her part of the work, plaintiff was not bound to a further performance of the contract and was entitled to recover the value of his and his wife's services for the time they actually worked. The trial court found for the plaintiff.

This court reversed and held that the defendant did not have to pay them anything. The court held that the rule is that performance is excused:

"... as where performance has been rendered impossible by an act of God, by the act of the law, or by the act of the other party ... the obligation is discharged if he is prevented by sickness or death from performing it ... sickness or death is generally recognized as an act of God in such a sense that it excuses the nonperformance, and a recovery is allowed upon a quantum merit. ..." 39 Wis. at 557.

This court said that since the husband must have known his wife was four months pregnant when they took the job and that she would be unable to complete the year of work, therefore no recovery was allowed. This court said "For when performance becomes impossible by reason of contingencies which should have been foreseen and provided against in the contract, the promisor is held answerable." 39 Wis. at 558. Nowhere did the *Jennings* court say "a health danger will not excuse nonperformance of a contractual obligation when the danger is caused by the nonperforming party."

The precedential value of *Jennings* is doubtful but to the extent the rules stated may still be valid it provides no support for the majority. Here there is an illness, "an act of God," there is nothing in the record to show that the severe increase in Elaine Lukaszewski's hypertension was foreseeable when she signed the contract. Thus, even under *Jennings*, the teacher should be excused from performance.

Hypertension is a health problem that when caused by stress, however induced, may require a job change. That is what occurred here.

But the majority has discovered what it apparently regards as a "fall back" position, that Elaine Lukaszewski really did not resign her teaching job for health reasons after all.

The majority says: "In short, the decisions [of the trial court] *indicate* that the court believed Lukaszewski resigned for reasons other than her health." (Emphasis added.) (*Supra*, p. 205.)

The word "indicate" has picked up increasing popularity in the jargon of the legal profession in the past few years mostly, I believe, because it does not say anything one can pin down precisely. *Webster's Third New International Dictionary* (1961) gives a wide range of possible meanings to the word "indicate," among them are: "SUGGEST, INTIMATE, HINT ... INDICATE signifies to serve as a sign or symptom pointing to (the inference or action), stressing only a general, unspecified connection between subject and object. . . ."

"Indicate" seems to fall short on the definiteness required for a "finding of fact" by a trial court.

The first time the case came to the court of appeals they sent it back for further "findings" and it is the "original" remarks from the bench plus additional written comments by the judge on remand that form the bases for the appeal and this review.

What the trial court said was that the desire to take the better job brought on the physical symptoms when release from her contract by the Board was refused.

If the trial court had found that she quit merely for the better job and *not* because of her health problems brought on by the high blood pressure, this would be an entirely different case. However, that is *not* what the trial court found in my opinion. The trial court found her medical problems were self induced and concluded they were therefore unworthy of consideration.

I would reverse the court of appeals decision that held she breached her contract. . . .

NOTES AND QUESTIONS

1. *Contrasts and distinctions:* Suppose a Wisconsin promoter contracted with the representative of Count Basie[41] on March 20, 1984. The contract called for Basie and his orchestra to appear in Milwaukee on June 1, 1984. Assume that the contract was silent about the risk of Basie's death. Basie was born in 1904. Although he had suffered a serious heart attack and had been ill for about five years, Basie continued to perform with his band. Basie and his orchestra appeared in a concert in Hollywood on March 17, 1984. This was Basie's last appearance with his band. He died of cancer on April 26, 1984. You can assume that the promoter would not have to accept an appearance of Basie's band without Basie. Does the *Lukaszewski* decision suggest that the Milwaukee promoter could sue Basie's estate successfully for the profits the promoter could prove it would have made from the band's Milwaukee appearance, or would Basie's death give his estate an impossibility excuse? Would the parties have to litigate Basie's personal habits to see if he were at fault for his death? Suppose, for example, as is likely, he had smoked cigarettes throughout the 1920s until sometime in the 1960s. Moreover, by playing in jazz clubs and dance halls during that period, he had been subject to a great deal of second-hand smoke. Would the promoter have to prove that Basie's smoking caused his death so that he could

---

[41] Some readers may know little about Count Basie. Along with Duke Ellington, he is one of the important figures in big band jazz. We prescribe listening to a recording as you contemplate this hypothetical. You might also want to follow up this with a biography such as Murray, GOOD MORNING BLUES: THE AUTOBIOGRAPHY OF COUNT BASIE (Random House 1985), which may change the way in which we hear the music—given its portrait of Basie's struggle, as a black musician with the burdens of segregation. (Is this footnote irrelevant to a contracts student? Construct an argument that it is not.)

not perform in Milwaukee on June 1, 1984? Or would Basie's estate's lawyer have to prove that Basie was not responsible for his own death?[42]

2. *Clear rules to avoid difficult questions of responsibility:* In *CNA International Reinsurance Co. v. Arlyn Phoenix*,[43] the actor River Phoenix had contracted to appear in two films. The agreement included a provision requiring Phoenix not to do anything that would deprive the film studio of the benefits of the contract. Phoenix took a large quantity of illegal drugs and died. As a result, one film had to be abandoned, while the other was completed with another actor playing Phoenix' part. The insurance company paid the film studio over $5.7 million. It was subrogated to the studio's rights, and it sued Phoenix' estate for breach of contract. The trial court dismissed the insurance company's complaint. The insurance company argued on appeal that Restatement (Second) of Contracts §§ 261 and 262, and *Handicapped Children's Education Board v. Lukaszewski* bar an impossibility excuse when a person has destroyed his or her own health. "Appellants also suggest a policy basis for the ruling they advocate, arguing that in a society dealing with increasing problems created by illegal drug abuse, such conduct should not excuse the performance of the contract."

The Florida appellate court declined to follow the *Lukaszewski* decision. It said:

> . . . [A]ny attempt to discern fault in a death case such as this one, or in a similar case, perhaps involving the use of tobacco or alcohol would create another case by case and hard to interpret rule of law. Being mindful that there are already too many of these in existence, we are not persuaded by the facts or the arguments presented to depart from the clear and unambiguous rule that death renders a personal services contract impossible to perform.

The court did say "we believe that the parties to the agreements could have provided specifically for the contingency of loss due to the use of illegal drugs. . . ."

Suppose the exact facts of the *Lukaszewski* case arose in Florida today. Would you expect the Florida court to excuse the teacher from performing her original contract so that she could take the better offer? If film studios started using clauses providing "specifically for the contingency of loss due to the use of illegal drugs, . . ." won't courts have to make case by case decisions about the degree of fault of the actor and whether his or her drug use caused the inability to perform?

We are informed by an experienced entertainment lawyer that there is too much money at stake in a film production to risk a significant exclusion from cast

---

[42] Our hypothetical case is an unlikely one. The written contracts used in the music business usually deal with situations where a performer cannot appear because of illness or death. You can never forget this problem when you draft a contract that calls for a service to be performed by a specific person. Indeed, you should also consider whether the services can be performed by anyone else and still satisfy the contract. For example, suppose the representative of Count Basie's estate tendered the services of the Count Basie Orchestra after Basie's death. Would the promoter have to accept this or did the contract require Basie himself to appear?

[43] 678 So. 2d 378 (Fla. App. 1996).

insurance on a starring or featured performer. Every studio's actor's employment contract provides that cast insurance coverage at a non-rated premium is an absolute condition of employment. The lawyer tries to get a clause in the contract that permits his actor clients to meet the condition by paying the premium when a non-standard premium is demanded by the cast insurer. He did know of one instance where a production company had accepted an insurer's refusal to cover losses caused by a particular actor's inability to perform caused by drugs. This is a big risk, and those who finance pictures typically would not accept it. When an independent film company produces a picture, the producer typically must obtain a guaranty of completion from a bonding company so that the lenders will be assured that the picture will in fact be completed. A completion guarantor almost certainly would not issue such a bond without unqualified cast insurance.

TRANSATLANTIC FINANCING
CORPORATION v. UNITED STATES
United States Court of Appeals, District of Columbia Circuit
363 F.2d 312 (1966)

J. SKELLY WRIGHT. [On July 26, 1956, Egypt had taken over operation of the Suez Canal. On October 2, 1956 the U.S. contracted with Transatlantic Financing Corporation for the shipment of a full cargo of wheat aboard the SS Christos, a ship operated by Transatlantic, to a port in Iran. On October 27th, the SS Christos sailed from Galveston headed for Iran on a course which would have taken it through Gibraltar and the Suez Canal. On October 29 Israel invaded Egypt. On October 31, Great Britain and France invaded the Suez Canal Zone. On November 2, Egypt obstructed the Canal with sunken vessels and closed it to traffic. On November 7 a representative of Transatlantic contacted the U.S. and sought a promise that if the shipment of grain were shipped around the Cape of Good Hope that additional compensation would be paid to Transatlantic. The U.S. representative advised Transatlantic that they were expected to complete the charter, but that they should expect no additional compensation. Transatlantic made a claim against the U.S. for the additional costs it incurred when it proceeded to Iran via the Cape of Good Hope. The District Court dismissed the claim, and the D.C. Cir. affirmed.]

. . . Transatlantic's claim is based on the following train of argument. The charter was a contract for a voyage from the Gulf Port to Iran. Admiralty principles and practices, especially stemming from the doctrine of deviation, require us to imply into the contract the term that the voyage was to be performed by the "usual and customary" route. The usual and customary route from Texas to Iran was, at the time of contract, via Suez, so the contract was for a voyage from Texas to Iran via Suez. When Suez was closed this contract became impossible to perform. Consequently, appellant's argument continues, when Transatlantic delivered the cargo by going around the Cape of Good Hope, in compliance with the Government's demand under claim of right, it conferred a benefit upon the United States for which it should be paid in *quantum meruit*.

The doctrine of impossibility of performance has gradually been freed from the earlier fictional and unrealistic strictures of such tests as the "implied term" and the parties' "contemplation." Page, *The Development of the Doctrine of Impossibility of Performance*, 18 Mich.L.Rev. 589, 596 (1920). See generally 6 Corbin, Contracts §§ 1320-1372 (rev. ed. 1962); 6 Williston, Contracts §§ 1931-1979 (rev. ed. 1938). It is now recognized that " 'A thing is impossible in legal contemplation when it is not practicable; and a thing is impracticable when it can only be done at an excessive and unreasonable cost.' " Mineral Park Land Co. v. Howard, 172 Cal. 289, 293, 156 P. 458, L.R.A. 1916F, 1 (1916). . . . Uniform Commercial Code (U.L.A.) § 2-615, comment 3. The doctrine ultimately represents the ever-shifting line, drawn by courts hopefully responsive to commercial practices and mores, at which the community's interest in having contracts enforced according to their terms is outweighed by the commercial senselessness of requiring performance.[44] When the issue is raised, the court is asked to construct a condition of performance based on the changed circumstances, a process which involves at least three reasonably definable steps. First, a contingency—something unexpected—must have occurred. Second, the risk of the unexpected occurrence must not have been allocated either by agreement or by custom. Finally, occurrence of the contingency must have rendered performance commercially impracticable.[45] Unless the court finds these three requirements satisfied, the plea of impossibility must fail.

The first requirement was met here. It seems reasonable, where no route is mentioned in a contract, to assume the parties expected performance by the usual and customary route at the time of contract. Since the usual and customary route from Texas to Iran at the time of contract was through Suez, closure of the Canal made impossible the expected method of performance. But this unexpected development raises rather than resolves the impossibility issue, which turns additionally on whether the risk of the contingency's occurrence had been allocated and, if not, whether performance by alternative routes was rendered impracticable.

Proof that the risk of a contingency's occurrence has been allocated may be expressed in or implied from the agreement. Such proof may also be found in the surrounding circumstances, including custom and usages of the trade. See 6 Corbin, *supra*, § 1339, at 394-397; 6 Williston, *supra*, § 1948, at 5457-5458. The

---

[44] [1] While the impossibility issue rarely arises, as it has here, in a suit to recover the cost of an alternative method of performance, compare Annot., 84 A.L.R.2d 12, 19 (1962), there is nothing necessarily inconsistent in claiming commercial impracticability for the method of performance actually adopted; the concept of impracticability assumes performance was physically possible. Moreover, a rule making nonperformance a condition precedent to recovery would unjustifiably encourage disappointment of expectations.

[45] [3] Compare Uniform Commercial code § 2-615(a), which provides that, in the absence of an assumption of greater liability, delay or non-delivery by a seller is not a breach if performance as agreed is made "impracticable" by the occurrence of a "contingency" the non-occurrence of which was a "basic assumption on which the contract was made." To the extent this limits relief to "unforeseen" circumstances, comment 1, see the discussion below, and compare Uniform Commercial Code § 2-614(1). There may be a point beyond which agreement cannot go, Uniform Commercial Code § 2-615, comment 8, presumably the point at which the obligation would be "manifestly unreasonable," § 1-102(3), in bad faith, § 1-203, or unconscionable, § 2-302. For an application of these provisions, see Judge Friendly's opinion in United States v. Wegematic Corporation, 2 Cir., 360 F.2d 674 (1966).

contract in this case does not expressly condition performance upon availability of the Suez route. Nor does it specify "via Suez" or, on the other hand, "via Suez or Cape of Good Hope."[46] Nor are there provisions in the contract from which we may properly imply that the continued availability of Suez was a condition of performance. Nor is there anything in custom or trade usage, or in the surrounding circumstances generally, which would support our constructing a condition of performance. The numerous cases requiring performance around the Cape when Suez was closed, see *e.g.*, Ocean Tramp Tankers Corp. v. V/O Sovfracht (The Eugenia), [1964] 2 Q.B. 226, and cases cited therein, indicate that the Cape route is generally regarded as an alternative means of performance. So the implied expectation that the route would be via Suez is hardly adequate proof of an allocation to the promisee of the risk of closure. In some cases, even an express expectation may not amount to a condition of performance.[47] The doctrine of deviation supports our assumption that parties normally expect performance by the usual and customary route, but it adds nothing beyond this that is probative of an allocation of the risk.

If anything, the circumstances surrounding this contract indicate that the risk of the Canal's closure may be deemed to have been allocated to Transatlantic. We know or may safely assume that the parties were aware, as were most commercial men with interests affected by the Suez situation . . . that the Canal might become a dangerous area. No doubt the tension affected freight rates, and it is arguable that the risk of closure became part of the dickered terms. Uniform Commercial Code § 2-615, comment 8. We do not deem the risk of closure so allocated, however. Foreseeability or even recognition of a risk does not necessarily prove its allocation. Compare Uniform Commercial Code § 2-615, Comment 1; Restatement, Contracts § 457 (1932). Parties to a contract are not always able to provide for all the possibilities of which they are aware, sometimes be-

---

[46] [7] In Glidden Company v. Hellenic Lines, Limited, 2 Cir. 275 F.2d 253 (1960), the charter was for transportation of materials from India to America "via Suez Canal or Cape of Good Hope, or Panama Canal," and the court held performance was not "frustrated." In his discussion of this case, Professor Corbin states: "Except for the provision for an alternative route, the defendant would have been discharged, for the reason that the parties contemplated an open Suez Canal as a specific condition or means of performance." 6 Corbin, *supra*, § 1339, at 399 n. 57. Appellant claims this supports its argument, since the Suez route was contemplated as usual and customary. But there is obviously a difference, in deciding whether a contract allocates the risk of a contingency's occurrence, between a contract specifying no route and a contract specifying Suez. We think that when Professor Corbin said, "Except for the provision for an alternative route," he was referring, not to the entire *provision*—"via Suez Canal or Cape of Good Hope" etc.—but to the fact that *an alternative route* had been provided for. Moreover, in determining what Corbin meant when he said "the parties contemplated an open Suez Canal as a specific condition or means of performance," consideration must be given to the fact, recited by Corbin, that in *Glidden* the parties were specifically aware when the contract was made the Canal might be closed, and the promisee had refused to include a clause excusing performance in the event of closure. Corbin's statement, therefore, is most accurately read as referring to cases in which a route is specified after negotiations reflecting the parties' awareness that the usual and customary route might become unavailable. Compare Held v. Goldsmith, 153 La. 598, 96 So. 272 (1919).

[47] [9] Uniform Commercial Code § 2-614(1) provides: "Where without fault of either party . . . the *agreed* manner of delivery . . . becomes commercially impracticable but a commercially reasonable substitute is available, such substitute performance must be tendered and accepted." (Emphasis added.)

cause they cannot agree, often simply because they are too busy. Moreover, that some abnormal risk was contemplated is probative but does not necessarily establish an allocation of the risk of the contingency which actually occurs. In this case, for example, nationalization by Egypt of the Canal Corporation and formation of the Suez Users Group did not necessarily indicate that the Canal would be blocked even if a confrontation resulted.[48] The surrounding circumstances do indicate, however, a willingness by Transatlantic to assume abnormal risks, and this fact should legitimately cause us to judge the impracticability of performance by an alternative route in stricter terms than we would were the contingency unforeseen.

We turn then to the question whether occurrence of the contingency rendered performance commercially impracticable under the circumstances of this case. The goods shipped were not subject to harm from the longer, less temperate Southern route. The vessel and crew were fit to proceed around the Cape.[49] Transatlantic was no less able than the United States to purchase insurance to cover the contingency's occurrence. If anything, it is more reasonable to expect owner-operators of vessels to insure against the hazards of war. They are in the best position to calculate the cost of performance by alternative routes (and therefore to estimate the amount of insurance required), and are undoubtedly sensitive to international troubles which uniquely affect the demand for and cost of their services. The only factor operating here in appellant's favor is the added expense, allegedly $43,972.00 above and beyond the contract price of $305,842.92, of extending a 10,000 mile voyage by approximately 3,000 miles. While it may be an overstatement to say that increased cost and difficulty of performance never constitute impracticability, to justify relief there must be more of a variation between expected cost and the cost of performing by an available alternative than is present in this case, where the promisor can legitimately be presumed to have accepted some degree of abnormal risk, and where impracticability is urged on the basis of added expense alone.[50]

We conclude, therefore, as have most other courts considering related issues arising out of the Suez closure, that performance of this contract was not rendered legally impossible. Even if we agreed with appellant, its theory of relief

---

[48] [12] Sources cited in the briefs indicate formation of the Suez Canal Users Association on October 1, 1956, was viewed in some quarters as an implied threat of force. See N.Y. Times, Oct. 2, 1956, p. 1, col. 1, noting, on the day the charter in this case was executed, that "Britain has declared her freedom to use force as a last resort if peaceful methods fail to achieve a satisfactory settlement." Secretary of State Dulles was able, however, to view the statement as evidence of the canal users' "dedication to a just and peaceful solution." The Suez Problem 369-370 (Department of State Pub. 1956).

[49] [13] The issue of impracticability should no doubt be "an objective determination of whether the promise can reasonably be performed rather than a subjective inquiry into the promisor's capability of performing as agreed." Symposium, The Uniform Commercial Code and Contract Law: Some Selected Problems, 105 U.Pa.L.Rev. 836, 880, 887 (1957). Dealers should not be excused because of less than normal capabilities. But if both parties are aware of a dealer's limited capabilities, no objective determination would be complete without taking into account this fact.

[50] [15] See Uniform Commercial Code § 2-615, comment 4: "Increased cost alone does not excuse performance unless the rise in cost is due to some unforeseen contingency which alters the essential nature of the performance." . . .

seems untenable. When performance of a contract is deemed impossible it is a nullity. . . . If the performance rendered has value, recovery in *quantum meruit* for the entire performance is proper. But here Transatlantic has collected its contract price, and now seeks *quantum meruit* relief for the additional expense of the trip around the Cape. If the contract is a nullity, Transatlantic's theory of relief should have been *quantum meruit* for the entire trip, rather than only for the extra expense. Transatlantic attempts to take its profit on the contract, and then force the Government to absorb the cost of the additional voyage.[51] When impracticability without fault occurs, the law seeks an equitable solution, see 6 Corbin, *supra*, § 1321, and *quantum meruit* is one of its potent devices to achieve this end. There is no interest in casting the entire burden of commercial disaster on one party in order to preserve the other's profit. Apparently the contract price in this case was advantageous enough to deter appellant from taking a stance on damages consistent with its theory of liability. In any event, there is no basis for relief. Affirmed.

NOTES AND QUESTIONS

1. *Comparing Transatlantic Finance and Lukaszewski:* In what ways are the cases of *Transatlantic Finance Corporation v. United States* and *Handicapped Children's Ed. Bd. of Sheboygan Co. v. Lukaszewski* alike? In what ways are they different? What about the opinions themselves—how do they compare? How do you account for the differences, whether stylistic or analytic, which you identify?

2. *The likely impact of UCC § 2-615:* If the *Transatlantic Financing Corp.* case reflects the way most courts will use § 2-615, is that statute likely to excuse performance very often? Does the statute as applied reflect *Paradine v. Jane*, *Taylor v. Caldwell* or something else?

A seller may have a better chance of an excuse under the second part of § 2-615(a) when its performance has been made impracticable "by compliance in good faith with any applicable foreign or domestic governmental regulation or order whether or not it later proves to be invalid." Official Comment 10 notes, however, that "governmental interference cannot excuse unless it truly 'supervenes' in such a manner as to be beyond the seller's assumption of risk. And any action by the party claiming excuse which causes or colludes in inducing the governmental action preventing his performance would be in breach of good faith and would destroy his exemption."

3. *The virtues of uniform and relatively certain law*: Is it important that the *Transatlantic Financing Corp.* case followed the British decisions denying relief based on the closing of the Suez Canal? Are there reasons in the international

---

[51] [17] The argument that the Uniform Commercial Code requires the buyer to pay the additional cost of performance by a commercially reasonable substitute was advanced and rejected in Symposium, *supra* Note 13, 105 U. Pa. L. Rev. at 884 n. 205. In Dillon v. United States, 156 F. Supp. 719, 140 Ct. Cl. 508 (1957), relief was afforded for some of the cost of delivering hay from a commercially unreasonable distance, but the suit was one in which the plaintiff had suffered losses far in excess of the relief given.

shipping area to have relatively certain uniform rules about such things as excuses?

3. *Industry response:* Goldberg[52] asserts: "Perusal of current shipping contracts indicates that the basic shipping form contracts were not altered after the *Suez* decisions. Closing of the canal is not an enumerated excuse in *force majeure clauses*. Hence, it would appear that the courts got it right." Why does Goldberg say that this failure to change standard form contract clauses means that the "courts got it right"? What does he assume that courts should do when one party seeks an excuse because of an event such as the closing of the Suez Canal?

7200 SCOTTSDALE ROAD GENERAL PARTNERS v. KUHN FARM MACHINERY, INC.
Court of Appeals of Arizona
184 Ariz. 341, 909 P.2d 408 (1995)

TOCI, J. Kuhn Farm Machinery, Inc. ("Kuhn") contracted with 7200 Scottsdale Road General Partners dba Scottsdale Plaza Resort (the "resort"), to use the resort's facilities for a convention at which Kuhn's European personnel were to present new products to Kuhn's dealers and employees. In this appeal from the granting of a summary judgment for Kuhn, we consider the following issue: did the risk to air travel to Scottsdale, Arizona, posed by the Gulf War and Saddam Hussein's threats of worldwide terrorism, substantially frustrate the purpose of the contract?

Reversing the trial court's grant of summary judgment for Kuhn, we hold as follows. First, the resort did not contract with the understanding that Kuhn's European personnel were crucial to the success of Kuhn's convention. Thus, even if the attendance of the Europeans at the Scottsdale convention was thwarted by the threat to international air travel, their nonattendance did not excuse Kuhn's performance under the contract. Neither did the risk to domestic air travel posed by the Gulf War entitle Kuhn to relief. Although that risk may have rendered the convention uneconomical for Kuhn, the threat to domestic air travel did not rise to the level of "substantial frustration." Finally, Kuhn's cancellation based on the perceived risk of terrorism was not an objectively reasonable response to an extraordinary and specific threat. Consequently, Kuhn is not entitled to relief on the theory of "apprehension of impossibility."

I.   FACTS AND PROCEDURAL HISTORY

A. Background

On February 9, 1990, the resort and Kuhn signed a letter agreement providing that Kuhn would hold its North American dealers' convention at the resort. The agreement required the resort to reserve, at group rates, a block of 190 guest rooms and banquet and meeting rooms for the period from March 26, 1991, to March 30, 1991. Kuhn, in turn, guaranteed rental of a minimum number of guest rooms and food and beverage revenue of at least $ 8,000 from the use of the meeting and banquet rooms.

---

[52] *Impossibility and Related Excuses*, 144 J. Inst. Theoretical Econ. 100 (1988).

The agreement contained remedies protecting the resort if Kuhn canceled the meeting. Kuhn was required to pay liquidated damages for any decrease after January 25, 1991, of ten percent or more in the reserved room block. Additionally, the resort agreed to accept individual room cancellations up to seventy-two hours prior to arrival without penalty so long as total attrition did not exceed five percent. The agreement also provided that, because the loss of food and beverage revenues and of room rentals resulting from cancellation were incapable of estimation, cancellation would result in assessment of liquidated damages.

Because Kuhn refused to hold its dealers' meeting at the resort at the time specified in the agreement, the resort sued for breach of contract, seeking the liquidated damages provided for in the agreement. The resort then moved for partial summary judgment to obtain a ruling in its favor on the issue of liability. Kuhn filed a cross motion for summary judgment, alleging that its performance was discharged or suspended pursuant to the doctrines of impracticability of performance and frustration of purpose.

B. Additional Facts Established by Kuhn's Motion

In support of its motion for summary judgment, Kuhn offered the following facts. Kuhn S.A., the parent of Kuhn, is headquartered in France, where it manufactures farm machinery. . . .

Kuhn and Kuhn S.A. planned to use the North American dealers' convention to introduce new products to Kuhn's sales people and dealers, stimulate enthusiasm for the new products, and provide its sales people and dealers with information to effectively market and sell the products. To accomplish these goals, Kuhn invited its top 200 independent dealers from the United States and Canada ("North Americans"), as well as some of its overseas suppliers, to attend the meeting. Approximately twenty-five Kuhn and Kuhn S.A. employees and suppliers from the United States, Europe, and Australia were to host the convention and present the new products.

Kuhn considered the overseas personnel ("Europeans") crucial to the presentation and success of the dealers' meeting. Of all of Kuhn's personnel, they were the most familiar with the design, manufacture, and production of the new products. Kuhn intended the Europeans to play the primary role in presenting the products and leading the discussions at the convention.

On August 2, 1990, Iraq invaded Kuwait. A few days later, the United States began sending troops to the Middle East. On January 16, 1991, the United States and allied forces, in Operation Desert Storm, engaged in war with Iraq. As a result, Saddam Hussein and other high-ranking Iraqi officials threatened terrorist acts against the countries that sought to prevent Iraq's takeover of Kuwait. Hussein stated, "hundreds of thousands of volunteers . . . [would become] missiles to be thrown against the enemy. . ." and "the theater of operations would [include] every freedom fighter who can reach out to harm the aggressors in the whole world. . . ."

Kuhn discovered that, apparently because of the war, convention attendance would not meet expectations. Many of Kuhn's employees who were to attend the meeting were concerned about the safety of air travel. . . . Because tentative registration was lower than Kuhn had anticipated when it signed the agreement, in late January—two months prior to the date of the planned convention—Kuhn reduced the reserved room block by more than twenty-five percent.

Interest in the proposed convention continued to wane. From February 4 to February 14, 1991, several of Kuhn's top dealerships who had won all-expense-paid trips to the convention canceled their plans to attend. By mid-February, eleven of the top fifty dealerships with expense-paid trips had either canceled their plans to send people to the convention or failed to sign up.

Kuhn S.A. wrote to the resort on February 14, 1991, requesting cooperation in rescheduling the meeting for a later date. Among other things, the letter stated that Kuhn was concerned with the safety of its people, that the dealers were reluctant to travel, and that attendance had decreased to a level making it uneconomical to hold the convention.

Without waiting for the resort's response, Kuhn decided to postpone the scheduled meeting. On February 18, 1991, Kuhn notified all potential convention participants that the dealers' meeting had been postponed. Although Kuhn and the resort did attempt to reschedule the meeting for the following year, the rescheduling negotiations broke down. The convention was never held at the resort.

C. The Resort's Response To Kuhn's Motion

The resort did not dispute Kuhn's description of the planned convention; rather, the resort contested the extent of the threat to air travel. Specifically, the resort noted that the articles cited by Kuhn indicated either that there was little risk or that the risk was primarily to overseas locations.

The resort also contested the inferences to be drawn from the facts presented by each party. The resort asserted that the facts did not establish that the threat of terrorism frustrated the ability of Kuhn associates to fly to Scottsdale. Although conceding that several dealers canceled because of fear of terrorism, the resort emphasized that nearly all of the approximately 150 dealers registered for the meeting signed up after the Operation Desert Storm attack on Iraq. In the resort's view, Kuhn's January 29, 1991, request for a reduction in the room block to 140 rooms impliedly reconfirmed the convention after the commencement of the war. . . .

The trial court granted summary judgment to Kuhn, ruling that Kuhn proved both of its defenses. . . . The resort appeals from the summary judgment ruling. . . .

II. IMPRACTICABILITY DISTINGUISHED FROM FRUSTRATION OF PURPOSE

The trial court held that the contract was discharged under the doctrines of impracticability of performance and frustration of purpose. These are similar but distinct doctrines. . . . Impracticability of performance is . . . utilized when certain events occurring after a contract is made constitute an impediment to performance by either party. See Restatement § 261. Traditionally, the doctrine has been applied to three categories of supervening events: death or incapacity of a person necessary for performance, destruction of a specific thing necessary for performance, and prohibition or prevention by law.

On the other hand, frustration of purpose deals with "the problem that arises when a change in circumstances makes one party's performance virtually worthless to the other. . . ." Restatement § 265 cmt. a. "Performance remains possible but the expected value of performance to the party seeking to be excused has been destroyed by a fortuitous event, which supervenes to cause an actual but not literal failure of consideration." Lloyd v. Murphy, 25 Cal. 2d 48, 153 P.2d 47, 50 (Cal. 1944). . . .

Turning to the contract between Kuhn and the resort, Kuhn clearly has no claim for impossibility or impracticability. . . . Kuhn does not allege that it was impossible or impracticable to perform its contractual duty to make payment for the reserved facilities. Rather, it contends that the value of the resort's counter-performance—the furnishing of convention facilities—was rendered worthless because of the Gulf War's effect on convention attendance. This is a claim of frustration of purpose.

III. FRUSTRATION OF PURPOSE

A. Krell v. Henry

The doctrine of frustration of purpose traces its roots to Krell v. Henry, [1903] 2 K.B. 740. There, the owner of a London apartment advertised it for rent to observe the King's coronation parade. Responding to the advertisement, the renter paid a deposit and agreed to rent the apartment for two days. When the coronation parade was postponed, the renter refused to pay the balance of the rent. The court held that the contract to rent the apartment was premised on an implied condition—the occurrence of the King's coronation parade. . . . Accordingly, when the parade was canceled, the renter's duty to perform was discharged by the frustration of his purpose in entering the contract. Several aspects of Krell are worth noting. First, the owner of the apartment was prepared to render the entire performance promised by him. . . . Second, the renter could have performed by simply paying the rental fee for the apartment. In other words, there was no impediment to the renter's performance of the contract. The renter's sole grievance was that his intended benefit from the contract had not been realized. . . .

The complaint that a contracting party did not realize the benefit he intended to realize from the contract has been described as "frustration-in-fact." Frustration-in-fact results when, because of events subsequent to formation of a contract, the desirability of the performance for which a party contracted diminishes. The issue then becomes: should legal consequences flow from a contracting party's failure to realize the expected benefit from a contract?

B. Frustration of Purpose and The Equitable Doctrine of Lloyd

. . . [M]any authorities, including the courts of Arizona, extend limited relief for frustration-in-fact through an extraordinary legal remedy closely resembling relief in equity. . . . As Justice Traynor pointed out in his frequently cited opinion in Lloyd:

> The question in cases involving frustration is whether the equities of the case, considered in the light of sound public policy, require placing the risk of a disruption or complete destruction of the contract equilibrium on defendant or plaintiff under the circumstances of a given case, and the

answer depends on whether an unanticipated circumstance, the risk of which should not be fairly thrown on the promisor, has made performance vitally different from what was reasonably to be expected.

153 P.2d at 50 (citations omitted). . . .

D. Standard of Review

The trial court granted Kuhn's cross-motion for summary judgment on the theory that the purpose of Kuhn's contract with the resort was frustrated. In reviewing an order granting summary judgment, we must determine whether there is a genuine issue of disputed material fact. . . . Where the facts are not in dispute, we analyze the record to determine if the trial court correctly applied the law to the undisputed facts. . . . Here, the underlying facts are undisputed. . . .

Whether a party to a contract is entitled to relief under the doctrine of frustration of purpose is generally treated as a question of law. . . . [F]rustration of purpose is essentially an equitable doctrine, and the power to grant relief under that doctrine is reserved to the court. Arizona courts have frequently followed this general rule. Thus, the issues to be considered here—principal purpose and substantial frustration—are questions of law for the court.

IV. RESOLUTION OF THIS CASE

A. Requirements for Relief

Restatement section 265 comment a lists four requirements that must exist before relief may be granted for frustration of purpose. First, "the purpose that is frustrated must have been a principal purpose of that party" and must have been so to the understanding of both parties. . . . Second, "the frustration must be substantial. . . ; [it] must be so severe that it is not to be regarded as within the risks assumed . . . under the contract." Third, "the non-occurrence of the frustrating event must have been a basic assumption. . . ." Finally, relief will not be granted if it may be inferred from either the language of the contract or the circumstances that the risk of the frustrating occurrence, or the loss caused thereby, should properly be placed on the party seeking relief. . . .

Kuhn contends that the Gulf War with its attendant threats of terrorism was an "event the non-occurrence of which was a basic assumption" of the contract. . . . Here, because we find no substantial frustration of a principal purpose entitling Kuhn to relief, we need not decide if the nonoccurrence of the Gulf war and Saddam Hussein's threats of terrorism was a basic assumption of the parties.

B. Principal Purpose

1. A Forum For European Personnel

Kuhn contends that its principal purpose in scheduling the convention was to provide a forum for its European personnel to introduce new and innovative products to its North American dealers. The resort acknowledged that the primary threat of terrorist activity was to the United States' international interests rather than domestic targets. Even if we take this as an implied concession by the resort that it was too dangerous for Kuhn's European personnel to fly to Scottsdale, Kuhn is not entitled to relief for frustration of purpose on this ground.

For Kuhn to obtain relief based on the frustration of its plans for its European employees to introduce new products, those plans must have been understood by the resort as Kuhn's "principal purpose" in entering the contract, As the court noted in Krell, to establish that "the object of the contract was frustrated," it must be shown that the frustrated purpose was "the subject of the contract. . ., and was so to the knowledge of both parties." It is not enough that the promisor "had in mind some specific object without which he would not have made the contract," Restatement § 265 cmt. a. . . . In Krell, for example, the "coronation procession and the relative position of the rooms [was] the basis of the contract as much for the lessor as the hirer," [1903] 2 K.B, at 751.

Here, Kuhn never established that both parties had a common understanding that Kuhn's principal purpose in entering the contract was a convention at which the European personnel would be present, First, the contract itself makes no mention of any particular purpose for the convention. Second, neither the deposition and affidavit of Timothy Harman—Kuhn's general sales manager responsible for scheduling the convention—nor the deposition of William Kilburg—the resort's vice president—raised any factual inference that the resort knew of Kuhn's plans concerning the European personnel. Harman's affidavit only related Kuhn's understanding of the purpose of the convention. The only other reference in the record to the purpose of the convention is Harman's deposition testimony that his role was to find a venue for a North American dealers' meeting. . . .

2.   Attendance Of Most Invited Personnel

Nevertheless, Kuhn argues that the parties contracted with the idea that "all or most" of Kuhn's employees and dealers would come to Scottsdale for the meeting. . . . [N]othing in this record establishes that the resort contracted with the understanding that all or most of Kuhn's dealers and employees would attend the convention. Kuhn's degree of success was not of primary concern to the resort. To the contrary, the resort clearly contemplated that the convention might not meet Kuhn's expectations. Not only does the contract include a provision for attrition in attendance and outright cancellation, it assigns the risk of such events to Kuhn. Thus, as with the attendance of the European employees, the attendance of all or most of Kuhn's dealers and employees was not so completely the basis of the contract, as understood by the resort, that without such attendance the transaction would make little sense.

Kuhn did establish, however, that the resort contracted with knowledge that a principal purpose of Kuhn was a convention at which some of Kuhn's employees and dealers would attend. If that purpose was substantially frustrated by the Gulf War, Kuhn is entitled to relief. Consequently, we next consider whether the Gulf War and Saddam Hussein's threats of terrorism substantially frustrated a convention for some of Kuhn's employees and dealers.

C.   Substantial Frustration

Kuhn argues that its purpose was effectively frustrated because air travel was unexpectedly rendered unreasonably dangerous. The resort, on the other hand, while essentially conceding that Kuhn's decision to cancel was made in good faith, contends that the general threat of terrorism was not sufficient to justify Kuhn's cancellation of the convention. We agree with the resort.

Preliminarily, as discussed above, Kuhn cannot rely on the absence of the Europeans as a basis for canceling the contract. Kuhn never established that both parties had a common understanding that Kuhn's principal purpose in entering the contract was a convention at which the European personnel would be present. Thus, in resolving this issue, we do not consider the threat posed to the European employees traveling internationally by air.

On the other hand, the threat to domestic air travel is a relevant consideration. Most of those invited to the convention resided in the United States and in Canada. Furthermore, the resort did not controvert Kuhn's assertion in its statement of facts that "the parties assumed that Kuhn personnel could and would travel to Scottsdale." Consequently, if the Gulf War effectively precluded domestic air travel, Kuhn could not have hosted a convention attended by even some of its dealers and employees. Under such circumstances, the resort's furnishing of its facilities would have been rendered valueless to Kuhn. We could then say that Kuhn's purpose in entering the contract was substantially frustrated. We conclude, however, that the contrary is true.

We begin our analysis on this point with the proposition that substantial frustration means frustration "so severe that it is not fairly to be regarded as within the risks . . . assumed under the contract." Restatement § 265 cmt. a. Furthermore, "it is not enough that the transaction has become less profitable for the affected party or even that he will sustain a loss." Id. The value of the counter-performance to be rendered by the promisee must be "totally or nearly totally destroyed" by the occurrence of the event. Lloyd, 153 P.2d at 50.

Here, the conduct of Kuhn and its dealers clearly demonstrates that the value of the resort's counter-performance—the furnishing of its facilities for Kuhn's convention—was not totally or nearly totally destroyed by terrorist threats. In late January, after the United States attacked Iraq and when the threat of terrorism was at its highest level, Kuhn implicitly confirmed the convention date by reducing the reserved room block from 190 to 140. Furthermore, although several dealers canceled in early February, the uncontroverted record demonstrates that over one hundred dealers registered for the convention after the commencement of Operation Desert Storm on January 16, 1991. Thus, the frustration was not so severe that it cannot fairly be regarded as one of the risks assumed by Kuhn under the contract.

Kuhn argues, however, that even if the jointly understood purpose in holding the convention was not substantially frustrated by the actual risk of terrorism, it was entitled to cancel the convention because of its perception of a serious risk to air travel. For this proposition, Kuhn relies primarily on the wartime shipping cases. . . . The wartime shipping cases essentially held that a ship captain is entitled to take reasonable precautions, including abandoning the voyage, in the face of a reasonable apprehension of danger. Read together, they establish that the promisor's decision not to perform must be an objectively reasonable response to an extraordinary, specific, and identifiable threat. . . . The degree of danger is judged in light of the facts available at the time, First Restatement section 465 comment b, but "mere good faith . . . will not excuse" cancellation of performance.

. . . Even though Kuhn canceled the convention in good faith, . . . Kuhn's cancellation did not excuse its performance of the contract with the resort. Press reports in circulation at the time Kuhn canceled the convention indicated that the risk to domestic air travel was slight. Moreover, the United States government announced that it was taking measures to insure the safety of domestic air travel and that travelers should not be put off by the threat of terrorist activity.

Furthermore, the record establishes that by the time Kuhn canceled the convention, the risk of terrorism, if any, was diminishing. First, the danger, publicized since October 1990, had failed to materialize. Second, Kuhn itself recognized that even its French employees could possibly travel as early as April. Finally, even after the commencement of Operation Desert Storm, more than 100 of Kuhn's dealers expressed their willingness to travel to Scottsdale. We conclude that Kuhn's cancellation of the convention because of the perceived threat of terrorism was not an objectively reasonable response to an extraordinary and specific threat. The slight risk to domestic air travel by vague threats of terrorism does not equate with the actual and substantial danger of running a naval blockade in time of war. . . .

Finally, we consider whether Kuhn is entitled to relief on the ground that fear of terrorist activities resulted in less than expected attendance, which in turn made the convention uneconomical. Although economic return may be characterized as the "principal purpose" of virtually all commercial contracts, mere economic impracticality is no defense to performance of a contract. . . . Thus, although the Gulf War's effect on the expected level of attendance may have rendered the convention uneconomical, Kuhn was not on this ground relieved of its contractual obligation.

V. PROCEDURAL DISPOSITION

The only issues raised by Kuhn in its response to the resort's motion for summary judgment on liability were its claims for relief under the doctrines of impracticability of performance and frustration of purpose. Because we conclude that Kuhn is not entitled to relief under these doctrines, partial summary judgment must be granted to the resort.

NOTES AND QUESTIONS

1. *What was the resort hotel selling to Kuhn Farm Machinery*? In *Krell v. Henry*, the person who owned an interest in the apartment was selling a place from which to watch a parade. It is very likely that he could not have sold seats from which people could look out the window of his apartment at the pigeons and people passing on the street absent a coronation parade. It is also likely that he was able to charge a premium price because of the happy coincidence that his apartment window faced the parade route. The Scottsdale Plaza Resort was selling a facility for a conference. It was not guaranteeing that Kuhn could run a successful conference; the contract put that burden on Kuhn. As far as we can tell, the Scottsdale Plaza Resort was ready to supply adequate conference facilities. Is this enough to distinguish the cases?

2. *Coming closer to Krell v. Henry*? A promoter of diving tours made a contract with twenty people for a tour that would allow participants to dive at Taveuni, one of the Fiji Islands in the Pacific. The tour was to be at Taveuni for a week that would include New Year's Eve at the end of 2000. The island lies on the 180 degree meridian line. Given the location of the island, it would be one of the very first places where the New Year would arrive and where dawn would come on January 1, 2001. Promoter's literature promoting the tour indicated that the members of the party would begin a dive at 11:30 p.m. on December 31 and surface 30 minutes into the New Year. Promoter made a contract with the Taveuni Island Resort to provide rooms for seven days for participants in his tour. The Resort's officials knew that the promoter was bringing people to their hotel who planned on diving at the reefs off the coast of Taveuni Island. These officials also knew of Promoter's plans to dive on New Year's Eve. All of the promotional literature published by the Resort featured stories about snorkeling and diving during the days and parties staged in the evenings. Local customs concerning New Year's Eve were described in this promotional literature, and they promised a grand party. While Taveuni Island is beautiful, it is sufficiently remote that relatively few people would travel there who were not interested in diving. Resort's officials knew this.

On November 1, 2000, Ratu Glanville Lalabalavu, the paramount chief of the Cakaudrove Province (which included the island of Taveuni) died. Local custom dictated that a period of mourning be observed for 100 days that began on November 4, 2000, and would end in mid-February 2001. During this period of mourning, custom established that there would be no parties and people would not dive near the many reefs around the islands in Cakaudrove Province. Ratu Tevita Vakalalabure, another chief, warned that he would use ancient rites to call up sharks to attack revelers. This threat had been used in the past as a way to keep both the local population and tourists from diving during the period of mourning.

Suppose Promoter sued the Taveuni Island Resort for his expectation and reliance losses caused by its breach of the contract it had made with him for his tour. The contract contains no express terms dealing with excuses for the performances promised by the Resort or by Promoter. Assume that the Fiji Islands once were a British colony, and its courts follow the common law. How likely is it that Promoter will recover for breach of the contract that he made with the resort? How would the Resort likely defend against Promoter's claim? What was the Resort selling to Promoter: hotel rooms from which you could do anything or rooms from which you could go diving?[53]

3. *Contract law and terrorism:* On September 11, 2001, terrorists destroyed the Word Trade Center towers in New York and damaged the Pentagon in Washington, D.C. by highjacking three passenger aircraft loaded with fuel for a trans-

---

[53] *See* Stuart Millar, *Shark Curse Threatens Party*, THE GUARDIAN (LONDON), Dec. 6, 1999, at 1; 36 CONDÉ NAST TRAVELER, January 2001, at 76.

continental trip and crashing them into these buildings. (A fourth plane was also highjacked, but did not reach its target). The federal government closed the airline system. Planes did not come to the United States from abroad and all domestic flights were canceled. Suppose Kuhn Farm Machinery's convention in Scottsdale, Arizona was scheduled to begin on September 13, 2001, during the period when all flights were canceled. The only Kuhn dealers who could get to the Scottsdale Plaza Resort were those who lived within driving distance from the resort. Would the Arizona court now recognize a frustration of purpose defense to any claim that the resort tried to make against Kuhn? Would it be enough to say that the Resort had promised to make available hotel and conference rooms on the specified dates, and it did exactly this? Absent a *force majeure* clause in the contract, why should we say that the Resort assumed the risk of the loss of the United States airline system?

4. *Force majeure clauses as the solution*? A California lawyer said: "The pattern has always been that people address these things with general language . . . and when some unexpected permutation occurs, they all rush to address that specifically." He expected more contract clauses to deal with terrorism explicitly as a result of the September 11th attacks in New York and Washington.[54] Some people did have contracts with clauses that they could argue governed the events of September 11th. In the same article, the managing partner of a large Los Angeles firm is quoted as saying:

> We had booked rooms for a couple hundred lawyers [at a partners' meeting in Phoenix a week after the attacks]. . . . We invoked our force majeure clause with the hotel [to avoid penalty fees], because no one could get there. If our meeting had been in December rather than Sept. 18th, we would have had a different argument. The further you get away from this Sept. 11 date, the harder it's going to be to make that claim.

2. *PARADINE v. JANE* OR *TAYLOR v. CALDWELL*?

EASTERN AIR LINES, INC. v. MCDONNELL DOUGLAS CORP.

United States Court of Appeals, Fifth Circuit
532 F.2d 957 (5th Cir. 1976)

[See the statement of facts *supra* page 448. This portion of the opinion begins on page 980 in the reporter.]

IV. *The Vietnam War as an Excuse for Delayed Deliveries*

Much of the trial below was devoted to McDonnell's defense that the delivery delays were the result of the escalation of the war in Vietnam and were therefore excusable under the contracts, the Defense Production Act, and the Uniform Commercial Code. To prove this contention, McDonnell introduced evidence of government pressure on its suppliers and subcontractors to accord military orders

---

[54] Lisa Girion, *Businesses Seek a Legal Escape from Terrorism*, LOS ANGELES TIMES, October 14, 2001, part 3, at 1.

priority over civilian projects. McDonnell asserts that its efforts to raise the defense of government "jawboning" was frustrated by the trial judge's ruling and subsequent instructions to the jury which held that the only excusable delays were those resulting from formal ratings and directives issued in strict compliance with the Defense Production Act. Issue is also taken by McDonnell with the lower court's rulings that it had the burden of proof in establishing its defenses, that the U.C.C. is not applicable to this question and that any excusing event must have been unforeseeable.

Because we find that the Government's "jawboning" policy in effect during the years 1966-1969 comes within the terms of the contracts' excusable delay clause and the exculpatory provision of the Defense Production Act, we hold that the District Judge committed reversible error on this issue. The jury should have been instructed that McDonnell was not liable for any delays proximately caused by this government policy. The trial judge also erred in instructing the jury both that these particular delays had to have been unforeseeable and that the Code's impracticability defense was not available to McDonnell.

A.   The Government's "Jawboning" Policy

Although the origins of American involvement in Vietnam can be traced back to World War II, direct military intervention did not begin on a significant scale until after the overthrow of the Diem Regime in November of 1963. During the ensuing year, the United States increased the number of its troops stationed in that country from 1,000 to 23,000. This American commitment, however, constituted a relatively insignificant part of our total military budget and had no substantial effect on the national economy. Even after the Gulf of Tonkin Resolution of August 2, 1964, our troop commitment in Vietnam remained stable with the total size of the army, in fact, declining. The massive American buildup did not begin in earnest until January of 1965,[55] and it was not until mid-1966 that the United States assumed the bulk of the combat role in Vietnam.

Thus, in February 1965, when Eastern and Douglas signed the letter of intent concerning all the agreements ultimately executed between them, the Vietnam conflict was having no significant effect on the American economy. There was, moreover, little indication at that time of the proportions which the war was quickly to assume.[56]

---

[55] [65] The bombing of North Vietnam did not officially begin until February 1966. As is indicated below, the number of American troops in Vietnam increased by 800 per cent during 1965:

Date	Number of troops
December 31, 1964	23,000
June 30, 1965	103,000
December 31, 1965	184,000
June 30, 1966	322,000
December 31, 1966	455,000

[56] [66] For example, Secretary of Defense McNamara announced in 1965 that "We have stopped losing the war." At the time, President Johnson estimated that the military budget for the fiscal year ending in 1965 would be lower than that of the previous year. As late as 1966, American fiscal policy was being formulated on the assumption that the war would be over by June 1967. In March of that year, therefore, Secretary of the Treasury Fowler publicly expressed the hope that "no one will base his economic decisions on the purely speculative assumption that our Vietnam needs will

It was not until 1966 that the war first began to have a substantial impact on the American economy. During that year, for example, the armed forces absorbed over two-fifths of the nation's available manpower. A substantial share of the remaining available work force was taken by firms confronted with a rising back-log of defense-related orders. As one expert testified at trial, this military buildup was superimposed on an economy which was rapidly approaching full employ-ment. . . .

> Hence there wasn't the available capacity in the American economy to absorb the Vietnam requirements on top of existing civilian require-ments.

This, of course, led to conflicts between already scheduled commercial pro-duction and sudden, unexpectedly-large military needs. Rather than abandoning entirely the "guns and butter" policy upon which the war had been predicated, the Government sought instead to have military suppliers accord first priority to war production.

The vehicle by which military orders gained precedence over civilian produc-tion was the Defense Production Act of 1950 ("D.P.A."). 50 App.U.S.C. § 2061 *et seq.* Section 101 of the D.P.A. grants the President broad authority to require that priority be given to "contracts or orders . . . which he deems necessary or appropriate to promote the national defense." Under section 704, the President is authorized further to "make such rules, regulations, and orders as he deems nec-essary or appropriate to carry out the provisions of this Act."

As provided under the D.P.A., the President in 1953 delegated his priority powers to the Director of what was then the Office of Emergency Planning ("O.E.P."), a part of the Executive Office of the President. Pursuant to this dele-gation, the O.E.P., in turn, delegated priority authority over the air transport and other industries to the Secretary of Commerce. Within the Commerce Depart-ment, the Business and Defense Services Administration ("B.D.S.A.") was charged with administering the Defense Production Act.

Pursuant to these delegations, the B.D.S.A. adopted rules and regulations gov-erning the precedence to be given certain civilian and military orders. The high-est priority under these regulations was achieved by "directives" issued by the B.D.S.A. or the Office of Emergency Preparedness to schedule production at a particular plant. "DX" ratings were intended to be used "to obtain products and materials in cases of extreme urgency," and were accorded precedence over "DO"-rated orders which, in turn, had priority over all unrated goods in a particu-lar area of production.

Because of its importance both to the economy and to national defense, pro-duction for civil air carriers, ever since the Korean War, had been accorded the same general "DO" priority rating given military aircraft. By having equal pref-erential status with military production, the manufacturers of commercial planes were guaranteed prior access to the hardware and vital raw materials also being sought by less essential industries.

---

exceed current expectations." The cost of the war in the fiscal year ending in 1967, however, ex-ceeded the Government's estimates by almost 100 per cent.

Occasionally, "DO"-rated civilian orders would delay military requirements with the same priority rating. Prior to 1966, these conflicts were usually resolved by a Defense Department application to the B.D.S.A. for a "bottleneck-breaking DX rating." After a number of weeks, the B.D.S.A. would issue the requested rating if it determined that civilian orders were in fact delaying military production.

By the end of 1965, however, the enormous increase in urgent military orders had made this process so unwieldy that the Defense Department sought to have the "DO" rating removed from commercial aircraft production. This request alarmed the entire aviation industry because it would have severely impeded its access to scarce raw materials and the heavy industry which was then processing these materials at full capacity. The airlines themselves were concerned that the loss of "DO" priority would further slow the production of planes already being delayed by a war-caused shortage of jet engines, and that non-urgent military orders would be filled at the expense of pressing commercial needs.

In the face of this widespread opposition, the military withdrew its request that the "DO" rating be removed from commercial aircraft production. As a *quid pro quo*, however, the Defense Department insisted that particular military orders be given preference on an individual and informal basis. It appears that the aviation industry agreed to the proposed arrangement. . . .

[The court summarized evidence showing that jawboning of aircraft manufacturers was government policy.] . . . Individual firms, moreover, were told that any resistance to informal requests by representatives of the military would result in a formal directive being issued against them. For example, Pratt & Whitney, the sole supplier of engines to Douglas, was "overwhelmed" in 1966 by government demands that its production of military engines be accelerated. These requests were being acceded to, in the words of one Pratt & Whitney executive, "to prevent the removal of the priority rating from the commercial [orders]."

Similar pressures were being applied to the manufacturers of Douglas' landing gear. Gerald Lynch, President and Chairman of Menasco, Inc., testified that the underlying reason for his firm's delay in delivering landing gear to Douglas was "the extraordinary unanticipated requirements for . . . military spares." . . . [Menasco felt obliged to give priority to military requirements.]

Cleveland Pneumatic Tool Company, the other supplier of landing gear to Douglas also gave military orders priority despite the "DO" rating given its civilian contracts. . . .

Taking the view that the jawboning policy described above was voluntarily acquiesced in by the aviation industry, the District Court ruled and subsequently instructed the jury during the liability phase of the trial that only delays resulting from the actual issuance of formal ratings or directives could be deemed excusable. Consistent with this approach, the trial judge either excluded or struck evidence concerning government jawboning of Douglas' suppliers.

In an effort to blunt McDonnell's attack on the trial judge's rulings and instructions, Eastern devoted a great deal of its briefs and oral argument to a recitation of purported management difficulties at Douglas during the years 1965-1966. Eastern implied that even if the District Court erred in its approach to the

Government's jawboning policy, there are no grounds for reversal because the delivery delays were in fact the product of Douglas mismanagement rather than the Vietnam conflict. . . .

. . . [H]owever, there is ample evidence in the record to make this issue one for the jury. Not only does it appear that there was a substantial war-caused labor shortage in Douglas' recruiting area, but Douglas' suppliers testified that their own delays were the product of similar labor shortages. There is also direct evidence indicating that the delivery schedules of the manufacturers of Douglas landing gear and engines were delayed by the war. In short, the proof indicating that there were at least some war-caused delivery delays is not so inadequate as to eliminate the prejudicial effect of the trial court's rulings on military jawboning. We turn, therefore, to an examination of the legal basis for those of the court's rulings and instructions to the jury which related to McDonnell's Vietnam War defense.

B. The "Excusable Delay" Clause

McDonnell Douglas contends that the trial judge's instructions to the jury undercut the defense available to it under the excusable delay clause found in all of the contracts at issue in this appeal. In relevant part, the provision reads as follows:

> Seller shall not be responsible nor deemed to be in default on account of delays in performance . . . due to causes beyond Seller's control and not occasioned by its fault or negligence, including but not being limited to . . . any act of government, governmental priorities, allocation regulations or orders affecting materials, equipment, facilities or completed aircraft, . . . failure of vendors (due to causes similar to those within the scope of this clause) to perform their contracts . . . , provided such cause is beyond Seller's control.

1. Ejusdem Generis and the Applicability of U.C.C. § 2-615

McDonnell's first contention in this regard is that the District Court unduly narrowed the scope of this clause by instructing the jury that an excusable delay must be the result of "one or more of the listed events in the excusable delay clause of the contracts, or . . . a similar cause beyond the defendant's control. . . ." This instruction, in McDonnell's view, effectively construes the specifically listed excusable causes of delay as restricting the application of the more general phrase which exempts Douglas from liability for delays beyond its control and not due to its negligence. McDonnell feels, therefore, that its affirmative defense was unjustifiably limited to delays caused by events similar to those specifically listed when, in fact, the contracts excused all delays which were not its fault.

The trial judge's construction of the clause, moreover, affords McDonnell Douglas a narrower range of excuses than is available under the modern view of impossibility as it is codified in U.C.C. § 2-615. Simply stated, section 2-615 excuses delay or nondelivery when the agreed upon performance has been rendered "commercially impracticable" by an unforeseen supervening event not within the contemplation of the parties at the time the contract was entered into.

Uniform Commercial Code § 2-615 [Cal. Comm. Code § 2615] Comments 1 & 8; *see* Restatement, Contracts §§ 454, 457 (1932); 6 A. Corbin, Contracts §§ 1321, 1339 (1962).

Under section 2-615, the impossibility defense is available to the seller only if he has not "assumed a greater obligation" than that imposed upon him by this provision. During the trial, the court below ruled that section 2-615 was not applicable for this reason. Although the trial judge failed to explain his holding, it must have been based upon his restrictive construction of the excusable delay clause. Presumably, then, the protections of section 2-615 were deemed to have been waived because the contracts were interpreted as limiting McDonnell's impossibility defense to delays caused by events similar to those specifically provided for in the excusable delay clause.

In support of this approach, Eastern argues that the District Court correctly applied *ejusdem generis*, a canon of judicial construction limiting the application of general terms which follow specific ones to matters similar in kind or classification to those specified. . . .

This maxim, however, "is only an instrumentality for ascertaining the correct meaning of the words when there is uncertainty." . . . Obviously, the application of the doctrine in this case would make superfluous the unambiguous words "including but not being limited to" which precede the specifically listed excuses for delay.[57] It is clear, then, that by excusing delays not within McDonnell's control nor due to its negligence, "including but not being limited to" governmental acts, priorities, or orders, the parties intended to excuse all delays coming within the general description regardless of their similarity to the listed excuses. Consequently, there is no basis for the trial judge's conclusion that McDonnell waived the protections of section 2-615 and that its contract excuses are narrower than those available under the doctrine of commercial impracticability.

2. *The Foreseeability Issue*

McDonnell also challenges the trial judge's jury instruction which limited excusable delivery delays to those resulting from events which were not "reasonably foreseeable" at the time a contract was executed. By writing a foreseeability requirement into the excusable delay clause, the District Court appeared to construe the contracts as constituting nothing more than an application of the Code's commercial impracticability rule to those particular events specified in the contracts.

Although there has been some doubt expressed as to whether the Code permits parties to bargain for exemptions broader than those available under section 2-615, this concern is ill-founded.

. . . Comment 8 to this provision plainly indicates that parties may "enlarge upon or supplant" section 2-615. *See United States v. Wegematic Corp.*, 2 Cir., 1966, 360 F.2d 674, 677 (Friendly, J.).

---

[57] [90] *Ejusdem generis*, by its very terms, applies only where the general terms of an exculpatory clause follow a more specific listing of excused events. Here, of course, the general terms of the excusable delay clause precede the more specific provisions. . . .

There appear to be, however, certain strictures imposed upon judicial interpretation of such agreements. Comment 8 provides:

> Generally, express agreements as to exemptions designed to enlarge upon or supplant the provisions of this section are to be read in light of mercantile sense and reason, for this section itself sets up the commercial standard for normal and reasonable interpretation and provides a minimum beyond which agreement may not go.

While this provision could have been drafted in less vague terms, we presume that Comment 8 establishes "mercantile sense and reason" as a general standard governing our construction of agreements enlarging upon the protections of section 2-615. As we understand Comment 8, where there is doubt concerning the parties' intention, exemption clauses should not be construed as broadening the excuses available under the Code's impracticability rule. Applying this standard to the excusable delay clause, we cannot, in the absence of evidence to the contrary, hold that McDonnell is exempt from liability for any delay, regardless of its foreseeability, that is due to causes beyond its control. Exculpatory provisions which are phrased merely in general terms have long been construed as excusing only unforeseen events which make performance impracticable. . . . Courts have often held, therefore, that if a promisor desires to broaden the protections available under the excuse doctrine he should provide for the excusing contingencies with particularity and not in general language. . . .

We realize, of course, that this rule of construction developed in the pre-U.C.C. era when the scope of the impossibility and frustration doctrines was unclear and varied from jurisdiction to jurisdiction. Because of the uncertainty surrounding the law of excuse, parties had good reason to resort to general contract provisions relieving the promisor of liability for breaches caused by events "beyond his control." Although the Uniform Commercial Code has ostensibly eliminated the need for such clauses, lawyers, either through an abundance of caution or by force of habit, continue to write them into contract. . . . Thus, even though our interpretation would render the general terms of the excusable delay clause merely duplicative of section 2-615, we will adhere to the established rule of construction because it continues to reflect prevailing commercial practices.

We reiterate, however, that we are applying only a canon of contract interpretation which generally reflects commercial standards of reasonableness. We disagree with the suggestion of one commentator that section 2-615 imposes a fixed standard governing the interpretation of exemption clauses. The Code establishes no absolute requirement that any agreement purporting to enlarge upon section 2-615 must do so in plain and specific language. Even in the absence of detailed wording, trade usage and the circumstances surrounding a particular agreement may indicate that the parties intended to accord the seller an exemption broader than is available under the U.C.C.

While we hold that the provision of the excusable delay clause exempting McDonnell from liability for delays beyond its control should be interpreted as incorporating the Code's commercial impracticability doctrine, we disagree with the trial judge's jury instruction on foreseeability insofar as it implies that the events specifically listed in the excusable delay clause in each contract must have been unforeseeable at the time the agreement was executed. The rationale for the doctrine of impracticability is that the circumstance causing the breach has made performance so vitally different from what was anticipated that the contract cannot reasonably be thought to govern. . . . However, because the purpose of a contract is to place the reasonable risk of performance on the promisor, he is presumed, in the absence of evidence to the contrary, to have agreed to bear any loss occasioned by an event which was foreseeable at the time of contracting. *Lloyd v. Murphy*, 1944, 25 Cal.2d 48, 54, 153 P.2d 47, 50 (Traynor, J.). . . . Underlying this presumption is the view that a promisor can protect himself against foreseeable events by means of an express provision in the agreement.

Therefore, when the promisor has anticipated a particular event by specifically providing for it in a contract, he should be relieved of liability for the occurrence of such event regardless of whether it was foreseeable. . . .

As Justice Traynor noted for the California Supreme Court under different but nonetheless analogous circumstances,

> the question whether a risk was foreseeable is quite distinct from the question whether it was contemplated by the parties. . . . When a risk has been contemplated and voluntarily assumed . . . foreseeability is not an issue and the parties will be held to the bargain they made.

Glenn R. Sewell Sheet Metal, Inc. v. Loverde, 1969, 70 Cal.2d 666, 451 P.2d 721, 728 n. 13; *see Lloyd v. Murphy, supra*, 153 P.2d at 50. In this case, it is clear that Eastern specifically "contemplated and voluntarily assumed" the risk that deliveries would be delayed by governmental acts, priorities, regulations or orders. Moreover, unlike the only case cited to us by Eastern which construes a similar provision, *United States v. Brooks-Callaway Co.*, 318 U.S. 120, 63 S.Ct. 474, 87 L.Ed. 653 (1943), there is no indication from the wording of the excusable delay clause that McDonnell's defenses are to be limited to breaches caused by unforeseeable events. Therefore, we must conclude that the trial judge erred in instructing the jury that the events specifically listed in the excusable delay clause must have been unforeseeable at the time the contracts were entered into for McDonnell to claim exemption from liability.

3.   *Informal Demands for Priority as an "Act of Government"*

Turning next to the question of whether the Government's informal priorities policy came within the ambit of the excusable delay clause, we have seen in Part IV-A of this opinion that McDonnell and its suppliers, in granting priority to the military, were cooperating with the established, publicly announced procurement policy of the Federal Government. Eastern contends, however, that this informal program did not come within the scope of the contract clause specifically excusing "any act of government, governmental priorities, allocations, or orders affecting materials." Asserting that the Defense Production Act authorizes the Government to obtain precedence for certain orders only by means of formal, published regulations, Eastern concludes that any other method is illegal, if not unconstitutional, and therefore cannot be deemed an act of Government. We disagree for the following reasons.

The Defense Production Act, in "a sweeping delegation of power," grants the President broad authority to require that defense-related contracts be given precedence over less essential orders. D.P.A. § 101(a), 50 App. U.S.C. § 2071(a). Congress created no detailed scheme by which this power was to be exercised, providing only that "[t]he President may make such rules, regulations, and orders as he deems necessary or appropriate." D.P.A. § 704, 50 App. U.S.C. § 2154. There is, moreover, nothing in either the legislative history of the D.P.A. or in the wording of the Act itself which gives any indication that the Government may not seek compliance with its priorities policies by informal means. It is reasonable to conclude, therefore, that Congress intended to accord the Executive Branch great flexibility in molding its priorities policies to the frequently unanticipated exigencies of national defense. . . .

We note, moreover, that this case precisely fits an established pattern of decisions rejecting the contention that breaches of contract are excused only by formal or technical acts of Government. Whether predicated on a contractual provision or simply on the common law defense of impossibility these decisions indicate in the clearest terms that fundamentally coercive acts of Government, whatever their form, constitute an excuse for breach. Thus, a promisor is not liable merely because the government order causing a breach is technically deficient. . . .

Consequently, we will not permit the form of the military priorities policy to disguise what was in substance a governmental act beyond the control of McDonnell Douglas. The excusable delay clause cannot be made to turn on a distinction which for so long has been held to be entirely artificial and unrealistic. . . .

This approach, moreover, is consistent with that required under the Uniform Commercial Code. In Comment 10 to section 615, the draftsmen of Article 2 stated:

> Following its basic policy of using commercial practicability as a test for excuse, this section . . . disregards any technical distinctions between "law," "regulation," "order" and the like. Nor does it make the present action of the seller depend upon the eventual judicial determination of the legality of the particular governmental action. The seller's good faith belief in the validity of the regulation is the test under this Article and the best evidence of this good faith is the general commercial acceptance of the regulation.

Given McDonnell's unquestioned good faith in complying with the Government's demands for priority and the uncontroverted evidence of the entire aviation industry's acceptance of the policy, we must hold as a matter of law that McDonnell is not liable for any delivery delay proximately resulting from the informal procurement program. . . .

NOTES AND QUESTIONS

1. *The impact of a contract clause*: While the courts generally have interpreted UCC § 2-615 very narrowly and offered few excuses, the *Eastern Air Lines* case reflects the very different approach that is common when a clause in a

contract deals with the problem. In many instances, of course, this is just a matter of free contract. If a seller or buyer wants to condition its obligation so that it is not liable for strikes, national emergency priority schemes, or anything else, and if the other party agrees, we might expect courts to honor their wishes. In the *Eastern Air Lines* case, the court deals with the view that the introductory clause to UCC §§ 2-615 and 2-616(3) regulates impracticability excuses greater than those that would be provided by the statute absent such a provision. Instead of regulation, the court reads the language as a principle of interpretation.

While the Court's interpretation may simply implement free contract in a bargained deal between a sophisticated seller and buyer, should courts uphold clauses in standard forms that go beyond § 2-615 so that a seller no longer is assuming the normal risks in business? Could courts make such decisions without extensive and expensive evidence about trade custom?

What does the introductory clause to § 2-615 mean? A literal reading suggests that the drafters of Article 2 were trying to preserve free contract so that parties could allocate risks as they pleased. Suppose, absent any provision in the contract, a court would find that if seller's plant burned down, this would be the occurrence of a contingency, the non-occurrence of which was a basic assumption on which the contract was made. When the parties are negotiating their deal, the buyer wants the seller to promise to deliver whether or not its plant burns down. This way, if there is such a fire, the buyer will get seller's best efforts to find substitute goods or the buyer will be able to recover damages from the seller to compensate the buyer for its losses. The introductory clause tells us that the buyer can make such a contract if it has the bargaining power to induce the seller to agree to it. The seller has "assumed a greater obligation" and so it cannot use the excuse that otherwise it would have had under § 2-615.

2. *Judicial control of force majeure clauses*: In *Nissho-Iwai Co., Ltd. v. Occidental Crude Sales, Inc.*,[58] Occidental agreed to supply a Japanese oil distributor with crude oil produced from Concession 102 in Libya. The contract excused performances that could not be rendered because of "executive or administrative orders of acts [of the Libyan Government] . . . or by any other event, whether or not similar to the causes specified above . . . which shall not reasonably be within the control of" Occidental. The Libyan government issued orders cutting back production of oil from this field.

The trial court charged that the jury had to find "the excusing event or events were not reasonably within the control of Occidental or its supplier." Occidental challenged this instruction on appeal. It argued that the "control" limitation only applied to "other events" and not actions of the Libyan government. The Court of Appeals, applying California law as specified in the contract, affirmed. It said,

> [T]he California law of force majeure requires us to apply a reasonable control limitation to each specified event, regardless of what generalized contract interpretation would suggest. . . .
>
> The term "reasonable control" has come to include two related notions. First, a party may not affirmatively cause the event that prevents

---

[58] 729 F.2d 1530 (5th Cir. 1984).

his performance. The rationale behind this requirement is obvious. If a contractor were able to escape his responsibilities merely by causing an excusing event to occur, he would have no effective "obligation to perform." . . .

The second aspect of reasonable control is more subtle. Some courts will not allow a party to rely on an excusing event if he could have taken reasonable steps to prevent it. . . . The rationale behind this requirement is that the force majeure did not actually prevent performance if a party could reasonably have prevented the event from occurring. The party has prevented performance and, again, breached his good faith obligation to perform by failing to exercise reasonable diligence. . . .

[Occidental's proposed jury] instruction would permit Occidental to rest on its legal rights and to refuse any demands by the Libyan Government that violated the contract between Libya and Occidental. When Libya imposed restrictions on Occidental's oil production in 1975, Occidental, acting on advice of counsel, withheld $117 million in payments that were due. The Government retaliated by imposing an embargo. Under Occidental's proposed instruction, the embargo would not have been within Occidental's reasonable control even if Occidental knew in advance that it could prevent the embargo by paying the $117 Million. . . .

It is clear Occidental was aware of the threatened embargo and could have prevented it by paying $117 million. This sum in [it]self was not unreasonable, since the entire figure represented back taxes, royalties, and oil costs that Occidental already owed the Libyan Government. Of course, even if Occidental had paid this sum and averted the embargo, it would still have faced production restrictions. A reasonable jury could have found, though, that Occidental would be able to recoup through arbitration or settlement any losses that might result from the restrictions. The company had already commenced arbitration proceedings against the Libyan Government; and, in December, it was able to reach a settlement. To be sure, the withheld payments and the resulting embargo were factors in producing that settlement. That is not to say, however, that a settlement would not have been reached in the absence of an embargo. In the past, Occidental had been able to convince the Government to back down from production restrictions. A reasonable jury might have found that Occidental would again have been able to negotiate a reasonable settlement, particularly given the threat of arbitration proceedings.[59]

How could Occidental show that the actions of the Libyan government were not within Occidental's reasonable control? Can it engage in aggressive negotiations without losing a defense under the court's construction? Can it seek to establish a reputation with the Libyan government as a hard bargainer willing to

---

[59] *Id.* at 1540-43.

risk an embargo? Could Occidental contract around this problem so that it would be free of this heavy burden of proof in the future?[60]

Is *Nissho-Iwai* consistent with the *Eastern Air Lines* opinion?

3. *A force majeure clause and foreseeable risks*: In the *Eastern Air Lines* case, the court said: "we disagree with the trial judge's jury instruction on fore-seeability insofar as it implies that the events specifically listed in the excusable delay clause in each contract must have been unforeseeable at the time the agreement was executed." If an event is foreseeable, and if a party specifically provides for an excuse if that event occurs, there is no reason not to carry out the risk allocation of the parties. However, in *Watson Laboratories, Inc. v. Rhone-Poulenc Rorer, Inc.,*[61] the court distinguished the situation in the *Eastern Air Lines* case. Rhone-Poulence Rorer (RPR) was to supply the drug Dilacor to Watson. The drug was to be produced by Centeon, a company partially owned by RPR, at Centeon's Kankakee, Illinois plant. However, at the time the parties signed the supply agreement, as both parties knew, Centeon was operating that plant under an FDA Consent Decree. The FDA had found that the Kankakee plant was in violation of many FDA regulations. The Consent Degree provided that if Centeon failed to comply with FDA regulations, the FDA could immediately order Centeon to stop all manufacturing of pharmaceutical products at the Kankakee plant. After the supply contract was signed, the FDA inspected the Kankakee plant and ordered it to cease manufacturing any drugs.

The supply contract provided:

> The obligations of RPR and Watson hereunder shall be subject to any de-lays or non-performance caused by: acts of God, earthquakes, fires, floods, explosion, sabotage, riot, accidents; regulatory, governmental, or military action or inaction; strikes, lockouts or labor trouble; perils of the sea; or failure or delay in performance by third parties, including suppli-ers and service providers; or any other cause beyond the reasonable con-trol of either party. . . . The party which is not performing its obligations under this Agreement as a result of any such event of Force Majeure

---

[60] Compare International Minerals & Chem. Corp. v. Llano, Inc. 770 F.2d 879 (10th Cir. 1985), where a buyer sought a declaratory judgment that it was excused from taking natural gas under the terms of a contract. It provided: "In the event . . . Buyer is unable to receive gas as provided in this contract for any reason beyond the reasonable control of the parties . . . an appropriate adjustment in the minimum purchase requirements . . . shall be made."

The New Mexico Environmental Improvement Board later issued a regulation requiring emissions from industrial plants to be reduced "as expeditiously as practicable." The buyer converted its plant to a chemical precipitation process that used about 50-60% less natural gas.

The trial court found that the buyer voluntarily complied with the regulation and had come into compliance earlier than required. Thus, there was no excuse. The Court of Appeals reversed and found the buyer excused. The regulation was an event beyond the reasonable control of the buyer that rendered it "unable" to receive its minimum amount of gas under the contract. The court said that "unable" was synonymous with "impracticable" as that term is used in UCC § 2-615. It concluded that as a matter of policy those who cooperate with regulatory agencies and comply with the letter and spirit of legally proper regulations are to be encouraged. The court noted that the buyer's power was limited by the requirement of good faith. A buyer may not collude or induce a governmental agency to act so that the buyer can avoid a contract. However, cooperation to eliminate pollution "can hardly be termed improper collusion."

[61] 178 F. Supp. 1099 (C.D. Calif 2001).

shall use commercially reasonable efforts to resume compliance with this Agreement as soon as possible.

The court found as a matter of law that the supplier could not rely on this clause to excuse nonperformance "because the shutdown of the Centeon plant was both entirely foreseeable and not encompassed within the force majeure clause."[62] It stated:

> The language referring to "regulatory, governmental . . . action" is vague and boilerplate. These words cannot reasonably be construed to reflect that the parties considered that the shutdown of the Centeon plant would be encompassed. In contract, the clause in the Eastern Airlines-McDonnell Douglas contract was specific. It referred to precisely the kind of governmental action that . . . caused the delay. . . .

The court explained: "when parties expressly contemplate a known risk of a regulatory prohibition, they should be expected to allocate that risk expressly, rather than rely upon a boilerplate clause enumerating a parade of horribles that are so unlikely to occur as to make them qualitatively different. In the absence of such allocation, only governmental action not previously contemplated could quality as force majeure." Does the *Eastern Air Lines* case differ from the situation in *Watson Laboratories,* if we assume that the goal of both courts was, in the words of UCC §1-201(3), to carry out "the bargain of the parties in fact"?

3. DO THE RULES CHANGE WHEN THE GAME GETS BIGGER?

Westinghouse Electric Corporation sold nuclear reactors to twenty-seven power companies in the '60s and early '70s. In order to persuade the utilities to buy the reactors, Westinghouse agreed to supply the uranium oxide which the reactors used as fuel. The contract price averaged $9.50 per pound. Westinghouse committed itself to supply 80 million pounds of fuel, though it owned at the time only about 15 million pounds; it was confident that it could buy fuel on the market as the need arose. Much to the dismay of Westinghouse the price of uranium oxide rose from about $6 per pound in 1972 to $44 per pound in 1978. It doesn't take a nuclear physicist to see that the financial implications of this to Westinghouse were significant, if not dire.

On September 8, 1975, Westinghouse shocked its utility customers, and others in the business community, by announcing that it would not honor its contracts to supply the nuclear fuel. It argued that it was excused from performance by § 2-615(a) of the Uniform Commercial Code. That section provides a defense to an action for breach if the non-performance is "the occurrence of a contingency the non-occurrence of which was a basic assumption on which the contract was made." Westinghouse argued that the extreme and unforeseen change in the market for uranium oxide amounted to just such a contingency. The power companies responded by bringing suits which charged that Westinghouse was simply

---

[62] The court also said that the supplier would have to establish that the closing of the Centeon plant was "beyond the reasonable control" of supplier, but this was a disputed question of fact and could not be established on a motion for summary judgment.

seeking to avoid responsibility for the risk it took when it promised to deliver fuel it didn't own, electing to rely on an inherently risky market. Their theory was that Westinghouse had made a business misjudgment by gambling on the market and was trying to avoid taking the consequences. The claims of the utilities aggregated approximately $2.6 billion. The net worth of Westinghouse was $2.3 billion at the end of 1977. Many of the utility suits were joined in a single suit in the federal court in Richmond, Virginia, presided over by Robert Merhige, Jr.

Question: How would you assess the strength of Westinghouse's § 2-615 claim, acknowledging of course that you have only the sketchiest description of a very complicated story?

In 1976, documents surfaced in Australia which revealed an international uranium cartel which had been organized in 1972 to control sales by producing governments, and so to raise prices. The United States producers apparently knew about the cartel, but had chosen not to participate. It was not clear whether or not such a cartel was legal under international law. Westinghouse argued that the cartel was the reason for the price run-up. A Canadian subsidiary of Gulf Oil was a participant in the cartel. Westinghouse brought suit in October of 1976 against Gulf Oil and 29 uranium producers for price fixing. It alleged that Gulf Oil's Canadian subsidiary provided the link between American uranium producers and the international cartel. Gulf Oil admitted the participation of its Canadian subsidiary, but said that the cartel's plans had carefully excluded the American market from its plans. In May of 1978 Gulf filed a countersuit, alleging that Westinghouse itself had been seeking to monopolize markets for nuclear reactors, fabricated fuel, and uranium.

Question: What is the relevance, to the § 2-615 dispute, of the discovery of the international cartel?

From the very beginning, Federal Judge Merhige urged the parties to the suits between the utilities and Westinghouse to settle. Although the potential liability of Westinghouse exceeded $2 billion, most observers expected settlements in most, if not all, of the disputes. In addition to the risks associated with litigating and losing, the utilities had an interest in the survival of Westinghouse. Someone would have to continue to provide engineering for the reactor projects, as well as parts and service. In addition, the utility industry had a general interest in the survival of competition in the reactor and power-generation industry; Westinghouse was an important player in that market. At one point after three months of trial hearings had been held, a Pittsburgh judge was asked about his efforts to convince the parties to settle:

> The fiscal well-being, possibly the survival, of one of the world's corporate giants is in jeopardy. Likewise, the future of thousands of jobs.
>
> Any decision I hand down will hurt somebody and because of that potential damage, I want to make it clear that it will happen only because certain captains of industry could not together work out their problems so that the hurt might have been held to a minimum. . . .
>
> Solomon-like as I want to be, I can't cut this baby in half. . .

There are also, of course, some pressures to proceed with the litigation. There is a chance that both parties over-estimate their chances for winning the lawsuit, and so see the other side's position as unreasonable. One or both of the parties may in fact *be* unreasonable, making it more difficult to get agreement. And some reasons are more subtle. Professor Macaulay[63] has pointed out:

> [L]itigation may legitimate concessions in the eyes of outsiders who audit decisions. For example, the customers of Westinghouse are utilities whose rates are regulated. Without some strong justification, they could not negotiate a settlement with Westinghouse and then ask for approval of a rate increase to cover the balance of the loss. The chance that Westinghouse might win may serve to rationalize settlement, and the act of bringing suit might show the regulators that the utilities are not just giving money away. Consumer and antinuclear power organizations filed petitions in eleven states asking state utility regulators to scrutinize any out-of-court settlements that utilities may reach with Westinghouse. These groups assert that if utilities do not hold Westinghouse to its contracts, consumers will have to pay the extra fuel costs. . . .

> The *Wall Street Journal* . . . points to . . . [an] assertion of norms that are not coterminous with the law of contract, in the Westinghouse cases:

> > [T]he electric utilities have canceled and stretched out contracts for atomic power plants, putting a financial squeeze on such companies as Westinghouse.

> > "You and I know that in the real world of business there's going to be some horse-trading," an industry person says. "You can bet that Westinghouse is reminding companies like Con Edison that it has gone along with them in stretching contracts."

> Conduct in prior transactions generally is legally irrelevant in contract law, which focuses on the particular contract under litigation. However, the claim of prior accommodation to the needs of the utilities was highly relevant if any settlement was to be reached.

> Although it would be hard to prove, the contract litigation process may also exert an indirect influence on the behavior of the managers of industrial enterprises even where they devote little thought to it. Those making bargains may tacitly rely on the law to fill gaps and provide sanctions, in order to avoid the costs of negotiating about unlikely contingencies or of constructing elaborate systems of security to insure performance. Contract law may crystallize business customs and provide a normative vocabulary, affecting expectations about what is fair. Westinghouse, for example, did not repudiate its uranium oxide contracts in the name of pure self-interest but sought to cloak its actions in the language of the Uniform Commercial Code. Its positions, in that guise, may have been more palatable to some of its customers. It may be easier to negotiate with someone asserting a plausible claim of right than with an

---

[63] Macaulay, *Elegant Models, Empirical Pictures, and the Complexities of Contract*, 11 Law & Soc'y Rev. 507 (1977). Reprinted with permission.

outlaw openly scorning those who had relied on its promise. (Perhaps the U.C.C. served as a means of self-justification so that executives at Westinghouse felt better about not honoring the commitment their firm had made.) We can only speculate about the situation had the drafters of the Uniform Commercial Code adopted a more rigorous standard that rarely excused nonperformance based on the occurrence of an unforeseen contingency. Suppose the rule had been that one who makes a promise must perform come hell or high water. Would Westinghouse have marched into bankruptcy trying to perform or would it have begged for mercy? Would the impact have been only on the amount of any settlement, since the likelihood of victory by Westinghouse would have been insignificant and thus worth little?

Ultimately, the cases brought by the utilities were settled. Judge Merhige, the federal judge presiding over most of the cases, pressed the parties to settle; the day the trial opened he told the assembled lawyers that "I don't ever expect to finish these cases. . . . I expect (them) to get settled."[64] There had been relatively little in the way of settlement negotiations up to that time. Lawyers for the utilities expressed surprise about this, but some who were following the case suggested that Westinghouse was digging up information about the international cartel, and didn't want to discuss settlement until it had compiled that information. It was also noted that the utilities themselves had to be careful in reaching a settlement. If a rate-setting regulatory agency concluded that the utility had been too accommodating in reaching a settlement, they might refuse to allow the utility to pass along the extra fuel costs associated with settlement to customers. A Westinghouse representative said, "If these were industrial customers, we could have arrived at settlements months ago."[65]

As a way of increasing the likelihood of settlement, Merhige appointed a law school dean to serve as a special master to "be utilized for purposes of encouraging and assisting the parties in reaching an amicable adjustment of the respective claims in these cases. . . ." He also required the parties to file proposals for settlement. Something worked; the cases settled. In most cases the settlements were not cash settlements, but instead involved a combination of cash and services. In one case involving the Texas Utilities Services, Inc. the settlement (embodied in a 350 page settlement agreement!) was estimated to be worth $65 to $80 million to the utility, whereas Westinghouse estimated the settlement had cost it only $27 million. While it may be that the magnitude of the gap between the estimates reflects both sides' need to feel good about the settlement, it is quite plausible for a bargain to generate a substantial surplus of value. In fact, of course, every truly free bargain leaves both parties better off than they would have been with no bargain.

The antitrust suits which were brought against the 29 uranium producers, including perhaps most prominently Gulf Oil, were settled in the summer of 1981.

---

[64] Pappas, *Westinghouse, Utilities Under Pressure to Settle Uranium Suit Before Court Does*, WALL STREET JOURNAL, June 2, 1978 at 32, cols. 1-3.
[65] WALL STREET JOURNAL, *op.cit.*

NOTES AND QUESTIONS

1. *The law firm's role:* James B. Stewart wrote a book about prominent American law firms.[66] Chapter Four is devoted to the Chicago firm of Kirkland & Ellis, whose partner, William Jentes, was principal outside counsel for Westinghouse. Stewart's book contains an interesting account of some aspects of the litigation between Westinghouse and the utilities:[67]

> One of the Uniform Commercial Code's most controversial provisions is one which provides an escape for sellers who would otherwise be locked into their contracts under common law principles, and Jentes had mentioned it as a possibility at the first meeting with the Westinghouse lawyers. . . . [T]he provision had almost never been invoked or upheld in a court decision excusing non-performance. Undaunted, Jentes assigned some associates to scour the case law for some support should Westinghouse assert the commercial impracticability clause.
>
> Legal research, and the related preparation of a memorandum of law, are among the relatively few tasks mastered during the course of law school, and part of that assignment at Kirkland & Ellis fell to James Goold, a law student at the University of Chicago who was working as a summer associate for the firm. . . .
>
> Eventually [Goold's] task of researching the question of impracticability would take a full year—he barely attended class at the University of Chicago in order to complete the research—and resulted in a 200-page memorandum. . . .
>
> There was considerable debate inside Kirkland & Ellis about whether the facts surrounding the Westinghouse uranium contracts satisfied [the] conditions [for relief under Section 2-615]. . . .
>
> As one general counsel for a major utility recalls, he found the Westinghouse default "almost unbelievable," given its scope; the legal opinion [of Kirkland & Ellis] he dismissed as "flimsy—obviously grasping at legal straws." The legal opinion may even have been a tactical error. Expected by Westinghouse to be interpreted by the utilities as an indication of how serious Westinghouse's plight had become, it was instead greeted as an audacious attempt by Westinghouse to wriggle out of the contracts rather than admit its own errors and ask the utilities to help restructure the deal. Jentes, however, doubts that the utilities would ever have expressed a conciliatory attitude. "They were not the least bit statesmanlike. They acted like we were repudiating the Bible." One by one, the utilities marched into courts across the country, all filing lawsuits against Westinghouse. . . .
>
> Meanwhile, another contingent of Kirkland & Ellis lawyers was assigned to shore up the legal positions. When he had been a student at the University of Chicago, Goold, who had now come to work full-time, had

---

[66] James B. Stewart, THE PARTNERS: INSIDE AMERICA'S MOST POWERFUL LAW FIRMS (Simon and Schuster 1983). Reprinted with permission.

[67] *Id.* at 152.

taken a class in contracts with Professor Soia Mentschikoff. Mentschikoff was the widow of Karl Llewellyn, the man who had actually drafted
the Uniform Commercial Code which formed the basis for Westinghouse's defense, and Mentschikoff had worked closely with him on the
project. Goold hired her as a consultant on the case, and together they
began to sift through Llewellyn's files for more clues about the meaning
of the impracticability provision.

Eventually they found a bundle of handwritten notes, some of them
nearly tattered beyond legibility, and after piecing them together, they
derived some small encouragement for the position that a price increase,
if it was the result of some unforeseeable event directly related to performance of the contract, might excuse performance. . . .

As Judge Merhige had urged, by 1980 all of the utilities had reached
out-of-court settlements with Westinghouse which eliminated the need
for the planned trial on the damages issue. . . . [The settlements] were
handled internally by Westinghouse executives and the company's legal
staff—and though non-monetary aspects of the agreements make them
difficult to value, it is estimated that they cost Westinghouse approximately $900 million, or about half of what the utilities had claimed. If
Westinghouse and the utilities had simply split their differences in 1975,
before resorting to litigation, the result would have been about the same.

In a review of Stewart's book, Peter W. Bernstein quotes this last paragraph
about the final result in the Westinghouse cases.[68] He continues by saying,

[Y]ou'd think that such details would spur some serious rethinking about
the possibly excessive use of corporate lawyers. Ironically, the Westinghouse case seems to have had almost the opposite effect. Stewart reports
that despite Kirkland & Ellis's setbacks, "it is the widespread perception
among members of the corporate bar—and in the firm itself—that it was
Kirkland & Ellis that saved Westinghouse." It would seem that lawyers
can convince themselves of anything.

Does the final result of these cases show "excessive use of corporate lawyers"?
Had the utilities and Westinghouse split their differences in 1975, the result
would have been roughly the same as reached in 1980 after a large amount was
paid in legal fees. But had Kirkland & Ellis not been called in and played the § 2-
615 card, would the utilities and Westinghouse have split their differences?

2. *Anticipating unforeseen risks at the drafting stage*: We sometimes forget
that there are different ways to proceed in the face of similar problems. Often the
participants in different business cultures, or subcultures, react differently to
problems. In the *Westinghouse* cases we have just read about, the parties were
reluctant to give up the gains they believed they had won by their bargain, and
which they believed were embodied in their agreement; they chose to litigate the
question of the contract's enforceability. Leon Trakman has written about the

---

[68] FORTUNE, April 4, 1983, at 189, 191.

way that the multinational oil sellers respond, at the drafting stage, to the risks of unforeseen changes in oil supply and prices.[69]

. . . We analyzed the contract practices of multinational oil sellers and their international oil buyers, as described by their inside legal counsel. . . .

[C]ivil lawyers differed from common lawyers in their construction of the laws of nonperformance. Civil lawyers were generally much more willing to permit excuses from performance in the face of circumstances occurring beyond control than were their common law counterparts. For instance, of the civil lawyers who replied to the questionnaire, 100 percent favored an excuse from performance if the performance obligation had become "radically different" since the date of contracting; whereas only 63 percent of the common lawyers agreed. This difference in attitude is attributable partly to the jurisprudential differences between civil and common law systems, and partly to the political-economic havoc that was experienced in European civil law jurisdictions during the post-world war eras. . . .

Crude oil contracts of sale provided for an array of performance risks and burdens in succinct language within their terms. The counsel structured their business obligations along predetermined lines. They established the contractual consequences that should ensue as a result of market and political unrest in the international crude oil market.

Nonperformance clauses in international crude oil contracts of sale were therefore the product of deliberate planning and compromise. As carefully formulated provisions, they constituted a means of avoiding deadlock and dissatisfaction over performance among oil companies. They summarized oil relations; and they embodied industry usages in their written terms. Most importantly, they ensured that crude oil transactors would not be left in doubt as to the nature and extent of their performance duties and as to their respective responsibilities in the event of nonperformance. . . .

[A]fter each severe disruption in oil supply, international contracts for the sale of crude oil were revised to take specific account of fluctuating oil prices and severely impeded oil supplies. After each Middle Eastern War, inside legal counsel gave particular attention to the expanding role of governments in relation to crude oil contracts. They evaluated the effects upon performance of "royalty taxes," "new and changed government directions," and "increased government take. . . ."

[A] majority of inside legal counsel who responded to the question indicated that, in their opinion, international oil contractors were not capable of foreseeing *all* categories of nonperformance risks. Nor were they capable of incorporating *all* such categories of nonperformance risks into their crude oil contracts of sale. They were even less likely to

---

[69] Trakman, *Nonperformance in Oil Contracts*, 29 Oil & Gas Q. 716 (1981). Copyright © 1981 by Matthew Bender & Co., Inc., and reprinted with permission from Oil and Gas Quarterly.

incorporate all categories of nonperformance risks into their agreements in an unambiguous manner. . . .

3. *Dealing with the problem by renegotiating the contract*: Another way in which the parties might respond to an unforeseen development, and again this may depend on the business culture in which the event occurs, is to renegotiate the agreement. Can such a response be successful? Doesn't renegotiation constitute a repudiation of the rationale for the contract itself? Jeswald Salacuse suggests that renegotiation is a common practice, at least in some international contexts.[70]

> . . . In recent years we have seen many examples of the phenomenon of renegotiations. Since the outbreak of the international debt crisis in 1982, Western commercial banks and their Third World borrowers have been engaged in a constant process of renegotiating loans that developing countries have been unable to repay, an exercise commonly known as "debt rescheduling." The dramatic fall in the price of oil and gas from the heights of the early 1980s has forced purchasers to seek renegotiation of long-term supply agreements that once seemed profitable but have now become ruinous. And the rapid decline in the value of the dollar, particularly against the Japanese yen, has since 1986 prompted attempts to renegotiate other long-term contractual relationships.
>
> Renegotiation in international business is by no means peculiar to the 1980s. For decades, host country governments, often with the threat of nationalization in the background, have periodically sought to revise investment arrangements which they had previously made with foreign corporations but later judged no longer advantageous. . . . These examples illustrate a traditional theme in international business circles: the lament over the "unstable contract," the profitable agreement that the other party refuses to respect. One common response to contractual instability is renegotiation. . . .
>
> Discussions of "renegotiation" apply the term to three fundamentally different situations, and it is important to distinguish each of them at the outset. . . .
>
> (1) Post-Deal Renegotiations
>
> In this context, negotiations may take place at the expiration of a contract, when the parties, though legally free to go their own ways, nonetheless seek to renew their previous relationship. . . .
>
> (2) Intra-Deal Renegotiations
>
> A second type of renegotiation occurs when the agreement itself provides that, during its life at specified times, the parties may renegotiate or at least review certain of its provisions. Here, renegotiation is anticipated as a legitimate activity in which both parties are to engage in good faith. . . .

---

[70] Jeswald W. Salacuse, *Renegotiations in International Business*, 4 Negotiation J. 347 (1988). Copyright © Negotiation Journal 1988. Reprinted with permission.

(3) Extra-Deal Renegotiations

The most difficult and emotional renegotiations are those undertaken in apparent violation of the agreement, or at least in the absence of a specific clause for redoing the deal. These renegotiations take place "extra-deal," for they occur outside the framework of the existing agreement. The renegotiations of the 1980s over Third World loans, petroleum prices, and currencies all fit within the category of extra-deal renegotiations, because in each case one of the participants was seeking relief from a legally binding obligation without any basis in the agreement itself for renegotiation. . . .

Beyond mere disappointed expectations, extra-deal renegotiations, by their very nature, can create bad feeling and mistrust. One side sees itself as being asked to give up something to which it has a legal and moral right, and it views the other side as having gone back on its word, as having acted in bad faith by reneging on the deal. Indeed, the reluctant party may even feel it is being coerced into participating in extra-deal renegotiations, since a refusal to do so would result in losing the investment already made in the transaction or joint venture. Thus, it is very difficult for the parties to see renegotiations as anything more than a "zero-sum game," where one side wins and the other side loses.

The extra-deal renegotiation of an established arrangement may also have significant implications beyond the transaction in question. The party being asked to give up a contractual right may feel obliged to show various political constituencies, both inside and outside its own organization, that it is not "weak," and cannot be taken advantage of. Moreover, a party will usually fear that yielding to a demand for the renegotiation of one contract may encourage other parties to seek renegotiation of their agreements as well. This concern for the potential "ripple" effect from renegotiations clearly contributed to the reluctance of the international commercial banks to yield to demands by individual developing countries for a revision of loan terms. Concessions to Mexico would inevitably lead Argentina to demand equal treatment in its own renegotiation. . . ."

While a request for extra-deal renegotiations may provoke bad feeling in one party, an outright refusal to renegotiate may also create ill will on the other side since it will be seen as an attempt to force adherence to a bargain that has become unreasonable.

Ultimately, the basic conflict between the parties in an extra-deal renegotiation will be over the type of changed circumstances justifying the negotiations. Such circumstances may cover a broad spectrum, ranging from sudden changes in objective conditions over which neither of the parties has control, such as rising exchange rates or closed trade routes, to conditions determined subjectively by one side alone. With regard to the latter, for example, host country governments often reassess their relations with foreign investors based on the country's current need for the investor's capital and technology. . . .

Today, most contracts explicitly or implicitly deny the possibility of change and therefore make no provision whatsoever for adjustments to meet changing circumstances. This assumption of contractual stability has proven false time and time again. For example, most mineral development agreements assume they will continue unchanged for periods of from 15 to 99 years, yet they rarely remain unmodified for more than a few years. . . . As Raymond Vernon . . . has argued, with reference to mineral investment agreements, a bargain, once struck, will inevitably become obsolete and issues once agreed upon will be reopened at a later time as circumstances change. Indeed, to borrow Vernon's phrase, international business negotiations should probably assume that most long-term deals are "obsolescing bargains."

4. *Arbitration as an alternative*: We have seen that the parties might deal with the unforseeable by attempting to anticipate it in their drafting of the agreement, or by permitting renegotiation, or by resorting to judicial litigation. We must not forget private arbitration as another option. We offer an example which seems particularly apt, since it deals with the continued volatility of the uranium market, after the changes which prompted Westinghouse to repudiate its duty to deliver fuel to the utilities.

According to a 1985 story in the NEW YORK TIMES,[71] "once again, uranium is making lawyers glow." In 1976, with uranium selling for $40 a pound, a Switzerland-based utility, Kernkraftwerk Graben A.G., contracted to purchase uranium oxide for a twelve-year period from a New York Company, Freeport-McMoran, Inc. Over the next several years, the uranium contract price jumped up to $60 a pound. During the same time period, the market price plummeted to $17 a pound. To make matters worse, the Swiss government denied Kernkraftwerk a permit to build the nuclear power plant, thereby evaporating the utility's need for the uranium oxide.

Kernkraftwerk contended that the contract was no longer binding because of unforeseen circumstances. In 1982, the matter went to arbitration. Under a choice of laws agreement, the arbitrators applied New York contract law. Apparently, Kernkraftwerk had contractually agreed that it would not be excused from performing "on account of force majeure or any other reasons whatsoever." Yet, in August of 1984 the arbitrators agreed with Kernkraftwerk's argument that the purpose of the contract had been frustrated. In a decision which saved the utility $100 million, the arbitrators found that the dramatic price change and the Swiss government's refusal to allow the nuclear power plant to be built, were events which the parties did not foresee and therefore the contract could not have been intended to cover these eventualities.

The NEW YORK TIMES reporter states that "the award illustrates the decline of the sanctity accorded to contracts since the heyday of laissez-faire in the last century." The reporter goes on to suggest that courts in Britain and the United States modify contracts, construe terms contrary to the parties' intention and help parties to evade duties and the like. Can you argue that the reporter doesn't under-

---

[71] NEW YORK TIMES, Jan. 8, 1985, at 2, col. 1.

stand what the arbitrators did? Would the arbitrators have to concede that they rewrote the contract in question here?

5. *Bankruptcy—another option*: Suppose that the parties to a contract failed to deal with the unforeseen in their drafting, they chose not to renegotiate, arbitration was not an option, and the law of contracts offered no excuses. What next? What are the consequences to letting the chips fall where they may? If a company cannot perform its contracts, we could award judgments for damages and leave salvage operations to the law of bankruptcy. This was the response followed when Braniff Airlines got into trouble. Braniff expanded its route structure after the airlines were deregulated. It ordered additional aircraft, hired pilots, flight attendants, maintenance workers, opened offices, rented space at airports and borrowed money. The officers who ran the company guessed wrong, and Braniff ran out of money needed to continue operations. After efforts to keep the airline flying failed, it ceased operations and attempted to reorganize under the federal bankruptcy laws. Undoubtedly, the experience will contribute some deterrence to officials of other airlines when they think about the risks they are willing to take. Undoubtedly, a case could be made that Braniff's failure will contribute to efficient allocation of resources. Braniff's creditors negotiated a limited resumption of service, but it was a far different, and smaller, airline.

While major surgery may prove beneficial in the long run, usually it is painful to many. What are the consequences to which groups of people of a collapse of a major corporation? Many people are likely to get hurt, and the injury often falls hardest on those free of fault and who had little choice in the matter. The following article from the WALL STREET JOURNAL[72] suggests the consequences likely to follow the collapse of any large business organization.

> Braniff officials won't comment on potential losses under current market conditions, but one lender says a confidential study by creditors confirms the general range of loss under such conditions. A source close to the carrier says the assumption of a one-third "haircut" is "in the ball park."

> Losers in that case are legion. First and foremost, Braniff's 33,657 shareholders will lose their entire stake . . .

> Next in line for a beating are Braniff's unsecured creditors. . . . As of Dec. 31, trade suppliers were owed an estimated $92.3 million. In a separate category, Boeing Co. is listed as an unsecured creditor to the tune of $84 million, partly because of the aborted sale of three 747s to Braniff. . . .

> The unsecured creditors also include Braniff's 9,500 employees, plus retirees. . . . The employees and current retirees probably will see their pension benefits reduced because Braniff's unfunded liability for five different pension plans amounts to $148.7 million. Federal insurance may make up close to half of that amount, but the employees and retirees will be out the rest unless they succeed in realizing special claims on Braniff's assets ahead of secured creditors. [Research by Wisconsin Law

---

[72] WALL STREET JOURNAL, May 17, 1982, at 4, cols. 2-4.

School Professors Whitford and LoPucki indicates that unsecured creditors ultimately received only about 5% of their claims in the bankruptcy.
Secured creditors did much better.]

One notable victim is likely to be Harding Lawrence, Braniff's former chairman who is widely blamed for engineering a rapid expansion
that partly led to Braniff's downfall. His pension of $306,000 a year is
apt to be slashed by $180,000, a source close to the company esti-
mates. . . .

While the collapse of Braniff had major negative consequences, the failure of
even larger corporations might have even more serious impacts. In the Westinghouse litigation, all of the federal judges involved seemed well aware of the costs
of destroying Westinghouse. Rather than using traditional contract doctrine in an
orthodox manner, they pushed for a settlement and achieved it.

During the Vietnam war, the Lockheed corporation ran into great financial
problems, and it looked s if it would not be able to perform its contracts to produce both civilian and military aircraft. A lawyer could have made a plausible
argument that Lockheed should have been excused under UCC § 2-615. The crisis could have driven Lockheed into bankruptcy. After much debate, however,
Congress passed a bill providing for the United States government to guarantee
loans which private financial institutions would make to keep Lockheed in business. Congress decided to make a similar bailout of the Chrysler Corporation in
1980. The United States Congress, rather than the courts, dealt with the Lockheed and Chrysler "failures" by guaranteeing loans to keep them alive while they
performed their obligations to many, if not all, concerned. However, there was a
gap between American free enterprise rhetoric and the reality of what many saw
the federal government doing. We can ask whether the federal courts did a better
job in the Westinghouse situation than the Congress managed in the Lockheed
and Chrysler cases. To what extent, if at all, does contract doctrine just get in the
way of understanding what is involved? To what extent, if at all, does contract
doctrine reflect an underlying world view that affects judgments in openly political settings?

The situations in the Westinghouse case, the "bailout" incidents involving
Lockheed and Chrysler, and the ALCOA case which you are about to read seem
structurally similar. In all these situations a company has voluntarily assumed
burdens that turn out to be potentially capable of destroying a major business enterprise. A government institution is asked to intervene: in some cases the courts,
and in others the legislature. What are the criteria which are used in such cases?
Should the criteria for intervention be the same for each governmental organ, or
can they legitimately differ?

The following article raises issues concerning contract rhetoric and assumptions in our legal culture. Then *ALCOA v. Essex Group* moves to the next question—if courts cannot persuade the parties to settle, what should courts do? Next,
Westinghouse pushes its way back onstage, showing a court refusing to adjust
contracts as such but tinkering with remedies to make things come out right. We
can ask who must bear the price of rapid unexpected economic change or unan-

ticipated costs of technological change. Does it make a difference which institutions confront these problems?

Rational Law and Boundary Maintenance: Legitimating the 1971 Lockheed Loan Guarantee
Gerald Turkel[73]

Background of Lockheed's Financial Crisis

On August 2, 1971, Lockheed Aircraft Corporation became the first private manufacturing corporation in the history of the United States to receive direct loan guarantees from the federal government. The $250 million loan guarantee was preceded by years of financial problems and, finally, by the corporation's apparently imminent bankruptcy. Lockheed's crisis involved contracts with the federal government, private airlines, major private banking institutions, and foreign corporations.

In October of 1965, Lockheed had been awarded a $2.2 billion contract by the Department of Defense for 81 C5 cargo transport aircraft. As is fairly typical with such contracts, Lockheed ran into cost overruns and was unable to meet the initial price per aircraft as specified in its contract with the Defense Department (*Business Week*, January 29, 1972: 72). By 1971, the cost overruns amounted to hundreds of millions of dollars.

In September of 1967, the board of directors of Lockheed decided to venture into the production and sale of commercial jetliners. The Chairman of the Board hoped that the L-1011 Tristar would enable Lockheed to capture a portion of the commercial jetliner market and relieve Lockheed's dependence on government contracts. . . . By 1970, $1.4 billion had been invested in the L-1011 Tristar program. . . . Since production of the L-1011 was not planned until 1972, Lockheed was faced with a massive debt to carry for several years before any revenues could be realized.

Throughout 1970 and early 1971, Lockheed's financial position grew increasingly perilous. First, the Department of Defense refused to honor cost overruns in its contracts with Lockheed. . . . [This cost Lockheed $190 million in 1970 alone.] A second major blow was the announcement in 1971 of the bankruptcy of Rolls-Royce Ltd., the corporation under contract with Lockheed to build the engines for its L-1011 commercial jetliner (*New York Times*, February 5, 1971: 3). . . . This meant that Lockheed was faced not only with the need for additional revenue, but also with marketing problems for its new, higher priced commercial aircraft.

During this period of mounting problems with government contracts and the L-1011, Lockheed became increasingly dependent on bank loans. By March of 1970, a total of $320 million had been borrowed from a consortium of 24 banks (Hearings, 1971: 151). . . .

---

[73] 15 Law & Soc'y Rev. 41 (1980-81). Permission to reprint granted by the Law and Society Association.

[Bank examiners raised doubts about Lockheed's ability to repay its loans and the Defense Department declined to finalize its cost-overrun settlement with Lockheed.] In this situation, the 24-bank consortium was no longer willing to proceed with the $600 million financial agreement it had been negotiating with Lockheed. By February of 1971, bankruptcy seemed imminent.

Particularizing a Legislative Solution

In response to Lockheed's financial crisis, the Nixon Administration proposed legislation guaranteeing loans of up to $250 million to companies experiencing severe financial difficulties. . . . Sending the proposed legislation to Congress in May of 1971, Treasury Secretary Connally supported it in the following terms:

> The failure of major business enterprises can have serious national and regional consequences, including the causing of substantial unemployment, as well as other business failures. To provide for credit to avoid such consequences, government guarantees may be warranted to avoid such consequences, government guarantees may be warranted (*Congressional Quarterly*, May 21, 1971: 1124).

The legislation proposed to the Congress had the following administrative and financial provisions:

1. Authorize the Treasury Secretary to guarantee up to $250 million in loans to major business enterprises.

2. Require as conditions of any guarantee that the business be essential to insure competition and productive capacity in an industry.

3. That assistance be necessary to prevent serious adverse effects on the economy and that credit be unavailable otherwise.

4. Require as additional conditions that there be reasonable assurance of repayment and reasonable protection from the government.

5. Limit a guarantee to five years duration but authorize the Secretary to extend it for an additional five years.

6. Prohibit declarations of dividends while a guaranteed loan was outstanding.

7. Prohibit, during the life of a guaranteed loan, any payment or other indebtedness to a guaranteed lender.

8. Authorize the Secretary to waive the two preceding conditions.

9. Secure payment with a first *lien* on the property of the borrower and give a guaranteed loan priority over all other debts in any bankruptcy proceedings.

10. The bill also provided for the creation of an Emergency Loan Guarantee Board made up of the Secretary of the Treasury, the Chairman of the Federal Reserve Board and the Chairman of the Securities and Exchange Commission. The purpose of this board was to execute any government guarantee approved by Congress.

These provisions defined both the boundaries of government intervention and the conflicts inherent in particularizing government support. . . .

[One of the problems with this approach arises by virtue of the specification of government officials to administer the program.] ... These provisions placed administrative control among high federal officials—specifically, the Secretary of the Treasury, the Chairman of the Federal Reserve Board, and the Chairman of the Security and Exchange Commission. If we accept the idea that high government officials generally embody the interests of dominant corporate financial interests, then the staffing of the loan control board suggests a substantive direction. Given that high government officials would be most cognizant of the interests of major corporations and financial institutions, the direction of the loan control board in being sensitive to large capital interests rather than other, smaller interests would appear to be likely. While this feature of the legislation served to insure that the range of claims to government assumption of financial risks would be limited, it also provided the most economically dominant sector of the private economy with more than equal access to a potential source of governmental financial assistance. The possible sensitivities of high government officials, moreover, do not constitute formal criteria for determining which loans to private business government should underwrite. ...

[Though written in general form, it is clear that the bill was tailored to fit the Lockheed situation.]

The bill submitted to Congress by the Nixon administration was highly divisive. During the course of the debate, proposed amendments to the bill attempted either to maintain a narrow qualification for federal loan guarantees or to expand the scope of the bill to small businesses. When the bill was finally passed by a vote of 49 to 48 in the Senate and 192 to 189 in the House, it was basically unchanged from its original version. By analyzing the Congressional debate, we can specify more fully the boundaries of discourse around the issue of particularizing the legislation. Table 1 presents major categories that bounded the debate and summarizes the range of favorable and unfavorable arguments in each category.

Table 1. Boundaries of Lockheed Loan Guarantee Debate

Bounding Categories	Range of Disagreement	Over Proposed Legislation
	Favorable Arguments	**Opposition Arguments**
Nationalism	Bill needed to maintain a viable U.S. Defense and aircraft industry	Really a bail-out for Rolls-Royce and Great Britain; engines should be manufactured in the U.S.
Effect on Market	Maintain market by building business confidence	Disrupt market by raising corporate expectations of reliance on government support

Generalizability	Limit to Lockheed and/or major corporations	Expand to small businesses, ghetto businesses, businesses in health and educations
Administration of Loan	Reasonable for all parties; would protect the government's investment	Lacked enforceable controls
Economic Welfare	Clearly needed to maintain high employment levels and investment opportunities	Negative impact of Lockheed's bankruptcy overstated; slack would be taken up by Lockheed's competitors
Financial Institutions	Bill required to insure credit	Bill would protect creditors from their own decisions; financial domination of airlines and manufacturers
Viability of Lockheed	Loan guarantee definitely needed to avoid bankruptcy	Lockheed would probably survive without loan guarantees because banks would continue to supply credit

As formulated in Table 1, the boundaries of the debate went far beyond legal rational and formal criteria to include political and economic arguments. Within each bounding category, favorable arguments tended to be particularistic, while unfavorable arguments tended to be more universalistic and rule oriented. . . .

. . . Senator William Proxmire (D., Wis.) was the only staunch opponent on the Banking, Housing, and Urban Affairs Committee. Senator Proxmire, whose Joint Economic Committee hearings in 1968 revealed the C-5A cost overruns, raised three major points of concern. First, he accused the Nixon administration of misleading Congress regarding the loss of jobs that Lockheed's failure would generate. He stated that "even if Lockheed cancelled the L-1011 project, the slack would be taken up by its competitors" (*Congressional Quarterly*, May 21, 1971: 1128). Second, he was critical of some of the international implications of the Lockheed loan guarantee. He called the government loan guarantee "really a bail-out of Rolls-Royce and the British government at the expense of the United States" (*Congressional Quarterly*, May 21, 1971: 1128). Finally, he questioned the likelihood of the 24-bank consortium allowing Lockheed to go bankrupt if the government did not provide the loan guarantee. He expressed his belief that "these bankers would be more than willing to loan an additional $250 million to protect their original investment if there was a reasonable prospect of repayment" (*Congressional Quarterly*, May 21, 1971: 1128).

When the Senate committee opened testimony on the bill, Senator Proxmire added another dimension to his opposition. He stated that in 1970 over 10,000 small businesses failed and that the economic impact of these failures was greater than the potential failure of Lockheed. He rhetorically posed the question of why government guarantees were not considered for these small businesses and answered the question by saying that "the 10,000 small firms do not have the political clout of the Lockheed Aircraft Corporation" (*Congressional Quarterly*, June 11, 1971: 1275). In summarizing his views, he said, "My opposition is against the general principle of insulating big business from failure."

On June 30, the Senate Banking, Housing and Urban Affairs Committee decided to hold further hearings that would focus on a broad government loan guarantee. . . . [The bill would go beyond just the $250 million to Lockheed.]

. . . Secretary of the Treasury Connally's testimony supported the economic arguments of the bill's proponents. According to Secretary Connally, the loan guarantee to Lockheed was necessary to maintain "confidence in a renewed business expansion." He pointed out that Lockheed was the largest defense contractor in the United States with $2.5 billion in annual sales, 72,000 employees, and earnings of $830 million annually. He stated that the government loan guarantee posed only a "small" risk to the taxpayers and that "there is a good chance that the guarantee will succeed in financing Lockheed's needs . . . during the . . . next couple of years." . . .

Deputy Secretary of Defense David Packard revealed two important discrepancies concerning Lockheed and the proposed government loan guarantee (*Congressional Quarterly*, June 18, 1971: 1309). First, he cited Defense Department studies revealing that Lockheed would have to sell over 300 L-1011s just to recover its development and production costs. This was in contrast to the view of Lockheed officials that the sale of between 195 and 205 planes would meet their break-even point. Second, despite the findings of the Defense Department, Secretary Packard supported the loan guarantee to Lockheed stating:

> I, personally, do not see how Lockheed can avoid bankruptcy if this loan guarantee is not provided. Substantial unemployment would be the immediate result.

While Packard supported the loan guarantee, he maintained that "it would not be desirable to establish a precedent with this legislation that the government would go to the assistance of every company that got into financial difficulty" (*Congressional Quarterly*, June 18, 1971: 1309). . . .

The issue of the role played by major banks in Lockheed's financial crisis was most fully articulated by Leonor K. Sullivan (D., Mo.). Rep. Sullivan was concerned with the "tremendous financial involvement" of the 24-bank consortium in the aircraft and airline industry (Hearings, 1971: 166). She pointed out that the willingness of these banks to loan $6.8 billion to the aircraft companies and airline companies not only rendered them financially dependent, but also resulted in unstable financial conditions in these sectors of the economy. . . .

Based upon this information, Rep. Sullivan argued that over-extension in the airline and aircraft industries could not have occurred without the concurrence of the major banks. They had financed the crisis by loaning the capital both for the production and purchase of the aircraft. . . .

[Amendments to the bill on the house floor] . . . essentially narrowed it to the original Administration bill (*Congressional Quarterly*, August 6, 1971: 1646). The two most important amendments limited the total loan guarantee to $250 million and deleted a provision that required Congressional review of proposed loan guarantees. The [amended] bill was . . . passed by a vote of 192 to 189.

. . . After a limited debate, the bill passed the Senate by one vote, 49 to 48.

Underlying Ideologies

. . . [One assumption which seemed unchallenged in the debate over the guarantees] is the private ownership and control of capital and the prerogative of private investment decisions. While the wisdom of particular corporate initiatives were questioned and while management was criticized to the point of Senator Cranston's demand for their resignation as a condition for government support, there was a total absence of proposals either for nationalization or direct government supervision of investment decisions. In this regard, the discussion of the involvement of major banks in the Lockheed financial crisis initiated by Representative Sullivan was directed at determining why the major banks were unable to foresee financial difficulties rather than as an effort to interfere with their prerogatives. Thus, the fundamental condition for private control of economic initiatives was left intact.

Maintaining corporate prerogatives over investment decisions affirmed a major limit to state intervention. The central role played by the market in the loan guarantee debate also limited state involvement and private control. As we have seen, participants in the debate argued that the loan guarantee would maintain competitive market conditions, that it would hinder the operation of the market, or that it would pose potential problems of government interference in market relations. Despite these differences in evaluating the impact of the loan on the market, the range of discussion indicates an underlying consensus on the importance of maintaining the market as the institutional nexus through which economic activity is regulated.

Yet in the case of the Lockheed loan guarantee, the affirmation of market control, when considered in light of structural relations, was largely without substance. . . . Thus, the state was not only overwhelmingly Lockheed's major customer, but also a major supplier of Lockheed capital before the loan guarantee was initiated. . . .

The belief that the market disciplines and directs the behavior of economic actors toward efficient use of resources underlay the limited character of state intervention specified in the loan guarantee bill. Yet the loan guarantee, since it involved government financial obligations, required a public presence. This presence took the form of public administration of the loan program. The administrative component of the loan guarantee bill supervised the allocation of funds beyond the "laws" of the market. . . .

While adherence to the market and private control over investment decisions demonstrates the continuity of principles of private enterprise in legitimating the loan guarantee, the administrative dimension of the loan control board and Congressional oversight demonstrate the continuity of principles of administrative rationality. Yet, as I suggested, the staffing of the loan control board with high government officials indicates substantive power rather than the application of purely administrative principles. Furthermore, as in the Lockheed case, state officials must base their proposals and actions on decisions they expect from private economic actors. In relying on these expectations, government officials are subject to pronouncements made by private corporate executives. Would the banks have refused to extend credit to Lockheed without government loan guarantees? Would the financial crisis of Lockheed, if the banks had refused more credit, have led to the anticipated economic dislocations? The answers to these questions, even if based on clear information about Lockheed's finances and its role in the U.S. economy, would require speculation about the behavior of private economic actors. Yet it is on the basis of this speculation that the government sought to legitimate its economic actions. This greatly diminishes the ability to use rules in making decisions, thereby further undercutting formal features or rationality and enhancing the privatized, particular character of legality.

NOTES AND QUESTIONS

1. *The rest of the story:* Well, what happened to Lockheed after it was bailed out? Did everyone live happily ever after? The WALL STREET JOURNAL wrote a follow-up story in 1983.[74] After briefly recapitulating the Congressional debate, the story notes that although Lockheed has reported record earnings, it is no longer among the top five U.S. defense contractors. David Packard, the deputy secretary of defense who ram rodded the Nixon administration effort to get the loan guarantees, indicated that, "Looking back on it, I don't think it would have been a disaster if Lockheed had gone under." Others note that the L-1011 project cost Lockheed $2.5 billion, and wasn't cancelled until 1981; it might have been better to have killed the jumbo jet project "in its cradle." Some company insiders suggested that Lockheed's competitive edge was dulled because executives became preoccupied with the task of just keeping the company alive. One former executive reports that Lockheed began "playing not to lose." Senator Proxmire noted that the loan guarantee didn't fulfill its promise of making Lockheed more diversified and stronger. Instead it simply hurt Boeing Co. and McDonnell Douglas because both would have benefited from the early demise of the L-1011.

On the other hand, the fears that failing companies would descend on Washington looking for help just didn't materialize. Until the terrorist attacks that hurt the airlines in 2001 the only other major bailout effort was the 1980 Chrysler loan guarantee. The official Lockheed position is that the bailout was a great success. The program didn't cost the taxpayers any money, and there was no interruption in production of the firms military programs. In fact, some have speculated that the real, though never acknowledged, reason for the loan guarantee was to satisfy the military's need for giant C-5A transport planes for use in Vietnam.

2. *Options*: Suppose a major corporation faced an economic disaster that threatens its survival. What could our society do? Our legal and political institu-

---

[74] Roy Harris Jr., *Survival Tactics: Back from the Brink, Lockheed Shows Signs of Prospering Again*, WALL STREET JOURNAL, May 12, at 1, col. 1.

tions *could* treat the situation as a matter of contract. The firm would have to perform its contracts, settle the claims of its creditors or seek some form of bankruptcy. In some instances this would mean that the firm would go out of business as its assets were liquidated to satisfy creditors. However, in other cases the firm would continue to exist. Creditors and shareholders would take some or all of the loss. Management might or might not continue in power. Labor would feel the pressure on management to cut wages and benefits or the number of jobs.

There are other possibilities as well. Courts might seek to save the corporation by finding excuses for performance or by refashioning terms of contracts to reflect changed conditions.[75] Legislatures could make loans to the sick corporation to give it time to deal with its problems. Of course, the threat of possible judicial or legislative relief could affect settlement negotiations. We also might nationalize the corporation and have it run by an agency of a state or the national government. Less drastically, we might condition any aid so the troubled corporation pursued certain goals rather than others. We could also subsidize a major corporation or a whole industry in our typically American way—that is, by such more or less hidden devices such as favorable tax treatment, formal or informal tariffs, or placing government procurement contracts with firms in economic difficulty.

Does it matter whether and how we offset large shocks to the economy? What should courts do when they face contracts cases involving major events that upset assumptions and expectations about the future? Is there any reason to think that legislatures will handle these problems better?

3. *An anecdote:* A successful real estate developer was asked if he could summarize the secret of his success. He is reported to have said, "Well, some of it I attribute to the recognition that if you owe the bank $10,000 and can't pay, you're in trouble. But if you owe the bank $10 million and can't pay, the bank's in trouble."

4. *Other examples*: Lockheed was not the only example of Congress protecting a large corporation in the face of major economic challenges. When the Chrysler Corporation approached bankruptcy in 1979, Congress passed the Chrysler Loan Guarantee Act. Various interests made concessions. A Loan Guarantee Board subjected Chrysler management to some oversight. Chrysler survived and was very successful during the early 1980s. Turkel and Costello[76] studied the arguments offered for the Chrysler arrangement and the acceptance of these ideas by laid-off Chrysler workers. The workers "overwhelmingly take basic features of capitalist market ideology, including competition, for granted." They felt that sacrifices made by workers had not produced satisfactory results. They felt that Chrysler management and various financial interests had been the beneficiaries of the loan guarantee. Reich and Donahue[77] analyzed the arguments for and against the results of the Chrysler Loan Guarantee Act. They say:

---

[75] For a more extended treatment of these alternatives than we can possibly offer here, see Robert Hillman, *Contract Excuse and Bankruptcy Discharge*, 43 Stan. L. Rev. 99-136 (1990).

[76] *Laid-Off Workers, the Chrysler Loan Guarantee and Corporatist Legitimacy: A Thematic Analysis,* 9 Contemp. Crisis 229 (1985).

[77] NEW DEALS: THE CHRYSLER REVIVAL AND THE AMERICAN SYSTEM (Times Books 1985). *See also*, Reich and Donahue, *Lessons from the Chrysler Bailout*, 27 Calif. Mgmt. Rev. 157 (1985).

The guaranteed loans were only a bargaining chip. What ultimately saved Chrysler was the sacrifice from labor, creditors, suppliers, and other constituents. The government's presence at the bargaining table radically changed the terms of the negotiations among claimants. It spurred greater sacrifice from these groups than they otherwise would have rendered. The government was able to broaden the terms of the bargain by threatening certain recalcitrant players, by verifying Chrysler's own threat to declare bankruptcy unless sacrifice was forthcoming, and by orchestrating a single grand bargain incorporating all major parties.[78]

However, Reich and Donahue conclude "[i]f we opt to replicate the Chrysler bailout, we will need to develop a clearer consensus on the proper limits of the government's power to coerce concessions."[79] Consider the judge's role in major contracts cases. How is it similar to the role played by all agencies of the federal government in the Chrysler situation? How do the situations differ?

Finally, Stewart describes the role of Debevoise, Plimpton, Lyons & Gates in the Chrysler rescue.[80] His story describes great efforts to get the statute passed and to comply with its terms. However, he concludes, "[u]ltimately, it was politics, not the law, that saved Chrysler." To what extent, if at all, is this conclusion also true of the cases that follow?

5. *September 11th:* On September 11, 2001, terrorists hijacked four commercial airliners and crashed three of them into the World Trade Center and the Pentagon. The airlines were shut down immediately. Once airline service resumed, airports and planes were relatively empty. Just eleven days after the attack, Congress agreed to $15 billion in aid as well as loan guarantees. However, the statute created the Air Transportation Stabilization Board, which was given broad discretion to determine the terms on which loan guarantees would be given. America West Airlines was the first airline to apply for a guaranteed loan of $400 million. The Stabilization Board insisted on two revisions of the proposed terms for the guarantee. The government got an option to buy up to one-third of the stock of the carrier. Most airlines found the government's terms unappealing and decided against applying for loan guarantees. Nonetheless, most airlines received some portion of the $5 billion in cash payments said to be designed to compensate the airlines for their losses when the air travel system was closed after the attacks.

ALUMINUM COMPANY OF AMERICA V. ESSEX GROUP, INC.
United States District Court, Western District of Pennsylvania
499 F. Supp. 53 (1980)

TEITELBAUM, J. Plaintiff, Aluminum Company of America (ALCOA), brought the instant action against defendant, Essex Group, Inc. (Essex), in three counts. The first count requests the Court to reform or equitably adjust an agreement en-

---

[78] Reich and Donahue, *supra*, at 174.

[79] *Id.* at 175.

[80] THE PARTNERS 201-244 (Warner Books 1984).

titled the Molten Metal Agreement entered into between ALCOA and Essex. The second count alleges that the Molten Metal Agreement was modified by oral amendment and that Essex has breached the amended agreement. The second count seeks a declaratory judgment that the alleged breach by Essex excuses ALCOA's further performance and seeks as well an award of damages caused by the alleged breach of Essex. The third count asks for a declaratory judgment that ALCOA's prior notice of termination of the Molten Metal Agreement was proper or, in the alternative, that ALCOA may terminate the Molten Metal Agreement if it be determined by this Court to be a contract for the sale of goods. Essex denies all of ALCOA's material allegations. Essex further counterclaims that ALCOA is liable to it for damages based on ALCOA's failure to deliver to Essex the amounts of molten metal ALCOA is contractually obligated to deliver under the Molten Metal Agreement and seeks entry of an order specifically enforcing its right to receive molten aluminum from ALCOA in the amounts requested.

Jurisdiction is based upon diversity of citizenship and amount in controversy and is one of the few issues in the case *sub judice* not in dispute.

In 1966 Essex made a policy decision to expand its participation in the manufacture of aluminum wire products. Thus, beginning in the spring of 1967, ALCOA and Essex negotiated with each other for the purpose of reaching an agreement whereby ALCOA would supply Essex with its long-term needs for aluminum that Essex could use in its manufacturing operations.

By December 26, 1967 the parties had entered into what they designated as a toll conversion service contract known as the Molten Metal Agreement under which Essex would supply ALCOA with alumina which ALCOA would convert by a smelting process into molten aluminum. Under the terms of the Molten Metal Agreement, Essex delivers alumina to ALCOA which ALCOA smelts (or toll converts) into molten aluminum at its Warrick, Indiana, smelting facility. Essex then picks up the molten aluminum for further processing.

The price provisions of the contract contained an escalation formula which indicates that $.03 per pound of the original price escalates in accordance with changes in the Wholesale Price Index-Industrial Commodities (WPI) and $.03 per pound escalates in accordance with an index based on the average hourly labor rates paid to ALCOA employees at the Warrick plant. The portion of the pricing formula which is in issue in this case under counts one and two is the production charge which is escalated by the WPI. ALCOA contends that this charge was intended by the parties to reflect actual changes in the cost of the non-labor items utilized by ALCOA in the production of aluminum from alumina at its Warrick, Indiana smelting plant. In count one of this suit ALCOA asserts that the WPI used in the Molten Metal Agreement was in fact incapable of reasonably reflecting changes in the non-labor costs at ALCOA's Warrick, Indiana smelting plant and has in fact failed to so reflect such changes.

It is ALCOA's contention in count one of its complaint that the shared objectives of the parties with respect to the use of the WPI have been completely and totally frustrated, that both ALCOA and Essex made a mutual mistake of fact in agreeing to use the WPI to escalate non-labor costs at Warrick. ALCOA is seeking reformation or equitable adjustment of the Molten Metal Agreement so that pursuant to count one of its complaint, the pricing formula with respect to the non-labor portion of the production charge will be changed to eliminate the WPI and substitute the actual costs incurred by ALCOA for the non-labor items used at its Warrick, Indiana smelting plant. Essex opposes relief under count one contending that: 1) ALCOA cannot obtain reformation of the Molten Metal Agreement on the grounds of mutual mistake since ALCOA has failed to establish any antecedent agreement on pricing not expressed in the Molten Metal Agreement; 2) ALCOA assumed the risk that its prediction as to future costs would be incorrect; 3) ALCOA has failed to prove that enforcement of the Molten Metal Agreement would be unconscionable. . . .

COUNT ONE

ALCOA's first count seeks an equitable modification of the contract price for its services. The pleadings, arguments and briefs frame the issue in several forms. ALCOA seeks reformation or modification of the price on the basis of mutual mistake of fact, unilateral mistake of fact, unconscionability, frustration of purpose, and commercial impracticability.

A. The facts pertinent to count one are few and simple. In 1967 ALCOA and Essex entered into a written contract in which ALCOA promised to convert specified amounts of alumina supplied by Essex into aluminum for Essex. The service is to be performed at the ALCOA works at Warrick, Indiana. The contract is to run until the end of 1983. Essex has the option to extend it until the end of 1988. The price for each pound of aluminum converted is calculated by a complex formula which includes three variable components based on specific indices. The initial contract price was set at fifteen cents per pound, computed as follows:

A.	Demand Charge	$0.05/lb.
B.	Production Charge	
	(i) Fixed component	.04/lb.
	(ii) Non-labor production cost component	.03/lb.
	(iii) Labor production cost component	.03/lb.
	Total initial charge	$0.15/lb.

The demand charge is to vary from its initial base in direct proportion to periodic changes in the Engineering News Record Construction Cost—20 Cities Average Index published in the Engineering News Record. The Non-labor Production Cost Component is to vary from its initial base in direct proportion to periodic changes in the Wholesale Price Index-Industrial Commodities (WPI-IC) published by the Bureau of Labor Statistics of the United States Department of Labor. The Labor Production Cost Component is to vary from its initial base in direct proportion to periodic changes in ALCOA's average hourly labor cost at the Warrick, Indiana works. The adjusted price is subject to an over-all "cap" price of 65% of the price of a specified type of aluminum sold on specified terms, as published in a trade journal, American Metal Market.

The indexing system was evolved by ALCOA. . . . ALCOA examined the non-labor production cost component to assure that the WPI-IC had not tended to deviate markedly from their non-labor cost experience in the years before the contract was executed. Essex agreed to the contract including the index provisions after an examination of the past record of the indices revealed an acceptable pattern of stability.

ALCOA sought, by the indexed price agreement, to achieve a stable net income of about 4 ovp(c)/per pound of aluminum converted. This net income represented ALCOA's return (i) on its substantial capital investment devoted to the performance of the contracted services, (ii) on its management, and (iii) on the risks of short-falls or losses it undertook over an extended period. The fact that the non-labor production cost component of ALCOA's costs was priced according to a surrogate, objective index opened the door to a foreseeable fluctuation of ALCOA's return due to deviations between ALCOA's costs and the performance of the WPI-IC. The range of foreseeable deviation was roughly three cents per pound. That is to say that in some years ALCOA's return might foreseeably (and did, in fact) rise to seven cents per pound, while in other years it might foreseeably (and did, in fact) fall to about one cent per pound. See Table I.

Essex sought to assure itself of a long term supply of aluminum at a favorable price. Essex intended to and did manufacture a new line of aluminum wire products. The long term supply of aluminum was important to assure Essex of the steady use of its expensive machinery. A steady production stream was vital to preserve the market position it sought to establish. The favorable price was important to allow Essex to compete with firms like ALCOA which produced the aluminum and manufactured aluminum wire products in an efficient, integrated operation.

In the early years of the contract, the price formula yielded prices related, within the foreseeable range of deviation, to ALCOA's cost figures. Beginning in 1973, OPEC actions to increase oil prices and unanticipated pollution control costs greatly increased ALCOA's electricity costs. Electric power is the principal non-labor cost factor in aluminum conversion, and the electric power rates rose much more rapidly than did the WPI-IC. As a result, ALCOA's production costs rose greatly and unforeseeably beyond the indexed increase in the contract price. Table I illustrates the relation between the WPI-IC and ALCOA's costs over the years of the contract, and the resulting consequences of ALCOA.

During the most recent years, the market price of aluminum has increased even faster than the production costs. At the trial ALCOA introduced the deposition of Mr. Wilfred Jones, an Essex employee whose duties included the sale of surplus metal. Mr. Jones stated that Essex had resold some millions of pounds of aluminum which ALCOA had refined. The cost of the aluminum to Essex (including the purchase price of the alumina and its transportation) was 36.35 cents per pound around June of 1979. Mr. Jones further stated that the resale price in June 1979 at one cent per pound under the market, was 73.313 cents per pound, yielding Essex a gross profit of 37.043 cents per pound. This margin of profit shows the tremendous advantage Essex enjoys under the contract as it is written and as both parties have performed it. A significant fraction of Essex's advantage is directly attributable to the corresponding out of pocket losses ALCOA suffers. ALCOA has sufficiently shown that without judicial relief or economic changes which are not presently foreseeable, it stands to lose in excess of $75,000,000 out of pocket, during the remaining term of the contract.

B. ALCOA's Warrick Works, located in Indiana, are the designated source of supply. The Essex plant, where the bulk of the aluminum is used, is also located in Indiana. Essex takes delivery at the Warrick Works.

TABLE I

YEAR	BASE WPI-IC[1]	WARRICK NON-LABOR PRODUCTION COSTS PER POUND[2]		PROFIT/ LOSS PER LB.	POUNDS DELIVERED	PROFIT/LOSS
		¢	%			
1968	102.5	4.371	110.5	5.799	25,300,000	$ 1,467,147
1969	106.0	4.010	101.4	7.097	54,694,317	3,881,656
1970	110.0	4.397	111.1	6.517	84,370,265	5,498,410
1971	114.1	5.215	131.8	5.267	65,522,280	3,516,581
1972	117.9	5.309	134.2	5.721	83,128,209	4,755,765
1973	125.9	5.819	147.1	4.535	82,201,940	3,727,857
1974	153.9	9.009	227.1	2.070	86,234,310	1,785,050
1975	171.5	11.450	289.4	.189	76,688,530	144,941
1976	182.4	13.949	352.6	(.301)[3]	83,363,502	250,924
1977	195.1	17.806	450.1	(4.725)[3]	72,289,722	(3,415,689)
1978	209.4	22.717	574.2	(10.484)[3]	82,235,337	(8,620,504)

[1]The contract calls for a recomputation of the WPI-IC, so that the "Base Wholesale Price Index" equals 100 in 1967.

[2]Warrick Non-Labor Production Costs 1967-100%.

[3]The profit (loss) shown in years 1976 through 1978 was affected by a temporary surcharge agreement. Without the temporary surcharge the loss in cents per pound would have been as follows: 1967 (1.699); 1977 (6.725); 1978 (10.984). The loss each year would have been as follows: 1976 ($1,416,346); 1977 ($4,861,484); 1978 ($9,031,631).

The contract declares "This Agreement shall be governed and interpreted in accordance with the laws of the State of Indiana." The parties surely have sufficient contacts with the State of Indiana and Pennsylvania courts would enforce their agreement respecting the application of Indiana law. Restatement 2d Conflict of Laws § 187; cf. 13 Pa.C.S.A. § 1105(1) (U.C.C.). This Court must enforce it as well. . . .

This case presents many issues which are governed by common law principles. Most fall within the interstices of the reported decisions of Indiana courts. Some touch principles announced in hoary Indiana decisions. Where the Indiana law remains undeclared, or where the declaration is far from current, the obligation of this Court is to discern the most probable state of current Indiana law for "the outcome of the litigation in the federal court should be substantially the same, so far as legal rules determine the outcome of a litigation, as it would be if tried in a State court." *Guaranty Trust Co. v. York*, 326 U.S. 99, 65 S.Ct. 1464, 89 L.Ed. 2079 (1945). . . . In connection with these observations, the Court notes that the appellate courts of Indiana appear to join in the habits of thought and in the assessments of policy which have lately prevailed in most of the fine courts in this nation. The Indiana courts have joined the throng of state courts in (i) declaring that residential landlords are bound by an implied warranty of habitability. *Old Town Development v. Langford*, 349 N.E.2d 744 (Ind.App.1976); (ii) adopting the rule of strict products liability from the Restatement 2d of Torts § 402A, *Perfection Paint & Color Co. v. Konduris*, 258 N.E.2d 681 (Ind.App.1970); (iii) adopting the increasing prevalent view that harsh or unconscionable provisions in contracts of adhesion may be refused enforcement, *Weaver v. American Oil Co.*, 276 N.E.2d 144 (Ind.1971).

C. ALCOA initially argues that it is entitled to relief on the theory of mutual mistake. ALCOA contends that both parties were mistaken in their estimate of the suitability of the WPI-IC as an objective index of ALCOA's non-labor production costs, and that their mistake is legally sufficient to warrant modification or avoidance of ALCOA's promise. Essex appropriately raised several defenses to these claims. Essex first argues that the asserted mistake is legally insufficient because it is essentially a mistake as to future economic events rather than a mistake of fact. Essex next argues that ALCOA assumed or bore the risk of the mistake. Essex finally argues that the requested remedy of reformation is not available under Indiana law.

The late Professor Corbin wrote the best modern analysis of the doctrine of mutual mistake. Corbin took pains to show the great number and variety of factors which must be considered in resolving claims for relief founded on the doctrine of mistake, and to show the inappropriateness of any single verbal rule to govern the decision of mistake cases. Corbin on Contracts § 597 at 582-83 (1960).

The present case involves a claimed mistake in the price indexing formula. This is clearly a mistake concerning a factor affecting the value of the agreed exchange. Of such mistakes Corbin concluded that the law must consider the character of the risks assumed by the parties. Id. at § 605. He further concluded:

> In these cases, the decision involves a judgment as to the materiality of the alleged factor, and as to whether the parties made a definite assumption that it existed and made their agreement in the belief that there was *no risk* with respect to it. Opinions are almost sure to differ on both of these matters, so that decisions must be, or appear to be, conflicting. The court's judgment on each of them is a judgment on a matter of fact, not a judgment as to law. No rule of thumb should be constructed for cases of this kind. 3 Corbin on Contracts § 605 at p. 643 (1960).

The new Restatement 2d of Contracts follows a similar approach.[81] After defining "mistake" as "a belief not in accord with the facts," § 151, the Restatement declares:

> § 152. WHEN MISTAKE OF BOTH PARTIES MAKES A CONTRACT VOIDABLE.
>
> (1) Where a mistake of both parties at the time a contract was made as to a basic assumption on which the contract was made has a material effect on the agreed exchange of performances the contract is voidable by the adversely affected party unless he bears the risk of the mistake under the rule stated in § 154.
>
> (2) In determining whether the mistake has a material affect on the agreed exchange of performances, account is taken of any relief by way of reformation, restitution, or otherwise.

Both Professor Corbin and the Restatement emphasize the limited place of the doctrine of mistake in the law of contracts. They, along with most modern commentators, emphasize the importance of contracts as devices to allocate the risks of life's uncertainties, particularly economic uncertainties. Where parties to a contract deliberately and expressly undertake to allocate the risk of loss attendant on those uncertainties between themselves or where they enter a contract of a customary kind which by common understanding, sense, and legal doctrine has the affect of allocating such risks, the commentators and the opinions are agreed that there is little room for judicial relief from resulting losses. Corbin on Contracts § 598 and authorities there cited. The new Restatement agrees, § 154. This is, in part, the function of the doctrine of assumption of the risk as a limitation of the doctrine of mistake. Whether ALCOA assumed the risk it seeks relief from is at issue in this case. The doctrine of assumption of the risk is therefore considered below. The important point to note here is that the doctrine of assumption of the risk is not the only risk allocating limitation on the doctrine of mistake. Other important risk allocating limitations are inherent in the doctrine of mistake itself. They find expression in the cases and treatises in declarations that there has been no mistake, or no legally cognizable mistake, or a mistake of the wrong part.

ALCOA claims that there was a mutual mistake about the suitability of the WPI-IC as an index to accomplish the purposes of the parties. Essex replies that the mistake, if any, was not a mistake of *fact*, but it was rather a mistake in predicting future economic conditions. Essex asserts that such a mistake does not justify legal relief for ALCOA. The conflicting claims require the Court to resolve three questions: (1) Was the mistake one of "fact" as the cases and commentators use that word? (2) If so, was it of the sort of fact for which relief could be granted? (3) If the mistake was not one of "fact," is relief necessarily foreclosed?

The initial question requires the characterization, as a matter of fact rather than of law, of the claimed mistake. The cases and commentaries contain useful

---

[81] Eds. note: The court, in its opinion, often cites to the Restatement (Second) of Contracts. The citations were to a tentative draft, with different numbers than the final published version. We have changed the numbers so that they refer to the final, published version.

thoughts and analogous problems which aid in this characterization. But the characterization is itself a question of fact. That it may have ultimate legal significance, and that it requires the exercise of judgment does not distinguish this determination from other determinations of fact. The distinction between questions of law and questions of fact is old. Its resolution is often doubtful. No simple and mechanical verbal formula can capture the distinction and resolve the hard cases. Factors affecting the characterization of a question include its suitability for jury or other fact finder determination and its analytical separability from the final determination of legal consequences. The separation of fact from things which are not fact—opinion, prediction, desire, and the like—is principally a question of common sense or epistemology rather than of law, even when the separation must be done by courts. So it is here. ALCOA calls the mistaken assumption that the index was suitable a factual assumption. Essex calls it a prediction. This is a dispute of facts, not law. Its resolution will affect the decision of this case as factual determinations usually do. The law must be applied to it to yield a result. Neither is this question beyond the usual function and capacity of a jury or other fact finder.

The first Restatement of Contracts notes, and the published Tentative Draft No. 10 of the Restatement Second stresses, the distinction between "existing fact" and prediction. See Restatement of Contracts § 502, comment a; Restatement 2d of Contracts [Tentative Draft] §293 [151 in published version]. The approved final form . . . modifies the emphasis by deleting the word "existing." The Reporter, Professor Farnsworth of the Columbia University School of Law, related the circumstances of that change to the Court when he appeared on behalf of ALCOA.

> . . . My clear recollection is that following the discussion of misrepresentation, a number of people came up to me and later saw me in the hallway and said that they agreed with the speaker that "existing" should be dropped.
>
> It would be fair to say that there were probably as many reasons for dropping it given to me as there were people who had advanced the opinion.
>
> I would suppose at the end at least a dozen people had said they didn't like "existing," and nobody had defended it. *The reporter has the authority to change even the black letter when it is a matter of style, and since I did not bring it back to the Institute for a vote as a matter of substance, I think one would have to say that any change made was considered by the reporter to be a matter of style.*
>
> In any event, in response to the small but unanimous body of opinion that didn't like "existing," it was deleted in the draft that I finally sent off to the editor and it now reads "Belief that is not in accord with the facts."
>
> *I think that there is in the comment still a statement with respect to "existing," but the deletion from the black letter is at least a change that perhaps permits more flexibility with respect to the line between what is an existing fact or what is a fact and what is a pure presumption which is an extremely difficult line to draw in both cases.*

Testimony of E. Allan Farnsworth 20-22 (Emphasis added).

The Comment Professor Farnsworth mentioned declares:

> [T]he erroneous belief must relate to the facts as they exist at the time of the making of the contract. A party's prediction or judgment as to events to occur in the future, even if erroneous, is not a "mistake" as that word is defined here. . . .

The Court finds the parties' mistake in this case to be one of fact rather than one of simple prediction of future events. Plainly the mistake is not wholly isolated from predictions of the future or from the searching illuminations of painful hindsight. But this is not the legal test. At the time the contract was made both parties were aware that the future was unknown, and their agreed contract was intended to bind them for many years to come. Both knew that Essex sought an objective pricing formula and that ALCOA sought a formula which would cover its out of pocket costs over the years and which would yield it a return of around four cents a pound. Both parties to the contract carefully examined the past performance of the WPI-IC before agreeing to its use. The testimony was clear that each assumed the Index was adequate to fulfill its purpose. This mistaken assumption was essentially a present actuarial error.

The parties took pains to avoid the full risk of future economic changes when they embarked on a twenty-one year contract involving services worth hundreds of millions of dollars. To this end they employed a customary business risk limiting device—price indexing—with more than customary sophistication and care. They chose not a single index formula but a complex one with three separate indices.

. . . Here the practical necessities of the very long term service contract demanded an agreed risk limiting device. Both parties understood this and adopted one. The capacity of their selected device to achieve the known purposes of the parties was not simply a matter of acknowledged uncertainty like the . . . prediction. It was more in the nature of an actuarial prediction of the outside limits of variation in the relation between two variable figures—the WPI-IC and the nonlabor production costs of ALCOA. Its capacity to work as the parties expected it to work was a matter of fact, existing at the time they made the contract.

This crucial fact was not known, and was scarcely knowable when the contract was made.[82] But this does not alter its status as an existing fact. The law of mistake has not distinguished between facts which are unknown but presently knowable, e.g. *Raffles v. Wichelhaus*, 2 H. & C. 906 (1864), and facts which presently exist but are unknowable, e.g. *Sherwood v. Walker*, 66 Mich. 568, 33 N.W. 919 (1887). Relief has been granted for mistakes of both kinds.

To conclude that the parties contracted upon a mistake of fact does not, by itself, justify an award of judicial relief to ALCOA. Relief can only follow if the

---

[82] [5] Clear hindsight suggests the flaw might have been anticipated and cured by a "floor" resembling the 65% "cap" that Essex wrote into the price formula. To the extent this possibility might be thought material to the case, the Court specifically finds that when the contract was made, even people of exceptional prudence and foresight would not have anticipated a need for this additional limitation to achieve the purpose of the parties.

mistake was mutual, if it related to a basic assumption underlying the contract, and if it caused a severe imbalance in the agreed exchange.

The doctrine of mistake has long distinguished claims of mutual mistake from claims of unilateral mistake. Corbin on Contracts § 608. The standards for judicial relief are higher where the proven mistake is unilateral than where it is mutual. Compare, *e.g.* Restatement 2d of Contracts § 152 with § 153.

Essex asserts that ALCOA's mistake was unilateral. Mr. O'Malley, Chairman of the board of Essex Corporation, testified at trial that he had no particular concern for ALCOA's well-being and that in the negotiations of the contract he sought only Essex's best interests. Essex claims this testimony tends to rebut any possible mutual mistake of fact between the parties. The Court disagrees. . . .

The law of mutual mistake is not addressed primarily to motivation or to desire to have a good bargain, such as that credibly testified to by Mr. O'Malley. As Mr. O'Malley struck the bargain for Essex, he understood the function of the Wholesale Price Index, as part of the pricing formula, to be the protection of ALCOA from foreseeable economic fluctuations. He further had every reason to believe that the formula was selected on the factual prediction that it would, within tolerable limits, serve its purpose. While he did not share the motive to protect ALCOA, he understood the functional purposes of the agreement. He therefore shared this mistake of fact. And his mistake was Essex's. The Court recognizes that Mr. O'Malley and Essex would cheerfully live with the benefit of their mistake, but the law provides otherwise. As a matter of law Mr. O'Malley's testimony of Essex's indifference concerning ALCOA's motivation for the use of the Wholesale Price Index as a gauge for tracking non-labor costs is immaterial.

Is it enough that one party is indifferent to avoid a mutual mistake? The Court thinks not. This situation resembles that in *Sherwood v. Walker, supra*, the celebrated case of Rose of Aberlone. There the owner of a prize breeding cow sold her for slaughter at the going rate for good slaughter cattle. The owner had unsuccessfully tried to breed her and had erroneously concluded she was sterile. In fact she was pregnant at the time of the sale and she was much more valuable for breeding than for slaughter. There as here, the buyer was indifferent to the unknown fact; he would have been pleased to keep the unexpected profit. But he understood the bargain rested on a presumed state of facts. The court let the seller avoid the contract because of mutual mistake of fact.

In *Sherwood*, the buyer didn't know the highly pedigreed Rose was with calf. He probably could not have discovered it at the time of the sale with due diligence. Here the parties could not possibly have known of the sudden inability of the Wholesale Price Index to reflect ALCOA's non-labor costs. If, over the previous twenty years, the Wholesale Price Index had tracked, within a 5% variation, pertinent costs to ALCOA, a 500% variation of costs to Index must be deemed to be unforeseeable, within any meaningful sense of the word.

Essex has not seriously argued that the mistake does not relate to an assumption which is basic to the contract. The relation is clear. The assumed capacity of the price formula in a long term service contract to protect against vast windfall profits to one party and vast windfall losses to the other is so clearly basic to the agreement as to repel dispute. While the cases often assert that a mistake as to price or as to future market conditions will not justify relief, this is not because price assumptions are not basic to the contracts. Instead, relief is denied because the parties allocated the risk of present price uncertainties or of uncertain future market values by their contract. Where a "price mistake" derives from a mistake about the nature or quantity of an object sold, the courts have allowed a remedy; they have found no contractual allocation of that sort of risk of price error. Indiana cases hold that where land is sold as a tract for a set price, and it later appears that there was a material error in the parties' estimate of the quantity of land conveyed, the court will correct the error by adjusting the price, *McMahan v. Terkhorn*, 67 Ind.App. 501, 116 N.E. 327 (1917), or by allowing rescission, *Earl v. VaNatta*, 29 Ind.App. 532, 64 N.E. 901 (1902). See Corbin on Contracts §§ 604-05. Similarly many cases allow relief from unilateral price errors by construction contractors. An Indiana decision reached this result. *Board of School Comm'rs v. Bender*, 36 Ind.App. 164, 72 N.E. 154 (1904). See Corbin on Contracts § 609. Restatement 2d of Contracts § 153, comment a. These cases demonstrate that price assumptions may be basic to the contract.

Essex concedes that the result of the mistake has a material effect on the contract and that it has produced a severe imbalance in the bargain. See Restatement 2d of Contracts § 152, comment c. The most that Essex argues is this: ALCOA has not proved that enforcement of the contract would be *unconscionable*. Essex correctly points out that at the time of the trial ALCOA had shown a net profit of $9 million on the contract. Essex further argues that ALCOA has failed to prove that it ever will lose money on the contract, and that such proof would require expert testimony concerning future economic values and costs. These arguments are insufficient.

The evidence shows that during the last three years ALCOA has suffered increasingly large out of pocket losses.[83] If the contract were to expire today that net profit of $9 million would raise doubts concerning the materiality of the parties' mistake. But even on that supposition, the court would find the mistake to be material because it would leave ALCOA dramatically short of the minimum return of one cent per pound which the parties had contemplated.

But the contract will not expire today. Essex has the power to keep it in force until 1988. The Court rejects Essex's objection to the absence of expert testimony concerning future costs and prices. The objection is essentially based on the traditional refusal of courts to award speculative damages. But Essex presses the argument too far. The law often requires courts to make awards to redress anticipated losses. The reports are filled with tort and contract cases where such a awards are made without the benefit of expert testimony concerning future economic trends. Awards are commonly denied because they are too speculative where there is a claim for lost future profits and there is insufficient evidence of present profits to form a basis for protecting future profits.

---

[83] [6] The Court recognizes that ALCOA has suffered even larger losses of potential profits which it might have earned, but for the contract, in the strong aluminum market in recent years. Essex, rather than ALCOA, has enjoyed those profits. But their existence is immaterial to the questions raised in this case.

Similarly the courts often decline to speculate concerning future economic trends in calculating awards for lost future earnings. Many states refuse to consider any possibility of future inflation in calculating such awards despite the presence of expert testimony and the teachings of common experience. . . . This demonstrates the law's healthy skepticism concerning the reliability of expert predictions of economic trends. Where future predictions are necessary, the law commonly accepts and applies a prediction that the future economy will be much like the present (except that inflation will cease). Since some prediction of the future is inescapable in this case, that commonly accepted one will necessarily apply. On that prediction, ALCOA has proved that over the entire life of the contract it will lose, out of pocket, in excess of $60 million, and the whole of this loss will be matched by an equal windfall profit to Essex.[84] This proof clearly establishes that the mistake had the required material effect on the agreed exchange. Indeed, if this case required a determination of the conscionability of enforcing this contract in the current circumstances, the Court would not hesitate to hold it unconscionable.

Essex next argues that ALCOA may not be relieved of the consequences of the mistake because it assumed or bore the risk of the market. . . .

The Restatements and these cases reveal four facets of risk assumption and risk allocation under the law of mistake. First, a party to a contract may expressly assume a risk. . . .

Customary dealing in a trade or common understanding may lead a court to impose a risk on a party where the contract is silent. Often the result corresponds to the expectation of both parties, but this will not always be true. *See* Berman, Excuse for Nonperformance in the Light of Contract Practices in International Trade, 63 *Colum. L. Rev.* 1413, 1420-24 (1963). At times legal rules may form the basis for the inferred common understanding. Equity traditionally put the risk of casualty losses on the purchaser of land while the purchase contract remained executory. This allocation was derived from the doctrine of equitable conversion. "Equity regards as done that which ought to be done." The rule could always be modified by express agreement. It survives today—where it does survive—largely by reason of its acceptance as part of the common expectations of real estate traders and their advisors.

Third, where neither express words nor some particular common understanding or trade usage dictate a result, the court must allocate the risk in some reasoned way. . . .

---

[84] [8] The equivalence of ALCOA's loss and Essex's gain may distinguish this case from the concededly more difficult "Suez cases." Transatlantic Financing Corp. v. United States, 363 F.2d 312 (D.C. Cir. 1966); American Trading and Production Corp. v. Shell International Marine, 453 F.2d 939 (2nd Cir. 1972); Glidden Co. v. Hellenic Lines, 275 F.2d 253 (2nd Cir. 1960); Ocean Tramp Tankers Corp. v. V/U Sorracht (The Eugenia), [1964] 1 All E.R. 161 (C.A. 1963). In those cases an unexpected closing of the canal materially increased the cost of performing the contract leaving the courts to determine the allocation of a loss not balanced by an equal profit. Those cases might also be distinguished in that they involved the doctrine of frustration of purpose rather than the doctrine of mistake. However, the similarity of these doctrines renders this distinction doubtful.

Fourth, where parties enter a contract in a state of conscious ignorance of the facts, they are deemed to risk the burden of having the facts turn out to be adverse, within very broad limits. Each party takes a calculated gamble in such a contract. Because information is often troublesome or costly to obtain, the law does not seek to discourage such contracts. Thus if parties agree to sell and purchase a stone which both know may be glass or diamond at a price which in some way reflects their uncertainty, the contract is enforceable whether the stone is in fact glass or diamond. If, by contrast, the parties both mistakenly believe it to be glass, the case is said not to be one of conscious ignorance but one of mutual mistake. Consequently, the vendor may avoid the contract.

In this case Essex raises two arguments. First, it asserts that ALCOA expressly or by fair implication assumed the risk that the WPI-IC would not keep up with ALCOA's non-labor production costs. Second, it asserts that the parties made a calculated gamble with full awareness that the future was uncertain, so the contract should be enforced despite the mutual mistake. Both arguments are correct within limits, and within those limits they affect the relief ALCOA may receive. Both arguments fail as complete defenses to ALCOA's claim.

Essex first asserts that ALCOA expressly or implicitly assumed the risk that the WPI-IC would not track ALCOA's non-labor production costs. Essex asserts that ALCOA drafted the index provision; that it did so on the basis of its superior knowledge of its cost experience at the Warrick Works; and that ALCOA's officials knew of the inherent risk that the index would not reflect cost changes. Essex emphasized that, during the negotiation of the contract, it insisted on the inclusion of a protective "ceiling" on the indexed price of ALCOA's services at 65% of a specified published market price. Essex implies that ALCOA could have sought a corresponding "floor" provision to limit its risks.

Essex' arguments rely on two ancient and powerful principles of interpretation. The first is reflected in the maxim "expressio unius est exclusio alterius." The second is the principle that a contract is to be construed against its drafter. To agree to an indexed price term subject to a ceiling but without a floor is to make a deliberate choice, Essex argues. It is to choose one principle and to reject another. The argument is plausible but not sufficient. The maxim rules no farther than its reason, and its reason is simply this: often an expression of a rule couched in one form reflects with high probability the rejection of a contradictory rule. Less often it reflects a probable rejection of a supplementary rule. To know if this is true of a particular case requires a scrupulous examination of the thing expressed, the thing not expressed, and the context of the expression. The question here is precisely this: By omitting a floor provision did ALCOA accept the risk of any and every deviation of the selected index from its costs, no matter how great or how highly improbable? The course of dealing between the parties repels the idea. Essex and ALCOA are huge industrial enterprises. The management of each is highly trained and highly responsible. The corporate officers have access to and use professional personnel including lawyers, accountants, economists and engineers. The contract was drafted by sophisticated, responsible businessmen who were intensely conscious of the risks inherent in long term contracts and who plainly sought to limit the risks of their undertaking. The parties' laudable attention to risk limitation appears in many ways: in the complex price formula, in the 65% ceiling, in the "most favored customer" clause which Essex wrote into the contract, and in the elaborate "force majeur" clause favoring AL-COA. It appears as well in the care and in the expense of the negotiations and drafting process. Essex negotiated with several aluminum producers, seeking a long term assured supply, before agreeing to the ALCOA contract. Its search for an assured long term supply for its aluminum product plants itself bespeaks a motive of limiting risks. Essex settled on ALCOA's offer rather than a proffered joint venture on the basis of many considerations including the required capital, engineering and management demands of the joint venture, the cost, and the comparative risks and burdens of the two arrangements. When ALCOA proposed the price formula which appears in the contract, Essex's management examined the past behavior of the indices for stability to assure they would not cause their final aluminum cost to deviate unacceptably from the going market rate. AL-COA's management was equally attentive to risk limitation. . . . They selected the WPI-IC as a pricing element for this long term contract only after they assured themselves that it had closely tracked ALCOA's non-labor production costs for many years in the past and was highly likely to continue to do so in the future. In the context of the formation of the contract, it is untenable to argue that ALCOA implicitly or expressly assumed a limitless, if highly improbable, risk. On this record, the absence of an express floor limitation can only be understood to imply that the parties deemed the risk too remote and their meaning too clear to trifle with additional negotiation and drafting.

The principle that a writing is to be construed against its maker will not aid Essex here. That principle once sounded as a clarion call to retrograde courts to pervert agreements if they could. Today it is happily domesticated as a rule with diverse uses. In cases involving issues of conscience or of strong policy, such as forfeiture cases, the principle complements the familiar doctrine of strict construction to favor lenient results. In other cases it serves as an aid in resolving otherwise intractable ambiguities. This case presents neither of these problems. The question of defining the risks ALCOA assumed is one of interpretation. It implicates no strong public policy. Neither does it present an intractable ambiguity.

Neither is this a case of "conscious ignorance" as Essex argues. Essex cites many cases which establish the general rule that mistaken assumptions about the future are not the sort of mistaken assumptions which lead to relief from contractual duties. . . . The general rule is in fact as Essex states it. but that rule has limited application. The new Restatement notes that the rule does not apply where both parties are unconscious of their ignorance—that is, where both mistakenly believe they know the vital facts. See § 154 Comment C. . . .

This distinction is sufficient to settle many cases but it is framed too crudely for sensible application to cases like the present one. The distinction posits two polar positions: certain belief that a vital fact is true and certain recognition that a vital fact is unknown. Such certainties are seldom encountered in human affairs. They are particularly rare in the understanding of sophisticated businessmen. . . .

The . . . notion of a range of uncertainty is not unknown to Indiana law. In *McMahan v. Terkhorn, supra*, the parties contracted to purchase and to sell a tract of land which they thought to contain 133 acres for $15,000. Before the date for performance the purchaser had the land surveyed. The surveyor reported the tract contained 104.52 acres. The parties then adjusted the purchase price to $12,000 and completed the conveyance on that basis. Later the vendor learned the survey was wrong; the tract contained 129 acres. He then sued for and won the value of the "excess" land conveyed. The court distinguished between the normal range of survey error which parties are deemed to expect and to risk, and gross errors for which a remedy is available. . . .

Once courts recognize that supposed specific values lie, and are commonly understood to lie, within a penumbra of uncertainty, and that the range of probability is subject to estimation, the principle of conscious uncertainty requires reformulation. The proper question is not simply whether the parties to a contract were conscious of uncertainty with respect to a vital fact, but whether they believed that uncertainty was effectively limited within a designated range so that they would deem outcomes beyond that range to be highly unlikely. In this case the answer is clear. Both parties knew that the use of an objective price index injected a limited range of uncertainty into their projected return on the contract. Both had every reason to predict that the likely range of variation would not exceed three cents per pound. That is to say both would have deemed deviations yielding ALCOA less of a return on its investment, work and risk of less than one cent a pound or of more than seven cents a pound to be highly unlikely. Both consciously undertook a closely calculated risk rather than a limitless one. Their mistake concerning its calculation is thus fundamentally unlike the limitless conscious undertaking of an unknown risk which Essex now posits.

What has been said to this point suffices to establish that ALCOA is entitled to some form of relief due to mutual mistake of fact. But the stakes in this case are large, and the chances of review by higher courts are high. Therefore the Court thinks it appropriate to rule on two other theories which ALCOA presented in support of its first count.

D. ALCOA argues that it is entitled to relief on the grounds of impracticability and frustration of purpose. The Court agrees.

In broad outline the doctrines of impracticability and of frustration of purpose resemble the doctrine of mistake. All three doctrines discharge an obligor from his duty to perform a contract where a failure of a basic assumption of the parties produces a grave failure of the equivalence of value of the exchange to the parties. And all three are qualified by the same notions of risk assumption and allocation. The doctrine of mistake of fact requires that the mistake relate to a basic assumption on which the contract was made. The doctrine of impracticability requires that the non-occurrence of the "event," Restatement 2d of Contracts § 261, or the non-existence of the "fact," Id. § 266, causing the impracticability be a basic assumption on which the contract is made. The doctrine of frustration of purpose similarly rests on the same "non-occurrence" or "non-existence," "basic assumption" equation. Id. §§ 265, 266.

The three doctrines further overlap in time. There may be some residual notion that the doctrine of frustration and impracticability relate to occurrences after the execution of the contract while the doctrine of mistake relates to facts as they stand at the time of execution. But that view has never won general acceptance. The first Restatement does not specifically limit the mistakes of fact for which relief may be granted to facts existing at the time of the contract. §§ 500, 502. Corbin and Williston do not suggest such a limitation. And the new Restatement equivocates on the point. Section 151 defines "mistake" as "a belief that is not in accord with the facts." The word "existing" modified the word "facts" in Tentative Draft Number 10 but was deleted by the Reporter. Comment a to the section does declare:

> [T]he erroneous belief must relate to the facts as they exist at the time of the making of the contract. A party's prediction or judgment as to events to occur in the future, even if erroneous, is not a 'mistake' as the word is defined here.

This declaration is anomalous and unexplained. The Court believes the definition rather than the comment expresses the better rule. The denial of relief for mistakes of future facts is better understood to rest on policies of risk allocation discussed above than to rest on the definition of "mistake."

National Presto Industries, Inc. v. United States, 338 F.2d 99 (Ct.Cl.1964), is a prime example of the application of the doctrine of mistake to developments after the execution of the contract. There the corporation contracted to produce artillery shells for the Army at a fixed price, using a new and only partially proven production method. The method was contrived to reduce wasted steel by eliminating the need for shaving excess metal from the shells. After the contract was signed, the corporation spent large sums of money in unsuccessful attempts to make the method work. Eventually it became clear that some shaving would be required. The corporation purchased the necessary equipment and paid for the materials and labor. Then it sought and obtained relief in the Court of Claims for its added expense. The court held that there had been an actionable mutual mistake of fact. The assumed capacity of the new method to produce shells without a shaving step proved to be mistaken.[85] The court based its decision solely on mistake of fact. It does not appear that frustration or impracticability were considered.

Conversely the notion that the doctrines of frustration and impracticability apply only to events occurring after the execution of a contract appear to be drawn more from common experience with their application than from any inherent limitation of those doctrines. Nothing in the language of the first Restatement limits the doctrine to events occurring after the execution of the contract, though all three illustrations involve such supervening events. § 288. The new Restatement recognizes that circumstances existing at the execution of a contract may render performance impracticable or they may frustrate the purpose of one of the parties so as to excuse his performance. § 266.

---

[85] [14] The court further held that the corporation had not assumed the risk of the experiment by entering into an unconditional fixed price contract. The court found that the parties did not contemplate the hazard and did not assign its risk. 338 F.2d at 109-110. The court further found that the actual cost of testing and development in attempting to perfect the new method exceeded the testing expense implicitly risked by the corporation. 338 F.2d at 109.

Thus there is a substantial area of similarity between the three doctrines. Within that area, the findings and holdings with respect to the claim of mistake also apply to the claims of impracticability and frustration. It requires no further discussion to establish that the non-occurrence of an extreme deviation of the WPI-IC and ALCOA's non-labor production costs was a basic assumption on which the contract was made. And it is clear that ALCOA neither assumed nor bore the risk of the deviation beyond the foreseeable limits of risk.

The court must still consider those aspects of doctrines of frustration and impracticability which differ from the doctrine of mistake. . . .

The focus of the doctrines of impracticability and of frustration is distinctly on hardship. Section 261 declares a party is discharged from performing a contract where a supervening event renders his performance impracticable. Comment d discusses the meaning of "impracticability." The comment states the word is taken from Uniform Commercial Code § 2-615(a). It declares that the word denotes an impediment to performance lying between "impossibility" and "impracticality."

Performance may be impracticable because *extreme and unreasonable difficulty, expense, injury, or loss to one of the parties will be involved.* . . .

A mere change in the degree of difficulty or expense due to such causes as increased wages, prices of raw materials, or costs of construction, unless well beyond the normal range, does not amount to impracticability since it is this sort of risk that a fixed-price contract is intended to cover. Restatement 2nd Contracts § 261 com. (d).

Similarly, § 265 declares a party is discharged from performing his contract where his principal purpose is *substantially* frustrated by the occurrence of a supervening event. The extent of the necessary frustration is further described in comment a: "[T]he frustration must be substantial. It is not enough that the transaction has become less profitable for the affected party or even that he will sustain a loss. The frustration must be so severe that it is not fairly to be regarded as within the risks that he assumed under the contract."

Professor Corbin explained this requirement of a severe disappointment by relating this doctrine to the broad public policies that parties should generally be required to perform their contracts.

> Variations in the value of a promised performance, caused by the constantly varying factors that affect the bargaining appetites of men, are the rule rather than the exception. Bargainers know this and swallow their losses and disappointments, meantime keeping their promises. Such being the business mores, court decisions that are not in harmony with them will not make for satisfaction or prosperity. Relief from duty, outside of the bankruptcy court, can safely be granted on the ground of frustration of purpose by the rise or fall of values, only when the variation in value is very great and is caused by a supervening event that was not in fact contemplated by the parties and the risk of which was not allocated by them. Corbin on Contracts § 1355.

This strict standard of severe disappointment is clearly met in the present case. ALCOA has sufficiently proved that it will lose well over $60 million dollars out of pocket over the life of the contract due to the extreme deviation of the WPI-IC from ALCOA's actual costs. [86]

Is this, then, a case of impracticability, of frustration, or both? The doctrine of impracticability and of frustration focus on different kinds of disappointment of a contracting party. Impracticability focuses on occurrences which greatly increase the costs, difficulty, or risk of the party's performance. Restatement 2d of Contracts § 261.

The doctrine of frustration, on the other hand, focuses on a party's severe disappointment which is caused by circumstances which frustrate his principal purpose for entering the contract. [87] Restatement 2d of Contracts § 265. The doctrine of frustration often applies to relieve a party of a contract which could be performed without impediment; relief is allowed because the performance would be of little value to the frustrated party. Illustration 1 of the new Restatement—abstracted from the Coronation Cases—typifies this aspect of the doctrine of frustration.

A and B make a contract under which B is to pay A $1,000 and is to have the use of A's window on January 10 to view a parade that has been scheduled for that day. Because of the illness of an important official, the parade is cancelled. B refuses to use the window or pay the $1,000. B's duty to pay $1,000 is discharged, and B is not liable to A for breach of contract.

Nothing impedes the full performance of this contract. B is able to pay $1,000 and to use the window despite the cancellation of the parade. But B's purpose—to observe the spectacle—has been frustrated.

In the present case ALCOA has satisfied the requirements of both doctrines. The impracticability of its performance is clear. The increase in its cost of performance is severe enough to warrant relief, and the other elements necessary for the granting of relief have been proven. Essex argues that the causes of AL-COA's losses are due to market price increases to which the doctrine of impracticability does not apply. The doctrine of impracticability of the new Restatement is one of recent evolution in the law. The first Restatement used the term as part of the definition of "impossibility." The interesting legal evolution from the strict standards of impossibility, evident at least by dictum in *Parradine v. Jane*, Aleyn, 26 (1647, K.B.), to modern standards of impracticability is traced in Professor Gilmore's The Death of Contract 35-90 (1974). The drafters of the Uniform Commercial Code adopted this line of development, particularly in § 2-615. The new Restatement expressly draws upon § 2-615 in defining the scope of the

[86] [15] The Court recognizes the additional requirement that the frustration or impracticability must not be the fault of the party who seeks relief. Restatement 2d of Contracts §§ 261, 265. Essex has not claimed or shown that ALCOA's dealings during the contract caused or contributed to AL-COA's losses. The record sufficiently proves that the great cost increases of some of the non-labor cost components (power, electrolytes, carbon) were beyond ALCOA's control. . . .

[87] [16] Professor Corbin primely observed, "A 'contract' never has a purpose or object. Only the contracting persons have purposes; and the purpose of any one of these persons is different from the purpose of any other. The hopes and purposes and objects of one of the parties may be frustrated by supervening events, although the purposes of the other party may not be at all affected by those events." Corbin on Contracts § 1353.

doctrine. § 261 comments reporter's notes. The official comment to § 2-615 lends strength to Essex's claim.

> 1.This section excuses a seller from timely delivery of goods contracted for, where his performance has become commercially impracticable because of unforeseen supervening circumstances not within the contemplation of the parties at the time of contracting. . . .

However,

> 4.Increased cost alone does not excuse performance unless the rise in cost is due to some unforeseen contingency which alters the essential nature of the performance. Neither is a rise or a collapse in the market in itself a justification, for that is exactly the type of business risk which business contracts made at fixed prices are intended to cover. But a severe shortage of raw materials or supplies due to a contingency such as war, embargo, local crop failure, unforeseen shutdown of major sources of supply or the like, which either causes a marked increase in cost or altogether prevents the seller from securing supplies necessary to his performance is within the contemplation of this section.

Several of the cases cited by Essex rely on comment 4 in denying claims for relief. [citations omitted]. . . Each is distinguishable from the present case in the absolute extent of the loss and in the proportion of loss involved.

In *Publicker Industries*, the defendant Union Carbide had contracted in 1972 to sell ethanol in specified quantities over a three year period to the plaintiff. The price was set by a formula, adjusted annually to reflect the seller's cost for raw materials, and subject to a ceiling on adjustment increases. The raw materials were derivatives of natural gas; their price soared beginning in 1973 as did ALCOA's energy costs. The seller's costs for ethanol rose from 21.2 cents a gallon in 1973 to 37.2 cents per gallon in mid-1974. The ceiling contract sales price was then 26.5 cents per gallon. The seller's loss of 10.7 cents per gallon led to a projected aggregate loss of $5.8 million. The court refused to relieve the seller. It found that the ceiling provision constituted an intentional allocation of the "risk of a substantial and unforeseen rise in cost" to the seller. It based this finding in part on the twenty-five percent rise in prices by OPEC in 1971 which made future cost increases highly foreseeable. The court addressed the degree of loss issue, declaring:

> We are not aware of any cases where something less than a 100% cost increase has been held to make a seller's performance 'impracticable.'
>
> . . . '[T]here must be more of a variation between expected cost and the cost of performing by an available alternative than is present in this case, where the promisor can legitimately be presumed to have accepted some degree of abnormal risk, and where impracticability is urged on the basis of added expense alone.'[88]

---

[88] [17] Quoting Transatlantic Financing Corp. v. United States, supra.

Publicker Industries is clearly distinguishable from the present case respecting the degree of loss which the seller suffered in comparison to what it foresaw at the time of contracting. The fact that the Publicker contract was made after the substantial price increase of 1971 may justify the court's finding that the seller had assumed the risk of further large price increases. The contract in the present case antedated the 1971 price increase. There is no similar factual basis for finding that ALCOA assumed the risk of the full loss which it is experiencing.

Transatlantic Financing Corp. v. United States, supra, was one of the "Suez" cases. The carrier had contracted to transport a cargo from the United States to Iran for a specified price. The contract did not specify the route, but both parties knew the most direct route was by way of Suez. When the Canal was closed the carrier had to divert its ships around Cape Horn, adding three thousand miles to the expected ten thousand mile voyage, and adding an expense of about $44,000 to the contract price of about $306,000. Judge J. Skelly Wright, for a unanimous panel, found that "circumstances surrounding the contract indicate that the risk of the Canal's closure may be deemed to have been allocated to Transatlantic." But he found this conclusion doubtful enough to cause him to reject a direct application of the risk allocation rule. He went on:

> The surrounding circumstances do indicate, however, a willingness by Transatlantic to assume abnormal risks, and this fact should legitimately cause us to judge the impracticability of performance by an alternate route in stricter terms than we would were the contingency unforeseen. *Id.* at 318-19.

Judge Wright then held, in the passage quoted in *Publicker Industries, supra,* that there must be more than a twelve percent cost increase to constitute impracticability.

Here ALCOA's loss is more than a thousand times greater than the carrier's loss. And the circumstances surrounding the contract show a deliberate avoidance of abnormal risks. . . .

Eastern Air Lines Inc. v. Gulf Oil Corp., supra, follows the pattern of these cases except in one detail. Gulf had contracted to furnish jet fuel to Eastern in designated cities from June 1972 until January 31, 1977. The price was tied to a specific trade journal report of posted prices for a specified type of domestic oil. During the contract the price of imported oil soared. Domestic oil was subjected to a complex and shifting body of regulations including a "two-tier" price control scheme regulating the price of "old oil" but not the price of "new oil." The specified trade journal reacted to the new system by publishing prices only for the regulated "old oil." Gulf sought to escape the burden of its contract and Eastern sued to compel Gulf to perform it.

The court required Gulf to perform the contract. It found that Gulf had failed to prove its defense. The "cost" figures in evidence included built in intra-company profits such that the court could not "determine how much it costs Gulf to produce a gallon of jet fuel for sale to Eastern, whether Gulf loses money or makes a profit on its sale of jet fuel to Eastern, either now or at the inception of the contract, or at any time in between." *Id.* at 440. Thus Gulf failed to prove it had suffered losses on the contract.

In the course of the decision the court declared that relief was available under § 2-615 for an *unforeseeable* failure of a pre-supposed condition. It inferred this requirement from Comment 8 to § 2-615[89] and from the Suez cases. If it were generally adopted, this requirement would reduce the occasions for excusing performance under § 2-615. Judge Wright rejected such a requirement in *Transatlantic Financing*, declaring:

> Foreseeability or even recognition of a risk does not necessarily prove its allocation. . . . Parties to a contract are not always able to provide for all the possibilities of which they are aware, sometimes because they cannot agree, often simply because they are too busy. Moreover, that some abnormal risk was contemplated is probative but does not necessarily establish an allocation of the risk of the contingency which actually occurs. 363 F.2d at 318.

The question is important in developing doctrine of impracticability. The Indiana cases are silent on it. The Court believes that Indiana courts would find Judge Wright's approach is more in keeping with the spirit and purpose of the Uniform Commercial Code than is the strict approach of Judge King in *Eastern Air Lines*. The Code, embodied in Title 26, Burns Ind.Stat.Ann. (1974) seeks to accommodate the law to sound commercial sense and practice. Courts must decide the point at which the community's interest in predictable contract enforcement shall yield to the fact that enforcement of a particular contract would be commercially senseless and unjust. The spirit of the Code is that such decisions cannot justly derive from legal abstractions. They must derive from courts sensitive to the mores, practices and habits of thought in the respectable commercial world.

If it were important to the decision of this case, the Court would hold that the foreseeability of a variation between the WPI-IC and ALCOA's costs would not preclude relief under the doctrine of impracticability. But the need for such a holding is not clear, for the Court has found that the risk of a wide variation between these values was unforeseeable in a commercial sense and was not allocated to ALCOA in the contract.

The Court holds that ALCOA is entitled to relief under the doctrine of impracticability. The cases Essex relies on and the other cases discovered by the Court are all distinguishable with respect to the gravity of harm which the aggrieved contracting party was liable to suffer. Except for *Transatlantic Financing*, they are also distinguishable with respect to the question of allocation of the risk, inferred from the circumstances known to the parties at the time of the contract and from the contract terms.

ALCOA's claim of frustration requires more discussion. ALCOA's "principal purpose" in making the contract was to earn money. This purpose has plainly been severely disappointed. The gravity of ALCOA's loss is undisputably suffi-

---

[89] [18] The provisions of this section are made subject to assumption of greater liability by agreement and such agreement is to be found not only in the expressed terms of the contract but in the circumstances surrounding the contracting, in trade usage and the like. Thus the exemptions of this section do not apply when the contingency in question is sufficiently foreshadowed at the time of contracting to be included among the business risks which are fairly to be regarded as part of the dickered terms, either consciously or as a matter of reasonable, commercial interpretation from the circumstances. . . .

cient to meet the stern standard for relief. But the question remains whether the law will grant relief for the serious frustration of this kind of purpose, *i.e.*, for the conversion of an expected profit into a serious loss. All of the new Restatement illustrations center on purposes other than making a profit. However most of them bear on some stage of a profit oriented activity. . . .

In § 1360 Professor Corbin demonstrates that at times courts should treat loss avoidance as a principal purpose of a party. That section deals with frustration of purpose caused by inflationary depreciation of money. Corbin demonstrates that the decisions are not uniform on this subject, but he rejects as reprehensible the nominalist rule that a dollar's a dollar no matter how small. The injustice of the nominalist position was clearly recognized in the case of *Anderson v. Equitable Life Assurance Society*, 134 L.T. 557, 42 T.L.R. 302 (1926). The facts in *Anderson* were these: In 1887 an Englishman in Russia took out a twenty-premium life insurance policy with premiums and benefits payable in German marks. The policy benefit was 60,000 marks. The premiums were paid from 1887 to 1907 and were converted, as both parties understood they would be, into pounds. Their value came to £2,377. The insured died in 1922 at the height of the German hyperinflation. At that time the value of 60,000 marks was less than an English penny. The insurer argued that it owed nothing on the contract, for it could not be required to pay a fraction of a cent. Astonishingly, the court agreed. Under English law the obligation to pay in foreign currency was absolute and unqualified by variations in exchange rates. The judges noted the harshness of the result and pressed upon the company its moral obligation to make some payment which they held the law would not compel.

Happily some American cases and the law of many foreign countries take a different view of the problem. The problem of serious, sustained inflation is not unique to modern America. During the Revolution and the Civil War, America witnessed serious inflation. And several other nations have recently experienced more severe inflation than America has. When the problem has arisen, here and abroad, courts and legislatures have repeatedly acted to relieve parties from great and unexpected losses. See Mann, The Legal Aspect of Money (1938); Corbin on Contracts § 1360 and cases there cited. The exact character of the relief granted is not important here. Neither is the exact explanation of the decisions found in the cases, because even the Civil War cases antedate the evolution of the distinct doctrine of frustration. What is important is this: first, the results of those decisions would be readily explained today in terms of frustration of purpose. Corbin discusses them in his chapter on Frustration of Purpose. And second, the frustration which they involved was a frustration of the purpose to earn money or to avoid losses. Thus it appears that there is no legitimate doctrinal problem which prevents relief for frustration of this sort. There remain the customary strictures concerning risk allocation and gravity of injury. Those have been addressed above and need not be considered again here. The Court holds ALCOA is entitled to relief on its claim of frustration of purpose.

E. This leaves the question of framing a remedy for ALCOA. Essex argues that reformation is not available. It cites many Indiana cases declaring that reformation is only available to correct writings which, through mistake, do not reflect the agreement of the parties. The declarations to that effect are clear. . . .

But the point is immaterial here. This case does not fall within reformation as a traditional head of equity jurisprudence. It does fall within the more general rules of equitable restitution. Courts have traditionally applied three remedial rules in cases of mistake, frustration and impracticability. In some cases courts declare that no contract ever arose because there was no true agreement between the parties, *Raffles v. Wichelhaus, supra*, or because the parties were ignorant of existing facts which frustrated the purpose of one party or made performance impracticable. Restatement 2d of Contracts § 266. In some other cases the courts hold that a contract is voidable on one of the three theories. In these cases the customary remedy is rescission. In both classes of cases where one or both parties have performed under the supposed contract, the courts award appropriate restitution in the light of the benefits the parties have conferred on each other. The aim is to prevent unjust enrichment. The courts in such cases often call this remedy "reformation" in the loose sense of "modification." See III Palmer, Law of Restitution § 13.9 (1978). In *Schwaderer v. Huron-Clinton Metropolitan Authority*, 329 Mich. 258, 45 N.W.2d 279 (1951), the plaintiff contracted to clear a tract of land of trees and brush. The parties mistakenly believed the tract contained 239 acres, and on that belief the plaintiff bid $59,000 for the job. In fact the land contained 545 acres. The court "reformed" the contract to award the plaintiff the value of the extra work it had performed. Professor Palmer says this of *Schwaderer* and similar cases:

> [T]he judgment is aimed at carving out and leaving intact an exchange that approximates or is in substance the one the parties had in mind, and at the same time readjusting the contract or its consequences so as to prevent unjust enrichment.

> The cases . . . demonstrate that many situations do not fit neatly into a general scheme of classification. There are many typical cases for which a standard remedy is appropriate; there are also cases for which the relief given should be responsible to the particular facts. III Palmer, Law of Restitution § 13.9 at 61-62.

Indiana has accepted this remedial theory. In *McMahan v. Terkhorn, supra*, the parties had purchased and sold a tract of land at a price less than their contract price in reliance on a survey which erroneously showed there was less land in the tract than the parties had believed. After the sale and before the survey error was discovered the purchaser resold part of the land, making rescission inappropriate. The court "reformed" or modified the contract to require the purchaser to pay for the extra land which had been conveyed. There, in a fully executed contract, a price adjustment was necessary to protect the fair expectation of the parties and to prevent unjust enrichment.

The same ends can be achieved under a long term executory contract by a similar remedy. To decree rescission in this case would be to grant ALCOA a windfall gain in the current aluminum market. It would at the same time deprive Essex of the assured long term aluminum supply which it obtained under the contract and of the gains it legitimately may enforce within the scope of the risk ALCOA bears under the contract. A remedy which merely shifts the windfall gains and losses is neither required nor permitted by Indiana law.

To frame an equitable remedy where frustration, impracticability or mistake prevent strict enforcement of a long term executory contract requires a careful examination of the circumstances of the contract, the purposes of the parties, and the circumstances which upset the contract. For some long term executory contracts rescission with or without restitution will be the only sensible remedy. Where developments make performance of the contract economically senseless or purposeless, to modify the contract and to enforce it as modified would be highly inappropriate. But in cases like the present one modification and enforcement may be the only proper remedy.[90] See *Parev Products Co. v. I. Rokeach and Sons, Inc.*, 124 F.2d 147 (2nd Cir. 1941). In this case Essex sought an assured long term supply of aluminum at a price which would let it earn a profit on its finished products. ALCOA, facing ordinary market risks in 1967, sought a long term, limited risk use for its Warrick Works. A remedy modifying the price term of the contract in light of the circumstances which upset the price formula will better preserve the purposes and expectations of the parties than any other remedy. Such a remedy is essential to avoid injustice in this case.

During the trial the parties agreed that a modification of the price term to require Essex to pay ALCOA the ceiling price specified in the contract would be an appropriate remedy if the Court held for ALCOA. The Court understands from the parties that ALCOA will continue to suffer a substantial but smaller out of pocket loss at this price level. But ALCOA has not argued that the ceiling price term is subject to the same basic assumptions about risk limitation as the indexed price term. Accordingly the Court adopts the ceiling price term as part of the remedy it grants to ALCOA.

The Court must recognize, though, that before the contract expires economic changes may make this remedy excessively favorable to ALCOA. To deal with that possibility, the Court must frame a remedy which is suitable to the expectation and to the original agreement of the parties. A price fixed at the contract ceiling could redound to ALCOA's great profit and to Essex's great loss in changed circumstances. Therefore the Court adopts the following remedial scheme. For the duration of the contract the price for each pound of aluminum converted by ALCOA shall be the lesser of the current Price A or Price B indicated below.

Price A shall be the contract ceiling price computed periodically as specified in the contract.

Price B shall be the greater of the current Price B1 or Price B2. *Price B1* shall be the price specified in the contract, computed according to the terms of the contract. *Price B2* shall be that price which yields ALCOA a profit of one cent per pound of aluminum converted. This will generally yield Essex the benefit of its favorable bargain, and it will reduce ALCOA's disappointment to the limit of risk the parties expected in making the contract. The profit shall be computed using the same accounting methods used for the production of plaintiff's exhibit 431. The profit and the resulting price shall be computed once each calendar quarter, as soon after the close of the quarter as the necessary information may be

---

[90] [21] The remedial provisions of the new Restatement agree. Section 272(2) declares that a court may frame a remedy by supplying a term which is reasonable in the circumstances to avoid injustice. The same provision appears in §158(2).

assembled. When Price B2 applies, ALCOA shall bill Essex periodically, as specified in the contract at the price specified at the last quarterly price computation. Essex shall pay those bills according to the payment terms previously observed by the parties. When the next quarterly price computation is completed, that price shall be applied retroactively to the aluminum converted during the previous quarter. ALCOA shall refund any surplus payment by Essex upon the computation of the price or shall bill Essex for any additional money due.

ALCOA shall keep detailed records of the pertinent costs, indices and computations used to calculate Prices A, B1 and B2 and shall preserve them for two years beyond the termination of the contract. ALCOA shall send Essex, in the manner and at the times specified in the contract, the price information called for in the contract, as well as a quarterly statement of Price B2 whether or not that price then applies. The statement of Price B2 need not specify the elements from which it was calculated. . . .

CONCLUSION

This case is novel. The sums of money involved are huge. The Court has been considerably aided by the thorough and commendable work of all of the counsel who have participated in the case. There remains a need for a few concluding remarks concerning the theory of Count One of this case and its limitations.

One of the principal themes in the development of commercial contract doctrines since the 1920s has been the need for a body of law compatible with responsible commercial practices and understandings. The old spirit of the law manifest in *Parradine v. Jane, supra*, is gone. The new spirit of commercial law in Indiana and elsewhere appears in the Uniform Commercial Code, in new developments of implied covenants, and in the new Restatement.[91]

At stake in this suit is the future of a commercially important device—the long term contract. Such contracts are common in many fields of commerce. Mineral leases, building and ground leases, and long term coal sales agreements are just three examples of such contracts. If the law refused an appropriate remedy when a prudently drafted long term contract goes badly awry, the risks attending such contracts would increase. Prudent business people would avoid using this sensible business tool. Or they would needlessly suffer the delay and expense of ever more detailed and sophisticated drafting in an attempt to approximate by agreement what the law could readily furnish by general rule. . . .

Corporate managers are fiduciaries. Law, founded on good sense, requires them to act with care in the management of businesses owned by other people. Attention to risk limitation is essential to the fiduciary duty of corporate managers. Courts must consider the fiduciary duty of management and the established practice of risk limitation in interpreting contracts and in the application of con-

---

[91] [34] The essential unity of the new spirit of commercial contract law appears in the recurring adoption of new statutory principles from the Code into the body of the common law by the Restatement and by the courts. See J. Murray, Intention Over Terms: An Exploration of UCC 2-207 and New Section 60, Restatement of Contracts, 37 Fordham L. Rev. 317 (1969); J. Murray, Behaviorism Under the Uniform Commercial Code, 51 Ore. L. Rev. 269, 272 (1972); J. Murray, Under the Spreading Analogy of Article 2 of the Uniform Commercial Code, 39 Fordham L. Rev. 447 (1971).

tract doctrines such as mistake, frustration and impracticability. Corporate managers should not gamble with corporate funds. Generally they do not. Courts should not presume that they do, nor should they frame rules founded on such a presumption. Instead, courts should be alert to indications that the parties to a commercial contract sought to limit their risks, and should interpret the contracts and frame remedies to protect that purpose.

Parev Products Co. v. I. Rokeach & Sons, Inc., supra, decided by Judges Clark, Frank and Learned Hand, illustrated an aspect of this point. There Parev, the plaintiff, by contract gave the defendant the exclusive right to produce and to market its product, Nyafat, a cooking oil, for fifty years for a specified royalty. The defendant had the option to cancel the contract at any time for a fee. The plaintiff agreed not to market the product or any similar product during the contract, and the defendant agreed not to market the product or any similar product after the end of the contract. In 1939 competitors began to sell Crisco and Spry, white semi-solid cooking oils which reduced the sales of the plaintiff's oil. The defendant responded to the falling sales by introducing a new product of its own, Kea, similar to Crisco and Spry. The plaintiff sued to enjoin this further competition with its product. Since the express negative covenants did not forbid this competition, the plaintiff argued that the court should imply a negative covenant to forbid it.

The court rejected the defendant's argument that only covenants intended by the parties may be implied. The court noted the then traditional "reluctance of courts to admit that they were to a considerable extent 'remaking' a contract in situations where it seemed necessary and appropriate to do so." 124 F.2d at 149. The court acknowledged that a discernible intent of the parties should control the case, but it found no sufficient indication of intent respecting this problem:

> Of course, where intent though obscure, is nevertheless discernible, it must be followed; but a certain sophistication must be recognized—if we are to approach the matter frankly—where we are dealing with changed circumstances, fifteen years later, with respect to a contract which does not touch this exact point and which has at most only points of departure for more or less pressing analogies. *Id.*

Thus the question of whether to imply some sort of covenant to protect the plaintiff did not rest on the parties' intent. It rested on the status, expectations and needs of the parties to preserve the mutual benefit of the long term contract under changed circumstances. . . .

The court protected the "status" of both parties by implying a term requiring the defendant to compensate the plaintiff for royalties lost due to competition with the defendant's new product.

The court gave close attention to the legitimate business aims of the parties, to their purpose of avoiding the risks of great losses, and to the need to frame a remedy to preserve the essence of the agreement. To that extent the decision exemplifies the new spirit of contract law.

This attitude toward contract law and toward the work of the courts will disturb some people even at this late date. It strains against half-remembered truths and remembered half-truths from the venerated first year course in Contract Law.

The core of the trouble lies in the hoary maxim that the courts will not make a contract for the parties. The maxim requires three replies. First, courts today can indeed make contracts for the parties. Given certain minimal indicators of an intent to contract, the courts are today directed to impose on the parties the necessary specific provisions to complete the process. See U.C.C. §§ 2-204, 2-207, 2-208; U.L.T.A. §§ 2-202-2-204. Second, a distinction has long been noted between judicial imposition of initial terms and judicial interpretations and implications of terms to resolve disputes concerning contracts the parties have made for themselves. The maxim bears less weight when it is applied to dispute resolution than it does when it is applied to questions of contract formation. This case is plainly one of dispute resolution. Third, the maxim rests on two sensible notions: (1) Liability under the law of contract rests on assent, not imposition; (2) Judges are seldom able business men; they seldom have the information, ability, or time to do a good job of contracting for the parties. Neither of these notions applies here. The parties have made their own contract. The Court's role here is limited to framing a remedy for a problem they did not foresee and provide for. And while the Court willingly concedes that the managements of ALCOA and Essex are better able to conduct their business than is the Court, in this dispute the court has information from hindsight far superior to that which the parties had when they made their contract. The parties may both be better served by an informed judicial decision based on the known circumstances than by a decision wrenched from words of the contract which were not chosen with a prevision of today's circumstances. The Court gladly concedes that the parties might today evolve a better working arrangement by negotiation than the Court can impose. But they have not done so, and a rule that the Court may not act would have the perverse effect of discouraging the parties from resolving this dispute or future disputes on their own. Only a rule which permits judicial action of the kind the Court has taken in this case will provide a desirable practical incentive for businessmen to negotiate their own resolution to problems which arise in the life of long term contracts. [92]

Finally, the Court notes that this case presents a problem of the appropriate legal response to problems of inflation. There are many long term contracts extant where inflation has upset the basic equivalence of the agreement. Courts will increasingly have to attend to problems like the present one. . . .

The limitation of judicial relief to cases where the parties evidence a desire to limit their risks, where one party suffers severe out of pocket losses not adequately foreseen and provided for by the parties seems adequate to prevent a general disruption of commercial life by inflation. This limitation also seems generally compatible with the fair needs and understanding of responsible businessmen. Little more can be asked of the courts in the development of the law.

The foregoing shall constitute findings of fact and conclusions of law as required by Federal Rule of Civil Procedure 52(a). An appropriate Order will issue.

---

[92] [35] The Court is aware of the practical incentive to negotiation which lies in the delay, expense and uncertainty of litigation. This case shows that at times these burdens are insufficient to prompt settlements.

NOTES AND QUESTIONS

1. *Judge Teitelbaum's background*: Judge Teitelbaum graduated from the University of Pittsburgh Law School in 1940. He was an FBI Special Agent and United States Attorney for the Western District of Pennsylvania. When he wrote his opinion in the *ALCOA* case, he was an Adjunct Professor at the Duquesne University Law School in Pittsburgh and a member of the American Law Institute. Perhaps he was more ready than many federal judges to consider the innovations of the Restatement (Second) of Contracts.

2. *Essex brief on appeal to the Third Circuit*: The case was appealed to the United States Court of Appeals for the Third Circuit. Lawyers for Essex Group argued:

> . . . the decision endangers the future of long term contracts. It does this by replacing the escalated fixed price formula in a long term contract involving in excess of $300,000,000 with a new formula drafted by the court and never discussed or intended by the parties, essentially converting the contract into a cost plus agreement. . . .

> . . . [Essex] contends that the trial court's decision is without precedent in American jurisprudence. It has charted a course which, unless reversed, will henceforth inextricably embroil courts in the constant supervision and administration of commercial contracts. For reasons hereinafter set forth, both the applicable law and the largely undisputed facts in this case require that the trial court's judgment be reversed and that judgment be entered for . . . Essex Group, Inc.

Essex charged that the escalated fixed price formula used in the contract had been developed by ALCOA's Department of Economic Analysis and Planning. According to Essex, ALCOA used the formula because it believed that its costs at the Warrick, Indiana plant were under control and the wholesale price index would increase faster than ALCOA's actual costs of aluminum production. Thus, the formula selected provided an opportunity to increase profits in a way a cost plus contract could not. During the period from 1960 when the plant opened to 1967 when the contract with the Essex Group was signed, while the wholesale price index was increasing, the actual cost of producing aluminum at the Warrick facility had declined dramatically. Moreover, ALCOA did not want to use an escalator clause based on actual costs because then it would have to reveal its costs to Essex (both a customer and a competitor) and questions of cost accounting could lead to disputes.

First, consider the assertions Essex Group's lawyers made about the trial court's opinion. Do they describe fairly Judge Teitelbaum's opinion? Second, consider the brief as an exercise in rhetoric. Note the use of the term "rewrite" and the phrase "without precedent." The Restatement (Second) of Contracts provisions are ignored here. Why? How many strands of classic contract ideology can you identify? Notice, too, the phrase "embroil courts in the constant supervision and administration of commercial contracts," with its image of burdening the judiciary.

3. *ALCOA's brief on appeal to the Third Circuit*: ALCOA's lawyers, supporting Judge Teitelbaum's opinion, responded as follows:

First, Alcoa proved a sufficient underlying agreement for reformation under Indiana law. . . .

Second, the fact situation here fits exactly with the Restatement 2d of Contracts definition of mutual mistake of fact (§ 152) for which the remedy of reformation (§§ 297 & 300) is provided. Professor Farnsworth, the Reporter of the Restatement 2d of Contracts, presented an oral brief at the trial, which brief is included in the transcript . . . Professor Farnsworth testified:

> In my opinion, it is entirely possible that Alcoa could show at the trial that both parties at the time of contracting made a mistake as to the fact that the wholesale price index was then suitable for an escalation clause in an energy-intensive contract. An analogy by way of example would be to a mistake of two parties to a contract using specified equipment that the equipment was suitable to the task.

Alcoa proved, and the trial court found, the facts to be as Professor Farnsworth suggested the evidence might show.

If there is any difference between the provisions in the Restatement 2d of Contracts on mutual mistake of fact and the Indiana cases cited (Essex relies on the 1896 *Citizens National Bank* case), then certainly one would expect the Supreme Court of Indiana now to follow the Restatement as it has repeatedly done.

Third, the trial court cited Restatement 2d of Contracts, § 300(2)[93] which allows a court to equitably adjust or supply a term that is reasonable in the circumstances to avoid injustice. As Professor Farnsworth stated in his oral brief, the Restatement has been liberalized to permit the formulation of a remedy to do justice and prevent an unconscionable result. . . .

Restatement 2d of Contracts § 300(2) which is entitled "RELIEF INCLUDING RESTITUTION; SUPPLYING A TERM" states at page 306 of Tentative Draft No. 14:

> In any case governed by the rules stated in this Chapter, if those rules together with the rules stated in prospective Chapter 16 will not avoid injustice, *the court may grant relief on such terms as justice requires* including protection of the parties' reliance interests. (Emphasis added).

Thus, Restatement 2d of Contracts § 300(2) constitutes an alternative theory of law for the trial court's remedy, even if reformation were somehow ruled inappropriate.

ALCOA's lawyers also responded to Essex Group's charge concerning the reasons the formula was used by saying: "the WPI was selected to meet Essex's desire for an objective and easily administered index to reflect ALCOA's Warrick non-labor costs, not to increase ALCOA's profits, and the trial court observing the testimony found it to be the fact."

---

[93] This is now § 158 in the final version of the Restatement.

Presumably, the *ALCOA* case was being tried under the law of Indiana as applied by federal courts. Whatever the merits of Judge Teitelbaum's opinion, did the ALCOA lawyers convince you that Indiana would adopt the new Restatement (Second) of Contracts approach? How would you argue this point for ALCOA or for Essex Group? As we have said several times in these materials, federal judges often develop state law dealing with contracts and statutes related to contracts problems. Federal judges must divine what a state court would do if it faced the problem. Yet diversity of citizenship jurisdiction keeps state courts from getting an opportunity to offer many modern clues.

4. *The outcome of the case*: The parties settled the case after oral argument to the United States Court of Appeals for the Third Circuit. Judge Arlin M. Adams, a member of the Third Circuit Court of Appeals, requested the parties to attend a conciliation session between the time briefs were filed and oral argument was scheduled, a relatively unusual procedure.

Following oral argument, ALCOA indicated an interest in settling the case. The parties conferred at length, with ALCOA giving ground in its demands. It appears that the case was settled on the basis that the original contract would continue in effect until December 31, 1981; that during the balance of the original time of the contract, ALCOA would sell at a more favorable price; and that ALCOA would extend the time of the contract for a period of five years on a favorable price basis, albeit not as favorable as during the contract period.

Judge Adams settlement conference might not have promoted a settlement. Something might have happened during oral argument to cause ALCOA to reevaluate its position, or it might have been waiting for what it thought was the right moment to strike a deal. There had been settlement discussions from time to time over a period of several years.

Why didn't the parties settle earlier and save all the investment in lawyering and judicial time? Did Judge Teitelbaum's opinion, work on the briefs, and the process before the Third Circuit serve some purpose?

5. *Scholarly criticism of the case*: The case provoked contracts scholars into print. The late Professor John Dawson was highly critical of the *ALCOA* decision. He said that the *ALCOA* approach "is the treatment that is now normally given frustrated contracts [in West Germany], a treatment described with the hope that our own courts can be dissuaded from a course so disastrous for the coherence and rationality of our law of contract." [94]

Professor Sheldon Halpern[95] notes that courts have not followed the *ALCOA* decision. He argues that Judge Teitelbaum's decision did not rest on an accepted theory of contract law. While the court rejected the often fictional search for the parties' intentions, all it could point to was the need to relieve hardship. Judge Teitelbaum went too far, too soon and with too little.

---

[94] See Dawson, *Judicial Revision of Frustrated Contracts: Germany*, 63 B.U. L. Rev. 1039 (1983); Dawson, *Judicial Revision of Frustrated Contracts: The United States*, 64 B.U. L. Rev. 1 (1984).

[95] *Applicability of the Doctrine of Commercial Impracticability: Searching for "The Wisdom of Solomon,"* 135 U. Pa. L. Rev. 1123 (1987).

Judge, and formerly Professor, Richard Posner offered the following comments in *Northern Indiana Public Service Co. v. Carbon County Coal Co.*:[96]

Since impossibility and related doctrines are devices for shifting risk in accordance with the parties' presumed intentions, which are to minimize the costs of contract performance, one of which is the disutility created by risk, they have no place when the contract explicitly assigns a particular risk to one party or the other. . . . *[A] fixed-price contract is an explicit assignment of the risk of market price increases to the seller and the risk of market price decreases to the buyer*, and the assignment of the latter risk to the buyer is even clearer where, as in this case, the contract places a floor under price but allows for escalation. If, as is also the case here, the buyer forecasts the market incorrectly and therefore finds himself locked into a disadvantageous contract, he has only himself to blame and so cannot shift the risk back to the seller by invoking impossibility or related doctrines. [Emphasis added].

6. *Scholarly defense of adjustment*: Several other scholars have defended judicial adjustment of contracts. For example, Professor Leon Trakman argues "[t]he need for a functional category of remedial adjustments, however, becomes more pressing when an all-or-nothing principle of law governs nonperformance and produces neither fairness nor economic efficiency."[97]

Professor Robert A. Hillman argues that a supplier is entitled to adjustment of a contractual obligation in at least some situations.[98] Hillman says the objective theory and interpretation seeking the reasonable expectations of the parties tell us whether there is a duty to adjust.[99] He points out that some contracts expressly provide for adjustment when the cost of performance is grossly inequitable. Such express provisions are common in some industries. Moreover, even if a supply contract contains no express agreement to adjust, the situation when the parties made the deal may show that they intended adjustments in light of changed circumstances. That they say nothing about adjustments in their written contract does not necessarily establish anything. Drafting a clause for what they see as unclear risks isn't worth the effort. Trade custom or the course of dealing or performance may establish a duty to adjust. Indeed, a party's duty of good faith may create an obligation to adjust a contract in light of changed circumstances.

Still, Professor Hillman recognizes that not every contract raises a duty to adjust if something goes awry. Large one-time deals involving standardized commodities usually involve assumption of the risk of market shifts. The parties may see adjustment as a matter of comity rather than legal obligation. Buyer may adjust seller's obligation as a favor which seller will return in the future. The parties may bargain about rising prices and shortages, and this suggests that the written contract reflects their risk assumption. However, even when this is true, they may

---

[96] 799 F.2d 265, 278 (7th Cir. 1986).

[97] *Winner Take Some: Loss Sharing and Commercial Impracticability*, 69 Minn. L. Rev. 471 (1985).

[98] Hillman, *Court Adjustment of Long-Term Contracts: An Analysis Under Modern Contract Law*, 1987 Duke L.J. 1.

[99] Contrast Professor Hillman's view with that of Judge Posner quoted above. Recall, too, the debates about the parol evidence rule. Do we read the words on paper or do we look at these words in full context seeking the parties' real deal?

not intend their written provision to govern an extreme shift in the market. Hillman recognizes that one of the most difficult questions is how much disruption triggers the duty to adjust.

Hillman also argues that parties may leave a gap in their agreement despite the appearance of settling their obligations in a formal writing. The evidence may not establish a duty to make adjustments, but a court may conclude that reasonable parties would not have expected the supplier to act as insurer. Courts could fill this gap in their agreement by finding a duty to adjust.

Are there any standards or must courts fly blind if they find a duty to adjust? Hillman argues there are standards. Courts may find that parties did not intend to allow a supplier to raise prices without a corresponding increase in its actual costs. They may find that parties did not intend buyers to be able to take advantage of a drastic market shift. Often they do not intend to allow buyers to raise their prices to third parties while insisting on seller's performance at a pre-inflationary price. Furthermore, courts can look to similar supply contracts made or adjusted under the changed conditions that provoked the problem. They can consider settlement offers. They can find large windfalls to be unjust enrichment. They can hold the supplier responsible to deliver at the old price only long enough to allow a buyer to cover its reliance losses based on this old price.

Professor Richard Speidel attempts to rationalize the approach, if not the result, of the court in the *ALCOA* case.

[C]an a case be made for imposing a duty on the advantaged party to accept a "fair and equitable" adjustment proposal made by the disadvantaged party? If so, what remedies are appropriate? Keeping the *ALCOA* facts in mind, a tentative case can be made that does not convert the law of contracts into a pervasive duty to be altruistic.

First, the disadvantaged party must propose a modification that would be enforceable if accepted by the advantaged party. Under the Restatement (Second), [§ 89] this occurs if the disrupted contract is not "fully performed on either side" and if the modification is "fair and equitable in view of circumstances not anticipated by the parties when the contract was made." The changed circumstances are similar to but less than those required to discharge a contract for impracticability. This first requirement both neutralizes any opportunism by the disadvantaged party, e.g., duress, and affirms that agreed adjustments are preferred—that contract is available to resolve the dilemma and has been employed by the disadvantaged party.

Second, it must be clear that the disadvantaged party did not assume the risk of the unanticipated event by agreement, or under the test stated in the U.C.C. in section 2-615(a), or otherwise. If the disadvantaged party did assume the risk, then the advantaged party has no duty to accept any proposed modification. The risk assumption question is complicated, and the answer will probably not be clear at the time that the adjustment is proposed. Why should the advantaged party be held to reject at his peril? Because it is in this precise situation—where there are substantial unbargained-for gains and losses caused by unanticipated events—that a case for the duty to rescue can be made. In this setting where the risk of changed circumstances has not been allocated to either party, a refusal to adjust by the advantaged party leaves all of the loss on the disadvantaged party and permits the advantaged party to salt away all of the gains. Short of discharging the contract and leaving the parties to restitution, a duty to adjust is necessary to avoid opportunism.

Thus, imposing the duty here is consistent with emerging notions of good faith performance and *ALCOA's* second peg in the "new" spirit, loss avoidance. More importantly, it is an imposition with little damage to the requirement of consent in contract law. . . .

Last, this conclusion is bolstered by what might be the imperatives of an emerging theory of relational contract law. In *ALCOA*, the parties, at the time of contracting, were unable adequately to deal with certain changed circumstances over the duration of a seventeen-year contract. Yet preserving the contract was important to the parties and to third parties dependent upon its performance but not represented in the litigation. Ian Macneil has argued that in situations such as this there are relational norms that the contract should be preserved and conflict harmonized by adjustment. These norms put a high premium upon developing mechanisms for adjustment over time and good faith efforts to adjust in the light of change. Thus, if in an ALCOA-type case, the court concludes that the disadvantaged party is entitled to "some relief" but not discharge, and the advantaged party has refused to accept a reasonable adjustment in light of risks that the disadvantaged party did not assume, relational theory also supports a court imposed adjustment to preserve the contract, to adjust the price and to avoid the twin devils of un-bargained for hardship and unjust enrichment.[100]

7. *The relational exchange approach to contracts*: The economist Victor Goldberg has written about price adjustment in long-term contracts.[101] He notes that business people often use "gross inequity" clauses in some long-term contracts. Under these clauses, parties leave to an arbitrator or judge the decision to adjust the contract or discharge the parties when performance would cause a gross inequity. Absent such clauses, courts will have to decide whether ever to grant any relief, what changes are sufficient to justify judicial action, and what relief they should grant.

Goldberg considers when parties might want a third party to make adjustments or award discharges. He says that the case for intervention is stronger "when the costs of a price dispute are high and the costs of settlement would be reduced by giving the disadvantaged party the right to call upon the court to revise the contract." There might be few such cases.

Goldberg points out that businesses have reason to use some form of price adjustment mechanism in their contracts. "Firms do not generally enter into multi-year contracts because of their concern for the future course of prices. Rather, they enter into the agreements to achieve the benefits of cooperation." Price ad-

---

[100] *See* Speidel, *The New Spirit of Contract*, 2 J. L. & Com. 193, 206-208 (1982); Speidel, *Court-Imposed Price Adjustments Under Long-Term Supply Contracts*, 76 Nw. U. L. Rev. 369 (1981). Reprinted with permission.

[101] Goldberg, *Price Adjustment in Long-Term Contracts*, 1985 Wis. L. Rev. 527. Copyright © The University of Wisconsin.

justment clauses often are used when the contract calls for a complex product constantly redefined over the life of the contract. Adjustment also discourages the parties from wasting assets. Without adjustment, the below-market price of an input might cause a buyer to use too much of it. In addition, an adjustment clause reduces the likelihood that a party who had been a big loser on a contractual "bet" will try to recapture losses by minimal performance, retaliate by failing to cooperate, make threats to breach, or search for arguments to minimize the nature of the obligation.

Those who drafted the contract in *ALCOA v. Essex* used a price adjustment mechanism, but it didn't work. What kind of mistake was this, and should it warrant relief? Lawyers often find it hard to fashion an effective acceptable price adjustment mechanism. Price indices are the easiest to use, but often in a long-term contract there is no unique external market price to use.

Goldberg notes that in the *ALCOA* case the failure of the price index to measure the change in fuel prices accounted for only about ten to twelve cents of the difference between the contract price and the market price for aluminum in 1979. The balance of the difference may have reflected demand-induced, rather than cost-driven, market price increases. The contract did not track changing demand conditions and the demand for aluminum was soaring in the late 1970s. Moreover, the contract was not designed to adjust to large changes in the overall price level. "Sixty percent of the initial contract price (the demand charge plus the fixed 'profit') was unadjusted for the life of the contract." Nonetheless, Goldberg says it is a close question whether ALCOA should have bargained to index the remaining 60% of costs. He says that parties do not necessarily confront the same external price, and this makes it hard to use a price index based on aluminum prices. It is as if they are dealing in two different, imperfectly connected, markets.

> Alcoa's opportunity cost is the net price it could receive by using the Warrick capacity to produce ingot for export to other customers. Essex's opportunity cost is the price of delivered aluminum ingot. There is no a priori reason to believe that these will be close to each other. However, for an index to work it is not necessary that the prices be close, only that they move together over time. Whether these two opportunity costs (and the market price for aluminum ingot) move together over time is an empirical question which I intend to explore in a later paper. [102]

If we assume that the parties would have had difficulty finding an acceptable price adjustment mechanism, was the burden on ALCOA great enough to makes its performance impracticable? Goldberg argues that in the *ALCOA* case, the court assumed something about future costs and prices and concluded that AL-COA stood to lose about $75 million.

> What does Alcoa lose if it must fulfill the contract? It loses the chance to sell aluminum to someone else. That is the true measure of the loss, and in this case it is considerably greater than the figure cited by the judge. In

the year the suit was brought the loss was over thirty cents per pound, over $20 million.

However, Goldberg says that we cannot define a magic number or percentage to allow us to judge whether relief should be granted. Even a very large difference between the market and contract prices for a standardized commodity might have little adverse effect on the expected value of the contract. On the other hand, at times a small difference might generate considerable joint costs and make revision valuable. However, if courts make relief too easy to get, this will generate additional joint costs as it will affect performance and demands for renegotiations. Part of the problem is that when the opportunity costs of buyer and seller differ, it is not clear how an arbitrator should set a new price.

Professor Thomas Palay commented on Goldberg's article. [103] Palay praised Goldberg's approach to the problem, but Palay cautioned that we cannot focus on the written document to tell us whether the parties in a long-term contract could benefit from or expect price adjustments. "Parties who have, or anticipate, strong relational ties with their contracting opposites are not particularly worried about initial terms of agreement."

Palay then discusses Oliver Williamson's approach to transactional governance structures. Williamson argues that three variables determine structural characteristics: (1) the degree to which uncertainty is present; (2) the frequency of exchange, and (3) the extent to which exchanges are supported by idiosyncratic capital that cannot be devoted elsewhere easily.

Williamson's third variable is particularly important. Those in idiosyncratic exchanges can protect themselves by demanding a price that compensates them for marginal costs and includes an insurance component covering opportunistic behavior. They also can gain credible commitments not to act opportunistically. This is done by the mutual exchange of hostages—investments of capital assets that will be destroyed if the contract falls apart.

Palay looks at the problems in *ALCOA v. Essex*:

> Alcoa's "hostage" was that portion of the Warwick capacity that was added for, or dedicated to, Essex. Alcoa might have believed that Essex had posted a similar hostage when it placed its fabricating facility near the Warwick smelter. The value of the fabricating facility, built specifically to receive aluminum from the Warwick plant, would diminish if the contractual relation failed. Alternatively, if Essex helped finance Alcoa's dedicated capacity, the arrangement could have led Alcoa to believe that Essex became tied to the aluminum manufacturer. After all, Essex could have lost its investment in Warwick if the contract failed.
>
> If these were the hostages Essex posted, imagining why they proved inadequate to force renegotiation of the contract is easy. Essex could receive aluminum from plenty of other sources if Alcoa were to breach, but any other source would entail additional transportation costs. This meant that as a hostage the plant was only worth the difference between its use

---

[103] Palay, *A Contract Does Not a Contract Make*, 1985 Wis. L. Rev. 561. Copyright © The University of Wisconsin.

in fabricating Warwick Aluminum and its use in fabricating aluminum that had to be transported from elsewhere. That is, as a hostage Essex's plant ranked right up there with giving the wicked king your lazy, shift-less third cousin. Using any of the financing aspects of the arrangement as a hostage would be similarly inadequate. Alcoa's pockets were simply too deep. Essex would know that Alcoa was never really in danger of de-faulting on the "loan."

Thus, under this scenario, Alcoa's problem was not so much a "mis-take" concerning the price term, but rather a mistake about the impor-tance that Essex would place on the preservation of the relationship. Admittedly, many of my observations are little more than speculation— but they are reasonable hypotheses that require the researcher to look be-yond the formal documents for confirmation. [104]

Assume Palay's speculation proved to be right. What significance would it have for our appraisal of Judge Teitelbaum's opinion? Would such a mistake fit into traditional notions of mistake or impossibility? Does it suggest what we should do?

8. *One economist offers a presumption as to the real deal:* Victor Gold-berg[105] argues:

Regardless of how the doctrine is labeled, courts, when considering a plea to excuse performance, should be constrained by the fundamental question: what would the parties have chosen? I will argue that, as a general rule, parties would not agree to excuse performance because of changed market conditions (neither supply nor demand shocks). The fact that market prices have doubled or tripled would be irrelevant. Parties are more likely to excuse performance if the supervening events adversely effect the costs of performing this particular contract for reasons that are essentially unrelated to overall market condi-tions. . . .

The crucial point is this. If the occurrence of a *force majeure* condition is not correlated with market conditions, the expected change in market price is zero, and therefore, the benefits anticipated at the contract formation stage from holding the promisor liable are likely to be low. However, if the seller re-fuses to perform because events subsequent to the formation of the contract have shown that the contract price is too low, the buyer does suffer. If the seller could perform, but would prefer not to, we can reasonably infer that the reason is that the contract price is too low; the seller could do better selling elsewhere. The changed conditions affect the market for the good or service involved. There is a widespread drought, the Suez Canal closes, etc. Discharg-ing the contract in this instance carries a greater cost. If a seller could be ex-cused simply because the contract price was below the market price, the sub-stantial benefits from entering into a contract in a timely manner are sacrificed. While this sacrifice might be acceptable in some cases, it is clear that the costs

[104] *Id.* at 564.
[105] *Impossibility and Related Excuses*, J. Inst'l & Theoretical Econ. Vol. 144, 100-116 (1988).

of excusing a seller's performance when the contract price is too low are greater than excusing its performance in the event of a fire or other act of God.

Goldberg does note: "This is not to say that parties would never adjust the contract price. Price concessions in the face of changed market conditions are commonplace. But the grantor of the concession often expects a quid pro quo, either express (e.g., an increase in the term of the contract) or implied (e.g., enhanced good will). The grantor, that is, maintains the right to make (or not make) price concessions." [106]

9. *A note on the law and economics notes*: The two previous notes both rely on the commentary of an economist, and draw to some extent on the vocabulary of economics. This can be frustrating for those with little or no training in economics. A great deal of legal scholarship in the last 15 or 20 years has drawn on economic analysis. It is often controversial. Many reject the analysis and assert that it is not to be trusted because it contains concealed substantive or ideological biases. Others reject it by suggesting that it is not to be trusted because it is incomplete, but is presented as if it were not. Either or both of these critiques may be right (or wrong). But it is *not*, it seems to the authors, appropriate to reject the analysis because we are unable to understand it—though that is a very human tendency. Such a rejection would be akin to an English speaker asserting that a poem, or novel, is no good because it wasn't written in English. We offer this note to acknowledge the discomfort which the law and economics notes might cause some. As non-economists ourselves, we often share your discomfort. But we do need to be aware of, and take seriously, the accounts of our subject matter which are presented to us, and which often seem to illuminate the issue, even if they are difficult and make us uncomfortable. To the extent that there are those among this book's readers who would offer suggestions about improving its clarity, we welcome such comments.

10. *The role of jurists in the American system*: Professor Farnsworth, the Reporter for Restatement (Second) of Contracts, gave Judge Teitelbaum an oral brief that favored *ALCOA*. Interestingly, Professor Dawson tells us in his article on the United States' approach to judicial revision of frustrated contracts, "counsel for Essex . . . had requested me to comment on the briefs that were being prepared for the appeal by Essex. I had thus had considerably earlier an opportunity to form a highly adverse opinion of the trial court's decision." Dawson calls the *ALCOA* opinion a "bizarre solution." Had the appeal gone forward, the Third Circuit might have had to choose between the views of Farnsworth and the Restatement (Second) and Dawson. The late Professor Dawson was a professor emeritus at Harvard Law School, and a recognized expert in contracts, comparative law and legal history. Thus, each side could have pointed to a distinguished academic in its corner.

In what sense, if at all, are Professors Farnsworth, Dawson, Hillman, Halpern, Speidel, Trakman or the authors of the *Contracts: Law in Action* "experts" on what contract law ought to be? Should we fashion some mechanism so courts could call on contracts professors for assistance in major cases? Do you see any

---

[106] *Id.* at n.3.

problem with Professor Farnsworth giving an "oral brief" to the court but being sponsored by ALCOA or Professor Dawson consulting with the Essex Group lawyers on their briefs in the case?

11. *Is ALCOA the law or is it only a case to provoke law professors?* In *United States v. Southwestern Electric Cooperative,* [107] the court commented that the *ALCOA* decision had faded into obscurity. A party cannot get out of a contract because of an error in judgment about the construction costs of a project. However, in *Unihealth v. U.S. Healthcare, Inc.,* [108] the court placed great reliance on *ALCOA.* Health maintenance organizations had contracted with a hospital for services to their members. The contract called for discounts from the hospital's usual rates. However, the hospital sought to limit the amounts of these discounts. It provided: "If the overall discount for all Inpatients exceeds 40% during a calendar year, U.S. Healthcare will reimburse Meadowlands Hospital and Medical Center monies beyond the 40% discount." However, "the term 'discount,' specifically, the lodestar from which the discount should be assessed, is not referred to or defined anywhere in the Agreement." The contract was negotiated in 1991. The State of New Jersey had a regulatory scheme, the Diagnostic Related Groups (DRG) system, which had been in place since 1979. It required all hospitals to bill for inpatient services at prices set by the New Jersey Department of Health. The state repealed the DRG system, effective January 1, 1993. The hospital had provided services in 1992 and 1993, but the parties never were able to agree on how to calculate the limit on the amount of discounts once the DRG was repealed.

The court decided that the repeal of the DRG system frustrated the contract as written. This repeal was not a risk that was assumed by either party. The court relied on *Aluminum Corporation of America v. Essex Group*, as showing its power to fashion a reasonable term to substitute for the one that the parties drafted which no longer could be applied. The court appointed a special master to act as a mediator. He was to try to help the parties reach an agreement about the compensation due. If agreement could not be reached, the master was to formulate a pricing system for medical services comparable to the former DRG system. Once this system was in place, then the discount clause could be applied.

---

[107] 869 F.2d 310 (7th Cir. 1989).
[108] 14 F. Supp. 2d 623 (D. N.J. 1998).

IN THE MATTER OF WESTINGHOUSE ELECTRIC CORP.
URANIUM CONTRACTS LITIGATION;
FLORIDA POWER AND LIGHT CO. V.
WESTINGHOUSE ELECTRIC CORP.

United States District Court, Eastern District of Virginia
517 F. Supp. 440 (1981)

MERHIGE, J. The instant issue arises out of an alleged breach by the defendant Westinghouse Electric Corporation (Westinghouse) of a contract executed by the parties in May of 1966 with an effective date of November 15, 1965, for the long term fueling of two nuclear steam supply systems manufactured by Westinghouse for . . . [Florida Power and Light Company]. The contract in issue was entered into as a consequence of plaintiff having, in the same year, agreed to purchase from defendant two nuclear steam supply systems for the generation of electric power. . . .

Florida seeks, in addition to monetary damages, an order requiring Westinghouse to comply with Section 27(a)(2) of the contract of May 1966 which reads as follows:

Section 27. Scope

(a) Westinghouse will: . . .

(2) Remove the irradiated fuel from the plant site and dispose of it as Westinghouse sees fit. . . .

On September 2, 1975 Westinghouse advised Florida by letter that it had no plans to remove the irradiated (spent) fuel from Florida's plant site, and this lawsuit followed.

The evidence reveals that in 1965 the nuclear industry was at an early stage in its evolution. In 1964 legislation had been enacted permitting, for the first time, private ownership of uranium, a necessary component of nuclear power. The sale of nuclear steam supply systems was in its infancy, and Westinghouse, a manufacturer of such systems, was most anxious to enter into a contract with Florida for its proposed plants designated as Turkey Point Units 3 and 4, located in Dade County, Florida. At the time, there were no nuclear plants operating in the south. Additionally, the opportunity was unique; for Florida contemplated the construction of two power plants at the same location. It was during a period when fossil fuels were relatively inexpensive, capital costs were down, and adequate gas, oil and other fuels were available. While the potential for nuclear powered plants for the production of electricity was considered bright, reactor sales were not abundant and few negotiations for nuclear power plants were in progress. Additionally, in the view of many, uncertainty existed during the period of 1965-66 as to whether nuclear power could compete economically in most areas of the country with fossil fuels.

The securing of a contract by Westinghouse with Florida for the sale of two pressurized water reactors was viewed by Westinghouse not only as a vote of confidence, but as an incentive for other utilities to seriously consider the use of nuclear power.

Florida, at the time, had no expertise in nuclear power, a fact well known to Westinghouse. Indeed, in March of 1965 Florida notified Westinghouse that it (Florida) lacked the manpower and knowledge needed to develop specifications and evaluate proposals for a nuclear plant. This lack of expertise resulted in Florida's continued insistence on the purchase of a complete package with a guaranteed maximum price. The evidence further reflects that Westinghouse actually encouraged Florida to rely on Westinghouse's professed nuclear knowledge and capability.

Ironically, Westinghouse was aided in inducing Florida to enter into the contracts by the fact that General Electric, a principal competitor, was also proposing that Florida convert to nuclear power, and in this effort provided much economic analysis tending to show its advantages. The competition between General Electric and Westinghouse was keen, and the form of Westinghouse's offer to Florida was influenced by its knowledge of General Electric's proposal. Westinghouse concluded that the form of its fuel offer, though not as it would have chosen in the absence of its knowledge of General Electric's position, was necessary in order to secure the contract. Coupled with this incentive was Westinghouse's knowledge that Florida's chief executive officer had expressed the view that the successful manufacturer of the contemplated units would have to assume responsibility for total fuel supply. He expressed the view most vividly in the following language:

> I do not want to buy a sheep to get a suit of clothes, and have the sheep sheared, dyed, treated, woven into cloth, cut, and sewn into a suit. I want to buy a suit, not go through all the procedures of having to acquire the wool that goes into the suit, nor the manufacture of the thread, nor the material or anything else. I want to buy a suit already made.

Florida's continued insistence on guaranteed fuel costs, for as long a period as possible, together with the extreme importance Westinghouse placed on obtaining the construction contracts, prompted Westinghouse's offer of a guaranteed ten year fuel cycle cost. This, of course, included the cost of uranium and the purchase and disposal of the spent fuel as a part of the fuel cycle. In short, Florida expressed a consistent desire to look at a complete package.

The cost assumptions upon which Westinghouse predicated its proffered fuel contract were based on what one witness described as "very little knowledge." In its contract with Florida, Westinghouse agreed to a contract price fixed solely by reference to the amount of electricity generated by Florida, and independent of the cost to Westinghouse of the purchase or disposal of uranium. Joseph Rengel, who was principally responsible within the Westinghouse organization for developing the terms of Westinghouse's fuel proposal to Florida, quite candidly testified that under the mills per kilowatt hour formula used in the contract between the parties, the risks taken by Westinghouse encompassed "the reprocessing of the fuel at the end of the project." Mr. Rengel's explanation for Westinghouse's assumption of the risks inherent in a long term, fixed price fuel contract was that Westinghouse assumed "that the risks were not very significant." Indeed, the evidence reflects that it was not until after the contract had been executed that Westinghouse examined in detail the fuel cycle, consisting of enrichment, conversion and reprocessing. [109]

Under the provisions of the contract, Florida had the right until "initial criticality" to elect one of three fuel purchase options. Initial criticality occurred at Turkey Point Unit 3 on October 20, 1972 and at Turkey Point Unit 4 on June 11, 1973. Under the option timely selected by Florida, option C, which includes the contested Section 27(a)(2), Westinghouse is required to furnish fuel until each plant goes off the line or "the first refueling after ten years from the date of initial criticality." Under that option Florida's obligation to pay for the power generated by the fuel it received began with "initial criticality," which is defined as the first time of self-sustaining chain reaction occurs in the core of a nuclear unit. It is a moment that may be determined with technical precision. It is an event which occurs only once in the life of a nuclear unit.

In its negotiations, Westinghouse endeavored, unsuccessfully, to convince Florida that its fuel cost would be lower if it undertook on its own to have the spent fuel reprocessed. Indeed, at one point Westinghouse offered to act as Florida's agent in obtaining reprocessing. Florida never seriously entered these suggestions, by virtue of its negotiator's insistence that it wished to purchase a complete package.

In view of the infancy of the commercial market in uranium at the time of the negotiations with Florida, Westinghouse had no way of determining whether the wholesale price index would be an accurate measure of increases in the price of uranium, yet it agreed to a specified price in reference to the cost to Florida for fuel based upon mills per kilowatt hour as a charge for the energy generated.

Westinghouse had full knowledge of Florida's hesitancy to use nuclear power but ultimately convinced Florida that the capital, fuel, and production costs of nuclear power would not exceed the costs that it was incurring for its fossil units, and would inure to the benefit of Florida's rate payers. Under the option which it exercised, if spent fuel were not reprocessed, Florida ran little risk, and though the parties contemplated that Westinghouse would remove the spent fuel and reprocess it, the contract by its terms requires Westinghouse to remove the spent fuel and "dispose of it as Westinghouse sees fit." Indeed, no witness for either party ever viewed Westinghouse's contractual obligation as encompassing a reprocessing of the irradiated (spent) fuel.

---

[109] [4] Irradiated, or spent fuel contains valuable fuel material. After the spent fuel has cooled for three or four months, it is loaded underwater into heavily shielded casks. These lead-lined casks are used to transport the fuel to a chemical reprocessing plant. At the reprocessing plant the fuel is unloaded into another underwater storage pool.

The first step in reprocessing is to transfer the fuel from the storage pool to a cell where the assembly can be mechanically disassembled. After the end fittings have been removed, the fuel rods are sheared into shore pieces. These pieces are placed in a dissolver where nitric acid selectively dissolves the fuel and leaves the cladding. The resultant fuel-bearing acid solution is treated by solvent extraction to separate the uranium and plutonium from the fission products. The uranium and plutonium are then subjected to further solvent extraction steps to purify them and remove nearly all of the fission products. Final products of the reprocessing are uranium and plutonium nitrate solutions.

Reprocessing is, according to those knowledgeable in the nuclear power industry, the appropriate method of disposing of spent nuclear fuel. Absent reprocessing, spent fuel is not only valueless, but represents a financial burden.

It is obvious to the Court that Westinghouse took a calculated risk in providing the guarantees demanded by Florida. Included in those guarantees was Westinghouse's obligation to remove the spent fuel. To a great extent Westinghouse's willingness to accept the risks involved was premised on its understandable desire to enter into a contract for the building of Florida's nuclear reactors. Additionally, a not insignificant consideration was that Westinghouse anticipated that the reprocessing of the spent fuel, with its consequent recovery of uranium nitrate and plutonium nitrate, would result in a financial gain to it of between sixteen and nineteen million dollars, as the estimated value of reusable uranium and production of plutonium. While the given dollar value was simply an estimate on the part of Westinghouse, unsupported by hard evidence or reference to sources with a background of precise costs or values, the Court is satisfied that Westinghouse in its business judgment concluded that there was substantial value to it in reprocessing. Of necessity, the contract price also encompassed a charge to Florida for Westinghouse's anticipated service in removing the spent fuel.

The Court concludes that while both parties understood that Westinghouse intended to reprocess the spent fuel if it would inure to Westinghouse's benefit, that fact, excepting for its effect on the price Westinghouse offered to charge for the energy which Florida was purchasing, had no influence on Florida's executing the contract.

The only reference to reprocessing in the final contract is a provision permitting Westinghouse to use "plutonium and reprocessed or depleted uranium in fuel loadings subsequent to the initial fuel loading. . . ."

Florida, unwilling to tie itself to reprocessing, was told by Westinghouse that as a consequence it was committing to pay a higher price for its fuel. In this regard, Westinghouse pointed out to Florida that it was its view that Florida's cost would be less if it would reprocess the spent fuel; for reprocessed fuel, which under the contract Westinghouse had the right to use in Florida's reloads, was contemplated to be less expensive than mined uranium. Nevertheless, Florida rejected a risk factor which Westinghouse was willing to take. The most logical conclusion in light of the nature of the negotiations is that Florida viewed Westinghouse's willingness to remove and dispose of the irradiated or spent fuel as inuring to Florida's benefit in the cost of energy and the completion of the "suit of clothes." That Westinghouse contemplated reprocessing, in light of its statements to Florida reference the beneficial economics of same, was simply viewed by Florida as a factor to which Westinghouse gave more weight than Florida was willing to, especially in view of Florida's desire to have the limits of its responsibilities and concomitant costs precisely defined. As one of counsel suggested, Westinghouse was, at least as to any risk factors, simply "out-negotiated." The Court finds no evidence which would support a conclusion that the parties ever understood or intended that Westinghouse be contractually obligated to reprocess the spent fuel. One would be hard pressed to construe the phrase ". . . dispose of it as Westinghouse sees fit" as imposing a duty to reprocess.

Admittedly, although the possibility was present in the contract, Westinghouse, having offered three options to Florida, had no way of knowing until Florida selected option C in 1972 that it, Westinghouse, would in fact have responsibility for removal of the spent fuel.

Option A of the contract would have foreclosed any responsibility on the part of Westinghouse to remove the spent fuel—options B and C placed that responsibility on Westinghouse. . . .

While, as the Court has concluded, both parties contemplated reprocessing, the fact remains that Westinghouse accepted the responsibility of removing the spent fuel and with that responsibility, to utilize that fuel as it saw fit. Its reliance on its own business judgment cannot in fairness impose on Florida greater burdens than it contracted for, absent what might be imposed by law, to which the Court addresses itself, *infra*.

That Westinghouse anticipated a monetary value is obvious. That Westinghouse took a calculated risk is just as obvious. No spent fuel had ever been commercially reprocessed as of the time of execution of the contract, and further, the first commercial reprocessing plant in the United States was not licensed until April 19, 1966; more than a year after negotiations between the parties had commenced. Additionally, Westinghouse fully understood that its offer to Florida was premised on what it deemed to be a reasonable business risk that commercial reprocessing would come to pass and would be economically feasible, conditions which had not, at the time of execution of the contract, been demonstrated. Florida, on the other hand, had its "suit of clothes" and had no financial interest in the spent fuel.

In short, Westinghouse was, in its eagerness to construct the power plants, willing to accept the risks which Florida was not willing to take. That Westinghouse fully appreciated this fact is evidenced by a Westinghouse proposal of November 3, 1965, which would effectively have placed responsibility for spent fuel on Florida, as well as the fact that other written suggestions of Westinghouse making reference to "reprocessing" were not incorporated into option C of the final contract. Florida simply refused to tie its cost to what it deemed at the time to be uncertain technology.

Except for eighteen spent fuel assemblies which Westinghouse arranged to be removed and which were sent to a governmental agency for experimental programs, Westinghouse has not removed the spent fuel, and as a consequence Florida at time of trial was storing 411 spent fuel assemblies.

The evidence discloses that over the life of the contract a total of 981 spent fuel assemblies will be generated. While no schedule for the removal of the spent fuel is set out in the contract, the Court finds that it was the intention of the parties that same be accomplished within six months to a year after the spent fuel is removed from the reactors, and as a consequence of Westinghouse's failure to remove same, Florida was compelled to expand its spent fuel storage pits to accommodate excess spent fuel.

Florida had, in anticipation of both temporarily storing spent fuel assemblies and in the event a problem occurred in the reactor vessel requiring an unloading of an entire core of fuel assemblies, caused to be constructed a storage pit for each reactor, each capable of holding 217 assemblies. The original expectation was that the pits would be sufficiently large enough to handle not only the anticipated annual discharge, but emergency unloadings as well. Each pit was intended for interim, temporary storage for the period between the time the fuel was taken out of the reactor and the time it was cool enough to be removed from the plant's site by Westinghouse. Had Florida not expanded its spent fuel storage pits, its operation of the nuclear units would have had to cease.

As a consequence of Westinghouse's refusal to remove the spent fuel assemblies, Florida has expended $9,473,242.04 in reracking—that is, adding additional spent fuel storage racks at a closer center-to-center spacing which permits each pit to have a larger capacity than contemplated in the original design. This of course has resulted in increased operating and maintenance costs, as well as potential environmental difficulties.

It is estimated that by the end of the year 1985 both storage pits will reach their potential capacity for storage. If such comes to pass, Florida's reactors will be forced to shut down with a consequent cost estimated to be approximately $500,000 per day, per unit, for replacement power.

While the government has announced plans to provide an interim storage facility during the 1980's, no capacity for a final disposal facility has been demonstrated, nor indeed is there any certainty that even the interim storage facility will come to pass.

Florida chose what it deemed to be a fixed cost contract and as a part thereof, Westinghouse was to remove the spent fuel and dispose of it as Westinghouse saw fit. That conclusion, in the Court's view, is unassailable.

Finally in this regard, it can be said that the evidence reflects that Westinghouse's entry into the contract came about at a time when Westinghouse fully anticipated, despite the lack of a binding contract for reprocessing the spent fuel, to reprocess Florida's spent fuel with the hope of making its agreement with Florida under option C economically more profitable. Such anticipation was, however, just that—an anticipation fueled by its desire to secure the contract for the building of two nuclear steam supply systems and its own enthusiasm for its view of the merits and future of nuclear power.

Regardless of how one views the business judgment of Westinghouse in this regard, the fact is that, as early as 1957 the United States Atomic Energy Commission adopted a policy of assuring the nuclear power industry that the government would, in the event that commercial reprocessing services were not available at reasonable times and conditions when irradiated power reactor fuels were discharged from their reactors, make financial settlement for the materials contained in those fuel elements, and reprocess them. Indeed, in 1965 the Government was actively urging reprocessing of spent fuel, was accepting fuel for reprocessing, and to a limited extent was underwriting a portion of the financial burden associated therewith. Notably, however, at that period in time the uranium was leased by the government and was in fact government material.

As a consequence of this policy of encouragement, reiterated in January of 1968, a number of companies expressed interest, and at least one, National Fuel

Services, Incorporated, built a plant which became operational in 1966, and operated until 1972.

It is to be noted, however, that the plant which became operational in 1966 was designed to operate at only about 300 tons per year. It is estimated that the Turkey Point plants will produce about 400 tons of spent fuel over the term of the contract with Westinghouse. Other companies, such as General Electric, which had expressed an interest in commercial reprocessing services, abandoned their plans.

Events occurring after formation of the contract, however, made Westinghouse's plans to reprocess—rather than merely remove—and dispose of Florida's spent fuel more difficult to accomplish than Westinghouse had anticipated. After the start of the small NFS reprocessing plant in 1966, no other commercial reprocessing concerns became operable. In 1970, four years after the execution of the contract, Westinghouse entered into a letter of intent with Allied-General Nuclear Services (AGNS), to contract with AGNS, subject to AGNS's receipt of a license, for the reprocessing of the Turkey Point spent fuel. At the time of the letter of intent, AGNS was not licensed to reprocess nuclear fuel; nor is it now. AGNS never executed a formal contract with Westinghouse, and in fact, in early 1974 AGNS advised Westinghouse that it was not prepared to execute a formal agreement. On September 2, 1975, Westinghouse notified Florida by letter that Westinghouse had no plans for removing the spent fuel from the Turkey Point site. Westinghouse assigned as its reason for not removing the spent fuel, the fact that the schedule for removing and reprocessing the discharged fuel was "of course, dependent on the Allied-General [Nuclear] Services' reprocessing schedule."

No stretch of the imagination nor the arguments of ingenious counsel could satisfy the Court that, regardless of whether reprocessing was an integral part of the contract, Florida ever agreed to condition Westinghouse's obligation to remove the spent fuel on "Allied-General Nuclear Services' (AGNS) reprocessing facility schedule."

In April 1977, two years after Westinghouse declared its unwillingness to fulfill the contract, President Carter, by Executive Order, precluded the development of domestic facilities for the commercial reprocessing of nuclear fuel and the exportation of nuclear fuel for reprocessing purposes. As a consequence of the presidential ban on reprocessing, licensing procedures for contemplated commercial reprocessing facilities have been terminated.

Two years after Westinghouse's breach, occurring because of its own failure to successfully negotiate a contract for the removal and storage of the spent fuel, or alternatively to have utilized the period between the date of Florida's exercise of Option C and its breach in 1975 to make other arrangements, the government's change of policy thwarted Westinghouse's hope for reprocessing. As a consequence of the ban on reprocessing, Westinghouse contends that it is faced with an effective bar to removal of the spent fuel.

Inexplicably, though Westinghouse introduced evidence to the effect that it and AGNS had reached a finalized agreement . . . [for] the removal and reprocessing of the spent fuel as early as March 1973, no action was taken, nor has any since been taken, by Westinghouse, to enforce what it contends was its contract with AGNS. The Court concludes that no action has been taken in this regard because of Westinghouse's failure to expend millions of dollars in expanding its storage pits. . . .

This, however, does not end the case. Florida seeks not only monetary damages as compensation for its having to expand its storage pits, but an order directing Westinghouse to remove the spent fuel.

The evidence does reflect that as a consequence of the presidential ban on reprocessing, licensing procedures for contemplated commercial reprocessing facilities have been terminated. There are, however, a number of facilities, including AGNS' Barnwell, South Carolina facility, where subject to appropriate licenses, spent fuel could be stored and perhaps ultimately reprocessed.

Finally in this regard, there are no commercial facilities, excepting for a few such as that of General Electric, which, because of the ban on reprocessing, has limited the use of its facility to taking spent fuel from its customers as an accommodation in lieu of being able to fulfill reprocessing commitments, that could be used for storage of spent fuel. Though there are eight government facilities with potential for storing spent fuel, which, theoretically, could store spent fuel produced beyond the year 2000, they would require extensive physical modifications to make them usable.

While there is now legislation pending to permit the U.S. Department of Energy to proceed to provide storage facilities, even if enacted, such facilities would not be available for a number of years.

It would appear that in the absence of a reversal of the government's policy against reprocessing or alternatively, facilities for the storage of spent fuel, if not presently available, becoming available, Florida's nuclear Turkey Point plants will be shut down by the year 1986 as to one plant, and 1988 as to the other.

LEGAL ISSUES

Westinghouse raises the following five defenses: (1) that its performance is excused by the common law doctrine of impossibility of performance; (2) that the government's change of policy concerning commercial reprocessing discharges its duty under the force majeure clause; (3) that performance by it has been rendered commercially impracticable under § 2-615 of the Uniform Commercial Code; (4) that the non-availability of reprocessing has frustrated the purpose of the contract; and (5) that the parties' erroneous expectation that the spent fuel would be reprocessed discharges Westinghouse's obligation under the doctrine of mutual mistake.

Both in conceptual terms and in terms of the facts to which they relate there is considerable similarity among the defenses, particularly defenses 1, 3, 4, and 5. Commercial impracticability under the UCC is basically a codification of the common law doctrine of impossibility of performance, which, in turn, is grounded in the doctrines of mutual mistake and frustration of purpose. The purpose of each of the defenses is to

> . . . discharge an obligor from his duty to perform a contract where a failure of
> a basic assumption of the parties produces a grave failure of the equivalence of

value of the exchange to the parties. And all [of the defenses] are qualified by the same notions of risk assumption and allocation.

Aluminum Co. of America v. Essex Group, Inc., 499 F.Supp. 53, 70 (W.D. Penn. 1980). The burden of proving the elements of each of these defenses is on the party seeking to avoid performance. *Ocean Air Tradeways, Inc. v. Arkay Realty Corp.*, 480 F.2d 1112, 1117 (9th Cir. 1973).

The bulk of the Court's analysis will proceed under the two most similar of the claimed defenses, common law impossibility and commercial impracticability under the UCC. . . .

I.   *Commercial Impracticability. . . .*

In the Court's view, Westinghouse's claim of commercial impracticability raises four issues: (1) Was performance as agreed rendered impracticable? (2) Did the claimed impracticability arise from an unforeseen contingency? (3) Was the non-occurrence of the contingency a basic assumption on which the contract was made? (4) Did the parties, explicitly or implicitly, allocate the risk that the contingency would occur.

There is nothing magical about these four questions: they are not, strictly speaking, elements of proof, or hurdles which Westinghouse must cross if it is to be excused for nonperformance. They merely provide, for purposes of the instant case, a useful method for structuring the inquiry.

It is further to be noted that the issues as framed are interrelated: the "answer" to each depends in part on the "answers" to the other three. . . .

1.   Was performance as agreed rendered impracticable?

Westinghouse contends that the reversal of the government's policy concerning reprocessing, and specifically the 1977 presidential order banning commercial reprocessing, has had the practical effect of rendering performance as contemplated impracticable. At the time the contract was executed, Westinghouse expected to recoup between 16 and 19 million dollars from the spent fuel. Now, however, the fuel is virtually valueless. Thus, Westinghouse's basic contention is that the government's actions have made commercial reprocessing unavailable, which in turn has massively increased the costs of removal of the spent fuel from Florida's plants.

In so arguing, Westinghouse relies in part on the sewage disposal cases discussed *supra*. There, as here, it is contended, a supervening governmental action rendered performance much more expensive than was contemplated at the time of execution.

The Court finds that the facts simply do not support the conclusion that Westinghouse's performance has been rendered impracticable. The short, albeit incomplete answer to Westinghouse's contentions is the plain language of the contract. The contract in unequivocal language requires Westinghouse to remove the spent fuel. It does not by any stretch of construction *require* Westinghouse to reprocess. The bargained for performance was removal; reprocessing was merely an option given to Westinghouse. . . .

In two very similar cases, *Transatlantic Financing Corp. v. U.S.*, 363 F.2d 312 (D.C. Cir. 1966) and *American Trading & Production Co. v. Shell International Marine, Ltd.*, 453 F.2d 939 (2d Cir. 1972), shipowners sought compensation for additional expenses incurred as a result of the fact that the Suez Canal was closed after they had begun their voyages. To reach their destinations the ships had to sail around the Cape of Good Hope, a much longer voyage than through the Suez. The shipowners claimed that the contemplated means of performance, *i.e.* passage through Suez, had been rendered impracticable. The courts rejected the shipowners' arguments: the fact that both parties to each of the contracts contemplated the Suez route "is not at all equivalent to an agreement that it be the exclusive method of performance." *American Trading*, 453 F.2d at 941. Because the promises to transport cargo from one point to another were unqualified, the shippers were not relieved of the obligation to perform by alternate means when the contemplated means became impracticable.

Thus, where the contract, explicitly or implicitly, provides for an exclusive means of performance, the impracticability of the specified means may release the promisor from his duty. Where, on the other hand, the promised performance is set forth in unqualified language, as was Westinghouse's promise to remove the spent fuel, the promisor may be required to perform by alternate means when the contemplated means become impracticable. . . .

There can be no doubt that both Westinghouse and Florida contemplated that the spent fuel would be reprocessed. But there is no indication in the contract itself or in the history of its negotiation to indicate that reprocessing was viewed as the exclusive means of performance. Indeed, reprocessing was not in actuality the contemplated "means" of performance at all; it was the contemplated disposition of the spent fuel *after* performance. The means of performance, of removal, were left unspecified. Further, as will be hereinafter discussed, the evidence indicates that the unqualified nature of the promise was a consciously bargained for term of the contract. Florida, in its negotiator's words, sought "a suit of clothes," without regard to the process necessary to achieve this.

Even if reprocessing could reasonably be viewed as an exclusive means of performance, or as an integral part of the exclusive means of performance, there is the additional question of whether the increased expense claimed by Westinghouse is sufficient to rise to the level of impracticability.

Promisors seeking to establish impracticability by reason of increased expense have not generally found a sympathetic ear in court. . . . Comment 4 to the Florida U.C.C. section on impracticability provides that increased cost alone may constitute impracticability where the increase is due to an "unforeseen contingency which alters the essential nature of the performance." Generally, however, "the fact that performance has become economically burdensome or unattractive is not sufficient for performance to be excused. . . . We will not allow a party to a contract to escape a bad bargain merely because it is burdensome." *Neal-Cooper Grain Co. v. Texas Gulf Sulpher Co.*, 508 F.2d 283, 293-294 (7th Cir. 1974). The strictness of this rule is based on a number of considerations: the fact, for example, that the very purpose of a fixed price agreement is to place the risk of increased costs on the promisor (and the risk of decreased costs on the promisee).

Further, enforcing the bargain struck encourages parties to attempt to foresee cost variations, and to structure their agreements accordingly.

Without doubt, the sum which Westinghouse is precluded from recouping as a result of the unavailability of reprocessing is substantial. But impracticability by reason of additional expense is not to be determined by reference to the loss, or failure to profit, from one particular contract term in isolation. Rather, it is to be judged from the perspective of the entire undertaking. *Eastern Air Lines v. Gulf Oil Corp.*, 415 F. Supp. 429 (S.D. Fla. 1975); *United States v. Wegematic*, 360 F.2d 674 (2d Cir. 1966). There has been no showing that Westinghouse lost money on the entire "package deal" of plant and fuel contracts for Florida. Further, Westinghouse sought benefits beyond whatever profits it may have anticipated from the contracts: it clearly hoped that the Turkey Point plants would demonstrate the benefits of nuclear power, and would promote its own position in the industry.

Admittedly, the additional cost of removal itself might be sufficient to constitute impracticability in another context. As will be discussed *infra*, however, the Court believes that to the extent that Westinghouse was aware of the uncertainties of reprocessing, it assumed the risk that reprocessing would prove to be more expensive than anticipated, or not available at any price.

2.   Did the claimed impracticability arise from an unforeseen contingency?

The success of a commercial impracticability defense often turns on whether the promisor foresaw, or should have foreseen, the contingency claimed to have made performance impracticable. Where the promisor had no reason to anticipate a supervening event which radically increases the difficulty of performance, or which renders performance impossible, it is manifestly unfair to hold him to the agreement. For instance, a seller of produce may be relieved because of a total crop failure. *Mitchell Canneries, Inc. v. United States*, 77 F. Supp. 498 (Ct. Cl. 1948). Conversely, where the contingency may reasonably be said to have been foreseeable, courts have generally taken the view that the promisor should not be released from his obligation. This rule is based on the notion that where the parties can reasonably anticipate events that may affect performance, the prudent course is to provide for such eventualities in their contract.

Because the future is by definition unknowable, a rule holding the obligor to performance only where he foresees, but fails to guard against, the *precise* event that renders performance more difficult, would be meaningless. As may be seen from the following cases, it may be enough that he is (or should be) aware of a certain trend, or that a given state of affairs is in flux, or that an assumption is more than usually uncertain.

In *Eastern Air Lines v. Gulf Oil Corp., supra*, the parties entered a requirements contract for jet fuel. They attempted to guard against price fluctuations through an escalator clause, which tied the price paid by Eastern for jet fuel to published prices of a certain type of domestic oil. In the year following the execution of the contract, the price of foreign oil rose substantially as a result of OPEC actions, including the 1973 embargo. In response, the United States government sought to control oil prices by implementing a "two tier" pricing system.

The indicator oil chosen by the parties was in the lower tier, and its price rose far less rapidly than did Gulf's oil costs.

The court held that Gulf's performance had not been rendered commercially impracticable. While Gulf could not reasonably have anticipated the embargo, the precise effect that OPEC's actions would have on worldwide oil prices, or the advent of the two tier pricing system, it was aware of the volatility of affairs in the Middle East, of the constantly changing government price regulations, and of the general upward trend in oil prices. As one witness in that case stated, "the handwriting was on the wall." Therefore, even though the indicator chosen did not accomplish its intended purpose, in that it proved to be a very poor measure of Gulf's costs, the contract was enforced.

The analogies to the instant case are manifest. It is a fact that government policy favored reprocessing at the time the contract was negotiated; it is also a fact that, just as Gulf could not anticipate the two tier pricing system, Westinghouse could not have anticipated in 1966 that eleven years later President Carter would ban commercial processing. But while Westinghouse could not have foreseen the precise eventuality claimed to excuse performance, its officers certainly knew that commercial reprocessing was, at best, a highly uncertain proposition. In fact, as a practical matter, there was no such thing as commercial reprocessing in 1966. Westinghouse's claim that the unavailability of reprocessing was an unforeseen contingency is belied by the fact that, even at the time the contract was executed, reprocessing for Florida's anticipated spent fuel was, for all practical purposes, unavailable.

Further, Westinghouse cannot, in the Court's view, rely on the 1977 presidential order banning commercial reprocessing as an excuse for its consistent refusal to perform beginning two years earlier. The unavailability of reprocessing or storage for Florida's spent fuel prior to 1977 is clearly attributable, at least in part, to Westinghouse's own less than zealous attempts to obtain a facility. Apart from the drawn out, ultimately unsuccessful negotiations with AGNS, Westinghouse made no significant attempts to secure storage or reprocessing facilities, and gave little, if any, serious consideration to building its own facility, in spite of its knowledge that failure to remove the spent fuel could ultimately result in a shut-down of the plants.

3.   Was the nonoccurrence of the contingency a basic assumption of the contract?

Westinghouse, pointing to the abundant evidence that both parties contemplated reprocessing, and to the fact that the price per kilowatt hour was calculated on the assumption that Westinghouse would obtain considerable value from the spent fuel, argues that the availability of reprocessing was a fundamental assumption of the contract, and therefore a condition of performance.

The Court finds, however, that notwithstanding the parties' expectation that reprocessing would occur, there is nothing in the evidence to evince any intention that Westinghouse was to be absolved from its responsibility to remove the spent fuel in the event that reprocessing would not be available. Indeed, it is difficult to discern how the availability of reprocessing could have been a basic assumption of the parties, given the fact that commercial reprocessing did not exist at the time the contract was executed, as well as the fact that the contract specifically calls for Westinghouse to do with the spent fuel as "it sees fit."

If there was a basic and mutual assumption in this regard, it was that Florida would have no involvement whatever with reprocessing, or with whatever alternate disposition Westinghouse might make of the spent fuel. Florida deemed reprocessing too speculative to undertake it. In light of Florida's rejection of formulas which tied its costs to reprocessing, it is inconceivable that Florida would have agreed to a term conditioning Westinghouse's performance on the availability of reprocessing.

Certainly, as the Court has found, the bargained for price per kilowatt hour reflected the parties' anticipation that the fuel would be reprocessed. This, however, is not sufficient to transform an expectation into a basic assumption or a condition of performance. Arguments akin to that urged by Westinghouse in this regard were rejected in the Suez closing cases. In *American Trading and Pro. Co., supra,* the shipowner contended that because the shipping rate was based on a Suez passage, the availability of that route was a basic assumption of the contract. The court responded that "all that the . . . rate establishes is that the parties obviously expected a Suez passage but there is no indication at all in the instrument or *dehors* that it was a condition of performance." 453 F.2d at 942. Here, not only is there an absence of evidence that reprocessing was a condition of performance, there are positive indications that the unqualified promise to remove the spent fuel was bargained for, and that reprocessing was a subject left entirely to Westinghouse. These facts are radically inconsistent with the contentions made by Westinghouse.

4. Did the parties, explicitly or implicitly, allocate the risk that the contingency would occur?

Generally, the risk of a contingency affecting performance is based on the promisor: "he is presumed, in the absence of evidence to the contrary, to have agreed to bear any loss occasioned by an event which was unforeseeable at the time of contracting." *Eastern Air Lines v. McDonnell Douglas Corp.,* 532 F.2d 957 (5th Cir. 1976). Comment 8 to Section 2-615 of the U.C.C. explains that the defense of commercial impracticability is not available where the risk may be deemed to have been allocated to the promisor:

> The provisions of this section are made subject to assumption of greater liability by agreement and such agreement is to be found not only in the expressed terms of the contract but in the circumstances surrounding the contracting, in trade usage, and the like. Thus the exemptions of this section do not apply when the contingency in question is sufficiently foreshadowed at the time of contracting to be included among the business risks which are fairly to be regarded as part of the dickered terms, either consciously or as a matter of reasonable, commercial interpretation from the circumstances. . . .

Thus, risk allocation is determined by the totality of the circumstances, including the comparative abilities of the parties to make informed judgments as to the extent of the risk; each party's interest in avoiding the risk; and the extent to which that interest was a factor in the negotiation of the contract. As indicated by the Comment, the foreseeability of the risk alone may well be sufficient for it to be regarded as implicitly assumed by the promisor.

Here, the record is replete with indications that Westinghouse, and not Florida, assumed the risk of any difficulties that might arise concerning reprocessing. As it made abundantly clear to Westinghouse throughout the negotiations, Florida, a public utility, had a strong interest in a low-risk, fixed price contract. Indeed, "strong interest" is too mild an expression: Florida's position throughout was that it would not agree to anything other than its finished "suit of clothes." Florida required, and Westinghouse agreed, that the means by which the "suit of clothes" would be made was to be left entirely to Westinghouse. As noted earlier, Florida's rejection of options under which the price of the fuel would depend on reprocessing renders it inconceivable that it would have accepted a contract term under which Westinghouse's performance was contingent upon the availability of reprocessing.

Westinghouse, by contrast, was in an entirely different situation as it met Florida across the bargaining table. As a giant in the then-nascent nuclear industry, it had a powerful interest in promoting both the viability of nuclear power, and its own position in the industry. In light of Florida's requirements, and of Westinghouse's knowledge that General Electric was actively seeking the contract, Westinghouse's goals, as it perceived them then, could not be achieved without taking substantial risks—the availability and cost of reprocessing being just one of many. Westinghouse was certainly in a position to know of the uncertainties, both technological and commercial, of reprocessing. Indeed, at the time it entered the contract, Westinghouse had not yet conducted a detailed study of the fuel cycle.

Knowing full well Florida's requirements, and knowing that reprocessing, not being available even then as a practical matter, was highly uncertain, Westinghouse agreed to a contract term which in plain, unequivocal, unqualified language, required it to remove the spent fuel from Florida's plants. If this is not assumption of risk, the Court confesses itself unable to discern what would be. Whatever opinion one might hold as to Westinghouse's wisdom in agreeing to such a term, it did agree to it. There is nothing to indicate that the language of the term did not reflect the parties' intentions. On the contrary, all of the evidence, including the history of the negotiations and the parties' interests and goals in entering into the contract, indicate that the unqualified promise made by Westinghouse to remove the spent fuel was precisely the bargained for performance.

II. *Mutual Mistake*

Westinghouse contends that the parties made two related assumptions: that reprocessing would be available, and that the spent fuel had value. These assumptions having proven to be erroneous, Westinghouse argues that its performance is excused under the doctrine of mutual mistake.

Section 152 of the Restatement of Contracts 2d provides as follows:

(1) Where a mistake of both parties at the time the contract was made as to a basic assumption on which the contract was made has a material ef-

fect on the agreed exchange of performances, the contract is voidable by the adversely affected party unless he bears the risk of the mistake. . . .

Section 151 defines "mistake" as a "belief not in accord with existing facts."

It is immediately apparent that the defense of mutual mistake includes two of the same elements as the doctrine of commercial impracticability: it requires the mistaken fact be as to a basic assumption, and it is qualified by the notion of risk allocation. The Court has already made findings as to these issues adverse to Westinghouse. However, in light of the magnitude of this dispute, the Court deems it appropriate to more fully address the issues as they arise under this defense.

The Court finds that the parties' anticipation that reprocessing of the spent fuel would occur was not a mutual mistake of fact, but rather an erroneous prediction. Indeed, Florida proved not to have been mistaken at all; it viewed reprocessing as too speculative a proposition to agree to any involvement in it, or to a contract under which either the price it would pay or Westinghouse's performance was in any way dependent upon it.

One recent case (decided after the parties' last briefing in this matter), *Aluminum Co. of America v. Essex Group, (Alcoa)*, 499 F. Supp. 53 (W.D. Penn. 1980), creates considerable tension in the distinction between a mistake as to a fact existing at the time the contract was executed, and an erroneous prediction of a future event. The Court addresses *Alcoa* not because it must distinguish it, but rather because its distinctions from the instant case are particularly enlightening.

In *Alcoa*, the parties entered a long term contract in which Alcoa agreed to process alumina for Essex. After a careful study, the parties developed a complex pricing formula. One component of the formula was designed to reflect Alcoa's labor costs; another component, intended to reflect Alcoa's non-labor costs, was tied to the Wholesale Price Index (WPI). The non-labor component was arrived at on the basis of a study showing that for many years, there had been a close correlation between the WPI and Alcoa's non-labor costs. However, after the contract was executed, the price of electricity, a major component of Alcoa's non-labor costs, rose enormously, far outpacing the rise in the WPI; as a result, Alcoa suffered substantial losses. Essex, on the other hand, obtained considerable windfall benefits by selling the aluminum it manufactured from alumina processed by Alcoa, because the rise in the market price of aluminum also far outstripped the WPI.

The court held that the parties' belief, at the time the contract was executed, that the WPI would reflect Alcoa's non-labor costs was a mutual mistake of fact rather than an erroneous prediction of future events, and that therefore Alcoa was entitled to relief under the doctrine of mutual mistake.

While the Court has, most respectfully, some difficulty with the holding in *Alcoa*, it has no difficulty in finding that, even under that court's expansive reading of mutual mistake, Westinghouse's reliance on that defense is misplaced. As the *Alcoa* court noted, there is an important difference between conscious and unconscious ignorance of a material fact: "where parties enter a contract in a state of conscious ignorance of the facts, they are deemed to risk the burden of having the facts turn out to be adverse, within very broad limits." 499 F. Supp.

53, 68. In the instant case, there can be no doubt that the parties entered the contract in a state of "conscious ignorance" as to the technology, costs, and even the availability of reprocessing for Florida's spent fuel, as indicated by the fact that commercial reprocessing was not then readily available, and by Westinghouse's candid admission that its price calculations were based on "very little knowledge."

A passage from *Alcoa* is particularly instructive as to the distinction between conscious and unconscious ignorance:

> [I]f parties agree to sell and purchase a stone which both know may be glass or diamond at a price which in some way reflects their uncertainty, the contract is enforceable whether the stone is in fact glass or diamond. If, by contrast, the parties both mistakenly believe it to be glass, the case is said not to be one of conscious ignorance but one of mutual mistake.

499 F. Supp. at 68. The instant case falls in the first category; Judge Teitelbaum held that *Alcoa* fell in the second. While the Court is convinced that the price per kilowatt hour charged to Florida was lower than it would have been if Westinghouse had known that it would not be able to reprocess, the Court is equally certain that the price was higher than it would have been had there been no uncertainty about reprocessing. Expressed another way, Westinghouse was wagering that the stone would turn out to be a diamond. That it misjudged the odds does not release it from its bargain.

A related distinction is the manner in which the mistake, or the erroneous prediction, affects the contemplated performances or the equivalence of value. To the extent that *Alcoa* was disadvantaged by the mistake, Essex was enriched. Here, by contrast, while the unavailability of reprocessing has the effect of making performance by Westinghouse more expensive, it in no way enriches Florida, or gives Florida any benefit it did not bargain for.

Westinghouse's own poor judgment and mistakes cannot alone excuse its performance.

III. *Force Majeure*

Westinghouse claims that its nonperformance is excused by the terms of the contract's force majeure clause, which reads as follows:

> Section 9. Force Majeure
>
> Except as otherwise specifically provided in this contract, neither Westinghouse nor Florida shall be liable for loss, damage, detention, or delay resulting from causes beyond its reasonable control, including but not limited to, fire, work stoppage, civil or military authority, restrictions of the United States Government, or any department, branch or representative thereof, insurrection, or riot, embargoes, car shortages, wrecks or delays in transportation, or inability to obtain necessary labor or manufacturing facilities due to such causes.

Westinghouse points to other contract provisions, which give Florida responsibility for the fuel from the time that it is delivered until Westinghouse removes it. Read together, it is contended, these provisions indicate that Florida assumed the risk of having to store the spent fuel in the event that Westinghouse was unable to remove it as a result of one of the contingencies listed in the fore majeure clause, and that therefore Westinghouse's performance is excused.

As noted earlier, the risk of a contingency that affects performance is presumed to rest on the promisor. However, the parties may agree to shift a particular risk to the promisee, or to allocate the various risks between them as they see fit.

For instance, in *Eastern Air Lines v. McDonnell Douglas*, 532 F.2d 957 (5th Cir. 1976), McDonnell Douglas urged both commercial impracticability and an "excusable delay" clause, exempting McDonnell Douglas from liability for delays beyond its control, in defense of Eastern's action for damages caused by late delivery. The late delivery was attributable to informal demands by the government that McDonnell Douglas accord priority to military aircraft for the Vietnam war. The court held that the excusable delay clause had the effect of broadening the protection afforded McDonnell Douglas under the U.C.C., and that the government's demands came within the terms of that clause.

Because of the same factors which compelled the Court to reject Westinghouse's defense of commercial impracticability, it is unable to view Westinghouse's obligation as discharged under the force majeure clause. To begin, Westinghouse's argument ignores the important fact that unlike the clause in *McDonnell Douglas*, which exempted only the seller, the force majeure clause at issue here *protects both Westinghouse and Florida*. To construe the clause as Westinghouse contends would, in effect, place the entire loss on Florida—a result not consonant with the clause itself, or with the parties' intentions concerning allocation of risk.

Further, the language of the clause is such that it is simply not applicable to the facts. The term reads "except as otherwise provided in the contract." Section 27 of the contract unequivocally places responsibility for removal of the spent fuel on Westinghouse. Westinghouse's contention that other contract terms place responsibility for the fuel on Florida until it is removed is not only misguided—it is cynical, in light of the fact that the fuel remains with Florida only because of Westinghouse's construction of the phrase "until it is removed" as a valid defense to its failure to perform, in the context of the whole contract, would, in the Court's opinion, denude the law of reason.

Finally, the force majeure clause applies only to losses resulting from causes beyond the parties' reasonable control, including actions of the government. As noted in the discussion of commercial impracticability, the Court is unable to conclude that Westinghouse's failure to perform was in any meaningful way caused by the government's actions. Reprocessing, not removal from Florida's site, was rendered illegal by presidential order. No representative of the government has ever forbidden Westinghouse to transport spent nuclear fuel from Florida's spent fuel storage site to some other site; nor has any government stricture prevented Westinghouse from accepting responsibility for the spent fuel from Florida, as required by the contract. Further, the presidential order was not issued until two years after Westinghouse's initial refusal to remove the first spent fuel. Finally, in light of the fact that Westinghouse's attempts to obtain reprocessing facilities prior to the presidential order were less than aggressive at best, it has not been shown that Westinghouse's failure to obtain reprocessing during that period, much less its failure to remove the spent fuel, resulted from causes beyond its reasonable control.

IV. *Frustration of Purpose*

Westinghouse contends that, insofar as its purpose in promising to remove the spent fuel was to obtain value from it through reprocessing, that purpose has been completely frustrated by supervening events.

The defense of frustration of purpose, like commercial impracticability and mistake of fact, is limited by the parties' allocation of the risk that the supervening event will occur. *See* Corbin, *Contracts*, § 1354 (1964). Having found overwhelming evidence that Westinghouse assumed the risk of the uncertainties of reprocessing, the Court cannot find that frustration of purpose excuses its nonperformance.

Additionally, it is to be noted that while in the narrow sense, Westinghouse's purpose in agreeing to remove the spent fuel was to reprocess it, Westinghouse's broader purpose was to secure the Florida contract. The Court has found that Florida would not have agreed to a contract which required it to reprocess the fuel, or which gave it responsibility for the spent fuel after the "cooling off" period. Knowing this, Westinghouse agreed to remove the fuel; and by so doing, it did indeed achieve its larger purpose of obtaining the Florida contracts for the construction of two nuclear stream supply systems. That its accomplishment in this regard may now be viewed by it as a commercial tragedy is unfortunate, yet one cannot but conclude that Westinghouse is to a great extent the architect of its own misfortune.

V. *Relief*

As the Court has previously noted, Florida has already been financially damaged in an amount in excess of nine million dollars, and any relief must, of course, call for reimbursement, at least to that extent. There has been some evidence to the effect that other utilities have been considering the construction of interim spent fuel storage facilities. The estimates of the cost of such facilities, depending on the site and capacity, range from 20 million dollars to 44 million dollars. Estimates of the cost to construct a storage facility, if one can be constructed, at the Turkey Point site, are in excess of 33 million dollars, with a further annual cost of approximately one million dollars.

In addition to monetary damages for expenses incurred thus far in storing the spent fuel, Florida seeks an order requiring Westinghouse to specifically perform its promise to remove the spent fuel. Westinghouse contends that Florida is not entitled to a decree of specific performance under Florida law on the following grounds: (1) that Florida has not shown that monetary damages would be an inadequate remedy; (2) that Westinghouse cannot be ordered to remove the spent fuel because its performance necessarily depends on the cooperation and assent of third parties (specifically, government agencies which regulate the nuclear industry), and (3) specific performance is inappropriate in light of the difficulty of fashioning a specific and workable decree, and of monitoring the parties' compliance therewith over the long term.

Under Florida law, specific performance is often said to lie within the "sound discretion" of the Court. *Buck v. McNab*, 139 So.2d 734 (Fla. App. 1962). It is discretionary in the sense that the Court may,—indeed, in many cases, must— make judgments based on equitable considerations. However, it is not "discretionary" in the sense that the Court's power is relatively unlimited:

> By saying that the exercise of discretion be 'sound' and 'judicial,' the courts should be understood as meaning that there are reasonably well established working rules and standards by which they are governed in granting and refusing the remedy.

Corbin, *Contracts*, § 1136. Because the Court does not possess current information as to a number of crucial factors bearing on the appropriateness of a decree of specific performance, and, more importantly, because it wishes to provide the parties an opportunity to reach agreement as to how Westinghouse's duty may best be discharged, it does not now decide which of the remedies available to it should be applied here. The Court deems it appropriate, however, to discuss briefly the factors relevant to the selection of a remedy in the hope that the Court may assist the parties in reaching agreement, or, if such should prove necessary, that the parties may better assist the Court by providing evidence bearing on the matter as expeditiously as possible.

Specific performance may be warranted where the plaintiff cannot be adequately compensated by an award of damages. *City Stores Co. v. Ammerman*, 266 F. Supp. 766 (D.D.C. 1967). Here, there is considerable uncertainty as to Florida's future damages. Its estimate as to the expense it will have to incur should it be forced to shut down its plant in 1985 is just that—an estimate. Given the volatility of the price of all forms of energy, its actual expenses may vary considerably from this projection. Florida will, if the spent fuel is not removed, doubtlessly suffer very large future damages as a result of Westinghouse's breach. While this uncertainty would not be sufficient to defeat a damages claim, *Twyman v. Roell*, 123 Fla. 2, 166 So. 215 (1936) the uncertainty of the estimate is to be noted as one factor tending to militate in favor of specific performance. A further uncertainty arises from the probable difficulty of Florida obtaining from another party performance substantially similar to that promised by Westinghouse. The Court does not have information concerning the current availability of storage facilities or the present government regulations and policies concerning transportation of spent fuel. At trial, there was evidence that it would be extremely difficult, if not impossible, for Florida to obtain a contract for removal by another party. To the extent that this remains true, it may be viewed as another factor favoring specific performance.

By the same token, however, the very factors which might render it difficult for Florida to contract for removal with a third party would, obviously, make performance by Westinghouse difficult. While the Court has concluded that Westinghouse's nonperformance is not excused by commercial impracticability, this is not to be construed as precluding the Court from giving consideration to the hardship of performance in deciding the question of remedy. There are "[f]acts that are not sufficient to invalidate a contract and that may nevertheless be sufficient to induce the refusal of a decree for specific enforcement." Corbin, *Contracts*, § 1162.

Finally, while the court is fully cognizant of the difficulty of fashioning a sufficiently specific degree should the parties be unable to reach agreement, and should the Court conclude that specific enforcement is appropriate considering the various other factors, the Court believes that, with the assistance of the parties, a workable and appropriate decree would be achieved.

The Court, however, fervently hopes that it will not be called upon to draft a decree, not because it would be difficult, but rather because the Court is convinced that the parties themselves are in a far better position to find an equitable solution. The future of nuclear energy is a political question upon which the Court expresses no view. Resolution of the issue may or may not assist the parties in reaching an agreement. Regardless, however, of the government's present or future policies and actions vis-a-vis nuclear power, it is clear that, under the law, Westinghouse is liable to Florida for its breach of contract. It must pay damages, or perform, or some combination thereof, whether by agreement of the parties or by order of the Court. The former is, in the Court's view, far preferable in light of the parties' greater ability to discern the best interests of both Florida's ratepayers and Westinghouse's shareholders, and their greater experience in solving complex practical problems.

The Court is not without some perspective as to the willingness and ability of the parties, with the assistance of the Court, to reach a fair agreement. Westinghouse has, in a series of cases which the multi-district panel transferred to this court along with the instant case, evidenced its good faith and willingness to work toward fair and equitable solutions of myriad complex problems. The agreements reached were, in the Court's view, beneficial to the parties and the public as well. Plaintiff, too, has shown its good faith as evidenced by the fair solution reached in another aspect of the instant case.

The solutions to which this court makes reference were reached after all parties, through their respective counsel, fairly, fully and vigorously litigated the issue of liability. The court is satisfied that no less a result may be attained here. In the event, however, that the Court's hope in this regard does not reach fruition, then the parties may present further evidence on the issue of specific performance, as well as evidence in reference to a fair monetary award. As mentioned *supra*, there is considerable uncertainty in the present record as to Florida's future damages. Further evidence will be necessary, to the end that Westinghouse pay no more, and Florida receive no less, than is fair.

Therefore, the parties will be granted ninety (90) days within which to attempt to reach agreement as to the form of the decree to be entered in this matter. Should they wish additional time, the Court may be willing to grant it, upon a showing that additional time would be productive.

In the interim, the Court will meet and confer with counsel, in an effort to assist them in reaching agreement, and for the purpose of more fully apprising the parties as to the further information which the Court deems necessary to draft an appropriate decree in the event that the parties fail to reach an agreement. At such a meeting the parties should be prepared to render assistance in the selection of an expert for the purpose of assisting the Court, should the court conclude that such assistance is necessary, in ascertaining the various alternatives, if any, leading to the removal and storage of the spent fuel.

In view of the fact that the interests of both parties and the public would best be served by an expeditious and final resolution of this matter, both parties are urged to use the initial time period in an intensive attempt to reach agreement, rather than in preparing to further litigate the issue of remedy.

An appropriate order shall issue.

NOTES AND QUESTIONS

1. *Judge Merhige's background*: In the early 1970s, Judge Merhige ordered the Richmond, Virginia schools integrated. In the mid-1980s, he heard about 350 of the Dalkon Shield contraceptive device claims against A. H. Robins Co. He helped about 140 of these cases settle out of court. He also was in charge of most of the Westinghouse uranium litigation.

The late Emily Couric told us more about Judge Merhige in the NATIONAL LAW JOURNAL:[110]

> U.S. District Judge Robert R. Merhige, Jr. of the Eastern District of Virginia tells a story: He privately brought together the two parties in a case before him. The case involved millions of dollars, and the trial, he predicted, would last at least six to eight weeks.
>
> "I sat the two of them down on a Sunday night in my [home's] sun-room," the judge recounts. "I pointed out to them the expense of the trial and the fact that it was a business decision they could make better than six people who know nothing about business."
>
> Then Judge Merhige left the room, and closed the door.
>
> "In 45 minutes they came out," he continues. "I was in my library. They thanked me for the effort. One said, 'We've tried, judge, but it's impossible.'"
>
> "For you to tell me it's impossible really frightens me," Judge Merhige recalls answering, "because I didn't think anything was impossible for American businessmen. I didn't think people got to be executive vice presidents by having 'impossible' in their vocabulary."
>
> One of the executives responded, "I guess that's not the right word. It's not impossible."
>
> "Why then, why don't you try again?" suggested Judge Merhige.
>
> The two men looked at each other, and retreated to the sun-room a second time.
>
> Fifteen minutes later they had reached a settlement. . . .
>
> "Not infrequently, I will insist that the lawyers [in a case] bring their principals here because I want to satisfy myself that both principals recognize what

---

[110] Copyright © 1986, THE NATIONAL LAW JOURNAL, August 4, 1986, at 1. Reprinted with permission.

[strong arguments] the other has," says the judge. "Even a pancake has two sides.". . .

Not everyone agrees that such an activist role in settling cases is appropriate for a judge. . . .

"Judges can't settle cases," says Judge Merhige. "I'm not worried about someone saying, 'He forced us to settle.' Good lawyers can't be forced to do anything."

2. *What happened next?* Despite Judge Merhige's efforts, the parties were unable to settle the case. The docket discloses that the parties filed joint reports of their efforts to resolve the dispute throughout 1981 and 1982. On October 10, 1983, there was a trial on the issue of damages that lasted almost six hours.

In *Florida Power and Light Co. v. Westinghouse Electric Co.*,[111] Judge Merhige reported "[t]he parties made a good faith effort to negotiate the remedy but failed." However, several things happened while the negotiations took place. The parties discovered that it was possible to "re-rack" the Turkey Point spent fuel storage pits a second time.[112] This would provide sufficient on-site storage for all the spent fuel that the reactors will discharge over their useful life. As a result, the reactors will not have to shut down. FP & L will not have to spend a half-million dollars a day on substitute power. Westinghouse agreed to do the second re-racking at Turkey Point at no cost to FP & L.

Furthermore, the United States Government passed the Nuclear Waste Policy Act of 1982.[113] The statute provides that the Department of Energy and the owners and generators of spent fuel are to enter into contracts. DOE takes title to the spent fuel and assumes full responsibility for it. The statute sets a time-table for the government to build a permanent storage facility. However, the site to receive spent fuel will not open until 1998 at the earliest (and indeed, as of 2002 it was still not open). The Act encourages interim storage at the reactor sites through the use of techniques such as re-racking. FP & L entered a contract with the DOE and agreed to pay a fee of $70 million.

FP & L argued that Westinghouse should pay the $70 million fee, roughly $13 million for the first re-racking, and roughly $12 million for the second re-racking. Judge Merhige found that the United States Government had not acted in a timely fashion in honoring its implied commitment regarding spent fuel.[114] This

---

[111] 597 F. Supp. 1456 (E.D. Va. 1984).

[112] Prompted by the settlement negotiations, both Westinghouse and FP & L appointed panels of experts. They found that a second re-racking was the only practical option for dealing with the spent fuel.

[113] 42 U.S.C. § 10101 *et seq.*

[114] Campbell, *The State and the Nuclear Waste Crisis: An Institutional Analysis of Policy Constraints*, 34 Soc. Probs. 18 (Feb. 1987), notes that the Atomic Energy Act of 1954 required the development of a private reprocessing industry. However, costs and environmental concerns made profitable operations extremely questionable. Some firms tried to enter the field, but those with superior technology could not get established. The Natural Resources Defense Council and the Sierra Club used their access to policy-makers to impose serious delays on the development of reprocessing. In 1976, President Ford imposed a three-year moratorium on reprocessing so that the risks associated with nuclear arms proliferation arising from the extraction of plutonium from spent fuel could be studied. In 1977, President Carter announced that reprocessing would be deferred

was a contingency, the non-occurrence of which was a basic assumption of the contract. It made performance of Westinghouse's implicit obligation to perform within a reasonable time impracticable under UCC § 2-615. "Both Florida and Westinghouse were aware that reprocessing might not be available, but neither of them anticipated that no alternative means of removal would be available until 1998 or after."

Judge Merhige said that an equitable allocation of the interim storage costs was in order. "In making the allocation, the Court must of necessity utilize its own sense of fairness." He said that there was "no reason to suspect that the costs of the permanent federal repository have been increased by the delays." As a result, he concluded that the $70 million DOE disposal fee should be borne entirely by Westinghouse. He then turned to the other costs caused by the delays. FP & L ratepayers had benefited enormously from the use of nuclear power during the era of high oil prices. However, Westinghouse should not be rewarded for its lack of diligence during the early 1970s. Thus, Judge Merhige ordered the costs divided. "Without attempting mathematical precision, the allocation will divide the costs roughly as if Westinghouse were absorbing the costs of the first re-racking and Florida absorbing the costs of the second." He refused to award FP & L compensation for increased property taxes and insurance premiums. He concluded:

> The sums aforementioned are not intended to be precise. The Court is satisfied that the parties, who have worked so diligently toward settling their differences, will not be unable to draft an appropriate decree in accord with the Court's view as expressed herein.

3. *Criticism of Judge Merhige's approach*: Duesenberg[115] says that the significance of the *Florida Power and Light* case is "enormous." "It takes its place in a growing line of decisions under section 2-615 in which the relief contem-

---

indefinitely. Campbell notes that the French, for example, subsidize reprocessing as a necessary part of their nuclear energy policy.

As of 2002, the problem of what to do with nuclear waste is still unsolved. In August 2001, the United States Department of Energy made a favorable safety assessment of a plan to build an underground storage dump for radioactive spent fuel in Nevada's Yucca Mountain. The plan was opposed by both of Nevada's senators and the governor of the state. Environmental groups are also opposed to the proposal. Among other things, they point to the dangers involved in shipping the spent nuclear fuel from locations around the United States to Yucca Mountain, and they question the long-term safety of storing the fuel there. In February 2002, President George W. Bush said that "a 57-year accumulation of nuclear waste from power plants and weapons should be buried in the Nevada desert at Yucca Mountain, declaring that an end to the 40-year search for a place to isolate radioactive waste was necessary." NEW YORK TIMES, Feb. 16, 2002, at A11. The *Times* commented: "What was seen in 1982 as a 16-year plan for finding a location and opening a repository is entering its 20th year and seems likely to last for at least 10 more."

Also as of 2002, there is no reprocessing of spent fuel in the United States. However, it is done in Europe by British Nuclear Fuels P.L.C., at its Sellafield plant in northwestern England. Irish and Danish activists have campaigned to shut down spent-fuel reprocessing at Sellafield because of radioactive emissions into the Irish Sea and the atmosphere. In 1999, BNF bought the former Westinghouse nuclear energy operations. There are more than 400 nuclear plants worldwide, and Westinghouse designed four out of ten of them. Fuel reprocessing also takes place in France and Japan.

[115] *Uniform Commercial Code Annual Survey: Sales and Bulk Transfers*, 37 Bus. Law. 949 (1982).

plated by the section has been denied. . . . [T]he language of the court is forbidding; taking a 2-615 route out of a contract is not an easy journey." He also says that "[t]he court's attitude on the force majeure provision contrasts remarkably from that of the Fifth Circuit in Eastern Air Lines v. McDonnell Douglas. . . ." Duesenberg has written a great deal about the UCC. Are his assertions about the original *Florida Power and Light* opinion correct? To the extent they are, why do the judges refuse to apply the statute? Does Judge Merhige's second opinion suggest that Duesenberg might be happier with the final result of the case?

4. ***The Court of Appeals neatens matters:*** The parties appealed Judge Merhige's decisions. The United States Court of Appeals for the Fourth Circuit rejected much of Judge Merhige's reasoning and reached a result more favorable to Westinghouse than his. [116]

First, the Fourth Circuit found that the situation was a classic case of impossibility. Both parties had assumed that the spent fuel would be reprocessed, and both had assumed that either commercial reprocessing would be available or the government would provide this service. Westinghouse had not assumed the risk that neither reprocessing nor storage would be available. Moreover, there was no evidence that Westinghouse could have mitigated any of the losses under the contract as no reprocessing facilities ever were available after Florida Power & Light exercised its option to have Westinghouse remove the spent fuel.

Second, the court said that it must consider the equities of the parties after Westinghouse established that performance was impracticable. The parties had not challenged on appeal the District Court's allocation of the costs of reracking the storage facilities (though the Fourth circuit suggested it would have freed Westinghouse from its share, if Westinghouse had appealed this issue). The Court of Appeals concluded that the ratepayers had enjoyed tremendous benefits (about $10 billion) because of the much lower costs of nuclear power. Thus, it would be fair to charge them with the entire cost of storing the spent fuel until the federal storage facility went into operation. Since the Florida Public Service Commission had given Florida Power & Light the right to pass along these costs for the life of the Turkey Point facility, there was no reason to charge any of the DOE disposal fees to Westinghouse.

To what extent, if at all, does the Fourth Circuit's decision differ from Judge Teitelbaum's approach in the *ALCOA* case? Is the Fourth Circuit writing the contract it thinks the parties should have written if they had known that nuclear power would produce great savings compared to oil but that reprocessing would not be available and storage would not be available until far into the future? Is the Fourth Circuit acting as an administrative agency seeking to balance the interests of power users, utilities and equipment manufacturers? Were the interests of the ratepayers adequately represented before the Fourth Circuit by FP & L's and Westinghouse's lawyers? [117]

---

[116] Florida Power & Light Co. v. Westinghouse Electric Corp., 826 F.2d 239 (4th Cir. 1987).

[117] Moreover, how broadly should we look into the relationship between FP & L and Westinghouse? In 1977, FP & L sued Westinghouse alleging defects in the design and construction of the Turkey Point nuclear plant. FP & L had to replace the tubes that carried the radioactive water to its six steam generators. The parties battled about whether FP & L could sue for negligent design or

Westinghouse and FP & L continued to do business. In 1989, they entered a risk sharing contract under which Westinghouse provided certain maintenance items to the Turkey Point plant. If costs were below a fixed amount, Westinghouse earned a bonus; if they were above this amount, Westinghouse would be paid less. It would be difficult to end the relationship: the Nuclear Regulatory Commission has ruled that replacing items in the reactor with Westinghouse parts does not require a new license while replacing items with a competitor's products would require a licensing procedure.

5. *The judge as mediator rather than as vindicator of rights*: Judge Merhige's solution to this Westinghouse problem was to (1) press the parties to settle; (2) find Westinghouse bound by the contract and not excused by changed circumstances; (3) ask the parties to agree on a settlement; and (4) limit the remedy so there was some sharing of the losses. In the *ALCOA* case, Judge Teitelbaum considered the purposes of the parties and drafted a new pricing clause in light of changed circumstances. However, Essex appealed, and the Court of Appeals pressed the parties to settle. Finally, Essex and ALCOA reworked their arrangement.

In both cases the parties gained a compromise settlement after one or more federal judges played the role of "coercive mediator." Judge Merhige made "suggestions" in a judicial opinion, and Judge Teitelbaum wrote an opinion which would stand if not overturned on appeal. The parties were pushed to work out matters rather than stand on their rights. While ultimately Judge Merhige's effort was unsuccessful, the parties spent almost two years attempting to resolve the issue. Does this pressure to settle produce better solutions than the application of law school contract law producing a decision about breach and an amount of damages?

Judge Teitelbaum adjusted ALCOA's obligations and offered several options. Judge Merhige refused to excuse Westinghouse but then used notions of foreseeability and fault to limit the remedy. The Court of Appeals found commercial impracticability, but then used its equitable powers to fashion a remedy it saw as fair. To what extent do these approaches differ in substance?

---

was confined to breach of warranty claims. The federal courts certified the question to the Supreme Court of Florida. It decided that where there was no personal injury all claims for defective products are limited to breach of warranty theories. *See* Florida Power & Light Co. v. Westinghouse Electric Corp. 785 F.2d 952 (11th Cir. 1986), 510 So. 2d 899 (S. Ct. Fla. 1987); 835 F.2d 817 (11th Cir. 1988). This decision will bring all of the warranty disclaimers and remedy limitations in the contract into play. Moreover, it triggers the contract's provisions limiting the time within which FP & L must make claims.

Westinghouse's failure to remove the spent fuel may have influenced the decision of FP & L officials to bring this suit. Recall that one reason the Court of Appeals refused to charge Westinghouse for the costs of storing spent fuel was the great benefits power users in the Miami enjoyed because of nuclear power. Expensive repairs to FP & L's Turkey Point plant could offset some of these benefits. Moreover, some of the losses suffered because of Westinghouse's inability to reprocess spent fuel might be recovered in the breach of warranty action if FP & L recovered a large sum which the jury did not calculate too precisely.

Westinghouse settled this suit, but the terms of the settlement were not made public. *See* 32 Nu-cleonics Week, May 9, 1991, at 2.

One important function of a mediator is to make a concrete proposal. The parties may accept it as a fair compromise. However, even when they do not accept it, often it moves along the process. Parties can offer variations on the mediator's solution. It serves as a new starting point. If the parties cannot find a better solution, they always can fall back on the mediator's compromise. How does a federal District Judge's decision differ from that of a mediator? Remember that in both cases the trial judges' solutions were not final. The parties could and did appeal, and appellate courts could reverse these decisions. Moreover, at any time before the appellate courts acted, the parties could reach their own settlement.

6. ***The rhetoric of the forum***: If Congress deals with a bad bargain (or a number of bad bargains) made by a major corporation, will the rhetoric and solutions reached differ from those used when courts try to cope with these problems? For example, in which forum would we expect negative views about nuclear power to play a role in dealing with contracts to build nuclear generating plants and dispose of the waste? Concern about the impact of a decision on the economy of Pittsburgh or another city? Concern about the jobs of the Braniff employees who lost so much when senior executives of the corporation wrecked the corporation? [118] What, if anything, does this say about the functions of contract doctrine? About the functions of various branches of the government? About politics?

---

[118] In Northern Indiana Public Service Co. v. Carbon County Coal Co., 799 F.2d 265, 280 (7th Cir. 1986), Judge Posner considered arguments about the appropriate remedy after he found that a buyer was not excused from a contract to supply coal. The supplier sought specific performance. It asserted the interest of workers and merchants in Hanna, Wyoming, where the supplier's coal mine was located. Judge Posner said that the workers and merchants had no legal interest in the contract. "Moreover, the workers and merchants in Hanna assumed the risk that the coal mine would have to close down if it turned out to be uneconomical. The contract with NIPSCO did not guarantee that the mine would operate throughout the life of the contract but only protected the owners of Carbon County [the mining company] against the financial consequences of a breach."

TABLE OF CASES

[References are to page and footnote numbers. Italicized page numbers indicate case excerpts.]

[References are to page and footnote numbers. Italicized page numbers indicate case excerpts.]

[References are to page and footnote numbers. Italicized page numbers indicate case excerpts.]

[References are to page and footnote numbers. Italicized page numbers indicate case excerpts.]

[References are to page and footnote numbers. Italicized page numbers indicate case excerpts.]

[References are to page and footnote numbers. Italicized page numbers indicate case excerpts.]

[References are to page and footnote numbers. Italicized page numbers indicate case excerpts.]

TABLE OF STATUTES

[References are to page numbers.]

[References are to page numbers.]

[References are to page numbers.]

INDEX

[References are to page numbers.]

[References are to page numbers.]

[References are to page numbers.]

[References are to page numbers.]

[References are to page numbers.]

[References are to page numbers.]

V

VAN IDERSTINE CO. V. BARNET LEATHER CO.
Forfeiture . . . 423

VICKERY V. RITCHIE
Unenforceable contracts, restitution and reliance . . . 77

W

WAIVERS
Modification of terms, waiver of conditions compared with . . . 390

WESTINGHOUSE ELECTRIC CORP.
Uranium contracts litigation involving 646; 704

WPC ENTERPRISES, INC. V. UNITED STATES
Ambiguity or misunderstanding . . . 23

WRITING
Modification of terms and "written modification only" clauses
  Central Illinois Public Service Company v. Atlas Minerals, Inc. . . . 376
  Universal Builders, Inc. v. Moon Motor Lodge, Inc. . . . 370